HAMMOND

New Century
World Atlas

Mapmakers for the 21st Century

Contents

ENTIRE CONTENTS
© COPYRIGHT 2000 BY
HAMMOND WORLD ATLAS CORPORATION
All rights reserved. No part of this book may be reproduced or utilized in any form or by any means, electronic or mechanical, including photocopying, recording or by any information storage and retrieval system, without permission in writing from the Publisher.
Printed in Canada

LIBRARY OF CONGRESS
CATALOGING-IN-PUBLICATION DATA

Hammond World Atlas Corporation.
 Hammond new century world atlas.
   p. cm.
Copyright 2000 Hammond World Atlas Corporation.
 Includes index.
  ISBN 0-8437-1371-2
  ISBN 0-8437-1356-9 (pbk.)
 1. Atlases. I. Title.
G1021. H2735   1999   <G&M>
912--DC21   99-28551
                          CIP
                          MAPS

Map Projections

Simply stated, the map-maker's challenge is to project the earth's curved surface onto a flat plane. To achieve this elusive goal, cartographers have developed map projections — equations which govern this conversion of geographic data.

This section explores some of the most widely used projections. It also introduces a new projection, Hammond's Optimal Conformal.

GENERAL PRINCIPLES AND TERMS

The earth rotates around its axis once a day. Its end points are the North and South poles; the line circling the earth midway between the poles is the equator. The arc from the equator to either pole is divided into 90 degrees of latitude. The equator represents 0° latitude. Circles of equal latitude, called parallels, are traditionally shown at every fifth or tenth degree.

The equator is divided into 360 degrees. Lines circling the globe from pole to pole through the degree points on the equator are called meridians, or great circles. All meridians are equal in length, but by international agreement the meridian passing through the Greenwich Observatory near London has been chosen as the prime meridian or 0° longitude. The distance in degrees from the prime meridian to any point east or west is its longitude.

While meridians are all equal in length, parallels become shorter as they approach the poles. Whereas one degree of latitude represents approximately 69 miles (112 km.) anywhere on the globe, a degree of longitude varies from 69 miles (112 km.) at the equator to zero at the poles. Each degree of latitude and longitude is divided into 60 minutes. One minute of latitude equals one nautical mile (1.15 land miles or 1.85 km.).

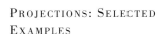

HOW TO FLATTEN A SPHERE: THE ART OF CONTROLLING DISTORTION

There is only one way to represent a sphere with absolute precision: on a globe. All attempts to project our planet's surface onto a plane unevenly stretch or tear the sphere as it flattens, inevitably distorting shapes, distances, area (sizes appear larger or smaller than actual size), angles or direction.

Since representing a sphere on a flat plane always creates distortion, only the parallels or the meridians (or some other set of lines) can maintain the same length as on a globe of corresponding scale. All other lines must be either too long or too short. Accordingly, the scale on a flat map cannot be true everywhere; there will always be different scales in different parts of a map. On world maps or very large areas, variations in scale may be extreme. Most maps seek to preserve either true area relationships (equal area projections) or true angles and shapes (conformal projections); some attempt to achieve overall balance.

PROJECTIONS: SELECTED EXAMPLES

Mercator (Fig. 1): This projection is especially useful because all compass directions appear as straight lines, making it a valuable navigation-al tool. Moreover, every small region conforms to its shape on a globe — hence the name conformal. But because its meridians are evenly-spaced vertical lines which never converge (unlike the globe), the horizontal parallels must be drawn farther and farther apart at higher latitudes to

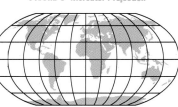

FIGURE 1 **Mercator Projection**

FIGURE 2 **Robinson Projection**

maintain a correct relationship. Only the equator is true to scale, and the size of areas in the higher latitudes is dramatically distorted.

Robinson (Fig. 2): To create the thematic maps in Global Relationships and the two-page world map in the Maps of the World section, the Robinson projection was used. It combines elements of both conformal and equal area projections to show the whole earth with relatively true shapes and reasonably equal areas.

Conic (Fig. 3): This projection has been used frequently for air navigation charts and to create most of the national and regional maps in this atlas. (See text in margin at left).

HAMMOND OPTIMAL CONFORMAL

As its name implies, this new conformal projection presents the optimal view of an area by reducing shifts in scale over an entire region to the minimum degree possible. While conformal maps generally preserve all small shapes, large shapes can become very distorted because of varying scales, causing considerable inaccuracy in distance measurements. The concept underlying the Optimal Conformal is that for any region on the globe, there is an ideal projection for which scale variation can be made as small as possible. Consequently, unlike other projections, the Optimal Conformal does not use one standard formula to construct a map. Each map is a unique projection — the optimal projection for that particular area.

In practice, the cartographer first defines the map subject, then, working on a computer, draws a band around the region to be mapped. Next, a sophisticated software program evaluates the size and shape of the region to determine the most accurate way to project it. The result is the most distortion-free conformal map possible, and the most

Optimal Conformal
Projection

ACCURACY COMPARED

CITIES	SPHERICAL (TRUE) DISTANCE	OPTIMAL CONFORMAL DISTANCE	LAMBERT AZIMUTHAL DISTANCE
CARACAS TO RIO GRANDE	4,443 MI. (7,149 KM.)	4,429 MI. (7,126 KM.)	4,316 MI. (6,944 KM.)
MARACAIBO TO RECIFE	2,834 MI. (4,560 KM.)	2,845 MI. (4,578 KM.)	2,817 MI. (4,533 KM.)
FORTALEZA TO PUNTA ARENAS	3,882 MI. (6,246 KM.)	3,907 MI. (6,266 KM.)	3,843 MI. (6,163 KM.)

Continent maps drawn using the Lambert Azimuthal Equal Area projection (Fig. 4) contain distortions ranging from 2.3 percent for Europe up to 15 percent for Asia. The Optimal Conformal cuts that distortion in half, improving distance measurements on these continent maps. Less distortion means greater visual fidelity, so the shape of a continent on an Optimal projection more closely represents its True shape. The table above compares measurements on the Optimal projection to those of the Lambert Azimuthal Equal Area projection for selected cities.

accurate projections that have ever been made. All of the continents maps in this atlas (with the exception of Antarctica) have been drawn using this projection.

PROJECTIONS COMPARED

Because the true shapes of earth's land-forms are unfamiliar to most people, distinguishing between various projections can be difficult. The following diagrams reveal the distortions introduced by several commonly used projections. By using a simple face with familiar shapes as the starting point (The Plan), it is easy to see the benefits — and drawbacks — of each. Think of the facial features as continents. Note that distortion appears not only in the features themselves, but in the changing shapes, angles and areas of the background grid, or graticule.

Figure 5: The Plan
The Plan indicates that the continents are either perfect concentric circles or are true straight lines *on the earth*. They should appear that way on a "perfect" map.

Figure 6: Orthographic Projection
This view shows the continents on the earth as seen from space. The facial features occupy half of the earth, which is all that you can see from this perspective. As you move outward towards the edge, note how the eyes become elliptical, the nose appears larger and less straight, and the mouth is curved into a smile.

Figure 7: Mercator
This cylindrical projection preserves angles exactly, but the mouth is now smiling broadly, and shows extreme distortion at the map's outer edge. This rapid expansion as you move away from the map's center is typified by the extreme enlargement of Greenland found on Mercator world maps (also see Fig. 1).

Figure 8: Peters
The Peters projection is a square equal area projection elongated, or stretched vertically, by a factor of two. While representing areas in their correct proportions, it does not closely resemble the Plan, and angles, local shapes and global relations are significantly distorted.

Figure 9: Hammond Optimal Conformal
As you can see, this projection minimizes inaccuracies between the angles and shapes of the Plan, yielding a near-perfect map of the given area, up to a complete hemisphere. Like all conformal maps, the Optimal projection preserves every angle exactly, but it is more successful than previous projections at spreading the inevitable curvature across the entire map. Note that the sides of the triangle appear almost straight while correctly containing more than 180°. And though the eyes are slightly too large, it is the only map with eyes which appear concentric. Both mathematically and visually, it offers the best conformal map that can be made of the ideal Plan. All continent maps in this atlas are drawn on this projection.

FIGURE 5
The Plan

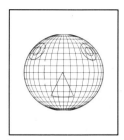

FIGURE 6
Orthographic Projection

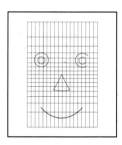

FIGURE 7
Mercator Projection

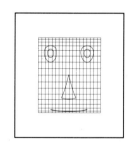

FIGURE 8
Peters Projection

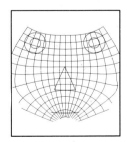

FIGURE 9
Optimal Conformal Projection

Using This Atlas

How to Locate Information Quickly

Our Maps of the World section is organized by continent. If you're looking for a major region of the world, consult the Contents on page two.

Australia
Page/Location:
Area: 2,966,136 sq
7,682,300 s
Population: 17,2
Capital: Canb
Largest C

World Reference Guide

This concise guide lists the countries of the world alphabetically. If you're looking for the largest scale map of any country, you'll find a page and alpha-numeric reference at a glance, as well as information about each country, including its flag.

Merlimont, Fran
.9/F4 **Mersch**, Luxembou
68/A3 **Mers-les-Bains**, France
69/F4 **Mertert**, Luxembourg
69/F4 **Mertesdorf**, Germany
69/G6 **Mertzwiller**, France
68/B5 **Méru**, France
68/B2 **Merville**, France
69/F2 **Merzenich**, Germany
59/F5 **Merzig**, Germany
C4 **Messancy**, Belo
Mattet, Rel

Master Index

When you're looking for a specific place or physical feature, your quickest route is the Master Index. This 45,000-entry alphabetical index lists both the page number and alpha-numeric reference for major places and features in Maps of the World.

T his completely new atlas has been thoughtfully designed for easy, enjoyable use. It is organized as both a general reference atlas and as a comparative tour of the world and its regions. A short time spent familiarizing yourself with its arrangement will help you to benefit fully from its use.

WORLD FLAGS AND REFERENCE GUIDE

This colorful section portrays each nation of the world with its flag and important geographical data including area, population, capital, largest city, highest point and monetary unit. The guide also serves as a quick reference to page and location in the detailed Maps of the World section.

GLOBAL RELATIONSHIPS

World thematic maps highlight important social, cultural, economic and geographic factors affecting today's world. Here, readers can explore complex relationships among such topics as population growth, environmental problems and land utilization or compare worldwide standards of living, energy, resources and manufacturing. Chapters on the Solar System and Structure of the Earth complete this thematic unit.

THE PHYSICAL WORLD

These relief maps of the continents are actual photographs of three-dimensional TerraScape™ models. They present the relationships of land and sea forms with startling realism.

MAPS OF THE WORLD

The largest part of the atlas, this section is subdivided into continental groupings. Each division is introduced with facing-page thematic and political maps of each continent, making topical relationships easier to compare. The thematic maps include topography, population distribution, land use and mineral resources.

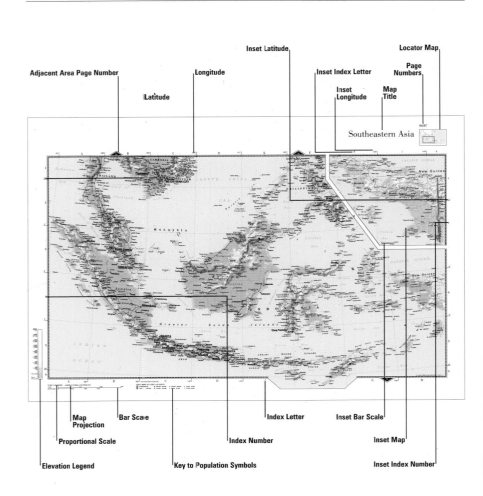

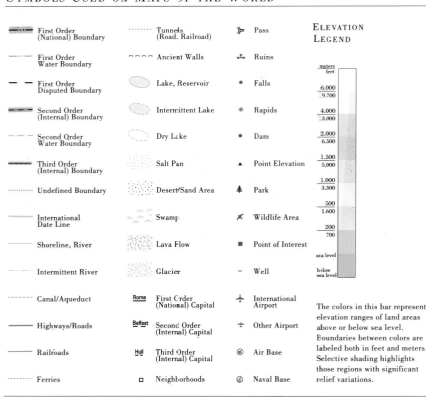

SYMBOLS USED ON MAPS OF THE WORLD

First Order (National) Boundary	Tunnels (Road, Railroad)	Pass	**ELEVATION LEGEND**
First Order Water Boundary	Ancient Walls	Ruins	
First Order Disputed Boundary	Lake, Reservoir	Falls	
Second Order (Internal) Boundary	Intermittent Lake	Rapids	
Second Order Water Boundary	Dry Lake	Dam	
Third Order (Internal) Boundary	Salt Pan	Point Elevation	
Undefined Boundary	Desert/Sand Area	Park	
International Date Line	Swamp	Wildlife Area	
Shoreline, River	Lava Flow	Point of Interest	
Intermittent River	Glacier	Well	
Canal/Aqueduct	**Rome** First Order (National) Capital	International Airport	
Highways/Roads	**Belfast** Second Order (Internal) Capital	Other Airport	
Railroads	**Hull** Third Order (Internal) Capital	Air Base	
Ferries	Neighborhoods	Naval Base	

The colors in this bar represent elevation ranges of land areas above or below sea level. Boundaries between colors are labeled both in feet and meters. Selective shading highlights those regions with significant relief variations.

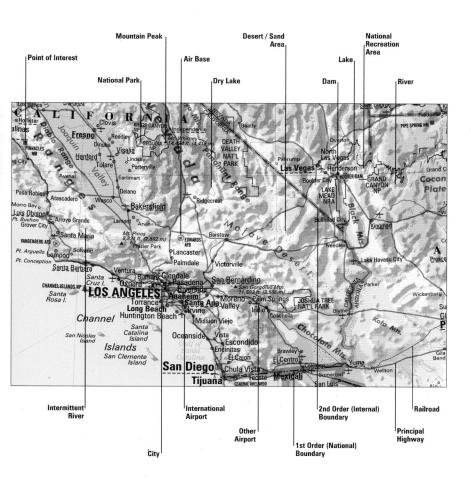

Point of Interest
Mountain Peak
National Park
Air Base
Dry Lake
Desert / Sand Area
Lake
Dam
River
National Recreation Area

Intermittent River
City
International Airport
Other Airport
1st Order (National) Boundary
2nd Order (Internal) Boundary
Railroad
Principal Highway

PRINCIPAL MAP ABBREVIATIONS

Abor. Rsv.	Aboriginal Reserve	Ind. Res.	Indian Reservation	NWR	National Wildlife Reserve
Admin.	Administration	Int'l	International		
AFB	Air Force Base	IR	Indian Reservation	Obl.	Oblast
Amm. Dep.	Ammunition Depot	Isth.	Isthmus	Occ.	Occupied
Arch.	Archipelago	Jct.	Junction	Okr.	Okrug
Arpt.	Airport	L.	Lake	Par.	Parish
Aut.	Autonomous	Lag.	Lagoon	Passg.	Passage
B.	Bay	Lakesh.	Lakeshore	Pen.	Peninsula
Bfld.	Battlefield	Mem.	Memorial	Pk.	Peak
Bk.	Brook	Mil.	Military	Plat.	Plateau
Bor.	Borough	Miss.	Missile	PN	Park National
Br.	Branch	Mon.	Monument	Pref.	Prefecture
C.	Cape	Mt.	Mount	Prom.	Promontory
Can.	Canal	Mtn.	Mountain	Prov.	Province
Cap.	Capital	Mts.	Mountains	Prsv.	Preserve
C.G.	Coast Guard	Nat.	Natural	Pt.	Point
Chan.	Channel	Nat'l	National	R.	River
Co.	County	Nav.	Naval	RA	Recreation Area
Cr.	Creek	NB	National Battlefield	Ra.	Range
Ctr.	Center			Rec.	Recreation(al)
Dep.	Depot	NBP	National Battlefield Park	Ref.	Refuge
Depr.	Depression			Reg.	Region
Dept.	Department	NBS	National Battlefield Site	Rep.	Republic
Des.	Desert			Res.	Reservoir, Reservation
Dist.	District	NHP	National Historical Park		
DMZ	Demilitarized Zone			Rvwy.	Riverway
Dpcy.	Dependency	NHPP	National Historical Park and Preserve	Sa.	Sierra
Eng.	Engineering			Sd.	Sound
Est.	Estuary	NHS	National Historic Site	Seash.	Seashore
Fd.	Fiord, Fjord			So.	Southern
Fed.	Federal	NL	National Lakeshore	SP	State Park
Fk.	Fork	NM	National Monument	Spr., Sprs.	Spring, Springs
Fld.	Field	NMEMP	National Memorial Park	St.	State
For.	Forest			Sta.	Station
Ft.	Fort	NMILP	National Military Park	Stm.	Stream
G.	Gulf			Str.	Strait
Gov.	Governor	No.	Northern	Terr.	Territory
Govt.	Government	NP	National Park	Tun.	Tunnel
Gd.	Grand	NPP	National Park and Preserve	Twp.	Township
Gt.	Great			Val.	Valley
Har.	Harbor	NPRSV	National Preserve	Vill.	Village
Hd.	Head	NRA	National Recreation Area	Vol.	Volcano
Hist.	Historic(al)			Wild.	Wildlife, Wilderness
Hts.	Heights	NRSV	National Reserve		
I., Is.	Island(s)	NS	National Seashore	Wtr.	Water

Completing the continental coverage, in-depth regional maps offer abundant detail including boundaries, cities, transportation networks, rivers and major mountain peaks. Map backgrounds are shown in a pleasing combination of elevation coloration and relief shading, with boundary bands identifying the extent of each country's national and internal limits.

In place of relief, colors on metropolitan area inset maps highlight cities, parks and other bounded areas. Population legends accompany all maps.

WORLD STATISTICS
These tables list the dimensions of the earth's principal mountains, islands, rivers and lakes, along with other useful geographical information.

MASTER INDEX
This is an A to Z listing of names found on the political maps in the Maps of the World section. It has its own abbreviation list which, along with an introduction, appears on page 138.

MAP SCALES
A map's scale is the relationship of any length on that map to an identical length on the earth's surface. A scale of 1:7,000,000 means that one inch on the map represents 7,000,000 inches (110 miles, 178 kilometers) on the earth's surface. Thus, a 1:7,000,000 scale is larger than a 1:14,000,000 scale just as 1/7 is larger than 1/14.

In addition to these proportional scales, each map is accompanied by a linear (bar) scale, useful in making accurate measurements between places on the maps.

In this atlas, the most densely populated areas are shown at a scale of 1:1,170,000. Other populous areas are presented at 1:3,500,000 and 1:7,000,000, allowing you to accurately compare areas and distances of similar regions. Remaining regions are scaled at 1:10,500,000. The continent maps, as well as the United States, Canada, Russia, Pacific and World have smaller scales.

World Flags and Reference Guide

Afghanistan
Page/Location: 73/H2
Area: 250,775 sq. mi.
649,507 sq. km.
Population: 26,668,251
Capital: Kabul
Largest City: Kabul
Highest Point: Noshaq
Monetary Unit: afghani

Albania
Page/Location: 61/F2
Area: 11,100 sq. mi.
28,749 sq. km.
Population: 3,401,126
Capital: Tiranë
Largest City: Tiranë
Highest Point: Korab
Monetary Unit: lek

Algeria
Page/Location: 96/F2
Area: 919,591 sq. mi.
2,381,740 sq. km.
Population: 31,787,647
Capital: Algiers
Largest City: Algiers
Highest Point: Tahat
Monetary Unit: Algerian dinar

Andorra
Page/Location: 59/F1
Area: 174 sq. mi.
450 sq. km.
Population: 67,673
Capital: Andorra la Vella
Largest City: Andorra la Vella
Highest Point: Coma Pedrosa
Monetary Unit: Fr. franc, Sp. peseta

Angola
Page/Location: 104/C3
Area: 481,351 sq. mi.
1,246,700 sq. km.
Population: 11,486,729
Capital: Luanda
Largest City: Luanda
Highest Point: Morro de Môco
Monetary Unit: new kwanza

Antigua and Barbuda
Page/Location: 117/J4
Area: 171 sq. mi.
443 sq. km.
Population: 64,461
Capital: St. John's
Largest City: St. John's
Highest Point: Boggy Peak
Monetary Unit: East Caribbean dollar

Argentina
Page/Location: 111/C4
Area: 1,068,296 sq. mi.
2,766,890 sq. km.
Population: 37,214,757
Capital: Buenos Aires
Largest City: Buenos Aires
Highest Point: Cerro Aconcagua
Monetary Unit: nuevo peso argentino

Armenia
Page/Location: 67/H5
Area: 11,506 sq. mi.
29,800 sq. km.
Population: 3,396,184
Capital: Yerevan
Largest City: Yerevan
Highest Point: Alagez
Monetary Unit: dram

Australia
Page/Location: 89
Area: 2,966,136 sq. mi.
7,682,300 sq. km.
Population: 18,950,108
Capital: Canberra
Largest City: Sydney
Highest Point: Mt. Kosciusko
Monetary Unit: Australian dollar

Austria
Page/Location: 57/L3
Area: 32,375 sq. mi.
83,851 sq. km.
Population: 8,148,007
Capital: Vienna
Largest City: Vienna
Highest Point: Grossglockner
Monetary Unit: schilling

Azerbaijan
Page/Location: 67/H4
Area: 33,436 sq. mi.
86,600 sq. km.
Population: 7,955,772
Capital: Baku
Largest City: Baku
Highest Point: Bazardyuzyu
Monetary Unit: manat

Bahamas
Page/Location: 117/F2
Area: 5,382 sq. mi.
13,939 sq. km.
Population: 287,548
Capital: Nassau
Largest City: Nassau
Highest Point: 207 ft. (63 m)
Monetary Unit: Bahamian dollar

Bahrain
Page/Location: 72/F3
Area: 240 sq. mi.
622 sq. km.
Population: 641,539
Capital: Manama
Largest City: Manama
Highest Point: Jabal Dukhān
Monetary Unit: Bahraini dinar

Bangladesh
Page/Location: 84/E3
Area: 55,598 sq. mi.
144,000 sq. km.
Population: 129,146,695
Capital: Dhākā
Largest City: Dhākā
Highest Point: Keokradong
Monetary Unit: taka

Barbados
Page/Location: 117/J5
Area: 166 sq. mi.
430 sq. km.
Population: 259,248
Capital: Bridgetown
Largest City: Bridgetown
Highest Point: Mt. Hillaby
Monetary Unit: Barbadian dollar

Belarus
Page/Location: 41/G3
Area: 80,154 sq. mi.
207,600 sq. km.
Population: 10,390,697
Capital: Minsk
Largest City: Minsk
Highest Point: Dzerzhinskaya
Monetary Unit: Belarusian ruble

Belgium
Page/Location: 52/C2
Area: 11,781 sq. mi.
30,513 sq. km.
Population: 10,185,894
Capital: Brussels
Largest City: Brussels
Highest Point: Botrange
Monetary Unit: Belgian franc

Belize
Page/Location: 116/D4
Area: 8,867 sq. mi.
22,966 sq. km.
Population: 241,546
Capital: Belmopan
Largest City: Belize City
Highest Point: Victoria Peak
Monetary Unit: Belize dollar

Benin
Page/Location: 99/F4
Area: 43,483 sq. mi.
112,620 sq. km.
Population: 6,516,630
Capital: Porto-Novo
Largest City: Cotonou
Highest Point: Nassoukou
Monetary Unit: CFA franc

Bhutan
Page/Location: 84/E2
Area: 18,147 sq. mi.
47,000 sq. km.
Population: 1,996,221
Capital: Thimphu
Largest City: Thimphu
Highest Point: Kula Kangri
Monetary Unit: ngultrum

Bolivia
Page/Location: 108/F7
Area: 424,163 sq. mi.
1,098,582 sq. km.
Population: 8,139,180
Capital: La Paz; Sucre
Largest City: La Paz
Highest Point: Nevado Ancohuma
Monetary Unit: boliviano

Bosnia and Herzegovina
Page/Location: 62/C3
Area: 19,940 sq. mi.
51,645 sq. km.
Population: 3,591,618
Capital: Sarajevo
Largest City: Sarajevo
Highest Point: Maglič
Monetary Unit: dinar

Botswana
Page/Location: 104/D5
Area: 231,803 sq. mi.
600,370 sq. km.
Population: 1,479,039
Capital: Gaborone
Largest City: Gaborone
Highest Point: Tsodilo Hills
Monetary Unit: pula

Brazil
Page/Location: 107/D3
Area: 3,286,470 sq. mi.
8,511,965 sq. km.
Population: 173,790,810
Capital: Brasília
Largest City: São Paulo
Highest Point: Pico da Neblina
Monetary Unit: real

Brunei
Page/Location: 86/D2
Area: 2,226 sq. mi.
5,765 sq. km.
Population: 330,689
Capital: Bandar Seri Begawan
Largest City: Bandar Seri Begawan
Highest Point: Bukit Pagon
Monetary Unit: Brunei dollar

Bulgaria
Page/Location: 63/G4
Area: 42,823 sq. mi.
110,912 sq. km.
Population: 8,155,828
Capital: Sofia
Largest City: Sofia
Highest Point: Musala
Monetary Unit: lev

Burkina Faso
Page/Location: 99/E3
Area: 105,869 sq. mi.
274,200 sq. km.
Population: 11,892,029
Capital: Ouagadougou
Largest City: Ouagadougou
Highest Point: 2,405 ft. (733 m)
Monetary Unit: CFA franc

Burundi
Page/Location: 101/A3
Area: 10,747 sq. mi.
27,835 sq. km.
Population: 5,930,805
Capital: Bujumbura
Largest City: Bujumbura
Highest Point: 8,760 ft. (2,671 m)
Monetary Unit: Burundi franc

Cambodia
Page/Location: 83/D3
Area: 69,898 sq. mi.
181,036 sq. km.
Population: 11,918,865
Capital: Phnom Penh
Largest City: Phnom Penh
Highest Point: Phnum Aoral
Monetary Unit: new riel

Cameroon
Page/Location: 96/H7
Area: 183,568 sq. mi.
475,441 sq. km.
Population: 15,891,531
Capital: Yaoundé
Largest City: Douala
Highest Point: Mt. Cameroon
Monetary Unit: CFA franc

Canada
Page/Location: 118
Area: 3,851,787 sq. mi.
9,976,139 sq. km.
Population: 31,330,255
Capital: Ottawa
Largest City: Toronto
Highest Point: Mt. Logan
Monetary Unit: Canadian dollar

Cape Verde
Page/Location: 38/H5
Area: 1,557 sq. mi.
4,033 sq. km.
Population: 411,487
Capital: Praia
Largest City: Praia
Highest Point: 9,282 ft. (2,829 m)
Monetary Unit: Cape Verde escudo

Central African Republic
Page/Location: 97/J6
Area: 240,533 sq. mi.
622,980 sq. km.
Population: 3,515,657
Capital: Bangui
Largest City: Bangui
Highest Point: Mt. Kayagangiri
Monetary Unit: CFA franc

Chad
Page/Location: 97/J4
Area: 495,752 sq. mi.
1,283,998 sq. km.
Population: 7,760,252
Capital: N'Djamena
Largest City: N'Djamena
Highest Point: Emi Koussi
Monetary Unit: CFA franc

Chile
Page/Location: 111/B3
Area: 292,257 sq. mi.
756,946 sq. km.
Population: 15,155,495
Capital: Santiago
Largest City: Santiago
Highest Point: Nevado Ojos del Salado
Monetary Unit: Chilean peso

China
Page/Location: 71/J6
Area: 3,705,386 sq. mi.
9,596,960 sq. km.
Population: 1,256,167,701
Capital: Beijing
Largest City: Shanghai
Highest Point: Mt. Everest
Monetary Unit: yuan

Colombia
Page/Location: 108/D3
Area: 439,513 sq. mi.
1,138,339 sq. km.
Population: 40,036,927
Capital: Bogotá
Largest City: Bogotá
Highest Point: Pico Cristóbal Colón
Monetary Unit: Colombian peso

Comoros
Page/Location: 103/G5
Area: 838 sq. mi.
2,170 sq. km.
Population: 580,509
Capital: Moroni
Largest City: Moroni
Highest Point: Karthala
Monetary Unit: Comorian franc

Congo, Dem. Rep. of the
Page/Location: 95/E5
Area: 905,563 sq. mi.
2,345,410 sq. km.
Population: 51,987,773
Capital: Kinshasa
Largest City: Kinshasa
Highest Point: Margherita Peak
Monetary Unit: zaire

Congo, Rep. of the
Page/Location: 95/D4
Area: 132,046 sq. mi.
342,000 sq. km.
Population: 2,775,659
Capital: Brazzaville
Largest City: Brazzaville
Highest Point: Lékéti Mts.
Monetary Unit: CFA franc

Costa Rica
Page/Location: 116/E5
Area: 19,730 sq. mi.
51,100 sq. km.
Population: 3,743,677
Capital: San José
Largest City: San José
Highest Point: Cerro Chirripó Grande
Monetary Unit: Costa Rican colón

Côte d'Ivoire
Page/Location: 98/D5
Area: 124,504 sq. mi.
322,465 sq. km.
Population: 16,190,105
Capital: Yamoussoukro
Largest City: Abidjan
Highest Point: Mt. Nimba
Monetary Unit: CFA franc

Croatia
Page/Location: 62/C3
Area: 22,050 sq. mi.
57,110 sq. km.
Population: 4,681,015
Capital: Zagreb
Largest City: Zagreb
Highest Point: Veliki Troglav
Monetary Unit: Croatian kuna

Cuba
Page/Location: 117/F3
Area: 42,803 sq. mi.
110,860 sq. km.
Population: 11,139,412
Capital: Havana
Largest City: Havana
Highest Point: Pico Turquino
Monetary Unit: Cuban peso

Cyprus
Page/Location: 72/B1
Area: 3,571 sq. mi.
9,250 sq. km.
Population: 759,048
Capital: Nicosia
Largest City: Nicosia
Highest Point: Olympus
Monetary Unit: Cypriot pound

Czech Republic
Page/Location: 49/H4
Area: 30,387 sq. mi.
78,703 sq. km.
Population: 10,283,762
Capital: Prague
Largest City: Prague
Highest Point: Sněžka
Monetary Unit: Czech koruna

Denmark
Page/Location: 42/C5
Area: 16,629 sq. mi.
43,069 sq. km.
Population: 5,374,554
Capital: Copenhagen
Largest City: Copenhagen
Highest Point: Yding Skovhøj
Monetary Unit: Danish krone

Djibouti
Page/Location: 97/P5
Area: 8,494 sq. mi.
22,000 sq. km.
Population: 454,294
Capital: Djibouti
Largest City: Djibouti
Highest Point: Moussa Ali
Monetary Unit: Djibouti franc

Dominica
Page/Location: 117/J4
Area: 290 sq. mi.
751 sq. km.
Population: 63,944
Capital: Roseau
Largest City: Roseau
Highest Point: Morne Diablotin
Monetary Unit: EC dollar

Dominican Republic
Page/Location: 117/H4
Area: 18,815 sq. mi.
48,730 sq. km.
Population: 8,261,536
Capital: Santo Domingo
Largest City: Santo Domingo
Highest Point: Pico Duarte
Monetary Unit: Dominican peso

Ecuador
Page/Location: 108/C4
Area: 109,483 sq. mi.
283,561 sq. km.
Population: 12,782,161
Capital: Quito
Largest City: Guayaquil
Highest Point: Chimborazo
Monetary Unit: sucre

Egypt
Page/Location: 100/L2
Area: 386,659 sq. mi.
1,001,447 sq. km.
Population: 68,494,584
Capital: Cairo
Largest City: Cairo
Highest Point: Mt. Catherine
Monetary Unit: Egyptian pound

El Salvador
Page/Location: 116/C5
Area: 8,124 sq. mi.
21,040 sq. km.
Population: 5,925,374
Capital: San Salvador
Largest City: San Salvador
Highest Point: Santa Ana
Monetary Unit: Salvadoran colón

Equatorial Guinea
Page/Location: 96/G7
Area: 10,831 sq. mi.
28,052 sq. km.
Population: 477,763
Capital: Malabo
Largest City: Malabo
Highest Point: Pico de Santa Isabel
Monetary Unit: CFA franc

Eritrea
Page/Location: 97/N5
Area: 46,842 sq. mi.
121,320 sq. km.
Population: 4,142,481
Capital: Asmara
Largest City: Asmara
Highest Point: Soira
Monetary Unit: nafka

Estonia
Page/Location: 64/E4
Area: 17,413 sq. mi.
45,100 sq. km.
Population: 1,398,140
Capital: Tallinn
Largest City: Tallinn
Highest Point: Munamägi
Monetary Unit: kroon

Ethiopia
Page/Location: 97/N5
Area: 435,184 sq. mi.
1,127,127 sq. km.
Population: 60,967,436
Capital: Addis Ababa
Largest City: Addis Ababa
Highest Point: Ras Dashen Terara
Monetary Unit: birr

Fiji
Page/Location: 92/G6
Area: 7,055 sq. mi.
18,272 sq. km.
Population: 823,376
Capital: Suva
Largest City: Suva
Highest Point: Tomaniivi
Monetary Unit: Fijian dollar

Finland
Page/Location: 42/H2
Area: 130,128 sq. mi.
337,032 sq. km.
Population: 5,164,825
Capital: Helsinki
Largest City: Helsinki
Highest Point: Kahperusvaara
Monetary Unit: markka

Unknown

France
Page/Location: 56/D3
Area: 211,208 sq. mi.
547,030 sq. km.
Population: 59,128,187
Capital: Paris
Largest City: Paris
Highest Point: Mont Blanc
Monetary Unit: French franc

Gabon
Page/Location: 96/H7
Area: 103,346 sq. mi.
267,666 sq. km.
Population: 1,244,192
Capital: Libreville
Largest City: Libreville
Highest Point: Mt. Iboundji
Monetary Unit: CFA franc

Gambia, The
Page/Location: 98/B3
Area: 4,363 sq. mi.
11,300 sq. km.
Population: 1,381,496
Capital: Banjul
Largest City: Banjul
Highest Point: 98 ft. (30 m)
Monetary Unit: dalasi

Georgia
Page/Location: 67/G4
Area: 26,911 sq. mi.
69,700 sq. km.
Population: 5,034,051
Capital: T'bilisi
Largest City: T'bilisi
Highest Point: Kazbek
Monetary Unit: lari

Germany
Page/Location: 48/E3
Area: 137,803 sq. mi.
356,910 sq. km.
Population: 82,081,365
Capital: Berlin
Largest City: Berlin
Highest Point: Zugspitze
Monetary Unit: Deutsche mark

Ghana
Page/Location: 99/E4
Area: 92,099 sq. mi.
238,536 sq. km.
Population: 19,271,744
Capital: Accra
Largest City: Accra
Highest Point: Afadjoto
Monetary Unit: new cedi

Unknown

Greece
Page/Location: 61/G3
Area: 50,944 sq. mi.
131,945 sq. km.
Population: 10,750,705
Capital: Athens
Largest City: Athens
Highest Point: Mt. Olympus
Monetary Unit: drachma

World Flags and Reference Guide

Grenada
Page/Location: 117/J5
Area: 133 sq. mi.
344 sq. km.
Population: 97,913
Capital: St. George's
Largest City: St. George's
Highest Point: Mt. St. Catherine
Monetary Unit: East Caribbean dollar

Guatemala
Page/Location: 116/C4
Area: 42,042 sq. mi.
108,889 sq. km.
Population: 12,669,576
Capital: Guatemala
Largest City: Guatemala
Highest Point: Tajumulco
Monetary Unit: quetzal

Guinea
Page/Location: 98/C4
Area: 94,925 sq. mi.
245,856 sq. km.
Population: 7,610,869
Capital: Conakry
Largest City: Conakry
Highest Point: Mt. Nimba
Monetary Unit: Guinea franc

Guinea-Bissau
Page/Location: 98/B3
Area: 13,948 sq. mi.
36,125 sq. km.
Population: 1,263,341
Capital: Bissau
Largest City: Bissau
Highest Point: 689 ft. (210 m)
Monetary Unit: Guinea-Bissau peso

Guyana
Page/Location: 108/G3
Area: 83,000 sq. mi.
214,970 sq. km.
Population: 703,399
Capital: Georgetown
Largest City: Georgetown
Highest Point: Mt. Roraima
Monetary Unit: Guyana dollar

Haiti
Page/Location: 117/G4
Area: 10,694 sq. mi.
27,697 sq. km.
Population: 6,991,589
Capital: Port-au-Prince
Largest City: Port-au-Prince
Highest Point: Pic la Selle
Monetary Unit: gourde

Honduras
Page/Location: 116/D4
Area: 43,277 sq. mi.
112,087 sq. km.
Population: 6,130,135
Capital: Tegucigalpa
Largest City: Tegucigalpa
Highest Point: Cerro de las Minas
Monetary Unit: lempira

Hungary
Page/Location: 62/D2
Area: 35,919 sq. mi.
93,030 sq. km.
Population: 10,167,182
Capital: Budapest
Largest City: Budapest
Highest Point: Kékes
Monetary Unit: forint

Iceland
Page/Location: 42/N7
Area: 39,768 sq. mi.
103,000 sq. km.
Population: 274,141
Capital: Reykjavík
Largest City: Reykjavík
Highest Point: Hvannadalshnúkur
Monetary Unit: króna

India
Page/Location: 84/C3
Area: 1,269,339 sq. mi.
3,287,588 sq. km.
Population: 1,017,645,163
Capital: New Delhi
Largest City: Calcutta
Highest Point: Nanda Devi
Monetary Unit: Indian rupee

Indonesia
Page/Location: 87/E4
Area: 741,096 sq. mi.
1,919,440 sq. km.
Population: 219,266,557
Capital: Jakarta
Largest City: Jakarta
Highest Point: Puncak Jaya
Monetary Unit: rupiah

Iran
Page/Location: 72/F2
Area: 636,293 sq. mi.
1,648,000 sq. km.
Population: 65,865,302
Capital: Tehrān
Largest City: Tehrān
Highest Point: Qolleh-ye Damāvand
Monetary Unit: Iranian rial

Iraq
Page/Location: 72/D2
Area: 168,753 sq. mi.
437,072 sq. km.
Population: 23,150,926
Capital: Baghdad
Largest City: Baghdad
Highest Point: Haji Ibrahim
Monetary Unit: Iraqi dinar

Ireland
Page/Location: 43/A4
Area: 27,136 sq. mi.
70,282 sq. km.
Population: 3,647,348
Capital: Dublin
Largest City: Dublin
Highest Point: Carrantuohill
Monetary Unit: Irish pound

Israel
Page/Location: 74/J5
Area: 8,019 sq. mi.
20,770 sq. km.
Population: 5,851,913
Capital: Jerusalem
Largest City: Tel Aviv-Yafo
Highest Point: Har Meron
Monetary Unit: new Israeli shekel

Italy
Page/Location: 41/F4
Area: 116,303 sq. mi.
301,225 sq. km.
Population: 56,686,568
Capital: Rome
Largest City: Rome
Highest Point: Monte Rosa
Monetary Unit: Italian lira

Jamaica
Page/Location: 117/F4
Area: 4,243 sq. mi.
10,990 sq. km.
Population: 2,668,740
Capital: Kingston
Largest City: Kingston
Highest Point: Blue Mountain Pk.
Monetary Unit: Jamaican dollar

Japan
Page/Location: 77/M4
Area: 145,882 sq. mi.
377,835 sq. km.
Population: 126,434,470
Capital: Tokyo
Largest City: Tokyo
Highest Point: Fujiyama
Monetary Unit: yen

Jordan
Page/Location: 72/C2
Area: 34,445 sq. mi.
89,213 sq. km.
Population: 4,700,843
Capital: Ammān
Largest City: Ammān
Highest Point: Jabal Ramm
Monetary Unit: Jordanian dinar

Kazakhstan
Page/Location: 68/G5
Area: 1,049,150 sq. mi.
2,717,300 sq. km.
Population: 16,816,150
Capital: Astana
Largest City: Almaty
Highest Point: Khan-Tengri
Monetary Unit: Kazakstani tenge

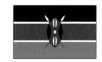

Kenya
Page/Location: 101/C2
Area: 224,960 sq. mi.
582,646 sq. km.
Population: 29,250,541
Capital: Nairobi
Largest City: Nairobi
Highest Point: Mt. Kenya
Monetary Unit: Kenya shilling

Kiribati
Page/Location: 92/H5
Area: 277 sq. mi.
717 sq. km.
Population: 87,025
Capital: Tarawa
Largest City: —
Highest Point: Banaba Island
Monetary Unit: Australian dollar

Korea, North
Page/Location: 80/D2
Area: 46,540 sq. mi.
120,539 sq. km.
Population: 21,687,550
Capital: P'yŏngyang
Largest City: P'yŏngyang
Highest Point: Paektu-san
Monetary Unit: North Korean won

Korea, South
Page/Location: 80/D4
Area: 38,023 sq. mi.
98,480 sq. km.
Population: 47,350,529
Capital: Seoul
Largest City: Seoul
Highest Point: Halla-san
Monetary Unit: South Korean won

Kuwait
Page/Location: 72/E3
Area: 6,880 sq. mi.
17,820 sq. km.
Population: 2,067,728
Capital: Kuwait
Largest City: Kuwait
Highest Point: 951 ft. (290 m)
Monetary Unit: Kuwaiti dinar

Kyrgyzstan
Page/Location: 75/B3
Area: 76,641 sq. mi.
198,500 sq. km.
Population: 4,584,341
Capital: Bishkek
Largest City: Bishkek
Highest Point: Pik Pobedy
Monetary Unit: som

Laos
Page/Location: 83/C2
Area: 91,428 sq. mi.
236,800 sq. km.
Population: 5,556,821
Capital: Vientiane
Largest City: Vientiane
Highest Point: Phou Bia
Monetary Unit: new kip

Latvia
Page/Location: 64/E4
Area: 24,749 sq. mi.
64,100 sq. km.
Population: 2,326,689
Capital: Riga
Largest City: Riga
Highest Point: Gaizina Kalns
Monetary Unit: Latvian lat

Lebanon
Page/Location: 74/K5
Area: 4,015 sq. mi.
10,399 sq. km.
Population: 3,619,971
Capital: Beirut
Largest City: Beirut
Highest Point: Qurnat as Sawdā'
Monetary Unit: Lebanese pound

Lesotho
Page/Location: 102/D3
Area: 11,720 sq. mi.
30,355 sq. km.
Population: 2,166,520
Capital: Maseru
Largest City: Maseru
Highest Point: Thabana-Ntlenyana
Monetary Unit: loti

Liberia
Page/Location: 98/C5
Area: 43,000 sq. mi.
111,370 sq. km.
Population: 3,089,980
Capital: Monrovia
Largest City: Monrovia
Highest Point: Mt. Wuteve
Monetary Unit: Liberian dollar

Libya
Page/Location: 97/J2
Area: 679,358 sq. mi.
1,759,537 sq. km.
Population: 5,114,032
Capital: Tripoli
Largest City: Tripoli
Highest Point: Picco Bette
Monetary Unit: Libyan dinar

Liechtenstein
Page/Location: 55/F3
Area: 61 sq. mi.
158 sq. km.
Population: 32,410
Capital: Vaduz
Largest City: Vaduz
Highest Point: Grauspitz
Monetary Unit: Swiss franc

Lithuania
Page/Location: 64/D5
Area: 25,174 sq. mi.
65,200 sq. km.
Population: 3,571,552
Capital: Vilnius
Largest City: Vilnius
Highest Point: Nevaišių
Monetary Unit: litas

Luxembourg
Page/Location: 53/E4
Area: 999 sq. mi.
2,587 sq. km.
Population: 432,577
Capital: Luxembourg
Largest City: Luxembourg
Highest Point: Ardennes Plateau
Monetary Unit: Luxembourg franc

Macedonia (F.Y.R.O.M.)
Page/Location: 61/G2
Area: 9,781 sq. mi.
25,333 sq. km.
Population: 2,035,044
Capital: Skopje
Largest City: Skopje
Highest Point: Korab
Monetary Unit: denar

Madagascar
Page/Location: 103/H8
Area: 226,657 sq. mi.
587,041 sq. km.
Population: 15,294,535
Capital: Antananarivo
Largest City: Antananarivo
Highest Point: Maromokotro
Monetary Unit: Malagasy franc

Malawi
Page/Location: 104/F3
Area: 45,747 sq. mi.
118, 485 sq. km.
Population: 10,154,299
Capital: Lilongwe
Largest City: Blantyre
Highest Point: Mulanje Mts.
Monetary Unit: Malawi kwacha

Malaysia
Page/Location: 86/C2
Area: 127,316 sq. mi.
329,750 sq. km.
Population: 21,820,143
Capital: Kuala Lumpur
Largest City: Kuala Lumpur
Highest Point: Gunung Kinabalu
Monetary Unit: ringgit

Maldives
Page/Location: 71/G9
Area: 115 sq. mi.
298 sq. km.
Population: 310,425
Capital: Male
Largest City: Male
Highest Point: 20 ft. (6 m)
Monetary Unit: rufiyaa

Mali
Page/Location: 96/E4
Area: 478,764 sq. mi.
1,240,000 sq. km.
Population: 10,750,686
Capital: Bamako
Largest City: Bamako
Highest Point: Hombori Tondo
Monetary Unit: CFA franc

Malta
Page/Location: 60/D5
Area: 122 sq. mi.
316 sq. km.
Population: 383,285
Capital: Valletta
Largest City: Sliema
Highest Point: 830 ft. (253 m)
Monetary Unit: Maltese lira

Marshall Islands
Page/Location: 92/G3
Area: 70 sq. mi.
181 sq. km.
Population: 68,088
Capital: Majuro
Largest City: —
Highest Point: 20 ft. (6 m)
Monetary Unit: U.S. dollar

Mauritania
Page/Location: 96/C4
Area: 397,953 sq. mi.
1,030,700 sq. km.
Population: 2,660,155
Capital: Nouakchott
Largest City: Nouakchott
Highest Point: Kediet Ijill
Monetary Unit: ouguiya

Mauritius
Page/Location: 103/S15
Area: 718 sq. mi.
1,860 sq. km.
Population: 1,196,172
Capital: Port Louis
Largest City: Port Louis
Highest Point: 2,713 ft. (827 m)
Monetary Unit: Mauritian rupee

Mexico
Page/Location: 116/A3
Area: 761,601 sq. mi.
1,972,546 sq. km.
Population: 102,026,691
Capital: Mexico
Largest City: Mexico
Highest Point: Citlaltépetl
Monetary Unit: new Mexican peso

Micronesia
Page/Location: 92/D4
Area: 271 sq. mi.
702 sq. km.
Population: 133,144
Capital: Palikir
Largest City: —
Highest Point: —
Monetary Unit: U.S. dollar

Moldova
Page/Location: 63/H2
Area: 13,012 sq. mi.
33,700 sq. km.
Population: 4,466,758
Capital: Chişinău
Largest City: Chişinău
Highest Point: 1,408 ft. (429 m)
Monetary Unit: leu

Monaco
Page/Location: 57/G5
Area: 0.7 sq. mi.
1.9 sq. km.
Population: 32,231
Capital: Monaco
Largest City: —
Highest Point: —
Monetary Unit: French franc

Mongolia
Page/Location: 76/D2
Area: 606,163 sq. mi.
1,569, 962 sq. km.
Population: 2,654,572
Capital: Ulaanbaatar
Largest City: Ulaanbaatar
Highest Point: Tavan Bogd Uul
Monetary Unit: tughrik

Morocco
Page/Location: 96/C1
Area: 172,414 sq. mi.
446,550 sq. km.
Population: 30,205,387
Capital: Rabat
Largest City: Casablanca
Highest Point: Jebel Toubkal
Monetary Unit: Moroccan dirham

Mozambique
Page/Location: 104/G4
Area: 309,494 sq. mi.
801,590 sq. km.
Population: 19,614,345
Capital: Maputo
Largest City: Maputo
Highest Point: Monte Binga
Monetary Unit: metical

Myanmar (Burma)
Page/Location: 85/G3
Area: 261,969 sq. mi.
678,500 sq. km.
Population: 48,852,098
Capital: Rangoon
Largest City: Rangoon
Highest Point: Hkakabo Razi
Monetary Unit: kyat

Namibia
Page/Location: 104/C5
Area: 318,694 sq. mi.
825,418 sq. km.
Population: 1,674,116
Capital: Windhoek
Largest City: Windhoek
Highest Point: Brandberg
Monetary Unit: Namibian dollar

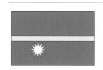

Nauru
Page/Location: 92/F5
Area: 7.7 sq. mi.
20 sq. km.
Population: 10,704
Capital: Yaren (district)
Largest City: —
Highest Point: 230 ft. (70 m)
Monetary Unit: Australian dollar

Nepal
Page/Location: 84/D2
Area: 54,663 sq. mi.
141,577 sq. km.
Population: 24,920,211
Capital: Kāthmāndu
Largest City: Kāthmāndu
Highest Point: Mt. Everest
Monetary Unit: Nepalese rupee

Netherlands
Page/Location: 50/B5
Area: 14,413 sq. mi.
37,330 sq. km.
Population: 15,878,304
Capital: The Hague; Amsterdam
Largest City: Amsterdam
Highest Point: Vaalserberg
Monetary Unit: Netherlands guilder

New Zealand
Page/Location: 89/H6
Area: 103,736 sq. mi.
268,676 sq. km.
Population: 3,697,850
Capital: Wellington
Largest City: Auckland
Highest Point: Mt. Cook
Monetary Unit: New Zealand dollar

Nicaragua
Page/Location: 116/D5
Area: 49,998 sq. mi.
129,494 sq. km.
Population: 4,850,976
Capital: Managua
Largest City: Managua
Highest Point: Pico Mogotón
Monetary Unit: gold cordoba

Niger
Page/Location: 96/G4
Area: 489,189 sq. mi.
1,267,000 sq. km.
Population: 10,260,316
Capital: Niamey
Largest City: Niamey
Highest Point: Bagzane
Monetary Unit: CFA franc

Nigeria
Page/Location: 96/G6
Area: 356,668 sq. mi.
923,770 sq. km.
Population: 117,170,948
Capital: Abuja
Largest City: Lagos
Highest Point: Dimlang
Monetary Unit: naira

Norway
Page/Location: 42/C3
Area: 125,053 sq. mi.
323,887 sq. km.
Population: 4,455,707
Capital: Oslo
Largest City: Oslo
Highest Point: Glittertjnden
Monetary Unit: Norwegian kror e

Oman
Page/Location: 73/G4
Area: 82,031 sq. mi.
212,460 sq. km.
Population: 2,532,556
Capital: Muscat
Largest City: Muscat
Highest Point: Jabal ash Shām
Monetary Unit: Omani rial

Pakistan
Page/Location: 73/H3
Area: 310,403 sq. mi.
803,944 sq. km.
Population: 141,145,344
Capital: Islāmābād
Largest City: Karāchi
Highest Point: K2 (Godwin Austen)
Monetary Unit: Pakistani rupee

Palau
Page/Location: 92/C4
Area: 177 sq. mi.
458 sq. km.
Population: 18,827
Capital: Koror
Largest City: Koror
Highest Point: 699 ft. (213m)
Monetary Unit: U.S. dollar

Panama
Page/Location: 115/E6
Area: 30,193 sq. mi.
78,200 sq. km.
Population: 2,821,085
Capital: Panamá
Largest City: Panamá
Highest Point: Barú
Monetary Unit: balboa

World Flags and Reference Guide

Papua New Guinea
Page/Location: 92/D5
Area: 178,259 sq. mi.
461,690 sq. km.
Population: 4,811,939
Capital: Port Moresby
Largest City: Port Moresby
Highest Point: Mt. Wilhelm
Monetary Unit: kina

Paraguay
Page/Location: 107/D5
Area: 157,047 sq. mi.
406,752 sq. km.
Population: 5,579,503
Capital: Asunción
Largest City: Asunción
Highest Point: Sierra de Amambay
Monetary Unit: guaraní

Peru
Page/Location: 108/C5
Area: 496,222 sq. mi.
1,285,215 sq. km.
Population: 27,135,689
Capital: Lima
Largest City: Lima
Highest Point: Nevado Huascarán
Monetary Unit: nuevo sol

Philippines
Page/Location: 82/D5
Area: 115,830 sq. mi.
300,000 sq. km.
Population: 80,961,430
Capital: Manila
Largest City: Manila
Highest Point: Mt. Apo
Monetary Unit: Philippine peso

Poland
Page/Location: 49/K2
Area: 120,725 sq. mi.
312,678 sq. km.
Population: 38,644,184
Capital: Warsaw
Largest City: Warsaw
Highest Point: Rysy
Monetary Unit: zloty

Portugal
Page/Location: 58/A3
Area: 35,549 sq. mi.
92,072 sq. km.
Population: 9,902,147
Capital: Lisbon
Largest City: Lisbon
Highest Point: Serra da Estrela
Monetary Unit: Portuguese escudo

Qatar
Page/Location: 72/F3
Area: 4,247 sq. mi.
11,000 sq. km.
Population: 749,542
Capital: Doha
Largest City: Doha
Highest Point: Dukhān Heights
Monetary Unit: Qatari riyal

Romania
Page/Location: 63/F3
Area: 91,699 sq. mi.
237,500 sq. km.
Population: 22,291,200
Capital: Bucharest
Largest City: Bucharest
Highest Point: Moldoveanul
Monetary Unit: leu

Russia
Page/Location: 68/H3
Area: 6,592,812 sq. mi.
17,075,400 sq. km.
Population: 145,904,542
Capital: Moscow
Largest City: Moscow
Highest Point: El'brus
Monetary Unit: Russian ruble

Rwanda
Page/Location: 101/A3
Area: 10,169 sq. mi.
26,337 sq. km.
Population: 8,336,995
Capital: Kigali
Largest City: Kigali
Highest Point: Karisimbi
Monetary Unit: Rwanda franc

Saint Kitts and Nevis
Page/Location: 117/J4
Area: 104 sq. mi.
269 sq. km.
Population: 43,441
Capital: Basseterre
Largest City: Basseterre
Highest Point: Mt. Misery
Monetary Unit: East Caribbean dollar

Saint Lucia
Page/Location: 117/J5
Area: 238 sq. mi.
616 sq. km.
Population: 155,678
Capital: Castries
Largest City: Castries
Highest Point: Mt. Gimie
Monetary Unit: East Caribbean dollar

Saint Vincent and the Grenadines
Page/Location: 117/J5
Area: 131 sq. mi.
340 sq. km.
Population: 121,188
Capital: Kingstown
Largest City: Kingstown
Highest Point: Soufrière
Monetary Unit: East Caribbean dollar

Samoa
Page/Location: 93/H6
Area: 1,104 sq. mi.
2,860 sq. km.
Population: 235,302
Capital: Apia
Largest City: Apia
Highest Point: Mt. Silisili
Monetary Unit: tala

San Marino
Page/Location: 57/K5
Area: 23.4 sq. mi.
60.6 sq. km.
Population: 25,215
Capital: San Marino
Largest City: San Marino
Highest Point: Monte Titano
Monetary Unit: Italian lira

São Tomé and Príncipe
Page/Location: 96/F7
Area: 371 sq. mi.
960 sq. km.
Population: 159,832
Capital: São Tomé
Largest City: São Tomé
Highest Point: Pico de São Tomé
Monetary Unit: dobra

Saudi Arabia
Page/Location: 72/D4
Area: 756,981 sq. mi.
1,960,582 sq. km.
Population: 22,245,751
Capital: Riyadh
Largest City: Riyadh
Highest Point: Jabal Sawdā'
Monetary Unit: Saudi riyal

Senegal
Page/Location: 98/B3
Area: 75,954 sq. mi.
196,720 sq. km.
Population: 10,390,296
Capital: Dakar
Largest City: Dakar
Highest Point: Fouta Djallon
Monetary Unit: CFA franc

Seychelles
Page/Location: 39/M6
Area: 176 sq. mi.
455 sq. km.
Population: 79,672
Capital: Victoria
Largest City: Victoria
Highest Point: Morne Seychellois
Monetary Unit: Seychelles rupee

Sierra Leone
Page/Location: 98/B4
Area: 27,699 sq. mi.
71,740 sq. km.
Population: 5,509,263
Capital: Freetown
Largest City: Freetown
Highest Point: Loma Mansa
Monetary Unit: leone

Singapore
Page/Location: 86/B3
Area: 244 sq. mi.
632.6 sq. km.
Population: 3,571,710
Capital: Singapore
Largest City: Singapore
Highest Point: Bukit Timah
Monetary Unit: Singapore dollar

Slovakia
Page/Location: 49/K4
Area: 18,924 sq. mi.
49,013 sq. km.
Population: 5,401,134
Capital: Bratislava
Largest City: Bratislava
Highest Point: Gerlachovský Štít
Monetary Unit: Slovak koruna

Slovenia
Page/Location: 62/B3
Area: 7,898 sq. mi.
20,456 sq. km.
Population: 1,970,056
Capital: Ljubljana
Largest City: Ljubljana
Highest Point: Triglav
Monetary Unit: tolar

Solomon Islands
Page/Location: 92/E6
Area: 11,500 sq. mi.
29,785 sq. km.
Population: 470,000
Capital: Honiara
Largest City: Honiara
Highest Point: Mt. Makarakomburu
Monetary Unit: Solomon Islands dollar

Somalia
Page/Location: 97/Q6
Area: 246,200 sq. mi.
637,658 sq. km.
Population: 7,433,922
Capital: Mogadishu
Largest City: Mogadishu
Highest Point: Shimber Berris
Monetary Unit: Somali shilling

South Africa
Page/Location: 102/C3
Area: 471,008 sq. mi.
1,219,912 sq. km.
Population: 43,981,758
Capital: Cape Town; Pretoria
Largest City: Johannesburg
Highest Point: Injasuti
Monetary Unit: rand

Spain
Page/Location: 58/C2
Area: 194,881 sq. mi.
504,742 sq. km.
Population: 39,208,236
Capital: Madrid
Largest City: Madrid
Highest Point: Pico de Teide
Monetary Unit: peseta

Sri Lanka
Page/Location: 84/D6
Area: 25,332 sq. mi.
65,610 sq. km.
Population: 19,355,053
Capital: Colombo
Largest City: Colombo
Highest Point: Pidurutalagala
Monetary Unit: Sri Lanka rupee

Sudan
Page/Location: 97/L5
Area: 967,494 sq. mi.
2,505,809 sq. km.
Population: 35,530,371
Capital: Khartoum
Largest City: Omdurman
Highest Point: Jabal Marrah
Monetary Unit: Sudanese pound

Suriname
Page/Location: 109/G3
Area: 63,039 sq. mi.
163,270 sq. km.
Population: 434,093
Capital: Paramaribo
Largest City: Paramaribo
Highest Point: Juliana Top
Monetary Unit: Suriname guilder

Swaziland
Page/Location: 103/E2
Area: 6,705 sq. mi.
17,366 sq. km.
Population: 1,004,072
Capital: Mbabane; Lobamba
Largest City: Mbabane
Highest Point: Emlembe
Monetary Unit: lilangeni

Sweden
Page/Location: 42/E3
Area: 173,665 sq. mi.
449,792 sq. km.
Population: 8,938,559
Capital: Stockholm
Largest City: Stockholm
Highest Point: Kebnekaise
Monetary Unit: krona

Switzerland
Page/Location: 54/D4
Area: 15,943 sq. mi.
41,292 sq. km.
Population: 7,288,715
Capital: Bern
Largest City: Zürich
Highest Point: Dufourspitze
Monetary Unit: Swiss franc

Syria
Page/Location: 72/C1
Area: 71,498 sq. mi.
185,180 sq. km.
Population: 17,758,925
Capital: Damascus
Largest City: Damascus
Highest Point: Jabal ash Shaykh
Monetary Unit: Syrian pound

Taiwan
Page/Location: 82/D3
Area: 13,971 sq. mi.
36,185 sq. km.
Population: 22,319,222
Capital: T'aipei
Largest City: T'aipei
Highest Point: Yü Shan
Monetary Unit: new Taiwan dollar

Tajikistan
Page/Location: 68/H6
Area: 55,251 sq. mi.
143,100 sq. km.
Population: 6,194,373
Capital: Dushanbe
Largest City: Dushanbe
Highest Point: Communism Peak
Monetary Unit: Tajikistani ruble

Tanzania
Page/Location: 101/B4
Area: 364,699 sq. mi.
945,090 sq. km.
Population: 31,962,769
Capital: Dar es Salaam
Largest City: Dar es Salaam
Highest Point: Kilimanjaro
Monetary Unit: Tanzanian shilling

Thailand
Page/Location: 83/C3
Area: 198,455 sq. mi.
513,998 sq. km.
Population: 61,163,833
Capital: Bangkok
Largest City: Bangkok
Highest Point: Doi Inthanon
Monetary Unit: baht

Togo
Page/Location: 99/F4
Area: 21,927 sq. mi.
56,790 sq. km.
Population: 5,262,611
Capital: Lomé
Largest City: Lomé
Highest Point: Mt. Agou
Monetary Unit: CFA franc

Tonga
Page/Location: 93/H7
Area: 289 sq. mi.
748 sq. km.
Population: 109,959
Capital: Nuku'alofa
Largest City: Nuku'alofa
Highest Point: Kao Island
Monetary Unit: pa'anga

Trinidad and Tobago
Page/Location: 117/J5
Area: 1,980 sq. mi.
5,128 sq. km.
Population: 1,086,908
Capital: Port-of-Spain
Largest City: Port-of-Spain
Highest Point: El Cerro del Aripo
Monetary Unit: Trin. & Tobago dollar

Tunisia
Page/Location: 96/G1
Area: 63,170 sq. mi.
163,610 sq. km.
Population: 9,645,499
Capital: Tūnis
Largest City: Tūnis
Highest Point: Jabal ash Sha'nabī
Monetary Unit: Tunisian dinar

Turkey
Page/Location: 74/C2
Area: 301,382 sq. mi.
780,580 sq. km.
Population: 66,620,120
Capital: Ankara
Largest City: Istanbul
Highest Point: Mt. Ararat
Monetary Unit: Turkish lira

Turkmenistan
Page/Location: 68/F6
Area: 188,455 sq. mi.
488,100 sq. km.
Population: 4,435,507
Capital: Ashgabat
Largest City: Ashgabat
Highest Point: Rize
Monetary Unit: manat

Tuvalu
Page/Location: 92/G5
Area: 9.78 sq. mi.
25.33 sq. km.
Population: 10,730
Capital: Funafuti
Largest City: —
Highest Point: 16 ft. (5 m)
Monetary Unit: Australian dollar

Uganda
Page/Location: 101/B2
Area: 91,076 sq. mi.
235,887 sq. km.
Population: 23,451,687
Capital: Kampala
Largest City: Kampala
Highest Point: Margherita Peak
Monetary Unit: Ugandan shilling

Ukraine
Page/Location: 66/D2
Area: 233,089 sq. mi.
603,700 sq. km.
Population: 49,506,779
Capital: Kiev
Largest City: Kiev
Highest Point: Goverla
Monetary Unit: hryvnia

United Arab Emirates
Page/Location: 72/F4
Area: 29,182 sq. mi.
75,581 sq. km.
Population: 2,386,472
Capital: Abu Dhabi
Largest City: Dubayy
Highest Point: Hajar Mts.
Monetary Unit: Emirian dirham

United Kingdom
Page/Location: 43
Area: 94,399 sq. mi.
244,493 sq. km.
Population: 59,247,439
Capital: London
Largest City: London
Highest Point: Ben Nevis
Monetary Unit: pound sterling

United States
Page/Location: 120
Area: 3,618,765 sq. mi.
9,372,610 sq. km.
Population: 274,943,496
Capital: Washington, D.C.
Largest City: New York
Highest Point: Mt. McKinley
Monetary Unit: U.S. dollar

Uruguay
Page/Location: 111/E3
Area: 68,039 sq. mi.
176,220 sq. km.
Population: 3,332,782
Capital: Montevideo
Largest City: Montevideo
Highest Point: Cerro Catedral
Monetary Unit: Uruguayan peso

Uzbekistan
Page/Location: 68/G5
Area: 172,741 sq. mi.
447,400 sq. km.
Population: 24,422,518
Capital: Tashkent
Largest City: Tashkent
Highest Point: Khodzha-Pir'yakh
Monetary Unit: som

Vanuatu
Page/Location: 92/F6
Area: 5,700 sq. mi.
14,763 sq. km.
Population: 192,848
Capital: Port-Vila
Largest City: Port-Vila
Highest Point: Tabwemasana
Monetary Unit: vatu

Vatican City
Page/Location: 60/C2
Area: 0.17 sq. mi.
0.44 sq. km.
Population: 870
Capital: —
Largest City: —
Highest Point: —
Monetary Unit: Vatican lira

Venezuela
Page/Location: 108/E2
Area: 352,143 sq. mi.
912,050 sq. km.
Population: 23,595,822
Capital: Caracas
Largest City: Caracas
Highest Point: Pico Bolívar
Monetary Unit: bolívar

Vietnam
Page/Location: 83/D2
Area: 127,243 sq. mi.
329,560 sq. km.
Population: 78,349,503
Capital: Hanoi
Largest City: Ho Chi Minh City
Highest Point: Fan Si Pan
Monetary Unit: new dong

Yemen
Page/Location: 72/E5
Area: 203,849 sq. mi.
527,970 sq. km.
Population: 17,521,085
Capital: Sanaa
Largest City: Aden
Highest Point: Nabī Shu'ayb
Monetary Unit: Yemeni rial

Yugoslavia
Page/Location: 62/E3
Area: 39,517 sq. mi.
102,350 sq. km.
Population: 11,210,243
Capital: Belgrade
Largest City: Belgrade
Highest Point: Daravica
Monetary Unit: Yugoslav new dinar

Zambia
Page/Location: 104/E3
Area: 290,586 sq. mi.
752,618 sq. km.
Population: 9,872,007
Capital: Lusaka
Largest City: Lusaka
Highest Point: Sunzu
Monetary Unit: Zambian kwacha

Zimbabwe
Page/Location: 104/E4
Area: 150,803 sq. mi.
390,580 sq. km.
Population: 11,272,013
Capital: Harare
Largest City: Harare
Highest Point: Inyangani
Monetary Unit: Zimbabwe dollar

The Solar System

Pluto

Neptune

Uranus

Mars

Jupiter

Sun

Mercury

Venus

Mercury

Mean Distance from Sun:
35,990,000 miles
Period of Revolution
around Sun: 87.97 days
Period of Rotation
on Axis: 59 days
Equatorial Diameter:
3,032 miles
Surface Gravity
(Earth=1): 0.38
Mass (Earth =1): 0.055
Mean Density:
(Water=1): 5.5
Satellites: 0

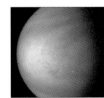

Venus

Mean Distance from Sun:
67,240,000 miles
Period of Revolution
around Sun: 224.70 days
Period of Rotation
on Axis: 243 days†
Equatorial Diameter:
7,523 miles
Surface Gravity
(Earth=1): 0.90
Mass (Earth =1): 0.815
Mean Density:
(Water=1): 5.25
Satellites: 0
† retrograde motion

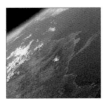

Earth

Mean Distance from Sun:
93,000,000 miles
Period of Revolution
around Sun: 365.26 days
Period of Rotation
on Axis: 23h 56m
Equatorial Diameter:
7,926 miles
Surface Gravity
(Earth=1): 1.00
Mass (Earth =1): 1.00
Mean Density:
(Water=1): 5.5
Satellites: 1

Mars

Mean Distance from Sun:
141,730,000 miles
Period of Revolution
around Sun: 687.00 days
Period of Rotation
on Axis: 24h 37m
Equatorial Diameter:
4,220 miles
Surface Gravity
(Earth=1): 0.38
Mass (Earth =1): 0.107
Mean Density:
(Water=1) 4.0
Satellites: 2

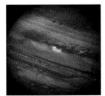

Jupiter

Mean Distance from Sun:
483,880,000 miles
Period of Revolution
around Sun: 11.86 years
Period of Rotation
on Axis: 9h 50m
Equatorial Diameter:
88,750 miles
Surface Gravity
(Earth=1): 2.87
Mass (Earth =1): 317.9
Mean Density:
(Water=1): 1.3
Satellites: 16

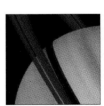

Saturn

Mean Distance from Sun:
887,130,000 miles
Period of Revolution
around Sun: 29.46 years
Period of Rotation
on Axis: 10h 39m
Equatorial Diameter:
74,580 miles
Surface Gravity
(Earth=1): 1.32
Mass (Earth =1): 95.2
Mean Density:
(Water=1): 0.7
Satellites: 23

Saturn

Moon

Earth

The solar system is comprised of a star, the Sun, and other matter such as planets, satellites, asteroids, comets, meteoroids, dust and gases. The Sun is the center of this system; its mass is more than 99 percent of the entire system.

Nine planets make up the next largest objects. The innermost ones, Mercury, Venus, Earth and Mars, are called terrestrial planets — they are primarily iron and rock in composition. The outer planets, Jupiter, Saturn, Uranus and Neptune have large components of hydrogen, helium, ammonia and methane gases and little iron and rock. Less is known about Pluto and it is not included in either grouping. All planets travel around the sun in elliptical orbits. Seven planets have natural satellites (moons) orbiting them.

Scattered in a belt between the orbits of Mars and Jupiter are many thousands of smaller planet-like bodies called asteroids. Ceres, the largest, has a diameter of 620 miles; a few others have diameters of more than 100 miles. Most asteroids are less than one mile wide.

Comets are made up of dust particles and frozen gases. Most move around the Sun in highly angular, elliptical orbits. Those that travel near to the Sun provide rare and spectacular sights with their distinct comas (heads) and long tails.

When asteroids collide or comets disintegrate into fragments, some resultant chunks of iron and rock may stray into eccentric orbits. These chunks are called meteoroids. If they enter the Earth's atmosphere they are termed meteors and are known as meteorites if they reach the Earth's surface.

THE SUN

Core: Source of the Sun's heat and light– generated by thermonuclear reactions.

Radiation Zone: Pass-through area which allows core energy to flow (radiate) toward the Sun's surface.

Energy Convection Zone: Region of extreme turbulence and shock waves which propel energy into the Sun's atmosphere.

Photosphere: The solar surface of stormy activity–the lowest part of the sun's atmosphere.

Chromosphere: The middle atmosphere of the Sun containing streams of flowing gases.

Corona: The Sun's upper atmosphere of expanding gases (solar wind) that whirl constantly away from the Sun.

Granules: Small patches of gas believed to be caused by waves in the photosphere.

Sunspots: Gases in a strong magnetic field that, due to lower temperatures, make them appear dark against the bright photosphere.

Solar Flares: short-lived radiation and particle emissions which are ejected from the Sun and shot into space.

Prominences: Bright arches of gas, thousands of miles long, that last from several hours to a few months in duration.

Uranus

Mean Distance from Sun:
1,783,700,000 miles
Period of Revolution
around Sun: 84.01 years
Period of Rotation
on Axis: 17h 24m†
Equatorial Diameter:
31,600 miles
Surface Gravity
(Earth = 1): 0.93
Mass (Earth = 1): 14.6
Mean Density:
(Water = 1): 1.3
Satellites: 15
† retrograde motion

Neptune

Mean Distance from Sun:
2,795,500,000 miles
Period of Revolution
around Sun: 164.79 years
Period of Rotation
on Axis: 17h 50m
Equatorial Diameter:
30,200 miles
Surface Gravity
(Earth = 1): 1.23
Mass (Earth = 1): 17.2
Mean Density:
(Water = 1): 1.8
Satellites: 8

Pluto

Mean Distance from Sun:
3,667,900,000 miles
Period of Revolution
around Sun: 247.70 years
Period of Rotation
on Axis: 6.39 days (?)
Equatorial Diameter:
1,500 miles
Surface Gravity
(Earth = 1): 0.03(?)
Mass (Earth = 1): 0.01(?)
Mean Density:
(Water = 1): 0.7(?)
Satellites: 1

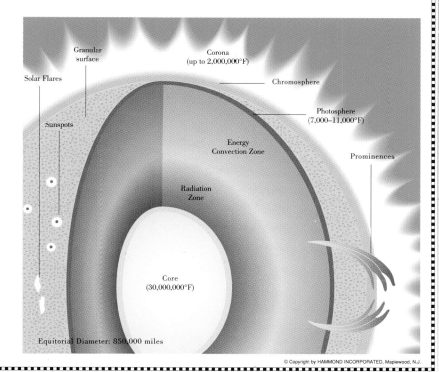

Granular surface

Corona (up to 2,000,000°F)

Solar Flares

Chromosphere

Sunspots

Photosphere (7,000–11,000°F)

Energy Convection Zone

Prominences

Radiation Zone

Core (30,000,000°F)

Equatorial Diameter: 850,000 miles

Structure of the

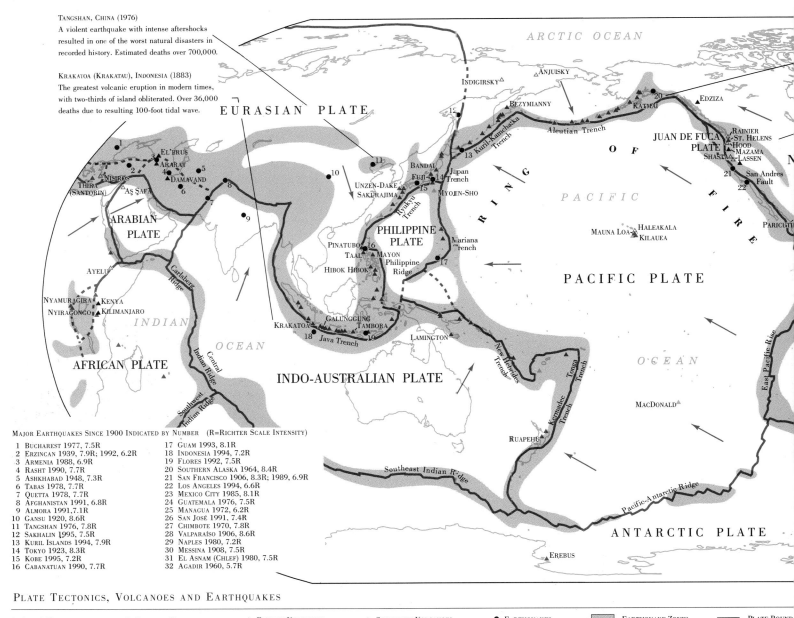

TANGSHAN, CHINA (1976)
A violent earthquake with intense aftershocks resulted in one of the worst natural disasters in recorded history. Estimated deaths over 700,000.

KRAKATOA (KRAKATAU), INDONESIA (1883)
The greatest volcanic eruption in modern times, with two-thirds of island obliterated. Over 36,000 deaths due to resulting 100-foot tidal wave.

EURASIAN PLATE

ARCTIC OCEAN

ANJUISKY
INDIGIRSKY
BEZYMIANNY
Aleutian Trench
KATMAI
EDZIZA

JUAN DE FUCA PLATE
RAINIER
ST. HELENS
HOOD
MAZAMA
SHASTA
LASSEN
San Andres Fault

O F

RING

PACIFIC

MAUNA LOA   HALEAKALA
KILAUEA

PACIFIC PLATE

F I R E

PARICUTI

Kuril Kamchatka Trench
Kuril Trench
BANDAI
FUJI   Japan Trench
UNZEN-DAKE
SAKURAJIMA
MYOJIN-SHO
Kyukyu Trench

PHILIPPINE PLATE
PINATUBO
TAAL   MAYON
HIBOK HIBOK   Philippine Ridge

Mariana Trench

EL'BRUS
ARARAT
DAMAVAND
NISIROS
THIRA (SANTORIN)
AS SAFA

ARABIAN PLATE

AYELU

NYAMURAGIRA   KENYA
NYIRAGONGO   KILIMANJARO

Carlsberg Ridge

INDIAN

OCEAN

AFRICAN PLATE

Central Indian Ridge

Southwest Indian Ridge

KRAKATOA
Java Trench
GALUNGGUNG
TAMBORA
LAMINGTON

INDO-AUSTRALIAN PLATE

New Hebrides Trench
Tonga Trench
Kermadec Trench

RUAPEHU

Southeast Indian Ridge

Pacific-Antarctic Ridge

MacDONALD

OCEAN

East Pacific Rise

ANTARCTIC PLATE

EREBUS

MAJOR EARTHQUAKES SINCE 1900 INDICATED BY NUMBER (R=RICHTER SCALE INTENSITY)

1 BUCHAREST 1977, 7.5R
2 ERZINCAN 1939, 7.9R; 1992, 6.2R
3 ARMENIA 1988, 6.9R
4 RASHT 1990, 7.7R
5 ASHKHABAD 1948, 7.3R
6 TABAS 1978, 7.7R
7 QUETTA 1978, 7.7R
8 AFGHANISTAN 1991, 6.8R
9 ALMORA 1991, 7.1R
10 GANSU 1920, 8.6R
11 TANGSHAN 1976, 7.8R
12 SAKHALIN 1995, 7.5R
13 KURIL ISLANDS 1994, 7.9R
14 TOKYO 1923, 8.3R
15 KOBE 1995, 7.2R
16 CABANATUAN 1990, 7.7R
17 GUAM 1993, 8.1R
18 INDONESIA 1994, 7.2R
19 FLORES 1992, 7.5R
20 SOUTHERN ALASKA 1964, 8.4R
21 SAN FRANCISCO 1906, 8.3R; 1989, 6.9R
22 LOS ANGELES 1994, 6.6R
23 MEXICO CITY 1985, 8.1R
24 GUATEMALA 1976, 7.5R
25 MANAGUA 1972, 6.2R
26 SAN JOSÉ 1991, 7.4R
27 CHIMBOTE 1970, 7.8R
28 VALPARAÍSO 1906, 8.6R
29 NAPLES 1980, 7.2R
30 MESSINA 1908, 7.5R
31 EL ASNAM (CHLEF) 1980, 7.5R
32 AGADIR 1960, 5.7R

PLATE TECTONICS, VOLCANOES AND EARTHQUAKES

▲ ACTIVE VOLCANOES   △ DORMANT VOLCANOES   ▲ EXTINCT VOLCANOES   ▲ SUBMARINE VOLCANOES   ● EARTHQUAKES   ▨ EARTHQUAKE ZONES   ▬ PLATE BOUND

The making of continents began more than 200 million years ago with the splitting of a gigantic landmass known as Pangaea. Two super continents, Laurasia and Gondwana, were formed by the initial division. Over a period of many millions of years these landmasses further subdivided into smaller parts and drifted across a single great ocean, forming the oceans and continents of today. In terms of current theory, called plate tectonics, the earth's crust is divided into at least 15 rigid rock segments, known as plates, that float on a semi-molten layer of upper mantle. Seven plates are of major size and, except for the vast Pacific

CONTINENTAL DRIFT

180 MILLION YEARS AGO

70 MILLION YEARS AGO

PRESENT TIME

Earth

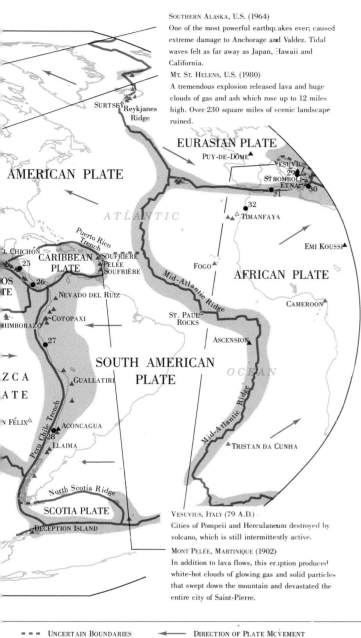

SOUTHERN ALASKA, U.S. (1964)
One of the most powerful earthquakes ever; caused extreme damage to Anchorage and Valdez. Tidal waves felt as far away as Japan, Hawaii and California.

MT. ST. HELENS, U.S. (1980)
A tremendous explosion released lava and huge clouds of gas and ash which rose up to 12 miles high. Over 230 square miles of scenic landscape ruined.

VESUVIUS, ITALY (79 A.D.)
Cities of Pompeii and Herculaneum destroyed by volcano, which is still intermittently active.

MONT PELÉE, MARTINIQUE (1902)
In addition to lava flows, this eruption produced white-hot clouds of glowing gas and solid particles that swept down the mountain and devastated the entire city of Saint-Pierre.

- - - UNCERTAIN BOUNDARIES　　←—— DIRECTION OF PLATE MOVEMENT

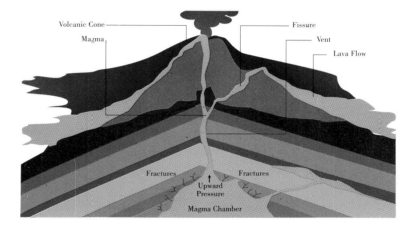

INTERIOR AND CRUST OF THE EARTH

Mantle
1800 miles thick
solid, mostly iron and
magnesium silicates

Outer Core
1350 miles thick
liquid, iron
and nickel

Inner Core
800 mile radius
solid, iron
and nickel

Continental Crust
25 miles thick
solid, mostly coarse
crystalline rock

Oceanic Crust
4 miles thick
solid, mostly fine
crystalline rock

By studying records of earthquakes, scientists have developed a fairly reasonable picture (cross section) of the earth's principal layers, including their composition. The inner core is a very dense, highly-pressurized, extremely hot (about 9,000° F.) sphere. Moving outward toward the crust, densities, pressures and temperatures decrease significantly.

Volcanic Cone　　Magma　　Fissure　　Vent　　Lava Flow

Fractures　　Fractures　　Upward Pressure　　Magma Chamber

VOLCANOES

One of the earth's most dynamic and colorful builders is the volcano. In the mantle, magma—molten rock containing compressed gases—probes for weak spots in the earth's crust and bursts forth through the ground in an eruption of fiery lava, ash, gas and steam. After a period of eruption, lasting from a few days to many years, the magma ceases to push upward and the volcano becomes dormant.

Plate, carry a continental landmass with surrounding ocean floor and island areas. The plates are slow-moving, driven by powerful forces within the mantle. At their boundaries they are either slowly separating with new material added from the mantle, converging, with one plate being forced down (subducted) and consumed under another, or sliding past each other. Almost all earthquake, volcanic and mountain-building activity closely follows these boundaries and is related to movements between them. Although these movements may be no more than inches per year, the destructive power unleashed can be cataclysmic.

PLATE TECTONICS

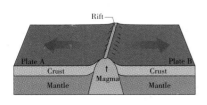

SEPARATING PLATES

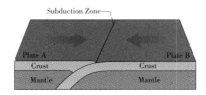

CONVERGING PLATES

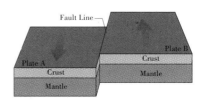

SLIDING PLATES

Environmental Concerns

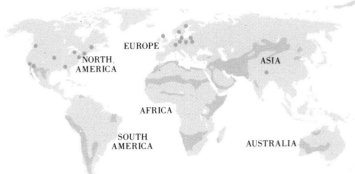

DESERTIFICATION AND ACID RAIN DAMAGE

AREAS OF PRODUCTIVE DRYLANDS
DESERTIFIED BY EARLY 1980'S

AREAS OF DAMAGE FROM ACID RAIN
AND OTHER AIRBORNE POLLUTANTS

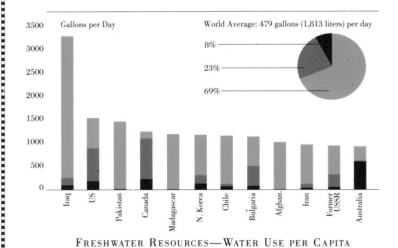

World Average: 479 gallons (1,813 liters) per day

8%
23%
69%

FRESHWATER RESOURCES—WATER USE PER CAPITA

DOMESTIC   INDUSTRY   AGRICULTURE

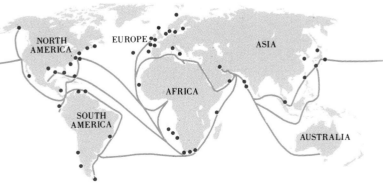

MAIN TANKER ROUTES AND MAJOR OIL SPILLS

ROUTES OF VERY LARGE CRUDE OIL CARRIERS   ● MAJOR OIL SPILLS

GRIZZLY BEAR
Much of Pacific temperate rain forest has been clear-cut. Remainder could be gone in 35 years.

WOODLAND CARIBOU

HUMPBACK WHALE

Hydroelectric power projects and development in Quebec are disrupting wildlife habitats.

Commercial fishing harvest in the northwest Atlantic has declined over 30 percent since 1970.

SPOTTED OWL

BLACK-FOOTED FERRET

BALD EAGLE

Fragile barrier beaches of the Atlantic coast have been damaged by agricultural runoff, sewage and overdevelopment.

CONDOR

WHOOPING CRANE

ATLANTIC RIDLEY TURTLE

MANATEE

Ecological balance in coral reefs of the Gulf and Caribbean area is being upset by a booming tourist industry.

At the present rate of clearing, half of Central America's rain forest will disappear by the year 2000.

One-third of Guinea's tropical forest is expected to disappear in the next decade.

HOWLER MONKEY

Erosion. the depletion of water resources for irrigation, and overgrazing have turned range and cropland into desert.

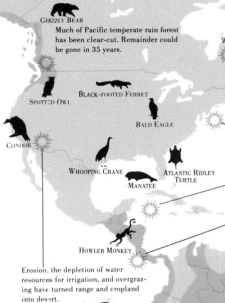

GALÁPAGOS TORTOISE

BLACK CAIMAN

JAGUAR

VICUNA

GOLDEN LION TAMARIN

CHINCHILLA

Every year over 5000 square miles (13,000 sq km) of rain forest is destroyed in Brazil's Amazon Basin.

GIANT ARMADILLO

Southern Chile's rain forest is threatened by development.

The Atlantic waters off Patagonia have suffered from over-fishing and oil spills.

BLUE WHALE

Acid Rain

Acid rain of nitric and sulfuric acids has killed all life in thousands of lakes, and over 15 million acres (6 million hectares) of virgin forest in Europe and North America are dead or dying.

Deforestation

Each year, 50 million acres (20 million hectares) of tropical rainforests are being felled by loggers. Trees remove carbon-dioxide from the atmosphere and are vital to the prevention of soil erosion.

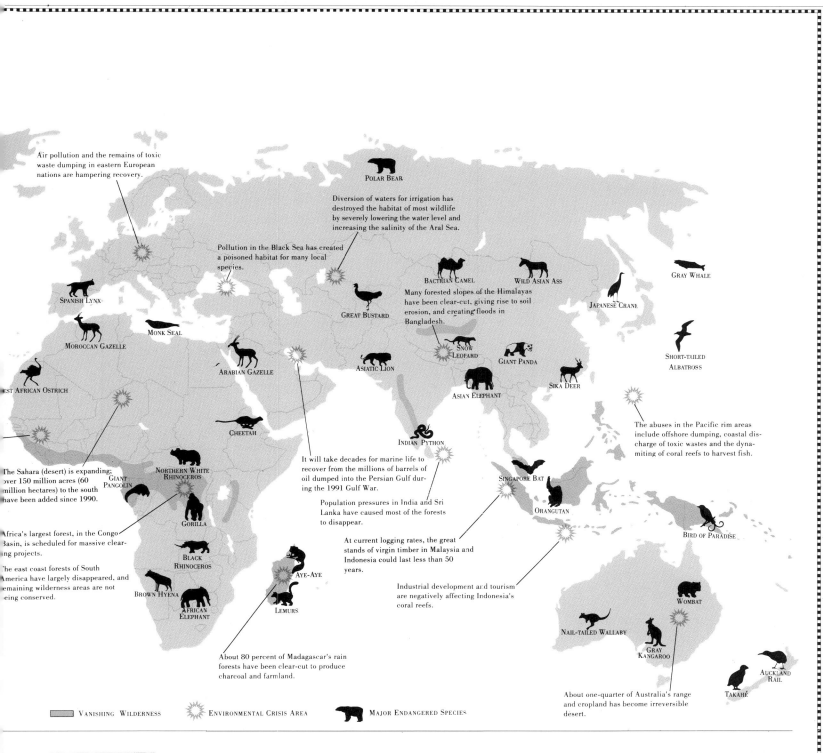

Air pollution and the remains of toxic waste dumping in eastern European nations are hampering recovery.

Diversion of waters for irrigation has destroyed the habitat of most wildlife by severely lowering the water level and increasing the salinity of the Aral Sea.

Pollution in the Black Sea has created a poisoned habitat for many local species.

Many forested slopes of the Himalayas have been clear-cut, giving rise to soil erosion, and creating floods in Bangladesh.

POLAR BEAR

BACTRIAN CAMEL   WILD ASIAN ASS

GRAY WHALE

SPANISH LYNX

GREAT BUSTARD

JAPANESE CRANE

MOROCCAN GAZELLE

MONK SEAL

SHORT-TAILED ALBATROSS

ARABIAN GAZELLE

ASIATIC LION

SNOW LEOPARD

GIANT PANDA

SIKA DEER

EST AFRICAN OSTRICH

ASIAN ELEPHANT

CHEETAH

INDIAN PYTHON

The abuses in the Pacific rim areas include offshore dumping, coastal discharge of toxic wastes and the dynamiting of coral reefs to harvest fish.

The Sahara (desert) is expanding; over 150 million acres (60 million hectares) to the south have been added since 1990.

GIANT PANGOLIN

NORTHERN WHITE RHINOCEROS

It will take decades for marine life to recover from the millions of barrels of oil dumped into the Persian Gulf during the 1991 Gulf War.

SINGAPORE BAT

ORANGUTAN

Africa's largest forest, in the Congo Basin, is scheduled for massive clearing projects.

GORILLA

Population pressures in India and Sri Lanka have caused most of the forests to disappear.

BIRD OF PARADISE

The east coast forests of South America have largely disappeared, and remaining wilderness areas are not being conserved.

BLACK RHINOCEROS

At current logging rates, the great stands of virgin timber in Malaysia and Indonesia could last less than 50 years.

WOMBAT

AYE-AYE

BROWN HYENA

AFRICAN ELEPHANT

LEMURS

Industrial development and tourism are negatively affecting Indonesia's coral reefs.

NAIL-TAILED WALLABY

GRAY KANGAROO

AUCKLAND RAIL

About 80 percent of Madagascar's rain forests have been clear-cut to produce charcoal and farmland.

TAKAHÉ

About one-quarter of Australia's range and cropland has become irreversible desert.

◻ VANISHING WILDERNESS   ✺ ENVIRONMENTAL CRISIS AREA   🐻 MAJOR ENDANGERED SPECIES

Extinction

Biologists estimate that over 50,000 plant and animal species inhabiting the world's rain forests are disappearing each year due to pollution, unchecked hunting and the destruction of natural habitats.

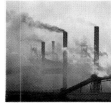

Air Pollution

Billions of tons of industrial emissions and toxic pollutants are released into the air each year, depleting our ozone layer, killing our forests and lakes with acid rain and threatening our health.

Water Pollution

Only 3 percent of the earth's water is fresh. Pollution from cities, farms and factories has made much of it unfit to drink. In the developing world, most sewage flows untreated into lakes and rivers.

Ozone Depletion

The layer of ozone in the stratosphere shields earth from harmful ultraviolet radiation. But man-made gases are destroying this vital barrier, increasing the risk of skin cancer and eye disease.

Population

WORLD'S LARGEST URBAN AREAS

MILLIONS OF INHABITANTS

TOKYO, Japan 26.5

NEW YORK, U.S. 18.0

SÃO PAULO, Brazil 16.9

OSAKA, Japan 16.9

SEOUL, Korea, 15.8

MEXICO, Mexico 15.5

SHANGHAI, China 14.7

MUMBAI, India 14.5

LOS ANGELES, U.S. 14.5

MOSCOW, Russia 13.1

BEIJING, China 12.0

CALCUTTA, India 11.4

LONDON, U.K. 11.1

RIO DE JANEIRO, Brazil 11.0

JAKARTA, Indonesia 11.0

URBAN & RURAL POPULATION COMPONENTS

SELECTED COUNTRIES

■ URBAN   ■ RURAL

Uruguay 87% / 13%

Australia 85% / 15%

Japan 77% / 23%

United States 74% / 26%

Russia 73% / 27%

Hungary 62% / 38%

Iran 54% / 46%

Egypt 44% / 56%

Philippines 37% / 63%

Portugal 30% / 70%

China 26% / 74%

Maldives 20% / 80%

Bangladesh 15% / 85%

Nepal 6% / 94%

AGE DISTRIBUTION

UNITED STATES

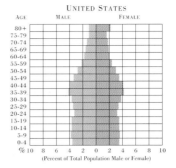

(Percent of Total Population Male or Female)

SWITZERLAND

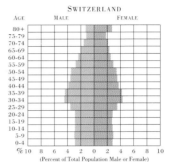

(Percent of Total Population Male or Female)

ANGOLA

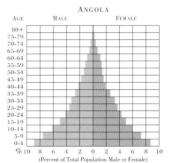

(Percent of Total Population Male or Female)

Source: U.S. Bureau of the Census, International Database

POPULATION DENSITY PER SQUARE MILE (SQ. KM.)

1,000 - 5,000 (390 - 2,000)	500 - 1,000 (195 - 390)	100 - 500 (39 - 195)	30 - 100 (12 - 39)	UNDER 30 (UNDER 12)

Source: U.S. Bureau of the Census, International Database

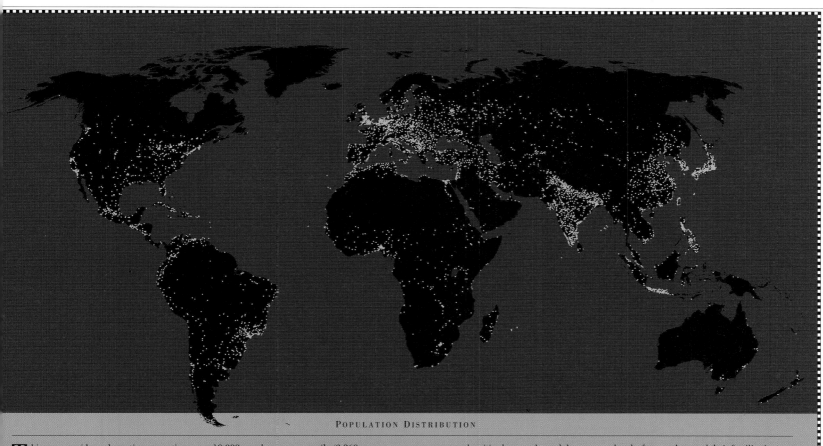

POPULATION DISTRIBUTION

This map provides a dramatic perspective by illuminating populated areas with one point of light for each city over 50,000 residents. Over 675 million people live in cities with populations in excess of 500,000. According to the latest census data, there are 10,000 people per square mile (3,860 per sq km) in London. In New York, there are 11,000 (4,250). Hong Kong has over 16,000 people per square mile (6,200 per sq km), and the Tokyo-Yokohama agglomeration includes over 25,000 (9,650). During the last decade, the movement to the cities has accelerated dramatically, particulary in developing nations. In Lagos, Nigeria, where there are over 24,000 people per square mile (9,290 per sq km), most live in shantytowns. In São Paulo, Brazil, 2,000 buses arrive each day, bringing field hands, farm workers and their families in search of a better life. Tokyo, Mexico and Mumbai are the world's largest urban agglomerations. According to the United Nations, 15 of the 20 largest urban agglomerations are located in less-industrialized nations.

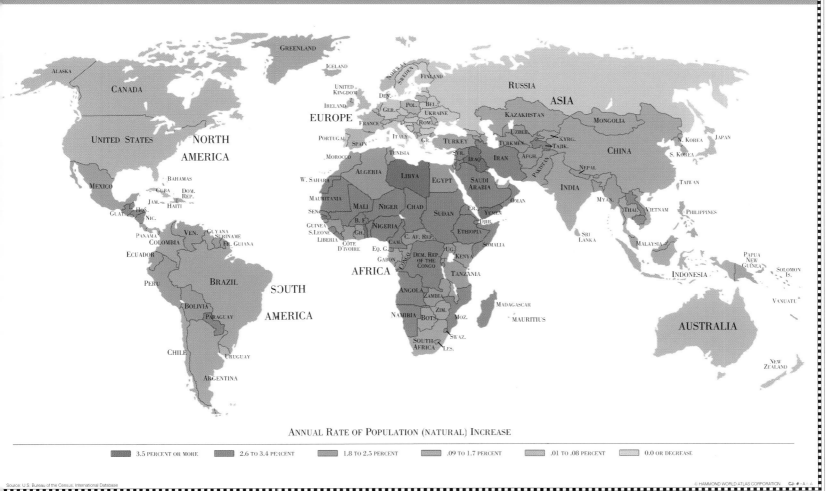

ANNUAL RATE OF POPULATION (NATURAL) INCREASE

| 3.5 PERCENT OR MORE | 2.6 TO 3.4 PERCENT | 1.8 TO 2.5 PERCENT | .09 TO 1.7 PERCENT | .01 TO .08 PERCENT | 0.0 OR DECREASE |

Languages
& Religions

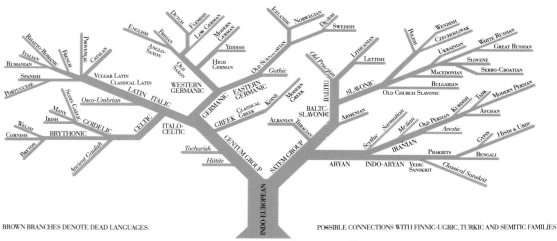

BROWN BRANCHES DENOTE DEAD LANGUAGES.

POSSIBLE CONNECTIONS WITH FINNIC-UGRIC, TURKIC AND SEMITIC FAMILIES

THE INDO-EUROPEAN LANGUAGE TREE

The most well-established family tree is Indo-European. Spoken by more than 2.5 billion people, it contains dozens of languages. Some linguists theorize that all people - and all languages - are descended from a tiny population that lived in Africa some 200,000 years ago.

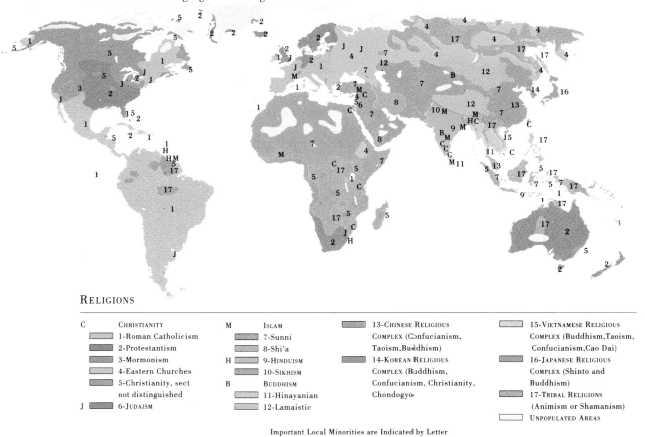

RELIGIONS

C	CHRISTIANITY	M	ISLAM		13-CHINESE RELIGIOUS COMPLEX (Confucianism, Taoism, Buddhism)
	1-Roman Catholicism		7-Sunni		
	2-Protestantism		8-Shi'a		
	3-Mormonism	H	9-HINDUISM		14-KOREAN RELIGIOUS COMPLEX (Buddhism, Confucianism, Christianity, Chondogyo
	4-Eastern Churches		10-SIKHISM		
	5-Christianity, sect not distinguished	B	BUDDHISM		
J	6-JUDAISM		11-Hinayanian		
			12-Lamaistic		

15-VIETNAMESE RELIGIOUS COMPLEX (Buddhism,Taoism, Confucianism,Cao Dai)	
16-JAPANESE RELIGIOUS COMPLEX (Shinto and Buddhism)	
17-TRIBAL RELIGIONS (Animism or Shamanism)	
UNPOPULATED AREAS	

Important Local Minorities are Indicated by Letter

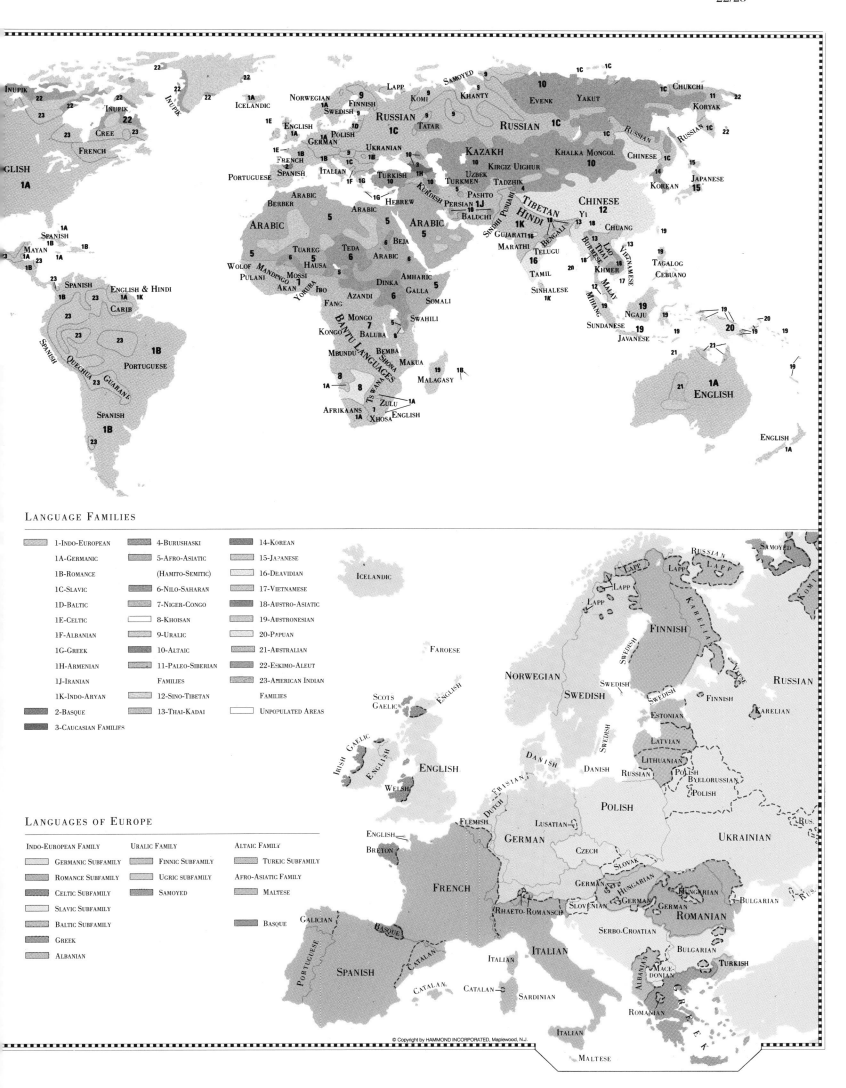

Standards of Living

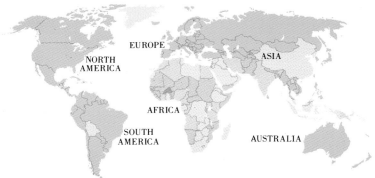

LITERATE PERCENT OF POPULATION

80 AND ABOVE	40-59	0-19
60-79	20-39	

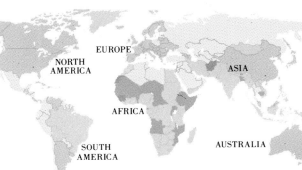

YEARS OF LIFE EXPECTANCY (MEN AND WOMEN)

70 AND ABOVE	50-59	0-39
60-69	40-49	

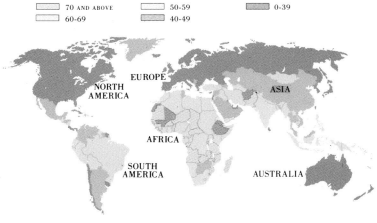

INFANT DEATHS PER 1,000 LIVE BIRTHS

150 AND MORE	50-99	0-24
100-149	25-49	

UNITED STATES
The economic and political influence of women has risen substantially. In a number of fields, women's salaries are now nearly equal to men's.

SOUTH AMERICA
Political unrest, rising inflation and slow economic growth continue to thwart efforts to bring unity and prosperity to the nations of South America.

LATIN AMERICA
The gulf between rich and poor continues to widen, despite efforts to reform oppressive governments, increase literacy and relieve overburdened cities.

COMPARISON OF EUROPEAN, U.S. AND JAPANESE WORKERS

COUNTRY	SCHEDULED WEEKLY HOURS	ANNUAL LEAVE DAYS/HOLIDAYS	ANNUAL HOURS WORKED
GERMANY	39	42	1708
NETHERLANDS	40	43.5	1740
BELGIUM	38	31	1748
AUSTRIA	39.3	38	1751
FRANCE	39	34	1771
ITALY	40	39	1776
UNITED KINGDOM	39	33	1778
LUXEMBOURG	40	37	1792
FINLAND	40	37	1792
SWEDEN	40	37	1792
SPAIN	40	36	1800
DENMARK	40	34	1816
NORWAY	40	30	1848
GREECE	40	28	1864
IRELAND	40	28	1864
UNITED STATES	40	22	1912
SWITZERLAND	41.5	30.5	1913
PORTUGAL	45	36	2025
JAPAN	44	23.5	2116

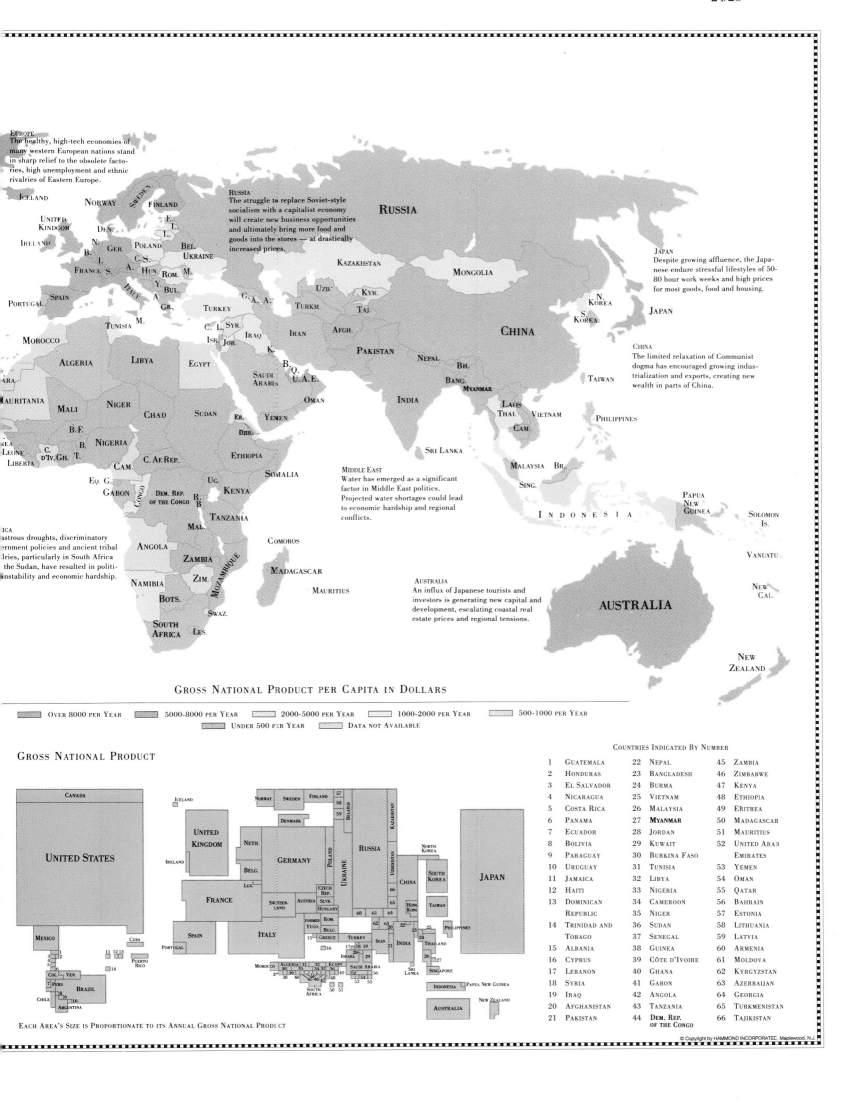

EUROPE
The healthy, high-tech economies of many western European nations stand in sharp relief to the obsolete factories, high unemployment and ethnic rivalries of Eastern Europe.

RUSSIA
The struggle to replace Soviet-style socialism with a capitalist economy will create new business opportunities and ultimately bring more food and goods into the stores — at drastically increased prices.

JAPAN
Despite growing affluence, the Japanese endure stressful lifestyles of 50-80 hour work weeks and high prices for most goods, food and housing.

CHINA
The limited relaxation of Communist dogma has encouraged growing industrialization and exports, creating new wealth in parts of China.

MIDDLE EAST
Water has emerged as a significant factor in Middle East politics. Projected water shortages could lead to economic hardship and regional conflicts.

AUSTRALIA
An influx of Japanese tourists and investors is generating new capital and development, escalating coastal real estate prices and regional tensions.

...ICA
...astrous droughts, discriminatory ...ernment policies and ancient tribal ...lries, particularly in South Africa ...the Sudan, have resulted in politi-...instability and economic hardship.

GROSS NATIONAL PRODUCT PER CAPITA IN DOLLARS

- OVER 8000 PER YEAR
- 5000-8000 PER YEAR
- 2000-5000 PER YEAR
- 1000-2000 PER YEAR
- 500-1000 PER YEAR
- UNDER 500 PER YEAR
- DATA NOT AVAILABLE

GROSS NATIONAL PRODUCT

EACH AREA'S SIZE IS PROPORTIONATE TO ITS ANNUAL GROSS NATIONAL PRODUCT

COUNTRIES INDICATED BY NUMBER

1	GUATEMALA	22	NEPAL	45	ZAMBIA		
2	HONDURAS	23	BANGLADESH	46	ZIMBABWE		
3	EL SALVADOR	24	BURMA	47	KENYA		
4	NICARAGUA	25	VIETNAM	48	ETHIOPIA		
5	COSTA RICA	26	MALAYSIA	49	ERITREA		
6	PANAMA	27	**MYANMAR**	50	MADAGASCAR		
7	ECUADOR	28	JORDAN	51	MAURITIUS		
8	BOLIVIA	29	KUWAIT	52	UNITED ARAB		
9	PARAGUAY	30	BURKINA FASO		EMIRATES		
10	URUGUAY	31	TUNISIA	53	YEMEN		
11	JAMAICA	32	LIBYA	54	OMAN		
12	HAITI	33	NIGERIA	55	QATAR		
13	DOMINICAN	34	CAMEROON	56	BAHRAIN		
	REPUBLIC	35	NIGER	57	ESTONIA		
14	TRINIDAD AND	36	SUDAN	58	LITHUANIA		
	TOBAGO	37	SENEGAL	59	LATVIA		
15	ALBANIA	38	GUINEA	60	ARMENIA		
16	CYPRUS	39	CÔTE D'IVOIRE	61	MOLDOVA		
17	LEBANON	40	GHANA	62	KYRGYZSTAN		
18	SYRIA	41	GABON	63	AZERBAIJAN		
19	IRAQ	42	ANGOLA	64	GEORGIA		
20	AFGHANISTAN	43	TANZANIA	65	TURKMENISTAN		
21	PAKISTAN	44	DEM. REP. OF THE CONGO	66	TAJIKISTAN		

Energy & Resources

TOP FIVE WORLD PRODUCERS OF SELECTED MINERAL COMMODITIES

MINERAL FUELS	1	2	3	4	5
CRUDE OIL	SAUDI ARABIA	UNITED STATES	RUSSIA	IRAN	CHINA
GASOLINE	UNITED STATES	RUSSIA	JAPAN	CHINA	UNITED KINGDOM
NATURAL GAS	RUSSIA	UNITED STATES	CANADA	NETHERLANDS	UNITED KINGDOM
HARD COAL	CHINA	UNITED STATES	INDIA	SOUTH AFRICA	AUSTRALIA
URANIUM-BEARING ORES	CANADA	NIGER	KAZAKHSTAN	RUSSIA	UZBEKISTAN

METALS	1	2	3	4	5
CHROMITE	SOUTH AFRICA	KAZAKHSTAN	INDIA	TURKEY	FINLAND
IRON ORE	CHINA	BRAZIL	RUSSIA	AUSTRALIA	UNITED STATES
MANGANESE ORE	SOUTH AFRICA	CHINA	UKRAINE	AUSTRALIA	BRAZIL
MINE NICKEL	RUSSIA	CANADA	NEW CALEDONIA	INDONESIA	AUSTRALIA
MINE SILVER	MEXICO	PERU	UNITED STATES	AUSTRALIA	CANADA
BAUXITE	AUSTRALIA	GUINEA	JAMAICA	BRAZIL	INDIA
ALUMINUM	UNITED STATES	RUSSIA	CANADA	AUSTRALIA	BRAZIL
MINE GOLD	SOUTH AFRICA	UNITED STATES	AUSTRALIA	CHINA	RUSSIA
MINE COPPER	CHILE	UNITED STATES	CANADA	RUSSIA	AUSTRALIA
MINE LEAD	AUSTRALIA	UNITED STATES	CHINA	PERU	CANADA
MINE TIN	CHINA	INDONESIA	BRAZIL	BOLIVIA	PERU
MINE ZINC	CANADA	AUSTRALIA	CHINA	PERU	UNITED STATES

NONMETALS	1	2	3	4	5
NATURAL DIAMOND	AUSTRALIA	BOTSWANA	RUSSIA	SOUTH AFRICA	DEM. REP. OF THE CONGO
POTASH	CANADA	GERMANY	BELARUS	RUSSIA	UNITED STATES
PHOSPHATE ROCK	UNITED STATES	CHINA	MOROCCO	RUSSIA	TUNISIA
SULFUR (ALL FORMS)	UNITED STATES	CANADA	CHINA	MEXICO	JAPAN

Names in Black Indicate More Than 10% of Total World Production

Source: U.S. Geological Survey, Mineral Commodity Summary; Handbook of International Economic Statistics

NUCLEAR POWER PRODUCTION

PERCENTAGE OF WORLD TOTAL

United States 27.4

France 15.1

Japan 11.4

Germany 8.6

Canada 4.6

Sweden 4.1

United Kingdom 3.3

Belgium 2.5

Spain 2.5

South Korea 2.4

Czech Republic 1.3

Switzerland 1.3

Finland 1.2

COMMERCIAL ENERGY CONSUMPTION/PRODUCTION

PERCENTAGE OF WORLD TOTAL
0.0 PRODUCTION   ■ 0.0 CONSUMPTION

Russia 23.2 / 19.3

United States 19.8 / 24.1

China 8.8 / 8.3

Canada 3.3 / 2.7

United Kingdom 3.3 / 3.0

Saudi Arabia 3.3 / 0.8

Mexico 2.5 / 1.5

Germany 2.5 / 4.9

India 2.1 / 2.3

Australia 1.9 / 1.1

Iran 1.9 / 0.7

Poland 1.8 / 1.9

Venezuela 1.7 / 0.6

Map legend

- OIL FIELDS
- NATURAL GAS FIELDS
- MAJOR COAL DEPOSITS
- OIL SANDS
- OIL SHALE
- MAJOR URANIUM DEPOSITS
- IMPORTANT PEAT DEPOSITS

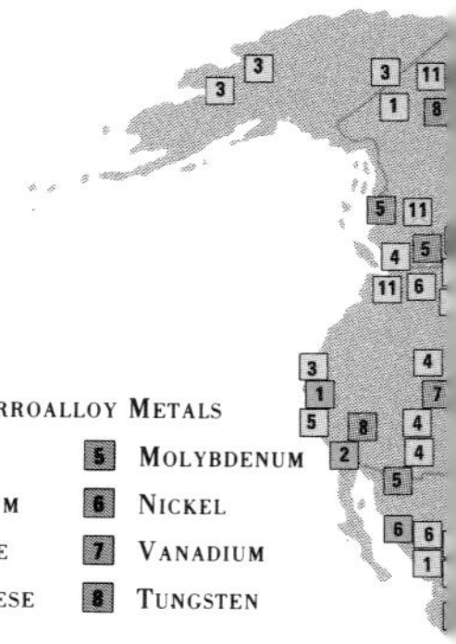

ALASKA

UNITED

MEXIC

IRON AND FERROALLOY METALS
1. COBALT
2. CHROMIUM
3. IRON ORE
4. MANGANESE
5. MOLYBDENUM
6. NICKEL
7. VANADIUM
8. TUNGSTEN

OTHER METALS
1. SILVER
2. BAUXITE
3. GOLD
4. COPPER
5. MERCURY
6. LEAD
7. PLATINUM
8. ANTIMONY
9. TIN
10. TITANIUM
11. ZINC

NONMETALS
1. ASBESTOS
2. BORAX
3. DIAMONDS
4. EMERALDS
5. FLUORSPAR
6. GRAPHITE
7. IODINE
8. JADE
9. POTASH
10. MICA
11. NITRATES
12. OPALS
13. PHOSPHATES
14. PEARLS
15. RUBIES
16. SULFUR
17. SAPPHIRES

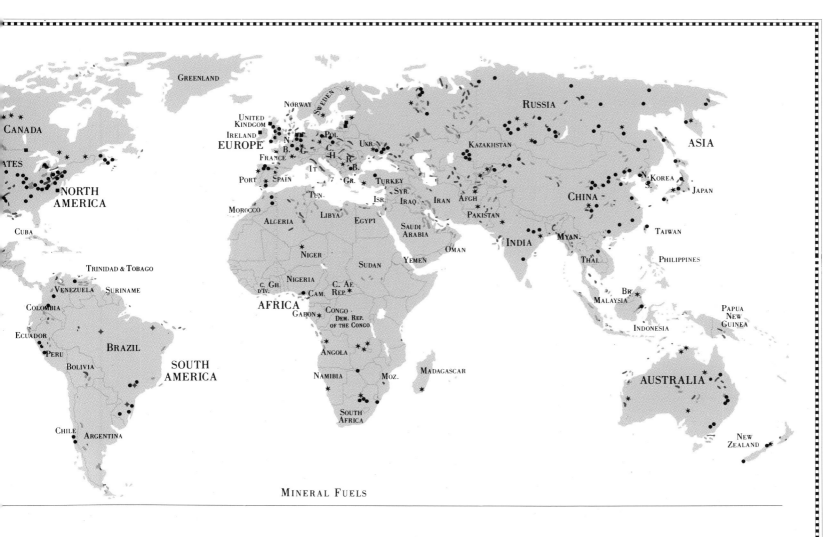

MINERAL FUELS

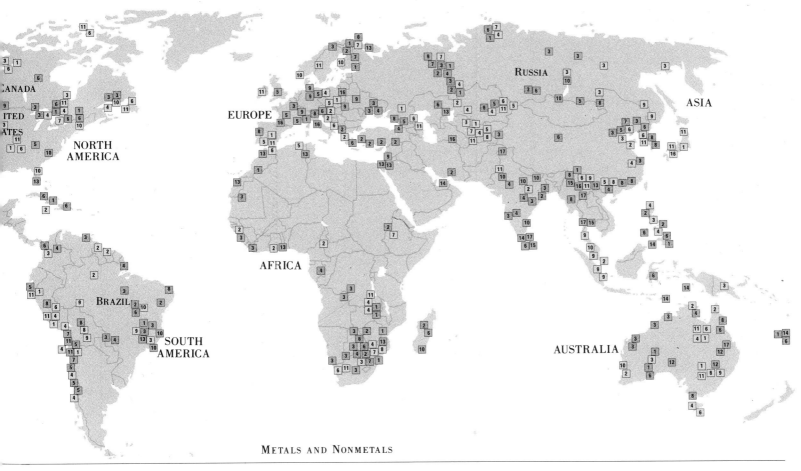

METALS AND NONMETALS

Agriculture & Manufacturing

TOP FIVE WORLD PRODUCERS OF SELECTED AGRICULTURAL COMMODITIES

	1	2	3	4	5
WHEAT	CHINA	INDIA	UNITED STATES	FRANCE	RUSSIA
RICE	CHINA	INDIA	INDONESIA	BANGLADESH	VIETNAM
OATS	RUSSIA	CANADA	UNITED STATES	GERMANY	AUSTRALIA
CORN (MAIZE)	UNITED STATES	CHINA	BRAZIL	MEXICO	FRANCE
SOYBEANS	UNITED STATES	BRAZIL	CHINA	ARGENTINA	INDIA
POTATOES	CHINA	RUSSIA	UNITED STATES	POLAND	UKRAINE
COFFEE	BRAZIL	COLOMBIA	INDONESIA	MEXICO	UGANDA
TEA	INDIA	CHINA	KENYA	SRI LANKA	INDONESIA
TOBACCO	CHINA	UNITED STATES	INDIA	BRAZIL	TURKEY
COTTON	UNITED STATES	CHINA	INDIA	PAKISTAN	UZBEKISTAN
SUGAR	INDIA	BRAZIL	CHINA	UNITED STATES	THAILAND
CATTLE (STOCK)	BRAZIL	CHINA	UNITED STATES	ARGENTINA	RUSSIA
SHEEP (STOCK)	CHINA	AUSTRALIA	IRAN	NEW ZEALAND	INDIA
HOGS (STOCK)	CHINA	UNITED STATES	BRAZIL	GERMANY	RUSSIA
COW'S MILK	UNITED STATES	RUSSIA	INDIA	GERMANY	FRANCE
HEN'S EGGS	CHINA	UNITED STATES	JAPAN	RUSSIA	INDIA
WOOL	AUSTRALIA	CHINA	NEW ZEALAND	RUSSIA	URUGUAY
ROUNDWOOD	UNITED STATES	INDIA	CHINA	BRAZIL	CANADA
NATURAL RUBBER	THAILAND	INDONESIA	MALAYSIA	INDIA	CHINA
FISH CATCHES	CHINA	PERU	JAPAN	CHILE	UNITED STATES

Names in Black Indicate More Than 10% of Total World Production

Source: United Nations, Food and Agriculture Organization

PERCENT OF TOTAL EMPLOYMENT IN AGRICULTURE, MANUFACTURING AND OTHER INDUSTRIES

Legend:
- AGRICULTURE (INCLUDES FORESTRY AND FISHING)
- MANUFACTURING
- CONSTRUCTION
- TRADE AND COMMERCE
- FINANCE, INSURANCE, REAL ESTATE
- SERVICES
- OTHER (INCLUDES MINING, UTILITIES, TRANSPORTATION)

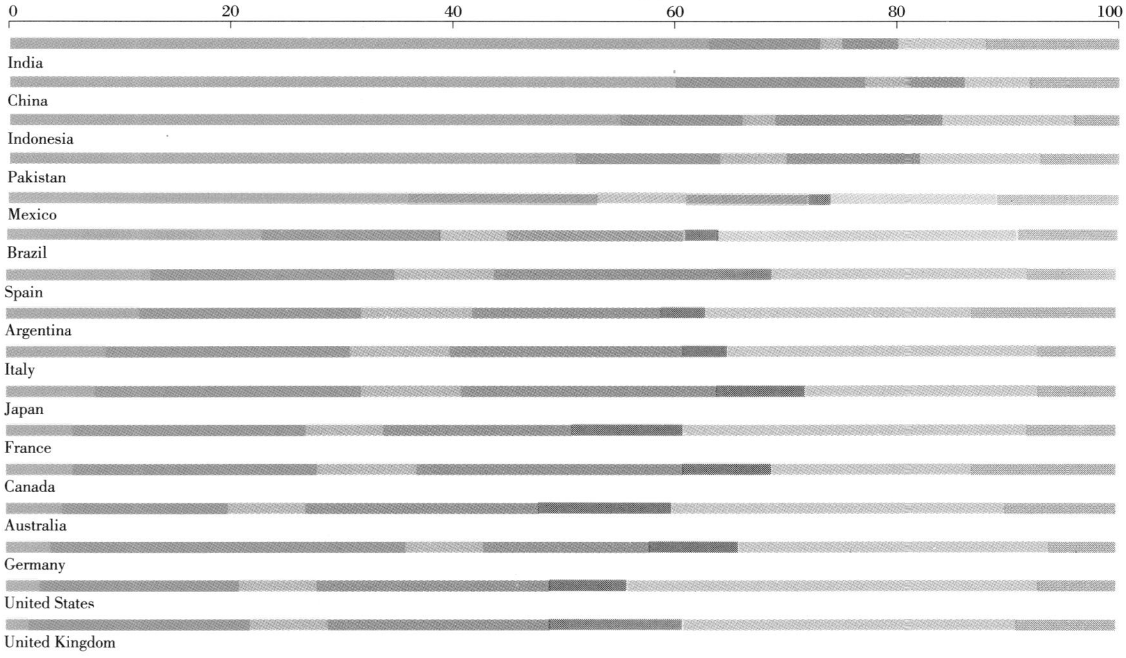

Scale: 0 — 20 — 40 — 60 — 80 — 100

India
China
Indonesia
Pakistan
Mexico
Brazil
Spain
Argentina
Italy
Japan
France
Canada
Australia
Germany
United States
United Kingdom

Finance, Insurance, Real Estate Data Included With "Other" for India, China, Indonesia and Pakistan

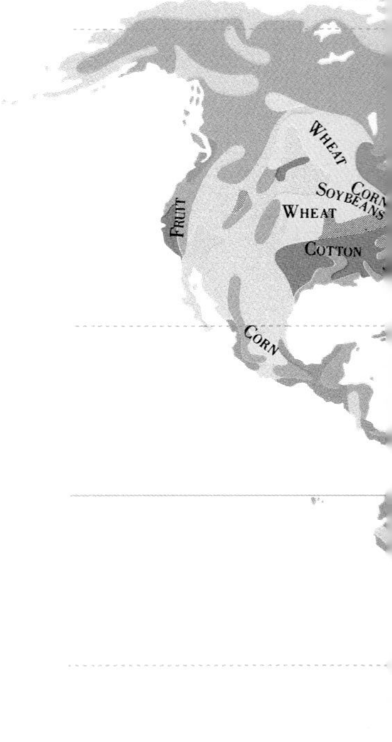

CEREALS, LIVESTOCK

LIVESTOCK RANCHING AND HE[...]

SEATTLE - TACOMA
SAN FRANCISCO - SAN JOSE
SOUTHERN CALIFORNIA
MEXICO - PUEBLA
DETR[...]
CHICAGO - G[...]
ST. LOU[...]
HOUS[...]
SANTIAGO - VALPAR[...]

- ▲ AIRCRAFT
- △ MOTOR VEHICLES
- ▽ SHIPBUILDING

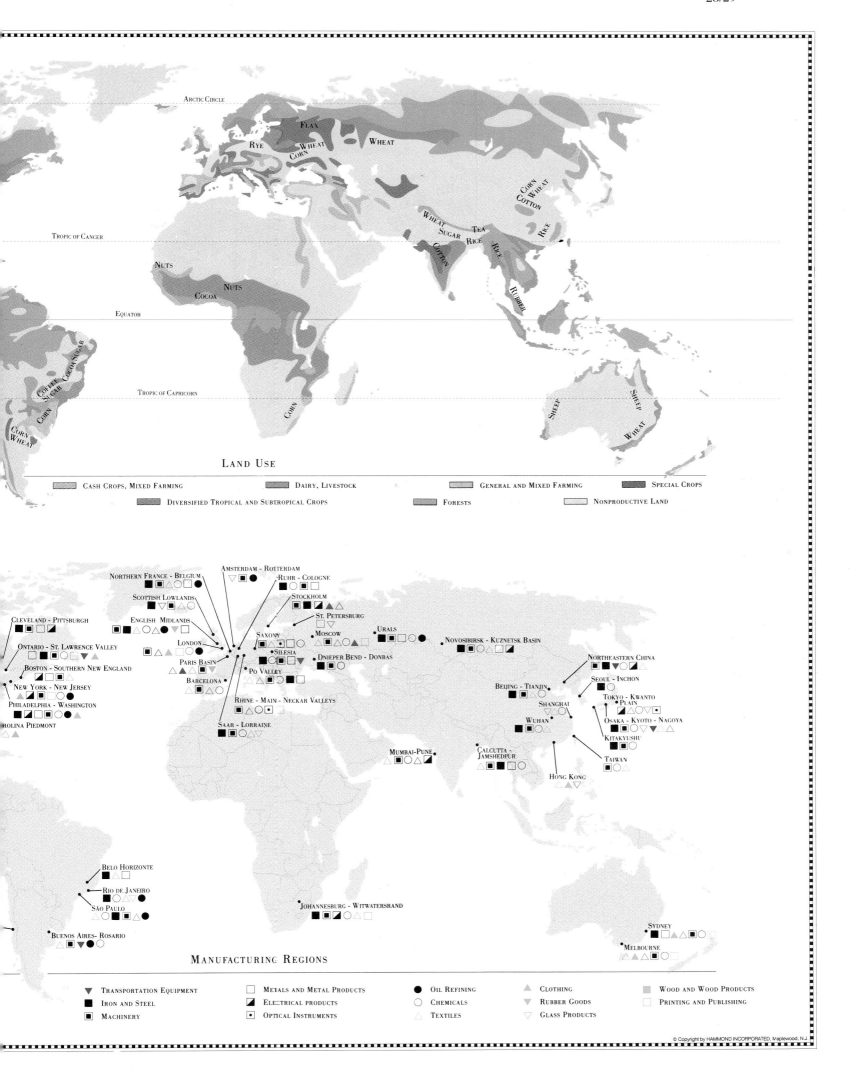

ARCTIC CIRCLE

FLAX

RYE
WHEAT
CORN
WHEAT

WHEAT

CORN
WHEAT
COTTON

TROPIC OF CANCER

WHEAT
SUGAR
COTTON
TEA
RICE
RICE
RICE

NUTS

NUTS
COCOA

RUBBER

EQUATOR

COFFEE
SUGAR COCOA SUGAR

CORN

TROPIC OF CAPRICORN

CORN

SHEEP
SHEEP

WHEAT

CORN
WHEAT

LAND USE

▨ CASH CROPS, MIXED FARMING	▨ DAIRY, LIVESTOCK	▨ GENERAL AND MIXED FARMING	▨ SPECIAL CROPS

▨ DIVERSIFIED TROPICAL AND SUBTROPICAL CROPS	▨ FORESTS	▨ NONPRODUCTIVE LAND

AMSTERDAM - ROTTERDAM
NORTHERN FRANCE - BELGIUM
RUHR - COLOGNE
SCOTTISH LOWLANDS
STOCKHOLM
CLEVELAND - PITTSBURGH
ENGLISH MIDLANDS
ST. PETERSBURG
ONTARIO - ST. LAWRENCE VALLEY
LONDON
SAXONY
MOSCOW
URALS
NOVOSIBIRSK - KUZNETSK BASIN
BOSTON - SOUTHERN NEW ENGLAND
PARIS BASIN
SILESIA
NEW YORK - NEW JERSEY
DNIEPER BEND - DONBAS
NORTHEASTERN CHINA
PHILADELPHIA - WASHINGTON
BARCELONA
PO VALLEY
SEOUL - INCHON
CAROLINA PIEDMONT
RHINE - MAIN - NECKAR VALLEYS
BEIJING - TIANJIN
TOKYO - KWANTO PLAIN
SHANGHAI
SAAR - LORRAINE
OSAKA - KYOTO - NAGOYA
WUHAN
KITAKYUSHU
MUMBAI-PUNE
CALCUTTA - JAMSHEDPUR
TAIWAN
HONG KONG
BELO HORIZONTE
RIO DE JANEIRO
SÃO PAULO
JOHANNESBURG - WITWATERSRAND
SYDNEY
BUENOS AIRES- ROSARIO
MELBOURNE

MANUFACTURING REGIONS

▼ TRANSPORTATION EQUIPMENT	▢ METALS AND METAL PRODUCTS	● OIL REFINING	▲ CLOTHING	▨ WOOD AND WOOD PRODUCTS
■ IRON AND STEEL	◪ ELECTRICAL PRODUCTS	○ CHEMICALS	▽ RUBBER GOODS	▢ PRINTING AND PUBLISHING
▣ MACHINERY	⊡ OPTICAL INSTRUMENTS	△ TEXTILES	▽ GLASS PRODUCTS	

A R C T I C
O C E A N

'−17,881 ft.
(−5450 m)

FRANZ JOSEF LAND

SVALBARD

SEVERNAYA
ZEMLYA

NEW SIBERIAN IS.

NOVAYA
ZEMLYA

Kara
Sea

Laptev
Sea

Wrangel I.

Nordkapp

Barents
Sea

Kola

Baltic Sea

L. Ladoga

S i b e r i a

Bering
Sea

ALEUTIAN
BASIN

Ural Mountains

Ob'

Yenisey

Lena

Aldan

Kamchatka
Pen.

ALEUTIAN ISLANDS

NEGIAN
BASIN

Angara

Sea
of
Okhotsk

ALEUTIAN TRENCH

E U R O P E

Volga

Dnieper

Irtysh

L. Baykal

A S I A

Amur

Sakhalin

KURIL-KAMCHATKA TRENCH

Danube

Black Sea

Caspian Sea

Aral
Sea

L. Balkhash

Gobi

Sea of
Japan

Honshu

JAPAN
TRENCH

NORTHWEST
PACIFIC
BASIN

Euphrates

Kunlun

Himalaya

Mt. Everest

Huang

East
China
Sea

P A C I F I C

editerranean Sea

Nile

Red Sea

Indus

Ganges

Chang

Taiwan

MARIANA

Tropic of Cancer

A F R I C A

Arabian
Sea

ARABIAN
BASIN

Mekong

South
China
Sea

PHILIPPINE
BASIN

Luzon

MARIANA IS.

MARSHALL IS.

CENTRAL
PACIFIC
BASIN

CARLSBERG
RIDGE

C. Comorin

Ceylon

Bay
of
Bengal

Borneo

Mindanao

TRENCH

Challenger Deep
−36,198 ft.
(−11,033 m)

CAROLINE IS.

Victoria

Kilimanjaro

SOMALI
BASIN

CENTRAL

CEYLON
PLAIN

Sumatra

Java

Celebes

New Guinea

MELANESIAN
BASIN

Equator

O C E A N

OLA

Zambezi

INDIAN

RIDGE

Madagascar

NINETYEAST RIDGE

24,443 ft.
(7450 m)
JAVA TRENCH

AUSTRALIA

Coral
Sea

Fiji Is.

RIDGE

Orange

I N D I A N

O C E A N

BROKEN
PLATEAU

C. Leeuwin

Ocean Barrier Reef

Tropic of Capricorn

CAPE
of Good Hope

BASIN

SOUTHEAST INDIAN RIDGE

S. Australia Basin

Tasman
Sea

North Cape

North I.

LHAS RIDGE

SOUTHWEST INDIAN RIDGE

KERGUELEN
PLATEAU

Tasmania

South I.

ENDERBY ABYSSAL PLAIN

AUSTRALIAN-ANTARCTIC BASIN

SOUTHEAST INDIAN RIDGE

Antarctic Circle

C. Adare

Amery
Ice Shelf

Ross Sea

A N T A R C T I C A

Europe

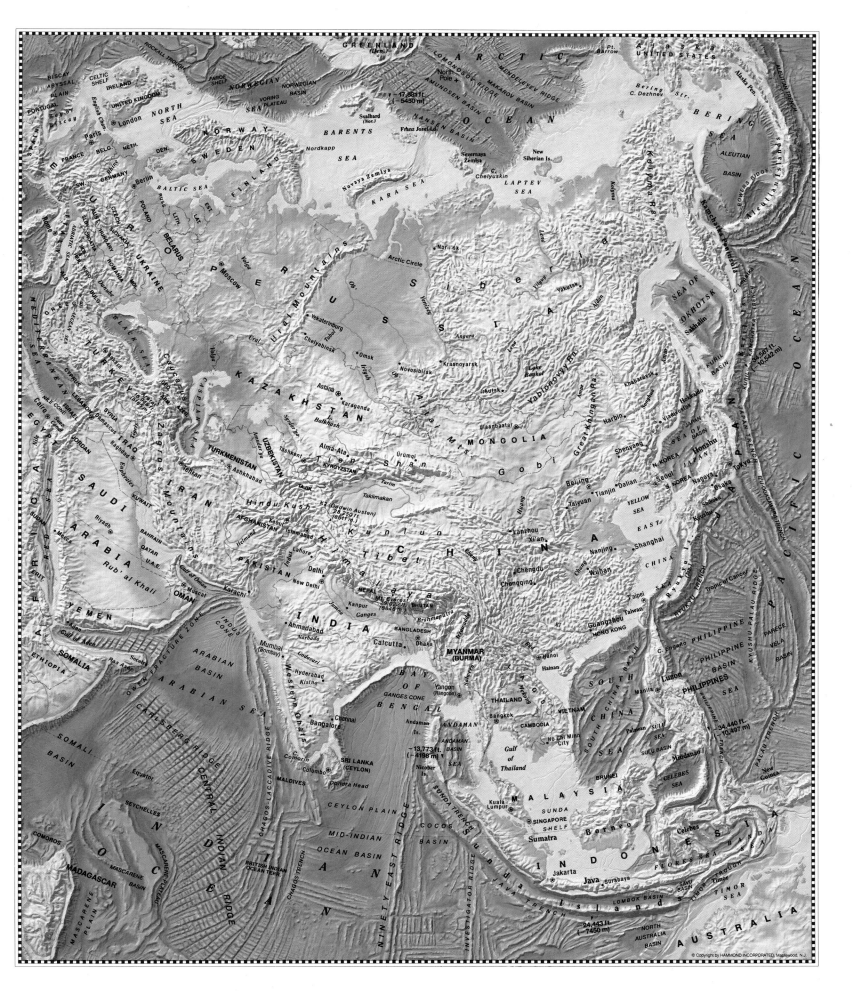

GREENLAND
(Den.)

ARCTIC
OCEAN

Pt. Barrow

Alaska
UNITED STATES

Lomonosov Ridge
North Pole
Makarov Basin
Mendeleyev Ridge

Amundsen Basin
−17,881 ft.
(−5450 m)

Nansen Basin

BERING
SEA

Svalbard
(Nor.)
Franz Josef Ld.

BARENTS
SEA

Severnaya
Zemlya

New
Siberian Is.

LAPTEV
SEA

Chelyuskin

C. Dezhnev
Bering
Str.

Alaska Pen.

ALEUTIAN
BASIN

BOWERS RIDGE

ALEUTIAN

KAMCHATKA TRENCH

BISCAY
ABYSSAL
PLAIN
CELTIC
SHELF
IRELAND
FAROE
SHELF
NORWEGIAN
SEA
PLATEAU
NORWEGIAN
BASIN
VORING
PLATEAU

Nordkapp

Novaya Zemlya

KARA SEA

Noril'sk

Arctic Circle

S i b e r i a

Kolyma Ra.

Kolyma

SEA OF
OKHOTSK

Sakhalin

PORTUGAL
Biscay
English Chan.
London
NORTH
SEA

NORWAY
SWEDEN
FINLAND

Ob'
Yenisey

Lena

Vilyuy
Yakutsk

Aldan

PACIFIC
OCEAN

FRANCE
Paris
BELG.
NETH.
DEN.
GERMANY
Berlin
Rhine

BALTIC SEA

EST.
LAT.
LITH.

Moscow

Volga

R U S S I A

Yekaterinburg

Chelyabinsk
Tobol

Omsk

Irtysh

Novosibirsk

Angara

Krasnoyarsk

Lake
Baykal

Irkutsk

Amur

Yablonovyy Ra.

Khabarovsk

Amur

Harbin

Vladivostok

N. KOREA

SEA OF
JAPAN

KURIL
BASIN

Hokkaido

JAPAN
KURIL IS.

−24,507 ft.
(−10,542 m)

JAPAN TRENCH

POL.
CZECH
SLOVAKIA
Vienna
AUSTRIA
HUNGARY
ROMANIA
BELARUS
UKRAINE

KAZAKHSTAN

Astana
Karaganda

Balkhash

Syr Darya

Alma-Ata

Ürümqi

MONGOLIA

Ulaanbaatar

Gobi

Great Khingan Ra.

Shenyang

Beijing

S. KOREA
Seoul

Dalian

JAPAN
Honshu
Tokyo

Nagoya
Osaka

IZU-OGASAWARA TRENCH

CROATIA
BOS.
SERBIA
BULGARIA
GREECE
ITALY
ADRIATIC SEA
MEDITERRANEAN SEA

BLACK SEA

TURKEY

Caucasus

Caspian Sea

Aral Sea

TURKMENISTAN

UZBEKISTAN
Tashkent

Ashkhabad

Amu Darya

Tien Shan

Tarim

Taklimakan

K u n l u n

Lanzhou

Xi'an

Tianjin

YELLOW
SEA

Taiyuan

C H I N A

EAST

Nanjing

Shanghai

Kyushu

Shikoku

RYUKYU TRENCH

CYPRUS
SYRIA
Damascus
LEBANON
ISRAEL
Cairo
JORDAN
IRAQ
Baghdad
Euphrates
Tigris
Zagros Mountains

IRAN
Tehran

KYRGYZSTAN

Kabul
AFGHANISTAN
Islamabad

Hindu Kush

K2
(Godwin Austen)
28,250 ft.
(8611 m)

T i b e t

H i m a l a y a

Chengdu

Chongqing

Chang

Wuhan

CHINA

Guangzhou
HONG KONG

Taipei

Taiwan

Tropic of Cancer

PHILIPPINE SEA

KYUSHU-PALAU RIDGE

PARECE
VELA
BASIN

EGYPT

Nile

SAUDI
ARABIA
Riyadh
Mecca
BAHRAIN
QATAR
U.A.E.

KUWAIT

Gulf of Oman

OMAN
Muscat

PAKISTAN

Helmand

Indus

Lahore

Delhi
New Delhi

Karachi

Jumna

NEPAL

Kanpur
Ganges

Mt. Everest
29,028 ft.
(8848 m)

BHUTAN

Brahmaputra

BANGLADESH

Dhaka

A1

Hanoi

Hainan

SOUTH

PHILIPPINE

BASIN

PHILIPPINES

Luzon

Manila

VELA
BASIN

RED SEA
ERITREA

YEMEN

Gulf of Aden
Ras Asir

Rub' al Khali

Socotra

LOWER FRACTURE ZONE

ARABIAN
BASIN

INDUS
CONE

Western Ghats

INDIA

Narbada

Ahmadabad

Mumbai
(Bombay)

Godavari

Hyderabad

Kistna

Calcutta

BAY
OF
BENGAL

GANGES CONE

MYANMAR
(BURMA)

Yangon
(Rangoon)

Irrawaddy

Salween

Mekong

THAILAND
Bangkok

VIETNAM

CAMBODIA

Gulf of
Thailand

SOUTH

CHINA

SEA

Palawan

SULU
SEA

SULU BASIN

Mindanao

34,440 ft.
(10,497 m)

MINDANAO TRENCH

PALAU TRENCH

ETHIOPIA

SOMALIA

CARLSBERG RIDGE

ARABIAN SEA

LACCADIVE RIDGE

Bangalore

Chennai

Comorin

Colombo

SRI LANKA
(CEYLON)

Dondra Head

Andaman
Is.

ANDAMAN

Nicobar
Is.

−13,773 ft.
(−4198 m)

ANDAMAN
BASIN

ANDAMAN
SEA

Ho Chi Minh
City

BRUNEI

CELEBES
SEA

Celebes

New
Guinea

SOMALI
BASIN

SEYCHELLES

Equator

MASCARENE
BASIN

CHAGOS-LACCADIVE RIDGE

MALDIVES

BRITISH INDIAN
OCEAN TERR.

CEYLON PLAIN

COCOS
BASIN

MID-INDIAN
OCEAN BASIN

SUNDA TRENCH

Kuala
Lumpur

MALAYSIA

SUNDA
SHELF

SINGAPORE

Borneo

INDONESIA

FLORES SEA

BANDA
SEA

SAVU
BASIN

Timor

TIMOR
SEA

COMOROS

MADAGASCAR

MASCARENE
PLATEAU

I N D I A N   O C E A N

NINETYEAST RIDGE

INVESTIGATOR RIDGE

Sumatra

Jakarta

Java
Surabaya

JAVA TRENCH

LOMBOK BASIN

S u n d a   I s l a n d s

24,443 ft.
(7450 m)

NORTH
AUSTRALIA
BASIN

AUSTRALIA

MASCARENE
PLAIN

Africa

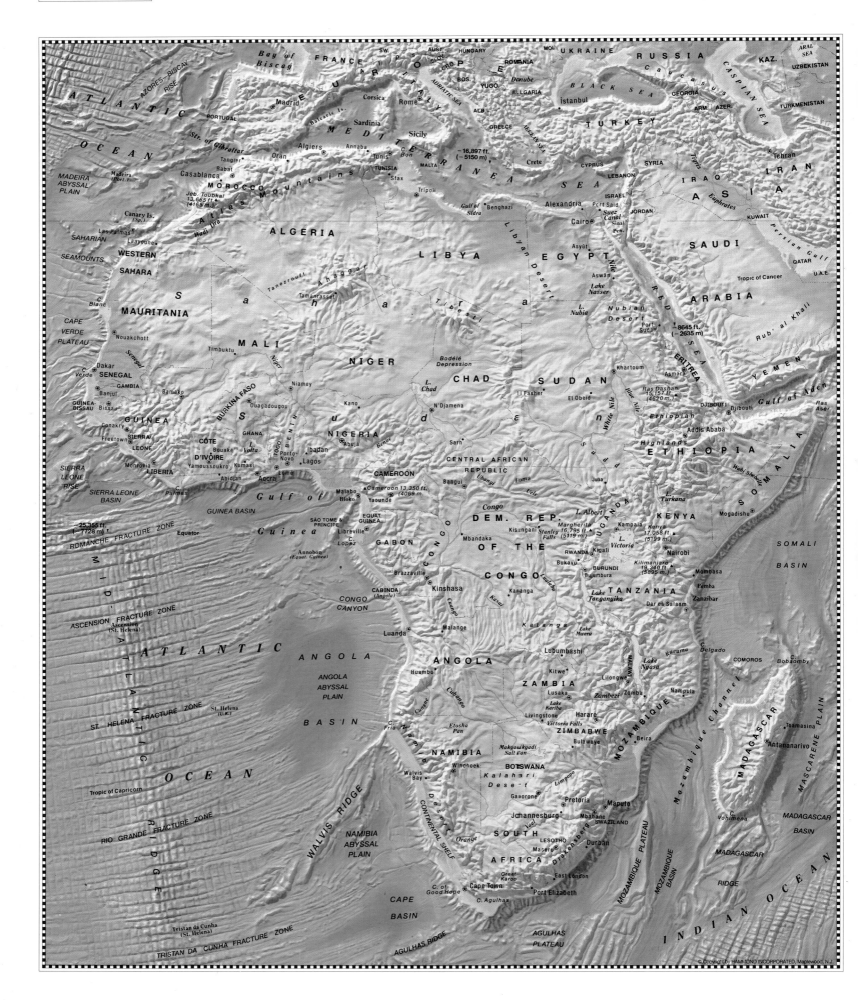

South America

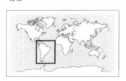

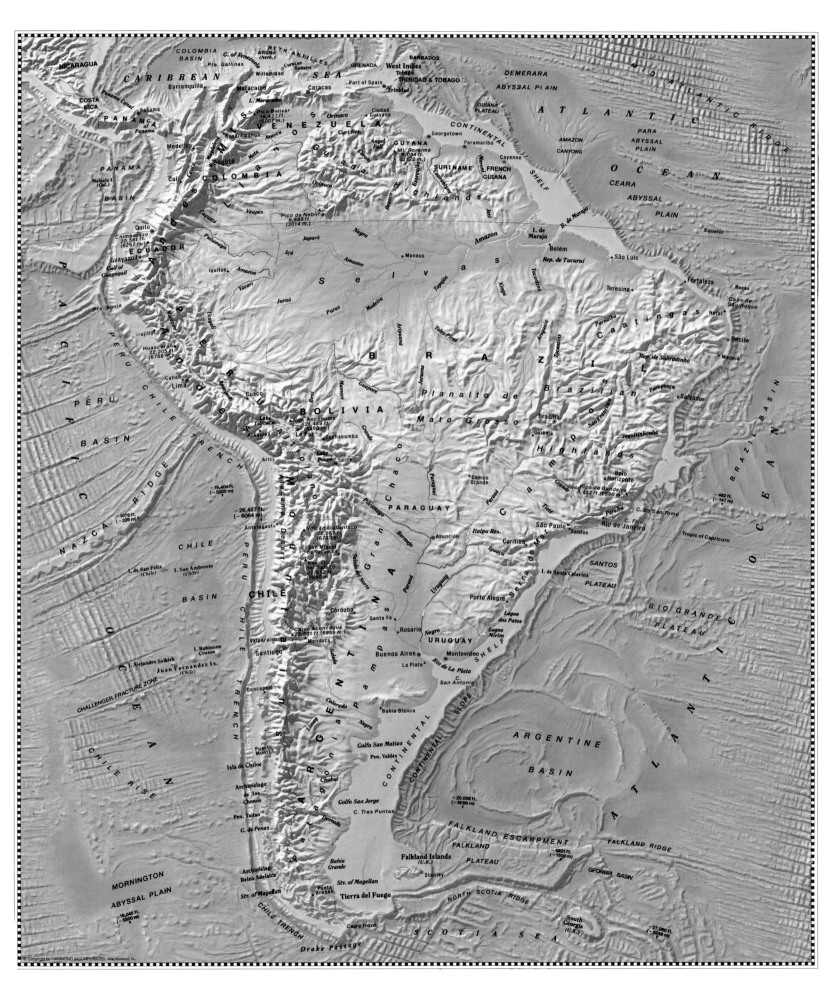

North America

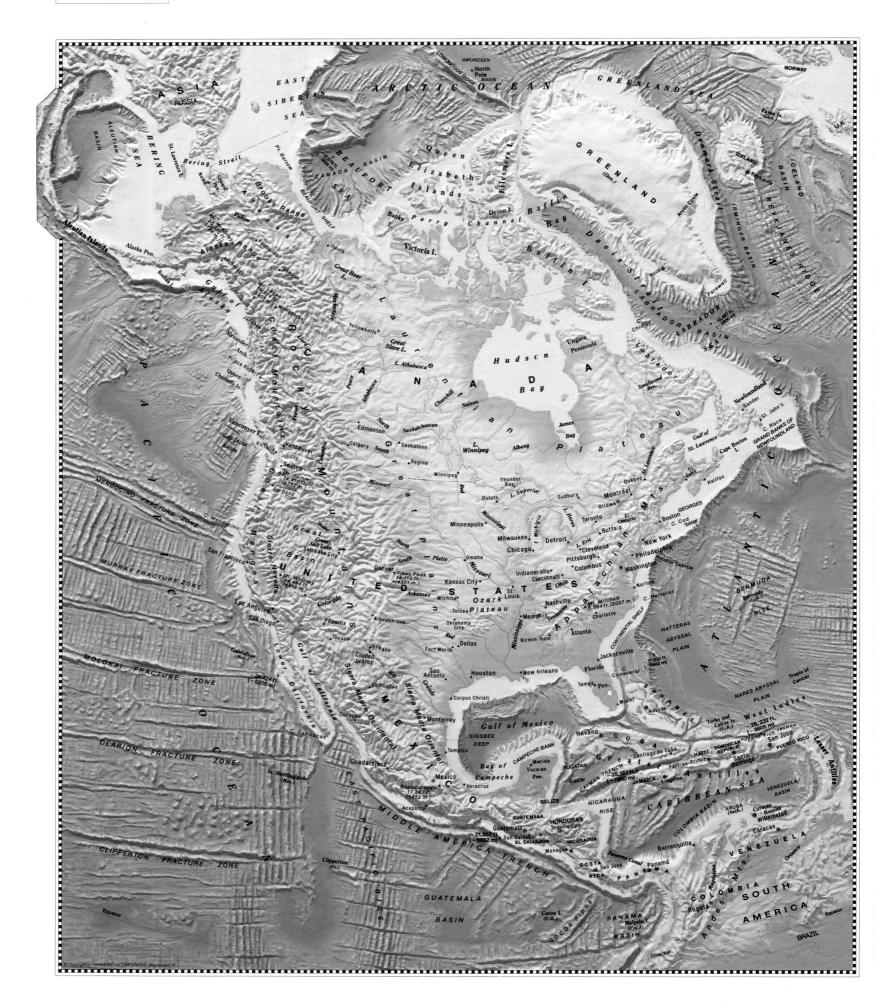

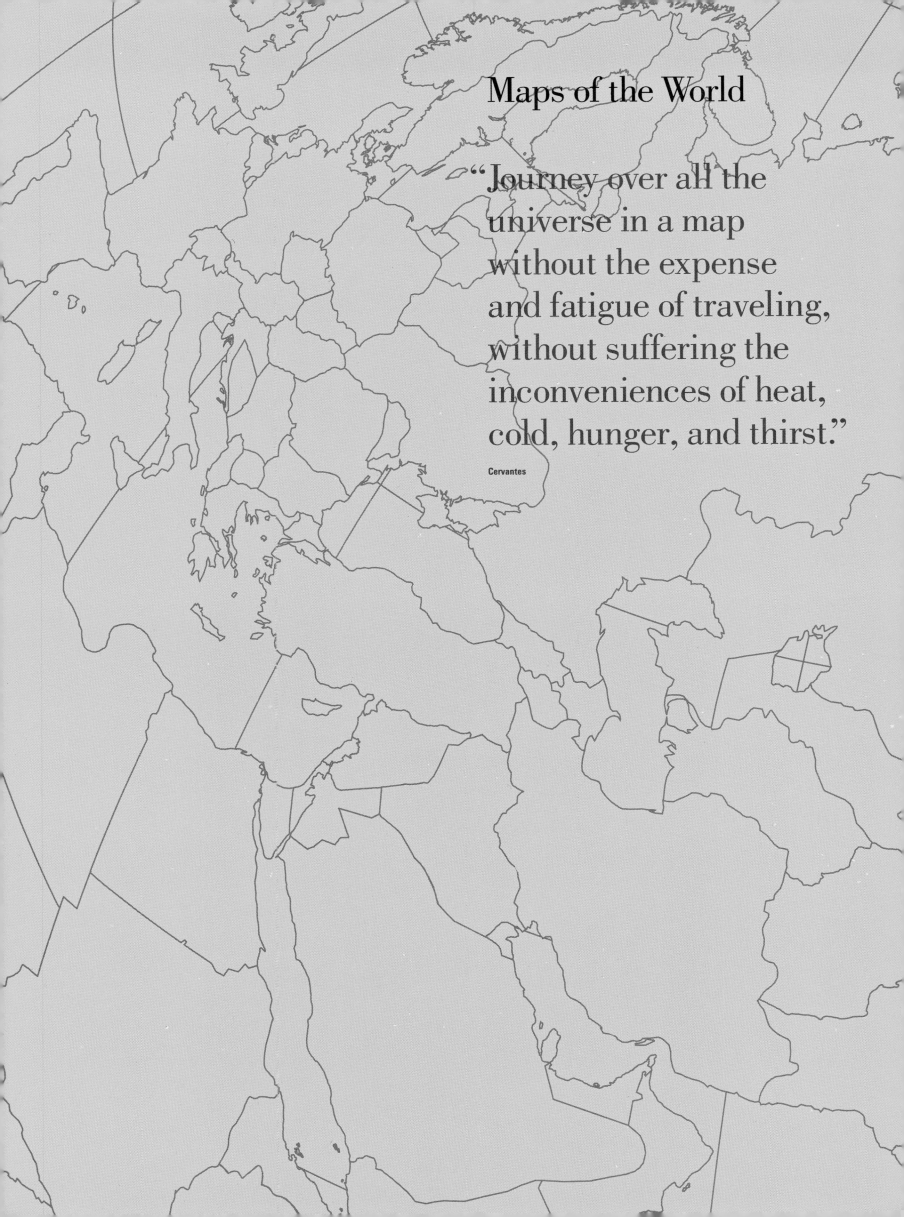

Maps of the World

"Journey over all the universe in a map without the expense and fatigue of traveling, without suffering the inconveniences of heat, cold, hunger, and thirst."

Cervantes

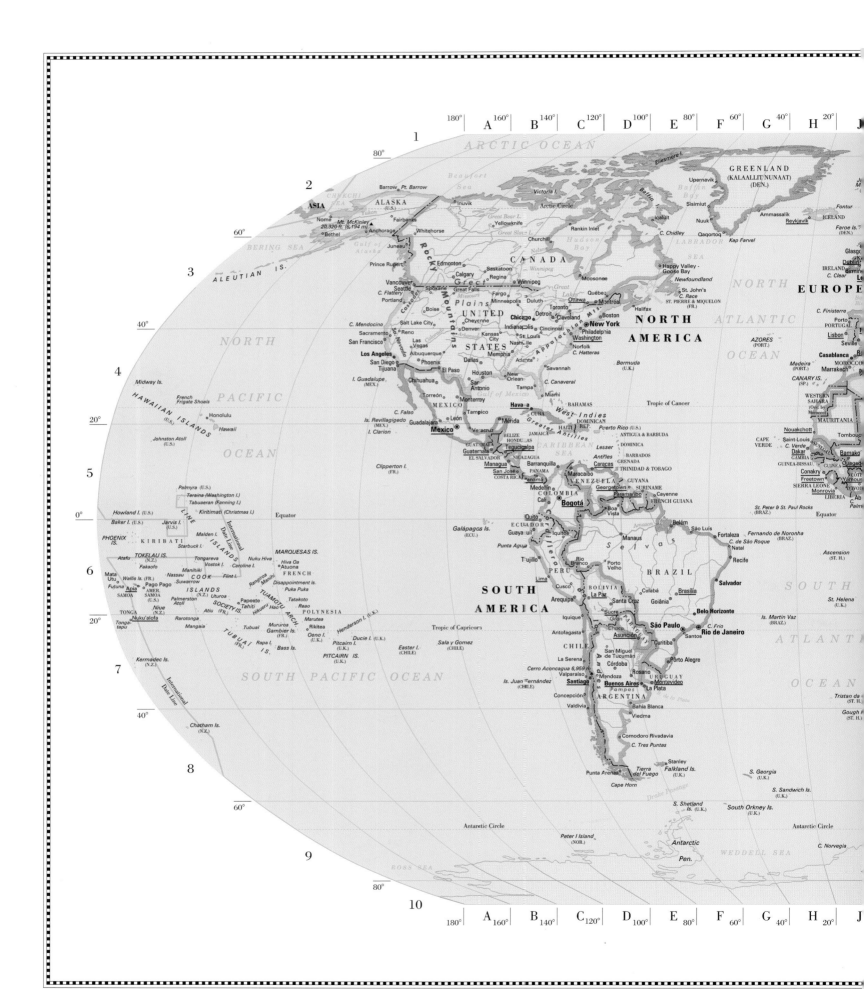

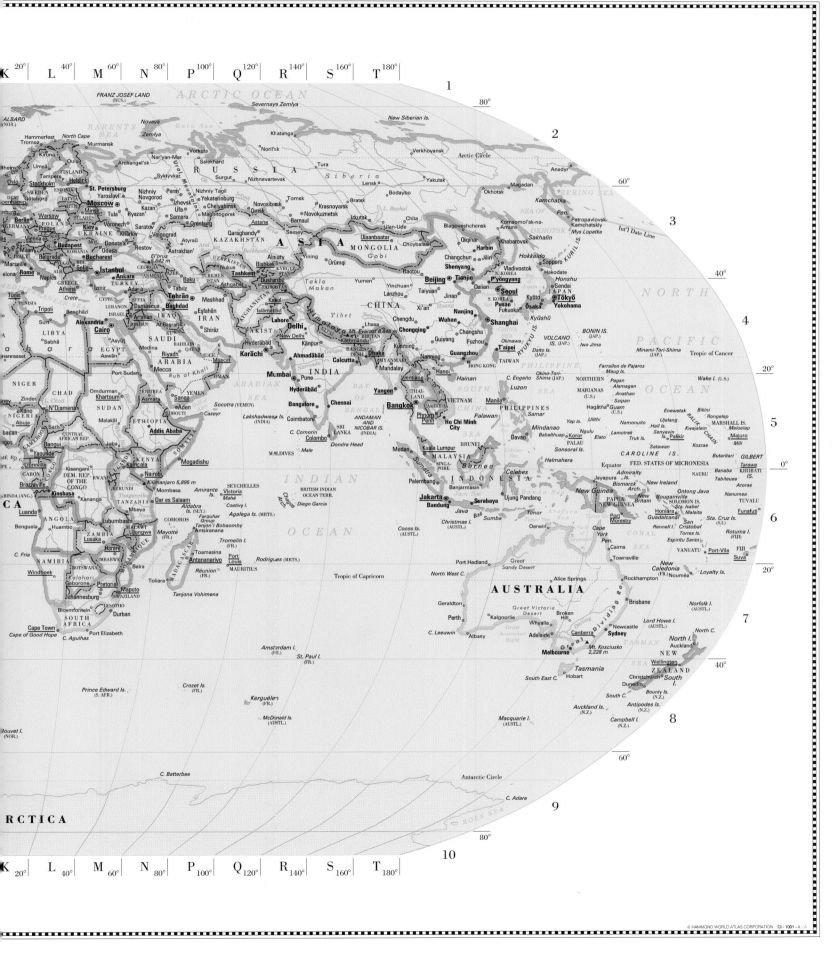

POPULATION OF CITIES AND TOWNS

◉ OVER 5,000,000   ⊙ 500,000 – 1,999,999
● 2,000,000 – 4,999,999   ○ UNDER 500,000

SCALE 1:81,700,000   ROBINSON PROJECTION   STANDARD PARALLELS 38°N AND 38°S

MILES   0   1000   2000   3000   4000
KILOMETERS   0   1000   2000   3000   4000

Europe - Comparisons

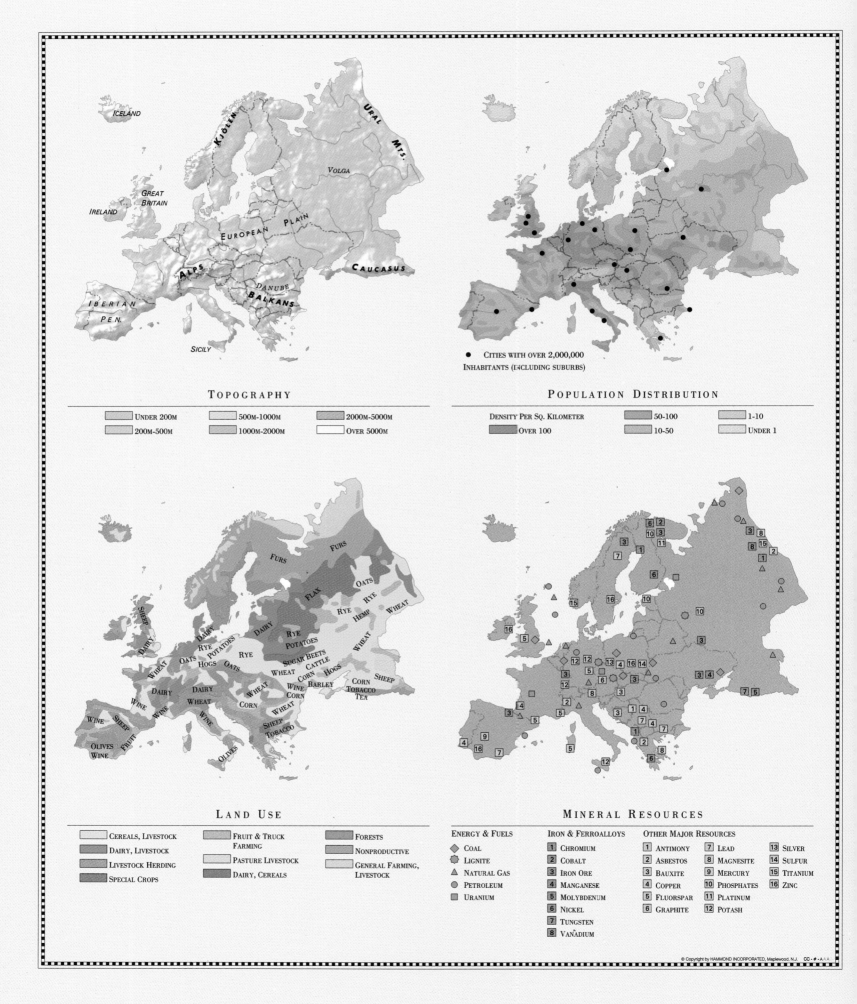

TOPOGRAPHY

- UNDER 200M
- 200M-500M
- 500M-1000M
- 1000M-2000M
- 2000M-5000M
- OVER 5000M

POPULATION DISTRIBUTION

● CITIES WITH OVER 2,000,000 INHABITANTS (INCLUDING SUBURBS)

DENSITY PER SQ. KILOMETER
- OVER 100
- 50-100
- 10-50
- 1-10
- UNDER 1

LAND USE

- CEREALS, LIVESTOCK
- DAIRY, LIVESTOCK
- LIVESTOCK HERDING
- SPECIAL CROPS
- FRUIT & TRUCK FARMING
- PASTURE LIVESTOCK
- DAIRY, CEREALS
- FORESTS
- NONPRODUCTIVE
- GENERAL FARMING, LIVESTOCK

MINERAL RESOURCES

ENERGY & FUELS
- ◆ COAL
- ⬡ LIGNITE
- △ NATURAL GAS
- ● PETROLEUM
- ▢ URANIUM

IRON & FERROALLOYS
- 1 CHROMIUM
- 2 COBALT
- 3 IRON ORE
- 4 MANGANESE
- 5 MOLYBDENUM
- 6 NICKEL
- 7 TUNGSTEN
- 8 VANADIUM

OTHER MAJOR RESOURCES
- 1 ANTIMONY
- 2 ASBESTOS
- 3 BAUXITE
- 4 COPPER
- 5 FLUORSPAR
- 6 GRAPHITE
- 7 LEAD
- 8 MAGNESITE
- 9 MERCURY
- 10 PHOSPHATES
- 11 PLATINUM
- 12 POTASH
- 13 SILVER
- 14 SULFUR
- 15 TITANIUM
- 16 ZINC

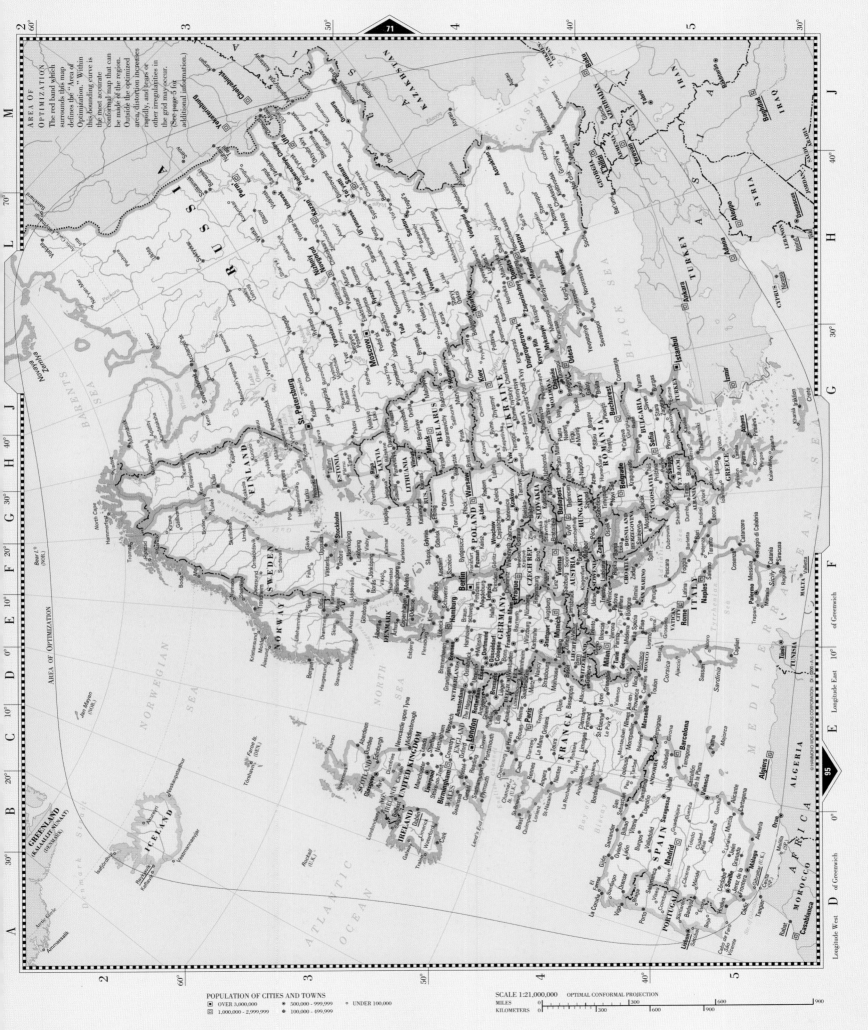

Scandinavia and
Finland, Iceland

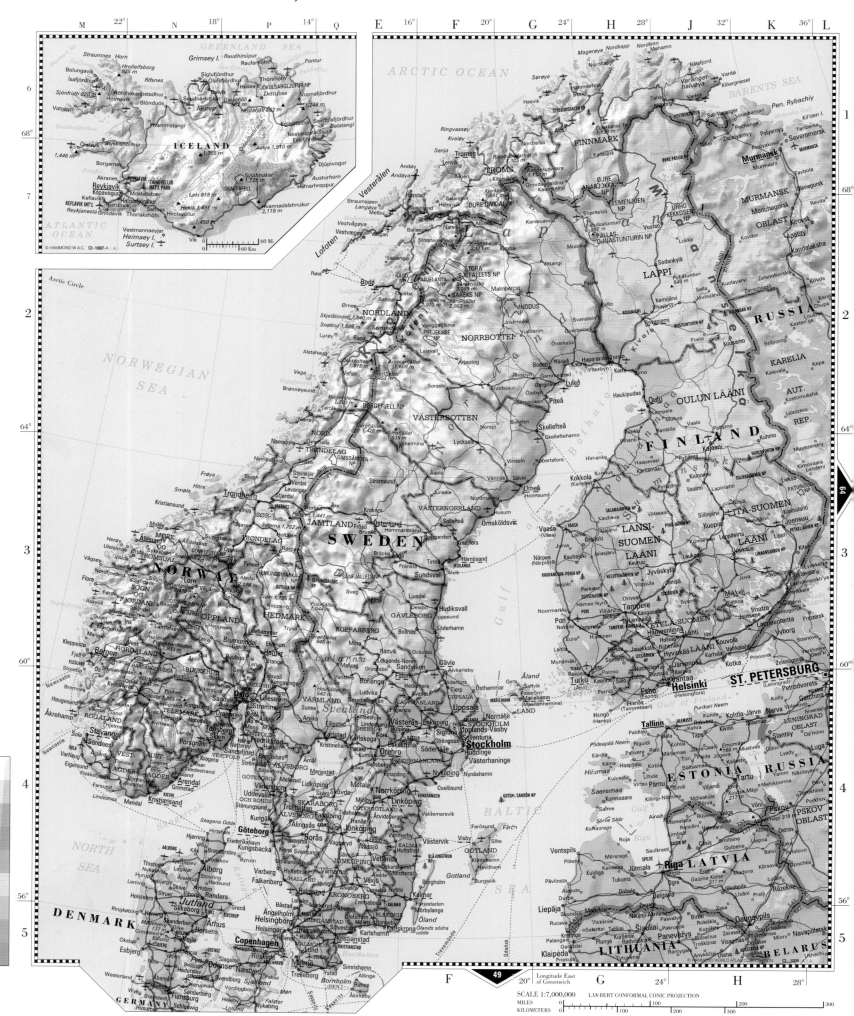

United Kingdom, Ireland

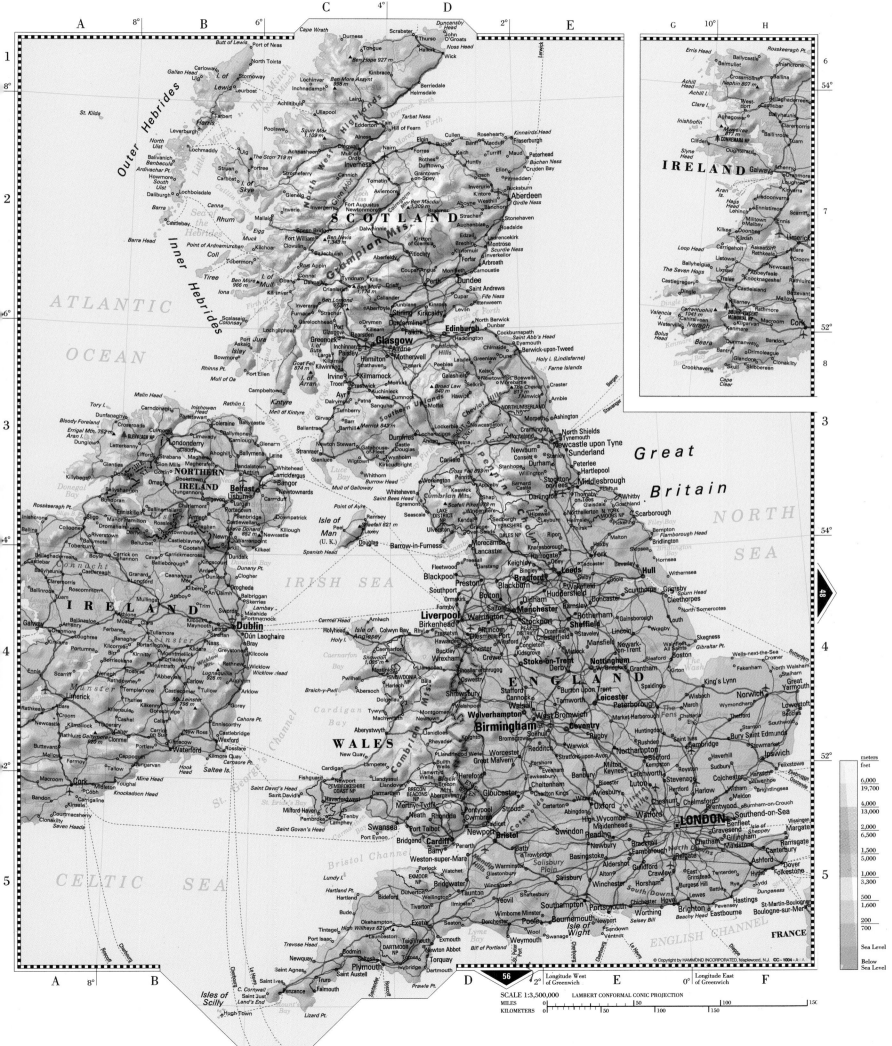

SCALE 1:3,500,000   LAMBERT CONFORMAL CONIC PROJECTION

© Copyright by HAMMOND INCORPORATED, Maplewood, N.J. CC-1004·A·A

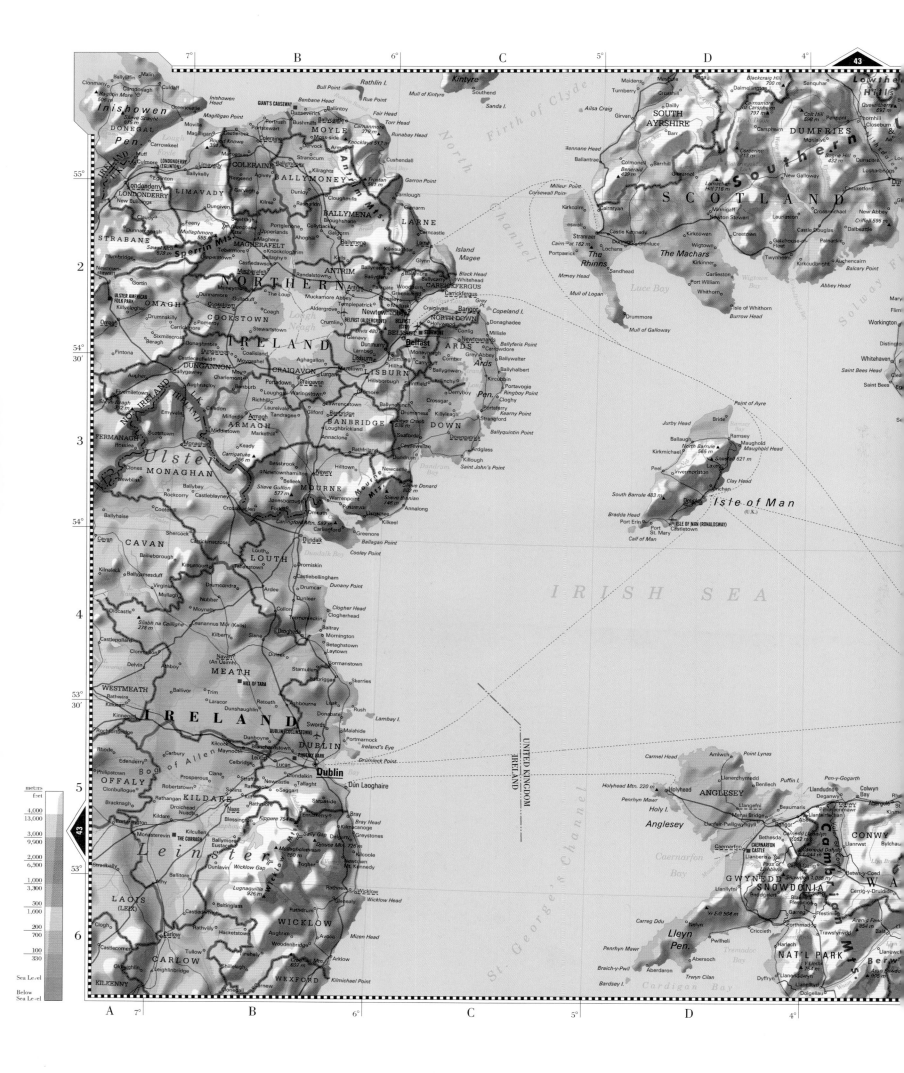

Northeastern Ireland, Northern England and Wales

POPULATION OF CITIES AND TOWNS

- ■ OVER 2,000,000
- ⊡ 1,000,000 - 1,999,999
- ◉ 500,000 - 999,999
- ◍ 250,000 - 499,999
- ● 100,000 - 249,999
- ◐ 30,000 - 99,999
- ○ 10,000 - 29,999
- ○ UNDER 10,000

SCALE 1:1,170,000   LAMBERT CONFORMAL CONIC PROJECTION

MILES
KILOMETERS

Southern England and Wales

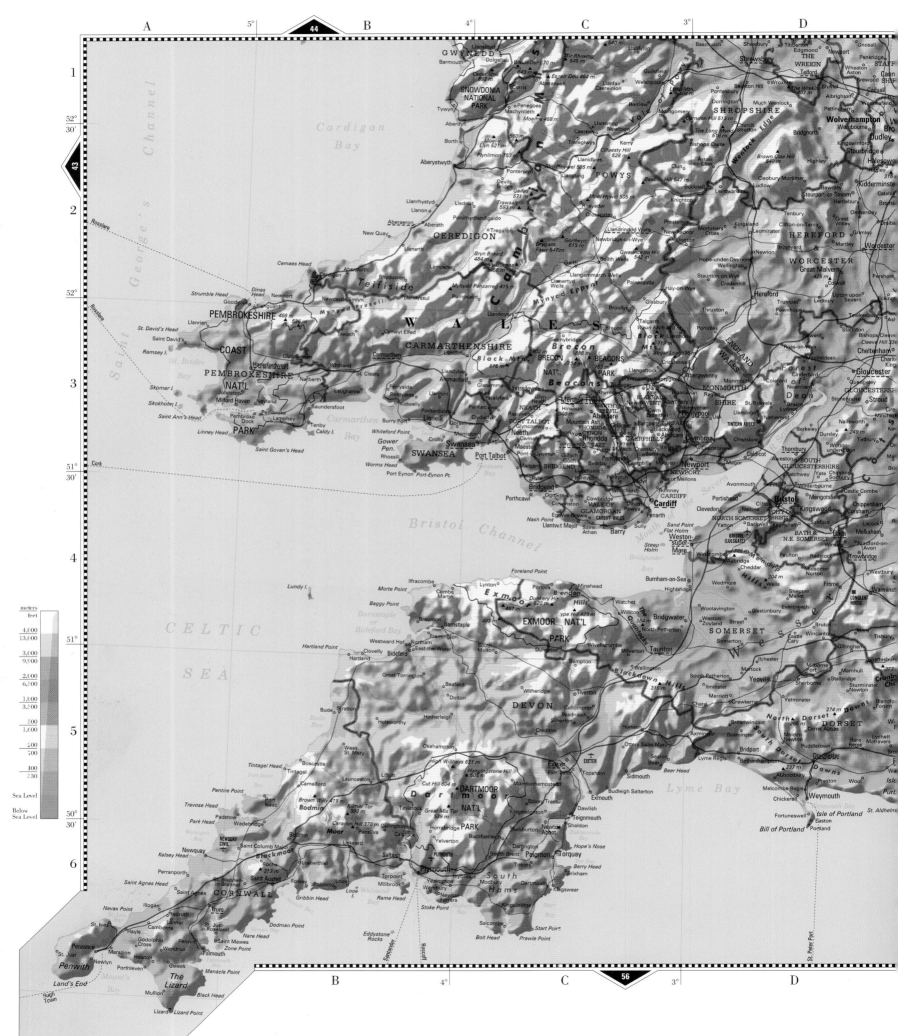

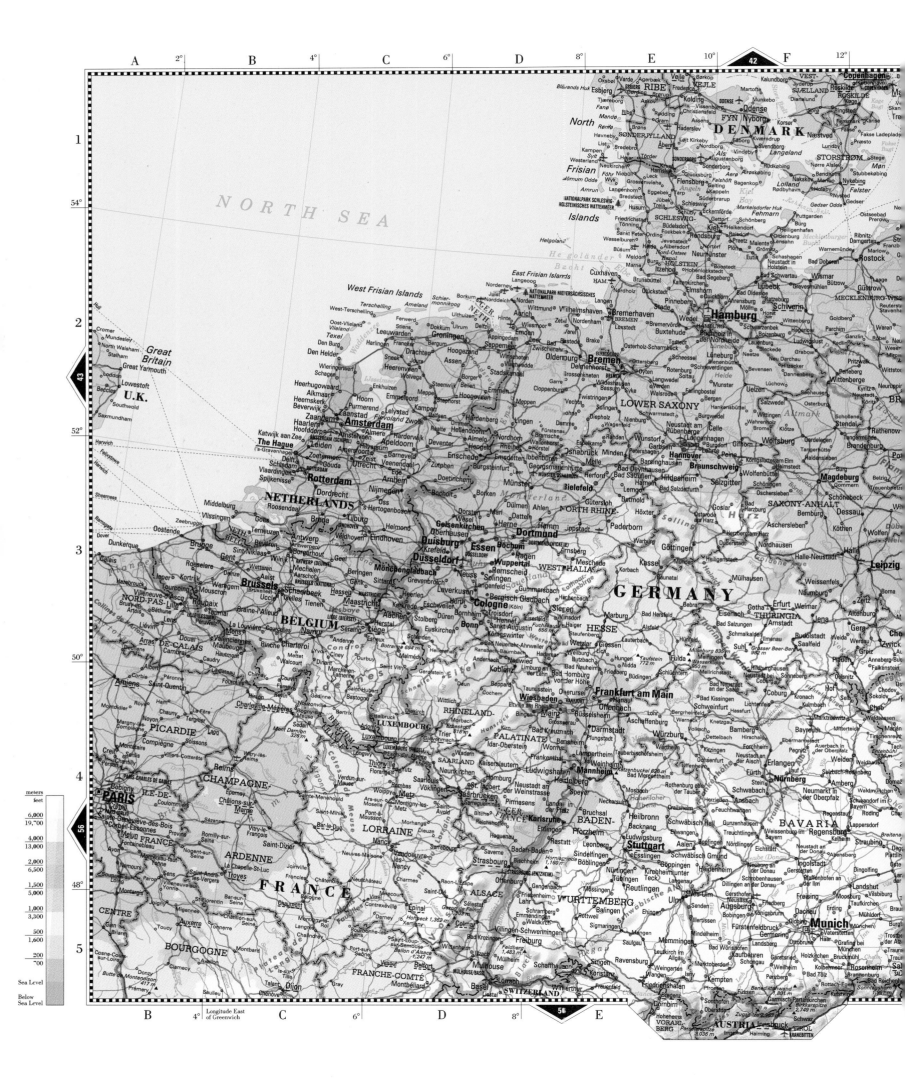

North Central Europe

SCALE 1:3,500,000   LAMBERT CONFORMAL CONIC PROJECTION

POPULATION OF CITIES AND TOWNS

■ OVER 2,000,000	◉ 500,000 - 999,999	● 100,000 - 249,999	○ 10,000 - 29,999
◻ 1,000,000 - 1,999,999	◉ 250,000 - 499,999	○ 30,000 - 99,999	· UNDER 10,000

MILES

KILOMETERS

Netherlands, Northwestern Germany

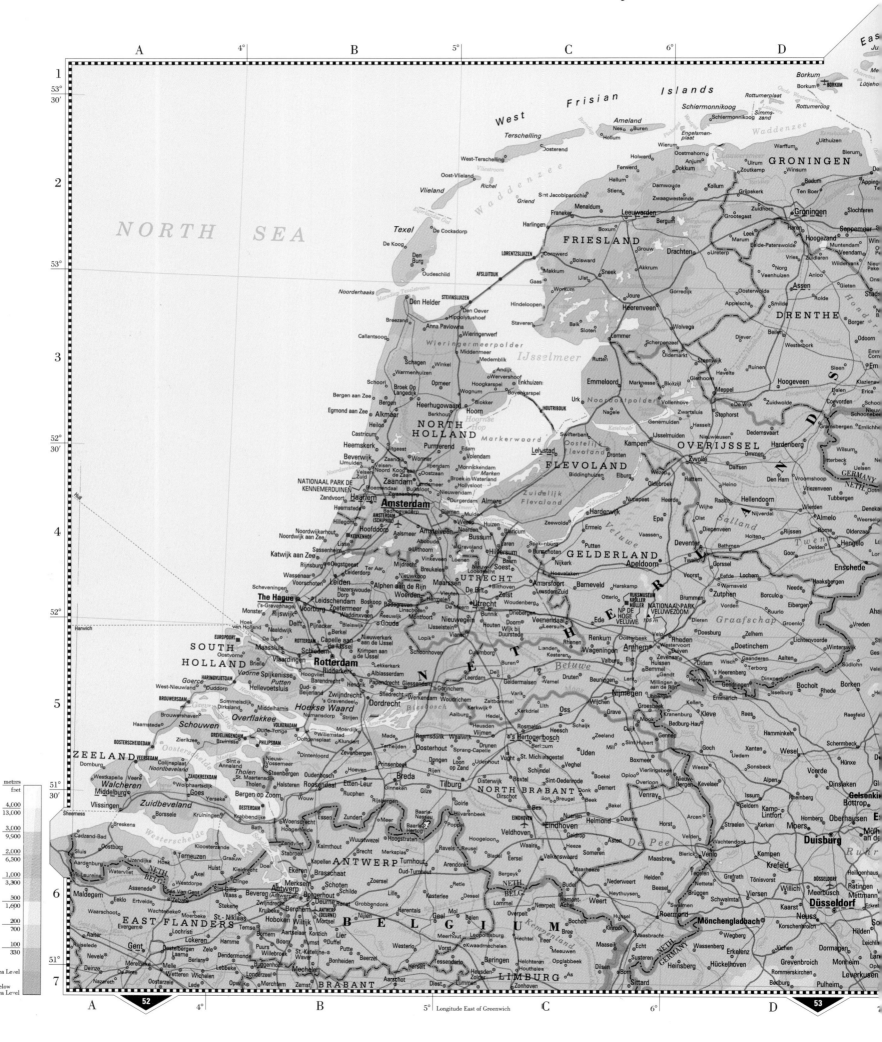

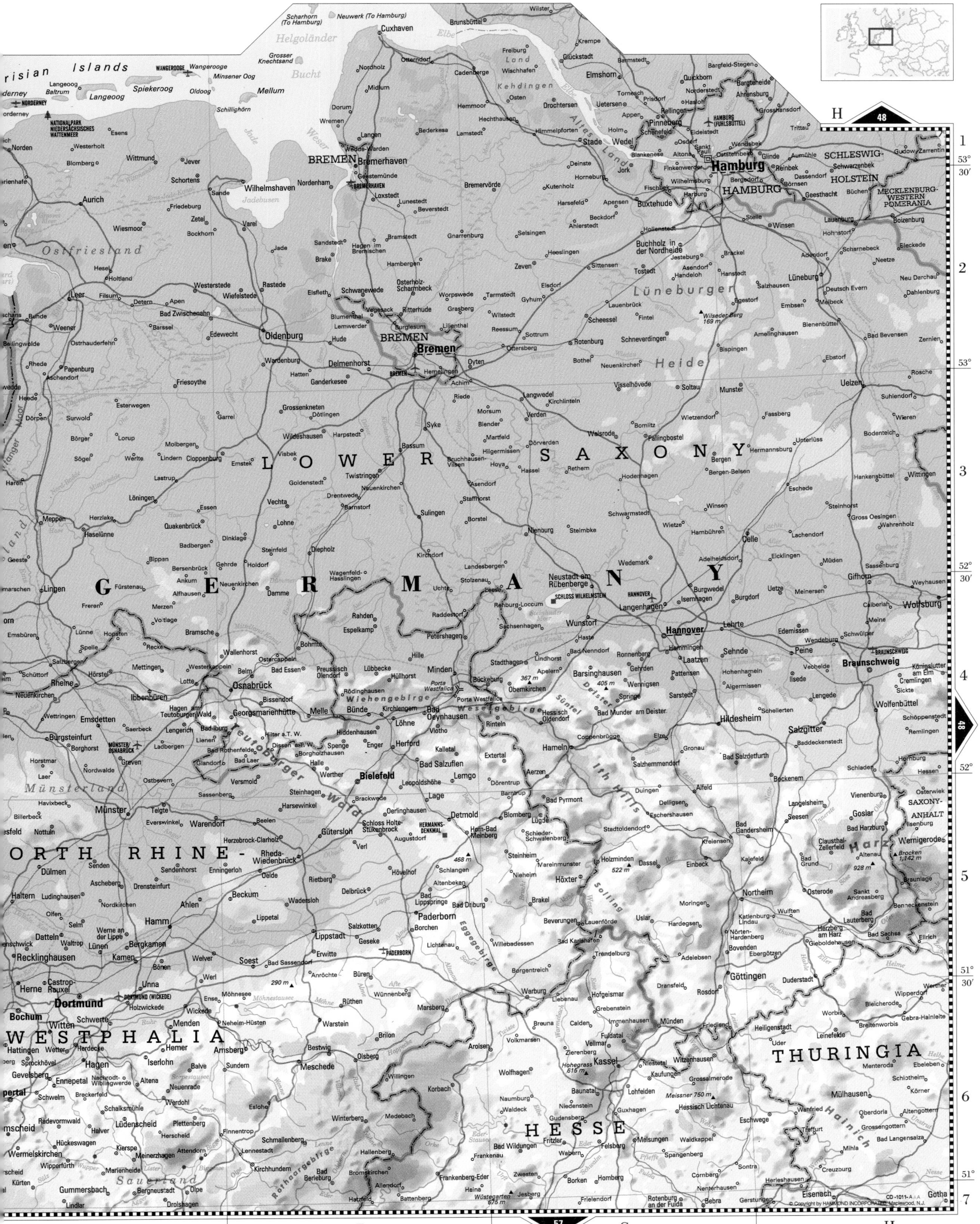

H 48

1
53° 30'

2
53°

3
52° 30'

4
48 52°

5
51° 30'

6
51°

7

GERMANY

LOWER SAXONY

NORTH RHINE-WESTPHALIA

THURINGIA

HESSE

SCHLESWIG-HOLSTEIN

MECKLENBURG-WESTERN POMERANIA

SAXONY-ANHALT

BREMEN

HAMBURG

Frisian Islands

Ostfriesland

Münsterland

Sauerland

Lüneburger Heide

Teutoburger Wald

Wiehengebirge · Wesergebirge

Eggegebirge

Rothaargebirge

Harz

Solling

Ith Hills

Helgoländer Bucht

National Park Niedersächsisches Wattenmeer

Hamburg · Bremen · Bremerhaven · Oldenburg · Osnabrück · Münster · Bielefeld · Paderborn · Dortmund · Bochum · Hannover · Braunschweig · Hildesheim · Salzgitter · Göttingen · Kassel · Wolfsburg · Goslar · Cuxhaven · Stade · Buxtehude · Lüneburg · Celle · Minden · Herford · Gütersloh · Hamm · Soest · Lippstadt

Brocken 1,142 m · Wilseder Berg 169 m · Meisner 750 m · Wüstegarten 675 m · Hohegrass 615 m

Elbe · Weser · Aller · Leine · Jade · Ems · Lippe · Ruhr · Fulda · Eder

POPULATION OF CITIES AND TOWNS

■ OVER 2,000,000   ● 500,000 – 999,999   ● 100,000 – 249,999   ○ 10,000 – 29,999
□ 1,000,000 – 1,999,999   ● 250,000 – 499,999   ○ 30,000 – 99,999   ○ UNDER 10,000

SCALE 1:1,170,000   LAMBERT CONFORMAL CONIC PROJECTION

MILES   0   10   20   30   40   50
KILOMETERS   0   10   20   30   40   50

E   8°   F   9°   57   G   10°   H

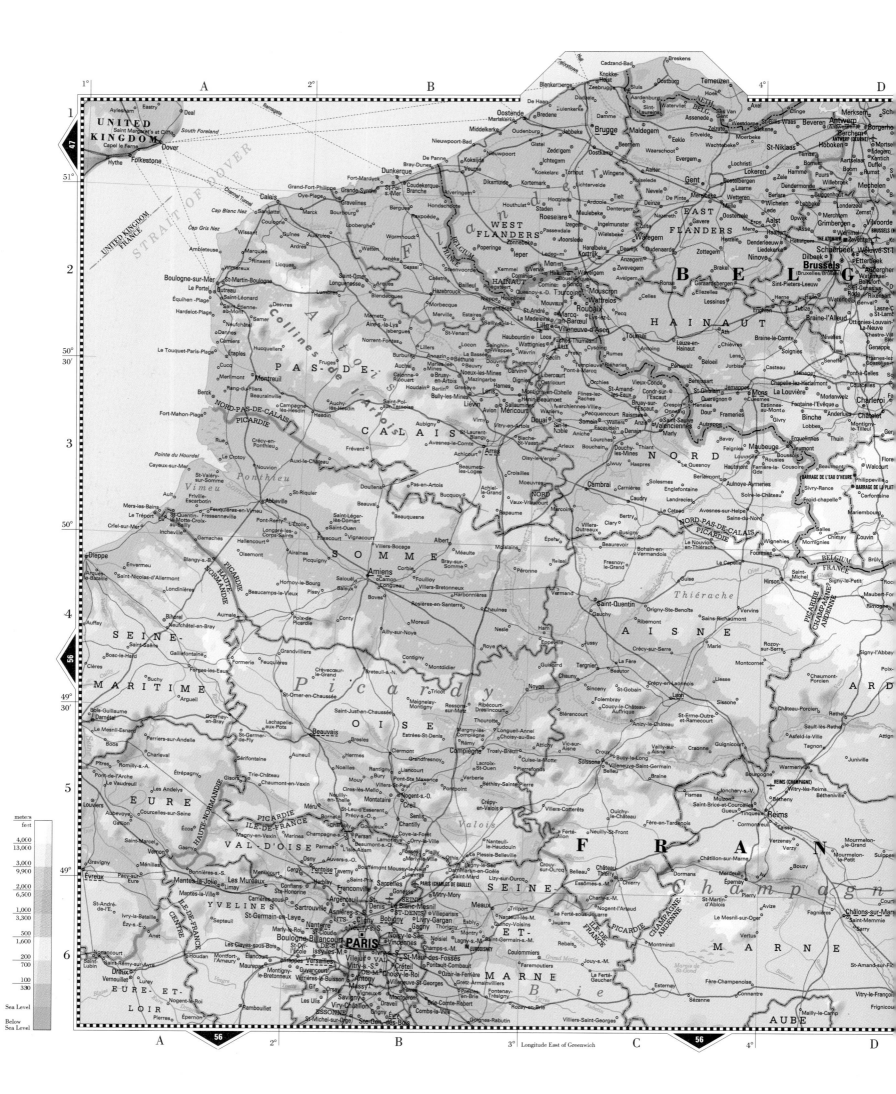

Belgium, Northern France, Western Germany

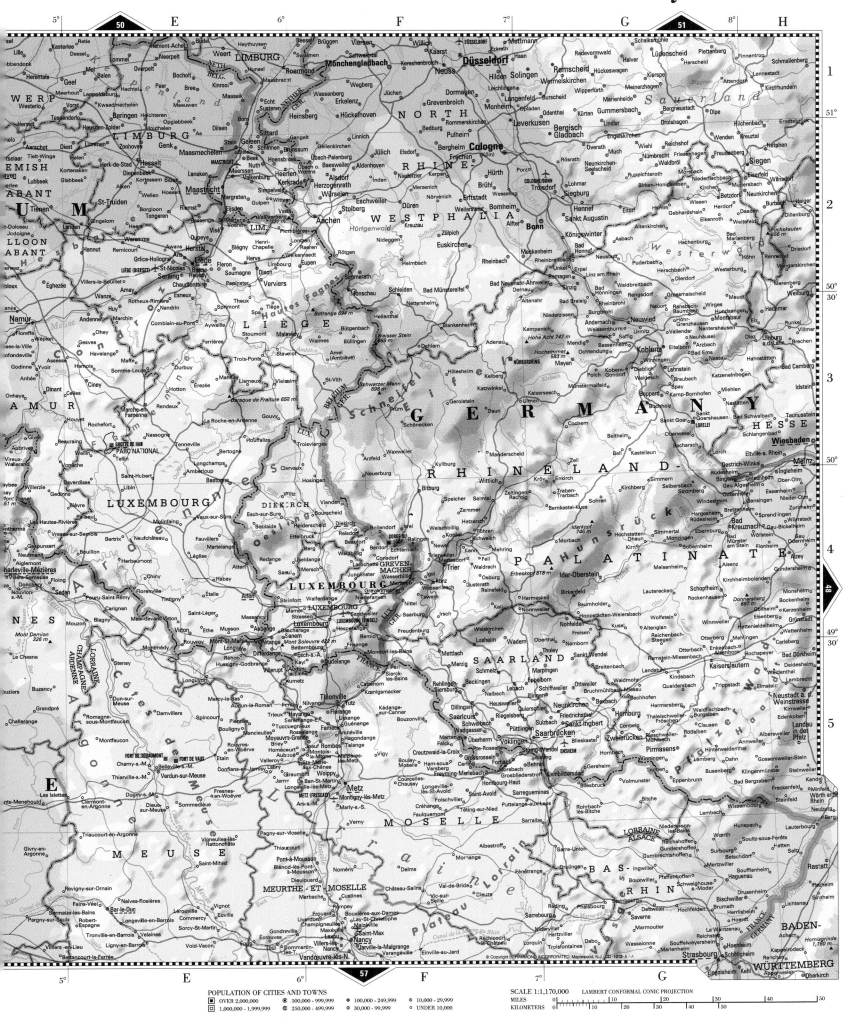

POPULATION OF CITIES AND TOWNS

■ OVER 2,000,000	◉ 500,000 - 999,999
▣ 1,000,000 - 1,999,999	◉ 250,000 - 499,999

● 100,000 - 249,999	● 10,000 - 29,999
● 30,000 - 99,999	○ UNDER 10,000

SCALE 1:1,170,000   LAMBERT CONFORMAL CONIC PROJECTION

MILES 0 ___ 10 ___ 20 ___ 30 ___ 40 ___ 50

KILOMETERS 0 __ 10 __ 20 __ 30 __ 40 __ 50

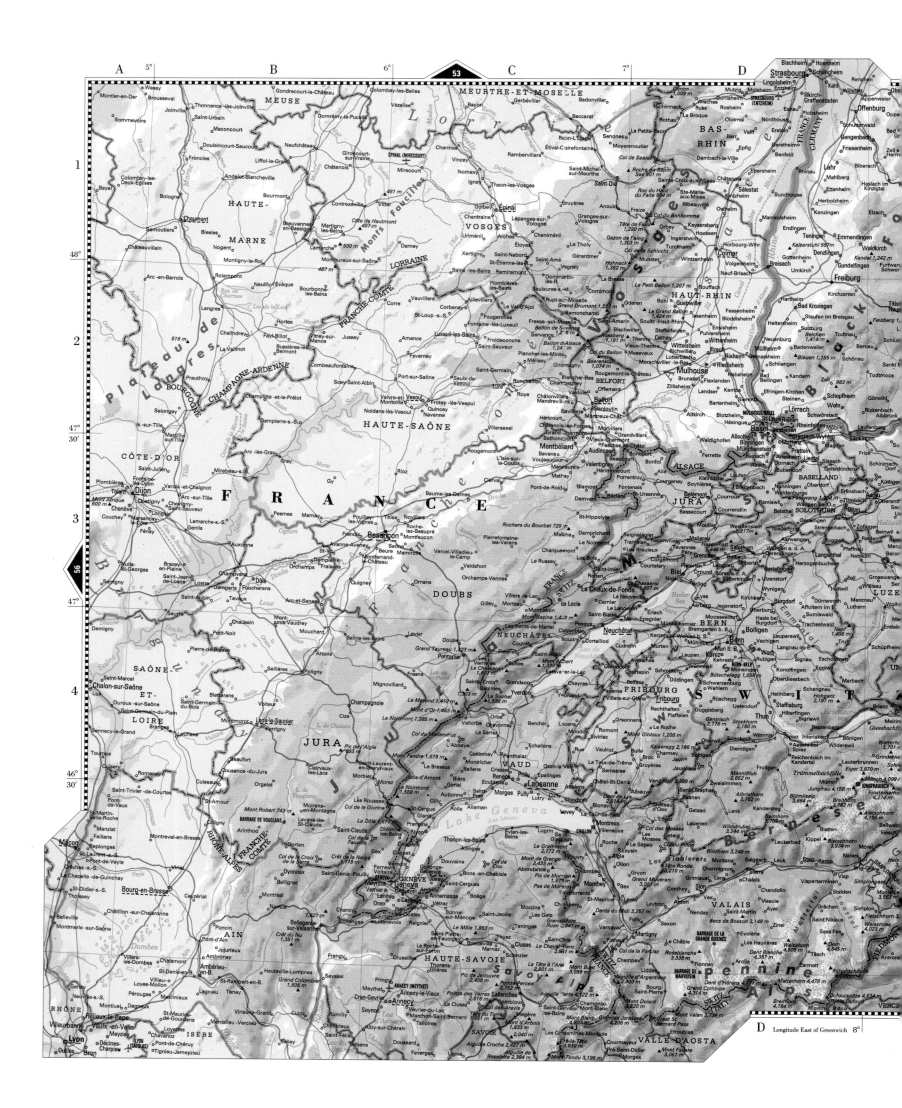

Central Alps Region

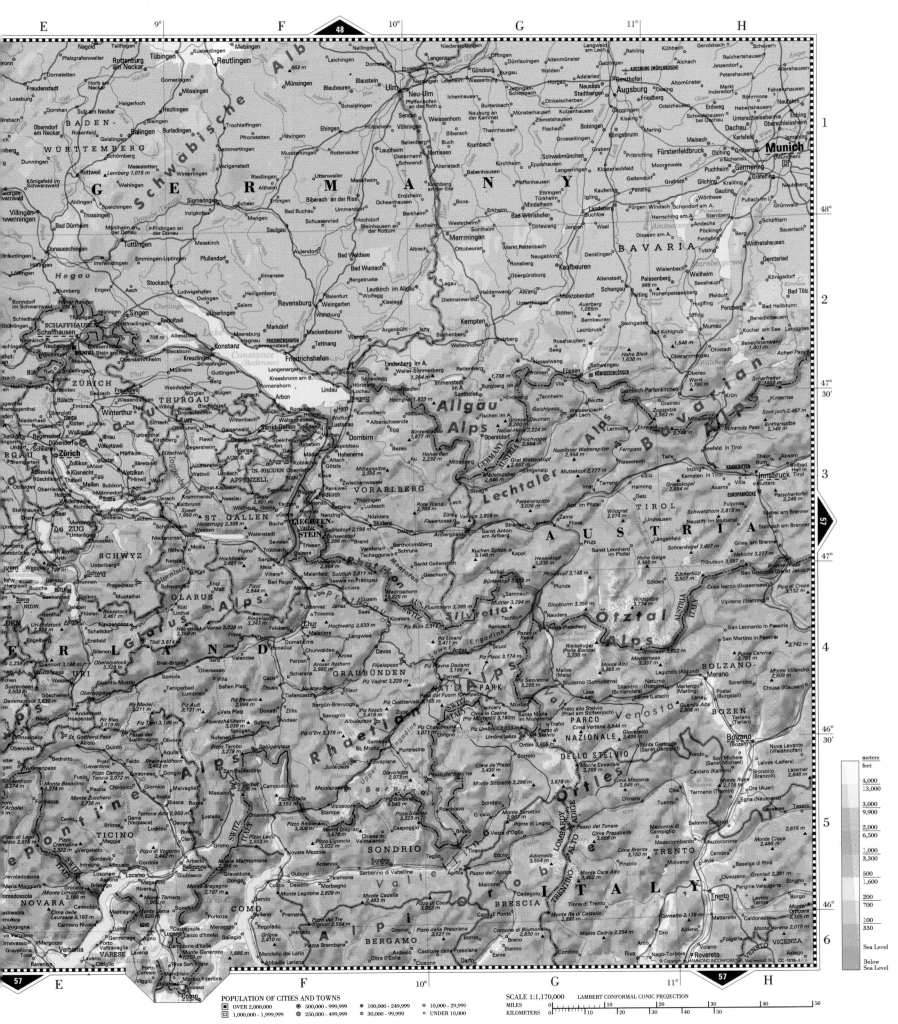

POPULATION OF CITIES AND TOWNS
- ■ OVER 2,000,000
- ⊡ 1,000,000 - 1,999,999
- ⊛ 500,000 - 999,999
- ⊛ 250,000 - 499,999
- ⊛ 100,000 - 249,999
- ⊛ 30,000 - 99,999
- ⊛ 10,000 - 29,999
- ○ UNDER 10,000

SCALE 1:1,170,000   LAMBERT CONFORMAL CONIC PROJECTION

MILES 0   10   20   30   40   50
KILOMETERS 0   10   20   30   40   50

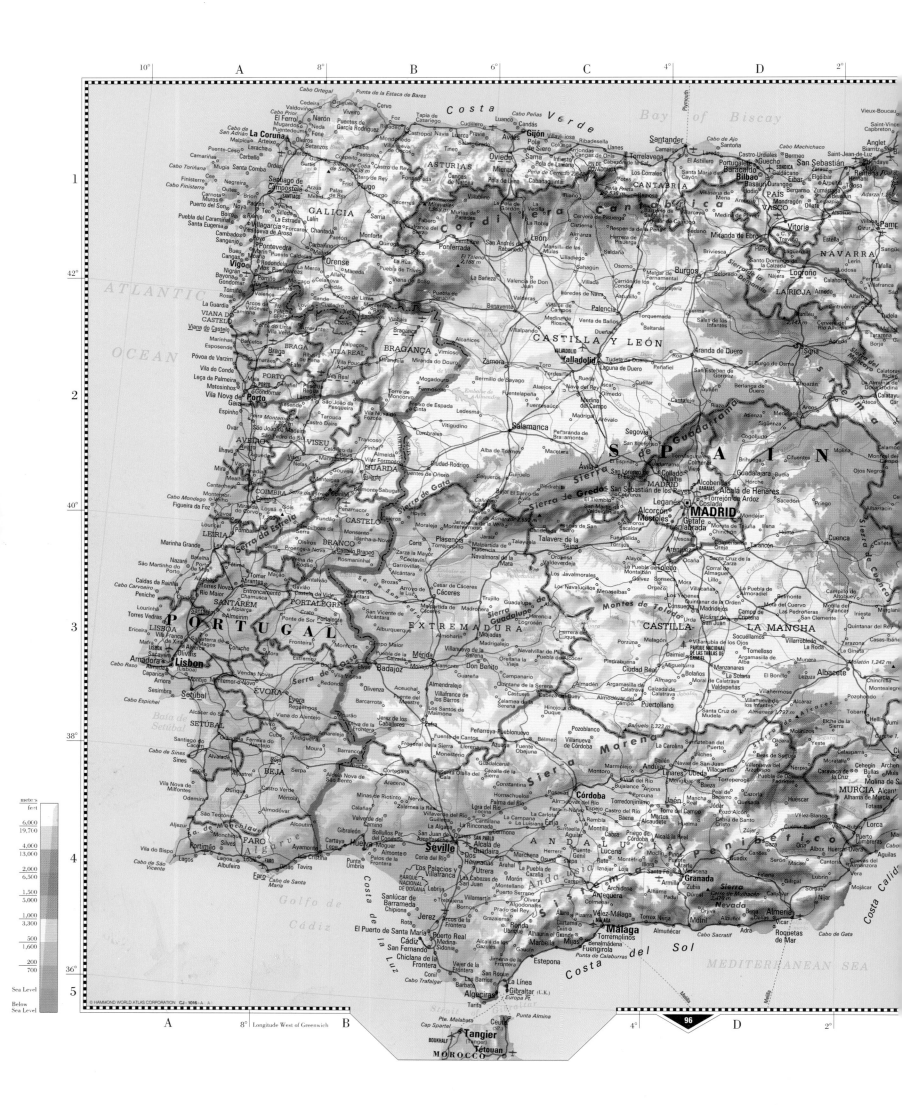

Spain, Portugal

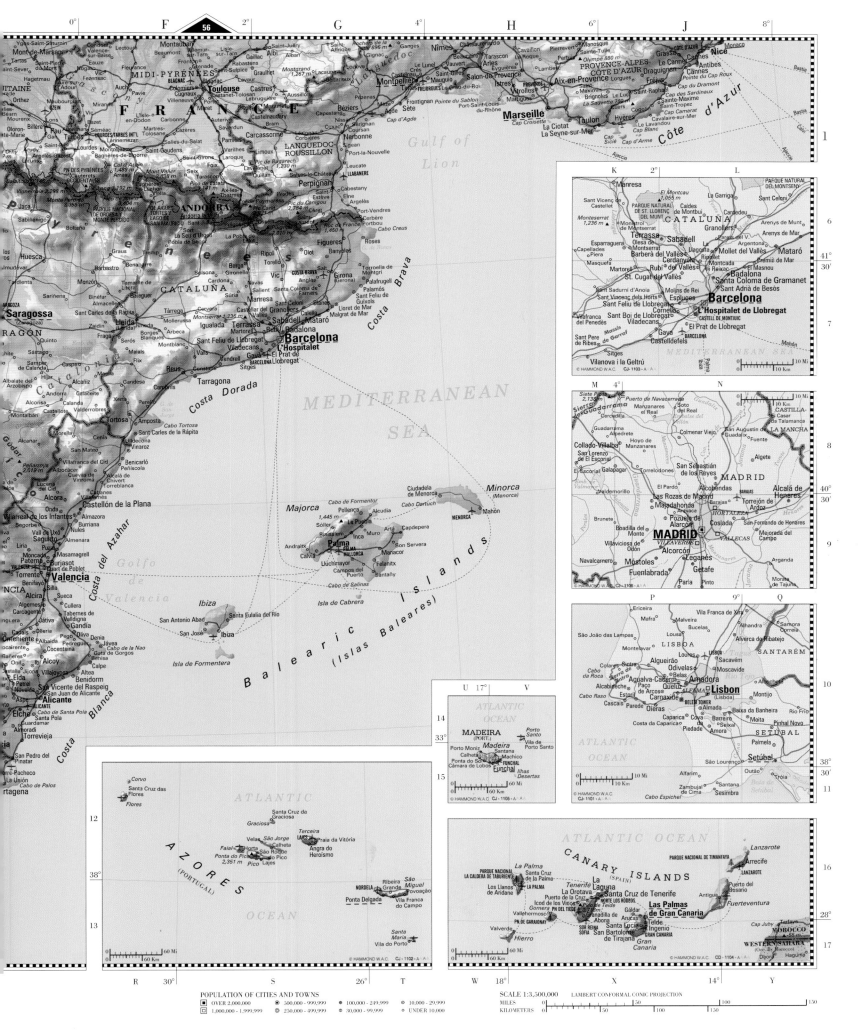

POPULATION OF CITIES AND TOWNS

■ OVER 2,000,000
□ 1,000,000 - 1,999,999
● 500,000 - 999,999
● 250,000 - 499,999
● 100,000 - 249,999
● 30,000 - 99,999
● 10,000 - 29,999
● UNDER 10,000

SCALE 1:3,500,000   LAMBERT CONFORMAL CONIC PROJECTION

MILES
KILOMETERS

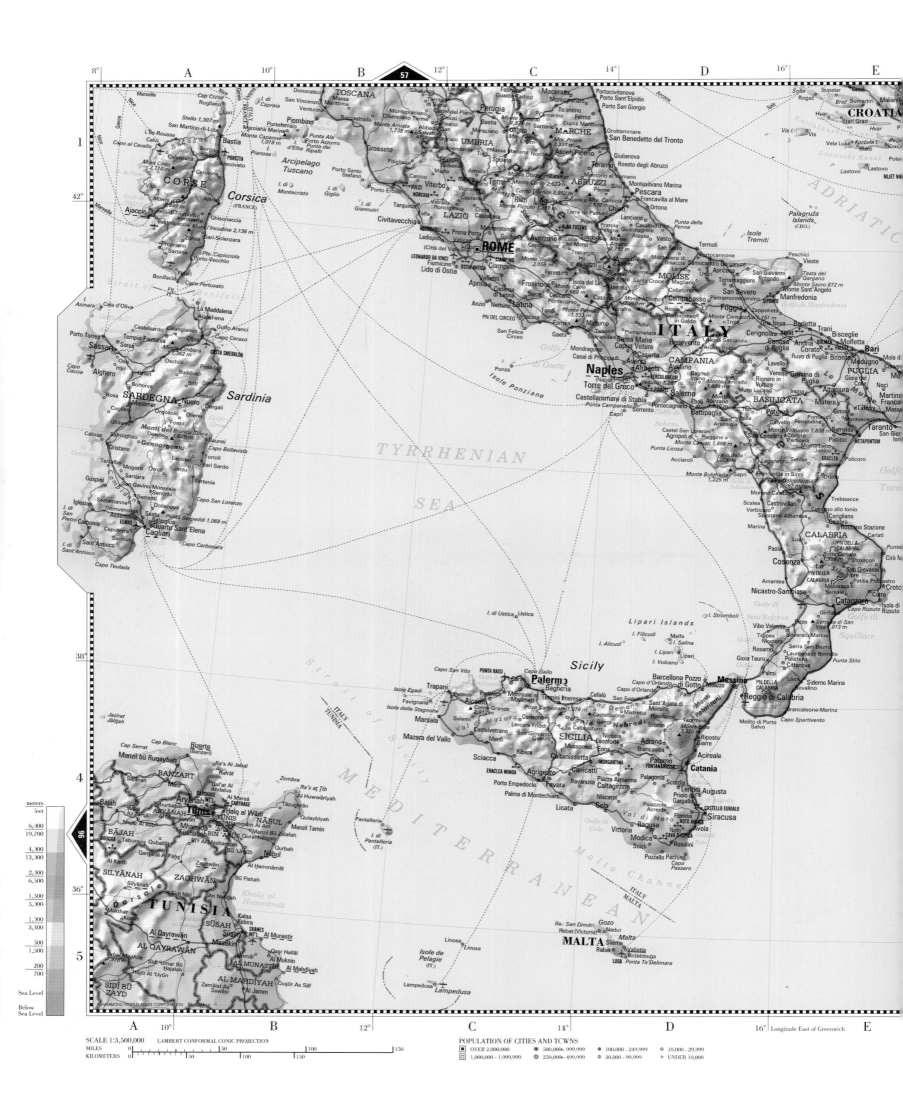

SCALE 1:3,500,000   LAMBERT CONFORMAL CONIC PROJECTION

MILES
KILOMETERS

POPULATION OF CITIES AND TOWNS

■ OVER 2,000,000
□ 1,000,000 - 1,999,999
● 500,000 - 999,999
◉ 250,000 - 499,999
● 100,000 - 249,999
● 30,000 - 99,999
◦ 10,000 - 29,999
◦ UNDER 10,000

Longitude East of Greenwich

Southern Italy, Albania, Greece

SCALE 1:3,500,000   LAMBERT CONFORMAL CONIC PROJECTION
MILES
KILOMETERS

POPULATION OF CITIES AND TOWNS
■ OVER 2,000,000   ● 500,000 - 999,999   ⊕ 100,000 - 249,999   ⊙ 10,000 - 29,999
▣ 1,000,000 - 1,999,999 ◉ 250,000 - 499,999   ⊙ 30,000 - 99,999   ∘ UNDER 10,000

Hungary, Northern Balkan States

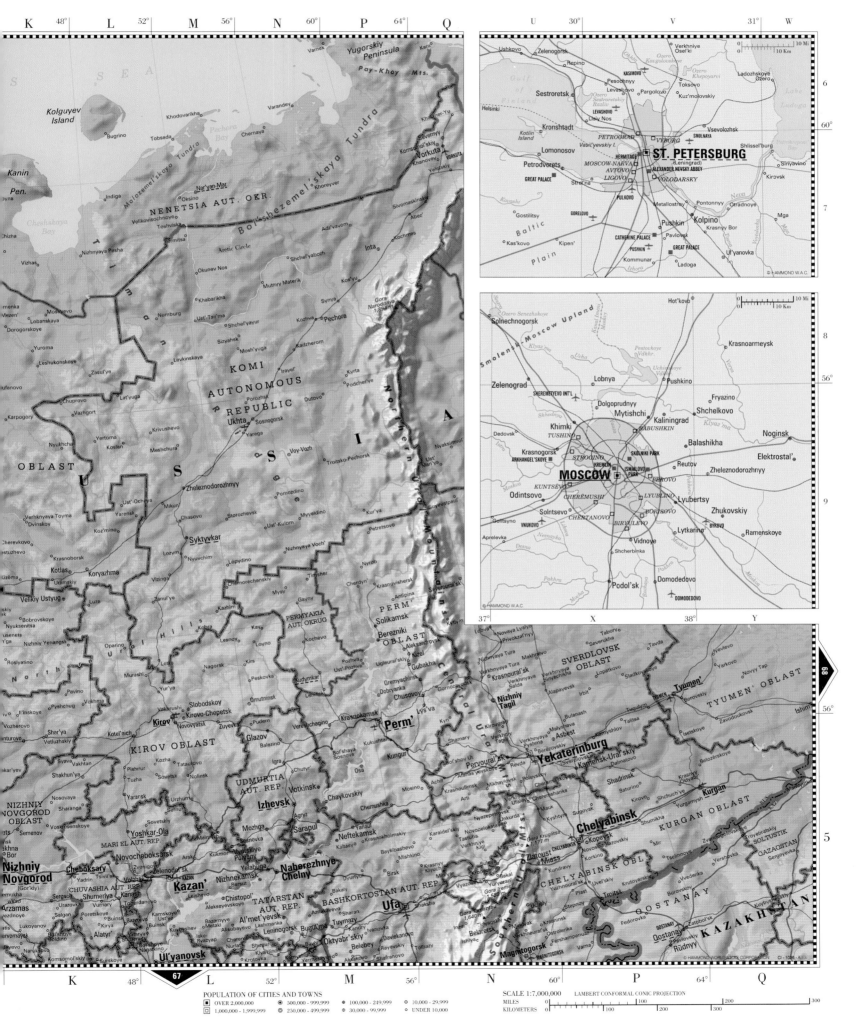

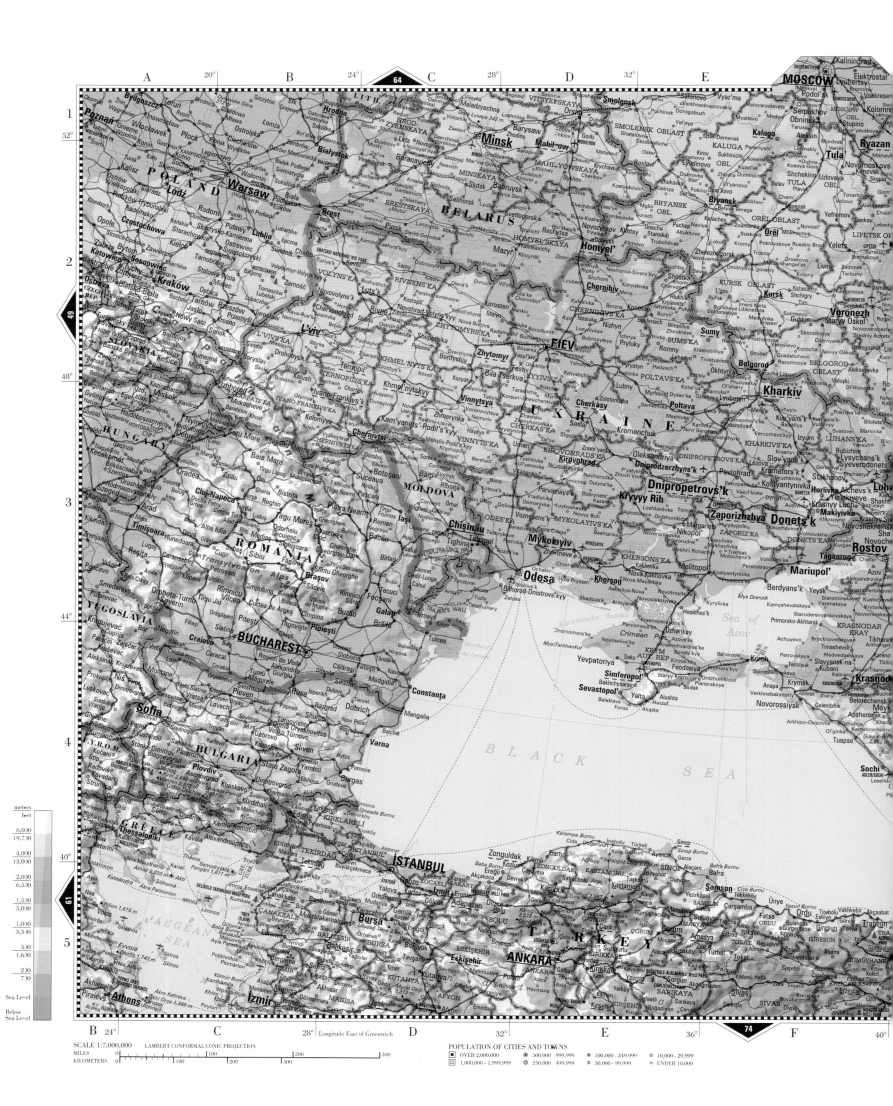

POPULATION OF CITIES AND TOWNS

| ■ | OVER 2,000,000 | ● | 500,000 - 999,999 | ● | 100,000 - 249,999 | ○ | 10,000 - 29,999 |
| □ | 1,000,000 - 1,999,999 | ● | 250,000 - 499,999 | ● | 30,000 - 99,999 | ○ | UNDER 10,000 |

Southeastern Europe

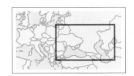

Russia and Neighboring Countries

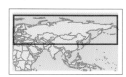

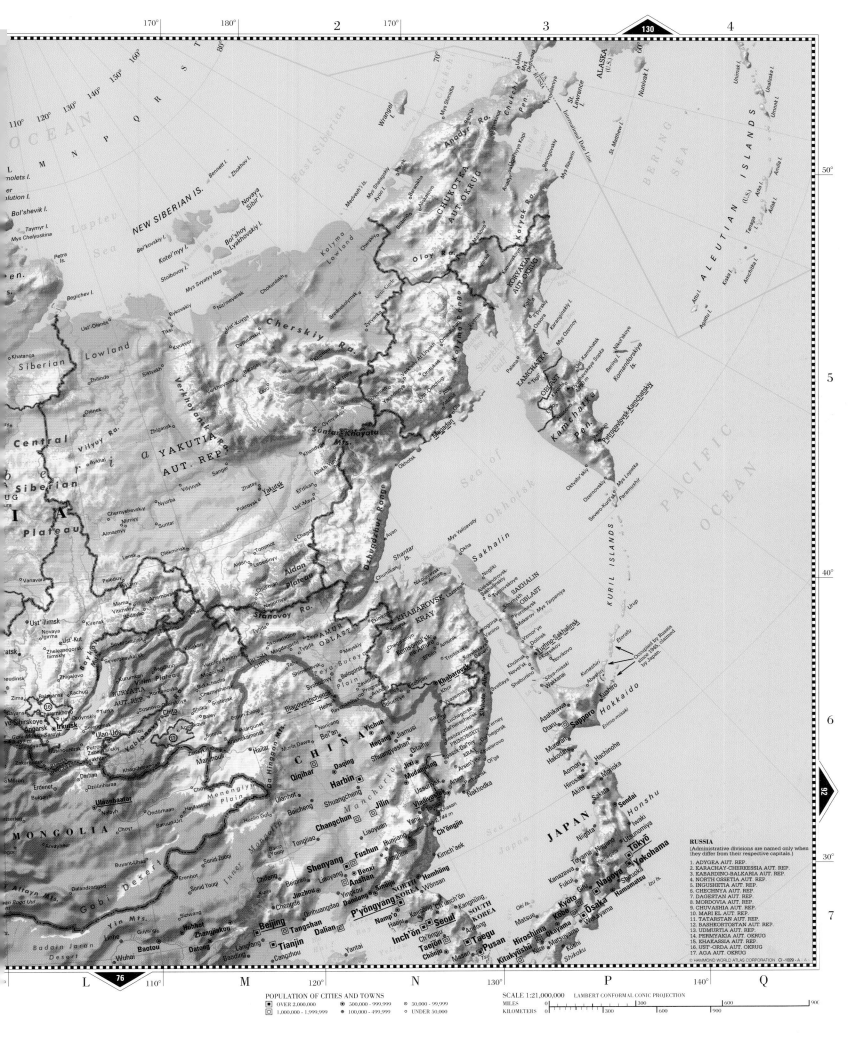

RUSSIA
(Administrative divisions are named only when they differ from their respective capitals.)

1. ADYGEA AUT. REP.
2. KARACHAY-CHERKESSIA AUT. REP.
3. KABARDINO-BALKARIA AUT. REP.
4. NORTH OSSETIA AUT. REP.
5. INGUSHETIA AUT. REP.
6. CHECHNYA AUT. REP.
7. DAGESTAN AUT. REP.
8. MORDOVIA AUT. REP.
9. CHUVASHIA AUT. REP.
10. MARI EL AUT. REP.
11. TATARSTAN AUT. REP.
12. BASHKORTOSTAN AUT. REP.
13. UDMURTIA AUT. REP.
14. PERMYAKIA AUT. OKRUG
15. KHAKASSIA AUT. REP.
16. UST'-ORDA AUT. OKRUG
17. AGA AUT. OKRUG

© HAMMOND WORLD ATLAS CORPORATION   CI -1029 -A· A

POPULATION OF CITIES AND TOWNS

- ■ OVER 2,000,000
- ◉ 500,000 - 999,999
- ● 50,000 - 99,999
- ▣ 1,000,000 - 1,999,999
- ● 100,000 - 499,999
- ○ UNDER 50,000

SCALE 1:21,000,000   LAMBERT CONFORMAL CONIC PROJECTION

MILES 0 ___ 300 ___ 600
KILOMETERS 0 ___ 300 ___ 600 ___ 900

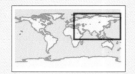

Asia - Comparisons

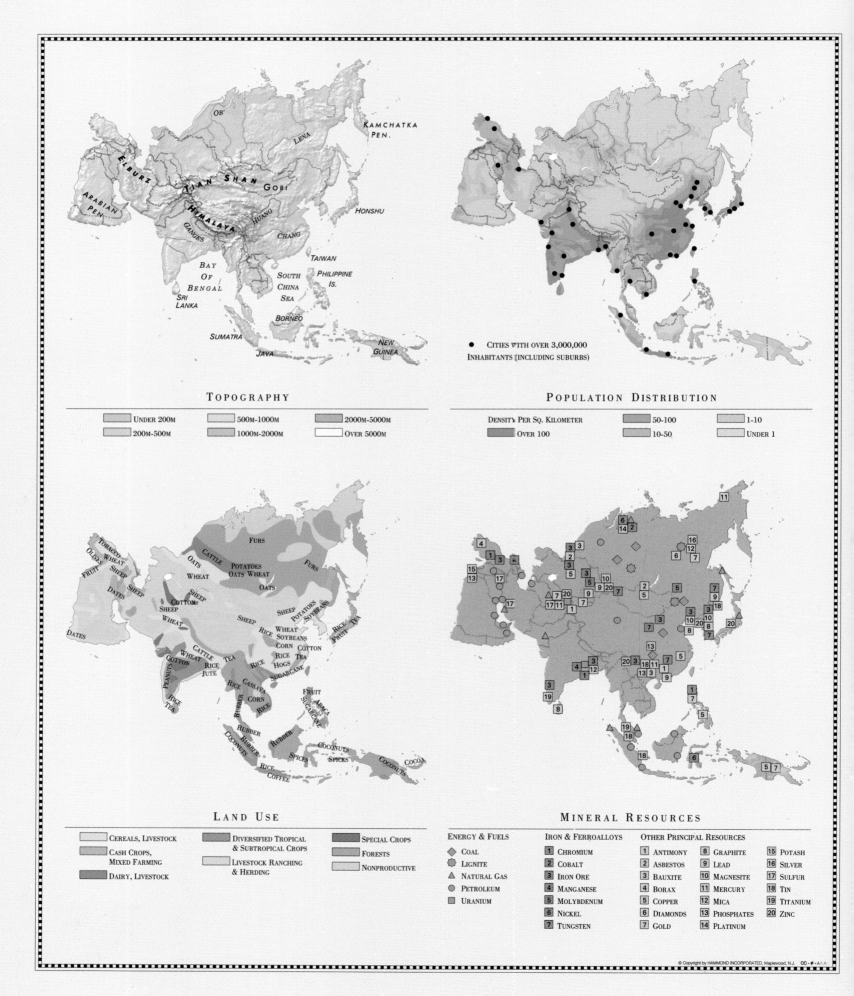

TOPOGRAPHY

UNDER 200M	500M-1000M	2000M-5000M
200M-500M	1000M-2000M	OVER 5000M

POPULATION DISTRIBUTION

- CITIES WITH OVER 3,000,000 INHABITANTS (INCLUDING SUBURBS)

DENSITY PER SQ. KILOMETER	50-100	1-10
OVER 100	10-50	UNDER 1

LAND USE

CEREALS, LIVESTOCK	DIVERSIFIED TROPICAL & SUBTROPICAL CROPS	SPECIAL CROPS
CASH CROPS, MIXED FARMING	LIVESTOCK RANCHING & HERDING	FORESTS
DAIRY, LIVESTOCK		NONPRODUCTIVE

MINERAL RESOURCES

ENERGY & FUELS
- ◇ COAL
- ⬡ LIGNITE
- △ NATURAL GAS
- ○ PETROLEUM
- ▢ URANIUM

IRON & FERROALLOYS
1 CHROMIUM
2 COBALT
3 IRON ORE
4 MANGANESE
5 MOLYBDENUM
6 NICKEL
7 TUNGSTEN

OTHER PRINCIPAL RESOURCES
1 ANTIMONY
2 ASBESTOS
3 BAUXITE
4 BORAX
5 COPPER
6 DIAMONDS
7 GOLD
8 GRAPHITE
9 LEAD
10 MAGNESITE
11 MERCURY
12 MICA
13 PHOSPHATES
14 PLATINUM
15 POTASH
16 SILVER
17 SULFUR
18 TIN
19 TITANIUM
20 ZINC

Asia

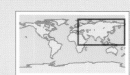

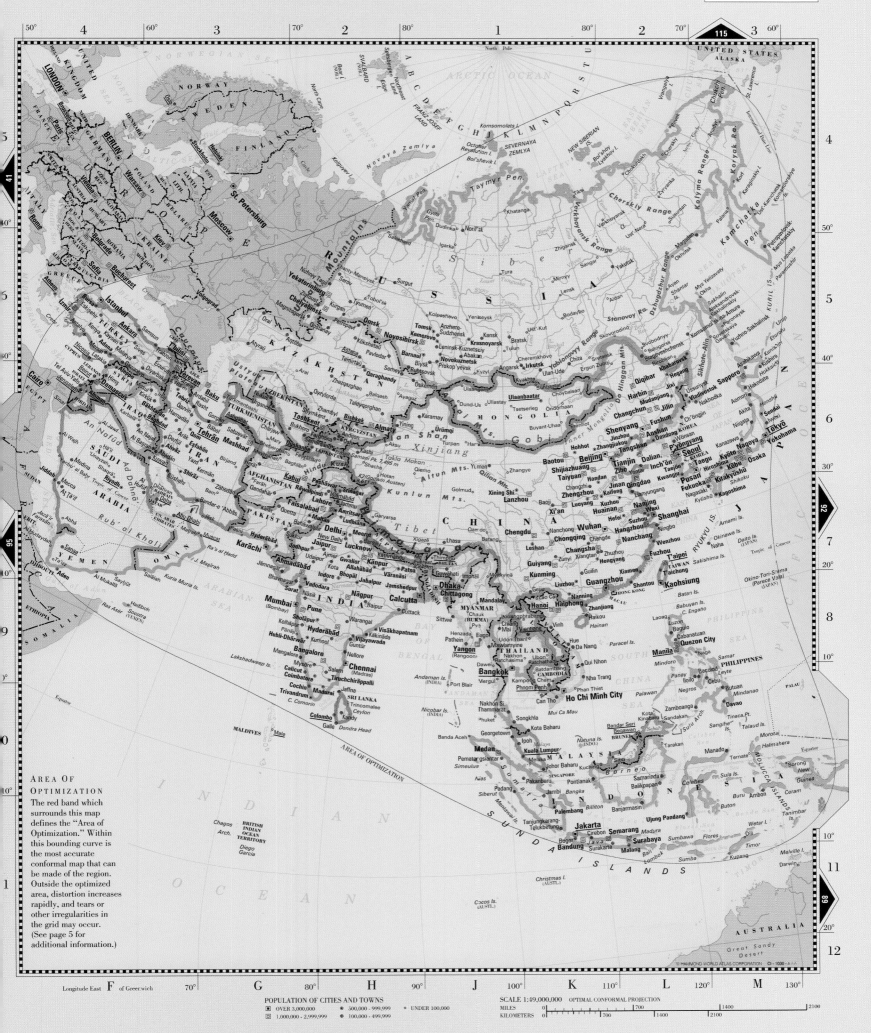

POPULATION OF CITIES AND TOWNS

- ⬛ OVER 3,000,000
- ⬛ 1,000,000 - 2,999,999
- ⬛ 500,000 - 999,999
- ⬛ 100,000 - 499,999
- ○ UNDER 100,000

SCALE 1:49,000,000   OPTIMAL CONFORMAL PROJECTION

MILES   0   700   1400   2100
KILOMETERS 0   700   1400   2100

© Hammond World Atlas Corporation   CI - 1030 - A - A

AREA OF OPTIMIZATION

The red band which surrounds this map defines the "Area of Optimization." Within this bounding curve is the most accurate conformal map that can be made of the region. Outside the optimized area, distortion increases rapidly, and tears or other irregularities in the grid may occur. (See page 5 for additional information.)

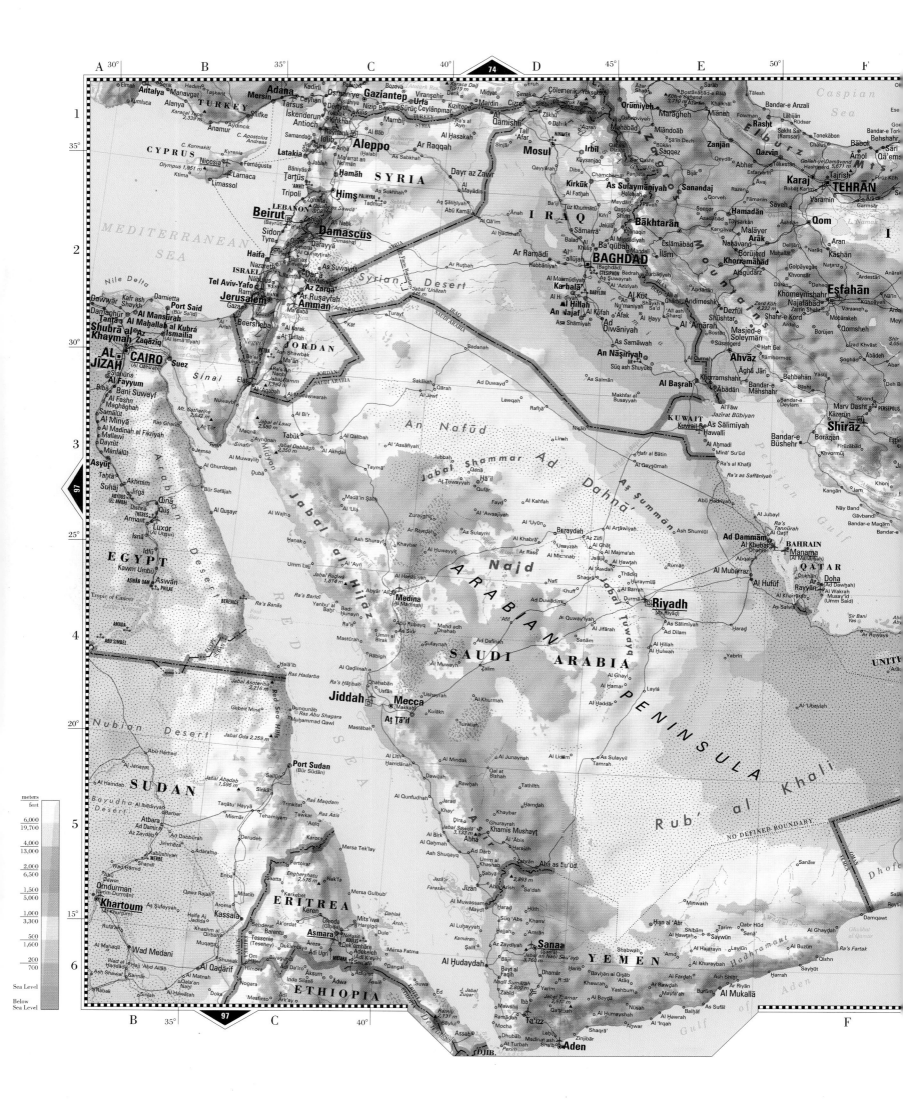

Southwestern Asia

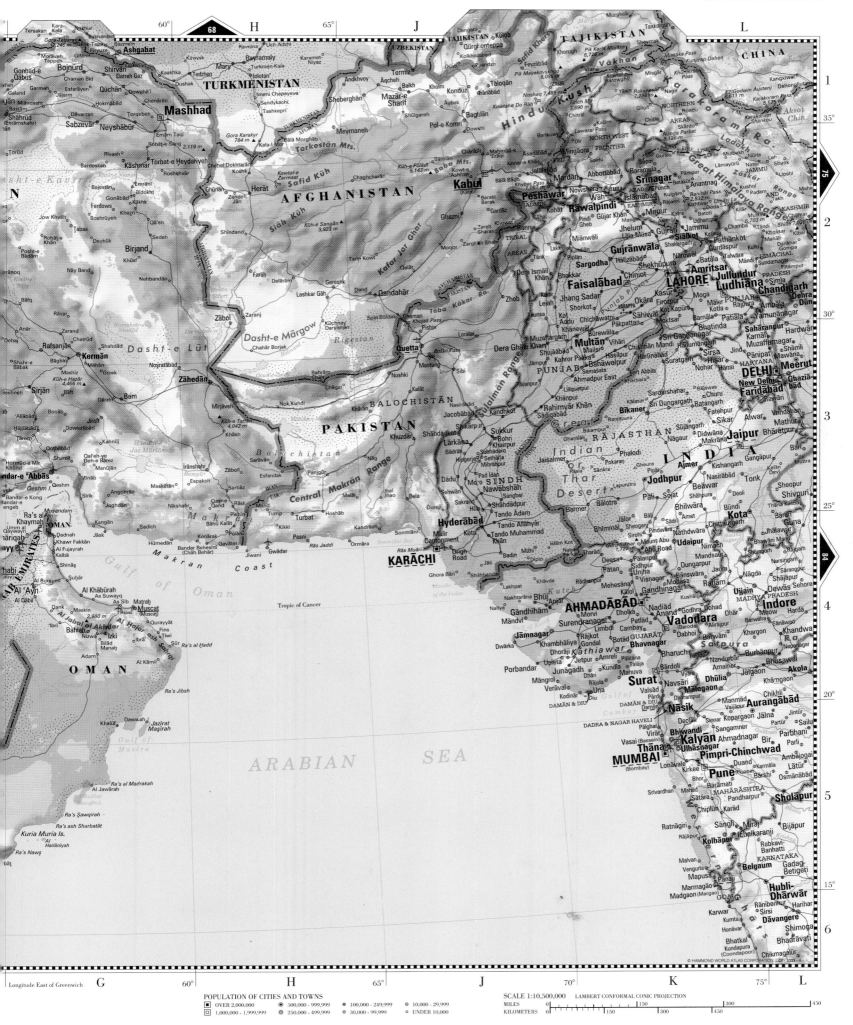

Eastern Mediterranean Region

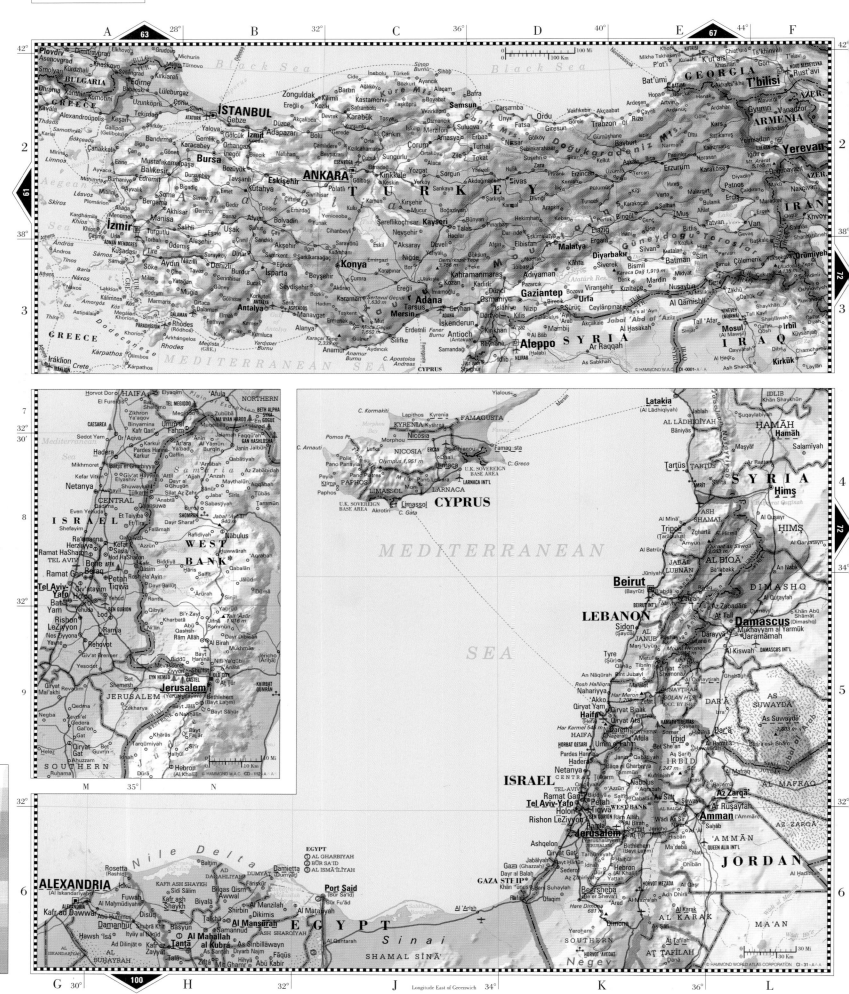

Central Asia

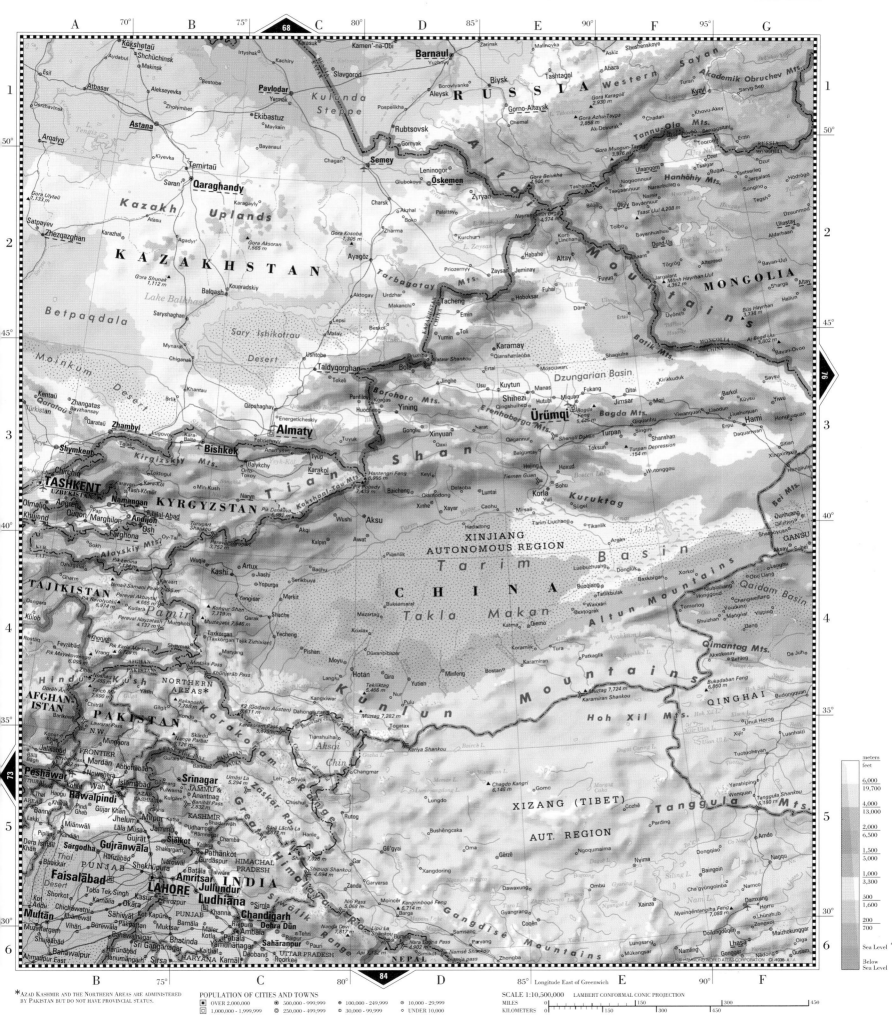

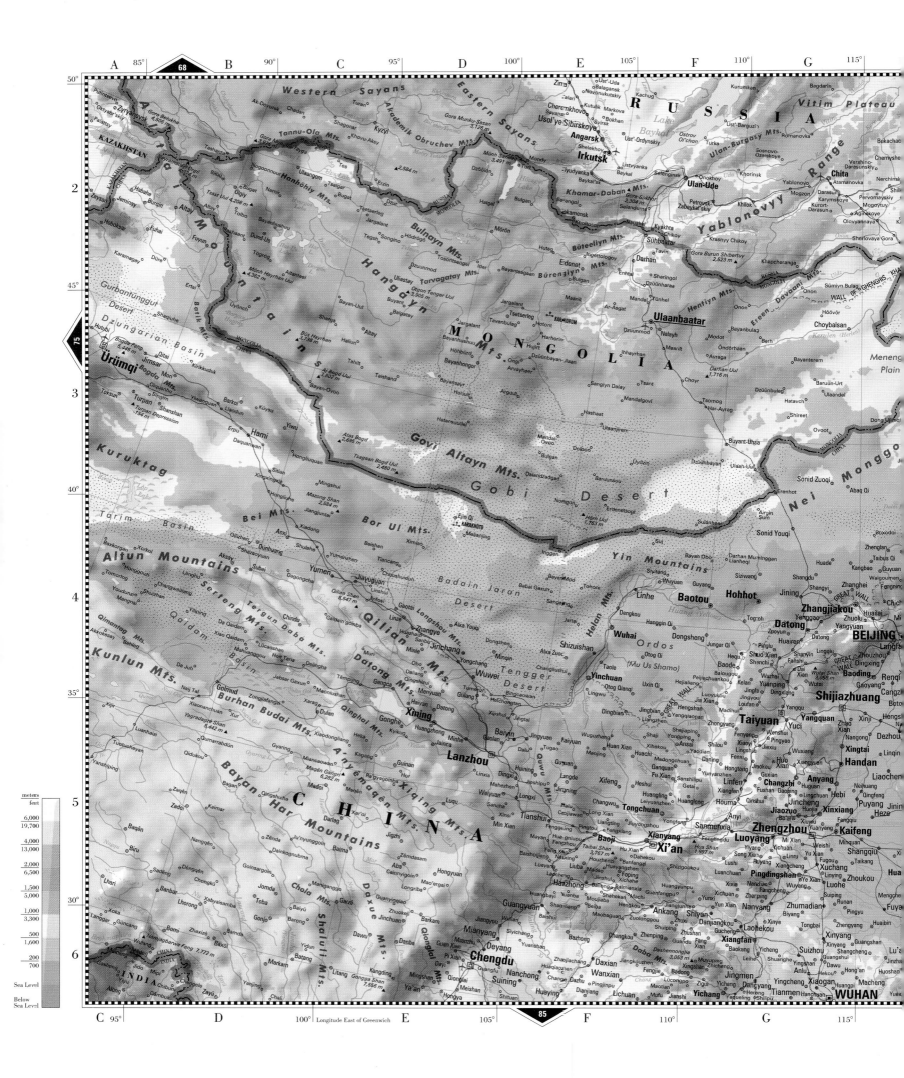

Eastern Asia

POPULATION OF CITIES AND TOWNS

■ OVER 2,000,000   ● 500,000 - 999,999   ● 100,000 - 249,999   ○ 10,000 - 29,999
□ 1,000,000 - 1,999,999   ● 250,000 - 499,999   ○ 30,000 - 99,999   ○ UNDER 10,000

SCALE 1:10,500,000   LAMBERT CONFORMAL CONIC PROJECTION

MILES   0   150   300   450
KILOMETERS   0   150   300   450

Central and Southern Japan

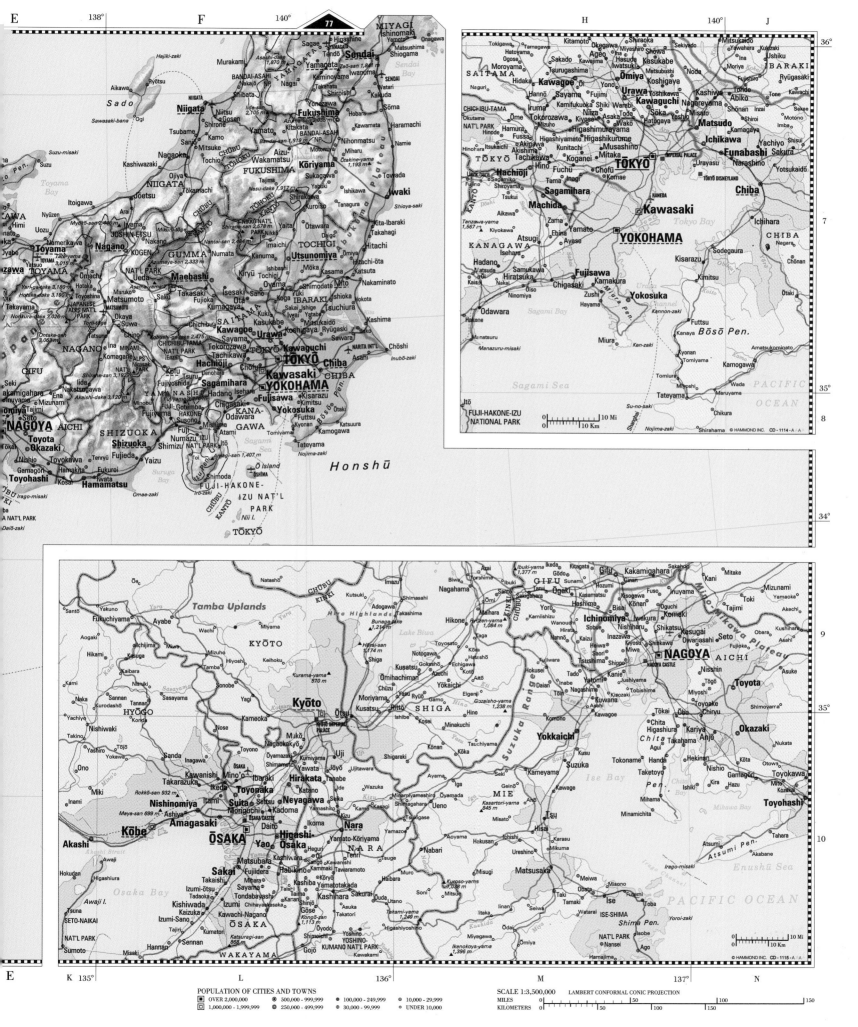

Korea

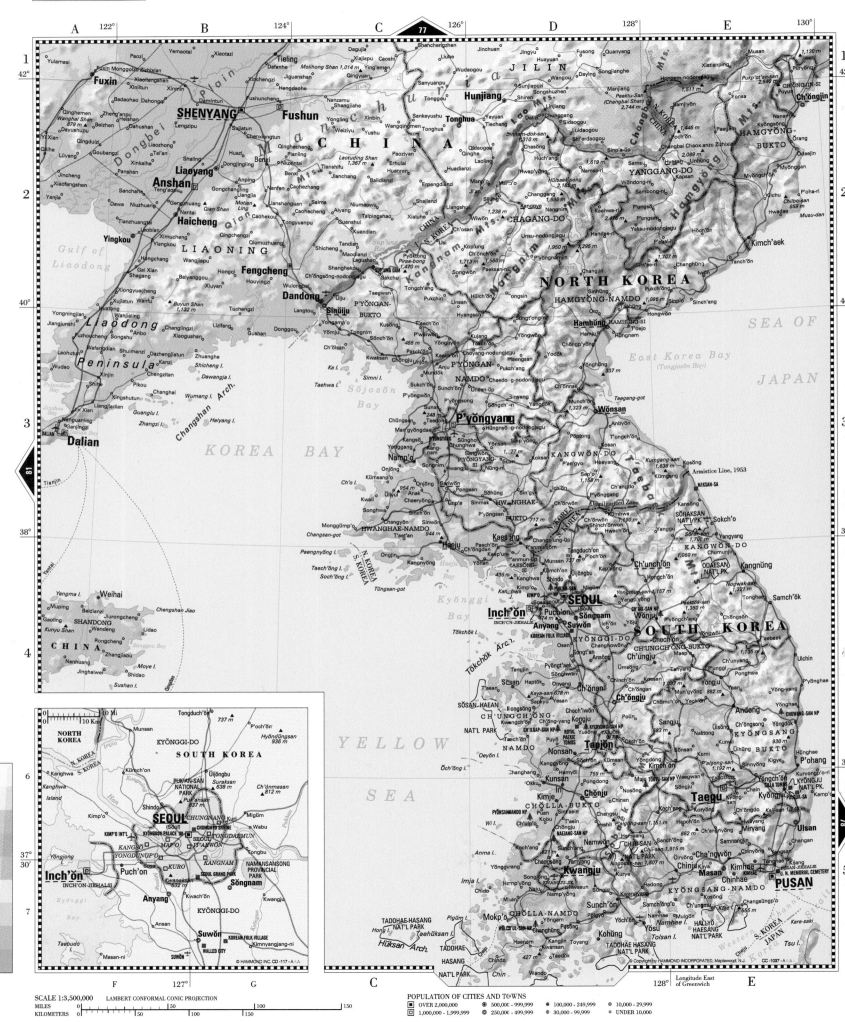

Northeastern China

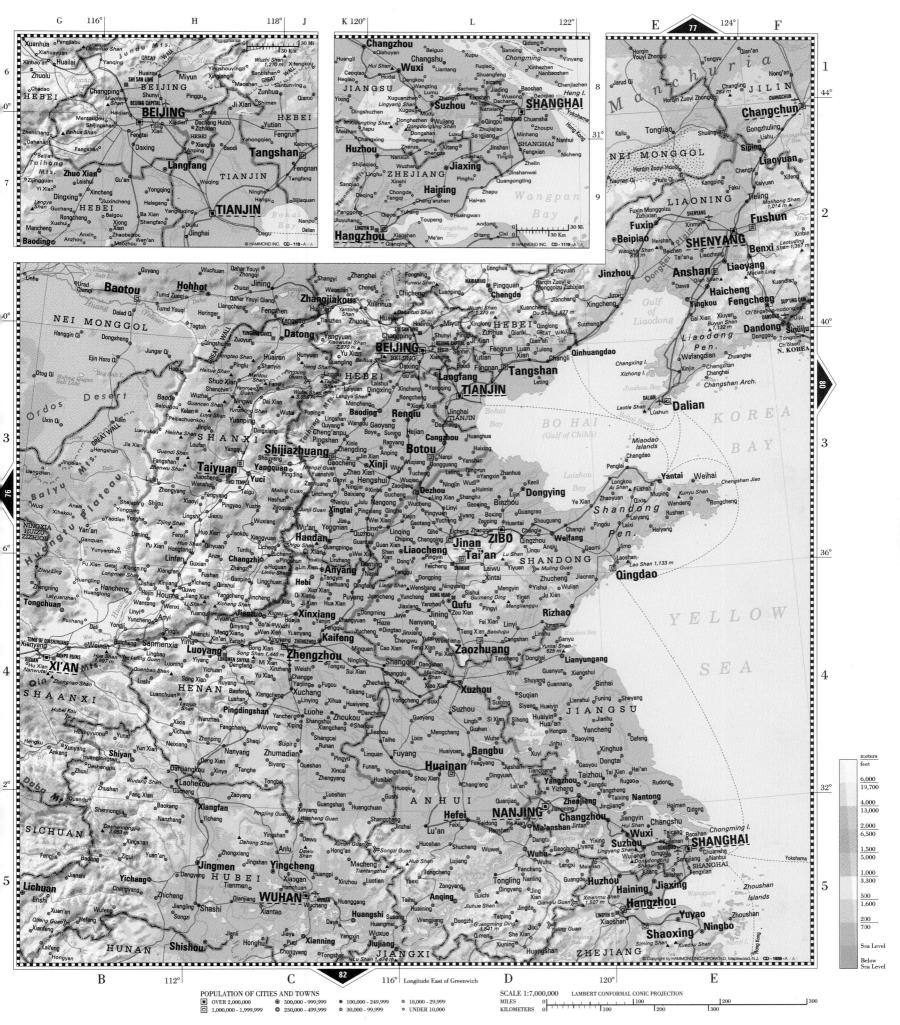

Southeastern China, Taiwan, Philippines

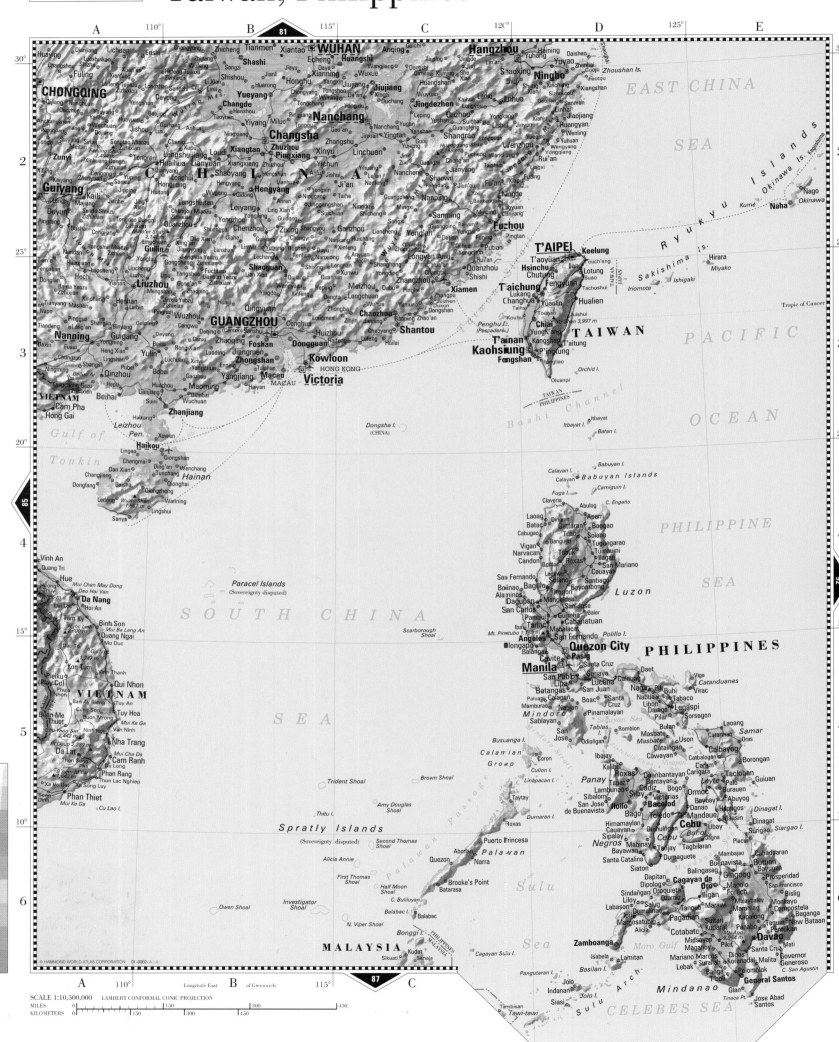

Indochina

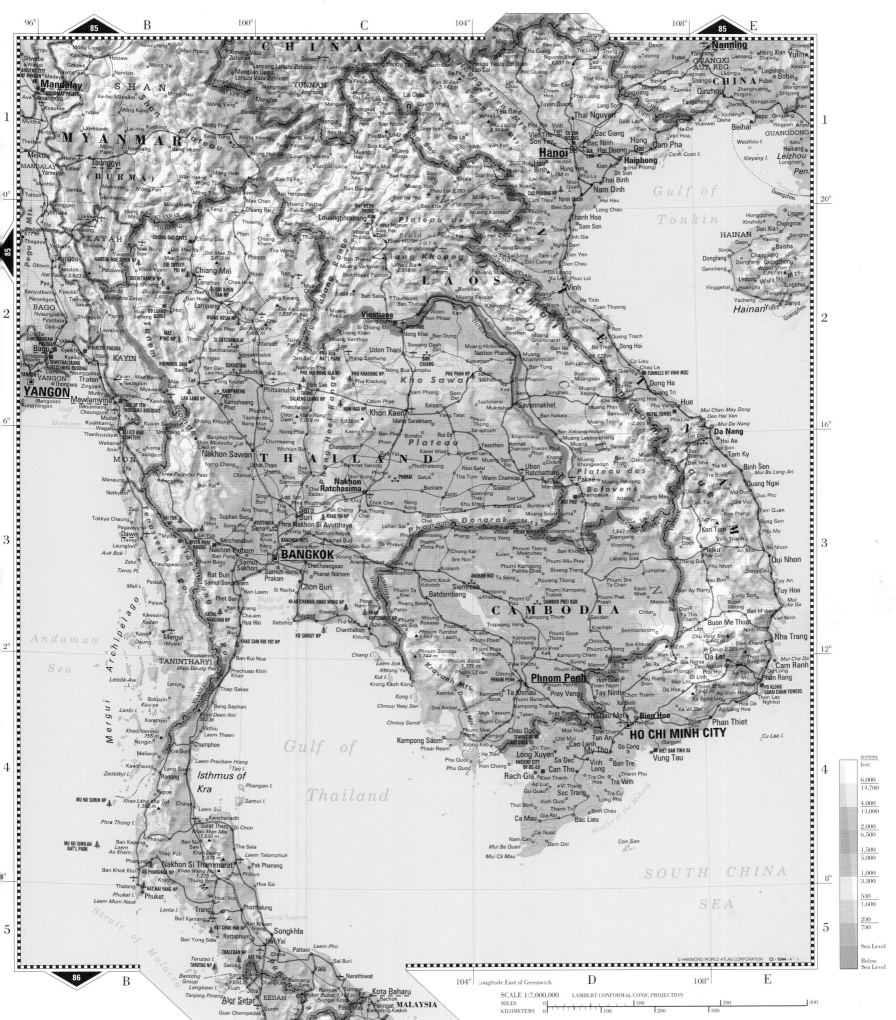

SCALE 1:7,000,000 LAMBERT CONFORMAL CONIC PROJECTION

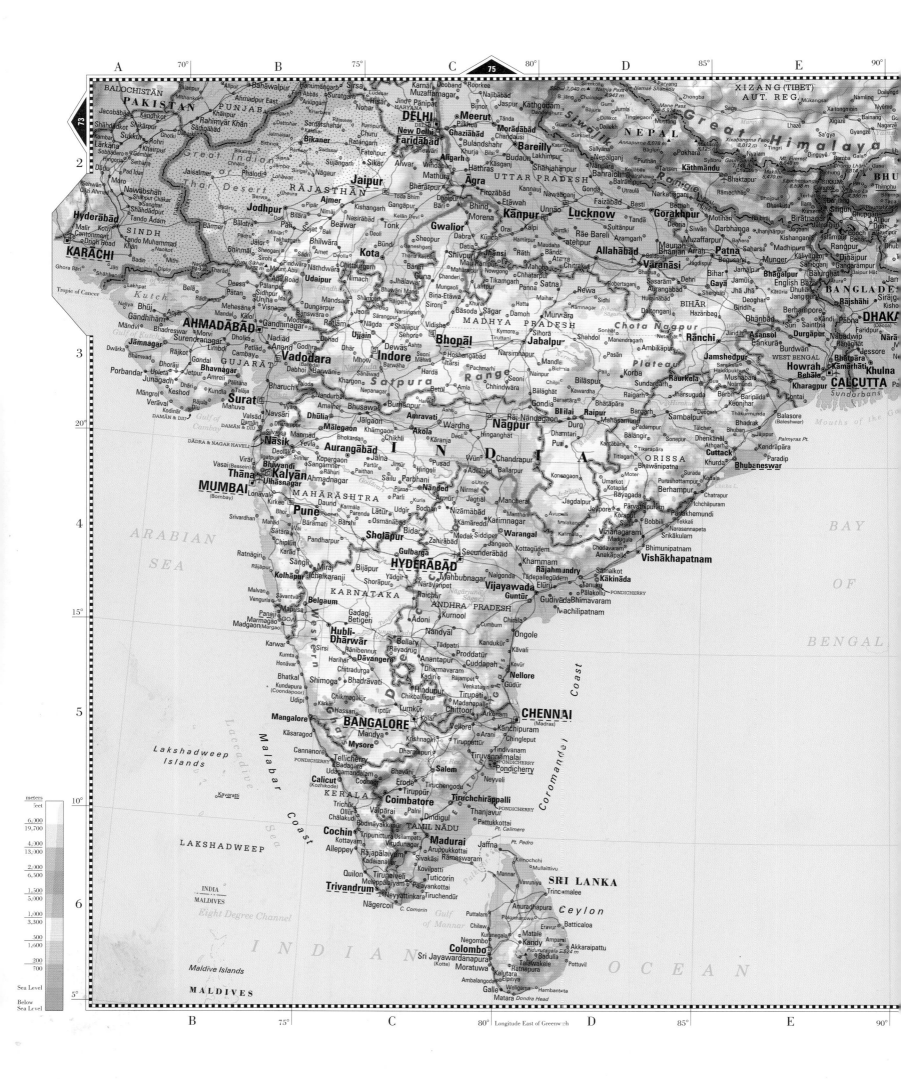

Southern Asia

POPULATION OF CITIES AND TOWNS

■ OVER 2,000,000   ● 500,000 - 999,999   ⊕ 100,000 - 249,999   ○ 10,000 - 29,999
□ 1,000,000 - 1,999,999   ⊙ 250,000 - 499,999   ● 30,000 - 99,999   ○ UNDER 10,000

SCALE 1:10,500,000   LAMBERT CONFORMAL CONIC PROJECTION
MILES 0   150   300   450
KILOMETERS 0   150   300   450

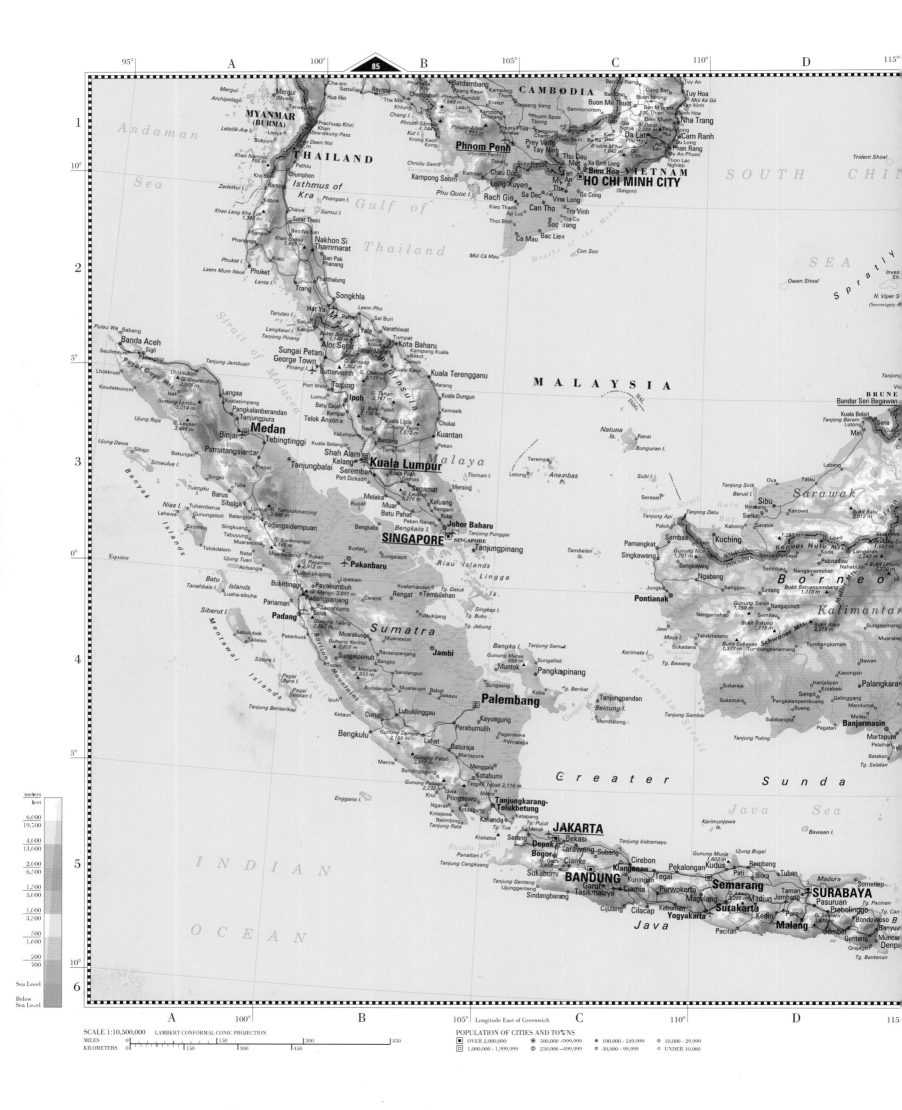

Map labels (from the cartographic image):

Andaman Sea

MYANMAR (BURMA)

THAILAND

Isthmus of Kra

Gulf of Thailand

CAMBODIA

Phnom Penh (Phnum Pénh)

VIETNAM

HO CHI MINH CITY (Saigon)

Bien Hoa

SOUTH CHINA SEA

Spratly

MALAYSIA

Strait of Malacca

Banda Aceh

George Town
Butterworth

Medan

Ipoh

Kuala Lumpur
Shah Alam
Kelang

SINGAPORE

Johor Baharu

Pakanbaru

Equator

Sumatra

Jambi

Palembang

Pontianak

Borneo

Kalimantan

Sarawak

BRUNEI
Bandar Seri Begawan

Kuching

Banjarmasin

Greater Sunda

Bengkulu

INDIAN OCEAN

Java Sea

JAKARTA
Bekasi
Depok
Bogor
BANDUNG

Semarang
Surakarta
Yogyakarta
SURABAYA
Malang

Java

MILES
KILOMETERS

POPULATION OF CITIES AND TOWNS

■ OVER 2,000,000
□ 1,000,000 –1,999,999
◉ 500,000 –999,999
◎ 250,000 –499,999
● 100,000 – 249,999
○ 30,000 – 99,999
◦ 10,000 – 29,999
· UNDER 10,000

Southeastern Asia

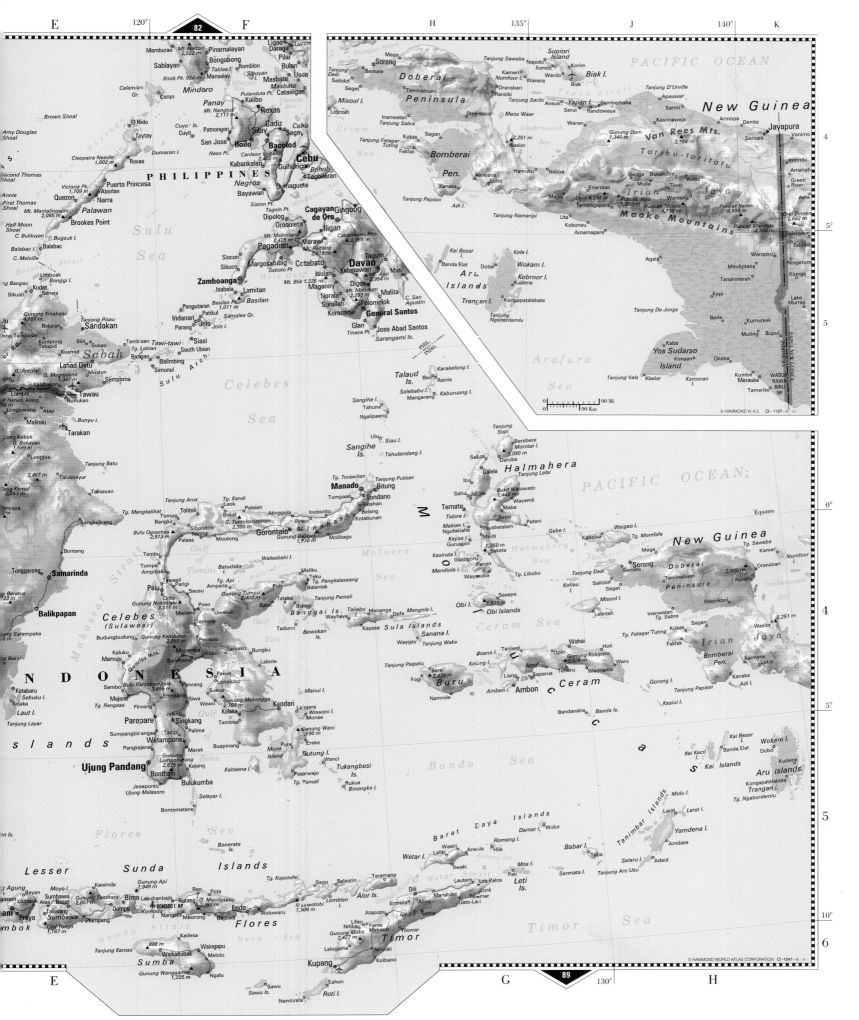

Australia and New Zealand - Comparisons

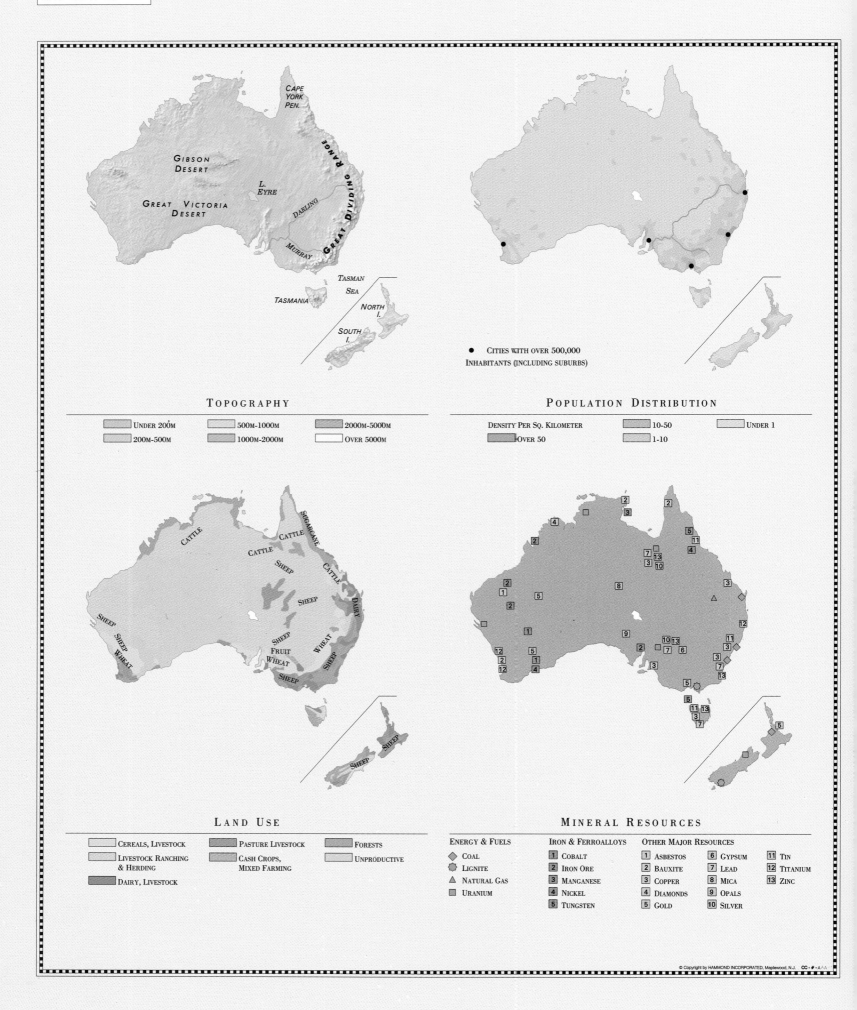

TOPOGRAPHY

	UNDER 200M		500M-1000M		2000M-5000M
	200M-500M		1000M-2000M		OVER 5000M

POPULATION DISTRIBUTION

● CITIES WITH OVER 500,000
INHABITANTS (INCLUDING SUBURBS)

DENSITY PER SQ. KILOMETER
	10-50		UNDER 1
OVER 50		1-10	

LAND USE

	CEREALS, LIVESTOCK		PASTURE LIVESTOCK		FORESTS
	LIVESTOCK RANCHING & HERDING		CASH CROPS, MIXED FARMING		UNPRODUCTIVE
	DAIRY, LIVESTOCK				

MINERAL RESOURCES

ENERGY & FUELS
◆ COAL
⬡ LIGNITE
▲ NATURAL GAS
▢ URANIUM

IRON & FERROALLOYS
1 COBALT
2 IRON ORE
3 MANGANESE
4 NICKEL
5 TUNGSTEN

OTHER MAJOR RESOURCES
1 ASBESTOS
2 BAUXITE
3 COPPER
4 DIAMONDS
5 GOLD

6 GYPSUM
7 LEAD
8 MICA
9 OPALS
10 SILVER

11 TIN
12 TITANIUM
13 ZINC

Australia, New Zealand

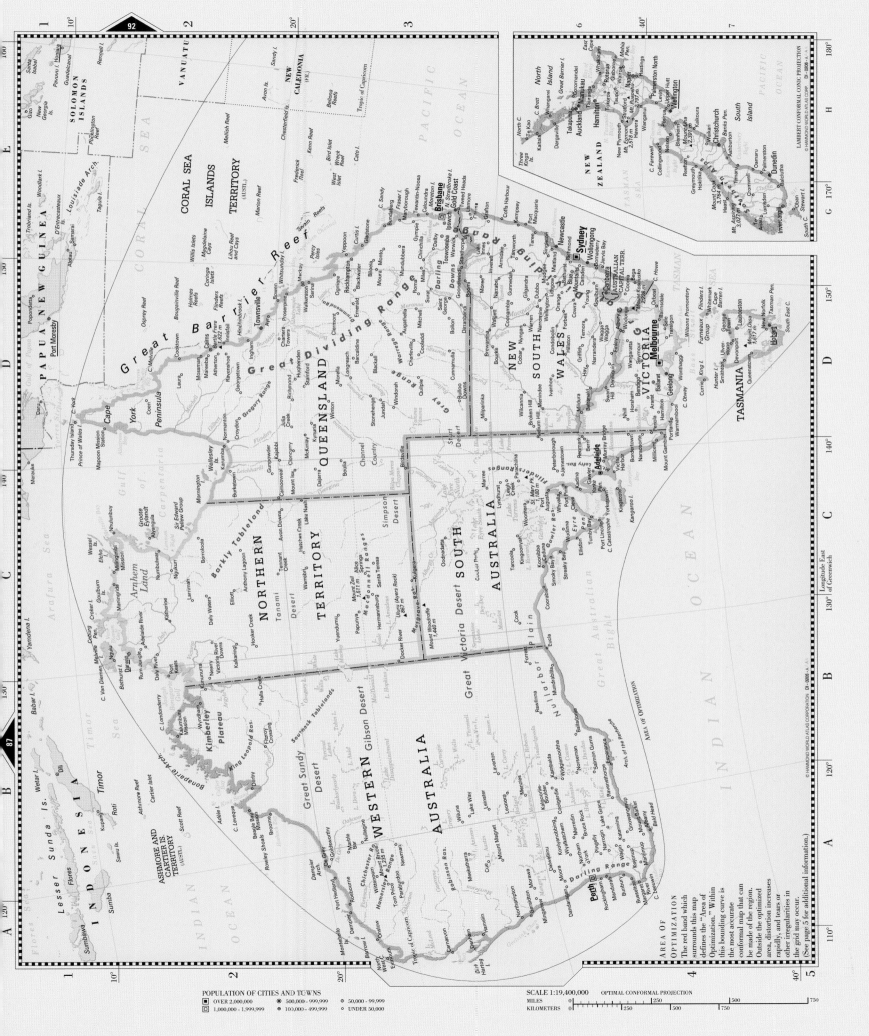

POPULATION OF CITIES AND TOWNS
- OVER 2,000,000
- 1,000,000 - 1,999,999
- 500,000 - 999,999
- 100,000 - 499,999
- 50,000 - 99,999
- UNDER 50,000

SCALE 1:19,400,000   OPTIMAL CONFORMAL PROJECTION

MILES   0   250   500   750
KILOMETERS   0   250   500   750

Northeastern Australia

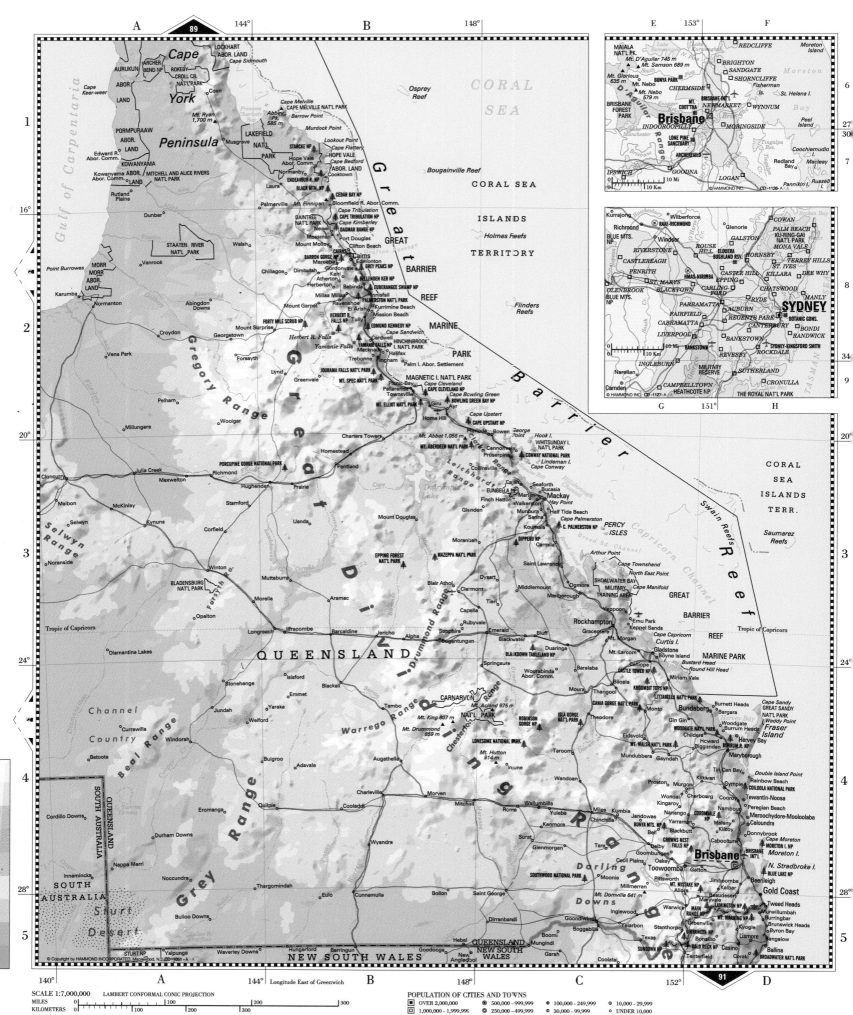

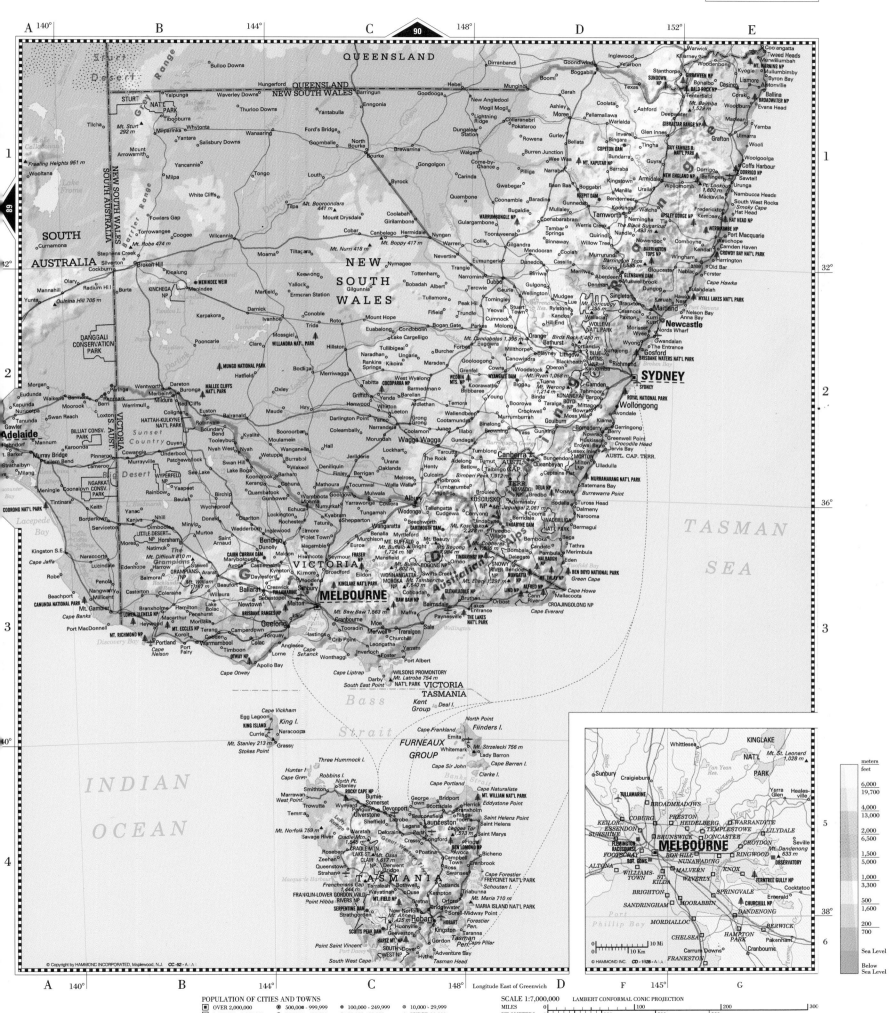

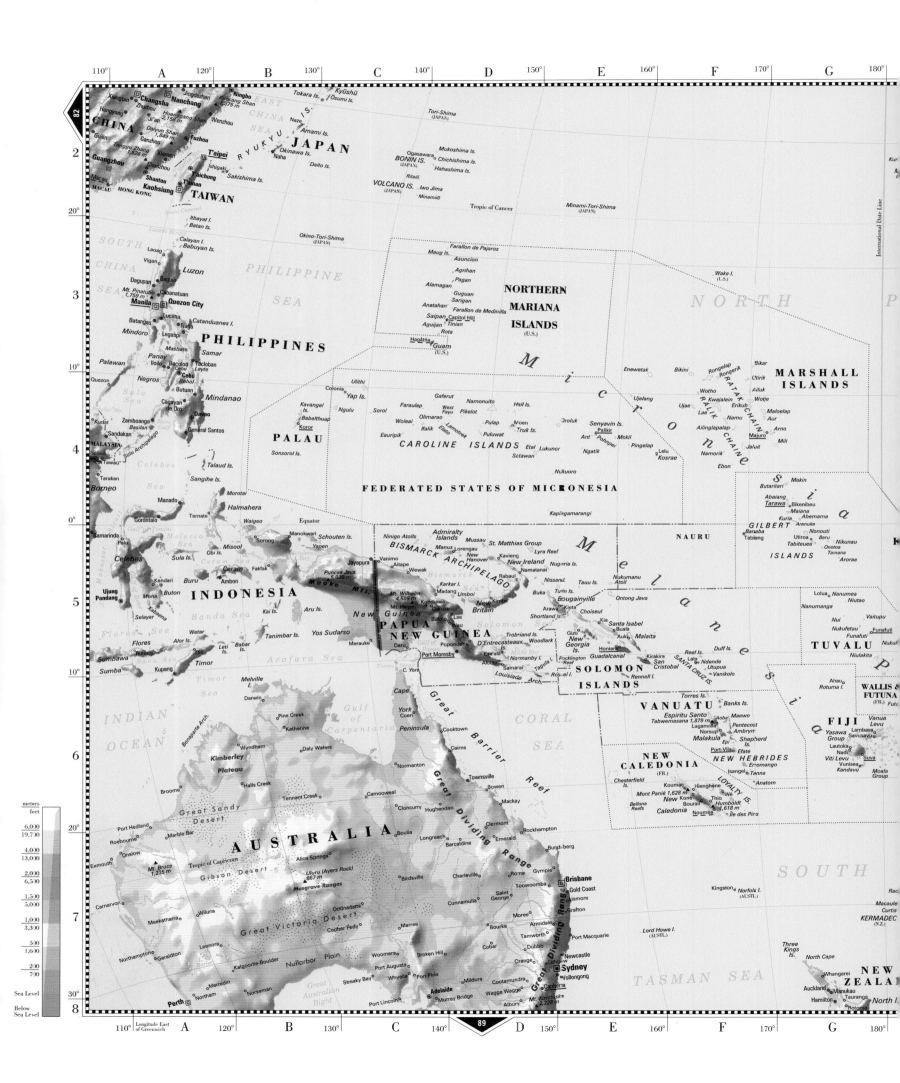

110° | A | 120° | B | 130° | C | 140° | D | 150° | E | 160° | F | 170° | G | 180°

CHINA

Xiangtan
Hengyang
Guilin
Guangzhou
Macau
MACAU HONG KONG

Changsha **Nanchang** Jingdezhen
Huangang Zhuzhou Gocang Shan
Ji'an 2,158 m
Huangshan Quzhou
Daiyun Shan 1,849 m Fuzhou
Ganzhou
Tonggu Zhang 1,608 m Xiamen
Shantou
Kaohsiung Tainan

Ningbo Wenzhou

Taipei
Taichung

TAIWAN

EAST
CHINA
SEA

Tokara Is.
Kyūshū
Ōsumi Is.
Naze Amami Is.

JAPAN

Tori-Shima
(JAPAN)

Mukoshima Is.
Ogasawara Chichishima Is.
BONIN IS. Hahashima Is.
(JAPAN)

Ritaiō

VOLCANO IS. Iwo Jima
(JAPAN)
Minamiiō

Minami-Tori-Shima
(JAPAN)

RYUKYU IS.
Okinawa I.
Naha
Ishigaki
Sakishima Is.
Daitō Is.

20°

Tropic of Cancer

Itbayat I.
Batan I.

Okino-Tori-Shima
(JAPAN)

Farallon de Pajaros
Maug Is.
Asuncion
Agrihan
Pagan

NORTHERN

Wake I.
(U.S.)

SOUTH
CHINA
SEA

Luzon Strait
Calayan I.
Babuyan Is.
Laoag
Vigan
Dagupan **Luzon**
Baguio
Mt. Pinatubo **Cabanatuan**
1,759 m
Manila **Quezon City**
Batangas Lucena
Lucena Naga Catanduanes I.
Legaspi
Mindoro
Masbate
Panay Samar
PHILIPPINES

PHILIPPINE

SEA

Alamagan
Guguan
Sarigan
Anatahan Farallon de Medinilla

Saipan Capitol Hill
Aguijan Tinian
Rota

MARIANA
ISLANDS
(U.S.)

Enewetak
Bikini
Rongelap
Rongerik
Utirik
Ailuk

Wotho
Ujelang
Ujae
Kwajalein
Lae
Erikub
Namu
Ailinglapalap
Namorik
Ebon

Bikar

MARSHALL
ISLANDS

Wotje
Maloelap
Aur
Arno
Majuro
Jaluit
Mili

3°

Quezon
Palawan
Iloilo Bacolod **Cebu** Leyte
Negros Bohol Tacloban
Butuan
Cagayan
de Oro **Mindanao**
Zamboanga **Davao**
Basilan General Santos

Hagåtña
Guam
(U.S.)

M
i
c
r
o

RATAK CHAIN
RAIK CHAIN

10°

MALAYSIA
Kudat
Sandakan
Tawau

Sulu Archipelago
Talaud Is.

Colonia
Ulithi
Kavangel Yap Is.
PALAU
Babelthuap
Koror Ngulu
Sonsorol Is.

Gaferut
Faraulep
Sorol West
Fayu Namonuito
Woleai Olimarao Pikelot
Ifalik Lamotrek
Eauripik Elato Puluwat
Satawan

Hall Is.

Pulap
Moen
Truk Is.

Oroluk

Senyavin Is.
Ant Pohnpei
Palikir
Ngatik Mokil
Pingelap

Makin
Butaritari
Abaiang Bikenibeu
Tarawa Maiana
Kuria Abemama
Aranuka

s
i
a

4°

Celebes Sea
Sangihe Is.

Morotai
Manado Halmahera
Gorontalo Ternate

FEDERATED STATES OF MICRONESIA

CAROLINE ISLANDS

Etal Lukunor
Setawan

Lelu Kosrae

Namorik

Nukuoro

Kapingamarangi

NAURU

n
e

Banaba
Tabiang

GILBERT

ISLANDS

Nonouti
Beru Nikunau
Tamana
Onotoa
Arorae

0° Equator

Samarinda
Palu
INDONESIA
Kendari
Ujung Pandang
Muna
Buton
Selayar
Kabaena

Celebes
Sula Is.
Obi Is.

Molucca
Sea

Ceram
Banda Sea

Waigeo
Misool Ceram
Ambon
Buru

Sorong Manokwari
Yapen Schouten Is.
Fakfak Puncak Jaya
5,036 m
Mooke Mts.
New Guinea

Ninigo Atolls
Admiralty
Islands Mussau
Manus Lorengau
Vanimo New
Aitape Hanover
Wewak

Bismarck
Sea

BISMARCK ARCHIPELAGO

St. Matthias Group
Kavieng
New Ireland
Namatanai

Lyra Reef

Nugaria Is.

M
e

Nukumanu
Atoll

Lolua Nanumea
Niutao
Nanumanga

Nui Vaitupu

a

TUVALU

5°

Aru Is.
Kai Is.
Tanimbar Is.
Yos Sudarso
Merauke

Mt. Wilhelm
4,509 m
Mt. Hagen Madang
Umboi
PAPUA
NEW GUINEA
Daru
Port Moresby

Karkar I.
Kundiawa **Kimbe**
Lae **New**
Bulolo **Britain**

Rabaul
Buka
Arawa
Kieta

Nissan I.
Tauu Is.
Bougainville
Shortland Is.

Tulin Is.

Choiseul

Ontong Java

Santa Isabel
Buala

l
i

Nukufetau Funafuti
Funafuti

Niulakita

6°

Indonesia
Timor

Kei Is.
Kupang

Arafura Sea

Wetar
Alor Is.
Leti Babar Is.
Dili Timor

Trobriand Is.
Esa'ala D'Entrecasteaux
Popondetta Woodlark I.
Normanby I.

Gizo
New
Georgia Honiara
New Georgia
Rennell I.
Reef

Kia
Malaita

Kirakira
San
Cristobal

Reef Is.

Lata Duff Is.
Ndende
Utupua
Vanikolo

Ahau
Rotuma I.

Vanua
FIJI Levu

n
e
s
i
a

WALLIS &
FUTUNA
(FR.) Fute

Nui
Nukufetau

Vaitupu

7°

C. York
York **Cape**
Coen **York**
Peninsula
Cooktown
Cairns

Samarai
Louisiade
Arch.

Torres Is.

Tagula I.

Rossel I.

SOLOMON
ISLANDS

P

Yasawa
Group
Lautoka
Nadi
Viti Levu
Suva

Lambasa
Savusavu

Vunisea
Kandavu

Moala
Group

AUSTRALIA

Melville I.
Darwin
Pine Creek
Katherine
Kimberley
Plateau
Wyndham
Broome
Halls Creek
Port Hedland
Marble Bar
Roebourne
Onslow
Exmouth Mt. Bruce
1,235 m
Carnarvon
Gibson Desert
Great Sandy
Desert
Tropic of Capricorn
Uluru (Ayers Rock)
867 m
Musgrave Ranges

Daly Waters

Tennant Creek

Alice Springs

Cooktown
Normanton
Camooweal
Cloncurry
Hughenden
Clermont
Longreach
Barcaldine
Emerald
Rockhampton
Bund-berg

Birdsville
Charleville
Roma
Gympie **Brisbane**
Gold Coast
Toowoomba

Gulf
of
Carpentaria

Townsville
Bowen
Mackay

Great

Barrier

Reef

CORAL

SEA

VANUATU
Banks Is.
Espiritu Santo
Tabwemasana 1,879 m
Luganville
Norsup
Malakula
Port-Vilao

Aoba Maewo
Pentecost
Ambrym
Shepherd
Epi
Efate
Erromango
Tanna

Chesterfield
NEW
CALEDONIA
(FR.)
Koumac
Mont Panie 1,628 m
Bellona New Kone
Reefs Bourail
Caledonia Nouméa

Hienghéne
Thio
Humboldt
1,618 m
Ile des Pins

NEW HEBRIDES
Isangel

LOYALTY IS.
Wé
Anatom

SOUTH

Kingston Norfolk I.
(AUSTL.)

Macaule
Curtis
KERMADEC
(N.Z.)

7°

Wiluna
Meekatharra
Northampton
Geraldton
Kalgoorlie-Boulder
Norseman
Merredin
Northam
Perth
Leonora

Great Victoria Desert

Coober Pedy
Marree
Woomera
Port Augusta
Whyalla
Port Pirie
Port Lincoln

Bourke
Cobar
Nyngan
Moree
Armidale
Tamworth
Dubbo
Orange
Newcastle
Lithgow **Sydney**
Wollongong

Broken Hill

Great Dividing Range

Grafton
Port Macquarie

Lord Howe I.
(AUSTL.)

Three
Kings
Is.

North Cape
Whangarei
Auckland Manukau
Hamilton Tauranga

NEW
ZEALA
North I.

30°

Carnarvon
Geraldton

Nullarbor Plain

Streaky Bay
Ceduna

Great
Australian
Bight

Murray Bridge
Adelaide
Mildura
Cootamundra
Wagga Wagga
Albury
Mt. Kosciusko
2,228 m
Canberra

TASMAN SEA

8°

110° Longitude East of Greenwich | A | 120° | B | 130° | C | 140° | D | 150° | E | 160° | F | 170° | G | 180°

meters feet
6,000 19,700
4,000 13,000
2,000 6,500
1,500 5,000
1,000 3,300
500 1,600
200 700
Sea Level
Below
Sea Level

Central Pacific Ocean

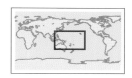

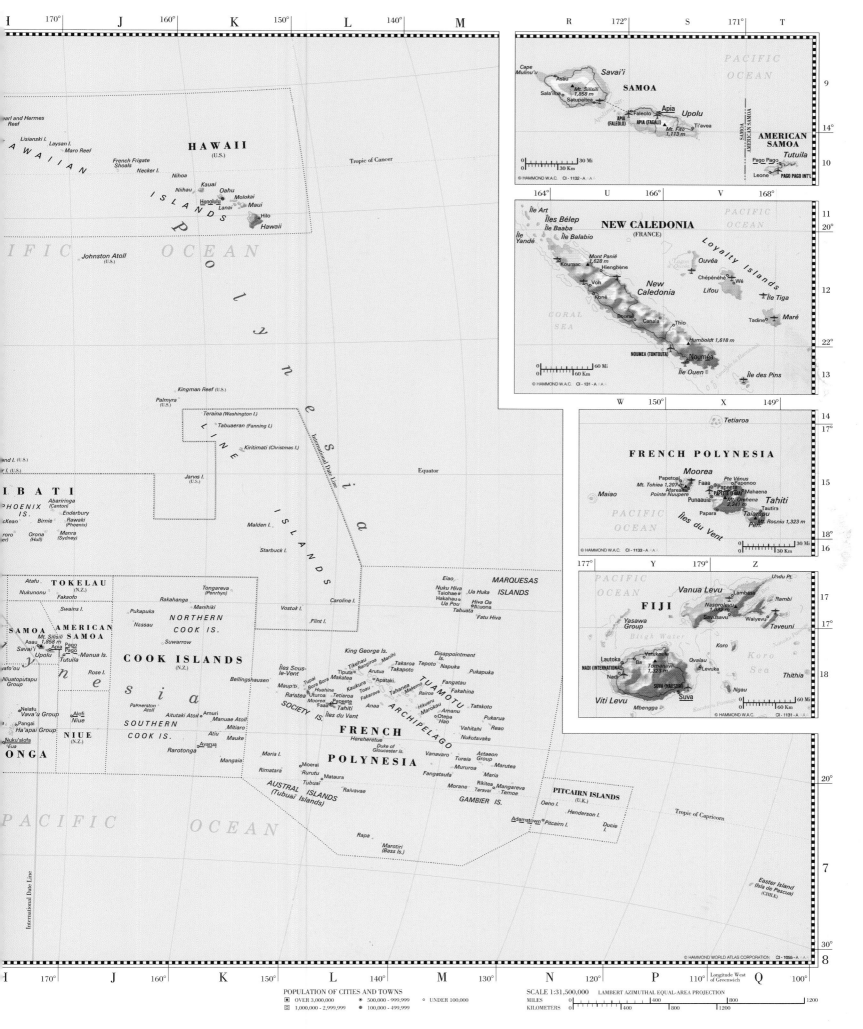

SAMOA

PACIFIC OCEAN

Cape Mulinu'u
Asau
Savai'i
Mt. Silisili 1,858 m
Sala'ilua
Satupaitea
Faleolo
APIA (FALEOLO)
APIA (FAGALI)
Apia
Upolu
Ti'avea
Mt. Fito 1,113 m

SAMOA / AMERICAN SAMOA

AMERICAN SAMOA
Tutuila
Pago Pago
Leone
PAGO PAGO INT'L

0 30 Mi
0 30 Km
© HAMMOND W.A.C.   CI-1132-A·A

9
14°
10

NEW CALEDONIA (FRANCE)

164° U 166° V 168°

PACIFIC OCEAN

Île Art
Îles Bélep
Île Baaba
Île Yandé
Île Balabio
Kournac
Mont Panié 1,628 m
Hienghène
Voh
Koné
New Caledonia
Loyalty Islands
Ouvéa
Chépénéhé
Wé
Lifou
Île Tiga

CORAL SEA

Bourail
Canala
Thio
Tadine
Maré
Humboldt 1,618 m

NOUMEA (TONTOUTA)
Nouméa
Île Ouen
Île des Pins

0 60 Mi
0 60 Km
© HAMMOND W.A.C.   CI-131-A·A

11
20°
12
22°
13

FRENCH POLYNESIA

W 150° X 149°

Tetiaroa

Maiao
Moorea
Papetoai
Taiohae
Mt. Tohiea 1,207 m
Faaa
Pte Vénus
Papenoo
Afareaitu
PAPEETE (FAAA)
Papeete
Mahena
Pointe Nuupere
Punaauia
Mt. Orohena 2,241 m
Tahiti
Papara
Taiarapu Pen.
Tautira
Mt. Roçniu 1,323 m
Îles du Vent

PACIFIC OCEAN

0 30 Mi
0 30 Km
© HAMMOND W.A.C.   CI-1133-A·A

14
17°
15
18°
16

FIJI

177° Y 179° Z

PACIFIC OCEAN
Vanua Levu
Undu Pt.
Lambasa
Rambi
Yasawa Group
Nasorolevu 1,032 m
Savusavu
Waiyevo
Taveuni
Koro
Koro Sea
Bligh Water
Lautoka
Vatukoula
Ovalau
Ba
Tomanivi 1,323 m
Levuka
Thithia
NADI (INTERNATIONAL)
Nadi
Ngau
SUVA (NAUSORI)
Suva
Viti Levu
Mbengga

0 60 Mi
0 60 Km
© HAMMOND W.A.C.   CI-1131-A·A

17
17°
18

HAWAII (U.S.)

Pearl and Hermes Reef
Lisianski I. Laysan I.
Maro Reef
Necker I.
French Frigate Shoals
Nihoa
Niihau Kauai Oahu Molokai
Honolulu Lanai Maui
Hilo
Hawaii

HAWAIIAN ISLANDS

Tropic of Cancer

PACIFIC OCEAN

Johnston Atoll (U.S.)

Kingman Reef (U.S.)
Palmyra (U.S.)
Teraina (Washington I.)
Tabuaeran (Fanning I.)
Kiritimati (Christmas I.)

LINE ISLANDS

Jarvis I. (U.S.)

International Date Line

Equator

KIRIBATI
PHOENIX IS.
Abariringa (Canton)
McKean Birnie
Enderbury
Rawaki (Phoenix)
Nikumaroro Orona (Hull) Manra (Sydney)
Malden I.
Starbuck I.
Vostok I.
Flint I.
Caroline I.

P o l y n e s i a

Atafu
TOKELAU (N.Z.)
Nukunonu
Fakaofo
Swains I.
Rakahanga
Manihiki
Tongareva (Penrhyn)
Pukapuka
Nassau
Suwarrow
NORTHERN COOK IS.

SAMOA
AMERICAN SAMOA
Asau
Mt. Silisili 1,858 m
Savai'i
Apia
Pago Pago
Upolu
Tutuila
Manua Is.
Rose I.
Niuafo'ou
Niuatoputapu Group
Neiafu
Vava'u Group
Palmerston Atoll
Aitutaki Atoll
Amuri
Manuae Atoll
COOK ISLANDS (N.Z.)
Bellingshausen
Îles Sous-le-Vent
Maupiti
Bora Bora
Tupai
Huahine
Ra'iatea
Tahaa
Tetiaroa
SOCIETY IS.
Uturoa
Moorea
Papeete
Tahiti
Îles du Vent
Pangai
Ha'apai Group
Mauke
Atiu
Mitiaro
Mauke
SOUTHERN COOK IS.
NIUE (N.Z.)
Niue
Alofi
Nuku'alofa
'Eua
TONGA
Avarua
Rarotonga
Mangaia

King George Is.
Tikehau
Rangiroa
Manihi
Disappointment Is.
Tiputa
Arutua
Takaroa
Takapoto
Napuka
Maupiti
Kaukura
Apataki
Tepoto
Pukapuka
Fangataro
Makatea
Fakarava
Makemo
Fangatau
Anaa
Tatakoto
Tahanea
Hikueru
Marokau
Reao
Otepa
Hao
Vahitahi
Pukarua
Nukutavake
TUAMOTU ARCHIPELAGO

FRENCH POLYNESIA

Eiao
Nuku Hiva
Ua Huka
MARQUESAS ISLANDS
Hakahau
Hiva Oa
Ua Pou
Atuona
Tahuata
Fatu Hiva

Hereheretue
Duke of Gloucester Is.
Maria I.
Moerai
Rurutu
Vanavaro
Tureia
Actaeon Group
Rimatara
Tubuai
Mataura
Mururoa
Marutea
Raivavae
Fangataufa
Maria
Morane
Rikitea
Mangareva
Temoe
AUSTRAL ISLANDS (Tubuai Islands)
GAMBIER IS.
Taravai
PITCAIRN ISLANDS (U.K.)
Oeno I.
Henderson I.
Rapa
Marotiri (Bass Is.)
Adamstown Pitcairn I.
Ducie I.

Tropic of Capricorn

PACIFIC OCEAN

Easter Island (Isla de Pascua) (CHILE)

M i c r o n e s i a

International Date Line

POPULATION OF CITIES AND TOWNS
■ OVER 3,000,000
⊡ 1,000,000 - 2,999,999
⊛ 500,000 - 999,999
⊙ 100,000 - 499,999
○ UNDER 100,000

SCALE 1:31,500,000   LAMBERT AZIMUTHAL EQUAL-AREA PROJECTION
MILES 0 400 800 1200
KILOMETERS 0 400 800 1200

Africa - Comparisons

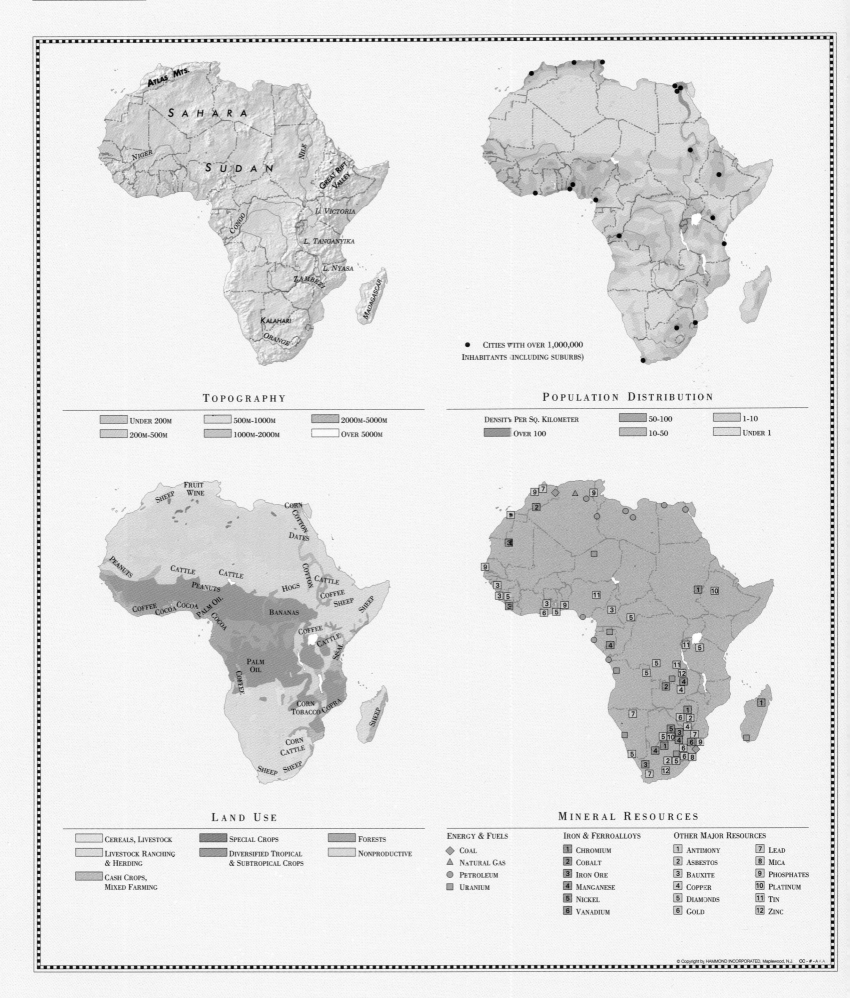

TOPOGRAPHY

UNDER 200M	500M-1000M	2000M-5000M
200M-500M	1000M-2000M	OVER 5000M

POPULATION DISTRIBUTION

DENSITY PER SQ. KILOMETER

	50-100	1-10
OVER 100	10-50	UNDER 1

● CITIES WITH OVER 1,000,000
INHABITANTS (INCLUDING SUBURBS)

LAND USE

CEREALS, LIVESTOCK	SPECIAL CROPS	FORESTS
LIVESTOCK RANCHING & HERDING	DIVERSIFIED TROPICAL & SUBTROPICAL CROPS	NONPRODUCTIVE
CASH CROPS, MIXED FARMING		

MINERAL RESOURCES

ENERGY & FUELS

◆ COAL
▲ NATURAL GAS
● PETROLEUM
▪ URANIUM

IRON & FERROALLOYS

1 CHROMIUM
2 COBALT
3 IRON ORE
4 MANGANESE
5 NICKEL
6 VANADIUM

OTHER MAJOR RESOURCES

1 ANTIMONY
2 ASBESTOS
3 BAUXITE
4 COPPER
5 DIAMONDS
6 GOLD

7 LEAD
8 MICA
9 PHOSPHATES
10 PLATINUM
11 TIN
12 ZINC

Africa

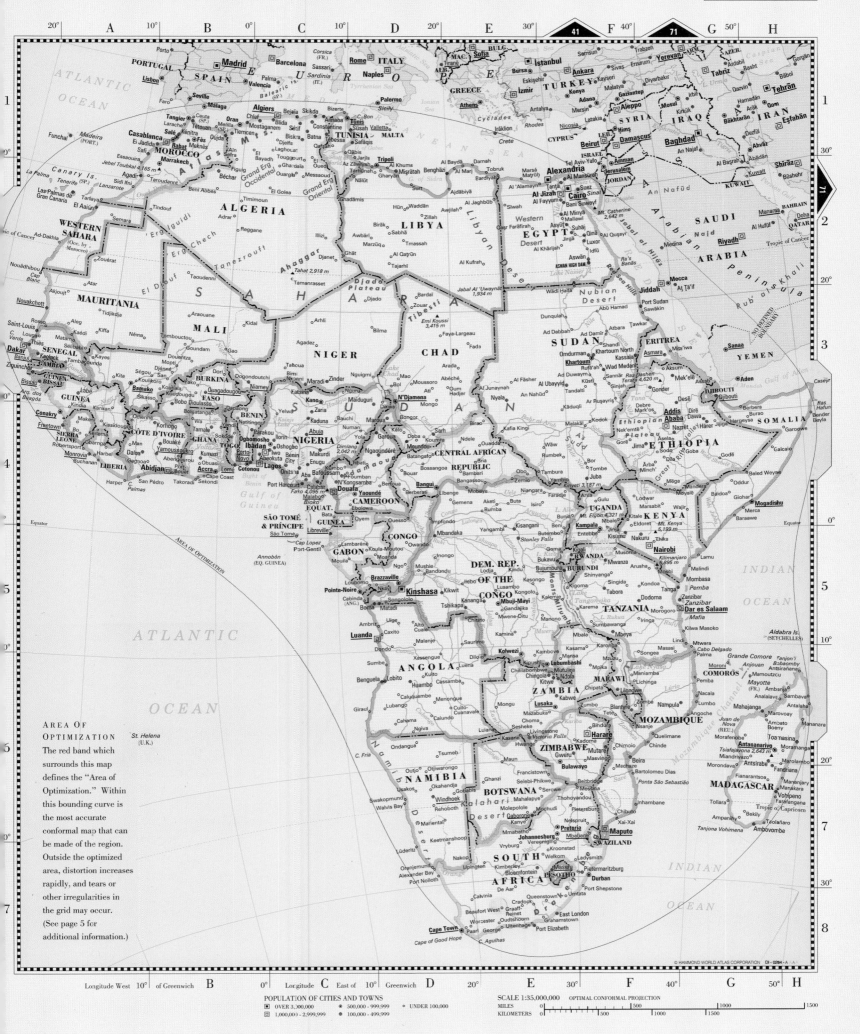

AREA OF
OPTIMIZATION
The red band which
surrounds this map
defines the "Area of
Optimization." Within
this bounding curve is
the most accurate
conformal map that can
be made of the region.
Outside the optimized
area, distortion increases
rapidly, and tears or
other irregularities in
the grid may occur.
(See page 5 for
additional information.)

POPULATION OF CITIES AND TOWNS

SCALE 1:35,000,000   OPTIMAL CONFORMAL PROJECTION

© HAMMOND WORLD ATLAS CORPORATION   DI - 0264 - A - A

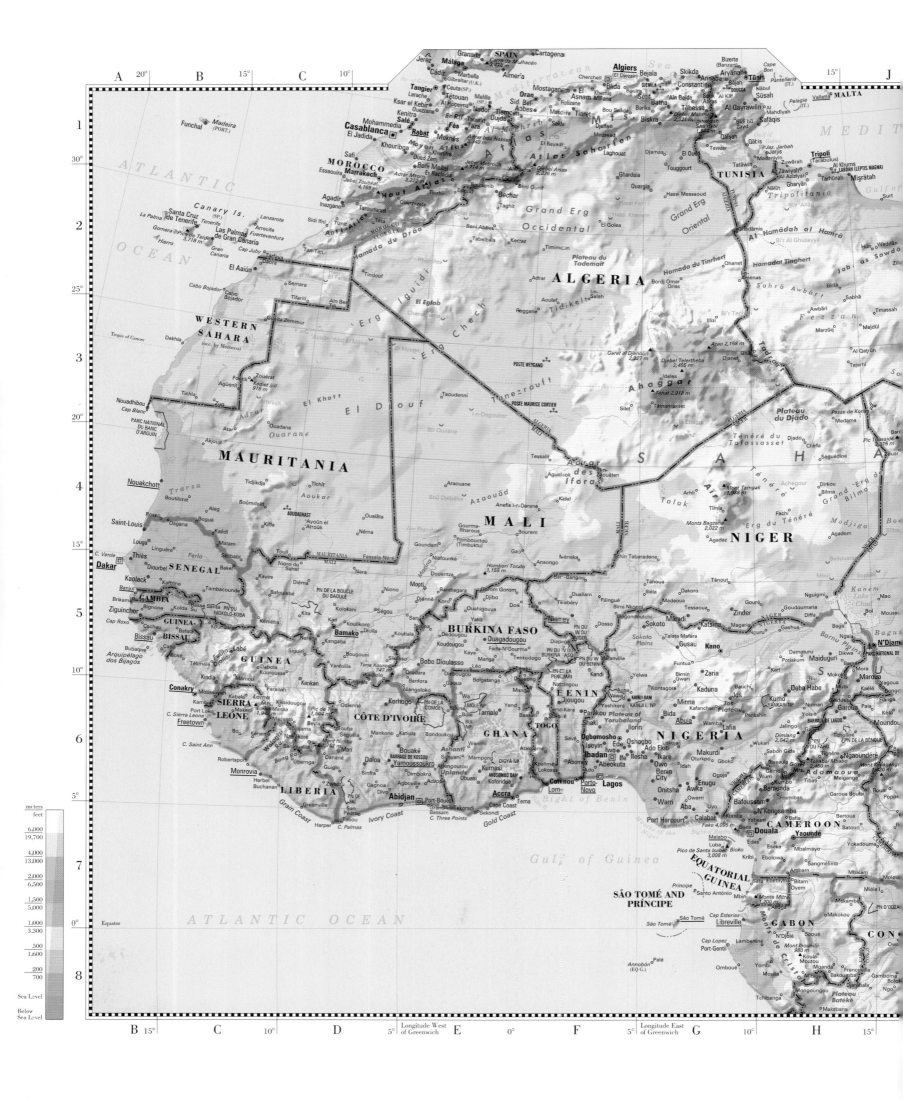

Northern Africa

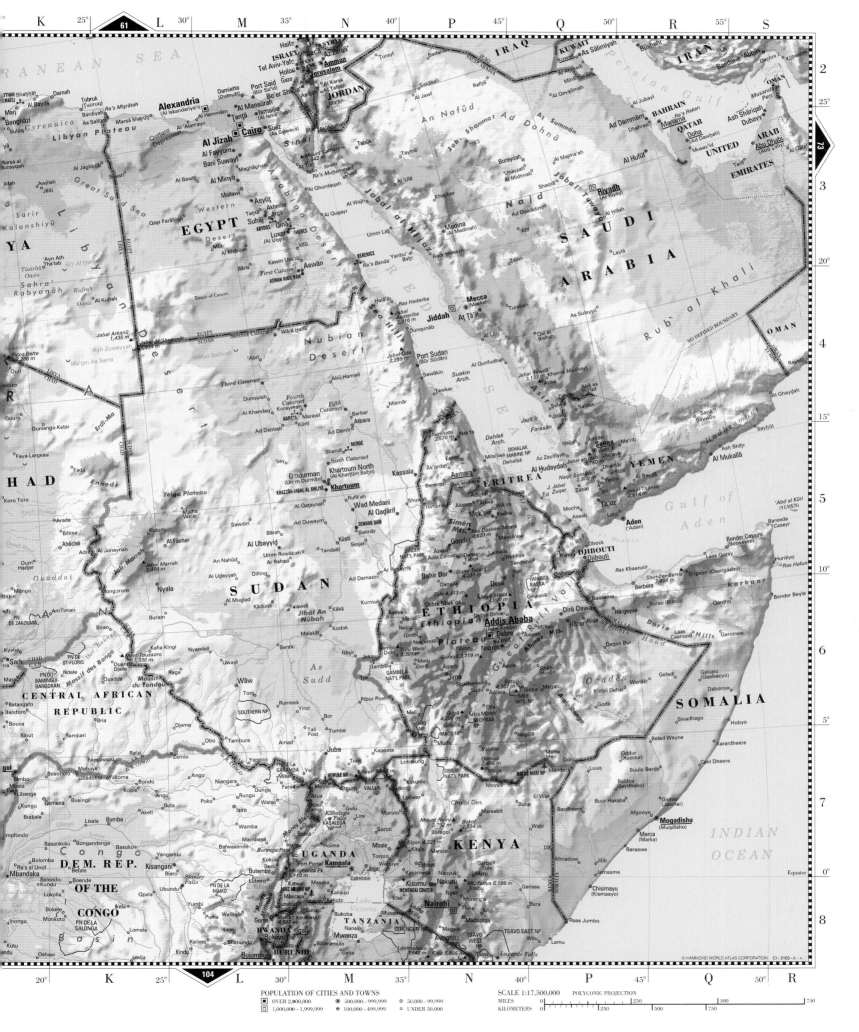

POPULATION OF CITIES AND TOWNS

■ OVER 2,000,000	● 500,000 - 999,999
▢ 1,000,000 - 1,999,999	● 100,000 - 499,999

● 50,000 - 99,999
○ UNDER 50,000

SCALE 1:17,500,000   POLYCONIC PROJECTION

MILES 0   250   500   750
KILOMETERS 0   250   500   750

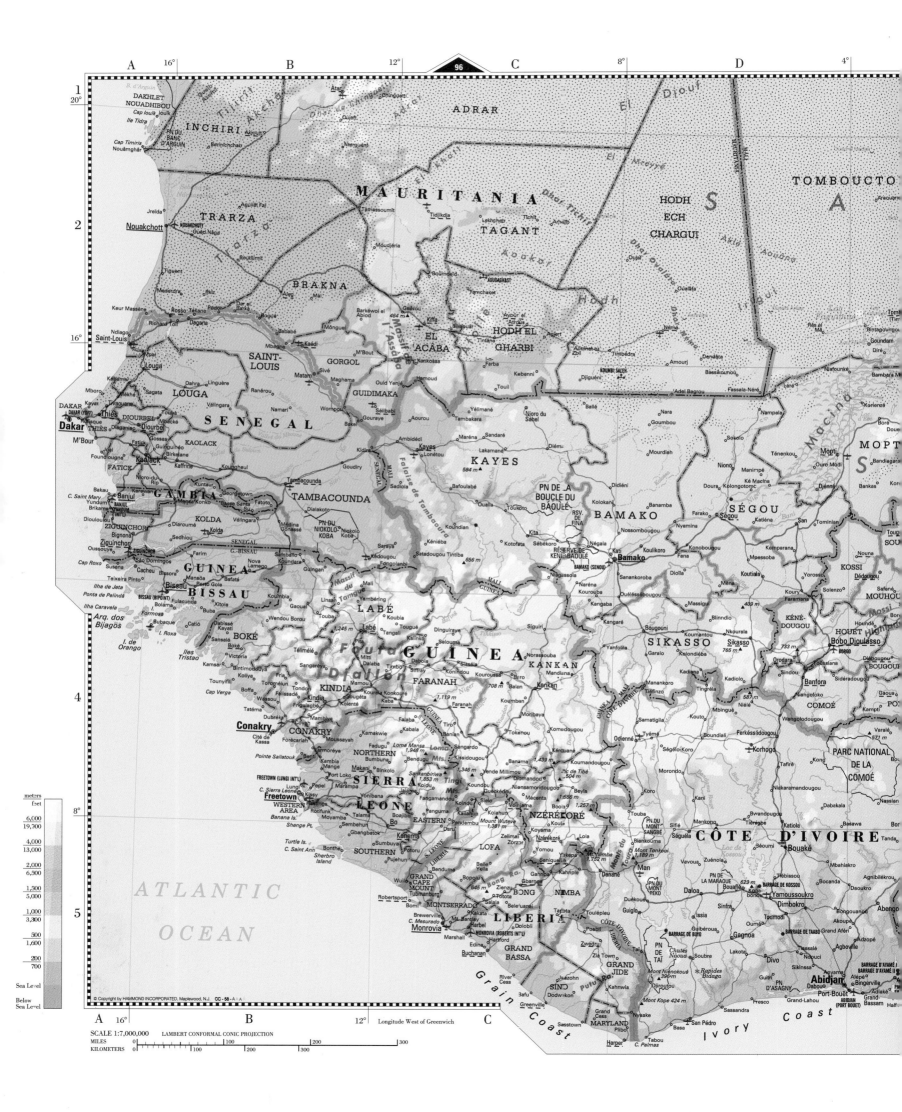

ATLANTIC

OCEAN

SCALE 1:7,000,000   LAMBERT CONFORMAL CONIC PROJECTION

MILES

KILOMETERS

Longitude West of Greenwich

meters
feet

6,000
19,700

4,000
13,000

2,000
6,500

1,300
5,000

1,000
3,300

300
1,600

200
700

Sea Level

Below
Sea Level

West Africa

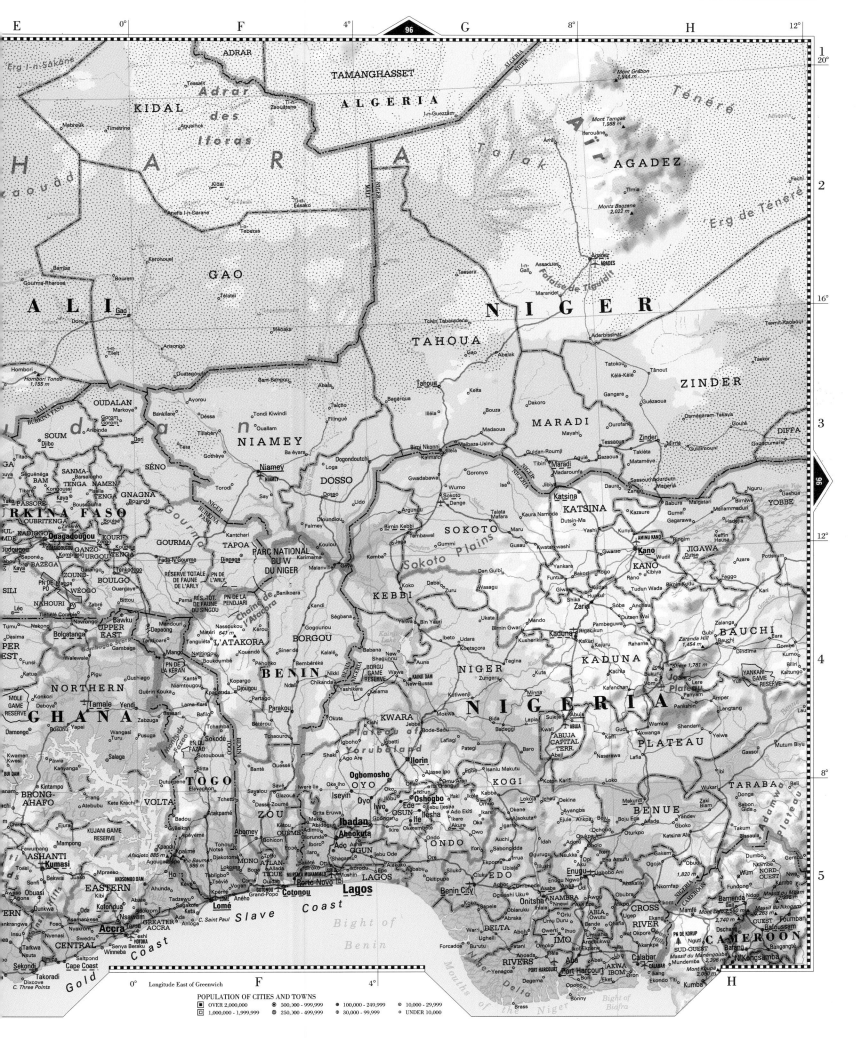

POPULATION OF CITIES AND TOWNS

■ OVER 2,000,000	● 500,000 - 999,999	● 100,000 - 249,999	○ 10,000 - 29,999		
□ 1,000,000 - 1,999,999	● 250,000 - 499,999	● 30,000 - 99,999	○ UNDER 10,000		

0°   Longitude East of Greenwich

Northeastern Africa

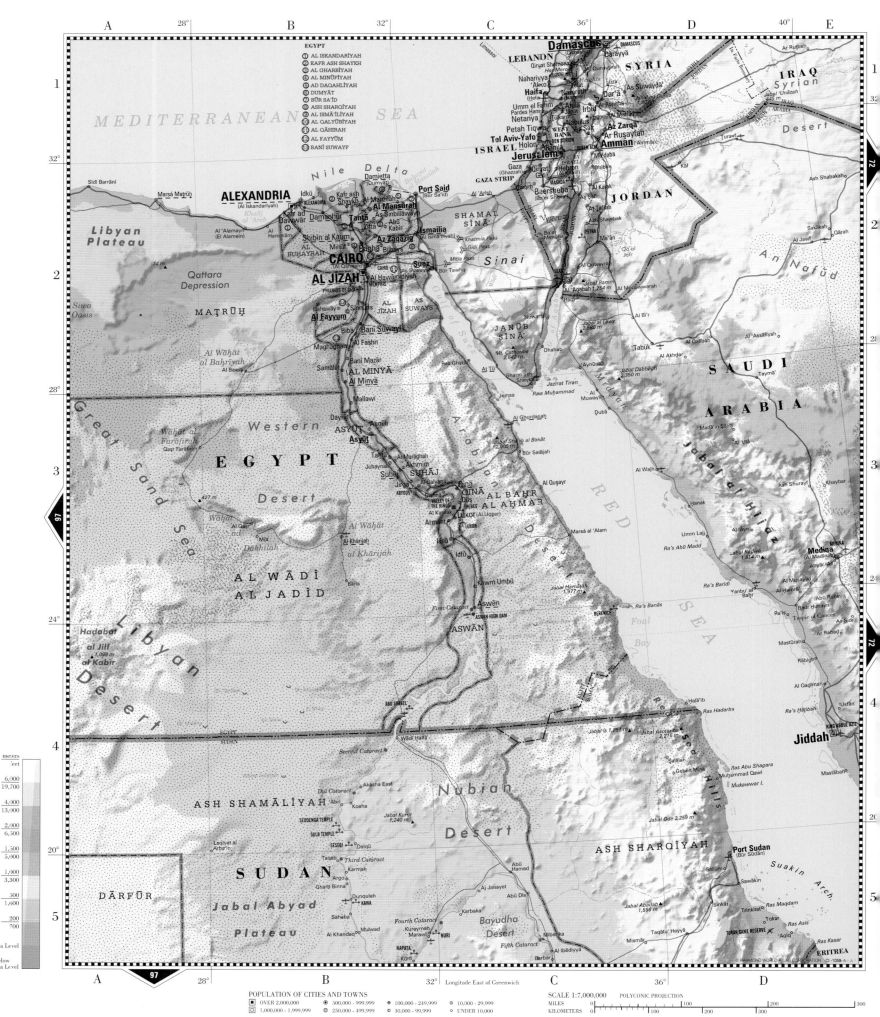

MEDITERRANEAN SEA

POPULATION OF CITIES AND TOWNS

■ OVER 2,000,000	⊛ 500,000 - 999,999	● 100,000 - 249,999	◦ 10,000 - 29,999
▣ 1,000,000 - 1,999,999	◉ 250,000 - 499,999	• 30,000 - 99,999	∘ UNDER 10,000

SCALE 1:7,000,000   POLYCONIC PROJECTION

MILES 0 · · · · · · 100 · · · 200 · · · 300

KILOMETERS 0 · · · 100 · · · 200 · · · 300

Longitude East of Greenwich

East Africa

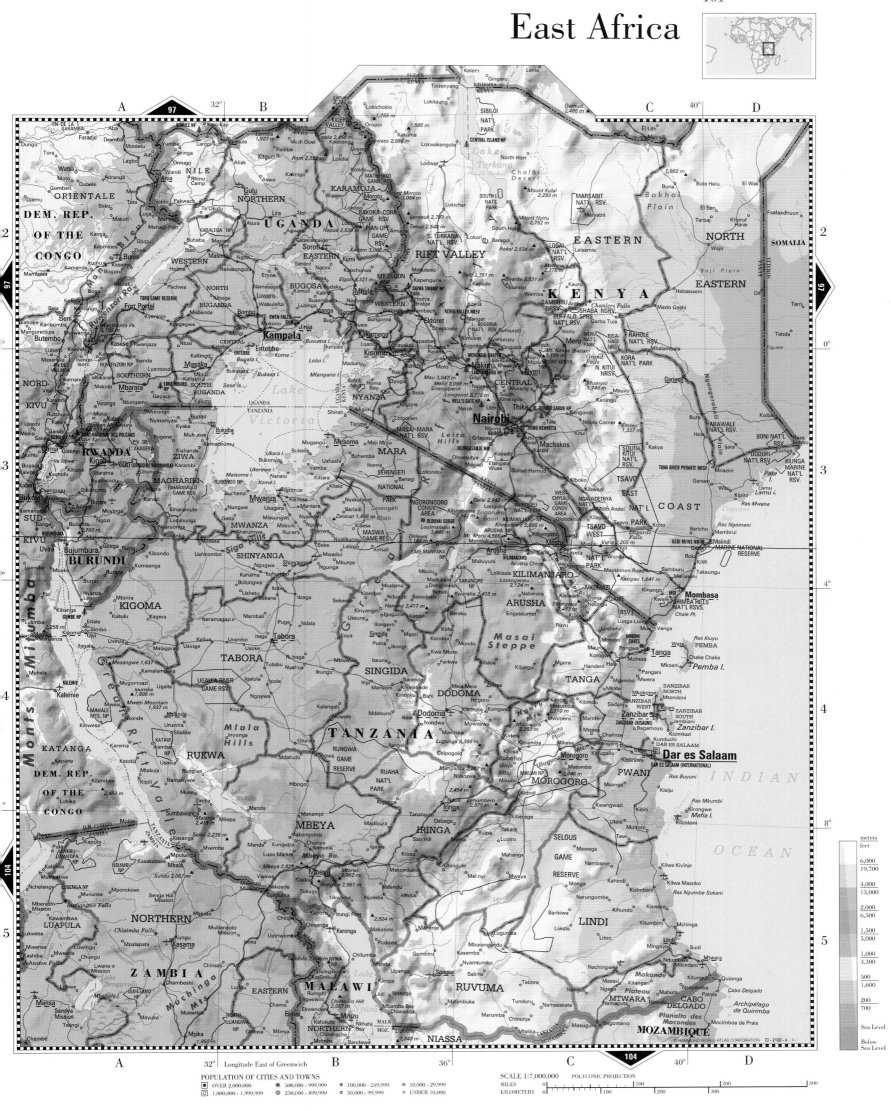

POPULATION OF CITIES AND TOWNS

■ OVER 2,000,000   ◉ 500,000 - 999,999   ● 100,000 - 249,999   ○ 10,000 - 29,999
□ 1,000,000 - 1,999,999   ◉ 250,000 - 499,999   ● 30,000 - 99,999   ○ UNDER 10,000

SCALE 1:7,000,000   POLYCONIC PROJECTION

MILES
KILOMETERS

meters	feet
6,000	19,700
4,000	13,000
2,000	6,500
1,500	5,000
1,000	3,300
500	1,600
200	700
Sea Level	Sea Level
Below Sea Level	Below Sea Level

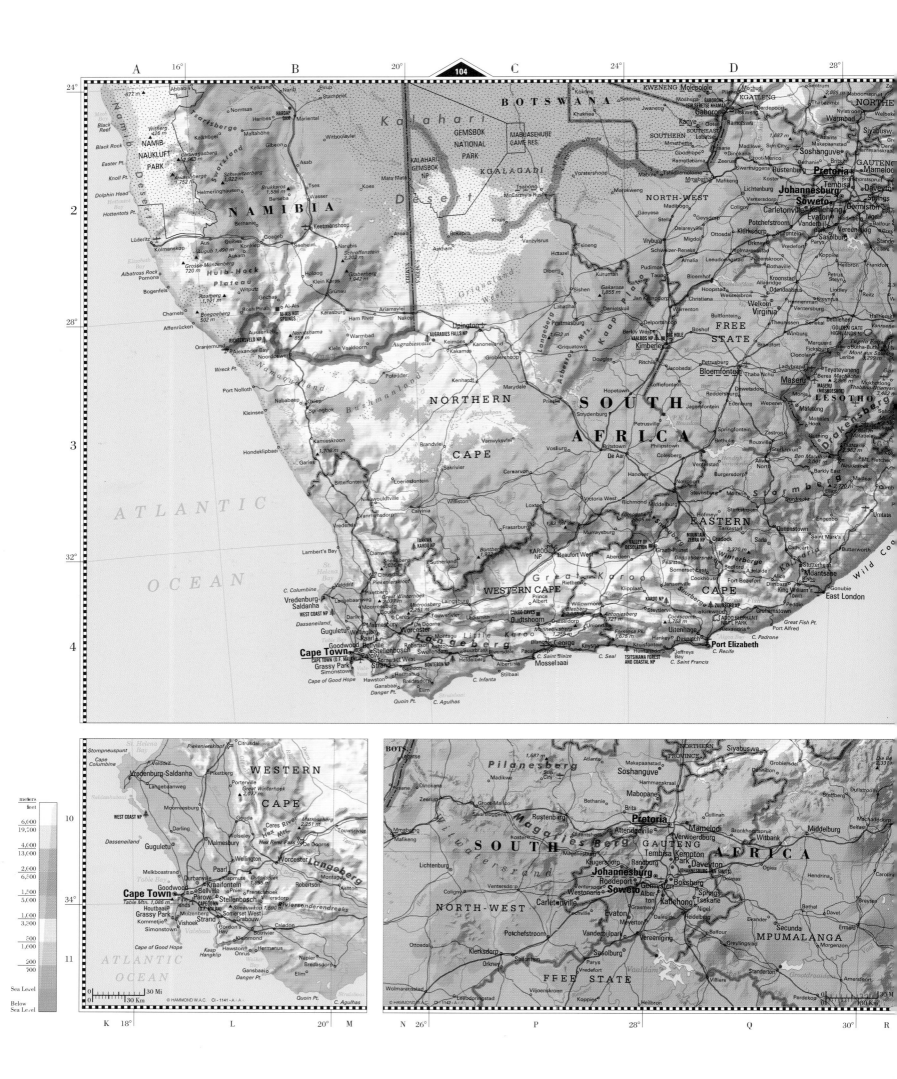

A 16° B 20° C 24° D 28°

24°

BOTSWANA

Kalahari

GEMSBOK
NATIONAL
PARK

MABUASEHUBE
GAME RES.

KGALAGADI

Desert

2

NAMIBIA

KALAHARI-
GEMSBOK
NP

Namib Desert

Tsarisberge

NAMIB-
NAUKLUFT
PARK

Huib-Hoch
Plateau

NORTH-WEST

GAUTENG

Pretoria

Johannesburg
Soweto

FREE
STATE

28°

NORTHERN

Namaqualand

Bushmanland

Griqualand
West

CAPE

SOUTH

AFRICA

Bloemfontein

Maseru

LESOTHO

Drakensberg

3

ATLANTIC

EASTERN

32°

OCEAN

WESTERN CAPE

Great Karoo

CAPE

East London

4

Cape Town

Port Elizabeth

C. Agulhas

St. Helena
Bay

Citrusdal

WESTERN

NORTHERN
PROVINCE

Siyabuswa

Pilanesberg

BOTS.

Soshanguve

10

Vredenburg-Saldanha

CAPE

Great Winterhoek
2,077 m

SOUTH

Pretoria

Mamelodi

AFRICA

Middelburg

WEST COAST NP

Ceres River
Mastroogberg
2,251 m

Tembisa

GAUTENG

Witbank

meters
feet
6,000
19,700
4,000
13,000
2,000
6,500
1,500
5,000
1,000
3,300
500
1,600
200
700

Sea Level

Below
Sea Level

Johannesburg

Soweto

34°

Cape Town

NORTH-WEST

Carletonville

Evaton

Stellenbosch

11

ATLANTIC

Klerksdorp

MPUMALANGA

OCEAN

30 Mi

Sasolburg

Vereeniging

30 Km

FREE STATE

Vanderbijlpark

K 18° L 20° M N 26° P 28° Q 30° R

South Africa

Southern Africa

Antarctica

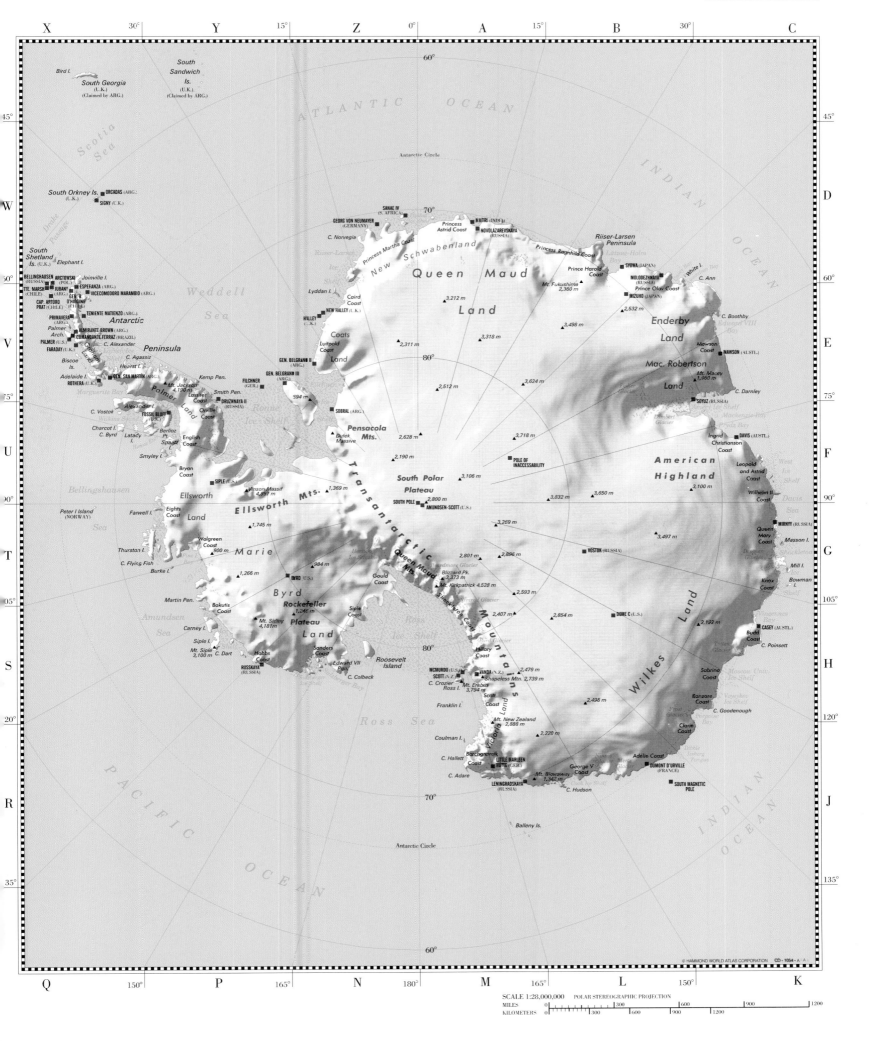

South America - Comparisons

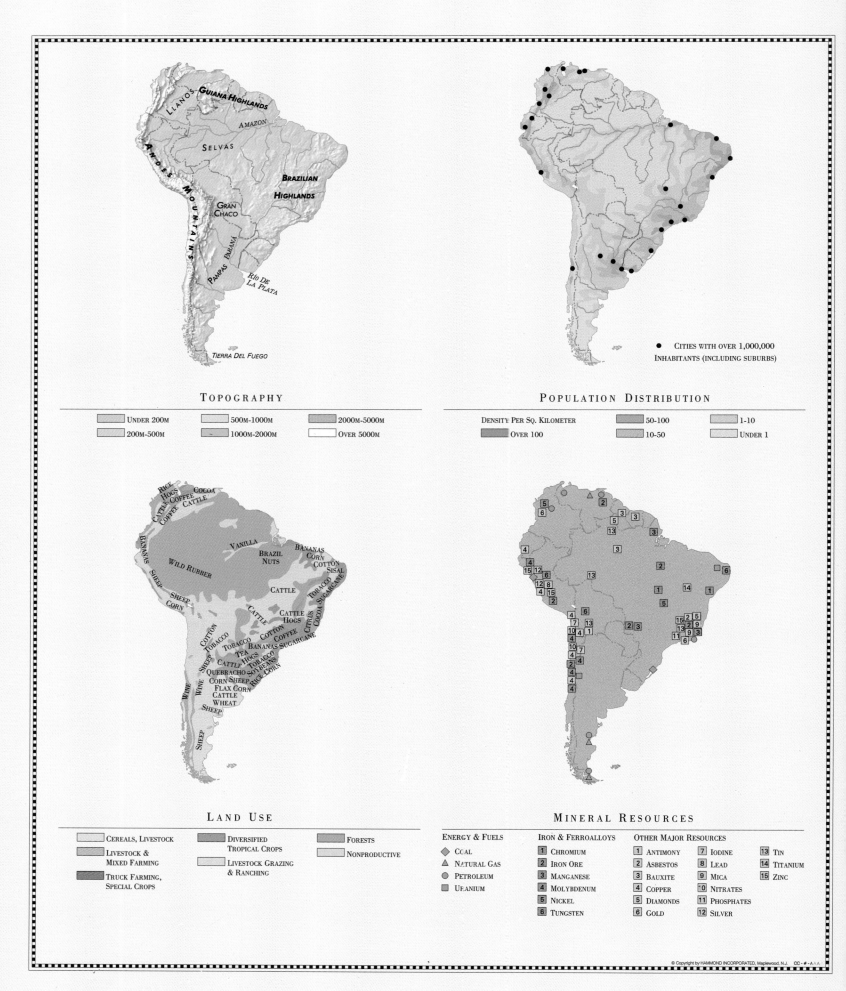

TOPOGRAPHY

UNDER 200M	500M-1000M	2000M-5000M
200M-500M	1000M-2000M	OVER 5000M

Llanos · Guiana Highlands · Amazon · Selvas · Brazilian Highlands · Gran Chaco · Parana · Pampas · Parana · Río de la Plata · Andes Mountains · Tierra del Fuego

POPULATION DISTRIBUTION

- CITIES WITH OVER 1,000,000 INHABITANTS (INCLUDING SUBURBS)

DENSITY PER SQ. KILOMETER		
OVER 100	50-100	1-10
	10-50	UNDER 1

LAND USE

CEREALS, LIVESTOCK	DIVERSIFIED TROPICAL CROPS	FORESTS
LIVESTOCK & MIXED FARMING	LIVESTOCK GRAZING & RANCHING	NONPRODUCTIVE
TRUCK FARMING, SPECIAL CROPS		

MINERAL RESOURCES

ENERGY & FUELS
- ◆ COAL
- ▲ NATURAL GAS
- ● PETROLEUM
- ▪ URANIUM

IRON & FERROALLOYS
1. CHROMIUM
2. IRON ORE
3. MANGANESE
4. MOLYBDENUM
5. NICKEL
6. TUNGSTEN

OTHER MAJOR RESOURCES
1. ANTIMONY
2. ASBESTOS
3. BAUXITE
4. COPPER
5. DIAMONDS
6. GOLD
7. IODINE
8. LEAD
9. MICA
0. NITRATES
11. PHOSPHATES
12. SILVER
13. TIN
14. TITANIUM
15. ZINC

South America

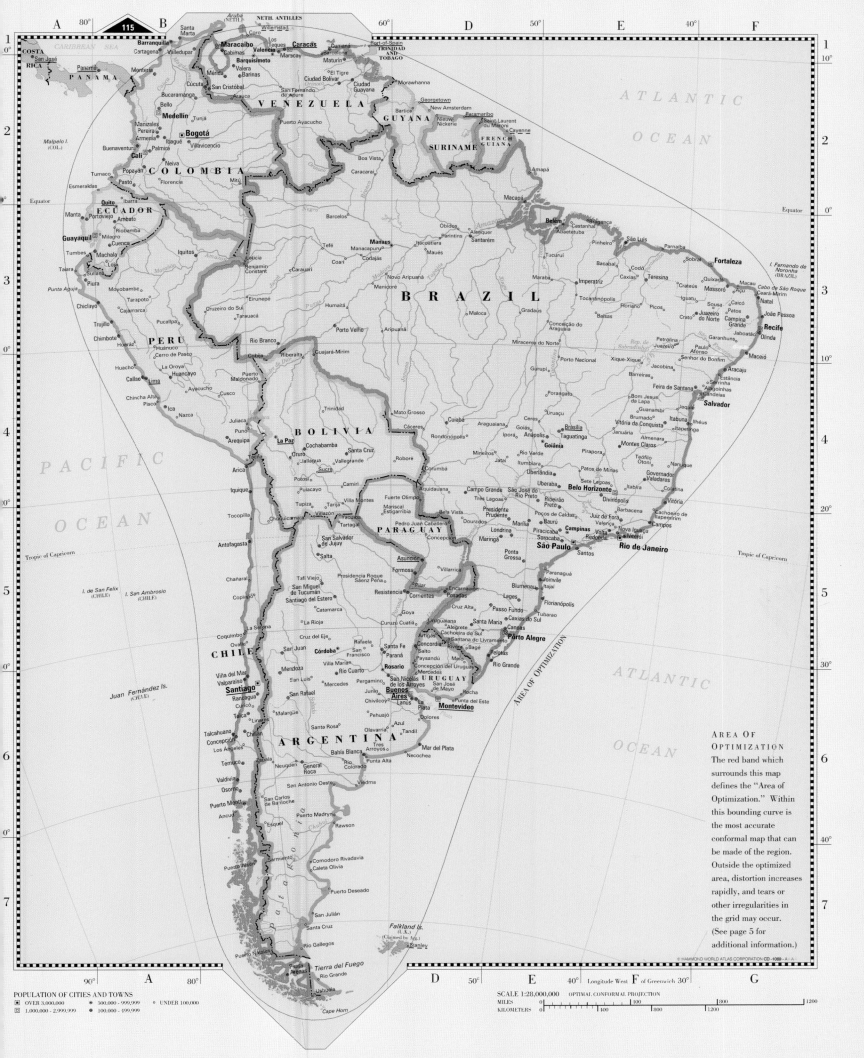

AREA OF OPTIMIZATION
The red band which surrounds this map defines the "Area of Optimization." Within this bounding curve is the most accurate conformal map that can be made of the region. Outside the optimized area, distortion increases rapidly, and tears or other irregularities in the grid may occur. (See page 5 for additional information.)

POPULATION OF CITIES AND TOWNS

SCALE 1:28,000,000   OPTIMAL CONFORMAL PROJECTION

Northern South America

POPULATION OF CITIES AND TOWNS

- OVER 2,000,000
- 1,000,000 - 1,999,999
- 500,000 - 999,999
- 100,000 - 499,999
- 50,000 - 99,999
- UNDER 50,000

SCALE 1:15,000,000   LAMBERT CONFORMAL CONIC PROJECTION

MILES   0   200   400   600

KILOMETERS   0   200   400   600

Southeastern Brazil

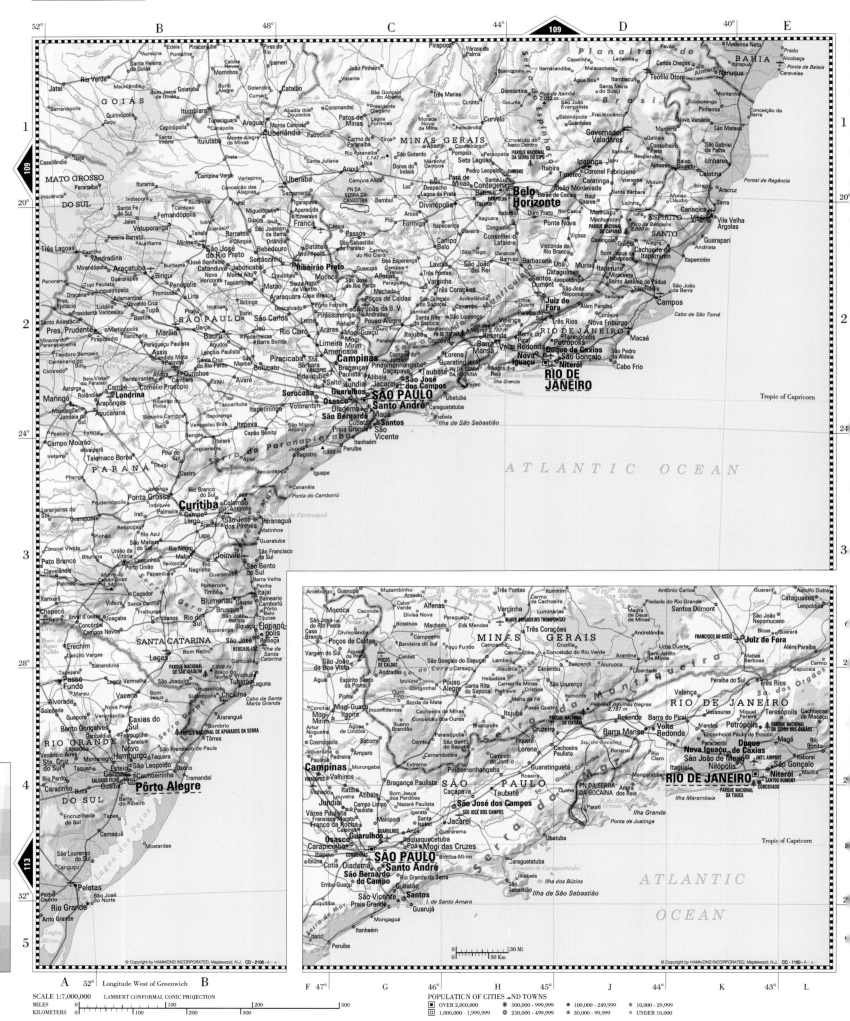

SCALE 1:7,000,000 LAMBERT CONFORMAL CONIC PROJECTION

MILES
KILOMETERS

POPULATION OF CITIES AND TOWNS

Southern South America

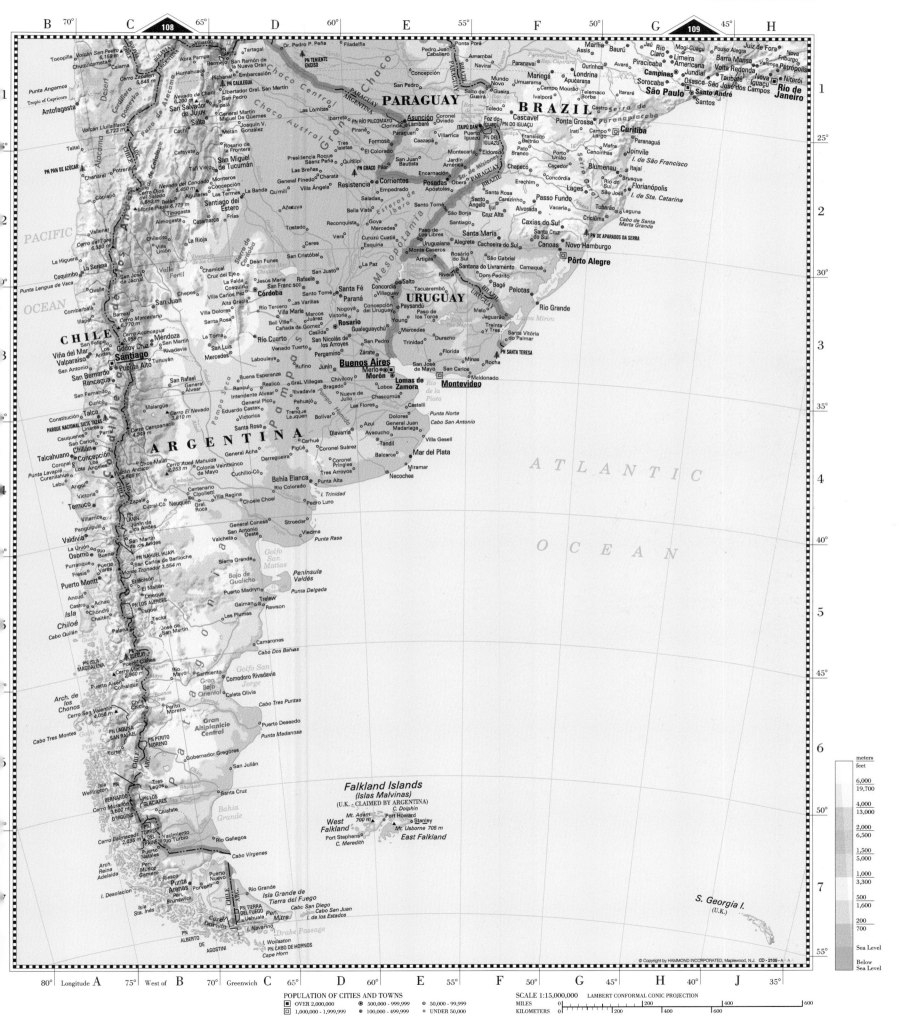

POPULATION OF CITIES AND TOWNS

■ OVER 2,000,000
▣ 1,000,000 - 1,999,999
◉ 500,000 - 999,999
◎ 100,000 - 499,999
◉ 50,000 - 99,999
○ UNDER 50,000

SCALE 1:15,000,000 LAMBERT CONFORMAL CONIC PROJECTION

MILES 0 | 200 | 400 | 600
KILOMETERS 0 | 200 | 400 | 600

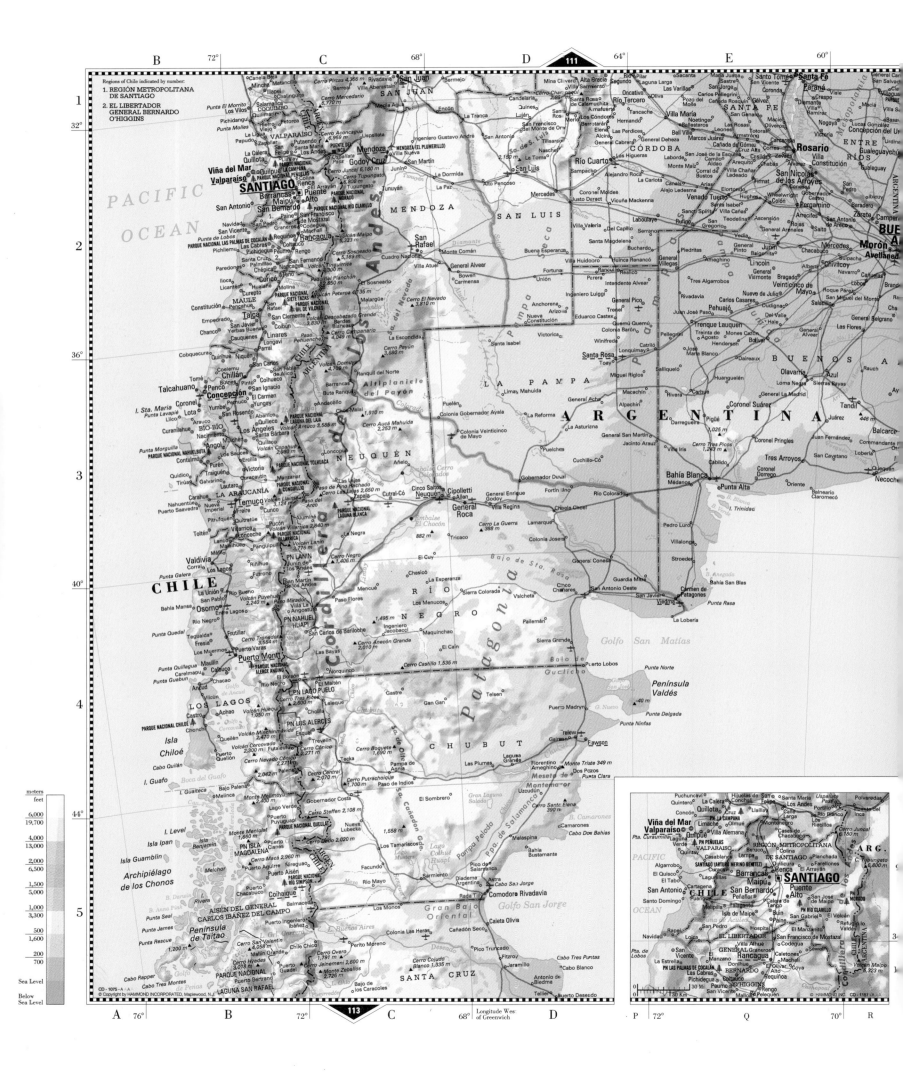

Southern Chile and Argentina

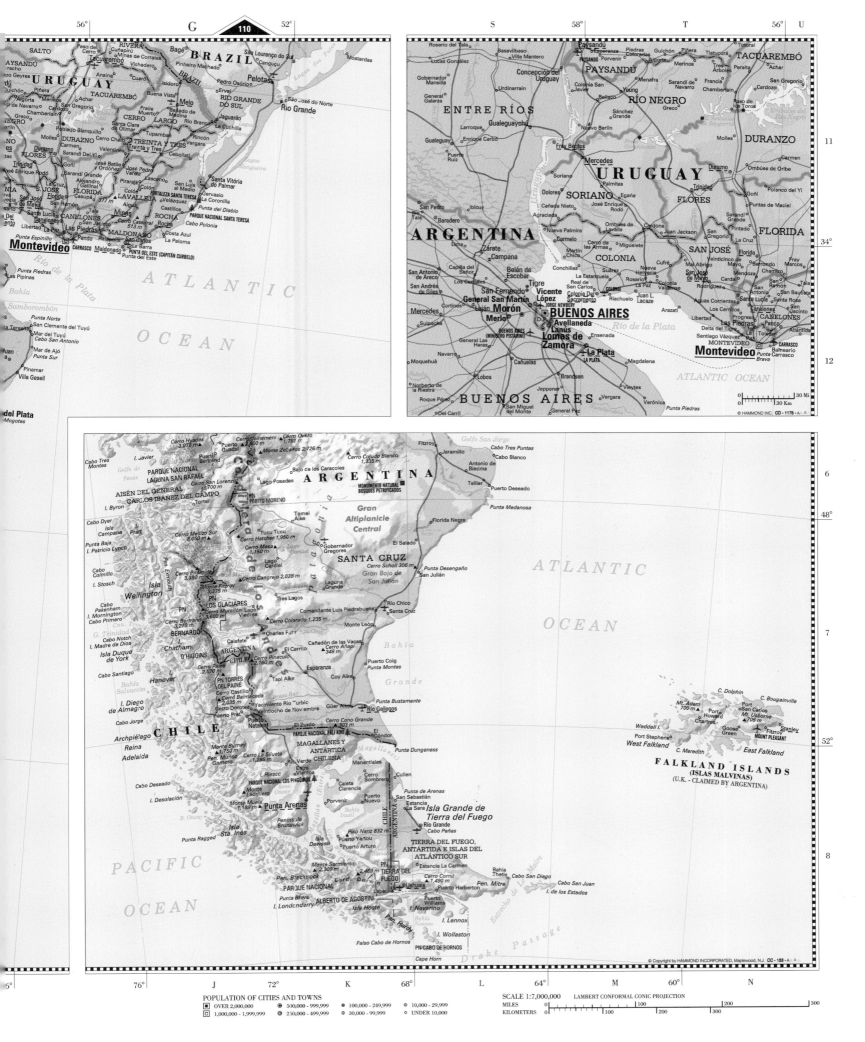

POPULATION OF CITIES AND TOWNS

■ OVER 2,000,000   ⬣ 500,000 - 999,999   ⬤ 100,000 - 249,999   ○ 10,000 - 29,999
▣ 1,000,000 - 1,999,999   ⬤ 250,000 - 499,999   ○ 30,000 - 99,999   ∘ UNDER 10,000

SCALE 1:7,000,000   LAMBERT CONFORMAL CONIC PROJECTION
MILES   0   100   200   300
KILOMETERS   0   100   200   300

North America - Comparisons

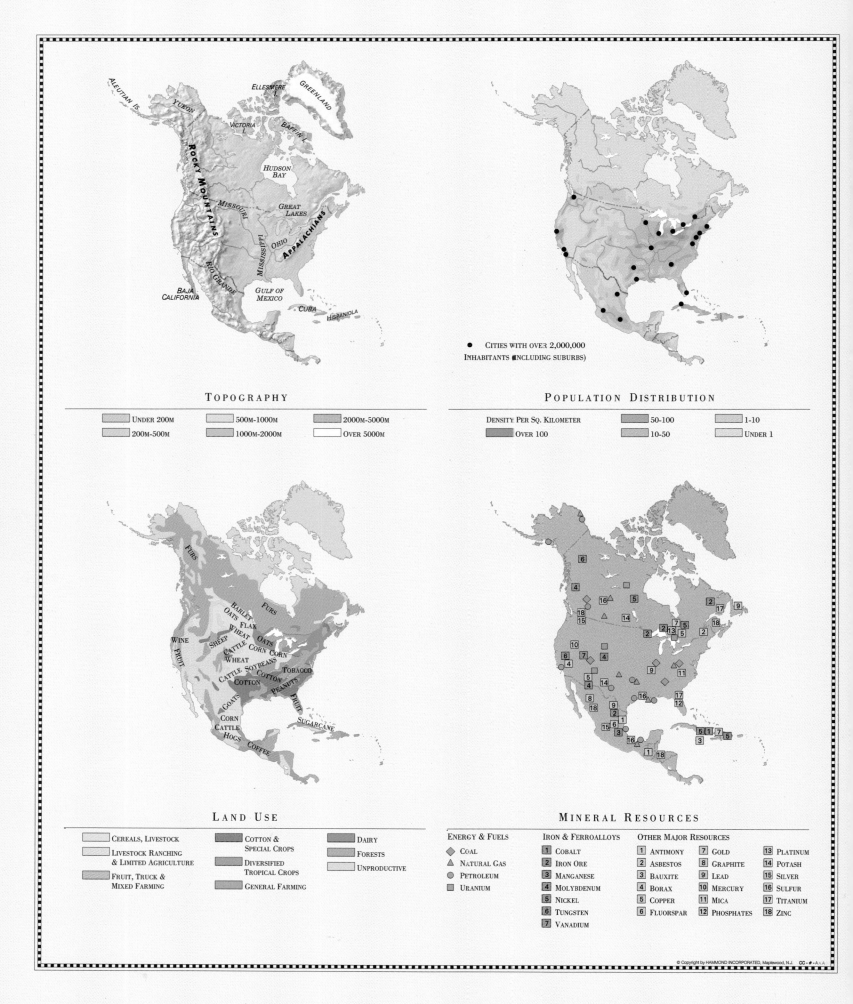

TOPOGRAPHY

- UNDER 200M
- 200M-500M
- 500M-1000M
- 1000M-2000M
- 2000M-5000M
- OVER 5000M

POPULATION DISTRIBUTION

- • CITIES WITH OVER 2,000,000 INHABITANTS (INCLUDING SUBURBS)

DENSITY PER SQ. KILOMETER
- OVER 100
- 50-100
- 10-50
- 1-10
- UNDER 1

LAND USE

- CEREALS, LIVESTOCK
- LIVESTOCK RANCHING & LIMITED AGRICULTURE
- FRUIT, TRUCK & MIXED FARMING
- COTTON & SPECIAL CROPS
- DIVERSIFIED TROPICAL CROPS
- GENERAL FARMING
- DAIRY
- FORESTS
- UNPRODUCTIVE

MINERAL RESOURCES

ENERGY & FUELS
- ◆ COAL
- ▲ NATURAL GAS
- ● PETROLEUM
- ■ URANIUM

IRON & FERROALLOYS
- 1 COBALT
- 2 IRON ORE
- 3 MANGANESE
- 4 MOLYBDENUM
- 5 NICKEL
- 6 TUNGSTEN
- 7 VANADIUM

OTHER MAJOR RESOURCES
- 1 ANTIMONY
- 2 ASBESTOS
- 3 BAUXITE
- 4 BORAX
- 5 COPPER
- 6 FLUORSPAR
- 7 GOLD
- 8 GRAPHITE
- 9 LEAD
- 10 MERCURY
- 11 MICA
- 12 PHOSPHATES
- 13 PLATINUM
- 14 POTASH
- 15 SILVER
- 16 SULFUR
- 17 TITANIUM
- 18 ZINC

North America

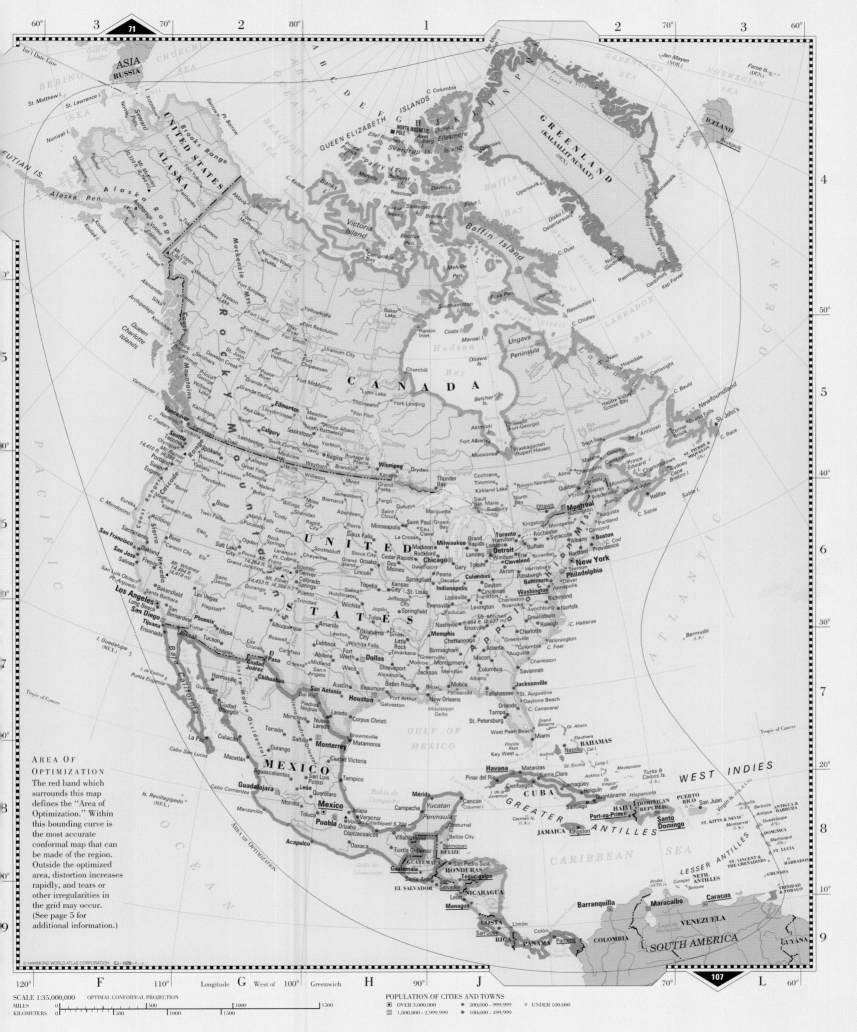

AREA OF
OPTIMIZATION
The red band which
surrounds this map
defines the "Area of
Optimization." Within
this bounding curve is
the most accurate
conformal map that can
be made of the region.
Outside the optimized
area, distortion increases
rapidly, and tears or
other irregularities in
the grid may occur.
(See page 5 for
additional information.)

SCALE 1:35,000,000   OPTIMAL CONFORMAL PROJECTION

MILES
KILOMETERS

POPULATION OF CITIES AND TOWNS
■ OVER 3,000,000   ✳ 500,000 - 999,999   ○ UNDER 100,000
▣ 1,000,000 - 2,999,999   ◉ 100,000 - 499,999

Middle America and Caribbean

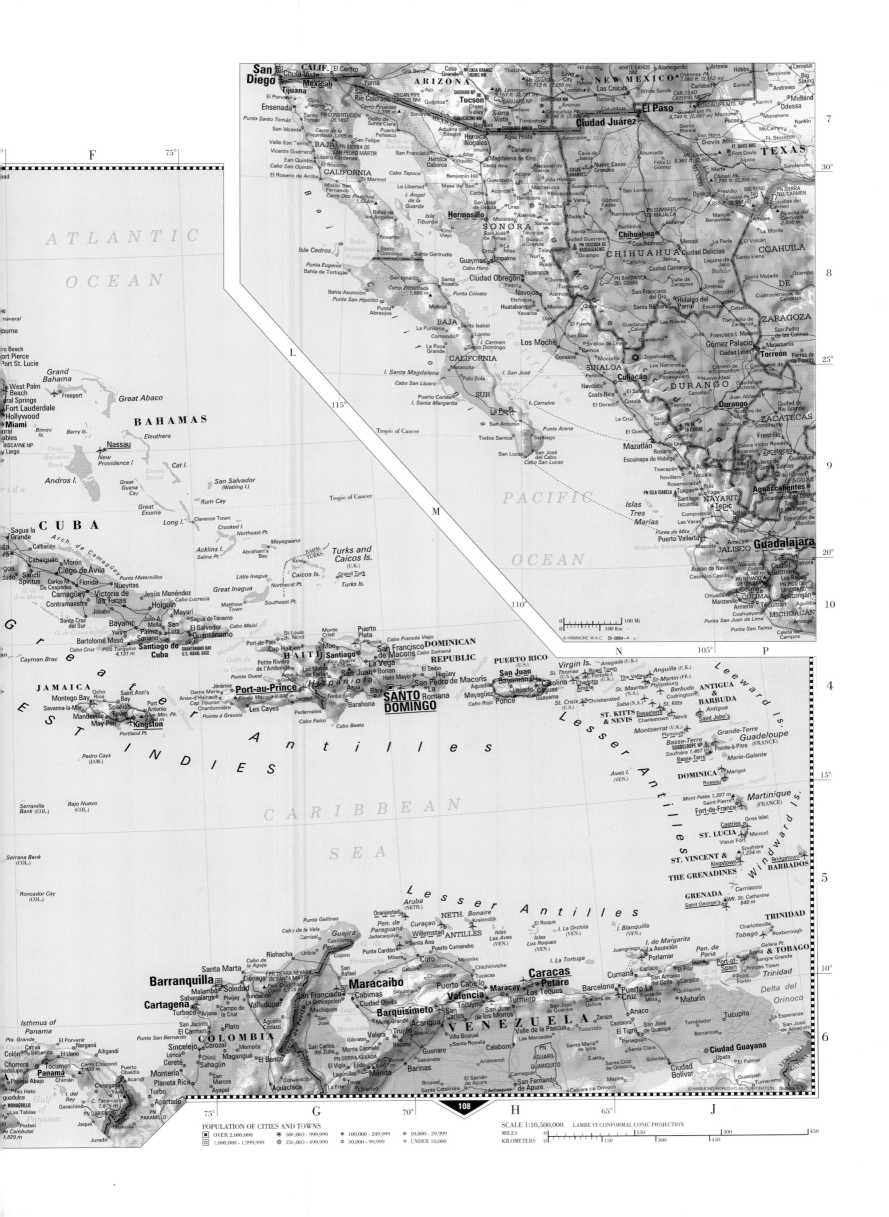

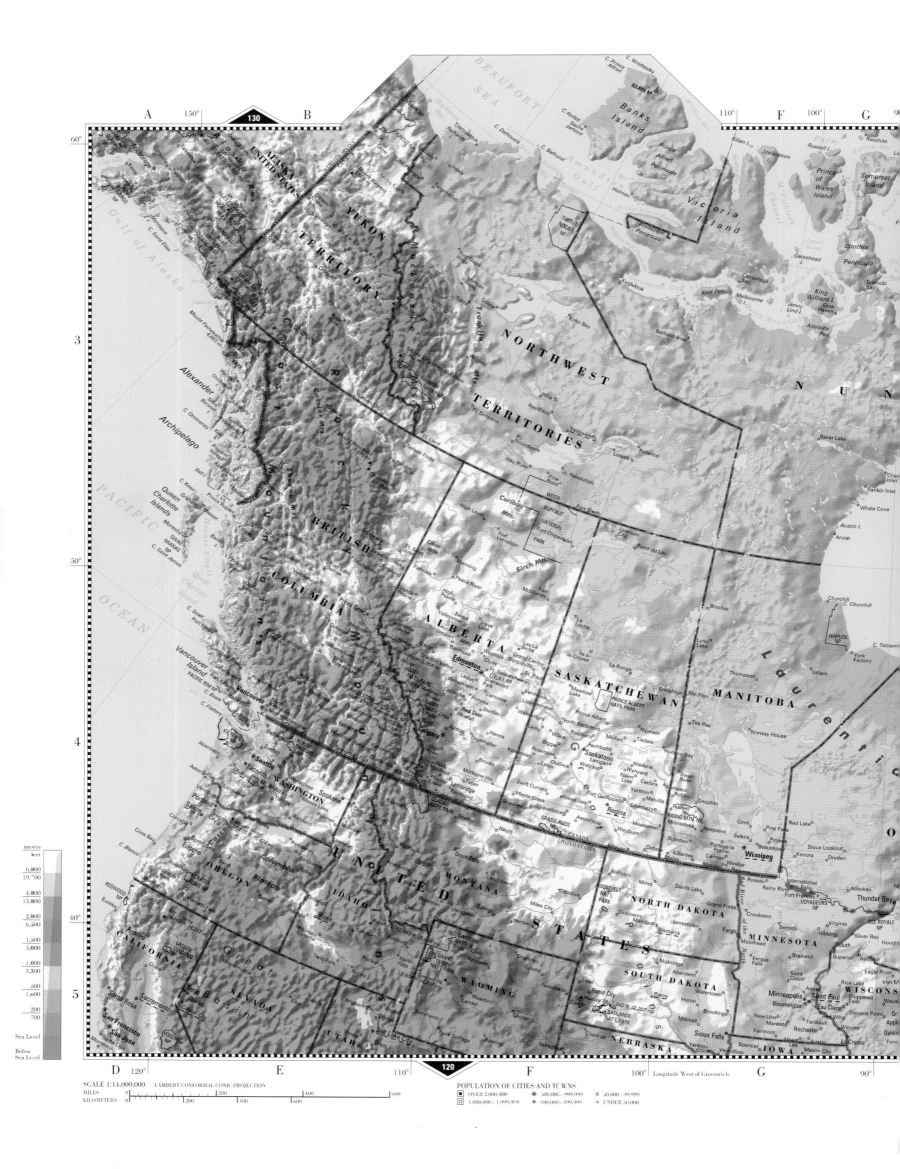

POPULATION OF CITIES AND TOWNS

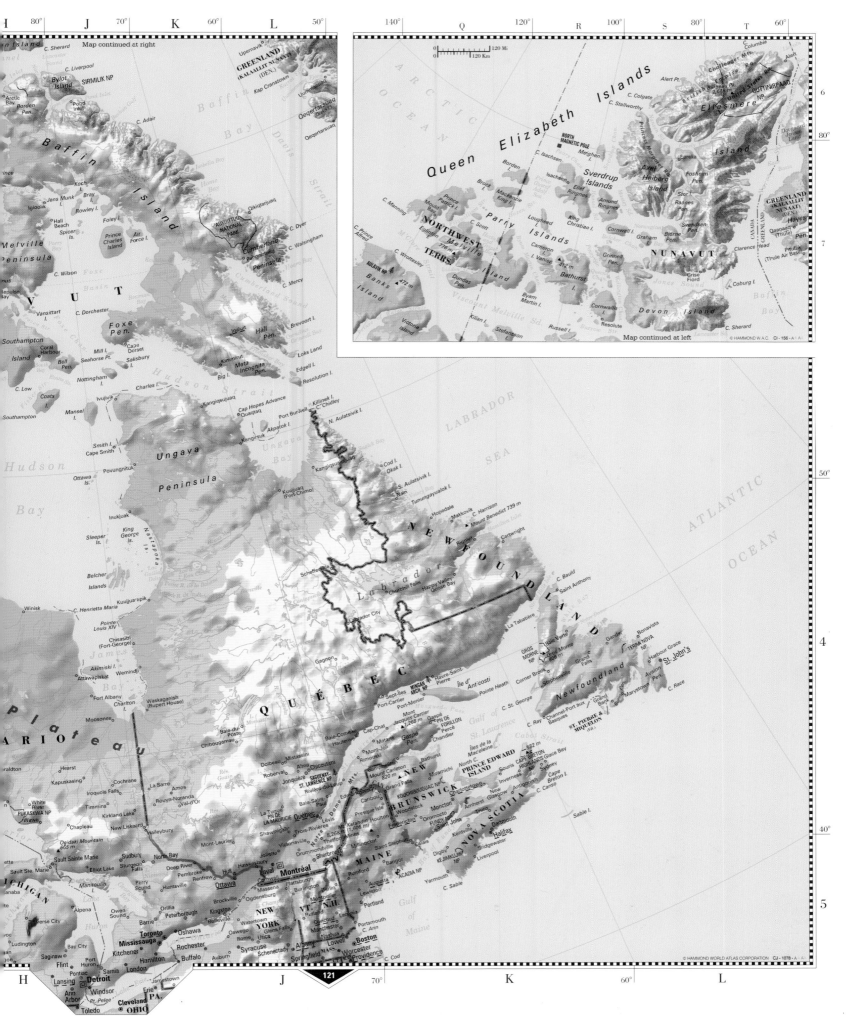

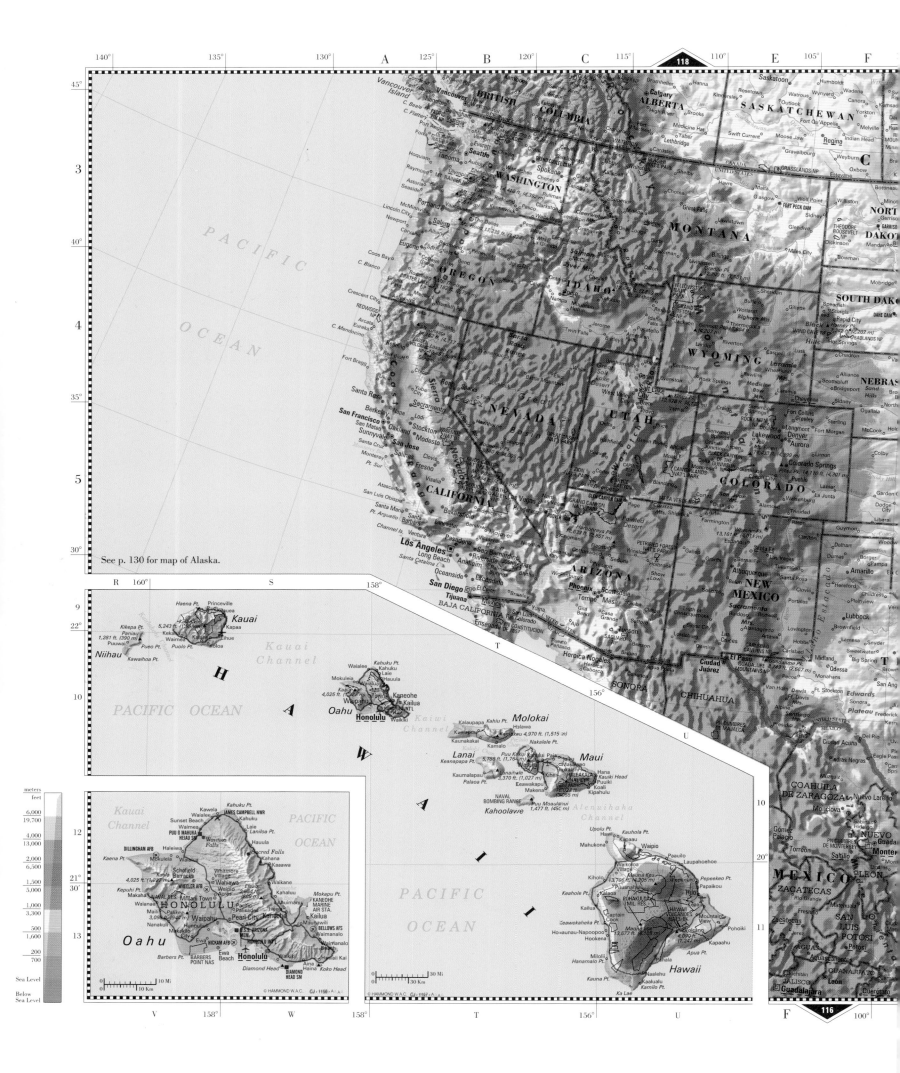

See p. 130 for map of Alaska.

© HAMMOND W.A.C.

meters feet
6,000 19,700
4,000 13,000
2,000 6,500
1,500 5,000
1,000 3,300
500 1,600
200 700
Sea Level
Below Sea Level

United States

Southwestern Canada, Northwestern United States

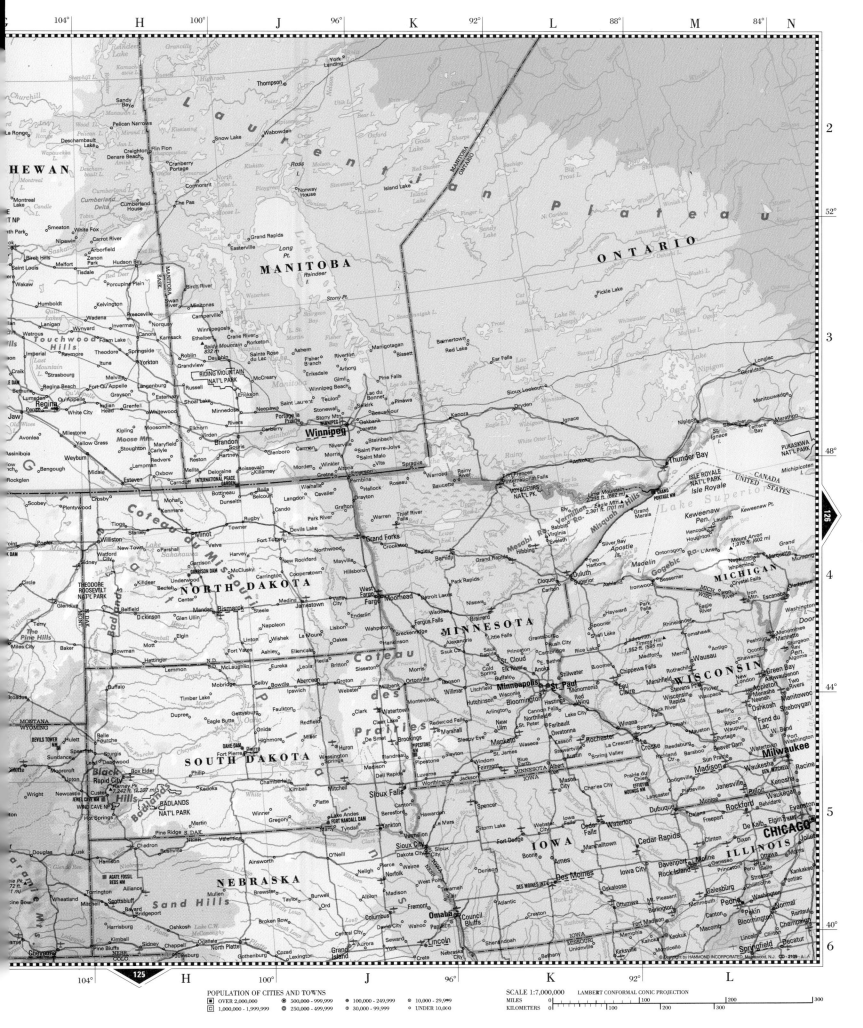

POPULATION OF CITIES AND TOWNS

■ OVER 2,000,000	● 500,000 - 999,999	● 100,000 - 249,999	○ 10,000 - 29,999
◻ 1,000,000 - 1,999,999	● 250,000 - 499,999	⊕ 30,000 - 99,999	○ UNDER 10,000

SCALE 1:7,000,000   LAMBERT CONFORMAL CONIC PROJECTION

MILES 0   100   200   300
KILOMETERS 0   100   200   300

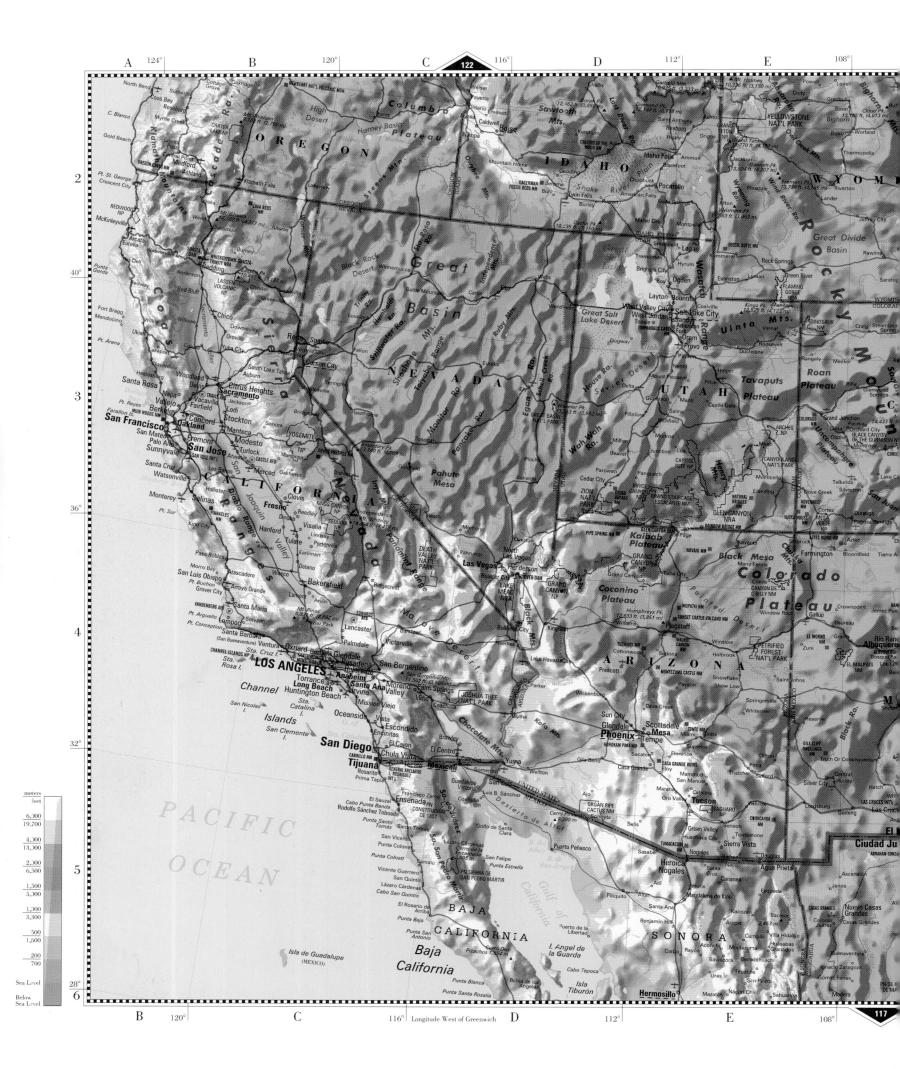

Southwestern United States

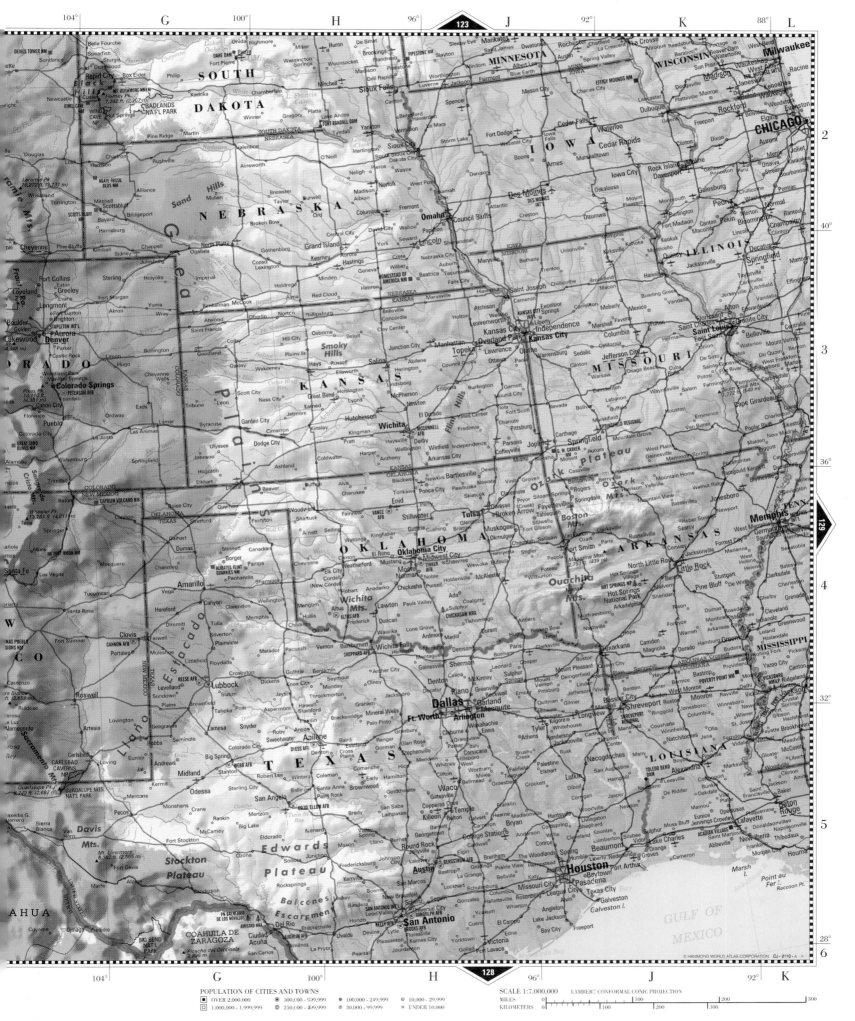

129

POPULATION OF CITIES AND TOWNS

| ■ | OVER 2,000,000 | ◉ | 500,000–999,999 | ● | 100,000–249,999 | ○ | 10,000–29,999 |
| □ | 1,000,000–1,999,999 | ◉ | 250,000–499,999 | ● | 30,000–99,999 | ∘ | UNDER 10,000 |

SCALE 1:7,000,000   LAMBERT CONFORMAL CONIC PROJECTION

MILES 0   100   200   300

KILOMETERS 0   100   200   300

© HAMMOND WORLD ATLAS CORPORATION   CJ–2110–A   A

Southeastern Canada, Northeastern United States

POPULATION OF CITIES AND TOWNS

■ OVER 2,000,000 ◉ 500,000 - 999,999 ● 100,000 - 249,999 ⊙ 10,000 - 29,999
◻ 1,000,000 - 1,999,999 ◉ 250,000 - 499,999 ● 30,000 - 99,999 ∘ UNDER 10,000

SCALE 1:7,000,000   LAMBERT CONFORMAL CONIC PROJECTION

MILES
KILOMETERS

© HAMMOND WORLD ATLAS CORPORATION CJ-2111-A-A

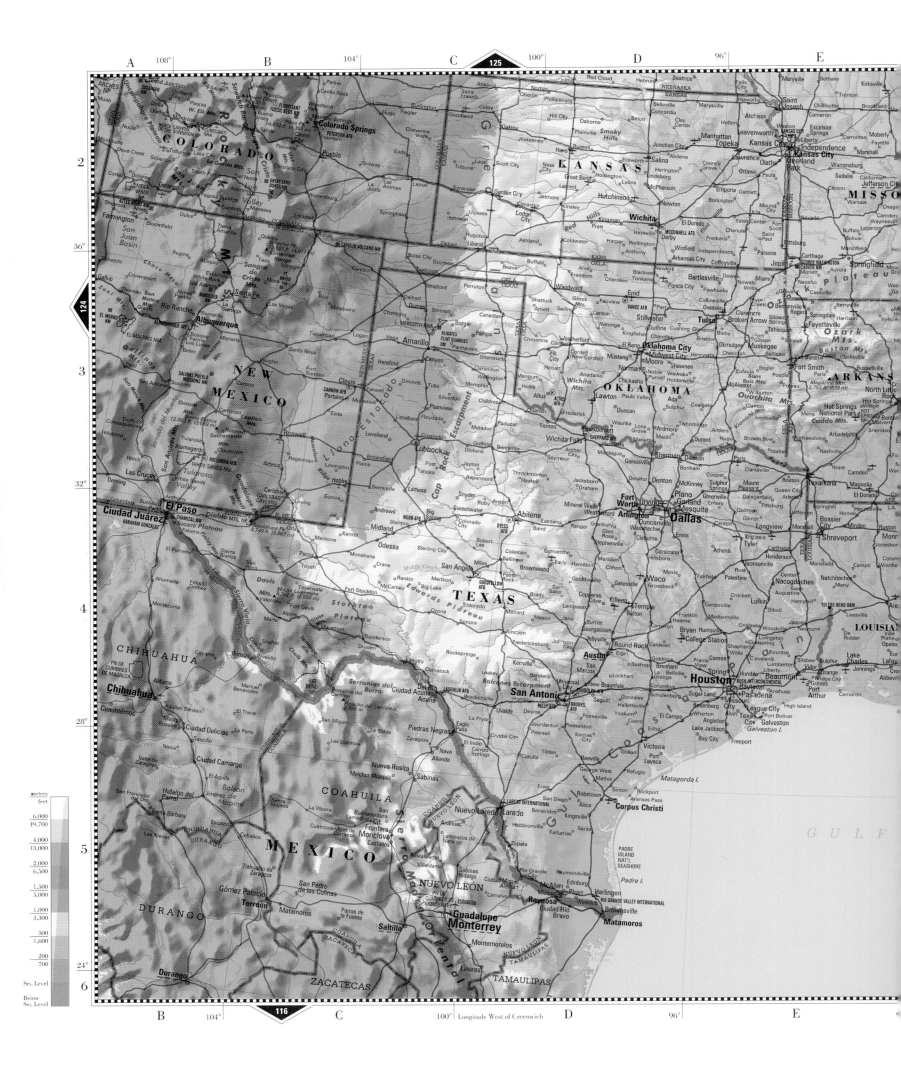

Southeastern United States

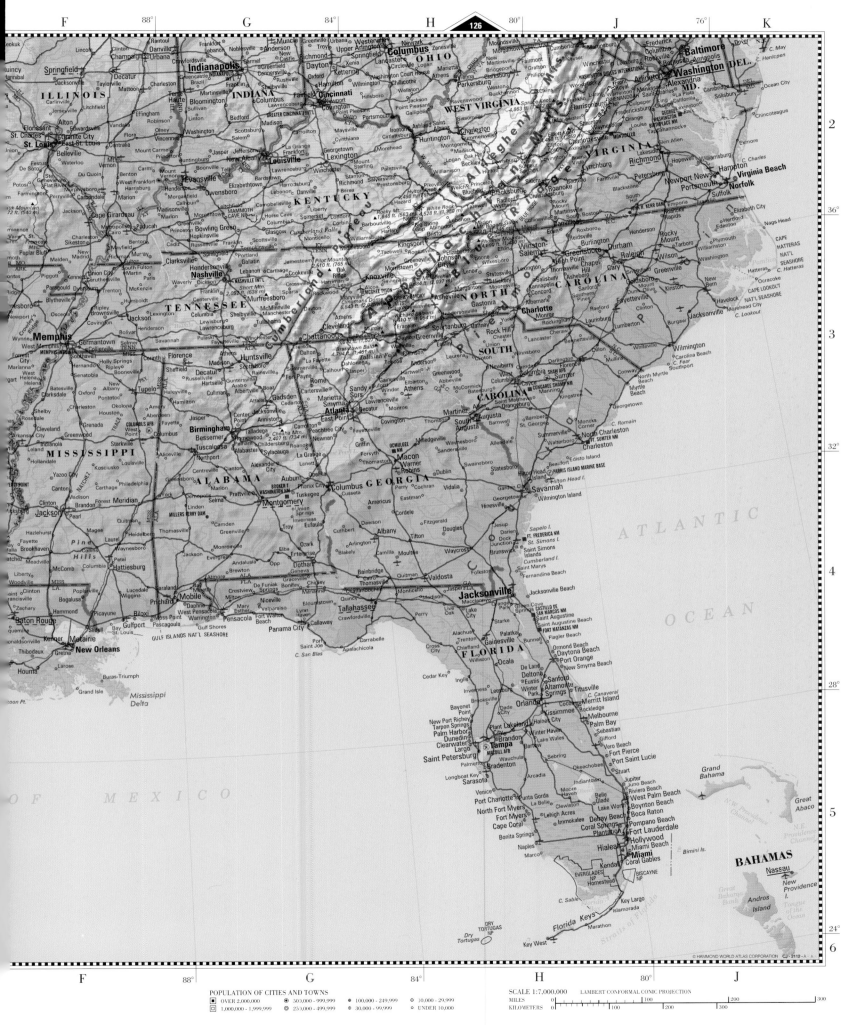

POPULATION OF CITIES AND TOWNS

■ OVER 2,000,000   ● 500,000 - 999,999   ● 100,000 - 249,999   ○ 10,000 - 29,999
□ 1,000,000 - 1,999,999   ● 250,000 - 499,999   ● 30,000 - 99,999   ○ UNDER 10,000

SCALE 1:7,000,000   LAMBERT CONFORMAL CONIC PROJECTION

MILES 0   100   200   300
KILOMETERS 0   100   200   300

© HAMMOND WORLD ATLAS CORPORATION   CJ-2112-A

Alaska

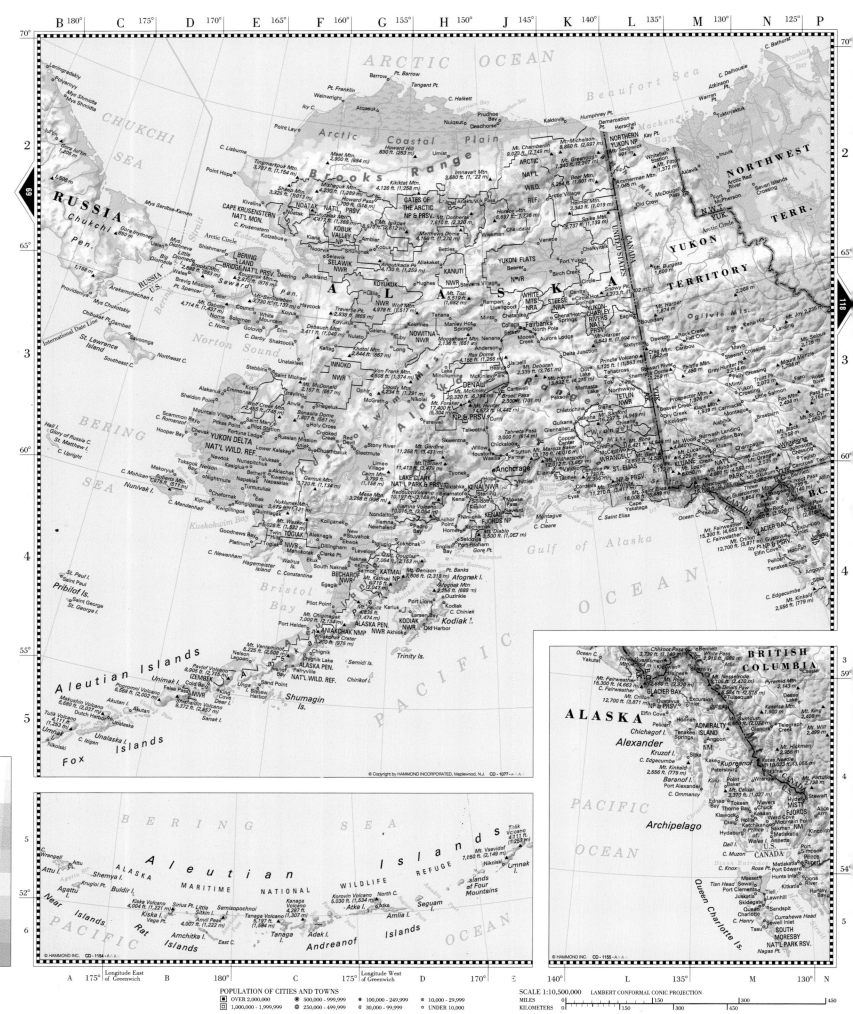

POPULATION OF CITIES AND TOWNS

- ■ OVER 2,000,000
- ▣ 1,000,000 - 1,999,999
- ● 500,000 - 999,999
- ◉ 250,000 - 499,999
- ● 100,000 - 249,999
- ◔ 30,000 - 99,999
- ◦ 10,000 - 29,999
- ○ UNDER 10,000

SCALE 1:10,500,000   LAMBERT CONFORMAL CONIC PROJECTION

MILES   0   150   300   450

KILOMETERS   0   150   300   450

Los Angeles, New York-Philadelphia-Washington

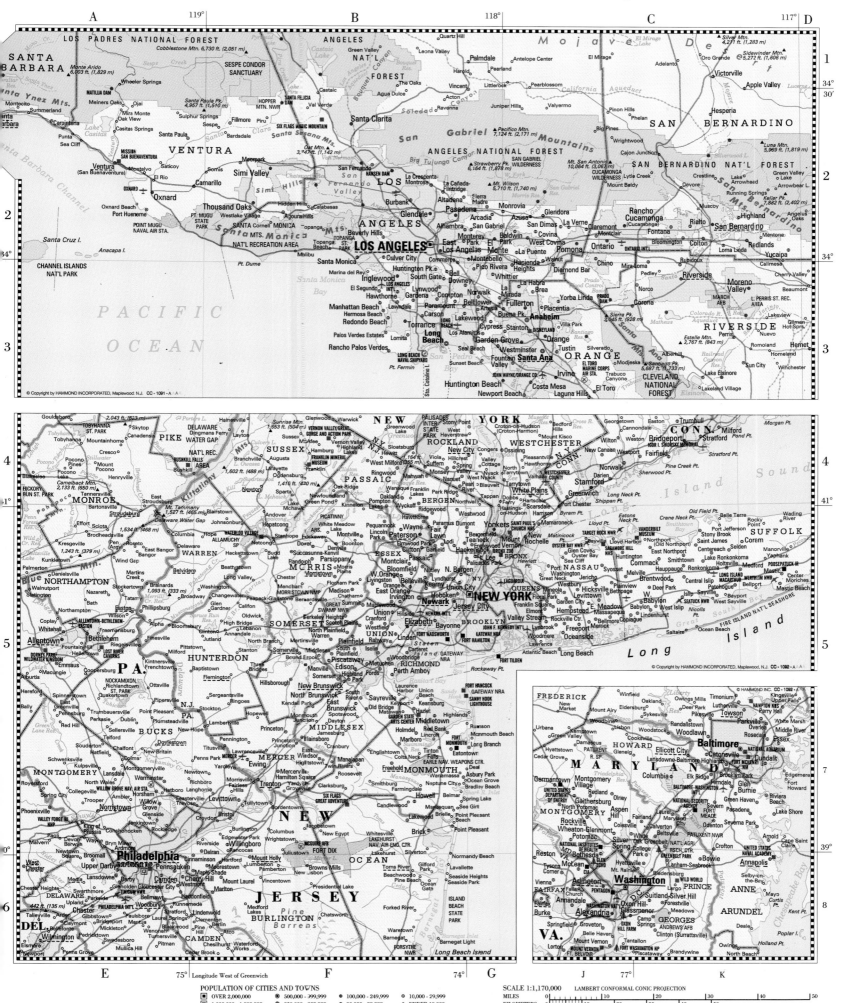

Seattle, San Francisco, Detroit, Chicago

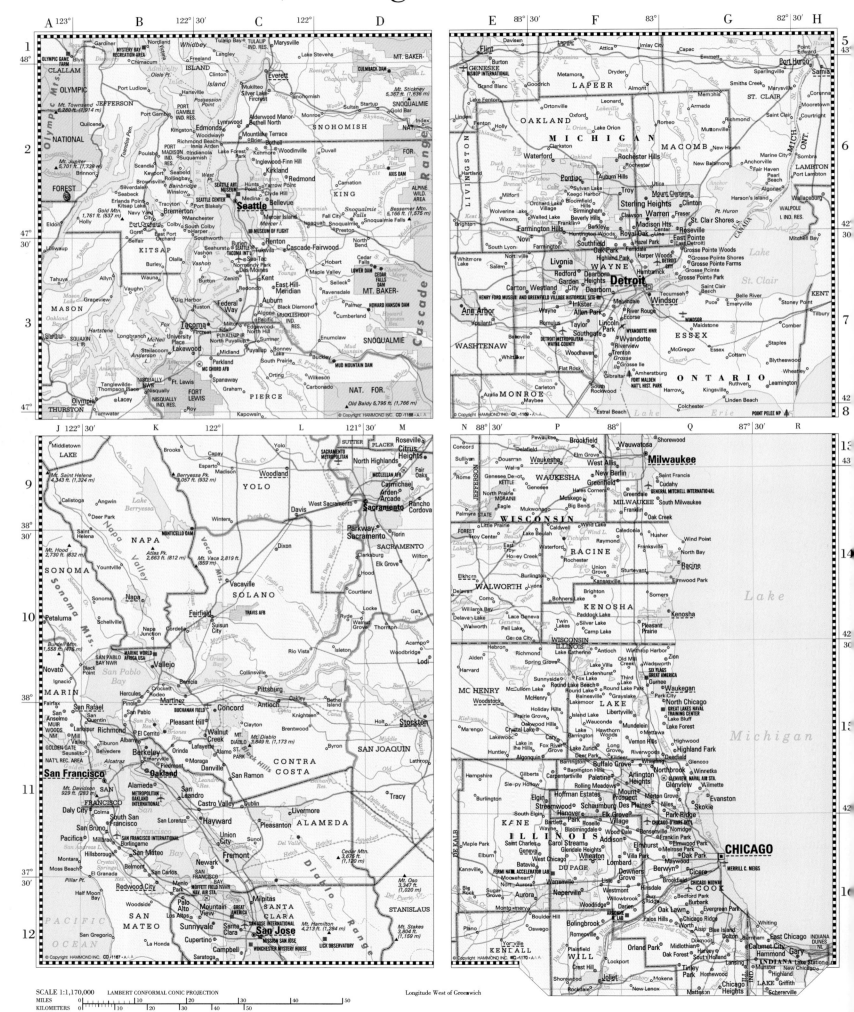

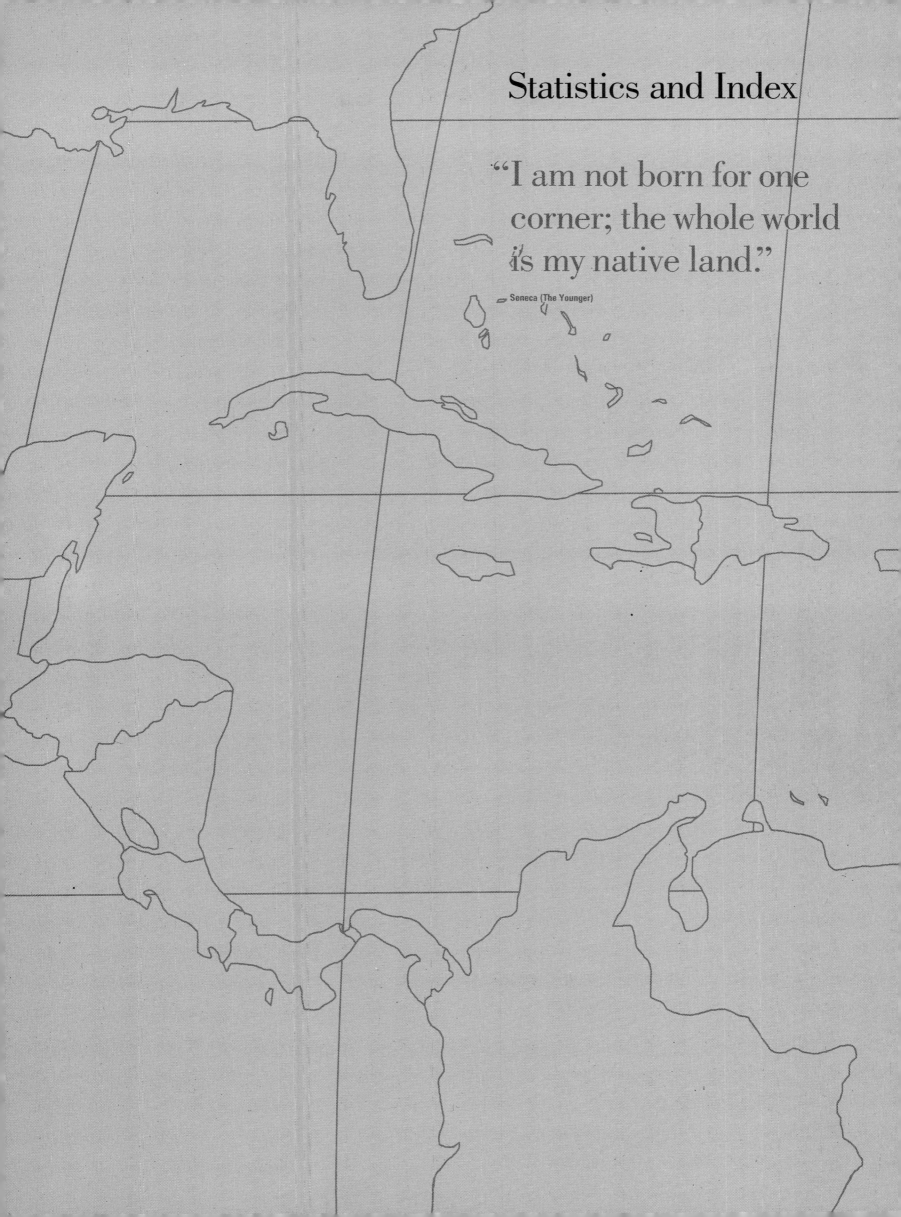

Statistics and Index

"I am not born for one corner; the whole world is my native land."

— Seneca (The Younger)

Time Zones of the World

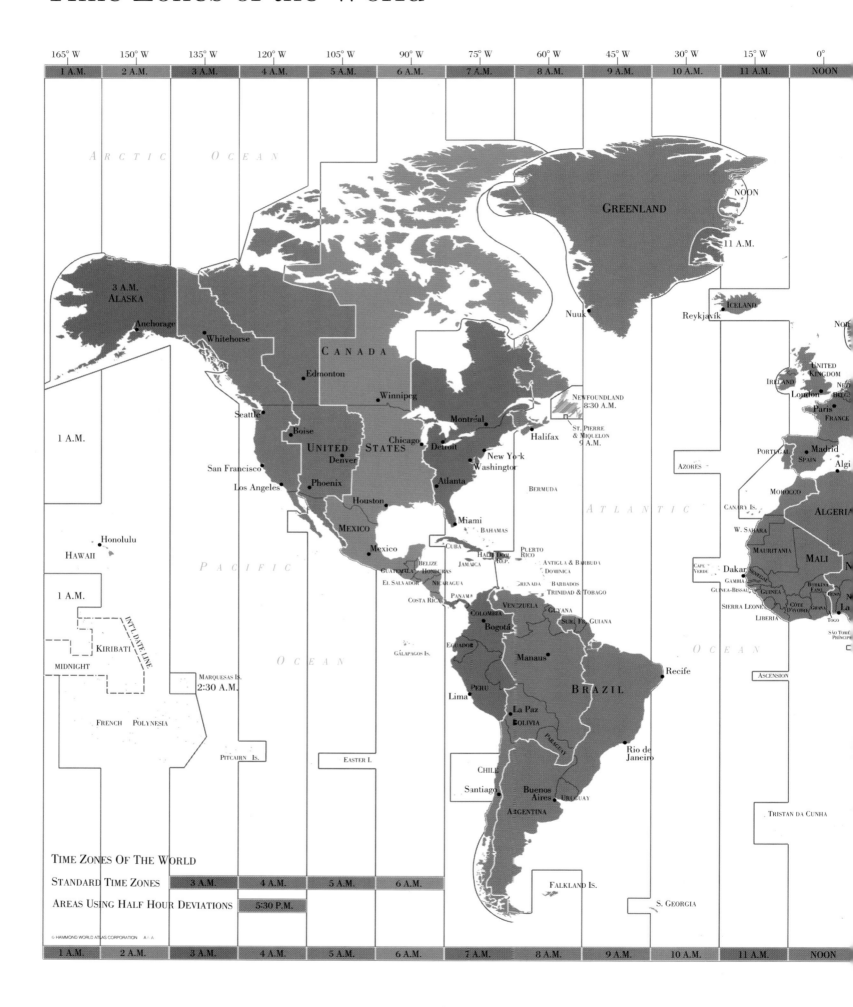

| 165° W | 150° W | 135° W | 120° W | 105° W | 90° W | 75° W | 60° W | 45° W | 30° W | 15° W | 0° |

| 1 A.M. | 2 A.M. | 3 A.M. | 4 A.M. | 5 A.M. | 6 A.M. | 7 A.M. | 8 A.M. | 9 A.M. | 10 A.M. | 11 A.M. | NOON |

ARCTIC   OCEAN

GREENLAND

NOON

11 A.M.

3 A.M.
ALASKA
• Anchorage

• Whitehorse

CANADA

Nuuk•

ICELAND
Reykjavík•

• Edmonton

NEWFOUNDLAND
8:30 A.M.

UNITED
KINGDOM
IRELAND
London•
Paris•
FRANCE

• Seattle
• Boise

• Winnipeg

• Montréal

ST. PIERRE
& MIQUELON
9 A.M.

Madrid
SPAIN
Algi

1 A.M.

San Francisco •
• Denver
Los Angeles •
• Phoenix

UNITED   STATES
• Chicago   Detroit•
• Denver
New York•
Washington•
Atlanta•

• Halifax

AZORES

PORTUGAL

MOROCCO

CANARY IS.

ATLANTIC

ALGERIA

BERMUDA

W. SAHARA

Honolulu •

HAWAII

MEXICO

Houston•

Miami•
BAHAMAS
CUBA

PUERTO
RICO
ANTIGUA & BARBUDA
DOMINICA

MAURITANIA

MALI

PACIFIC

Mexico•

HAITI DOM.
JAMAICA   REP.
BELIZE
GUATEMALA   HONDURAS
EL SALVADOR   NICARAGUA
COSTA RICA   PANAMA

GRENADA   BARBADOS
TRINIDAD & TOBAGO

CAPE
VERDE   Dakar•   SENEGAL
GAMBIA
GUINEA-BISSAU   GUINEA
SIERRA LEONE
LIBERIA

BURKINA
FASO
CÔTE
D'IVOIRE   GHANA

TOGO

SÃO TOMÉ
PRÍNCIPE

1 A.M.

COLOMBIA
Bogotá•

VENEZUELA   GUYANA
SURI.   FR. GUIANA

OCEAN

MIDNIGHT

INT'L DATE LINE

KIRIBATI

ECUADOR•

GALÁPAGOS IS.

Manaus•

BRAZIL

Recife•

ASCENSION

MARQUESAS IS.
2:30 A.M.

FRENCH   POLYNESIA

OCEAN

Lima•   PERU

La Paz•
BOLIVIA

PARAGUAY

Rio de
Janeiro•

PITCAIRN IS.

EASTER I.

CHILE

Santiago•

Buenos
Aires•   URUGUAY

ARGENTINA

TRISTAN DA CUNHA

FALKLAND IS.

S. GEORGIA

TIME ZONES OF THE WORLD

STANDARD TIME ZONES | 3 A.M. | 4 A.M. | 5 A.M. | 6 A.M. |

AREAS USING HALF HOUR DEVIATIONS | 5:30 P.M. |

© HAMMOND WORLD ATLAS CORPORATION   A^A

| 1 A.M. | 2 A.M. | 3 A.M. | 4 A.M. | 5 A.M. | 6 A.M. | 7 A.M. | 8 A.M. | 9 A.M. | 10 A.M. | 11 A.M. | NOON |

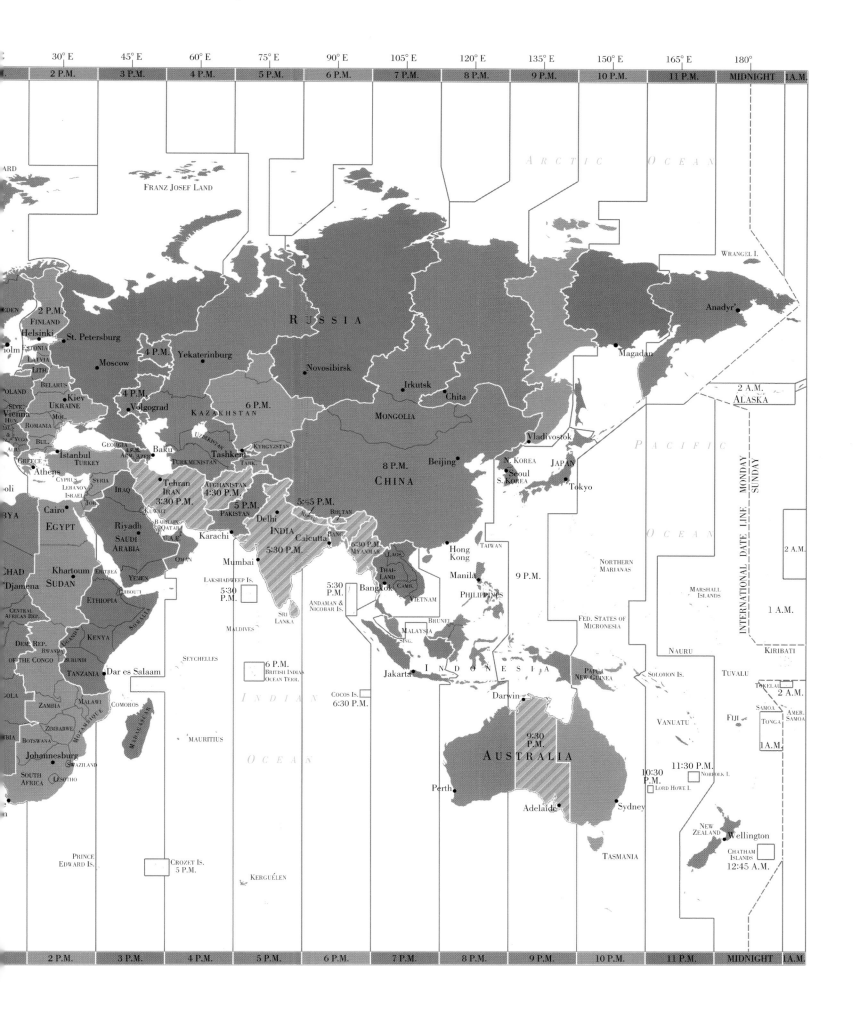

World Statistics

Elements of the Solar System

	Mean Distance from Sun: in Miles	in Kilometers	Period of Revolution around Sun	Period of Rotation on Axis	Equatorial Diameter in Miles	in Kilometers	Surface Gravity (Earth = 1)	Mass (Earth = 1)	Mean Density (Water = 1)	Number of Satellites
Mercury	35,990,000	57,900,000	87.97 days	58.7 days	3,032	4,880	0.38	0.055	5.4	0
Venus	67,240,000	108,200,000	224.70 days	243.7 days†	7,521	12,104	0.91	0.815	5.2	0
Earth	93,000,000	149,700,000	365.26 days	23h 56m	7,926	12,755	1.00	1.00	5.5	1
Mars	141,610,000	227,900,000	686.98 days	24h 37m	4,221	6,794	0.38	0.107	3.9	2
Jupiter	483,675,000	778,400,000	11.86 years	9h 55m	88,846	142,984	2.36	317.8	1.3	16
Saturn	886,572,000	1,426,800,000	29.46 years	10h 30m	74,898	120,536	0.92	95.2	0.7	18
Uranus	1,783,957,000	2,871,000,000	84.01 years	17h 14m†	31,763	51,118	0.89	14.5	1.3	15
Neptune	2,795,114,000	4,498,300,000	164.79 years	13h 6m	30,778	49,532	1.13	17.1	1.6	8
Pluto	3,670,000,000	5,906,400,000	247.70 years	6.4 days†	1,413	2,274	0.07	0.002	2.1	1

† Retrograde motion

Source: NASA, National Space Science Data Center

Dimensions of the Earth

	Area in: Sq. Miles	Sq. Kilometers
Superficial area	196,939,000	510,072,000
Land surface	57,506,000	148,940,000
Water surface	139,433,000	361,132,000

	Distance in: Miles	Kilometers
Equatorial circumference	24,902	40,075
Polar circumference	24,860	40,007
Equatorial diameter	7,926.4	12,756.4
Polar diameter	7,899.8	12,713.6
Equatorial radius	3,963.2	6,378.2
Polar radius	3,949.9	6,356.8

Volume of the Earth	2.6×10^{11} cubic miles	10.84×10^{11} cubic kilometers
Mass or weight	6.6×10^{21} short tons	6.0×10^{21} metric tons
Maximum distance from Sun	94,600,000 miles	152,000,000 kilometers
Minimum distance from Sun	91,300,000 miles	147,000,000 kilometers

Oceans and Major Seas

	Area in: Sq. Miles	Sq. Kms.	Greatest Depth in: Feet	Meters
Pacific Ocean	63,855,000	166,241,000	36,198	11,033
Atlantic Ocean	31,744,000	82,217,000	28,374	8,648
Indian Ocean	28,417,000	73,600,000	25,344	7,725
Arctic Ocean	5,427,000	14,056,000	17,880	5,450
Caribbean Sea	970,000	2,512,300	24,720	7,535
Mediterranean Sea	969,000	2,509,700	16,896	5,150
South China Sea	895,000	2,318,000	15,000	4,600
Bering Sea	875,000	2,266,250	15,800	4,800
Gulf of Mexico	600,000	1,554,000	12,300	3,750
Sea of Okhotsk	590,000	1,528,100	11,070	3,370
East China Sea	482,000	1,248,400	9,500	2,900
Yellow Sea	480,000	1,243,200	350	107
Sea of Japan	389,000	1,007,500	12,280	3,740
Hudson Bay	317,500	822,300	846	258
North Sea	222,000	575,000	2,200	670
Black Sea	185,000	479,150	7,365	2,245
Red Sea	169,000	437,700	7,200	2,195
Baltic Sea	163,000	422,170	1,506	459

The Continents

	Area in: Sq. Miles	Sq. Kms.	Percent of World's Land
Asia	17,128,500	44,362,815	29.5
Africa	11,707,000	30,321,130	20.2
North America	9,363,000	24,250,170	16.2
South America	6,879,725	17,818,505	11.9
Antarctica	5,405,000	14,000,000	9.4
Europe	4,057,000	10,507,630	7.0
Australia	2,967,893	7,686,850	5.1

Major Ship Canals

	Length in: Miles	Kms.	Minimum Depth in: Feet	Meters
Volga-Baltic, Russia	225	362	–	–
Baltic-White Sea, Russia	140	225	16	5
Suez, Egypt	100.76	162	42	13
Albert, Belgium	80	129	16.5	5
Moscow-Volga, Russia	80	129	18	6
Volga-Don, Russia	62	100	–	–
Göta, Sweden	54	87	10	3
Kiel (Nord-Ostsee), Germany	53.2	86	38	12
Panama Canal, Panama	50.72	82	41.6	13
Houston Ship, U.S.A.	50	81	36	11

Largest Islands

	Area in: Sq. Miles	Sq. Kms.
Greenland	840,000	2,175,600
New Guinea	305,000	789,950
Borneo	286,000	740,740
Madagascar	226,656	587,040
Baffin, Canada	195,928	507,454
Sumatra, Indonesia	164,000	424,760
Honshu, Japan	88,000	227,920
Great Britain	84,400	218,896
Victoria, Canada	83,896	217,290
Ellesmere, Canada	75,767	196,236
Celebes, Indonesia	72,986	189,034
South I., New Zealand	58,393	151,238
Java, Indonesia	48,842	126,501
North I., New Zealand	44,187	114,444
Cuba	42,803	110,860
Newfoundland, Canada	42,031	108,860
Luzon, Philippines	40,420	104,688
Iceland	39,768	103,000
Mindanao, Philippines	36,537	94,631
Ireland	32,589	84,406
Hokkaidō, Japan	30,436	78,829
Sakhalin, Russia	29,500	76,405

	Area in: Sq. Miles	Sq. Kms.
Hispaniola, Haiti & Dom. Rep.	29,399	76,143
Banks, Canada	27,038	70,028
Ceylon, Sri Lanka	25,332	65,610
Tasmania, Australia	24,600	63,710
Svalbard, Norway	23,957	62,049
Devon, Canada	21,331	55,247
Novaya Zemlya (north isl.), Russia	18,600	48,200
Marajó, Brazil	17,991	46,597
Tierra del Fuego, Chile & Argentina	17,900	46,360
Alexander, Antarctica	16,700	43,250
Axel Heiberg, Canada	16,671	43,178
Melville, Canada	16,274	42,150
Southhampton, Canada	15,913	41,215
New Britain, Papua New Guinea	14,100	36,519
Taiwan, China	13,836	35,835
Kyushu, Japan	13,770	35,664
Hainan, China	13,127	33,999
Prince of Wales, Canada	12,872	33,338
Spitsbergen, Norway	12,355	31,999
Vancouver, Canada	12,079	31,285
Timor, Indonesia	11,527	29,855
Sicily, Italy	9,926	25,708

	Area in: Sq. Miles	Sq. Kms.
Somerset, Canada	9,570	24,786
Sardinia, Italy	9,301	24,090
Shikoku, Japan	6,860	17,767
New Caledonia, France	6,530	16,913
Nordaustlandet, Norway	6,409	16,599
Samar, Philippines	5,050	13,080
Negros, Philippines	4,906	12,707
Palawan, Philippines	4,550	11,785
Panay, Philippines	4,446	11,515
Jamaica	4,232	10,961
Hawaii, United States	4,038	10,458
Viti Levu, Fiji	4,010	10,386
Cape Breton, Canada	3,981	10,311
Mindoro, Philippines	3,759	9,736
Kodiak, Alaska, U.S.A.	3,670	9,505
Cyprus	3,572	9,251
Puerto Rico, U.S.A.	3,435	8,897
Corsica, France	3,352	8,682
New Ireland, Papua New Guinea	3,340	8,651
Crete, Greece	3,218	8,335
Anticosti, Canada	3,066	7,941
Wrangel, Russia	2,819	7,301

PRINCIPAL MOUNTAINS

	Height in: Feet	Meters		Height in: Feet	Meters		Height in: Feet	Meters
Everest, Nepal-China	29,028	8,848	Pissis, Argentina	22,241	6,779	Margherita (Ruwenzori), Africa	16,795	5,119
K2 (Godwin Austen), Pakistan-China	28,250	8,611	Mercedario, Argentina	22,211	6,770	Kazbek, Georgia-Russia	16,558	5,047
Kanchenjunga, Nepal-India	28,208	8,598	Huascarán, Peru	22,205	6,768	Puncak Jaya, Indonesia	16,503	5,030
Lhotse, Nepal-China	27,923	8,511	Llullaillaco, Chile-Argentina	22,057	6,723	Blanc, France	15,771	4,807
Makalu, Nepal-China	27,789	8,470	Nevada Ancohuma, Bolivia	21,489	6,550	Klyuchevskaya Sopka, Russia	15,584	4,750
Dhaulagiri, Nepal	26,810	8,172	Chimborazo, Ecuador	20,561	6,267	Fairweather, Br. Col., Canada	15,300	4,663
Nanga Parbat, Pakistan	26,660	8,126	McKinley, Alaska	20,320	6,194	Dufourspitze (Mte. Rosa), Italy-Switzerland	15,203	4,634
Annapurna, Nepal	26,504	8,078	Logan, Yukon, Canada	19,524	5,951	Ras Dashen, Ethiopia	15,157	4,620
Nanda Devi, India	25,645	7,817	Cotopaxi, Ecuador	19,347	5,897	Matterhorn, Switzerland	14,691	4,478
Rakaposhi, Pakistan	25,550	7,788	Kilimanjaro, Tanzania	19,340	5,895	Whitney, California, U.S.A.	14,494	4,418
Kongur Shan, China	25,325	7,719	El Mist, Peru	19,101	5,322	Elbert, Colorado, U.S.A.	14,433	4,399
Tirich Mir, Pakistan	25,230	7,690	Pico Cristóbal Colón, Colombia	18,947	5,775	Rainier, Washington, U.S.A.	14,410	4,392
Gongga Shan, China	24,790	7,556	Huila, Colombia	18,865	5,750	Shasta, California, U.S.A.	14,162	4,317
Ismail Samani Peak, Tajikistan	24,590	7,495	Citlaltépetl (Orizaba), Mexico	18,700	5,700	Pikes Peak, Colorado, U.S.A.	14,110	4,301
Pobedy Peak, Kyrgyzstan	24,406	7,439	Damavand, Iran	18,605	5,671	Finsteraarhorn, Switzerland	14,022	4,274
Chomo Lhari, Bhutan-China	23,997	7,314	El'brus, Russia	18,510	5,642	Mauna Kea, Hawaii, U.S.A.	13,796	4,205
Muztag, China	23,891	7,282	St. Elias, Alaska, U.S.A.-Yukon, Canada	18,008	5,489	Mauna Loa, Hawaii, U.S.A.	13,677	4,169
Cerro Aconcagua, Argentina	22,831	6,959	Dykh-tau, Russia	17,070	5,203	Jungfrau, Switzerland	13,642	4,158
Ojos del Salado, Chile-Argentina	22,572	6,880	Batian (Kenya), Kenya	17,058	5,199	Grossglockner, Austria	12,457	3,797
Bonete, Chile-Argentina	22,546	6,872	Ararat, Turkey	16,946	5,165	Fujiyama, Japan	12,389	3,776
Tupungato, Chile-Argentina	22,310	6,800	Vinson Massif, Antarctica	16,864	5,140	Cook, New Zealand	12,349	3,764

LONGEST RIVERS

	Length in: Miles	Kms.		Length in: Miles	Kms.		Length in: Miles	Kms.
Nile, Africa	4,145	6,671	Rio Grande, Mexico-U.S.A.	1,885	3,034	Kama, Russia	1,252	2,031
Amazon, S. America	4,007	6,448	Syrdar'ya-Naryn, Asia	1,859	2,992	Don, Russia	1,222	1,967
Mississippi-Missouri-Red Rock, U.S.A.	3,710	5,971	Indus, Asia	1,800	2,897	Red, U.S.A.	1,222	1,966
Chang Jiang (Yangtze), China	3,500	5,633	Danube, Europe	1,775	2,857	Columbia, U.S.A.-Canada	1,214	1,953
Ob'-Irtysh, Russia-Kazakhstan	3,362	5,411	Brahmaputra, Asia	1,700	2,736	Tigris, Asia	1,181	1,901
Yenisey-Angara, Russia	3,100	4,989	Tocantins, Brazil	1,677	2,699	Darling, Australia	1,160	1,867
Huang He (Yellow), China	2,950	4,747	Salween, Asia	1,675	2,696	Angara, Russia	1,135	1,827
Congo (Zaire), Africa	2,780	4,474	Euphrates, Asia	1,650	2,655	Sungari, Russia	1,130	1,819
Amur-Shilka-Onon, Asia	2,744	4,416	Xi (Si), China	1,650	2,655	Pechora, Russia	1,124	1,809
Lena, Russia	2,734	4,400	Amu Darya, Asia	1,616	2,601	Snake, U.S.A.	1,038	1,670
Mackenzie-Peace-Finlay,Canada	2,635	4,241	Nelson-Saskatchewan, Canada	1,600	2,575	Churchill, Canada	1,000	1,609
Paraná-La Plata, S. America	2,630	4,232	Orinoco, S. America	1,600	2,575	Pilcomayo, S. America	1,000	1,609
Mekong, Asia	2,610	4,200	Paraguay, S. America	1,584	2,549	Uruguay, S. America	994	1.600
Niger, Africa	2,580	4,152	Kolyma, Russia	1,562	2,514	Platte-N. Platte, U.S.A.	990	1,593
Missouri-Red Rock, U.S.A.	2,564	4,125	Ganges, Asia	1,550	2,494	Ohio, U.S.A.	981	1,578
Yenisey, Russia	2,500	4,028	Ural, Russia-Kazakhstan	1,509	2,428	Magdalena, Colombia	956	1,538
Mississippi, U.S.A.	2,348	3,778	Japurá S. America	1,500	2,414	Pecos, U.S.A.	926	1,490
Murray-Darling, Australia	2,310	3,718	Arkansas, U.S.A.	1,450	2,334	Oka, Russia	918	1,477
Volga, Russia	2,290	3,685	Colorado, U.S.A.-Mexico	1.450	2,334	Canadian, U.S.A.	906	1,458
Madeira, S. America	2,013	3,240	Negro, S. America	1,400	2,253	Colorado, Texas, U.S.A.	894	1,439
Purus, S. America	1,995	3,211	Dnepr, Russia-Belarus-Ukraine	1,368	2,202	Dniester, Ukraine-Moldova	876	1,410
Yukon, Alaska-Canada	1,979	3,185	Orange, Africa	1,350	2,173	Fraser, Canada	850	1,369
Zambezi, Africa	1,950	3,138	Irrawaddy, Myanmar	1,325	2,132	Rhine, Europe	820	1,319
São Francisco, Brazil	1,930	3,106	Brazos U.S.A.	1,309	2,107	Northern Dvina, Russia	809	1,302
St. Lawrence, Canada-U.S.A.	1,900	3,058	Ohio-Allegheny, U.S.A.	1,306	2,102	Ottawa, Canada	790	1,271

PRINCIPAL NATURAL LAKES

	Area in: Sq. Miles	Sq. Kms.	Max. Depth in: Feet	Meters		Area in: Sq. Miles	Sq. Kms.	Max. Depth in: Feet	Meters
Caspian Sea, Asia	143,243	370,999	3,264	995	Lake Eyre, Australia*	3,500-0	9,000-0	–	–
Lake Superior, U.S.A.-Canada	31,820	82,414	1,329	405	Lake Titicaca, Peru-Bolivia	3,200	8,288	1,000	305
Lake Victoria, Africa	26,628	69,215	270	82	Lake Nicaragua, Nicaragua	3,100	8,029	230	70
Lake Huron, U.S.A.-Canada	23,010	59,596	748	228	Lake Athabasca, Canada	3,064	7,936	400	122
Lake Michigan, U.S.A.	22,400	58,016	923	281	Reindeer Lake, Canada*	2,568	6,651		
Aral Sea, Kazakhstan-Uzbekistan	15,830	41,000	213	65	Lake Turkana (Rudolf), Africa	2,463	6,379	240	73
Lake Tanganyika, Africa	12,650	32,764	4,700	1,433	Ysyk-Köl, Kyrgyzstan	2,425	6,281	2,303	702
Lake Baykal, Russia	12,162	31,500	5,316	1,620	Lake Torrens, Australia*	2,230	5,776	–	–
Great Bear Lake, Canada	12,096	31,328	1,356	413	Vänern, Sweden	2,156	5,584	328	100
Lake Nyasa (Malawi), Africa	11,555	29,928	2,320	707	Nettilling Lake, Canada*	2,140	5,543	–	–
Great Slave Lake, Canada	11,031	28,570	2,015	614	Lake Winnipegosis, Canada	2,075	5,374	38	12
Lake Erie, U.S.A.-Canada	9,940	25,745	210	64	Lake Mobutu Sese Seko (Albert), Africa	2,075	5,374	160	49
Lake Winnipeg, Canada	9,417	24,390	60	18	Kariba Lake, Zambia-Zimbabwe	2,050	5,310	295	90
Lake Ontario, U.S.A.-Canada	7,540	19,529	775	244	Lake Nipigon, Canada	1,872	4,848	540	165
Lake Balkhash, Kazakhstan	7,081	18,340	87	27	Lake Mweru, Dem. Rep. of the Congo-Zambia	1,800	4,662	60	18
Lake Ladoga, Russia	6,900	17,871	738	225	Lake Manitoba, Canada	1,799	4,659	12	4
Lake Maracaibo, Venezuela	5,120	13,261	100	31	Lake Taymyr, Russia	1,737	4,499	85	26
Lake Chad, Africa*	10,000 –	25,900 –			Lake Khanka, China-Russia	1,700	4,403	33	10
	4,000	10,360	25	8	Lake Kioga, Uganda	1,700	4,403	25	8
Lake Onega, Russia	3,761	9,741	377	115	Lake of the Woods, U.S.A.-Canada	1,679	4,349	70	21

* Area and depth figures subject to great seasonal variations.

Index of the World

This index is a comprehensive listing of the places and geographic features found in the atlas. Names are arranged in strict alphabetical order, without regard to hyphens or spaces. Every name is followed by the country or area to which it belongs. Except for cities, towns, countries and cultural areas, all entries include a reference to feature type, such as province, river, island, peak, and so on. The page number and alpha-numeric code appear in green to the left of each listing. The page number directs you to the largest scale map on which the name can be found. The code refers to the grid squares formed by the horizontal and vertical lines of latitude and longitude on each map. Following the letters from left to right and the numbers from top to bottom helps you to locate quickly the square containing the place or feature. Inset maps have their own alpha-numeric codes. Names that are accompanied by a point symbol are indexed to the symbol's location on the map. Other names are indexed to the initial letter of the name. When a map name contains a subordinate or alternate name, both names are listed in the index. To conserve space and provide room for more entries, many abbreviations are used in this index. The primary abbreviations are listed below.

Index Abbreviations

A Ab,Can	Alberta		Cap. Terr.	Capital Territory
Abor.	Aboriginal		Cay.	Cayman Islands
Acad.	Academy		C.d'Iv.	Côte d'Ivoire
ACT	Australian Capital Territory		C.G.	Coast Guard
A.F.B.	Air Force Base		Chan.	Channel
Afld.	Airfield		Chl.	Channel Islands
Afg.	Afghanistan		Co.	County
Afr.	Africa		Co,US	Colorado
Ak,US	Alaska		Col.	Colombia
Al,US	Alabama		Com.	Comoros
Alb.	Albania		Cont.	Continent
Alg.	Algeria		CpV.	Cape Verde Islands
Amm. Dep.	Ammunition Depot		CR	Costa Rica
And.	Andorra		Cr.	Creek
Ang.	Angola		Cro.	Croatia
Angu.	Anguilla		CSea.	Coral Sea Islands Territory
Ant.	Antarctica		Ct,US	Connecticut
Anti.	Antigua and Barbuda		Ctr.	Center
Ar,US	Arkansas		Ctry.	Country
Arch.	Archipelago		Cyp.	Cyprus
Arg.	Argentina		Czh.	Czech Republic
Arm.	Armenia		**D** DC,US	District of Columbia
Arpt.	Airport		De,US	Delaware
Aru.	Aruba		Den.	Denmark
ASam.	American Samoa		Depr.	Depression
Ash.	Ashmore and Cartier Islands		Dept.	Department
Aus.	Austria		Des.	Desert
Austl.	Australia		DF	Distrito Federal
Aut.	Autonomous		Dist.	District
Az,US	Arizona		Djib.	Djibouti
Azer.	Azerbaijan		Dom.	Dominica
Azor.	Azores		Dpcy.	Dependency
B Bahm.	Bahamas, The		D.R.Congo	Democratic Republic of the Congo
Bahr.	Bahrain		DRep.	Dominican Republic
Bang.	Bangladesh		**E** Ecu.	Ecuador
Bar.	Barbados		Emb.	Embankment
BC,Can	British Columbia		Eng.	Engineering
Bela.	Belarus		Eng,UK	England
Belg.	Belgium		EqG.	Equatorial Guinea
Belz.	Belize		Erit.	Eritrea
Ben.	Benin		ESal.	El Salvador
Berm.	Bermuda		Est.	Estonia
Bfld.	Battlefield		Eth.	Ethiopia
Bhu.	Bhutan		Eur.	Europe
Bol.	Bolivia		**F** Falk.	Falkland Islands
Bor.	Borough		Far.	Faroe Islands
Bosn.	Bosnia and Herzegovina		Fed. Dist.	Federal District
Bots.	Botswana		Fin.	Finland
Braz.	Brazil		Fl,US	Florida
Brln.	British Indian Ocean Territory		For.	Forest
Bru.	Brunei		Fr.	France
Bul.	Bulgaria		FrAnt.	French Southern and Antarctic Lands
Burk.	Burkina Faso		FrG.	French Guiana
Buru.	Burundi		FrPol.	French Polynesia
BVI	British Virgin Islands		FYROM	Former Yugoslav Rep. of Macedonia
C Ca,US	California		**G** Ga,US	Georgia
CAfr.	Central African Republic		Galp.	Galapagos Islands
Camb.	Cambodia			
Camr.	Cameroon			
Can.	Canada			
Can.	Canal			
Canl.	Canary Islands			
Cap.	Capital			
Cap. Dist.	Capital District			

G Gam.	Gambia, The		**M** Me,US	Maine
Gaza	Gaza Strip		Mem.	Memorial
GBis.	Guinea-Bissau		Mex.	Mexico
Geo.	Georgia		Mi,US	Michigan
Ger.	Germany		Micr.	Micronesia, Federated States of
Gha.	Ghana		Mil.	Military
Gib.	Gibraltar		Mn,US	Minnesota
Glac.	Glacier		Mo,US	Missouri
Gov.	Governorate		Mol.	Moldova
Govt.	Government		Mon.	Monument
Gre.	Greece		Mona.	Monaco
Grld.	Greenland		Mong.	Mongolia
Gren.	Grenada		Mnts.	Montserrat
Grsld.	Grassland		Mor.	Morocco
Guad.	Guadeloupe		Moz.	Mozambique
Guat.	Guatemala		Mrsh.	Marshall Islands
Gui.	Guinea		Mrta.	Mauritania
Guy.	Guyana		Mrts.	Mauritius
H Har.	Harbor		Ms,US	Mississippi
Hi,US	Hawaii		Mt.	Mount
Hist.	Historic(al)		Mt,US	Montana
Hon.	Honduras		Mtn., Mts.	Mountain, Mountains
Hts.	Heights		Mun. Arpt.	Municipal Airport
Hun.	Hungary		Myan.	Myanmar
I Ia,US	Iowa		**N** NAm.	North America
Ice.	Iceland		Namb.	Namibia
Id,US	Idaho		NAnt.	Netherlands Antilles
Il,US	Illinois		Nat'l	National
IM	Isle of Man		Nav.	Naval
In,US	Indiana		NB,Can	New Brunswick
Ind. Res.	Indian Reservation		Nbrhd.	Neighborhood
Indo.	Indonesia		NC,US	North Carolina
Int'l	International		NCal.	New Caledonia
Ire.	Ireland		ND,US	North Dakota
Isl., Isls.	Island, Islands		Ne,US	Nebraska
Isr.	Israel		Neth.	Netherlands
Isth.	Isthmus		Nf,Can	Newfoundland
It.	Italy		Nga.	Nigeria
J Jam.	Jamaica		NH,US	New Hampshire
Jor.	Jordan		NIre.	Northern Ireland
K Kaz.	Kazakhstan		Nic.	Nicaragua
Kiri.	Kiribati		NJ,US	New Jersey
Ks,US	Kansas		NKor.	North Korea
Kuw.	Kuwait		NM,US	New Mexico
Ky,US	Kentucky		NMar.	Northern Mariana Islands
Kyr.	Kyrgyzstan		Nor.	Norway
L La,US	Louisiana		NS,Can	Nova Scotia
Lab.	Laboratory		Nv,US	Nevada
Lag.	Lagoon		Nun.,Can	Nunavut
Lakesh.	Lakeshore		NW,Can	Northwest Territories
Lat.	Latvia		NY,US	New York
Lcht.	Liechtenstein		NZ	New Zealand
Ldg.	Landing		**O** Obl.	Oblast
Leb.	Lebanon		Oh,US	Ohio
Les.	Lesotho		Ok,US	Oklahoma
Libr.	Liberia		On,Can	Ontario
Lith.	Lithuania		Or,US	Oregon
Lux.	Luxembourg		**P** Pa,US	Pennsylvania
M Ma,US	Massachusetts		Pac,US	Pacific Islands, U.S.
Madg.	Madagascar		Pak.	Pakistan
Madr.	Madeira		Pan.	Panama
Malay.	Malaysia		Par.	Paraguay
Mald.	Maldives		Par.	Parish
Malw.	Malawi			
Mart.	Martinique			
May.	Mayotte			
Mb,Can	Manitoba			
Md,US	Maryland			

P PE,Can	Prince Edward Island		Swaz.	Swaziland
Pen.	Peninsula		Swe.	Sweden
Phil.	Philippines		Swi.	Switzerland
Phys. Reg.	Physical Region		**T** Tah.	Tahiti
Pitc.	Pitcairn Islands		Tai.	Taiwan
Plat.	Plateau		Taj.	Tajikistan
PNG	Papua New Guinea		Tanz.	Tanzania
Pol.	Poland		Ter.	Terrace
Port.	Portugal		Terr.	Territory
Poss.	Possession		Thai.	Thailand
Pkwy.	Parkway		Tn,US	Tennessee
PR	Puerto Rico		Tok.	Tokelau
Pref.	Prefecture		Trg.	Training
Prov.	Province		Trin.	Trinidad and Tobago
Prsv.	Preserve		Trkm.	Turkmenistan
Pt.	Point		Trks.	Turks and Caicos Islands
Q Qu,Can	Quebec		Tun.	Tunisia
R Rec.	Recreation(al)		Tun.	Tunnel
Ref.	Refuge		Turk.	Turkey
Reg.	Region		Tuv.	Tuvalu
Rep.	Republic		Tx,US	Texas
Res.	Reservoir, Reservation		**U** UAE	United Arab Emirates
Reun.	Réunion		Ugan.	Uganda
RI,US	Rhode Island		UK	United Kingdom
Riv.	River		Ukr.	Ukraine
Rom.	Romania		Uru.	Uruguay
Rsv.	Reserve		US	United States
Rus.	Russia		USVI	U.S. Virgin Islands
Rvwy.	Riverway		Ut,US	Utah
Rwa.	Rwanda		Uzb.	Uzbekistan
S SAfr.	South Africa		**V** Va,US	Virginia
Sam.	Samoa		Val.	Valley
SAm.	South America		Van.	Vanuatu
SaoT.	São Tomé and Príncipe		VatC.	Vatican City
SAr.	Saudi Arabia		Ven.	Venezuela
Sc,UK	Scotland		Viet.	Vietnam
SC,US	South Carolina		Vill.	Village
SD,US	South Dakota		Vol.	Volcano
Seash.	Seashore		Vt,US	Vermont
Sen.	Senegal		**W** Wa,US	Washington
Sey.	Seychelles		Wal,UK	Wales
SGeo.	South Georgia and Sandwich Islands		Wall.	Wallis and Futuna
Sing.	Singapore		WBnk.	West Bank
Sk,Can	Saskatchewan		Wi,US	Wisconsin
SKor.	South Korea		Wild.	Wildlife, Wilderness
SLeo.	Sierra Leone		WSah.	Western Sahara
Slov.	Slovenia		WV,US	West Virginia
Slvk.	Slovakia		Wy,US	Wyoming
SMar.	San Marino		**Y** Yem.	Yemen
Sol.	Solomon Islands		Yk,Can	Yukon Territory
Som.	Somalia		Yugo.	Yugoslavia
Sp.	Spain		**Z** Zam.	Zambia
Spr., Sprs.	Spring, Springs		Zim.	Zimbabwe
SrL.	Sri Lanka			
Sta.	Station			
StH.	Saint Helena			
Str.	Strait			
StK.	Saint Kitts and Nevis			
StL.	Saint Lucia			
StP.	Saint Pierre and Miquelon			
StV.	Saint Vincent and the Grenadines			
Sur.	Suriname			
Sval.	Svalbard			

A

52/B2 **Aa** (riv.), Fr.
50/D5 **Aa** (riv.), Ger.
51/G5 **Aa** (riv.), Ger.
53/F2 **Aachen**, Ger.
50/C5 **Aalburg**, Neth.
57/J2 **Aalen**, Ger.
50/B4 **Aalsmeer**, Neth.
52/D2 **Aalst**, Belg.
50/D5 **Aalten**, Neth.
52/C1 **Aalter**, Belg.
54/E3 **Aarau**, Swi.
54/D3 **Aare** (riv.), Swi.
54/E3 **Aargau** (canton), Swi.
53/D2 **Aarschot**, Belg.
52/D1 **Aartselaar**, Belg.
76/E5 **Aba**, China
99/G5 **Aba**, Nga.
101/A2 **Aba**, D.R. Congo
72/D5 **Abā as Su'ūd**, SAr.
108/G5 **Abacaxis** (riv.), Braz.
100/C5 **Abadab, Jabal** (peak), Sudan
72/E2 **Ābādān**, Iran
72/F2 **Ābādeh**, Iran
110/C1 **Abaeté**, Braz.
109/J4 **Abaetetuba**, Braz.
92/G4 **Abaiang** (atoll), Kiri.
120/D4 **Abajo** (mts.), Ut,US
68/K4 **Abakan**, Rus.
108/D6 **Abancay**, Peru
76/G3 **Abaq Qi**, China
58/E3 **Abarán**, Sp.
93/H5 **Abariringa** (Canton) (atoll), Kiri.
72/F2 **Abar Kūh**, Iran
77/N3 **Abashiri**, Japan
68/H5 **Abay**, Kaz.
97/N6 **Ābaya Hayk'** (lake), Eth.
75/F1 **Abaza**, Rus.
60/B1 **Abbadia San Salvatore**, It.
52/A3 **Abbeville**, Fr.
128/E4 **Abbeville**, La,US
129/H3 **Abbeville**, SC,US
44/E2 **Abbey Head** (pt.), Sc,UK
90/B3 **Abbot** (mt.), Austl.
105/T **Abbot Ice Shelf**, Ant.
45/G6 **Abbots Bromley**, Eng,UK
46/D5 **Abbotsbury**, Eng,UK
73/K2 **Abbottābād**, Pak.
50/B4 **Abcoude**, Neth.
74/E3 **'Abd al 'Azīz, Jabal** (mts.), Syria
67/K1 **Abdulino**, Rus.
97/K5 **Abéché**, Chad
103/E2 **Abel Erasmuspas** (pass), SAfr.
92/G4 **Abemama** (atoll), Kiri.
98/E5 **Abengourou**, IvC.
48/E3 **Åbenrå**, Den.
57/J2 **Abens** (riv.), Ger.
99/F5 **Abeokuta**, Nga.
44/D5 **Aber**, Wal,UK
46/C2 **Aberaeron**, Wal,UK
46/C1 **Aberangell**, Wal,UK
46/B2 **Aberath**, Wal,UK
46/C3 **Abercarn**, Wal,UK
46/C3 **Aberdare**, Wal,UK
44/D6 **Aberdaron**, Wal,UK
118/G2 **Aberdeen** (lake), Nun.,Can
43/D2 **Aberdeen**, Sc,UK
129/F3 **Aberdeen**, Ms,US
123/J4 **Aberdeen**, SD,US
122/C4 **Aberdeen**, Wa,US
46/B1 **Aberdyfi**, Wal,UK
43/D2 **Aberfeldy**, Sc,UK
43/C2 **Aberfoyle**, Sc,UK
46/C3 **Abergavenny**, Wal,UK
44/E5 **Abergele**, Wal,UK
46/B2 **Aberporth**, Wal,UK
44/D6 **Abersoch**, Wal,UK
46/C3 **Abersychan**, Wal,UK
124/B2 **Abert** (lake), Or,US
46/C3 **Abertillery**, Wal,UK
46/B2 **Aberystwyth**, Wal,UK
72/D5 **Abhā**, SAr.
72/E1 **Abhar**, Iran
97/P5 **Abhe Bad** (lake), Djib., Eth.
98/D5 **Abidjan**, IvC.
79/J7 **Abiko**, Japan
125/H3 **Abilene**, Ks,US
128/D3 **Abilene**, Tx,US
47/E3 **Abingdon**, Eng,UK
126/D4 **Abingdon**, Va,US
127/R10 **Abino** (pt.), On,Can
125/F3 **Abiquiu**, NM,US
126/E1 **Abitibi** (lake), On,Can
126/D1 **Abitibi** (riv.), On,Can
67/G4 **Abkhaz Aut. Rep.**, Geo.
100/B3 **Abnūb**, Egypt
98/E5 **Aboisso**, IvC.
99/F5 **Abomey**, Ben.
62/E2 **Abony**, Hun.
87/E2 **Aborlan**, Phil.
42/G3 **Åbo** (Turku), Fin.
43/D2 **Aboyne**, Sc,UK
82/D4 **Abra** (riv.), Phil.
117/G3 **Abraham's Bay**, Bahm.
58/A3 **Abrantes**, Port.
111/C1 **Abra Pampa**, Arg.
100/B4 **'Abrī**, Sudan
62/F2 **Abrud**, Rom.
60/C1 **Abruzzi** (reg.), It.
60/C2 **Abruzzo Nat'l Park**, It.
122/F4 **Absaroka** (range), Mt, Wy,US
72/F4 **Abū al Abyaḍ** (isl.), UAE
73/F4 **Abu Dhabi** (Abū Ẓaby) (cap.), UAE
100/C5 **Abū Dīs**, Sudan
100/B4 **Abu el-Husein, Bîr** (well), Egypt
100/C5 **Abū Hamad**, Sudan
100/C4 **Abū Hashim, Bi'r** (well), Egypt
74/H6 **Abū Ḥummuṣ**, Egypt
99/G4 **Abuja** (cap.), Nga.
99/G4 **Abuja Cap. Terr.**, Nga.
74/H6 **Abū Kabīr**, Egypt
72/D2 **Abū Kamāl**, Syria
79/G2 **Abukuma** (hills), Japan
79/G2 **Abukuma** (riv.), Japan
82/D4 **Abulog**, Phil.
100/A3 **Abu Minqâr, Bîr** (well), Egypt
84/C4 **Ābu**, India
108/E6 **Abuná** (riv.), Bol.
108/E5 **Abunã** (riv.), Braz.
84/B3 **Abu Road**, India
100/D4 **Abu Shagara, Ras** (cape), Sudan
100/B4 **Abu Simbel** (ruins), Egypt
97/N5 **Ābuyē Mēda** (peak), Eth.
82/E5 **Abuyog**, Phil.
73/F4 **Abū Ẓaby** (Abu Dhabi) (cap.), UAE
60/A4 **Abyaḍ, Ar Ra's al** (cape), Tun.
100/B3 **Abydos** (ruins), Egypt
127/G2 **Acadia Nat'l Park**, Me,US
117/N9 **Acaponeta**, Mex.
116/B4 **Acapulco**, Mex.
108/G5 **Acari** (riv.), Braz.
117/H6 **Acarigua**, Ven.
116/B4 **Acatlán**, Mex.
99/E5 **Accra** (cap.), Gha.
45/F4 **Accrington**, Eng,UK
112/B4 **Achao**, Chile
99/H2 **Achegour** (well), Niger
77/K2 **Acheng**, China
52/B3 **Achicourt**, Fr.
52/B3 **Achiel-le-Grand**, Fr.
127/N6 **Achigan** (riv.), Qu,Can
68/K4 **Achinsk**, Rus.
98/D2 **Achmîm** (well), Mrta.
43/C2 **Achnasheen**, Sc,UK
53/G3 **Acht, Hohe** (peak), Ger.
60/D4 **Acireale**, It.
117/G3 **Acklins** (isl.), Bahm.
45/G4 **Ackworth Moor Top**, Eng,UK
90/C4 **Acland** (peak), Austl.
47/H1 **Acle**, Eng,UK
112/C2 **Aconcagua, Cerro** (peak), Arg.
109/L5 **Acopiara**, Braz.
57/H4 **Acqui Terme**, It.
108/E6 **Acre** (riv.), Braz., Peru
110/B1 **Acreúna**, Braz.
61/L7 **Acropolis**, Gre.
93/M7 **Actaeon Group** (isls.), FrPol.
131/B2 **Acton**, Ca,US
109/L5 **Açu**, Braz.
112/Q9 **Aculeo** (lake), Chile
126/D3 **Ada**, Oh,US
125/H4 **Ada**, Ok,US
62/E3 **Ada**, Yugo.
119/J1 **Adair** (cape), Nun.,Can
58/C2 **Adaja** (riv.), Sp.
130/C6 **Adak** (isl.), Ak,US
130/C6 **Adak** (str.), Ak,US
113/M7 **Adam** (peak), Falk.
110/B2 **Adamantina**, Braz.
99/H5 **Adamawa** (plat.), Camr., Nga.
122/D3 **Adams** (lake), BC,Can
122/C4 **Adams** (peak), Wa,US
74/C3 **Adana**, Turk.
63/K5 **Adapazarı**, Turk.
105/M **Adare** (cape), Ant.
56/C5 **Adarza** (mtn.), Fr.
57/H4 **Adda** (riv.), It.
97/M4 **Ad Dabbah**, Sudan
72/D3 **Ad Dahnā'** (des.), SAr.
97/M5 **Ad Damazin**, Sudan
97/M4 **Ad Dāmir**, Sudan
72/F3 **Ad Dammām**, SAr.
74/H6 **Ad Daqahlīyah** (gov.), Egypt
72/F3 **Ad Dawḥah** (Doha) (cap.), Qatar
74/H6 **Ad Dilinjāt**, Egypt
97/N6 **Addis Ababa** (cap.), Eth.
132/Q16 **Addison**, Il,US
72/D2 **Ad Dīwānīyah**, Iraq
102/D4 **Addo Elephant Nat'l Park**, SAfr.
97/M5 **Ad Duwaym**, Sudan
105/V **Adelaide** (isl.), Ant.
91/A2 **Adelaide**, Austl.
118/G2 **Adelaide** (pen.), Nun.,Can
102/D4 **Adelaide**, SAfr.
131/C1 **Adelanto**, Ca,US
51/G5 **Adelebsen**, Ger.
105/K **Adélie** (coast), Ant.
97/Q5 **Aden** (gulf), Afr., Asia
72/D6 **Aden**, Yem.
51/H2 **Adendorf**, Ger.
87/H4 **Adi** (isl.), Indo.
57/J4 **Adige** (Etsch) (riv.), It.
97/N5 **Ādīgrat**, Eth.
84/C4 **Adilābād**, India
99/E2 **Adiora** (well), Mali
126/F2 **Adirondack** (mts.), NY,US
97/N6 **Ādīs Ābeba** (Addis Ababa) (cap.), Eth.
97/N5 **Ādīs Zemen**, Eth.
72/C6 **Ādī Ugri**, Erit.
74/D3 **Adıyaman**, Turk.
63/H2 **Adjud**, Rom.
116/B3 **Adjuntas** (res.), Mex.
45/F4 **Adlington**, Eng,UK
119/H1 **Admiralty** (inlet), Nun.,Can
92/D5 **Admiralty** (isls.), PNG
132/B2 **Admiralty** (inlet), Wa,US
130/M4 **Admiralty I. Nat'l Mon.**, Ak,US
79/L9 **Ado** (riv.), Japan
99/F5 **Ado**, Nga.
79/M9 **Adogawa**, Japan
84/C4 **Ādoni**, India
56/C5 **Adour** (riv.), Fr.
58/D4 **Adra**, Sp.
60/D4 **Adrano**, It.
96/E2 **Adrar**, Alg.
98/B1 **Adrar** (reg.), Mrta.
96/E1 **Adrar bou Nasser** (peak), Mor.
99/F1 **Adrar des Iforas** (mts.), Mali
97/K5 **Adré**, Chad
57/K4 **Adria**, It.
126/C3 **Adrian**, Mi,US
47/F5 **Adur** (riv.), Eng,UK
97/N5 **Ādwa**, Eth.
45/G4 **Adwick le Street**, Eng,UK
69/P3 **Adycha** (riv.), Rus.
67/G4 **Adzhar Aut. Rep.**, Geo.
65/N2 **Adz'va** (riv.), Rus.
61/J3 **Aegean** (sea), Gre., Turk.
48/F1 **Aerø** (isl.), Den.
46/B2 **Aeron** (riv.), Wal,UK
44/E1 **Ae, Water of** (riv.), Sc,UK
99/F5 **Afadjoto** (peak), Gha.
93/X15 **Afareaitu**, FrPol.
74/M8 **Afek Nat'l Park**, Isr.
56/B3 **Aff** (riv.), Fr.
73/H2 **Afghanistan**
97/Q7 **Afgooye**, Som.
130/H4 **Afognak** (isl.), Ak,US
130/H4 **Afognak** (mtn.), Ak,US
98/C2 **Afollé** (reg.), Mrta.
110/D2 **Afonso Cláudio**, Braz.
60/D2 **Afragola**, It.
95/* **Africa**
74/D2 **Afşin**, Turk.
50/C2 **Afsluitdijk** (IJsselmeer) (dam), Neth.
51/F5 **Afte** (riv.), Ger.
122/F5 **Afton**, Wy,US
74/K5 **'Afula**, Isr.
74/B2 **Afyon**, Turk.
96/H4 **Agadem**, Niger
99/G2 **Agadez**, Niger
99/H2 **Agadez** (dept.), Niger
96/D1 **Agadir**, Mor.
39/M6 **Agalega** (isls.), Mrts.
99/F2 **Agamor** (well), Mali
79/F2 **Agano** (riv.), Japan
97/N6 **Āgaro**, Eth.
85/F3 **Agartala**, India
105/V **Agassiz** (cape), Ant.
119/T6 **Agassiz** (ice field), Nun.,Can
125/F2 **Agate Fossil Beds Nat'l Mon.**, Ne,US
130/A5 **Agattu** (isl.), Ak,US
130/A5 **Agattu** (str.), Ak,US
99/G5 **Agbor**, Nga.
98/D5 **Agboville**, IvC.
67/H5 **Agdam**, Azer.
56/E5 **Agde**, Fr.
56/E5 **Agde, Cap d'** (cape), Fr.
56/D4 **Agen**, Fr.
79/H7 **Ageo**, Japan
48/E1 **Agerbæk**, Den.
51/E6 **Agger** (riv.), Ger.
62/E1 **Aggteleki Nat'l Park**, Hun.
44/B3 **Aghagallon**, NI,UK
72/E2 **Āghā Jārī**, Iran
117/N8 **Agiabampo, Estero de** (bay), Mex.
76/G1 **Aginskoye**, Rus.
44/B1 **Agivey**, NI,UK
56/E5 **Agly** (riv.), Fr.
63/G3 **Agnita**, Rom.
79/M10 **Ago**, Japan
57/H4 **Agogna** (riv.), It.
131/B2 **Agoura Hills**, Ca,US
56/D5 **Agout** (riv.), Fr.
84/C2 **Āgra**, India
60/E2 **Agri** (riv.), It.
67/H5 **Ağrı** (Ararat) (peak), Turk.
60/C4 **Agrigento**, It.
92/D3 **Agrihan** (isl.), NMar.
61/G3 **Agrinion**, Gre.
112/C3 **Agrio** (riv.), Arg.
60/D2 **Agropoli**, It.
65/M4 **Agryz**, Rus.
117/G6 **Aguachica**, Col.
117/H4 **Aguadilla**, PR
116/C4 **Agua Dulce**, Mex.
117/E6 **Aguadulce**, Pan.
110/F7 **Aguaí**, Braz.
59/P10 **Agualva-Cacém**, Port.
116/D4 **Aguan** (riv.), Hon.
110/B2 **Aguapeí** (riv.), Braz.
117/N7 **Agua Prieta**, Mex.
117/H6 **Aguaro-Guariquito Nat'l Park**, Ven.
110/H6 **Águas** (hills), Braz.
116/A3 **Aguascalientes**, Mex.
116/A3 **Aguascalientes** (state), Mex.
110/G6 **Águas da Prata**, Braz.
110/G7 **Águas de Lindóia**, Braz.
110/B1 **Aguavermelha** (res.), Braz.
110/B2 **Agudos**, Braz.
58/A2 **Águeda**, Port.
58/B2 **Agueda** (riv.), Sp.
96/C3 **Agüenit**, WSah.
79/M10 **Agui**, Japan
92/D3 **Aguijan** (isl.), NMar.
58/C4 **Aguilar**, Sp.
58/C1 **Aguilar de Campóo**, Sp.
111/C2 **Aguilares**, Arg.
58/E4 **Águilas**, Sp.
117/P10 **Aguililla de Iturbide**, Mex.
59/X17 **Agüimes**, Canl.,Sp.
117/G5 **Aguja** (cape), Col.
102/M11 **Agulhas** (cape), SAfr.
110/C2 **Agulhas Negras** (peak), Braz.
87/E5 **Agung** (vol.), Indo.
82/E6 **Agusan** (riv.), Phil.
117/G5 **Agustín Codazzi**, Col.
96/G3 **Ahaggar** (plat.), Alg.
50/E4 **Ahaus**, Ger.
53/F3 **Ahbach** (riv.), Ger.
74/E2 **Ahlat**, Turk.
51/E5 **Ahlen**, Ger.
84/B3 **Ahmadābād**, India
84/B4 **Ahmadnagar**, India
73/K3 **Ahmadpur East**, Pak.
97/P6 **Ahmar** (mts.), Eth.
44/B2 **Ahoghill**, NI,UK
53/F3 **Ahr** (riv.), Ger.
51/H1 **Ahrensburg**, Ger.
51/F5 **Ahse** (riv.), Ger.
117/P9 **Ahuacatlán**, Mex.
120/W13 **Ahuimanu**, Hi,US
117/N7 **Ahumada**, Mex.
72/E2 **Ahvāz**, Iran
42/F4 **Ahvenanmaa** (prov.), Fin.
102/B2 **Ai-Ais Hot Springs**, Namb.
81/B2 **Aibag Gol** (riv.), China
79/E3 **Aichi** (pref.), Japan
120/W13 **Aiea**, Hi,US
56/E4 **Aigoual** (mtn.), Fr.
56/F4 **Aigues** (riv.), Fr.
59/F1 **Aigues Tortes y Lago de San Mauricio Nat'l Park**, Sp.
79/F1 **Aikawa**, Japan
129/H3 **Aiken**, SC,US
117/F6 **Ailigandí**, Pan.
92/F4 **Ailinglapalap** (atoll), Mrsh.
44/C1 **Ailsa Craig** (isl.), Sc,UK
92/G3 **Ailuk** (atoll), Mrsh.
81/C5 **Aimen Guan** (pass), China
110/D1 **Aimorés**, Braz.
54/B5 **Ain** (dept.), Fr.
56/F4 **Ain** (riv.), Fr.
96/G1 **'Aïn Beïda**, Alg.
96/D2 **'Aïn Ben Tili**, Mrta.
61/G3 **Aínos** (peak), Gre.
61/G3 **Aínos Nat'l Park**, Gre.
45/E4 **Ainsdale**, Eng,UK
96/E1 **'Aïn Sefra**, Alg.
125/H2 **Ainsworth**, Ne,US
99/G2 **Aïr** (plat.), Niger
122/E3 **Airdrie**, Ab,Can
43/D3 **Airdrie**, Sc,UK
52/D5 **Aire** (riv.), Fr.
45/G4 **Aire** (riv.), Eng,UK
52/B2 **Aire, Canal de** (can.), Fr.
45/E5 **Aire, Point of** (pt.), Wal,UK
52/B2 **Aire-sur-la-Lys**, Fr.
119/J2 **Air Force** (isl.), Nun.,Can
45/F3 **Airton**, Eng,UK
57/J2 **Aisch** (riv.), Ger.
52/D3 **Aiseau-Presles**, Belg.
112/B5 **Aisén del General Carlos Ibáñez del Campo** (reg.), Chile
81/E3 **Ai Shan** (mtn.), China
130/L3 **Aishihik**, Yk,Can
53/E3 **Aisne** (riv.), Belg.
52/C4 **Aisne** (dept.), Fr.
52/C5 **Aisne** (riv.), Fr.
96/E1 **Aïssa** (peak), Alg.
79/M9 **Aitō**, Japan
93/J6 **Aitutaki** (atoll), Cookls.
63/F2 **Aiud**, Rom.
110/J7 **Aiuruoca** (riv.), Braz.
56/F5 **Aix-en-Provence**, Fr.
56/F4 **Aix-les-Bains**, Fr.
61/H4 **Aíyina**, Gre.
61/H3 **Aíyion**, Gre.
79/F2 **Aizu-Wakamatsu**, Japan
85/F3 **Aīzwal**, India
60/A2 **Ajaccio**, Fr.
60/A2 **Ajaccio** (gulf), Fr.
127/R8 **Ajax**, On,Can
76/D3 **Aj Bogd** (peak), Mong.
96/K1 **Ajdābiyā**, Libya
100/C5 **Aj Janayet**, Sudan
62/C2 **Ajka**, Hun.
84/B2 **Ajmer**, India
124/D4 **Ajo**, Az,US
58/D1 **Ajo, Cabo de** (cape), Sp.
116/A4 **Ajuchitlán**, Mex.
79/F1 **Aka** (riv.), Japan
79/N10 **Akabane**, Japan
75/F1 **Akademik Obruchev** (mts.), Rus.
79/F3 **Akaishi-dake** (mtn.), Japan
100/B4 **Akasha East**, Sudan
78/D3 **Akashi**, Japan
79/K10 **Akashi** (str.), Japan
75/B4 **Akbaytal** (pass), Taj.
74/D2 **Akçaabat**, Turk.
74/D3 **Akçakale**, Turk.
63/K5 **Akçakoca**, Turk.
98/B2 **Akchâr** (reg.), Mrta.
74/C2 **Akdağmadeni**, Turk.
72/G4 **Akdar, Al Jabal** (mts.), Oman
79/N9 **Akechi**, Japan
42/D3 **Akershus** (co.), Nor.
97/K7 **Aketi**, D.R. Congo
67/G4 **Akhaltsikhe**, Geo.
61/H3 **Akharnaí**, Gre.
61/G3 **Akhelóos** (riv.), Gre.
74/A2 **Akhisar**, Turk.
100/B3 **Akhmīm**, Egypt
67/H3 **Akhtuba** (riv.), Rus.
67/H2 **Akhtubinsk**, Rus.
66/E2 **Akhtyrka**, Ukr.
78/C4 **Aki**, Japan
79/H7 **Aki** (riv.), Japan
79/H7 **Akigawa**, Japan
119/H3 **Akimiski** (isl.), NW,Can
79/H7 **Akishima**, Japan
77/N4 **Akita**, Japan
98/B2 **Akjoujt**, Mrta.
84/D6 **Akkaraipattu**, SrL.
74/K5 **'Akko**, Isr.
98/D2 **'Aklé 'Aouâna** (dune), Mali, Mrta.
78/D3 **Akō**, Japan
96/H7 **Akoga**, Gabon
84/C3 **Akola**, India
97/N4 **Ak'ordat**, Erit.
99/F5 **Akosombo** (dam), Gha.
119/K2 **Akpatok** (isl.), Nun.,Can
75/C3 **Akqi**, China
61/J2 **Akrathos, Ákra** (cape), Gre.
42/C4 **Akrehamn**, Nor.
61/G4 **Akrítas, Ákra** (cape), Gre.
125/G2 **Akron**, Co,US
126/D3 **Akron**, Oh,US
75/C4 **Aksai Chin** (reg.), China, India
74/C2 **Aksaray**, Turk.
76/C4 **Aksay**, China
67/K2 **Aksay**, Kaz.
74/B2 **Akşehir**, Turk.
74/B2 **Akşehir** (lake), Turk.
75/C2 **Aksoran** (peak), Kaz.
75/D3 **Aksu**, China
75/C3 **Aksu** (riv.), China
75/C2 **Aksu** (riv.), Kaz.
97/N5 **Āksum**, Eth.
61/J2 **Akti** (pen.), Gre.
78/B4 **Akune**, Japan
42/N6 **Akureyri**, Ice.
130/E5 **Akutan** (isl.), Ak,US
130/E5 **Akutan** (passg.), Ak,US
99/G5 **Akwa Ibom** (state), Nga.
85/F3 **Akyab** (Sittwe), Myan.
67/L2 **Ak"yar**, Rus.
63/K5 **Akyazı**, Turk.
76/B3 **Ala** (riv.), China
129/G3 **Alabama** (state), US
129/G4 **Alabama** (riv.), Al,US
129/G3 **Alabaster**, Al,US
74/C2 **Alaca**, Turk.
74/C2 **Alaçam**, Turk.
129/H4 **Alachua**, Fl,US
67/H4 **Alagir**, Rus.
56/E4 **Alagnon** (riv.), Fr.
109/L6 **Alagoinhas**, Braz.
58/B2 **Alagón** (riv.), Sp.
42/G3 **Alajärvi**, Fin.
116/E5 **Alajuela**, CR
75/D2 **Alakol'** (lake), Kaz.
100/B2 **Al 'Alamayn** (El Alamein), Egypt
92/D3 **Alamagan** (isl.), NMar.
72/E2 **Al 'Amārah**, Iraq
72/F2 **'Alāmarvdasht** (riv.), Iran
132/K11 **Alameda**, Ca,US
116/E5 **Alamikamba**, Nic.
116/B3 **Alamo**, Mex.
124/D4 **Alamo** (lake), Az,US
132/K11 **Alamo**, Ca,US
124/D3 **Alamo**, Nv,US
124/F4 **Alamogordo**, NM,US
117/N8 **Álamos**, Mex.
125/F3 **Alamosa**, Co,US
42/G3 **Åland** (isls.), Fin.
48/F2 **Aland** (riv.), Ger.
74/C3 **Alanya**, Turk.
103/J7 **Alaotra** (lake), Madg.
129/H4 **Alapaha** (riv.), Ga,US
63/K5 **Alaplı**, Turk.
58/D3 **Alarcón** (res.), Sp.
74/B2 **Alaşehir**, Turk.
74/L6 **Al 'Āsimah** (gov.), Jor.
130/* **Alaska** (state), US
130/J4 **Alaska** (gulf), Ak,US
130/J4 **Alaska** (pen.), Ak,US
130/H3 **Alaska** (range), Ak,US
130/B5 **Alaska Maritime Nat'l Wild. Ref.**, Ak,US
130/G4 **Alaska Pen. Nat'l Wild. Ref.**, Ak,US
57/H5 **Alassio**, It.
65/K5 **Alatyr'**, Rus.
67/H4 **Alaverdi**, Arm.
42/G3 **Alavus**, Fin.
44/D5 **Alaw** (riv.), Wal,UK
44/D5 **Alaw, Llyn** (lake), Wal,UK
75/B4 **Alayskiy** (mts.), Kyr.
69/R3 **Alazeya** (riv.), Rus.
72/E2 **Al 'Azīzīyah**, Iraq
96/H1 **Al 'Azīzīyah**, Libya
57/H4 **Alba**, It.
63/F2 **Alba** (co.), Rom.
74/D3 **Al Bāb**, Syria
58/E3 **Albacete**, Sp.
100/C3 **Al Baḥr al Aḥmar** (gov.), Egypt
63/F2 **Alba Iulia**, Rom.
74/K5 **Al Balqā'** (gov.), Jor.
100/C3 **Al Balyanā**, Egypt
127/F1 **Albanel** (lake), Qu,Can
61/F2 **Albania**
89/A4 **Albany**, Austl.
119/H3 **Albany** (riv.), On,Can
132/K11 **Albany**, Ca,US
129/G4 **Albany**, Ga,US
126/C4 **Albany**, Ky,US
126/F3 **Albany** (cap.), NY,US
122/C4 **Albany**, Or,US
72/E2 **Al Başrah**, Iraq
102/A2 **Albatross** (pt.), Namb.
100/B2 **Al Bawīṭī**, Egypt
97/K1 **Al Bayḍā**, Libya
129/H3 **Albemarle**, NC,US
129/J2 **Albemarle** (sound), NC,US
57/H4 **Albenga**, It.
58/C2 **Alberche** (riv.), Sp.
91/A2 **Albert** (inlet), Austl.
53/E2 **Albert** (can.), Belg.
52/B4 **Albert**, Fr.
101/A2 **Albert** (lake), D.R. Congo, Ugan.
118/E3 **Alberta** (prov.), Can
112/E2 **Alberti**, Arg.
62/D2 **Albertirsa**, Hun.
123/K5 **Albert Lea**, Mn,US
101/A2 **Albert Nile** (riv.), Ugan.
113/J8 **Alberto de Agostini Nat'l Park**, Chile
102/Q13 **Alberton**, SAfr.
57/G4 **Albertville**, Fr.
129/G3 **Albertville**, Al,US
56/E5 **Albi**, Fr.
57/H4 **Albino**, It.
126/C3 **Albion**, Mi,US
125/H2 **Albion**, Ne,US
74/L4 **Al Biqā'** (gov.), Leb.
74/K5 **Al Biqā'** (Bekaa) (val.), Leb.
74/K6 **Al Bīrah**, WBnk.
50/B5 **Alblasserdam**, Neth.
42/D4 **Ålborg**, Den.
58/D4 **Albox**, Sp.
46/D1 **Albrighton**, Eng,UK
58/A4 **Albufeira**, Port.
74/H6 **Al Buḥayrah** (gov.), Egypt
55/F4 **Albula** (riv.), Swi.
124/F4 **Albuquerque**, NM,US
58/B3 **Alburquerque**, Sp.
91/C3 **Albury**, Austl.
59/P10 **Alcabideche**, Port.
58/A3 **Alcácer do Sal**, Port.
58/C4 **Alcalá de Guadaira**, Sp.
58/D2 **Alcalá de Henares**, Sp.
58/D4 **Alcalá la Real**, Sp.
60/C4 **Alcamo**, It.
59/E2 **Alcanadre** (riv.), Sp.
59/E2 **Alcanar**, Sp.
59/E2 **Alcañiz**, Sp.
58/B3 **Alcantara** (res.), Sp.
58/E4 **Alcantarilla**, Sp.
58/D3 **Alcarez** (range), Sp.
132/K11 **Alcatraz** (isl.), Ca,US
58/C4 **Alcaudete**, Sp.
58/D3 **Alcázar de San Juan**, Sp.
47/E2 **Alcester**, Eng,UK
59/E3 **Alcira**, Sp.
129/H3 **Alcoa**, Tn,US
58/D2 **Alcobendas**, Sp.
59/Q10 **Alcochete**, Port.
59/E2 **Alcora**, Sp.
58/D2 **Alcorcón**, Sp.
129/H3 **Alcovy** (riv.), Ga,US
59/E3 **Alcoy**, Sp.
95/G5 **Aldabra** (isls.), Sey.
128/B4 **Aldama**, Mex.
69/N4 **Aldan**, Rus.
69/N4 **Aldan** (plat.), Rus.
69/P3 **Aldan** (riv.), Rus.
75/G2 **Aldarhaan**, Mong.
47/E4 **Aldbourne**, Eng,UK
45/H4 **Aldbrough**, Eng,UK
47/H2 **Alde** (riv.), Eng,UK
47/H2 **Aldeburgh**, Eng,UK
104/B2 **Aldeia Viçosa**, Ang.
53/F2 **Aldenhoven**, Ger.
44/B2 **Aldergrove**, NI,UK
45/F5 **Alderley Edge**, Eng,UK
47/E4 **Aldermaston**, Eng,UK
127/Q9 **Aldershot**, On,Can
47/F4 **Aldershot**, Eng,UK
132/C2 **Alderwood Manor-Bothell North**, Wa,US
128/E4 **Aldine**, Tx,US
47/E1 **Aldridge**, Eng,UK
98/B2 **Aleg**, Mrta.
110/D2 **Alegre**, Braz.
111/E2 **Alegrete**, Braz.
107/A6 **Alejandro Selkirk** (isl.), Chile
66/E2 **Aleksandriya**, Ukr.
64/H4 **Aleksandrov**, Rus.
65/N4 **Aleksandrovsk**, Rus.
77/N1 **Aleksandrovsk-Sakhalinskiy**, Rus.
49/K2 **Aleksandrów Kujawski**, Pol.
49/K3 **Aleksandrów Łódzki**, Pol.
75/B1 **Alekseyevka**, Kaz.
66/F2 **Alekseyevka**, Rus.
64/H5 **Aleksin**, Rus.
62/E4 **Aleksinac**, Yugo.
110/L6 **Além Paraíba**, Braz.
56/D2 **Alençon**, Fr.
109/H4 **Alenquer**, Braz.
120/T10 **Alenuihaha** (chan.), Hi,US
74/D3 **Aleppo** (Ḥalab), Syria
112/B4 **Alerce Andino Nat'l Park**, Chile
119/S6 **Alert** (pt.), Nun.,Can
62/F2 **Aleşd**, Rom.
57/H4 **Alessandria**, It.
42/C3 **Ålesund**, Nor.
130/E5 **Aleutian** (isls.), Ak,US
130/G4 **Aleutian** (range), Ak,US
105/V **Alexander** (cape), Ant.
105/V **Alexander** (isl.), Ant.
130/L4 **Alexander** (arch.), Ak,US
129/G3 **Alexander City**, Al,US
61/H2 **Alexándria**, Gre.
63/G4 **Alexandria**, Rom.
128/E4 **Alexandria**, La,US
123/K4 **Alexandria**, Mn,US
131/J8 **Alexandria**, Va,US
74/G6 **Alexandria** (Al Iskandarīyah), Egypt
91/A2 **Alexandrina** (lake), Austl.
61/J2 **Alexandroúpolis**, Gre.
122/C2 **Alexis Creek**, BC,Can
75/D1 **Aley** (riv.), Rus.
75/D1 **Aleysk**, Rus.
59/E3 **Alfafar**, Sp.
72/D2 **Al Fallūjah**, Iraq
59/P10 **Alfama**, Port.
59/P11 **Alfarim**, Port.
58/E1 **Alfaro**, Sp.
97/L5 **Al Fāsher**, Sudan
100/B2 **Al Fashn**, Egypt
72/D1 **Al Fatḥah**, Iraq
72/E3 **Al Fāw**, Iraq
100/B2 **Al Fayyum**, Egypt
53/F3 **Alfbach** (riv.), Ger.
51/G5 **Alfeld**, Ger.
110/H6 **Alfenas**, Braz.
61/G4 **Alfiós** (riv.), Gre.
45/J5 **Alford**, Eng,UK
91/D3 **Alfred Nat'l Park**, Austl.
45/G5 **Alfreton**, Eng,UK
47/G5 **Alfriston**, Eng,UK
53/G2 **Alfter**, Ger.
67/L2 **Alga**, Kaz.
42/C4 **Ålgård**, Nor.
58/C4 **Algeciras**, Sp.
59/E3 **Algemesí**, Sp.
96/F2 **Algeria**
51/G4 **Algermissen**, Ger.
59/N8 **Algete**, Sp.
100/B2 **Al Gharbīyah** (gov.), Egypt
60/A2 **Alghero**, It.
100/C3 **Al Ghurdaqah**, Egypt
96/F1 **Algiers** (cap.), Alg.
59/E3 **Alginet**, Sp.
102/D4 **Algoa** (bay), SAfr.
108/D4 **Algodón** (riv.), Peru
132/P15 **Algonquin**, Il,US
59/P10 **Algueirão**, Port.
72/D2 **Al Ḥadīthah**, Iraq
74/E3 **Al Ḥaḍr**, Iraq
73/G4 **Al Ḥajar ash Sharqī** (mts.), Oman
73/G5 **Al Ḥallānīyah** (isl.), Oman
58/D4 **Alhama de Granada**, Sp.
58/E4 **Alhama de Murcia**, Sp.
131/B2 **Alhambra**, Ca,US
100/B2 **Al Ḥammām**, Egypt
59/Q10 **Alhandra**, Port.
74/E3 **Al Ḥasakah**, Syria
58/C4 **Alhaurín el Grande**, Sp.
100/B2 **Al Ḥawāmidīyah**, Egypt
72/E2 **Al Ḥayy**, Iraq
72/D2 **Al Ḥillah**, Iraq
72/D2 **Al Hindīyah**, Iraq
96/E1 **Al Hoceima**, Mor.
72/E3 **Al Hufūf**, SAr.
74/A2 **Aliağa**, Turk.
61/G2 **Aliákmon** (riv.), Gre.
61/G2 **Aliákmonos** (lake), Gre.
72/E2 **'Alī al Gharbī**, Iraq
72/E2 **'Alī ash Sharqī**, Iraq
128/C3 **Alibates Flint Quarries Nat'l Mon.**, Tx,US
67/J5 **Āli-Bayramlı**, Azer.
100/C5 **Al Ibēdiyya**, Sudan
63/J5 **Alibeyköy**, Turk.
59/E3 **Alicante**, Sp.
90/A1 **Alice** (riv.), Austl.
60/E3 **Alice** (pt.), It.
128/D5 **Alice**, Tx,US
89/C3 **Alice Springs**, Austl.
129/F3 **Aliceville**, Al,US
82/D6 **Alicia**, Phil.
82/C6 **Alicia Annie** (shoal)
60/D3 **Alicudi** (isl.), It.
84/C2 **Alīgarh**, India
72/E2 **Alīgudarz**, Iran
96/J8 **Alima** (riv.), Congo
42/E4 **Alingsås**, Swe.
84/B2 **Alīpur**, Pak.
84/E2 **Alīpur Duār**, India
74/G6 **Al Iskandarīyah** (gov.), Egypt
74/G6 **Al Iskandarīyah** (Alexandria), Egypt
100/C2 **Al Ismā'īlīyah** (gov.), Egypt
100/C2 **Al Ismā'īlīyah** (Ismalia), Egypt
102/D3 **Aliwal North**, SAfr.
97/K2 **Al Jaghbūb**, Libya
60/B5 **Al Jamm**, Tun.
74/K5 **Al Janūb** (gov.), Leb.
100/B2 **Al Jīzah**, Egypt
100/B2 **Al Jīzah** (gov.), Egypt
97/L5 **Al Junaynah**, Sudan
58/A4 **Aljustrel**, Port.
74/K6 **Al Karak**, Jor.
74/L6 **Al Karak** (gov.), Jor.
100/C3 **Al Karnak**, Egypt
53/E2 **Alken**, Belg.
73/G4 **Al Khābūrah**, Oman
74/K6 **Al Khalīl** (Hebron), WBnk.
72/D2 **Al Khāliṣ**, Iraq
100/B5 **Al Khandaq**, Sudan
100/B3 **Al Khārijah**, Egypt
97/M4 **Al Kharṭūm Baḥrī** (Khartoum North), Sudan
72/F3 **Al Khobar**, SAr.
96/H1 **Al Khums**, Libya
50/B3 **Alkmaar**, Neth.
96/H3 **Alkoum** (well), Alg.
72/D2 **Al Kūfah**, Iraq
97/K3 **Al Kufrah**, Libya
72/E2 **Al Kūt**, Iraq
74/K4 **Al Lādhiqīyah** (Latakia), Syria
84/D2 **Allahābād**, India
123/G3 **Allan**, Sk,Can
123/G3 **Allan** (hills), Sk,Can
127/R9 **Allanburg**, On,Can
85/G4 **Allanmyo**, Myan.
123/L3 **Allan Water** (riv.), On,Can
96/H1 **'Allāq** (well), Libya
100/C4 **'Allāqi, Wādī al** (dry riv.), Egypt
126/C3 **Allegan**, Mi,US
121/K4 **Allegheny** (mts.), US
126/E3 **Allegheny** (plat.), Pa,US
126/E3 **Allegheny** (riv.), Pa,US
112/D3 **Allen**, Arg.
46/B5 **Allen** (riv.), Eng,UK
44/B5 **Allen, Bog of** (swamp), Ire.
45/F2 **Allendale**, Eng,UK
129/H3 **Allendale**, SC,US
116/A2 **Allende**, Mex.
132/F7 **Allen Park**, Mi,US
131/E5 **Allentown**, Pa,US
84/C6 **Alleppey**, India
53/G3 **Aller** (riv.), Ger.
51/H4 **Allerkanal** (can.), Ger.
55/G3 **Allgäu** (mts.), Aus., Ger.
125/G2 **Alliance**, Ne,US
126/D3 **Alliance**, Oh,US
56/E3 **Allier** (riv.), Fr.
56/D3 **Allones**, Fr.
127/G1 **Alma**, Qu,Can
126/C3 **Alma**, Mi,US
125/H2 **Alma**, Ne,US
58/A3 **Almada**, Port.
58/C3 **Almadén**, Sp.
72/B3 **Al Madīnah al Fikrīyah**, Egypt
60/B5 **Al Madīyah**, Tun.
60/B5 **Al Madīyah** (gov.), Tun.
74/L5 **Al Mafraq**, Jor.
112/D2 **Almafuerte**, Arg.
96/E1 **Al Maghrib** (reg.), Alg., Mor.
58/D3 **Almagro**, Sp.
74/H6 **Al Maḥallah al Kubrá**, Egypt
74/H6 **Al Maḥmūdīyah**, Egypt
72/D2 **Al Maḥmūdīyah**, Iraq
74/L4 **Al Mālikīyah**, Syria
75/A3 **Almalyk**, Uzb.
72/F3 **Al Manāmah** (Manama) (cap.), Bahr.
124/B2 **Almanor** (lake), Ca,US
59/E3 **Almansa**, Sp.
74/H6 **Al Manṣūra**, Egypt
74/H6 **Al Manzilah**, Egypt
58/D4 **Almanzora** (riv.), Sp.
58/C2 **Almanzor, Pico de** (peak), Sp.
100/B3 **Al Marāghah**, Egypt
96/K1 **Al Marj**, Libya
109/J6 **Almas** (riv.), Braz.
74/J6 **Al Maṭarīyah**, Egypt
75/C3 **Almaty**, Kaz.
74/E3 **Al Mawṣil** (Mosul), Iraq
72/D1 **Al Mayādin**, Syria

140

Almaz – Arma

59/E3 Almazora, Sp.
51/F5 Alme (riv.), Ger.
58/A3 Almeirim, Port.
50/D4 Almelo, Neth.
109/K7 Almenara, Braz.
58/D3 Almenara (mtn.), Sp.
58/B2 Almendra (res.), Sp.
58/B3 Almendralejo, Sp.
50/C4 Almere, Neth.
58/D4 Almería, Sp.
59/D4 Almería (gulf), Sp.
65/M5 Al'met'yevsk, Rus.
42/E4 Älmhult, Swe.
58/C5 Almina (pt.), Sp.
100/B2 Al Minūfīyah (gov.), Egypt
100/B2 Al Minyā, Egypt
100/B3 Al Minyā (gov.), Egypt
72/D2 Al Miqdādiyah, Iraq
113/J7 Almirante Montt (gulf), Chile
61/H3 Almirós, Gre.
61/J5 Almiroú (gulf), Gre.
58/C3 Almodóvar del Campo, Sp.
58/C4 Almodóvar del Río, Sp.
43/D2 Almond (riv.), Sc,UK
126/E2 Almonte, On,Can
58/B4 Almonte, Sp.
59/E3 Almoradí, Sp.
110/D1 Almores (range), Braz.
72/E3 Al Mubarraz, SAr.
97/L5 Al Muglad, Sudan
60/B5 Al Muknīn, Tun.
60/B5 Al Munastīr, Tun.
60/B5 Al Munastīr (gov.), Tun.
58/D4 Almuñécar, Sp.
43/C2 Alness, Sc,UK
93/J6 Alofi (cap.), Niue
92/H6 Alofi (isl.), Wall.
85/G2 Along, India
61/H3 Alónnisos (isl.), Gre.
87/F5 Alor (isls.), Indo.
58/C4 Álora, Sp.
86/B2 Alor Setar, Malay.
92/E6 Alotau, PNG
50/D5 Alpen, Ger.
126/D2 Alpena, Mi,US
109/J5 Alpercatas (mts.), Braz.
50/B4 Alphen aan de Rijn, Neth.
58/A3 Alpiarça, Port.
128/C4 Alpine, Tx,US
122/F5 Alpine, Wy,US
58/B4 Alportel, Port.
41/E4 Alps (mts.), Eur.
79/F3 Alps-Minami Nat'l Park, Japan
73/G4 Al Qābil, Oman
97/N5 Al Qaḍārif, Sudan
100/B2 Al Qāhirah (Cairo) (cap.), Egypt
74/E3 Al Qāmishlī, Syria
100/B3 Al Qaşr, Egypt
97/M5 Al Qaţaynah, Sudan
96/H3 Al Qaţrūn, Libya
60/A5 Al Qayrawān, Tun.
60/A5 Al Qayrawān (gov.), Tun.
74/K5 Al Qunayţirah (prov.), Syria
100/C3 Al Quşayr, Egypt
74/L4 Al Quşayr, Syria
74/L5 Al Quţayfah, Syria
47/E1 Alrewas, Eng,UK
48/F1 Als (isl.), Den.
54/D2 Alsace (reg.), Fr.
54/C2 Alsace, Ballon d' (mtn.), Fr.
45/F5 Alsager, Eng,UK
122/F3 Alsask, Sk,Can
58/D1 Alsasua, Sp.
53/F2 Alsdorf, Ger.
48/E3 Alsfeld, Ger.
132/Q16 Alsip, Il,US
51/H1 Alster (riv.), Ger.
45/F2 Alston, Eng,UK
45/F4 Alt (riv.), Eng,UK
42/G1 Alta, Nor.
131/B2 Altadena, Ca,US
109/G5 Alta Floresta, Braz.
112/D1 Alta Gracia, Arg.
116/D5 Alta Gracia, Nic.
75/D1 Altai (mts.), Asia
129/H4 Altamaha (riv.), Ga,US
109/H4 Altamira, Braz.
116/B3 Altamira, Mex.
129/H4 Altamonte Springs, Fl,US
60/E2 Altamura, It.
116/C4 Altar de los Sacrificios (ruins), Guat.
76/B2 Altay, China
68/J4 Altay (kray), Rus.
55/E4 Altdorf, Swi.
57/J2 Altdorf bei Nürnberg, Ger.
59/E3 Altea, Sp.
51/E6 Altena, Ger.
51/F5 Altenau (riv.), Ger.
51/F5 Altenbeken, Ger.
48/G3 Altenburg, Ger.
49/G2 Altentreptow, Ger.
117/P8 Alteres, Mex.
50/D5 Alter Rhein (riv.), Ger.
51/G1 Altes Land (reg.), Ger.
45/H4 Althorpe, Eng,UK
108/E7 Altiplano (plat.), Bol., Peru
48/F2 Altmark (reg.), Ger.
57/J2 Altmühl (riv.), Ger.
57/K3 Altmünster, Aus.
109/J6 Alto (peak), Braz.
109/H7 Alto Araguaia, Braz.
104/C2 Alto Cuale, Ang.
47/F4 Alton, Eng,UK
126/B4 Alton, Il,US
91/F5 Altona, Austl.
123/J3 Altona, Mb,Can
126/E3 Altoona, Pa,US
108/D6 Alto Purús (riv.), Peru
109/K5 Altos, Braz.
45/F5 Altrincham, Eng,UK
76/C4 Altun (mts.), China
116/D4 Altun Ha (ruins), Belz.
124/B2 Alturas, Ca,US
125/H4 Altus, Ok,US
125/H4 Altus (res.), Ok,US
125/H4 Altus A.F.B., Ok,US
97/M5 Al Ubayyiḑ, Sudan
97/L5 Al Uḑayyah, Sudan
44/E5 Alun (riv.), Wal,UK
100/C3 Al Uqşur (Luxor), Egypt
66/E3 Alushta, Ukr.
97/L3 Al 'Uwaynāt (peak), Sudan
125/H3 Alva, Ok,US
47/E2 Alvechurch, Eng,UK
58/A3 Alverca, Port.
59/P10 Alverca do Ribatejo, Port.
42/E4 Alvesta, Swe.
46/D4 Alveston, Eng,UK
128/E4 Alvin, Tx,US
42/F3 Älvkarleby, Swe.
42/E4 Älvsborg (co.), Swe.
42/G2 Älvsbyn, Swe.
100/B3 Al Wādī al Jadīd (gov.), Egypt
84/C2 Alwar, India
76/E4 Alxa Youqi, China
76/F4 Alxa Zuoqi, China
49/N1 Alytus, Lith.
57/K2 Alz (riv.), Ger.
57/H4 Alzano Lombardo, It.
53/F4 Alzette (riv.), Lux.
100/C2 Al `Aqabah, Jor.
108/D4 Amacayacú Nat'l Park, Col.
72/B4 Amada (ruins), Egypt
97/M6 Amadi, Sudan
119/J2 Amadjuak (lake), Nun.,Can
58/A3 Amadora, Port.
79/L10 Amagasaki, Japan
78/B4 Amagi, Japan
79/F3 Amagi-san (mtn.), Japan
87/G4 Amahai, Indo.
78/A4 Amakusa (sea), Japan
42/E4 Åmål, Swe.
76/G1 Amalat (riv.), Rus.
61/G4 Amaliás, Gre.
84/C3 Amalner, India
111/E1 Amambaí, Braz.
109/H8 Amambaí (riv.), Braz.
92/B2 Amami (isls.), Japan
60/E3 Amantea, It.
93/L6 Amanu (atoll), FrPol.
58/A2 Amarante, Port.
83/B1 Amarapura, Myan.
124/C3 Amargosa (dry riv.), Ca, Nv,US
128/C3 Amarillo, Tx,US
60/D1 Amaro (peak), It.
74/C2 Amasya, Turk.
79/J7 Amatsukominato, Japan
53/E2 Amay, Belg.
109/H4 Amazon (riv.), SAm.
109/G4 Amazônia (Tapajós) Nat'l Park, Braz.
84/C4 Ambajogai, India
73/L2 Ambāla, India
84/D6 Ambalangoda, SrL.
103/H8 Ambalavao, Madg.
103/J6 Ambanja, Madg.
103/H6 Ambaro (bay), Madg.
108/C4 Ambato, Ecu.
103/H7 Ambato Boeny, Madg.
103/H8 Ambatofinandrahana, Madg.
103/H7 Ambatolampy, Madg.
103/J7 Ambatondrazaka, Madg.
61/H4 Ámbelos, Ákra (cape), Gre.
57/J2 Amberg, Ger.
45/G5 Ambergate, Eng,UK
84/D3 Ambikāpur, India
103/J6 Ambilobe, Madg.
103/J7 Ambinaninony, Madg.
45/G1 Amble, Eng,UK
131/E5 Ambler, Pa,US
45/F3 Ambleside, Eng,UK
52/A2 Ambleteuse, Fr.
53/F3 Amblève (riv.), Belg.
103/H9 Amboasary, Madg.
103/J6 Ambohitra, Tampon (peak), Madg.
87/G4 Ambon, Indo.
87/G4 Ambon (isl.), Indo.
103/H8 Ambositra, Madg.
103/H9 Ambovombe, Madg.
104/B2 Ambriz, Ang.
92/F6 Ambrym (isl.), Van.
130/B6 Amchitka (isl.), Ak,US
130/B6 Amchitka (passg.), Ak,US
117/P9 Ameca, Mex.
53/F3 Amel, Belg.
50/C2 Ameland (isl.), Neth.
50/B5 Amer (chan.), Neth.
105/F American (highland), Ant.
132/M9 American (riv.), Ca,US
132/B3 American (lake), Wa,US
110/C2 Americana, Braz.
122/E5 American Falls, Id,US
124/D2 American Falls (res.), Id,US
124/E2 American Fork, Ut,US
93/J6 American Samoa (terr.), US
129/G3 Americus, Ga,US
57/L3 Ameringkogel (peak), Aus.
50/C4 Amersfoort, Neth.
47/F3 Amersham, Eng,UK
105/E Amery Ice Shelf, Ant.
123/K5 Ames, Ia,US
47/E4 Amesbury, Eng,UK
61/H3 Ámfissa, Gre.
69/N3 Amga (riv.), Rus.
69/T3 Amguema (riv.), Rus.
77/M1 Amgun' (riv.), Rus.
127/H2 Amherst, NS,Can
132/F7 Amherstburg, On,Can
60/B1 Amiata (peak), It.
52/B4 Amiens, Fr.
69/U4 Amila (isl.), Ak,US
39/M6 Amirante (isls.), Sey.
123/H2 Amisk (lake), Sk,Can
128/C4 Amistad (res.), Mex., US
125/G5 Amistad Nat'l Rec. Area, Tx,US
125/K5 Amite (riv.), La,US
84/C3 Amla, India
130/D6 Amlia (isl.), Ak,US
44/D5 Amlwch, Wal,UK
74/K6 Amman (cap.), Jor.
46/C3 Amman (riv.), Wal,UK
46/C3 Ammanford, Wal,UK
42/E2 Ammarfjället (peak), Swe.
130/K2 Ammerman (mtn.), Yk,Can
55/H2 Ammersee (lake), Ger.
122/F5 Ammon, Id,US
83/D3 Amnat Charoen, Thai.
53/F5 Amnéville, Fr.
72/F1 Āmol, Iran
59/P10 Amora, Port.
61/J4 Amorgós (isl.), Gre.
129/F3 Amory, Ms,US
126/E1 Amos, Qu,Can
103/J8 Ampangalana (can.), Madg.
103/H9 Ampanihy, Madg.
84/D6 Amparai, SrL.
110/G7 Amparo, Braz.
103/J6 Ampasindava (bay), Madg.
59/F2 Amposta, Sp.
47/F2 Ampthill, Eng,UK
127/H1 Amqui, Qu,Can
84/C3 Amravati, India
84/B3 Amreli, India
72/C2 'Amrīt (ruins), Syria
73/K2 Amritsar, India
48/E1 Amrum (isl.), Ger.
50/B4 Amstel (riv.), Neth.
50/B4 Amstelveen, Neth.
39/N7 Amsterdam (isl.), FrAnt.
50/B4 Amsterdam (cap.), Neth.
126/F3 Amsterdam, NY,US
50/C5 Amsterdam-Rijnkanaal (can.), Neth.
57/L2 Amstetten, Aus.
97/K5 Am Timan, Chad
71/F5 Amudar'ya (riv.), Asia
130/D5 Amukta (passg.), Ak,US
119/S7 Amund Rignes (isl.), Nun.,Can
105/D Amundsen (bay), Ant.
105/S Amundsen (sea), Ant.
118/D1 Amundsen (gulf), NW,Can
105/A Amundsen-Scott, Ant.
77/M1 Amur (riv.), China, Rus.
93/K6 Amuri, CookIs.
69/N4 Amur Obl., Rus.
58/D1 Amurrio, Sp.
77/M1 Amursk, Rus.
100/C5 'Amur, Wādī (dry riv.), Sudan
82/C5 Amy Douglas (shoal)
74/K4 Amyūn, Leb.
93/L6 Anaa (atoll), FrPol.
69/L3 Anabar (riv.), Rus.
131/A2 Anacapa (isl.), Ca,US
117/J6 Anaco, Ven.
122/E4 Anaconda, Mt,US
125/H4 Anadarko, Ok,US
69/T3 Anadyr', Rus.
69/U3 Anadyr' (gulf), Rus.
69/T3 Anadyr' (range), Rus.
71/S3 Anadyr' (riv.), Rus.
61/J4 Anáfi (isl.), Gre.
72/D2 'Ānah, Iraq
131/C3 Anaheim, Ca,US
122/B2 Anahim Lake, BC,Can
116/A2 Anáhuac, Mex.
128/E4 Anahuac, Tx,US
84/D4 Anakāpalle, India
103/H6 Analalava, Madg.
103/J7 Analamaitso (plat.), Madg.
117/F3 Ana María (gulf), Cuba
86/C3 Anambas (isls.), Indo.
95/G5 Anambra (state), Nga.
74/C3 Anamur, Turk.
74/C3 Anamur (pt.), Turk.
78/D4 Anan, Japan
84/B3 Anand, India
84/C5 Anantapur, India
73/L2 Anantnag, India
75/C3 Anan'yevo, Kyr.
66/F3 Anapa, Rus.
113/K7 Añapi (peak), Arg.
105/J7 Anápolis, Braz.
109/H4 Anapu (riv.), Braz.
109/G8 Anastácio, Braz.
92/D3 Anathan (isl.), NMar.
74/B2 Anatolia (reg.), Turk.
111/D2 Añatuya, Arg.
108/F3 Anauá (riv.), Braz.
127/Q9 Ancaster, On,Can
82/A2 Anchangzhen, China
132/G6 Anchor (bay), Mi,US
130/J3 Anchorage, Ak,US
127/G2 Ancienne-Lorette, Qu,Can
108/E7 Ancohuma (peak), Bol.
57/K5 Ancona, It.
112/B4 Ancud, Chile
112/B4 Ancud (gulf), Chile
77/K2 Anda, China
108/D6 Andahuaylas, Peru
103/J7 Andaingo Gara, Madg.
42/C3 Åndalsnes, Nor.
58/C4 Andalusia (aut. comm.), Sp.
129/G4 Andalusia, Al,US
85/F5 Andaman (sea), Asia
85/F5 Andaman (isls.), India
85/F5 Andaman & Nicobar Is. (terr.), India
103/J6 Andapa, Madg.
52/A4 Andelle (riv.), Fr.
42/F1 Andenes, Nor.
53/E3 Andenne, Belg.
42/F1 Ånderdalen Nat'l Park, Nor.
52/D3 Anderlues, Belg.
53/G3 Andernach, Ger.
130/N2 Anderson (riv.), NW,Can
124/B2 Anderson, Ca,US
126/C3 Anderson, In,US
129/H3 Anderson, SC,US
128/E4 Anderson, Tx,US
132/B3 Anderson (isl.), Wa,US
107/C4 Andes (mts.), SAm.
42/F1 Andfjorden (fjord), Nor.
84/C4 Andhra Pradesh (state), India
61/H5 Andikíthira (isl.), Gre.
103/J7 Andilamena, Madg.
72/E2 Andīmeshk, Iran
61/J4 Andíparos (isl.), Gre.
110/B2 Andira, Braz.
75/B3 Andizhan, Uzb.
58/D1 Andoain, Sp.
80/E4 Andong, SKor.
80/E4 Andong (lake), SKor.
59/F1 Andorra
59/E2 Andorra, Sp.
59/F1 Andorra la Vella (cap.), And.
47/E4 Andover, Eng,UK
131/F5 Andover, NJ,US
42/E1 Andøya (isl.), Nor.
110/E7 Andradas, Braz.
110/B2 Andradina, Braz.
59/G3 Andraitx, Sp.
103/H7 Andranomavo (riv.), Madg.
130/C6 Andreanof (isls.), Ak,US
110/J6 Andrelândia, Braz.
128/C3 Andrews, Tx,US
60/E2 Andria, It.
103/H8 Andringitra (mts.), Madg.
103/J6 Androntany (cape), Madg.
117/F3 Andros (isl.), Bahm.
61/J4 Ándros (isl.), Gre.
126/G2 Androscoggin (riv.), Me, NH,US
58/C3 Andújar, Sp.
112/C4 Anecón Grande (peak), Arg.
112/E4 Anegada (bay), Arg.
117/J4 Anegada (isl.), BVI.
117/J4 Anegada (passage), NAm.
99/F5 Anécho, Togo
92/G7 Aneityum (isl.), Van.
59/F1 Aneto, Pico de (peak), Sp.
82/E2 Anfu, China
111/E1 Angamos (pt.), Chile
76/E1 Angara (riv.), Rus.
76/E1 Angarsk, Rus.
42/E3 Ånge, Swe.
51/E5 Angel (riv.), Ger.
117/M8 Ángel de la Guarda (isl.), Mex.
82/D4 Angeles, Phil.
131/B2 Angeles Nat'l Forest, Ca,US
128/E4 Angelina (riv.), Tx,US
48/E1 Angeln (reg.), Ger.
108/F2 Angel, Salto (falls), Ven.
132/F6 Angelus (lake), Mi,US
87/J4 Angemuk (mtn.), Indo.
42/E2 Ångermanälven (riv.), Swe.
49/H2 Angermünde, Ger.
56/C3 Angers, Fr.
83/C3 Angkor (ruins), Camb.
83/D4 Angk Tasaom, Camb.
44/D5 Anglesey (co.), Wal,UK
44/D5 Anglesey (isl.), Wal,UK
56/C5 Anglet, Fr.
128/E4 Angleton, Tx,US
56/D3 Anglin (riv.), Fr.
83/C2 Ang Nam Ngum (lake), Laos
97/L7 Ango, D.R. Congo
112/B3 Angol, Chile
104/C3 Angola
126/C3 Angola, In,US
116/C4 Angostura (res.), Mex.
56/D4 Angoulême, Fr.
59/S12 Angra do Heroísmo, Azor.,Port.
110/J8 Angra dos Reis, Braz.
75/B3 Angren, Uzb.
83/C3 Ang Thong, Thai.
97/K7 Angu, D.R. Congo
117/J4 Anguilla (isl.), UK
130/G2 Angutikada (peak), Ak,US
109/H8 Anhanduí (riv.), Braz.
53/D3 Anhée, Belg.
85/K2 Anhua, China
81/D4 Anhui (prov.), China
130/G4 Aniakchak (crater), Ak,US
130/G4 Aniakchak Nat'l Mon. & Prsv., Ak,US
52/C3 Aniche, Fr.
124/F3 Animas (riv.), Co, NM,US
62/E3 Anina, Rom.
77/N2 Aniva (bay), Rus.
42/H3 Anjalamkoski, Fin.
84/B3 Anjār, India
79/N10 Anjō, Japan
127/N6 Anjou, Qu,Can
56/C3 Anjou (hist. reg.), Fr.
103/H6 Anjouan (isl.), Com.
74/C2 Ankara (cap.), Turk.
103/H7 Ankaratra, Massif (plat.), Madg.
128/C2 Ankaree (riv.), Co,US
103/H8 Ankazoabo, Madg.
83/E3 An Khe, Viet.
49/G2 Anklam, Ger.
83/D3 Anlong Veng, Camb.
50/D2 Anloo, Neth.
81/C5 Anlu, China
105/D Ann (cape), Ant.
127/G3 Ann (cape), Ma,US
126/E4 Anna (lake), Va,US
96/G1 Annaba, Alg.
57/K1 Annaberg-Buchholz, Ger.
74/L4 An Nabk, Syria
44/B3 Annaclone, NI,UK
72/C3 An Nafūd (des.), SAr.
97/L5 An Nahūd, Sudan
72/D2 An Najaf, Iraq
43/B3 Annalee (riv.), Ire.
44/C3 Annalong, NI,UK
83/D2 Annamitique, Chaîne (mts.), Laos, Viet.
45/E2 Annan, Sc,UK
43/D3 Annan (riv.), Sc,UK
131/J8 Annandale, Va,US
50/B3 Anna Pavlowna, Neth.
112/B5 Anna Pink (bay), Chile
131/K8 Annapolis (cap.), Md,US
84/D2 Annapurna (mtn.), Nepal
72/C3 An Naqb, Ra's, Jor.
132/E7 Ann Arbor, Mi,US
72/E2 An Nāşirīyah, Iraq
91/C4 Anne (peak), Austl.
57/G4 Annecy, Fr.
83/E3 An Nhon, Viet.
129/G3 Anniston, Al,US
96/F8 Annobón (isl.), EqG.
56/F4 Annonay, Fr.
72/E2 An Nu'manīyah, Iraq
79/M10 Anō, Japan
59/K7 Anoia (riv.), Sp.
123/K4 Anoka, Mn,US
103/J7 Anosibe an' Ala, Madg.
99/G2 Anou-Zeggarene (wadi), Niger
83/E4 An Phuoc, Viet.
81/D5 Anqing, China
51/F5 Anröchte, Ger.
53/E2 Ans, Belg.
57/J2 Ansbach, Ger.
117/G4 Anse-d'Hainault, Haiti
57/L2 Ansfelden, Aus.
85/J2 Anshun, China
128/D3 Anson, Tx,US
80/D4 Ansŏng, SKor.
92/E4 Ant (atoll), Micr.
47/H1 Ant (riv.), Eng,UK
74/D3 Antakya (Antioch), Turk.
103/J6 Antalaha, Madg.
74/B3 Antalya, Turk.
74/B3 Antalya (gulf), Turk.
103/H7 Antananarivo (cap.), Madg.
103/H7 Antananarivo (prov.), Madg.
105/W Antarctic (pen.), Ant.
105/* Antarctica
110/B4 Antas (riv.), Braz.
52/D5 Ante (riv.), Fr.
58/C4 Antequera, Sp.
125/H3 Anthony, Ks,US
124/F4 Anthony, NM,US
96/D2 Anti-Atlas (mts.), Mor.
57/G5 Antibes, Fr.
127/J1 Anticosti (isl.), Qu,Can
56/D2 Antifer, Cap d' (cape), Fr.
126/B2 Antigo, Wi,US
127/J2 Antigonish, NS,Can
117/J4 Antigua (isl.), Ant. & Barb.
117/J4 Antigua and Barbuda
74/K5 Anti-Lebanon (mts.), Leb.
132/L10 Antioch, Ca,US
132/P15 Antioch, Il,US
74/D3 Antioch (Antakya), Turk.
39/T8 Antipodes (isls.), NZ
125/J4 Antlers, Ok,US
111/B1 Antofagasta, Chile
52/C2 Antoing, Belg.
103/J6 Antongil (bay), Madg.
102/C4 Antoniesberg (peak), SAfr.
110/B3 Antonina, Braz.
125/F3 Antonito, Co,US
116/B4 Anton Lizardo (pt.), Mex.
52/B6 Antony, Fr.
44/B2 Antrim, NI,UK
44/B2 Antrim (dist.), NI,UK
44/B1 Antrim (mts.), NI,UK
103/H7 Antsalova, Madg.
103/H7 Antsirabe, Madg.
103/J6 Antsiranana, Madg.
103/J6 Antsiranana (prov.), Madg.
103/H6 Antsohihy, Madg.
112/C3 Antuco (vol.), Chile
53/E1 Antwerp (prov.), Belg.
52/D1 Antwerp (Antwerpen), Belg.
84/D6 Anuradhapura, SrL.
130/B6 Anvil (vol.), Ak,US
82/C2 Anxi, China
81/C3 Anyang, China
76/D4 A'nyêmaqên (mts.), China
81/B4 Anyi, China
77/M2 Anyuy (riv.), Rus.
52/C2 Anzegem, Belg.
68/J4 Anzhero-Sudzhensk, Rus.
52/C3 Anzin, Fr.
60/C2 Anzio, It.
79/L9 Aogaki, Japan
83/B4 Ao Kham (pt.), Thai.
77/N3 Aomori, Japan
61/G2 Aóos (riv.), Gre.
83/B4 Ao Phangnga Nat'l Park, Thai.
83/D3 Aoral (peak), Camb.
57/G4 Aosta, It.
98/C2 Aoudaghost (ruins), Mrta.
97/K5 Aouk (riv.), CAfr., Chad
98/C2 Aoukar (reg.), Mrta.
96/F2 Aoulef, Alg.
79/M10 Aoyama, Japan
96/J3 Aozou, Chad
128/B4 Apache (mts.), Tx,US
129/G4 Apalachicola, Fl,US
110/B4 Aparados da Serra Nat'l Park, Braz.
110/C2 Aparecida, Braz.
110/B2 Aparecida do Taboado, Braz.
82/D4 Aparri, Phil.
117/F6 Apartadó, Col.
93/L6 Apataki, FrPol.
62/D3 Apatin, Yugo.
64/G2 Apatity, Rus.
117/P10 Apatzingán, Mex.
116/B4 Apaxtla, Mex.
83/D4 Ap Binh Chau, Viet.
50/D4 Apeldoorn, Neth.
50/C4 Apeldoornsch (can.), Neth.
51/E2 Apen, Ger.
41/F4 Apennines (mts.), It.
86/C3 Api (cape), Indo.
87/E5 Api (peak), Indo.
75/D5 Api (mtn.), Nepal
93/H6 Apia (cap.), Samoa
109/G6 Apiacás (mts.), Braz.
110/B3 Apiaí, Braz.
83/D4 Ap Loc Thanh, Viet.
83/E4 Ap Long Hoa, Viet.
83/D4 Ap Luc, Viet.
82/E6 Apo (mt.), Phil.
93/R9 Apolima (str.), Samoa
110/B1 Aporé (riv.), Braz.
126/B2 Apostle (isls.), Wi,US
111/E2 Apóstoles, Arg.
74/C3 Apostolos Andreas (cape), Cyp.
121/K4 Appalachian (mts.), US
55/F3 Appenzell Ausser Rhoden (canton), Swi.
55/F3 Appenzell Inner Rhoden (canton), Swi.
50/D2 Appingedam, Neth.
45/F2 Appleby, Eng,UK
47/E1 Appleby Magna, Eng,UK
127/S9 Appleton, NY,US
126/B2 Appleton, Wi,US
131/C1 Apple Valley, Ca,US
60/D2 Apricena, It.
60/C2 Aprilia, It.
66/F3 Apsheronsk, Rus.
91/E1 Apsley Gorge Nat'l Park, Austl.
83/E4 Ap Tan My, Viet.
120/U11 Apua (pt.), Hi,US
57/J4 Apuane (mts.), It.
110/B2 Apucarana, Braz.
117/H6 Apure (riv.), Ven.
108/D6 Apurímac (riv.), Peru
83/E4 Ap Vinh Hao, Viet.
100/C2 Aqaba (gulf), Asia
72/B3 Aqaba (gulf), Egypt, SAr.
100/D5 'Aqīq, Sudan
75/E4 Aqqikkol (lake), China
72/D1 'Aqrah, Iraq
67/J4 Aqtaū, Kaz.
67/L2 Aqtöbe, Kaz.
67/L3 Aqtöbe Obl., Kaz.
109/G8 Aquidauana, Braz.
109/G8 Aquidauana (riv.), Braz.
56/C4 Aquitaine (reg.), Fr.
76/D4 Ar (riv.), China
79/F2 Ara (riv.), Japan
97/L5 'Arab (riv.), Sudan
129/G3 Arab, Al,US
100/C2 'Arabah, Wādī (dry riv.), Egypt
72/D3 Arabian (pen.), Asia
73/H5 Arabian (sea), Asia
100/C3 Arabian (des.), Egypt
74/L5 'Arab, Jabal al (mts.), Syria
100/B2 'Arab, Kalīj al (gulf), Egypt
66/E4 Araç (riv.), Turk.
109/L6 Aracaju, Braz.
109/L4 Aracati, Braz.
110/B2 Araçatuba, Braz.
58/B4 Aracena, Sp.
110/D1 Aracruz, Braz.
109/K7 Araçuaí, Braz.
62/E2 Arad, Rom.
62/E2 Arad (co.), Rom.
97/K4 Arada, Chad
72/F1 Ārādān, Iran
72/D4 'Arafāt, Jabal (mtn.), SAr.
92/C5 Arafura (sea), Austl., Indo.
109/H7 Aragarças, Braz.
67/H4 Aragats, Gora (peak), Arm.
59/E2 Aragon (aut. comm.), Sp.
58/E1 Aragón (riv.), Sp.
109/J5 Araguaia (riv.), Braz.
109/H5 Araguaia Nat'l Park, Braz.
109/J5 Araguaína, Braz.
110/B1 Araguari, Braz.
109/H3 Araguari (riv.), Braz.
109/J7 Araguari (riv.), Braz.
110/C1 Araguari (Valhas) (riv.), Braz.
109/J5 Araguatins, Braz.
79/F2 Arai, Japan
72/E2 Arāk, Iran
130/D3 Arakamchechan (isl.), Rus.
85/F3 Arakan (mts.), Myan.
61/G3 Arakhthos (riv.), Gre.
67/H5 Araks (Aras) (riv.), Eur., Asia
68/G5 Aral (sea), Uzb., Kaz.
68/G5 Aral'sk, Kaz.
67/H2 Aralsor (lake), Kaz.
72/F2 Ārān, Iran
43/H7 Aran (isl.), Ire.
43/A4 Aran (isls.), Ire.
58/D2 Aranda de Duero, Sp.
62/E3 Arandelovac, Yugo.
58/D2 Aranjuez, Sp.
44/E6 Aran Mawddwy (mtn.), Wal,UK
128/D5 Aransas Pass, Tx,US
92/G4 Aranuka (atoll), Kiri.
109/L5 Arapiraca, Braz.
74/D2 Arapkir, Turk.
110/B2 Arapongas, Braz.
110/B4 Araranguá, Braz.
110/B2 Araraquara, Braz.
110/C2 Araras, Braz.
91/B3 Ararat, Austl.
109/K5 Araripina, Braz.
67/H5 Aras (riv.), Asia
98/C2 Aratane (well), Mrta.
108/F4 Arauá (riv.), Braz.
108/D2 Arauca, Col.
110/B3 Araucária, Braz.
92/E5 Arawa, PNG
110/C1 Araxá, Braz.
97/N6 Ārba Minch', Eth.
123/H2 Arborfield, Sk,Can
123/J3 Arborg, Mb,Can
43/D2 Arbroath, Sc,UK
56/F5 Arc (riv.), Fr.
57/G4 Arc (riv.), Fr.
56/C4 Arcachon, Fr.
56/C4 Arcachon (lag.), Fr.
56/C4 Arcachon, Pointe d' (pt.), Fr.
131/B2 Arcadia, Ca,US
129/H5 Arcadia, Fl,US
124/A2 Arcata, Ca,US
64/H3 Archangel Obl., Rus.
64/J2 Archangel'sk, Rus.
58/E3 Archena, Sp.
90/A1 Archer (riv.), Austl.
90/A1 Archer Bend Nat'l Park, Austl.
128/D3 Archer City, Tx,US
124/E3 Arches Nat'l Park, Ut,US
58/C4 Archidona, Sp.
112/C3 Arco (pass), Arg.
57/J4 Arco, It.
122/E5 Arco, Id,US
110/C2 Arcos, Braz.
58/C4 Arcos de la Frontera, Sp.
109/L5 Arcoverde, Braz.
38/A1 Arctic (ocean)
130/F2 Arctic (coast. pl.), Ak,US
130/J2 Arctic Nat'l Wild. Ref., Ak,US
130/M2 Arctic Red River, NW,Can
63/G5 Arda (riv.), Bul.
74/E2 Ardahan, Turk.
72/F2 Ardakān, Iran
42/C3 Årdalstangen, Nor.
74/E2 Ardanuç, Turk.
45/E6 Arddleen, Wal,UK
56/F4 Ardèche (riv.), Fr.
132/M9 Arden-Arcade, Ca,US
53/E4 Ardennes (for.), Eur.
52/D4 Ardennes (dept.), Fr.
53/D4 Ardennes, Canal des (can.), Fr.
74/E2 Ardeşen, Turk.
44/C3 Ardglass, NI,UK
58/B3 Ardila (riv.), Sp.
125/H4 Ardmore, Ok,US
131/E5 Ardmore, Pa,US
52/C2 Ardooie, Belg.
44/C2 Ards (dist.), NI,UK
44/C3 Ards (pen.), NI,UK
42/E3 Åre, Swe.
110/G6 Areado, Braz.
110/C3 Areia Branca, Braz.
117/N9 Arena (pt.), Mex.
124/B3 Arena (pt.), Ca,US
109/G6 Arenápolis, Braz.
58/C2 Arenas de San Pedro, Sp.
113/K8 Arenas, Punta de (pt.), Arg.
42/D4 Arendal, Nor.
50/C6 Arendonk, Belg.
44/E6 Arenig Fawr (mtn.), Wal,UK
59/L6 Arenys de Mar, Sp.
59/L6 Arenys de Munt, Sp.
108/D7 Arequipa, Peru
58/C2 Arévalo, Sp.
57/J5 Arezzo, It.
56/C5 Arga (riv.), Sp.
58/D3 Argamasilla de Alba, Sp.
58/C3 Argamasilla de Calatrava, Sp.
59/N9 Arganda, Sp.
57/G5 Argens (riv.), Fr.
56/C2 Argentan, Fr.
57/G4 Argentera (peak), It.
52/B6 Argenteuil, Fr.
111/C4 Argentina
113/J7 Argentino (lake), Arg.
59/L6 Argentona, Sp.
63/G3 Argeş (co.), Rom.
63/G3 Argeş (riv.), Rom.
73/J2 Arghandab (riv.), Afg.
100/B5 Argo, Sudan
61/H4 Argolís (gulf), Gre.
53/E5 Argonne (for.), Fr.
61/H4 Árgos, Gre.
61/G3 Argostólion, Gre.
52/A4 Argueil, Fr.
124/B4 Arguello (pt.), Ca,US
98/A1 Arguin (bay), Mrta.
77/H1 Argun (riv.), China, Rus.
75/E2 Argut (riv.), Rus.
96/C3 Arhreijît (well), Mrta.
42/D4 Århus, Den.
60/D2 Ariano Irpino, It.
58/C1 Arianza (riv.), Sp.
108/D7 Arica, Chile
78/D3 Arida, Japan
131/A1 Arido (mt.), Ca,US
56/D5 Ariège (riv.), Fr.
63/K5 Arifiye, Turk.
74/K6 Arīḩā (Jericho), WBnk.
125/G3 Arikaree (riv.), Co,US
117/J5 Arima, Trin.
109/G6 Arinos (riv.), Braz.
109/G6 Aripuanã (riv.), Braz.
108/F5 Ariquemes, Braz.
100/C2 'Arīsh, Wādī al (dry riv.), Egypt
103/H7 Arivonimamo, Madg.
59/F1 Arize (riv.), Fr.
124/D4 Arizona (state), US
117/F5 Arjona, Col.
58/C4 Arjona, Sp.
128/E3 Arkadelphia, Ar,US
43/C2 Arkaig, Loch (lake), Sc,UK
75/A1 Arkalyk, Kaz.
125/K4 Arkansas (riv.), US
128/E3 Arkansas (state), US
129/F3 Arkansas City, Ar,US
125/H3 Arkansas City, Ks,US
97/K3 Arkanū (peak), Libya
44/B6 Arklow, Ire.
49/G1 Arkona, Kap (cape), Ger.
84/C5 Arkonam, India
45/G4 Arksey, Eng,UK
68/H2 Arkticheskiy Institut (isls.), Rus.
58/C1 Arlanza (riv.), Sp.
58/C1 Arlanzón (riv.), Sp.
56/F5 Arles, Fr.
52/C3 Arleux, Fr.
129/G4 Arlington, Ga,US
123/K4 Arlington, Mn,US
128/D3 Arlington, Tx,US
131/J8 Arlington, Va,US
132/Q15 Arlington Heights, Il,US
53/E4 Arlon, Belg.
99/F4 Arly Nat'l Park, Burk.
132/G6 Armada, Mi,US

141

Armag – Balei

44/B3 **Armagh**, NI,UK
44/B3 **Armagh** (dist.), NI,UK
56/F3 **Armançon** (riv.), Fr.
110/B2 **Armando Laydner** (res.), Braz.
100/C3 **Armant**, Egypt
67/G3 **Armavir**, Rus.
57/G5 **Arme, Cap d'** (cape), Fr.
67/H4 **Armenia**
108/C3 **Armenia**, Col.
52/B2 **Armentières**, Fr.
117/P10 **Armería**, Mex.
91/D1 **Armidale**, Austl.
58/D4 **Armilla**, Sp.
44/B1 **Armoy**, NI,UK
112/E2 **Armstrong**, Arg.
122/D3 **Armstrong**, BC,Can
45/G4 **Armthorpe**, Eng,UK
84/C4 **Ārmūr**, India
119/J3 **Arnaud** (riv.), Qu,Can
74/J4 **Arnauti** (cape), Cyp.
47/E3 **Arncott**, Eng,UK
58/D1 **Arnedo**, Sp.
52/B2 **Arnèke**, Fr.
125/H3 **Arnett**, Ok,US
50/C5 **Arnhem**, Neth.
84/C5 **Arni**, India
57/J5 **Arno** (riv.), It.
92/G4 **Arno** (atoll), Mrsh.
45/G5 **Arnold**, Eng,UK
57/K3 **Arnoldstein**, Aus.
56/E3 **Arnon** (riv.), Fr.
126/E2 **Arnprior**, On,Can
51/F6 **Arnsberg**, Ger.
45/F3 **Arnside**, Eng,UK
48/F3 **Arnstadt**, Ger.
51/G6 **Arolsen**, Ger.
56/E3 **Aron** (riv.), Fr.
59/X16 **Arona**, Canl.
52/B4 **Aronde** (riv.), Fr.
92/G5 **Arorae** (atoll), Kiri.
87/H5 **Aro Usu** (cape), Indo.
52/B2 **Arques**, Fr.
84/D2 **Arrah**, India
97/M5 **Ar Rahad**, Sudan
109/H6 **Arraias** (riv.), Braz.
45/H4 **Arram**, Eng,UK
72/D2 **Ar Ramādī**, Iraq
74/L5 **Ar Ramthā**, Jor.
43/C3 **Arran** (isl.), Sc,UK
74/D3 **Ar Raqqah**, Syria
52/B3 **Arras**, Fr.
74/L4 **Ar Rastan**, Syria
59/F1 **Arrats** (riv.), Fr.
59/Y16 **Arrecife**, Canl.
112/E2 **Arrecifes**, Arg.
56/B2 **Arrée** (mts.), Fr.
116/C4 **Arriaga**, Mex.
110/A5 **Arrio Grande**, Braz.
72/E4 **Ar Riyāḑ** (Riyadh) (cap.), SAr.
56/F3 **Arroux** (riv.), Fr.
58/B3 **Arroyo de la Luz**, Sp.
124/B4 **Arroyo Grande**, Ca,US
74/L5 **Ar Ruşayfah**, Jor.
97/M5 **Ar Ruşayriş**, Sudan
72/F4 **Ar Ruways**, SAr.
77/L3 **Arsen'yev**, Rus.
93/T11 **Art** (isl.), NCal.
61/G3 **Árta**, Gre.
61/G3 **Arta** (gulf), Gre.
58/A1 **Arteijo**, Sp.
77/L3 **Artem**, Rus.
116/E3 **Artemisa**, Cuba
131/B3 **Artesia**, Ca,US
125/F4 **Artesia**, NM,US
90/C3 **Arthur** (pt.), Austl.
111/E3 **Artigas**, Uru.
52/A2 **Artois** (reg.), Fr.
52/B2 **Artois, Collines de l'** (hills), Fr.
110/F7 **Artur Nogueira**, Braz.
75/C4 **Artux**, China
74/E2 **Artvin**, Turk.
87/H5 **Aru** (isls.), Indo.
101/A2 **Arua**, Ugan.
117/H5 **Aruba** (isl.), Neth.
110/G8 **Arujá**, Braz.
47/F5 **Arun** (riv.), Eng,UK
85/F2 **Arunachal Pradesh** (state), India
47/F5 **Arundel**, Eng,UK
84/C6 **Aruppukkottai**, India
87/F3 **Arus** (cape), Indo.
101/C3 **Arusha**, Tanz.
101/C4 **Arusha** (prov.), Tanz.
93/L6 **Arutua** (atoll), FrPol.
97/L7 **Aruwimi** (riv.), D.R. Congo
76/E2 **Arvayheer**, Mong.
42/F2 **Arvidsjaur**, Swe.
42/E4 **Arvika**, Swe.
124/C4 **Arvin**, Ca,US
126/B2 **Arvon** (peak), Mi,US
60/A4 **Aryānah** (gov.), Tun.
75/A3 **Arys'**, Kaz.
56/B3 **Arz** (riv.), Fr.
65/J5 **Arzamas**, Rus.
51/G4 **Arzen**, Ger.
53/F3 **Arzfeld**, Ger.
58/A1 **Arzúa**, Sp.
53/E1 **As**, Belg.
57/K1 **Aš**, Czh.
42/D4 **Ås**, Nor.
72/E2 **Asadābād**, Iran
98/D5 **Asagny Nat'l Park**, IvC.
86/A3 **Asahan** (riv.), Indo.
78/C3 **Asahi** (riv.), Japan
79/G2 **Asahi-Bandai Nat'l Park**, Japan
77/N3 **Asahi-dake** (mtn.), Japan
77/N3 **Asahikawa**, Japan
79/H7 **Asaka**, Japan
79/M9 **Asake** (riv.), Japan
97/P5 **Āsalē**, Erit.
79/F2 **Asama-yama** (mtn.), Japan
84/E3 **Asansol**, India
96/J3 **Asawanwah** (well), Libya
65/P4 **Asbest**, Rus.
102/C3 **Asbestos** (mts.), SAfr.
131/F5 **Asbury Park**, NJ,US
116/D4 **Ascención** (bay), Mex.
38/J6 **Ascension** (isl.), StH.
51/E5 **Ascheberg**, Ger.
48/F3 **Aschersleben**, Ger.
60/A1 **Asco** (riv.), Fr.
60/C1 **Ascoli Piceno**, It.
60/D2 **Ascoli Satriano**, It.
47/F4 **Ascot**, Eng,UK
97/P5 **Āseb**, Erit.
97/N6 **Āsela**, Eth.
63/G4 **Asenovgrad**, Bul.
76/G2 **Asgat**, Mong.
47/G4 **Ash**, Eng,UK
47/E4 **Ashampstead**, Eng,UK
99/E5 **Ashanti** (reg.), Gha.
99/E5 **Ashanti** (uplands), Gha.
45/G5 **Ashbourne**, Eng,UK
89/H7 **Ashburton**, NZ
46/C5 **Ashburton**, Eng,UK
47/E1 **Ashby** (can.), Eng,UK
45/G6 **Ashby-de-la-Zouch**, Eng,UK
46/D3 **Ashchurch**, Eng,UK
122/C3 **Ashcroft**, BC,Can
129/J3 **Asheboro**, NC,US
123/J3 **Ashern**, Mb,Can
129/H3 **Asheville**, NC,US
123/M2 **Asheweig** (riv.), On,Can
47/F1 **Ashfordby**, Eng,UK
73/G1 **Ashgabat** (cap.), Trkm.
127/Q8 **Ashgrove**, On,Can
45/G3 **Ashington**, Eng,UK
79/L10 **Ashiya**, Japan
78/C4 **Ashizuri-misaki** (cape), Japan
125/H3 **Ashland**, Ks,US
126/D4 **Ashland**, Ky,US
126/D3 **Ashland**, Oh,US
122/C5 **Ashland**, Or,US
126/B2 **Ashland**, Wi,US
123/J4 **Ashley**, ND,US
89/B2 **Ashmore and Cartier Is.** (terr.), Austl.
74/L4 **Ash Shamāl** (gov.), Leb.
72/D2 **Ash Shāmīyah**, Iraq
73/G3 **Ash Shāriqah**, UAE
74/E3 **Ash Sharqāţ**, Iraq
74/H6 **Ash Sharqīyah** (gov.), Egypt
84/C3 **Ashta**, India
126/D3 **Ashtabula**, Oh,US
122/F4 **Ashton**, Id,US
45/F5 **Ashton-in-Makerfield**, Eng,UK
45/F5 **Ashton-under-Lyne**, Eng,UK
126/B2 **Ashwaubenon**, Wi,US
47/F2 **Ashwell**, Eng,UK
71/* **Asia**
60/A2 **Asinara** (gulf), It.
60/A2 **Asinara** (isl.), It.
68/J4 **Asino**, Rus.
72/D5 **'Asīr** (mts.), SAr., Yemen
100/D5 **Asis, Ras** (cape), Sudan
74/E2 **Aşkale**, Turk.
45/E3 **Askam in Furness**, Eng,UK
42/D4 **Asker**, Nor.
45/G4 **Askern**, Eng,UK
42/D4 **Askim**, Nor.
61/G2 **Áskion** (peak), Gre.
42/P6 **Askja** (crater), Ice.
97/N4 **Asmara** (cap.), Erit.
52/B6 **Asnières-sur-Seine**, Fr.
78/B4 **Aso Nat'l Park**, Japan
97/M5 **Āsosa**, Eth.
78/B4 **Aso-san** (mtn.), Japan
100/D4 **Asoteriba, Jabal** (peak), Sudan
45/E2 **Aspatria**, Eng,UK
59/E3 **Aspe**, Sp.
124/F3 **Aspen**, Co,US
131/J7 **Aspen Hill**, Md,US
128/C3 **Aspermont**, Tx,US
59/F1 **Aspin, Col d'** (pass), Fr.
61/H3 **Asprópirgos**, Gre.
122/G2 **Asquith**, Sk,Can
98/C2 **'Assâba, Massif de l'** (reg.), Mrta.
74/D3 **As Sabkhah**, Syria
74/K6 **Aş Şāfī**, Jor.
72/E3 **As Sālimīyah**, Kuw.
72/E4 **As Sālimīyah**, SAr.
97/L1 **As Sallūm**, Egypt
74/K5 **As Salţ**, Jor.
85/F2 **Assam** (state), India
72/E2 **As Samāwah**, Iraq
74/H6 **As Santah**, Egypt
74/K5 **Aş Şarīḩ**, Jor.
52/D2 **Asse**, Belg.
60/A3 **Assemini**, It.
50/D2 **Assen**, Neth.
52/C1 **Assenede**, Belg.
96/J1 **As Sidr**, Libya
74/H6 **As Sinbillāwayn**, Egypt
123/G3 **Assiniboia**, Sk,Can
122/E3 **Assiniboine** (peak), BC,Can
123/J3 **Assiniboine** (riv.), Mb,Can
126/F1 **Assinika** (lake), Qu,Can
110/B2 **Assis**, Braz.
59/G1 **Assou** (riv.), Fr.
97/M6 **As Sudd** (reg.), Sudan
72/E1 **As Sulaymānīyah**, Iraq
72/E3 **Aş Şummān** (mts.), SAr.
74/L5 **As Suwaydā'**, Syria
74/L5 **As Suwaydā'** (dist.), Syria
72/D2 **Aş Şuwayrah**, Iraq
100/C2 **As Suways** (gov.), Egypt
100/C2 **As Suways** (Suez), Egypt
75/B1 **Astana** (cap.), Kaz.
50/C6 **Asten**, Neth
57/H4 **Asti**, It.
110/L6 **Astolfo Dutra**, Braz.
47/E2 **Aston**, Eng,UK
46/D2 **Aston on Clun**, Eng,UK
110/B2 **Astorga**, Braz.
122/C4 **Astoria**, Or,US
67/J3 **Astrakhan'**, Rus.
67/H3 **Astrakhan Obl.**, Rus.
58/B1 **Asturias** (aut. comm.), Sp.
47/E2 **Astwood Bank**, Eng,UK
79/L10 **Asuka**, Japan
79/N9 **Asuke**, Japan
92/D3 **Asuncion** (isl.), NMar.
111/E2 **Asunción** (cap.), Par.
116/B4 **Asunción Ixcaltepec**, Mex.
101/B2 **Aswa** (riv.), Ugan.
100/C3 **Aswān**, Egypt
100/C4 **Aswān** (gov.), Egypt
100/C4 **Aswan High** (dam), Egypt
100/B3 **Asyūt**, Egypt
100/B3 **Asyūt** (gov.), Egypt
100/C2 **Asyūţī, Wādī al** (dry riv.), Egypt
111/C2 **Atacama** (des.), Chile
111/C1 **Atacama, Puna de** (plat.), Arg.
99/F4 **Atacora** (range), Ben.
95/E5 **Atafu** (atoll), Tok.
99/F5 **Atakpamé**, Togo
79/F3 **Atami**, Japan
98/B1 **Atar**, Mrta.
58/D4 **Atarfe**, Sp.
84/D2 **Atarra**, India
76/D3 **Atas Bogd** (peak), Mong.
124/B4 **Atascadero**, Ca,US
74/D3 **Atatürk** (res.), Turk.
97/M4 **Atbara**, Sudan
97/M4 **Atbara** (Atbarah) (riv.), Eth., Sudan
75/A1 **Atbasar**, Kaz.
125/K5 **Atchafalaya** (bay), La,US
129/F4 **Atchafalaya** (riv.), La,US
125/J3 **Atchison**, Ks,US
99/E5 **Atebubu**, Gha.
42/G1 **Ateelva** (riv.), Nor.
117/P9 **Atengo** (riv.), Mex.
60/C1 **Aterno** (riv.), It.
52/C2 **Ath**, Belg.
122/E2 **Athabasca**, Ab,Can
118/E3 **Athabasca** (riv.), Ab,Can
118/F3 **Athabasca** (lake), Ab, Sk,Can
123/H2 **Athapapuskow** (lake), Mb,Can
96/K1 **Athār Ţulmaythah** (Ptolemaïs) (ruins), Libya
129/G3 **Athens**, Al,US
129/H3 **Athens**, Ga,US
126/D4 **Athens**, Oh,US
129/G3 **Athens**, Tn,US
128/E3 **Athens**, Tx,US
61/L7 **Athens** (Athínai) (cap.), Gre.
47/E1 **Atherstone**, Eng,UK
45/F4 **Atherton**, Eng,UK
43/B4 **Athlone**, Ire.
61/J2 **Áthos** (peak), Gre.
96/J5 **Ati**, Chad
110/G8 **Atibaia**, Braz.
110/G7 **Atibaia** (riv.), Braz.
126/B1 **Atikokan**, On,Can
93/K7 **Atiu** (isl.), CookIs.
130/C5 **Atka** (isl.), Ak,US
67/H2 **Atkarsk**, Rus.
130/M2 **Atkinson** (pt.), NW,Can
129/G3 **Atlanta** (cap.), Ga,US
128/E3 **Atlanta**, Tx,US
38/G3 **Atlantic** (ocean)
131/G5 **Atlantic Beach**, NY,US
99/F5 **Atlantique** (prov.), Ben.
96/E2 **Atlas** (mts.), Afr.
132/K10 **Atlas** (peak), Ca,US
96/E1 **Atlas Saharien** (mts.), Alg., Mor.
130/M4 **Atlin** (lake), BC,Can
116/B4 **Atlixco**, Mex.
129/G4 **Atmore**, Al,US
96/B3 **Atoui** (dry riv.), Mrta.
73/J1 **Atrak** (riv.), Iran
108/C2 **Atrato** (riv.), Col.
79/H7 **Atsugi**, Japan
79/N10 **Atsumi**, Japan
79/N10 **Atsumi** (pen.), Japan
74/K6 **Aţ Ţafīlah**, Jor.
72/D4 **Aţ Ţā'if**, SAr.
74/L5 **At Tall**, Syria
129/G3 **Attalla**, Al,US
119/H3 **Attawapiskat** (riv.), On,Can
51/E6 **Attendorn**, Ger.
57/K3 **Attersee** (lake), Aus.
52/C5 **Attichy**, Fr.
47/E2 **Attleborough**, Eng,UK
47/H2 **Attleborough**, Eng,UK
130/A5 **Attu** (isl.), Ak,US
100/C2 **Aţ Ţūr**, Egypt
74/K6 **Aţ Ţūr**, WBnk.
72/D6 **At Turbah**, Yem.
112/D2 **Atuel** (riv.), Arg.
42/F4 **Åtvidaberg**, Swe.
124/B3 **Atwater**, Ca,US
125/G3 **Atwood**, Ks,US
67/J3 **Atyraū**, Kaz.
67/J3 **Atyraū Obl.**, Kaz.
116/E4 **Auas**, Hon.
53/E4 **Aubange**, Belg.
52/D6 **Aube** (dept.), Fr.
56/F2 **Aube** (riv.), Fr.
56/F4 **Aubenas**, Fr.
52/C6 **Aubetin** (riv.), Fr.
52/A5 **Aubette** (riv.), Fr.
56/E4 **Aubin**, Fr.
56/E4 **Aubrac** (mts.), Fr.
129/G3 **Auburn**, Al,US
124/B3 **Auburn**, Ca,US
126/C3 **Auburn**, In,US
127/G2 **Auburn**, Me,US
125/J2 **Auburn**, Ne,US
126/E3 **Auburn**, NY,US
132/C3 **Auburn**, Wa,US
132/F6 **Auburn Hills**, Mi,US
112/C3 **Aucá Mahuida** (peak), Arg.
56/D5 **Auch**, Fr.
52/B3 **Auchel**, Fr.
43/D2 **Auchenblae**, Sc,UK
44/E2 **Auchencairn**, Sc,UK
43/C3 **Auchinleck**, Sc,UK
89/H6 **Auckland**, NZ
39/S8 **Auckland** (isls.), NZ
56/E5 **Aude** (riv.), Fr.
52/D2 **Auderghem**, Belg.
56/A3 **Audierne** (bay), Fr.
45/F6 **Audlem**, Eng,UK
45/F5 **Audley**, Eng,UK
97/P6 **Audo** (range), Eth.
53/E5 **Audun-le-Tiche**, Fr.
57/K1 **Aue**, Ger.
51/E2 **Aue** (riv.), Ger.
51/F3 **Aue** (riv.), Ger.
57/K1 **Auerbach**, Ger.
57/J2 **Auerbach in der Oberpfalz**, Ger.
44/A3 **Augher**, NI,UK
44/B3 **Aughnacloy**, NI,UK
102/C3 **Augrabies Falls Nat'l Park**, SAfr.
102/C3 **Augrabiesvalle** (falls), SAfr.
55/G1 **Augsburg**, Ger.
102/A2 **Augub** (peak), Namb.
60/D4 **Augusta**, It.
60/D4 **Augusta** (gulf), It.
129/H3 **Augusta**, Ga,US
127/G2 **Augusta** (cap.), Me,US
51/F5 **Augustdorf**, Ger.
49/M2 **Augustów**, Pol.
83/B3 **Auk Bok** (isl.), Myan.
59/M9 **Aulencia** (riv.), Sp.
56/B2 **Aulne** (riv.), Fr.
52/C3 **Aulnoye-Aymeries**, Fr.
52/B5 **Aunette** (riv.), Fr.
102/B2 **Auob** (dry riv.), Namb.
102/C2 **Auobrivier** (dry riv.), SAfr.
92/G4 **Aur** (atoll), Mrsh.
84/C4 **Aurangābād**, India
84/D3 **Aurangābād**, India
56/B3 **Auray**, Fr.
56/D5 **Aureilhan**, Fr.
51/E2 **Aurich**, Ger.
110/B2 **Auriflama**, Braz.
56/E4 **Aurillac**, Fr.
125/F3 **Aurora**, Co,US
132/P16 **Aurora**, Il,US
125/J3 **Aurora**, Mo,US
125/H2 **Aurora**, Ne,US
90/A1 **Aurukun Abor. Land**, Austl.
126/C2 **Au Sable** (riv.), Mi,US
49/K3 **Auschwitz** (Oświęcim), Pol.
56/E5 **Aussillon**, Fr.
42/C4 **Aust-Agder** (co.), Nor.
118/G2 **Austin** (isl.), Nun.,Can
123/K5 **Austin**, Mn,US
124/C3 **Austin**, Nv,US
128/D4 **Austin** (cap.), Tx,US
89/* **Australia**
91/C3 **Australian Alps** (mts.), Austl.
91/D3 **Australian Cap. Terr.**, Austl.
57/L3 **Austria**
42/P7 **Austurhorn** (pt.), Ice.
52/B3 **Authie** (riv.), Fr.
117/P10 **Autlán de Navarro**, Mex.
52/B5 **Automne** (riv.), Fr.
56/F3 **Autun**, Fr.
56/E4 **Auvergne** (reg.), Fr.
52/B5 **Auvers-sur-Oise**, Fr.
56/D4 **Auvézère** (riv.), Fr.
56/E3 **Auxerre**, Fr.
54/B3 **Auxonne**, Fr.
126/D2 **Aux Sables** (riv.), On,Can
119/K2 **Auyuittuq Nat'l Park**, Nun.,Can
108/D6 **Auzangate** (peak), Peru
56/E3 **Avallon**, Fr.
127/K2 **Avalon** (pen.), Nf,Can
110/B2 **Avaré**, Braz.
47/E4 **Avebury**, Eng,UK
58/A2 **Aveiro**, Port.
58/A2 **Aveiro** (dist.), Port.
52/C2 **Avelgem**, Belg.
112/F2 **Avellaneda**, Arg.
60/D2 **Avellino**, It.
52/A4 **Avelon** (riv.), Fr.
124/B3 **Avenal**, Ca,US
52/A58 **Aver** (riv.), Fr.
60/D2 **Aversa**, It.
117/J4 **Aves** (isl.), Ven.
42/F3 **Avesta**, Swe.
56/D4 **Aveyron** (riv.), Fr.
60/C1 **Avezzano**, It.
43/D2 **Aviemore**, Sc,UK
56/F5 **Avignon**, Fr.
58/C2 **Ávila de los Caballeros**, Sp.
58/C1 **Avilés**, Sp.
52/B3 **Avion**, Fr.
58/B3 **Avis**, Port.
44/B6 **Avoca**, Ire.
44/B6 **Avoca** (riv.), Ire.
60/D4 **Avola**, It.
56/E2 **Avon**, Fr.
46/C6 **Avon** (riv.), Eng,UK
46/D4 **Avon** (riv.), Eng,UK
47/E2 **Avon** (riv.), Eng,UK
47/E5 **Avon** (riv.), Eng,UK
44/B6 **Avonbeg** (riv.), Ire.
123/G3 **Avonlea**, Sk,Can
44/B6 **Avonmore** (riv.), Ire.
46/D4 **Avonmouth**, Eng,UK
56/C2 **Avranches**, Fr.
52/B4 **Avre** (riv.), Fr.
56/C3 **Avrillé**, Fr.
79/L10 **Awaji**, Japan
78/D3 **Awaji** (isl.), Japan
74/L5 **A'waj, Nahr al** (riv.), Syria
53/E2 **Awans**, Belg.
97/N6 **Āwasa**, Eth.
97/P5 **Āwash Wenz** (riv.), Eth.
102/A2 **Awasibberge** (peak), Namb.
96/H2 **Awbārī**, Libya
43/C2 **Awe, Loch** (lake), Sc,UK
97/K2 **Awjilah**, Libya
42/P6 **Axarfjördhur** (bay), Ice.
46/D4 **Axbridge**, Eng,UK
46/D4 **Axe** (riv.), Eng,UK
46/D5 **Axe** (riv.), Eng,UK
50/A6 **Axel**, Neth.
119/S7 **Axel Heiberg** (isl.), Nun.,Can
99/E5 **Axim**, Gha.
61/H2 **Axios** (riv.), Gre.
46/D5 **Axminster**, Eng,UK
65/N5 **Ay** (riv.), Rus.
78/D3 **Ayabe**, Japan
112/F3 **Ayacucho**, Arg.
108/D6 **Ayacucho**, Peru
75/D2 **Ayaguz**, Kaz.
75/D2 **Ayaguz** (riv.), Kaz.
75/E4 **Ayakkum** (lake), China
79/M10 **Ayama**, Japan
98/E5 **Ayamé, Barrage d'** (dam), IvC.
58/B4 **Ayamonte**, Sp.
74/C2 **Ayancık**, Turk.
117/F6 **Ayapel**, Col.
79/H7 **Ayase**, Japan
108/D6 **Ayaviri**, Peru
73/J1 **Āybak**, Afg.
74/N8 **'Aybāl, Jabal** (Har Eval) (mtn.), WBnk.
74/A3 **Aydın**, Turk.
74/C3 **Aydıncık**, Turk.
92/C7 **Ayers Rock** (Uluru) (peak), Austl.
85/G4 **Ayeyarwady** (riv.), Myan.
61/J3 **Áyios Evstrátios** (isl.), Gre.
61/J5 **Áyios Ioánnis, Ákra** (cape), Gre.
61/J5 **Áyios Nikólaos**, Gre.
47/F3 **Aylesbury**, Eng,UK
47/G4 **Aylesford**, Eng,UK
47/H4 **Aylesham**, Eng,UK
118/F2 **Aylmer** (lake), NW,Can
47/H1 **Aylsham**, Eng,UK
74/D3 **'Ayn al 'Arab**, Syria
97/K2 **'Ayn Ath Tha'lab**, Libya
72/D1 **'Ayn, Ra's al**, Syria
97/K3 **'Ayn Zuwayyah** (well), Libya
69/S3 **Ayon** (isl.), Rus.
59/E3 **Ayora**, Sp.
96/D3 **'Ayoûn 'Abd el Mâlek** (well), Mrta.
90/B2 **Ayr**, Austl.
43/C3 **Ayr**, Sc,UK
44/D3 **Ayre, Point of** (pt.), Eng,UK
45/H3 **Ayton**, Eng,UK
63/H4 **Aytos**, Bul.
56/C3 **Aytré**, Fr.
116/B4 **Ayutla**, Mex.
83/C3 **Ayutthaya** (ruins), Thai.
74/A2 **Ayvacık**, Turk.
74/A2 **Ayvalık**, Turk.
53/E3 **Aywaille**, Belg.
59/E3 **Azahar** (coast), Sp.
79/M9 **Azaj**, Japan
122/C5 **Azalea**, Or,US
84/D2 **Azamgarh**, India
108/D6 **Azángaro**, Peru
96/G2 **Azao** (peak), Alg.
99/E2 **Azaouâd** (reg.), Mali
99/G2 **Azaouak, Vallée de l'** (wadi), Mali, Niger
74/D3 **A'zāz**, Syria
67/H4 **Azerbaijan**
97/N5 **Āzezo**, Eth.
75/E1 **Azhu-Tayga, Gora** (peak), Rus.
108/C4 **Azogues**, Ecu.
59/R12 **Azores** (aut. reg.), Port.
59/R12 **Azores** (isls.), Port.
66/F3 **Azov**, Rus.
66/E3 **Azov** (sea), Rus., Ukr.
58/D1 **Azpeitia**, Sp.
124/F3 **Aztec**, NM,US
124/E3 **Aztec Ruins Nat'l Mon.**, NM,US
117/G4 **Azua**, DRep.
58/C3 **Azuaga**, Sp.
79/M9 **Azuchi**, Japan
117/F6 **Azuero** (pen.), Pan.
112/F3 **Azul**, Arg.
79/G2 **Azuma-san** (mtn.), Japan
79/F2 **Azumaya-san** (mtn.), Japan
57/G5 **Azur, Côte d'** (coast), Fr.
131/C2 **Azuza**, Ca,US
74/L5 **Az Zabadānī**, Syria
100/B2 **Az Zaqāzīq**, Egypt
57/K4 **Azzano Decimo**, It.
74/L5 **Az Zarqā'**, Jor.
96/H1 **Az Zāwiyah**, Libya

B

93/Y18 **Ba**, Fiji
83/E3 **Ba** (riv.), Viet.
93/U11 **Baaba** (isl.), NCal.
74/N9 **Ba'al Hazor** (Tall 'Āsūr) (mtn.), WBnk.
55/E3 **Baar**, Swi.
50/C4 **Baarn**, Neth.
76/D2 **Baatsagaan**, Mong.
73/J2 **Baba** (mts.), Afg.
63/F4 **Baba** (peak), Bul.
66/D4 **Baba Burnu** (pt.), Turk.
63/J3 **Babadag**, Rom.
63/H5 **Babaeski**, Turk.
108/C4 **Babahoyo**, Ecu.
87/G5 **Babar** (isl.), Indo.
101/B4 **Babati**, Tanz.
46/C5 **Babbacombe** (bay), Eng,UK
123/L4 **Babbitt**, Mn,US
124/C3 **Babbitt**, Nv,US
97/P5 **Bab el Mandeb** (str.), Afr., Asia
92/C4 **Babelthuap** (isl.), Palau
66/A2 **Babia Gora** (peak), Pol.
85/H3 **Babian** (riv.), China
122/B2 **Babine** (lake), BC,Can
118/D3 **Babine** (riv.), BC,Can
72/F1 **Bābol**, Iran
66/D1 **Babruysk**, Bela.
82/D4 **Babuyan** (isls.), Phil.
72/D2 **Babylon** (ruins), Iraq
131/G5 **Babylon**, NY,US
109/J4 **Bacabal**, Braz.
109/H4 **Bacajá** (riv.), Braz.
87/G4 **Bacan** (isl.), Indo.
63/H2 **Bacău**, Rom.
63/H2 **Bacău** (co.), Rom.
83/D1 **Bac Can**, Viet.
83/D1 **Bac Giang**, Viet.
118/G2 **Back** (riv.), Nun.,Can
126/E2 **Back** (lake), On,Can
131/K7 **Back** (riv.), Md,US
62/D3 **Bačka** (reg.), Yugo.
62/D3 **Bačka Palanka**, Yugo.
62/D3 **Bačka Topola**, Yugo.
57/H2 **Backnang**, Ger.
46/D4 **Backwell**, Eng,UK
83/D4 **Bac Lieu**, Viet.
83/D1 **Bac Ninh**, Viet.
82/D5 **Bacolod**, Phil.
83/D1 **Bac Quang**, Viet.
62/D2 **Bácsalmás**, Hun.
62/D2 **Bács-Kiskun** (co.), Hun.
47/H1 **Bacton**, Eng,UK
45/F4 **Bacup**, Eng,UK
123/H4 **Bad** (riv.), SD,US
84/C5 **Badagara**, India
76/E3 **Badain Jaran** (des.), China
58/B3 **Badajoz**, Sp.
59/L7 **Badalona**, Sp.
126/D3 **Bad Axe**, Mi,US
51/F6 **Bad Berleberg**, Ger.
53/G2 **Bad Breisig**, Ger.
48/F1 **Bad Doberan**, Ger.
51/G5 **Bad Driburg**, Ger.
57/M2 **Baden**, Aus.
57/H2 **Baden-Baden**, Ger.
55/E1 **Baden-Württemberg** (state), Ger.
51/F4 **Bad Essen**, Ger.
49/H2 **Bad Freienwalde**, Ger.
51/H5 **Bad Gandersheim**, Ger.
57/K3 **Bad Goisern**, Aus.
51/H5 **Bad Harzburg**, Ger.
48/E3 **Bad Hersfeld**, Ger.
57/H1 **Bad Homburg vor der Höhe**, Ger.
53/G2 **Bad Honnef**, Ger.
73/J4 **Badīn**, Pak.
57/K3 **Bad Ischl**, Aus.
57/G2 **Bad Kreuznach**, Ger.
54/D2 **Bad Krozingen**, Ger.
123/H4 **Badlands** (uplands), ND,US
123/H5 **Badlands** (hills), SD,US
123/H5 **Badlands Nat'l Park**, SD,US
51/H6 **Bad Langensalza**, Ger.
51/H5 **Bad Lauterberg**, Ger.
51/F3 **Bad Lippspringe**, Ger.
57/H2 **Bad Mergentheim**, Ger.
51/G4 **Bad Munder am Deister**, Ger.
53/F2 **Bad Münstereifel**, Ger.
57/H1 **Bad Nauheim**, Ger.
51/G4 **Bad Nenndorf**, Ger.
53/G2 **Bad Neuenahr-Ahrweiler**, Ger.
57/J1 **Bad Neustadt an der Saale**, Ger.
51/F4 **Bad Oeynhausen**, Ger.
48/F2 **Bad Oldesloe**, Ger.
51/G5 **Bad Pyrmont**, Ger.
73/J3 **Bādrāh**, Pak.
48/G5 **Bad Reichenhall**, Ger.
51/H5 **Bad Sachsa**, Ger.
51/H4 **Bad Salzdetfurth**, Ger.
51/F4 **Bad Salzuflen**, Ger.
48/F3 **Bad Salzungen**, Ger.
51/F5 **Bad Sassendorf**, Ger.
48/F2 **Bad Schwartau**, Ger.
48/F2 **Bad Segeberg**, Ger.
51/G6 **Bad Sooden-Allendorf**, Ger.
55/H2 **Bad Tölz**, Ger.
84/D6 **Badulla**, SrL.
57/M3 **Bad Vöslau**, Aus.
51/G6 **Bad Wildungen**, Ger.
51/E2 **Bad Zwischenahn**, Ger.
58/C4 **Baena**, Sp.
110/J6 **Baependi**, Braz.
53/F2 **Baesweiler**, Ger.
58/D4 **Baeza**, Sp.
99/H5 **Bafang**, Camr.
119/H1 **Baffin** (isl.), Nun.,Can
119/K1 **Baffin** (bay), Can.,Grld.
128/D5 **Baffin** (bay), Tx,US
96/H7 **Bafia**, Camr.
98/D4 **Bafing** (riv.), Gui., IvC.
98/C3 **Bafing** (riv.), Gui., Mali
99/H5 **Bafoussam**, Camr.
74/C2 **Bafra**, Turk.
98/B2 **Bafrechié** (well), Mrta.
97/L7 **Bafwasende**, D.R. Congo
81/B3 **Bag** (salt lake), China
96/H5 **Baga**, Nga.
82/E6 **Baganga**, Phil.
99/G3 **Bagaroua**, Niger
75/E3 **Bagda** (mts.), China
113/G1 **Bagé**, Braz.
82/D4 **Bagao**, Phil.
46/B4 **Baggy** (pt.), Eng,UK
72/D2 **Baghdad** (Baghdād) (cap.), Iraq
60/C3 **Bagheria**, It.
73/J1 **Baghlān**, Afg.
46/C3 **Baglan**, Wal,UK
123/K4 **Bagley**, Mn,US
56/D5 **Bagnères-de-Bigorre**, Fr.
56/F4 **Bagnols-sur-Cèze**, Fr.
82/D5 **Bago**, Phil.
98/D3 **Bagoe** (riv.), IvC., Mali
83/B2 **Bago** (Pegu) (div.), Myan.
82/D4 **Baguio**, Phil.
96/J5 **Baguirmi** (reg.), Chad
99/H2 **Bagzane** (peak), Niger
117/F2 **Bahamas**
84/E3 **Baharampur**, India
75/B6 **Bahāwalnagar**, Pak.
73/K3 **Bahāwalpur**, Pak.
101/B4 **Bahi**, Tanz.
116/D4 **Bahía** (isls.), Hon.
117/M8 **Bahia Asunción**, Mex.
112/E3 **Bahía Blanca**, Arg.
117/M8 **Bahía de los Angeles**, Mex.
84/D3 **Bahía Honda**, Cuba
117/M8 **Bahía Kino**, Mex.
117/M8 **Bahía Tortugas**, Mex.
97/N5 **Bahir Dar**, Eth.
73/G4 **Bahlah**, Oman
84/D2 **Bahraich**, India
72/F3 **Bahrain**
72/F3 **Bahrain** (gulf), Bahr., SAr.
72/D2 **Baḩr al Milḩ** (lake), Iraq
97/K6 **Bahr Aouk** (riv.), CAfr., Chad
100/B2 **Baḩrīyah, Al Wāḩāt al** (oasis), Egypt
81/C2 **Bai** (riv.), China
81/C4 **Bai** (riv.), China
63/F2 **Baia Mare**, Rom.
63/F2 **Baia Sprie**, Rom.
96/J6 **Baïbokoum**, Chad
77/J2 **Baicheng**, China
75/D3 **Baicheng**, China
63/G3 **Băicoi**, Rom.
97/P7 **Baidoa**, Som.
81/D5 **Baidong** (lake), China
127/G1 **Baie-Comeau**, Qu,Can
119/J3 **Baie-du-Poste**, Qu,Can
127/G2 **Baie-Saint-Paul**, Qu,Can
127/K1 **Baie Verte**, Nf,Can
81/G7 **Baigou** (riv.), China
81/C3 **Baihua Shan** (mtn.), China
72/D2 **Ba'ījī**, Iraq
69/L4 **Baikal** (Baykal) (lake), Rus.
45/G4 **Baildon**, Eng,UK
58/D3 **Bailén**, Sp.
63/F3 **Băileşti**, Rom.
52/B2 **Bailleul**, Fr.
76/E5 **Bailong** (riv.), China
81/C4 **Bailu** (riv.), China
45/H5 **Bain** (riv.), Eng,UK
129/G4 **Bainbridge**, Ga,US
132/B2 **Bainbridge** (isl.), Wa,US
75/D4 **Bairab** (lake), China
130/F3 **Baird** (inlet), Ak,US
128/D3 **Baird**, Tx,US
91/C3 **Bairnsdale**, Austl.
74/L6 **Bā'ir, Wādī** (riv.), Jor.
56/D5 **Baïse** (riv.), Fr.
84/D2 **Baitadi**, Nepal
83/D2 **Bai Thuong**, Viet.
59/P10 **Baixa de Banheira**, Port.
110/D1 **Baixo Guandu**, Braz.
76/E4 **Baiyin**, China
81/B3 **Baiyu** (mts.), China
82/C2 **Baiyun**, China
113/J7 **Baja** (pt.), Chile
62/D2 **Baja**, Hun.
117/L8 **Baja California** (pen.), Mex.
117/L7 **Baja California** (state), Mex.
117/M8 **Baja California Sur** (state), Mex.
60/A4 **Bājah**, Tun.
60/A4 **Bājah** (gov.), Tun.
87/F5 **Bajawa**, Indo.
62/D4 **Bajina Bašta**, Yugo.
91/E1 **Bajmba** (peak), Austl.
62/D3 **Bajmok**, Yugo.
117/F4 **Bajo Nuevo** (isl.), Col.
75/C2 **Bakanas** (riv.), Kaz.
87/E3 **Bakayan** (peak), Indo.
98/B3 **Bakel**, Sen.
118/G2 **Baker** (lake), Nun.,Can
113/J6 **Baker** (riv.), Chile
93/H4 **Baker** (isl.), PacUS
124/C4 **Baker**, Ca,US
123/G4 **Baker**, Mt,US
124/D3 **Baker**, Nv,US
122/D4 **Baker**, Or,US
122/C3 **Baker** (peak), Wa,US
124/C4 **Bakersfield**, Ca,US
45/G5 **Bakewell**, Eng,UK
66/E3 **Bakhchisaray**, Ukr.
66/E2 **Bakhmach**, Ukr.
72/E2 **Bākhtarān**, Iran
72/F3 **Bakhtegān** (lake), Iran
42/P6 **Bakkaflói** (bay), Ice.
104/B1 **Bakoumba**, Gabon
98/C4 **Bakoye** (riv.), Gui., Mali
67/J4 **Baku** (cap.), Azer.
105/S **Bakutis** (coast), Ant.
108/E6 **Bala** (mts.), Bol.
44/E6 **Bala**, Wal,UK
87/E2 **Balabac** (str.), Malay., Phil.
82/C6 **Balabac**, Phil.
82/C6 **Balabac** (isl.), Phil.
74/L5 **Ba'labakk**, Leb.
93/U12 **Balabio** (isl.), NCal.
72/D2 **Balad**, Iraq
84/D3 **Bālāghāt**, India
60/A1 **Balagne** (range), Fr.
59/F2 **Balaguer**, Sp.
56/C5 **Balaïtous** (mtn.), Fr.
104/F3 **Balaka**, Malw.
65/J4 **Balakhna**, Rus.
67/H1 **Balakovo**, Rus.
73/H1 **Bālā Morghab**, Afg.
63/G2 **Bălan**, Rom.
116/C4 **Balancán**, Mex.
82/D5 **Balanga**, Phil.
83/E3 **Ba Lang An** (cape), Viet.
84/D3 **Balāngir**, India
65/X9 **Balashikha**, Rus.
67/G2 **Balashov**, Rus.
62/D1 **Balassagyarmat**, Hun.
62/C2 **Balaton** (lake), Hun.
62/C2 **Balatonfüred**, Hun.
112/F3 **Balcarce**, Arg.
44/E2 **Balcary** (pt.), Sc,UK
63/J4 **Balchik**, Bul.
89/J7 **Balclutha**, NZ
47/F4 **Balcombe**, Eng,UK
128/D4 **Balcones Escarpment** (plat.), Tx,US
129/H2 **Bald** (peak), Va,US
47/F3 **Baldock**, Eng,UK
91/E1 **Bald Rock Nat'l Park**, Austl.
131/C2 **Baldwin Park**, Ca,US
123/H3 **Baldy** (peak), Mb,Can
59/F3 **Balearic** (Baleares) (isls.), Sp.
110/E1 **Baleia, Ponta da** (pt.), Braz.
119/K3 **Baleine** (riv.), Qu,Can

142

Balei – Belm

119/J3 Baleine, Grande Rivière de la (riv.), Qu,Can
119/J3 Baleine, Petite Rivière de la (riv.), Qu,Can
97/N6 Bale Mountains Nat'l Park, Eth.
53/E1 Balen, Belg.
82/D4 Baler, Phil.
84/E3 Baleshwar, India
76/H1 Baley, Rus.
84/B2 Bali, India
86/D5 Bali (isl.), Indo.
86/D5 Bali (sea), Indo.
74/A2 Balıkesir, Turk.
87/E4 Balikpapan, Indo.
82/D6 Balingasag, Phil.
55/E1 Balingen, Ger.
63/F4 Balkan (mts.), Eur.
67/K4 Balkhan Obl., Trkm.
75/C2 Balkhash, Kaz.
75/B2 Balkhash (lake), Kaz.
44/B4 Ballagan (pt.), Ire.
44/C1 Ballantrae, Sc,UK
91/B3 Ballarat, Austl.
84/C4 Ballarpur, India
44/D3 Ballaugh, IM,UK
105/L Balleny (isls.), Ant.
91/E1 Ballina, Austl.
43/A3 Ballina, Ire.
43/A4 Ballinasloe, Ire.
44/B2 Ballinderry (riv.), NI,UK
128/D4 Ballinger, Tx,US
44/B1 Ballintoy, NI,UK
44/C2 Ballycarry, NI,UK
44/B1 Ballycastle, NI,UK
44/B2 Ballyclare, NI,UK
44/C2 Ballyeaston, NI,UK
44/A3 Ballygawley, NI,UK
44/C3 Ballygowan, NI,UK
44/C3 Ballyhalbert, NI,UK
44/A1 Ballykelly, NI,UK
44/B2 Ballymena, NI,UK
44/B2 Ballymena (dist.), NI,UK
44/B1 Ballymoney, NI,UK
44/B1 Ballymoney (dist.), NI,UK
44/C3 Ballynahinch, NI,UK
44/C2 Ballynure, NI,UK
44/C3 Ballyquintin (pt.), NI,UK
44/C2 Ballywalter, NI,UK
113/J7 Balmaceda (peak), Chile
62/E2 Balmazújváros, Hun.
123/K3 Balmertown, On,Can
110/B3 Balneario Camboriú, Braz.
113/T12 Balneario Carras, Uru.
90/C4 Balonne (riv.), Austl.
84/B2 Bālotra, India
81/B3 Balougou, China
84/D2 Balrāmpur, India
63/G3 Balş, Rom.
47/E2 Balsall Common, Eng,UK
109/J5 Balsas, Braz.
109/J5 Balsas (riv.), Braz.
116/A4 Balsas (riv.), Mex.
42/F4 Baltic (sea), Eur.
49/K1 Baltic (spit), Pol., Rus.
74/H6 Baltīm, Egypt
131/K7 Baltimore, Md,US
131/K7 Baltimore Highlands-Lansdown, Md,US
49/K1 Baltiysk, Rus.
51/E1 Baltrum (isl.), Ger.
73/H3 Baluchistan (reg.), Iran, Pak.
84/E2 Bālurghāt, India
51/E6 Balve, Ger.
67/J3 Balykshi, Kaz.
99/E3 Bam (prov.), Burk.
75/F5 Bam (lake), China
73/G3 Bam, Iran
96/H5 Bama, Nga.
126/A1 Bamaji (lake), On,Can
98/D3 Bamako (cap.), Mali
98/D3 Bamako (reg.), Mali
108/C5 Bambamarca, Peru
97/K6 Bambari, CAfr.
57/J2 Bamberg, Ger.
129/H3 Bamberg, SC,US
45/F4 Bamber Bridge, Eng,UK
42/D4 Bamble, Nor.
110/C2 Bambuí, Braz.
99/H5 Bamenda, Camr.
73/J2 Bāmiān, Afg.
97/K6 Bamingui-Bangoran Nat'l Park, CAfr.
117/N8 Bamoa, Mex.
46/C5 Bampton, Eng,UK
73/H3 Bampūr (riv.), Iran
92/F5 Banaba (isl.), Kiri.
98/D3 Banamba, Mali
98/B4 Banana (isls.), SLeo.
104/B2 Banana, D.R. Congo
84/B2 Banās (riv.), India
100/C4 Banās, Ra's (pt.), Egypt
62/E3 Banatsko Novo Selo, Yugo.
74/B2 Banaz, Turk.
44/B3 Banbridge, NI,UK
44/B3 Banbridge (dist.), NI,UK
47/E2 Banbury, Eng,UK
96/B3 Banc d'Arguin Nat'l Park, Mrta.
83/C2 Ban Chiang (ruins), Thai.
43/D2 Banchory, Sc,UK
116/D4 Banco Chinchorro (isls.), Mex.
126/E2 Bancroft, On,Can
87/H4 Banda (isls.), Indo.
87/G5 Banda (sea), Indo.
86/A2 Banda Aceh, Indo.
79/G2 Bandai-Asahi Nat'l Park, Japan
79/G2 Bandai-san (mtn.), Japan
98/D5 Bandama (riv.), IvC.
98/D4 Bandama Blanc (riv.), IvC.
98/D4 Bandama Rouge (riv.), IvC.
73/H3 Bandar Beheshtī (Chāh Bahār), Iran
73/G3 Bandar-e 'Abbās, Iran
72/E1 Bandar-e Anzalī, Iran
72/F3 Bandar-e Būshehr, Iran
72/E2 Bandar-e Māhshahr, Iran
72/F1 Bandar-e Torkeman, Iran
86/D3 Bandar Seri Begawan (cap.), Bru.
110/D2 Bandeira (peak), Braz.
124/F4 Bandelier Nat'l Mon., NM,US
128/D4 Bandera, Tx,US
117/N9 Banderas (bay), Mex.
98/E3 Bandiagara, Mali
75/B5 Bandipura, India
63/H5 Bandırma, Turk.
63/J5 Bandirma (gulf), Turk.
85/J5 Ban Don, Viet.
104/C1 Bandundu, D.R. Congo
86/C5 Bandung, Indo.
59/E3 Bañeres, Sp.
43/D2 Banff, Sc,UK
122/E3 Banff Nat'l Park, Ab, BC,Can
98/D4 Banfora, Burk.
82/D6 Bañga, Phil.
84/C5 Bangalore, India
99/H5 Bangangté, Camr.
97/K7 Bangassou, CAfr.
87/E2 Bangau, Tanjong (cape), Malay.
87/F4 Banggai (isls.), Indo.
75/C5 Banggong (lake), China
83/D2 Banghiang (riv.), Laos
86/C4 Bangka (isl.), Indo.
86/B4 Bangka (str.), Indo.
83/C3 Bangkok (bight), Thai.
83/C3 Bangkok (Krung Thep) (cap.), Thai.
84/E3 Bangladesh
83/C5 Bang Lang (res.), Thai.
44/C2 Bangor, NI,UK
44/D5 Bangor, Wal,UK
127/G2 Bangor, Me,US
45/F6 Bangor-is-y-Coed, Wal,UK
104/D2 Bangu, D.R. Congo
82/D4 Bangued, Phil.
97/J7 Bangui (cap.), CAfr.
100/B2 Banhā, Egypt
104/F5 Banhine Nat'l Park, Moz.
117/G4 Baní, DRep.
98/D3 Bani (riv.), Mali
98/D3 Banifing (riv.), Burk., Mali
73/L2 Banihāl (pass), India
100/B2 Banī Mazār, Egypt
129/J2 Banister (riv.), Va,US
74/K6 Banī Suhaylah, Gaza
100/B2 Banī Suwayf, Egypt
100/B2 Banī Suwayf (gov.), Egypt
74/K4 Bāniyās, Syria
62/C3 Banja Luka, Bosn.
86/D4 Banjarmasin, Indo.
98/A3 Banjul (cap.), Gam.
83/B5 Ban Kantang, Thai.
85/J4 Ban Kengkok, Laos
82/C2 Bankengting, China
83/D3 Ban Khampho, Laos
83/C5 Ban Khuan Niang, Thai.
91/B3 Banks (cape), Austl.
91/C4 Banks (str.), Austl.
118/C3 Banks (isl.), BC,Can
118/D1 Banks (isl.), NW,Can
130/H4 Banks (pt.), Ak,US
122/D4 Banks (lake), Wa,US
92/F6 Banks (isls.), Van.
90/H8 Bankstown, Austl.
84/E3 Bānkura, India
61/H1 Bankya, Bul.
83/D2 Ban Loboy, Laos
83/E3 Ban Mdrack, Viet.
83/D2 Ban Mong, Viet.
83/D2 Ban Muangsen, Laos
43/B4 Bann (riv.), Ire.
44/B2 Bann (riv.), NI,UK
83/D2 Ban Nape, Laos
73/K2 Bannu, Pak.
62/D3 Banovići, Bosn.
83/C4 Ban Pak Phanang, Thai.
83/D3 Ban Phon, Laos
81/B4 Banpo (ruins), China
83/C2 Ban Sieou, Laos
49/K4 Banská Bystrica, Slvk.
63/F5 Bansko, Bul.
47/F4 Banstead, Eng,UK
84/B3 Bānswāra, India
82/D5 Bantayan, Phil.
86/D5 Bantenan (cape), Indo.
83/C2 Ban Thabok, Laos
83/B5 Bantong Group (isls.), Thai.
58/C3 Bañuelo (mtn.), Sp.
83/D3 Ban Xebang-Nouan, Laos
86/A3 Banyak (isls.), Indo.
59/G1 Banyoles, Sp.
86/D5 Banyuwangi, Indo.
105/J Banzare (coast), Ant.
60/A4 Banzart (gov.), Tun.
60/A4 Banzart (lake), Tun.
60/A4 Banzart (Bizerte), Tun.
81/B3 Baode, China
81/D3 Baodi, China
81/C3 Baoding, China
81/D4 Baodugu (mtn.), China
83/D1 Bao Ha, Viet.
76/F5 Baoji, China
85/J2 Baojing, China
83/D1 Bao Lac, Viet.
83/D4 Bao Loc, Viet.
81/E5 Baoshan, China
85/G2 Baoshan, China
81/B2 Baotou, China
98/D4 Baoulé (riv.), IvC., Mali
98/C3 Baoulé (riv.), Mali
84/D4 Bāpatla, India
74/K5 Bāqa el Gharbiyya, Isr.
83/D4 Ba Quan (cape), Viet.
72/D2 Ba'qūbah, Iraq
52/D5 Bar (riv.), Fr.
62/D4 Bar, Yugo.
83/D4 Ba Ra, Viet.
97/P7 Baraawe, Som.
86/E4 Barabai, Indo.
68/H4 Barabinsk, Rus.
126/B3 Baraboo, Wi,US
58/D1 Baracaldo, Sp.
74/L5 Baradá (riv.), Syria
112/F2 Baradero, Arg.
97/M5 Bārah, Sudan
117/G4 Barahona, DRep.
75/C5 Bārā Lācha La (pass), India
86/D3 Baram (cape), Malay.
86/D3 Baram (riv.), Malay.
108/G2 Barama (riv.), Guy.
84/B4 Bārāmati, India
73/K2 Bāramula, India
84/C2 Bāran, India
66/C1 Baranavichy, Bela.
130/L4 Baranof (isl.), Ak,US
62/C3 Baranya (co.), Hun.
110/D1 Barão de Cocais, Braz.
63/G2 Baraolt, Rom.
53/E3 Baraque de Fraiture (hill), Belg.
87/G5 Barat Daya (isls.), Indo.
110/D2 Barbacena, Braz.
117/J5 Barbados
100/C5 Barbar, Sudan
59/F1 Barbastro, Sp.
58/C4 Barbate de Franco, Sp.
119/T6 Barbeau (peak), Nun.,Can
59/L6 Barbera del Valles, Sp.
120/V13 Barbers (pt.), Hi,US
103/E2 Barberton, SAfr.
126/D3 Barberton, Oh,US
56/C4 Barbezieux-Saint-Hilaire, Fr.
84/E3 Barbil, India
45/F3 Barbon, Eng,UK
126/D4 Barbourville, Ky,US
117/J4 Barbuda (isl.), Ant. & Barb.
62/F2 Barcău (riv.), Rom.
60/D3 Barcellona Pozzo di Gotto, It.
59/L7 Barcelona, Sp.
117/J5 Barcelona, Ven.
58/A2 Barcelos, Port.
49/J2 Barcin, Pol.
90/A4 Barcoo (riv.), Austl.
62/C3 Barcs, Hun.
49/L2 Barczewo, Pol.
96/J3 Bardaï, Chad
74/J6 Bardawīl, Sabkhat al (lag.), Egypt
49/L4 Bardejov, Slvk.
97/P7 Bardheere, Som.
45/H5 Bardney, Eng,UK
84/B3 Bārdoli, India
44/D6 Bardsey (isl.), Wal,UK
126/C4 Bardstown, Ky,US
97/R5 Bareeda, Som.
84/C2 Bareilly, India
50/B5 Barendrecht, Neth.
56/D2 Barentin, Fr.
58/J2 Barents (sea)
97/N4 Barentu, Erit.
56/C2 Barfleur, Pointe de (pt.), Fr.
84/D3 Bargarh, India
46/C3 Bargoed, Wal,UK
51/H1 Bargteheide, Ger.
76/F1 Barguzin (riv.), Rus.
84/D2 Barhaj, India
127/G2 Bar Harbor, Me,US
47/G2 Bar Hill, Eng,UK
84/C2 Bāri, India
60/E2 Bari, It.
96/F1 Barika, Alg.
116/C4 Barillas, Guat.
117/G6 Barinas, Ven.
104/C2 Baringa-Twana, D.R. Congo
84/E3 Baripāda, India
110/B2 Bariri, Braz.
100/B3 Bārīs, Egypt
84/F3 Barisāl, Bang.
86/B4 Barisan (mts.), Indo.
86/D4 Barito (riv.), Indo.
111/C1 Baritu Nat'l Park, Arg.
127/S9 Barker, NY,US
122/B3 Barkley (sound), BC,Can
126/C4 Barkley (lake), Ky,US
45/F6 Barlaston, Eng,UK
45/G4 Barlby, Eng,UK
53/E6 Bar-le-Duc, Fr.
60/E2 Barletta, It.
52/B3 Barlin, Fr.
49/H2 Barlinek, Pol.
111/E2 Barmejo (riv.), Arg.
84/B2 Barmer, India
46/B1 Barmouth, Wal,UK
51/G1 Barmstedt, Ger.
73/L2 Barnāla, India
45/G2 Barnard Castle, Eng,UK
75/D1 Barnaul, Rus.
131/F6 Barnegat (bay), NJ,US
50/C4 Barneveld, Neth.
49/G2 Barnim (reg.), Ger.
45/F4 Barnoldswick, Eng,UK
45/G4 Barnsley, Eng,UK
46/B4 Barnstaple, Eng,UK
46/B4 Barnstaple (Bideford) (bay), Eng,UK
46/E2 Barnt Green, Eng,UK
51/G5 Barntrup, Ger.
129/H3 Barnwell, SC,US
84/B3 Baroda, India
73/K1 Barowghīl (Khyber) (pass), Afg.
84/F2 Barpeta, India
117/H5 Barquisimeto, Ven.
44/D1 Barr, Sc,UK
109/K6 Barra, Braz.
110/B2 Barra Bonita, Braz.
110/B2 Barra Bonita (res.), Braz.
116/E5 Barra del Colorado Nat'l Park, CR
116/E5 Barra de Río Grande, Nic.
109/G7 Barra do Bugres, Braz.
109/J5 Barra do Corda, Braz.
109/H7 Barra do Garças, Braz.
110/K7 Barra do Piraí, Braz.
110/B4 Barra do Ribeiro, Braz.
110/J7 Barra Mansa, Braz.
108/C4 Barranca, Peru
108/C6 Barranca, Peru
108/D2 Barrancabermeja, Col.
117/N8 Barranca del Cobre Nat'l Park, Mex.
112/C2 Barrancas, Chile
117/G5 Barranquilla, Col.
110/B3 Barra Velha, Braz.
109/J6 Barreiras, Braz.
58/A3 Barreiro, Port.
103/G7 Barren, Nosy (isls.), Madg.
110/B2 Barretos, Braz.
122/E2 Barrhead, Ab,Can
44/D1 Barrhill, Sc,UK
126/E2 Barrie, On,Can
91/B1 Barrier (range), Austl.
122/C3 Barrière, BC,Can
132/P15 Barrington, Il,US
132/P15 Barrington Hills, Il,US
91/D1 Barrington Tops (peak), Austl.
91/D1 Barrington Tops Nat'l Park, Austl.
90/B2 Barron Gorge Nat'l Park, Austl.
110/D2 Barroso, Braz.
90/B1 Barrow (pt.), Austl.
118/G1 Barrow (str.), Nun.,Can
43/B4 Barrow (riv.), Ire.
130/G1 Barrow (pt.), Ak,US
45/H6 Barrowby, Eng,UK
45/F4 Barrowford, Eng,UK
45/E3 Barrow-in-Furness, Eng,UK
46/C4 Barry, Wal,UK
67/L4 Barsakel'mes (salt pan), Uzb.
73/L5 Bārshi, India
51/G4 Barsinghausen, Ger.
51/E2 Barssel, Ger.
124/C4 Barstow, Ca,US
56/F2 Bar-sur-Aube, Fr.
75/B4 Bartang (riv.), Taj.
48/G1 Barth, Ger.
63/L5 Bartın, Turk.
125/J3 Bartlesville, Ok,US
132/P16 Bartlett, Il,US
117/F3 Bartolomé Masó, Cuba
104/G5 Bartolomeu Dias, Moz.
47/F3 Barton in the Clay, Eng,UK
47/E5 Barton on Sea, Eng,UK
47/E1 Barton under Needwood, Eng,UK
45/H4 Barton-upon-Humber, Eng,UK
49/L1 Bartoszyce, Pol.
129/H5 Bartow, Fl,US
116/E6 Barú (vol.), Pan.
86/B3 Barumun (riv.), Indo.
86/A3 Barus, Indo.
76/C2 Baruun Huuray (reg.), Mong.
76/G2 Baruun-Urt, Mong.
84/C3 Barwāha, India
84/B3 Barwāni, India
91/D1 Barwon (riv.), Austl.
49/J3 Barycz (riv.), Pol.
64/F5 Barysaw, Bela.
67/H1 Barysh, Rus.
97/J7 Basankusu, D.R. Congo
58/D1 Basauri, Sp.
112/F2 Basavilbaso, Arg.
46/D1 Baschurch, Eng,UK
54/D2 Basel, Swi.
54/D3 Baselland (canton), Swi.
60/E2 Basento (riv.), It.
102/E3 Bashee (riv.), SAfr.
82/D3 Bashi (chan.), Phil., Tai.
75/E1 Bashkaus (riv.), Rus.
65/M5 Bashkortostan Aut. Rep., Rus.
82/D6 Basilan (isl.), Phil.
87/F2 Basilan (peak), Phil.
47/G3 Basildon, Eng,UK
60/D2 Basilicata (reg.), It.
84/C3 Bāsim, India
122/F4 Basin, Wy,US
47/E4 Basingstoke, Eng,UK
74/F2 Başkale, Turk.
126/F2 Baskatong (res.), Qu,Can
84/C3 Bāsoda, India
97/K7 Basoko, D.R. Congo
58/D1 Basque Provinces (aut. comm.), Sp.
54/D1 Bas-Rhin (dept.), Fr.
91/C3 Bass (str.), Austl.
93/L7 Bass (isls.), FrPol.
61/G4 Bassae (ruins), Gre.
122/E3 Bassano, Ab,Can
57/J4 Bassano del Grappa, It.
104/G5 Bassas da India (isl.), Reun.
85/F4 Bassein, Myan.
85/F4 Bassein (riv.), Myan.
84/B4 Bassein, India
53/E2 Bassenge, Belg.
56/C2 Basse-Normandie (reg.), Fr.
44/E2 Bassenthwaite (lake), Eng,UK
117/J4 Basse-Terre (cap.), Guad.
117/J4 Basse-Terre (isl.), Guad.
117/J4 Basseterre (cap.), StK.
51/F3 Bassum, Ger.
126/B1 Basswood (lake), On,Can, Mn,US
42/E4 Båstad, Swe.
84/D2 Bastī, India
60/A1 Bastia, Fr.
60/C1 Bastia, It.
53/E3 Bastogne, Belg.
110/B2 Bastos, Braz.
128/F3 Bastrop, La,US
128/D4 Bastrop, Tx,US
74/H6 Basyūn, Egypt
96/G7 Bata, EqG.
116/E3 Batabanó (gulf), Cuba
82/D4 Batac, Phil.
69/P3 Batagay, Rus.
73/L2 Batāla, India
58/A3 Batalha, Port.
82/D3 Batan (isl.), Phil.
97/J6 Batangafo, CAfr.
82/D5 Batangas, Phil.
87/H4 Batanta (mtn.), Indo.
110/C2 Batatais, Braz.
132/P16 Batavia, Il,US
126/E3 Batavia, NY,US
66/F3 Bataysk, Rus.
85/H5 Batdambang, Camb.
90/H9 Bate (bay), Austl.
96/H8 Batéké (plat.), Congo
91/D2 Batemans Bay, Austl.
129/H3 Batesburg, SC,US
129/F3 Batesville, Ar,US
129/F3 Batesville, Ms,US
46/D4 Bath, Eng,UK
46/D4 Bath and Northeast Somerset (co.), Eng,UK
127/G3 Bath, Me,US
126/E3 Bath, NY,US
91/D2 Bathurst, Austl.
127/H2 Bathurst, NB,Can
130/N1 Bathurst (cape), NW,Can
118/F2 Bathurst (inlet), Nun.,Can
119/R7 Bathurst (isl.), Nun.,Can
97/P5 Batī, Eth.
75/F2 Batik (mts.), China
72/E3 Bāţin, Wādī al (dry riv.), SAr.
45/G4 Batley, Eng,UK
74/E3 Batman, Turk.
96/G1 Batna, Alg.
127/F4 Baton Rouge (cap.), La,US
96/H7 Batouri, Camr.
127/F2 Batiscan (riv.), Qu,Can
131/F6 Batsto (riv.), NJ,US
76/F2 Batsümber, Mong.
39/M9 Batterbee (cape), Ant.
45/G3 Battersby, Eng,UK
84/D6 Batticaloa, SrL.
122/F2 Battle (riv.), Ab, Sk,Can
47/G5 Battle, Eng,UK
122/F3 Battle (cr.), Mt,US
126/C3 Battle Creek, Mi,US
122/F2 Battleford, Sk,Can
124/C2 Battle Mountain, Nv,US
62/E2 Battonya, Hun.
76/E2 Battsengel, Mong.
97/N6 Batu (peak), Eth.
87/E3 Batu (cape), Indo.
86/A4 Batu (isls.), Indo.
86/D3 Batu (bay), Malay.
86/D3 Batu (peak), Malay.
87/F4 Batudaka (isl.), Indo.
86/D3 Batuensambang (peak), Indo.
86/B3 Batu Gajah, Malay.
67/G4 Bat'umi, Geo.
86/B3 Batu Pahat, Malay.
86/B3 Batu Puteh (peak), Malay.
86/B4 Baturaja, Indo.
109/L4 Baturité, Braz.
74/M8 Bat Yam, Isr.
99/H4 Bauchi (state), Nga.
123/K3 Baudette, Mn,US
119/L1 Bauld (cape), Nf,Can
99/F5 Bauman (peak), Togo
51/G6 Baunatal, Ger.
110/B2 Bauru, Braz.
49/H3 Bautzen, Ger.
55/G2 Bavaria (state), Ger.
55/G3 Bavarian Alps (mts.), Aus., Ger.
86/C4 Bawang (cape), Indo.
91/C3 Baw Baw (peak), Austl.
91/C3 Baw Baw Nat'l Park, Austl.
86/D5 Bawean (isl.), Indo.
99/E4 Bawku, Gha.
117/F3 Bayamo, Cuba
117/H4 Bayamón, PR
76/D5 Bayan Har (mts.), China
76/E2 Bayanhongor, Mong.
76/E3 Bayanleg, Mong.
75/F2 Bayannur, Mong.
76/E2 Bayan-Ovoo, Mong.
76/D2 Bayan-Uul, Mong.
125/G2 Bayard, Ne,US
82/D6 Bayawan, Phil.
53/G3 Baybach (riv.), Ger.
82/D5 Baybay, Phil.
74/E2 Bayburt, Turk.
126/D3 Bay City, Mi,US
128/E4 Bay City, Tx,US
68/G2 Baydaratskaya (bay), Rus.
76/D2 Baydrag (riv.), Mong.
57/K2 Bayerischer Wald Nat'l Park, Ger.
109/M5 Bayeux, Braz.
56/C2 Bayeux, Fr.
113/T11 Baygorria, Artificial de (res.), Uru.
72/E6 Bayḩān al Qisāb, Yem.
69/L4 Baykal (mts.), Rus.
76/F1 Baykal (Baikal) (lake), Rus.
129/G4 Bay Minette, Al,US
82/D4 Bayombong, Phil.
83/A1 Bayona, Sp.
129/H4 Bayonet Point, Fl,US
56/C5 Bayonne, Fr.
131/F5 Bayonne, NJ,US
131/G5 Bayport, NY,US
73/H1 Bayram-Ali, Trkm.
63/H5 Bayramiç, Turk.
57/J2 Bayreuth, Ger.
74/K5 Bayrūt (Beirut) (cap.), Leb.
126/E2 Bays (lake), On,Can
129/F4 Bay Saint Louis, Ms,US
59/E1 Bayse (riv.), Fr.
46/D1 Bayston Hill, Eng,UK
74/K6 Bayt Laḩm (Bethlehem), WBnk.
128/E4 Baytown, Tx,US
100/C5 Bayudha (des.), Sudan
82/E6 Bayugan, Phil.
131/G5 Bayville, NY,US
58/D4 Baza, Sp.
67/H4 Bazardyuzyu, Gora (peak), Rus.
104/G5 Bazaruto (isl.), Moz.
99/E4 Bazèga (prov.), Burk.
126/F2 Bazin (riv.), Qu,Can
131/F6 Beachwood, NJ,US
47/G5 Beachy Head (pt.), Eng,UK
46/C2 Beacon (hill), Wal,UK
127/N7 Beaconsfield, Qu,Can
47/F3 Beaconsfield, Eng,UK
46/B5 Beaford, Eng,UK
90/A4 Beal (mts.), Austl.
103/J6 Bealanana, Madg.
122/B3 Beale (cape), BC,Can
125/G4 Beals (cr.), Tx,US
46/D5 Beaminster, Eng,UK
103/H9 Beampingaratra (ridge), Madg.
127/R9 Beamsville, On,Can
123/K2 Bear (lake), Mb,Can
68/C2 Bear (isl.), Nor.
130/K2 Bear (mtn.), Ak,US
130/K3 Bear (mtn.), Ak,US
122/F5 Bear (lake), Id, Ut,US
122/F5 Bear (riv.), Id, Ut,US
105/M Beardmore (glac.), Ant.
122/F3 Bearpaw (mts.), Mt,US
43/C3 Bearsden, Sc,UK
122/F4 Beartooth (mts.), Mt, Wy,US
129/F4 Bear Town, Ms,US
58/D1 Beasain, Sp.
58/D3 Beas de Segura, Sp.
117/G4 Beata (cape), DRep.
125/H2 Beatrice, Ne,US
44/E1 Beattock, Sc,UK
124/C3 Beatty, Nv,US
56/F5 Beaucaire, Fr.
115/C2 Beaufort (sea), Can., US
129/H3 Beaufort, SC,US
102/C4 Beaufort West, SAfr.
56/D3 Beaugency, Fr.
127/N7 Beauharnois, Qu,Can
56/F4 Beaujolais (mts.), Fr.
47/E5 Beaulieu, Eng,UK
44/D5 Beaumaris, Wal,UK
52/B3 Beaumetz-les-Loges, Fr.
131/C3 Beaumont, Ca,US
128/E4 Beaumont, Tx,US
52/B5 Beaumont-sur-Oise, Fr.
56/F3 Beaune, Fr.
56/C3 Beaupréau, Fr.
53/D3 Beauraing, Belg.
123/J3 Beauséjour, Mb,Can
52/B5 Beauvais, Fr.
122/G2 Beauval, Sk,Can
122/F2 Beaver (riv.), Ab, Sk,Can
118/D2 Beaver (riv.), Yk,Can
125/G3 Beaver (riv.), Co,US
125/G3 Beaver (riv.), Ks, Ne,US
126/C2 Beaver (isl.), Mi,US
125/G3 Beaver (riv.), NM, Ok,US
125/G3 Beaver, Ok,US
124/D3 Beaver, Ut,US
130/K3 Beaver Creek, Yk,Can
126/B3 Beaver Dam, Wi,US
122/E4 Beaverhead (riv.), Mt,US
122/D2 Beaverlodge, Ab,Can
123/L2 Beaver Stone (riv.), On,Can
84/B2 Beāwar, India
110/B2 Bebedouro, Braz.
45/E5 Bebington, Eng,UK
51/G7 Bebra, Ger.
47/H2 Beccles, Eng,UK
62/E3 Bečej, Yugo.
96/E1 Bechar, Alg.
130/G4 Becharof (lake), Ak,US
130/G4 Becharof Nat'l Wild. Ref., Ak,US
53/F5 Beckingen, Ger.
45/H5 Beckingham, Eng,UK
126/D4 Beckley, WV,US
51/F5 Beckum, Ger.
63/G2 Beclean, Rom.
45/G3 Bedale, Eng,UK
50/D7 Bedburg, Ger.
50/D5 Bedburg-Hau, Ger.
46/C3 Beddau, Wal,UK
44/D5 Beddgelert, Wal,UK
90/B1 Bedford (cape), Austl.
127/F2 Bedford, Qu,Can
47/F2 Bedford, Eng,UK
126/C4 Bedford, In,US
126/E4 Bedford, Va,US
47/G2 Bedford Level (reg.), Eng,UK
47/F2 Bedfordshire (co.), Eng,UK
45/G1 Bedlington, Eng,UK
96/H4 Bedouaram (well), Niger
50/D2 Bedum, Neth.
46/C3 Bedwas, Wal,UK
47/E2 Bedworth, Eng,UK
90/D4 Beenleigh, Austl.
46/C5 Beer, Eng,UK
46/C5 Beer Head (pt.), Eng,UK
52/C1 Beernem, Belg.
74/K6 Beersheba (Be'er Sheva'), Isr.
53/D1 Beerzel, Belg.
50/D6 Beesel, Neth.
45/G6 Beeston, Eng,UK
128/D4 Beeville, Tx,US
97/K7 Befale, D.R. Congo
51/F5 Bega (riv.), Ger.
84/C3 Begamganj, India
67/K4 Begarslan (peak), Trkm.
62/E3 Bega Veche (riv.), Rom.
69/M2 Begichev (isl.), Rus.
44/B2 Beg, Lough (lake), NI,UK
42/D3 Begna (riv.), Nor.
84/E2 Begusarai, India
109/H3 Béhague (pt.), FrG.
86/B4 Behala (str.), Indo.
72/F2 Behbahān, Iran
53/F5 Behren-lès-Forbach, Fr.
72/F1 Behshahr, Iran
75/F3 Bei (mts.), China
82/A2 Bei (riv.), China
77/K2 Bei'an, China
76/D4 Beida (riv.), China
83/E1 Beihai, China
81/H7 Beijing (cap.), China
81/H6 Beijing (prov.), China
50/D3 Beilen, Neth.
76/C5 Beilu (riv.), China
83/D1 Beilun (pass), China
81/E2 Beipiao, China
104/F4 Beira, Moz.
81/C4 Beiru (riv.), China
74/K5 Beirut (Bayrūt) (cap.), Leb.
104/E5 Beitbridge, Zim.
62/F2 Beiuş, Rom.
58/B3 Beja, Port.
58/A4 Beja (dist.), Port.
96/F1 Bejaïa, Alg.
58/C2 Béjar, Sp.
73/J3 Bejhi (riv.), Pak.
74/K5 Bekaa (Al Biqā') (val.), Leb.
86/C5 Bekasi, Indo.
62/E2 Békés, Hun.
62/E2 Békés (co.), Hun.
62/E2 Békéscsaba, Hun.
103/H8 Bekily, Madg.
99/E5 Bekwai, Gha.
84/B3 Bela, India
73/J3 Bela, Pak.
62/E3 Bela Crkva, Yugo.
62/F4 Bela Palanka, Yugo.
41/G3 Belarus
59/P10 Belas, Port.
109/G8 Bela Vista, Braz.
110/B2 Bela Vista do Paraiso, Braz.
65/M5 Belaya (riv.), Rus.
67/G2 Belaya Kalitva, Rus.
66/D2 Belaya Tserkov', Ukr.
49/K3 Bełchatów, Pol.
119/S7 Belcher (chan.), Nun.,Can
119/H3 Belcher (isls.), Nun.,Can
123/J3 Belcourt, ND,US
65/M5 Belebey, Rus.
97/Q7 Beled Weyne, Som.
111/C2 Belén, Arg.
124/F4 Belen, NM,US
113/S12 Belén de Escobar, Arg.
63/G4 Belene, Bul.
58/B1 Belesar (res.), Sp.
97/N5 Beles Wenz (riv.), Eth.
66/F1 Belev, Rus.
44/C2 Belfast (cap.), NI,UK
44/C2 Belfast (dist.), NI,UK
127/G2 Belfast, Me,US
44/C2 Belfast Lough (inlet), NI,UK
123/H4 Belfield, ND,US
54/C2 Belfort, Fr.
54/C2 Belfort (dept.), Fr.
84/B4 Belgaum, India
48/C3 Belgium
66/F2 Belgorod, Rus.
66/D3 Belgorod-Dnestrovskiy, Ukr.
66/F2 Belgorod Obl., Rus.
122/F4 Belgrade, Mt,US
62/E3 Belgrade (Beograd) (cap.), Yugo.
62/E4 Beli Drim (riv.), Yugo.
62/D3 Beli Manastir, Cro.
62/F4 Beli Timok (riv.), Yugo.
86/C4 Belitung (isl.), Indo.
116/D4 Belize
116/D4 Belize City, Belz.
62/E3 Beljanica (peak), Yugo.
69/P2 Bel'kovskiy (isl.), Rus.
119/H2 Bell (pen.), Nun.,Can
126/E1 Bell (riv.), Qu,Can
131/B3 Bell, Ca,US
122/B2 Bella Coola, BC,Can
44/B2 Bellaghy, NI,UK
84/C4 Bellary, India
111/E2 Bella Vista, Arg.
60/A3 Bellavista (cape), It.
132/G7 Belle (riv.), On,Can
132/G6 Belle (riv.), Mi,US
52/C5 Belleau, Fr.
44/B3 Belleek, NI,UK
126/D3 Bellefontaine, Oh,US
123/G4 Belle Fourche (riv.), SD, Wy,US
54/B5 Bellegarde-sur-Valserine, Fr.
129/H5 Belle Glade, Fl,US
131/B2 Belle Haven, Va,US
56/B3 Belle-Île (isl.), Fr.
127/K1 Belle Isle (str.), Nf, Qu,Can
90/B2 Bellenden Ker Nat'l Park, Austl.
56/E3 Bellerive-sur-Allier, Fr.
126/E2 Belleville, On,Can
126/B4 Belleville, Il,US
125/H3 Belleville, Ks,US
131/F5 Belleville, NJ,US
132/C2 Bellevue, Wa,US
131/B3 Bellflower, Ca,US
45/F1 Bellingham, Eng,UK
122/C3 Bellingham, Wa,US
105/U Bellingshausen (sea), Ant.
93/K6 Bellingshausen (isl.), FrPol.
51/E2 Bellingwolde, Neth.
55/E5 Bellinzona, Swi.
131/E6 Bellmawr, NJ,US
131/G5 Bellmore, NY,US
108/C2 Bello, Col.
92/F7 Bellona (reefs), NCal.
118/G1 Bellot (str.), Nun.,Can
120/W13 Bellows A.F.B., Hi,US
131/H5 Bellport, NY,US
43/C3 Bellshill, Sc,UK
57/K3 Belluno, It.
112/E2 Bell Ville, Arg.
102/B4 Bellville, SAfr.
128/D4 Bellville, Tx,US
51/F4 Belm, Ger.

131/F5 **Belmar**, NJ,US
132/K11 **Belmont**, Ca,US
116/D4 **Belmopan** (cap.), Belz.
52/C2 **Beloeil**, Belg.
127/P6 **Beloeil**, Qu,Can
77/K1 **Belogorsk**, Rus.
62/F4 **Belogradchik**, Bul.
110/D1 **Belo Horizonte**, Braz.
125/H3 **Beloit**, Ks,US
126/B3 **Beloit**, Wi,US
109/L5 **Belo Jardim**, Braz.
64/G2 **Belomorsk**, Rus.
104/C1 **Belondo-Kundu**, D.R. Congo
66/F3 **Belorechensk**, Rus.
65/N5 **Beloretsk**, Rus.
62/E4 **Beloševac**, Yugo.
63/H4 **Beloslav**, Bul.
68/J4 **Belovo**, Rus.
64/H3 **Beloye** (lake), Rus.
45/G5 **Belper**, Eng,UK
45/G1 **Belsay**, Eng,UK
122/F4 **Belt**, Mt,US
50/D3 **Belterwijde** (lake), Neth.
47/H1 **Belton**, Eng,UK
128/D4 **Belton**, Tx,US
131/K7 **Beltsville**, Md,US
63/H2 **Bel'tsy**, Mol.
131/E5 **Beltzville** (lake), Pa,US
75/E2 **Belukha, Gora** (peak), Rus.
126/B3 **Belvidere**, Il,US
90/B3 **Belyando** (riv.), Austl.
68/G2 **Belyy** (isl.), Rus.
48/G2 **Belzig**, Ger.
49/M3 **Bełżyce**, Pol.
103/H7 **Bemaraha** (plat.), Madg.
103/H7 **Bemarivo** (riv.), Madg.
58/B1 **Bembibre**, Sp.
47/E5 **Bembridge**, Eng,UK
123/K4 **Bemidji**, Mn,US
50/C5 **Bemmel**, Neth.
45/H3 **Bempton**, Eng,UK
91/C3 **Benalla**, Austl.
58/C4 **Benalmádena**, Sp.
58/C2 **Benavente**, Sp.
128/D5 **Benavides**, Tx,US
44/B1 **Benbane Head** (pt.), NI,UK
91/D3 **Ben Boyd Nat'l Park**, Austl.
44/B3 **Benburb**, NI,UK
122/C4 **Bend**, Or,US
99/G5 **Bendel** (state), Nga.
130/F2 **Bendeleben** (mtn.), Ak,US
63/J2 **Bendery**, Mol.
91/C3 **Bendigo**, Austl.
74/M8 **Bene Beraq**, Isr.
119/L3 **Benedict** (mtn.), Nf,Can
44/D1 **Beneraid** (hill), Sc,UK
57/L2 **Benešov**, Czh.
60/D2 **Benevento**, It.
47/G3 **Benfleet**, Eng,UK
84/E4 **Bengal** (bay), Asia
81/D4 **Bengbu**, China
97/K1 **Benghāzī**, Libya
83/D3 **Ben Giang**, Viet.
86/B3 **Bengkalis**, Indo.
86/B3 **Bengkalis** (isl.), Indo.
86/C3 **Bengkayang**, Indo.
86/B4 **Bengkulu**, Indo.
123/G3 **Bengough**, Sk,Can
42/E4 **Bengtsfors**, Swe.
104/B3 **Benguela**, Ang.
101/A5 **Bengweulu** (lake), Zam.
108/E6 **Beni** (riv.), Bol.
101/A2 **Beni**, D.R. Congo
96/E1 **Beni Abbes**, Alg.
59/F2 **Benicarló**, Sp.
132/K10 **Benicia**, Ca,US
59/E3 **Benidorm**, Sp.
59/E3 **Benifayó**, Sp.
96/D1 **Beni Mellal**, Mor.
99/F4 **Benin**
99/F5 **Benin** (bight), Ben., Nga.
99/G5 **Benin City**, Nga.
96/E1 **Beni Ounif**, Alg.
59/F3 **Benisa**, Sp.
112/B5 **Benjamin** (isl.), Chile
128/D3 **Benjamin**, Tx,US
108/D4 **Benjamin Constant**, Braz.
117/M7 **Benjamín Hill**, Mex.
125/G2 **Benkelman**, Ne,US
44/D5 **Benllech**, Wal,UK
43/C2 **Ben Lomond** (mtn.), Sc,UK
91/C4 **Ben Lomond Nat'l Park**, Austl.
43/D2 **Ben Macdui** (mtn.), Sc,UK
43/C2 **Ben More** (mtn.), Sc,UK
44/C1 **Bennane Head** (pt.), Sc,UK
69/R2 **Bennett** (isl.), Rus.
129/J3 **Bennettsville**, SC,US
43/C2 **Ben Nevis** (mtn.), Sc,UK
127/F3 **Bennington**, Vt,US
102/Q13 **Benoni**, SAfr.
103/J6 **Be, Nosy** (isl.), Madg.
96/H6 **Bénoue Nat'l Park**, Camr.
83/D2 **Ben Quang**, Viet.
132/Q16 **Bensenville**, Il,US
57/H2 **Bensheim**, Ger.
124/E5 **Benson**, Az,US
123/K4 **Benson**, Mn,US
45/F3 **Bentham**, Eng,UK
51/E4 **Bentheim**, Ger.
97/L6 **Bentiu**, Sudan
45/G4 **Bentley**, Eng,UK
110/B4 **Bento Gonçalves**, Braz.
128/E3 **Benton**, Ar,US
126/B4 **Benton**, Il,US
126/B4 **Benton**, Ky,US
86/B3 **Bentong**, Malay.
126/C3 **Benton Harbor**, Mi,US
128/E2 **Bentonville**, Ar,US
83/D4 **Ben Tre**, Viet.
99/G4 **Benue** (riv.), Nga.
99/G5 **Benue** (state), Nga.
62/D3 **Beočin**, Yugo.
62/E3 **Beograd** (Belgrade) (cap.), Yugo.
78/B4 **Beppu**, Japan
78/B4 **Beppu** (bay), Japan
96/E1 **Beraber** (well), Alg.
44/A2 **Beragh**, NI,UK
61/F2 **Berat**, Alb.
87/E4 **Beratus** (peak), Indo.
87/H4 **Berau** (bay), Indo.
87/E3 **Berau** (riv.), Indo.
97/Q5 **Berbera**, Som.
96/J7 **Berberati**, CAfr.
108/G2 **Berbice** (riv.), Guy.
52/D1 **Berchem**, Belg.
57/K3 **Berchtesgaden**, Ger.
57/K3 **Berchtesgaden Nat'l Park**, Ger.
52/A3 **Berck**, Fr.
66/D2 **Berdichev**, Ukr.
68/J4 **Berdsk**, Rus.
66/F3 **Berdyansk**, Ukr.
126/C4 **Berea**, Ky,US
66/B2 **Beregovo**, Ukr.
99/E5 **Berekum**, Gha.
100/C4 **Berenice** (ruins), Egypt
46/D5 **Bere Regis**, Eng,UK
127/H2 **Beresford**, NB,Can
123/J5 **Beresford**, SD,US
62/E2 **Berettyo** (riv.), Hun.
62/E2 **Berettyóújfalu**, Hun.
65/N4 **Berezniki**, Rus.
102/B4 **Berg** (riv.), SAfr.
74/A2 **Bergama**, Turk.
57/H4 **Bergamo**, It.
50/B3 **Bergen**, Neth.
42/C3 **Bergen**, Nor.
51/G3 **Bergen-Belsen**, Ger.
131/F5 **Bergenfield**, NJ,US
50/B6 **Bergen op Zoom**, Neth.
56/D4 **Bergerac**, Fr.
50/C6 **Bergeyk**, Neth.
53/F2 **Bergheim**, Ger.
51/E6 **Bergisch Gladbach**, Ger.
51/E5 **Bergkamen**, Ger.
51/E6 **Bergneustadt**, Ger.
50/C2 **Bergum**, Neth.
50/D2 **Bergumermeer** (lake), Neth.
84/D4 **Berhampur**, India
86/C4 **Berikat** (cape), Indo.
69/S4 **Bering** (isl.), Rus.
130/E3 **Bering** (str.), Rus., Ak,US
53/E1 **Beringen**, Belg.
130/E2 **Bering Land Bridge Nat'l Prsv.**, Ak,US
86/B4 **Beritarikap** (cape), Indo.
58/D4 **Berja**, Sp.
50/D4 **Berkel** (riv.), Ger.
50/B5 **Berkel**, Neth.
46/D3 **Berkeley**, Eng,UK
132/K11 **Berkeley**, Ca,US
131/F5 **Berkeley Heights**, NJ,US
47/F3 **Berkhamsted**, Eng,UK
132/F6 **Berkley**, Mi,US
105/W **Berkner** (isl.), Ant.
63/F4 **Berkovitsa**, Bul.
47/E4 **Berkshire** (co.), Eng,UK
47/E4 **Berkshire Downs** (uplands), Eng,UK
52/C1 **Berlare**, Belg.
50/C5 **Berlicum**, Neth.
49/G2 **Berlin** (cap.), Ger.
127/G2 **Berlin**, NH,US
105/V **Berlioz** (pt.), Ant.
107/C5 **Bermejo** (riv.), Arg.
111/D1 **Bermejo**, Bol.
58/D1 **Bermeo**, Sp.
115/L6 **Bermuda** (isl.), UK
54/D3 **Bern** (canton), Swi.
54/D4 **Bern** (cap.), Swi.
108/B5 **Bernal**, Peru
60/E2 **Bernalda**, It.
124/F4 **Bernalillo**, NM,US
118/D1 **Bernard** (riv.), NW,Can
113/J7 **Bernardo O'Higgins Nat'l Park**, Chile
131/G5 **Bernardsville**, NJ,US
56/D2 **Bernay**, Fr.
48/F3 **Bernburg**, Ger.
51/F2 **Berne** (riv.), Ger.
54/D5 **Bernese Alps** (range), Swi.
118/G1 **Bernier** (bay), Nun.,Can
55/G5 **Bernina, Passo del** (pass), Swi.
52/C3 **Bernissart**, Belg.
53/G4 **Bernkastel-Kues**, Ger.
103/H8 **Beroroha**, Madg.
57/L2 **Beroun**, Czh.
57/K2 **Berounka** (riv.), Czh.
62/F5 **Berovo**, FYROM
56/F5 **Berre** (lag.), Fr.
46/C1 **Berriew**, Wal,UK
117/F2 **Berry** (isls.), Bahm.
56/D3 **Berry** (hist. reg.), Fr.
132/K9 **Berryessa** (lake), Ca,US
132/K9 **Berryessa** (peak), Ca,US
46/C6 **Berry Head** (pt.), Wal,UK
128/E2 **Berryville**, Ar,US
96/H7 **Bertoua**, Camr.
113/J7 **Bertrand** (peak), Arg.
53/E4 **Bertrix**, Belg.
92/G5 **Beru** (atoll), Kiri.
86/D3 **Beruit** (isl.), Malay.
91/G5 **Berwick**, Austl.
127/H2 **Berwick**, NB,Can
43/D3 **Berwick-upon-Tweed**, Eng,UK
44/E6 **Berwyn** (mts.), Wal,UK
132/Q16 **Berwyn**, Il,US
131/E5 **Berwyn-Devon**, Pa,US
56/E4 **Bès** (riv.), Fr.
103/H7 **Besalampy**, Madg.
54/B3 **Besançon**, Fr.
87/E4 **Besar** (peak), Indo.
56/E3 **Besbre** (riv.), Fr.
68/F6 **Beshahr**, Iran
62/E3 **Beška**, Yugo.
49/K4 **Beskids** (mts.), Pol.
67/H4 **Beslan**, Rus.
62/F4 **Besna Kobila** (peak), Yugo.
123/G2 **Besnard** (lake), Sk,Can
45/G4 **Bessacarr**, Eng,UK
63/J2 **Bessarabia** (reg.), Mol.
44/B3 **Bessbrook**, NI,UK
129/G3 **Bessemer**, Al,US
126/B2 **Bessemer**, Mi,US
132/D2 **Bessemer** (mtn.), Wa,US
67/K3 **Besshoky, Gora** (peak), Kaz.
50/C6 **Best**, Neth.
51/F6 **Bestwig**, Ger.
58/A1 **Betanzos**, Sp.
74/N7 **Beth Alpha Synagogue Nat'l Park**, Isr.
125/J2 **Bethany**, Mo,US
44/D5 **Bethesda**, Wal,UK
131/J8 **Bethesda**, Md,US
102/E3 **Bethlehem**, SAfr.
131/E5 **Bethlehem**, Pa,US
74/K6 **Bethlehem** (Bayt Laḩm), WBnk.
131/G5 **Bethpage**, NY,US
123/G3 **Bethune**, Sk,Can
52/B2 **Béthune**, Fr.
52/A4 **Béthune** (riv.), Fr.
110/C1 **Betim**, Braz.
103/H8 **Betioky**, Madg.
75/A2 **Betpak-Dala** (des.), Kaz.
53/G6 **Betschdorf**, Fr.
74/K5 **Bet She'an**, Isr.
74/M9 **Bet Shemesh**, Isr.
127/G1 **Betsiamites** (riv.), Qu,Can
103/H7 **Betsiboka** (riv.), Madg.
97/J3 **Bette** (peak), Libya
53/F4 **Bettembourg**, Lux.
84/D2 **Bettiah**, India
84/C3 **Betūl**, India
50/C5 **Betuwe** (reg.), Neth.
44/E5 **Betws-y-Coed**, Wal,UK
53/G2 **Betzdorf**, Ger.
123/H4 **Beulah**, ND,US
50/D3 **Beulakerwijde** (lake), Neth.
47/G4 **Beult** (riv.), Eng,UK
50/C5 **Beuningen**, Neth.
56/D3 **Beuvron** (riv.), Fr.
52/B2 **Beuvry**, Fr.
51/H2 **Bevensen**, Ger.
51/E4 **Bever** (riv.), Ger.
52/D1 **Beveren**, Belg.
45/H4 **Beverley**, Eng,UK
131/B2 **Beverly Hills**, Ca,US
132/F6 **Beverly Hills**, Mi,US
51/G5 **Beverungen**, Ger.
50/B4 **Beverwijk**, Neth.
45/F1 **Bewcastle**, Eng,UK
46/D2 **Bewdley**, Eng,UK
47/G4 **Bewl Bridge** (res.), Eng,UK
53/G5 **Bexbach**, Ger.
47/G5 **Bexhill**, Eng,UK
63/J5 **Beykoz**, Turk.
53/E2 **Beyne-Heusay**, Belg.
63/K5 **Beypazarı**, Turk.
74/B3 **Beyşehir**, Turk.
74/B3 **Beyşehir** (lake), Turk.
62/D3 **Bezdan**, Yugo.
57/L1 **Bezděz** (peak), Czh.
64/H4 **Bezhetsk**, Rus.
56/E5 **Béziers**, Fr.
84/D2 **Bhabua**, India
84/E3 **Bhadrak**, India
84/C5 **Bhadrāvati**, India
84/A3 **Bhadreswar**, India
84/E2 **Bhāgalpur**, India
73/K2 **Bhakkar**, Pak.
84/E2 **Bhaktapur**, Nepal
85/G3 **Bhamo**, Myan.
84/C2 **Bharātpur**, India
84/B3 **Bharuch**, India
84/D3 **Bhātāpāra**, India
73/K2 **Bhatinda**, India
84/B5 **Bhatkal**, India
84/E3 **Bhātpāra**, India
84/C5 **Bhavāni**, India
84/B3 **Bhavnagar**, India
84/C3 **Bhawāni Mandi**, India
84/D4 **Bhawānipatna**, India
84/D3 **Bhilai**, India
84/B2 **Bhīlwāra**, India
84/C4 **Bhīma** (riv.), India
84/D4 **Bhīmavaram**, India
84/D4 **Bhimunipatnam**, India
84/C2 **Bhind**, India
84/B3 **Bhīnmāl**, India
84/B4 **Bhiwandi**, India
84/E2 **Bhojpur**, Nepal
84/C3 **Bhopāl**, India
84/B4 **Bhor**, India
84/E3 **Bhuban**, India
84/E3 **Bhubaneswar**, India
84/A3 **Bhūj**, India
83/B2 **Bhumibol** (dam), Thai.
84/C3 **Bhusawal**, India
84/E2 **Bhutan**
75/F5 **Bi** (riv.), China
108/E4 **Biá** (riv.), Braz.
98/E5 **Bia** (riv.), Gui., IvC.
52/B3 **Biache-Saint-Vaast**, Fr.
96/G7 **Biafra** (bight), Afr.
87/J4 **Biak** (isl.), Indo.
49/M2 **Biała Podlaska**, Pol.
49/M3 **Biała Podlaska** (prov.), Pol.
49/L3 **Białobrzegi**, Pol.
49/J2 **Białogard**, Pol.
49/K4 **Białowieski Nat'l Park**, Pol.
49/M2 **Białystok**, Pol.
49/M2 **Białystok** (prov.), Pol.
55/G4 **Bianca** (peak), It.
60/D4 **Biancavilla**, It.
97/L7 **Biaro**, D.R. Congo
56/C5 **Biarritz**, Fr.
100/B2 **Bibā**, Egypt
110/K6 **Bicas**, Braz.
63/H2 **Bicaz**, Rom.
47/E3 **Bicester**, Eng,UK
62/D2 **Bicske**, Hun.
98/D5 **Bidaga** (rapids), IvC.
84/C4 **Bīdar**, India
127/G3 **Biddeford**, Me,US
45/F5 **Biddulph**, Eng,UK
46/B4 **Bideford**, Eng,UK
46/B4 **Bideford** (Barnstaple) (bay), Eng,UK
47/E2 **Bidford on Avon**, Eng,UK
83/E3 **Bi Doup** (peak), Viet.
59/E1 **Bidouze** (riv.), Fr.
104/B4 **Bíe** (plat.), Ang.
49/M2 **Biebzra** (riv.), Pol.
54/D3 **Biel**, Swi.
49/J3 **Bielawa**, Pol.
51/F4 **Bielefeld**, Ger.
119/J1 **Bieler** (lake), Nun.,Can
49/K4 **Bielsko** (prov.), Pol.
49/K4 **Bielsko-Biała**, Pol.
49/M2 **Bielsk Podlaski**, Pol.
83/D4 **Bien Hoa**, Viet.
83/D1 **Bien Son**, Viet.
119/J3 **Bienville** (lake), Qu,Can
50/B5 **Biesbosch** (reg.), Neth.
50/D5 **Biesme** (riv.), Fr.
54/D5 **Bietschhorn** (peak), Swi.
60/D2 **Biferno** (riv.), It.
91/B2 **Big** (des.), Austl.
119/J2 **Big** (isl.), Nun.,Can
118/D1 **Big** (riv.), NW,Can
63/H5 **Biga**, Turk.
74/B2 **Bigadiç**, Turk.
122/F4 **Big Belt** (mts.), Mt,US
128/C4 **Big Bend Nat'l Park**, Tx,US
125/K4 **Big Black** (riv.), Ms,US
125/H2 **Big Blue** (riv.), Ks, Ne,US
46/C6 **Bigbury** (bay), Eng,UK
130/D2 **Big Diomede** (isl.), Rus.
123/K4 **Big Fork** (riv.), Mn,US
122/G2 **Biggar**, Sk,Can
53/G1 **Biggasee** (lake), Ger.
51/E6 **Bigge** (riv.), Ger.
51/E6 **Biggesee** (res.), Ger.
47/F2 **Biggleswade**, Eng,UK
102/D3 **Big Hole**, SAfr.
122/E4 **Big Hole** (riv.), Mt,US
122/F4 **Bighorn** (lake), Mt, Wy,US
122/G4 **Bighorn** (mts.), Mt, Wy,US
122/G4 **Bighorn** (riv.), Mt, Wy,US
124/E1 **Bighorn** (basin), Wy,US
118/F4 **Bighorn Canyon Nat'l Rec. Area**, Mt,US
128/C4 **Big Lake**, Tx,US
124/D2 **Big Lost** (riv.), Id,US
132/P14 **Big Muskego** (lake), Wi,US
98/A3 **Bignona**, Sen.
126/C3 **Big Rapids**, Mi,US
122/G2 **Big River**, Sk,Can
132/N16 **Big Rock** (cr.), Il,US
129/H4 **Big Saltilla** (cr.), Ga,US
125/G3 **Big Sandy** (cr.), Co,US
129/F2 **Big Sandy** (riv.), Tn,US
124/E2 **Big Sandy** (riv.), Wy,US
123/J5 **Big Sioux** (riv.), Ia, SD,US
128/C3 **Big Spring**, Tx,US
123/J4 **Big Stone** (lake), Mn, SD,US
126/D4 **Big Stone Gap**, Va,US
122/F4 **Big Timber**, Mt,US
118/H3 **Big Trout** (lake), On,Can
131/B2 **Big Tujunga** (canyon), Ca,US
110/B3 **Biguaçu**, Braz.
124/D2 **Big Wood** (riv.), Id,US
62/B3 **Bihać**, Yugo.
84/E2 **Bihār**, India
84/D3 **Bihār** (state), India
62/F2 **Bihor** (co.), Rom.
52/A4 **Bihorel**, Fr.
98/A4 **Bijagós** (isls.), GBis.
84/C4 **Bijāpur**, India
72/E1 **Bījār**, Iran
62/D3 **Bijeljina**, Bosn.
62/D4 **Bijelo Polje**, Yugo.
84/C2 **Bijnor**, India
84/B2 **Bīkaner**, India
92/G3 **Bikar** (atoll), Mrsh.
77/L2 **Bikin**, Rus.
77/M2 **Bikin** (riv.), Rus.
92/F3 **Bikini** (atoll), Mrsh.
104/C4 **Bikuar Nat'l Park**, Moz.
83/B3 **Bilauktaung** (range), Myan., Thai.
58/D1 **Bilbao**, Sp.
100/B2 **Bilbays**, Egypt
62/D4 **Bileća**, Bosn.
74/B2 **Bilecik**, Turk.
63/K5 **Bilecik** (prov.), Turk.
49/M3 **Biłgoraj**, Pol.
69/S3 **Bilibino**, Rus.
83/B2 **Bilin** (riv.), Myan.
91/C2 **Billabong** (cr.), Austl.
51/H1 **Bille** (riv.), Ger.
51/E5 **Billerbeck**, Ger.
56/C5 **Billère**, Fr.
47/G3 **Billericay**, Eng,UK
91/B2 **Billiat Consv. Park**, Austl.
45/F5 **Billinge**, Eng,UK
45/G2 **Billingham**, Eng,UK
122/F4 **Billings**, Mt,US
47/F4 **Billingshurst**, Eng,UK
71/K10 **Billiton** (isl.), Indo.
124/D4 **Bill Williams** (riv.), Az,US
90/C4 **Biloela**, Austl.
129/F4 **Biloxi**, Ms,US
84/C2 **Bilsi**, India
53/E2 **Bilzen**, Belg.
87/E5 **Bima**, Indo.
91/D2 **Bimberi** (peak), Austl.
117/F2 **Bimini** (isls.), Bahm.
84/C3 **Bina-Etāwa**, India
60/B4 **Bin 'Arūs** (gov.), Tun.
127/Q9 **Binbrook**, On,Can
45/H5 **Binbrook**, Eng,UK
52/D3 **Binche**, Belg.
76/G2 **Binder**, Mong.
84/D2 **Bindki**, India
104/C2 **Bindu**, D.R. Congo
104/F4 **Bindura**, Zim.
59/F2 **Binéfar**, Sp.
47/F4 **Binfield**, Eng,UK
104/F4 **Binga** (mtn.), Moz.
57/G2 **Bingen**, Ger.
98/E5 **Bingerville**, IvC.
45/H6 **Bingham**, Eng,UK
126/F3 **Binghamton**, NY,US
45/G4 **Bingley**, Eng,UK
74/E2 **Bingöl**, Turk.
81/D4 **Binhai**, China
83/D4 **Binh Chanh**, Viet.
83/D4 **Binh Chau**, Viet.
85/G4 **Binhon** (peak), Myan.
83/E3 **Binh Son**, Viet.
86/A3 **Binjai**, Indo.
87/F5 **Binongko** (isl.), Indo.
86/B2 **Bintang** (peak), Malay.
85/J3 **Binyang**, China
81/D3 **Binzhou**, China
112/B3 **Bío-Bío** (reg.), Chile
112/B3 **Bío-Bío** (riv.), Chile
62/B4 **Biograd**, Cro.
62/D4 **Biogradska Nat'l Park**, Yugo.
96/G7 **Bioko** (isl.), EqG.
84/C4 **Bīr**, India
96/H2 **Birāk**, Libya
96/H2 **Bi'r al Ghuzayyil** (well), Libya
97/K2 **Bi'r al Ḩarash** (well), Libya
84/E2 **Birātnagar**, Nepal
118/E3 **Birch** (mts.), Ab,Can
123/G2 **Birch Hills**, Sk,Can
123/H2 **Birch River**, Mb,Can
105/X **Bird** (isl.), Ant.
91/D2 **Birds Rock** (peak), Austl.
74/D3 **Birecik**, Turk.
110/B2 **Birigui**, Braz.
110/G8 **Biritiba-Mirim**, Braz.
73/G2 **Bīrjand**, Iran
92/G4 **Birkenebeu**, Kiri.
45/E5 **Birkenhead**, Eng,UK
55/H3 **Birkkarspitze** (peak), Aus.
63/H2 **Bîrlad**, Rom.
63/H2 **Bîrlad** (riv.), Rom.
75/B3 **Birlik**, Kaz.
47/E2 **Birmingham**, Eng,UK
129/G3 **Birmingham**, Al,US
132/F6 **Birmingham**, Mi,US
57/K3 **Birnhorn** (peak), Aus.
93/H5 **Birnie** (isl.), Kiri.
99/G3 **Birni Nkonni**, Niger
77/L2 **Birobidzhan**, Rus.
96/E3 **Bîr Ounâne** (well), Mali
54/D3 **Birs** (riv.), Swi.
65/M5 **Birsk**, Rus.
64/E4 **Biržai**, Lith.
63/F4 **Bis** (lake), Rom.
79/M9 **Bisai**, Japan
124/E5 **Bisbee**, Az,US
56/C4 **Biscarrosse**, Fr.
56/C4 **Biscarrosse** (lag.), Fr.
56/B4 **Biscay** (bay), Eur.
129/H5 **Biscayne Nat'l Park**, Fl,US
60/E2 **Bisceglie**, It.
54/D1 **Bischheim**, Fr.
57/K3 **Bischofshofen**, Aus.
53/G6 **Bischwiller**, Fr.
105/V **Biscoe** (isls.), Ant.
117/H6 **Biscucuy**, Ven.
72/D4 **Bīshah** (dry riv.), SAr.
75/B3 **Bishkek** (cap.), Kyr.
124/C3 **Bishop**, Ca,US
45/G2 **Bishop Auckland**, Eng,UK
46/D2 **Bishops Castle**, Eng,UK
46/D3 **Bishops Cleeve**, Eng,UK
127/L1 **Bishop's Falls**, Nf,Can
47/G3 **Bishop's Stortford**, Eng,UK
47/E5 **Bishops Waltham**, Eng,UK
45/H4 **Bishop Wilton**, Eng,UK
96/G1 **Biskra**, Alg.
49/L2 **Biskupiec**, Pol.
82/E6 **Bislig**, Phil.
127/Q9 **Bismarck**, On,Can
92/D5 **Bismarck** (arch.), PNG
92/D5 **Bismarck** (sea), PNG
123/H4 **Bismarck** (cap.), ND,US
74/E3 **Bismil**, Turk.
98/B4 **Bissau** (cap.), GBis.
51/F4 **Bissendorf**, Ger.
123/K3 **Bissett**, Mb,Can
63/G2 **Bistrița**, Rom.
63/G2 **Bistrița-Năsăud** (co.), Rom.
108/E2 **Bita** (riv.), Col.
96/H7 **Bitam**, Gabon
53/F4 **Bitburg**, Ger.
53/G5 **Bitche**, Fr.
96/J5 **Bitkin**, Chad
74/E2 **Bitlis**, Turk.
62/E5 **Bitola**, FYROM
62/C5 **Bitonto**, It.
63/G2 **Bitrița** (riv.), Rom.
100/C2 **Bitter** (lakes), Egypt
122/E4 **Bitterroot** (range), Id, Mt,US
87/G3 **Bitung**, Indo.
96/H5 **Biu**, Nga.
79/M9 **Biwa**, Japan
78/E3 **Biwa** (lake), Japan
125/J4 **Bixby**, Ok,US
74/H6 **Biyalā**, Egypt
75/E1 **Biysk**, Rus.
127/N7 **Bizard** (isl.), Qu,Can
60/A4 **Bizerte** (Banzart), Tun.
42/M6 **Bjargtangar** (pt.), Ice.
48/G1 **Bjärred**, Swe.
62/C3 **Bjelovar**, Cro.
119/S7 **Bjorne** (pen.), Nun.,Can
47/E1 **Blaby**, Eng,UK
49/K3 **Blachownia**, Pol.
66/D4 **Black** (sea), Asia, Eur.
126/B1 **Black** (bay), On,Can
123/L2 **Black** (riv.), On,Can
130/M3 **Black** (mtn.), Yk,Can
83/C1 **Black** (riv.), China
66/D4 **Black** (sea), Eur.
54/D2 **Black** (for.), Ger.
102/A2 **Black** (pt.), Namb.
46/A6 **Black** (pt.), Eng,UK
46/C3 **Black** (mtn.), Wal,UK
46/C3 **Black** (mts.), Wal,UK
125/K3 **Black** (riv.), Ar, Mo,US
124/D4 **Black** (mts.), Az,US
124/E4 **Black** (riv.), Az,US
132/L11 **Black** (hills), Ca,US
132/G5 **Black** (riv.), Mi,US
124/F4 **Black** (range), NM,US
126/F3 **Black** (riv.), NY,US
123/H5 **Black** (hills), SD, Wy,US
123/L4 **Black** (riv.), Wi,US
47/E3 **Black Bourton**, Eng,UK
45/F4 **Blackburn**, Eng,UK
44/D1 **Blackcraig** (hill), Sc,UK
83/C1 **Black** (Da) (riv.), Viet.
144/F3 **Black Canyon of the Gunnison NP**, Co,US
122/E3 **Black Diamond**, Ab,Can
47/F4 **Blackdown** (hill), Eng,UK
46/C5 **Blackdown** (hills), Eng,UK
90/C3 **Blackdown Tableland Nat'l Park**, Austl.
122/F4 **Black Eagle**, Mt,US
122/E5 **Blackfoot**, Id,US
122/F5 **Blackfoot** (res.), Id,US
45/G2 **Blackhall Rocks**, Eng,UK
44/C2 **Black Head** (pt.), NI,UK
124/E3 **Black Mesa** (upland), Az,US
46/B6 **Blackmoor** (upland), Eng,UK
90/B1 **Black Mountain Nat'l Park**, Austl.
45/E4 **Blackpool**, Eng,UK
102/A2 **Black Reef** (pt.), Namb.
126/B2 **Black River Falls**, Wi,US
124/C2 **Black Rock** (des.), Nv,US
45/F4 **Blackrod**, Eng,UK
126/D4 **Blacksburg**, Va,US
129/H3 **Blackshear** (lake), Ga,US
126/E4 **Blackstone**, Va,US
91/D1 **Black Sugarloaf** (peak), Austl.
90/G8 **Blacktown**, Austl.
127/H2 **Blackville**, NB,Can
98/E4 **Black Volta** (riv.), Afr.
129/G3 **Black Warrior** (riv.), Al,US
90/C3 **Blackwater**, Austl.
44/B4 **Blackwater** (riv.), Ire.
43/A4 **Blackwater** (riv.), Ire.
47/G3 **Blackwater** (riv.), Eng,UK
44/B3 **Blackwater** (riv.), NI,UK
125/J3 **Blackwater** (riv.), Mo,US
125/H3 **Blackwell**, Ok,US
46/C3 **Blackwood**, Wal,UK
131/K8 **Bladensburg**, Md,US
90/A3 **Bladensburg Nat'l Park**, Austl.
44/D2 **Bladnoch** (riv.), Sc,UK
44/E6 **Blaenau-Ffestiniog**, Wal,UK
46/C3 **Blaenau Gwent** (co.), Wal,UK
46/C3 **Blaenavon**, Wal,UK
56/D5 **Blagnac**, Fr.
63/F4 **Blagoevgrad**, Bul.
77/K1 **Blagoveshchensk**, Rus.
122/G2 **Blaine Lake**, Sk,Can
127/N6 **Blainville**, Qu,Can
125/H2 **Blair**, Ne,US
122/E3 **Blairmore**, Ab,Can
131/F5 **Blairstown**, NJ,US
54/A1 **Blaise** (riv.), Fr.
63/F2 **Blaj**, Rom.
129/G4 **Blakely**, Ga,US
96/B3 **Blanc** (cape), Mrta.
112/E3 **Blanca** (bay), Arg.
108/C5 **Blanca** (range), Peru
58/E3 **Blanca**, Sp.
59/E4 **Blanca** (coast), Sp.
125/F4 **Blanca** (peak), NM,US
57/G4 **Blanc, Mont** (mtn.), Fr., It.
52/A2 **Blanc Nez** (cape), Fr.
113/K6 **Blanco** (riv.), Arg.
113/K8 **Blanco** (lake), Chile
112/C1 **Blanco** (riv.), Chile
116/D6 **Blanco** (cape), CR
108/B4 **Blanco** (cape), Peru
122/B5 **Blanco** (cape), Or,US
125/H5 **Blanco** (riv.), Tx,US
46/D5 **Blandford Forum**, Eng,UK
124/E3 **Blanding**, Ut,US
59/G2 **Blanes**, Sp.
59/G1 **Blanes, Serre de** (mtn.), Fr.
49/G4 **Blanice** (riv.), Czh.
52/C1 **Blankenberge**, Belg.
53/F3 **Blankenheim**, Ger.
117/J5 **Blanquilla** (isl.), Ven.
49/J4 **Blansko**, Czh.
104/G4 **Blantyre**, Malw.
56/F3 **Blanzy**, Fr.
50/C4 **Blaricum**, Neth.
48/E1 **Blåvands Huk** (pt.), Den.
56/B2 **Blavet** (riv.), Fr.
51/H2 **Bleckede**, Ger.
53/E2 **Blégny**, Belg.
52/C2 **Bléharies**, Belg.
62/B2 **Bleiburg**, Aus.
51/H6 **Bleicherode**, Ger.
50/B4 **Bleiswijk**, Neth.
42/E4 **Blekinge** (co.), Swe.
89/H7 **Blenheim**, NZ
47/E3 **Blenheim Palace**, Eng,UK
57/G4 **Bléone** (riv.), Fr.
52/C4 **Blérancourt**, Fr.
102/C4 **Blesberg** (peak), SAfr.
47/F2 **Bletchley**, Eng,UK
101/A2 **Bleus** (mts.), D.R. Congo
47/E3 **Blewbury**, Eng,UK
96/F1 **Blida**, Alg.
45/G5 **Blidworth**, Eng,UK
53/G5 **Blies** (riv.), Fr., Ger.
53/G5 **Bliesbruck**, Fr.
53/G5 **Blieskastel**, Ger.
93/Y18 **Bligh Water** (sound), Fiji
87/F2 **Blik** (mt.), Phil.
45/G6 **Blithfield** (res.), Eng,UK
105/L **Blizzard** (peak), Ant.
50/B4 **Bloemendaal**, Neth.
102/D3 **Bloemfontein**, SAfr.
102/D2 **Bloemhofdam** (res.), SAfr.
56/D3 **Blois**, Fr.
50/C3 **Blokker**, Neth.
123/J3 **Bloodvein** (riv.), Mb, On,Can
43/A3 **Bloody Foreland** (pt.), Ire.
126/B2 **Bloomer**, Wi,US
131/F5 **Bloomfield**, NJ,US
124/F3 **Bloomfield**, NM,US
132/F6 **Bloomfield Hills**, Mi,US
132/P16 **Bloomingdale**, Il,US
131/C2 **Bloomington**, Ca,US
126/B3 **Bloomington**, Il,US
126/C4 **Bloomington**, In,US
123/K4 **Bloomington**, Mn,US
86/D5 **Blora**, Indo.
129/G4 **Blountstown**, Fl,US
105/L **Blowaway** (peak), Ant.
47/E3 **Bloxham**, Eng,UK
46/E1 **Bloxwich**, Eng,UK
57/K1 **Blšanka** (riv.), Czh.
55/F3 **Bludenz**, Aus.
85/F3 **Blue** (mtn.), India
128/D3 **Blue** (riv.), Ok,US
122/D4 **Blue** (mts.), Or, Wa,US
123/K5 **Blue Earth**, Mn,US
126/D4 **Bluefield**, Va,US
126/D4 **Bluefield**, WV,US
116/E5 **Bluefields**, Nic.
132/Q16 **Blue Island**, Il,US
124/C2 **Bluejoint** (lake), Or,US
90/D4 **Blue Lake Nat'l Park**, Austl.
124/F3 **Blue Mesa** (res.), Co,US
117/F4 **Blue Mountain** (pk.), Jam.
89/D4 **Blue Mountains**, Austl.
91/D2 **Blue Mountains Nat'l Park**, Austl.
97/M5 **Blue Nile** (riv.), Eth., Sudan
118/E2 **Bluenose** (lake), Nun.,Can
129/G3 **Blue Ridge**, Ga,US
129/H2 **Blue Ridge** (mts.), NC, Va,US
126/C3 **Bluffton**, In,US
110/B3 **Blumenau**, Braz.
45/G1 **Blyth**, Eng,UK
45/G5 **Blyth**, Eng,UK
47/H2 **Blyth** (riv.), Eng,UK
45/F6 **Blythe** (riv.), Eng,UK
124/D4 **Blythe**, Ca,US
45/F6 **Blythe Bridge**, Eng,UK
129/F3 **Blytheville**, Ar,US
83/D4 **B'nom M'hai** (peak), Viet.
98/C5 **Bo**, SLeo.
82/D5 **Boac**, Phil.
116/D5 **Boaco**, Nic.
110/C2 **Boa Esperança**, Braz.
109/J5 **Boa Esperança** (res.), Braz.
87/G4 **Boano** (isl.), Indo.
119/H2 **Boas** (riv.), Nun.,Can
109/K4 **Boa Viagem**, Braz.
108/F3 **Boa Vista**, Braz.
129/G3 **Boaz**, Al,US
85/J3 **Bobai**, China
103/J5 **Bobaomby** (cape), Madg.
84/D4 **Bobbili**, India
52/B6 **Bobigny**, Fr.
57/H2 **Böblingen**, Ger.
98/D4 **Bobo Dioulasso**, Burk.
62/D4 **Bobotov Kuk** (peak), Yugo.
62/F4 **Bobovdol**, Bul.
49/H3 **Bóbr** (riv.), Pol.
66/G2 **Bobrov**, Rus.
103/H8 **Boby** (peak), Madg.
108/E5 **Boca do Acre**, Braz.
110/J7 **Bocaina** (mts.), Braz.
109/K7 **Bocaiúva**, Braz.
129/H5 **Boca Raton**, Fl,US
116/D5 **Bocay**, Nic.
49/L4 **Bochnia**, Pol.
53/E1 **Bocholt**, Belg.
50/D5 **Bocholt**, Ger.
51/E6 **Bochum**, Ger.
51/H4 **Bockenem**, Ger.
47/G3 **Bocking**, Eng,UK
117/G6 **Boconó**, Ven.
53/D3 **Bocq** (riv.), Belg.
96/J7 **Boda**, CAfr.
69/M4 **Bodaybo**, Rus.
48/F3 **Bode** (riv.), Ger.
124/B3 **Bodega** (bay), Ca,US
50/B4 **Bodegraven**, Neth.
96/J4 **Bodélé** (depr.), Chad
42/G2 **Boden**, Swe.
55/F2 **Bodensee** (Constance) (lake), Ger., Swi.
84/C4 **Bodhan**, India
84/C5 **Bodināyakkanūr**, India
46/B6 **Bodmin**, Eng,UK
46/B5 **Bodmin Moor** (upland), Eng,UK
42/E2 **Bodø**, Nor.
76/C2 **Bodonchiyn** (riv.), Mong.
62/E1 **Bodrog** (riv.), Hun.
74/A3 **Bodrum**, Turk.
83/D4 **Bo Duc**, Viet.
102/A2 **Boegoeberg** (peak), Namb.
50/C5 **Boekel**, Neth.
104/D1 **Boende**, D.R. Congo
125/K4 **Boeuf** (riv.), Ar, La,US
129/F4 **Bogalusa**, La,US
91/C1 **Bogan** (riv.), Austl.
99/E3 **Bogandé**, Burk.

Bogat - Büdel

62/D3 **Bogatić**, Yugo.
49/H3 **Bogatynia**, Pol.
74/C2 **Boğazlıyan**, Turk.
75/E5 **Bogcang** (riv.), China
76/E2 **Bogd**, Mong.
76/B3 **Bogda** (mts.), China
75/E3 **Bogda Feng** (peak), China
47/F5 **Bognor Regis**, Eng,UK
53/D4 **Bogny-sur-Meuse**, Fr.
82/D5 **Bogo**, Phil.
91/C3 **Bogong** (peak), Austl.
91/C3 **Bogong Nat'l Park**, Austl.
86/C5 **Bogor**, Indo.
108/D3 **Bogotá** (cap.), Col.
62/E5 **Bogovinje**, FYROM
84/E3 **Bogra**, Bang.
44/E1 **Bogrie** (hill), Sc,UK
98/B2 **Bogué**, Mrta.
81/D3 **Bohai** (bay), China
81/E3 **Bohai** (str.), China
81/D3 **Bo Hai (Chihli)** (gulf), China
52/C4 **Bohain-en-Vermandois**, Fr.
57/K1 **Bohemia** (reg.), Czh.
51/G3 **Böhme** (riv.), Ger.
51/F4 **Bohmte**, Ger.
82/D6 **Bohol** (isl.), Phil.
85/J4 **Bo Ho Su**, Viet.
60/D2 **Boiano**, It.
58/A1 **Boiro**, Sp.
110/B1 **Bois** (riv.), Braz.
122/D5 **Boise** (cap.), Id,US
122/E5 **Boise** (riv.), Id,US
125/G3 **Boise City**, Ok,US
52/A5 **Bois-Guillaume**, Fr.
123/H3 **Boissevain**, Mb,Can
51/H2 **Boizenburg**, Ger.
96/C2 **Bojador** (cape), WSah.
49/J4 **Bojkovice**, Czh.
73/G1 **Bojnūrd**, Iran
98/B4 **Boké** (comm.), Gui.
104/D1 **Bokele**, D.R. Congo
42/C4 **Boknafjorden** (fjord), Nor.
101/C2 **Bokol** (peak), Kenya
96/J5 **Bokoro**, Chad
102/E2 **Boksburg**, SAfr.
98/B4 **Bolama**, GBis.
73/J3 **Bolān** (pass), Pak.
58/D3 **Bolaños de Calatrava**, Sp.
56/D2 **Bolbec**, Fr.
63/H3 **Boldeşti-Scăeni**, Rom.
45/G2 **Boldon**, Eng,UK
99/E4 **Bole**, Gha.
49/H3 **Bolesławiec**, Pol.
99/E4 **Bolgatanga**, Gha.
132/P16 **Bolingbrook**, Il,US
112/E3 **Bolívar**, Arg.
125/J3 **Bolivar**, Mo,US
126/B5 **Bolivar**, Tn,US
117/G6 **Bolívar** (pk.), Ven.
108/F7 **Bolivia**
53/F4 **Bollendorf**, Ger.
56/F4 **Bollène**, Fr.
54/D4 **Bolligen**, Swi.
45/F5 **Bollin** (riv.), Eng,UK
45/F5 **Bollington**, Eng,UK
42/F3 **Bollnäs**, Swe.
58/B4 **Bollullos Par del Condado**, Sp.
47/F5 **Bolney**, Eng,UK
104/C1 **Bolobo**, D.R. Congo
57/J4 **Bologna**, It.
64/G4 **Bologoye**, Rus.
97/J7 **Bolomba**, D.R. Congo
77/M2 **Bolon'** (lake), Rus.
104/C2 **Bolongongo**, Ang.
83/D3 **Bolovens** (plat.), Laos
60/B1 **Bolsena** (lake), It.
67/K2 **Bol'shaya Khobda** (riv.), Kaz.
67/K1 **Bol'shaya Kinel'** (riv.), Rus.
65/P2 **Bol'shaya Rogovaya** (riv.), Rus.
65/N2 **Bol'shaya Synya** (riv.), Rus.
77/L2 **Bol'shaya Ussurka** (riv.), Rus.
69/L2 **Bol'shevik** (isl.), Rus.
65/M2 **Bol'shezemel'skaya** (tundra), Rus.
68/F2 **Bol'shoy Bolvanskiy Nos** (pt.), Rus.
67/H2 **Bol'shoy Irgiz** (riv.), Rus.
69/Q2 **Bol'shoy Lyakhovskiy** (isl.), Rus.
67/J2 **Bol'shoy Uzen'** (riv.), Kaz., Rus.
76/D1 **Bol'shoy Yenisey** (riv.), Rus.
45/G5 **Bolsover**, Eng,UK
50/C2 **Bolsward**, Neth.
46/C6 **Bolt Head** (pt.), Wal,UK
127/Q8 **Bolton**, On,Can
45/F4 **Bolton**, Eng,UK
45/G4 **Bolton Abbey**, Eng,UK
63/K5 **Bolu**, Turk.
63/K5 **Bolu** (prov.), Turk.
74/B2 **Bolvadin**, Turk.
55/H5 **Bolzano** (Bozen), It.
55/H4 **Bolzano-Bozen** (prov.), It.
104/B2 **Boma**, D.R. Congo
91/D2 **Bomaderry**, Austl.
84/B4 **Bombay** (Mumbai), India
87/H4 **Bomberai** (pen.), Indo.
110/C1 **Bom Despacho**, Braz.
85/G2 **Bomi**, China
110/J6 **Bom Jardim de Minas**, Braz.
110/B4 **Bom Jesus**, Braz.
109/K5 **Bom Jesus da Gurguéia** (mts.), Braz.
109/K6 **Bom Jesus da Lapa**, Braz.
110/B1 **Bom Jesus de Goiás**, Braz.
110/D2 **Bom Jesus do Itabapoana**, Braz.
110/G8 **Bom Jesus dos Perdões**, Braz.
51/G3 **Bomlitz**, Ger.
110/B3 **Bom Retiro**, Braz.
97/L6 **Bomu** (riv.), D.R. Congo
60/B4 **Bon** (cape), Tun.
130/K3 **Bona** (mtn.), Ak,US
117/H5 **Bonaire** (isl.), NAnt.
116/C4 **Bonampak** (ruins), Mex.
117/G4 **Bonao**, DRep.
92/B6 **Bonaparte** (arch.), Austl.
130/F3 **Bonasila** (mtn.), Ak,US
127/H1 **Bonaventure**, Qu,Can
127/H1 **Bonaventure** (riv.), Qu,Can
127/L1 **Bonavista** (bay), Nf,Can
127/L1 **Bonavista** (cape), Nf,Can
57/J4 **Bondeno**, It.
97/K7 **Bondo**, D.R. Congo
98/E4 **Bondoukou**, IvC.
86/D5 **Bondowoso**, Indo.
87/F4 **Bone** (gulf), Indo.
51/E5 **Bönen**, Ger.
87/F5 **Bonerate** (isls.), Indo.
75/F5 **Bong** (lake), China
98/C5 **Bong** (co.), Libr.
98/C5 **Bong** (range), Libr.
87/F1 **Bongabong**, Phil.
97/K7 **Bongandanga**, D.R. Congo
87/E2 **Bongao**, Phil.
87/E2 **Bonggi** (isl.), Malay.
87/F4 **Bongka** (riv.), Indo.
103/H7 **Bongolava** (uplands), Madg.
96/J5 **Bongor**, Chad
97/K6 **Bongos** (mts.), CAfr.
83/E3 **Bong Son**, Viet.
128/D3 **Bonham**, Tx,US
52/D1 **Bonheiden**, Belg.
60/A2 **Bonifacio** (str.), Fr., It.
129/G4 **Bonifay**, Fl,US
92/D2 **Bonin** (isls.), Japan
129/H5 **Bonita Springs**, Fl,US
116/D4 **Bonito** (pk.), Hon.
53/G2 **Bonn**, Ger.
122/D3 **Bonners Ferry**, Id,US
122/E4 **Bonner-West Riverside**, Mt,US
123/K3 **Bonnet** (lake), Mb,Can
54/C5 **Bonneville**, Fr.
122/C4 **Bonneville** (dam), Or, Wa,US
132/C3 **Bonney Lake**, Wa,US
122/F2 **Bonnyville**, Ab,Can
102/C4 **Bontberg** (peak), SAfr.
102/C4 **Bontebok Nat'l Park**, SAfr.
87/E5 **Bonthain**, Indo.
98/B5 **Bonthe**, SLeo.
82/D4 **Bontoc**, Phil.
62/D2 **Bonyhád**, Hun.
105/J **Bonzare** (coast), Ant.
52/D1 **Boom**, Belg.
123/K5 **Boone**, Ia,US
129/H2 **Boone**, NC,US
129/F3 **Booneville**, Ms,US
131/F5 **Boonton**, NJ,US
76/D2 **Böōntsagaan** (lake), Mong.
126/C4 **Boonville**, In,US
91/C1 **Booroondara** (peak), Austl.
52/A5 **Boos**, Fr.
127/G3 **Boothbay Harbor**, Me,US
105/D **Boothby** (cape), Ant.
118/G1 **Boothia** (gulf), Nun.,Can
118/G1 **Boothia** (pen.), Nun.,Can
45/E5 **Bootle**, Eng,UK
96/H8 **Booué**, Gabon
53/G3 **Boppard**, Ger.
91/C1 **Boppy** (peak), Austl.
112/C4 **Boquete** (peak), Arg.
101/C2 **Bor** (dry riv.), Kenya
65/K4 **Bor**, Rus.
97/M6 **Bor**, Sudan
74/C3 **Bor**, Turk.
62/F3 **Bor**, Yugo.
93/K6 **Bora Bora** (isl.), FrPol.
122/E4 **Borah** (peak), Id,US
42/E4 **Borås**, Swe.
72/F3 **Borāzjān**, Iran
108/G4 **Borba**, Braz.
56/D3 **Borbonnais** (hist. reg.), Fr.
109/L5 **Borborema** (plat.), Braz.
62/E3 **Borča**, Yugo.
51/F5 **Borchen**, Ger.
105/M **Borchgrevink** (coast), Ant.
74/E2 **Borçka**, Turk.
50/D4 **Borculo**, Neth.
110/G7 **Borda da Mata**, Braz.
56/C4 **Bordeaux**, Fr.
119/R7 **Borden** (isl.), NW,Can
119/H2 **Borden** (pen.), Nun.,Can
131/F5 **Bordentown**, NJ,US
59/G4 **Bordj el Bahri** (cape), Alg.
96/G2 **Bordj Omar Driss**, Alg.
47/F4 **Bordon**, Eng,UK
47/F3 **Borehamwood**, Eng,UK
42/E2 **Børgefjell Nat'l Park**, Nor.
51/G5 **Borgentreich**, Ger.
50/D3 **Borger**, Neth.
128/C3 **Borger**, Tx,US
52/D1 **Borgerhout**, Belg.
42/F4 **Borgholm**, Swe.
51/F4 **Borgholzhausen**, Ger.
51/E4 **Borghorst**, Ger.
57/G4 **Borgo San Dalmazzo**, It.
99/F4 **Borgou** (prov.), Ben.
99/F4 **Borgu Game Rsv.**, Nga.
66/B2 **Borislav**, Ukr.
67/G2 **Borisoglebsk**, Rus.
103/H6 **Boriziny**, Madg.
50/D5 **Borken**, Ger.
50/D1 **Borkum** (isl.), Ger.
42/E3 **Borlänge**, Swe.
57/H4 **Bormida** (riv.), It.
50/C6 **Born**, Neth.
48/G3 **Borna**, Ger.
50/C2 **Borndiep** (chan.), Neth.
50/D4 **Borne**, Neth.
52/D1 **Bornem**, Belg.
86/E3 **Borneo** (isl.), Asia
53/F2 **Bornheim**, Ger.
49/H1 **Bornholm** (co.), Den.
49/H1 **Bornholm** (isl.), Den.
49/H1 **Bornholmsgat** (chan.), Swe.
99/H3 **Borno** (state), Nga.
58/C4 **Bornos**, Sp.
96/H5 **Bornu** (plains), Nga.
97/L6 **Boro** (riv.), Sudan
75/D3 **Borohoro** (mts.), China, Kaz.
82/E5 **Borongan**, Phil.
45/G3 **Boroughbridge**, Eng,UK
64/G4 **Borovichi**, Rus.
62/D3 **Borovo**, Cro.
66/B3 **Borşa**, Rom.
77/H1 **Borshchovochnyy** (mts.), Rus.
62/E1 **Borsod-Abaúj-Zemplén** (co.), Hun.
50/A6 **Borssele**, Neth.
75/D3 **Bortala** (riv.), China
46/B2 **Borth**, Wal,UK
72/F2 **Borūjen**, Iran
72/E2 **Borūjerd**, Iran
76/D3 **Bor Ul** (mts.), China
76/H1 **Borzya**, Rus.
60/A2 **Bosa**, It.
62/C3 **Bosanska Dubica**, Bosn.
62/C3 **Bosanska Gradiška**, Bosn.
62/C3 **Bosanska Kostajnica**, Bosn.
62/C3 **Bosanska Krupa**, Bosn.
62/D3 **Bosanski Brod**, Bosn.
62/C3 **Bosanski Petrovac**, Bosn.
62/D3 **Bosanski Šamac**, Bosn.
97/Q5 **Bosaso** (Bender Cassim), Som.
46/B5 **Boscastle**, Eng,UK
85/J3 **Bose**, China
47/F5 **Bosham**, Eng,UK
50/B4 **Boskoop**, Neth.
49/J4 **Boskovice**, Czh.
62/D3 **Bosna** (riv.), Bosn.
62/C3 **Bosnia and Herzegovina**
79/G3 **Bōsō** (pen.), Japan
97/J7 **Bosobolo**, D.R. Congo
63/J5 **Bosporus** (str.), Turk.
124/F4 **Bosque Farms**, NM,US
113/K6 **Bosques Petrificados Natural Mon.**, Arg.
96/J6 **Bossangoa**, CAfr.
128/E3 **Bossier City**, La,US
75/E3 **Bosten** (lake), China
45/H6 **Boston**, Eng,UK
128/E3 **Boston** (mts.), Ar,US
127/G3 **Boston** (cap.), Ma,US
128/E3 **Boston**, Tx,US
62/D3 **Bosut** (riv.), Cro.
84/B3 **Botād**, India
90/H8 **Botany** (bay), Austl.
129/H3 **Boteler** (peak), NC,US
103/F2 **Botelerpunt** (pt.), SAfr.
110/G6 **Botelhos**, Braz.
61/J1 **Botev** (peak), Bul.
63/F4 **Botevgrad**, Bul.
103/E2 **Bothaspas** (pass), SAfr.
45/E2 **Bothel**, Eng,UK
132/C2 **Bothell**, Wa,US
46/D5 **Bothenhampton**, Eng,UK
42/G2 **Bothnia** (gulf), Fin., Swe.
66/C3 **Botoşani**, Rom.
63/H2 **Botoşani** (co.), Rom.
81/D3 **Botou**, China
83/D2 **Bo Trach**, Viet.
53/F3 **Botrange** (mtn.), Belg.
104/D5 **Botswana**
60/E3 **Botte Donato** (peak), It.
45/H4 **Bottesford**, Eng,UK
45/H6 **Bottesford**, Eng,UK
123/H3 **Bottineau**, ND,US
50/D5 **Bottrop**, Ger.
110/B2 **Botucatu**, Braz.
127/L1 **Botwood**, Nf,Can
98/D4 **Bou** (riv.), IvC.
98/D5 **Bouaflé**, IvC.
98/D5 **Bouaké**, IvC.
96/J6 **Bouar**, CAfr.
57/K2 **Boubín** (peak), Czh.
97/J6 **Bouca**, CAfr.
127/P6 **Boucherville**, Qu,Can
98/C3 **Boucle du Baoulé Nat'l Park**, Mali
96/E1 **Boudenib**, Mor.
99/E2 **Boû Djébéha** (well), Mali
52/B5 **Bouffémont**, Fr.
90/B1 **Bougainville** (reef), Austl.
113/N7 **Bougainville** (cape), Falk.
92/E5 **Bougainville** (isl.), PNG
98/D4 **Bougouni**, Mali
98/E4 **Bougouriba** (prov.), Burk.
56/C3 **Bouguenais**, Fr.
96/F1 **Bouira**, Alg.
92/B8 **Boulder**, Austl.
125/F2 **Boulder**, Co,US
122/E4 **Boulder**, Mt,US
124/D4 **Boulder City**, Nv,US
132/P16 **Boulder Hill**, Il,US
99/E4 **Boulgo** (prov.), Burk.
99/E3 **Boulkiemde** (prov.), Burk.
56/C3 **Boulogne** (riv.), Fr.
52/B6 **Boulogne-Billancourt**, Fr.
52/A2 **Boulogne-sur-Mer**, Fr.
45/F4 **Boulsworth** (hill), Eng,UK
59/F1 **Boumort** (mtn.), Sp.
130/K3 **Boundary**, Yk,Can
124/C3 **Boundary** (peak), Nv,US
131/F5 **Bound Brook**, NJ,US
98/D4 **Boundiali**, IvC.
124/E2 **Bountiful**, Ut,US
39/T8 **Bounty** (isls.), NZ
131/B2 **Bouquet** (canyon), Ca,US
126/C3 **Bourbonnais**, Il,US
52/B2 **Bourbourg**, Fr.
99/F2 **Bouressa** (wadi), Mali
54/B5 **Bourg-en-Bresse**, Fr.
56/E3 **Bourges**, Fr.
56/F4 **Bourg-lès-Valence**, Fr.
56/B3 **Bourgneuf** (bay), Fr.
52/D5 **Bourgogne**, Fr.
56/E3 **Bourgogne** (reg.), Fr.
56/F4 **Bourgoin-Jallieu**, Fr.
47/F1 **Bourne**, Eng,UK
47/F3 **Bourne End**, Eng,UK
47/E5 **Bournemouth**, Eng,UK
47/E2 **Bournville**, Eng,UK
43/A4 **Bourn-Vincent Mem. Nat'l Park**, Ire.
51/E3 **Bourtanger Moor** (reg.), Ger.
47/E3 **Bourton on the Water**, Eng,UK
98/B2 **Boutilimit**, Mrta.
39/K8 **Bouvet** (isl.), Nor.
52/C5 **Bouzy**, Fr.
51/G5 **Bovenden**, Ger.
50/D3 **Bovenwijde** (lake), Neth.
46/C5 **Bovey Tracey**, Eng,UK
57/J4 **Bovolone**, It.
122/E3 **Bow** (riv.), Ab,Can
123/J4 **Bowdle**, SD,US
45/F5 **Bowdon**, Eng,UK
90/C3 **Bowen**, Austl.
50/C5 **Bowen Merwede** (can.), Neth.
45/G3 **Bowes**, Eng,UK
124/E4 **Bowie**, Az,US
131/K8 **Bowie**, Md,US
122/F3 **Bow Island**, Ab,Can
90/B2 **Bowling Green** (cape), Austl.
126/C4 **Bowling Green**, Ky,US
125/K3 **Bowling Green**, Mo,US
126/D3 **Bowling Green**, Oh,US
90/B2 **Bowling Green Bay Nat'l Park**, Austl.
105/G **Bowman** (isl.), Ant.
119/J2 **Bowman** (bay), Nun.,Can
123/H4 **Bowman**, ND,US
127/S8 **Bowmanville**, Nf,Can
45/E2 **Bowness-on-Solway**, Eng,UK
87/F4 **Bowokan** (isls.), Indo.
91/D2 **Bowral**, Austl.
122/C2 **Bowron** (riv.), BC,Can
123/H4 **Box Elder**, SD,US
91/C3 **Box Hill**, Austl.
91/G5 **Box Hill**, Austl.
50/C5 **Boxmeer**, Neth.
50/C5 **Boxtel**, Neth.
74/C2 **Boyabat**, Turk.
91/D2 **Boyd-Konangra Nat'l Park**, Austl.
123/K5 **Boyer** (riv.), Ia,US
122/E2 **Boyle**, Ab,Can
44/B4 **Boyne** (riv.), Ire.
126/C2 **Boyne City**, Mi,US
129/H5 **Boynton Beach**, Fl,US
122/F5 **Boysen** (res.), Wy,US
61/J3 **Bozcaada** (isl.), Turk.
122/F4 **Bozeman**, Mt,US
74/C3 **Bozkir**, Turk.
96/J6 **Bozoum**, CAfr.
74/B2 **Bozüyük**, Turk.
57/G4 **Bra**, It.
52/D2 **Brabant** (prov.), Belg.
47/G4 **Brabourne Lees**, Eng,UK
62/C4 **Brač** (isl.), Cro.
60/B1 **Bracciano** (lake), It.
126/E2 **Bracebridge**, On,Can
64/B3 **Bräcke**, Swe.
128/C4 **Brackettville**, Tx,US
47/E2 **Brackley**, Eng,UK
47/F4 **Bracknell**, Eng,UK
110/B4 **Braço do Norte**, Braz.
62/F2 **Brad**, Rom.
60/D2 **Bradano** (riv.), It.
44/D3 **Bradda Head** (pt.), IM,UK
129/H5 **Bradenton**, Fl,US
45/G4 **Bradford**, Eng,UK
126/E3 **Bradford**, Pa,US
46/D4 **Bradford on Avon**, Eng,UK
47/E5 **Brading**, Eng,UK
131/F5 **Bradley Beach**, NJ,US
46/C5 **Bradninch**, Eng,UK
128/D4 **Brady**, Tx,US
130/L3 **Braeburn**, Yk,Can
43/D2 **Braemar**, Sc,UK
58/A2 **Braga**, Port.
58/A2 **Braga** (dist.), Port.
112/E2 **Bragado**, Arg.
109/J4 **Bragança**, Braz.
58/B2 **Bragança**, Port.
58/B2 **Bragança** (dist.), Port.
110/G7 **Bragança Paulista**, Braz.
71/J7 **Brahmaputra** (riv.), Asia
44/D6 **Braich-y-Pwll** (pt.), Wal,UK
44/B2 **Braid** (riv.), NI,UK
63/H3 **Brăila**, Rom.
63/H3 **Brăila** (co.), Rom.
52/D2 **Braine-l'Alleud**, Belg.
52/D2 **Braine-le-Comte**, Belg.
123/K4 **Brainerd**, Mn,US
47/G3 **Braintree**, Eng,UK
102/C3 **Brak** (riv.), SAfr.
51/F2 **Brake**, Ger.
52/C2 **Brakel**, Belg.
51/G5 **Brakel**, Ger.
98/B2 **Brakna** (reg.), Mrta.
127/Q8 **Bramalea**, On,Can
45/G4 **Bramhope**, Eng,UK
127/Q8 **Brampton**, On,Can
45/F2 **Brampton**, Eng,UK
51/E4 **Bramsche**, Ger.
108/F4 **Branco** (riv.), Braz.
104/B5 **Brandberg** (peak), Namb.
48/G2 **Brandenburg**, Ger.
48/G2 **Brandenburg** (state), Ger.
45/H4 **Brandesburton**, Eng,UK
123/J3 **Brandon**, Mb,Can
47/G2 **Brandon**, Eng,UK
129/H5 **Brandon**, Fl,US
129/F3 **Brandon**, Ms,US
112/F2 **Brandsen**, Arg.
49/K1 **Braniewo**, Pol.
47/E5 **Bransgore**, Eng,UK
127/J2 **Bras d'Or** (lake), NS,Can
109/J7 **Brasília** (cap.), Braz.
109/J7 **Brasília Nat'l Park**, Braz.
110/D1 **Brasil, Planalto do** (plat.), Braz.
63/G3 **Braşov**, Rom.
63/G3 **Braşov** (co.), Rom.
50/B6 **Brasschaat**, Belg.
129/H3 **Brasstown Bald** (peak), Ga,US
49/J4 **Bratislava** (cap.), Slvk.
49/J4 **Bratislava** (reg.), Slvk.
69/L4 **Bratsk**, Rus.
127/F3 **Brattleboro**, Vt,US
116/E5 **Braulio Carrillo**, CR
57/H5 **Braunau am Inn**, Aus.
51/H5 **Braunlage**, Ger.
51/H4 **Braunschweig** (Brunswick), Ger.
46/B4 **Braunton**, Eng,UK
59/G2 **Brava** (coast), Sp.
113/T12 **Brava** (pt.), Uru.
108/F7 **Bravo** (peak), Bol.
124/D4 **Brawley**, Ca,US
119/J2 **Bray** (isl.), Nun.,Can
44/B5 **Bray**, Ire.
56/D3 **Braye** (riv.), Fr.
44/B5 **Bray Head** (pt.), Ire.
52/B4 **Bray-sur-Somme**, Fr
107/D3 **Brazil**
126/C4 **Brazil**, In,US
107/E4 **Brazilian** (plat.), Braz.
110/H7 **Brazópolis**, Braz.
128/D4 **Brazos** (riv.), Tx,US
113/K7 **Brazo Sur** (riv.), Arg.
104/C1 **Brazzaville** (cap.), Congo
62/D3 **Brčko**, Bosn.
48/J2 **Brda** (riv.), Pol.
57/K2 **Brdy** (mts.), Czh.
131/C3 **Brea**, Ca,US
46/D3 **Bream**, Eng,UK
63/G3 **Breaza**, Rom.
43/D2 **Brechin**, Sc,UK
50/B6 **Brecht**, Belg.
123/J4 **Breckenridge**, Mn,US
51/E6 **Breckerfeld**, Ger.
47/G2 **Breckland** (reg.), Eng,UK
113/K8 **Brecknock** (pen.), Chile
49/J4 **Břeclav**, Czh.
46/C3 **Brecon**, Wal,UK
46/C3 **Brecon Beacons** (mts.), Wal,UK
46/C3 **Brecon Beacons Nat'l Park**, Wal,UK
50/B5 **Breda**, Neth.
52/B1 **Bredene**, Belg.
53/E1 **Bree**, Belg.
102/L10 **Breë** (riv.), SAfr.
62/F5 **Bregalinca** (riv.), FYROM
55/F2 **Bregenz**, Aus.
42/M6 **Breidhafjördhur** (bay), Ice.
51/F2 **Bremen**, Ger.
51/F2 **Bremen** (state), Ger.
90/E7 **Bremer** (riv.), Austl.
51/F1 **Bremerhaven**, Ger.
132/B2 **Bremerton**, Wa,US
51/G2 **Bremervörde**, Ger.
46/C4 **Brendon** (hills), Eng,UK
128/D4 **Brenham**, Tx,US
44/E5 **Brenig, Llyn** (lake), Wal,UK
54/B4 **Brenne** (riv.), Fr.
55/H4 **Brenner** (Brennerpass) (pass), Aus.
57/J4 **Brenta** (riv.), It.
47/G3 **Brentwood**, Eng,UK
132/L11 **Brentwood**, Ca,US
131/G5 **Brentwood**, NY,US
57/J4 **Brescia**, It.
55/G5 **Brescia** (prov.), It.
52/A4 **Bresle** (riv.), Fr.
57/J3 **Bressanone**, It.
56/C3 **Bressuire**, Fr.
49/M2 **Brest**, Bela.
56/A2 **Brest**, Fr.
49/M2 **Brestskaya** (prov.), Bela.
56/B2 **Bretagne** (mts.), Fr.
56/B2 **Bretagne** (reg.), Fr.
103/R15 **Bretagne** (pt.), Reun.
122/E2 **Breton**, Ab,Can
127/K2 **Breton** (cape), NS,Can
50/B4 **Breukelen**, Neth.
109/H4 **Breves**, Braz.
119/K2 **Brevoort** (isl.), Nun.,Can
127/G2 **Brewer**, Me,US
46/D1 **Brewood**, Eng,UK
125/H2 **Brewster**, Ne,US
122/D3 **Brewster**, Wa,US
129/G4 **Brewton**, Al,US
62/B3 **Brežice**, Slov.
63/G3 **Brezoi**, Rom.
97/K6 **Bria**, CAfr.
57/G4 **Briançon**, Fr.
46/C2 **Brianne, Lyn** (res.), Wal,UK
131/F5 **Brick**, NJ,US
43/A4 **Bride** (riv.), Ire.
44/D3 **Bride**, IM,UK
128/E4 **Bridge City**, Tx,US
46/C4 **Bridgend**, Wal,UK
46/C4 **Bridgend** (co.), Wal,UK
124/C3 **Bridgeport**, Ca,US
127/F3 **Bridgeport**, Ct,US
125/G2 **Bridgeport**, Ne,US
126/D4 **Bridgeport**, WV,US
122/F4 **Bridger**, Mt,US
117/K5 **Bridgetown** (cap.), Bar.
91/C4 **Bridgewater**, Austl.
127/H2 **Bridgewater**, NS,Can
126/E4 **Bridgewater**, Va,US
46/D1 **Bridgnorth**, Eng,UK
127/G2 **Bridgton**, Me,US
46/D4 **Bridgwater**, Eng,UK
46/C4 **Bridgwater** (bay), Eng,UK
45/H3 **Bridlington**, Eng,UK
45/H3 **Bridlington** (bay), Eng,UK
46/D5 **Bridport**, Eng,UK
52/C6 **Brie** (reg.), Fr.
52/B6 **Brie-Comte-Robert**, Fr.
49/J3 **Brieg Brzeg**, Pol.
50/B5 **Brielle**, Neth.
131/F5 **Brielle**, NJ,US
45/F4 **Brierfield**, Eng,UK
45/H4 **Brigg**, Eng,UK
54/D5 **Brig-Glis**, Swi.
124/D2 **Brigham City**, Ut,US
45/G4 **Brighouse**, Eng,UK
47/E5 **Brighstone**, Eng,UK
47/H3 **Brightlingsea**, Eng,UK
90/F6 **Brighton**, Austl.
91/F5 **Brighton**, Austl.
47/F5 **Brighton**, Eng,UK
125/F3 **Brighton**, Co,US
56/F4 **Brignais**, Fr.
56/G5 **Brignoles**, Fr.
98/A3 **Brikama**, Gam.
47/E3 **Brill**, Eng,UK
109/H8 **Brillante** (riv.), Braz.
51/F6 **Brilon**, Ger.
45/G5 **Brimington**, Eng,UK
61/E2 **Brindisi**, It.
46/E3 **Brinkworth**, Eng,UK
58/A1 **Brion**, Sp.
132/K11 **Briones** (res.), Ca,US
90/F6 **Brisbane** (riv.), Austl.
90/E6 **Brisbane For. Park**, Austl.
90/E6 **Brisbane**, Austl.
91/C3 **Brisbane Ranges Nat'l Park**, Austl.
91/D2 **Brisbane Waters Nat'l Park**, Austl.
46/B4 **Bristol** (chan.), UK
46/D4 **Bristol**, Eng,UK
46/D4 **Bristol** (co.), Eng,UK
130/F4 **Bristol** (bay), Ak,US
131/F5 **Bristol**, Pa,US
129/H2 **Bristol**, Tn,US
125/H4 **Bristow**, Ok,US
130/K2 **British** (mts.), Yk,Can, Ak,US
118/D3 **British Columbia** (prov.), Can.
119/S6 **British Empire** (range), Nun.,Can
71/G10 **British Indian Ocean Terr.**
102/P12 **Brits**, SAfr.
56/B2 **Brittany** (reg.), Fr.
123/J4 **Britton**, SD,US
56/D4 **Brive-la-Gaillarde**, Fr.
46/C6 **Brixham**, Eng,UK
47/F2 **Brixworth**, Eng,UK
49/J4 **Brno**, Czh.
90/C3 **Broad** (sound), Austl.
130/J3 **Broad** (pass), Ak,US
129/H3 **Broad** (riv.), NC, SC,US
126/E1 **Broadback** (riv.), Qu,Can
43/D3 **Broad Law** (mtn.), Sc,UK
91/F5 **Broadmeadows**, Austl.
90/C3 **Broad Sound** (chan.), Austl.
47/H4 **Broadstairs**, Eng,UK
47/E5 **Broadstone**, Eng,UK
123/G4 **Broadus**, Mt,US
91/E1 **Broadwater Nat'l Park**, Austl.
47/E2 **Broadway**, Eng,UK
47/E2 **Broadway** (hill), Eng,UK
46/D5 **Broadwindsor**, Eng,UK
119/R7 **Brock** (isl.), NW,Can
51/H5 **Brocken** (peak), Ger.
47/E5 **Brockenhurst**, Eng,UK
127/G3 **Brockton**, Ma,US
126/F2 **Brockville**, On,Can
118/G1 **Brodeur** (pen.), Nun.,Can
131/E4 **Brodhead** (cr.), Pa,US
49/K2 **Brodnica**, Pol.
50/B3 **Broek Op Langedijk**, Neth.
91/D2 **Broken** (bay), Austl.
125/J3 **Broken Arrow**, Ok,US
125/H2 **Broken Bow**, Ne,US
125/J4 **Broken Bow**, Ok,US
125/J4 **Broken Bow** (lake), Ok,US
91/B1 **Broken Hill**, Austl.
128/B3 **Brokeoff** (mts.), NM,US
46/D2 **Bromsgrove**, Eng,UK
46/D2 **Bromyard**, Eng,UK
56/F4 **Bron**, Fr.
42/D4 **Brønderslev**, Den.
99/E5 **Brong-Ahafo** (reg.), Gha.
57/H4 **Broni**, It.
46/C3 **Bronllys**, Wal,UK
42/E2 **Brønnøysund**, Nor.
127/Q9 **Bronte**, On,Can
60/D4 **Bronte**, It.
131/G5 **Bronx** (co.), NY,US
82/C6 **Brooke's Point**, Phil.
132/Q16 **Brookfield**, Il,US
125/J3 **Brookfield**, Mo,US
132/P13 **Brookfield**, Wi,US
129/F4 **Brookhaven**, Ms,US
131/H5 **Brookhaven**, NY,US
123/J4 **Brookings**, SD,US
131/G5 **Brooklyn (Kings)** (co.), NY,US
131/K7 **Brooklyn Park**, Md,US
47/F3 **Brookmans Park**, Eng,UK
122/F3 **Brooks**, Ab,Can
130/E2 **Brooks** (mtn.), Ak,US
130/F2 **Brooks** (range), Ak,US
129/H4 **Brooksville**, Fl,US
131/E6 **Broomall**, Pa,US
127/P7 **Brossard**, Qu,Can
45/H2 **Brotton**, Eng,UK
45/F2 **Brough**, Eng,UK
127/R8 **Brougham**, On,Can
44/B2 **Broughshane**, NI,UK
47/F2 **Broughton**, Eng,UK
45/E3 **Broughton in Furness**, Eng,UK
47/G4 **Broughton Street**, Eng,UK
50/A5 **Brouwersdam** (dam), Neth.
82/C5 **Brown** (shoal)
46/D2 **Brown Clee** (hill), Eng,UK
128/C3 **Brownfield**, Tx,US
47/E1 **Brownhills**, Eng,UK
122/E3 **Browning**, Mt,US
47/E5 **Brownsea** (isl.), Eng,UK
131/F6 **Browns Mills**, NJ,US
129/F3 **Brownsville**, Tn,US
128/D5 **Brownsville**, Tx,US
46/B5 **Brown Willy** (hill), Eng,UK
128/D4 **Brownwood**, Tx,US
52/B3 **Bruay-en-Artois**, Fr.
52/C3 **Bruay-sur-l'Escaut**, Fr.
92/A7 **Bruce** (peak), Austl.
126/D2 **Bruce** (pen.), On,Can
54/D1 **Bruche** (riv.), Fr.
53/G5 **Bruchmühlbach-Miesau**, Ger.
57/H2 **Bruchsal**, Ger.
51/G5 **Brucht** (riv.), Ger.
57/K3 **Bruck an der Grossglockner-strasse**, Aus.
62/C1 **Bruck an der Leitha**, Aus.
57/L3 **Bruck an der Mur**, Aus.
48/F5 **Bruckmühl**, Ger.
46/D4 **Brue** (riv.), Eng,UK
52/C1 **Bruges** (Brugge), Belg.
50/D6 **Brüggen**, Ger.
53/F2 **Brühl**, Ger.
102/B2 **Brukkaros** (peak), Namb.
109/K6 **Brumado**, Braz.
53/G6 **Brumath**, Fr.
50/D4 **Brummen**, Neth.
42/D3 **Brumunddal**, Nor.
60/A2 **Bruncu Spina** (peak), It.
47/H1 **Brundall**, Eng,UK
52/D4 **Brune** (riv.), Fr.
124/D2 **Bruneau** (riv.), Id, Nv,US
86/D2 **Brunei**
57/J3 **Brunico**, It.
51/G1 **Brunsbüttel**, Ger.
53/E2 **Brunssum**, Neth.
91/F5 **Brunswick**, Austl.
113/J8 **Brunswick** (pen.), Chile
129/H4 **Brunswick**, Ga,US
127/G3 **Brunswick**, Me,US
126/D3 **Brunswick**, Oh,US
51/H4 **Brunswick** (Braunschweig), Ger.
110/B3 **Brusque**, Braz.
52/D2 **Brussels** (Bruxelles) (cap.), Belg.
46/D4 **Bruton**, Eng,UK
56/C2 **Bruz**, Fr.
105/U **Bryan** (coast), Ant.
126/C3 **Bryan**, Oh,US
128/D4 **Bryan**, Tx,US
66/E1 **Bryansk**, Rus.
66/E1 **Bryansk Obl.**, Rus.
124/D3 **Bryce Canyon Nat'l Park**, Ut,US
45/E5 **Brymbo**, Wal,UK
46/C2 **Bryn Brawd** (mtn.), Wal,UK
46/C3 **Brynithel**, Wal,UK
46/C3 **Brynmawr**, Wal,UK
49/J3 **Brzeg Dolny**, Pol.
49/L4 **Brzesko**, Pol.
49/M4 **Brzozów**, Pol.
83/C3 **Bua Yai**, Thai.
98/B4 **Buba**, GBis.
98/B4 **Bubaque**, GBis.
72/E3 **Būbiyan** (isl.), Kuw.
74/B3 **Bucak**, Turk.
108/D2 **Bucaramanga**, Col.
59/P10 **Bucelas**, Port.
119/J1 **Buchan** (gulf), Nun.,Can
98/C5 **Buchanan**, Libr.
125/H5 **Buchanan** (lake), Tx,US
127/K1 **Buchans**, Nf,Can
63/H3 **Bucharest** (Bucureşti) (cap.), Rom.
51/G2 **Buchholz in der Nordheide**, Ger.
124/B4 **Buchon** (pt.), Ca,US
45/F3 **Buckden Pike** (mtn.), Eng,UK
51/G4 **Bückeburg**, Ger.
46/C6 **Buckfastleigh**, Eng,UK
126/D4 **Buckhannon**, WV,US
43/D2 **Buckie**, Sc,UK
126/F2 **Buckingham**, Qu,Can
47/F3 **Buckingham**, Eng,UK
47/F3 **Buckinghamshire** (co.), Eng,UK
45/E5 **Buckley**, Wal,UK
46/D2 **Bucknell**, Eng,UK
43/D2 **Bucksburn**, Sc,UK
127/H2 **Buctouche**, NB,Can
63/H3 **Bucureşti** (Bucharest) (cap.), Rom.
126/D3 **Bucyrus**, Oh,US
62/D2 **Budaörs**, Hun.
62/D2 **Budapest** (cap.), Hun.
84/C2 **Budaun**, India
105/H **Budd** (coast), Ant.
132/B3 **Budd** (inlet), Wa,US
131/F5 **Budd Lake**, NJ,US
46/B5 **Bude**, Eng,UK
46/B5 **Bude** (bay), Eng,UK
50/C6 **Budel**, Neth.
48/E1 **Büdelsdorf**, Ger.

145
Büdin – Carav

57/H1 **Büdingen,** Ger.
97/J7 **Budjala,** D.R. Congo
46/C5 **Budleigh Salterton,** Eng,UK
62/D4 **Budva,** Yugo.
63/J2 **Budzhak** (reg.), Mol., Ukr.
96/G7 **Buea,** Camr.
131/C3 **Buena Park,** Ca,US
108/C3 **Buenaventura,** Col.
125/F3 **Buena Vista,** Co,US
126/E4 **Buena Vista,** Va,US
112/B4 **Bueno** (riv.), Chile
113/S12 **Buenos Aires** (cap.), Arg.
112/C5 **Buenos Aires** (lake), Arg.
112/E3 **Buenos Aires** (prov.), Arg.
58/A1 **Bueu,** Sp.
91/C3 **Buffalo** (peak), Austl.
122/E2 **Buffalo** (lake), Ab,Can
103/E2 **Buffalo** (riv.), SAfr.
128/E2 **Buffalo** (riv.), Ar,US
123/K4 **Buffalo,** Mn,US
125/J3 **Buffalo,** Mo,US
127/S10 **Buffalo,** NY,US
125/H3 **Buffalo,** Ok,US
123/H4 **Buffalo,** SD,US
129/G3 **Buffalo** (riv.), Tn,US
122/G4 **Buffalo,** Wy,US
132/Q15 **Buffalo Grove,** Il,US
122/F2 **Buffalo Narrows,** Sk,Can
91/B1 **Buffalo Riv. Overflow** (swamp), Austl.
102/B3 **Buffelsrivier** (dry riv.), SAfr.
129/G3 **Buford,** Ga,US
63/G3 **Buftea,** Rom.
66/B1 **Bug** (riv.), Eur.
63/K2 **Bug** (estuary), Ukr.
108/C3 **Buga,** Col.
116/E6 **Bugaba,** Pan.
56/E5 **Bugarach, Pic de** (peak), Fr.
47/E2 **Bugbrooke,** Eng,UK
86/D5 **Bugel** (pt.), Indo.
52/D1 **Buggenhout,** Belg.
62/C3 **Bugojno,** Bosn.
101/B2 **Bugosa** (prov.), Ugan.
87/E2 **Bugsuk** (isl.), Phil.
65/M5 **Bugul'ma,** Rus.
67/K1 **Buguruslan,** Rus.
76/D4 **Buh** (riv.), China
74/D3 **Buḩayrat al Asad** (lake), Turk.
72/D2 **Buḩayrat ath Tharthār** (lake), Iraq
122/E5 **Buhl,** Id,US
63/H2 **Buhuşi,** Rom.
99/E4 **Bui** (dam), Gha.
99/E4 **Bui Gorge** (res.), Gha.
46/C2 **Builth Wells,** Wal,UK
112/Q9 **Buin,** Chile
58/C4 **Bujalance,** Sp.
62/E4 **Bujanovac,** Yugo.
63/H3 **Bujor,** Rom.
101/A3 **Bujumbura** (cap.), Buru.
49/J2 **Buk,** Pol.
92/E5 **Buka** (isl.), PNG
76/H1 **Bukachacha,** Rus.
75/F4 **Bukadaban Feng** (peak), China
72/E1 **Būkān,** Iran
101/A3 **Bukavu,** D.R. Congo
83/C5 **Buket Bubat** (peak), Malay.
68/G6 **Bukhara,** Uzb.
76/A2 **Bukhtarma** (riv.), Kaz.
86/B4 **Bukittinggi,** Indo.
62/E1 **Bükki Nat'l Park,** Hun.
101/A3 **Bukoba,** Tanz.
86/B4 **Buku** (cape), Indo.
82/D5 **Bulan,** Phil.
84/C2 **Bulandshahr,** India
74/E2 **Bulanık,** Turk.
87/F3 **Bulawa** (peak), Indo.
104/E5 **Bulawayo,** Zim.
130/B5 **Buldir** (isl.), Ak,US
76/C2 **Bulgan** (riv.), Mong.
63/G4 **Bulgaria**
60/D2 **Bulgheria** (peak), It.
82/C6 **Buliluyan** (cape), Phil.
90/F7 **Bulimba** (cr.), Austl.
47/E2 **Bulkington,** Eng,UK
122/B2 **Bulkley** (riv.), BC,Can
44/B1 **Bull** (pt.), NI,UK
58/E3 **Bullas,** Sp.
91/C3 **Buller** (peak), Austl.
124/D4 **Bullhead City,** Az,US
53/F3 **Büllingen,** Belg.
90/A5 **Bulloo** (riv.), Austl.
125/J3 **Bull Shoals** (lake), Ar, Mo,US
52/B3 **Bully-les-Mines,** Fr.
76/D2 **Bulnayn** (mts.), Mong.
112/B3 **Bulnes,** Chile
92/D5 **Bulolo,** PNG
87/F5 **Bulukumba,** Indo.
104/D2 **Bulungu,** D.R. Congo
97/K7 **Bumba,** D.R. Congo
101/C2 **Buna,** Kenya
79/L9 **Bunaga-take** (peak), Japan
101/A3 **Bunazi,** Tanz.
89/A4 **Bunbury,** Austl.
90/D4 **Bundaberg,** Austl.
51/F4 **Bünde,** Ger.
84/C2 **Būndi,** India
47/H2 **Bungay,** Eng,UK
86/C3 **Bunguran** (isl.), Indo.
101/A2 **Bunia,** D.R. Congo
129/H4 **Bunnell,** Fl,US
50/C4 **Bunnik,** Neth.
59/E3 **Buñol,** Sp.
50/C4 **Bunschoten,** Neth.
47/F3 **Buntingford,** Eng,UK
90/C4 **Bunya Mountains Nat'l Park,** Austl.
74/C2 **Bünyan,** Turk.
90/E6 **Bunya Park,** Austl.
87/E3 **Bunyu** (isl.), Indo.
83/E3 **Buon Me Thuot,** Viet.
83/E3 **Buon Mrong,** Viet.
101/C3 **Bura,** Kenya
97/L5 **Buram,** Sudan
97/M7 **Buranga** (pass), Ugan.
97/Q6 **Burao** (Burco), Som.
129/F4 **Buras-Triumph,** La,US
82/D5 **Burauen,** Phil.
72/D3 **Buraydah,** SAr.
53/H2 **Burbach,** Ger.
131/B2 **Burbank,** Ca,US
132/Q16 **Burbank,** Il,US
97/Q6 **Burco** (Burao), Som.
90/B3 **Burdekin** (riv.), Austl.
132/J10 **Burdell** (mtn.), Ca,US
74/B3 **Burdur,** Turk.
84/E3 **Burdwān,** India
47/H1 **Bure** (riv.), Eng,UK
51/F5 **Büren,** Ger.
50/C5 **Buren,** Neth.
76/E2 **Bürengiyn** (mts.), Mong.
73/K2 **Būrewāla,** Pak.
77/L1 **Bureya** (mts.), Rus.
77/L1 **Bureya** (riv.), Rus.
47/E3 **Burford,** Eng,UK
63/H4 **Burgas,** Bul.
63/H4 **Burgas** (bay), Bul.
63/H4 **Burgas** (reg.), Bul.
51/H4 **Burgdorf,** Ger.
57/M3 **Burgenland** (prov.), Aus.
127/K2 **Burgeo,** Nf,Can
102/D3 **Burgersdorp,** SAfr.
130/L2 **Burgess** (mtn.), Yk,Can
47/F5 **Burgess Hill,** Eng,UK
42/E2 **Burgfjället** (peak), Swe.
45/J5 **Burgh le Marsh,** Eng,UK
57/K2 **Burglengenfeld,** Ger.
58/D1 **Burgos,** Sp.
51/E4 **Burgsteinfurt,** Ger.
54/A3 **Burgundy** (hist. reg.), Fr.
51/G3 **Burgwedel,** Ger.
76/D4 **Burhan Budai** (mts.), China
74/A2 **Burhaniye,** Turk.
84/C3 **Burhānpur,** India
116/E6 **Burica** (pen.), CR, Pan.
116/E6 **Burica** (pt.), Pan.
132/C3 **Burien,** Wa,US
127/L2 **Burin,** Nf,Can
127/K2 **Burin** (pen.), Nf,Can
83/C3 **Buriram,** Thai.
110/B2 **Buritama,** Braz.
110/B1 **Buriti Alegre,** Braz.
110/C1 **Buritizeiro,** Braz.
59/E3 **Burjasot,** Sp.
128/D3 **Burkburnett,** Tx,US
105/S **Burke** (isl.), Ant.
131/J8 **Burke,** Va,US
122/B2 **Burke Channel** (inlet), BC,Can
99/E3 **Burkina Faso**
122/E5 **Burley,** Id,US
132/K11 **Burlingame,** Ca,US
127/Q9 **Burlington,** On,Can
125/G3 **Burlington,** Co,US
123/L5 **Burlington,** Ia,US
125/J3 **Burlington,** Ks,US
129/J2 **Burlington,** NC,US
131/F5 **Burlington,** NJ,US
127/F2 **Burlington,** Vt,US
132/P14 **Burlington,** Wi,US
63/K3 **Burnas** (lake), Ukr.
128/D4 **Burnet,** Tx,US
113/J8 **Burney** (peak), Chile
124/B2 **Burney,** Ca,US
47/G3 **Burnham on Crouch,** Eng,UK
46/D4 **Burnham on Sea,** Eng,UK
91/C4 **Burnie-Somerset,** Austl.
45/F4 **Burnley,** Eng,UK
122/D5 **Burns,** Or,US
118/E2 **Burnside** (riv.), Nun.,Can
122/B2 **Burns Lake,** BC,Can
123/J2 **Burntwood** (riv.), Mb,Can
47/E1 **Burntwood,** Eng,UK
91/B2 **Buronga,** Austl.
76/B2 **Burqin** (riv.), China
61/G2 **Burrel,** Alb.
91/D2 **Burrendong** (res.), Austl.
91/D2 **Burrewarra** (pt.), Austl.
59/E3 **Burriana,** Sp.
91/D2 **Burrinjuck** (res.), Austl.
90/A2 **Burrowes** (pt.), Austl.
44/D2 **Burrow Head** (pt.), Sc,UK
132/Q16 **Burr Ridge,** Il,US
90/D4 **Burrum River Nat'l Park,** Austl.
46/B3 **Burry** (inlet), Wal,UK
46/B3 **Burry Port,** Wal,UK
63/J5 **Bursa,** Turk.
63/J5 **Bursa** (prov.), Turk.
100/C3 **Būr Safājah,** Egypt
74/J6 **Būr Sa'īd** (gov.), Egypt
74/J6 **Būr Sa'īd** (Port Said), Egypt
51/E6 **Burscheid,** Ger.
45/F4 **Burscough Bridge,** Eng,UK
100/D5 **Būr Sūdān** (Port Sudan), Sudan
127/S9 **Burt,** NY,US
100/C2 **Būr Tawfīq,** Egypt
47/E5 **Burton,** Eng,UK
132/E6 **Burton,** Mi,US
47/F2 **Burton Latimer,** Eng,UK
47/E1 **Burton upon Trent,** Eng,UK
87/G4 **Buru** (isl.), Indo.
74/H6 **Burullus, Buḩayrat al** (lag.), Egypt
101/A3 **Burundi**
76/F2 **Burun Shibertuy** (peak), Rus.
130/L3 **Burwash Landing,** Yk,Can
47/G2 **Burwell,** Eng,UK
125/H2 **Burwell,** Ne,US
47/F5 **Bury,** Eng,UK
69/M4 **Buryat Aut. Rep.,** Rus.
67/J3 **Burynshyk** (pt.), Kaz.
47/G2 **Bury Saint Edmunds,** Eng,UK
57/H4 **Busalla,** It.
44/B1 **Bush** (riv.), NI,UK
76/C2 **Büs Hayrhan** (peak), Mong.
47/F3 **Bushey,** Eng,UK
131/E4 **Bushkill** (falls), Pa,US
102/B3 **Bushmanland** (reg.), SAfr.
44/B1 **Bushmills,** NI,UK
97/K7 **Businga,** D.R. Congo
42/D3 **Buskerud** (co.), Nor.
49/L3 **Busko-Zdrój,** Pol.
89/A4 **Busselton,** Austl.
97/L6 **Busseri** (riv.), Sudan
50/C4 **Bussum,** Neth.
113/K7 **Bustamente** (pt.), Arg.
90/C4 **Bustard** (pt.), Austl.
63/G3 **Buşteni,** Rom.
57/H4 **Busto Arsizio,** It.
82/C5 **Busuanga** (isl.), Phil.
97/K7 **Buta,** D.R. Congo
101/A3 **Butare,** Rwa.
92/G4 **Butaritari** (atoll), Kiri.
122/B3 **Bute** (inlet), BC,Can
43/C3 **Bute** (isl.), Sc,UK
76/E2 **Büteeliyn** (mts.), Mong.
101/A2 **Butembo,** D.R. Congo
110/B4 **Butiá,** Braz.
122/E3 **Butler,** Pa,US
87/F5 **Buton** (isl.), Indo.
122/E4 **Butte,** Mt,US
86/B2 **Butterworth,** Malay.
87/F5 **Butung** (isl.), Indo.
67/G2 **Buturlinovka,** Rus.
57/H1 **Butzbach,** Ger.
48/F2 **Bützow,** Ger.
97/Q7 **Buulo Berde,** Som.
97/P7 **Buur Hakaba,** Som.
51/G2 **Buxtehude,** Ger.
45/G5 **Buxton,** Eng,UK
64/J4 **Buy,** Rus.
67/H4 **Buynaksk,** Rus.
98/D5 **Buyo, Barrage de** (dam), IvC.
77/H2 **Buyr** (lake), Mong.
63/J5 **Büyükçekmece,** Turk.
74/B3 **Büyük Menderes** (riv.), Turk.
81/E2 **Buyun Shan** (peak), China
67/J3 **Buzachi** (pen.), Kaz.
63/H3 **Buzău,** Rom.
63/H3 **Buzău** (co.), Rom.
63/H3 **Buzău** (riv.), Rom.
62/E3 **Buziaş,** Rom.
110/H8 **Búzios** (isl.), Braz.
67/K1 **Buzuluk,** Rus.
63/F4 **Byala Slatina,** Bul.
119/R7 **Byam Martin** (chan.), Nun.,Can
119/R7 **Byam Martin** (isl.), Nun.,Can
66/D1 **Byarezina** (riv.), Bela.
49/J2 **Bydgoszcz,** Pol.
49/J2 **Bydgoszcz** (prov.), Pol.
47/E2 **Byfield,** Eng,UK
66/D1 **Bykhov,** Bela.
44/E5 **Bylchau,** Wal,UK
119/J1 **Bylot** (isl.), Nun.,Can
131/G5 **Byram** (pt.), NY,US
105/U **Byrd** (cape), Ant.
105/L **Byrd** (glac.), Ant.
113/J6 **Byron** (isl.), Chile
68/K2 **Byrranga** (mts.), Rus.
49/K4 **Bystrá** (peak), Slvk.
69/N3 **Bytantay** (riv.), Rus.
49/K3 **Bytom,** Pol.
49/J1 **Bytów,** Pol.

C

83/D2 **Ca** (riv.), Viet.
104/C3 **Caála,** Ang.
109/K5 **Caatingas** (reg.), Braz.
82/E6 **Cabadbaran,** Phil.
117/F3 **Cabaiguán,** Cuba
124/F4 **Caballo** (res.), NM,US
58/C1 **Cabañaquinta,** Sp.
82/D4 **Cabanatuan,** Phil.
46/C2 **Caban Coch** (res.), Wal,UK
127/G2 **Cabano,** Qu,Can
56/E5 **Cabestany,** Fr.
58/C3 **Cabeza del Buey,** Sp.
58/C1 **Cabezón de la Sal,** Sp.
117/G5 **Cabimas,** Ven.
104/B2 **Cabinda,** Ang.
96/C2 **Cabo Bojador,** WSah.
101/C5 **Cabo Delgado** (prov.), Moz.
110/D2 **Cabo Frio,** Braz.
126/E2 **Cabonga** (res.), Qu,Can
90/D4 **Caboolture,** Austl.
109/H3 **Cabo Orange Nat'l Park,** Braz.
104/F4 **Cabora Bassa** (lake), Moz.
127/J2 **Cabot** (str.), Nf, NS,Can
110/G6 **Cabo Verde,** Braz.
58/C4 **Cabra,** Sp.
90/G8 **Cabramatta,** Austl.
60/A3 **Cabras,** It.
59/G3 **Cabrera** (isl.), Sp.
122/F3 **Cabri,** Sk,Can
58/E3 **Cabriel** (riv.), Sp.
82/D4 **Cabugao,** Phil.
117/H5 **Cabure,** Ven.
110/B3 **Caçador,** Braz.
62/E4 **Čačak,** Yugo.
110/H8 **Caçapava,** Braz.
60/A2 **Caccia** (cape), It.
108/G7 **Cáceres,** Braz.
58/B3 **Cáceres,** Sp.
112/Q10 **Cachapoal** (riv.), Chile
124/B3 **Cache** (cr.), Ca,US
122/E5 **Cache** (peak), Id,US
122/C3 **Cache Creek,** BC,Can
98/A3 **Cacheu,** GBis.
109/G5 **Cachimbo** (mts.), Braz.
110/A4 **Cachoeira do Sul,** Braz.
110/J7 **Cachoeira Paulista,** Braz.
110/L7 **Cachoeiras de Macacu,** Braz.
110/B4 **Cachoeirinha,** Braz.
110/D2 **Cachoeiro de Itapemirim,** Braz.
110/G6 **Caconde,** Braz.
110/B1 **Caçu,** Braz.
104/B3 **Cacula,** Ang.
109/K6 **Caculé,** Braz.
59/G1 **Cadaqués,** Sp.
49/K4 **Čadca,** Slvk.
128/E3 **Caddo** (mts.), Ar,US
46/C1 **Cader Idris** (mtn.), Wal,UK
126/C2 **Cadillac,** Mi,US
82/D5 **Cadiz,** Phil.
58/B4 **Cádiz,** Sp.
58/B4 **Cádiz** (gulf), Sp.
126/C4 **Cadiz,** Ky,US
47/E5 **Cadnam,** Eng,UK
56/C2 **Caen,** Fr.
46/D3 **Caerleon,** Wal,UK
44/D5 **Caernarfon,** Wal,UK
44/D5 **Caernarfon** (bay), Wal,UK
46/C3 **Caerphilly,** Wal,UK
46/C3 **Caerphilly** (co.), Wal,UK
46/C1 **Caersws,** Wal,UK
74/M7 **Caesarea Nat'l Park,** Isr.
52/B2 **Caëstre,** Fr.
111/C2 **Cafayate,** Arg.
82/D6 **Cagayan de Oro,** Phil.
82/C6 **Cagayan Sulu** (isl.), Phil.
60/A3 **Cagliari,** It.
60/A3 **Cagliari** (gulf), It.
57/G5 **Cagnes-sur-Mer,** Fr.
108/D3 **Caguán** (riv.), Col.
117/H4 **Caguas,** PR
104/B4 **Cahama,** Ang.
43/B4 **Cahore** (pt.), Ire.
56/D4 **Cahors,** Fr.
110/B4 **Caí** (riv.), Braz.
109/H7 **Caiapó** (mts.), Braz.
109/H7 **Caiapó** (riv.), Braz.
117/F3 **Caibarién,** Cuba
109/L5 **Caicó,** Braz.
117/G3 **Caicos** (isls.), Trks.
110/G8 **Caieiras,** Braz.
52/A4 **Cailly** (riv.), Fr.
83/D4 **Cai Nuoc,** Viet.
105/Y **Caird** (coast), Ant.
130/G3 **Cairn** (mtn.), Ak,US
91/B3 **Cairn Curran** (dam), Austl.
43/D2 **Cairngorm** (mts.), Sc,UK
44/C2 **Cairn Pat** (hill), Sc,UK
44/C2 **Cairnryan,** Sc,UK
90/B2 **Cairns,** Austl.
44/D1 **Cairnsmore of Carsphairn** (mtn.), Sc,UK
129/G4 **Cairo,** Ga,US
126/B4 **Cairo,** Il,US
100/B2 **Cairo** (Al Qāhirah) (cap.), Egypt
47/H1 **Caister on Sea,** Eng,UK
45/H5 **Caistor,** Eng,UK
127/Q9 **Caistor Centre,** On,Can
127/Q9 **Caistorville,** On,Can
104/C4 **Caiundo,** Ang.
81/C5 **Caizi** (lake), China
108/C5 **Cajabamba,** Peru
108/C5 **Cajamarca,** Peru
116/E3 **Cajón** (pt.), Cuba
99/H5 **Calabar,** Nga.
117/H6 **Calabozo,** Ven.
60/E3 **Calabria** (reg.), It.
60/E3 **Calabria Nat'l Park,** It.
58/C4 **Calaburras, Punta de** (pt.), Sp.
62/F4 **Calafat,** Rom.
58/E1 **Calahorra,** Sp.
52/A2 **Calais,** Fr.
127/H2 **Calais,** Me,US
52/A2 **Calais, Canal de** (can.), Fr.
111/C2 **Calalaste** (mts.), Arg.
111/C1 **Calama,** Chile
82/C5 **Calamian Group** (isls.), Phil.
62/F3 **Călan,** Rom.
82/D5 **Calapan,** Phil.
63/H3 **Călăraşi,** Rom.
63/H3 **Călăraşi** (co.), Rom.
58/E3 **Calasparra,** Sp.
58/E2 **Calatayud,** Sp.
132/L12 **Calaveras** (res.), Ca,US
82/D4 **Calayan,** Phil.
82/D4 **Calayan** (isl.), Phil.
82/D5 **Calbayog,** Phil.
112/B4 **Calbuco,** Chile
108/D6 **Calca,** Peru
128/E4 **Calcasieu** (riv.), La,US
126/F2 **Calcium,** NY,US
84/E3 **Calcutta,** India
58/A3 **Caldas da Rainha,** Port.
110/B1 **Caldas Novas,** Braz.
45/E2 **Caldbeck,** Eng,UK
51/G6 **Calden,** Ger.
45/G4 **Calder** (riv.), Eng,UK
130/M4 **Calder** (mtn.), Ak,US
59/L6 **Caldes de Montbui,** Sp.
45/F2 **Caldew** (riv.), Eng,UK
46/D3 **Caldicot,** Wal,UK
122/D5 **Caldwell,** Id,US
128/D4 **Caldwell,** Tx,US
46/B3 **Caldy** (isl.), Wal,UK
102/D3 **Caledon** (riv.), Les., SAfr.
127/Q8 **Caledon East,** On,Can
127/H2 **Caledonia** (hills), NB,Can
59/G2 **Calella,** Sp.
112/Q9 **Calera de Tango,** Chile
117/P9 **Calera Víctor Rosales,** Mex.
117/P10 **Caleta de Campos Chutla,** Mex.
112/D5 **Caleta Olivia,** Arg.
124/D4 **Calexico,** Ca,US
45/E3 **Calf, The** (mtn.), Eng,UK
122/E3 **Calgary,** Ab,Can
59/S12 **Calheta,** Azor.,Port.
59/U15 **Calheta,** Madr.,Port.
129/G3 **Calhoun,** Ga,US
126/C4 **Calhoun,** Ky,US
108/C3 **Cali,** Col.
84/C5 **Calicut** (Kozhikode), India
58/E4 **Calida, Costa** (coast), Sp.
124/D3 **Caliente,** Nv,US
117/M8 **California** (gulf), Mex.
124/B3 **California** (state), US
126/E4 **California,** Md,US
125/J3 **California,** Mo,US
111/D1 **Calilegua Nat'l Park,** Arg.
63/G3 **Călimăneşti,** Rom.
84/C5 **Calimere** (pt.), India
131/C2 **Calimesa,** Ca,US
116/C3 **Calkiní,** Mex.
91/A1 **Callabonna** (lake), Austl.
43/C2 **Callander,** Sc,UK
108/C6 **Callao,** Peru
129/G4 **Callaway,** Fl,US
112/Q9 **Calle Larga,** Chile
46/B6 **Callington,** Eng,UK
59/E3 **Callosa de Ensarriá,** Sp.
59/E3 **Callosa de Segura,** Sp.
46/D4 **Calne,** Eng,UK
52/B3 **Calonne-Ricouart,** Fr.
60/D2 **Calore** (riv.), It.
90/D4 **Caloundra,** Austl.
59/F3 **Calpe,** Sp.
46/B6 **Calstock,** Eng,UK
60/D4 **Caltagirone,** It.
60/D4 **Caltanissetta,** It.
56/F4 **Caluire-et-Cuire,** Fr.
132/Q16 **Calumet** (riv.), Il,US
132/Q16 **Calumet City,** Il,US
104/B3 **Caluquembe,** Ang.
122/A3 **Calvert** (isl.), BC,Can
45/G5 **Calverton,** Eng,UK
131/K7 **Calverton,** Md,US
131/H5 **Calverton,** NY,US
59/G3 **Calviá,** Sp.
102/B3 **Calvinia,** SAfr.
58/C2 **Calvitero** (mtn.), Sp.
47/G2 **Cam** (riv.), Eng,UK
109/L6 **Camaçari,** Braz.
104/C3 **Camacupa,** Ang.
117/F3 **Camagüey,** Cuba
117/F3 **Camagüey** (arch.), Cuba
57/J5 **Camaiore,** It.
108/D7 **Camaná,** Peru
110/B4 **Camaquã,** Braz.
110/A4 **Camaquã** (riv.), Braz.
59/V15 **Câmara de Lobos,** Madr.,Port.
57/G5 **Camarat** (cape), Fr.
58/D1 **Camargo,** Sp.
131/A2 **Camarillo,** Ca,US
58/A1 **Camariñas,** Sp.
116/D4 **Camarón** (cape), Hon.
112/D5 **Camarones** (bay), Arg.
58/B4 **Camas,** Sp.
83/D4 **Ca Mau,** Viet.
83/D4 **Ca Mau** (cape), Viet.
58/A1 **Cambados,** Sp.
110/B2 **Cambará,** Braz.
84/B3 **Cambay,** India
84/B3 **Cambay** (gulf), India
110/B2 **Cambé,** Braz.
47/F4 **Camberley Frimley,** Eng,UK
83/D3 **Cambodia**
110/C3 **Camboriú, Ponta do** (pt.), Braz.
46/A6 **Camborne,** Eng,UK
52/C3 **Cambrai,** Fr.
46/C2 **Cambrian** (mts.), Wal,UK
126/D3 **Cambridge,** On,Can
47/G2 **Cambridge,** Eng,UK
127/G3 **Cambridge,** Ma,US
126/E4 **Cambridge,** Md,US
123/K4 **Cambridge,** Mn,US
126/D3 **Cambridge,** Oh,US
47/G2 **Cambridgeshire** (co.), Eng,UK
59/F2 **Cambrils,** Sp.
110/G7 **Cambuí,** Braz.
110/H6 **Cambuquira,** Braz.
117/E6 **Cambutal** (mt.), Pan.
91/D2 **Camden,** Austl.
129/G4 **Camden,** Al,US
128/E3 **Camden,** Ar,US
127/G2 **Camden,** Me,US
131/E6 **Camden,** NJ,US
129/H3 **Camden,** SC,US
125/J3 **Camdenton,** Mo,US
104/D3 **Cameia Nat'l Park,** Ang.
46/B6 **Camel** (riv.), Eng,UK
131/E4 **Camelback** (mtn.), Pa,US
46/B5 **Camelford,** Eng,UK
119/R7 **Cameron** (isl.), Nun.,Can
124/E4 **Cameron,** Az,US
128/E4 **Cameron,** La,US
125/J3 **Cameron,** Mo,US
128/D4 **Cameron,** Tx,US
96/H7 **Cameroon**
109/J4 **Cametá,** Braz.
52/A2 **Camiers,** Fr.
82/D4 **Camiguin** (isl.), Phil.
129/G4 **Camilla,** Ga,US
108/F8 **Camiri,** Bol.
104/F5 **Camo-Camo,** Moz.
109/K4 **Camocim,** Braz.
85/F6 **Camorta** (isl.), India
52/A3 **Campagne,** Fr.
112/F2 **Campana,** Arg.
113/J7 **Campana** (isl.), Chile
112/C2 **Campanario** (peak), Arg.
60/D2 **Campanella** (cape), It.
110/H6 **Campanha,** Braz.
60/D2 **Campania** (reg.), It.
39/T8 **Campbell** (isl.), NZ
132/L12 **Campbell,** Ca,US
122/A2 **Campbell Island,** BC,Can
122/B3 **Campbell River,** BC,Can
126/C4 **Campbellsville,** Ky,US
127/H2 **Campbellton,** NB,Can
90/G9 **Campbelltown,** Austl.
127/Q9 **Campbellville,** On,Can
127/R9 **Campden,** On,Can
116/C4 **Campeche,** Mex.
116/C4 **Campeche** (bay), Mex.
116/C4 **Campeche** (state), Mex.
123/H3 **Camperville,** Mb,Can
110/G6 **Campestre,** Braz.
60/A3 **Campidano** (range), It.
58/C4 **Campillos,** Sp.
109/L5 **Campina Grande,** Braz.
110/F7 **Campinas,** Braz.
110/B1 **Campina Verde,** Braz.
108/C3 **Campoalegre,** Col.
60/D2 **Campobasso,** It.
110/C2 **Campo Belo,** Braz.
58/D3 **Campo de Criptana,** Sp.
117/G5 **Campo de la Cruz,** Col.
109/K6 **Campo Formoso,** Braz.
109/H8 **Campo Grande,** Braz.
111/G2 **Campo Largo,** Braz.
110/G8 **Campo Limpo Paulista,** Braz.
109/K4 **Campo Maior,** Braz.
58/B3 **Campo Maior,** Port.
57/H4 **Campomorone,** It.
110/A3 **Campo Mourão,** Braz.
58/C1 **Camporredondo** (res.), Sp.
110/D2 **Campos,** Braz.
109/J7 **Campos** (reg.), Braz.
110/C1 **Campos Altos,** Braz.
59/G3 **Campos del Puerto,** Sp.
110/H7 **Campos do Jordão,** Braz.
110/C2 **Campos Gerais,** Braz.
110/B3 **Campos Novos,** Braz.
131/K8 **Camp Springs,** Md,US
128/E4 **Campti,** La,US
83/E4 **Cam Ranh,** Viet.
122/E2 **Camrose,** Ab,Can
83/D1 **Cam Thuy,** Viet.
118/* **Canada**
112/E2 **Cañada de Gómez,** Arg.
125/H4 **Canadian** (riv.), US
128/C3 **Canadian,** Tx,US
112/C5 **Cañadon Grande** (mts.), Arg.
117/G6 **Canagua,** Ven.
108/F2 **Canaima Nat'l Park,** Ven.
63/H5 **Çanakkale,** Turk.
63/H5 **Çanakkale** (prov.), Turk.
93/U12 **Canala,** NCal.
112/E2 **Canals,** Arg.
59/E3 **Canals,** Sp.
126/E3 **Canandaigua,** NY,US
117/M7 **Cananea,** Mex.
110/C3 **Cananéia,** Braz.
59/X16 **Canary Islands** (aut. comm.), Sp.
116/D5 **Cañas,** CR
117/P9 **Canatlán,** Mex.
129/H4 **Canaveral** (cape), Fl,US
109/L7 **Canavieiras,** Braz.
91/D2 **Canberra** (cap.), Austl.
52/A3 **Canche** (riv.), Fr.
116/D3 **Cancún,** Mex.
58/C1 **Candás,** Sp.
127/N7 **Candiac,** Qu,Can
110/B2 **Candido Mota,** Braz.
86/D5 **Canding** (cape), Indo.
123/G2 **Candle** (lake), Sk,Can
123/J3 **Cando,** ND,US
82/D4 **Candon,** Phil.
110/B4 **Canela,** Braz.
57/H4 **Canelli,** It.
113/F2 **Canelones,** Uru.
113/F2 **Canelones** (dept.), Uru.
58/A1 **Cangas,** Sp.
58/B1 **Cangas de Narcea,** Sp.
58/C1 **Cangas de Onís,** Sp.
86/C5 **Cangkuang** (cape), Indo.
102/C4 **Cango Caves,** SAfr.
104/D3 **Cangombe,** Ang.
113/J7 **Cangrejo** (peak), Arg.
110/A4 **Canguçu,** Braz.
81/D3 **Cangzhou,** China
83/D1 **Canh Cuoc** (isl.), Viet.
104/B3 **Canhoca,** Ang.
90/C4 **Cania Gorge Nat'l Park,** Austl.
119/K3 **Caniapiscau** (lake), Qu,Can
119/K3 **Caniapiscau** (riv.), Qu,Can
60/C4 **Canicatti,** It.
56/E5 **Canigou, Pic de** (peak), Fr.
74/D2 **Canik** (mts.), Turk.
58/D4 **Caniles,** Sp.
109/L4 **Canindé,** Braz.
109/K5 **Canindé** (riv.), Braz.
74/C2 **Çankırı,** Turk.
87/F1 **Canlaon** (vol.), Phil.
122/E3 **Canmore,** Ab,Can
84/C5 **Cannanore,** India
60/E2 **Canne** (ruins), It.
53/F5 **Canner** (riv.), Fr.
57/G5 **Cannes,** Fr.
43/C2 **Cannich,** Sc,UK
46/D1 **Cannock,** Eng,UK
123/H4 **Cannonball** (riv.), ND,US
123/K4 **Cannon Falls,** Mn,US
110/B4 **Canoas,** Braz.
110/B3 **Canoas** (riv.), Braz.
91/D2 **Canobolas** (peak), Austl.
122/F2 **Canoe** (lake), Sk,Can
110/B3 **Canoinhas,** Braz.
45/F1 **Canonbie,** Sc,UK
125/F3 **Canon City,** Co,US
123/H3 **Canora,** Sk,Can
127/J2 **Canso** (cape), Can.
58/C1 **Cantabria** (aut. comm.), Sp.
56/E4 **Cantal** (plat.), Fr.
58/A2 **Cantanhede,** Port.
117/J6 **Cantaura,** Ven.
90/H8 **Canterbury,** Austl.
47/H4 **Canterbury,** Eng,UK
83/D4 **Can Tho,** Viet.
58/C4 **Cantillana,** Sp.
126/B3 **Canton,** Il,US
132/E7 **Canton,** Mi,US
129/F3 **Canton,** Ms,US
126/F2 **Canton,** NY,US
126/D3 **Canton,** Oh,US
125/H3 **Canton,** Ok,US
123/J5 **Canton,** SD,US
128/E3 **Canton,** Tx,US
93/H5 **Canton** (Abariringa) (atoll), Kiri.
82/B3 **Canton** (Guangzhou), China
57/H4 **Cantù,** It.
112/F2 **Cañuelas,** Arg.
91/B3 **Canunda Nat'l Park,** Austl.
47/G3 **Canvey Island,** Eng,UK
122/G2 **Canwood,** Sk,Can
128/C3 **Canyon,** Tx,US
124/E3 **Canyon de Chelly Nat'l Mon.,** Az,US
124/E3 **Canyonlands Nat'l Park,** Ut,US
83/D1 **Cao Bang,** Viet.
82/A2 **Caodu** (riv.), China
83/D4 **Cao Lanh,** Viet.
108/E2 **Capanaparo** (riv.), Ven.
109/J4 **Capanema,** Braz.
60/B1 **Capanne** (peak), It.
57/J5 **Capannori,** It.
110/B3 **Capão Bonito,** Braz.
110/D2 **Caparaó Nat'l Park,** Braz.
58/A3 **Caparica,** Port.
127/H1 **Cap-Chat,** Qu,Can
127/F2 **Cap-de-la-Madeleine,** Qu,Can
90/B1 **Cape** (riv.), Austl.
91/D4 **Cape Barren** (isl.), Austl.
127/J2 **Cape Breton** (highlands), NS,Can
127/J2 **Cape Breton** (isl.), NS,Can
127/J2 **Cape Breton Highlands Nat'l Park,** NS,Can
90/B2 **Cape Cleveland Nat'l Park,** Austl.
39/E5 **Cape Coast,** Gha.
127/G3 **Cape Cod Nat'l Seashore,** Ma,US
129/H5 **Cape Coral,** Fl,US
129/J3 **Cape Fear** (riv.), NC,US
125/K3 **Cape Girardeau,** Mo,US
129/K3 **Cape Hatteras Nat'l Seashore,** NC,US
130/E2 **Cape Krusenstern Nat'l Mon.,** Ak,US
44/E5 **Capel-Curig,** Wal,UK
110/D1 **Capelinha,** Braz.
59/K6 **Capellades,** Sp.
47/H4 **Capel le Ferne,** Eng,UK
129/J3 **Cape Lookout Nat'l Seashore,** NC,US
47/H2 **Capel Saint Mary,** Eng,UK
90/B1 **Cape Melville Nat'l Park,** Austl.
90/C3 **Cape Palmerston Nat'l Park,** Austl.
131/K7 **Cape Saint Claire,** Md,US
102/B4 **Cape Town** (cap.), SAfr.
90/B2 **Cape Tribulation Nat'l Park,** Austl.
90/B2 **Cape Upstart Nat'l Park,** Austl.
33/H5 **Cape Verde**
90/A1 **Cape York** (pen.), Austl.
117/G4 **Cap-Haïtien,** Haiti
60/A2 **Capicciola** (pt.), Fr.
109/J4 **Capim** (riv.), Braz.
110/B1 **Capinópolis,** Braz.
110/B2 **Capirara** (res.), Braz.
128/B3 **Capitan** (mts.), NM,US
109/J4 **Capitão Poco,** Braz.
92/D3 **Capitol Hill** (cap.), NMar.
124/E3 **Capitol Reef Nat'l Park,** Ut,US
109/H8 **Capivara** (res.), Braz.
110/J6 **Capivari** (riv.), Braz.
62/C4 **Čapljina,** Bosn.
60/D3 **Capo d'Orlando,** It.
60/A3 **Capoterra,** It.
60/A1 **Capraia** (isl.), It.
126/D2 **Capreol,** On,Can
60/D2 **Capri,** It.
90/C3 **Capricorn** (cape), Austl.
90/C3 **Capricorn** (chan.), Austl.
104/D4 **Caprivi Strip** (reg.), Namb.
128/C3 **Cap Rock Escarpment** (cliffs), Tx,US
128/C3 **Caprock, The** (cliffs), NM,US
127/G2 **Cap-Rouge,** Qu,Can
57/G5 **Cap Roux, Pointe du** (pt.), Fr.
125/G3 **Capulin Volcano Nat'l Mon.,** NM,US
108/D4 **Caquetá** (riv.), Col.
59/N9 **Carabanchel** (nrbhd.), Sp.
63/G3 **Caracal,** Rom.
117/H5 **Caracas** (cap.), Ven.
46/B5 **Caradon** (hill), Eng,UK
110/H8 **Caraguatatuba,** Braz.
110/H8 **Caraguatatuba** (bay), Braz.
112/B3 **Carahue,** Chile
109/H5 **Carajás** (mts.), Braz.
110/D2 **Carandaí,** Braz.
110/D2 **Carangola,** Braz.
62/F3 **Caransebeş,** Rom.
60/D2 **Carapelle** (riv.), It.
110/G8 **Carapicuíba,** Braz.
127/H2 **Caraquet,** NB,Can
62/E3 **Caraş-Severin** (co.), Rom.
116/E4 **Caratasca** (lag.), Hon.
110/D1 **Caratinga,** Braz.
108/E4 **Carauari,** Braz.
58/E3 **Caravaca de la Cruz,** Sp.

146

Carav – Chern

98/A4 **Caravela** (isl.), GBis.
111/F2 **Carazinho**, Braz.
58/A1 **Carballino**, Sp.
58/A1 **Carballo**, Sp.
123/J3 **Carberry**, Mb,Can
132/C3 **Carbon** (riv.), Wa,US
60/A3 **Carbonara** (cape), It.
60/D4 **Carbonara, Pizzo** (peak), It.
126/B4 **Carbondale**, Il,US
126/F3 **Carbondale**, Pa,US
60/A3 **Carbonia**, It.
59/E3 **Carcagente**, Sp.
112/E2 **Carcarañá**, Arg.
56/E5 **Carcassonne**, Fr.
59/P10 **Carcavelos**, Port.
58/E3 **Carche** (mtn.), Sp.
118/C2 **Carcross**, Yt,Can
59/L6 **Cardedeu**, Sp.
113/K7 **Cardiel** (lake), Arg.
46/C4 **Cardiff** (cap.), Wal,UK
46/B2 **Cardigan**, Wal,UK
59/F2 **Cardona**, Sp.
110/B2 **Cardoso**, Braz.
122/E3 **Cardston**, Ab,Can
62/F2 **Carei**, Rom.
56/C2 **Carentan**, Fr.
62/F4 **Carev vrh** (peak), FYROM
56/B2 **Carhaix-Plouguer**, Fr.
112/E3 **Carhué**, Arg.
110/D2 **Cariacica**, Braz.
117/J5 **Cariaco**, Ven.
108/C4 **Cariamanga**, Ecu.
60/E3 **Cariati**, It.
117/G5 **Caribbean** (sea)
122/C2 **Cariboo** (mts.), BC,Can
118/E3 **Caribou** (mts.), Ab,Can
126/B1 **Caribou** (lake), On,Can
130/L3 **Caribou**, Yk,Can
122/F5 **Caribou** (range), Id,US
127/G2 **Caribou**, Me,US
82/D5 **Carigara**, Phil.
109/K6 **Carinhanha**, Braz.
60/C3 **Carini**, It.
57/K3 **Carinthia** (prov.), Aus.
117/J5 **Caripito**, Ven.
125/G3 **Carizzo** (cr.), NM, Tx,US
59/E3 **Carlet**, Sp.
127/H2 **Carleton** (peak), NB,Can
127/H2 **Carleton** (riv.), NS,Can
127/H1 **Carleton**, Qu,Can
102/D2 **Carletonville**, SAfr.
124/C2 **Carlin**, Nv,US
90/H8 **Carlingford**, Austl.
44/B3 **Carlingford** (mtn.), Ire.
44/B3 **Carlingford Lough** (inlet), Ire.
126/B4 **Carlinville**, Il,US
127/Q9 **Carlisle**, On,Can
45/F2 **Carlisle**, Eng,UK
56/D5 **Carlit** (peak), Fr.
112/E2 **Carlos Casares**, Arg.
110/D1 **Carlos Chagas**, Braz.
117/F3 **Carlos M. De Cespedes**, Cuba
44/B6 **Carlow**, Ire.
44/B6 **Carlow** (co.), Ire.
125/F4 **Carlsbad**, NM,US
125/F4 **Carlsbad Caverns Nat'l Park**, NM,US
45/G6 **Carlton**, Eng,UK
123/K4 **Carlton**, Mn,US
127/Q9 **Carluke**, On,Can
123/H3 **Carlyle**, Sk,Can
125/K3 **Carlyle** (lake), Il,US
118/C2 **Carmacks**, Yk,Can
57/G4 **Carmagnola**, It.
123/J3 **Carman**, Mb,Can
46/B3 **Carmarthen**, Wal,UK
46/B3 **Carmarthen** (bay), Wal,UK
46/B3 **Carmarthenshire** (co.), Wal,UK
56/E4 **Carmaux**, Fr.
126/C4 **Carmel**, In,US
44/D5 **Carmel Head** (pt.), Wal,UK
74/K5 **Carmel, Mount** (Har Karmel) (mtn.), Isr.
112/F2 **Carmelo**, Uru.
117/M8 **Carmen** (isl.), Mex.
117/N7 **Carmen** (riv.), Mex.
126/B4 **Carmi**, Il,US
132/M9 **Carmichael**, Ca,US
110/L6 **Carmo**, Braz.
110/C1 **Carmo do Paranaíba**, Braz.
110/C2 **Carmo do Rio Claro**, Braz.
58/C4 **Carmona**, Sp.
44/B1 **Carnanmore** (mtn.), NI,UK
89/A3 **Carnarvon**, Austl.
102/C3 **Carnarvonleegte** (dry riv.), SAfr.
90/B4 **Carnarvon Nat'l Park**, Austl.
59/P10 **Carnaxide**, Port.
44/C2 **Carncastle**, NI,UK
123/H3 **Carnduff**, Sk,Can
44/D5 **Carnedd Dafydd** (mtn.), Wal,UK
44/E5 **Carnedd Llewelyn** (mtn.), Wal,UK
105/S **Carney** (isl.), Ant.
45/F3 **Carnforth**, Eng,UK
52/C3 **Carnières**, Fr.
44/B2 **Carnlough**, NI,UK
96/J7 **Carnot**, CAfr.
58/A1 **Carnota**, Sp.
43/D2 **Carnoustie**, Sc,UK
43/B4 **Carnsore** (pt.), Ire.
118/D2 **Carnwath** (riv.), NW,Can
126/D3 **Caro**, Mi,US
117/H4 **Carolina**, PR
93/K5 **Caroline** (isl.), Kiri.
92/D4 **Caroline** (isls.), Micr.
132/P16 **Carol Stream**, Il,US
41/G4 **Carpathian** (mts.), Eur.
57/J4 **Carpenedolo**, It.
89/C2 **Carpentaria** (gulf), Austl.
132/P15 **Carpentersville**, Il,US
56/F4 **Carpentras**, Fr.
57/J4 **Carpi**, It.
131/A2 **Carpinteria**, Ca,US
132/B3 **Carr** (inlet), Wa,US
129/G4 **Carrabelle**, Fl,US
57/J4 **Carrara**, It.
44/D6 **Carreg Ddu** (pt.), Wal,UK
117/J5 **Carriacou** (isl.), Gren.
44/C2 **Carrickfergus**, NI,UK
44/C2 **Carrickfergus** (dist.), NI,UK
44/A2 **Carrickmore**, NI,UK
52/B6 **Carrières-sous-Poissy**, Fr.
44/B3 **Carrigatuke** (mtn.), NI,UK
123/J4 **Carrington**, ND,US
58/C1 **Carrión** (riv.), Sp.
117/G5 **Carrizal**, Col.
120/E4 **Carrizo** (mts.), Az,US
128/C2 **Carrizo** (cr.), NM,US
128/D4 **Carrizo Springs**, Tx,US
125/F4 **Carrizozo**, NM,US
129/G3 **Carrollton**, Ga,US
126/C4 **Carrollton**, Ky,US
125/J3 **Carrollton**, Mo,US
123/H2 **Carrot** (riv.), Sk,Can
123/H2 **Carrot River**, Sk,Can
44/C2 **Carrowdore**, NI,UK
44/C2 **Carryduff**, NI,UK
74/D2 **Çarşamba**, Turk.
131/B3 **Carson**, Ca,US
124/C3 **Carson** (riv.), Nv,US
124/C3 **Carson** (sink), Nv,US
124/C3 **Carson City** (cap.), Nv,US
44/D1 **Carsphairn**, Sc,UK
122/E3 **Carstairs**, Ab,Can
112/Q9 **Cartagena**, Chile
112/F3 **Cartagena**, Col.
59/E4 **Cartagena**, Sp.
108/C3 **Cartago**, Col.
116/E6 **Cartago**, CR
58/C4 **Cártama**, Sp.
58/A3 **Cartaxo**, Port.
58/B4 **Cartaya**, Sp.
90/A1 **Carter** (peak), Austl.
131/F5 **Carteret**, NJ,US
129/G3 **Cartersville**, Ga,US
47/E3 **Carterton**, Eng,UK
60/B4 **Carthage** (ruins), Tun.
125/J3 **Carthage**, Mo,US
129/F3 **Carthage**, Ms,US
129/G2 **Carthage**, Tn,US
128/E3 **Carthage**, Tx,US
119/L3 **Cartwright**, Nf,Can
109/L5 **Caruaru**, Braz.
108/F1 **Carúpano**, Ven.
125/K3 **Caruthersville**, Mo,US
52/B2 **Carvin**, Fr.
58/A3 **Carvoeiro** (cape), Port.
132/P15 **Cary**, Il,US
129/J3 **Cary**, NC,US
96/D1 **Casablanca**, Mor.
110/F6 **Casa Branca**, Braz.
117/N7 **Casa de Janos**, Mex.
124/E4 **Casa Grande**, Az,US
124/E4 **Casa Grande Nat'l Mon.**, Az,US
60/D2 **Casal di Principe**, It.
57/J4 **Casalecchio di Reno**, It.
57/H4 **Casale Monferrato**, It.
98/A3 **Casamance** (riv.), Sen.
109/L4 **Casa Nova**, Braz.
61/F3 **Casarano**, It.
117/N7 **Casas Grandes** (ruins), Mex.
117/N8 **Cascada de Bassaseachic Nat'l Park**, Mex.
122/C5 **Cascade** (range), Can., US
122/D4 **Cascade** (res.), Id,US
132/C3 **Cascade-Fairwood**, Wa,US
103/R15 **Cascades** (pt.), Reun.
59/P10 **Cascais**, Port.
127/H1 **Cascapédia** (riv.), Qu,Can
57/J5 **Cascina-Navacchio**, It.
132/B3 **Case** (inlet), Wa,US
60/D2 **Caserta**, It.
105/H **Casey**, Ant.
105/D **Casey** (bay), Ant.
97/R5 **Caseyr** (cape), Som.
122/C4 **Cashmere**, Wa,US
112/E2 **Casilda**, Arg.
117/P10 **Casimiro Castillo**, Mex.
91/E1 **Casino**, Austl.
131/A2 **Casitas** (lake), Ca,US
108/C5 **Casma**, Peru
59/E2 **Caspe**, Sp.
123/G5 **Casper**, Wy,US
68/F6 **Caspian** (sea), Eur., Asia
59/G2 **Cassà de la Selva**, Sp.
104/D3 **Cassai** (riv.), Ang.
104/D3 **Cassamba**, Ang.
60/E3 **Cassano allo Ionio**, It.
126/D3 **Cass City**, Mi,US
110/C2 **Cássia**, Braz.
118/C3 **Cassiar** (mts.), BC,Can
110/B1 **Cassilândia**, Braz.
60/C2 **Cassino**, It.
125/J3 **Cassville**, Mo,US
131/B2 **Castaic**, Ca,US
131/B1 **Castaic** (lake), Ca,US
59/E3 **Castalla**, Sp.
109/J4 **Castanhal**, Braz.
60/D4 **Castelbuono**, It.
57/K5 **Castelfidardo**, It.
60/C3 **Castellammare** (gulf), It.
60/D2 **Castellammare di Stabia**, It.
57/G4 **Castellamonte**, It.
59/G2 **Castellar del Vallès**, Sp.
59/K7 **Castelldefels**, Sp.
59/L7 **Castell de Montjuïc**, Sp.
60/D4 **Castello Eurialo** (ruins), It.
59/E3 **Castellón de la Plana**, Sp.
74/N9 **Castel Nat'l Park**, Isr.
56/D5 **Castelnaudary**, Fr.
56/E5 **Castelnau-le-Lez**, Fr.
58/B3 **Castelo Branco**, Port.
58/B2 **Castelo Branco** (dist.), Port.
56/D4 **Castelsarrasin**, Fr.
60/C4 **Castelvetrano**, It.
110/B2 **Castilho**, Braz.
108/B5 **Castilla**, Peru
58/C2 **Castilla and León** (aut. comm.), Sp.
58/D3 **Castille-La Mancha** (aut. comm.), Sp.
117/G5 **Castilletes**, Col.
112/C4 **Castillo** (peak), Arg.
129/H4 **Castillo de San Marcos Nat'l Mon.**, Fl,US
113/G2 **Castillos**, Uru.
47/G1 **Castle Acre**, Eng,UK
43/A4 **Castlebar**, Ire.
46/D4 **Castle Cary**, Eng,UK
44/B3 **Castlecaulfield**, NI,UK
46/D4 **Castle Combe**, Eng,UK
124/E3 **Castle Dale**, Ut,US
44/B2 **Castledawson**, NI,UK
45/G6 **Castle Donnington**, Eng,UK
44/E2 **Castle Douglas**, Sc,UK
45/G4 **Castleford**, Eng,UK
122/D3 **Castlegar**, BC,Can
90/H8 **Castle Hill**, Austl.
44/D2 **Castle Kennedy**, Sc,UK
91/C3 **Castlemaine**, Austl.
90/G8 **Castlereagh**, Austl.
44/B1 **Castlerock**, NI,UK
125/F3 **Castle Rock**, Co,US
123/L5 **Castle Rock** (lake), Wi,US
90/C4 **Castle Tower Nat'l Park**, Austl.
44/D3 **Castletown**, IM,UK
44/C3 **Castlewellan**, NI,UK
122/F2 **Castor**, Ab,Can
96/D6 **Castos** (riv.), Libr.
56/E5 **Castres**, Fr.
50/B3 **Castricum**, Neth.
117/J5 **Castries** (cap.), StL.
110/B3 **Castro**, Braz.
112/B4 **Castro**, Chile
58/C4 **Castro del Río**, Sp.
58/B1 **Castro de Rey**, Sp.
51/E5 **Castrop-Rauxel**, Ger.
58/D1 **Castro-Urdiales**, Sp.
132/K11 **Castro Valley**, Ca,US
60/E3 **Castrovillari**, It.
58/C3 **Castuera**, Sp.
117/F3 **Cat** (isl.), Bahm.
123/K3 **Cat** (lake), On,Can
92/B3 **Catanduanes** (isl.), Phil.
110/L6 **Cataguases**, Braz.
82/D5 **Catainghan**, Phil.
87/F1 **Catainghan**, Phil.
63/K5 **Çatalağzı**, Turk.
110/C1 **Catalão**, Braz.
63/J5 **Çatalca**, Turk.
124/E4 **Catalina**, Az,US
59/F2 **Catalonia** (aut. comm.), Sp.
111/C2 **Catamarca**, Arg.
82/D5 **Catanduanes** (isl.), Phil.
110/B2 **Catanduva**, Braz.
60/D4 **Catania**, It.
60/D4 **Catania** (gulf), It.
60/E3 **Catanzaro**, It.
87/F1 **Catarman**, Indo.
82/D5 **Catarman**, Phil.
59/E3 **Catarroja**, Sp.
117/G6 **Catatumbo** (riv.), Col., Ven.
87/F2 **Catatungan** (mtn.), Phil.
129/H3 **Catawba** (riv.), NC, SC,US
82/D5 **Catbalogan**, Phil.
113/G2 **Catedral** (peak), Uru.
47/F4 **Caterham and Warlingham**, Eng,UK
100/C2 **Catherine, Mount** (Jabal Katrīnah) (mtn.), Egypt
117/F6 **Cativá**, Pan.
126/D4 **Catlettsburg**, Ky,US
116/D3 **Catoche** (cape), Mex.
57/K5 **Catria** (peak), It.
108/F3 **Catrimani** (riv.), Braz.
46/D2 **Catshill**, Eng,UK
126/F3 **Catskill** (mts.), NY,US
53/F5 **Cattenom**, Fr.
45/G3 **Catterick**, Eng,UK
82/D4 **Cauayan**, Phil.
82/D6 **Cauayan**, Phil.
108/C2 **Cauca** (riv.), Col.
109/L4 **Caucaia**, Braz.
108/C2 **Caucasia**, Col.
66/G4 **Caucasus** (mts.), Eur.
59/E3 **Caudete**, Sp.
52/C3 **Caudry**, Fr.
45/F1 **Cauldcleuch** (mtn.), Sc,UK
112/B2 **Cauquenes**, Chile
56/D4 **Caussade**, Fr.
60/D4 **Cava d'Ispica** (ruins), It.
58/B2 **Cávado** (riv.), Port.
56/F5 **Cavaillon**, Fr.
123/J3 **Cavalier**, ND,US
96/D6 **Cavalla** (riv.), IvC., Libr.
98/D5 **Cavalla** (Cavally) (riv.), IvC., Libr.
60/A1 **Cavallo, Capo al** (cape), Fr.
44/A4 **Cavan** (co.), Ire.
124/E4 **Cave Creek**, Az,US
109/J3 **Caviana**, Braz.
63/F2 **Cavnic**, Rom.
82/D5 **Cawayan**, Phil.
91/B2 **Cawndilla** (lake), Austl.
45/G4 **Cawood**, Eng,UK
47/H1 **Cawston**, Eng,UK
110/J6 **Caxambu**, Braz.
109/K4 **Caxias**, Braz.
110/B4 **Caxias do Sul**, Braz.
116/D4 **Caxinas** (pt.), Hon.
104/B2 **Caxito**, Ang.
74/B2 **Çay**, Turk.
108/C3 **Cayambe** (vol.), Ecu.
129/H3 **Cayce**, SC,US
63/L5 **Çaycuma**, Turk.
74/E2 **Çayeli**, Turk.
109/H3 **Cayenne** (cap.), FrG.
117/F4 **Cayman Brac** (isl.), Cay.
116/E4 **Cayman Islands**, UK
116/E4 **Cayos Cajones** (isls.), Hon.
116/E5 **Cayos Miskitos** (isls.), Nic.
62/B3 **Cazin**, Bosn.
58/D4 **Cazorla**, Sp.
58/C1 **Cea** (riv.), Sp.
109/L5 **Ceará-Mirim**, Braz.
113/G2 **Cebollatí** (riv.), Uru.
82/D5 **Cebu**, Phil.
82/D6 **Cebu** (isl.), Phil.
60/C2 **Ceccano**, It.
103/E2 **Cecil Macks** (pass), Swaz.
57/J5 **Cecina**, It.
60/E3 **Cecita** (lake), It.
123/H2 **Cedar** (lake), Mb,Can
126/E2 **Cedar** (lake), On,Can
132/L11 **Cedar** (mtn.), Ca,US
123/L5 **Cedar** (riv.), Ia,US
131/F6 **Cedar** (cr.), NJ,US
132/C3 **Cedar** (riv.), Wa,US
90/B1 **Cedar Bay Nat'l Park**, Austl.
125/G3 **Cedar Bluff** (res.), Ks,US
124/D3 **Cedar Breaks Nat'l Mon.**, Ut,US
124/D3 **Cedar City**, Ut,US
128/D3 **Cedar Creek** (res.), Tx,US
123/K5 **Cedar Falls**, Ia,US
131/F5 **Cedar Grove**, NJ,US
129/H4 **Cedar Key**, Fl,US
123/L5 **Cedar Rapids**, Ia,US
129/G3 **Cedartown**, Ga,US
124/B2 **Cedarville**, Ca,US
58/A1 **Cedeira**, Sp.
109/L5 **Cedro**, Braz.
117/L8 **Cedros** (isl.), Mex.
58/A1 **Cee**, Sp.
97/Q7 **Ceel Dheere**, Som.
97/Q5 **Ceerigaabo** (Erigabo), Som.
60/D3 **Cefalù**, It.
44/D5 **Cefni** (riv.), Wal,UK
45/E6 **Cefn-mawr**, Wal,UK
58/C2 **Cega** (riv.), Sp.
62/D2 **Cegléd**, Hun.
58/E3 **Cehegín**, Sp.
63/F2 **Cehu Silvaniei**, Rom.
45/E6 **Ceiriog** (riv.), Wal,UK
66/F4 **Çekerek** (riv.), Turk.
58/B1 **Celanova**, Sp.
116/D3 **Celarain** (pt.), Mex.
116/A3 **Celaya**, Mex.
44/B5 **Celbridge**, Ire.
87/F3 **Celebes** (sea), Asia
87/E4 **Celebes** (Sulawesi) (isl.), Indo.
126/C3 **Celina**, Oh,US
62/B2 **Celje**, Slov.
62/C2 **Celldömölk**, Hun.
56/E2 **Celle** (riv.), Fr.
51/H3 **Celle**, Ger.
46/A4 **Celtic** (sea), Eur.
46/B2 **Cemaes Head** (pt.), Wal,UK
86/D3 **Cemaru** (peak), Indo.
58/E3 **Cenajo** (res.), Sp.
87/H4 **Cenderawasih** (bay), Indo.
111/C4 **Centenario**, Arg.
110/B2 **Centenario do Sul**, Braz.
124/D4 **Centennial** (wash), Az,US
122/E4 **Centennial** (mts.), Id,US
123/H4 **Center**, ND,US
128/E4 **Center**, Tx,US
131/G5 **Centereach**, NY,US
132/F7 **Center Line**, Mi,US
131/H5 **Center Moriches**, NY,US
129/G3 **Center Point**, Al,US
129/G3 **Centerville**, Tn,US
128/E4 **Centerville**, Tx,US
57/J4 **Cento**, It.
112/C4 **Central** (peak), Arg.
99/E5 **Central** (reg.), Gha.
74/K5 **Central** (dist.), Isr.
101/C3 **Central** (prov.), Kenya
101/A2 **Central** (prov.), Ugan.
97/J6 **Central African Republic**
122/G3 **Central Butte**, Sk,Can
125/H2 **Central City**, Ne,US
108/C5 **Central, Cordillera** (range), SAm.
126/B4 **Centralia**, Il,US
122/C4 **Centralia**, Wa,US
131/G5 **Central Islip**, NY,US
73/H3 **Central Makrān** (range), Pak.
56/E4 **Central, Massif** (plat.), Fr.
109/J7 **Central, Planalto** (plat.), Braz.
122/C5 **Central Point**, Or,US
69/L3 **Central Siberian** (plat.), Rus.
65/N4 **Central Ural** (mts.), Rus.
56/D3 **Centre** (reg.), Fr.
129/G3 **Centreville**, Al,US
56/D4 **Céou** (riv.), Fr.
62/D3 **Čepin**, Cro.
87/G4 **Ceram** (isl.), Indo.
87/G4 **Ceram** (sea), Indo.
60/A2 **Ceraso** (cape), It.
59/L7 **Cerdanyola del Vallès**, Sp.
56/D4 **Cère** (riv.), Fr.
57/J4 **Cerea**, It.
46/B2 **Ceredigion** (co.), Wal.,UK
111/D2 **Ceres**, Arg.
109/J7 **Ceres**, Braz.
102/B4 **Ceres**, SAfr.
117/F6 **Cereté**, Col.
52/B5 **Cergy**, Fr.
60/D2 **Cerignola**, It.
63/J5 **Çerkezköy**, Turk.
63/J3 **Cernavodă**, Rom.
46/D5 **Cerne Abbas**, Eng,UK
117/N9 **Cerralvo** (isl.), Mex.
44/E5 **Cerrig-y-Druidion**, Wal,UK
61/F2 **Cërrik**, Alb.
116/A3 **Cerritos**, Mex.
116/B3 **Cerro Azul**, Mex.
112/C3 **Cerro Colorados** (res.), Arg.
117/L7 **Cerro de la Encantada** (peak), Mex.
117/M8 **Cerro Dos Picachos** (peak), Mex.
117/M8 **Cerro Encantada** (peak), Mex.
113/G2 **Cerro Largo** (dept.), Uru.
117/M7 **Cerro Pinacote** (peak), Mex.
60/D2 **Cervaro** (riv.), It.
60/D2 **Cervati** (peak), It.
59/F2 **Cervera**, Sp.
57/K4 **Cervia**, It.
60/D2 **Cervialto** (peak), It.
57/K4 **Cervignano del Friuli**, It.
110/H7 **Cervo** (hills), Braz.
58/B1 **Cervo**, Sp.
117/G5 **César** (riv.), Col.
57/K4 **Cesena**, It.
57/K4 **Cesenatico**, It.
64/E4 **Cēsis**, Lat.
57/L2 **České Budějovice**, Czh.
49/H4 **Českomoravská Vysočina** (upland), Czh.
57/L2 **Český Krumlov**, Czh.
62/C3 **Česma** (riv.), Cro.
61/K3 **Çeşme**, Turk.
74/A2 **Çeşme**, Turk.
56/C2 **Cesson-Sévigné**, Fr.
98/C5 **Cestos** (riv.), Libr.
62/C4 **Cetina** (riv), Cro.
62/D4 **Cetinje**, Yugo.
58/D2 **Ceurda del Pozo** (res.), Sp.
58/C5 **Ceuta**, Sp.
56/E5 **Cévennes** (mts.), Fr.
56/E4 **Cévennes Nat'l Park**, Fr.
74/C3 **Ceyhan**, Turk.
74/E3 **Ceylânpınar**, Turk.
84/D6 **Ceylon** (isl.), SrL.
56/F4 **Cèze** (riv.), Fr.
56/C5 **Chabarrou** (peak), Fr.
112/E2 **Chacabuco**, Arg.
108/C5 **Chachapoyas**, Peru
83/C3 **Chachoengsao**, Thai.
134/F3 **Chaco** (dry riv.), NM,US
128/B3 **Chaco** (mesa), NM,US
111/D2 **Chaco Austral** (plain), Arg.
108/G8 **Chaco Boreal** (plain), Par.
111/D1 **Chaco Central** (plain), Arg.
111/E2 **Chaco Nat'l Park**, Arg.
116/D4 **Chacujal** (ruins), Guat.
97/J4 **Chad**
96/H5 **Chad** (lake), Afr.
83/E4 **Cha Da** (cape), Viet.
47/E3 **Chadlington**, Eng,UK
125/G2 **Chadron**, Ne,US
63/J2 **Chadyr-Lunga**, Mol.
80/D2 **Chagang-Do** (prov.), NKor.
75/D5 **Chagdo Kangri** (peak), China
71/G10 **Chagos** (arch.), BrIn.
73/H3 **Chāh Behār** (Bandar Beheshtī), Iran
116/C4 **Chahuites**, Mex.
83/C3 **Chainat**, Thai.
83/C3 **Chaiyaphum**, Thai.
84/C5 **Chālakudi**, India
116/D5 **Chalatenango**, ESal.
101/C2 **Chalbi** (des.), Kenya
77/H2 **Chalchyn** (riv.), Mong.
127/H2 **Chaleur** (bay), NB, Qu,Can
47/F3 **Chalfont Saint Peter**, Eng,UK
47/E3 **Chalgrove**, Eng,UK
28/C4 **Chalk** (mts.), Tx,US
56/C3 **Challans**, Fr.
19/T6 **Challenger** (mts.), Nun.,Can
53/D5 **Challerange**, Fr.
122/E4 **Challis**, Id,US
47/G4 **Challock**, Eng,UK
52/D6 **Châlons-sur-Marne**, Fr.
54/A4 **Chalon-sur-Saône**, Fr.
72/F1 **Chālūs**, Iran
57/K2 **Cham**, Ger.
124/F3 **Chama** (riv.), Co, NM,US
86/B2 **Chamah** (peak), Malay.
73/J2 **Chaman**, Pak.
73/L2 **Chamba**, India
84/C2 **Chambal** (riv.), India
56/F4 **Chambaran** (plat.), Fr.
127/G2 **Chamberlain** (lake), Me,US
123/J5 **Chamberlain**, SD,US
130/K2 **Chamberlin** (mtn.), Ak,US
126/E4 **Chambersburg**, Pa,US
56/F4 **Chambéry**, Fr.
101/A5 **Chambeshi** (riv.), Zam.
127/P7 **Chambly**, Qu,Can
52/B5 **Chambly**, Fr.
74/F3 **Chamchamāl**, Iraq
56/F4 **Chamechaude** (mtn.), Fr.
111/C3 **Chamical**, Arg.
57/G4 **Chamonix-Mont-Blanc**, Fr.
130/L3 **Champagne**, Yk,Can
52/C6 **Champagne** (reg.), Fr.
56/F2 **Champagne-Ardennes** (reg.), Fr.
52/B5 **Champagne-sur-Oise**, Fr.
126/B3 **Champaign**, Il,US
112/D1 **Champaquí** (peak), Arg.
53/F6 **Champigneulles**, Fr.
126/F2 **Champlain** (lake), Can., US
116/C4 **Champotón**, Mex.
52/B6 **Champs-sur-Marne**, Fr.
111/B2 **Chañaral**, Chile
58/B4 **Chança** (riv.), Port.
108/C5 **Chan Chan** (ruins), Peru
112/B2 **Chanco**, Chile
130/J2 **Chandalar** (riv.), Ak,US
84/C2 **Chandausi**, India
84/C3 **Chanderi**, India
73/L2 **Chandigarh**, India
127/H1 **Chandler**, Qu,Can
130/H2 **Chandler** (riv.), Ak,US
128/D3 **Chandler**, Ok,US
84/C4 **Chandrapur**, India
81/C5 **Chang** (lake), China
81/L8 **Chang** (riv.), China
83/C3 **Chang** (isl.), Thai.
77/K3 **Changbai** (peak), China
80/D2 **Changbai** (mts.), China, NKor.
81/F2 **Changchun**, China
81/D5 **Changdang** (lake), China
82/B2 **Changde**, China
77/K4 **Changgi-ap** (cape), SKor.
82/D3 **Changhua**, Tai.
80/D5 **Changhŭng**, SKor.
81/D3 **Changli**, China
81/D2 **Changping**, China
80/C3 **Changsan-got** (cape), NKor.
82/B2 **Changsha**, China
81/E5 **Changshu**, China
85/J2 **Changshun**, China
80/D5 **Changsŏng**, SKor.
116/E6 **Changuinola**, Pan.
80/E5 **Ch'angwŏn**, SKor.
81/E3 **Changxing** (isl.), China
81/D5 **Chang** (Yangtze) (riv.), China
81/C3 **Changzhi**, China
81/D5 **Changzhou**, China
83/E2 **Chan May Dong** (cape), Viet.
47/H4 **Channel** (tunnel), UK, Fr.
124/C4 **Channel** (isls.), Ca,US
90/A4 **Channel Country** (plain), Austl.
56/B2 **Channel Islands**, UK
124/B4 **Channel Islands Nat'l Park**, Ca,US
127/K2 **Channel-Port aux Basques**, Nf,Can
58/B1 **Chantada**, Sp.
83/C3 **Chanthaburi**, Thai.
52/B5 **Chantilly**, Fr.
118/G2 **Chantrey** (inlet), Nun.,Can
125/J3 **Chanute**, Ks,US
81/D5 **Chao** (lake), China
77/H4 **Chaobai** (riv.), China
83/C3 **Chao Phraya** (riv.), Thai.
77/J2 **Chaor** (riv.), China
82/C3 **Chaoyang**, China
82/C3 **Chaozhou**, China
109/K6 **Chapada Diamantina Nat'l Park**, Braz.
109/J6 **Chapada dos Veadeiros Nat'l Park**, Braz.
126/F1 **Chapais**, Qu,Can
117/P9 **Chapala** (lake), Mex.
67/J1 **Chapayevsk**, Rus.
110/A3 **Chapecó**, Braz.
45/G5 **Chapel en le Frith**, Eng,UK
45/F2 **Chapelfell Top** (mtn.), Eng,UK
129/J3 **Chapel Hill**, NC,US
52/D3 **Chapelle-Lez-Herlaimont**, Belg.
45/J5 **Chapel Saint Leonards**, Eng,UK
45/G5 **Chapeltown**, Eng,UK
132/D2 **Chaplain** (lake), Wa,US
83/D2 **Chap Le**, Viet.
126/D2 **Chapleau**, On,Can
122/G3 **Chaplin**, Sk,Can
125/G2 **Chappell**, Ne,US
69/M4 **Chara** (riv.), Rus.
108/C3 **Charambirá** (pt.), Col.
61/L6 **Charandra** (riv.), Gre.
111/D2 **Charata**, Arg.
116/A3 **Charcas**, Mex.
105/U **Charcot** (isl.), Ant.
46/D5 **Chard**, Eng,UK
68/G6 **Chardzhou**, Trkm.
56/C4 **Charente** (riv.), Fr.
96/J5 **Chari** (riv.), Chad
73/J1 **Chārīkār**, Afg.
47/G4 **Charing**, Eng,UK
125/J2 **Chariton** (riv.), Ia, Mo,US
47/E3 **Charlbury**, Eng,UK
44/B3 **Charlemont**, NI,UK
52/D3 **Charleroi**, Belg.
52/D2 **Charleroi à Bruxelles, Canal de** (can.), Belg.
119/J2 **Charles** (isl.), Nun.,Can
126/F4 **Charles** (cape), Va,US
123/K5 **Charles City**, Ia,US
126/B4 **Charleston**, Il,US
125/K3 **Charleston**, Mo,US
129/F3 **Charleston**, Ms,US
124/D2 **Charleston**, Nv,US
129/J3 **Charleston**, SC,US
126/D4 **Charleston** (cap.), WV,US
53/D4 **Charleville-Mézières**, Fr.
126/C2 **Charlevoix**, Mi,US
122/B2 **Charlotte** (lake), BC,Can
126/C3 **Charlotte**, Mi,US
129/H3 **Charlotte**, NC,US
117/J4 **Charlotte Amalie** (cap.), USVI
126/E4 **Charlottesville**, Va,US
127/J2 **Charlottetown** (cap.), PE,Can
117/J5 **Charlotteville**, Trin.
119/H3 **Charlton** (isl.), Nun.,Can
46/D3 **Charlton Kings**, Eng,UK
56/F3 **Charolais** (mts.), Fr.
75/D2 **Charsk**, Kaz.
90/B3 **Charters Towers**, Austl.
56/D2 **Chartres**, Fr.
75/C3 **Charyn** (riv.), Kaz.
75/D1 **Charysh** (riv.), Rus.
112/F2 **Chascomús**, Arg.
122/D3 **Chase**, BC,Can
56/F4 **Chassezac** (riv.), Fr.
56/C3 **Chassiron, Pointe de** (pt.), Fr.
56/C3 **Châteaubriant**, Fr.
56/C3 **Château-d'Olonne**, Fr.
56/D2 **Châteaudun**, Fr.
127/N7 **Châteauguay**, Qu,Can
56/F5 **Châteaurenard-Provence**, Fr.
56/D3 **Château-Renault**, Fr.
56/D3 **Châteauroux**, Fr.
52/C5 **Château-Thierry**, Fr.
52/D3 **Châtelet**, Belg.
56/D3 **Châtellerault**, Fr.
125/J2 **Chatfield**, Mn,US
126/D3 **Chatham**, On,Can
113/J7 **Chatham** (isl.), Chile
47/G4 **Chatham**, Eng,UK
131/F5 **Chatham**, NJ,US
56/F3 **Châtillon-sur-Seine**, Fr.
84/D4 **Chatrapur**, India
90/H8 **Chatswood**, Austl.
131/B2 **Chatsworth** (res.), Ca,US
129/G3 **Chatsworth**, Ga,US
129/G4 **Chattahoochee**, Fl,US
129/G4 **Chattahoochee** (riv.), Fl, Ga,US
129/G3 **Chattanooga**, Tn,US
47/G2 **Chatteris**, Eng,UK
53/E2 **Chaudfontaine**, Belg.
127/G2 **Chaudière** (riv.), Qu,Can
83/D4 **Chau Doc**, Viet.
85/F3 **Chauk**, Myan.
85/G2 **Chaukan** (pass), India
52/B4 **Chaulnes**, Fr.
54/B1 **Chaumont**, Fr.
52/A5 **Chaumont-en-Vexin**, Fr.
52/D4 **Chaumont-Porcien**, Fr.
69/T3 **Chaunskaya** (bay), Rus.
52/C4 **Chauny**, Fr.
126/E3 **Chautauqua** (lake), NY,US
56/D3 **Chauvigny**, Fr.
58/B2 **Chaves**, Port.
83/D1 **Chay** (isl.), Viet.
108/E7 **Chayana** (riv.), Bol.
65/M4 **Chaykovskiy**, Rus.
45/G6 **Cheadle**, Eng,UK
129/G3 **Cheaha** (peak), Al,US
57/K1 **Cheb**, Czh.
65/K4 **Cheboksary**, Rus.
65/K4 **Cheboksary** (res.), Rus.
126/C2 **Cheboygan**, Mi,US
67/H4 **Chechen'** (isl.), Rus.
67/H4 **Chechnya Aut. Rep.**, Rus.
96/D3 **Chech, 'Erg** (des.), Afr.
80/E4 **Chech'ŏn**, SKor.
125/J4 **Checotah**, Ok,US
127/J2 **Chedabucto** (bay), NS,Can
46/D4 **Cheddar**, Eng,UK
85/F4 **Cheduba** (isl.), Myan.
127/S10 **Cheektowaga**, NY,US
126/D1 **Cheepash** (riv.), On,Can
126/D1 **Cheepay** (riv.), On,Can
77/L1 **Chegdomyn**, Rus.
104/F4 **Chegutu**, Zim.
122/C4 **Chehalis**, Wa,US
57/G5 **Cheiron, Cime du** (peak), Fr.
77/K5 **Cheju**, SKor.
77/K5 **Cheju** (isl.), SKor.
77/K5 **Cheju** (str.), SKor.
122/C4 **Chelan**, Wa,US
122/C4 **Chelan** (lake), Wa,US
45/F5 **Chelford**, Eng,UK
67/L3 **Chelkar**, Kaz.
49/M3 **Chełm**, Pol.
49/M3 **Chełm** (prov.), Pol.
47/G3 **Chelmer** (riv.), Eng,UK
49/K2 **Chełmno**, Pol.
47/G3 **Chelmsford**, Eng,UK
49/K2 **Chełmża**, Pol.
91/G6 **Chelsea**, Austl.
127/Q8 **Cheltenham**, On,Can
46/D3 **Cheltenham**, Eng,UK
65/P5 **Chelyabinsk**, Rus.
65/P5 **Chelyabinsk Obl.**, Rus.
69/L2 **Chelyuskina** (cape), Rus.
101/A5 **Chembe**, Zam.
48/G3 **Chemnitz**, Ger.
82/A2 **Chen** (riv.), China
73/K2 **Chenāb** (riv.), India, Pak.
96/E2 **Chenachane** (well), Alg.
122/D4 **Cheney**, Wa,US
81/C3 **Cheng'anpu**, China
81/D2 **Chengde**, China
76/E5 **Chengdu**, China
81/E3 **Chengshan Jiao** (cape), China
84/D5 **Chennai** (Madras), India
54/A3 **Chenôve**, Fr.
82/B2 **Chenzhou**, China
63/G5 **Chepelare**, Bul.
93/V12 **Chépénéhé**, NCal.
112/C2 **Chépica**, Chile
117/F6 **Chepigana**, Pan.
46/D3 **Chepstow**, Wal,UK
65/M4 **Cheptsa** (riv.), Rus.
56/D3 **Cher** (riv.), Fr.
129/J3 **Cheraw**, SC,US
56/C2 **Cherbourg**, Fr.
96/F1 **Cherchell**, Alg.
76/E1 **Cheremkhovo**, Rus.
64/H4 **Cherepovets**, Rus.
66/D2 **Cherkas'ka Obl.**, Ukr.
66/E2 **Cherkasy**, Ukr.
67/G3 **Cherkessk**, Rus.
90/E6 **Chermside**, Austl.
65/M2 **Chernaya** (riv.), Rus.
66/D2 **Chernihiv**, Ukr.
66/D2 **Chernihivs'ka Obl.**, Ukr.
63/H4 **Cherni Lom** (riv.), Bul.

147
Chern – Conak

63/F4 Cherni Vrŭkh (peak), Bul.
66/C2 Chernivtsi, Ukr.
66/C2 Chernivets'ka Obl., Ukr.
65/N4 Chernushka, Rus.
76/H1 Chernyshevsk, Rus.
125/H3 Cherokee, Ok,US
128/E2 Cherokees (lake), Ok,US
85/F2 Cherrapunjee, India
124/D3 Cherry Creek, Nv,US
131/E6 Cherry Hill, NJ,US
131/D3 Cherry Valley, Ca,US
69/Q3 Cherskiy (range), Rus.
47/F4 Chertsey, Eng,UK
63/G4 Cherven Bryag, Bul.
66/C2 Chervonograd, Ukr.
47/E3 Cherwell (riv.), Eng,UK
126/C3 Chesaning, Mi,US
126/E4 Chesapeake (bay), Md, Va,US
47/F3 Chesham, Eng,UK
45/F5 Cheshire (co.), Eng,UK
45/F5 Cheshire (plain), Eng,UK
65/K2 Cheshskaya (bay), Rus.
47/F3 Cheshunt, Eng,UK
45/F5 Chester, Eng,UK
124/B2 Chester, Ca,US
122/F3 Chester, Mt,US
131/F5 Chester, NJ,US
131/E6 Chester, Pa,US
129/H3 Chester, SC,US
118/G2 Chesterfield (inlet), Nun.,Can
92/E7 Chesterfield (isls.), NCal.
45/G5 Chesterfield, Eng,UK
103/H7 Chesterfield, Nosy (isl.), Madg.
45/G2 Chester-le-Street, Eng,UK
90/B3 Chesterton (range), Austl.
127/G2 Chesuncook (lake), Me,US
116/D4 Chetumal (bay), Belz., Mex.
116/D4 Chetumal, Mex.
122/C2 Chetwynd, BC,Can
46/D4 Chew (riv.), Eng,UK
122/D3 Chewelah, Wa,US
46/D4 Chew Valley (lake), Eng,UK
125/H4 Cheyenne, Ok,US
123/H4 Cheyenne (riv.), SD, Wy,US
123/G5 Cheyenne (cap.), Wy,US
125/G3 Cheyenne Wells, Co,US
84/C3 Chhatarpur, India
84/C3 Chhindwāra, India
83/D3 Chhlong, Camb.
81/D4 Chi (riv.), China
83/C2 Chi (riv.), Thai.
83/B2 Chiang Dao (caves), Thai.
83/B2 Chiang Mai, Thai.
83/B2 Chiang Rai, Thai.
60/C1 Chiani (riv.), It.
116/C4 Chiapas (state), Mex.
67/G4 Chiatura, Geo.
57/H4 Chiavari, It.
55/F5 Chiavenna, It.
82/D3 Chiayi, Tai.
79/G3 Chiba, Japan
79/G3 Chiba (pref.), Japan
126/F1 Chibougamau, Qu,Can
126/F1 Chibougamau (lake), Qu,Can
126/F1 Chibougamau (riv.), Qu,Can
130/D3 Chibukak (pt.), Ak,US
103/F2 Chibuto, Moz.
132/Q16 Chicago, Il,US
132/Q16 Chicago Heights, Il,US
132/Q16 Chicago Ridge, Il,US
130/L4 Chichagof (isl.), Ak,US
73/K2 Chīchāwatni, Pak.
81/C2 Chicheng, China
116/D3 Chichén Itzá (ruins), Mex.
47/F5 Chichester, Eng,UK
79/F3 Chichibu, Japan
79/F3 Chichibu-Tama Nat'l Park, Japan
116/D5 Chichigalpa, Nic.
92/D2 Chichishima (isls.), Japan
129/G3 Chickamauga (lake), Tn,US
125/H4 Chickasha, Ok,US
46/D5 Chickerell, Eng,UK
58/B4 Chiclana de la Frontera, Sp.
108/C5 Chiclayo, Peru
112/C4 Chico (riv.), Arg.
112/D5 Chico (riv.), Arg.
124/B3 Chico, Ca,US
127/F3 Chicopee, Ma,US
104/D4 Chicote, Ang.
127/G1 Chicoutimi, Qu,Can
119/K2 Chidley (cape), Nf,Can
129/H4 Chiefland, Fl,US
83/D1 Chiem Hoa, Viet.
57/K3 Chiemsee (lake), Ger.
60/C1 Chienti (riv.), It.
83/B4 Chieo Lan (res.), Thai.
53/E5 Chiers (riv.), Fr.
55/G6 Chiese (riv.), It.
60/D1 Chieti, It.
47/E4 Chieveley, Eng,UK
77/H3 Chifeng, China
109/K7 Chifre (mts.), Braz.
79/F3 Chigasaki, Japan
130/G4 Chiginagak (mtn.), Ak,US
127/H2 Chignecto (bay), NB,Can
47/G3 Chigwell, Eng,UK
79/L10 Chihayaakasaka, Japan
81/D3 Chihli (Bo Hai) (gulf), China
117/N8 Chihuahua, Mex.
117/N8 Chihuahua (state), Mex.
125/H3 Chikaskia (riv.), Ks,US
84/C5 Chikballāpur, India
84/C3 Chikhli, India
84/C5 Chikmagalūr, India
76/G1 Chikoy (riv.), Rus.
78/B4 Chikugo (riv.), Japan
79/F2 Chikuma (riv.), Japan
79/H8 Chikura, Japan
84/D4 Chilakalūrupet, India
116/B4 Chilapa, Mex.
84/C6 Chilaw, SrL.
122/C3 Chilcotin (riv.), BC,Can
129/G3 Childersburg, Al,US
128/C3 Childress, Tx,US
107/B6 Chile
116/D5 Chile (mt.), Hon.
111/C2 Chilecito, Arg.
104/E3 Chililabombwe, Zam.
84/E4 Chilka (lake), India
122/C3 Chilko (lake), BC,Can
130/L4 Chilkoot (pass), BC,Can, Ak,US
112/B3 Chillán, Chile
126/B3 Chillicothe, Il,US
125/J3 Chillicothe, Mo,US
126/D4 Chillicothe, Oh,US
122/C3 Chilliwack, BC,Can
112/B4 Chiloé (isl.), Chile
112/B4 Chiloé Nat'l Park, Chile
122/C5 Chiloquin, Or,US
116/B4 Chilpancingo, Mex.
47/F3 Chiltern (hills), Eng,UK
104/G4 Chilwa (lake), Malw.
117/F6 Chimán, Pan.
52/D3 Chimay, Belg.
68/F5 Chimbay, Uzb.
108/C4 Chimborazo (vol.), Ecu.
108/C5 Chimbote, Peru
75/A3 Chimkent, Kaz.
117/N7 Chimney (peak), NM.,US
85/F3 Chin (state), Myan.
80/D5 Chin (isl.), SKor.
71/J6 China
116/D5 Chinandega, Nic.
128/B4 Chinati (mts.), Tx,US
117/P8 Chinati (peak), Tx.,US
108/C6 Chincha Alta, Peru
118/E3 Chinchaga (riv.), Ab,Can
126/F4 Chincoteague, Va,US
87/F5 Chindwin (riv.), Myan.
108/D3 Chingaza Nat'l Park, Col.
84/C5 Chingleput, India
104/E3 Chingola, Zam.
98/B1 Chinguetti, Dhar de (hills), Mrta.
80/E5 Chinhae, SKor.
104/F4 Chinhoyi, Zim.
130/H4 Chiniak (cape), Ak,US
73/K2 Chiniot, Pak.
83/D3 Chinit (riv.), Camb.
97/K6 Chinko (riv.), CAfr.
124/E3 Chinle (dry riv.), Az, Ut,US
47/F3 Chinnor, Eng,UK
79/F3 Chino, Japan
131/C2 Chino, Ca,US
122/F3 Chinook, Mt,US
117/F6 Chinú, Col.
104/F3 Chipata, Zam.
81/D3 Chiping, China
58/B4 Chipiona, Sp.
129/G4 Chipley, Fl,US
84/B4 Chiplūn, India
129/G4 Chipola (riv.), Fl,US
46/D4 Chippenham, Eng,UK
123/K4 Chippewa (riv.), Mn,US
126/B2 Chippewa (riv.), Wi,US
126/B2 Chippewa Falls, Wi,US
47/E2 Chipping Campden, Eng,UK
47/E3 Chipping Norton, Eng,UK
47/G3 Chipping Ongar, Eng,UK
46/D3 Chipping Sodbury, Eng,UK
127/H2 Chiputneticook (lakes), NB,Can, Me,US
116/D5 Chiquimula, Guat.
108/D2 Chiquinquirá, Col.
107/C6 Chiquita, Mar (lake), Arg.
107/A3 Chira (riv.), Peru
84/D4 Chīrāla, India
75/A3 Chirchik, Uzb.
96/H3 Chirfa, Niger
117/N7 Chiricahua (peak), Az.,US
124/E4 Chiricahua Nat'l Mon., Az,US
130/G4 Chirikof (isl.), Ak,US
116/E6 Chiriquí (gulf), Pan.
45/E6 Chirk, Eng,UK
43/D3 Chirnside, Sc,UK
63/G4 Chirpan, Bul.
116/E6 Chirripó Grande (mt.), CR
116/E6 Chirripó Nat'l Park, CR
79/N10 Chiryu, Japan
119/J3 Chisasibi (Fort-George), Qu,Can
116/C4 Chisec, Guat.
47/E3 Chiseldon, Eng,UK
126/A2 Chisholm, Mn,US
73/K3 Chishtiān Mandi, Pak.
97/P8 Chisimayu, Som.
63/J2 Chişinău (cap.), Mol.
62/E2 Chişineu Criş, Rom.
65/L5 Chistopol', Rus.
47/F3 Chiswell Green, Eng,UK
79/M10 Chita, Japan
79/M10 Chita (bay), Japan
79/M10 Chita (pen.), Japan
76/G1 Chita, Rus.
104/B4 Chitado, Ang.
101/B5 Chitipa, Malw.
84/B3 Chitorgarh, India
77/N3 Chitose, Japan
84/C5 Chitradurga, India
84/D2 Chitrakut, India
117/E6 Chitré, Pan.
85/F3 Chittagong, Bang.
84/C5 Chittoor, India
104/D4 Chiume, Ang.
57/G4 Chivasso, It.
117/M8 Chivato (pt.), Mex.
112/E2 Chivilcoy, Arg.
83/D3 Choam Khsant, Camb.
112/C1 Choapa (riv.), Chile
104/D4 Chobe Nat'l Park, Bots.
49/K4 Choč (peak), Slvk.
49/J4 Choceň, Czh.
49/H3 Chocianów, Pol.
124/D4 Chocolate (mts.), Ca,US
57/K1 Chodov, Czh.
49/J2 Chodzież, Pol.
79/F3 Chōfu, Japan
79/H7 Chōfu, Japan
92/E5 Choiseul (isl.), Sol.
52/B6 Choisy-le-Roi, Fr.
49/H2 Chojna, Pol.
49/J2 Chojnice, Pol.
49/H3 Chojnów, Pol.
77/N4 Chokai-san (mtn.), Japan
128/D4 Choke Canyon (res.), Tx,US
76/D5 Chola (mts.), China
56/C3 Cholet, Fr.
80/D5 Chŏlla-Bukto (prov.), SKor.
80/D5 Chŏlla-Namdo (prov.), SKor.
47/E3 Cholsey, Eng,UK
116/D5 Choluteca (riv.), Hon.
116/D5 Choluteca, Hon.
104/E4 Choma, Zam.
80/E4 Chŏmch'on, SKor.
84/E2 Chomo Lhāri (mtn.), Bhu.
57/K1 Chomutov, Czh.
79/J7 Chōnan, Japan
80/D4 Ch'ŏnan, SKor.
83/C3 Chon Buri, Thai.
112/B4 Chonchi, Chile
108/B4 Chone, Ecu.
80/E2 Ch'ŏngjin, NKor.
80/E2 Ch'ŏngjin-Si (prov.), NKor.
80/D4 Ch'ŏngju, SKor.
83/C3 Chong Kal, Camb.
81/L8 Chongming (isl.), China
82/A2 Chongqing, China
80/E4 Ch'ŏngsong, SKor.
80/D5 Chŏnju, SKor.
112/A5 Chonos (arch.), Chile
83/D4 Chon Thanh, Viet.
45/F4 Chorley, Eng,UK
47/F3 Chorleywood, Eng,UK
66/C2 Chortkov, Ukr.
49/K3 Chorzów, Pol.
79/G3 Chōshi, Japan
49/H2 Choszczno, Pol.
108/C5 Chota, Peru
122/E4 Choteau, Mt,US
102/A2 Chowagasberg (peak), Namb.
129/J2 Chowan (riv.), NC,US
76/G2 Choybalsan, Mong.
89/H7 Christchurch, NZ
47/E5 Christchurch, Eng,UK
47/E5 Christchurch (bay), Eng,UK
130/L4 Christian (sound), Ak,US
102/D2 Christiana, SAfr.
126/D4 Christiansburg, Va,US
122/F2 Christine (riv.), Ab,Can
71/K11 Christmas (isl.), Austl.
93/K4 Christmas (Kiritimati) (atoll), Kiri.
49/H4 Chrudim, Czh
49/K3 Chrzanów, Pol.
75/B3 Chu (riv.), Kaz.
83/D2 Chu (riv.), Viet.
81/E4 Chuanchang (riv.), China
122/E5 Chubbuck, Id,US
79/F2 Chūbu (prov.), Japan
112/C4 Chubut (prov.), Arg.
112/D4 Chubut (riv.), Arg.
117/F6 Chucanti (mt.), Pan.
78/C3 Chūgoku (mts.), Japan
78/C3 Chūgoku (prov.), Japan
86/B3 Chukai, Malay.
77/M1 Chukchagirskoye (lake), Rus.
69/U3 Chukchi (pen.), Rus.
69/S3 Chukotka Aut. Okr., Rus.
130/D3 Chukotskiy, Mys (pt.), Rus.
124/C4 Chula Vista, Ca,US
108/B5 Chulucanas, Peru
68/J4 Chulym (riv.), Rus.
75/E1 Chulyshman (riv.), Rus.
63/G4 Chumerna (peak), Bul.
83/B4 Chumphon, Thai.
68/K4 Chuna (riv.), Rus.
80/D4 Ch'unch'ŏn, SKor.
80/D4 Ch'ungch'ŏng-Bukto (prov.), SKor.
80/D4 Ch'ungch'ŏng-Namdo (prov.), SKor.
80/D4 Ch'ungju, SKor.
80/E5 Ch'ungmu, SKor.
69/L3 Chunya (riv.), Rus.
111/C1 Chuquicamata, Chile
55/F4 Chur, Swi.
85/F3 Churachandpur, India
45/F4 Church, Eng,UK
118/D3 Churchill (peak), BC,Can
118/G3 Churchill, Mb,Can
118/G3 Churchill (cape), Mb,Can
118/G3 Churchill (riv.), Mb, Sk,Can
119/K3 Churchill (riv.), Nf,Can
122/F1 Churchill (lake), Sk,Can
118/G3 Churchill (riv.), Mb, Sk,Can
91/G5 Churchill Nat'l Park, Austl.
46/D1 Church Stretton, Eng,UK
45/G6 Churnet (riv.), Eng,UK
84/B2 Churu, India
117/H5 Churuguara, Ven.
124/E3 Chuska (mts.), Az, NM,US
65/N4 Chusovaya (riv.), Rus.
65/N4 Chusovoy, Rus.
65/K5 Chuvash Aut. Rep., Rus.
80/E4 Chuwang-san Nat'l Park, SKor.
85/H2 Chuxiong, China
76/B1 Chuya (riv.), Rus.
83/E3 Chu Yang Sin (peak), Viet.
79/M9 Chūzu, Japan
86/C5 Ciamis, Indo.
60/C2 Ciampino, It.
86/C5 Cianjur, Indo.
132/Q16 Cicero, Il,US
109/L6 Cícero Dantas, Braz.
60/C2 Cicero Nat'l Park, It.
74/C2 Cide, Turk.
49/L2 Ciechanów, Pol.
49/K2 Ciechanów (prov.), Pol.
49/K2 Ciechocinek, Pol.
117/F3 Ciego de Avilla, Cuba
117/G5 Ciénaga, Col.
117/E3 Cienfuegos, Cuba
49/H3 Cieplice Śląskie Zdrój, Pol.
49/K4 Cieszyn, Pol.
58/E3 Cieza, Sp.
74/B2 Çifteler, Turk.
58/D3 Cigüela (riv.), Sp.
74/C2 Cihanbeyli, Turk.
117/P10 Cihuatlán, Mex.
58/C3 Cijara (res.), Sp.
86/C5 Cijulang, Indo.
86/C5 Cilacap, Indo.
46/C2 Cilfaesty (hill), Wal,UK
125/G3 Cimarron, Ks,US
125/H3 Cimarron (riv.), Ks, Ok,US
128/B2 Cimarron (range), NM,US
62/F2 Cîmpeni, Rom.
63/F2 Cîmpia Turzii, Rom.
63/G3 Cîmpina, Rom.
63/G3 Cîmpulung, Rom.
63/G2 Cîmpulung Moldovenesc, Rom.
59/F1 Cinca (riv.), Sp.
62/C4 Cincar (peak), Bosn.
126/C4 Cincinnati, Oh,US
112/C3 Cinco Saltos, Arg.
46/D3 Cinderford, Eng,UK
63/F3 Cîndrelu (peak), Rom.
74/B3 Çine, Turk.
53/E3 Ciney, Belg.
131/F6 Cinnaminson, NJ,US
116/C4 Cintalapa, Mex.
60/A1 Cinto (mtn.), Fr.
62/C4 Čiovo (isl.), Cro.
112/D3 Cipolletti, Arg.
123/G4 Circle, Mt,US
126/D4 Circleville, Oh,US
86/C5 Cirebon, Indo.
46/E3 Cirencester, Eng,UK
60/E3 Cirò Marina, It.
56/C4 Ciron (riv.), Fr.
63/G3 Cisnădie, Rom.
112/B5 Cisnes (riv.), Chile
56/D3 Cisse (riv.), Fr.
60/C2 Cisterna di Latina, It.
116/B4 Citlaltépetl (mt.), Mex.
132/M9 Citrus Heights, Ca,US
57/K5 Città di Castello, It.
60/E3 Cittanova, It.
116/A2 Ciudad Acuna, Mex.
117/J6 Ciudad Bolívar, Ven.
117/N8 Ciudad Camargo, Mex.
116/C4 Ciudad del Carmen, Mex.
117/N8 Ciudad Delicias, Mex.
117/P9 Ciudad de Río Grande, Mex.
59/G3 Ciudadela, Sp.
117/J6 Ciudad Guayana, Ven.
117/N8 Ciudad Guerrero, Mex.
117/P10 Ciudad Guzmán, Mex.
117/N7 Ciudad Juárez, Mex.
117/P8 Ciudad Lerdo, Mex.
116/B3 Ciudad Madero, Mex.
116/B3 Ciudad Mante, Mex.
116/B2 Ciudad Miguel Alemán, Mex.
117/N8 Ciudad Obregón, Mex.
117/G5 Ciudad Ojeda, Ven.
58/D3 Ciudad Real, Sp.
116/B2 Ciudad Río Bravo, Mex.
58/B2 Ciudad-Rodrigo, Sp.
116/B3 Ciudad Valles, Mex.
116/B3 Ciudad Victoria, Mex.
66/F4 Civa Burnu (pt.), Turk.
57/K3 Cividale del Friuli, It.
60/C1 Civita Castellana, It.
60/B1 Civitavecchia, It.
74/B2 Çivril, Turk.
81/C3 Ci Xian, China
74/E3 Cizre, Turk.
58/E1 Cizur, Sp.
47/H3 Clacton on Sea, Eng,UK
46/C2 Claerwen (res.), Wal,UK
56/D3 Clain (riv.), Fr.
118/E3 Claire (lake), Ab,Can
124/B2 Clair Engle (lake), Ca,US
56/D3 Claise (riv.), Fr.
47/F5 Clanfield, Eng,UK
129/G3 Clanton, Al,US
127/Q9 Clappison's Corners, On,Can
112/D4 Clara (pt.), Arg.
43/A4 Clare (riv.), Ire.
126/C3 Clare, Mi,US
131/C2 Claremont, Ca,US
127/F3 Claremont, NH,US
125/J3 Claremore, Ok,US
91/E1 Clarence (riv.), Austl.
119/T7 Clarence (pt.), Nun.,Can
127/S9 Clarence, NY,US
117/G3 Clarence Town, Bahm.
128/C3 Clarendon, Tx,US
122/E3 Claresholm, BC,Can
105/J Clarie (coast), Ant.
123/J4 Clark, SD,US
91/D4 Clarke (isl.), Austl.
90/B3 Clarke (range), Austl.
122/E3 Clark Fork (riv.), Id, Mt,US
129/H3 Clark Hill (lake), Ga, SC,US
126/D4 Clarksburg, WV,US
129/F3 Clarksdale, Ms,US
127/Q8 Clarkson, On,Can
132/F6 Clarkston, Mi,US
122/D4 Clarkston, Wa,US
128/E3 Clarksville, Ar,US
129/G2 Clarksville, Tn,US
128/E3 Clarksville, Tx,US
110/B1 Claro (riv.), Braz.
52/C3 Clary, Fr.
44/D1 Clatteringshaws Loch (lake), Sc,UK
44/A2 Claudy, NI,UK
51/H5 Clausthal-Zellerfeld, Ger.
82/D4 Claveria, Phil.
132/F6 Clawson, Mi,US
125/H3 Clay Center, Ks,US
45/G5 Clay Cross, Eng,UK
47/H2 Claydon, Eng,UK
44/D3 Clay Head (pt.), IM,UK
131/E6 Claymont, De,US
132/L11 Clayton, Ca,US
129/H3 Clayton, Ga,US
125/G3 Clayton, NM,US
125/J4 Clayton, Ok,US
45/F4 Clayton-le-Moors, Eng,UK
113/S11 Clé (stream), Arg.
118/E3 Clear (hills), Ab,Can
43/H8 Clear (cape), Ire.
124/B3 Clear (lake), Ca,US
130/J4 Cleare (cape), Ak,US
123/J4 Clear Lake, SD,US
122/C3 Clearwater, BC,Can
129/H5 Clearwater, Fl,US
122/D4 Clearwater (mts.), Id,US
123/K4 Clearwater (riv.), Mn,US
44/E2 Cleator Moor, Eng,UK
128/D3 Cleburne, Tx,US
45/H4 Cleethorpes, Eng,UK
46/D3 Cleeve (hill), Eng,UK
129/H3 Clemson, SC,US
46/D2 Cleobury Mortimer, Eng,UK
87/E1 Cleopatra Needle (mtn.), Phil.
52/A4 Clères, Fr.
53/E3 Clerf (riv.), Belg., Lux.
52/B5 Clermont, Fr.
46/D4 Clevedon, Eng,UK
90/B2 Cleveland (cape), Austl.
45/G3 Cleveland (hills), Eng,UK
129/F3 Cleveland, Ms,US
122/E3 Cleveland (peak), Mt,US
126/D3 Cleveland, Oh,US
129/G3 Cleveland, Tn,US
128/E4 Cleveland, Tx,US
110/A3 Clevelândia, Braz.
43/A4 Clew (bay), Ire.
129/H5 Clewiston, Fl,US
52/B6 Clichy, Fr.
46/D4 Clifton, Eng,UK
124/E4 Clifton, Az,US
131/F5 Clifton, NJ,US
128/D4 Clifton, Tx,US
129/J2 Clifton Forge, Va,US
46/D2 Clifton upon Teme, Eng,UK
52/C5 Clignon (riv.), Fr.
129/H3 Clingmans (mtn.), Tn,US
122/C3 Clinton, BC,Can
123/L5 Clinton, Ia,US
126/B3 Clinton, Il,US
129/F4 Clinton, La,US
132/G6 Clinton, Mi,US
132/F6 Clinton (riv.), Mi,US
125/J3 Clinton, Mo,US
129/F3 Clinton, Ms,US
129/J3 Clinton, NC,US
131/F5 Clinton, NJ,US
131/F4 Clinton (res.), NJ,US
125/H4 Clinton, Ok,US
129/H3 Clinton, SC,US
118/F2 Clinton-Colden (lake), NW,Can
118/B2 Clinton Creek, Yk,Can
131/K8 Clinton (Surratts-ville), Md,US
126/D3 Clio, Mi,US
38/D5 Clipperton (isl.), Fr.
47/F2 Clipston, Eng,UK
45/F4 Clitheroe, Eng,UK
44/B4 Clogherhead, Ire.
44/B4 Clogher Head (pt.), Ire.
44/C3 Cloghy, NI,UK
43/B4 Clonmel, Ire.
51/F3 Cloppenburg, Ger.
123/K4 Cloquet, Mn,US
111/E2 Clorinda, Arg.
44/E1 Closeburn, Sc,UK
122/G4 Cloud (peak), Wy,US
128/B3 Cloudcroft, NM,US
130/G3 Cloudy (mtn.), Ak,US
44/B2 Cloughmills, NI,UK
45/H3 Cloughton, Eng,UK
46/B4 Clovelly, Eng,UK
124/B3 Cloverdale, Ca,US
124/C3 Clovis, Ca,US
125/G4 Clovis, NM,US
43/C2 Clovullin, Sc,UK
45/G5 Clowne, Eng,UK
63/F2 Cluj (co.), Rom.
63/F2 Cluj-Napoca, Rom.
46/C2 Clun, Eng,UK
46/B3 Clunderwen, Wal,UK
54/C5 Cluses, Fr.
57/H4 Clusone, It.
45/E5 Clwyd (riv.), Wal,UK
45/E5 Clwydian (range), Wal,UK
46/C3 Clydach, Wal,UK
127/H2 Clyde (riv.), NS,Can
122/E2 Clyde, Ab,Can
43/C3 Clyde (riv.), Sc,UK
43/C3 Clyde, Firth of (inlet), Sc,UK
46/C2 Clywedog (riv.), Wal,UK
127/R8 CN Tower, On,Can
58/B2 Côa (riv.), Port.
124/C4 Coachella, Ca,US
44/B2 Coagh, NI,UK
116/A2 Coahuila (state), Mex.
122/E3 Coaldale, Ab,Can
125/H4 Coalgate, Ok,US
122/E3 Coalhurst, Ab,Can
44/B2 Coalisland, NI,UK
47/E1 Coalville, Eng,UK
124/E2 Coalville, Ut,US
108/F4 Coari, Braz.
108/F5 Coari (riv.), Braz.
118/C2 Coast (mts.), BC, Yk,Can
101/C3 Coast (prov.), Kenya
120/B4 Coast (ranges), Ca,US
129/H4 Coastal (plain), US
116/B4 Coatepec, Mex.
127/G2 Coaticook, Qu,Can
119/H2 Coats (isl.), Nun.,Can
105/Y Coats Land (reg.), Ant.
116/C4 Coatzacoalcos, Mex.
116/D3 Coba (ruins), Mex.
58/B1 Coba de Serpe, Sierra de (mts.), Sp.
116/C4 Cobán, Guat.
91/D3 Cobberas (peak), Austl.
131/B1 Cobblestone (mtn.), Ca,US
123/K2 Cobham (riv.), Mb, On,Can
47/F4 Cobham, Eng,UK
89/C2 Cobourg (pen.), Austl.
126/E3 Cobourg, On,Can
112/B3 Cobquecura, Chile
91/F5 Coburg, Austl.
119/T7 Coburg (isl.), Nun.,Can
57/J1 Coburg, Ger.
59/E3 Cocentaina, Sp.
108/E7 Cochabamba, Bol.
84/C6 Cochin, India
129/H3 Cochran, Ga,US
122/E3 Cochrane, Ab,Can
126/D1 Cochrane, On,Can
113/J8 Cockburn (chan.), Chile
43/D3 Cockburnspath, Sc,UK
45/E2 Cockermouth, Eng,UK
102/D4 Cockscomb (peak), SAfr.
108/A2 Coco (isl.), CR
116/E5 Coco (riv.), Hon.
129/H4 Cocoa, Fl,US
124/D4 Coconino (plat.), Az,US
91/C2 Cocoparra Nat'l Park, Austl.
71/J11 Cocos (Keeling) (isls.), Austl.
119/K3 Cod (isl.), Nf,Can
45/G3 Cod Beck (riv.), Eng,UK
112/C2 Codegua, Chile
63/G3 Codlea, Rom.
109/K4 Codó, Braz.
57/H4 Codogno, It.
117/J4 Codrington, Anti.
57/K4 Codroipo, It.
46/D1 Codsall, Eng,UK
122/F4 Cody, Wy,US
109/K4 Coelho Neto, Braz.
51/E5 Coesfeld, Ger.
39/M6 Coetivy (isl.), Sey.
122/D4 Coeur d'Alene, Id,US
122/D4 Coeur d'Alene (lake), Id,US
50/D3 Coevorden, Neth.
125/J3 Coffeyville, Ks,US
91/E1 Coffs Harbour, Austl.
47/G3 Coggeshall, Eng,UK
60/A2 Coghinas (lake), It.
56/C4 Cognac, Fr.
116/E6 Coiba (isl.), Pan.
113/K7 Coig (riv.), Arg.
112/B5 Coihaique, Chile
112/C3 Coihueco, Chile
84/C5 Coimbatore, India
58/A2 Coimbra, Port.
58/A2 Coimbra (dist.), Port.
58/C4 Coín, Sp.
59/P10 Coina (riv.), Port.
56/F4 Coise (riv.), Fr.
108/E2 Cojedes (riv.), Ven.
117/G5 Cojoro, Ven.
112/C5 Cojudo Blanco (peak), Arg.
116/D5 Cojutepeque, ESal.
125/G3 Cokeville, Wy,US
91/B3 Colac, Austl.
125/H2 Colamus (riv.), Ne,US
59/P10 Colares, Port.
110/D1 Colatina, Braz.
105/P Colbeck (cape), Ant.
112/C2 Colbún, Chile
125/G3 Colby, Ks,US
47/G3 Colchester, Eng,UK
122/F2 Cold (lake), Ab, Sk,Can
45/F2 Cold Fell (mtn.), Eng,UK
122/F2 Cold Lake, Ab,Can
123/K4 Cold Spring, Mn,US
128/E4 Coldspring, Tx,US
125/H3 Coldwater, Ks,US
126/C3 Coldwater, Mi,US
47/E3 Cole (riv.), Eng,UK
46/D3 Coleford, Eng,UK
128/D4 Coleman, Tx,US
74/E3 Çölemerik, Turk.
44/B1 Coleraine, NI,UK
44/B1 Coleraine (dist.), NI,UK
102/D3 Colesberg, SAfr.
47/E2 Coleshill, Eng,UK
131/J7 Colesville, Md,US
122/D4 Colfax, Wa,US
119/S6 Colgate (cape), Nun.,Can
112/C5 Colhué Huapí (lake), Arg.
83/D2 Co Lieu, Viet.
117/P10 Colima, Mex.
117/P10 Colima (state), Mex.
112/C2 Colina, Chile
109/K5 Colinas, Braz.
58/D2 Collado-Villalba, Sp.
130/J3 College, Ak,US
131/K8 College Park, Md,US
128/D4 College Station, Tx,US
57/G4 Collegno, It.
91/D1 Collie, Austl.
45/G2 Collier Law (hill), Eng,UK
129/F3 Collierville, Tn,US
46/B6 Colliford (res.), Eng,UK
45/G4 Collingham, Eng,UK
126/D2 Collingwood, On,Can
89/H7 Collingwood, NZ
129/F4 Collins, Ms,US
125/J3 Collinsville, Ok,US
126/E4 Collinsville, Va,US
54/D1 Colmar, Fr.
58/D2 Colmenar Viejo, Sp.
113/J7 Colmillo (cape), Chile
44/D1 Colmonell, Sc,UK
47/E3 Coln (riv.), Eng,UK
45/F4 Colne, Eng,UK
47/G3 Colne (riv.), Eng,UK
53/F2 Cologne (Köln), Ger.
108/D3 Colombia
110/B3 Colombo, Braz.
84/C6 Colombo (cap.), SrL.
56/D5 Colomiers, Fr.
112/E2 Colón, Arg.
112/F2 Colón, Arg.
117/F6 Colón, Pan.
92/C4 Colonia, Micro.
113/F2 Colonia (dept.), Uru.
113/F2 Colonia Del Sacramento, Uru.
113/K7 Colorado (peak), Arg.
112/D3 Colorado (riv.), Arg.
110/B2 Colorado, Braz.
124/D4 Colorado (riv.), Mex., US
124/E3 Colorado (plat.), US
124/F3 Colorado (state), US
128/D4 Colorado (riv.), Tx,US
125/F3 Colorado City, Co,US
128/C3 Colorado City, Tx,US
124/E3 Colorado Nat'l Mon., Co,US
111/C2 Colorados, Desagües de los (marsh), Arg.
125/F3 Colorado Springs, Co,US
108/E7 Colquiri, Bol.
122/G4 Colstrip, Mt,US
44/D1 Colt (hill), Sc,UK
112/C2 Coltauco, Chile
47/H1 Coltishall, Eng,UK
131/C2 Colton, Ca,US
131/F5 Colts Neck, NJ,US
107/D4 Coluene (riv.), Braz.
118/E3 Columbia (mtn.), Ab,Can
122/C2 Columbia (mts.), BC,Can
119/T6 Columbia (cape), Nun.,Can
122/C4 Columbia (riv.), Can., US
122/D4 Columbia (plat.), US
126/C4 Columbia, Ky,US
128/E3 Columbia, La,US
131/K7 Columbia, Md,US
125/J3 Columbia, Mo,US
129/F4 Columbia, Ms,US
129/H3 Columbia (cap.), SC,US
129/G3 Columbia, Tn,US
122/E3 Columbia Falls, Mt,US
102/B4 Columbine (cape), SAfr.
129/G3 Columbus, Ga,US
126/C4 Columbus, In,US
129/F3 Columbus, Ms,US
122/F4 Columbus, Mt,US
125/H2 Columbus, Ne,US
131/F5 Columbus, NJ,US
124/F5 Columbus, NM,US
126/D4 Columbus (cap.), Oh,US
128/D4 Columbus, Tx,US
124/B3 Colusa, Ca,US
118/D2 Colville (lake), NW,Can
130/H2 Colville (riv.), Ak,US
122/D3 Colville, Wa,US
132/B3 Colvos (passg.), Wa,US
46/D2 Colwall, Eng,UK
46/C4 Colwinston, Wal,UK
44/E5 Colwyn Bay, Wal,UK
57/K4 Comacchio, It.
57/K4 Comacchio, Valli di (lag.), It.
128/D4 Comanche, Tx,US
112/F3 Comandante Nicanor Otamendi, Arg.
63/H2 Comănești, Rom.
63/G3 Comarnic, Rom.
116/D5 Comayagua, Hon.
111/B3 Combarbalá, Chile
46/B4 Combe Martin, Eng,UK
44/C2 Comber, NI,UK
52/B6 Combs-la-Ville, Fr.
90/C4 Comet (riv.), Austl.
85/F3 Comilla, Bang.
52/B2 Comines, Belg.
52/C2 Comines, Fr.
131/G5 Commack, NY,US
56/E3 Commentry, Fr.
131/B2 Commerce, Ca,US
53/E6 Commercy, Fr.
119/H2 Committee (bay), Nun.,Can
57/H4 Como, It.
55/F5 Como (lake), It.
55/F5 Como (prov.), It.
132/P14 Como (lake), Wi,US
112/D5 Comodoro Rivadavia, Arg.
98/D4 Comoé (prov.), Burk.
98/E4 Comoé Nat'l Park, IvC.
84/C6 Comorin (cape), India
103/G5 Comoros
122/B3 Comox, BC,Can
52/B5 Compiègne, Fr.
117/P9 Compostela, Mex.
131/B3 Compton, Ca,US
128/C4 Comstock, Tx,US
98/B4 Conakry (cap.), Gui.

98/B4 **Conakry** (comm.), Gui.
56/B3 **Concarneau**, Fr.
110/E1 **Conceição da Barra**, Braz.
110/B1 **Conceição das Alagoas**, Braz.
109/J5 **Conceição do Araguaia**, Braz.
110/D1 **Conceição do Mato Dentro**, Braz.
110/H6 **Conceição do Rio Verde**, Braz.
108/F7 **Concepción** (lake), Bol.
112/B3 **Concepción**, Chile
111/E1 **Concepción**, Par.
108/C6 **Concepción**, Peru
116/A3 **Concepción del Oro**, Mex.
112/F2 **Concepción del Uruguay**, Arg.
124/B4 **Conception** (pt.), Ca,US
110/F7 **Conchal**, Braz.
125/F4 **Conchas** (lake), NM,US
125/G5 **Concho** (riv.), Tx,US
117/N8 **Conchos** (riv.), Mex.
132/K11 **Concord**, Ca,US
129/H3 **Concord**, NC,US
127/G3 **Concord** (cap.), NH,US
111/E3 **Concordia**, Arg.
110/A3 **Concórdia**, Braz.
125/H3 **Concordia**, Ks,US
122/C3 **Concrete**, Wa,US
83/D2 **Con Cuong**, Viet.
117/F3 **Condado**, Cuba
52/C3 **Condé-sur-L'Escaut**, Fr.
56/C2 **Condé-sur-Noireau**, Fr.
90/C4 **Condomine** (riv.), Austl.
122/C4 **Condon**, Or,US
53/D3 **Condroz** (plat.), Belg.
129/G4 **Conecuh** (riv.), Al,US
57/K4 **Conegliano**, It.
128/B2 **Conejos**, Co,US
52/B6 **Conflans-Sainte-Honorine**, Fr.
131/G4 **Congers**, NY,US
82/B3 **Conghua**, China
45/F5 **Congleton**, Eng,UK
95/E5 **Congo, Dem. Rep. of the**
95/D4 **Congo, Rep. of the**
97/K7 **Congo** (basin), Afr.
104/C1 **Congo** (riv.), Afr.
110/D2 **Congonhas**, Braz.
112/C3 **Conguillio Nat'l Park**, Chile
112/C4 **Cónico, Cerro** (Nevado) (peak), Arg., Chile
58/B4 **Conil de la Frontera**, Sp.
45/H5 **Coningsby**, Eng,UK
45/G5 **Conisbrough**, Eng,UK
45/E3 **Coniston**, Eng,UK
45/E3 **Coniston Water** (lake), Eng,UK
44/C2 **Conlig**, NI,UK
119/J1 **Conn** (lake), Nun.,Can
43/A4 **Connacht** (prov.), Ire.
45/E5 **Connah's Quay**, Wal,UK
126/D3 **Conneaut**, Oh,US
127/G2 **Connecticut** (riv.), US
127/F3 **Connecticut** (state), US
43/C2 **Connel**, Sc,UK
126/E3 **Connellsville**, Pa,US
43/H7 **Connemara Nat'l Park**, Ire.
126/C4 **Connersville**, In,US
43/A3 **Conn, Lough** (lake), Ire.
113/K7 **Cono Grande** (peak), Arg.
90/D4 **Conondale Nat'l Park**, Austl.
56/E4 **Conques**, Fr.
122/F3 **Conrad**, Mt,US
116/B1 **Conroe**, Tx.,US
128/E4 **Conroe**, Tx,US
110/D2 **Conselheiro Lafaiete**, Braz.
110/D1 **Conselheiro Pena**, Braz.
45/G2 **Consett**, Eng,UK
131/E5 **Conshohocken**, Pa,US
116/E3 **Consolación del Sur**, Cuba
83/D4 **Con Son** (isl.), Viet.
55/F2 **Constance** (Bodensee) (lake), Ger., Swi.
63/J3 **Constanţa**, Rom.
63/J3 **Constanţa** (co.), Rom.
59/F2 **Constantí**, Sp.
58/C4 **Constantina**, Sp.
96/G1 **Constantine**, Alg.
130/G4 **Constantine** (cape), Ak,US
112/B2 **Constitución**, Chile
113/T11 **Constitución** (res.), Uru.
117/L7 **Constitución de 1997 Nat'l Park**, Mex.
58/D3 **Consuegra**, Sp.
84/E3 **Contai**, India
57/K4 **Contarina**, It.
109/K6 **Contas** (riv.), Braz.
110/C1 **Contegem**, Braz.
52/B4 **Contigny**, Fr.
122/C2 **Continental** (ranges), Ab, BC,Can
132/L11 **Contra Costa** (can.), Ca,US
117/F3 **Contramaestre**, Cuba
58/E3 **Contreras** (res.), Sp.
130/J3 **Controller** (bay), Ak,US
112/B3 **Contulmo**, Chile
118/E2 **Contwoyto** (lake), Nun.,Can
52/B4 **Conty**, Fr.
117/G6 **Convención**, Col.
60/E2 **Conversano**, It.
90/C3 **Conway** (cape), Austl.
128/E3 **Conway**, Ar,US
127/G3 **Conway**, NH,US
129/J3 **Conway**, SC,US
90/C3 **Conway Range Nat'l Park**, Austl.
44/E5 **Conway, Vale of** (val.), Wal,UK
44/E5 **Conwy**, Wal,UK
44/D5 **Conwy** (bay), Wal,UK
44/E5 **Conwy** (co.), Wal,UK
44/E5 **Conwy** (riv.), Wal,UK
84/E2 **Cooch Behār**, India
90/F7 **Coochiemudlo** (isl.), Austl.
113/K8 **Cook** (bay), Chile
89/H7 **Cook** (str.), NZ
130/H3 **Cook** (inlet), Ak,US
129/G2 **Cookeville**, Tn,US
105/L **Cook Ice Shelf**, Ant.
93/J6 **Cook Islands** (terr.), NZ
44/B2 **Cookstown**, NI,UK
44/B2 **Cookstown** (dist.), NI,UK
91/B3 **Coola Coola** (swamp), Austl.
44/B4 **Cooley** (pt.), Ire.
90/D4 **Cooloola Nat'l Park**, Austl.
91/D3 **Cooma**, Austl.
84/B5 **Coondapoor**, India
84/C5 **Coonoor**, India
128/E3 **Cooper**, Tx,US
123/J4 **Cooperstown**, ND,US
91/A3 **Coorong Nat'l Park**, Austl.
129/G3 **Coosa** (riv.), Al,US
122/B5 **Coos Bay**, Or,US
91/D2 **Cootamundra**, Austl.
131/G5 **Copague**, NY,US
112/C3 **Copahué** (vol.), Chile
116/D5 **Copán** (ruins), Hon.
58/E4 **Cope** (cape), Sp.
44/C2 **Copeland** (isl.), NI,UK
48/G1 **Copenhagen** (København) (cap.), Den.
61/F2 **Copertino**, It.
91/D1 **Copeton** (dam), Austl.
111/B2 **Copiapó**, Chile
57/J4 **Copparo**, It.
51/G4 **Coppenbrügge**, Ger.
128/D4 **Copperas Cove**, Tx,US
118/E2 **Coppermine** (riv.), NW,Nun.,Can
45/F4 **Coppull**, Eng,UK
63/G2 **Copşa Mică**, Rom.
45/F1 **Coquet** (riv.), Eng,UK
45/G1 **Coquet Dale** (val.), Eng,UK
111/B2 **Coquimbo**, Chile
112/C1 **Coquimbo** (reg.), Chile
63/G4 **Corabia**, Rom.
90/C1 **Coral** (sea)
129/H5 **Coral Gables**, Fl,US
89/E2 **Coral Sea Is.** (terr.), Austl.
129/H5 **Coral Springs**, Fl,US
131/H5 **Coram**, NY,US
56/E2 **Corbeil-Essonnes**, Fr.
52/B4 **Corbie**, Fr.
56/E5 **Corbieres** (mts.), Fr.
126/C4 **Corbin**, Ky,US
45/F2 **Corbridge**, Eng,UK
47/F2 **Corby**, Eng,UK
110/K7 **Corcovado** (mon.), Braz.
112/B4 **Corcovado** (gulf), Chile
112/B4 **Corcovado** (vol.), Chile
116/E6 **Corcovado Nat'l Park**, CR
110/D2 **Cordeiro**, Braz.
129/H4 **Cordele**, Ga,US
125/H4 **Cordell** (New Cordell), Ok,US
57/K4 **Cordenons**, It.
108/D3 **Cordillera de los Picachos Nat'l Park**, Col.
111/D3 **Córdoba**, Arg.
111/D3 **Córdoba** (mts.), Arg.
112/E2 **Córdoba** (prov.), Arg.
116/B4 **Córdoba**, Mex.
58/C4 **Córdoba**, Sp.
130/J3 **Cordova** (peak), Ak,US
58/E1 **Corella**, Sp.
108/G3 **Corentyne** (riv.), Guy.
61/F3 **Corfu** (Kérkira) (isl.), Gre.
58/B3 **Coria**, Sp.
58/B4 **Coria del Río**, Sp.
91/D2 **Coricudgy** (peak), Austl.
60/E3 **Corigliano Calabro**, It.
61/H4 **Corinth** (ruins), Gre.
129/F3 **Corinth**, Ms,US
61/H4 **Corinth** (Kórinthos), Gre.
110/C1 **Corinto**, Braz.
116/D5 **Corinto**, Nic.
58/A1 **Coristanco**, Sp.
60/C4 **Corleone**, It.
63/H5 **Çorlu**, Turk.
52/D5 **Cormontreuil**, Fr.
123/H2 **Cormorant**, Mb,Can
123/H2 **Cormorant** (lake), Mb,Can
46/C1 **Corndon** (hill), Wal,UK
110/B2 **Cornélio Procópio**, Braz.
119/K2 **Cornelius Grinnell** (bay), Nun.,Can
59/L7 **Cornella**, Sp.
91/C3 **Corner** (inlet), Austl.
127/K1 **Corner Brook**, Nf,Can
126/E3 **Corning**, NY,US
90/B3 **Cornish** (cr.), Austl.
57/J4 **Corno alle Scale** (peak), It.
113/L8 **Cornú** (peak), Arg.
119/S7 **Cornwall** (isl.), Nun.,Can
126/F2 **Cornwall**, On,Can
127/J2 **Cornwall**, PE,Can
46/B6 **Cornwall** (co.), Eng,UK
119/S7 **Cornwallis** (isl.), Nun.,Can
117/H5 **Coro**, Ven.
109/K4 **Coroatá**, Braz.
108/E7 **Corocoro**, Bol.
110/C1 **Coromandel**, Braz.
84/D5 **Coromandel** (coast), India
89/H6 **Coromandel**, NZ
82/D5 **Coron**, Phil.
131/C3 **Corona**, Ca,US
125/F4 **Corona**, NM,US
116/E6 **Coronado** (bay), CR
122/F2 **Coronation**, Ab,Can
118/E2 **Coronation** (gulf), Nun.,Can
112/E1 **Coronda**, Arg.
112/B3 **Coronel**, Chile
112/E3 **Coronel Dorrego**, Arg.
110/D1 **Coronel Fabriciano**, Braz.
112/D2 **Coronel Moldes**, Arg.
111/E2 **Coronel Oviedo**, Par.
112/E3 **Coronel Pringles**, Arg.
112/E3 **Coronel Suárez**, Arg.
110/A3 **Coronel Vivida**, Braz.
108/D7 **Coropuna** (peak), Peru
117/F6 **Corozal**, Col.
116/D4 **Corozal Town**, Belz.
128/D5 **Corpus Christi**, Tx,US
58/D3 **Corral de Almaguer**, Sp.
112/E2 **Corral de Bustos**, Arg.
59/Y16 **Corralejo**, Canl.
91/B3 **Corrangamite** (lake), Austl.
116/E6 **Corredor**, CR
109/J6 **Corrente**, Braz.
110/B1 **Corrente** (riv.), Braz.
43/A4 **Corrib, Lough** (lake), Ire.
111/E2 **Corrientes**, Arg.
116/E3 **Corrientes** (cape), Cuba
108/C4 **Corrientes** (riv.), Ecu., Peru
46/C1 **Corris**, Wal,UK
60/A1 **Corse** (cape), Fr.
60/A1 **Corse** (reg.), Fr.
44/D1 **Corserine** (mtn.), Sc,UK
44/C1 **Corsewall** (pt.), Sc,UK
46/D4 **Corsham**, Eng,UK
60/A1 **Corsica** (Corse) (isl.), Fr.
128/D3 **Corsicana**, Tx,US
60/A1 **Corte**, Fr.
124/E3 **Cortez**, Co,US
57/K3 **Cortina d'Ampezzo**, It.
126/E3 **Cortland**, NY,US
98/B4 **Corubal** (riv.), GBis.
58/A3 **Coruche**, Port.
74/E2 **Çoruh** (riv.), Turk.
108/G7 **Corumbá**, Braz.
110/B1 **Corumbá** (riv.), Braz.
122/C4 **Corvallis**, Or,US
46/D2 **Corve** (riv.), Eng,UK
59/R12 **Corvo** (isl.), Azor.
60/C1 **Corvo** (peak), It.
45/E6 **Corwen**, Wal,UK
60/E3 **Cosenza**, It.
126/D3 **Coshocton**, Oh,US
116/D5 **Cosigüina** (pt.), Nic.
58/D2 **Coslada**, Sp.
110/F7 **Cosmópolis**, Braz.
56/E3 **Cosne-Cours-sur-Loire**, Fr.
58/B1 **Cospeito**, Sp.
111/D3 **Cosquín**, Arg.
56/D3 **Cosson** (riv.), Fr.
131/C3 **Costa Mesa**, Ca,US
116/E5 **Costa Rica**
117/N9 **Costa Rica**, Mex.
47/H1 **Costessey**, Eng,UK
63/G3 **Costeşti**, Rom.
132/M10 **Cosumnes** (riv.), Ca,US
82/D6 **Cotabato**, Phil.
98/D5 **Côte d'Ivoire** (Ivory Coast)
98/D5 **Côte d'Ivoire** (Ivory Coast)
54/A3 **Côte d'Or** (dept.), Fr.
127/N7 **Côte-Saint-Luc**, Qu,Can
46/B3 **Cothi** (riv.), Wal,UK
110/G8 **Cotia**, Braz.
99/F5 **Cotonou**, Ben.
46/D4 **Cotswolds** (hills), Eng,UK
122/C5 **Cottage Grove**, Or,US
49/H3 **Cottbus**, Ger.
47/G2 **Cottenham**, Eng,UK
124/D4 **Cottonwood**, Az,US
128/D2 **Cottonwood** (riv.), Ks,US
125/F5 **Cottonwood** (dry riv.), Tx,US
128/D4 **Cotulla**, Tx,US
56/C4 **Coubre, Pointe de la** (pt.), Fr.
52/C5 **Coucy-le-Château-Auffrique**, Fr.
52/B1 **Coudekerque-Branche**, Fr.
56/E5 **Couguille, Pic de** (peak), Fr.
56/D2 **Coulaines**, Fr.
122/D4 **Coulee City**, Wa,US
105/M **Coulman** (isl.), Ant.
52/C6 **Coulommiers**, Fr.
126/E2 **Coulonge** (riv.), Qu,Can
56/D4 **Coulounieix-Chamiers**, Fr.
122/D4 **Council**, Id,US
123/K5 **Council Bluffs**, Ia,US
125/H3 **Council Grove**, Ks,US
43/D2 **Coupar Angus**, Sc,UK
52/D3 **Courcelles**, Belg.
53/F5 **Courcelles-Chaussy**, Fr.
56/E4 **Cournon-d'Auvergne**, Fr.
118/D4 **Courtenay**, BC,Can
127/S8 **Courtice**, On,Can
52/C2 **Courtrai** (Kortrijk), Belg.
56/C2 **Coutances**, Fr.
122/F3 **Coutts**, Ab,Can
52/D3 **Couvin**, Belg.
59/P10 **Cova da Piedade**, Port.
58/C1 **Covadonga Nat'l Park**, Sp.
63/H3 **Covasna**, Rom.
63/G3 **Covasna** (co.), Rom.
47/E2 **Coventry**, Eng,UK
47/E1 **Coventry** (can.), Eng,UK
58/B2 **Covilhã**, Port.
131/C2 **Covina**, Ca,US
129/H3 **Covington**, Ga,US
126/C4 **Covington**, Ky,US
129/F3 **Covington**, Tn,US
126/E4 **Covington**, Va,US
90/H8 **Cowan**, Austl.
46/C4 **Cowbridge**, Wal,UK
47/E5 **Cowes**, Eng,UK
45/F2 **Cow Green** (res.), Eng,UK
122/C4 **Cowlitz** (riv.), Wa,US
129/H3 **Cowpens Nat'l Bfld.**, SC,US
91/D2 **Cowra**, Austl.
45/G2 **Coxhoe**, Eng,UK
109/H7 **Coxim**, Braz.
52/B5 **Coye-la-Forêt**, Fr.
125/H2 **Cozad**, Ne,US
116/D3 **Cozumel**, Mex.
116/D3 **Cozumel** (isl.), Mex.
91/C4 **Cradle** (peak), Austl.
91/C4 **Cradle Mountain-Lake Saint Clair Nat'l Park**, Austl.
102/D4 **Cradock**, SAfr.
130/K3 **Crag** (mtn.), Yk,Can
45/F3 **Crag** (hill), Eng,UK
124/F2 **Craig**, Co,US
44/C2 **Craigavad**, NI,UK
44/B3 **Craigavon**, NI,UK
44/B3 **Craigavon** (dist.), NI,UK
91/F5 **Craigieburn**, Austl.
123/G3 **Craik**, Sk,Can
57/J2 **Crailsheim**, Ger.
63/F3 **Craiova**, Rom.
45/G1 **Cramlington**, Eng,UK
44/A1 **Crana** (riv.), Ire.
123/H2 **Cranberry Portage**, Mb,Can
46/D5 **Cranborne Chase** (for.), Eng,UK
91/C3 **Cranbourne**, Austl.
122/E3 **Cranbrook**, BC,Can
47/G4 **Cranbrook**, Eng,UK
131/F5 **Cranbury**, NJ,US
128/C4 **Crane**, Tx,US
123/J3 **Crane River**, Mb,Can
131/F5 **Cranford**, NJ,US
47/F4 **Cranleigh**, Eng,UK
52/C5 **Craonne**, Fr.
63/F2 **Crasna** (riv.), Rom.
122/C5 **Crater** (lake), Or,US
122/C5 **Crater Lake Nat'l Park**, Or,US
122/E5 **Craters of the Moon Nat'l Mon.**, Id,US
109/K5 **Crateús**, Braz.
60/E3 **Crati** (riv.), It.
109/L5 **Crato**, Braz.
110/C2 **Cravinhos**, Braz.
126/C3 **Crawfordsville**, In,US
129/G4 **Crawfordville**, Fl,US
47/F4 **Crawley**, Eng,UK
122/F4 **Crazy** (mts.), Mt,US
52/A3 **Crécy-en-Ponthieu**, Fr.
56/C2 **Cotentin** (pen.), Fr.
46/D2 **Credenhill**, Eng,UK
127/Q8 **Credit** (riv.), On,Can
46/C5 **Crediton**, Eng,UK
118/F3 **Cree** (lake), Sk,Can
118/F3 **Cree** (riv.), Sk,Can
44/D2 **Cree** (riv.), Sc,UK
44/D2 **Creetown**, Sc,UK
123/H2 **Creighton**, Sk,Can
52/B5 **Creil**, Fr.
57/H4 **Crema**, It.
51/H4 **Cremlingen**, Ger.
57/J4 **Cremona**, It.
52/B5 **Crépy-en-Valois**, Fr.
62/B3 **Cres** (isl.), Cro.
124/A2 **Crescent City**, Ca,US
112/E2 **Crespo**, Arg.
56/F4 **Crest**, Fr.
132/P16 **Crest Hill**, Il,US
131/C2 **Crestline**, Ca,US
122/D3 **Creston**, BC,Can
123/K5 **Creston**, Ia,US
129/G4 **Crestview**, Fl,US
45/G5 **Creswell**, Eng,UK
61/J5 **Crete** (isl.), Gre.
61/J5 **Crete** (sea), Gre.
125/H2 **Crete**, Ne,US
52/B6 **Créteil**, Fr.
59/G1 **Creus** (cape), Sp.
56/D3 **Creuse** (riv.), Fr.
53/F5 **Creutzwald-la-Croix**, Fr.
57/J4 **Crevalcore**, It.
59/E3 **Crevillente**, Sp.
45/F5 **Crewe**, Eng,UK
46/D5 **Crewkerne**, Eng,UK
43/C2 **Crianlarich**, Sc,UK
44/D6 **Criccieth**, Wal,UK
110/B4 **Criciúma**, Braz.
46/C3 **Crickhowell**, Wal,UK
47/E3 **Cricklade**, Eng,UK
43/D2 **Crieff**, Sc,UK
52/A3 **Criel-sur-Mer**, Fr.
44/E2 **Criffell** (hill), Eng,UK
66/E3 **Crimean** (pen.), Ukr.
96/H7 **Cristal** (mts.), Gabon
109/J7 **Cristalina**, Braz.
117/G5 **Cristóbal** (pk.), Col.
62/F2 **Criştul Alb** (riv.), Rom.
63/G2 **Cristuru Secuiesc**, Rom.
62/E2 **Crişul Negru** (riv.), Rom.
109/H6 **Crixás-Açu** (riv.), Braz.
61/G2 **Crna Reka** (riv.), FYROM
91/D3 **Croajingolong Nat'l Park**, Austl.
62/B3 **Croatia**
127/F2 **Croche** (riv.), Qu,Can
86/E3 **Crocker** (range), Malay.
44/E1 **Crocketford**, Sc,UK
128/E4 **Crockett**, Tx,US
91/D2 **Crocodile** (pt.), Austl.
131/K7 **Crofton**, Md,US
46/B3 **Crofty**, Wal,UK
44/B6 **Croghan** (mtn.), Ire.
56/F5 **Croisette** (cape), Fr.
123/L3 **Croix** (lake), Can., US
47/H1 **Cromer**, Eng,UK
89/G7 **Cromwell**, NZ
83/E3 **Crong A Na** (riv.), Viet.
90/H9 **Cronulla**, Austl.
45/G2 **Crook**, Eng,UK
117/G3 **Crooked** (isl.), Bahm.
123/J4 **Crookston**, Mn,US
45/E5 **Crosby**, Eng,UK
123/H3 **Crosby**, ND,US
128/C3 **Crosbyton**, Tx,US
99/H5 **Cross** (riv.), Camr., Nga.
123/J2 **Cross** (lake), Mb,Can
129/H4 **Cross City**, Fl,US
128/F3 **Crossett**, Ar,US
45/F2 **Cross Fell** (mtn.), Eng,UK
122/E3 **Crossfield**, Ab,Can
44/C3 **Crossgar**, NI,UK
46/C2 **Crossgates**, Wal,UK
44/D1 **Crosshill**, Sc,UK
46/C3 **Crosskeys**, Wal,UK
44/B3 **Crossmaglen**, NI,UK
44/E2 **Crossmichael**, Sc,UK
99/H5 **Cross River** (state), Nga.
129/G3 **Crossville**, Tn,US
45/F4 **Croston**, Eng,UK
60/E3 **Crotone**, It.
47/G3 **Crouch** (riv.), Eng,UK
52/C5 **Crouy-sur-Ourcq**, Fr.
122/G4 **Crow Agency**, Mt,US
47/G4 **Crowborough**, Eng,UK
91/E1 **Crowdy Bay Nat'l Park**, Austl.
126/E2 **Crowe** (riv.), On,Can
122/F5 **Crowheart**, Wy,US
47/F1 **Crowland**, Eng,UK
45/H4 **Crowle**, Eng,UK
128/E4 **Crowley**, La,US
129/F3 **Crowley's** (ridge), Ar,US
123/K4 **Crow, North Fork** (riv.), Mn,US
126/C3 **Crown Point**, In,US
124/E4 **Crownpoint**, NM,US
119/H1 **Crown Prince Frederik** (isl.), Nun.,Can
90/D4 **Crows Nest Falls Nat'l Park**, Austl.
47/F4 **Crowthorne**, Eng,UK
47/F3 **Croxley Green**, Eng,UK
91/G5 **Croydon**, Austl.
39/M8 **Crozet** (isls.), FrAnt.
105/M **Crozier** (cape), Ant.
56/A2 **Crozon**, Fr.
43/E2 **Cruden Bay**, Sc,UK
44/B2 **Crumlin**, NI,UK
45/E2 **Crummock Water** (lake), Eng,UK
53/E5 **Crusnes** (riv.), Fr.
117/F4 **Cruz** (cape), Cuba
112/E2 **Cruz Alta**, Arg.
111/F2 **Cruz Alta**, Braz.
59/P10 **Cruz Alta** (mtn.), Port.
109/L6 **Cruz das Almas**, Braz.
111/D3 **Cruz del Eje**, Arg.
110/J7 **Cruzeiro**, Braz.
108/D5 **Cruzeiro do Sul**, Braz.
110/J6 **Cruzília**, Braz.
62/D3 **Crvenka**, Yugo.
45/E5 **Cryn-y-Brain** (mtn.), Wal,UK
124/C3 **Crystal Bay**, Nv,US
128/D4 **Crystal City**, Tx,US
126/B2 **Crystal Falls**, Mi,US
132/P15 **Crystal Lake**, Il,US
62/E2 **Csongrád**, Hun.
62/E2 **Csongrád** (co.), Hun.
62/C2 **Csorna**, Hun.
62/E2 **Csorvás**, Hun.
62/D2 **Csóványos** (peak), Hun.
72/D2 **Ctesiphon** (ruins), Iraq
104/D4 **Cuando** (riv.), Ang.
104/C4 **Cuangar**, Ang.
104/C2 **Cuango** (riv.), Ang.
104/B2 **Cuanza** (riv.), Ang.
59/E3 **Cuart de Poblet**, Sp.
112/D2 **Cuarto** (riv.), Arg.
116/A2 **Cuatrociénagas**, Mex.
117/F3 **Cuba**
125/K3 **Cuba**, Mo,US
104/C4 **Cubango** (riv.), Ang.
110/G8 **Cubatão**, Braz.
74/C2 **Çubuk**, Turk.
131/C2 **Cucamonga** (Rancho Cucamonga), Ca,US
108/E2 **Cuchivero** (riv.), Ven.
47/F4 **Cuckfield**, Eng,UK
47/G5 **Cuckmere** (riv.), Eng,UK
83/D1 **Cuc Phuong Nat'l Park**, Viet.
108/D2 **Cúcuta**, Col.
132/Q14 **Cudahy**, Wi,US
84/C5 **Cuddalore**, India
84/C5 **Cuddapah**, India
45/F5 **Cuddington**, Eng,UK
58/B1 **Cudillero**, Sp.
45/G4 **Cudworth**, Eng,UK
58/C2 **Cuéllar**, Sp.
108/C4 **Cuenca**, Ecu.
58/D2 **Cuenca**, Sp.
58/E2 **Cuenca** (range), Sp.
116/B4 **Cuernavaca**, Mex.
128/D4 **Cuero**, Tx,US
56/G5 **Cuers**, Fr.
108/C3 **Cueva de los Guarcharos Nat'l Park**, Col.
58/E4 **Cuevas del Almanzora**, Sp.
63/F3 **Cugir**, Rom.
56/D5 **Cugnaux-Vingtcasses**, Fr.
109/G7 **Cuiabá**, Braz.
109/G7 **Cuiabá** (riv.), Braz.
50/C5 **Cuijk**, Neth.
104/C2 **Cuilo** (riv.), Ang.
104/C3 **Cuima**, Ang.
104/C4 **Cuito** (riv.), Ang.
104/C4 **Cuito-Cuanavale**, Ang.
108/F4 **Cuiuni** (riv.), Braz.
74/E3 **Çukurca**, Turk.
83/E4 **Cu Lao** (isl.), Viet.
44/A1 **Culdaff** (riv.), Ire.
50/C5 **Culemborg**, Neth.
109/H6 **Culene** (riv.), Braz.
91/C1 **Culgoa** (riv.), Austl.
117/N9 **Culiacán**, Mex.
82/D5 **Culion** (isl.), Phil.
58/D4 **Cúllar Baza**, Sp.
43/D2 **Cullen**, Sc,UK
59/E3 **Cullera**, Sp.
58/A1 **Culleredo**, Sp.
129/G3 **Cullman**, Al,US
46/C5 **Cullompton**, Eng,UK
44/B2 **Cullybackey**, NI,UK
44/A1 **Culmore**, NI,UK
90/B5 **Culoga** (riv.), Austl.
126/E4 **Culpeper**, Va,US
131/B2 **Culver City**, Ca,US
117/J5 **Cumaná**, Ven.
119/K2 **Cumberland** (pen.), Nun.,Can
119/K2 **Cumberland** (sound), Nun.,Can
123/H2 **Cumberland** (lake), Sk,Can
129/G3 **Cumberland** (plat.), US
129/H4 **Cumberland** (isl.), Ga,US
129/G2 **Cumberland** (falls), Ky,US
126/C4 **Cumberland** (lake), Ky,US
129/G2 **Cumberland** (riv.), Ky, Tn,US
126/E4 **Cumberland**, Md,US
126/D4 **Cumberland Gap Nat'l Hist. Park**, Tn,US
123/H2 **Cumberland House**, Sk,Can
117/N8 **Cumbres de Majalca Nat'l Park**, Mex.
116/A2 **Cumbres de Monterrey Nat'l Park**, Mex.
45/F2 **Cumbria** (co.), Eng,UK
45/E3 **Cumbrian** (mts.), Eng,UK
84/C4 **Cumbum**, India
74/C3 **Çumra**, Turk.
130/M5 **Cumshewa** (pt.), BC,Can
112/B3 **Cunco**, Chile
104/B4 **Cunene** (riv.), Ang.
57/G4 **Cuneo**, It.
83/E3 **Cung Son**, Viet.
110/J8 **Cunha**, Braz.
42/H1 **Čuokkaraš'ša** (peak), Nor.
57/G4 **Cuorgnè**, It.
43/D2 **Cupar**, Sc,UK
132/K12 **Cupertino**, Ca,US
62/E4 **Ćuprija**, Yugo.
117/H5 **Curaçao** (isl.), NAnt.
112/C3 **Curacautín**, Chile
112/B3 **Curanilahue**, Chile
108/C4 **Curaray** (riv.), Ecu., Peru
112/Q9 **Curaumilla** (pt.), Chile
62/F2 **Curcubăta** (peak), Rom.
56/E3 **Cure** (riv.), Fr.
103/S15 **Curepipe**, Mrts.
112/B2 **Curepto**, Chile
112/C2 **Curicó**, Chile
110/B3 **Curitiba**, Braz.
110/B3 **Curitibanos**, Braz.
44/B5 **Curragh, The**, Ire.
109/L5 **Currais Novos**, Braz.
125/K3 **Current** (riv.), Ar, Mo,US
124/D2 **Currie**, Nv,US
63/G3 **Curtea de Argeş**, Rom.
62/E2 **Curtici**, Rom.
90/C3 **Curtis** (isl.), Austl.
92/H8 **Curtis** (isl.), NZ
109/G4 **Curuá** (riv.), Braz.
109/H5 **Curuá** (riv.), Braz.
108/D5 **Curuçá** (riv.), Braz.
86/B4 **Curup**, Indo.
109/K4 **Cururupu**, Braz.
111/E2 **Curuzú Cuatiá**, Arg.
110/C1 **Curvelo**, Braz.
121/J2 **Curwood** (mtn.), Mi,US
108/D6 **Cusco**, Peru
44/B1 **Cushendall**, NI,UK
44/B3 **Cusher** (riv.), NI,UK
125/H4 **Cushing**, Ok,US
56/E3 **Cusset**, Fr.
129/G3 **Cusseta**, Ga,US
122/G4 **Custer**, Mt,US
125/H5 **Custer**, SD,US
46/C5 **Cut** (hill), Eng,UK
122/E3 **Cut Bank**, Mt,US
108/C5 **Cutervo**, Peru
129/G4 **Cuthbert**, Ga,US
122/F2 **Cut Knife**, Sk,Can
112/C3 **Cutral-Có**, Arg.
84/E3 **Cuttack**, India
51/F1 **Cuxhaven**, Ger.
124/C4 **Cuyama** (riv.), Ca,US
87/F1 **Cuyo**, Phil.
87/F1 **Cuyo** (isls.), Phil.
108/F2 **Cuyuni** (riv.), Guy., Ven.
46/C3 **Cwm**, Wal,UK
46/C3 **Cwmafan**, Wal,UK
46/C3 **Cwmbran**, Wal,UK
123/H5 **C.W. McConaughy** (lake), Ne,US
61/J4 **Cyclades** (isls.), Gre.
126/C4 **Cynthiana**, Ky,US
46/B3 **Cynwyl Elfed**, Wal,UK
122/F3 **Cypress** (hills), Ab, Sk,Can
131/B3 **Cypress**, Ca,US
74/J4 **Cyprus**
97/K1 **Cyrenaica** (reg.), Libya
46/B3 **Cywyn** (riv.), Wal,UK
49/J2 **Czaplinek**, Pol.
49/M2 **Czarna Białostocka**, Pol.
49/J2 **Czarnków**, Pol.
49/H4 **Czech Republic**
49/K3 **Częstochowa**, Pol.
49/K3 **Czestochowa** (prov.), Pol.
49/J2 **Człuchów**, Pol.

D

82/D2 **Da** (riv.), China
81/B4 **Daba** (mts.), China
62/D2 **Dabas**, Hun.
72/C3 **Dabbāgh, Jabal** (mtn.), SAr.
108/C2 **Dabeiba**, Col.
84/B3 **Dabhoi**, India
83/D1 **Da** (Black) (riv.), Viet.
132/B2 **Dabob** (bay), Wa,US
97/Q6 **Daborow**, Som.
98/D5 **Dabou**, IvC.
84/C2 **Dabra**, India
49/M2 **Dąbrowa Białostocka**, Pol.
49/K3 **Dąbrowa Górnicza**, Pol.
55/H1 **Dachau**, Ger.
83/D3 **Dac Sut**, Viet.
83/D3 **Dac To**, Viet.
129/H4 **Dade City**, Fl,US
87/H4 **Dadi** (cape), Indo.
84/B4 **Dadra & Nagar Haveli** (terr.), India
73/J3 **Dādu**, Pak.
84/D6 **Daduru** (riv.), SrL.
83/B4 **Daen Noi** (peak), Thai.
82/D5 **Daet**, Phil.
85/J2 **Dafang**, China
98/B2 **Dagana**, Sen.
67/H3 **Dagestan Aut. Rep.**, Rus.
102/D4 **Daggaboersnek** (pass), SAfr.
90/B2 **Dagmar Range Nat'l Park**, Austl.
85/H2 **Daguan**, China
90/E6 **D'Aguilar** (mtn.), Austl.
90/E6 **D'Aguilar** (range), Austl.
77/K2 **Daguokui** (peak), China
82/D4 **Dagupan**, Phil.
75/E5 **Dagzê** (lake), China
81/C2 **Dahaituo Shan** (mtn.), China
71/D7 **Dahana** (des.), SAr.
84/B4 **Dahānu**, India
84/A2 **Daharki**, Pak.
81/B2 **Dahei** (riv.), China
77/K2 **Daheiding** (peak), China
77/J2 **Da Hinggan** (mts.), China
97/N4 **Dahlak** (arch.), Erit.
129/H3 **Dahlonega**, Ga,US
49/G3 **Dahme** (riv.), Ger.
83/D4 **Da Hoa**, Viet.
81/C5 **Dahong** (mtn.), China
74/E3 **Dahūk**, Iraq
81/C2 **Dai** (lake), China
79/M9 **Daian**, Japan
79/G2 **Daigo**, Japan
84/D2 **Dailekh**, Nepal
44/D1 **Dailly**, Sc,UK
83/E3 **Dai Loc**, Viet.
58/D3 **Daimiel**, Sp.
128/E3 **Daingerfield**, Tx,US
90/B2 **Daintree Nat'l Park**, Austl.
79/E3 **Daiō-zaki** (pt.), Japan
112/E3 **Daireaux**, Arg.
78/C3 **Dai-sen** (mtn.), Japan
78/C3 **Daisen-Oki Nat'l Park**, Japan
79/L10 **Daitō**, Japan
92/C2 **Daito** (isls.), Japan
98/A3 **Dakar** (cap.), Sen.
98/A3 **Dakar** (reg.), Sen.
100/B3 **Dākhilah, Wāḥāt ad** (oasis), Egypt
96/B3 **Dakhla**, WSah.
98/A1 **Dakhlet Nouadhibou** (reg.), Mrta.
83/D3 **Dak Nhe**, Viet.
99/G3 **Dakoro**, Niger
125/H2 **Dakota City**, Ne,US
62/E4 **Dakovica**, Yugo.
62/D3 **Dakovo**, Yugo.
76/H3 **Dalai** (salt lake), China
74/B3 **Dalaman**, Turk.
76/F2 **Dalanjargalan**, Mong.
42/E3 **Dalarna** (reg.), Swe.
83/E4 **Da Lat**, Viet.
42/Q6 **Dalatangi** (pt.), Ice.
44/E2 **Dalbeattie**, Sc,UK
90/C4 **Dalby**, Austl.
100/B4 **Dal Cataract** (falls), Sudan
50/D4 **Dalfsen**, Neth.
128/C2 **Dalhart**, Tx,US
127/H1 **Dalhousie**, NB,Can
130/N1 **Dalhousie** (cape), NW,Can
85/H2 **Dali**, China
81/B3 **Dali** (riv.), China
58/D4 **Dalías**, Sp.
77/H3 **Daling** (riv.), China
62/D3 **Dalj**, Cro.
130/M4 **Dall** (isl.), Ak,US
130/F3 **Dall** (lake), Ak,US
128/D3 **Dallas**, Tx,US
122/C4 **Dalles, The**, Or,US
99/F3 **Dallol Bosso** (wadi), Mali, Niger
43/C2 **Dalmally**, Sc,UK
62/C4 **Dalmatia** (reg.), Cro.
44/D1 **Dalmellington**, Sc,UK
77/M3 **Dal'negorsk**, Rus.
77/L2 **Dal'nerechensk**, Rus.
98/D5 **Daloa**, IvC.
100/B4 **Dalqū**, Sudan
90/B3 **Dalrymple** (lake), Austl.
43/C2 **Dalrymple**, Sc,UK
129/G3 **Dalton**, Ga,US
84/D3 **Daltonganj**, India
45/E3 **Dalton-in-Furness**, Eng,UK
43/C2 **Dalwhinnie**, Sc,UK
118/H2 **Daly** (bay), Nun.,Can
132/K11 **Daly City**, Ca,US
75/F5 **Dam** (riv.), China
84/B3 **Damān**, India
84/B3 **Damān & Diu** (terr.), India
74/H6 **Damanhūr**, Egypt
87/G5 **Damar** (isl.), Indo.
131/J7 **Damascus**, Md,US
74/L5 **Damascus** (Dimashq) (cap.), Syria
96/H5 **Damaturu**, Nga.
72/F1 **Damāvand** (mtn.), Iran
83/D4 **Dam Doi**, Viet.
47/E5 **Damerham**, Eng,UK
73/F1 **Dāmghān**, Iran
74/H6 **Damietta** (Dumyāţ), Egypt

81/C3 Daming, China
53/D4 Damion (mtn.), Fr.
52/B5 Dammartin-en-Goële, Fr.
52/C1 Damme, Belg.
51/F3 Damme, Ger.
84/C3 Damoh, India
99/E4 Damongo, Gha.
87/H4 Dampier (str.), Indo.
83/C4 Damrei (mts.), Camb.
50/D2 Damsterdiep (riv.), Neth.
53/E5 Damvillers, Fr.
81/B4 Dan (riv.), China
129/H2 Dan (riv.), NC,US
97/P5 Danakil (reg.), Djib.
98/C5 Danané, IvC.
83/E2 Da Nang, Viet.
82/D5 Danao, Phil.
47/G3 Danbury, Eng,UK
91/G5 Dandenong, Austl.
91/G5 Dandenong (cr.), Austl.
91/G5 Dandenong (mtn.), Austl.
45/F5 Dane (riv.), Eng,UK
76/D4 Dang (riv.), China
102/B4 Danger (pt.), SAfr.
91/B2 Danggali Consv. Park, Austl.
97/N5 Dangila, Eth.
116/D4 Dangriga, Belz.
64/J4 Danilov, Rus.
81/B4 Danjiangkou, China
81/B4 Danjiangkou (res.), China
66/F1 Dankov, Rus.
75/C3 Dankova, Pik (peak), Kyr.
129/G3 Dannelly (res.), Al,US
48/F2 Dannenberg, Ger.
41/G4 Danube (riv.), Eur.
63/J3 Danube (delta), Rom.
63/H3 Danube, Borcea Branch (riv.), Rom.
63/J3 Danube, Mouths of the, Rom.
63/J3 Danube, Sfîntu Gheorghe Branch (riv.), Rom.
63/J3 Danube, Sulina Branch (riv.), Rom.
132/L11 Danville, Ca,US
126/C3 Danville, Il,US
126/C4 Danville, Ky,US
126/E4 Danville, Va,US
99/F4 Dapaong, Togo
129/G4 Daphne, Al,US
82/D6 Dapitan, Phil.
77/K2 Daqing, China
81/H7 Daqing (riv.), China
73/H2 Daqq-e Patargān (lake), Afg., Iran
74/L5 Dar'ā, Syria
73/F3 Dārāb, Iran
63/H1 Darabani, Rom.
82/D5 Daraga, Phil.
82/D5 Daram, Phil.
62/E4 Daravica (peak), Yugo.
74/L5 Dārayyā, Syria
84/E2 Darbhanga, India
130/F3 Darby (cape), Ak,US
131/E6 Darby, Pa,US
62/D3 Darda, Cro.
125/J4 Dardanelle (lake), Ar,US
63/H5 Dardanelles (str.), Turk.
91/G5 Darebin (cr.), Austl.
74/D2 Darende, Turk.
101/C4 Dar es Salaam (cap.), Tanz.
101/C4 Dar es Salaam (prov.), Tanz.
57/J4 Darfo, It.
89/H6 Dargaville, NZ
44/B5 Dargle (riv.), Ire.
76/F2 Darhan (peak), Mong.
97/Q6 Darie (hills), Som.
131/G4 Darien, Ct,US
129/H4 Darien, Ga,US
132/Q16 Darien, Il,US
117/F6 Darien Nat'l Park, Pan.
76/G2 Dariganga, Mong.
84/E2 Darjiling, India
91/B2 Darling (riv.), Austl.
90/C4 Darling Downs (upland), Austl.
45/G2 Darlington, Eng,UK
45/G2 Darlington, (co.), Eng,UK
129/J3 Darlington, SC,US
49/J1 Darłowo, Pol.
57/H2 Darmstadt, Ger.
97/K1 Darnah, Libya
52/A5 Darnétal, Fr.
105/E Darnley (cape), Ant.
118/D2 Darnley (bay), NW,Can
45/G1 Darras Hall, Eng,UK
73/G1 Darreh Gaz, Iran
97/K6 Dar Rounga (reg.), CAfr.
105/R Dart (cape), Ant.
46/C6 Dart (riv.), Eng,UK
47/G4 Dartford, Eng,UK
46/C6 Dartington, Eng,UK
46/B5 Dartmoor (upland), Eng,UK
46/C5 Dartmoor Nat'l Park, Eng,UK
91/C3 Dartmouth (res.), Austl.
127/J2 Dartmouth, NS,Can
46/C6 Dartmouth, Eng,UK
45/G4 Darton, Eng,UK
59/G3 Dartuch (cape), Sp.
92/D5 Daru, PNG
62/C3 Daruvar, Cro.
87/E3 Darvel (bay), Malay.
45/F4 Darwen, Eng,UK
89/C2 Darwin, Austl.
112/B5 Darwin (bay), Chile
113/K8 Darwin (mts.), Chile
73/H2 Daryācheh-ye Sīstān (lake), Iran
77/H3 Dashengtang (peak), China
81/B5 Dashennongjia (peak), China
97/N5 Dashen, Ras (peak), Eth.
73/F2 Dasht-e Kavīr (des.), Iran
73/G2 Dasht-e Lūt (des.), Iran
73/H2 Dasht-e Mārgow (des.), Afg.
73/H3 Dasht Kaur (riv.), Pak.
51/G5 Dassel, Ger.
102/B4 Dasseneiland (isl.), SAfr.
83/D4 Dat Do, Viet.
84/C2 Datia, India
124/F4 Datil, NM,US
81/C2 Datong, China
76/D4 Datong (mts.), China
76/D4 Datong (riv.), China
51/E5 Datteln, Ger.
86/C3 Datu (cape), Malay.
86/B3 Datuk (cape), Indo.
42/H4 Daugava (riv.), Lat.
64/E4 Daugava (riv.), Lat.
64/E5 Daugavpils, Lat.
53/F3 Daun, Ger.
83/B3 Daung (isl.), Myan.
123/H3 Dauphin, Mb,Can
123/J3 Dauphin (lake), Mb,Can
84/C5 Dāvangere, India
82/E6 Davao, Phil.
123/L5 Davenport, Ia,US
122/D4 Davenport, Wa,US
47/E2 Daventry, Eng,UK
119/T6 Davgaard-Jensen (reg.), Grld.
116/E6 David, Pan.
125/H2 David City, Ne,US
123/G3 Davidson, Sk,Can
132/K11 Davidson (mtn.), Ca,US
105/F Davis (sea), Ant.
105/F Davis (sta.), Ant.
115/M3 Davis (str.), Can., Grld.
132/L9 Davis, Ca,US
126/E4 Davis (peak), Pa,US
128/B4 Davis (mts.), Tx,US
65/M5 Davlekanovo, Rus.
98/D5 Davo (riv.), IvC.
55/F4 Davos, Swi.
76/C1 Davst, Mong.
97/N7 Dawa Wenz (riv.), Eth.
81/D4 Dawen (riv.), China
46/C5 Dawlish, Eng,UK
90/C4 Dawson (riv.), Austl.
130/L3 Dawson, Yk,Can
113/K8 Dawson (isl.), Chile
129/G4 Dawson, Ga,US
122/D2 Dawson Creek, BC,Can
81/C5 Dawu Shan (mtn.), China
72/G4 Dawwah, Oman
56/C5 Dax, Fr.
81/D3 Daxing, China
85/G3 Daying (riv.), China
113/F1 Dayman (riv.), Uru.
82/B2 Dayong, China
74/K6 Dayr al Balaḥ, Gaza
72/D1 Dayr az Zawr, Syria
100/B3 Dayrūt, Egypt
122/E2 Daysland, Ab,Can
126/C4 Dayton, Oh,US
129/G3 Dayton, Tn,US
122/D4 Dayton, Wa,US
129/H4 Daytona Beach, Fl,US
102/D3 De Aar, SAfr.
74/K6 Dead (sea), Isr., Jor.
123/H4 Deadwood, SD,US
91/C3 Deal (isl.), Austl.
47/H4 Deal, Eng,UK
131/G5 Deal, NJ,US
122/B2 Dean (riv.), BC,Can
46/D3 Dean, Forest of (for.), Eng,UK
111/D3 Deán Funes, Arg.
132/F7 Dearborn, Mi,US
132/F7 Dearborn Heights, Mi,US
45/G4 Dearne, Eng,UK
45/G4 Dearne (riv.), Eng,UK
130/N4 Dease (riv.), BC,Can
118/F2 Dease (str.), Nun.,Can
124/C3 Death Valley Nat'l Park, Ca, Nv,US
62/E5 Debar, FYROM
130/G3 Debauch (mtn.), Ak,US
47/H2 Deben (riv.), Eng,UK
47/H2 Debenham, Eng,UK
49/L3 Dębica, Pol.
50/C4 De Bilt, Neth.
49/L3 Dęblin, Pol.
49/H2 Dębno, Pol.
130/J3 Deborah (mtn.), Ak,US
97/N6 Debre Birhan, Eth.
62/E2 Debrecen, Hun.
97/N5 Debre Mark'os, Eth.
97/N5 Debre Tabor, Eth.
97/N6 Debre Zeyit, Eth.
129/G3 Decatur, Al,US
129/G3 Decatur, Ga,US
126/B4 Decatur, Il,US
126/C3 Decatur, In,US
128/D3 Decatur, Tx,US
56/E4 Decazeville, Fr.
84/C5 Deccan (plat.), India
49/H3 Děčín, Czh.
56/E3 Decize, Fr.
47/E3 Deddington, Eng,UK
50/D3 Dedemsvaart, Neth.
112/C5 Dedo (peak), Arg.
98/E3 Dédougou, Burk.
104/F3 Dedza, Malw.
44/B4 Dee (riv.), Ire.
44/D1 Dee (riv.), Sc,UK
43/D2 Dee (riv.), Sc,UK
45/E5 Dee (riv.), Wal,UK
44/A4 Deel (riv.), Ire.
47/F1 Deeping Saint James, Eng,UK
126/E2 Deep River, On,Can
130/F5 Deer (isl.), Ak,US
132/Q15 Deerfield, Il,US
127/K1 Deer Lake, Nf,Can
52/C2 Deerlijk, Belg.
122/E4 Deer Lodge, Mt,US
131/G5 Deer Park, NY,US
122/D4 Deer Park, Wa,US
84/B3 Deesa, India
90/H8 Dee Why, Austl.
97/Q6 Deex Nugaaleed (dry river), Som.
108/F8 Defensores del Chaco Nat'l Park, Par.
126/C3 Defiance, Oh,US
129/G4 De Funiak Springs, Fl,US
44/E5 Deganwy, Wal,UK
97/P6 Degeh Bur, Eth.
127/G2 Dégelis, Qu,Can
57/K2 Deggendorf, Ger.
52/C1 De Haan, Belg.
97/P4 Dehalak (isl.), Erit.
97/P4 Dehalak Marine Nat'l Park, Erit.
73/L2 Dehra Dūn, India
84/D3 Dehri, India
52/C2 Deinze, Belg.
51/G4 Deister (mts.), Ger.
63/F2 Dej, Rom.
126/B3 De Kalb, Il,US
97/N4 Dek'emhāre, Erit.
129/H4 De Land, Fl,US
124/C4 Delano, Ca,US
73/H2 Delārām, Afg.
122/G2 Delaronde (lake), Sk,Can
132/N14 Delavan, Wi,US
126/F3 Delaware (riv.), US
126/F4 Delaware (state), US
126/D3 Delaware, Oh,US
131/F4 Delaware Water Gap Nat'l Rec. Area, NJ, Pa,US
51/F5 Delbrück, Ger.
112/D2 Del Campillo, Arg.
62/F5 Delčevo, FYROM
50/D4 Delden, Neth.
50/D2 De Leijen (lake), Neth.
54/D3 Delémont, Swi.
50/B5 Delft, Neth.
50/D2 Delfzijl, Neth.
112/E4 Delgada (pt.), Arg.
101/D5 Delgado (cape), Moz.
76/D2 Delger (riv.), Mong.
76/F2 Delgerhaan, Mong.
76/E2 Delgerhangay, Mong.
84/C2 Delhi, India
66/E5 Delice (riv.), Turk.
50/B5 De Lier, Neth.
60/D5 Delimara, Fonta Ta' (pt.), Malta
122/G3 Delisle, Sk,Can
51/G5 Delligsen, Ger.
123/J5 Dell Rapids, SD,US
102/Q13 Delmas, SAfr.
53/F6 Delme, Fr.
51/F3 Delme (riv.), Ger.
51/F2 Delmenhorst, Ger.
125/F3 Del Norte, Co,US
123/H3 Deloraine, Mb,Can
61/J4 Delos (ruins), Gre.
61/H3 Delphi (ruins), Gre.
126/C3 Delphos, Oh,US
131/F5 Delran, NJ,US
129/H5 Delray Beach, Fl,US
128/C4 Del Rio, Tx,US
123/E4 Delta, Co,US
124/D3 Delta, Ut,US
113/T12 Delta del Tigre, Uru.
132/M11 Delta-Mendota (can.), Ca,US
129/H4 Deltona, Fl,US
76/C2 Delüün, Mong.
132/L11 Del Valle (lake), Ca,US
65/M5 Dēma (riv.), Rus.
58/D1 Demanda (range), Sp.
130/K2 Demarcation (pt.), Ak,US
104/D2 Demba, D.R. Congo
97/M6 Dembī Dolo, Eth.
50/B7 Demer (riv.), Belg.
124/F4 Deming, NM,US
108/F3 Demini (riv.), Braz.
48/G2 Demmin, Ger.
129/G3 Demopolis, Al,US
86/B4 Dempo (peak), Indo.
52/C3 Denain, Fr.
97/P5 Denakil (reg.), Erit., Eth.
130/H3 Denali Nat'l Park & Prsv., Ak,US
123/H2 Denare Beach, Sk,Can
45/E5 Denbigh, Wal,UK
45/E5 Denbighshire (co.), Wal,UK
50/B2 Den Burg, Neth.
45/G4 Denby Dale, Eng,UK
52/D2 Dender (riv.), Belg.
52/D2 Denderleeuw, Belg.
52/D1 Dendermonde, Belg.
50/D4 Denekamp, Neth.
50/D4 Den Ham, Neth.
50/B3 Den Helder, Neth.
45/G4 Denholme, Eng,UK
59/F3 Denia, Sp.
91/C2 Deniliquin, Austl.
124/C2 Denio, Nv,US
130/H4 Denison (mtn.), Ak,US
123/K5 Denison, Ia,US
128/D3 Denison, Tx,US
74/B3 Denizli, Turk.
105/G Denman (glac.), Ant.
42/C5 Denmark
115/Q3 Denmark (str.), NAm
86/E5 Denpasar, Indo.
52/C2 Dentergem, Belg.
47/G5 Denton, Eng,UK
128/D3 Denton, Tx,US
92/D5 D'Entrecasteaux (isls.), PNG
125/F3 Denver (cap.), Co,US
131/F5 Denville, NJ,US
84/C2 Deoband, India
84/D3 Deogarh, India
84/E3 Deoghar, India
84/B4 Deolāli, India
84/C2 Deoli, India
56/D3 Déols, Fr.
84/D2 Deoria, India
52/B1 De Panne, Belg.
50/C6 De Peel (reg.), Neth.
127/S10 Depew, NY,US
52/C2 De Pinte, Belg.
97/P7 Dera (dry riv.), Som.
73/K2 Dera Ghāzi Khān, Pak.
73/K2 Dera Ismā'īl Khān, Pak.
67/J4 Derbent, Rus.
45/G6 Derby, Eng,UK
45/G6 Derby City (co.), Eng,UK
125/H3 Derby, Ks,US
45/G6 Derbyshire (co.), Eng,UK
63/F3 Đerdap Nat'l Park, Yugo.
62/E2 Derecske, Hun.
76/F2 Deren, Mong.
43/A4 Derg, Lough (lake), Ire.
128/E4 De Ridder, La,US
74/E3 Derik, Turk.
56/B2 Déroute (passg.), Fr., Chl,UK
44/A4 Derravaragh, Lough (lake), Ire.
44/B6 Derry (riv.), Ire.
127/G3 Derry, NH,US
44/C3 Derryboy, NI,UK
43/B3 Derrylin, NI,UK
47/G1 Dersingham, Eng,UK
62/C3 Derventa, Bosn.
44/B1 Dervock, NI,UK
91/C4 Derwent (riv.), Austl.
45/F2 Derwent (res.), Eng,UK
45/E2 Derwent (riv.), Eng,UK
45/G5 Derwent (riv.), Eng,UK
45/H4 Derwent (riv.), Eng,UK
44/E2 Derwent Water (lake), Eng,UK
112/D2 Desaguadero (riv.), Arg.
108/E7 Desaguadero (riv.), Bol.
47/F2 Desborough, Eng,UK
112/C2 Descabezado Grande (vol.), Chile
110/C2 Descalvado, Braz.
123/H2 Deschambault Lake, Sk,Can
124/B2 Deschutes (riv.), Or,US
97/N5 Desē, Eth.
111/C6 Deseado (riv.), Arg.
113/J8 Deseado (cape), Chile
113/L7 Desengaño (pt.), Arg.
59/V15 Desertas (isl.), Madr.,Port.
81/B4 Deshengpu, China
123/J4 De Smet, SD,US
123/K5 Des Moines (cap.), Ia,US
123/K5 Des Moines (riv.), Ia, Mo,US
132/C3 Des Moines, Wa,US
66/D2 Desna (riv.), Rus., Ukr.
113/J8 Desolación (isl.), Chile
102/D4 Desolation, Valley of (val.), SAfr.
125/K3 De Soto, Mo,US
102/D4 Despatch, SAfr.
132/Q15 Des Plaines, Il,US
132/P16 Des Plaines (riv.), Il,US
48/G3 Dessau, Ger.
53/E1 Dessel, Belg.
52/C1 Destelbergen, Belg.
130/L3 Destruction Bay, Yk,Can
62/E3 Deta, Rom.
51/F5 Detmold, Ger.
132/F7 Detroit, Mi,US
132/F7 Detroit (riv.), On,Can, Mi,US
123/K4 Detroit Lakes, Mn,US
42/P6 Dettifoss (falls), Ice.
91/D2 Deua Nat'l Park, Austl.
52/B2 Deûle (riv.), Fr.
50/B6 Deurne, Belg.
50/C6 Deurne, Neth.
57/L3 Deutschlandsberg, Aus.
127/N6 Deux-Montagnes, Qu,Can
127/M7 Deux-Montagnes (lake), Qu,Can
62/F3 Deva, Rom.
62/E2 Dévaványa, Hun.
74/C2 Develi, Turk.
50/D4 Deventer, Neth.
43/D2 Deveron (riv.), Sc,UK
109/H2 Devil's (isl.), FrG.
125/G5 Devils (riv.), Tx,US
123/J3 Devils Lake, ND,US
130/M4 Devils Paw (mtn.), BC,Can, Ak,US
124/C3 Devils Postpile Nat'l Mon., Ca,US
123/G4 Devils Tower Nat'l Mon., Wy,US
63/G5 Devin, Bul.
128/D4 Devine, Tx,US
47/E4 Devizes, Eng,UK
63/H4 Devnya, Bul.
61/G2 Devoll (riv.), Alb.
122/E2 Devon, Ab,Can
119/S7 Devon (isl.), Nun.,Can
46/C5 Devon (co.), Eng,UK
91/C4 Devonport, Austl.
63/K5 Devrek, Turk.
66/D4 Devrek (riv.), Turk.
66/E4 Devrez (riv.), Turk.
86/A3 Dewa (pt.), Indo.
84/C3 Dewās, India
128/E2 Dewey, Ok,US
125/H2 De Witt, Ne,US
45/G4 Dewsbury, Eng,UK
127/G2 Dexter, Me,US
72/E2 Dez (riv.), Iran
72/E2 Dezfūl, Iran
130/E2 Dezhneva, Mys (pt.), Rus.
81/D3 Dezhou, China
100/C2 Dhahab, Egypt
84/F3 Dhaka (Dacca) (cap.), Bang.
84/D3 Dhamtari, India
84/E3 Dhānbād, India
84/E2 Dhankuta, Nepal
84/C3 Dhār, India
84/B3 Dharampur, India
84/B3 Dhāri, India
84/C5 Dharmapuri, India
84/C5 Dharmavaram, India
84/D2 Dhaulāgiri (peak), Nepal
61/H3 Dhelfoí (Delphi) (ruins), Gre.
84/E3 Dhenkānāl, India
61/K2 Dhidhimótikhon, Gre.
61/H3 Dhírfis (peak), Gre.
72/F5 Dhofar (reg.), Oman
84/B3 Dholka, India
84/C2 Dholpur, India
84/B4 Dhond, India
61/J4 Dhonoúsa (isl.), Gre.
84/B3 Dhorāji, India
61/J2 Dhráma, Gre.
53/F4 Dhronbach (riv.), Ger.
84/E2 Dhubri, India
84/B3 Dhūlia, India
84/E3 Dhuliān, India
84/E2 Dhupgāri, India
61/J5 Día (isl.), Gre.
57/G4 Diable, Cime du (peak), Fr.
130/H4 Diablo (mtn.), Ak,US
132/L11 Diablo (mt.), Ca,US
124/B3 Diablo (range), Ca,US
128/B4 Diablo (plat.), Tx,US
113/G2 Diablo, Punta del (pt.), Uru.
110/G8 Diadema, Braz.
112/E2 Diamante, Arg.
112/D2 Diamante (riv.), Arg.
110/D1 Diamantina, Braz.
109/K6 Diamantina (mts.), Braz.
109/G6 Diamantino, Braz.
91/G5 Diamond (cr.), Austl.
122/E4 Diamond (peak), Id,US
131/C3 Diamond Bar, Ca,US
120/W13 Diamond Head (crater), Hi,US
81/L8 Dianshan (lake), China
99/F3 Diapaga, Burk.
105/J Dibble Iceberg Tongue, Ant.
104/E5 Dibete, Bots.
100/B4 Dibis, Bīr (well), Egypt
128/E4 Diboll, Tx,US
85/F2 Dibrugarh, India
74/F3 Dibs, Iraq
128/C3 Dickens, Tx,US
123/H4 Dickinson, ND,US
129/G2 Dickson, Tn,US
74/E3 Dicle (riv.), Turk.
50/D5 Didam, Neth.
47/E3 Didcot, Eng,UK
122/E3 Didsbury, Ab,Can
73/K3 Didwāna, India
103/E2 Die Berg (peak), SAfr.
98/E4 Diébougou, Burk.
118/F3 Diefenbaker (lake), Sk,Can
113/J7 Diego de Almagro (isl.), Chile
71/G10 Diego Garcia (isl.), BrIn.
53/E4 Diekirch (dist.), Lux.
51/F5 Diemel (riv.), Ger.
50/B4 Diemen, Neth.
83/C1 Dien Bien Phu, Viet.
83/D2 Dien Chau, Viet.
83/E3 Dien Khanh, Viet.
53/E2 Diepenbeek, Belg.
50/D4 Diepenveen, Neth.
51/F3 Diepholz, Ger.
52/A4 Dieppe, Fr.
53/E2 Diest, Belg.
101/D2 Dif, Kenya
99/H3 Diffa (dept.), Niger
53/E4 Differdange, Lux.
91/B3 Difficult (peak), Austl.
85/G2 Digboi, India
127/H2 Digby, NS,Can
57/G4 Digne, Fr.
56/E3 Digoin, Fr.
82/E6 Digos, Phil.
84/C3 Digras, India
52/D2 Dijle (Dyle) (riv.), Belg.
54/B3 Dijon, Fr.
97/P5 Dikhil, Djib.
74/H6 Dikirnis, Egypt
67/H4 Diklosmta, Gora (peak), Geo.
52/B1 Diksmuide, Belg.
96/H5 Dikwa, Nga.
97/N6 Dīla, Eth.
52/D2 Dilbeek, Belg.
87/G5 Dili, Indo.
53/H2 Dillenburg, Ger.
97/L5 Dilling, Sudan
53/F5 Dillingen, Ger.
129/J3 Dillon, SC,US
104/D3 Dilolo, D.R. Congo
53/E1 Dilsen, Belg.
85/F2 Dimāpur, India
74/L5 Dimashq (Damascus) (cap.), Syria
98/D5 Dimbokro, IvC.
63/G3 Dîmbovița (co.), Rom.
69/P2 Dimitriya Lapteva (str.), Rus.
63/G4 Dimitrovgrad, Bul.
67/J1 Dimitrovgrad, Rus.
62/F4 Dimitrovgrad, Yugo.
96/H6 Dimlang (peak), Nga.
74/K6 Dimona, Isr.
74/K6 Dimona, Hare (mtn.), Isr.
82/E6 Dinagat, Phil.
82/E5 Dinagat (isl.), Phil.
84/E2 Dinājpur, Bang.
56/B2 Dinan, Fr.
53/D3 Dinant, Belg.
74/B2 Dinar, Turk.
56/B2 Dinard, Fr.
61/E1 Dinaric Alps (range), Bosn., Cro.
46/B2 Dinas (pt.), Wal,UK
46/C4 Dinas Powys, Wal,UK
97/N5 Dinder Nat'l Park, Eth.
84/C5 Dindigul, India
57/K2 Dingolfing, Ger.
82/D4 Dingras, Phil.
43/C2 Dingwall, Sc,UK
81/C3 Dingxing, China
81/D4 Dingyuan, China
83/D1 Dinh Lap, Viet.
51/E5 Dinkel (riv.), Ger.
51/F3 Dinklage, Ger.
45/G1 Dinnington, Eng,UK
124/E2 Dinosaur, Co,US
124/E2 Dinosaur Nat'l Mon., Co, Ut,US
50/D5 Dinslaken, Ger.
122/G3 Dinsmore, Sk,Can
50/B5 Dintel Mark (riv.), Neth.
124/C3 Dinuba, Ca,US
50/D5 Dinxperlo, Neth.
98/C4 Dion (riv.), Gui.
98/A3 Diourbel, Sen.
98/A3 Diourbel (reg.), Sen.
85/F2 Diphu, India
73/J4 Diplo, Pak.
82/D6 Dipolog, Phil.
90/C3 Dipperu Nat'l Park, Austl.
98/E2 Diré, Mali
97/P6 Dirē Dawa, Eth.
116/D5 Diriamba, Nic.
96/H4 Dirkou, Niger
50/B5 Dirksland, Neth.
124/E3 Dirty Devil (riv.), Ut,US
93/L6 Disappointment (isls.), FrPol.
91/B3 Discovery (bay), Austl.
100/C3 Dishnā, Egypt
119/L2 Disko (isl.), Grld.
45/F5 Disley, Eng,UK
131/C3 Disneyland, Ca,US
53/E2 Dison, Belg.
84/F2 Dispur, India
127/G2 Disraëli, Qu,Can
47/H2 Diss, Eng,UK
51/F4 Dissen am Teutoburger Wald, Ger.
44/E2 Distington, Eng,UK
131/J8 District of Columbia (cap.), US
113/S12 Distrito Federal (fed. dist.), Arg.
116/B4 Distrito Federal (state), Mex.
74/H6 Disūq, Egypt
47/F5 Ditchling Beacon (hill), Eng,UK
60/D4 Dittaino (riv.), It.
73/K4 Diu (isl.), India
84/B3 Diu, Damān and (terr.), India
62/D4 Diva (riv.), Yugo.
56/D3 Dive (riv.), Fr.
110/C2 Divinópolis, Braz.
44/B2 Divis (mtn.), NI,UK
108/D5 Divisor (mts.), Braz.
98/D5 Divo, IvC.
74/D2 Divriği, Turk.
130/M4 Dixon (chan.), Ak,US
132/L10 Dixon, Ca,US
126/B3 Dixon, Il,US
118/C3 Dixon Entrance (chan.), BC,Can
74/E2 Diyadin, Turk.
74/E3 Diyarbakır, Turk.
74/H6 Diyarb Najm, Egypt
96/H3 Djado, Niger
96/H3 Djado (plat.), Niger
96/G1 Djamaa, Alg.
104/B1 Djambala, Congo
96/G3 Djanet, Alg.
96/F1 Djelfa, Alg.
96/G1 Djemila (ruins), Alg.
98/D3 Djénné, Mali
99/E3 Djibo, Burk.
97/P5 Djibouti
97/P5 Djibouti (cap.), Djib.
44/B5 Djouce (mtn.), Ire.
99/F4 Djougou, Ben.
101/A2 Djugu, D.R. Congo
41/H3 Dnipro (riv.), Eur.
66/E2 Dniprodzerzhyns'k, Ukr.
66/E2 Dnipropetrovs'k, Ukr.
66/E2 Dnipropetrovs'ka Obl., Ukr.
66/D3 Dnister (riv.), Eur.
76/E5 Do (riv.), China
99/E3 Do (lake), Mali
96/J6 Doba, Chad
131/G4 Dobbs Ferry, NY,US
64/D4 Dobele, Lat.
48/G3 Döbeln, Ger.
87/H4 Doberai (pen.), Indo.
62/D3 Doboj, Bosn.
49/L2 Dobre Miasto, Pol.
63/H4 Dobruja (reg.), Bul., Rom.
66/D1 Dobrush, Bela.
65/N4 Dobryanka, Rus.
110/D1 Doce (riv.), Braz.
47/G1 Docking, Eng,UK
129/H4 Dock Junction, Ga,US
111/D1 Doctor Pedro P. Peña, Par.
62/F2 Doctor Petru Groza, Rom.
126/F1 Doda (lake), Qu,Can
44/B5 Dodder (riv.), Ire.
74/A3 Dodecanese (isls.), Gre.
125/G3 Dodge City, Ks,US
126/B3 Dodgeville, Wi,US
46/B6 Dodman (pt.), Wal,UK
101/B4 Dodoma, Tanz.
101/B4 Dodoma (prov.), Tanz.
61/G3 Dodoni (ruins), Gre.
122/F3 Dodsland, Sk,Can
45/G4 Dodworth, Eng,UK
50/D4 Doesburg, Neth.
50/D5 Doetinchem, Neth.
75/E5 Dogai Coring (lake), China
74/D2 Doğankent (riv.), Turk.
78/C2 Dōgo (isl.), Japan
99/G3 Dogondoutchi, Niger
74/F2 Doğubayazıt, Turk.
74/E2 Doğukaradeniz (mts.), Turk.
72/F3 Doha (Ad Dawḥah) (cap.), Qatar
84/B3 Dohad, India
83/B2 Doi Inthanon Nat'l Park, Thai.
83/B2 Doi Khun Tan Nat'l Park, Thai.
58/B1 Doiras (res.)
109/K5 Dois Irmãos (mts.), Braz.
83/B2 Doi Suthep-Pui Nat'l Park, Thai.
50/D2 Dokkum, Neth.
50/C2 Dokkumer Ee (riv.), Neth.
127/F1 Dolbeau, Qu,Can
54/B3 Dôle, Fr.
46/C1 Dolgellau, Wal,UK
60/A3 Dolianova, It.
77/N2 Dolinsk, Rus.
63/F3 Dolj (co.), Rom.
127/N7 Dollard-des-Ormeaux, Qu,Can
51/E2 Dollard (Dollart) (bay), Ger., Neth.
48/D5 Doller (riv.), Fr.
62/C5 Dolmen (ruins), It.
57/J3 Dolomite Alps (Alpi Dolomitiche) (range), It.
113/F3 Dolores, Arg.
116/D4 Dolores, Guat.
59/E3 Dolores, Sp.
112/F2 Dolores, Uru.
124/E3 Dolores, Co,US
124/E3 Dolores (riv.), Co, Ut,US
116/A3 Dolores Hidalgo, Mex.
113/N7 Dolphin (cape), Falk.
102/A2 Dolphin (pt.), Namb.
118/E1 Dolphin and Union (str.), Nun.,Can
45/F4 Dolphinholme, Eng,UK
46/B5 Dolton, Eng,UK
132/Q16 Dolton, Il,US
83/D2 Do Luong, Viet.
87/J4 Dom (peak), Indo.
55/F4 Domat-Ems, Swi.
57/K2 Domažlice, Czh.
57/G2 Dombasle-sur-Meurthe, Fr.
67/G4 Dombay-Ul'gen, Gora (peak), Geo.
62/D2 Dombóvár, Hun.
56/E3 Domérat, Fr.
111/C1 Domeyko (mts.), Chile
117/J4 Dominica
117/H4 Dominican Republic
50/C6 Dommel (riv.), Belg., Neth.
83/D3 Dom Noi (res.), Thai.
65/X9 Domodedovo, Rus.
55/E5 Domodossola, It.
111/F3 Dom Pedrito, Braz.
87/E5 Dompu, Indo.
62/D2 Dömsöd, Hun.
60/A3 Domusnovas, It.
112/C3 Domuyo (vol.), Arg.
90/C5 Domville (peak), Austl.
62/B2 Domžale, Slov.
56/C3 Don (riv.), Fr.
117/N8 Don, Mex.
67/G2 Don (ridge), Rus.
67/G3 Don (riv.), Rus.
45/G5 Don (riv.), Eng,UK
43/D2 Don (riv.), Sc,UK
44/C2 Donaghadee, NI,UK
44/B2 Donaghmore, NI,UK
129/F4 Donaldsonville, La,US
58/B4 Doñana Nat'l Park, Sp.
56/E5 Dona, Pic de la (peak), Fr.
49/H4 Donau (Danube) (riv.), Aus., Ger.
58/C3 Don Benito, Sp.
91/G5 Doncaster, Austl.
45/G4 Doncaster, Eng,UK
104/B2 Dondo, Ang.
84/D6 Dondra Head (pt.), SrL.
43/A3 Donegal (bay), Ire.
44/A1 Donegal (co.), Ire.
66/F3 Donets'k, Ukr.
66/F3 Donets'ka Obl., Ukr.
82/B3 Dong (riv.), China
85/J5 Dong (riv.), Viet.
99/H5 Donga (riv.), Camr., Nga.
85/H2 Dongchuan, China
85/J3 Dong Dang, Viet.
81/E5 Dongdongting Shan (mtn.), China
50/B5 Dongen, Neth.
82/B3 Dongguan, China
83/D2 Dong Ha, Viet.
83/D2 Donghen, Laos
83/D2 Dong Hoi, Viet.
81/E2 Dongliao (riv.), China
83/D4 Dong Noi (riv.), Viet.
81/D3 Dongping (lake), China
82/C3 Dongsha (isl.), China
81/E4 Dongtai, China
81/L9 Dongtiao (riv.), China
83/D2 Dong Tau, Viet.
82/B2 Dongting (lake), China
81/D3 Dongying, China
112/Q10 Donihue, Chile
45/H6 Donington, Eng,UK
118/D2 Donjek (riv.), Yk,Can
62/C3 Donji Vakuf, Bosn.
44/D1 Doon (riv.), Sc,UK
130/H2 Doonerak (mtn.), Ak,US
44/D1 Doon, Loch (lake), Sc,UK
126/C2 Door (pen.), Wi,US
50/C4 Doorn, Neth.
102/B3 Doorn (riv.), SAfr.
59/F2 Dorada (coast), Sp.
73/K1 Do Rāh (pass), Afg.
75/B4 Dorāh Ān (pass), Pak.
57/G4 Dora Riparia (riv.), It.
127/H2 Dorchester, NB,Can
119/J2 Dorchester (cape), Nun.,Can
46/D5 Dorchester, Eng,UK
56/D4 Dordogne (riv.), Fr.
50/B5 Dordrecht, Neth.
122/G2 Doré (lake), Sk,Can
56/E4 Dore (mts.), Fr.
56/E4 Dore (riv.), Fr.
110/C1 Dores do Indaiá, Braz.
60/A2 Dorgali, It.
76/C2 Dörgön (lake), Mong.
99/E3 Dori, Burk.
127/M7 Dorion, Qu,Can
47/F4 Dorking, Eng,UK
50/D6 Dormagen, Ger.
55/F3 Dornbirn, Aus.
62/D2 Dorog, Hun.
63/H2 Dorohoi, Rom.
47/E2 Dorridge, Eng,UK
91/E1 Dorrigo Nat'l Park, Austl.
46/D1 Dorrington, Eng,UK
124/B2 Dorris, Ca,US
60/A5 Dorsale (mts.), Tun.
46/D5 Dorset (co.), Eng,UK
50/D5 Dorsten, Ger.
51/E5 Dortmund, Ger.
51/E4 Dortmund-Ems (can.), Ger.
74/D3 Dörtyol, Turk.
127/N7 Dorval, Qu,Can
51/G3 Dörverden, Ger.
112/D5 Dos Bahias (cape), Arg.
132/A2 Dosewallips (riv.), Wa,US

151

Emery – Fonte

132/K11 **Emeryville,** Ca,US
74/B2 **Emet,** Turk.
57/J4 **Emilia-Romagna** (reg.), It.
75/D2 **Emin** (riv.), China
125/K3 **Eminence,** Mo,US
63/H4 **Emine, Nos** (cape), Bul.
74/B2 **Emirdağ,** Turk.
74/C3 **Emirgazi,** Turk.
103/E2 **Emlembe** (peak), Swaz.
50/D3 **Emlichheim,** Ger.
42/E4 **Emmaboda,** Swe.
131/E5 **Emmaus,** Pa,US
50/C3 **Emmeloord,** Neth.
50/D3 **Emmen,** Neth.
54/D1 **Emmendingen,** Ger.
51/G5 **Emmer** (riv.), Ger.
51/E5 **Emmerbach** (riv.), Ger.
50/D5 **Emmerich,** Ger.
122/D5 **Emmett,** Id,US
47/G1 **Emneth,** Eng,UK
128/E3 **Emory,** Tx,US
117/P8 **Emory** (peak), Tx.,US
117/M8 **Empalme,** Mex.
103/E3 **Empangeni,** SAfr.
111/E2 **Empedrado,** Arg.
112/B2 **Empedrado,** Chile
125/H3 **Emporia,** Ks,US
126/E4 **Emporia,** Va,US
51/E4 **Emsbüren,** Ger.
51/E4 **Emsdetten,** Ger.
50/D2 **Ems** (Eems) (riv.), Ger., Neth.
51/E2 **Ems-Jade** (can.), Ger.
51/E3 **Emsland** (reg.), Ger.
51/F3 **Emstek,** Ger.
42/H4 **Emumägi** (hill), Est.
77/J1 **Emur** (riv.), China
79/E3 **Ena,** Japan
122/G5 **Encampment,** Wy,US
117/L7 **Encantada** (mt.), Mex.
117/M8 **Encantado** (mt.), Mex.
111/E2 **Encarnación,** Par.
117/P9 **Encarnación de Díaz,** Mex.
98/E5 **Enchi,** Gha.
124/C4 **Encinitas,** Ca,US
91/A2 **Encounter** (bay), Austl.
110/A4 **Encruzilhada do Sul,** Braz.
87/F5 **Ende,** Indo.
90/B1 **Endeavour River Nat'l Park,** Austl.
93/H5 **Enderbury** (atoll), Kiri.
122/D3 **Enderby,** BC,Can
105/D **Enderby Land** (reg.), Ant.
123/J4 **Enderlin,** ND,US
126/E3 **Endicott,** NY,US
108/D6 **Ene** (riv.), Peru
92/F3 **Enewetak** (atoll), Mrsh.
82/D4 **Engaño** (cape), Phil.
67/H2 **Engel's,** Rus.
53/G2 **Engelskirchen,** Ger.
50/D2 **Engelsmanplaat** (isl.), Neth.
110/K7 **Engenheiro Paulo de Froutin,** Braz.
51/F4 **Enger,** Ger.
86/B5 **Enggano** (isl.), Indo.
97/N4 **Enghershatu** (peak), Erit.
52/D2 **Enghien,** Belg.
43/D4 **England,** UK
126/E2 **Englehart,** On,Can
131/F5 **Englewood,** NJ,US
131/G5 **Englewood,** NJ,US
105/V **English** (coast), Ant.
123/K3 **English** (riv.), On,Can
56/B2 **English** (chan.), Eur.
84/E3 **English Bāzār,** India
131/F5 **Englishtown,** NJ,US
125/H3 **Enid,** Ok,US
50/C3 **Enkhuizen,** Neth.
42/F4 **Enköping,** Swe.
60/D4 **Enna,** It.
97/K4 **Ennedi** (plat.), Chad
51/E6 **Ennepe** (riv.), Ger.
51/E6 **Ennepetal,** Ger.
51/F5 **Enningerloh,** Ger.
122/F4 **Ennis,** Mt,US
128/D3 **Ennis,** Tx,US
57/L3 **Enns** (riv.), Aus.
90/E6 **Enoggera** (res.), Austl.
129/H3 **Enoree** (riv.), SC,US
50/D4 **Enschede,** Neth.
51/E6 **Ense,** Ger.
117/L7 **Ensenada,** Mex.
81/B5 **Enshi,** China
101/B2 **Entebbe,** Ugan.
57/K2 **Entenbühl** (peak), Ger.
129/G4 **Enterprise,** Al,US
112/F2 **Entre Ríos** (prov.), Arg.
58/A3 **Entroncamento,** Port.
99/G5 **Enugu,** Nga.
132/D3 **Enumclaw,** Wa,US
79/N10 **Enushū** (sea), Japan
52/A4 **Envermeu,** Fr.
57/H2 **Enz** (riv.), Ger.
79/F3 **Enzan,** Japan
53/F4 **Enzbach** (riv.), Ger.
50/C4 **Epe,** Neth.
52/C5 **Épernay,** Fr.
92/F6 **Epi** (isl.), Van.
61/H4 **Epidaurus** (ruins), Gre.
54/C1 **Épinal,** Fr.
61/G3 **Epirus** (reg.), Gre.
53/F5 **Eppelborn,** Ger.
90/H8 **Epping,** Austl.
47/G3 **Epping,** Eng,UK
90/B3 **Epping Forest Nat'l Park,** Austl.
47/F4 **Epsom and Ewell,** Eng,UK
45/H4 **Epworth,** Eng,UK
96/G7 **Equatorial Guinea**
85/H2 **Er** (lake), China
60/E2 **Eraclea** (ruins), It.
60/C4 **Eraclea Minoa** (ruins), It.
84/D6 **Eravur,** SrL.
83/B3 **Erawan Nat'l Park,** Thai.
57/H4 **Erba,** It.
74/D2 **Erbaa,** Turk.
53/F4 **Erbeskopf** (peak), Ger.
112/B3 **Ercilla,** Chile
74/E2 **Erciş,** Turk.
52/C3 **Erclin** (riv.), Fr.
62/D2 **Érd,** Hun.
77/K3 **Erdao** (riv.), China
63/H5 **Erdek,** Turk.
63/H5 **Erdek** (gulf), Turk.
74/C3 **Erdemli,** Turk.
76/G3 **Erdene,** Mong.
76/E2 **Erdenedalay,** Mong.
97/K4 **Erdi-Ma** (plat.), Chad
57/J2 **Erding,** Ger.
56/C3 **Erdre** (riv.), Fr.
105/M **Erebus** (vol.), Ant.
110/A3 **Erechim,** Braz.
76/G2 **Ereen Davaanï** (mts.), Mong.
63/K5 **Ereğli,** Turk.
74/C3 **Ereğli,** Turk.
75/D3 **Erenhaberga** (mts.), China
76/G3 **Erenhot,** China
63/K5 **Erenler,** Turk.
109/G4 **Erepecu** (lake), Braz.
58/C2 **Eresma** (riv.), Sp.
96/E1 **Erfoud,** Mor.
53/F1 **Erft** (riv.), Ger.
53/F2 **Erftstadt,** Ger.
48/F3 **Erfurt,** Ger.
74/D2 **Ergani,** Turk.
96/D3 **'Erg Chech** (des.), Afr.
96/H4 **'Erg du Ténéré** (des.), Niger
63/H5 **Ergene Nehri** (riv.), Turk.
96/D2 **'Erg Iguidi** (des.), Afr.
96/J5 **Erguig** (riv.), Chad
77/H1 **Ergun** (riv.), China, Rus.
122/D3 **Erickson,** BC,Can
123/J3 **Erickson,** Mb,Can
126/D3 **Erie** (lake), Can., US
127/S9 **Erie** (can.), NY,US
126/D3 **Erie,** Pa,US
97/Q5 **Erigabo,** Som.
123/J3 **Eriksdale,** Mb,Can
92/F4 **Erikub** (atoll), Mrsh.
61/G4 **Erímanthos** (peak), Gre.
77/N3 **Erimo-misaki** (cape), Japan
97/N4 **Eritrea**
50/D6 **Erkelenz,** Ger.
49/G2 **Erkner,** Ger.
50/D6 **Erkrath,** Ger.
57/J2 **Erlangen,** Ger.
81/F2 **Erlongshan** (res.), China
46/C6 **Erme** (riv.), Eng,UK
50/C4 **Ermelo,** Neth.
103/E2 **Ermelo,** SAfr.
74/C3 **Ermenek,** Turk.
61/J4 **Ermoúpolis,** Gre.
53/H2 **Erndtebrück,** Ger.
56/C2 **Ernée** (riv.), Fr.
84/C5 **Erode,** India
52/D3 **Erquelinnes,** Belg.
96/E1 **Er Rachidīa,** Mor.
96/D1 **Er Rif** (mts.), Mor.
43/A3 **Errigal** (mtn.), Ire.
92/F6 **Erromango** (isl.), Van.
51/H4 **Erse** (riv.), Ger.
76/B2 **Ertix** (riv.), China
110/B3 **Erval d'Oeste,** Braz.
126/D4 **Erwin,** Tn,US
51/F5 **Erwitte,** Ger.
61/F2 **Erzen** (riv.), Alb.
57/K1 **Erzgebirge** (Krušné Hory) (mts.), Czh., Ger.
74/D2 **Erzincan,** Turk.
74/E2 **Erzurum,** Turk.
92/D5 **Esa'ala,** PNG
104/D1 **Esambo,** D.R. Congo
77/N3 **Esashi,** Japan
42/D5 **Esbjerg,** Den.
52/B6 **Esbly,** Fr.
42/H3 **Esbo** (Espoo), Fin.
124/E3 **Escalante** (riv.), Ut,US
129/G4 **Escambia** (riv.), Fl,US
126/C2 **Escanaba,** Mi,US
52/C3 **Escaudain,** Fr.
52/C3 **Escaut** (riv.), Belg., Fr.
53/E6 **Esch** (riv.), Fr.
52/B5 **Esches** (riv.), Fr.
53/E5 **Esch-sur-Alzette,** Lux.
51/H6 **Eschwege,** Ger.
53/F2 **Eschweiler,** Ger.
124/C4 **Escondido,** Ca,US
117/N9 **Escuinapa de Hidalgo,** Mex.
116/C5 **Escuintla,** Guat.
74/N7 **Esdraelon, Plain of** (plain), Isr.
96/H7 **Eséka,** Camr.
51/E1 **Esens,** Ger.
59/F1 **Esera** (riv.), Sp.
72/F2 **Eşfahān,** Iran
46/C1 **Esgair Ddu** (mtn.), Wal,UK
45/G2 **Esh,** Eng,UK
47/F4 **Esher,** Eng,UK
104/D2 **Eshimba,** D.R. Congo
45/G2 **Esh Winning,** Eng,UK
45/E2 **Esk** (riv.), Eng,UK
45/H3 **Esk** (riv.), Eng,UK
45/E1 **Eskdale** (val.), Sc,UK
74/C2 **Eskil,** Turk.
42/F4 **Eskilstuna,** Swe.
74/D2 **Eskimalatya,** Turk.
130/M2 **Eskimo** (lakes), NW,Can
74/B2 **Eskişehir,** Turk.
58/C1 **Esla** (riv.), Sp.
72/E2 **Eslāmābād,** Iran
51/F6 **Eslohe,** Ger.
74/B2 **Eşme,** Turk.
108/C3 **Esmeraldas,** Ecu.
53/E2 **Esneux,** Belg.
126/D2 **Espanola,** On,Can
125/F4 **Española,** NM,US
59/K6 **Esparreguera,** Sp.
51/F4 **Espelkamp,** Ger.
89/B4 **Esperance,** Austl.
122/B3 **Esperanza** (inlet), BC,Can
58/A3 **Espichel** (cape), Port.
108/D3 **Espinal,** Col.
95/D1 **Espinhaço** (mts.), Braz.
58/A2 **Espinho,** Port.
113/F2 **Espinillo** (pt.), Uru.
109/K6 **Espinosa,** Braz.
110/D1 **Espírito Santo** (state), Braz.
110/G7 **Espírito Santo do Pinhal,** Braz.
92/F6 **Espiritu Santo** (isl.), Van.
109/L6 **Esplanada,** Braz.
59/L7 **Espluges,** Sp.
42/H3 **Espoo** (Esbo), Fin.
112/C4 **Esquel,** Arg.
111/E3 **Esquina,** Arg.
96/D1 **Essaouira,** Mor.
51/G5 **Esse** (riv.), Ger.
50/B6 **Essen,** Belg.
50/E6 **Essen,** Ger.
91/F5 **Essendon,** Austl.
108/G2 **Essequibo** (riv.), Guy.
132/G7 **Essex,** On,Can
47/G3 **Essex** (co.), Eng,UK
131/K7 **Essex,** Md,US
57/H2 **Esslingen,** Ger.
52/B6 **Essonne** (dept.), Fr.
113/L8 **Estados** (isl.), Arg.
72/F3 **Eşţahbān,** Iran
109/L6 **Estância,** Braz.
113/L8 **Estancia La Carmen,** Arg.
113/L8 **Estancia La Sera,** Arg.
59/F1 **Estats, Pico de** (peak), Sp.
103/E3 **Estcourt,** SAfr.
116/E3 **Este** (pt.), Cuba
51/G2 **Este** (riv.), Ger.
57/J4 **Este,** It.
110/B4 **Esteio,** Braz.
116/D5 **Estelí,** Nic.
58/D1 **Estella,** Sp
131/C3 **Estelle** (mtn.), Ca,US
58/C4 **Estepa,** Sp.
58/C4 **Estepona,** Sp.
123/H3 **Esterhazy,** Sk,Can
96/G7 **Esterias** (cape), Gabon
57/G5 **Estéron** (riv.), Fr.
123/H3 **Estevan,** Sk,Can
52/D3 **Estinnes-Au-Mont,** Belg.
45/G2 **Eston,** Eng,UK
64/E4 **Estonia**
58/A3 **Estoril,** Port.
58/B2 **Estrela, Serra da** (mtn.), Port
58/A3 **Estrela, Serra da** (range), Port.
58/B3 **Estremadura** (aut. comm.), Sp
58/B3 **Estremoz,** Port.
109/J5 **Estrondo** (mts.), Braz.
62/D2 **Esztergom,** Hun.
92/E4 **Etal** (atoll), Micr.
42/H3 **Etalä-Suomen** (prov.) Fin.
52/A2 **Étaples,** Fr.
84/C2 **Etāwah,** India
123/H3 **Ethelbert,** Mb,Can
97/N5 **Ethiopia**
97/N6 **Ethiopian** (plat.), Eth.
79/M9 **Eti** (riv.), Japan
60/D4 **Etna, Monte** (Mount Etna) (vol.), It.
127/Q8 **Etobicoke,** On,Can
130/E3 **Etolin** (str.), Ak,US
77/P2 **Etorofu** (isl.), Rus.
104/C4 **Etosha Nat'l Park,** Namb.
104/C4 **Etosha Pan** (salt pan), Namb.
63/G4 **Etropole,** Bul.
79/F2 **Etsu-Joshin Kogen Nat'l Park,** Japan
74/M8 **Et Taiyiba,** Isr.
53/F4 **Ettelbruck,** Lux.
50/B5 **Etten-Leur,** Neth.
52/D2 **Etterbeek,** Belg.
74/M8 **Et Tīra,** Isr.
57/H2 **Ettlingen,** Ger.
45/E1 **Ettrick Pen** (mtn.), Sc,UK
52/A3 **Eu,** Fr.
93/H7 **Eua** (isl.), Tonga
90/B2 **Eubenangee Swamp Nat'l Park,** Austl.
126/D3 **Euclid,** Oh,US
129/F3 **Eudora,** Ar,US
129/G4 **Eufaula,** Al,US
125/J4 **Eufaula,** Ok,US
125/H4 **Eufaula** (lake), Ok,US
122/C4 **Eugene,** Or,US
117/L8 **Eugenia** (pt.), Mex.
58/B1 **Eume** (lake), Sp.
90/C3 **Eungella Nat'l Park,** Austl.
128/E4 **Eunice,** La,US
125/G4 **Eunice,** NM,US
53/F2 **Eupen,** Belg.
71/D6 **Euphrates** (riv.), Asia
56/D2 **Eure** (riv.), Fr.
119/S6 **Eureka,** Nun.,Can
119/S7 **Eureka** (sound), Nun.,Can
124/A2 **Eureka,** Ca,US
122/E3 **Eureka,** Mt,US
124/D3 **Eureka,** Nv,US
123/J4 **Eureka,** SD,US
52/B6 **Eurodisney,** Fr.
104/G5 **Europa** (isl.), Reun.
41/* **Europe**
50/B5 **Europoort,** Neth.
53/F2 **Euskirchen,** Ger.
129/H4 **Eustis,** Fl,US
48/F1 **Eutin,** Ger.
101/B5 **Eutini,** Malw.
122/B2 **Eutsuk** (lake), BC,Can
45/F4 **Euxton,** Eng,UK
126/E1 **Évain,** Qu,Can
119/H2 **Evans** (str.), Nun.,Can
126/E1 **Evans** (lake), Qu,Can
125/F2 **Evans,** Co,US
125/F3 **Evans** (mtn.), Co,US
132/Q15 **Evanston,** Il,US
122/F5 **Evanston,** Wy,US
126/C4 **Evansville,** In,US
125/F2 **Evansville,** Wy,US
126/C3 **Evart,** Mi,US
102/D2 **Evaton,** SAfr.
72/F3 **Evaz,** Iran
123/K4 **Eveleth,** Mn,US
69/L3 **Evenki Aut. Okr.,** Rus.
47/E3 **Evenlode** (riv.), Eng,UK
91/D3 **Everard** (cape), Austl.
46/D4 **Evercreech,** Eng,UK
132/C2 **Everett,** Wa,US
52/C1 **Evergem,** Belg.
129/H5 **Everglades Nat'l Park,** Fl,US
129/G4 **Evergreen,** Al,US
132/Q16 **Evergreen Park,** Il,US
47/F3 **Eversholt,** Eng,UK
51/E5 **Everswinkel,** Ger.
47/E2 **Evesham,** Eng,UK
61/G3 **Évinos** (riv.), Gre.
58/B3 **Évora,** Port.
58/A3 **Évora** (dist.), Port.
52/A5 **Évreux,** Fr.
56/C2 **Évron,** Fr.
61/H4 **Evrótas** (riv.), Gre.
52/B6 **Évry,** Fr.
61/H3 **Évvoia** (gulf), Gre.
61/H3 **Évvoia** (isl.), Gre.
120/V13 **Ewa,** Hi,US
120/V13 **Ewa Beach,** Hi,US
131/F5 **Ewing,** NJ,US
125/J3 **Excelsior Springs,** Mo,US
46/C5 **Exe** (riv.), Eng,UK
46/C5 **Exeter,** Eng,UK
127/G3 **Exeter,** NH,US
46/C5 **Exminster,** Eng,UK
46/C4 **Exmoor Nat'l Park,** Eng,UK
126/F4 **Exmore,** Va,US
113/J7 **Exmouth** (pen.), Chile
46/C5 **Exmouth,** Eng,UK
119/L4 **Exploits** (riv.), Nf,Can
110/G7 **Extrema,** Braz.
117/F3 **Exuma** (sound), Bahm.
45/G5 **Eyam,** Eng,UK
101/B3 **Eyasi** (lake), Tanz.
47/H2 **Eye,** Eng,UK
47/F1 **Eye** (brook), Eng,UK
43/D3 **Eyemouth,** Sc,UK
74/N9 **Eyn Hemed Nat'l Park,** Isr.
47/G4 **Eynsford,** Eng,UK
89/C4 **Eyre** (pen.), Austl.
89/C3 **Eyre North** (lake), Austl.
61/K3 **Ezine,** Turk.
96/H3 **Ezzane** (well), Alg.

F

93/L6 **Faaa,** FrPol.
128/B4 **Fabens,** Tx,US
58/B1 **Fabero,** Sp.
48/F1 **Fåborg,** Den.
57/K5 **Fabriano,** It.
108/D3 **Facatativá,** Col.
52/C2 **Faches-Thumesnil,** Fr.
97/K4 **Fada,** Chad
99/F3 **Fada-N'Gourma,** Burk.
57/J4 **Faenza,** It.
97/J6 **Fafa** (riv.), CAfr.
58/A2 **Fafe,** Port.
97/P6 **Fafen Shet'** (riv.), Eth.
63/G3 **Făgăraş,** Rom.
42/E4 **Fagersta,** Swe.
113/L8 **Fagnano** (lake), Arg.
98/D2 **Faguibine** (lake), Mali
59/S12 **Faial** (isl.), Azor.,Port.
45/F4 **Failsworth,** Eng,UK
130/J3 **Fairbanks,** Ak,US
132/J11 **Fairfax,** Ca,US
131/J8 **Fairfax,** Va,US
90/G8 **Fairfield,** Austl.
132/K10 **Fairfield,** Ca,US
131/G4 **Fairfield,** Ct,US
122/F4 **Fairfield,** Mt,US
126/C4 **Fairfield,** Oh,US
128/D4 **Fairfield,** Tx,US
47/E3 **Fairford,** Eng,UK
127/F3 **Fair Haven,** Vt,US
44/B1 **Fair Head** (pt.), NI,UK
131/K7 **Fairland,** Md,US
131/F5 **Fair Lawn,** NJ,US
131/F5 **Fairless Hills,** Pa,US
47/G5 **Fairlight,** Eng,UK
123/K5 **Fairmont,** Mn,US
126/D4 **Fairmont,** WV,US
132/M9 **Fair Oaks,** Ca,US
128/B2 **Fairplay,** Co,US
122/D1 **Fairview,** Ab,Can
125/H3 **Fairview,** Ok,US
130/L4 **Fairweather** (cape), Ak,US
130/L4 **Fairweather** (mtn.), BC,Can, Ak,US
132/C3 **Fairwood-Cascade,** Wa,US
73/K2 **Faisalabad,** Pak.
61/J5 **Faistós** (ruins), Gre.
84/D2 **Faizābād,** India
93/M6 **Fakahina** (isl.), FrPol.
93/H5 **Fakaofo** (atoll), Tok.
93/L6 **Fakarava** (atoll), FrPol.
47/G1 **Fakenham,** Eng,UK
96/G7 **Fako** (peak), Camr.
48/G1 **Fakse Bugt** (bay), Den.
46/B6 **Fal** (riv.), Eng,UK
128/D5 **Falcon** (res.), Mex., US
57/K5 **Falconara Marittima,** It.
98/C3 **Falémé** (riv.), Mali, Sen.
93/S9 **Faleolo,** Samoa
128/D5 **Falfurrias,** Tx,US
122/D2 **Falher,** Ab,Can
42/E4 **Falkenberg,** Swe.
47/H2 **Falkenham,** Eng,UK
113/M8 **Falkland Islands** (Islas Malvinas) (dpcy.), UK
42/E4 **Falköping,** Swe.
51/G3 **Fallingbostel,** Ger.
124/C3 **Fallon,** Nv,US
127/G3 **Fall River,** Ma,US
131/J8 **Falls Church,** Va,US
125/J2 **Falls City,** Ne,US
46/A6 **Falmouth,** Eng,UK
46/A6 **Falmouth** (bay), Eng,UK
117/G4 **Falso** (cape), DRep.
113/K8 **Falso Cabo de Hornos** (cape), Chile
48/G1 **Falster** (isl.), Den.
63/H2 **Fălticeni,** Rom.
42/E3 **Falun,** Swe.
74/J4 **Famagusta,** Cyp.
53/F5 **Fameck,** Fr.
53/E3 **Famenne** (reg.), Belg.
81/D5 **Fanchang,** China
103/H8 **Fandriana,** Madg.
44/B4 **Fane** (riv.), Ire.
93/L6 **Fangatau** (isl.), FrPol.
93/L7 **Fangataufa** (isl.), FrPol.
82/C2 **Fangcun,** China
82/C2 **Fangdao,** China
82/D3 **Fangliao,** Tai.
82/A2 **Fanjing** (peak), China
93/K4 **Fanning** (Tabuaeran) (atoll), Kiri.
48/E1 **Fanø** (isl.), Den.
57/K5 **Fano,** It.
83/C1 **Fan Si Pan** (peak), Viet.
74/H6 **Fāqūs,** Egypt
101/A2 **Faradje,** D.R. Congo
103/H8 **Farafangana,** Madg.
100/A3 **Farāfirah, Wāḩāt al** (oasis), Egypt
73/H2 **Farāh,** Afg.
73/H2 **Farāh** (riv.), Afg.
124/B3 **Farallon** (isls.), Ca,US
92/D3 **Farallon de Medinilla** (isl.), NMar.
92/D2 **Farallon de Pajaros** (isl.), NMar.
108/C3 **Farallones de Cali Nat'l Park,** Col.
98/C4 **Faranah** (comm.), Gui.
103/H8 **Faraony** (riv.), Madg.
92/D4 **Faraulep** (atoll), Micr.
52/D3 **Farciennes,** Belg.
47/E5 **Fareham,** Eng,UK
123/J4 **Fargo,** ND,US
123/K4 **Faribault,** Mn,US
84/C2 **Farīdābād,** India
84/E3 **Farīdpur,** Bang.
47/E3 **Faringdon,** Eng,UK
74/H6 **Fāriskūr,** Egypt
127/G2 **Farmington,** Me,US
132/F7 **Farmington,** Mi,US
125/K3 **Farmington,** Mo,US
124/E3 **Farmington,** NM,US
132/F7 **Farmington Hills,** Mi,US
126/E4 **Farmville,** Va,US
47/F4 **Farnborough,** Eng,UK
47/F4 **Farnham,** Eng,UK
45/F4 **Farnworth,** Eng,UK
118/C2 **Faro,** Yk,Can
58/B4 **Faro,** Port.
58/A4 **Faro** (dist.), Port.
41/D2 **Faroe** (isls.), Den.
42/F4 **Fårön** (isl.), Swe.
96/H6 **Faro Nat'l Park,** Camr.
39/M6 **Farquhar** (isls.), Sey.
110/B4 **Farroupilha,** Braz.
84/C2 **Farrukhābād,** India
61/H3 **Fársala,** Gre.
122/F5 **Farson,** Wy,US
42/C4 **Farsund,** Nor.
72/F5 **Fartak, Ra's** (pt.), Yem.
115/N4 **Farvel** (cape), Grld.
105/T **Farwell** (isl.), Ant.
72/F3 **Fasā,** Iran
60/E2 **Fasano,** It.
51/H3 **Fassberg,** Ger.
66/D2 **Fastov,** Ukr.
87/H4 **Fatagar Tuting** (cape), Indo.
39/T6 **Fataka** (isl.), Sol.
84/B2 **Fatehpur,** India
84/D2 **Fatehpur,** India
98/A3 **Fatick** (reg.), Sen.
58/A3 **Fátima,** Port.
72/C4 **Fāţimah** (dry riv.), SAr.
74/D2 **Fatsa,** Turk.
93/M6 **Fatu Hiva** (isl.), FrPol.
54/B1 **Faucilles** (mts.), Fr.
44/A2 **Faughan** (riv.), NI,UK
123/J4 **Faulkton,** SD,US
42/E2 **Fauske,** Nor.
60/C4 **Favara,** It.
47/G4 **Faversham,** Eng,UK
47/E5 **Fawley,** Eng,UK
118/H3 **Fawn** (riv.), On,Can
42/M7 **Faxaflói** (bay), Ice.
110/B2 **Faxinal,** Braz.
97/J4 **Faya-Largeau,** Chad
129/G3 **Fayette,** Al,US
125/J3 **Fayette,** Mo,US
129/F4 **Fayette,** Ms,US
128/E2 **Fayetteville,** Ar,US
129/G3 **Fayetteville,** Ga,US
129/J3 **Fayetteville,** NC,US
129/G3 **Fayetteville,** Tn,US
99/F4 **Fazao** (mts.), Gha., Togo
99/F4 **Fazao Nat'l Park,** Togo
43/A4 **Feale** (riv.), Ire.
129/J3 **Fear** (cape), NC,US
124/B3 **Feather** (riv.), Ca,US
45/G4 **Featherstone,** Eng,UK
56/D2 **Fécamp,** Fr.
132/C3 **Federal Way,** Wa,US
44/A2 **Feeny,** NI,UK
62/F2 **Fehérgyarmat,** Hun.
48/F1 **Fehmarn** (isl.), Ger.
48/F1 **Fehmarn Belt** (str.), Ger., Den.
81/D4 **Fei** (riv.), China
110/D2 **Feia** (lake), Braz.
52/C3 **Feignies,** Fr.
81/D4 **Fei Huang** (riv.), China
109/L6 **Feira de Santana,** Braz.
57/L3 **Feistritz** (riv.), Aus.
62/D2 **Fejér** (co.), Hun.
59/G3 **Felanitx,** Sp.
54/E2 **Feldberg** (peak), Ger.
55/F3 **Feldkirch,** Aus.
57/L3 **Feldkirchen in Kärnten,** Aus.
47/H3 **Felixstowe,** Eng,UK
117/N7 **Félix U. Gómez,** Mex.
45/G2 **Felling,** Eng,UK
51/G6 **Felsberg,** Ger.
47/G2 **Feltwell,** Eng,UK
81/C4 **Fen** (riv.), China
58/A1 **Fene,** Sp.
74/C3 **Fener** (pt.), Turk.
53/G6 **Fénétrange,** Fr.
61/J2 **Fengári** (peak), Gre.
77/J3 **Fengcheng,** China
81/D5 **Fengle** (riv.), China
81/D3 **Fengnan,** China
81/D3 **Fengrun,** China
77/J1 **Fengshui** (peak), China
81/C2 **Fengzhen,** China
130/C5 **Fenimore** (passg.), Ak,US
47/G2 **Fens, The** (reg.), Eng,UK
132/E6 **Fenton,** Mi,US
66/E3 **Feodosiya,** Ukr.
73/G2 **Ferdows,** Iran
60/C2 **Ferentino,** It.
60/C1 **Ferento** (ruins), It.
75/B3 **Fergana,** Uzb.
123/J4 **Fergus Falls,** Mn,US
118/F2 **Ferguson** (lake), Nun.,Can
98/D4 **Ferkéssédougou,** IvC.
57/L3 **Ferlach,** Aus.
96/C4 **Ferlo** (reg.), Sen.
98/B3 **Ferlo, Vallée du** (wadi), Sen.
44/A3 **Fermanagh** (dist.), NI,UK
131/B3 **Fermin** (pt.), Ca,US
60/C1 **Fermo,** It.
129/H4 **Fernandina Beach,** Fl,US
109/M4 **Fernando de Noronha** (isl.), Braz.
110/B2 **Fernandópolis,** Braz.
58/C4 **Fernán-Núñez,** Sp.
131/K7 **Ferndale,** Md,US
132/F7 **Ferndale,** Mi,US
47/E5 **Ferndown,** Eng,UK
122/E3 **Fernie,** BC,Can
91/G5 **Ferntree Gully Nat'l Park,** Austl.
60/E2 **Ferrandina,** It.
57/J4 **Ferrara,** It.
58/A3 **Ferreira do Alentejo,** Port.
56/C4 **Ferret** (cape), Fr.
128/F4 **Ferriday,** La,US
129/F4 **Ferriday,** La,US
45/G2 **Ferryhill,** Eng,UK
46/B3 **Ferryside,** Wal,UK
57/M3 **Fertő** (Neusiedler See) (lake), Aus., Hun.
50/C2 **Ferwerd,** Neth.
96/E1 **Fès,** Mor.
104/C2 **Feshi,** D.R. Congo
129/F2 **Festus,** Mo,US
47/F4 **Fetcham,** Eng,UK
63/H3 **Feteşti,** Rom.
57/J2 **Feucht,** Ger.
119/J3 **Feuilles** (lake), Qu,Can
119/J3 **Feuilles** (riv.), Qu,Can
56/F4 **Feurs,** Fr.
73/K1 **Feyẕābād,** Afg.
96/H2 **Fezzan** (reg.), Libya
44/E6 **Ffestiniog,** Wal,UK
103/H8 **Fianarantsoa,** Madg.
103/H8 **Fianarantsoa** (prov.), Madg.
96/J6 **Fianga,** Chad
102/D3 **Ficksburg,** SAfr.
57/J4 **Fidenza,** It.
98/C4 **Fié** (riv.), Gui., Mali
63/G3 **Fieni,** Rom.
61/F2 **Fier,** Alb.
61/G1 **Fierzë** (lake), Alb.
43/D2 **Fife Ness** (pt.), Sc,UK
56/E4 **Figeac,** Fr.
58/A2 **Figueira da Foz,** Port.
59/G1 **Figueres,** Sp.
96/E1 **Figuig,** Mor.
103/G8 **Fiherenana** (riv.), Madg.
92/G6 **Fiji**
105/X **Filchner Ice Shelf,** Ant.
45/H3 **Filey,** Eng,UK
45/H3 **Filey** (bay), Eng,UK
63/F3 **Filiaşi,** Rom.
60/D3 **Filicudi** (isl.), It.
99/F3 **Filingué,** Niger
61/J2 **Fílippoi** (ruins), Gre.
42/E4 **Filipstad,** Swe.
131/B2 **Fillmore,** Ca,US
124/D3 **Fillmore,** Ut,US
93/S9 **Filo** (peak), Samoa
46/D3 **Filton,** Eng,UK
105/Z **Fimbul Ice Shelf,** Ant.
96/J8 **Fimi** (riv.), D.R. Congo
57/H4 **Finale Ligure,** It.
98/C3 **Fina Rsv.,** Mali
43/D2 **Findhorn** (riv.), Sc,UK
126/D3 **Findlay,** Oh,US
91/D4 **Fingal,** Austl.
119/K2 **Finger** (lake), On,Can
126/E3 **Finger** (lakes), NY,US
56/E4 **Finiels, Sommet de** (peak), Fr.
74/B3 **Finike,** Turk.
58/A1 **Finisterre** (cape), Sp.
57/K3 **Finkenstein,** Aus.
42/H2 **Finland**
64/E4 **Finland** (gulf), Eur.
118/D3 **Finlay** (riv.), BC,Can
128/B4 **Finlay** (mts.), Tx,US
51/E6 **Finnentrop,** Ger.
132/C2 **Finn Hill-Inglewood,** Wa,US
90/B1 **Finnigan** (peak), Austl.
42/G1 **Finnmark** (co.), Nor.
42/E4 **Finspång,** Swe.
44/A3 **Fintona,** NI,UK
60/B1 **Fiora** (riv.), It.
57/H4 **Fiorenzuola d'Arda,** It.
132/C2 **Fircrest-Silver Lake,** Wa,US
57/J5 **Firenze** (Florence), It.
112/E2 **Firmat,** Arg.
56/F4 **Firminy,** Fr.
84/C2 **Firozābād,** India
73/K2 **Firozpur,** India
72/F3 **Fīrūzābād,** Iran
57/L3 **Fischbacher** (mts.), Aus.
102/B2 **Fish** (riv.), Namb.
102/C3 **Fish** (riv.), SAfr.
45/G2 **Fishburn,** Eng,UK
105/E **Fisher** (glac.), Ant.
123/J3 **Fisher** (bay), Mb,Can
119/H2 **Fisher** (str.), Nun.,Can
123/J3 **Fisher Branch,** Mb,Can
90/F6 **Fisherman** (isl.), Austl.
46/B3 **Fishguard,** Wal,UK
66/F4 **Fisht, Gora** (peak), Rus.
45/J6 **Fishtoft,** Eng,UK
93/S8 **Fito** (peak), Samoa
130/L2 **Fitton** (mtn.), Yk,Can
129/H4 **Fitzgerald,** Ga,US
122/B3 **Fitz Hugo** (sound), BC,Can
113/J7 **Fitzroy** (peak), Arg.
90/C3 **Fitzroy** (riv.), Austl.
119/R7 **Fitzwilliam** (str.), NW,Can
60/C2 **Fiumicino,** It.
44/A3 **Fivemiletown,** NI,UK
42/C3 **Fjell,** Nor.
47/F3 **Flackwell Heath,** Eng,UK
125/G3 **Flagler,** Co,US
129/H4 **Flagler Beach,** Fl,US
124/E4 **Flagstaff,** Az,US
126/B2 **Flambeau** (riv.), Wi,US
127/Q9 **Flamborough,** On,Can
45/H3 **Flamborough,** Eng,UK
45/H3 **Flamborough Head** (pt.), Eng,UK
48/G2 **Fläming** (hills), Ger.
122/F5 **Flaming Gorge Nat'l Rec. Area,** Ut, Wy,US
123/K2 **Flanagan** (riv.), On,Can
52/B2 **Flanders** (reg.), Belg., Fr.
123/J4 **Flandreau,** SD,US
130/L3 **Flat Creek,** Yk,Can
122/E4 **Flathead** (lake), Mt,US
122/E4 **Flathead** (riv.), Mt,US
46/C4 **Flat Holm** (isl.), Eng,UK
125/K3 **Flat River,** Mo,US
132/F7 **Flat Rock,** Mi,US
90/B1 **Flattery** (cape), Austl.
122/B3 **Flattery** (cape), Wa,US
47/F4 **Fleet,** Eng,UK
45/E4 **Fleetwood,** Eng,UK
42/C4 **Flekkefjord,** Nor.
131/F5 **Flemington,** NJ,US
48/E1 **Flensburg,** Ger.
53/E2 **Fleron,** Belg.
56/C2 **Flers,** Fr.
52/D3 **Fleurus,** Belg.
56/D3 **Fleury-les-Aubrais,** Fr.
50/C4 **Flevoland** (prov.), Neth.
44/E2 **Flimby,** Eng,UK
91/D3 **Flinders** (isl.), Austl.
90/C2 **Flinders** (reefs), Austl.
90/A2 **Flinders** (riv.), Austl.
123/L3 **Flindt** (riv.), On,Can
123/H2 **Flin Flon,** Mb,Can
119/J2 **Flint** (lake), Nun.,Can
93/K6 **Flint** (isl.), Kiri.
45/E5 **Flint,** Wal,UK
129/G4 **Flint** (riv.), Ga,US
125/H3 **Flint** (hills), Ks,US
132/E5 **Flint,** Mi,US
45/E5 **Flintshire** (co.), Wal.,UK
47/F3 **Flitwick,** Eng,UK
51/F1 **Flögelner See** (lake), Ger.
49/G3 **Flöha** (riv.), Ger.
126/B4 **Flora,** Il,US
131/G5 **Floral Park,** NY,US
53/F5 **Florange,** Fr.
53/D3 **Floreffe,** Belg.
129/G3 **Florence,** Al,US
124/E4 **Florence,** Az,US
125/F3 **Florence,** Co,US
129/J3 **Florence,** SC,US
57/J5 **Florence** (Firenze), It.
108/C3 **Florencia,** Col.
52/D3 **Florennes,** Belg.
112/E3 **Flores** (riv.), Arg.
122/B3 **Flores** (isl.), BC,Can
116/D4 **Flores,** Guat.
87/F5 **Flores** (isl.), Indo.
87/E5 **Flores** (sea), Indo.
59/R12 **Flores** (isl.), Azor.,Port.
113/F2 **Flores** (dept.), Uru.
109/L5 **Floresta,** Braz.
128/D4 **Floresville,** Tx,US
131/F5 **Florham Park,** NJ,US
109/K5 **Floriano,** Braz.
110/B3 **Florianópolis,** Braz.
117/F3 **Florida,** Cuba
117/E3 **Florida** (str.), NAm.
113/F2 **Florida,** Uru.
113/F2 **Florida** (dept.), Uru.
129/H4 **Florida** (state), US
129/H5 **Florida** (bay), Fl,US
129/H5 **Florida Keys** (isls.), Fl,US
60/D4 **Floridia,** It.
132/M10 **Florin,** Ca,US
61/G2 **Flórina,** Gre.
125/K3 **Florissant,** Mo,US
42/C3 **Florø,** Nor.
128/C3 **Floydada,** Tx,US
50/C3 **Fluessen** (lake), Neth.
60/A3 **Flumendosa** (riv.), It.
126/D3 **Flushing,** Mi,US
50/A6 **Flushing** (Vlissingen), Neth.
92/D5 **Fly** (riv.), PNG
105/T **Flying Fish** (cape), Ant.
42/P6 **Fnjóská** (riv.), Ice.
123/H3 **Foam Lake,** Sk,Can
62/D4 **Foča,** Bosn.
63/H3 **Focşani,** Rom.
60/D2 **Foggia,** It.
57/L3 **Fohnsdorf,** Aus.
48/E1 **Föhr** (isl.), Ger.
56/D5 **Foix,** Fr.
42/C3 **Folarskardnuten** (peak), Nor.
42/D2 **Folda** (fjord), Nor.
61/J4 **Folégandros** (isl.), Gre.
119/J2 **Foley** (isl.), Nun.,Can
60/C1 **Foligno,** It.
47/H4 **Folkestone,** Eng,UK
129/H4 **Folkston,** Ga,US
60/B1 **Follonica** (gulf), It.
118/F3 **Fond du Lac** (riv.), Sk,Can
126/B3 **Fond du Lac,** Wi,US
60/C2 **Fondi,** It.
42/D3 **Fongen** (peak), Nor.
58/B1 **Fonsagrada,** Sp.
116/D5 **Fonseca** (gulf), NAm.
56/F4 **Fontaine,** Fr.
56/E2 **Fontainebleau,** Fr.
52/D3 **Fontaine-L'Evêque,** Belg.
131/C2 **Fontana,** Ca,US
56/C3 **Fontenay-le-Comte,** Fr.
52/B6 **Fontenay-Trésigny,** Fr.
122/F5 **Fontenelle** (res.), Wy,US

152

Font S – Gez

57/G4 Font Sancte, Pic de la (peak), Fr.
42/P6 Fontur (pt.), Ice.
91/F5 Footscray, Austl.
130/H3 Foraker (mtn.), Ak,US
53/F5 Forbach, Fr.
91/D2 Forbes, Austl.
58/A1 Forcarey, Sp.
57/J2 Forchheim, Ger.
132/E7 Ford (lake), Mi,US
47/E5 Fordingbridge, Eng,UK
128/E3 Fordyce, Ar,US
46/C4 Foreland (pt.), Eng,UK
47/E5 Foreland, The (pt.), Eng,UK
122/F3 Foremost, Ab,Can
47/H4 Foreness (pt.), Eng,UK
129/F3 Forest, Ms,US
91/D4 Forestier (cape), Austl.
127/G1 Forestville, Qu,Can
131/K8 Forestville, Md,US
56/E4 Forez (mts.), Fr.
43/D2 Forfar, Sc,UK
127/H1 Forillon Nat'l Park, Qu,Can
44/B3 Forkill, NI,UK
57/K4 Forlì, It.
45/E4 Formby, Eng,UK
45/E4 Formby (pt.), Eng,UK
59/F3 Formentera (isl.), Sp.
59/G3 Formentor, Cabo de (cape), Sp.
60/C2 Formia, It.
110/C2 Formiga, Braz.
111/E2 Formosa, Arg.
109/J7 Formosa, Braz.
109/G6 Formosa (mts.), Braz.
98/A4 Formosa (isl.), GBis.
102/C4 Formosa (peak), SAfr.
109/J6 Formoso (riv.), Braz.
57/J5 Fornacelle, It.
43/D2 Forres, Sc,UK
129/F3 Forrest City, Ar,US
42/G3 Forssa, Fin.
90/A3 Forsyth (range), Austl.
129/H3 Forsyth, Ga,US
122/G4 Forsyth, Mt,US
73/K3 Fort Abbās, Pak.
109/L4 Fortaleza, Braz.
113/G2 Fortaleza Santa Teresa, Uru.
102/D4 Fort Beaufort, SAfr.
122/F4 Fort Benton, Mt,US
124/B3 Fort Bragg, Ca,US
125/H4 Fort Cobb (res.), Ok,US
125/F2 Fort Collins, Co,US
128/C4 Fort Davis, Tx,US
53/E5 Fort de Douaumont, Fr.
117/J5 Fort-de-France (cap.), Mart.
53/E5 Fort de Vaux, Fr.
123/K5 Fort Dodge, Ia,US
104/D3 Forte Cameia, Ang.
127/S10 Fort Erie, On,Can
92/A7 Fortescue (riv.), Austl.
126/A1 Fort Frances, On,Can
129/F4 Fort Gaines, Al,US
127/R9 Fort George, On,Can
119/J3 Fort-George (Chisasibi), Qu,Can
125/J4 Fort Gibson, Ok,US
128/E2 Fort Gibson (lake), Ok,US
96/C3 Fort-Gouraud, Mrta.
43/C2 Forth (riv.), Sc,UK
43/D2 Forth, Firth of (inlet), Sc,UK
127/G2 Fort Kent, Me,US
129/H5 Fort Lauderdale, Fl,US
131/F5 Fort Lee, NJ,US
125/F2 Fort Lupton, Co,US
122/E3 Fort Macleod, Ab,Can
123/L5 Fort Madison, Ia,US
129/H4 Fort Matanzas Nat'l Mon., Fl,US
118/E3 Fort McMurray, Ab,Can
126/C2 Fort Michilimackinac, Mi,US
125/G2 Fort Morgan, Co,US
129/J3 Fort Moultrie, SC,US
129/H5 Fort Myers, Fl,US
118/D3 Fort Nelson (riv.), BC,Can
45/F4 Forton, Eng,UK
60/D2 Fortore (riv.), It.
129/G3 Fort Payne, Al,US
122/G4 Fort Peck (lake), Mt,US
129/H5 Fort Pierce, Fl,US
123/H4 Fort Pierre, SD,US
101/A2 Fort Portal, Ugan.
123/H3 Fort Qu'Appelle, Sk,Can
123/J5 Fort Randall (dam), SD,US
122/B2 Fort Saint James, BC,Can
118/D3 Fort Saint John, BC,Can
122/E2 Fort Saskatchewan, Ab,Can
125/J3 Fort Scott, Ks,US
67/J3 Fort-Shevchenko, Kaz.
128/E3 Fort Smith, Ar,US
128/C4 Fort Stockton, Tx,US
125/F4 Fort Sumner, NM,US
123/J4 Fort Totten, ND,US
127/L2 Fortune, Nf,Can
127/L2 Fortune (bay), Nf,Can
46/D5 Fortuneswell, Eng,UK
125/F4 Fort Union Nat'l Mon., NM,US
129/G4 Fort Walton Beach, Fl,US
131/J8 Fort Washington Park, Md,US
126/C3 Fort Wayne, In,US
43/C2 Fort William, Sc,UK
128/D3 Fort Worth, Tx,US
123/H4 Fort Yates, ND,US
90/B2 Forty Mile Scrub Nat'l Park, Austl.
82/B3 Foshan, China
119/S7 Fosheim (pen.), Nun.,Can
45/G3 Foss (riv.), Eng,UK
57/G4 Fossano, It.
52/B5 Fosses, Fr.
53/D3 Fosses-la-Ville, Belg.
122/C4 Fossil, Or,US
122/F5 Fossil Butte Nat'l Mon., Wy,US
126/D3 Fostoria, Oh,US
56/C2 Fougères, Fr.
97/N3 Foul (bay), Egypt, Sudan
47/G3 Foulness (isl.), Eng,UK
47/G3 Foulness (pt.), Eng,UK
45/H4 Foulness (riv.), Eng,UK
47/H1 Foulsham, Eng,UK
99/H5 Foumban, Camr.
125/F3 Fountain, Co,US
131/C3 Fountain Valley, Ca,US
128/E3 Fourche La Fave (riv.), Ar,US
47/E4 Four Marks, Eng,UK
52/D4 Fourmies, Fr.
130/D5 Four Mountains (isls.), Ak,US
103/R15 Fournaise, Piton de la (peak), Reun.
98/B4 Fouta Djallon (reg.), Gha.
46/B6 Fowey, Eng,UK
46/B6 Fowey (riv.), Eng,UK
91/B1 Fowlers Gap, Austl.
72/E1 Fowman, Iran
130/M3 Fox (mtn.), Yk,Can
130/E5 Fox (isls.), Ak,US
126/B3 Fox (riv.), Il, Wi,US
122/D2 Fox Creek, Ab,Can
119/H2 Foxe (chan.), Nun.,Can
119/J2 Foxe (pen.), Nun.,Can
119/J2 Foxe Basin (sound), Nun.,Can
132/P15 Fox Lake, Il,US
47/G2 Foxton, Eng,UK
122/F3 Fox Valley, Sk,Can
44/A2 Foyle (riv.), NI,UK
44/A1 Foyle, Lough (inlet), Ire., NI,UK
58/B1 Foz, Sp.
104/B4 Foz do Cunene, Ang.
111/F2 Foz do Iguaçu, Braz.
59/F2 Fraga, Sp.
110/B3 Fraiburgo, Braz.
108/E7 Frailes (range), Bol.
52/C3 Frameries, Belg.
47/H2 Framlingham, Eng,UK
110/C2 Franca, Braz.
61/E2 Francavilla Fontana, It.
56/D3 France
56/E5 France, Roc de (mtn.), Fr.
118/C2 Frances (lake), Yk,Can
116/E3 Frances (cape), Cuba
117/H4 Francés Viejo (cape), DRep.
104/B1 Franceville, Gabon
54/C3 Franche-Comté (reg.), Fr.
123/J5 Francis Case (lake), SD,US
116/C4 Francisco Escárcega, Mex.
117/P8 Francisco I. Madero, Mex.
104/E5 Francistown, Bots.
110/G8 Franco da Rocha, Braz.
122/B2 Francois (lake), BC,Can
52/B6 Franconville, Fr.
50/C2 Franeker, Neth.
51/F6 Frankenberg-Eder, Ger.
126/D3 Frankenmuth, Mi,US
126/C3 Frankfort, In,US
126/C4 Frankfort (cap.), Ky,US
49/H2 Frankfurt, Ger.
57/H1 Frankfurt am Main, Ger.
57/J2 Fränkische Alb (mts.), Ger.
57/H1 Fränkische Saale (riv.), Ger.
57/J2 Fränkische Schweiz (reg.), Ger.
91/C3 Frankland (cape), Austl.
105/M Franklin (isl.), Ant.
130/N1 Franklin (bay), NW,Can
118/D2 Franklin (mts.), NW,Can
130/G1 Franklin (pt.), Ak,US
126/C4 Franklin, In,US
126/C4 Franklin, Ky,US
129/H3 Franklin, NC,US
129/G3 Franklin, Tn,US
128/D4 Franklin, Tx,US
126/E4 Franklin, Va,US
132/P14 Franklin, Wi,US
126/E4 Franklin, WV,US
122/D3 Franklin D. Roosevelt (lake), Wa,US
131/F4 Franklin Lakes, NJ,US
91/C4 Franklin-Lower Gordon Wild Rivers Nat'l Park, Austl.
132/Q16 Franklin Park, Il,US
131/G5 Franklin Square, NY,US
111/F2 Fransisco Beltrão, Braz.
110/G8 Fransisco Morato, Braz.
68/F2 Franz Josef Land (arch.), Rus.
90/D4 Fraser (isl.), Austl.
122/B2 Fraser (lake), BC,Can
122/C3 Fraser (riv.), BC,Can
132/G6 Fraser, Mi,US
43/D2 Fraserburgh, Sc,UK
122/B2 Fraser Lake, BC,Can
91/C3 Fraser Nat'l Park, Austl.
55/E2 Frauenfeld, Swi.
112/F2 Fray Bentos, Uru.
124/C4 Frazier Park, Ca,US
53/F2 Frechen, Ger.
102/E3 Fred (mtn.), SAfr.
48/E1 Fredericia, Den.
126/E4 Frederick, Md,US
125/H4 Frederick, Ok,US
128/D4 Fredericksburg, Tx,US
126/E4 Fredericksburg, Va,US
127/H2 Fredericton (cap.), NB,Can
42/D4 Frederikshavn, Den.
124/D3 Fredonia, Az,US
125/J3 Fredonia, Ks,US
126/E3 Fredonia, NY,US
42/D4 Fredrikstad, Nor.
125/H3 Freedom, Ok,US
131/F5 Freehold, NJ,US
91/A1 Freeling Heights (peak), Austl.
117/F2 Freeport, Bahm.
126/B3 Freeport, Il,US
131/G5 Freeport, NY,US
128/E4 Freeport, Tx,US
128/D5 Freer, Tx,US
102/D3 Free State (prov.), SAfr.
98/B4 Freetown (cap.), SLeo.
56/B2 Fréhel (cape), Fr.
48/G3 Freib (riv.), Ger.
49/G3 Freiberg, Ger.
54/D2 Freiburg, Ger.
48/G3 Freiberger Mulde (riv.), Ger.
110/D1 Frei Inocêncio, Braz.
112/B3 Freire, Chile
53/G4 Freisen, Ger.
57/J2 Freising, Ger.
57/L2 Freistadt, Aus.
49/G3 Freital, Ger.
57/G5 Fréjus, Fr.
46/B4 Fremington, Eng,UK
132/L11 Fremont, Ca,US
126/C3 Fremont, Mi,US
125/H2 Fremont, Ne,US
126/D3 Fremont, Oh,US
124/E3 Fremont (riv.), Ut,US
122/F5 Fremont (peak), Wy,US
126/D2 French (riv.), On,Can
93/J2 French Frigate (shoals), Hi,US
109/H3 French Guiana (dpcy.), Fr.
122/G3 Frenchman (riv.), Can., US
125/G2 Frenchman (cr.), Ne,US
127/R8 Frenchman's (bay), On,Can
91/C4 Frenchmans Cap (peak), Austl.
93/M6 French Polynesia (terr.), Fr.
109/H5 Fresco (riv.), Braz.
47/E5 Freshwater, Eng,UK
112/B4 Fresia, Chile
117/P9 Fresnillo de González Echeverría, Mex.
124/C3 Fresno, Ca,US
91/D4 Freycinet Nat'l Park, Austl.
53/F5 Freyming-Merlebach, Fr.
57/K2 Freyung, Ger.
104/B4 Fria (cape), Namb.
111/C2 Frías, Arg.
54/D4 Fribourg, Swi.
54/D4 Fribourg (canton), Swi.
57/H1 Friedberg, Ger.
51/E2 Friedeburg, Ger.
57/H1 Friedrichsdorf, Ger.
55/F2 Friedrichshafen, Ger.
53/G5 Friedrichsthal, Ger.
51/G7 Frielendorf, Ger.
54/D1 Friesenheim, Ger.
50/C2 Friesland (prov.), Neth.
51/E2 Friesoythe, Ger.
47/F4 Frimley, Eng,UK
47/H3 Frinton, Eng,UK
38/G7 Frio (cape), Braz.
125/H5 Frio (riv.), Tx,US
51/G6 Fritzlar, Ger.
57/K3 Friuli-Venezia Giulia (reg.), It.
44/E2 Frizington, Eng,UK
119/K2 Frobisher (bay), Nun.,Can
122/F1 Frobisher (lake), Sk,Can
45/F5 Frodsham, Eng,UK
42/D3 Frohavet (bay), Nor.
52/D3 Froidchapelle, Belg.
67/G2 Frolovo, Rus.
91/B1 Frome (lake), Austl.
46/D4 Frome, Eng,UK
46/D2 Frome (riv.), Eng,UK
46/D5 Frome (riv.), Eng,UK
125/F2 Front (range), Co,US
56/E5 Frontignan, Fr.
126/E4 Front Royal, Va,US
60/C2 Frosinone, It.
42/E3 Frösö, Swe.
105/J Frost (glac.), Ant.
53/F6 Frouard, Fr.
42/D3 Frøya (isl.), Nor.
119/H2 Frozen (str.), Nun.,Can
127/Q9 Fruitland, On,Can
62/D3 Fruška Gora Nat'l Park, Yugo.
110/B2 Frutal, Braz.
112/B4 Frutillar, Chile
49/K4 Frýdek-Místek, Czh.
81/C5 Fu (riv.), China
81/D3 Fucheng, China
48/E3 Fuchskaute (peak), Ger.
53/H2 Fuchskauten (peak), Ger.
78/C3 Fuchū, Japan
81/D5 Fuchun (riv.), China
87/H4 Fudi (mtn.), Indo.
82/D2 Fuding, China
59/Y16 Fuenaventura (isl.), Canl.
58/C4 Fuengirola, Sp.
58/D2 Fuenlabrada, Sp.
59/N8 Fuente, Sp.
59/E4 Fuente-Álamo, Sp.
58/B3 Fuente del Maestre, Sp.
58/C3 Fuente Obejuna, Sp.
58/E1 Fuenterrabiá, Sp.
58/C4 Fuentes de Andalucía, Sp.
117/N8 Fuerte (riv.), Mex.
82/D4 Fuga (isl.), Phil.
48/F3 Fuhne (riv.), Ger.
51/H4 Fuhse (riv.), Ger.
79/F3 Fuji, Japan
79/F3 Fuji (riv.), Japan
79/F3 Fujieda, Japan
79/F3 Fuji-Hakone-Izu Nat'l Park, Japan
79/L10 Fujiidera, Japan
79/H7 Fujimi, Japan
79/H7 Fujino, Japan
79/F3 Fujinomiya, Japan
79/F2 Fujioka, Japan
79/F3 Fujisawa, Japan
79/J7 Fujishiro, Japan
79/M9 Fujiwara, Japan
79/F3 Fujiyama (mtn.), Japan
79/F3 Fujiyoshida, Japan
78/D3 Fukuchiyama, Japan
78/A4 Fukue, Japan
78/A4 Fukue (isl.), Japan
78/E2 Fukui, Japan
78/E3 Fukui (pref.), Japan
78/B4 Fukuoka, Japan
78/B4 Fukuoka (pref.), Japan
79/E3 Fukuroi, Japan
105/C Fukushima (peak), Ant.
79/G2 Fukushima, Japan
79/F2 Fukushima (pref.), Japan
78/C3 Fukuyama, Japan
73/J2 Fūlādī (mtn.), Afg.
47/G2 Fulbourn, Eng,UK
57/H1 Fulda, Ger.
45/G4 Fulford, Eng,UK
82/A2 Fuling, China
131/C3 Fullerton, Ca,US
131/E5 Fullerton (Whitehall), Pa,US
127/Q9 Fulton, On,Can
126/B4 Fulton, Ky,US
125/K3 Fulton, Mo,US
126/E3 Fulton, NY,US
42/E3 Fulufjället (peak), Swe.
45/F4 Fulwood, Eng,UK
56/D4 Fumel, Fr.
79/H7 Funabashi, Japan
92/G5 Funafuti (atoll), Tuv.
92/G5 Funafuti (cap.), Tuv.
117/G5 Fundación, Col.
127/H2 Fundy (bay), NB, NS,Can
127/H2 Fundy Nat'l Park, NB,Can
104/F5 Funhalouro, Moz.
64/J4 Furmanov, Rus.
43/C2 Furnace, Sc,UK
110/H6 Furnas (res.), Braz.
91/C4 Furneaux Group (isls.), Austl.
51/E3 Fürstenau, Ger.
62/C2 Fürstenfeld, Aus.
55/H1 Fürstenfeldbruck, Ger.
49/H2 Fürstenwalde, Ger.
57/K2 Furth im Wald, Ger.
77/N4 Furukawa, Japan
119/H2 Fury and Hecla (str.), Nun.,Can
81/B4 Fushan, China
81/E3 Fushan, China
77/J3 Fushun, China
79/M9 Fuso, Japan
79/H7 Fussa, Japan
55/G2 Füssen, Ger.
79/M10 Futami, Japan
62/D3 Futog, Yugo.
112/B4 Futrono, Chile
79/F3 Futtsu, Japan
92/H6 Futuna (isl.), Wall.
74/H6 Fuwah, Egypt
85/H3 Fuxian (lake), China
77/J3 Fuxin, China
81/C4 Fuyang, China
82/B2 Fuyi (riv.), China
77/J2 Fuyu, China
49/L5 Füzesabony, Hun.
82/C2 Fuzhou, China
48/F1 Fyn (co.), Den.
42/D5 Fyn (isl.), Den.

G

97/Q6 Gaalkacyo (Galcaio), Som.
50/D5 Gaanderen, Neth.
50/C2 Gaast, Neth.
56/C5 Gabas (riv.), Fr.
124/C3 Gabbs, Nv,US
104/B3 Gabela, Ang.
96/H1 Gabès (gulf), Tun.
96/H7 Gabon
102/D2 Gaborone (cap.), Bots.
63/G4 Gabrovo, Bul.
62/D4 Gacko, Bosn.
84/C4 Gadag-Betgeri, India
129/G3 Gadsden, Al,US
63/G3 Găești, Rom.
60/C2 Gaeta, It.
60/C2 Gaeta (gulf), It.
129/H3 Gaffney, SC,US
64/G5 Gagarin, Rus.
98/D5 Gagnoa, IvC.
127/G1 Gagnon, Qu,Can
52/B6 Gagny, Fr.
66/G4 Gagra, Geo.
62/A2 Gail (riv.), Aus.
56/D5 Gaillac, Fr.
57/K3 Gailtaler Alps (mts.), Aus.
112/D4 Gaiman, Arg.
129/H4 Gainesville, Fl,US
129/H3 Gainesville, Ga,US
125/J3 Gainesville, Mo,US
128/D3 Gainesville, Tx,US
45/G2 Gainford, Eng,UK
45/H5 Gainsborough, Eng,UK
131/J7 Gaithersburg, Md,US
64/E4 Gaizina Kalns (peak), Lat.
102/C2 Gakarosa (peak), SAfr.
58/D2 Galapagar, Sp.
43/D3 Galashiels, Sc,UK
63/J3 Galați, Rom.
63/H3 Galați (co.), Rom.
61/F2 Galatina, It.
61/F2 Galatone, It.
126/D4 Galax, Va,US
61/H3 Galaxidhiou, Gre.
87/G3 Galela, Indo.
126/B3 Galena, Il,US
112/B3 Galera (pt.), Chile
108/B3 Galera (pt.), Ecu.
117/J5 Galera (pt.), Trin.
126/B3 Galesburg, Il,US
43/A4 Galey (riv.), Ire.
44/B2 Galgorm, NI,UK
64/J4 Galich, Rus.
49/L3 Galicia (reg.), Pol., Ukr.
58/A1 Galicia (aut. comm.), Sp.
62/E5 Galičica Nat'l Park, FYROM
74/K5 Galilee, Sea of (Tiberias) (lake), Isr.
126/D3 Galion, Oh,US
129/G2 Gallatin, Tn,US
84/D6 Galle, SrL.
113/K7 Gallegos (riv.), Arg.
117/G5 Gallinas (pt.), Col.
128/B3 Gallinas (mts.), NM,US
61/E2 Gallipoli, It.
63/H5 Gallipoli (pen.), Turk.
63/H5 Gallipoli (Gelibolu), Turk.
126/D4 Gallipolis, Oh,US
42/G2 Gällivare, Swe.
60/C3 Gallo (cape), It.
44/D2 Galloway, Mull of (pt.), Sc,UK
124/E4 Gallup, NM,US
76/D2 Galt, Mong.
132/M10 Galt, Ca,US
43/A4 Galtymore (mtn.), Ire.
76/E2 Galuut, Mong.
112/B3 Galvarino, Chile
128/E4 Galveston, Tx,US
128/E4 Galveston (bay), Tx,US
128/E4 Galveston (isl.), Tx,US
112/E2 Gálvez, Arg.
43/A4 Galway, Ire.
43/A4 Galway (bay), Ire.
83/D1 Gam (riv.), Viet.
102/C2 Gamagara (dry riv.), SAfr.
79/E3 Gamagōri, Japan
84/E2 Gamba, China
99/E4 Gambaga Scarp (escarp.), Gha., Togo
84/A2 Gambat, Pak.
97/M6 Gambēla, Eth.
97/M6 Gambela Nat'l Park, Eth.
98/B3 Gambia
98/A3 Gambia (Gambie) (riv.), Afr.
93/M7 Gambier (isls.), FrPol.
127/L1 Gambo, Nf,Can
104/C1 Gamboma, Congo
102/C4 Gamka (riv.), SAfr.
102/B3 Gamkab (dry riv.), Namb.
47/F2 Gamlingay, Eng,UK
64/D2 Gammelstad, Swe.
79/M9 Gamo, Japan
49/G5 Gamsfeld (peak), Aus.
101/C1 Gamud (peak), Eth.
82/C2 Gan (riv.), China
126/E2 Gananoque, On,Can
67/H4 Gäncä, Arm.
104/D2 Gandajika, D.R. Congo
127/L1 Gander, Nf,Can
127/L1 Gander (lake), Nf,Can
51/F2 Ganderkesee, Ger.
84/B3 Gāndhīhām, India
84/B3 Gandhinagar, India
84/B3 Gāndhi Sāgar (res.), India
59/E3 Gandía, Sp.
96/C4 Ganeb (well), Mrta.
84/C2 Gangāpur, India
84/E2 Gangārāmpur, India
75/D5 Gangdisê (mts.), China
53/F2 Gangelt, Ger.
84/E3 Ganges (riv.), India
60/D4 Gangi, It.
84/E2 Gangtok, India
74/N8 Gan Hashlosha Nat'l Park, Isr.
122/F5 Gannett (peak), Wy,US
75/F4 Gansu (prov.), China
96/H6 Ganye, Nga.
82/B2 Ganzhou, China
99/E3 Ganzourgou (prov.), Burk.
99/E2 Gao, Mali
99/E2 Gao (reg.), Mali
81/C3 Gaocheng, China
82/D2 Gaojian, China
98/E4 Gaoua, Burk.
81/C3 Gaoyang, China
81/D4 Gaoyou (lake), China
57/G4 Gap, Fr.
76/D5 Gar (riv.), China
67/K4 Garabogazköl (gulf), Trkm.
84/E3 Garai (riv.), Bang.
101/A2 Garamba Nat'l Park, D.R. Congo
109/L5 Garanhuns, Braz.
101/C2 Garba Tula, Kenya
48/E2 Garbsen, Ger.
110/B2 Garça, Braz.
58/C3 Garcia de Sota (res.), Sp.
56/F5 Gard (riv.), Fr.
57/J4 Garda (lake), It.
48/F2 Gardelegen, Ger.
131/B3 Gardena, Ca,US
129/H3 Garden City, Ga,US
125/G3 Garden City, Ks,US
132/F7 Garden City, Mi,US
131/G5 Garden City, NY,US
122/A2 Gardener Canal (inlet), BC,Can
131/C3 Garden Grove, Ca,US
73/J2 Gardēz, Afg.
127/G2 Gardiner, Me,US
122/F4 Gardiner, Mt,US
93/H5 Gardner (Nikumaroro) (atoll), Kiri.
43/C2 Garelochhead, Sc,UK
96/G2 Garet el Djenoun (peak), Alg.
122/E4 Garfield (peak), Mt,US
131/F5 Garfield, NJ,US
45/G4 Garforth, Eng,UK
56/D4 Gargan (mtn.), Fr.
45/F4 Gargrave, Eng,UK
84/C3 Garhākotā, India
110/B4 Garibaldi, Braz.
101/C3 Garissa, Kenya
128/D3 Garland, Tx,US
44/D2 Garlieston, Sc,UK
55/H3 Garmisch-Partenkirchen, Ger.
125/J3 Garnett, Ks,US
91/B2 Garnpung (lake), Austl.
56/D4 Garonne (riv.), Fr.
99/E2 Garou (lake), Mali
96/H6 Garoua, Camr.
96/H6 Garoua Boulaï, Camr.
59/K7 Garraf (range), Sp.
46/D4 Garreg, Wal,UK
51/F3 Garrel, Ger.
123/H4 Garrison, ND,US
123/H4 Garrison (dam), ND,US
44/C1 Garron (pt.), NI,UK
119/H2 Garry (bay), Nun.,Can
118/F2 Garry (lake), Nun.,Can
45/F4 Garstang, Eng,UK
57/L2 Garsten, Aus.
51/H6 Garte (riv.), Ger.
56/D3 Gartempe (riv.), Fr.
46/C2 Garth, Wal,UK
86/C5 Garut, Indo.
44/B2 Garvagh, NI,UK
49/L3 Garwolin, Pol.
132/R16 Gary, In,US
108/C3 Garzón, Col.
75/F4 Gas (lake), China
42/P6 Gæsafjöll (peak), Ice.
126/C3 Gas City, In,US
125/J3 Gasconade (riv.), Mo,US
56/C5 Gascony (reg.), Fr.
110/B3 Gaspar, Braz.
86/C4 Gaspar (riv.), Indo.
127/H1 Gaspé, Qu,Can
127/H1 Gaspé (pen.), Qu,Can
127/H1 Gaspé, Cap de (cape), Qu,Can
127/S9 Gasport, NY,US
129/J2 Gaston (lake), NC, Va,US
129/H3 Gastonia, NC,US
74/J4 Gata (cape), Cyp.
58/B2 Gata (range), Sp.
58/D4 Gata, Cabo de (cape), Sp.
64/F4 Gatchina, Rus.
44/D2 Gatehouse-of-Fleet, Sc,UK
118/F1 Gateshead (isl.), Nun.,Can
45/G2 Gateshead, Eng,UK
130/H2 Gates of the Arctic Nat'l Pk. & Prsv., Ak,US
128/D4 Gatesville, Tx,US
131/G5 Gateway Nat'l Rec. Area, NJ, NY,US
56/C3 Gâtine (hills), Fr.
126/F2 Gatineau, Qu,Can
126/F2 Gatineau (riv.), Qu,Can
53/H4 Gau-Bickelheim, Ger.
85/F2 Gauhāti, India
45/G2 Gaunless (riv.), Eng,UK
84/E2 Gauripur, India
84/E2 Gauri Sankar (mtn.), Nepal
42/D4 Gausta (peak), Nor.
102/E2 Gauteng (prov.), SAfr.
64/E4 Gauya Nat'l Park, Lat.
59/G2 Gavà, Sp.
61/J5 Gávdhos (isl.), Gre.
58/E1 Gave de Pau (riv.), Fr.
52/C2 Gavere, Belg.
42/F3 Gävle, Swe.
42/E3 Gävleborg (co.), Swe.
91/A2 Gawler, Austl.
76/D3 Gaxun (lake), China
67/L2 Gay, Rus.
126/D4 Gay (peak), WV,US
77/K3 Gaya (riv.), China
84/E3 Gayā, India
99/F4 Gaya, Niger
126/C2 Gaylord, Mi,US
66/D2 Gaysin, Ukr.
74/K6 Gaza (Ghazzah), Gaza
74/J6 Gaza Strip
74/D3 Gaziantep, Turk.
77/H1 Gazimur (riv.), Rus.
54/C1 Gazon de Faing (peak), Fr.
97/K7 Gbadolite, D.R. Congo
98/C5 Gbarnga, Libr.
49/K1 Gdańsk, Pol.
49/K1 Gdańsk (prov.), Pol.
49/K1 Gdańsk (gulf), Pol., Rus.
49/K1 Gdynia, Pol.
81/D5 Ge (lake), China
57/J1 Gebaberg (peak), Ger.
87/G3 Gebe (isl.), Indo.
100/D4 Gebeit Mine, Sudan
63/J5 Gebze, Turk.
86/C5 Gede (peak), Indo.
74/M9 Gedera, Isr.
74/B2 Gediz, Turk.
74/A2 Gediz (riv.), Turk.
53/E1 Geel, Belg.
91/C3 Geelong, Austl.
51/E3 Geeste, Ger.
51/F2 Geeste (riv.), Ger.
51/H2 Geesthacht, Ger.
75/D5 Gê'gyai, China
51/G4 Gehrden, Ger.
46/C2 Geifas (mtn.), Wal,UK
118/F3 Geikie (riv.), Sk,Can
53/F2 Geilenkirchen, Ger.
79/M10 Geinō, Japan
57/H2 Geislingen an der Steige, Ger.
85/H3 Gejiu, China
97/L6 Gel (riv.), Sudan
60/D4 Gela, It.
60/D4 Gela (gulf), It.
97/Q6 Geladī, Eth.
50/C4 Gelderland (prov.), Neth.
50/C5 Geldermalsen, Neth.
50/D5 Geldern, Ger.
50/C6 Geldrop, Neth.
53/E2 Geleen, Neth.
66/F3 Gelendzhik, Rus.
63/H5 Gelibolu (Gallipoli), Turk.
46/C3 Gelligaer, Wal,UK
50/E5 Gelsenkirchen, Ger.
53/D2 Gembloux, Belg.
97/J7 Gemena, D.R. Congo
50/C5 Gemert, Neth.
63/J5 Gemlik, Turk.
63/J5 Gemlik (gulf), Turk.
57/K3 Gemona del Friuli, It.
102/C2 Gemsbok-Kalahari Nat'l Park, SAfr.
102/C2 Gemsbok Nat'l Park, Bots.
130/G3 Gemuk (mtn.), Ak,US
77/J1 Gen (riv.), China
97/N6 Genalē Wenz (riv.), Eth.
52/D2 Genappe, Belg.
60/A3 Genargentu (mts.), It.
74/E2 Genç, Turk.
50/D5 Gendringen, Neth.
50/C5 Gendt, Neth.
50/D3 Genemuiden, Neth.
112/D3 General Acha, Arg.
112/D2 General Alvear, Arg.
112/F2 General Belgrano, Arg.
112/E2 General Cabrera, Arg.
112/B5 General Carrera (lake), Chile
113/F3 General Juan Madariaga, Arg.
113/S12 General Las Heras, Arg.
111/C1 General Martín Miguel de Güemes, Arg.
112/E2 General Pico, Arg.
111/D2 General Pinedo, Arg.
82/E6 General Santos, Phil.
63/J4 General-Toshevo, Bul.
112/E2 General Viamonte, Arg.
112/E2 General Villegas, Arg.
126/E3 Genesee (riv.), NY,US
123/L5 Geneseo, Il,US
126/E3 Geneseo, NY,US
129/G4 Geneva, Al,US
132/P16 Geneva, Il,US
125/H2 Geneva, Ne,US
126/E3 Geneva, NY,US
132/P14 Geneva (lake), Wi,US
54/C5 Geneva (Genève), Swi.
54/C5 Geneva (Léman) (lake), Fr., Swi.
54/C5 Genève (canton), Swi.
54/E1 Gengenbach, Ger.
66/E3 Genichesk, Ukr.
58/C4 Genil (riv.), Sp.
53/E2 Genk, Belg.
50/C5 Gennep, Neth.
57/H4 Genoa (Genova), It.
57/H4 Genoa (gulf), It.
52/C1 Gent-Brugge (can.), Belg.
86/C5 Genteng (cape), Indo.
52/C1 Gent (Ghent), Belg.
91/D2 George (lake), Austl.
90/C3 George (pt.), Austl.
119/K3 George (riv.), Qu,Can
102/C4 George, SAfr.
129/H4 George (lake), Fl,US
68/E1 George Land (isl.), Rus.
90/G9 Georges (riv.), Austl.
127/Q8 Georgetown, On,Can
116/E4 George Town (cap.), Cay.
108/G2 Georgetown (cap.), Guy.
129/H4 Georgetown, Ga,US
126/C4 Georgetown, Ky,US
129/J3 Georgetown, SC,US
128/D4 Georgetown, Tx,US
105/L George V (coast), Ant.
105/V George VI (sound), Ant.
128/D4 George West, Tx,US
67/G4 Georgia
122/B3 Georgia (str.), Can., US
129/G3 Georgia (state), US
126/D2 Georgian Bay Islands Nat'l Park, On,Can
63/H4 Georgi Traykov, Bul.
51/F4 Georgsmarienhütte, Ger.
48/G3 Gera, Ger.
52/C2 Geraardsbergen, Belg.
109/J6 Geral de Goiás (Espigão Mestre) (range), Braz.
89/A3 Geraldton, Austl.
126/C1 Geraldton, On,Can
56/F4 Gerbier de Jonc (mtn.), Fr.
51/H3 Gerdau (riv.), Ger.
130/H3 Gerdine (mtn.), Ak,US
63/L5 Gerede, Turk.
73/H2 Gereshk, Afg.
55/H2 Geretsried, Ger.
124/C2 Gerlach, Nv,US
49/L4 Gerlachovský Štít (peak), Slvk.
131/J7 Germantown, Md,US
129/F3 Germantown, Tn,US
48/E3 Germany
55/H1 Germering, Ger.
102/E2 Germiston, SAfr.
53/F3 Gerolstein, Ger.
59/G2 Gerona (Girona), Sp.
59/E1 Ger, Pic du (peak), Fr.
52/D3 Gerpinnes, Belg.
56/D5 Gers (riv.), Fr.
53/G5 Gersheim, Ger.
50/E5 Gescher, Ger.
51/F5 Geseke, Ger.
97/P6 Gestro Wenz (riv.), Eth.
58/D2 Getafe, Sp.
53/E2 Gete (riv.), Belg.
123/J4 Gettysburg, SD,US
110/A3 Getúlio Vargas, Braz.
105/S Getz Ice Shelf, Ant.
53/E2 Geul (riv.), Belg., Neth.
86/A3 Geureudong (peak), Indo.
74/E2 Gevaş, Turk.
51/E6 Gevelsberg, Ger.
62/F5 Gevgelija, FYROM
97/P5 Gewanē, Eth.
103/H6 Geyser (reef), Madg.
63/K5 Geyve, Turk.
75/B4 Gez (riv.), China

153
Ghad – Griqu

96/G1 **Ghadāmis**, Libya
100/C3 **Ghadir, Bi'r** (well), Egypt
99/E4 **Ghana**
104/D5 **Ghanzi**, Bots.
100/B5 **Gharb Binna**, Sudan
96/F1 **Ghardaïa**, Alg.
96/H1 **Gharyān**, Libya
96/H3 **Ghāt**, Libya
96/J5 **Ghazal** (riv.), Chad
84/C2 **Ghaziābād**, India
73/J2 **Ghaznī**, Afg.
74/K6 **Ghazzah** (Gaza), Gaza
76/G2 **Ghengis Khan Wall** (ruins), Mong.
52/C1 **Ghent** (Gent), Belg.
63/H2 **Gheorghe Gheorghiu-Dej**, Rom.
63/G2 **Gheorgheni**, Rom.
63/F2 **Gherla**, Rom.
112/C5 **Ghio** (lake), Arg.
84/A2 **Ghotki**, Pak.
73/H2 **Ghūrīān**, Afg.
83/D4 **Gia Nghia**, Viet.
102/E3 **Giant's Castle** (peak), SAfr.
60/D4 **Giarre**, It.
83/E3 **Gia Vuc**, Viet.
122/E2 **Gibbons**, Ab,Can
58/B4 **Gibraleón**, Sp.
58/B4 **Gibraltar** (str.), Afr., Eur.
127/R8 **Gibraltar** (pt.), On,Can
58/C4 **Gibraltar** (dpcy.), UK
132/F7 **Gibraltar**, Mi,US
91/E1 **Gibraltar Range Nat'l Park**, Austl.
92/B7 **Gibson** (des.), Austl.
128/D4 **Giddings**, Tx,US
100/C2 **Gidi** (pass), Egypt
97/N6 **Gīdolē**, Eth.
56/E3 **Gien**, Fr.
57/J2 **Giengen an der Brenz**, Ger.
56/F4 **Gier** (riv.), Fr.
57/H1 **Giessen**, Ger.
50/B5 **Giessendam**, Neth.
52/B6 **Gif**, Fr.
119/H1 **Gifford** (riv.), Nun.,Can
129/H5 **Gifford**, Fl,US
51/H4 **Gifhorn**, Ger.
79/E3 **Gifu**, Japan
79/E3 **Gifu** (pref.), Japan
45/F3 **Giggleswick**, Eng,UK
60/B1 **Giglio** (isl.), It.
58/C1 **Gijón**, Sp.
124/D4 **Gila** (riv.), Az, NM,US
124/D4 **Gila Bend**, Az,US
124/E4 **Gila Cliff Dwellings Nat'l Mon.**, NM,US
45/H4 **Gilberdyke Newport**, Eng,UK
90/A2 **Gilbert** (riv.), Austl.
92/G5 **Gilbert** (isls.), Kiri.
126/A2 **Gilbert**, Mn,US
112/C2 **Gil de Vilches Nat'l Park**, Chile
46/C3 **Gilfach Goch**, Wal,UK
44/B3 **Gilford**, NI,UK
131/F6 **Gilford Park**, NJ,US
73/K1 **Gilgit** (riv.), Pak.
123/G4 **Gillette**, Wy,US
122/B3 **Gillies Bay**, BC,Can
46/D4 **Gillingham**, Eng,UK
47/G4 **Gillingham**, Eng,UK
128/E3 **Gilmer**, Tx,US
73/K1 **Gilgit** (riv.), Pak.
77/K1 **Gilyuy** (riv.), Rus.
50/B5 **Gilze**, Neth.
97/N6 **Gīmbī**, Eth.
123/J3 **Gimli**, Mb,Can
59/F1 **Gimone** (riv.), Fr.
79/M9 **Ginan**, Japan
53/E2 **Gingelom**, Belg.
82/E6 **Gingoog**, Phil.
60/E2 **Ginosa**, It.
58/B1 **Ginzo de Limia**, Sp.
97/Q7 **Giohar**, Som.
60/D3 **Gioia** (gulf), It.
60/E2 **Gioia del Colle**, It.
60/D3 **Gioia Tauro**, It.
61/J3 **Gioŭra** (isl.), Gre.
47/G2 **Gipping** (riv.), Eng,UK
108/D3 **Girardot**, Col.
104/B4 **Giraul**, Ang.
74/D2 **Giresun**, Turk.
84/E3 **Girīdīh**, India
60/E3 **Girifalco**, It.
59/G2 **Girona** (Gerona), Sp.
56/C4 **Gironde** (riv.), Fr.
91/D1 **Girraween Nat'l Park**, Austl.
47/G2 **Girton**, Eng,UK
44/D1 **Girvan**, Sc,UK
44/D1 **Girvan, Water of** (riv.), Sc,UK
89/H6 **Gisborne**, NZ
52/A5 **Gisors**, Fr.
52/B1 **Gistel**, Belg.
101/A3 **Gitega**, Buru.
64/B2 **Gittsfjället** (peak), Swe.
55/F5 **Giubiasco**, Swi.
60/C1 **Giulianova**, It.
63/G4 **Giurgiu**, Rom.
63/G3 **Giurgiu** (co.), Rom.
74/M8 **Giv'atayim**, Isr.
53/D3 **Givet**, Fr.
56/F4 **Givors**, Fr.
53/D6 **Givry-en-Argonne**, Fr.
104/F5 **Giyani**, SAfr.
97/N6 **Giyon**, Eth.
100/B2 **Giza, Pyramids of** (Jīzah) (ruins), Egypt
69/R3 **Gizhiga** (bay), Rus.
49/L1 **Giżycko**, Pol.
61/G2 **Gjirokastër**, Alb.
42/D3 **Gjøvik**, Nor.
61/F2 **Gjuhëzës, Kep i** (cape), Alb.
127/K2 **Glace Bay**, NS,Can
122/D3 **Glacier**, BC,Can
122/C3 **Glacier** (peak), Wa,US
130/L4 **Glacier Bay Nat'l Park & Prsv.**, Ak,US
122/D3 **Glacier Nat'l Park**, Can., US
50/D5 **Gladbeck**, Ger.
90/C3 **Gladstone**, Austl.
126/C3 **Gladwin**, Mi,US
45/H3 **Glaisdale**, Eng,UK
53/G4 **Glan** (riv.), Ger.
82/E6 **Glan**, Phil.
46/C3 **Glanamman**, Wal,UK
52/D4 **Gland** (riv.), Fr.
55/F4 **Glarus** (canton), Swi.
55/E4 **Glarus Alps** (range), Swi.
46/C2 **Glasbury**, Wal,UK
43/C3 **Glasgow**, Sc,UK
126/C4 **Glasgow**, Ky,US
122/G3 **Glasgow**, Mt,US
44/D6 **Glaslyn** (riv.), Wal,UK
44/D3 **Glass** (riv.), IM,UK
128/D2 **Glass** (mts.), Ok,US
128/C4 **Glass** (mts.), Tx,US
131/K8 **Glassmanor-Oxon Hill**, Md,US
46/D4 **Glastonbury**, Eng,UK
65/M4 **Glazov**, Rus.
47/G2 **Glemsford**, Eng,UK
45/H6 **Glen** (riv.), Eng,UK
91/C3 **Glenaladale Nat'l Park**, Austl.
126/E4 **Glen Allen**, Va,US
44/C2 **Glenarm**, NI,UK
44/C2 **Glenarm** (riv.), NI,UK
44/B2 **Glenavy**, NI,UK
91/D2 **Glenbawn** (dam), Austl.
123/J3 **Glenboro**, Mb,Can
90/G8 **Glenbrook**, Austl.
131/K7 **Glen Burnie**, Md,US
124/E3 **Glen Canyon Nat'l Rec. Area**, Az, Ut,US
44/E1 **Glencaple**, Sc,UK
103/E3 **Glencoe**, SAfr.
132/Q15 **Glencoe**, Il,US
131/G5 **Glen Cove**, NY,US
124/D4 **Glendale**, Az,US
131/B2 **Glendale**, Ca,US
122/C5 **Glendale**, Or,US
132/P16 **Glendale Heights**, Il,US
123/G4 **Glendive**, Mt,US
125/F2 **Glendo** (res.), Wy,US
131/C2 **Glendora**, Ca,US
44/B1 **Glendun** (riv.), NI,UK
91/B3 **Glenelg** (riv.), Austl.
44/A2 **Glenelly** (riv.), NI,UK
44/D2 **Glenluce**, Sc,UK
43/C2 **Glen Mor** (val.), Sc,UK
131/E6 **Glenolden**, Pa,US
130/M4 **Glenora**, BC,Can
90/H8 **Glenorie**, Austl.
125/H4 **Glenpool**, Ok,US
128/D3 **Glen Rose**, Tx,US
126/F3 **Glens Falls**, NY,US
44/B2 **Glenshane** (pass), NI,UK
131/E5 **Glenside**, Pa,US
44/D1 **Glentrool**, Sc,UK
123/H4 **Glen Ullin**, ND,US
132/Q15 **Glenview**, Il,US
127/Q8 **Glen Williams**, On,Can
124/F3 **Glenwood Springs**, Co,US
61/L7 **Glifáda**, Gre.
51/H1 **Glinde**, Ger.
42/D3 **Glittertinden** (peak), Nor.
49/K3 **Gliwice**, Pol.
124/E4 **Globe**, Az,US
49/H5 **Gloggnitz**, Aus.
49/J3 **Głogów**, Pol.
49/J3 **Głogówek**, Pol.
42/D3 **Glomma** (riv.), Nor.
103/H5 **Glorieuses, Iles** (isls.), Reun.
90/E6 **Glorious** (mtn.), Austl.
130/D3 **Glory of Russia** (cape), Ak,US
45/G5 **Glossop**, Eng,UK
126/F2 **Gloucester**, On,Can
46/D3 **Gloucester**, Eng,UK
131/E6 **Gloucester City**, NJ,US
46/D3 **Gloucestershire** (co.), Eng,UK
46/D3 **Gloucester, Vale of** (val.), Eng,UK
127/L1 **Glovertown**, Nf,Can
49/K3 **Głowno**, Pol.
49/J3 **Głubczyce**, Pol.
49/J3 **Głuchołazy**, Pol.
48/E1 **Glücksburg**, Ger.
51/G1 **Glückstadt**, Ger.
66/E2 **Glukhov**, Ukr.
44/B4 **Glyde** (riv.), Ire.
46/C3 **Glyncorrwg**, Wal,UK
44/C2 **Glynn**, NI,UK
46/C3 **Glyn Neath**, Wal,UK
49/H4 **Gmünd**, Aus.
99/E3 **Gnagna** (prov.), Burk.
51/G2 **Gnarrenburg**, Ger.
49/J2 **Gniezno**, Pol.
62/E4 **Gnjilane**, Yugo.
46/D1 **Gnosall**, Eng,UK
78/C3 **Gō** (riv.), Japan
84/B4 **Goa** (state), India
84/F2 **Goālpāra**, India
43/C3 **Goat Fell** (mtn.), Sc,UK
45/H3 **Goathland**, Eng,UK
97/N6 **Goba**, Eth.
104/C5 **Gobabeb**, Namb.
76/E3 **Gobi** (des.), China, Mong.
78/D4 **Gobō**, Japan
45/E6 **Gobowen**, Eng,UK
50/D5 **Goch**, Ger.
83/D4 **Go Cong**, Viet.
47/F4 **Godalming**, Eng,UK
83/D4 **Go Dau Ha**, Viet.
84/D4 **Godāvari** (riv.), India
97/P6 **Godē**, Eth
62/F3 **Godeanu** (peak), Rom.
126/D3 **Goderich**, On,Can
84/B3 **Godhra**, India
47/F2 **Godmanchester**, Eng,UK
87/F4 **Godo** (mtn.), Indo.
79/M9 **Gōdo**, Japan
62/D2 **Gödöllő**, Hun.
46/A6 **Godolphin Cross**, Eng,UK
112/C3 **Godoy Cruz**, Arg.
123/K2 **Gods** (lake), Mb,Can
123/K2 **Gods** (riv.) Mb,Can
119/H2 **Gods Mercy** (bay), Nun.,Can
115/M3 **Godthåb** (Nuuk), Grld.
75/C4 **Godwin Austen** (K2) (peak), China, Pak.
126/E1 **Goéland** (lake), Qu,Can
50/A5 **Goerce**, Neth.
50/A6 **Goes**, Neth.
126/B2 **Gogebic** (range), Mi,US
84/D2 **Gogra** (riv.), India
51/G3 **Gohbach** (riv.), Ger.
109/M5 **Goiana**, Braz.
109/J7 **Goiânia**, Braz.
109/H7 **Goiás**, Braz.
110/B1 **Goiás** (state), Braz.
110/B1 **Goiatuba**, Braz.
50/C5 **Goirle**, Neth.
78/D3 **Gojō**, Japan
66/E4 **Gok** (riv.), Turk.
78/B4 **Gokase** (riv.), Japan
79/M9 **Gokashō**, Japan
63/G5 **Gökçeada** (isl.), Turk.
74/D2 **Göksun**, Turk.
74/K5 **Golan Heights** (reg.), Syria
74/C2 **Gölbaşı**, Turk.
74/D3 **Gölbaşı**, Turk.
45/F5 **Golborne**, Eng,UK
132/B2 **Gold** (mtn.) Wa,US
49/M1 **Gołdap**, Pol.
122/B5 **Gold Beach**, Or,US
90/D4 **Gold Coast**, Austl.
99/E5 **Gold Coast** (reg.), Gha.
122/D3 **Golden**, BC Can
125/F3 **Golden**, Co,US
122/C4 **Goldendale**, Wa,US
48/E3 **Goldene Aue** (reg.), Ger.
132/J11 **Golden Gate** (chan.), Ca,US
102/E3 **Golden Gate Highlands Nat'l Park**, SAfr.
122/B3 **Golden Hinde** (peak), BC,Can
51/F3 **Goldenstedt**, Ger.
124/C3 **Goldfield**, Nv,US
122/B3 **Gold River**, BC,Can
129/J3 **Goldsboro**, NC,US
128/D4 **Goldthwaite**, Tx,US
74/E2 **Göle**, Turk.
49/H2 **Goleniów**, Pol.
74/B3 **Gölhisar**, Turk.
128/D4 **Goliad**, Tx,US
74/D2 **Gölköy**, Turk.
76/C4 **Golmud**, China
72/F2 **Golpāyegān**, Iran
63/K5 **Gölpazarı**, Turk.
49/K2 **Golub-Dobrzyń**, Pol.
63/H4 **Golyama Kamchiya** (riv.), Bul.
63/G5 **Golyama Syutkya** (peak), Bul.
63/G5 **Golyam Perelik** (peak), Bul.
101/A3 **Goma**, D.R. Congo
59/X16 **Gomera** (isl.), Canl.
52/B6 **Gometz-le-Châtel**, Fr.
117/P8 **Gómez Palacio**, Mex.
48/F2 **Gommern**, Ger.
47/F4 **Gomshall**, Eng,UK
73/G2 **Gonābād**, Iran
104/F5 **Gonarezhou Nat'l Park**, Zim.
117/G4 **Gonâve** (gulf), Haiti
73/G1 **Gonbad-e Qābūs**, Iran
84/D2 **Gonda**, India
84/B3 **Gondal**, India
97/N5 **Gonder**, Eth.
84/D3 **Gondia**, India
58/A2 **Gondomar**, Port.
58/A1 **Gondomar**, Sp.
63/H5 **Gönen**, Turk.
85/F2 **Gongbo'gyamda**, China
85/H2 **Gongga** (peak), China
76/E4 **Gonghe**, China
99/H4 **Gongola** (riv.), Nga.
99/H4 **Gongola** (state), Nga.
91/C1 **Gongolgon**, Austl.
81/F2 **Gongzhuling**, China
128/D4 **Gonzales**, Tx US
116/B3 **González**, Mex.
105/J **Goodenough** (cape), Ant.
102/B4 **Good Hope, Cape of** (cape), SAfr.
122/E5 **Gooding**, Id,US
125/G3 **Goodland**, Ks,US
90/E7 **Goodna**, Austl.
46/B3 **Goodwick**, Wal,UK
102/B4 **Goodwood**, SAfr.
50/C4 **Gooimeer** (lake), Neth.
45/H4 **Goole**, Eng,UK
50/D4 **Goor**, Neth.
123/H2 **Goose** (lake), Mb,Can
120/B3 **Goose** (lake), Ca, Or,US
119/K3 **Goose Bay-Happy Valley**, Nf,Can
45/F5 **Goostrey**, Eng,UK
57/H2 **Göppingen**, Ger.
83/D4 **Go Quao**, Viet.
49/J3 **Góra**, Pol.
49/L3 **Góra Kalwaria**, Pol.
84/D2 **Gorakhpur**, India
62/D4 **Goražde**, Bosn.
116/E5 **Gorda** (pt.), Nic.
124/A2 **Gorda** (pt.), Ca,US
91/C4 **Gordon** (lake), Austl.
96/J6 **Goré**, Chad
97/N6 **Gorē**, Eth.
47/G1 **Gore** (pt.), Eng,UK
130/H4 **Gore** (pt.), Ak,US
74/D2 **Görele**, Turk.
56/B2 **Gorey**, Chl,UK
73/F1 **Gorgān**, Iran
53/F4 **Gorge du Loup**, Lux.
98/B3 **Gorgol** (reg.), Mrta.
98/B2 **Gorgol** (riv.), Mrta.
67/H4 **Gori**, Geo.
50/B5 **Gorinchem**, Neth.
47/E3 **Goring**, Eng,UK
47/F5 **Goring by Sea**, Eng,UK
57/K4 **Gorizia**, It.
63/F3 **Gorj** (co.), Rom.
66/D1 **Gorki**, Bela.
64/J4 **Gor'kiy** (res.), Rus.
65/K4 **Gor'kiy** (Nizhniy Novgorod), Rus.
49/L4 **Gorlice**, Pol.
49/H3 **Görlitz**, Ger.
46/C2 **Gorllwyn** (mtn.), Wal,UK
44/B4 **Gormanston**, Ire.
127/R8 **Gormley**, On,Can
63/G4 **Gorna Oryakhovitsa**, Bul.
62/E3 **Gornji Milanovac**, Yugo.
62/C4 **Gornji Vakuf**, Bosn.
68/J4 **Gorno-Altay Aut. Obl.**, Rus.
75/E1 **Gorno-Altaysk**, Rus.
68/H6 **Gorno-Badakhstan Aut. Obl.**, Taj.
65/J4 **Gorodets**, Rus.
92/D5 **Goroka**, PNG
87/H4 **Gorong** (isl.), Indo.
87/G3 **Gorontalo**, Indo.
46/B3 **Gorseinon**, Wal,UK
50/D4 **Gorssel**, Neth.
44/A2 **Gortin**, NI,UK
66/C2 **Goryn'** (riv.), Bela., Ukr.
49/H2 **Gorzów** (prov.), Pol.
49/H2 **Gorzów Wielkopolski**, Pol.
78/D3 **Gōse**, Japan
79/F2 **Gosen**, Japan
45/G2 **Gosforth**, Eng,UK
77/N3 **Goshogawara**, Japan
51/H5 **Goslar**, Ger.
62/B3 **Gospić**, Cro.
47/E5 **Gosport**, Eng,UK
62/E5 **Gostivar**, FYROM
49/J3 **Gostyń**, Pol.
49/K2 **Gostynin**, Pol.
42/D4 **Göteborg**, Swe.
42/D4 **Göteborg och Bohus** (co.), Swe.
96/H6 **Gotel** (mts.), Camr., Nga.
79/F3 **Gotemba**, Japan
51/H7 **Gotha**, Ger.
125/G2 **Gothenburg**, Ne,US
42/F4 **Gotland** (isl.), Swe.
78/A4 **Gotō** (isls.), Japan
63/F5 **Gotse Delchev**, Bul.
42/F4 **Gotska Sandön Nat'l Park**, Swe.
78/C3 **Gōtsu**, Japan
51/G5 **Göttingen**, Ger.
50/B4 **Gouda**, Neth.
38/J8 **Gough** (isl.), StH.
126/F1 **Gouin** (res.), Qu,Can
126/C2 **Goulais** (riv.), On,Can
91/D2 **Goulburn**, Austl.
91/D2 **Goulburn** (riv.), Austl.
105/P **Goulburn** (coast), Ant.
128/F3 **Gould**, Ar,US
98/E2 **Goundam**, Mali
99/H3 **Gouré**, Niger
102/C4 **Gourits** (riv.), SAfr.
99/F3 **Gourma** (prov.), Burk.
99/F3 **Gourma** (reg.), Burk.
99/E2 **Gourma-Rharous**, Mali
52/A5 **Gournay-en-Bray**, Fr.
97/J4 **Gouro**, Chad
74/D2 **Goušu** (riv.), Turk.
110/D1 **Gouvêa**, Braz.
52/B5 **Gouvieux**, Fr.
66/C2 **Goverla** (peak), Ukr.
110/D1 **Governador Valadares**, Braz.
76/D3 **Govī Altayn** (mts.), Mong.
73/H3 **Gowd-e-Zereh** (lake), Afg.
46/B3 **Gower** (pen.), Wal,UK
45/H4 **Goxhill**, Eng.UK
111/E2 **Goya**, Arg.
45/F5 **Goyt** (riv.), Eng,UK
79/M9 **Gozaisho-yama** (peak), Japan
75/D4 **Gozha** (lake), China
60/D4 **Gozo** (isl.), Malta
102/D4 **Graaff-Reinet**, SAfr.
50/D4 **Graafschap** (reg.), Neth.
102/B2 **Graberberg** (peak), Namb.
48/F2 **Grabow**, Ger.
62/B3 **Gračac**, Cro.
62/D3 **Gračanica**, Bosn.
129/G4 **Graceville**, Fl,US
116/E5 **Gracias a Dios** (cape), Nic.
59/S12 **Graciosa** (isl.), Azor.,Port.
62/D3 **Gradačac**, Bosn.
109/H5 **Gradaús**, Braz.
58/B1 **Grado**, Sp.
47/F2 **Grafham Water** (lake), Eng,UK
91/E1 **Grafton**, Austl.
90/B2 **Grafton** (passg.), Austl.
123/J3 **Grafton**, ND,US
126/D4 **Grafton**, WV,US
118/C3 **Graham** (isl.), BC,Can
119/S7 **Graham** (isl.), Nun.,Can
117/N7 **Graham** (peak), Az.,US
128/D3 **Graham**, Tx,US
132/C3 **Graham**, Wa,US
68/G1 **Graham Bell** (isl.), Rus.
105/V **Graham Land** (reg.), Ant.
102/D4 **Grahamstown**, SAfr.
47/G4 **Grain**, Eng,UK
98/C5 **Grain Coast** (reg.), Libr.
109/J5 **Grajaú**, Braz.
109/J4 **Grajaú** (riv.), Braz.
49/M2 **Grajewo**, Pol.
56/D4 **Gramat** (plat.), Fr.
43/C2 **Grampian** (mts.), Sc,UK
91/B3 **Grampians Nat'l Park**, Austl.
50/D3 **Gramsbergen**, Neth.
42/D3 **Gran**, Nor.
108/D3 **Granada**, Col.
116/D5 **Granada**, Nic.
58/D4 **Granada**, Sp.
113/K7 **Gran Altiplanicie Central** (plat.), Arg.
113/K7 **Gran Bajo de San Julián** (val.), Arg.
112/C5 **Gran Bajo Oriental** (val.), Arg.
128/D3 **Granbury**, Tx,US
125/F2 **Granby**, Co,US
59/X17 **Gran Canaria** (isl.), Canl.
107/C5 **Gran Chaco** (plain), SAm.
127/H2 **Grand** (lake), NB,Can
127/K1 **Grand** (lake), Nf,Can
119/J3 **Grand** (riv.), Qu,Can
81/D4 **Grand** (can.), China
44/B5 **Grand** (can.), Ire.
124/D3 **Grand** (canyon), Az,US
125/J3 **Grand** (riv.), Ia, Mo,US
125/J5 **Grand** (lake), La,US
126/C2 **Grand** (isl.), Mi,US
128/E2 **Grand** (riv.), Mo,US
127/S9 **Grand** (isl.), NY,US
123/H4 **Grand** (riv.), SD,US
117/F2 **Grand Bahama** (isl.), Bahm.
127/L2 **Grand Bank**, Nf,Can
98/C5 **Grand Bassa** (co.), Libr.
98/E5 **Grand-Bassam**, IvC.
127/H2 **Grand Bay**, NB,Can
132/E6 **Grand Blanc**, Mi,US
124/D3 **Grand Canyon Nat'l Park**, Az,US
98/C5 **Grand Cape Mount** (co.), Libr.
116/E4 **Grand Cayman** (isl.), Cay.
122/F2 **Grand Centre**, Ab,Can
122/D4 **Grand Coulee** (dam), Wa,US
113/K7 **Grande** (bay), Arg.
113/K8 **Grande** (riv.), Arg.
108/F7 **Grande** (riv.), Bol.
110/K8 **Grande** (isl.), Braz.
110/J7 **Grande** (riv.), Braz.
117/F6 **Grande** (pt.), Pan.
113/T11 **Grande** (stream), Uru.
122/D2 **Grande Cache**, Ab,Can
103/G5 **Grande Comore** (isl.), Com.
60/C1 **Grande, Corno** (peak), It.
109/H4 **Grande de Gurupá**, Braz.
60/C4 **Grande, Monte** (peak), It.
122/D2 **Grande Prairie**, Ab,Can
96/H4 **Grand 'Erg de Bilma** (des.), Niger
96/E1 **Grand Erg Occidental** (des.), Alg.
96/G1 **Grand Erg Oriental** (des.), Alg.
128/C4 **Grande, Río** (riv.), Mex., US
52/B1 **Grande-Synthe**, Fr.
117/J4 **Grande-Terre** (isl.), Guad.
127/H2 **Grand Falls**, NB,Can
127/L1 **Grand Falls**, Nf,Can
122/D3 **Grand Forks**, BC,Can
123/J4 **Grand Forks**, ND,US
52/B2 **Grand-Fort-Philippe**, Fr.
126/C3 **Grand Haven**, Mi,US
125/H2 **Grand Island**, Ne,US
129/F4 **Grand Isle**, La,US
98/D5 **Grand Jide** (co.), Libr.
124/E3 **Grand Junction**, Co,US
125/J3 **Grand Lake O'The Cherokees** (lake), Ok,US
127/H2 **Grand Manan** (isl.), NB,Can
123/L4 **Grand Marais**, Mn,US
52/C6 **Grand Marin** (riv.), Fr.
127/F2 **Grand-Mère**, Qu,Can
127/K2 **Grand Miquelon** (isl.), StP.
54/C5 **Grand Mont Ruan** (mtn.), Fr.
58/A3 **Grândola**, Port.
123/L4 **Grand Portage Nat'l Mon.**, Mn,US
53/D5 **Grandpré**, Fr.
123/J2 **Grand Rapids**, Mb,Can
126/C3 **Grand Rapids**, Mi,US
123/K4 **Grand Rapids**, Mn,US
56/F5 **Grand Rhône** (riv.), Fr.
122/F5 **Grand Teton Nat'l Park**, Wy,US
117/G3 **Grand Turk**, Trks.
47/F3 **Grand Union** (can.), Eng,UK
123/H3 **Grandview**, Mb,Can
122/D4 **Grandview**, Wa,US
112/C2 **Graneros**, Chile
42/E3 **Granfjället** (peak), Swe.
45/F3 **Grange**, Eng,UK
130/L3 **Granger** (mtn.), Yk,Can
122/D4 **Grangeville**, Id,US
122/B2 **Granisle**, BC,Can
122/F4 **Granite** (peak), Mt,US
126/B4 **Granite City**, Il,US
109/K4 **Granja**, Braz.
112/D5 **Gran Laguna Salada** (lake), Arg.
59/G2 **Granollers**, Sp.
57/G4 **Gran Paradiso Nat'l Park**, It.
57/J3 **Gran Pilastro** (peak), It.
59/Y16 **Gran Tarajal**, Canl.,Sp.
45/H6 **Grantham**, Eng,UK
43/D2 **Grantown-on-Spey**, Sc,UK
124/F4 **Grants**, NM,US
126/A2 **Grantsburg**, Wi,US
122/C5 **Grants Pass**, Or,US
108/C5 **Gran Vilaya** (ruins), Peru
123/H1 **Granville** (lake), Mb,Can
56/C2 **Granville**, Fr.
132/B3 **Grapeview-Allyn**, Wa,US
51/F2 **Grasberg**, Ger.
45/E3 **Grasmere**, Eng,UK
57/G5 **Grasse**, Fr.
127/Q9 **Grassie**, On,Can
45/G3 **Grassington**, Eng,UK
122/G3 **Grasslands Nat'l Park**, Sk,Can
62/B2 **Gratkorn**, Aus.
55/F4 **Graubünden** (canton), Swi.
56/E5 **Graulhet**, Fr.
50/C5 **Grave**, Neth.
122/G3 **Gravelbourg**, Sk,Can
52/B2 **Gravelines**, Fr.
126/E2 **Gravenhurst**, On,Can
47/G4 **Gravesend**, Eng,UK
52/A5 **Gravigny**, Fr.
60/E2 **Gravina di Puglia**, It.
117/G4 **Gravois** (pt.), Haiti
56/B3 **Gray**, Fr.
126/C2 **Grayling**, Mi,US
47/G4 **Grays**, Eng,UK
122/F5 **Grays** (lake), Id,US
122/B4 **Grays** (har.), Wa,US
132/P15 **Grayslake**, Il,US
123/H3 **Grayson**, Sk,Can
57/L3 **Graz**, Aus.
91/C4 **Great** (lake), Austl.
123/G3 **Great** (plains), Can., US
38/E3 **Great** (lakes), NAm.
124/C2 **Great** (basin), US
117/F2 **Great Abaco** (isl.), Bahm.
49/L5 **Great Alföld** (plain), Hun.
89/B4 **Great Australian** (bight), Austl.
117/F3 **Great Bahama** (bank), Bahm.
47/F2 **Great Barford**, Eng,UK
90/B2 **Great Barrier Reef Marine Park**, Austl.
47/G2 **Great Barton**, Eng,UK
124/D3 **Great Basin Nat'l Park**, Nv,US
118/D2 **Great Bear** (lake), NW,Can
125/H3 **Great Bend**, Ks,US
102/C3 **Great Brak** (riv.), SAfr.
43/E3 **Great Britain** (isl.), UK
39/P5 **Great Coco** (isl.), Myan.
47/G2 **Great Cornard**, Eng,UK
122/F5 **Great Divide** (basin), Wyo,US
91/B3 **Great Dividing** (range), Austl.
45/H4 **Great Driffield**, Eng,UK
47/G3 **Great Dunmow**, Eng,UK
99/F5 **Greater Accra** (reg.), Gha.
117/G4 **Greater Antilles** (arch.), NAm.
67/L3 **Greater Barsuki** (des.), Kaz.
47/F3 **Greater London** (co.), Eng,UK
45/F5 **Greater Manchester** (co.), Eng,UK
86/C4 **Greater Sunda** (isls.), Indo.
117/F3 **Great Exuma** (isl.), Bahm.
122/F4 **Great Falls**, Mt,US
102/D4 **Great Fish** (pt.), SAfr.
102/D4 **Great Fish** (riv.), SAfr.
47/F2 **Great Gransden**, Eng,UK
117/F3 **Great Guana Cay** (isl.), Bahm.
45/G2 **Greatham**, Eng,UK
45/F4 **Great Harwood**, Eng,UK
84/D2 **Great Himalaya** (range), Asia
117/G3 **Great Inagua** (isl.), Bahm.
84/A2 **Great Indian** (des.), India, Pak.
102/C3 **Great Karoo** (reg.), SAfr.
102/D4 **Great Kei** (riv.), SAfr.
46/D2 **Great Malvern**, Eng,UK
47/E3 **Great Milton**, Eng,UK
46/B5 **Great Mis Tor** (hill), Eng,UK
131/G5 **Great Neck**, NY,US
85/F6 **Great Nicobar** (isl.), India
47/G1 **Great Ouse** (riv.), Eng,UK
91/C4 **Great Oyster** (bay), Austl.
129/J3 **Great Pee Dee** (riv.), SC,US
101/A4 **Great Rift** (val.), Afr.
101/B4 **Great Ruaha** (riv.), Tanz.
124/D2 **Great Salt** (lake), Ut,US
124/D2 **Great Salt Lake** (des.), Ut,US
125/F3 **Great Sand Dunes Nat'l Mon.**, Co,US
100/A3 **Great Sand Sea** (des.), Egypt, Libya
92/B6 **Great Sandy** (des.), Austl.
124/B2 **Great Sandy** (des.), Or,US
90/D4 **Great Sandy Nat'l Park**, Austl.
98/B4 **Great Scarcies** (riv.), Gui., SLeo.
47/G2 **Great Shelford**, Eng,UK
45/F3 **Great Shunner Fell** (mtn.), Eng,UK
118/E2 **Great Slave** (lake), NW,Can
129/H3 **Great Smoky Mts. Nat'l Park**, NC, Tn,US
131/G5 **Great South** (bay), NY,US
47/G4 **Great Stour** (riv.), Eng,UK
83/B3 **Great Tenasserim** (riv.), Myan.
46/B5 **Great Torrington**, Eng,UK
92/B7 **Great Victoria** (des.), Austl.
81/B3 **Great Wall** (ruins), China
91/C4 **Great Western Tiers** (mts.), Austl.
102/B4 **Great Winterhoek** (peak), SAfr.
46/D2 **Great Witley**, Eng,UK
47/H1 **Great Yarmouth**, Eng,UK
74/F3 **Great Zab** (riv.), Iraq, Turk.
104/F5 **Great Zimbabwe** (ruins), Zim.
99/H2 **Grébon** (peak), Niger
74/K4 **Greco** (cape), Cyp.
60/D2 **Greco** (peak), It.
58/C2 **Gredos** (range), Sp.
41/G5 **Greece**
125/F2 **Greeley**, Co,US
119/S6 **Greely** (fjord), Nun.,Can
91/D3 **Green** (cape), Austl.
126/C4 **Green** (riv.), Ky,US
123/M4 **Green** (bay), Mi, Wi,US
124/E3 **Green** (riv.), Ut, Wy,US
127/G3 **Green** (mts.), Vt,US
126/B2 **Green Bay**, Wi,US
131/K7 **Greenbelt**, Md,US
126/C4 **Greencastle**, In,US
129/H4 **Green Cove Springs**, Fl,US
132/Q14 **Greendale**, Wi,US
129/H2 **Greeneville**, Tn,US
126/C4 **Greenfield**, In,US
127/F3 **Greenfield**, Ma,US
132/P14 **Greenfield**, Wi,US
127/P7 **Greenfield Park**, Qu,Can
131/K7 **Green Haven**, Md,US
44/C2 **Greenisland**, NI,UK
115/R2 **Greenland** (sea)
115/N2 **Greenland** (Kalaallit Nunaat) (dpcy.), Den.
43/D3 **Greenlaw**, Sc,UK
43/C3 **Greenock**, Sc,UK
130/K2 **Greenough** (mtn.), Ak,US
127/R8 **Green River**, On,Can
124/E3 **Green River**, Ut,US
122/F5 **Green River**, Wy,US
129/G3 **Greensboro**, Al,US
129/J2 **Greensboro**, NC,US
126/C4 **Greensburg**, In,US
126/E3 **Greensburg**, Pa,US
127/Q9 **Greensville**, On,Can
124/E5 **Green Valley**, Az,US
131/J7 **Green Valley**, Md,US
98/C5 **Greenville**, Libr.
129/G4 **Greenville**, Al,US
124/B2 **Greenville**, Ca,US
126/C4 **Greenville**, Ky,US
126/C3 **Greenville**, Mi,US
129/F3 **Greenville**, Ms,US
129/J3 **Greenville**, NC,US
126/C3 **Greenville**, Oh,US
129/H3 **Greenville**, SC,US
128/D3 **Greenville**, Tx,US
132/D3 **Greenwater** (riv.), Wa,US
131/G4 **Greenwich**, Ct,US
127/R8 **Greenwood**, On,Can
129/F3 **Greenwood**, Ms,US
131/F4 **Greenwood** (lake), NJ, NY,US
129/H3 **Greenwood**, SC,US
129/H3 **Greenwood** (lake), SC,US
125/J4 **Greers Ferry** (lake), Ar,US
44/B6 **Greese** (riv.), Ire.
50/D6 **Grefrath**, Ger.
108/D5 **Gregório** (riv.), Braz.
90/A2 **Gregory** (range), Austl.
123/J5 **Gregory**, SD,US
49/G1 **Greifswald**, Ger.
49/G1 **Greifswalder Bodden** (bay), Ger.
62/B2 **Greimberg** (peak), Aus.
48/G3 **Greiz**, Ger.
65/N4 **Gremyachinsk**, Rus.
42/D4 **Grenå**, Den.
117/J5 **Grenada**
129/F3 **Grenada**, Ms,US
54/D3 **Grenchen**, Swi.
123/H3 **Grenfell**, Sk,Can
56/F4 **Grenoble**, Fr.
42/E2 **Gressåmoen Nat'l Park**, Nor.
45/E2 **Greta** (riv.), Eng,UK
45/F3 **Greta** (riv.), Eng,UK
123/J3 **Gretna**, Mb,Can
45/E2 **Gretna**, Sc,UK
129/F4 **Gretna**, La,US
47/F1 **Gretton**, Eng,UK
52/B6 **Gretz-Armainvilliers**, Fr.
50/B5 **Grevelingendam** (dam), Neth.
51/E4 **Greven**, Ger.
61/G2 **Grevená**, Gre.
50/D6 **Grevenbroich**, Ger.
53/F4 **Grevenmacher** (dist.), Lux.
48/F2 **Grevesmühlen**, Ger.
50/A5 **Grevlingen** (chan.), Neth.
90/A5 **Grey** (range), Austl.
127/K2 **Grey** (riv.), Nf,Can
44/C2 **Grey** (pt.), NI,UK
44/C2 **Grey Abbey**, NI,UK
122/F4 **Greybull**, Wy,US
130/L3 **Grey Hunter** (peak), Yk,Can
89/H7 **Greymouth**, NZ
90/B2 **Grey Peaks Nat'l Park**, Austl.
45/F2 **Greystoke**, Eng,UK
44/B5 **Greystones**, Ire.
103/E3 **Greytown**, SAfr.
53/D2 **Grez-Doiceau**, Belg.
46/B6 **Gribbin** (pt.), Eng,UK
50/C2 **Griend** (isl.), Neth.
129/G3 **Griffin**, Ga,US
91/C2 **Griffith**, Austl.
132/R16 **Griffith**, In,US
52/B6 **Grigny**, Fr.
91/C4 **Grim** (cape), Austl.
53/D2 **Grimbergen**, Belg.
46/D2 **Grimley**, Eng,UK
48/G1 **Grimmen**, Ger.
127/Q9 **Grimsby**, On,Can
45/H4 **Grimsby**, Eng,UK
42/N6 **Grimsey** (isl.), Ice.
42/D4 **Grimstad**, Nor.
119/S7 **Grinnel** (pen.), Nun.,Can
62/B2 **Grintavec** (peak), Slov.
102/E3 **Griqualand East** (reg.), SAfr.
102/C2 **Griqualand West** (reg.), SAfr.

52/A2 **Gris Nez** (cape), Fr.
132/K10 **Grizzly** (bay), Ca,US
62/C3 **Grmeč** (mtn.), Bosn.
53/D1 **Grobbendonk,** Belg.
49/J3 **Grodków,** Pol.
49/J2 **Grodzisk Wielkopolski,** Pol.
50/D4 **Groenlo,** Neth.
128/D4 **Groesbeck,** Tx,US
50/C5 **Groesbeek,** Neth.
56/B3 **Groix** (isl.), Fr.
49/L3 **Grójec,** Pol.
48/F1 **Grömitz,** Ger.
50/E4 **Gronau,** Ger.
50/D2 **Groningen,** Neth.
50/D2 **Groningen** (prov.), Neth.
55/H5 **Gronlait** (peak), It.
102/C4 **Groot** (riv.), SAfr.
50/D2 **Grootegast,** Neth.
104/C4 **Grootfontein,** Namb.
102/D2 **Groot-Marico** (riv.), SAfr.
102/C3 **Grootvloer** (salt pan), SAfr.
117/J5 **Gros Islet,** StL.
127/K1 **Gros Morne** (peak), Nf,Can
127/K1 **Gros Morne Nat'l Park,** Nf,Can
56/F3 **Grosne** (riv.), Fr.
51/G6 **Grossalmerode,** Ger.
51/E3 **Grosse Aa** (riv.), Ger.
132/F7 **Grosse Ile,** Mi,US
102/A2 **Grosse Münzenberg** (peak), Namb.
53/G2 **Grosse Nister** (riv.), Ger.
51/F3 **Grossenkneten,** Ger.
132/G7 **Grosse Pointe,** Mi,US
132/G7 **Grosse Pointe Farms,** Mi,US
132/G7 **Grosse Pointe Park,** Mi,US
132/G7 **Grosse Pointe Shores,** Mi,US
132/G7 **Grosse Pointe Woods,** Mi,US
57/K2 **Grosser Arber** (peak), Ger.
51/G3 **Grosser Aue** (riv.), Ger.
48/F3 **Grosser Beer-Berg** (peak), Ger.
57/L3 **Grosser Bösenstein** (peak), Aus.
51/F1 **Grosser Knechtsand** (isl.), Ger.
49/H4 **Grosser Peilstein** (peak), Aus.
57/L3 **Grosser Priel** (peak), Aus.
49/H5 **Grosser Pyhrgas** (peak), Aus.
57/K2 **Grosser Rachel** (peak), Ger.
51/E2 **Grosses Meer** (lake), Ger.
62/A2 **Grosses Wiesbachhorn** (peak), Aus.
60/B1 **Grosseto,** It.
57/H2 **Grossgerau,** Ger.
57/K3 **Grossglockner** (peak), Aus.
51/H1 **Grosshansdorf,** Ger.
57/H5 **Grosso** (cape), Fr.
53/F5 **Grossrosseln,** Ger.
53/E2 **Grote Gete** (riv.), Belg.
53/D1 **Grote Nete** (riv.), Belg.
123/J4 **Groton,** SD,US
60/E2 **Grottaglie,** It.
53/E3 **Grotte de Han,** Belg.
59/E1 **Grottes de Bétharram,** Fr.
122/D2 **Grouard Mission,** Ab,Can
126/D1 **Groundhog** (riv.), On,Can
50/C2 **Grouw,** Neth.
47/E3 **Grove,** Eng,UK
125/J3 **Grove,** Ok,US
124/B4 **Grover City,** Ca,US
128/E4 **Groves,** Tx,US
131/J8 **Groveton,** Va,US
67/H4 **Groznyy,** Rus.
63/H4 **Grudovo,** Bul.
49/K2 **Grudziądz,** Pol.
45/E2 **Grune** (pt.), Eng,UK
66/F1 **Gryazi,** Rus.
49/H2 **Gryfice,** Pol.
49/H2 **Gryfino,** Pol.
112/B4 **Guabun** (pt.), Chile
117/F3 **Guacanayabo** (gulf), Cuba
110/D2 **Guaçuí,** Braz.
117/P9 **Guadalajara,** Mex.
58/D2 **Guadalajara,** Sp.
92/E6 **Guadalcanal** (isl.), Sol.
58/E4 **Guadalentín** (riv.), Sp.
58/D3 **Guadalimlar** (riv.), Sp.
59/N8 **Guadalix** (riv.), Sp.
59/E2 **Guadalope** (riv.), Sp.
58/D4 **Guadalquivir** (riv.), Sp.
117/F6 **Guadalupe,** Pan.
58/C3 **Guadalupe** (range), Sp.
128/B4 **Guadalupe** (peak), Tx,US
128/D4 **Guadalupe** (riv.), Tx,US
128/B4 **Guadalupe Mts. Nat'l Park,** Tx,US
59/M8 **Guadarrama** (pass), Sp.
58/C2 **Guadarrama** (range), Sp.
58/C3 **Guadarrama** (riv.), Sp.
117/J4 **Guadeloupe** (dpcy.), Fr.
117/J4 **Guadeloupe** (passage), NAm.
58/B4 **Guadiana** (riv.), Sp., Port.
58/D4 **Guadiana Menor** (riv.), Sp.
58/D4 **Guadix,** Sp.
112/B4 **Guafo** (chan.), Chile
112/B4 **Guafo** (isl.), Chile
110/B4 **Guaíba,** Braz.
110/B4 **Guaiba** (riv.), Braz.
108/F2 **Guaiquinima** (peak), Ven.
110/B2 **Guaíra,** Braz.
112/B4 **Guaiteca** (isl.), Chile
108/E6 **Guajará-Mirim,** Braz.
117/G5 **Guajira** (pen.), Col., Ven.
124/B3 **Gualala,** Ca,US
60/C1 **Gualdo Tadino,** It.
112/F2 **Gualeguay,** Arg.
112/F2 **Gualeguay** (riv.), Arg.
112/F2 **Gualeguaychú,** Arg.
112/D4 **Gualicho** (val.), Arg.
92/D3 **Guam** (isl.), PacUS
112/B5 **Guamblin** (isl.), Chile
110/K7 **Guanabara** (bay), Braz.
116/A3 **Guanajuato,** Mex.
116/A3 **Guanajuato** (state), Mex.
109/K6 **Guanambi,** Braz.
117/H6 **Guanare,** Ven.
117/H6 **Guanare** (riv.), Ven.
81/C3 **Guancen Shan** (mtn.), China
81/B3 **Guandi Shan** (mtn.), China
85/K3 **Guangdong** (prov.), China
81/D5 **Guangming Ding** (peak), China
85/J3 **Guangxi Zhuangzu Zizhiqu** (aut. reg.), China
82/C2 **Guangze,** China
82/B3 **Guangzhou** (Canton), China
110/D1 **Guanhães,** Braz.
117/J6 **Guanipa** (riv.), Ven.
117/F3 **Guantánamo,** Cuba
81/G6 **Guanting** (res.), China
81/D4 **Guanyun,** China
110/B4 **Guaporé,** Braz.
108/F6 **Guaporé** (riv.), Braz.
59/E1 **Guara** (peak), Sp.
109/L5 **Guarabira,** Braz.
109/J5 **Guaraí,** Braz.
110/B3 **Guaramirim,** Braz.
108/C4 **Guaranda,** Ecu.
110/D2 **Guarapari,** Braz.
110/B3 **Guarapuava,** Braz.
110/B2 **Guararapes,** Braz.
110/G8 **Guararema,** Braz.
110/H7 **Guaratinguetá,** Braz.
110/B3 **Guaratuba,** Braz.
58/B2 **Guarda,** Port.
58/B2 **Guarda** (dist.), Port.
58/B3 **Guareña,** Sp.
108/E2 **Guárico** (res.), Ven.
117/H6 **Guárico** (riv.), Ven.
110/G9 **Guarujá,** Braz.
110/G8 **Guarulhos,** Braz.
117/N8 **Guasave,** Mex.
116/C4 **Guatemala**
116/C5 **Guatemala** (cap.), Guat.
110/G6 **Guaxupé,** Braz.
117/H4 **Guayama,** PR
108/C4 **Guayaquil,** Ecu.
108/B4 **Guayaquil** (gulf), Ecu.
108/E6 **Guayaramerín,** Bol.
117/M8 **Guaymas,** Mex.
65/N4 **Gubakha,** Rus.
49/H3 **Guben,** Ger.
49/H3 **Gubin,** Pol.
66/F2 **Gubkin,** Rus.
76/E2 **Guchin-Us,** Mong.
59/E2 **Gúdar** (range), Sp.
51/G6 **Gudensberg,** Ger.
67/H4 **Gudermes,** Rus.
84/D4 **Gudivāda,** India
84/C5 **Gūdūr,** India
58/D1 **Guecho,** Sp.
98/B1 **Guelb Azefal** (mts.), Mrta.
126/D3 **Guelph,** On,Can
96/C2 **Guelta Zemmur,** WSah.
53/F5 **Guénange,** Fr.
56/B3 **Guérande,** Fr.
56/D3 **Guéret,** Fr.
58/D1 **Guernica y Luno,** Sp.
56/B2 **Guernsey** (isl.), Chl,UK
116/B4 **Guerrero** (state), Mex.
56/F3 **Gueugnon,** Fr.
99/H3 **Guézaoua,** Niger
97/N6 **Gugē** (peak), Eth.
92/D3 **Guguan** (isl.), NMar.
82/B3 **Gui** (riv.), China
59/X16 **Guía de Isora,** Sp.
108/F2 **Guiana Highlands** (mts.), SAm.
116/B4 **Guichicovi,** Mex.
96/H6 **Guidder,** Camr.
98/B3 **Guidimaka** (reg.), Mrta.
60/C2 **Guidonia,** It.
98/D5 **Guiglo,** IvC.
52/B6 **Guignes,** Fr.
52/C5 **Guignicourt,** Fr.
82/D5 **Guihulngan,** Phil.
47/F4 **Guildford,** Eng,UK
56/F4 **Guilherand,** Fr.
85/K2 **Guilin,** China
119/J3 **Guillaume-Delisle** (lake), Qu,Can
58/B4 **Guillena,** Sp.
46/C1 **Guilsfield,** Wal,UK
58/A2 **Guimarães,** Port.
81/D4 **Guimeng Ding** (mtn.), China
98/C4 **Guinea**
96/F7 **Guinea** (gulf), Afr.
98/B3 **Guinea-Bissau**
56/B2 **Guingamp,** Fr.
56/A2 **Guipavas,** Fr.
109/H7 **Guiratinga,** Braz.
117/J5 **Güiria,** Ven.
45/G2 **Guisborough,** Eng,UK
52/C4 **Guise,** Fr.
45/G4 **Guiseley,** Eng,UK
58/B1 **Guitiriz,** Sp.
82/B2 **Guiyang,** China
85/J2 **Guiyang,** China
85/J2 **Guizhou** (prov.), China
56/C4 **Gujan-Mestras,** Fr.
84/B3 **Gujarāt** (state), India
73/K2 **Gūjar Khān,** Pak.
73/K2 **Gujrānwāla,** Pak.
73/K2 **Gujrāt,** Pak.
66/F2 **Gukovo,** Rus.
76/E4 **Gulang,** China
84/C4 **Gulbarga,** India
53/G3 **Guldenbach** (riv.), Ger.
82/C3 **Guleitou,** China
129/F4 **Gulfport,** Ms,US
129/G4 **Gulf Shores,** Al,US
68/G5 **Gulistan,** Uzb.
77/J2 **Guliya** (peak), China
44/B2 **Gulladuff,** NI,UK
122/F3 **Gull Lake,** Sk,Can
74/C3 **Gülnar,** Turk.
53/E2 **Gulpen,** Neth.
101/B2 **Gulu,** Ugan.
63/G4 **Gŭlŭbovo,** Bul.
104/D4 **Gumare,** Bots.
79/F2 **Gumma** (pref.), Japan
51/E6 **Gummersbach,** Ger.
66/E4 **Gümüşhacıköy,** Turk.
74/D2 **Gümüşhane,** Turk.
97/N5 **Guna** (peak), Eth.
84/C3 **Guna,** India
74/E2 **Güneydogu Toroslar** (mts.), Turk.
123/J2 **Gunisao** (lake), Mb,Can
123/J2 **Gunisao** (riv.), Mb,Can
91/D1 **Gunnedah,** Austl.
124/F3 **Gunnison,** Co,US
124/F3 **Gunnison** (riv.), Co,US
124/E3 **Gunnison,** Ut,US
75/B4 **Gunt** (riv.), Taj.
129/G3 **Guntersville,** Al,US
129/G3 **Guntersville** (lake), Al,US
84/D4 **Guntūr,** India
55/G1 **Günz** (riv.), Ger.
57/J2 **Gunzenhausen,** Ger.
81/C4 **Guo** (riv.), China
97/N6 **Guragē** (peak), Eth.
63/G2 **Gura Humorului,** Rom.
111/F2 **Gural** (mts.), Braz.
76/B2 **Gurbantünggut** (des.), China
73/L2 **Gurdāspur,** India
109/K6 **Gurguéia** (riv.), Braz.
117/J6 **Guri, Embalse de** (res.), Ven.
57/L3 **Gurk** (riv.), Aus.
57/K3 **Gurkthaler** (mts.), Aus.
132/Q15 **Gurnee,** Il,US
63/J5 **Gürsu,** Turk.
109/J6 **Gurupi,** Braz.
109/J4 **Gurupi** (mts.), Braz.
109/J4 **Gurupi** (riv.), Braz.
84/B3 **Guru Sikhar** (mtn.), India
76/G2 **Gurvandzagal,** Mong.
64/J5 **Gus'-Khrustal'nyy,** Rus.
60/A3 **Guspini,** It.
48/G2 **Güstrow,** Ger.
51/F5 **Gütersloh,** Ger.
125/H4 **Guthrie,** Ok,US
125/G4 **Guthrie,** Tx,US
42/E3 **Gutulia Nat'l Park,** Nor.
108/G3 **Guyana**
52/B6 **Guyancourt,** Fr.
129/H2 **Guyandotte** (riv.), WV,US
81/B2 **Guyang,** China
56/C4 **Guyenne** (reg.), Fr.
91/E1 **Guy Fawkes Riv. Nat'l Park,** Austl.
47/G1 **Guyhirn,** Eng,UK
125/G3 **Guymon,** Ok,US
76/F4 **Guyuan,** China
76/H3 **Guyuan,** China
117/N7 **Guzmán** (lake), Mex.
73/H3 **Gwādar,** Pak.
84/C2 **Gwalior,** India
104/E5 **Gwanda,** Zim.
47/F1 **Gwash** (riv.), Eng,UK
46/C2 **Gwaunceste** (mtn.), Wal,UK
49/J2 **Gwda** (riv.), Pol.
46/A6 **Gweek,** Eng,UK
45/E5 **Gwersyllt,** Wal,UK
104/E4 **Gweru,** Zim.
91/D1 **Gwydir** (riv.), Austl.
44/D5 **Gwynedd** (co.), Wal,UK
77/D5 **Gyaring** (lake), China
99/F5 **Gyasikan,** Gha.
68/H2 **Gyda** (pen.), Rus.
90/D4 **Gympie,** Austl.
85/G4 **Gyobingauk,** Myan.
62/E2 **Gyoma,** Hun.
62/D2 **Gyöngyös,** Hun.
62/C2 **Győr,** Hun.
62/C2 **Győr-Sopron** (co.), Hun.
62/E2 **Gyula,** Hun.
67/G4 **Gyumri,** Arm.

H

52/D2 **Haacht,** Belg.
50/D4 **Haaksbergen,** Neth.
52/D2 **Haaltert,** Belg.
50/E6 **Haan,** Ger.
93/H6 **Ha'apai Group** (isls.), Tonga
42/H2 **Haapavesi,** Fin.
64/D4 **Haapsalu,** Est.
57/J2 **Haar,** Ger.
57/G2 **Haardt** (mts.), Ger.
50/B4 **Haarlem,** Neth.
89/G7 **Haast,** NZ
73/J3 **Hab** (riv.), Pak.
53/E4 **Habay,** Belg.
72/D2 **Habbānīyah,** Iraq
85/F3 **Habiganj,** Bang.
79/L10 **Habikino,** Japan
77/N3 **Haboro,** Japan
51/F3 **Hache** (riv.), Ger.
77/N5 **Hachijō** (isl.), Japan
79/F3 **Hachiōji,** Japan
131/C3 **Hacienda Heights,** Ca,US
74/C2 **Hacılar,** Turk.
131/F5 **Hackensack,** NJ,US
131/F5 **Hackettstown,** NJ,US
83/D1 **Ha Coi,** Viet.
57/H1 **Hadamar,** Ger.
79/F3 **Hadano,** Japan
100/D4 **Hadarba, Ras** (cape), Sudan
97/J4 **Haddad** (wadi), Chad
47/F3 **Haddenham,** Eng,UK
43/D3 **Haddington,** Sc,UK
131/E6 **Haddonfield,** NJ,US
131/E6 **Haddon** (Westmont), NJ,US
73/G4 **Ḩadd, Ra's al** (pt.), Oman
99/H3 **Hadejia** (riv.), Nga.
51/F1 **Hadelner** (can.), Ger.
74/K5 **Hadera,** Isr.
48/E1 **Haderslev,** Den.
74/C3 **Hadım,** Turk.
62/E2 **Hadjú-Bihar** (co.), Hun.
118/F1 **Hadley** (bay), Nun.,Can
45/F1 **Hadrian's Wall** (ruins), Eng,UK
42/E1 **Hadselfjorden** (fjord), Nor.
80/C3 **Haeju,** NKor.
120/S9 **Haena** (pt.), Hi,US
74/D2 **Hafik,** Turk.
73/K2 **Hāfizābād,** Pak.
42/N7 **Hafnarfjördhur,** Ice.
72/E3 **Ḩafr al Bāţin,** SAr.
72/E2 **Haft Gel,** Iran
97/R5 **Hafun, Ras** (pt.), Som.
92/D3 **Hagåtña** (cap.), Guam
130/F4 **Hagemeister** (isl.), Ak,US
51/E6 **Hagen,** Ger.
51/E4 **Hagen am Teutoburger Wald,** Ger.
48/F2 **Hagenow,** Ger.
125/F4 **Hagerman,** NM,US
126/E4 **Hagerstown,** Md,US
78/B3 **Hagi,** Japan
83/D1 **Ha Giang,** Viet.
46/D2 **Hagley,** Eng,UK
53/F5 **Hagondange,** Fr.
43/A4 **Hags Head** (pt.), Ire.
123/G2 **Hague,** Sk,Can
56/C2 **Hague, Cap de la** (cape), Fr.
53/G6 **Haguenau,** Fr.
50/B4 **Hague, The** ('s-Gravenhage) (cap.), Neth.
92/D2 **Hahashima** (isl.), Jap.
51/H6 **Hahle** (riv.), Ger.
53/G3 **Hahnenbach** (riv.), Ger.
81/D3 **Hai** (riv.), China
79/L10 **Haibara,** Japan
77/J3 **Haicheng,** China
83/D1 **Hai Duong,** Viet.
74/K5 **Haifa** (dist.), Isr.
74/K5 **Haifa** (Hefa), Isr.
53/H2 **Haiger,** Ger.
83/D1 **Hai Hau,** Viet.
82/B3 **Haikou,** China
77/H2 **Hailar,** China
77/J2 **Hailar** (riv.), China
126/E2 **Haileybury,** On,Can
47/G5 **Hailsham,** Eng,UK
85/J4 **Hainan** (prov.), China
82/B3 **Hainan** (str.), China
52/B2 **Hainaut** (prov.), Belg.
57/H1 **Hainburg,** Ger.
129/H4 **Haines City,** Fl,US
130/L3 **Haines Junction,** Yk,Can
51/H6 **Hainich** (mts.), Ger.
81/L9 **Haining,** China
83/D1 **Haiphong** (Hai Phong), Viet.
117/G4 **Haiti**
83/E2 **Hai Van** (pass), Viet.
85/K3 **Haixia** (str.), China
81/D4 **Haizhou** (bay), China
49/L5 **Hajdú-Bihar** (co.), Hun.
62/E2 **Hajdúboszormény,** Hun.
62/E2 **Hajdúdorog,** Hun.
62/E2 **Hajdúhadház,** Hun.
62/E2 **Hajdúnánás,** Hun.
62/E2 **Hajdúszoboszló,** Hun.
79/F1 **Hajiki-zaki** (pt.), Japan
49/M2 **Hajnówka,** Pol.
85/F2 **Hājo,** India
93/L5 **Hakahau,** Fr.Pol.
78/D3 **Hakken-san** (mtn.), Japan
77/N3 **Hakodate,** Japan
79/H7 **Hakone,** Japan
79/H8 **Hakone-Fuji-Izu Nat'l Park,** Japan
79/E2 **Hakui,** Japan
79/M10 **Hakusan,** Japan
79/E2 **Haku-san** (mtn.), Japan
79/E2 **Hakusan Nat'l Park,** Japan
73/J3 **Hāla,** Pak.
74/D3 **Ḩalab** (Aleppo), Syria
72/E1 **Ḩalabjah,** Iraq
100/D4 **Ḩalā'ib,** Sudan
42/D4 **Halden,** Nor.
48/F2 **Haldensleben,** Ger.
127/Q10 **Haldimand,** On,Can
76/G2 **Haldzan,** Mong.
101/C4 **Hale,** Tanz.
45/F5 **Hale,** Eng,UK
120/T10 **Haleakala Nat'l Park,** Hi,US
53/E2 **Halen,** Belg.
132/P14 **Hales Corners,** Wi,US
46/D2 **Halesowen,** Eng,UK
47/H2 **Halesworth,** Eng,UK
129/G3 **Haleyville,** Al,US
98/E5 **Half Assini,** Gha.
82/C6 **Half Moon** (shoal)
132/K12 **Half Moon Bay,** Ca,US
74/K6 **Ḩalḩūl,** WBnk.
126/E2 **Haliburton** (hills), On,Can
90/B2 **Halifax** (bay), Austl.
127/J2 **Halifax** (cap.), NS,Can
45/G4 **Halifax,** Eng,UK
73/G3 **Halīl** (riv.), Iran
130/H1 **Halkett** (cape), Ak,US
119/K2 **Hall** (pen.), Nun.,Can
92/E4 **Hall** (isls.), Micr.
130/D3 **Hall** (isl.), Ak,US
42/E4 **Halland** (co.), Swe.
77/K5 **Halla-san** (mtn.), SKor.
52/D2 **Halle,** Belg.
51/F4 **Halle,** Ger.
42/E4 **Hällefors,** Swe.
57/K3 **Hallein,** Aus.
52/A4 **Hallencourt,** Fr.
48/F3 **Halle-Neustadt,** Ger.
105/M **Hallett** (cape), Ant.
128/D4 **Hallettsville,** Tx,US
123/J3 **Hallock,** Mn,US
48/B4 **Hallu** (riv.), Fr.
52/B3 **Hallue** (riv.), Fr.
52/C2 **Halluin,** Fr.
80/E5 **Hallyŏ Haesang Nat'l Park,** SKor.
87/G3 **Halmahera** (isl.), Indo.
87/G4 **Halmahera** (sea), Indo.
42/E4 **Halmstad,** Swe.
60/B4 **Ḩalq al Wādī,** Tun.
42/E4 **Hälsingborg,** Swe.
47/G3 **Halstead,** Eng,UK
50/B5 **Halsteren,** Neth.
76/C4 **Haltang** (riv.), China
45/H4 **Haltemprice,** Eng,UK
51/E5 **Haltern,** Ger.
127/Q8 **Halton Hills,** On,Can
45/F2 **Haltwhistle,** Eng,UK
51/E6 **Halver,** Ger.
51/E3 **Halverder Aa** (riv.), Ger.
52/C4 **Ham,** Fr.
78/C3 **Hamada,** Japan
72/E2 **Hamadān,** Iran
74/L4 **Ḩamāh,** Syria
79/M10 **Hamajima,** Japan
79/E3 **Hamakita,** Japan
79/E3 **Hamamatsu,** Japan
42/D3 **Hamar,** Nor.
100/C3 **Ḩamāţah, Jabal** (mtn.), Egypt
84/D6 **Hambantota,** SrL.
47/E5 **Hamble,** Eng,UK
45/G3 **Hambleton** (hills), Eng,UK
51/G3 **Hambühren,** Ger.
51/G1 **Hamburg,** Ger.
51/H1 **Hamburg** (state), Ger.
128/F3 **Hamburg,** Ar,US
126/E3 **Hamburg,** NY,US
42/G3 **Hämeenkyrö,** Fin.
42/H3 **Hämeenlinna,** Fin.
51/G4 **Hameln,** Ger.
47/H3 **Hamford Water** (inlet), Eng,UK
80/E2 **Hamgyŏng** (mts.), NKor.
80/E2 **Hamgyŏng-Bukto** (prov.), NKor.
80/D2 **Hamgyŏng-Namdo** (prov.), NKor.
80/D3 **Hamhŭng,** NKor.
80/D3 **Hamhŭng-Si** (prov.), NKor.
76/C3 **Hami,** China
119/L3 **Hamilton** (inlet), Nf,Can
127/Q9 **Hamilton,** On,Can
89/H6 **Hamilton,** NZ
43/C3 **Hamilton,** Sc,UK
129/G3 **Hamilton,** Al,US
32/L12 **Hamilton** (mt.), Ca,US
122/E4 **Hamilton,** Mt,US
126/C4 **Hamilton,** Oh,US
128/D4 **Hamilton,** Tx,US
84/D2 **Hamīrpur,** India
60/B4 **Hammāmāt** (gulf), Tun.
52/D1 **Hamme,** Belg.
51/F2 **Hamme** (riv.), Ger.
42/G1 **Hammerfest,** Nor.
50/D5 **Hamminkeln,** Ger.
132/R16 **Hammond,** In,US
129/F4 **Hammond,** La,US
53/E1 **Hamont-Achel,** Belg.
47/E4 **Hampshire** (co.), Eng,UK
47/E4 **Hampshire Downs** (hills), Eng,UK
126/E4 **Hampton,** Va,US
91/G6 **Hampton Park,** Austl.
96/H1 **Ḩamrā** (upland), Libya
132/F7 **Hamtramck,** Mi,US
79/H7 **Hamura,** Japan
81/C5 **Han** (riv.), China
82/C3 **Han** (riv.), China
80/D4 **Han** (riv.), SKor.
77/N4 **Hanamaki,** Japan
120/U11 **Hanamalo** (pt.), Hi,US
77/M5 **Hanamatsu,** Japan
101/B4 **Hanang** (peak), Tanz.
126/B2 **Hancock,** Mi,US
79/M10 **Handa,** Japan
81/C3 **Handan,** China
47/E1 **Handsworth,** Eng,UK
124/C3 **Hanford,** Ca,US
76/D2 **Hangayn** (mts.), Mong.
46/C5 **Hangingstone** (hill), Eng,UK
102/L11 **Hangklip** (cape), SAfr.
75/B5 **Hangu,** Pak.
81/L9 **Hangzhou,** China
76/C2 **Hanhöhiy** (mts.), Mong.
74/E2 **Hani,** Turk.
123/J4 **Hankinson,** ND,US
123/G3 **Hanley,** Sk,Can
122/F3 **Hanna,** Ab,Can
122/G5 **Hanna,** Wy,US
79/L10 **Hannan,** Japan
125/K3 **Hannibal,** Mo,US
79/H7 **Hannō,** Japan
51/G4 **Hannover,** Ger.
53/E2 **Hannut,** Belg.
42/E5 **Hanöbukten** (bay), Swe.
83/D1 **Hanoi** (Ha Noi) (cap.), Viet.
126/D2 **Hanover,** On,Can
113/J7 **Hanover** (isl.), Chile
127/F3 **Hanover,** NH,US
132/P16 **Hanover Park,** Il,US
84/C2 **Hānsi,** India
75/D3 **Hantengri Feng** (peak), China
119/J2 **Hantzsch** (riv.), Nun.,Can
84/B2 **Hanumāngarh,** India
76/E2 **Hanuy** (riv.), Mong.
76/F5 **Hanzhong,** China
93/L6 **Hao** (atoll), FrPol.
42/H2 **Haparanda,** Swe.
119/K3 **Happy Valley-Goose Bay,** Nf,Can
76/D4 **Har** (lake), China
76/C2 **Har** (lake), Mong.
76/F2 **Haraa** (riv.), Mong.
79/G2 **Haramachi,** Japan
73/K2 **Harappa** (ruins), Pak.
104/F4 **Harare** (cap.), Zim.
76/F2 **Har-Ayrag,** Mong.
98/C5 **Harbel,** Libr.
77/K2 **Harbin,** China
127/L2 **Harbour Breton,** Nf,Can
47/E2 **Harbury,** Eng,UK
84/C3 **Hardā,** India
42/C3 **Hardangervidda Nat'l Park,** Nor.
102/B2 **Hardap** (dam), Namb.
51/H3 **Hardau** (riv.), Ger.
51/G5 **Hardegsen,** Ger.
50/D3 **Hardenberg,** Neth.
50/C4 **Harderwijk,** Neth.
122/G4 **Hardin,** Mt,US
73/L3 **Hardwār,** India
113/K8 **Hardy** (pen.), Chile
127/L1 **Hare** (bay), Nf,Can
52/C2 **Harelbeke,** Belg.
51/E3 **Haren,** Ger.
50/D2 **Haren,** Neth.
97/P6 **Hārer,** Eth.
74/N8 **Har Eval** (Jabal 'Aybāl) (mtn.), WBnk.
97/P6 **Hargeysa,** Som.
63/G2 **Harghita** (co.), Rom.
63/G2 **Harghita** (peak), Rom.
86/B4 **Hari** (riv.), Indo.
84/C5 **Harihar,** India
78/D3 **Harima** (sound), Japan
50/B5 **Haringvliet** (chan.), Neth.
73/H2 **Harīrūd** (riv.), Afg.
126/D4 **Harlan,** Ky,US
44/D6 **Harlech,** Wal,UK
47/H2 **Harleston,** Eng,UK
50/C2 **Harlingen,** Neth.
128/D5 **Harlingen,** Tx,US
47/F3 **Harlington,** Eng,UK
122/F4 **Harlowton,** Mt,US
50/B4 **Harmelen,** Neth.
52/B3 **Harnes,** Fr.
122/D5 **Harney** (lake), Or,US
122/D5 **Harney** (val.), Or,US
123/H5 **Harney** (peak), SD,US
42/F3 **Härnösand,** Swe.
117/M8 **Haro** (cape), Mex.
58/D1 **Haro,** Sp.
47/F3 **Harpenden,** Eng,UK
130/L3 **Harper** (mtn.), Yk,Can
98/D5 **Harper,** Libr.
130/K3 **Harper** (mtn.), Ak,US
128/D2 **Harper,** Ks,US
132/G7 **Harper Woods,** Mi,US
126/E1 **Harricana** (riv.), Qu,Can
129/G3 **Harriman,** Tn,US
126/B4 **Harrisburg,** Il,US
125/G2 **Harrisburg,** Ne,US
126/E3 **Harrisburg** (cap.), Pa,US
48/E1 **Harrislee,** Ger.
102/E3 **Harrismith,** SAfr.
122/C3 **Harrison** (lake), BC,Can
119/L3 **Harrison** (cape), Nf,Can
130/H1 **Harrison** (bay), Ak,US
128/E2 **Harrison,** Ar,US
125/G2 **Harrison,** Ne,US
131/G5 **Harrison,** NY,US
126/E4 **Harrisonburg,** Va,US
126/C4 **Harrodsburg,** Ky,US
45/G4 **Harrogate,** Eng,UK
125/J3 **Harry S Truman** (res.), Mo,US
51/G2 **Harsefeld,** Ger.
51/F5 **Harsewinkel,** Ger.
42/F1 **Harstad,** Nor.
118/C2 **Hart** (riv.), Yk,Can
124/C2 **Hart** (lake), Or,US
102/C3 **Hartbeesrivier** (dry riv.), SAfr.
42/C3 **Hårteigen** (peak), Nor.
50/B5 **Hartelkanaal** (can.), Neth.
127/F3 **Hartford** (cap.), Ct,US
126/C3 **Hartford City,** In,US
125/H2 **Hartington,** Ne,US
46/B5 **Hartland,** Eng,UK
46/B4 **Hartland** (pt.), Eng,UK
46/D2 **Hartlebury,** Eng,UK
45/G2 **Hartlepool,** Eng,UK
45/G2 **Hartlepool** (co.), Eng,UK
47/G4 **Hartley,** Eng,UK
123/H3 **Hartney,** Mb,Can
102/D3 **Harts** (riv.), SAfr.
131/G4 **Hartsdale,** NY,US
129/G3 **Hartselle,** Al,US
47/E1 **Hartshill,** Eng,UK
132/B3 **Hartstene** (isl.), Wa,US
129/H3 **Hartwell,** Ga,US
129/H3 **Hartwell** (lake), Ga, SC,US
91/C4 **Hartz Mtn. Nat'l Park,** Austl.
53/G6 **Hartzviller,** Fr.
73/K3 **Hārūnābād,** Pak.
87/E3 **Harun, Bukit** (peak), Indo.
75/F2 **Har Us** (lake), Mong.
76/D2 **Har-Us** (riv.), Mong.
73/H2 **Hārūt** (riv.), Afg.
132/Q16 **Harvey,** Il,US
123/J4 **Harvey,** ND,US
47/H3 **Harwich,** Eng,UK
45/G5 **Harworth,** Eng,UK
84/C2 **Haryana** (state), India
51/H5 **Harz** (mts.), Ger.
51/E3 **Hase** (riv.), Ger.
51/E3 **Haselünne,** Ger.
79/M9 **Hashima,** Japan
78/D3 **Hashimoto,** Japan
96/D2 **Hasi el Farsía** (well), WSah.
73/K3 **Hāsilpur,** Pak.
128/D3 **Haskell,** Tx,US
47/F4 **Haslemere,** Eng,UK
45/F4 **Haslingden,** Eng,UK
45/F5 **Haslington,** Eng,UK
84/C5 **Hassan,** India
119/S7 **Hassel** (sound), Nun.,Can
53/E2 **Hasselt,** Belg.
50/D3 **Hasselt,** Neth.
57/J1 **Hassfurt,** Ger.
96/G1 **Hassi Messaoud,** Alg.
42/E4 **Hässleholm,** Swe.
89/H6 **Hastings,** NZ
47/G5 **Hastings,** Eng,UK
126/C3 **Hastings,** Mi,US
123/K4 **Hastings,** Mn,US
125/H2 **Hastings,** Ne,US
131/G4 **Hastings-on-Hudson,** NY,US
79/H7 **Hasuda,** Japan
79/M9 **Hatashō,** Japan
131/E5 **Hatboro,** Pa,US
124/F4 **Hatch,** NM,US
83/B5 **Hat Chao Mai Nat'l Park,** Thai.
113/J7 **Hatcher** (peak), Arg.
62/F3 **Haţeg,** Rom.
47/F3 **Hatfield,** Eng,UK
91/E1 **Hat Head Nat'l Park,** Austl.
45/G5 **Hathersage,** Eng,UK
84/C2 **Hāthras,** India
72/C4 **Ḩāţibah, Ra's** (pt.), SAr.
83/D4 **Ha Tien,** Viet.
83/D2 **Ha Tinh,** Viet.
83/B5 **Hat Nai Yang Nat'l Park,** Thai.
79/H7 **Hatogaya,** Japan
117/H4 **Hato Mayor,** DRep.
79/H7 **Hatoyama,** Japan
84/C3 **Hatta,** India
91/B2 **Hattah-Kulkyne Nat'l Park,** Austl.
50/D4 **Hattem,** Neth.
51/F2 **Hatten,** Ger.
129/K3 **Hatteras** (cape), NC,US
129/F4 **Hattiesburg,** Ms,US
51/E6 **Hattingen,** Ger.
45/G6 **Hatton,** Eng,UK
62/D2 **Hatvan,** Hun.
83/C5 **Hat Yai,** Thai.
83/E3 **Hau Bon,** Viet.
52/B2 **Haubourdin,** Fr.
97/Q6 **Haud** (reg.), Eth., Som.
42/C4 **Haugesund,** Nor.
83/D4 **Hau Giang** (riv.), Viet.
42/H2 **Haukipudas,** Fin.
131/G5 **Hauppauge,** NY,US
59/E1 **Hauskoa** (mtn.), Fr.
96/D1 **Haut Atlas** (mts.), Mor.
54/B1 **Haute-Marne** (dept.), Fr.
56/D2 **Haute-Normandie** (reg.), Fr.
127/G1 **Hauterive,** Qu,Can
54/B2 **Haute-Saône** (dept.), Fr.
54/C5 **Haute-Savoie** (dept.), Fr.
53/E3 **Hautes Fagnes** (uplands), Belg.
52/C3 **Hautmont,** Fr.
54/D2 **Haut-Rhin** (dept.), Fr.
52/B6 **Hauts-de-Seine** (dept.), Fr.
116/E3 **Havana** (La Habana) (cap.), Cuba
93/V13 **Havannah** (chan.), NCal.
47/F5 **Havant,** Eng,UK
124/D4 **Havasu** (lake), Az, Ca,US
49/G2 **Havel** (riv.), Ger.
48/G2 **Havelland** (reg.), Ger.
129/J3 **Havelock,** NC,US
47/G3 **Havengore** (isl.), Eng,UK
46/B3 **Haverfordwest,** Wal,UK
47/G2 **Haverhill,** Eng,UK
127/G3 **Haverhill,** Ma,US
49/K4 **Havířov,** Czh.
51/E5 **Havixbeck,** Ger.
49/H4 **Havlíčkuv Brod,** Czh.
122/F3 **Havre,** Mt,US
127/J1 **Havre-Saint-Pierre,** Qu,Can
63/H5 **Havsa,** Turk.
120/S10 **Hawaii** (state), US
120/U11 **Hawaii** (isl.), Hi,US
93/H2 **Hawaiian** (isls.), Hi,US
120/U11 **Hawaii Volcanoes Nat'l Park,** Hi,US
72/E3 **Ḩawallī,** Kuw.
45/E5 **Hawarden,** Wal,UK
123/J5 **Hawarden,** Ia,US
89/H6 **Hawera,** NZ
45/F3 **Hawes,** Eng,UK
45/F2 **Haweswater** (res.), Eng,UK
43/D3 **Hawick,** Sc,UK
91/E2 **Hawke** (cape), Austl.
90/G8 **Hawkesbury** (riv.), Austl.
122/A2 **Hawkesbury** (isl.), BC,Can
126/F2 **Hawkesbury,** On,Can
72/E2 **Hawr al Ḩammār** (lake), Iraq
74/H6 **Ḩawsh 'Isá,** Egypt
131/B3 **Hawthorne,** Ca,US
124/C3 **Hawthorne,** Nv,US
45/G3 **Haxby,** Eng,UK
90/C3 **Hay** (pt.), Austl.
118/E3 **Hay** (riv.), Ab, NW,Can
79/H7 **Hayama,** Japan
53/F5 **Hayange,** Fr.
45/F5 **Haydock,** Eng,UK
45/F2 **Haydon Bridge,** Eng,UK
118/G3 **Hayes** (riv.), Mb,Can
118/G2 **Hayes** (riv.), Nun.,Can
119/T7 **Hayes** (pen.), Grld.
130/J3 **Hayes** (mtn.), Ak,US
46/A6 **Hayle,** Eng,UK
46/A6 **Hayle** (riv.), Eng,UK
47/F5 **Hayling** (isl.), Eng,UK
128/E3 **Haynesville,** La,US
46/C2 **Hay on Wye,** Wal,UK
63/H5 **Hayrabolu,** Turk.
125/H3 **Hays,** Ks,US
125/H3 **Haysville,** Ks,US
132/K11 **Hayward,** Ca,US
126/B2 **Hayward,** Wi,US
47/F5 **Haywards Heath,** Eng,UK
73/G3 **Hazār** (mtn.), Iran
126/D4 **Hazard,** Ky,US
84/E3 **Hazāribag,** India
52/B2 **Hazebrouck,** Fr.
45/F5 **Hazel Grove,** Eng,UK
132/F7 **Hazel Park,** Mi,US
119/R7 **Hazen** (str.), NW,Nun.,Can
130/E3 **Hazen** (bay), Ak,US

50/B4 Hazerswoude-Dorp, Neth.
129/F4 Hazlehurst, Ms,US
47/F3 Hazlemere, Eng,UK
131/F5 Hazlet, NJ,US
122/B2 Hazleton (mts.), BC,Can
126/F3 Hazleton, Pa,US
79/N10 Hazu, Japan
47/G1 Heacham, Eng,UK
47/G4 Headcorn, Eng,UK
45/G4 Headingley, Eng,UK
124/B3 Healdsburg, Ca,US
91/G5 Healesville, Austl.
45/G6 Heanor, Eng,UK
39/P8 Heard (isl.), Austl.
128/D4 Hearne, Tx,US
105/V Hearst (isl.), Ant.
126/D1 Hearst, On,Can
123/H4 Heart (riv.), ND,US
127/J1 Heath (pt.), Qu,Can
90/G9 Heathcote Nat'l Park, Austl.
47/G5 Heathfield, Eng,UK
128/D5 Hebbronville, Tx,US
45/F4 Hebden Bridge, Eng,UK
81/G6 Hebei (prov.), China
128/E3 Heber Springs, Ar,US
81/C4 Hebi, China
43/B2 Hebrides (isls.), Sc,UK
43/A2 Hebrides, Outer (isls.), Sc,UK
125/H2 Hebron, Ne,US
74/K6 Hebron (Al Khalīl), WBnk.
130/M5 Hecate (str.), BC,Can
85/J3 Hechi, China
53/E1 Hechtel, Belg.
45/H6 Heckington, Eng,UK
123/J4 Hecla, SD,US
119/R7 Hecla and Griper (bay), NW,Can
122/D3 Hector (peak), Ab,Can
42/E3 Hedemora, Swe.
42/D3 Hedmark (co.), Nor.
45/H4 Hedon, Eng,UK
51/E4 Heek, Ger.
50/B3 Heemskerk, Neth.
50/B4 Heemstede, Neth.
50/D4 Heerde, Neth.
50/C3 Heerenveen, Neth.
50/B3 Heerhugowaard, Neth.
53/E2 Heerlen, Neth.
53/E2 Heers, Belg.
50/C5 Heesch, Neth.
50/C6 Heeze, Neth.
74/K5 Ḩefa (Haifa), Isr.
81/D5 Hefei, China
77/L2 Hegang, China
55/E2 Hegau (reg.), Ger.
79/L10 Heguri, Japan
76/D4 Hei (riv.), China
81/B3 Heicha Shan (mtn.), China
48/E1 Heide, Ger.
91/G5 Heidelberg, Austl.
57/H2 Heidelberg, Ger.
103/E2 Heidelberg, SAfr.
129/F4 Heidelberg, Ms,US
50/D5 Heiden, Ger.
77/K1 Heihe, China
48/F1 Heikendorf, Ger.
102/D2 Heilbron, SAfr.
57/H2 Heilbronn, Ger.
48/F1 Heiligenhafen, Ger.
50/D6 Heiligenhaus, Ger.
51/H6 Heiligenstadt, Ger.
77/L2 Heilong (Amur) (riv.), China
50/B3 Heiloo, Neth.
42/N7 Heimaey (isl.), Ice.
50/D4 Heino, Neth.
42/H3 Heinola, Fin.
50/D6 Heinsberg, Ger.
81/C3 Heituo Shan (mtn.), China
79/M9 Heiwa, Japan
81/D3 Hejian, China
74/D2 Hekimhan, Turk.
79/M10 Hekinan, Japan
42/N7 Hekla (vol.), Ice.
76/F4 Helan (mts.), China
50/D6 Helden, Neth.
129/F3 Helena, Ar,US
122/E4 Helena (cap.), Mt,US
48/D1 Helgoland (isl.), Ger.
48/D1 Helgoländer Bucht (bay), Ger.
72/F3 Ḩelleh (riv.), Iran
50/D4 Hellendoorn, Neth.
53/F3 Hellenthal, Ger.
50/B5 Hellevoetsluis, Neth.
58/E3 Hellín, Sp.
122/D4 Hells Canyon Nat'l Rec. Area, Id, Or,US
73/H2 Helmand (riv.), Afg.
48/F3 Helme (riv.), Ger.
130/K2 Helmet (mtn.), Ak,US
50/C6 Helmond, Neth.
45/G3 Helmsley, Eng,UK
48/F2 Helmstedt, Ger.
124/E3 Helper, Ut,US
45/F5 Helsby, Eng,UK
42/E4 Helsingør, Den.
42/H3 Helsinki (Helsingfors) (cap.), Fin.
46/A6 Helston, Eng,UK
42/G3 Helvetinjärven Nat'l Park, Fin.
52/C2 Hem, Fr.
52/B2 Hem (riv.), Fr.
47/F3 Hemel Hempstead, Eng,UK
51/E6 Hemer, Ger.
131/D3 Hemet, Ca,US
51/G4 Hemmingen, Ger.
51/G1 Hemmoor, Ger.
128/E4 Hemphill, Tx,US
131/G5 Hempstead, NY,US
47/H1 Hemsby, Eng,UK
45/G4 Hemsworth, Eng,UK
81/B4 Henan (prov.), China
58/D2 Henares (riv.), Sp.
56/C5 Hendaye, Fr.
63/K5 Hendek, Turk.
112/E3 Henderson, Arg.
93/N7 Henderson (isl.), Pitc.
126/C4 Henderson, Ky,US
129/J2 Henderson, NC,US
124/D3 Henderson, Nv,US
129/F3 Henderson, Tn,US
128/E3 Henderson, Tx,US
129/H3 Hendersonville, NC,US
129/G2 Hendersonville, Tn,US
50/B5 Hendrik-Ido-Ambacht, Neth.
102/D3 Hendrik Verwoerdam (res.), SAfr.
47/F5 Henfield, Eng,UK
81/L8 Heng (isl.), China
85/G2 Hengduan (mts.), China
50/D4 Hengelo, Neth.
81/C3 Heng Shan (mtn.), China
81/C3 Hengshui, China
82/B2 Hengyang, China
52/B3 Hénin-Beaumont, Fr.
47/E2 Henley-in-Arden, Eng,UK
47/F3 Henley-on-Thames, Eng,UK
56/B3 Hennebont, Fr.
53/G2 Hennef, Ger.
53/E2 Henri-Chapelle, Belg.
128/D3 Henrietta, Tx,US
119/H3 Henrietta Maria (cape), On,Can
130/M5 Henry (cape), BC,Can
124/E3 Henry (mts.), Ut,US
125/J4 Henryetta, Ok,US
52/C3 Hensies, Belg.
76/F2 Hentiyn (mts.), Mong.
85/G4 Henzada, Myan.
42/N6 Heradhsvötn (riv.), Ice.
73/H2 Herāt, Afg.
59/G1 Hérault (riv.), Fr.
90/B2 Herbert (riv.), Austl.
122/G3 Herbert, Sk,Can
90/B2 Herbert Riv. Falls Nat'l Park, Austl.
52/B5 Herblay, Fr.
62/D4 Hercegnovi, Yugo.
132/K10 Hercules, Ca,US
51/E6 Herdecke, Ger.
53/G2 Herdorf, Ger.
116/E6 Heredia, CR
46/D2 Hereford, Eng,UK
128/C3 Hereford, Tx,US
46/D2 Hereford & Worcester (co.), Eng,UK
93/L6 Hereheretue (isl.), FrPol.
63/J5 Hereke, Turk.
58/C3 Herencia, Sp.
53/D1 Herentals, Belg.
51/F4 Herford, Ger.
125/H3 Herington, Ks,US
55/F3 Herisau, Swi.
53/E2 Herk (riv.), Belg.
53/E2 Herk-de-Stad, Belg.
76/G2 Herlen (riv.), Mong.
129/F2 Hermann, Mo,US
51/H3 Hermannsburg, Ger.
52/B5 Hermes, Fr.
122/D4 Hermiston, Or,US
74/K5 Hermon (mtn.), Leb., Syria
131/B3 Hermosa Beach, Ca,US
117/M8 Hermosillo, Mex.
112/E2 Hernando, Arg.
129/F3 Hernando, Ms,US
58/E1 Hernani, Sp.
52/D2 Herne, Belg.
51/E5 Herne, Ger.
47/H4 Herne Bay, Eng,UK
42/D4 Herning, Den.
74/N9 Herodian (ruins), WBnk.
74/N9 Herodion Nat'l Park, WBnk.
117/M7 Heroica Caborca, Mex.
117/M7 Heroica Nogales, Mex.
116/D4 Herrero (pt.), Mex.
56/D5 Hers (riv.), Fr.
51/E6 Herscheid, Ger.
130/L2 Herschel, Yk,Can
53/D1 Herselt, Belg.
53/E2 Herstal, Belg.
47/G5 Herstmonceux, Eng,UK
51/E5 Herten, Ger.
47/F3 Hertford, Eng,UK
47/F3 Hertfordshire (co.), Eng,UK
53/E2 Herve, Belg.
90/D4 Hervey Bay, Austl.
51/H5 Herzberg am Harz, Ger.
51/F5 Herzebrock-Clarholz, Ger.
52/C2 Herzele, Belg.
74/M8 Herzliyya, Isr.
57/J2 Herzogenaurach, Ger.
62/B1 Herzogenburg, Aus.
53/F2 Herzogenrath, Ger.
53/D3 Hesbaye (plat.), Belg.
85/J3 Heshan, China
53/F4 Hesperange, Lux.
131/C2 Hesperia, Ca,US
130/M3 Hess (riv.), Yk,Can
51/G6 Hesse (state), Ger.
51/F5 Hessel (riv.), Ger.
51/G6 Hessisch Lichtenau, Ger.
51/G4 Hessisch Oldendorf, Ger.
45/H4 Hessle, Eng,UK
45/E5 Heswall, Eng,UK
123/H4 Hettinger, ND,US
45/G2 Hetton-le-Hole, Eng,UK
51/E5 Heubach (riv.), Ger.
49/H5 Heukuppe (peak), Aus.
53/E1 Heusden-Zolder, Belg.
53/F5 Heusweiler, Ger.
56/D2 Hève, Cap de la (cape), Fr.
62/E2 Heves, Hun.
49/L5 Heves (co.), Hun.
131/G5 Hewlett (pt.), NY,US
45/F2 Hexham, Eng,UK
77/H3 Hexigten Qi, China
102/L10 Hex River (mts.), SAfr.
102/L10 Hex River (pass), SAfr.
45/F3 Heysham, Eng,UK
50/C6 Heythuysen, Neth.
45/F4 Heywood, Eng,UK
81/C4 Heze, China
129/H5 Hialeah, Fl,US
125/J3 Hiawatha, Ks,US
123/K4 Hibbing, Mn,US
91/C4 Hibbs (pt.), Austl.
130/M4 Hickman (mtn.), BC,Can
126/B4 Hickman, Ky,US
129/H3 Hickory, NC,US
131/G5 Hicksville, NY,US
79/E3 Hida (riv.), Japan
79/H7 Hidaka, Japan
78/D4 Hidaka (riv.), Japan
116/B3 Hidalgo (state), Mex.
117/N8 Hidalgo de Parral, Mex.
51/F4 Hiddenhausen, Ger.
59/W17 Hierro (isl.), Canl.
51/E2 Hieve (lake), Ger.
79/H7 Higashikurume, Japan
79/H7 Higashimurayama, Japan
79/G1 Higashine, Japan
79/L10 Higashi-Ōsaka, Japan
79/K10 Higashiura, Japan
79/H7 Higashiyamato, Japan
122/C5 High (des.), Or,US
47/F2 Higham Ferrers, Eng,UK
46/D4 Highbridge, Eng,UK
131/F5 High Bridge, NJ,US
128/E4 High Island, Tx,US
131/C2 Highland, Ca,US
132/R16 Highland, Il,US
132/Q15 Highland Park, Il,US
132/F7 Highland Park, Mi,US
131/F5 Highland Park, NJ,US
46/D2 Highley, Eng,UK
123/J4 Highmore, SD,US
129/H3 High Point, NC,US
122/D2 High Prairie, Ab,Can
123/H2 Highrock (lake), Mb,Can
45/F3 High Street (mtn.), Eng,UK
45/E4 Hightown, Eng,UK
131/F5 Hightstown, NJ,US
46/B5 High Willhays (hill), Eng,UK
47/E3 Highworth, Eng,UK
47/F3 High Wycombe, Eng,UK
117/H4 Higüey, DRep.
74/H6 Hihyā, Egypt
42/J3 Hiidenportin Nat'l Park, Fin.
64/D4 Hiiumaa (isl.), Est.
72/C3 Hijāz, Jabal al (mts.), SAr.
78/B4 Hiji, Japan
112/Q9 Hijuelas de Conchali, Chile
79/L9 Hikami, Japan
78/E3 Hikone, Japan
93/L6 Hikueru (atoll), FrPol.
53/H2 Hilchenbach, Ger.
57/J1 Hildburghausen, Ger.
50/D6 Hilden, Ger.
51/G4 Hildesheim, Ger.
105/L Hillary (coast), Ant.
125/H3 Hill City, Ks,US
131/F4 Hillcrest, NY US
51/F4 Hille, Ger.
50/B4 Hillegom, Neth.
42/E5 Hillerød, Den.
44/B2 Hillhall, NI,UK
43/D2 Hill of Fearn, Sc,UK
123/J4 Hillsboro, ND,US
124/F4 Hillsboro, NM,US
126/D4 Hillsboro, Oh,US
122/C4 Hillsboro, Or,US
128/D3 Hillsboro, Tx,US
44/B3 Hillsborough (chan.), Austl.
44/B3 Hillsborough, NI,UK
132/K11 Hillsborough, Ca,US
131/F5 Hillsborough, NJ,US
126/C3 Hillsdale, Mi,US
131/F5 Hillside, NJ,US
44/B3 Hilltown, NI,UK
120/U11 Hilo, Hi,US
82/D5 Hilongos, Phil.
45/E3 Hilpsford (pt.), Eng,UK
129/H3 Hilton Head Island, SC,US
50/C6 Hilvarenbeek, Neth.
50/C4 Hilversum, Neth.
75/C5 Himachal Pradesh (state), India
84/D2 Himalaya, Great (range), Asia
82/D5 Himamaylan, Phil.
78/D3 Himeji, Japan
79/E2 Himi, Japan
97/N5 Himora, Eth.
74/L4 Ḩimş, Syria
130/J3 Hinchinbrook (chan.), Ak,US
90/B2 Hinchinbrook I. Nat'l Park, Austl.
47/E1 Hinckley, Eng,UK
45/H2 Hinderwell, Eng,UK
45/F4 Hindley, Eng,UK
91/B2 Hindmarsh (lake), Austl.
73/J1 Hindu Kush (mts.), Afg., Pak.
84/C5 Hindupur, India
129/H4 Hinesville, Ga,US
84/C3 Hinganghāt, India
73/J3 Hingol (riv.), Pak.
84/C4 Hingoli, India
73/J3 Hingorja, Pak.
74/E2 Hınıs, Turk.
79/H7 Hino, Japan
79/M9 Hino (riv.), Japan
79/H7 Hinode, Japan
58/C3 Hinojosa del Duque, Sp.
78/C3 Hino-misaki (cape), Japan
132/Q16 Hinsdale, Il,US
45/F6 Hinstock, Eng,UK
51/E2 Hinte, Ger.
122/D2 Hinton, Ab,Can
126/D4 Hinton, WV,US
50/B3 Hippolytushoef, Neth.
45/G3 Hipswell, Eng,UK
79/L9 Hira (mts.), Japan
78/A4 Hirado, Japan
78/D3 Hirakata, Japan
84/D3 Hirakud (res.), India
78/C3 Hirata, Japan
79/H7 Hiratsuka, Japan
63/H2 Hirlău, Rom.
77/N3 Hirosaki, Japan
78/C3 Hiroshima, Japan
78/C3 Hiroshima (pref.), Japan
57/J2 Hirschau, Ger.
52/D4 Hirson, Fr.
63/H3 Hirşova, Rom.
42/D4 Hirtshals, Den.
46/C3 Hirwaun, Wal,UK
78/E3 Hisai, Japan
84/C2 Hisār, India
76/E2 Hishig-Öndör, Mong.
117/G4 Hispaniola (isl.), DRep., Haiti
79/G2 Hitachi, Japan
79/G2 Hitachi-ōta, Japan
47/F3 Hitchin, Eng,UK
78/B4 Hitoyoshi, Japan
42/C3 Hitra (isl.), Nor.
93/M5 Hiva Oa (isl.), FrPol.
64/B2 Hjartfjellet (peak), Nor.
83/B1 Hka (riv.), Myan.
85/G2 Hkakabo (peak), Myan.
49/J4 Hlohovec, Slvk.
90/G8 Hmas-Nirimba, Austl.
85/G4 Hmawbi, Myan.
99/F5 Ho, Gha.
83/D1 Hoa Bin, Viet.
83/E4 Hoa Da, Viet.
83/C1 Hoang Lien (mts.), Viet.
119/K2 Hoare (bay), Nun.,Can
79/G2 Hobara, Japan
91/C4 Hobart, Austl.
125/H4 Hobart, Ok,US
105/Q Hobbs (coast), Ant.
125/G4 Hobbs, NM,US
52/D1 Hoboken, Belg.
131/F5 Hoboken, NJ,US
97/Q6 Hobyo, Som.
62/A2 Hochalmspitze (peak), Aus.
83/D4 Ho Chi Minh City (Saigon), Viet.
57/K3 Hochkönig (peak), Aus.
57/L3 Hochschwab (peak), Aus.
53/G3 Hochsimmer (peak), Ger.
47/G3 Hockley, Eng,UK
45/F4 Hodder (riv.), Eng,UK
47/F3 Hoddesdon, Eng,UK
122/G3 Hodgeville, Sk,Can
98/C2 Hodh (reg.), Mrta.
74/M8 Hod HaSharon, Isr.
98/D2 Hodh ech Chargui (reg.), Mrta.
98/C2 Hodh el Gharbi (reg.), Mrta.
62/E2 Hódmezővásárhely, Hun.
45/F6 Hodnet, Eng,UK
49/J4 Hodonín, Czh.
53/E2 Hoegnel (riv.), Belg.
50/B5 Hoekse Waard (polder), Neth.
53/G6 Hoenheim, Fr.
53/E2 Hoensbroek, Neth.
53/E2 Hoeselt, Belg.
50/C4 Hoevelaken, Neth.
50/B5 Hoeven, Neth.
57/J1 Hof, Ger.
132/P15 Hoffman Estates, Il,US
51/G6 Hofgeismar, Ger.
81/B3 Hofong Qagan (salt lake), China
42/P6 Hofsá (riv.), Ice.
42/N7 Hofsjökull (glac.), Ice.
78/B3 Hōfu, Japan
50/C4 Hoge Veluwe Nat'l Park, Neth.
51/G6 Hohegrass (peak), Ger.
55/F3 Hohenems, Aus.
51/H4 Hohenhameln, Ger.
57/H2 Hohenloher Ebene (plain), Ger.
57/K3 Hoher Dachstein (peak), Aus.
57/K3 Hohe Tauern (mts.), Aus.
57/K3 Hohe Tauern Nat'l Park, Aus.
81/B2 Hohhot, China
54/C1 Hohneck (mtn.), Fr.
53/G3 Höhr-Grenzhausen, Ger.
75/F4 Hoh Sai (lake), China
75/F4 Hoh Xil (lake), China
75/E4 Hoh Xil (mts.), China
83/E3 Hoi An, Viet.
128/D2 Hoisington, Ks,US
83/D1 Hoi Xuan, Viet.
78/C4 Hōjō, Japan
89/H7 Hokitika, NZ
77/N3 Hokkaidō (isl.), Japan
79/G2 Hokota, Japan
79/K10 Hokudan, Japan
79/M9 Hokusei, Japan
45/J6 Holbeach, Eng,UK
47/H3 Holbrook, Eng,UK
124/E4 Holbrook, Az,US
125/H4 Holdenville, Ok,US
45/H4 Holderness (pen.), Eng,UK
125/H2 Holdrege, Ne,US
117/F3 Holguín, Cuba
130/G3 Holitna (riv.), Ak,US
126/C3 Holland, Mi,US
129/F3 Hollandale, Ms,US
50/B4 Hollandse IJssel (riv.), Neth.
47/H2 Hollesley, Eng,UK
125/H4 Hollis, Ok,US
124/B3 Hollister, Ca,US
53/E2 Hollogne-aux-Pierres, Belg.
42/H3 Hollola, Fin.
129/F3 Holly Springs, Ms,US
129/H5 Hollywood, Fl,US
42/F3 Holm, Swe.
118/E1 Holman, NW,Can
131/F5 Holmdel, NJ,US
90/C2 Holmes (reefs), Austl.
122/F4 Holmes (peak), Wy,US
45/F5 Holmes Chapel, Eng,UK
45/H4 Holme upon Spalding Moor, Eng,UK
45/G4 Holmfirth, Eng,UK
105/C Holm-Lützow (bay), Ant.
42/F3 Holmsjön (lake), Swe.
74/K5 Ḩolon, Isr.
42/D4 Holstebro, Den.
129/H2 Holston (riv.), Tn,US
46/B5 Holsworthy, Eng,UK
47/H1 Holt, Eng,UK
50/D4 Holten, Neth.
125/J3 Holton, Ks,US
131/G5 Holtsville, NY,US
44/D5 Holy (isl.), Wal,UK
44/D5 Holyhead, Wal,UK
44/D5 Holyhead (mtn.), Wal,UK
43/E3 Holy (Lindisfarne) (isl.), Eng,UK
125/G2 Holyoke, Co,US
127/F3 Holyoke, Ma,US
45/E5 Holywell, Wal,UK
44/C2 Holywood, NI,UK
48/F5 Holzkirchen, Ger.
51/G5 Holzminden, Ger.
51/E6 Holzwickede, Ger.
102/B3 Hom (dry riv.), Namb.
50/D6 Homberg, Ger.
51/G6 Homberg, Ger.
99/E3 Hombori Tondo (peak), Mali
53/F5 Hombourg-Haut, Fr.
53/G5 Homburg, Ger.
119/K2 Home (bay), Nun.,Can
53/E5 Homécourt, Fr.
128/E3 Homer, La,US
129/H5 Homestead, Fl,US
129/G3 Homewood, Al,US
132/Q16 Homewood, Il,US
129/F4 Homochitto (riv.), Ms,US
66/D1 Homyel', Bela.
66/C2 Homyel'skaya (prov.), Bela.
84/B5 Honāvar, India
83/D4 Hon Chong, Viet.
46/C3 Honddu (riv.), Wal,UK
78/B4 Hondo, Japan
125/F4 Hondo (dry riv.), NM,US
128/D4 Hondo, Tx,US
50/D3 Hondsrug (reg.), Neth.
116/D4 Honduras
116/D4 Honduras (gulf), NAm.
124/B2 Honey (lake), Ca,US
47/E2 Honeybourne, Eng,UK
81/C5 Hong (lake), China
81/C4 Hong (riv.), China
85/J2 Hongdu (riv.), China
83/D1 Hong Gai, Viet.
81/C5 Honghu, China
85/J2 Hongjiang, China
82/B3 Hong Kong, China
81/B3 Hongliu (riv.), China
83/C1 Hong (Red) (riv.), Viet.
85/J3 Hongshui (riv.), China
81/C3 Hongtao Shan (mtn.), China
127/H1 Honguedo (passg.), Qu,Can
81/D4 Hongze (lake), China
92/E5 Honiara (cap.), Sol.
46/C5 Honiton, Eng,UK
120/T10 Honolulu (cap.), Hi,US
83/D4 Hon Quan, Viet.
77/M5 Honshu (isl.), Japan
132/J10 Hood (mt.), Ca,US
122/C4 Hood (mt.), Or,US
122/C4 Hood Canal (inlet), Wa,US
50/B4 Hoofddorp, Neth.
50/C6 Hoogeloon, Neth.
50/B6 Hoogerheide, Neth.
50/D3 Hoogeveen, Neth.
50/D3 Hoogeveense Vaart (can.), Neth.
50/D2 Hoogezand, Neth.
84/E3 Hooghly-Chinsura, India
52/C2 Hooglede, Belg.
50/B6 Hoogstraten, Belg.
90/C3 Hook (isl.), Austl.
47/F4 Hook, Eng,UK
43/B4 Hook Head (pt.), Ire.
126/C3 Hoopeston, Il,US
50/C3 Hoorn, Neth.
50/C3 Hoornse Hop (bay), Neth.
124/D3 Hoover (dam), Az,US
74/E2 Hopa, Turk.
131/F5 Hopatcong, NJ,US
131/F5 Hopatcong (lake), NJ,US
122/C3 Hope, BC,Can
45/E5 Hope, Wal,UK
128/E3 Hope, Ar,US
119/K2 Hopes Advance (cape), Qu,Can
46/C6 Hope's Nose (pt.), Eng,UK
46/D2 Hope under Dinmore, Eng,UK
131/F5 Hopewell, NJ,US
126/E4 Hopewell, Va,US
91/B3 Hopkins (riv.), Austl.
126/C4 Hopkinsville, Ky,US
51/F6 Hoppecke (riv.), Ger.
51/E4 Hopsten, Ger.
122/C4 Hoquiam, Wa,US
130/J2 Horace (mtn.), Ak,US
79/L9 Hōrai-san (peak), Japan
74/E2 Horasan, Turk.
74/K5 Ḩorbat Qesari (ruins), Isr.
45/G4 Horbury, Eng,UK
42/C3 Hordaland (co.), Nor.
45/G2 Horden, Eng,UK
63/G3 Horezu, Rom.
76/F3 Hörh (peak), Mong.
39/S6 Horiara (cap.), Sol.
47/F4 Horley, Eng,UK
66/F2 Horlivka, Ukr.
57/L2 Horn, Aus.
42/M6 Horn (pt.), Ice.
49/L4 Hornád (riv.), Slvk.
42/E2 Hornavan (lake), Swe.
51/F5 Horn-Bad Meinberg, Ger.
127/Q8 Hornby, On,Can
45/H5 Horncastle, Eng,UK
126/E3 Hornell, NY,US
126/C1 Hornepayne, On,Can
113/L8 Horn (Hornos) (cape), Chile
113/L8 Hornos Nat'l Park, Cabo de, Chile
52/A4 Hornoy-le-Bourg, Fr.
90/H8 Hornsby, Austl.
45/H4 Hornsea, Eng,UK
48/E1 Hornum Odde (cape), Ger.
77/N3 Horoshiri-dake (mtn.), Japan
46/B6 Horrabridge, Eng,UK
125/F2 Horse (cr.), Ne, Wy,US
126/C4 Horse Cave, Ky,US
122/C2 Horsefly (lake), BC,Can
42/D5 Horsens, Den.
47/H3 Horsey (isl.), Eng,UK
45/G4 Horsforth, Eng,UK
91/B3 Horsham, Austl.
47/F4 Horsham, Eng,UK
131/E5 Horsham, Pa,US
50/D6 Horst, Neth.
51/E4 Hörstel, Ger.
51/E4 Horstmar, Ger.
59/S12 Horta, Azor.,Port.
59/N9 Hortaleza, Sp.
62/E2 Hortobágyi Nat'l Park, Hun.
130/N2 Horton (riv.), NW,Can
74/K6 Ḩorvot 'Avedat (ruins), Isr.
74/K6 Ḩorvot Mezada (Masada) (ruins), Isr.
45/F4 Horwich, Eng,UK
126/D2 Horwood (lake), On,Can
84/C3 Hoshangābād, India
84/C4 Hospet, India
113/K8 Hoste (isl.), Chile
79/E2 Hotaka, Japan
79/E2 Hotaka-dake (mtn.), Japan
75/D4 Hotan (riv.), China
123/H5 Hot Springs, SD,US
128/E3 Hot Springs Nat'l Park, Ar,US
118/E2 Hottah (lake), NW,Can
102/A2 Hottentot (bay), Namb.
102/A2 Hottentots (pt.), Namb.
52/B3 Houdain, Fr.
98/D4 Houet (prov.), Burk.
126/B2 Houghton, Mi,US
126/C2 Houghton Lake, Mi,US
45/G2 Houghton-le-Spring, Eng,UK
127/H2 Houlton, Me,US
81/B4 Houma, China
129/F4 Houma, La,US
52/B2 Houplines, Fr.
52/A3 Hourdel, Pointe du (pt.), Fr.
124/D3 House (range), Ut,US
122/B2 Houston, BC,Can
125/K3 Houston, Mo,US
129/F3 Houston, Ms,US
128/E4 Houston, Tx,US
50/C4 Houten, Neth.
52/B2 Houthulst, Belg.
50/C3 Houtribdijk (dam), Neth.
47/F5 Hove, Eng,UK
51/F5 Hövelhof, Ger.
124/E3 Hovenweep Nat'l Mon., Co,US
47/H1 Hoveton, Eng,UK
42/E3 Hovfjället (peak), Swe.
45/H3 Hovingham, Eng,UK
76/E1 Hövsgöl (lake), Mong.
130/H2 Howard (hill), Ak,US
130/G2 Howard (pass), Ak,US
45/H4 Howden, Eng,UK
91/D3 Howe (cape), Austl.
126/D3 Howell, Mi,US
131/F5 Howell, NJ,US
103/E3 Howick, SAfr.
93/H4 Howland (isl.), PacUS
84/E3 Howrah, India
48/E3 Höxter, Ger.
49/H3 Hoyerswerda, Ger.
45/E5 Hoylake, Eng,UK
45/G5 Hoyland Nether, Eng,UK
59/N8 Hoyo-de-Manzanares, Sp.
53/E3 Hoyoux (riv.), Belg.
76/E2 Hoyt Tamir (riv.), Mong.
79/M9 Hozumi, Japan
49/H3 Hradec Králové, Czh.
62/D4 Hrasnica, Bosn.
62/B2 Hrastnik, Slov.
49/M2 Hrodna, Bela.
64/E5 Hrodzyenskaya (prov.), Bela.
42/M6 Hrolleifsborg (peak), Ice.
49/K4 Hron (riv.), Slvk.
49/J3 Hronov, Czh.
49/M3 Hrubieszów, Pol.
49/J3 Hrubý Jeseník (mts.), Czh.
42/P6 Hrútafjöll (peak), Ice.
76/G5 Hua (peak), China
108/C6 Huacho, Peru
83/B3 Hua Hin, Thai.
93/K6 Huahine (isl.), FrPol.
81/C4 Huai (riv.), China
81/D4 Huai'an, China
76/H5 Huaibei, China
82/A2 Huaihua, China
81/C2 Huailai, China
81/D4 Huainan, China
81/C3 Huairen, China
81/D4 Huaiyin, China
116/B4 Huajuapan de León, Mex.
112/C2 Hualañé, Chile
82/D3 Hualien, Tai.
108/C5 Huallaga (riv.), Peru
108/C5 Huamachuco, Peru
104/C3 Huambo, Ang.
81/C5 Huan (riv.), China
108/C6 Huancavelica, Peru
108/C6 Huancayo, Peru
108/E8 Huanchaca (peak), Bol.
83/C2 Huang (riv.), Laos, Thai.
81/C4 Huangchuan, China
82/C2 Huanggang (peak), China
81/C2 Huangqi (lake), China
81/D5 Huangshan, China
81/C5 Huangshi, China
81/C5 Huangtang (lake), China
81/B4 Huangtu (plat.), China
77/H4 Huang (Yellow) (riv.), China
108/C5 Huánuco, Peru
108/E7 Huanuni, Bol.
108/C6 Huaral, Peru
108/C5 Huaráz, Peru
108/C6 Huarmey, Peru
108/C5 Huascarán (peak), Peru
108/C5 Huascarán Nat'l Park, Peru
81/B4 Hua Shan (peak), China
117/N8 Huatabampo, Mex.
108/E6 Huatunas (lake), Bol.
82/A1 Huaying, China
130/L3 Hubbard (mtn.), Ak,US, Yk,Can
125/H4 Hubbard Creek (res.), Tx,US
81/C5 Hubei (prov.), China
81/B4 Hubei Kou (pass), China
84/C4 Hubli-Dhārwār, India
50/D6 Hückelhoven, Ger.
51/E6 Hückeswagen, Ger.
45/G5 Hucknall Torkard, Eng,UK
52/A2 Hucqueliers, Fr.
45/G4 Huddersfield, Eng,UK
64/C4 Huddinge, Swe.
51/F2 Hude, Ger.
42/F3 Hudiksvall, Swe.
105/L Hudson (cape), Ant.
119/H2 Hudson (bay), Can.
119/J2 Hudson (str.), Nun., Qu,Can
127/M7 Hudson, Qu,Can
126/F3 Hudson (riv.), NJ, NY,US
126/F3 Hudson, NY,US
123/H2 Hudson Bay, Sk,Can
118/D3 Hudson's Hope, BC,Can
83/D2 Hue, Viet.
62/F2 Huedin, Rom.
116/C4 Huehuetenango, Guat.
116/B3 Huejutla, Mex.
58/B4 Huelva, Sp.
58/B3 Huelva (riv.), Sp.
112/B4 Huequi (vol.), Chile
58/E4 Huercal-Overa, Sp.
125/F3 Huerfano (riv.), Co,US
59/E1 Huesca, Sp.
58/D4 Huéscar, Sp.
112/F3 Huesos (riv.), Arg.
116/A4 Huetamo de Nuñez, Mex.
84/E3 Hugli (riv.), India
125/G3 Hugo, Co,US
125/J4 Hugo, Ok,US
125/G3 Hugoton, Ks,US
76/H2 Hui (riv.), China
102/B2 Huib-Hock (plat.), Namb.
104/B4 Huila (plat.), Ang.
112/D2 Huinca Renancó, Arg.
81/E5 Hui Shan (mtn.), China
56/D2 Huisne (riv.), Fr.
50/C5 Huissen, Neth.
64/D3 Huittinen, Fin.
116/C4 Huixtla, Mex.
50/C4 Huizen, Neth.
82/B3 Huizhou, China
80/C5 Hŭksan (arch.), SKor.
76/K2 Hulan (riv.), China
76/F2 Huld, Mong.
123/G4 Hulett, Wy,US
126/F2 Hull, Qu,Can
45/H4 Hull, Eng,UK
45/H4 Hull (riv.), Eng,UK
51/F4 Hüllhorst, Ger.
93/H5 Hull (Orona) (atoll), Kiri.
50/B6 Hulst, Neth.
81/B3 Hulu (riv.), China
76/H2 Hulun (lake), China
77/K1 Huma (riv.), China
108/F5 Humaitá, Braz.
117/N8 Humaya (riv.), Mex.
104/B4 Humbe, Ang.
127/K2 Humber (riv.), Nf,Can
127/R8 Humber (bay), On,Can
127/Q8 Humber (riv.), On,Can
45/H4 Humber (riv.), Eng,UK
45/H4 Humberston, Eng,UK
128/E4 Humble, Tx,US
123/G2 Humboldt, Sk,Can
92/F7 Humboldt (peak), NCal.
124/C2 Humboldt (range), Nv,US
124/D2 Humboldt (riv.), Nv,US
129/F3 Humboldt, Tn,US
91/C2 Hume (lake), Austl.
49/L4 Humenné, Slvk.
130/K2 Humphrey (pt.), Ak,US
124/E4 Humphreys (peak), Az,US
45/F1 Humshaugh, Eng,UK
77/J3 Hun (riv.), China
77/K3 Hun (riv.), China
42/N6 Húnaflói (bay), Ice.
85/K2 Hunan (prov.), China
77/L3 Hunchun, China
62/F3 Hunedoara, Rom.
62/F2 Hunedoara (co.), Rom.
48/E3 Hünfeld, Ger.
62/D2 Hungary
57/H1 Hungen, Ger.
47/E4 Hungerford, Eng,UK
76/C2 Hüngüy (riv.), Mong.
83/D1 Hung Yen, Viet.
77/K3 Hunjiang, China
45/H3 Hunmanby, Eng,UK
53/G1 Hunspatch, Fr.
53/G4 Hunsrück (mts.), Ger.
47/G1 Hunstanton, Eng,UK
51/F2 Hunte (riv.), Ger.
91/C4 Hunter (isl.), Austl.

91/D2 Hunter (riv.), Austl.
122/A3 Hunter (isl.), BC,Can
130/H3 Hunter (mtn.), Ak,US
126/C4 Huntingburg, In,US
47/F2 Huntingdon, Eng,UK
45/G4 Huntington, Eng,UK
126/C3 Huntington, In,US
131/G5 Huntington, NY,US
126/D4 Huntington, WV,US
131/C3 Huntington Beach, Ca,US
131/B3 Huntington Park, Ca,US
132/F7 Huntington Woods, Mi,US
43/D2 Huntly, Sc,UK
130/M4 Hunts Inlet, BC,Can
126/E2 Huntsville, On,Can
129/G3 Huntsville, Al,US
128/E4 Huntsville, Tx,US
50/D5 Hünxe, Ger.
77/H2 Huolin Gol, China
83/D2 Huong Hoa, Viet.
83/D2 Huong Khe, Viet.
83/D2 Huong Son, Viet.
85/J4 Huong Thuy, Viet.
81/B3 Huo Shan (mtn.), China
97/R5 Hurdiyo, Som.
124/E4 Hurley, NM,US
126/D2 Huron (lake), Can., US
132/F7 Huron (riv.), Mi,US
123/J4 Huron, SD,US
126/D4 Hurricane, WV,US
47/F5 Hurstpierpoint, Eng,UK
52/D4 Hurtaut (riv.), Fr.
53/F2 Hürth, Ger.
45/G3 Hurworth, Eng,UK
84/D3 Husainābād, India
47/E2 Husbands Bosworth, Eng,UK
63/J2 Huşi, Rom.
48/E1 Husum, Ger.
125/H3 Hutchinson, Ks,US
123/K4 Hutchinson, Mn,US
45/J5 Huttoft, Eng,UK
90/C4 Hutton (peak), Austl.
45/H4 Hutton Cranswick, Eng,UK
45/G3 Hutton Rudby, Eng,UK
127/Q8 Huttonville, On,Can
81/C3 Hutuo (riv.), China
53/E2 Huy, Belg.
45/F5 Huyton-with-Roby, Eng,UK
81/E5 Huzhou, China
42/P7 Hvannadalshnúkur (peak), Ice.
62/C4 Hvar (isl.), Cro.
42/N7 Hvítá (riv.), Ice.
104/E4 Hwange, Zim.
104/E4 Hwange (Wankie) Nat'l Park, Zim.
80/D3 Hwanghae-Bukto (prov.), NKor.
80/C3 Hwanghae-Namdo (prov.), NKor.
112/B5 Hyades (peak), Chile
76/C2 Hyargas, Mong.
76/C2 Hyargas (lake), Mong.
131/K8 Hyattsville, Md,US
45/F5 Hyde, Eng,UK
84/C4 Ḩyderābād, India
73/J3 Hyderābād, Pak.
57/G5 Hyères, Fr.
57/G5 Hyères (isls.), Fr.
118/D2 Hyland (riv.), Yk,Can
78/D3 Hyōgo (pref.), Japan
78/D3 Hyō-no-sen (mtn.), Japan
124/E2 Hyrum, Ut,US
47/E5 Hythe, Eng,UK
47/H4 Hythe, Eng,UK
78/B4 Hyūga, Japan
42/H3 Hyvinkää, Fin.

I

62/A2 Iâf di Montasio (peak), It.
63/H3 Ialomiţa (riv.), Rom.
110/D1 Iapu, Braz.
63/H2 Iaşi, Rom.
63/H2 Iaşi (co.), Rom.
82/C4 Iba, Phil.
99/F5 Ibadan, Nga.
108/C3 Ibagué, Col.
110/B2 Ibaiti, Braz.
82/D5 Ibajay, Phil.
124/D2 Ibapah, Ut,US
62/E4 Ibar (riv.), Yugo.
78/C3 Ibara, Japan
79/L10 Ibaraki, Japan
79/F2 Ibaraki (pref.), Japan
108/C3 Ibarra, Ecu.
111/E2 Ibarreta, Arg.
97/L6 Ibba (riv.), Sudan
51/E4 Ibbenbüren, Ger.
99/F2 Ibdekhene (wadi), Mali
111/E2 Ibera, Esteros de (marshes), Arg.
58/D2 Ibérico, Sistema (range), Sp.
127/P7 Iberville, Qu,Can
78/E3 Ibi (riv.), Japan
59/E3 Ibi, Sp.
110/C1 Ibiá, Braz.
109/L6 Ibicaraí, Braz.
110/B2 Ibitinga, Braz.
110/F8 Ibiúna, Braz.
59/F3 Ibiza, Sp.
59/F3 Ibiza (isl.), Sp.
78/D3 Ibo (riv.), Japan
109/K6 Ibotirama, Braz.
96/H8 Iboundji (peak), Gabon
49/L4 Ibrány, Hun.
100/B2 Ibshawāy, Egypt
47/E1 Ibstock, Eng,UK
87/G3 Ibu (mtn.), Indo.
79/M9 Ibuki, Japan
79/M9 Ibuki-yama (peak), Japan
108/C6 Ica, Peru
42/N7 Iceland
84/B4 Ichalkaranji, India
84/D4 Ichchāpuram, India
79/J7 Ichihara, Japan
79/L9 Ichijima, Japan
79/H7 Ichikawa, Japan
78/E3 Ichinomiya, Japan
77/N4 Ichinoseki, Japan
79/M10 Ichishi, Japan
52/C1 Ichtegem, Belg.
109/L5 Icó, Braz.
130/K4 Icy (bay), Ak,US
130/F1 Icy (cape), Ak,US
130/L4 Icy (str.), Ak,US
125/J4 Idabel, Ok,US
122/E5 Idaho (state), US
122/E5 Idaho Falls, Id,US
84/B3 Idar, India
53/G4 Idarkopf (peak), Ger.
53/G4 Idar-Oberstein, Ger.
79/L10 Ide, Japan
76/D2 Ider (riv.), Mong.
100/C3 Idfū, Egypt
61/J5 Ídhi (peak), Gre.
74/H6 Idkū, Egypt
45/H5 Idle (riv.), Eng,UK
74/D3 Idlib, Syria
62/B3 Idrija, Slov.
52/B2 Ieper, Belg.
61/J5 Ierápetra, Gre.
101/C5 Ifakara, Tanz.
92/D4 Ifalik (isl.), Micr.
103/H8 Ifanadiana, Madg.
99/G5 Ife, Nga.
79/M10 Iga, Japan
79/M10 Iga (riv.), Japan
110/C2 Igarapava, Braz.
109/J4 Igarapé-Miri, Braz.
68/J3 Igarka, Rus.
84/B4 Igatpuri, India
74/F2 Iğdır, Turk.
130/H2 Igikpak (mtn.), Ak,US
60/A3 Iglesias, It.
126/B1 Ignace, On,Can
63/J5 Iğneada (cape), Turk.
65/M4 Igra, Rus.
110/B3 Iguaçu (riv.), Braz.
111/F2 Iguaçu Nat'l Park, Braz.
116/B4 Iguala, Mex.
59/F2 Igualada, Sp.
111/E2 Iguapa (riv.), Braz.
110/C3 Iguape, Braz.
110/C3 Iguape (riv.), Braz.
109/L5 Iguatu, Braz.
111/F2 Iguazu Nat'l Park, Arg.
96/D2 Iguidi, 'Erg (des.), Afr.
103/H8 Ihosy, Madg.
103/G8 Ihotry (lake), Madg.
68/C3 Ii (riv.), Fin.
79/E3 Iida, Japan
79/F2 Iide-san (mtn.), Japan
64/E2 Iijoki (riv.), Fin.
79/M10 Iinan, Japan
42/H3 Iisalmi, Fin.
79/M10 Iitaka, Japan
64/E3 Iitti, Fin.
79/F2 Iiyama, Japan
78/B4 Iizuka, Japan
96/C3 Ijill (peak), Mrta.
50/C4 IJmeer (bay), Neth.
50/B4 IJmuiden, Neth.
98/B2 Ijnaoun (well), Mrta.
42/H2 Ijoki (riv.), Fin.
50/C4 IJssel (riv.), Neth.
50/C3 IJsselmeer (lake), Neth.
50/C3 IJsselmuiden, Neth.
50/C4 IJsselstein, Neth.
111/F2 Ijuí, Braz.
78/B5 Ijūin, Japan
52/B2 Ijzer (riv.), Belg.
65/M5 Ik (riv.), Rus.
103/H7 Ikahavo (plat.), Madg.
61/J4 Ikaría (isl.), Gre.
104/D1 Ikela, D.R. Congo
79/M10 Ikenokoya-yama (peak), Japan
63/F4 Ikhtiman, Bul.
78/A4 Iki (chan.), Japan
78/A4 Iki (isl.), Japan
79/L10 Ikoma, Japan
103/H7 Ikopa (riv.), Madg.
82/D4 Ilagan, Phil.
72/E2 Īlām, Iran
84/E2 Ilam, Nepal
82/D3 Ilan, Tai.
49/K2 Iława, Pol.
97/M4 'Ilay, Sudan
46/D4 Ilchester, Eng,UK
122/G2 Ile-à-la-Crosse, Sk,Can
123/G2 Ile-a-la-Crosse (lake), Sk,Can
104/D1 Ilebo, D.R. Congo
56/E2 Ile-de-France (reg.), Fr.
67/K2 Ilek (riv.), Kaz., Rus.
127/N7 Ile-Perrot, Qu,Can
98/E5 Iles Ehotilés Nat'l Park, IvC.
99/G5 Ilesha, Nga.
90/B3 Ilfracombe, Austl.
46/B4 Ilfracombe, Eng,UK
66/E4 Ilgaz, Turk.
74/B2 Ilgın, Turk.
110/H8 Ilhabela, Braz.
110/J8 Ilha Grande (bay), Braz.
110/B1 Ilha Solteira (res.), Braz.
58/A2 Ilhavo, Port.
109/L6 Ilhéus, Braz.
75/C3 Ili (riv.), China, Kaz.
130/G4 Iliamna (lake), Ak,US
130/H3 Iliamna (vol.), Ak,US
82/D6 Iligan, Phil.
74/E3 Ilısu (res.), Turk.
63/H6 Ilium (Troy) (ruins), Turk.
45/G6 Ilkeston, Eng,UK
45/G4 Ilkley, Eng,UK
55/F3 Ill (riv.), Aus.
54/D1 Ill (riv.), Fr.
112/C1 Illapel, Chile
99/G3 Illéla, Niger
55/G1 Iller (riv.), Ger.
58/D2 Illescas, Sp.
108/E7 Illimani (peak), Bol.
53/G5 Illingen, Ger.
126/B4 Illinois (state), US
126/B3 Illinois (riv.), Il,US
46/A6 Illogan, Eng,UK
58/D4 Illora, Sp.
54/D2 Illzach, Fr.
57/J2 Ilm (riv.), Ger.
42/G3 Ilmajoki, Fin.
51/G5 Ilme (riv.), Ger.
64/F4 Il'men' (lake), Rus.
48/F3 Ilmenau, Ger.
51/H2 Ilmenau (riv.), Ger.
46/D5 Ilminster, Eng,UK
108/D7 Ilo, Peru
82/D5 Iloilo, Phil.
99/G4 Ilorin, Nga.
67/H2 Ilovlya (riv.), Rus.
51/H4 Ilse (riv.), Ger.
51/H4 Ilsede, Ger.
51/H5 Ilsenburg, Ger.
63/H5 Ilyas (pt.), Turk.
65/N3 Ilych (riv.), Rus.
57/K2 Ilz (riv.), Ger.
78/C3 Imabari, Japan
79/F2 Imaichi, Japan
103/H8 Imaloto (riv.), Madg.
74/C3 İmamoğlu, Turk.
64/F2 Imandra (lake), Rus.
78/A4 Imari, Japan
42/J3 Imatra, Fin.
78/E3 Imazu, Japan
79/J7 Imba, Japan
110/B4 Imbituba, Braz.
97/P6 Īmī, Eth.
67/J5 Imishli, Azer.
61/L7 Imittós (mtn.), Gre.
124/C2 Imlay, Nv,US
51/G6 Immenhausen, Ger.
55/G2 Immenstadt im Allgäu, Ger.
45/H4 Immingham, Eng,UK
129/H5 Immokalee, Fl,US
130/J2 Imnavait (mtn.), Ak,US
99/G5 Imo (state), Nga.
57/J4 Imola, It.
109/J5 Imperatriz, Braz.
57/H5 Imperia, It.
123/G3 Imperial, Sk,Can
125/G2 Imperial, Ne,US
96/J7 Impfondo, Congo
85/F3 Imphāl, India
63/J5 İmrali (isl.), Turk.
74/D2 İmranlı, Turk.
55/G3 Imst, Aus.
79/E3 Ina, Japan
79/L10 Ina (riv.), Japan
49/H2 Ina (riv.), Pol.
79/M9 Inabe, Japan
79/L10 Inagawa, Japan
79/H7 Inagi, Japan
96/G2 I-n-Amenas, Alg.
79/K10 Inami, Japan
42/H1 Inari (lake), Fin.
63/G2 Inău (peak), Rom.
79/G2 Inawashiro (lake), Japan
79/M9 Inazawa, Japan
59/G3 Inca, Sp.
99/F2 I-n-Chaouâg (wadi), Mali
43/C3 Inchinnan, Sc,UK
98/B2 Inchiri (reg.), Mrta.
80/D4 Inch'ŏn, SKor.
80/D4 Inch'on-Jikhalsi (prov.), SKor.
96/E3 I-n-Dagouber (well), Mali
110/C1 Indaiá (riv.), Braz.
110/C2 Indaiatuba, Braz.
82/D6 Indanan, Phil.
53/F2 Inde (riv.), Ger.
53/F2 Inden, Ger.
116/D4 Independence, Belz.
124/C3 Independence, Ca,US
125/J3 Independence, Ks,US
125/J3 Independence, Mo,US
124/C2 Independence (mts.), Nv,US
131/E6 Independence Nat'l Hist. Park, Pa,US
67/J2 Inder (lake), Kaz.
71/G7 India
39/N6 Indian (ocean)
126/C3 Indiana (state), US
126/E3 Indiana, Pa,US
132/R16 Indiana Dunes Nat'l Lakesh., In,US
126/C4 Indianapolis (cap.), In,US
123/H3 Indian Head, Sk,Can
129/F3 Indianola, Ms,US
129/H5 Indiantown, Fl,US
110/B1 Indiaporã, Braz.
69/Q3 Indigirka (riv.), Rus.
62/E3 Inđija, Yugo.
124/C4 Indio, Ca,US
83/C1 Indochina (reg.), Asia
87/E4 Indonesia
90/E6 Indooroopilly, Austl.
84/C3 Indore, India
86/B4 Indragiri (riv.), Indo.
86/C5 Indramayu (cape), Indo.
84/D4 Indrāvati (riv.), India
56/D3 Indre (riv.), Fr.
56/D3 Indrois (riv.), Fr.
71/F7 Indus (riv.), Asia
73/J4 Indus, Mouths of the, Pak.
74/C2 İnebolu, Turk.
99/E1 I-n-Echaï (well), Mali
74/B2 İnegöl, Turk.
62/E2 Ineu, Rom.
96/D1 Inezgane, Mor.
102/C4 Infanta (cape), SAfr.
116/A4 Infiernillo (res.), Mex.
58/C1 Infiesto, Sp.
108/C4 Ingapirca, Ecu.
52/C2 Ingelmunster, Belg.
90/G8 Ingleburn, Austl.
45/G2 Ingleton, Eng,UK
127/Q8 Inglewood, On,Can
131/B3 Inglewood, Ca,US
132/C2 Inglewood-Finn Hill, Wa,US
129/H4 Inglis, Fl,US
76/G1 Ingoda (riv.), Rus.
45/J5 Ingoldmells, Eng,UK
57/J2 Ingolstadt, Ger.
105/E Ingrid Christianson (coast), Ant.
99/G2 I-n-Guezzâm, Alg.
66/E3 Ingulets (riv.), Ukr.
67/G4 Inguri (riv.), Geo.
109/J7 Inhumas, Braz.
44/A1 Inishowen (pen.), Ire.
44/B1 Inishowen Head (pt.), Ire.
132/F7 Inkster, Mi,US
78/C3 Inland (sea), Japan
85/G3 Inle (lake), Myan.
99/E2 I-n-Milach (well), Mali
57/K2 Inn (riv.), Eur.
76/G3 Inner Mongolia (reg.), China
51/H4 Innerste (riv.), Ger.
57/K3 Innichen (San Candido), It.
90/B2 Innisfail, Austl.
122/E2 Innisfail, Ab,Can
130/G3 Innoko (riv.), Ak,US
55/H3 Innsbruck, Aus.
46/B5 Inny (riv.), Eng,UK
78/C4 Ino, Japan
104/C1 Inongo, D.R. Congo
49/K4 Inovec (peak), Slvk.
49/K2 Inowrocław, Pol.
99/E1 I-n-Sâkâne, Erg (des.), Mali
96/F2 I-n-Salah, Alg.
43/D2 Insch, Sc,UK
85/G4 Insein, Myan.
122/A2 Inside (passg.), BC,Can
65/P2 Inta, Rus.
99/F2 I-n-Tassik (well), Mali
122/B2 Interior (plat.), BC,Can
123/K3 International Falls, Mn,US
83/B2 Inthanon (peak), Thai.
63/H3 Intorsura Buzăului, Rom.
79/G3 Inubō-zaki (pt.), Japan
119/J3 Inukjuak, Qu,Can
113/K8 Inútil (bay), Chile
79/E3 Inuyama, Japan
43/C2 Inveraray, Sc,UK
89/G7 Invercargill, NZ
91/D1 Inverell, Austl.
43/C2 Invergarry, Sc,UK
43/D2 Inverkeilor, Sc,UK
123/H3 Invermay, Sk,Can
127/J2 Inverness, NS,Can
43/C2 Inverness, Sc,UK
129/G3 Inverness, Al,US
129/H4 Inverness, Fl,US
43/D2 Inverurie, Sc,UK
82/B6 Investigator (shoal)
104/F4 Inyangani (peak), Zim.
130/D2 Inymney, Gora (mtn.), Rus.
124/C3 Inyo (mts.), Ca,US
67/H1 Inza, Rus.
79/J7 Inzai, Japan
61/G3 Ioánnina, Gre.
125/J3 Iola, Ks,US
73/H1 Iolotan', Trkm.
104/B4 Iona Nat'l Park, Ang.
126/C3 Ionia, Mi,US
61/F3 Ionian (sea), Eur.
61/F3 Ionian (isls.), Gre.
61/J4 Íos (isl.), Gre.
98/A2 Iouîk (cape), Mrta.
123/K5 Iowa (state), US
123/L5 Iowa (riv.), Ia,US
123/L5 Iowa City, Ia,US
123/K5 Iowa Falls, Ia,US
110/B1 Ipameri, Braz.
112/B5 Ipan (isl.), Chile
110/D1 Ipanema, Braz.
110/D1 Ipatinga, Braz.
49/K4 Ipel' (Ipoly) (riv.), Hun., Slvk.
108/C3 Ipiales, Col.
109/L6 Ipiaú, Braz.
86/B3 Ipoh, Malay.
49/K4 Ipoly (Ipel') (riv.), Hun., Slvk.
109/H7 Iporá, Braz.
61/K2 Ipsala, Turk.
90/E7 Ipswich, Austl.
47/H2 Ipswich, Eng,UK
123/J4 Ipswich, SD,US
109/K4 Ipu, Braz.
110/B2 Ipuã, Braz.
119/K2 Iqaluit (cap.), Nun.
108/D8 Iquique, Chile
108/D4 Iquitos, Peru
79/M10 Irago (chan.), Japan
79/E3 Irago-misaki (cape), Japan
61/J4 Iráklia (isl.), Gre.
61/J5 Iráklion, Gre.
72/F2 Iran
86/D3 Iran (mts.), Indo., Malay.
73/H3 Īrānshahr, Iran
116/A3 Irapuato, Mex.
72/D2 Iraq
110/B3 Irati, Braz.
87/H4 Irau (mtn.), Indo.
74/K5 Irbid, Jor.
74/L5 Irbid (gov.), Jor.
74/F3 Irbīl, Iraq
109/K6 Irecê, Braz.
43/A4 Ireland
43/B3 Ireland, Northern, UK
44/B5 Ireland's Eye (isl.), Ire.
65/N5 Iremel', Gora (peak), Rus.
46/C2 Irfon (riv.), Wal,UK
99/G2 Irhazer Oua-n-Agadez (wadi), Niger
80/D5 Iri, SKor.
87/H4 Irian Jaya (reg.), Indo.
98/D2 Irîgui (reg.), Mali, Mrta.
67/L2 Iriklinskiy (res.), Rus.
101/B4 Iringa, Tanz.
101/B5 Iringa (prov.), Tanz.
82/D3 Iriomote (isl.), Japan
109/H4 Iriri (riv.), Braz.
44/C4 Irish (sea), Ire., UK
76/E1 Irkut (riv.), Rus.
76/E1 Irkutsk, Rus.
45/F5 Irlam, Eng,UK
46/D1 Iron Bridge, Eng,UK
62/F3 Iron Gate (gorge), Eur.
126/B2 Iron Mountain, Mi,US
126/B2 Iron River, Mi,US
126/D4 Ironton, Oh,US
126/B2 Ironwood, Mi,US
126/D1 Iroquois Falls, On,Can
79/F3 Irō-zaki (pt.), Japan
66/E1 Irput' (riv.), Bela., Rus.
53/F4 Irrel, Ger.
53/F3 Irsen (riv.), Ger.
45/E3 Irt (riv.), Eng,UK
45/F1 Irthing (riv.), Eng,UK
47/F2 Irthlingborough, Eng,UK
68/G4 Irtysh (riv.), Kaz., Rus
79/H7 Iruma, Japan
101/A2 Irumu, D.R. Congo
58/E1 Irún, Sp.
43/C3 Irvine, Sc,UK
131/C3 Irvine, Ca,US
128/D3 Irving, Tx,US
131/F5 Irvington, NJ,US
90/C3 Isaac (riv.), Austl.
82/D6 Isabela, Phil.
119/K2 Isabella (bay), Nun.,Can
119/R7 Isachsen (cape), Nun.,Can
42/M6 Ísafjardhardjúp (fjord), Ice.
78/B4 Isahaya, Japan
103/H8 Isalo Nat'l Park, Madg.
103/H8 Isalo Ruiniform, Massif (plat.), Madg.
48/G4 Isar (riv.), Aus., Ger.
55/H4 Isarco (Eisack) (riv.), It.
60/C2 Ischia, It.
51/H3 Ise (riv.), Ger.
79/E3 Ise, Japan
79/M10 Ise (bay), Japan
47/F2 Ise (riv.), Eng,UK
79/F3 Isehara, Japan
131/F5 Iselin, NJ,US
57/K2 Isen (riv.), Ger.
57/J4 Iseo (lake), It.
56/F4 Isère (riv.), Fr.
51/E6 Iserlohn, Ger.
60/D2 Isernia, It.
79/F3 Isesaki, Japan
79/E3 Ise-Shima Nat'l Park, Japan
65/Q4 Iset' (riv.), Rus.
99/F5 Iseyin, Nga.
79/L10 Ishi (riv.), Japan
79/F2 Ishibashi, Japan
79/M9 Ishibe, Japan
92/B2 Ishigaki, Japan
82/D3 Ishigaki (isl.), Japan
79/F2 Ishige, Japan
79/G2 Ishikawa, Japan
79/E2 Ishikawa (pref.), Japan
79/N10 Ishiki, Japan
68/H4 Ishim (riv.), Kaz., Rus.
65/R4 Ishim, Rus.
67/L1 Ishimbay, Rus.
79/G1 Ishinomaki, Japan
79/G2 Ishioka, Japan
78/C4 Ishizuchi-san (mtn.), Japan
75/B4 Ismail Samani (peak), Taj.
126/C2 Ishpeming, Mi,US
108/E7 Isiboro Securé Nat'l Park, Bol.
113/G1 Isidoro, Uru.
68/H4 Isil'kul', Rus.
97/L7 Isiro, D.R. Congo
100/C4 Is, Jabal (peak), Sudan
74/D3 İskenderun, Turk.
74/C2 İskilip, Turk.
61/H1 Iskŭr (res.), Bul.
61/H1 Iskŭr (riv.), Bul.
43/D2 Isla (riv.), Sc,UK
58/B4 Isla Cristina, Sp.
112/Q9 Isla de Maipo, Chile
90/C4 Isla Gorge Nat'l Park, Austl.
117/N9 Isla Isabella Nat'l Park, Mex.
73/K2 Islāmābād (cap.), Pak.
112/B5 Isla Magdalena Nat'l Park, Chile
84/E2 Islāmpur, India
116/D3 Isla Mujeres, Mex.
123/K2 Island Lake, Mb,Can
127/K1 Islands (bay), Nf,Can
56/D4 Isle (riv.), Fr.
47/G2 Isleham, Eng,UK
44/D3 Isle of Man, UK
44/D2 Isle of Whithorn, Sc,UK
47/E5 Isle of Wight, (co.), Eng,UK
126/B2 Isle Royale Nat'l Park, Mi,US
131/G5 Islip, NY,US
65/X9 Ismailovo Park, Rus.
100/C2 Ismalia (Al Ismāʿīlīyah), Egypt
100/C3 Isnā, Egypt
55/G2 Isny, Ger.
79/M10 Isobe, Japan
42/H3 Isojärven Nat'l Park, Fin.
101/B5 Isoka, Zam.
60/C2 Isola del Liri, It.
60/E3 Isola di Capo Rizzuto, It.
74/B3 Isparta, Turk.
56/C5 Ispéguy, Col d' (pass), Fr.
63/H4 Isperikh, Bul.
74/E2 İspir, Turk.
74/J5 Israel
132/C2 Issaquah, Wa,US
50/D5 Issel (riv.), Ger.
50/D5 Isselburg, Ger.
98/D5 Issia, IvC.
56/E4 Issoire, Fr.
56/E3 Issoudun, Fr.
50/D5 Issum, Ger.
75/C3 Issyk-Kul' (lake), Kyr.
52/B6 Issy-les-Moulineaux, Fr.
62/E1 Istállós-kő (peak), Hun.
63/J5 İstanbul, Turk.
63/J5 İstanbul (prov.), Turk.
63/H5 Istranca (mts.), Turk.
56/F5 Istres, Fr.
62/A3 Istria (pen.), Cro.
87/F2 Isulan, Phil.
109/L6 Itabaiana, Braz.
110/D2 Itabapoana (riv.), Braz.
109/K6 Itaberaba, Braz.
110/D1 Itabira, Braz.
110/D2 Itabirito, Braz.
110/L7 Itaboraí, Braz.
109/L7 Itabuna, Braz.
109/H5 Itacaiunas (riv.), Braz.
108/G4 Itacoatiara, Braz.
108/D5 Itacuaí (riv.), Braz.
110/K7 Itaguaí, Braz.
108/C2 Itagüí, Col.
110/B2 Itaí, Braz.
110/B3 Itaiópolis, Braz.
111/F1 Itaipu (res.), Braz., Par.
109/G4 Itaituba, Braz.
110/B3 Itajaí, Braz.
110/B3 Itajaí (riv.), Braz.
110/H7 Itajubá, Braz.
79/G3 Itako, Japan
41/F4 Italy
109/L7 Itamaraju, Braz.
110/D1 Itamarandiba, Braz.
110/D1 Itambacuri, Braz.
110/D1 Itambé (peak), Braz.
79/L10 Itami, Japan
85/F2 Itanagar, India
110/G9 Itanhaém, Braz.
110/C2 Itanhandu, Braz.
110/D1 Itanhém (riv.), Braz.
110/D1 Itanhomi, Braz.
109/K7 Itaobim, Braz.
110/D2 Itaocara, Braz.
109/L4 Itapagé, Braz.
110/C2 Itapecerica, Braz.
109/K4 Itapecuru-Mirim, Braz.
110/D2 Itapemirim, Braz.
110/D2 Itaperuna, Braz.
109/K7 Itapetinga, Braz.
110/B2 Itapetininga, Braz.
110/B2 Itapeva, Braz.
110/G8 Itapevi, Braz.
109/K6 Itapicuru (riv.), Braz.
109/L4 Itapipoca, Braz.
110/G7 Itapira, Braz.
110/B2 Itaporanga, Braz.
110/G8 Itaquaquecetuba, Braz.
110/B3 Itararé, Braz.
84/C3 Itārsi, India
110/C2 Itatinga (res.), Braz.
42/J3 Itä-Suomen (prov.), Fin.
110/C2 Itatiaia Nat'l Park, Braz.
110/G8 Itatiba, Braz.
110/C2 Itatinga (res.), Braz.
109/K5 Itaueira (riv.), Braz.
110/C2 Itaúna, Braz.
77/N3 Itayanagi, Japan
82/D3 Itbayat (isl.), Phil.
47/E4 Itchen (riv.), Eng,UK
97/K7 Itembiri (riv.), D.R. Congo
108/F6 Iténez (riv.), Bol.
104/E4 Itezhi-Tezhi (dam), Zam.
126/E3 Ithaca, NY,US
61/G3 Ithaca (Itháki) (isl.), Gre.
51/G5 Ith Hils (ridge), Ger.
46/C2 Ithon (riv.), Wal,UK
101/B4 Itigi, Tanz.
79/F3 Itō, Japan
79/E2 Itoigawa, Japan
56/D2 Iton (riv.), Fr.
79/H7 Itsukaichi, Japan
51/F6 Itter (riv.), Ger.
60/A2 Ittiri, It.
110/C2 Itu, Braz.
108/D5 Ituí (riv.), Braz.
110/B1 Ituiutaba, Braz.
110/B1 Itumbiara, Braz.
110/B1 Itumbiara (res.), Braz.
123/H3 Ituna, Sk,Can
110/B3 Ituporanga, Braz.
110/B1 Iturama, Braz.
110/J6 Itutinga (res.), Braz.
110/C2 Ituverava, Braz.
108/E5 Ituxi (riv.), Braz.
74/H6 Ityāy al Bārūd, Egypt
48/E2 Itzehoe, Ger.
130/C2 Iul'tin, Gora (mtn.), Rus.
110/D2 Iuna, Braz.
110/B3 Ivaí (riv.), Braz.
110/B3 Ivaiporã, Braz.
42/H1 Ivalojoki (riv.), Fin.
57/M2 Ivančice, Czh.
62/D4 Ivangrad, Yugo.
126/D1 Ivanhoe (riv.), On,Can
62/E4 Ivanjica, Yugo.
66/C2 Ivano-Frankivs'k, Ukr.
66/C2 Ivano-Frankivs'ka (obl.), Ukr.
64/J4 Ivanovo, Rus.
65/J4 Ivanovo Obl., Rus.
61/J2 Ivaylovgrad (res.), Bul.
65/P3 Ivdel, Rus.
96/H7 Ivindo (riv.), Gabon
103/H8 Ivohibe, Madg.
103/J7 Ivondro (riv.), Madg.
57/G4 Ivrea, It.
52/B6 Ivry-sur-Seine, Fr.
130/K2 Ivvavik Nat'l Park, Yk,Can
46/C6 Ivybridge, Eng,UK
79/F2 Iwai, Japan
79/G2 Iwaki, Japan
78/C3 Iwakuni, Japan
79/M9 Iwakura, Japan
78/D3 Iwami, Japan
77/N3 Iwamizawa, Japan
79/G1 Iwanuma, Japan
79/E3 Iwata, Japan
77/N4 Iwate-san (mtn.), Japan
79/H7 Iwatsuki, Japan
99/G5 Iwo, Nga.
92/D2 Iwo Jima (isl.), Japan
48/C3 Ixelles, Belg.
116/B4 Ixtaltepec, Mex.
117/P9 Ixtlán del Río, Mex.
47/G2 Ixworth, Eng,UK
76/D1 Iya (riv.), Rus.
78/C4 Iyo, Japan
78/C4 Iyo (sea), Japan
116/D4 Izabal (lake), Guat.
67/H4 Izberbash, Rus.
52/C2 Izegem, Belg.
130/F4 Izembek Nat'l Wild. Ref., Ak,US
65/M4 Izhevsk, Rus.
65/M2 Izhma (riv.), Rus.
130/E5 Izigan (cape), Ak,US
73/G4 Izkī, Oman
63/J3 Izmail, Ukr.
74/A2 İzmir, Turk.
63/J5 İzmit, Turk.
63/J5 İzmit (gulf), Turk.
58/C4 Íznájar, Sp.
63/J5 İznik, Turk.
63/H5 İznik (lake), Turk.
74/L5 Izra', Syria
62/D2 Izsák, Hun.
77/M5 Izu (isls.), Japan
79/F3 Izu (pen.), Japan
116/B4 Izúcar de Matamoros, Mex.
79/H8 Izu-Fuji-Hakone Nat'l Park, Japan
78/A3 Izuhara, Japan
78/D3 Izumi, Japan
79/L10 Izumi-ōtsu, Japan
79/L10 Izumi-Sano, Japan
78/C3 Izumo, Japan
66/F2 Izyum, Ukr.

J

100/B5 Jabal Abyad (plat.), Sudan
74/K4 Jabal Lubnān (gov.), Leb.
58/D3 Jabalón (riv.), Sp.
84/C3 Jabalpur, India
74/K6 Jabālyah, Gaza
52/C1 Jabbeke, Belg.
100/C4 Jabjabah, Wādī (dry riv.), Egypt, Sudan
74/K4 Jablah, Syria
61/G2 Jablanica (mts.), Alb.
49/H3 Jablonec nad Nisou, Czh.
109/L5 Jaboatão, Braz.
110/B2 Jaboticabal, Braz.
62/E3 Jabuka, Yugo.
86/B4 Jabung (cape), Indo.
59/E1 Jaca, Sp.
110/C2 Jacareí, Braz.
97/Q5 Jaceel (riv.), Som.
127/G2 Jackman, Me,US
124/D2 Jackpot, Nv,US
128/D3 Jacksboro, Tx,US
129/G4 Jackson, Al,US
124/B3 Jackson, Ca,US
126/C3 Jackson, Mi,US
123/K5 Jackson, Mn,US
125/K3 Jackson, Mo,US
129/F3 Jackson (cap.), Ms,US
122/D5 Jackson (mts.), Nv,US
126/D4 Jackson, Oh,US
129/F3 Jackson, Tn,US
122/F5 Jackson, Wy,US
122/F4 Jackson (lake), Wy,US
129/G3 Jacksonville, Al,US
128/E3 Jacksonville, Ar,US
129/H4 Jacksonville, Fl,US
126/B4 Jacksonville, Il,US
129/J3 Jacksonville, NC,US
128/E4 Jacksonville, Tx,US
129/H4 Jacksonville Beach, Fl,US
117/G4 Jacmel, Haiti
73/J3 Jacobābād, Pak.
109/K6 Jacobina, Braz.
127/H1 Jacques-Cartier (mtn.), Qu,Can
127/G2 Jacques-Cartier (riv.), Qu,Can
111/F2 Jacuí (riv.), Braz.
109/L6 Jacuipe (riv.), Braz.
110/C3 Jacupiranga, Braz.
73/H3 Jaddi (pt.), Pak.
48/E2 Jade (bay), Ger.
51/F2 Jade (riv.), Ger.
51/F2 Jadebusen (bay), Ger.
58/D4 Jaén, Sp.
91/A3 Jaffa (cape), Austl.
84/D6 Jaffna, SrL.
84/D4 Jagdalpur, India
84/D2 Jagdīspur, India
82/D6 Jagna, Phil.
75/C5 Jagraon, India
57/J2 Jagst (riv.), Ger.
84/C4 Jagtiāl, India
109/K6 Jaguaquara, Braz.
113/G2 Jaguarão, Braz.
113/F2 Jaguarão (riv.), Braz.
110/G7 Jaguari (riv.), Braz.
110/B3 Jaguariaíva, Braz.
109/L5 Jaguaribe (riv.), Braz.
110/G7 Jaguariúna, Braz.
91/D3 Jagungal (peak), Austl.
72/F3 Jahrom, Iran
87/G3 Jailolo, Indo.
84/C2 Jaipur, India
84/B2 Jaisalmer, India
62/C3 Jajce, Bosn.
84/E3 Jājpur, India
86/C5 Jakarta (cap.), Indo.
42/G3 Jakobstad, Fin.
125/G4 Jal, NM,US
73/K2 Jalālābād, Afg.
42/G3 Jalasjärvi, Fin.
110/B2 Jales, Braz.
84/C3 Jālgaon, India
96/H6 Jalingo, Nga.
117/P9 Jalisco (state), Mex.
60/A4 Jaliṭah, Jazīrat (isl.), Tun.
84/C4 Jālna, India
58/E2 Jalón (riv.), Sp.
84/B2 Jālor, India
84/E2 Jalpaiguri, India
97/K2 Jālū, Libya
92/F4 Jaluit (atoll), Mrsh.
72/E2 Jalūlā', Iraq
97/P7 Jamaame, Som.
99/H4 Jamaare (riv.), Nga.
117/F4 Jamaica
117/F4 Jamaica (chan.), NAm.
84/E3 Jamālpur, Bang.
84/E2 Jamālpur, India
109/G5 Jamanxim (riv.), Braz.
108/F5 Jamari (riv.), Braz.
86/B4 Jambi, Indo.
86/A2 Jambuair (cape), Indo.
121/K1 James (lake), On,Can
119/H3 James (bay), On, Qu,Can
112/B5 James (pt.), Chile
123/J4 James (riv.), ND, SD,US
126/E4 James (riv.), Va,US
131/F5 Jamesburg, NJ,US
118/G1 James Ross (str.), Nun.,Can
123/J4 Jamestown, ND,US
126/E3 Jamestown, NY,US
129/G2 Jamestown, Tn,US
116/B4 Jamiltepec, Mex.
75/B5 Jammu, India
75/C5 Jammu and Kashmīr (state), India
84/B3 Jāmnagar, India
73/K3 Jāmpur, Pak.
42/H3 Jämsä, Fin.

84/E3 Jamshedpur, India
42/E3 Jämtland (co.), Swe.
84/E3 Jamūi, India
123/H2 Jan (lake), Sk,Can
64/E3 Janakkala, Fin.
109/K7 Janaúba, Braz.
109/J3 Janaucu (isl.), Braz.
110/B2 Jandaia do Sul, Braz.
58/C4 Jándula (riv.), Sp.
126/B3 Janesville, Wi,US
84/C4 Jangaon, India
84/E3 Jangipur, India
49/K2 Janikowo, Pol.
74/K5 Janīn, WBnk.
62/D3 Janja, Bosn.
41/D1 Jan Mayen (isl.), Nor.
62/D2 Jánoshalma, Hun.
49/M3 Janów Lubelski, Pol.
109/K7 Januária, Braz.
100/C2 Janūb Sīnā' (gov.), Egypt
84/C3 Jaora, India
77/M4 Japan
77/L4 Japan (sea), Asia
79/E3 Japanese Alps (range), Japan
79/E2 Japanese Alps Nat'l Park, Japan
108/E4 Japurá (riv.), Braz.
74/D3 Jarābulus, Syria
58/C2 Jaraíz de la Vera, Sp.
74/K5 Jarash, Jor.
96/H1 Jarbah (isl.), Tun.
111/E2 Jardín América, Arg.
110/C2 Jardinópolis, Braz.
109/H3 Jari (riv.), Braz.
84/E3 Jaridih, India
96/H1 Jarjīs, Tun.
53/E5 Jarny, Fr.
49/J3 Jarocin, Pol.
49/H3 Jaroměř, Czh.
49/M3 Jarosław, Pol.
45/G2 Jarrow, Eng,UK
83/C2 Jars (plain), Laos
53/F6 Jarville-la-Malgrange, Fr.
93/J5 Jarvis (isl.), PacUS
49/L4 Jasło, Pol.
122/D2 Jasper, Ab,Can
129/G3 Jasper, Al,US
129/H4 Jasper, Fl,US
129/G3 Jasper, Ga,US
126/C4 Jasper, In,US
128/E4 Jasper, Tx,US
122/D2 Jasper Nat'l Park, Ab, BC,Can
84/C2 Jaspur, India
49/J2 Jastrowie, Pol.
49/K4 Jastrzębie Zdroj, Pol.
62/E2 Jászapáti, Hun.
62/D2 Jászárokszállás, Hun.
62/D2 Jászberény, Hun.
62/E2 Jászladány, Hun.
62/E2 Jász-Nagykun-Szolnok (co.), Hun.
110/B1 Jataí, Braz.
108/G4 Jatapu (riv.), Braz.
59/E3 Játiva, Sp.
110/B2 Jaú, Braz.
108/F4 Jaú (riv.), Braz.
108/F3 Jauaperi (riv.), Braz.
109/H4 Jauaru (mts.), Braz.
108/F3 Jaua Sarisarinama Nat'l Park, Ven.
108/C6 Jauja, Peru
54/D4 Jaunpass (pass), Swi.
86/C5 Java (isl.), Indo.
86/D5 Java (sea), Indo.
108/D5 Javari (riv.), Braz.
59/F3 Jávea, Sp.
113/J6 Javier (isl.), Chile
62/D1 Javorie (peak), Slvk.
97/Q7 Jawhar (Giohar), Som.
49/J3 Jawor, Pol.
87/J4 Jaya (peak), Indo.
87/K4 Jayapura, Indo.
128/C3 Jayton, Tx,US
47/H3 Jaywick, Eng,UK
72/D5 Jazā'ir Farasān (isls.), SAr.
49/L3 Jędrzejów, Pol.
48/F2 Jeetze (riv.), Ger.
122/C4 Jefferson (peak), Or,US
128/E3 Jefferson, Tx,US
125/J3 Jefferson City (cap.), Mo,US
126/C4 Jeffersonville, In,US
122/G5 Jeffrey City, Wy,US
112/B5 Jeinemeni (peak), Chile
64/E4 Jēkabpils, Lat.
49/J3 Jelcz-Laskowice, Pol.
49/H3 Jelenia Góra, Pol.
49/H3 Jelenia Góra (prov.), Pol.
84/E2 Jelep (pass), China
64/D4 Jelgava, Lat.
52/C3 Jemappes, Belg.
86/D5 Jember, Indo.
124/F4 Jemez Pueblo, NM,US
87/E4 Jempang (riv.), Indo.
100/C3 Jemsa, Egypt
48/F3 Jena, Ger.
128/E4 Jena, La,US
87/E5 Jeneponto, Indo.
128/E4 Jennings, La,US
118/F2 Jenny Lind (isl.), Nun.,Can
119/H2 Jens Muck (isl.), Nun.,Can
109/L6 Jequié, Braz.
109/K7 Jequitinhonha, Braz.
109/K7 Jequitinhonha (riv.), Braz.
117/G4 Jérémie, Haiti
117/P9 Jerez de García Salinas, Mex.
58/B4 Jerez de la Frontera, Sp.
58/B3 Jerez de los Caballeros, Sp.
131/G5 Jericho, NY,US
74/K6 Jericho (Arīḥā), WBnk.
122/E5 Jerome, Id,US
131/F5 Jersey City, NJ,US
126/B4 Jerseyville, Il,US
74/M9 Jerusalem (dist.), Isr.
74/N9 Jerusalem Walls Nat'l Park, Isr.
74/K6 Jerusalem (Yerushalayim) (cap.), Isr.
122/C3 Jervis (inlet), BC,Can
62/B2 Jesenice, Slov.
57/K5 Jesi, It.
84/E3 Jessore, Bang.
129/H4 Jesup, Ga,US
127/N6 Jésus (isl.), Qu,Can
111/D3 Jesús María, Arg.
117/F3 Jesús Menéndez, Cuba
98/A4 Jeta (isl.), GBis.
125/H3 Jetmore, Ks,US
84/B3 Jetpur, India
52/D3 Jeumont, Fr.
51/E1 Jever, Ger.
123/G5 Jewel Cave Nat'l Mon., SD,US
84/D4 Jeypore, India
61/F1 Jezerce (peak), Alb.
49/K2 Jeziorák (lake), Pol.
84/E3 Jhā Jhā, India
84/C3 Jhālawār, India
73/K2 Jhang Sadar, Pak.
84/C2 Jhānsi, India
84/D3 Jhārsuguda, India
73/K2 Jhelum (riv.), India, Pak.
73/K2 Jhelum, Pak.
84/E3 Jiāganj, India
76/F5 Jialing (riv.), China
81/C4 Jialu (riv.), China
77/L2 Jiamusi, China
82/B2 Ji'an, China
82/B3 Jian (riv.), China
83/E1 Jiang (riv.), China
82/B3 Jiangmen, China
81/D4 Jiangsu (prov.), China
81/D5 Jiangxi (prov.), China
81/E5 Jiangyin, China
82/C2 Jianyang, China
82/D2 Jiaojiang, China
77/J3 Jiaolai (riv.), China
81/C4 Jiaozuo, China
75/C4 Jiashi, China
81/E5 Jiaxing, China
76/D4 Jiayuguan, China
63/F2 Jibou, Rom.
73/G4 Jibsh, Ra's (pt.), Oman
49/H3 Jičín, Czh.
72/C4 Jiddah, SAr.
49/H4 Jihlava, Czh.
57/L2 Jihočeský (reg.), Czh.
49/H4 Jihomoravský (reg.), Czh.
96/G1 Jijel, Alg.
63/H2 Jijia (riv.), Rom.
97/P6 Jijiga, Eth.
53/E3 Jijona, Sp.
100/A4 Jilf al Kabīr, Ḩadabat al (upland), Egypt
110/B2 Jilhá (res.), Braz.
49/J4 Jilhava (riv.), Czh.
75/E2 Jili (lake), China
77/K3 Jilin, China
77/J1 Jiliu (riv.), China
59/E2 Jiloca (riv.), Sp.
97/N6 Jīma, Eth.
62/E3 Jimbolia, Rom.
58/C4 Jimena de la Frontera, Sp.
76/B3 Jimsar, China
82/C2 Jin (riv.), China
85/K2 Jin (riv.), China
81/D3 Jinan, China
84/C2 Jīnd, India
49/H4 Jindřichuv Hradec, Czh.
81/B4 Jing (riv.), China
82/C2 Jingdezhen, China
82/B2 Jinggangshan, China
81/D3 Jinghai, China
81/C5 Jingmen, China
82/C2 Jinhua, China
81/C2 Jining, China
81/D4 Jining, China
101/B2 Jinja, Ugan.
116/D5 Jinotega, Nic.
116/D5 Jinotepe, Nic.
81/B4 Jinqian (riv.), China
81/E5 Jinshan, China
85/K2 Jinshi, China
82/D5 Jintotolo (chan.), Phil.
84/C4 Jintūr, India
81/E2 Jinxi, China
82/C2 Jinxi, China
81/E2 Jinzhou, China
108/F6 Ji-Paraná, Braz.
108/F5 Jiparaná (riv.), Braz.
108/B4 Jipijapa, Ecu.
100/B3 Jirgā, Egypt
82/A2 Jishou, China
74/D3 Jisr ash Shughūr, Syria
63/F4 Jiu (riv.), Rom.
82/C2 Jiujiang, China
82/A2 Jiuwan (mts.), China
81/D5 Jixi, China
81/C4 Ji Xian, China
81/D2 Ji Xian, China
100/B2 Jīzah, Pyramids of (Giza) (ruins), Egypt
81/C3 Jize, China
57/L1 Jizera (riv.), Czh.
78/C3 Jizō-zaki (pt.), Japan
72/F5 Jiz', Wādī al (dry riv.), Yem.
110/B3 Joaçaba, Braz.
110/D1 João Monlevade, Braz.
109/M5 João Pessoa, Braz.
110/C1 João Pinheiro, Braz.
111/D2 Joaquín V. González, Arg.
117/F3 Jobabo, Cuba
58/D4 Jódar, Sp.
84/B2 Jodhpur, India
53/D2 Jodoigne, Belg.
42/J3 Joensuu, Fin.
79/F2 Jōetsu, Japan
53/F5 Joeuf, Fr.
102/E2 Johannesburg, SAfr.
124/C4 Johannesburg, Ca,US
122/D4 John Day, Or,US
122/C4 John Day (riv.), Or,US
122/C4 John Day Fossil Beds Nat'l Mon., Or,US
128/C2 John Martin (res.), Co,US
129/H2 Johnson City, Tn,US
128/D4 Johnson City, Tx,US
125/G3 Johnson (Johnson City), Ks,US
130/M3 Johnsons Crossing, Yk,Can
93/J3 Johnston (atoll), PacUS
46/B3 Johnston, Wal,UK
126/E3 Johnstown, Pa,US
86/B3 Johor Baharu, Malay.
56/E3 Joigny, Fr.
110/B3 Joinville, Braz.
105/W Joinville (isl.), Ant.
97/M6 Jokau, Sudan
42/F2 Jokkmokk, Swe.
42/P6 Jökulsargljúfur Nat'l Park, Ice.
132/P16 Joliet, Il,US
126/F2 Joliette, Qu,Can
128/D4 Jollyville, Tx,US
82/D6 Jolo, Phil.
82/D6 Jolo (isl.), Phil.
86/D5 Jombang, Indo.
55/E3 Jona, Swi.
49/N1 Jonava, Lith.
119/S7 Jones (sound), Nun.,Can
129/F3 Jonesboro, Ar,US
128/E3 Jonesboro, La,US
44/B3 Jonesborough, NI,UK
42/E4 Jönköping, Swe.
42/E4 Jönköping (co.), Swe.
127/G1 Jonquière, Qu,Can
125/J3 Joplin, Mo,US
72/D2 Jordan
127/R9 Jordan, On,Can
74/K6 Jordan (riv.), Jor., WBnk.
122/G4 Jordan, Mt,US
124/E2 Jordan (riv.), Ut,US
127/R9 Jordan Station, On,Can
122/D5 Jordan Valley, Or,US
113/J7 Jorge (cape), Chile
85/F2 Jorhāt, India
51/G1 Jork, Ger.
128/B3 Jornada del Muerto (val.), NM,US
99/H4 Jos (plat.), Nga.
82/E6 Jose Abad Santos, Phil.
110/B2 José Bonifácio, Braz.
79/F2 Joshin-Etsu Kogen Nat'l Park, Japan
124/D4 Joshua Tree Nat'l Park, Ca,US
42/C3 Jotunheimen Nat'l Park, Nor.
56/E2 Jouanne (riv.), Fr.
52/C6 Jouarre, Fr.
56/D3 Joué-lès-Tours, Fr.
90/B2 Jourama Falls Nat'l Park, Austl.
128/D4 Jourdanton, Tx,US
50/C3 Joure, Neth.
42/J3 Joutseno, Fin.
72/G1 Joveyn (riv.), Iran
85/F2 Jowai, India
130/M3 Joy (mtn.), Yk,Can
79/L10 Jōyō, Japan
98/A2 Jreïda, Mrta.
81/B5 Ju (riv.), China
117/P9 Juan Aldama, Mex.
122/B3 Juan de Fuca (str.), Can., US
103/G7 Juan de Nova (isl.), Reun.
107/A6 Juan Fernández (isls.), Chile
117/J5 Juangriego, Ven.
108/C5 Juanjuí, Peru
113/T12 Juan L. Lacaze, Uru.
112/F3 Juárez, Arg.
110/J8 Juatinga (pt.), Braz.
109/K5 Juazeiro, Braz.
109/L5 Juazeiro do Norte, Braz.
97/M7 Juba, Sudan
97/P7 Jubba (riv.), Eth., Som.
59/Y17 Juby (cape), Mor.
58/D3 Júcar (riv.), Sp.
50/D6 Jüchen, Ger.
74/N9 Judaea (reg.), WBnk.
57/L3 Judenburg, Aus.
122/F4 Judith (riv.), Mt,US
100/B3 Juhaynah, Egypt
116/D5 Juigalpa, Nic.
56/E2 Juine (riv.), Fr.
82/D3 Juishui, Tai.
50/D1 Juist (isl.), Ger.
110/K6 Juiz de Fora, Braz.
125/G2 Julesburg, Co,US
108/D7 Juliaca, Peru
57/K3 Julian Alps (mts.), It., Slov.
53/F2 Jülich, Ger.
117/F3 Julio A. Mella, Cuba
73/L2 Jullundur, India
81/C3 Juma (riv.), China
58/E3 Jumilla, Sp.
84/D2 Jumla, Nepal
51/E2 Jümme (riv.), Ger.
84/B3 Junāgadh, India
112/C2 Juncal (peak), Arg., Chile
128/D4 Junction, Tx,US
124/D3 Junction, Ut,US
125/H3 Junction City, Ks,US
122/C4 Junction City, Or,US
110/G8 Jundiaí, Braz.
81/H6 Jundu (mts.), China
130/M4 Juneau (cap.), Ak,US
54/D4 Jungfrau (peak), Swi.
108/C6 Junín, Peru
52/D5 Juniville, Fr.
81/C3 Junji Guan (pass), China
129/H5 Juno Beach, Fl,US
110/B2 Junqueirópolis, Braz.
110/E1 Juparanã (lake), Braz.
127/J1 Jupiter (riv.), Qu,Can
129/H5 Jupiter, Fl,US
132/A2 Jupiter (mtn.), Wa,US
110/C3 Juquiá, Braz.
110/F8 Juquitiba, Braz.
97/L6 Jur (riv.), Sudan
54/B4 Jura (dept.), Fr.
54/B4 Jura (mts.), Fr.
54/D3 Jura (canton), Swi.
56/C5 Jurançon, Fr.
52/C2 Jurbise, Belg.
44/D3 Jurby Head (pt.), IM,UK
64/D4 Jūrmala, Lat.
108/E4 Juruá (riv.), Braz.
108/G6 Juruena (riv.), Braz.
109/G4 Juruti, Braz.
79/M9 Jushiyama, Japan
112/D2 Justo Daract, Arg.
108/E4 Jutaí (riv.), Braz.
116/D4 Jutiapa, Guat.
116/D5 Juticalpa, Hon.
42/D4 Jutland (pen.), Den.
42/H3 Juva, Fin.
116/E3 Juventud (Pinos) (isl.), Cuba
81/D4 Juye, China
81/C5 Juzhang (riv.), China
62/E4 Južna Morava (riv.), Yugo.
42/H3 Jyväskylä, Fin.

K

75/C4 K2 (Godwin Austen) (mtn.), China, Pak.
96/F5 Ka (riv.), Nga.
102/C3 Kaap (plat.), SAfr.
64/D3 Kaarina, Fin.
50/D6 Kaarst, Ger.
62/E2 Kaba, Hun.
87/F5 Kabaena (isl.), Indo.
116/D3 Kabah (ruins), Mex.
101/A3 Kabale, Ugan.
101/A2 Kabalega Nat'l Park, Ugan.
101/A2 Kabalo, D.R. Congo
101/A2 Kabamba (lake), D.R. Congo
87/F2 Kabankalan, Phil.
67/G4 Kabardin-Balkar Aut. Rep., Rus.
126/C1 Kabinakagani (lake), On,Can
104/D2 Kabinda, D.R. Congo
60/A5 Kabī'yah (lag.), Tun.
104/D3 Kabompo (riv.), Zam.
104/E2 Kabongo, D.R. Congo
73/J2 Kabul (riv.), Afg.
73/J2 Kabul (Kābol) (cap.), Afg.
87/G3 Kaburuang (isl.), Indo.
104/E3 Kabwe, Zam.
62/E4 Kačanik, Yugo.
130/H4 Kachemak (bay), Ak,US
85/G2 Kachin (state), Myan.
84/C6 Kadaianallur, India
83/B3 Kadan (isl.), Myan.
57/K1 Kadaň, Czh.
92/G6 Kadavu (isl.), Fiji
96/J7 Kadeï (riv.), CAfr., Congo
63/H5 Kadıköy, Turk.
74/C2 Kadınhanı, Turk.
99/E3 Kadiogo (prov.), Burk.
84/C5 Kadiri, India
74/D3 Kadirli, Turk.
123/H5 Kadoka, SD,US
79/L10 Kadoma, Japan
104/E4 Kadoma, Zim.
99/G4 Kaduna, Nga.
99/G4 Kaduna (riv.), Nga.
99/G4 Kaduna (state), Nga.
97/L5 Kāduqlī, Sudan
98/B2 Kaédi, Mrta.
96/H5 Kaélé, Camr.
83/C2 Kaeng Khlo, Thai.
83/B3 Kaeng Krachan Nat'l Park, Thai.
80/D3 Kaesŏng, NKor.
80/D4 Kaesŏng-Si (prov.), NKor.
67/H5 Kafan, Arm.
73/J2 Kafar Jar Ghar (mts.), Afg.
102/D4 Kaffraria (reg.), SAfr.
98/B3 Kaffrine, Sen.
97/K6 Kafia Kingi, Sudan
61/J3 Kafirévs, Ákra (cape), Gre.
74/H6 Kafr ad Dawwār, Egypt
74/H6 Kafr ash Shaykh, Egypt
74/H6 Kafr ash Shaykh (gov.), Egypt
74/H6 Kafr az Zayyāt, Egypt
74/N8 Kafr Qari', Isr.
74/M8 Kafr Qāsim, Isr.
104/E4 Kafue, Zam.
104/E4 Kafue (riv.), Zam.
104/E4 Kafue Nat'l Park, Zam.
78/E2 Kaga, Japan
96/J6 Kaga Bandoro, CAfr.
68/G6 Kagan, Uzb.
78/D3 Kagawa (pref.), Japan
63/J5 Kağıthane, Turk.
74/E2 Kağızman, Turk.
78/B5 Kagoshima, Japan
78/B5 Kagoshima (bay), Japan
78/B5 Kagoshima (pref.), Japan
63/J3 Kagul, Mol.
86/D4 Kahayan (riv.), Indo.
104/C2 Kahemba, D.R. Congo
76/D1 Kahmsara (riv.), Rus.
125/K2 Kahoka, Mo,US
120/T10 Kahoolawe (isl.), Hi,US
42/G1 Kahperusvaara (peak), Fin.
74/D3 Kahramanmaraş, Turk.
73/K3 Kahror Pakka, Pak.
74/D3 Kâhta, Turk.
120/T10 Kahuku (pt.), Hi,US
120/T10 Kahului, Hi,US
104/E1 Kahuzi-Biega Nat'l Park, D.R. Congo
87/H5 Kai (isls.), Indo.
124/D3 Kaibab (plat.), Az,US
79/L9 Kaibara, Japan
87/H5 Kai Besar (isl.), Indo.
75/E3 Kaidu (riv.), China
76/G5 Kaifeng, China
78/D4 Kaifu, Japan
87/H5 Kai Kecil (isl.), Indo.
89/H7 Kaikoura, NZ
85/J2 Kaili, China
120/U11 Kailua, Hi,US
102/B2 Kainab (dry riv.), Namb.
62/B2 Kainach (riv.), Aus.
78/D3 Kainan, Japan
99/G4 Kainji (lake), Nga.
79/H7 Kaisei, Japan
53/G5 Kaiserslautern, Ger.
89/H6 Kaitaia, NZ
75/C6 Kaithal, India
120/T10 Kaiwi (chan.), Hi,US
81/F2 Kaiyuan, China
85/H3 Kaiyuan, China
79/M9 Kaizu, Japan
79/L10 Kaizuka, Japan
42/H2 Kajaani, Fin.
80/E5 Kaji-san (mtn.), SKor.
97/M5 Kākā, Sudan
42/G3 Kakaanpää, Fin.
101/B2 Kakamega, Kenya
79/E3 Kakamigahara, Japan
62/D3 Kakanj, Bosn.
130/M4 Kaketsa (mtn.), BC,Can
66/E3 Kakhovka, Ukr.
66/E3 Kakhovs'ke (res.), Ukr.
84/D4 Kākināda, India
79/L9 Kako (riv.), Japan
98/B4 Kakrima (riv.), Gui.
79/G2 Kakuda, Japan
101/B2 Kakuma, Kenya
101/A3 Kakuto, Ugan.
60/B5 Kalaa-Kebira, Tun.
115/N2 Kalaallit Nunaat (Greenland) (dpcy.), Den.
104/D3 Kalabo, Zam.
67/G2 Kalach, Rus.
68/H4 Kalachinsk, Rus.
67/G2 Kalach-na-Donu, Rus.
85/F3 Kaladan (riv.), Myan.
120/U11 Ka Lae (cape), Hi,US
104/D5 Kalahari (des.), Afr.
102/C2 Kalahari-Gemsbok Nat'l Park, SAfr.
61/L7 Kalamáki, Gre.
96/H5 Kalamaloué Nat'l Park, Camr.
61/H2 Kalamariá, Gre.
61/H4 Kalamáta, Gre.
126/C3 Kalamazoo, Mi,US
83/C2 Kalasin, Thai.
73/J3 Kalāt, Pak.
60/B5 Kalbīyah (lake), Tun.
42/N7 Kaldakvísl (riv.), Ice.
51/H5 Kalefeld, Ger.
101/A4 Kalemie, D.R. Congo
49/K3 Kalety, Pol.
89/B4 Kalgoorlie-Boulder, Austl.
63/J4 Kaliakra, Nos (pt.), Bul.
86/C5 Kalianda, Indo.
82/D5 Kalibo, Phil.
104/E1 Kalima, D.R. Congo
86/D4 Kalimantan (reg.), Indo.
74/A3 Kálimnos, Gre.
49/L1 Kaliningrad, Rus.
64/H5 Kaliningrad, Rus.
49/K1 Kaliningrad (lag.), Rus.
64/D5 Kaliningrad Obl., Rus.
67/H2 Kalininsk, Rus.
66/D1 Kalinkovichi, Bela.
101/A3 Kalisizo, Ugan.
122/E3 Kalispell, Mt,US
49/K3 Kalisz, Pol.
49/J3 Kalisz (prov.), Pol.
42/G2 Kalix, Swe.
42/G2 Kalixälv (riv.), Swe.
84/E2 Kāliyāganj, India
126/C2 Kalkaska, Mi,US
61/L7 Kallithea, Gre.
42/E3 Kallsjön (lake), Swe.
42/F4 Kalmar, Swe.
42/E4 Kalmar (co.), Swe.
50/B6 Kalmthout, Belg.
67/H3 Kalmykia, Rus.
62/D2 Kalocsa, Hun.
120/T10 Kalohi (chan.), Hi,US
84/B3 Kālol, India
104/E4 Kalomo, Zam.
84/C2 Kālpi, India
48/E2 Kaltenkirchen, Ger.
57/F4 Kaltern (Caldaro), It.
84/D6 Kalu (riv.), SrL.
64/H5 Kaluga, Rus.
64/G5 Kaluga Obl., Rus.
48/F1 Kalundborg, Den.
66/C2 Kalush, Ukr.
84/C6 Kalutara, SrL.
84/B4 Kalyān, India
65/M4 Kama (res.), Rus.
65/M3 Kama (riv.), Rus.
104/E1 Kama, D.R. Congo
79/J7 Kamagaya, Japan
77/N4 Kamaishi, Japan
120/T10 Kamakou (peak), Hi,US
79/H7 Kamakura, Japan
75/B5 Kamālia, Pak.
74/C2 Kaman, Turk.
98/E2 Kamango (lake), Mali
84/C4 Kāmāreddi, India
84/E3 Kāmārhāti, India
84/A2 Kambar, Pak.
104/E3 Kambove, D.R. Congo
87/F4 Kambuno (peak), Indo.
69/R4 Kamchatka (pen.), Rus.
69/R4 Kamchatka Obl., Rus.
63/H4 Kamchiya (riv.), Bul.
51/E5 Kamen, Ger.
66/C2 Kam'yanets'-Podil's'kyy, Ukr.
62/A3 Kamenjak, Rt (cape), Cro.
67/H1 Kamenka, Rus.
75/D1 Kamen'-na-Obi, Rus.
66/G2 Kamensk-Shakhtinskiy, Rus.
65/P4 Kamensk-Ural'skiy, Rus.
78/D3 Kameoka, Japan
79/M10 Kameyama, Japan
122/D4 Kamiah, Id,US
49/H2 Kamień Pomorski, Pol.
79/H7 Kamifukuoka, Japan
77/N3 Kamiisco, Japan
79/M9 Kamiishizu, Japan
120/U11 Kamilo (pt.), Hi,US
104/E2 Kamina, D.R. Congo
79/G1 Kaminoyama, Japan
130/H4 Kamishak (bay), Ak,US
78/B5 Kamiyaku, Japan
122/C3 Kamloops, BC,Can
83/C4 Kamlot, Camb.
79/L10 Kammaki, Japan
62/B2 Kamnik, Slov.
79/J7 Kamo (riv.), Japan
79/G2 Kamogawa, Japan
78/D3 Kamojima, Japan
57/L2 Kamp (riv.), Aus.
101/B2 Kampala (cap.), Ugan.
86/B3 Kampar (riv.), Indo.
86/B3 Kampar, Malay.
50/C3 Kampen, Neth.
83/B2 Kamphaeng Phet, Thai.
49/L2 Kampinoski Nat'l Park, Pol.
50/D6 Kamp-Lintfort, Ger.
83/D4 Kampong Cham, Camb.
83/D3 Kampong Chhnang, Camb.
83/D3 Kampong Khleang, Camb.
83/C4 Kampong Saom, Camb.
83/C4 Kampong Saom (bay), Camb.
83/D4 Kampong Spoe, Camb.
83/D3 Kampong Thum, Camb.
83/D4 Kampong Trabek, Camb.
83/D4 Kampot, Camb.
87/H4 Kamrau (bay), Indo.
123/H3 Kamsack, Sk,Can
123/H1 Kamuchawie (lake), Sk,Can
116/E6 Kámuk (mt.), CR
67/H2 Kamyshin, Rus.
119/J3 Kanaaupscow (riv.), Qu,Can
124/D3 Kanab (riv.), Az, Ut,US
124/D3 Kanab, Ut,US
130/C6 Kanaga (isl.), Ak,US
130/C6 Kanaga (vol.), Ak,US
79/F3 Kanagawa (pref.), Japan
119/K3 Kanairiktok (riv.), Nf,Can
79/L10 Kanan, Japan
104/D2 Kananga, D.R. Congo
65/K5 Kanash, Rus.
126/D4 Kanawha (riv.), WV,US
79/E2 Kanazawa, Japan
83/B3 Kanchanaburi, Thai.
84/C5 Kānchīpuram, India
64/G2 Kandalaksha, Rus.
64/G2 Kandalaksha (gulf), Rus.
93/Y18 Kandavu (passg.), Fiji
73/J3 Kandhkot, Pak.
84/E3 Kāndi, India
87/F3 Kandi (cape), Indo.
63/K5 Kandıra, Turk.
84/C4 Kandukūr, India
84/D6 Kandy, SrL.
119/T7 Kane Basin (sound), Nun.,Can
96/H5 Kanem (reg.), Chad
120/W13 Kaneohe, Hi,US
120/W13 Kaneohe (bay), Hi,US
104/D5 Kang, Bots.
74/D2 Kangal, Turk.
86/B2 Kangar, Malay.
72/E2 Kangāvar, Iran
87/E5 Kangean (isls.), Indo.
119/K3 Kangiqsualujjuaq, Qu,Can
119/J2 Kangiqsujuaq, Qu,Can
119/J2 Kangirsuk, Qu,Can
80/E4 Kangnŭng, SKor.
75/D5 Kangrinboqê Feng (peak), China
85/F2 Kangto (peak), China
80/D3 Kangwŏn-Do (prov.), NKor.
80/D4 Kangwŏn-Do (prov.), SKor.
84/C3 Kanhān (riv.), India
79/M9 Kani, Japan
65/K2 Kanin (pen.), Rus.
64/J1 Kanin Nos (pt.), Rus.
62/E2 Kanjiiža, Yugo.
126/C3 Kankakee, Il,US
126/C3 Kankakee (riv.), Il, In,Us
98/C4 Kankan, Gui.
98/C4 Kankan (comm.), Gui.
84/D3 Kānker, India
78/C3 Kanmuri-yama (mtn.), Japan
129/H3 Kannapolis, NC,US
84/C2 Kannauj, India
79/H7 Kannon-zaki (pt.), Japan
99/H4 Kano, Nga.
99/H3 Kano (state), Nga.
78/C3 Kan'onji, Japan
78/B5 Kanoya, Japan
84/D2 Kānpur, India
125/H3 Kansas (state), US
125/H3 Kansas (riv.), Ks,US
125/J3 Kansas City, Ks, Mo,US
68/K4 Kansk, Rus.
84/D3 Kantābānji, India
79/F2 Kantō (prov.), Japan
108/G3 Kanuku (mts.), Guy.
79/F2 Kanuma, Japan
130/H2 Kanuti Nat'l Wild. Ref., Ak,US
102/D2 Kanye, Bots.
83/D3 Kaoh Nhek, Camb.
82/D3 Kaohsiung, Tai.
104/B4 Kaokoveld (reg.), Namb.
98/A3 Kaolack, Sen.
98/B3 Kaolack (reg.), Sen.
104/D3 Kaoma, Zam.
120/S9 Kapaa, Hi,US
82/E6 Kapalong, Phil.
104/D2 Kapanga, D.R. Congo
62/E4 Kapaonik (upland), Yugo.
75/C3 Kapchagay, Kaz.
75/C3 Kapchagay (res.), Kaz.
50/B6 Kapellen, Belg.
57/L3 Kapfenberg, Aus.
63/H5 Kapidaği (pen.), Turk.
92/E4 Kapingamarangi (isl.), Micr.
104/E3 Kapiri Mposhi, Zam.
119/H3 Kapiskau (riv.), On,Can
97/M7 Kapoeta, Sudan
62/C2 Kapos (riv.), Hun.
62/C2 Kaposvár, Hun.
49/M1 Kapsukas, Lith.
86/C4 Kapuas (riv.), Indo.
86/D3 Kapuas Hulu (mts.), Indo., Malay.
126/D1 Kapuskasing, On,Can
126/D1 Kapuskasing (riv.), On,Can
62/C2 Kapuvár, Hun.
67/H5 Kapydzhik, Gora (peak), Azer.
65/Q1 Kara (riv.), Rus.
68/G2 Kara (sea), Rus.
87/H4 Karabra (riv.), Indo.
74/C2 Karabük, Turk.
74/D3 Karaca (peak), Turk.
74/B2 Karacabey, Turk.
67/G4 Karachay-Cherkass Aut. Obl., Rus.
66/E1 Karachev, Rus.
73/J4 Karāchi, Pak.
84/B4 Karād, India
71/R4 Karaginskiy (isl.), Rus.
75/E1 Karagoš (peak), Rus.
84/C5 Kāraikkudi, India
72/F1 Karaj, Iran
67/L3 Karakalpak Aut. Rep., Uzb.
75/C4 Karakax (riv.), China
74/D2 Karakaya (res.), Turk.
87/G3 Karakelong (isl.), Indo.
75/E3 Karakhoto (ruins), China
74/E2 Karakoçan, Turk.
75/C4 Karakoram (range), Asia
75/C4 Karakoram (pass), China, India
98/C3 Karakoro (riv.), Mali, Mrta.
76/E2 Karakorum (ruins), Mong.
74/E2 Karaköse, Turk.
75/B4 Karakul' (lake), Taj.
67/L5 Karakumy (des.), Trkm.
67/K4 Karakyon, Gora (peak), Trkm.
73/H1 Karakyr (peak), Trkm.
87/E4 Karam (riv.), Indo.
74/C3 Karaman, Turk.
75/D2 Karamay, China
75/D4 Karamiran (riv.), China
75/E4 Karamiran Shankou (pass), China
101/B2 Karamoja (prov.), Ugan.
63/J5 Karamürsel, Turk.
85/G4 Karan (state), Myan.
87/E5 Karangasem, Indo.
69/S4 Karanginskiy (bay), Rus.
69/S4 Karanginskiy (isl.), Rus.
84/C3 Kāranja, India
83/B2 Karan (Kayin) (state), Myan.
74/C3 Karapınar, Turk.
78/A3 Kara-saki (pt.), Japan
79/M10 Karasu, Japan
63/K5 Karasu, Turk.
75/C1 Karasuk, Rus.
75/C2 Karatal (riv.), Kaz.
75/B3 Karatau, Kaz.
75/A3 Karatau (mts.), Kaz.
78/A4 Karatsu, Japan
61/G3 Karáva (peak), Gre.
75/B2 Karazhal, Kaz.
100/C5 Karbaka, Sudan
72/D2 Karbalā', Iraq
62/E2 Karcag, Hun.
61/G3 Kardhitsa, Gre.
68/D3 Karelian Aut. Rep., Rus.
101/A4 Karema, Tanz.
76/H1 Karenga (riv.), Rus.
104/E4 Kariba (lake), Zam., Zim.
104/E4 Kariba, Zim.
86/C4 Karimata (isl.), Indo.
86/C4 Karimata (str.), Indo.
84/C4 Karīmnagar, India
101/A3 Karisimbi (vol.), Rwa.
79/M10 Kariya, Japan
97/Q6 Karkaar (mts.), Som.
84/B5 Kārkāl, India
92/D5 Karkar (isl.), PNG
66/E3 Karkinitsk (gulf), Ukr.
75/B4 Karla Marksa, Pik (peak), Taj.
62/B3 Karlovac, Slov.
63/G4 Karlovo, Bul.
57/K1 Karlovy Vary (Karlsbad), Czh.
42/E4 Karlshamn, Swe.
42/E4 Karlskoga, Swe.
42/E4 Karlskrona, Swe.
57/H2 Karlsruhe, Ger.
42/E4 Karlstad, Swe.
100/B5 Karmah, Sudan
84/D4 Karmāla, India
74/K5 Karmel, Har (Mount Carmel) (mtn.), Isr.
84/C2 Karnāl, India
84/C4 Karnataka (state), India
128/D4 Karnes City, Tx,US
63/H4 Karnobat, Bul.
62/A2 Kärnten (prov.), Aus.
101/B5 Karonga, Malw.
102/C4 Karoo Nat'l Park, SAfr.
73/K2 Karor, Pak.
87/E5 Karoso (cape), Indo.
74/A3 Kárpathos (isl.), Gre.
102/C3 Kars (riv.), SAfr.
74/E2 Kars, Turk.
68/G6 Karshi, Uzb.
67/M1 Kartaly, Rus.
63/L3 Kartinitsk (gulf), Ukr.
49/K1 Kartuzy, Pol.
72/E2 Kārūn (riv.), Iran
49/K4 Karviná, Czh.
84/B5 Karwar, India

Kasab – Knox

123/L2 **Kasabonika** (lake), On,Can
84/E3 **Kāsai** (riv.), India
78/D3 **Kasai**, Japan
104/C1 **Kasai** (riv.), D.R. Congo
79/G2 **Kasama**, Japan
101/A5 **Kasama**, Zam.
79/M9 **Kasamatsu**, Japan
104/E4 **Kasane**, Bots.
78/C3 **Kasaoka**, Japan
84/C5 **Kāsaragod**, India
100/D5 **Kasar, Ras** (cape), Sudan
79/M10 **Kasartori-yama** (peak), Japan
118/F2 **Kasba** (lake), NW,Nun.Can
78/B5 **Kaseda**, Japan
84/C2 **Kāsganj**, India
73/H1 **Kashaf** (riv.), Iran
72/F2 **Kāshān**, Iran
75/C4 **Kashi**, China
79/L10 **Kashiba**, Japan
78/D3 **Kashihara**, Japan
78/B4 **Kashima**, Japan
79/G3 **Kashima**, Japan
64/H4 **Kashin**, Rus.
79/H7 **Kashiwa**, Japan
79/L10 **Kashiwara**, Japan
79/F2 **Kashiwazaki**, Japan
73/G1 **Kāshmar**, Iran
84/A2 **Kashmor**, Pak.
64/J5 **Kasimov**, Rus.
87/G4 **Kasiruta** (isl.), Indo.
87/H4 **Kasiui** (isl.), Indo.
126/B4 **Kaskaskia** (riv.), Il,US
122/D3 **Kaslo**, BC,Can
104/E1 **Kasongo**, D.R. Congo
104/C2 **Kasongo-Lunda**, D.R. Congo
67/H4 **Kaspiysk**, Rus.
97/N4 **Kassala**, Sudan
61/H3 **Kassándra** (pen.), Gre.
51/G6 **Kassel**, Ger.
123/K4 **Kasson**, Mn,US
74/C2 **Kastamonu**, Turk.
53/D1 **Kasterlee**, Belg.
61/G2 **Kastoría**, Gre.
61/G3 **Kastrakíou** (lake), Gre.
79/E3 **Kasugai**, Japan
79/F3 **Kasukabe**, Japan
101/A4 **Kasulu**, Tanz.
79/G2 **Kasumiga** (lake), Japan
104/F3 **Kasungu**, Malw.
73/K2 **Kasūr**, Pak.
104/E4 **Kataba**, Zam.
127/G2 **Katahdin** (mtn.), Me,US
101/A4 **Katanga** (prov.), D.R. Congo
104/E2 **Katanga** (reg.), D.R. Congo
79/L10 **Katano**, Japan
101/A4 **Katavi Nat'l Park**, Tanz.
85/F6 **Katchall** (isl.), India
104/D2 **Katea**, D.R. Congo
104/E2 **Katea**, D.R. Congo
61/H2 **Kateríni**, Gre.
130/M4 **Kates Needle** (mtn.), Ak,US
104/F3 **Katete**, Zam.
85/G3 **Katha**, Myan.
84/C2 **Kāthgodām**, India
73/K4 **Kathiawar** (pen.), India
84/E2 **Kāthmāndu** (cap.), Nepal
73/L2 **Kathua**, India
98/C3 **Kati**, Mali
98/D4 **Katiola**, IvC.
51/H5 **Katlenburg-Lindau**, Ger.
130/H4 **Katmai** (vol.), Ak,US
130/G4 **Katmai Nat'l Park & Prsv.**, Ak,US
49/K3 **Katowice**, Pol.
49/K3 **Katowice** (prov.), Pol.
97/M2 **Kātrīnā, Jabal** (Mt. Catherine) (peak), Egypt
43/C2 **Katrine, Loch** (lake), Sc,UK
99/G3 **Katsina**, Nga.
99/G3 **Katsina** (state), Nga.
99/H5 **Katsina Ala** (riv.), Camr., Nga.
79/L9 **Katsura** (riv.), Japan
78/D3 **Katsuragi**, Japan
79/L10 **Katsuragi-san** (peak), Japan
79/G2 **Katsuta**, Japan
79/G3 **Katsuura**, Japan
126/E1 **Kattawagami** (riv.), On,Can
101/B5 **Katumbi**, Malw.
75/E1 **Katun'** (riv.), Rus.
75/E1 **Katun'chuya** (riv.), Rus.
50/B4 **Katwijk aan Zee**, Neth.
57/H2 **Katzenbuckel** (peak), Ger.
120/S10 **Kauai** (chan.), Hi,US
120/S9 **Kauai** (isl.), Hi,US
55/G2 **Kaufbeuren**, Ger.
128/D3 **Kaufman**, Tx,US
51/G6 **Kaufungen**, Ger.
42/G3 **Kauhajoki**, Fin.
42/G3 **Kauhanevan-Pohjankankaan Nat'l Park**, Fin.
42/G3 **Kauhava**, Fin.
120/U10 **Kauhola** (pt.), Hi,US
120/U10 **Kauiki Head** (pt.), Hi,US
104/C5 **Kaukaveld** (mts.), Namb.
93/L6 **Kaukura** (atoll), FrPol.
120/R9 **Kaulakahi** (chan.), Hi,US
49/M1 **Kaunas**, Lith.
49/N1 **Kaunas** (res.), Lith.
83/B4 **Kau-ye** (isl.), Myan.
62/F5 **Kavadarci**, FYROM
61/F2 **Kavajë**, Alb.
61/J2 **Kavála**, Gre.
77/M3 **Kavalerovo**, Rus.
84/C5 **Kāvali**, India
92/C4 **Kavangel** (isls.), Palau
84/B5 **Kavaratti**, India
63/J4 **Kavarna**, Bul.
92/E5 **Kavieng**, PNG
128/D2 **Kaw** (lake), Ok,US
100/B5 **Kawa** (ruins), Sudan
79/L10 **Kawachi-Nagano**, Japan
79/M10 **Kawage**, Japan
79/F3 **Kawagoe**, Japan
79/M9 **Kawagoe**, Japan
79/F3 **Kawaguchi**, Japan
120/R10 **Kawaihoa** (pt.), Hi,US
120/S9 **Kawaikini** (peak), Hi,US
79/H7 **Kawajima**, Japan
79/G2 **Kawamata**, Japan
101/A5 **Kawambwa**, Zam.
79/L10 **Kawanishi**, Japan
84/D3 **Kawardha**, India
126/E2 **Kawartha** (lakes), On,Can
79/F3 **Kawasaki**, Japan
79/M9 **Kawashima**, Japan
120/V12 **Kawela Bay** (Kawela), Hi,US
100/C3 **Kawm Umbū**, Egypt
75/D3 **Kax** (riv.), China
75/C3 **Kaxgar** (riv.), China
130/L2 **Kay** (pt.), Yk,Can
99/E4 **Kaya**, Burk.
96/J6 **Kayagangiri** (peak), CAfr.
83/B2 **Kayah** (state), Myan.
87/E3 **Kayan** (riv.), Indo.
98/B3 **Kayanga** (riv.), Sen.
122/G5 **Kaycee**, Wy,US
124/E3 **Kayenta**, Az,US
98/C3 **Kayes**, Mali
98/C3 **Kayes** (reg.), Mali
83/B2 **Kayin (Karan)** (state), Myan.
53/F5 **Kayl**, Lux.
87/G3 **Kayoa** (isl.), Indo.
74/C2 **Kayseri**, Turk.
86/B4 **Kayuagung**, Indo.
75/B2 **Kazakh** (uplands), Kaz.
68/G5 **Kazakhstan**
118/F2 **Kazan** (riv.), Nun.,Can
65/L5 **Kazan'**, Rus.
63/G4 **Kazanlŭk**, Bul.
66/D2 **Kazatin**, Ukr.
67/H4 **Kazbek** (peak), Geo.
72/F3 **Kāzerūn**, Iran
49/L3 **Kazimierza Wielka**, Pol.
62/E1 **Kazincbarcika**, Hun.
77/N3 **Kazuno**, Japan
61/J4 **Kéa** (isl.), Gre.
44/B3 **Keady**, NI,UK
131/F5 **Keansburg**, NJ,US
125/H2 **Kearney**, Ne,US
44/C3 **Kearny** (pt.), NI,UK
131/F5 **Kearny**, NJ,US
120/U11 **Keawekaheka** (pt.), Hi,US
74/D2 **Keban** (res.), Turk.
42/F2 **Kebnekaise** (peak), Swe.
97/P6 **K'ebrī Dehar**, Eth.
86/C5 **Kebumen**, Indo.
62/D2 **Kecel**, Hun.
62/D2 **Kecskemét**, Hun.
49/M1 **Kėdainiai**, Lith.
53/F5 **Kédange-sur Canner**, Fr.
86/D5 **Kediri**, Indo.
98/B3 **Kédougou**, Sen.
49/K3 **Kędzierzyn-Koźle**, Pol.
132/F6 **Keego Harbor**, Mi,US
118/D2 **Keele** (riv.), NW,Can
118/C2 **Keele** (peak), Yk,Can
82/D2 **Keelung**, Tai.
127/F3 **Keene**, NH,US
90/A1 **Keer-weer** (cape), Austl.
102/B2 **Keetmanshoop**, Namb.
61/G3 **Kefallinía** (isl.), Gre.
74/M8 **Kefar Sava**, Isr.
42/M7 **Keflavík**, Ice.
85/J5 **Ke Ga** (cape), Viet.
84/D6 **Kegalla**, SrL.
45/G6 **Kegworth**, Eng,UK
53/G6 **Kehl**, Ger.
45/G4 **Keighley**, Eng,UK
79/L9 **Keihoku**, Japan
91/F5 **Keilor**, Austl.
97/J6 **Kéita** (riv.), Chad
43/D2 **Keith**, Sc,UK
127/H2 **Kejimkujik Nat'l Park**, NS,Can
62/D2 **Kékes** (peak), Hun.
87/G4 **Kelang** (isl.), Indo.
86/B3 **Kelang**, Malay.
99/H3 **Kélé-Kélé**, Niger
57/J2 **Kelheim**, Ger.
74/D2 **Kelkit**, Turk.
74/D2 **Kelkit** (riv.), Turk.
118/D2 **Keller** (lake), NW,Can
131/C2 **Keller** (peak), Ca,US
118/D1 **Kellett** (cape), NW,Can
122/D4 **Kellogg**, Id,US
44/B2 **Kells**, NI,UK
128/D4 **Kelly A.F.B.**, Tx,US
96/J6 **Kélo**, Chad
122/D3 **Kelowna**, BC,Can
45/F5 **Kelsall**, Eng,UK
46/A6 **Kelsey Head** (pt.), UK
43/D3 **Kelso**, Sc,UK
122/C4 **Kelso**, Wa,US
86/B3 **Keluang**, Malay.
47/G3 **Kelvedon**, Eng,UK
123/H2 **Kelvington**, Sk,Can
64/G2 **Kem'**, Rus.
64/G2 **Kem'** (riv.), Rus.
46/D3 **Kemble**, Eng,UK
86/D3 **Kemena** (riv.), Malay.
68/J4 **Kemerovo**, Rus.
42/H2 **Kemi**, Fin.
42/H2 **Kemijärvi**, Fin.
42/H2 **Kemijoki** (riv.), Fin.
52/B2 **Kemmel**, Belg.
122/F5 **Kemmerer**, Wy,US
105/W **Kemp** (pen.), Ant.
125/H4 **Kemp** (lake), Tx,US
42/H2 **Kempele**, Fin.
50/D6 **Kempen**, Ger.
50/C6 **Kempenland** (reg.), Belg.
50/B6 **Kempisch** (can.), Belg.
91/E1 **Kempsey**, Austl.
47/F2 **Kempston**, Eng,UK
126/F2 **Kempt** (lake), Qu,Can
55/G2 **Kempten**, Ger.
102/E2 **Kempton Park**, SAfr.
87/E3 **Kemul** (peak), Indo.
130/H3 **Kenai**, Ak,US
130/J3 **Kenai Fjords Nat'l Park**, Ak,US
45/F3 **Kendal**, Eng,UK
129/H5 **Kendall**, Fl,US
126/C3 **Kendallville**, In,US
87/F4 **Kendari**, Indo.
50/D5 **Kendel** (riv.), Neth., Ger.
84/E3 **Kendrāpāra**, India
98/D4 **Kénédougou** (prov.), Burk.
98/C5 **Kenema**, SLeo.
85/J4 **Keng Deng**, Laos
104/C1 **Kenge**, D.R. Congo
83/B1 **Kēng Tung**, Myan.
98/C3 **Kenié-Baoulé Rsv.**, Mali
47/E2 **Kenilworth**, Eng,UK
96/D1 **Kenitra**, Mor.
44/D1 **Ken, Loch** (lake), Sc,UK
123/H3 **Kenmare**, ND,US
127/S10 **Kenmore**, NY,US
132/C2 **Kenmore**, Wa,US
127/G2 **Kennebec** (riv.), Me,US
127/G3 **Kennebunk**, Me,US
119/T6 **Kennedy** (chan.), Nun.,Can
130/H4 **Kennedy** (str.), Ak,US
50/B4 **Kennemerduinen Nat'l Park**, Neth.
129/F4 **Kenner**, La,US
46/D4 **Kennet** (can.), Eng,UK
47/E4 **Kennet** (riv.), Eng,UK
126/B4 **Kennett**, Mo,US
122/D4 **Kennewick**, Wa,US
126/C1 **Kenogami** (riv.), On,Can
130/L3 **Keno Hill**, Yk,Can
126/A1 **Kenora**, On,Can
132/Q14 **Kenosha**, Wi,US
118/F2 **Kent** (pen.), Nun.,Can
47/G4 **Kent** (co.), Eng,UK
45/F3 **Kent** (riv.), Eng,UK
126/D3 **Kent**, Oh,US
132/C3 **Kent**, Wa,US
75/A3 **Kentau**, Kaz.
91/C3 **Kent Group** (isls.), Austl.
126/D3 **Kenton**, Oh,US
126/C4 **Kentucky** (state), US
126/C4 **Kentucky** (riv.), Ky,US
129/F2 **Kentucky** (lake), Ky, Tn,US
47/G4 **Kent, Vale of** (val.), Eng,UK
127/H2 **Kentville**, NS,Can
44/D1 **Ken, Water of** (riv.), Sc,UK
101/C2 **Kenya**
101/C3 **Kenya** (mtn.), Kenya
79/H7 **Ken-zaki** (pt.), Japan
123/L5 **Keokuk**, Ia,US
84/E3 **Keonjhar**, India
49/J3 **Kępno**, Pol.
84/C5 **Kerala** (state), India
99/F4 **Kéran Nat'l Park**, Togo
61/H4 **Keratéa**, Gre.
66/F3 **Kerch'** (str.), Rus., Ukr.
66/F3 **Kerch'**, Ukr.
122/D3 **Keremeos**, BC,Can
97/N4 **Keren**, Erit.
64/G2 **Keret'** (lake), Rus.
39/N8 **Kerguélen** (isl.), FrAnt.
86/B4 **Kerinci** (peak), Indo.
75/D4 **Keriya** (riv.), China
75/D4 **Keriya Shankou** (pass), China
50/C5 **Kerkdriel**, Neth.
50/D6 **Kerken**, Ger.
68/G6 **Kerki**, Trkm.
61/H2 **Kerkínis** (lake), Gre.
61/F3 **Kérkira** (Corfu), Gre.
53/F2 **Kerkrade**, Neth.
50/C5 **Kerkwijk**, Neth.
92/G7 **Kermadec** (isls.), NZ
73/G2 **Kermān**, Iran
128/C4 **Kermit**, Tx,US
124/C4 **Kern** (riv.), Ca,US
61/J4 **Kéros** (isl.), Gre.
129/J2 **Kerr** (res.), NC, Va,US
125/J4 **Kerr** (lake), Ok,US
122/F3 **Kerrobert**, Sk,Can
128/D4 **Kerrville**, Tx,US
46/C2 **Kerry**, Wal,UK
76/G2 **Kerulen** (riv.), China, Mong.
126/D1 **Kesagami** (riv.), On,Can
63/H5 **Keşan**, Turk.
77/N4 **Kesen'numa**, Japan
47/H2 **Kesgrave**, Eng,UK
84/B3 **Keshod**, India
74/C2 **Keskin**, Turk.
42/H3 **Khersons'ka** (obl.), Fin.
47/H2 **Kessingland**, Eng,UK
50/C5 **Kesteren**, Neth.
45/E2 **Keswick**, Eng,UK
62/C2 **Keszthely**, Hun.
68/J4 **Ket'** (riv.), Rus.
99/F5 **Keta**, Gha.
68/K2 **Keta** (riv.), Rus.
130/M4 **Ketchikan**, Ak,US
122/E5 **Ketchum**, Id,US
99/E5 **Kete Krachi**, Gha.
50/C3 **Ketelmeer** (lake), Neth.
49/L1 **Kętrzyn**, Pol.
47/F2 **Kettering**, Eng,UK
126/C4 **Kettering**, Oh,US
122/D3 **Kettle** (riv.), Can., US
45/F3 **Kettlewell**, Eng,UK
50/B4 **Keukenhof**, Neth.
42/H3 **Keuruu**, Fin.
50/D5 **Kevelaer**, Ger.
117/G3 **Kew**, Trks.
126/B2 **Keweenaw** (bay), Mi,US
126/B2 **Keweenaw** (pen.), Mi,US
129/H5 **Key Largo**, Fl,US
46/D4 **Keynsham**, Eng,UK
131/F5 **Keyport**, NJ,US
126/E4 **Keyser**, WV,US
128/D2 **Keystone** (lake), Ok,US
129/H5 **Key West**, Fl,US
45/G6 **Keyworth**, Eng,UK
49/L4 **Kežmarok**, Slvk.
97/Q5 **Khaanziir** (cape), Som.
77/M2 **Khabarovsk**, Rus.
67/J4 **Khachmas**, Azer.
72/E3 **Khafjī, Ra's al**, SAr.
84/D2 **Khairābād**, India
73/J3 **Khairpur**, Pak.
61/H3 **Khalándrion**, Gre.
61/H2 **Khalkhidhikhi** (pen.), Gre.
61/H3 **Khalkís**, Gre.
76/E1 **Khamar-Daban** (mts.), Rus.
84/D3 **Khamaria**, India
73/J4 **Khambaliya**, India
84/C3 **Khāmgaon**, India
72/D5 **Khamīs Mushayţ**, SAr.
84/D4 **Khammam**, India
73/J1 **Khānābād**, Afg.
72/E2 **Khānaqīn**, Iraq
84/C3 **Khandwa**, India
96/F1 **Khanem** (well), Alg.
73/K2 **Khānewāl**, Pak.
61/J5 **Khaniá**, Gre.
77/L3 **Khanka** (lake), Rus.
76/E1 **Khankh**, Mong.
75/C5 **Khanna**, India
73/K3 **Khānpur**, Pak.
68/G3 **Khanty-Mansiysk**, Rus.
68/G3 **Khanty-Mansiysk Aut. Okr.**, Rus.
74/K6 **Khān Yūnus**, Gaza
83/C3 **Khao Chamao-Khao Wong Nat'l Park**, Thai.
83/C3 **Khao Khitchakut Nat'l Park**, Thai.
83/B3 **Khao Laem** (res.), Thai.
83/B3 **Khao Sam Roi Yot Nat'l Park**, Thai.
83/C3 **Khao Yai Nat'l Park**, Thai.
84/E3 **Kharagpur**, India
75/B5 **Kharak**, Pak.
73/J3 **Khārān**, Pak.
84/C3 **Khargon**, India
100/B3 **Khārijah, Al Wāḩāt al** (oasis), Egypt
100/C3 **Kharīt, Wādī al** (dry riv.), Egypt
66/F2 **Kharkiv**, Ukr.
66/F2 **Kharkivs'ka** (obl.), Ukr.
63/G5 **Kharmanli**, Bul.
64/J4 **Kharovsk**, Rus.
97/M4 **Khartoum (Kharţūm)** (cap.), Sudan
97/M4 **Khartoum North**, Sudan
67/H4 **Khasavyurt**, Rus.
73/H2 **Khāsh** (riv.), Afg.
73/H3 **Khāsh**, Iran
67/G4 **Khashuri**, Geo.
63/G5 **Khaskovo**, Bul.
63/G5 **Khaskovo** (reg.), Bul.
69/L2 **Khatanga** (gulf), Rus.
69/L2 **Khatanga** (riv.), Rus.
100/C2 **Khatmia** (pass), Egypt
73/G3 **Khaymah, Ra's al**, UAE
97/M4 **Khazzān Jabal Al Awliyā** (dam), Sudan
96/F1 **Khemis Miliana**, Alg.
96/D1 **Khenifra**, Mor.
72/F2 **Khersān** (riv.), Iran
66/E3 **Kherson**, Ukr.
66/E3 **Khersons'ka** (obl.), Ukr.
76/G1 **Khilok**, Rus.
76/F1 **Khilok** (riv.), Rus.
61/K3 **Khíos**, Gre.
61/J3 **Khíos** (isl.), Gre.
63/G4 **Khisarya**, Bul.
68/G5 **Khiva**, Uzb.
66/C2 **Khmel'nyts'kyy**, Ukr.
73/J2 **Khojak** (pass), Pak.
83/C3 **Khok Samrong**, Thai.
73/J1 **Kholm**, Afg.
77/N2 **Kholmsk**, Rus.
72/F2 **Khomeynī shahr**, Iran
83/C2 **Khon Kaen**, Thai.
67/G2 **Khopër** (riv.), Rus.
77/M2 **Khor** (riv.), Rus.
75/B4 **Khorog**, Taj.
72/E2 **Khorramābād**, Iran
72/E2 **Khorramshahr**, Iran
83/C2 **Kho Sawai** (plat.), Thai.
130/G3 **Khotol** (mtn.), Ak,US
96/D1 **Khouribga**, Mor.
85/F3 **Khowai**, India
73/J2 **Khowst**, Afg.
61/J2 **Khrisoúpolis**, Gre.
67/L2 **Khromtau**, Kaz.
61/J5 **Khrysi** (isl.), Gre.
83/C2 **Khuan Ubon Ratana** (res.), Thai.
75/A3 **Khudzhand**, Taj.
84/E3 **Khulna**, Bang.
73/L1 **Khūnjerāb** (pass), Pak.
84/C3 **Khurai**, India
84/E3 **Khurda**, India
84/C2 **Khurja**, India
66/B2 **Khust**, Ukr.
73/J3 **Khuzdār**, Pak.
77/L3 **Khvalynka**, Rus.
72/F2 **Khvonsār**, Iran
74/F2 **Khvoy**, Iran
75/B5 **Khyber** (pass), Afg., Pak.
91/D2 **Kiama**, Austl.
128/E3 **Kiamichi** (mts.), Ok,US
45/G2 **Kibblesworth**, Eng,UK
42/J1 **Kibergneset** (pt.), Nor.
101/A3 **Kibondo**, Tanz.
62/E5 **Kičevo**, FYROM
87/F2 **Kidapawan**, Phil.
46/D2 **Kidderminster**, Eng,UK
101/B2 **Kidepo Valley Nat'l Park**, Ugan.
45/F5 **Kidsgrove**, Eng,UK
46/B3 **Kidwelly**, Wal,UK
48/F1 **Kiel** (bay), Den., Ger.
48/F1 **Kiel**, Ger.
49/L3 **Kielce**, Pol.
49/L3 **Kielce** (prov.), Pol.
45/F1 **Kielder**, Eng,UK
45/F1 **Kielder** (res.), Eng,UK
83/D1 **Kien An**, Viet.
83/D4 **Kien Duc**, Viet.
83/D4 **Kien Thanh**, Viet.
51/E6 **Kierspe**, Ger.
66/D2 **Kiev (Kyyiv)** (cap.), Ukr.
66/D2 **Kiev Obl.**, Ukr.
98/C2 **Kiffa**, Mrta.
61/L6 **Kifisiá**, Gre.
72/D2 **Kifrī**, Iraq
101/A3 **Kigali** (cap.), Rwa.
101/A4 **Kigoma**, Tanz.
101/A4 **Kigoma** (prov.), Tanz.
120/T10 **Kihei**, Hi,US
78/D4 **Kii** (chan.), Japan
78/D4 **Kii** (mts.), Japan
75/D3 **Kiines** (riv.), China
120/R9 **Kikepa** (pt.), Hi,US
130/H2 **Kikiktat** (mtn.), Ak,US
62/E3 **Kikinda**, Yugo.
104/C2 **Kikwit**, D.R. Congo
43/C3 **Kilbirnie**, Sc,UK
127/Q9 **Kilbride**, On,Can
44/B5 **Kildare** (co.), Ire.
64/G1 **Kil'den** (isl.), Rus.
128/E3 **Kilgore**, Tx,US
45/H3 **Kilham**, Eng,UK
119/R7 **Kilian** (isl.), Nun.,Can
101/C3 **Kilimanjaro** (prov.), Tanz.
63/K5 **Kilimli**, Turk.
101/C4 **Kilindoni**, Tanz.
74/D3 **Kilis**, Turk.
66/D3 **Kiliya**, Ukr.
44/B3 **Kilkeel**, NI,UK
43/B4 **Kilkenny**, Ire.
44/A6 **Kilkenny** (co.), Ire.
61/H2 **Kilkís**, Gre.
122/F2 **Killam**, Ab,Can
45/G5 **Killamarsh**, Eng,UK
90/B8 **Killara**, Austl.
123/J3 **Killarney**, Mb,Can
43/A4 **Killarney**, Ire.
123/H4 **Killdeer**, ND,US
43/C2 **Killearn**, Sc,UK
128/D4 **Killeen**, Tx,US
43/C2 **Killin**, Sc,UK
44/C3 **Killinchy**, NI,UK
119/K2 **Killinek** (isl.), Nun.,Can
61/H4 **Killíni** (peak), Gre.
44/C3 **Killough**, NI,UK
44/A2 **Killyclogher**, NI,UK
44/C3 **Killyleagh**, NI,UK
44/B5 **Kilmacanoge**, Ire.
43/C3 **Kilmarnock**, Sc,UK
46/B5 **Kilmar Tor** (hill), Eng,UK
44/B6 **Kilmichael** (pt.), Ire.
44/B1 **Kilraghts**, NI,UK
44/B2 **Kilrea**, NI,UK
101/C5 **Kilwa Masoko**, Tanz.
44/C2 **Kilwaughter**, NI,UK
43/C3 **Kilwinning**, Sc,UK
123/H5 **Kimball**, Ne,US
123/J5 **Kimball**, SD,US
92/E5 **Kimbe**, PNG
90/B2 **Kimberley** (cape), Austl.
92/B6 **Kimberley** (plat.), Austl.
122/E3 **Kimberley**, BC,Can
102/D3 **Kimberley**, SAfr.
80/E2 **Kimch'aek**, NKor.
80/D4 **Kimch'ŏn**, SKor.
80/E5 **Kimhae**, SKor.
79/F3 **Kimitsu**, Japan
80/D5 **Kimje**, SKor.
61/J4 **Kímolos** (isl.), Gre.
66/F1 **Kimovsk**, Rus.
104/D2 **Kimpanga**, D.R. Congo
64/H4 **Kimry**, Rus.
87/E2 **Kinabalu, Gunung** (peak), Malay.
87/E2 **Kinabatangan** (riv.), Malay.
122/D2 **Kinbasket** (lake), BC,Can
122/G3 **Kincaid**, Sk,Can
126/D2 **Kincardine**, On,Can
91/B2 **Kinchega Nat'l Park**, Austl.
104/D2 **Kindambi**, D.R. Congo
57/L3 **Kindberg**, Aus.
45/G5 **Kinder Scout** (mtn.), Eng,UK
98/B4 **Kindia**, Gui.
98/B4 **Kindia** (comm.), Gui.
104/E1 **Kindu**, D.R. Congo
67/J1 **Kinel'**, Rus.
64/J4 **Kineshma**, Rus.
47/E2 **Kineton**, Eng,UK
91/C3 **King** (isl.), Austl.
90/B4 **King** (peak), Austl.
122/B2 **King** (isl.), BC,Can
130/N4 **King** (mtn.), BC,Can
130/K3 **King** (peak), Yk,Can
90/C4 **Kingaroy**, Austl.
119/R7 **King Christian** (isl.), Nun.,Can
115/P3 **King Christian IX Land** (reg.), Grld.
115/Q2 **King Christian X Land** (reg.), Grld.
127/Q8 **King City**, On,Can
124/B3 **King City**, Ca,US
125/H4 **Kingfisher**, Ok,US
115/N3 **King Frederik VI Coast** (reg.), Grld.
115/Q2 **King Frederik VIII Land** (reg.), Grld.
93/L6 **King George** (isl.), FrPol.
126/E4 **King George**, Va,US
91/C3 **Kinglake Nat'l Park**, Austl.
93/J4 **Kingman** (reef), PacUS
124/D4 **Kingman**, Az,US
125/H3 **Kingman**, Ks,US
131/E5 **King of Prussia**, Pa,US
124/C3 **Kings** (riv.), Ca,US
124/E2 **Kings** (peak), Ut,US
46/C6 **Kingsbridge**, Eng,UK
124/C3 **Kings Canyon Nat'l Park**, Ca,US
47/E4 **Kingsclere**, Eng,UK
47/F1 **King's Cliffe**, Eng,UK
46/D2 **Kingsland**, Eng,UK
47/F3 **Kings Langley**, Eng,UK
47/G1 **King's Lynn**, Eng,UK
129/H2 **Kingsport**, Tn,US
47/E2 **Kings Sutton**, Eng,UK
46/C5 **Kingsteignton**, Eng,UK
91/C4 **Kingston**, Austl.
126/E2 **Kingston**, On,Can
117/F4 **Kingston** (cap.), Jam.
92/F7 **Kingston**, Norfl.
127/F3 **Kingston**, NY,US
91/A3 **Kingston South East**, Austl.
45/H4 **Kingston upon Hull** (co.), Eng,UK
47/F4 **Kingston upon Thames**, Eng,UK
117/J5 **Kingstown** (cap.), StV.
129/J3 **Kingstree**, SC,US
100/B3 **Kings, Valley of the**, Egypt
128/D5 **Kingsville**, Tx,US
46/D2 **Kingswinford**, Eng,UK
46/D4 **Kingswood**, Eng,UK
46/C2 **Kington**, Eng,UK
118/G2 **King William** (isl.), Nun.,Can
102/D4 **King William's Town**, SAfr.
130/L4 **Kinkaid** (mtn.), Ak,US
104/B1 **Kinkala**, Congo
78/D3 **Kinki** (prov.), Japan
98/B4 **Kinkon, Chutes de** (falls), Gui.
44/E5 **Kinmel**, Wal,UK
42/E4 **Kinna**, Swe.
43/E2 **Kinnairds Head** (pt.), Sc,UK
78/D3 **Kino** (riv.), Japan
53/E1 **Kinrooi**, Belg.
43/D2 **Kinross**, Sc,UK
127/R8 **Kinsale**, On,Can
104/C1 **Kinshasa** (cap.), D.R. Congo
125/H3 **Kinsley**, Ks,US
129/J3 **Kinston**, NC,US
99/E4 **Kintampo**, Gha.
43/D2 **Kintore**, Sc,UK
44/C1 **Kintyre, Mull of** (pt.), Sc,UK
79/F2 **Kinu** (riv.), Japan
97/M7 **Kinyeti** (peak), Sudan
61/G4 **Kiparissia** (gulf), Gre.
126/E2 **Kipawa** (lake), Qu,Can
101/A4 **Kipili**, Tanz.
123/H3 **Kipling**, Sk,Can
44/B5 **Kippure** (mtn.), Ire.
104/E3 **Kipushi**, D.R. Congo
79/N10 **Kira**, Japan
61/H3 **Kira Panayía** (isl.), Gre.
51/F6 **Kirchhundem**, Ger.
51/F4 **Kirchlengern**, Ger.
51/G3 **Kirchlinteln**, Ger.
44/C3 **Kircubbin**, NI,UK
44/D2 **Kircudbright** (bay), Sc,UK
69/L4 **Kirensk**, Rus.
75/B3 **Kirgizskiy** (mts.), Kyr.
68/F5 **Kirgiz Steppe** (grsld.), Kaz., Rus.
92/H5 **Kiribati**
74/D3 **Kırıkhan**, Turk.
74/C2 **Kırıkkale**, Turk.
76/C3 **Kirikkuduk**, China
64/G4 **Kirishi**, Rus.
78/B5 **Kirishima-Yaku Nat'l Park**, Japan
78/B5 **Kirishima-yama** (mtn.), Japan
93/K4 **Kiritimati** (Christmas) (atoll), Kiri.
45/G4 **Kirkburton**, Eng,UK
45/F5 **Kirkby**, Eng,UK
45/G5 **Kirkby in Ashfield**, Eng,UK
45/F3 **Kirkby Lonsdale**, Eng,UK
45/H3 **Kirkbymoorside**, Eng,UK
45/F3 **Kirkby Stephen**, Eng,UK
43/D2 **Kirkcaldy**, Sc,UK
44/C2 **Kirkcolm**, Sc,UK
44/D2 **Kirkcowan**, Sc,UK
44/D2 **Kirkcudbright**, Sc,UK
84/B4 **Kirkee**, India
42/J1 **Kirkenes**, Nor.
45/F4 **Kirkham**, Eng,UK
44/D2 **Kirkinner**, Sc,UK
127/N7 **Kirkland**, Qu,Can
132/C2 **Kirkland**, Wa,US
126/D1 **Kirkland Lake**, On,Can
63/H5 **Kırklareli**, Turk.
63/H5 **Kırklareli** (prov.), Turk.
44/D3 **Kirkmichael**, IM,UK
63/L2 **Kirkovgrad Obl.**, Ukr.
105/M **Kirkpatrick** (mtn.), Ant.
125/J2 **Kirksville**, Mo,US
43/D2 **Kirkton of Glenisla**, Sc,UK
74/F3 **Kirkūk**, Iraq
53/G4 **Kirn**, Ger.
66/E1 **Kirov**, Rus.
65/L4 **Kirov**, Rus.
65/L4 **Kirov Obl.**, Rus.
65/L4 **Kirovo-Chepetsk**, Rus.
66/E2 **Kirovohrad**, Ukr.
66/D2 **Kirovohrads'ka** (obl.), Ukr.
43/D2 **Kirriemuir**, Sc,UK
67/G1 **Kirsanov**, Rus.
74/C2 **Kırşehir**, Turk.
45/H6 **Kirton**, Eng,UK
45/H5 **Kirton in Lindsey**, Eng,UK
42/G2 **Kiruna**, Swe.
79/F2 **Kiryū**, Japan
97/L7 **Kisangani**, D.R. Congo
79/F3 **Kisarazu**, Japan
49/K5 **Kisbér**, Hun.
68/J4 **Kiselevsk**, Rus.
84/E2 **Kishanganj**, India
84/B2 **Kishangarh**, India
78/D3 **Kishiwada**, Japan
84/F3 **Kishorganj**, Bang.
73/L2 **Kishtwar**, India
132/N15 **Kishwaukee** (riv.), Il,US
101/B3 **Kisii**, Kenya
130/B6 **Kiska** (isl.), Ak,US
130/B5 **Kiska** (vol.), Ak,US
122/C2 **Kiskatinaw** (riv.), BC,Can
123/J2 **Kiskitto** (lake), Mb,Can
62/D2 **Kiskőrös**, Hun.
62/D2 **Kiskunfélegyháza**, Hun.
62/D2 **Kiskunhalas**, Hun.
62/D2 **Kiskunmajsa**, Hun.
62/D2 **Kiskunsági Nat'l Park**, Hun.
67/G4 **Kislovodsk**, Rus.
79/E3 **Kiso** (riv.), Japan
79/M9 **Kisogawa**, Japan
129/H4 **Kissimmee**, Fl,US
129/H4 **Kissimmee** (lake), Fl,US
123/H2 **Kississing** (lake), Mb,Can
62/E2 **Kisújszállás**, Hun.
101/B3 **Kisumu**, Kenya
62/F1 **Kisvárda**, Hun.
79/G2 **Kita** (inlet), Japan
98/C3 **Kita**, Mali
79/M9 **Kitagata**, Japan
79/G2 **Kita-Ibaraki**, Japan
79/F2 **Kitakata**, Japan
78/B4 **Kitakyūshū**, Japan
101/B2 **Kitale**, Kenya
77/N3 **Kitami**, Japan
77/N2 **Kitami** (mts.), Japan
79/H6 **Kitamoto**, Japan
126/D3 **Kitchener**, On,Can
42/J3 **Kitee**, Fin.
61/H4 **Kithira** (isl.), Gre.
61/J4 **Kithnos** (isl.), Gre.
122/A2 **Kitimat**, BC,Can
122/A2 **Kitimat Arm** (inlet), BC,Can
132/B2 **Kitsap Lake-Erlands Point**, Wa,US
131/E4 **Kittatinny** (mts.), NJ, Pa,US
127/G3 **Kittery**, Me,US
104/E3 **Kitwe**, Zam.
57/K3 **Kitzbühel**, Aus.
57/J2 **Kitzingen**, Ger.
42/H3 **Kiuruvesi**, Fin.
42/H2 **Kivalo** (mts.), Fin.
64/E4 **Kiviõli**, Est.
101/A3 **Kivu** (lake), Rwa., D.R. Congo
79/H7 **Kiyose**, Japan
79/M9 **Kiyosu**, Japan
104/C2 **Kizamba**, D.R. Congo
65/N4 **Kizel**, Rus.
75/B4 **Kizil** (riv.), China
74/C2 **Kızılcahamam**, Turk.
74/C2 **Kızılırmak** (riv.), Turk.
74/E3 **Kızıltepe**, Turk.
67/H4 **Kizlyar**, Rus.
79/L10 **Kizu**, Japan
78/E3 **Kizu** (riv.), Japan
67/L5 **Kizyl-Arvat**, Trkm.
64/C1 **Kjerkestinden** (peak), Nor.
42/E2 **Kjølen (Kölen)** (mts.), Nor., Swe.
62/D3 **Kladanj**, Bosn.
57/L1 **Kladno**, Czh.
62/F3 **Kladovo**, Yugo.
57/L3 **Klagenfurt**, Aus.
64/D5 **Klaipėda**, Lith.
122/C5 **Klamath** (mts.), Ca, Or,US
122/C5 **Klamath** (riv.), Ca, Or,US
122/C5 **Klamath Falls**, Or,US
68/B3 **Klar** (riv.), Swe.
42/E3 **Klarälven** (riv.), Swe.
50/E3 **Klazienaveen**, Neth.
53/G5 **Kleinblittersdorf**, Ger.
127/Q8 **Kleinburg**, On,Can
49/G3 **Kleine Elster** (riv.), Ger.
53/E2 **Kleine Gete** (riv.), Belg.
50/B6 **Kleine Nete** (riv.), Belg.
102/Q12 **Kleinolifants** (riv.), SAfr.
42/C3 **Kleppestø**, Nor.
102/D2 **Klerksdorp**, SAfr.
50/D5 **Kleve**, Ger.
66/E1 **Klintsy**, Rus.
102/E2 **Klip** (riv.), SAfr.
62/C3 **Ključ**, Bosn.
49/K2 **Kłodawa**, Pol.
49/J3 **Kłodzko**, Pol.
51/F3 **Klosterbach** (riv.), Ger.
57/M2 **Klosterneuburg**, Aus.
57/L3 **Klosterwappen** (peak), Aus.
48/F2 **Klötze**, Ger.
130/L3 **Kluane**, Yk,Can
130/K3 **Kluane Nat'l Park**, Yk,Can
49/K3 **Kluczbork**, Pol.
130/L3 **Klukshu**, Yk,Can
50/B5 **Klundert**, Neth.
51/E3 **Klüstenkanal** (can.), Ger.
64/J4 **Klyaz'ma** (riv.), Rus.
69/S4 **Klyuchevskaya** (peak), Rus.
45/G3 **Knaresborough**, Eng,UK
47/F3 **Knebworth**, Eng,UK
123/K2 **Knee** (lake), Mb,Can
63/G4 **Knezha**, Bul.
122/B3 **Knight** (inlet), BC,Can
46/C2 **Knighton**, Wal,UK
62/C3 **Knin**, Cro.
57/L3 **Knittelfeld**, Aus.
62/F4 **Knjaževac**, Yugo.
87/F1 **Knob** (peak), Phil.
44/B2 **Knockcloghrim**, NI,UK
44/B1 **Knocklayd** (mtn.), NI,UK
52/C1 **Knokke-Heist**, Belg.
102/A2 **Knoll** (pt.), Namb.
61/J5 **Knosós (Knossos)** (ruins), Gre.
45/F4 **Knott End**, Eng,UK
45/G4 **Knottingley**, Eng,UK
105/G **Knox** (coast), Ant.
91/G5 **Knox**, Austl.
130/M4 **Knox** (cape), BC,Can

129/H3 Knoxville, Tn,US
45/F5 Knutsford, Eng,UK
102/C4 Knysna, SAfr.
77/M2 Ko (peak), Rus.
78/B5 Kobayashi, Japan
78/D3 Kōbe, Japan
48/G1 København (Copenhagen) (cap.), Den.
87/G4 Kobipato (peak), Indo.
53/G3 Koblenz, Ger.
49/N2 Kobrin, Bela.
130/G2 Kobuk (riv.), Ak,US
130/G2 Kobuk Valley Nat'l Park, Ak,US
79/F3 Kobushi-ga-take (mtn.), Japan
63/J5 Kocaeli (prov.), Turk.
62/F5 Kočani, FYROM
62/B3 Kočevje, Slov.
119/J2 Koch (isl.), Nun.,Can
57/H2 Kocher (riv.), Ger.
78/C4 Kōchi, Japan
78/C4 Kōchi (pref.), Japan
130/H4 Kodiak, Ak,US
130/H4 Kodiak (isl.), Ak,US
130/H4 Kodiak Nat'l Wild. Ref., Ak,US
84/B3 Kodīnār, India
97/M6 Kodok, Sudan
63/H2 Kodry (hills), Mol.
52/B1 Koekelare, Belg.
84/D3 Koel (riv.), India
53/F5 Koenigsmacker, Fr.
124/D4 Kofa (mts.), Az,US
87/G4 Kofiau (isl.), Indo.
99/E5 Koforidua, Gha.
79/F3 Kōfu, Japan
79/F2 Koga, Japan
79/H7 Koganei, Japan
48/G1 Køge, Den.
48/G1 Køge Bugt (bay), Den.
98/B4 Kogon (riv.), Gui.
73/K2 Kohāt, Pak.
85/F2 Kohīma, India
64/E4 Kohtla-Järve, Est.
80/D5 Kohŭng, SKor.
116/D4 Kohunlich (ruins), Mex.
102/A2 Koichab (dry riv.), Namb.
130/K3 Koidern, Yk,Can
80/E5 Kōje (isl.), SKor.
49/L4 Kojšovská Hol'a (peak), Slvk.
83/B1 Kok (riv.), Myan.
79/M10 Koka, Japan
79/J7 Kokai (riv.), Japan
75/B3 Kokand, Uzb.
42/G3 Kokkola, Fin.
98/C3 Kokofata, Mali
120/W13 Koko Head (crater), Hi,US
101/A2 Kokola, D.R. Congo
126/C3 Kokomo, In,US
84/F2 Kokrajhar, India
75/C3 Kokshaal-Tau (mts.), Kyr.
52/B1 Koksijde, Belg.
119/K3 Koksoak (riv.), Qu,Can
75/A1 Kökshetaū, Kaz.
102/E3 Kokstad, SAfr.
78/B5 Kokubu, Japan
64/H1 Kola (pen.), Rus.
64/G1 Kola (riv.), Rus.
87/F4 Kolaka, Indo.
84/C5 Kolār, India
62/D4 Kolašin, Yugo.
48/G5 Kolbermoor, Ger.
49/L3 Kolbuszowa, Pol.
98/B3 Kolda, Sen.
98/B3 Kolda (reg.), Sen.
48/E1 Kolding, Den.
42/E2 Kölen (Kjølen) (mts.), Nor., Swe.
92/C5 Kolepom (isl.), Indo.
64/F4 Kolgompya (cape), Rus.
65/K1 Kolguyev (isl.), Rus.
84/B4 Kolhāpur, India
98/B3 Koliba (riv.), Gui.
49/H3 Kolín, Czh.
64/D4 Kolkasrags (pt.), Lat.
50/D2 Kollum, Neth.
50/D7 Köln (Cologne), Ger.
49/L2 Kolno, Pol.
66/A1 Koło, Pol.
101/B4 Kolo, Tanz.
49/H1 Kołobrzeg, Pol.
98/C3 Kolokani, Mali
66/F1 Kolomna, Rus.
66/C2 Kolomyya, Ukr.
84/C6 Kolonnawa, SrL.
98/D3 Kolossa (riv.), Mali
68/J4 Kolpashevo, Rus.
64/F4 Kolpino, Rus.
62/E3 Kolubara (riv.), Yugo
49/K3 Koluszki, Pol.
75/A1 Koluton (riv.), Kaz.
65/N2 Kolva (riv.), Rus.
104/E3 Kolwezi, D.R. Congo
69/R2 Kolyma (lowland), Rus.
69/R3 Kolyma (range), Rus.
69/R3 Kolyma (riv.), Rus.
62/F4 Kom (peak), Bul.
79/H7 Koma (riv.), Japan
62/E2 Komádi, Hun.
99/H4 Komadugu Gana (riv.), Nga.
99/H3 Komadugu Yobé (riv.), Nga.
79/H7 Komae, Japan
79/E3 Komagane, Japan
79/M9 Komaki, Japan
69/S4 Komandorskiye (isls.), Rus.
49/K5 Komárno, Slvk.
62/D2 Komárom, Hun.
62/D2 Komárom-Esztergom (co.), Hun.
78/E2 Komatsu, Japan
78/D4 Komatsushima, Japan
65/L2 Komi Aut. Rep., Rus.
65/M3 Komi-Permyak Aut. Okr., Rus.
62/D2 Komló, Hun.
66/F2 Kommunarsk, Ukr.
87/E5 Komodo Isl. Nat'l Park, Indo.
98/E5 Komoé (riv.), IvC.
78/E3 Komono, Japan
61/J2 Komotiní, Gre.
102/D3 Kompasberg (peak), SAfr.
63/J2 Komrat, Mol.
69/L1 Komsomolets (isl.), Rus.
65/P2 Komsomol'skiy, Rus.
77/M1 Komsomol'sk-na-Amure, Rus.
61/K3 Kömür (pt.), Turk.
75/A2 Kon (riv.), Kaz.
64/H4 Konakovo, Rus.
79/M10 Kōnan, Japan
79/M9 Kōnan, Japan
91/D2 Konangra-Boyd Nat'l Park, Austl.
87/F4 Konaweha (riv.), Indo.
76/G1 Konda (riv.), Rus.
64/G3 Kondopoga, Rus.
73/J1 Kondūz, Afg.
83/C4 Kong (isl.), Camb.
83/D3 Kong (riv.), Laos
80/D4 Kongju, SKor.
104/E2 Kongolo, D.R. Congo
79/L10 Kongō-zan (peak), Japan
42/D4 Kongsberg, Nor.
42/E3 Kongsvinger, Nor.
75/C4 Kongur Shan (peak), China
101/C4 Kongwa, Tanz.
49/K3 Koniecpol, Pol.
51/H4 Königslutter am Elm, Ger.
53/G2 Königswinter, Ger.
49/G2 Königs Wusterhausen, Ger.
49/K2 Konin, Pol.
49/K2 Konin (prov.), Pol.
54/D4 Köniz, Swi.
62/C4 Konjic, Bosn.
102/B2 Konkiep (dry riv.), Namb.
98/B4 Konkouré (riv.), Gui.
66/E2 Konotop, Ukr.
75/E3 Konqi (riv.), China
49/L3 Końskie, Pol.
49/L2 Konstancin-Jeziorna, Pol.
66/F2 Konstantinovka, Ukr.
49/K3 Konstantynów Łódzki, Pol.
55/F2 Konstanz, Ger.
52/D1 Kontich, Belg.
42/J3 Kontiolahti, Fin.
83/E3 Kon Tum, Viet.
74/C3 Konya, Turk.
53/F4 Konz, Ger.
122/E3 Koocanusa (lake), Can., US
122/D3 Kootenai (riv.), Id, Mt,US
122/D3 Kootenay (lake), BC,Can
122/D3 Kootenay Nat'l Park, BC,Can
84/B4 Kopargaon, India
42/N7 Kópavogur, Ice.
98/D5 Kope (peak), IvC.
49/G2 Köpenick, Ger.
65/P5 Kopeysk, Rus.
66/G4 Kop Gecidi (pass), Turk.
97/K7 Kopia, D.R. Congo
64/C4 Köping, Swe.
87/F5 Kopondei (cape), Indo.
42/E3 Kopparberg (co.), Swe.
77/M2 Koppi (riv.), Rus.
62/C2 Koprivnica, Cro.
72/F2 Kor (riv.), Iran
79/M9 Kōra, Japan
61/G2 Korab (peak), Alb.
57/L4 Korana (riv.), Bosn., Cro.
84/D4 Koraput, India
84/D3 Korba, India
51/F6 Korbach, Ger.
61/G2 Korçë, Alb.
62/C4 Korčula (isl.), Cro.
62/C4 Korčulanski (chan.), Cro.
72/F1 Kord Kūy, Iran
80/B3 Korea (bay), China, NKor.
78/A4 Korea (str.), Japan, SKor.
80/D2 Korea, North
80/D4 Korea, South
66/F3 Korenovsk, Rus.
98/D4 Korhogo, IvC.
61/H4 Kórinthos (Corinth), Gre.
62/C2 Kőris-hegy (peak), Hun.
79/G2 Kōriyama, Japan
96/J3 Korizo, Passe de (pass), Chad
69/R3 Korkodon (riv.), Rus.
74/B3 Korkuteli, Turk.
75/E3 Korla, China
74/J4 Kormakiti (cape), Cyp.
62/B4 Kornat (isl.), Cro.
93/Z18 Koro (isl.), Fiji
92/G6 Koro (sea), Fiji
63/K5 Köroğlu (peak), Turk.
101/C4 Korogwe, Tanz.
82/E6 Koronadal, Phil.
61/H2 Korónia (lake), Gre.
49/J2 Koronowo, Pol.
61/L7 Koropí, Gre.
92/C4 Koror (cap.), Palau
62/E2 Körös (riv.), Hun.
66/D2 Korosten', Ukr.
66/D2 Korostyshev, Ukr.
65/P1 Korotaikha (riv.), Rus.
96/J4 Koro Toro, Chad
130/D5 Korovin (vol.), Ak,US
77/N2 Korsakov, Rus.
50/D6 Korschenbroich, Ger.
48/F1 Korsør, Den.
52/C1 Kortemark, Belg.
53/E2 Kortenaken, Belg.
52/D2 Kortenberg, Belg.
53/E2 Kortessem, Belg.
52/C2 Kortrijk, Belg.
99/H5 Korup Nat'l Park, Camr.
71/R3 Koryak (range), Rus.
69/S3 Koryak Aut. Okr., Rus.
65/K3 Koryazhma, Rus.
79/L10 Kōryō, Japan
74/A3 Kós (isl.), Gre.
79/E3 Kosai, Japan
78/A3 Ko-saki (pt.), Japan
83/C3 Ko Samut Nat'l Park, Thai.
49/J2 Kościan, Pol.
49/J1 Kościerzyna, Pol.
91/D3 Kosciusko (mt.), Austl.
129/F3 Kosciusko, Ms,US
91/D3 Kosciusko Nat'l Park, Austl.
79/M10 Kosei, Japan
100/B4 Kosha, Sudan
79/F3 Koshigaya, Japan
73/H2 Koshk, Afg.
84/E2 Kosi (riv.), India
49/L4 Košice, Slvk.
75/C2 Kosoba, Gora (peak), Kaz.
62/E4 Kosovo (aut. reg.), Yugo.
62/E4 Kosovo Polje, Yugo.
62/E4 Kosovska Mitrovica, Yugo.
92/F4 Kosrae (isl.), Micr.
98/D3 Kossi (prov.), Burk.
98/D5 Kossou (lake), IvC.
67/K3 Kostinbrod, Bul.
66/C2 Kostopol', Ukr.
64/J4 Kostroma, Rus.
64/J4 Kostroma (riv.), Rus.
64/J4 Kostroma Obl., Rus.
49/H2 Kostrzyn, Pol.
49/J2 Kostrzyn, Pol.
65/N4 Kos'va (riv.), Rus.
65/N2 Kos'yu (riv.), Rus.
49/J1 Koszalin, Pol.
49/J2 Koszalin (prov.), Pol.
84/C2 Kota, India
79/N10 Kōta, Japan
86/B5 Kotaagung, Indo.
86/B2 Kota Baharu, Malay.
87/E4 Kotabaru, Indo.
86/C4 Kotabumi, Indo.
73/K2 Kot Addu, Pak.
63/H4 Kotel, Bul.
65/L4 Kotel'nich, Rus.
67/G3 Kotel'nikovo, Rus.
69/P2 Kotel'nyy (isl.), Rus.
48/F3 Köthen, Ger.
42/H3 Kotka, Fin.
64/E3 Kotka, Fin.
73/K2 Kot Kapūra, India
65/K3 Kotlas, Rus.
79/M9 Kotō, Japan
62/D4 Kotor, Yugo.
67/H2 Kotovo, Rus.
67/G1 Kotovsk, Rus.
73/J3 Kotri, Pak.
84/D4 Kottagūdem, India
84/C6 Kottayam, India
84/C6 Kotte, SrL.
97/K6 Kotto (riv.), CAfr.
69/L3 Kotuy (riv.), Rus.
130/E2 Kotzebue (sound), Ak,US
127/H2 Kouchibouguac Nat'l Park, NB,Can
99/E3 Koudougou, Burk.
61/J5 Koufonision (isl.), Gre.
130/E2 Kougarok (mtn.), Ak,US
82/D3 Kouhu, Tai.
119/J2 Koukdjuak (riv.), Nun.,Can
104/B1 Koula-Moutou, Gabon
98/D3 Koulikoro, Mali
98/B3 Koulountou (riv.), Gui., Sen.
98/D3 Koumbi Saleh (ruins), Mrta.
96/J6 Koumra, Chad
75/C2 Kounradskiy, Kaz.
125/E4 Kountze, Tx,US
99/H5 Koupé (peak), Camr.
99/E3 Koupela, Burk.
99/E3 Kouritenga (prov.), Burk.
109/H2 Kourou, FrG.
96/J4 Koussi (peak), Chad
98/D3 Koutiala, Mali
42/H3 Kouvola, Fin.
62/E3 Kovačica, Yugo.
64/F2 Kovdozero (lake), Rus.
66/C2 Kovel', Ukr.
84/C6 Kovilpatti, India
64/J4 Kovrov, Rus.
84/C5 Kovūr, India
67/G1 Kovylkino, Rus.
73/J1 Kowkcheh (riv.), Afg.
73/H2 Kowl-e Namaksār (lake), Afg., Iran
82/B3 Kowloon, China
78/B5 Kōyama, Japan
63/G4 Koynare, Bul.
130/H2 Koyukuk (riv.), Ak,US
79/N10 Kozakai, Japan
74/C3 Kozan, Turk.
61/G2 Kozáni, Gre.
62/C3 Kozara Nat'l Park, Bosn.
84/C5 Kozhikode (Calicut), India
64/H3 Kozhozero (lake), Rus.
65/M2 Kozhva (riv.), Rus.
49/L3 Kozienice, Pol.
63/F4 Kozloduy, Bul.
74/E2 Kozluk, Turk.
49/J3 Koźmin, Pol.
63/F4 Koznitsa (peak), Bul.
49/H3 Kożuchów, Pol.
99/F5 Kpalimé, Togo
99/F5 Kpandu, Gha.
83/B4 Kra (isth.), Myan., Thai.
102/D3 Kraai (riv.), SAfr.
102/L10 Kraaifontein, SAfr.
83/B4 Krabi, Thai.
83/D3 Kracheh, Camb.
42/D4 Kragerø, Nor.
62/E3 Kragujevac, Yugo.
57/H2 Kraichgau (reg.), Ger.
86/C5 Krakatoa (vol.), Indo.
83/D3 Krakor, Camb.
49/K3 Kraków, Pol.
49/K3 Kraków (prov.), Pol.
83/C3 Kralanh, Camb.
117/H5 Kralendijk, NAnt.
62/E4 Kraljevo, Yugo.
57/L1 Kralupy nad Vltavou, Czh.
66/F2 Kramators'k, Ukr.
42/F3 Kramfors, Swe.
50/B5 Krammer (chan.), Neth.
50/D5 Kranenburg, Ger.
62/B2 Kranj, Slov.
49/J3 Krapkowice, Pol.
49/M3 Kraśnik, Pol.
49/M3 Kraśnik Fabryczny, Pol.
67/H2 Krasnoarmeysk, Rus.
66/F3 Krasnodar, Rus.
66/F3 Krasnodar (kray), Rus.
66/F1 Krasnogorsk, Rus.
66/E2 Krasnograd, Ukr.
77/H1 Krasnokamensk, Rus.
65/M4 Krasnokamsk, Rus.
67/H2 Krasnoslobodsk, Rus.
68/G4 Krasnotur'insk, Rus.
65/P4 Krasnoural'sk, Rus.
68/K4 Krasnoyarsk, Rus.
49/M3 Krasnystaw, Pol.
67/H2 Krasnyy Kut, Rus.
66/F2 Krasnyy Luch, Ukr.
66/G3 Krasnyy Sulin, Rus.
83/C4 Kravanh (mts.), Camb.
86/C5 Krawang, Indo.
50/D6 Krefeld, Ger.
51/G5 Kreiensen, Ger.
61/G3 Kremastón (lake), Gre.
66/E2 Kremenchuk, Ukr.
66/E2 Kremenchuts'ke (res.), Ukr.
124/F2 Kremmling, Co,US
57/L2 Krems an der Donau, Aus.
69/T3 Kresta (gulf), Rus.
42/G5 Kretinga, Lith.
53/F2 Kreuzau, Ger.
53/G2 Kreuztal, Ger.
96/G7 Kribi, Camr.
66/D1 Krichev, Bela.
77/N2 Kril'on, Mys (cape), Rus.
50/B5 Krimpen aan de IJssel, Neth.
84/D4 Krishna (riv.), India
84/C5 Krishnagiri, India
42/C4 Kristiansand, Nor.
42/E4 Kristianstad, Swe.
49/H1 Kristianstad (co.), Swe.
42/C3 Kristiansund, Nor.
42/E4 Kristinehamn, Swe.
62/F4 Kriva Palanka, FYROM
62/B3 Krk, Cro.
62/C3 Krka (riv.), Cro.
49/J3 Krnov, Czh.
103/E2 Krokodil (riv.), SAfr.
102/D2 Krokodilrivier (riv.), SAfr.
66/E2 Krolovets, Ukr.
49/J4 Kroměříž, Czh.
57/J1 Kronach, Ger.
83/C4 Krong Kaoh Kong, Camb.
83/D4 Krong Keb, Camb.
42/E4 Kronoberg (co.), Swe.
64/F4 Kronshtadt, Rus.
90/C4 Kroombit Tops Nat'l Park, Austl.
102/D2 Kroonstad, SAfr.
67/G3 Kropotkin, Rus.
49/L4 Krosno, Pol.
49/L4 Krosno (prov.), Pol.
49/H2 Krosno Odrzańskie, Pol.
49/J3 Krotoszyn, Pol.
62/B3 Krško, Slov.
51/G1 Kruckau (riv.), Ger.
104/F5 Kruger Nat'l Park, SAfr.
102/P13 Krugersdorp, SAfr.
65/N5 Kruglitsa, Gora (peak), Rus.
130/A5 Krugloi (pt.), Ak,US
50/B6 Kruibeke, Belg.
62/D5 Krujë, Alb.
63/G5 Krumovgrad, Bul.
83/C3 Krung Thep (Bangkok) (cap.), Thai.
49/K4 Krupina, Slvk.
130/F2 Krusenstern (cape), Ak,US
62/E4 Kruševac, Yugo.
57/K1 Krušné Hory (Erzgebirge) (mts.), Czh., Ger.
49/K2 Kruszwica, Pol.
130/L4 Kruzof (isl.), Ak,US
66/E3 Krym Aut. Rep., Ukr.
66/F3 Krymsk, Rus.
49/L4 Krynica, Pol.
66/E3 Kryvyy Rih, Ukr.
49/M3 Krzna (riv.), Pol.
49/J2 Krzyż, Pol.
81/D4 Kuai (riv.), China
86/D3 Kuala Belait, Bru.
86/B3 Kuala Dungun, Malay.
86/B3 Kuala Lipis, Malay.
86/B3 Kuala Lumpur (cap.), Malay.
86/B3 Kuala Pilah, Malay.
86/B2 Kuala Terengganu, Malay.
86/B3 Kuantan, Malay.
67/J4 Kuba, Azer.
66/F3 Kuban' (riv.), Rus.
64/H4 Kubenskoye (lake), Rus.
78/C4 Kubokawa, Japan
63/H4 Kubrat, Bul.
86/D3 Kuching, Malay.
61/F2 Kuçovë, Alb.
78/B4 Kudamatsu, Japan
86/D5 Kudus, Indo.
65/M4 Kudymkar, Rus.
97/K3 Kufrah (oasis), Libya
74/K5 Kufrinjah, Jor.
57/K3 Kufstein, Aus.
42/J2 Kuhmo, Fin.
50/D3 Kuinder of Tjonger (riv.), Neth.
83/E1 Kuishan (mtn.), China
104/C3 Kuito, Ang.
130/M4 Kuiu (isl.), Ak,US
99/E5 Kujani Game Rsv., Gha.
49/K2 Kujawy (reg.), Pol.
77/N3 Kuji, Japan
78/B4 Kujū-san (mtn.), Japan
61/G1 Kukës, Alb.
79/F2 Kuki, Japan
79/J7 Kukizaki, Japan
73/G3 Kūl (riv.), Iran
62/D3 Kula, Yugo.
86/B3 Kulai, Malay.
67/J3 Kulaly (isl.), Kaz.
67/K4 Kulandag (mts.), Trkm.
67/G4 Kulashi, Geo.
64/D4 Kuldīga, Lat.
64/J5 Kulebaki, Rus.
83/D3 Kulen, Camb.
91/B2 Kulkyne-Hattah Nat'l Park, Austl.
73/L2 Kullu, India
57/J1 Kulmbach, Ger.
65/J2 Kuloy (riv.), Rus.
67/K3 Kul'sary, Kaz.
74/C2 Kulu, Turk.
68/H4 Kulunda, Rus.
75/C1 Kulunda (lake), Rus.
75/D1 Kulunda (riv.), Rus.
75/C1 Kulunda Steppe (grsld.), Kaz., Rus.
73/J1 Kulyab, Taj.
67/H3 Kuma (riv.), Rus.
79/F2 Kumagaya, Japan
78/B4 Kumamoto, Japan
78/B4 Kumamoto (pref.), Japan
78/E4 Kumano, Japan
78/D4 Kumano (riv.), Japan
62/E4 Kumanovo, FYROM
99/E5 Kumasi, Gha.
79/L10 Kumatori, Japan
99/H5 Kumba, Camr.
99/H5 Kumbo, Camr.
67/K5 Kum-Dag, Trkm.
82/E2 Kume (isl.), Japan
67/K1 Kumertau, Rus.
80/E4 Kumi, SKor.
79/L10 Kumiyama, Japan
42/E4 Kumla, Swe.
74/B3 Kumluca, Turk.
85/G2 Kumon (range), Myan.
84/B5 Kumta, India
120/U11 Kumukahi (cape), Hi,US
77/P3 Kunashiri (isl.), Rus.
84/C2 Kūnch, India
104/E3 Kundelungu Nat'l Park, D.R. Congo
73/K2 Kundiān, Pak.
84/B3 Kundla, India
42/E4 Kungsbacka, Swe.
97/J7 Kungu, D.R. Congo
65/N4 Kungur, Rus.
62/E2 Kunhegyes, Hun.
78/B4 Kunimi-dake (mtn.), Japan
86/C5 Kuningan, Indo.
79/H7 Kunitachi, Japan
75/C4 Kunjirap Daban (pass), China
75/C4 Kunlun (mts.), China
62/E2 Kunmadaras, Hun.
85/H2 Kunming, China
80/D5 Kunsan, SKor.
81/E5 Kunshan, China
62/E2 Kunszentmárton, Hun.
81/E3 Kunyu Shan (mtn.), China
42/H3 Kuopio, Fin.
62/B3 Kupa (riv.), Cro., Slov.
87/F6 Kupang, Indo.
68/H4 Kupino, Rus.
130/M4 Kupreanof (isl.), Ak,US
66/F2 Kupyansk, Ukr.
77/L1 Kur (riv.), Rus.
67/J5 Kura (riv.), Azer., Geo.
79/L9 Kurama-yama (peak), Japan
78/C3 Kurashiki, Japan
100/B5 Kuraymah, Sudan
78/C3 Kurayoshi, Japan
72/D1 Kurdistan (reg.), Asia
63/G5 Kŭrdzhali, Bul.
61/J2 Kŭrdzhali (res.), Bul.
78/C3 Kure, Japan
74/C2 Küre (mts.), Turk.
92/H2 Kure (isl.), Hi,US
64/D4 Kuressaare, Est.
68/K3 Kureyka (riv.), Rus.
65/Q5 Kurgan, Rus.
65/Q5 Kurgan Obl., Rus.
73/J1 Kurgan-Tyube, Taj.
92/G4 Kuria (isl.), Kiri.
72/G5 Kuria Muria (isls.), Oman
69/Q5 Kuril (isls.), Rus.
90/H8 Ku-Ring-Gai Nat'l Park, Austl.
97/M5 Kurmuk, Sudan
84/C4 Kurnool, India
79/K9 Kurodashō, Japan
79/G2 Kuroiso, Japan
79/M10 Kuroso-yama (peak), Japan
73/K2 Kurram (riv.), Pak.
64/D5 Kuršėnai, Lith.
84/E2 Kurseong, India
66/F2 Kursk, Rus.
49/L1 Kurskaya (spit), Lith., Rus.
49/L1 Kurskiy (lag.), Rus.
66/E2 Kursk Obl., Rus.
62/E4 Kuršumlija, Yugo.
74/E3 Kurtalan, Turk.
51/E6 Kürten, Ger.
100/B5 Kurtī, Sudan
97/L6 Kuru (riv.), Sudan
67/G4 Kuruçay (riv.), Turk.
75/E3 Kuruktag (mts.), China
78/B4 Kurume, Japan
84/D6 Kurunegala, SrL.
100/B4 Kurur, Jabal (peak), Sudan
90/E6 Kurwongbah (lake), Austl.
74/A3 Kuşadası, Turk.
83/C2 Ku Sathan (peak), Thai.
79/L9 Kusatsu, Japan
79/M9 Kusatsu, Japan
79/M10 Kushida (riv.), Japan
78/B5 Kushikino, Japan
78/B5 Kushima, Japan
78/D4 Kushimoto, Japan
77/N3 Kushiro, Japan
65/Q5 Kushmurun (lake), Kaz.
76/F4 Kushui (riv.), China
67/J2 Kushum (riv.), Kaz.
130/F4 Kuskokwim (bay), Ak,US
130/G3 Kuskokwim (mts.), Ak,US
130/F3 Kuskokwim (riv.), Ak,US
67/M2 Kustanay Obl., Kaz.
75/F1 Kūstī, Sudan
79/M10 Kusu, Japan
83/C4 Kut (isl.), Thai.
74/B2 Kütahya, Turk.
67/G4 K'ut'aisi, Geo.
84/A3 Kutch (gulf), India
84/A3 Kutch (reg.), India
73/J4 Kutch, Rann of (swamp), India, Pak.
49/H4 Kutná Hora, Czh.
49/K2 Kutno, Pol.
104/C1 Kutu, D.R. Congo
97/K5 Kutum, Sudan
118/E1 Kuujjua (riv.), NW,Can
119/K3 Kuujjuaq (Fort-Chimo), Qu,Can
119/J3 Kuujjuarapik, Qu,Can
42/J2 Kuusamo, Fin.
42/H3 Kuusankoski, Fin.
42/H4 Kuutse Mägi (mt.), Est.
67/L2 Kuvandyk, Rus.
72/E3 Kuwait
72/E3 Kuwait (cap.), Kuw.
84/D2 Kuwāna (riv.), India
78/E3 Kuwana, Japan
65/L5 Kuybyshev (res.), Rus.
81/B3 Kuye (riv.), China
74/F3 Küysanjaq, Iraq
64/F2 Kuyto (lake), Rus.
75/E3 Kuytun, China
75/D2 Kuytun (riv.), China
116/E5 Kuyu Tingni, Nic.
130/E2 Kuzitrin (riv.), Ak,US
67/H1 Kuznetsk, Rus.
42/F1 Kvaløy (isl.), Nor.
62/B3 Kvarner (chan.), Cro.
62/B3 Kvarnerić (chan.), Cro.
42/E2 Kvigtinden (peak), Nor.
42/C4 Kvinnherad, Nor.
104/C1 Kwa (riv.), D.R. Congo
83/B3 Kwai, River (bridge), Thai.
92/F4 Kwajelein (atoll), Mrsh.
80/D5 Kwangju, SKor.
80/D5 Kwangju-Jikhalsi (prov.), SKor.
104/C1 Kwango (riv.), D.R. Congo
101/B2 Kwania (lake), Ugan.
99/G4 Kwara (state), Nga.
126/D1 Kwataboahegan (riv.), On,Can
103/E7 KwaZulu Natal (prov.), SAfr.
104/E4 Kwekwe, Zim.
49/K2 Kwidzyn, Pol.
97/N5 Kwīha, Eth.
96/J6 Kyabé, Chad
83/B2 Kyaikkami, Myan.
83/B2 Kyaikto, Myan.
76/F1 Kyakhta, Rus.
85/G4 Kyangin, Myan.
83/D2 Ky Anh, Viet.
83/B1 Kyaukme, Myan.
85/F4 Kyaukpyu, Myan.
83/B1 Kyaukse, Myan.
49/J4 Kyjov, Czh.
122/F3 Kyle, Sk,Can
53/F3 Kyll (riv.), Ger.
53/F3 Kyllburg, Ger.
47/F2 Kym (riv.), Eng,UK
84/C3 Kymore, India
101/B2 Kyoga (lake), Ugan.
78/D3 Kyōga-misaki (cape), Japan
79/F3 Kyonan, Japan
80/C4 Kyŏnggi (bay), SKor.
80/D4 Kyŏnggi-Do (prov.), SKor.
80/E5 Kyŏngju, SKor.
80/E5 Kyŏngju Nat'l Park, SKor.
80/E4 Kyŏngsang-bukto (prov.), SKor.
80/E5 Kyŏngsang-namdo (prov.), SKor.
78/D3 Kyōto, Japan
78/D3 Kyōto (pref.), Japan
74/J4 Kyrenia (dist.), Cyp.
75/B3 Kyrgyzstan
48/G2 Kyritz, Ger.
85/H4 Ky Son, Viet.
78/B5 Kyūshū (isl.), Japan
78/B4 Kyūshū (mts.), Japan
78/B4 Kyūshū (prov.), Japan
62/F4 Kyustendil, Bul.
66/D2 Kyyiv (Kiev) (cap.), Ukr.
66/D2 Kyyivs'ke (res.), Ukr.
67/G1 Kyzyl, Rus.
68/G5 Kyzylkum (des.), Kaz.,Uzb.

L

48/G2 Laage, Ger.
57/K3 Laakirchen, Aus.
58/B4 La Algaba, Sp.
116/E6 La Amistad Int'l Park
112/B3 La Araucanía (reg.), Chile
52/C1 Laarne, Belg.
117/N7 La Ascensión, Mex.
117/J5 La Asunción, Ven.
51/G4 Laatzen, Ger.
96/C2 Laayoune, WSah.
127/G1 La Baie, Qu,Can
58/A1 La Baña, Sp.
111/D2 La Banda, Arg.
58/C1 La Bañeza, Sp.
82/D6 Labason, Phil.
52/B2 La Bassée, Fr.
56/B3 La Baule-Escoublac, Fr.
60/B1 Labbro (peak), It.
96/H1 Labdah (Leptis Magna) (ruins), Libya
98/B4 Labé, Gui.
98/B4 Labé (comm.), Gui.
49/H3 Labe (Elbe) (riv.), Czh.
129/H5 La Belle, Fl,US
62/B3 Labin, Cro.
67/G3 Labinsk, Rus.
59/G2 La Bisbal, Sp.
116/D3 Labná (ruins), Mex.
49/L4 Laborec (riv.), Slvk.
112/E2 Laboulaye, Arg.
119/K3 Labrador (reg.), Nf,Can
115/M4 Labrador (sea), Can., Grld.
119/K3 Labrador City, Nf,Can
108/F5 Lábrea, Braz.
87/E2 Labuk (bay), Malay.
87/E2 Labuk (riv.), Malay.
85/F4 Labutta, Myan.
61/F2 Laç, Alb.
112/C2 La Calera, Chile
127/N6 Lac-Alouette, Qu,Can
112/C2 La Campana Nat'l Park, Chile
131/B2 La Cañada-Flintridge, Ca,US
112/E2 La Carlota, Arg.
58/C4 La Carlota, Sp.
58/D3 La Carolina, Sp.
84/B5 Laccadive (sea), India
123/J3 Lac du Bonnet, Mb,Can
116/D4 La Ceiba, Hon.
91/A3 Lacepede (bay), Austl.
132/B3 Lacey, Wa,US
64/H3 Lacha (lake), Rus.
52/A5 Lachapelle-aux-Pots, Fr.
56/F2 La Chapelle-Saint-Luc, Fr.
56/C3 La Chapelle-sur-Erdre, Fr.
127/N6 Lachenaie, Qu,Can
127/N7 Lachine, Qu,Can
91/C2 Lachlan (riv.), Austl.
117/F6 La Chorrera, Pan.
51/H3 Lachte (riv.), Ger.
125/F4 La Cienega, NM,US
58/A1 La Ciñiza, Sp.
56/F5 La Ciotat, Fr.
117/N9 La Ciudad Nat'l Park, Mex.
127/S10 Lackawanna, NY,US
122/F2 Lac La Biche, Ab,Can
127/G2 Lac-Mégantic, Qu,Can
46/D4 Lacock, Eng,UK
122/E2 Lacombe, Ab,Can
116/E6 La Concepción, Pan.
117/G5 La Concepcion, Ven.
127/G3 Laconia, NH,US
58/A1 La Coruña, Sp.
56/D4 La Couronne, Fr.
123/L5 La Crescent, Mn,US
131/B2 La Crescenta-Montrose, Ca,US
126/B3 La Crosse, Wi,US
112/Q9 La Cruz, Chile
116/D5 La Cruz, CR
117/N9 La Cruz, Mex.
83/D1 Lac Son, Viet.
86/C1 Lac Thien, Viet.
73/L2 Ladakh (mts.), Pak., India
91/B3 Laddon (riv.), Austl.
49/J3 Lądek-Zdrój, Pol.
60/C2 Ladispoli, It.
64/F3 Ladoga (lake), Rus.
108/D2 La Dorada, Col.
113/J8 Ladrillero (mtn.), Chile
102/D3 Ladybrand, SAfr.
103/E3 Ladysmith, SAfr.
126/B2 Ladysmith, Wi,US
92/F4 Lae (atoll), Mrsh.
92/D5 Lae, PNG
116/D5 La Esperanza, Hon.
117/J6 La Esperanza, Ven.
58/B1 La Estaca de Bares, Punta de (cape), Sp.
58/A1 La Estrada, Sp.
111/D3 La Falda, Arg.
132/K11 Lafayette, Ca,US
129/G3 La Fayette, Ga,US
126/C3 Lafayette, In,US
128/E4 Lafayette, La,US
56/D2 La Ferté-Bernard, Fr.
56/C2 La Ferté-Macé, Fr.
52/C6 La Ferté-sous-Jouarre, Fr.
126/E1 Laflamme (riv.), Qu,Can
56/C3 La Flèche, Fr.
57/L3 Lafnitz (riv.), Aus.
127/M6 Lafontaine, Qu,Can
57/G4 La Font Sancte, Pic de (peak), Fr.
117/G6 La Fría, Ven.
85/F6 Lāfūl, India
44/B3 Lagan (riv.), NI,UK
128/B2 La Garita (mts.), Co,US
59/L6 La Garriga, Sp.
109/L6 Lagarto, Braz.
82/D4 Lagawe, Phil.
96/H6 Lagdo (riv.), Camr.
51/F5 Lage, Ger.
110/B3 Lages, Braz.
50/C4 Lage Vaart (can.), Neth.
96/F1 Laghouat, Alg.
52/B5 Lagny-le-Sec, Fr.
52/B6 Lagny-sur-Marne, Fr.
110/C2 Lagoa da Prata, Braz.
110/C1 Lagoa Formosa, Braz.
110/B4 Lagoa Vermelha, Braz.
112/C4 Lago Puelo Nat'l Park, Arg.
99/F5 Lagos, Nga.
99/F5 Lagos (state), Nga.
58/A4 Lagos, Port.
116/A3 Lagos de Moreno, Mex.
115/K4 La Grande (riv.), Can.
122/D4 La Grande, Or,US
57/G4 La Grande Ruine (mtn.), Fr.
129/G3 La Grange, Ga,US
126/C4 La Grange, Ky,US
128/D4 La Grange, Tx,US
108/F2 La Gran Sabana (plain), Ven.
58/A2 La Guardia, Sp.
112/D3 La Guerra (peak), Arg.
110/B4 Laguna, Braz.
132/M10 Laguna (cr.), Ca,US
112/C3 Laguna Blanca Nat'l Park, Chile
58/C2 Laguna de Duero, Sp.

160

Lagun – Lice

112/C3 Laguna del Laja Nat'l Park, Chile
131/C3 Laguna Hills, Ca,US
113/J6 Laguna San Rafael Nat'l Park, Chile
116/C4 Lagunas de Montebello Nat'l Park, Mex.
117/G6 Lagunillas, Ven.
131/C3 La Habra, Ca,US
86/B4 Lahat, Indo.
127/H2 La Have (riv.), NS,Can
111/B2 La Higuera, Chile
72/F1 Lāhījān, Iran
48/E3 Lahn (riv.), Ger.
53/G3 Lahnstein, Ger.
42/E4 Laholm, Swe.
73/K2 Lahore, Pak.
54/D1 Lahr, Ger.
42/H3 Lahti, Fin.
96/J6 Laï, Chad
83/C1 Lai Chau, Viet.
82/A2 Laifeng Tujiazu Zizhixian, China
56/D2 L'Aigle, Fr.
42/G3 Laihia, Fin.
42/G2 Lainioälven (riv.), Swe.
42/G3 Laitila, Fin.
55/H5 Laives (Leifers), It.
81/D3 Laiwu, China
81/D3 Laizhou (bay), China
112/C3 Laja (lake), Chile
110/B4 Lajeado, Braz.
59/S12 Lajes do Pico, Azor.,Port.
110/D2 Lajinha, Braz.
62/D2 Lajosmizse, Hun.
125/G3 La Junta, Co,US
123/J5 Lake Andes, SD,US
131/C2 Lake Arrowhead, Ca,US
128/E4 Lake Charles, La,US
124/F3 Lake City, Co,US
129/H4 Lake City, Fl,US
123/K4 Lake City, Mn,US
130/H3 Lake Clark Nat'l Park & Prsv., Ak,US
45/E2 Lake District Nat'l Park, Eng,UK
131/C3 Lake Elsinore, Ca,US
90/B1 Lakefield Nat'l Park, Austl.
132/Q15 Lake Forest, Il,US
128/E3 Lake Fork (res.), Tx,US
124/D4 Lake Havasu City, Az,US
131/F5 Lakehurst, NJ,US
128/E4 Lake Jackson, Tx,US
129/H4 Lakeland, Fl,US
122/D3 Lake Louise, Ab,Can
104/F3 Lake Malawi Nat'l Park, Malw.
101/A3 Lake Mburo Nat'l Park, Ugan.
124/D4 Lake Mead Nat'l Rec. Area, Az, Nv,US
61/G2 Lake Mikri Prespa Nat'l Park, Gre.
131/F4 Lake Mohawk, NJ,US
47/G2 Lakenheath, Eng,UK
125/J3 Lake of the Ozarks (lake), Mo,US
123/K3 Lake of the Woods (lake), Can., US
132/F6 Lake Orion, Mi,US
124/B3 Lakeport, Ca,US
128/F3 Lake Providence, La,US
131/G5 Lake Ronkonkoma, NY,US
91/C4 Lake Saint Clair-Cradle Mountain Nat'l Park, Austl.
42/H1 Lakesfjorden (fjord), Nor.
131/K7 Lake Shore, Md,US
126/E4 Lakeside, Va,US
132/R16 Lake Station, In,US
122/C5 Lakeview, Or,US
132/F6 Lakeville (lake), Mi,US
129/H5 Lake Wales, Fl,US
131/B3 Lakewood, Ca,US
125/F3 Lakewood, Co,US
132/P15 Lakewood, Il,US
131/F5 Lakewood, NJ,US
122/C3 Lakewood, Wa,US
129/H5 Lake Worth, Fl,US
132/P15 Lake Zurich, Il,US
84/D2 Lakhīmpur, India
42/N7 Laki (vol.), Ice.
73/K2 Lakki, Pak.
61/H4 Lakonía (gulf), Gre.
84/B5 Lakshadweep (isls.), India
84/B6 Lakshadweep (terr.), India
59/X16 La Laguna, Canl.
73/K2 Lāla Mūsa, Pak.
103/H8 Lalana (riv.), Madg.
86/B4 Lalang (riv.), Indo.
84/E3 Lālgola, India
97/N5 Lalībela, Eth.
108/B4 La Libertad, Ecu.
116/C4 La Libertad, Guat.
117/M8 La Libertad, Mex.
112/C2 La Ligua, Chile
77/K3 Lalin (riv.), China
58/A1 Lalín, Sp.
58/C4 La Línea de la Concepción, Sp.
84/C3 Lalitpur, India
59/L6 La Llagosta, Sp.
122/F1 La Loche, Sk,Can
52/D3 La Louvière, Belg.
58/C4 La Luisiana, Sp.
58/B4 La Luz, Costa de (coast), Sp.
44/D1 Lamachan (mtn.), Sc,UK
60/A2 La Maddalena, It.
52/C2 La Madeleine, Fr.
99/F4 Lama-Kara, Togo
127/G2 La Malbaie, Qu,Can
116/D4 Lamanai (ruins), Belz.
86/D4 Lamandau (riv.), Indo.
125/G3 Lamar, Co,US
118/E2 La Martre (lake), NW,Can
56/B2 Lamballe, Fr.
111/E2 Lambaré, Par.
104/B1 Lambaréné, Gabon
110/H6 Lambari, Braz.
44/B5 Lambay (isl.), Ire.
108/C5 Lambayeque, Peru
44/B3 Lambeg, NI,UK
98/C3 Lambé Koba (riv.), Mali
105/E Lambert (glac.), Ant.
126/D3 Lambertville, Mi,US
131/F5 Lambertville, NJ,US
47/E3 Lambourn, Eng,UK
58/B2 Lamego, Port.
127/H2 Lamèque (isl.), NB,Can
108/C6 La Merced, Peru
56/F3 La Mère Boitier, Signal de (mtn.), Fr.
128/C3 Lamesa, Tx,US
61/H3 Lamía, Gre.
90/D5 Lamington Nat'l Park, Austl.
131/B3 La Mirada, Ca,US
117/M8 La Misa, Mex.
82/D6 Lamitan, Phil.
126/B3 La Moine (riv.), Il,US
57/J4 Lamone (riv.), It.
124/C4 Lamont, Ca,US
108/D5 La Montaña (reg.), Peru
59/K7 La Morella (peak), Sp.
117/P8 La Morita, Mex.
52/B5 Lamorlaye, Fr.
92/D4 Lamotrek (isl.), Micr.
123/J4 La Moure, ND,US
112/Q9 Lampa, Chile
83/B2 Lampang, Thai.
83/C2 Lam Pao (res.), Thai.
128/D4 Lampasas, Tx,US
128/D4 Lampasas (riv.), Tx,US
60/C5 Lampedusa (isl.), It.
57/H2 Lampertheim, Ger.
46/B2 Lampeter, Wal,UK
46/B2 Lamphey, Wal,UK
83/B2 Lamphun, Thai.
123/H3 Lampman, Sk,Can
101/D3 Lamu, Kenya
120/T10 Lanai (isl.), Hi,US
120/T10 Lanaihale (peak), Hi,US
53/E2 Lanaken, Belg.
59/F3 La Nao, Cabo de (cape), Sp.
43/D3 Lanark, Sc,UK
83/B4 Lanbi (isl.), Myan.
76/D5 Lancang (riv.), China
45/F4 Lancashire (co.), Eng,UK
45/F4 Lancashire (plain), Eng,UK
119/H1 Lancaster (sound), Nun.,Can
45/F3 Lancaster, Eng,UK
124/C4 Lancaster, Ca,US
127/S10 Lancaster, NY,US
126/D4 Lancaster, Oh,US
129/H3 Lancaster, SC,US
126/B3 Lancaster, Wi,US
45/G2 Lanchester, Eng,UK
60/D1 Lanciano, It.
49/M3 Łańcut, Pol.
57/K2 Landau an der Isar, Ger.
57/H2 Landau in der Pfalz, Ger.
55/G3 Landeck, Aus.
53/E2 Landen, Belg.
122/F5 Lander, Wy,US
56/A2 Landerneau, Fr.
56/C4 Landes (reg.), Fr.
56/B3 Landes de Lanvaux (reg.), Fr.
122/F2 Landis, Sk,Can
56/A2 Landivisiau, Fr.
51/G1 Land Kehdingen (reg.), Ger.
90/B3 Landsborough (cr.), Austl.
46/A6 Land's End (pt.), Eng,UK
57/K2 Landshut, Ger.
50/B4 Landsmeer, Neth.
53/G5 Landstuhl, Ger.
45/F2 Lanercost, Eng,UK
56/B3 Lanester, Fr.
129/G3 Lanett, Al,US
123/J3 Langdon, ND,US
102/C3 Langeberg (mts.), SAfr.
102/L10 Langeberg (mts.), SAfr.
48/F1 Langeland (isl.), Den.
51/H5 Langelsheim, Ger.
51/F1 Langen, Ger.
51/E6 Langenberg, Ger.
123/H3 Langenburg, Sk,Can
50/D6 Langenfeld, Ger.
51/G4 Langenhagen, Ger.
49/H4 Langenlois, Aus.
54/D3 Langenthal, Swi.
51/E1 Langeoog (isl.), Ger.
81/D3 Langfang, China
122/G2 Langham, Sk,Can
47/F1 Langham, Eng,UK
45/F1 Langholm, Sc,UK
131/F5 Langhorne, Pa,US
42/N7 Langjökull (glac.), Ice.
86/A2 Langkawi (isl.), Malay.
83/B4 Lang Kha Tuk (peak), Thai.
47/G5 Langney (pt.), UK
42/E1 Langøya (isl.), Nor.
75/C5 Langqên (riv.), China
54/B2 Langres, Fr.
54/A2 Langres (plat.), Fr.
86/A3 Langsa, Indo.
83/D1 Lang Son, Viet.
127/R8 Langstaff, On,Can
128/C4 Langtry, Tx,US
59/G1 Languedoc (hist. reg.), Fr.
56/E5 Languedoc-Roussillon (reg.), Fr.
51/G3 Langwedel, Ger.
81/C3 Langya Shan (mtn.), China
131/K8 Lanham-Seabrook, Md,US
123/G3 Lanigan, Sk,Can
112/C3 Lanin (vol.), Chile
112/C3 Lanín Nat'l Park, Arg.
67/J5 Länkäran, Azer.
56/D5 Lannemezan, Fr.
56/D5 Lannemezan (plat.), Fr.
46/A6 Lanner, Eng,UK
56/B2 Lannion, Fr.
56/B2 Lannion (bay), Fr.
83/B2 Lan Sang Nat'l Park, Thai.
131/E5 Lansdale, Pa,US
131/E6 Lansdowne, Pa,US
131/K7 Lansdowne-Baltimore Highlands, Md,US
126/B2 L'Anse, Mi,US
130/M3 Lansing, Yk,Can
132/Q16 Lansing, Il,US
126/C3 Lansing (cap.), Mi,US
42/H3 Länsi-Suomen (prov.), Fin.
83/B5 Lanta (isl.), Thai.
113/S12 Lanús, Arg.
60/A3 Lanusei, It.
82/C2 Lanxi, China
59/Y16 Lanzarote (isl.), Canl.
76/E4 Lanzhou, China
82/D4 Laoag, Phil.
82/E5 Laoang, Phil.
83/C1 Lao Cai, Viet.
77/H3 Laoha (riv.), China
81/B4 Laohekou, China
44/A6 Laois (Leix) (co.), Ire.
81/B4 Laojun Shan (mtn.), China
52/C4 Laon, Fr.
117/H5 La Orchila (isl.), Ven.
108/C6 La Oroya, Peru
83/C2 Laos
81/E3 Lao Shan (peak), China
81/E3 Laotie Shan (mtn.), China
81/F2 Laotuding Shan (peak), China
110/B3 Lapa, Braz.
99/G4 Lapai, Nga.
59/X16 La Palma (isl.), Canl.
112/D3 La Pampa (prov.), Arg.
108/E7 La Paz (cap.), Bol.
116/D5 La Paz, Hon.
117/M9 La Paz, Mex.
117/M9 La Paz (bay), Mex.
113/F2 La Paz, Uru.
126/F2 La Pêche, Qu,Can
64/F3 Lapeenranta, Fin.
132/F5 Lapeer, Mi,US
116/E6 La Peña, Pan.
117/P8 La Perla, Mex.
116/A3 La Piedad Cavadas, Mex.
42/H3 Lapinlahti, Fin.
42/F1 Lapland (reg.), Eur.
113/F2 La Plata, Arg.
108/C3 La Plata, Col.
128/B2 La Plata (peak), Co,US
126/E4 La Plata, Md,US
52/D3 La Plate Taille, Barrage de (dam), Belg.
127/G2 La Pocatière, Qu,Can
58/C1 La Pola de Gordón, Sp.
126/C3 La Porte, In,US
77/N1 Lapotina (mtn.), Rus.
62/E3 Lapovo, Yugo.
117/M8 La Poza Grande, Mex.
42/J3 Lappeenranta, Fin.
57/K2 Lappersdorf, Ger.
42/H2 Lappi (prov.), Fin.
127/N7 La Prairie, Qu,Can
128/D4 La Pryor, Tx,US
69/N2 Laptev (sea), Rus.
42/G3 Lapua, Fin.
59/G3 La Puebla, Sp.
58/C4 La Puebla de Cazalla, Sp.
58/B4 La Puebla del Río, Sp.
58/C3 La Puebla de Montalbán, Sp.
131/C2 La Puente, Ca,US
108/B4 La Puntilla (pt.), Ecu.
117/M8 La Purísima, Mex.
49/M2 Łapy, Pol.
100/B4 Laqiyat al Arba'īn, Sudan
108/E8 La Quiaca, Arg.
60/C1 L'Aquila, It.
73/F3 Lār, Iran
58/A1 Laracha, Sp.
96/D1 Larache, Mor.
58/C4 La Rambla, Sp.
125/F2 Laramie (riv.), Co, Wy,US
123/G5 Laramie, Wy,US
122/G5 Laramie (mts.), Wy,US
123/G5 Laramie (peak), Wy,US
110/A3 Laranjeiras do Sul, Braz.
87/H5 Larat (isl.), Indo.
56/B2 L'Arcouest, Pointe de (pt.), Fr.
122/A2 Laredo (sound), BC,Can
58/D1 Laredo, Sp.
128/D5 Laredo, Tx,US
50/C4 Laren, Neth.
129/H5 Largo, Fl,US
131/K8 Largo, Md,US
43/C3 Largs, Sc,UK
87/F4 Lariang (riv.), Indo.
58/C4 La Rinconada, Sp.
111/C2 La Rioja, Arg.
58/D1 La Rioja (aut. comm.), Sp.
61/H3 Lárisa, Gre.
47/G2 Lark (riv.), Eng,UK
73/J3 Lārkāna, Pak.
47/E4 Larkhill, Eng,UK
132/J11 Larkspur, Ca,US
56/B3 Larmor-Plage, Fr.
74/J4 Larnaca, Cyp.
44/C2 Larne, NI,UK
44/C2 Larne (dist.), NI,UK
125/H3 Larned, Ks,US
44/C2 Larne Lough (inlet), NI,UK
122/F1 La Roche (lake), Sk,Can
56/C3 La Rochelle, Fr.
54/C5 La Roche-sur-Foron, Fr.
56/C3 La Roche-sur-Yon, Fr.
58/D3 La Roda, Sp.
117/H4 La Romana, DRep.
123/G2 La Ronge, Sk,Can
123/G2 La Ronge (lake), Sk,Can
129/F4 Larose, La,US
118/G1 Larsen (sound), Nun.,Can
105/V Larsen Ice Shelf, Ant.
48/A3 L'Artois, Collines de (hills), Fr.
58/B1 La Rúa, Sp.
127/N7 La Salle, Qu,Can
126/B3 La Salle, Il,US
125/G3 Las Animas, Co,US
126/E1 La Sarre, Qu,Can
57/G5 La Sauvette (mtn.), Fr.
117/H5 Las Aves (isls.), Ven.
111/D2 Las Breñas, Arg.
58/C4 Las Cabezas de San Juan, Sp.
112/C2 Las Cabras, Chile
116/D5 Las Cañas, CR
113/G2 Lascano, Uru.
116/C4 Las Choapas, Mex.
127/L1 La Scie, Nf,Can
124/F4 Las Cruces, NM,US
111/B2 La Serena, Chile
59/F1 La Seu d'Urgell, Sp.
56/F5 La Seyne-sur-Mer, Fr.
112/F3 Las Flores, Arg.
85/G3 Lashio, Myan.
73/H2 Lashkar Gāh, Afg.
60/E3 La Sila (mts.), It.
113/J8 La Silueta (peak), Chile
112/C3 Las Lajas (peak), Arg.
111/D1 Las Lomitas, Arg.
117/G4 Las Matas de Farfán, DRep.
117/H6 Las Mercedes, Ven.
52/D2 Lasne-Chapelle-Saint-Lambert, Belg.
117/N8 Las Nieves, Mex.
58/D3 La Solana, Sp.
87/F4 Lasolo (riv.), Indo.
52/B4 La Somme, Canal de (can.), Fr.
112/C2 Las Palmas de Cocalán Nat'l Park, Chile
59/X16 Las Palmas de Gran Canaria (cap.), Canl.
58/D3 Las Pedroñeras, Sp.
57/H4 La Spezia, It.
113/F2 Las Piedras, Uru.
112/E2 Las Rosas, Arg.
59/N9 Las Rozas, Sp.
124/B2 Lassen Volcanic Nat'l Park, Ca,US
105/V Lassiter (coast), Ant.
117/E6 Las Tablas, Pan.
58/D3 Las Tablas de Daimiel Nat'l Park, Sp.
111/D2 Las Termas, Arg.
123/G3 Last Mountain (lake), Sk,Can
62/C4 Lastovo (isl.), Cro.
62/C4 Lastovski (chan.), Cro.
117/N8 Las Varas, Mex.
117/N9 Las Varas, Mex.
112/E1 Las Varillas, Arg.
125/F4 Las Vegas, NM,US
124/D3 Las Vegas, Nv,US
127/K1 La Tabatière, Qu,Can
108/C4 Latacunga, Ecu.
105/U Latady (isl.), Ant.
74/K4 Latakia (Al Lādhiqīyah), Syria
99/F4 L'Atakora (prov.), Ben.
60/E2 Laterza, It.
56/C4 La Teste-de-Buch, Fr.
56/C3 Lathan (riv.), Fr.
132/M11 Lathrop, Ca,US
60/C2 Latina, It.
49/L4 Latorica (riv.), Slvk.
117/H5 La Tortuga (isl.), Ven.
91/C3 Latrobe (peak), Austl.
91/C3 Latrobe (riv.), Austl.
56/E5 Lattes, Fr.
127/F2 La Tuque, Qu,Can
84/C4 Lātūr, India
64/E4 Latvia
108/E7 Lauca Nat'l Park, Chile
57/G3 Lauch (riv.), Fr.
43/D3 Lauder, Sc,UK
132/N14 Lauderdale (lakes), Wi,US
51/H2 Lauenburg, Ger.
57/J2 Lauf, Ger.
46/B3 Laugharne, Wal,UK
128/C4 Laughlin A.F.B., Tx,US
92/H6 Lau Group (isls.), Fiji
42/G3 Lauhanvuoren Nat'l Park, Fin.
42/H3 Laukaa, Fin.
91/C4 Launceston, Austl.
46/B5 Launceston, Eng,UK
112/B4 La Unión, Chile
116/D5 La Unión, ESal.
59/E4 La Unión, Sp.
131/K7 Laurel, Md,US
129/F4 Laurel, Ms,US
122/F4 Laurel, Mt,US
44/B3 Laurelvale, NI,UK
43/D2 Laurencekirk, Sc,UK
129/H3 Laurens, SC,US
126/C1 Laurentian (plat.), Can.
44/D2 Laurieston, Sc,UK
129/J3 Laurinburg, NC,US
126/B2 Laurium, Mi,US
54/C4 Lausanne, Swi.
87/E4 Laut (isl.), Indo.
112/B3 Lautaro, Chile
57/H2 Lauter (riv.), Fr., Ger.
48/E3 Lauterbach, Ger.
92/G6 Lautoka, Fiji
50/D2 Lauwers (chan.), Neth.
50/D2 Lauwersmeer (lake), Neth.
124/B2 Lava Beds Nat'l Mon., Ca,US
127/N6 Laval, Qu,Can
56/C2 Laval, Fr.
113/G2 Lavalleja (dept.), Uru.
57/L3 Lavant (riv.), Aus.
112/B3 Lavapié (pt.), Chile
56/D5 Lavelanet, Fr.
60/D2 Lavello, It.
131/C2 La Verne, Ca,US
108/E1 La Victoria, Ven.
110/C2 Lavras, Braz.
61/J4 Lávrion, Gre.
73/K1 Lawarai (pass), Pak.
86/D3 Lawit (mtn.), Indo.
131/B3 Lawndale, Ca,US
125/J3 Lawrence, Ks,US
127/G3 Lawrence, Ma,US
126/C4 Lawrenceburg, In,US
129/G2 Lawrenceburg, Ky,US
129/G3 Lawrenceburg, Tn,US
44/B3 Lawrencetown, NI,UK
129/H3 Lawrenceville, Ga,US
131/F5 Lawrenceville, NJ,US
125/H4 Lawton, Ok,US
86/D5 Lawu (peak), Indo.
72/C3 Lawz, Jabal al (mtn.), SAr.
44/D3 Laxey, IM,UK
53/F6 Laxou, Fr.
56/C3 Lay (riv.), Fr.
65/N2 Laya (riv.), Rus.
87/E4 Layar (cape), Indo.
93/H2 Laycan (isl.), Hi,US
72/E4 Laylā, SAr.
56/C3 Layon (riv.), Fr.
124/E2 Layton, Ut,US
62/E3 Lazarevac, Yugo.
116/A4 Lazaro Cardenas, Mex.
60/C1 Lazio (reg.), It.
45/F2 Lazonby, Eng,UK
47/F3 Lea (riv.), Eng,UK
83/C3 Leach, Camb.
47/E3 Leach (riv.), Eng,UK
123/H4 Lead, SD,US
45/H5 Leadenham, Eng,UK
122/F3 Leader, Sk,Can
46/D2 Leadon (riv.), Eng,UK
128/B2 Leadville, Co,US
129/F4 Leaf (riv.), Ms,US
91/B2 Leaghur (lake), Austl.
125/J5 League City, Tx,US
128/D4 Leakey, Tx,US
47/E2 Leam (riv.), Eng,UK
132/G7 Leamington, On,Can
47/F4 Leatherhead, Eng,UK
52/D3 L'Eau d'Heure (riv.), Belg.
125/J3 Leavenworth, Ks,US
122/C4 Leavenworth, Wa,US
53/F5 Lebach, Ger.
62/E4 Lebane, Yugo.
74/K5 Lebanon
74/K5 Lebanon (mts.), Leb.
126/C3 Lebanon, In,US
126/C4 Lebanon, Ky,US
125/J3 Lebanon, Mo,US
127/F3 Lebanon, NH,US
122/C4 Lebanon, Or,US
129/G2 Lebanon, Tn,US
126/D4 Lebanon, Va,US
52/D2 Lebbeke, Belg.
66/E2 Lebedin, Ukr.
126/E1 Lebel-sur-Quévillon, Qu,Can
56/D3 Le Blanc, Fr.
52/B6 Le Blanc-Mesnil, Fr.
49/J1 Lębork, Pol.
58/B4 Lebrija, Sp.
111/B4 Lebu, Chile
58/A2 Leça da Palmeira, Port.
57/G5 Le Cannet, Fr.
52/C3 Le Cateau, Fr.
61/F2 Lecce, It.
57/H4 Lecco, It.
55/G1 Lech (riv.), Aus., Ger.
82/B2 Lechang, China
47/E3 Lechlade, Eng,UK
55/G3 Lechtaler Alps (mts.), Aus.
48/E1 Leck, Ger.
57/J5 Le Cornate (peak), It.
56/F3 Le Creusot, Fr.
49/M3 Łęczna, Pol.
51/E2 Leda (riv.), Ger.
86/B3 Ledang (peak), Malay.
46/D2 Ledbury, Eng,UK
52/C2 Lede, Belg.
52/C2 Ledegem, Belg.
122/E2 Leduc, Ab,Can
123/K4 Leech (lake), Mn,US
45/G4 Leeds, Eng,UK
45/G4 Leeds and Liverpool (can.), Eng,UK
50/D2 Leek, Neth.
45/F5 Leek, Eng,UK
51/E2 Leer, Ger.
50/C5 Leerdam, Neth.
50/C4 Leersum, Neth.
129/H4 Leesburg, Fl,US
126/E4 Leesburg, Va,US
128/E4 Leesville, La,US
91/C2 Leeton, Austl.
102/L10 Leeu (riv.), SAfr.
50/C2 Leeuwarden, Neth.
89/A4 Leeuwin (cape), Austl.
124/C3 Lee Vining, Ca,US
117/J4 Leeward (isls.), NAm.
56/B2 Leff (riv.), Fr.
99/H5 Lefo (peak), Camr.
58/D2 Leganés, Sp.
58/D1 Legazpia, Sp.
91/C4 Legges Tor (peak), Austl.
49/L2 Legionowo, Pol.
57/J4 Legnago, It.
57/H4 Legnano, It.
49/J3 Legnica, Pol.
49/H3 Legnica (prov.), Pol.
75/C5 Leh, India
56/D2 Le Havre, Fr.
131/E5 Lehigh (riv.), Pa,US
129/H5 Lehigh Acres, Fl,US
51/G4 Lehrte, Ger.
82/B2 Lei (riv.), China
73/K2 Leiah, Pak.
57/L3 Leibnitz, Aus.
47/E1 Leicester, Eng,UK
47/E1 Leicester (co.), Eng,UK
47/E1 Leicestershire (co.), Eng,UK
90/B3 Leichhardt (mts.), Austl.
50/E6 Leichlingen, Ger.
50/B4 Leiden, Neth.
50/B4 Leiderdorp, Neth.
50/B4 Leidschendam, Neth.
50/A7 Leie (riv.), Belg.
47/F3 Leighton Buzzard, Eng,UK
51/G5 Leine (riv.), Ger.
51/H6 Leinefelde, Ger.
43/B4 Leinster (mtn.), Ire.
43/B4 Leinster (prov.), Ire.
46/D2 Leintwardine, Eng,UK
48/G3 Leipzig, Ger.
52/C2 Leir (riv.), Belg.
58/A3 Leiria, Port.
58/A3 Leiria (dist.), Port.
47/H2 Leiston cum Sizewell, Eng,UK
126/C4 Leitchfield, Ky,US
47/F4 Leith (hill), Eng,UK
62/C2 Leitha (riv.), Aus.
44/A6 Leix (Laois) (co.), Ire.
44/B5 Leixlip, Ire.
81/B2 Leiyang, China
81/B4 Leiyuanzhen, China
82/A3 Leizhou (pen.), China
50/B5 Lek (riv.), Neth.
50/B5 Lekkerkerk, Neth.
99/G5 Lekki (lag.), Nga.
42/E3 Leksands-Noret, Swe.
64/F3 Leksozero (lake), Rus.
87/G3 Lelai (cape), Indo.
129/F3 Leland, Ms,US
92/F4 Lelu, Micro.
57/G5 Le Luc, Fr.
50/C3 Lelystad, Neth.
113/L8 Le Maire (str.), Arg.
54/C5 Léman (Geneva) (lake), Fr., Swi.
56/D3 Le Mans, Fr.
123/J5 Le Mars, Ia,US
53/G5 Lembach, Fr.
86/A3 Lembu (peak), Indo.
110/C2 Leme, Braz.
42/H1 Lemenjoen Nat'l Park, Fin.
51/F4 Lemgo, Ger.
50/C3 Lemmer, Neth.
117/M7 Lemmon (peak), Az.,US
123/H4 Lemmon, SD,US
56/E4 Le Moure de la Gardille (mtn.), Fr.
60/E2 Le Murge (upland), It.
65/P2 Lemva (riv.), Rus.
51/F2 Lemwerder, Ger.
42/D3 Lena, Nor.
69/N3 Lena (riv.), Rus.
109/K4 Lençóis Maranhenses Nat'l Park, Braz.
110/B2 Lençóis Paulista, Braz.
57/J4 Lendinara, It.
51/H4 Lengede, Ger.
51/E4 Lengerich, Ger.
82/B2 Lengshuijiang, China
82/B2 Lengshuitan, China
111/B3 Lengua de Vaca (pt.), Chile
75/B4 Lenina, Pik (peak), Kyr.
64/F4 Leningrad (Saint Petersburg), Rus.
64/G3 Leningrad Obl., Rus.
105/L Leningradskaya, Ant.
75/D1 Leninogorsk, Kaz.
65/M5 Leninogorsk, Rus.
68/J4 Leninsk-Kuznetskiy, Rus.
62/E2 Leninváros, Hun.
51/E6 Lenne (riv.), Ger.
51/F6 Lennestadt, Ger.
113/L8 Lennox (isl.), Chile
129/H3 Lenoir, NC,US
129/G3 Lenoir City, Tn,US
52/B3 Lens, Fr.
69/M3 Lensk, Rus.
42/F1 Lenvik, Nor.
99/E4 Léo, Burk.
57/L3 Leoben, Aus.
52/B2 Leoberghe, Fr.
123/J4 Leola, SD,US
46/D2 Leominster, Eng,UK
56/C4 Leon (lag.), Fr.
116/A3 León, Mex.
116/D5 León, Nic.
58/C1 León, Sp.
128/D3 Leon (riv.), Tx,US
132/F6 Leonard, Mi,US
57/L2 Leonding, Aus.
112/E2 Leones, Arg.
60/D4 Leonforte, It.
105/F Leopold and Astrid (coast), Ant.
110/L6 Leopoldina, Braz.
52/C1 Leopoldkanaal (can.), Belg.
53/E1 Leopoldsburg, Belg.
51/F4 Leopoldshöhe, Ger.
125/G3 Leoti, Ks,US
122/G2 Leoville, Sk,Can
56/D4 Le Passage, Fr.
58/B4 Lepe, Sp.
62/F3 Lepenski Vir, Yugo.
52/B5 Le Plessis-Belleville, Fr.
55/E5 Lepontine Alps (mts.), It., Swi.
103/R15 Le Port, Reun.
52/A2 Le Portel, Fr.
42/H3 Leppävirta, Fin.
75/C2 Lepsy (riv.), Kaz.
56/E4 Le Puy, Fr.
82/D5 Leqaspi, Phil.
98/D4 Léraba (riv.), Burk., IvC.
60/C4 Lercara Friddi, It.
57/H4 Lerici, It.
59/F2 Lérida (Lleida), Sp.
102/D3 Le Rouxdam, P. K. (res.), SAfr.
52/A5 Les Andelys, Fr.
117/G4 Les Cayes, Haiti
127/M7 Les Cèdres, Qu,Can
52/A6 Les Clayes-sous-Bois, Fr.
85/H2 Leshan, China
56/C3 Les Herbiers, Fr.
62/E4 Leskovac, Yugo.
43/D2 Leslie, Sc,UK
52/A6 Les Mureaux, Fr.
52/A2 Lesneven, Fr.
103/D3 Lesotho
77/L2 Lesozavodsk, Rus.
59/G1 L'Espinouse, Sommet de (peak), Fr.
56/C3 Les Sables-d'Olonne, Fr.
53/E4 Lesse (riv.), Belg.
42/E4 Lessebo, Swe.
117/H4 Lesser Antilles (arch.), NAm.
67/G4 Lesser Kavkaz (mts.), Eur.
122/D2 Lesser Slave (lake), Ab,Can
87/E5 Lesser Sunda (isls.), Indo.
52/C2 Lessines, Belg.
53/E5 L'Est, Canal de (can.), Fr.
54/C4 Le Suchet (peak), Swi.
52/B6 Les Ulis, Fr.
86/D3 Lesung (peak), Indo.
61/J3 Lésvos (isl.), Gre.
44/C2 Leswalt, Sc,UK
49/J3 Leszno, Pol.
49/J3 Leszno (prov.), Pol.
103/R15 Le Tampon, Reun.
47/F3 Letchworth, Eng,UK
122/E3 Lethbridge, Ab,Can
51/F2 Lethe (riv.), Ger.
87/G5 Leti (isls.), Indo.
108/E4 Leticia, Col.
104/E5 Letlhakane, Bots.
104/D5 Letlhakeng, Bots.
85/G4 Letpadan, Myan.
52/A3 Le Tréport, Fr.
83/B4 Letsôk-Aw (isl.), Myan.
50/C4 Leusden-Zuid, Neth.
86/A3 Leuser (peak), Indo.
55/F2 Leutkirch im Allgäu, Ger.
53/D2 Leuven (Louvain), Belg.
52/C2 Leuze-en-Hainaut, Belg.
61/H3 Levádhia, Gre.
42/D3 Levanger, Nor.
112/B5 Level (isl.), Chile
128/C3 Levelland, Tx,US
103/F2 Leven (pt.), SAfr.
45/H4 Leven, Eng,UK
45/F3 Leven (riv.), Eng,UK
45/G3 Leven (riv.), Eng,UK
43/D2 Leven, Sc,UK
50/D6 Leverkusen, Ger.
49/K4 Levice, Slvk.
89/H7 Levin, NZ
127/G2 Lévis, Qu,Can
131/G5 Levittown, NY,US
131/F5 Levittown, Pa,US
61/G3 Levkás, Gre.
61/G3 Levkás (isl.), Gre.
49/L4 Levoča, Slvk.
63/G4 Levski, Bul.
47/G5 Lewes, Eng,UK
127/K1 Lewis (hills), Nf,Can
122/E3 Lewis (range), Mt,US
122/C4 Lewis (riv.), Wa,US
123/J5 Lewis & Clark (lake), Ne, SD,US
129/G3 Lewisburg, Tn,US
126/D4 Lewisburg, WV,US
127/L1 Lewisporte, Nf,Can
129/G3 Lewis Smith (lake), Al,US
122/D4 Lewiston, Id,US
127/G2 Lewiston, Me,US
127/R9 Lewiston, NY,US
122/F4 Lewistown, Mt,US
126/E3 Lewistown, Pa,US
87/F5 Lewotobi (peak), Indo.
126/C4 Lexington, Ky,US
129/H3 Lexington, NC,US
125/H2 Lexington, Ne,US
129/H3 Lexington, SC,US
129/F3 Lexington, Tn,US
126/E4 Lexington, Va,US
126/E4 Lexington Park, Md,US
45/G3 Leyburn, Eng,UK
45/F4 Leyland, Eng,UK
82/D5 Leyte (isl.), Phil.
56/F4 Lez (riv.), Fr.
49/M3 Leżajsk, Pol.
61/F2 Lezhë, Alb.
56/E5 Lézignan-Corbières, Fr.
66/E2 L'gov, Rus.
84/F2 Lhasa, China
84/E2 Lhazê, China
59/G2 L'Hospitalet, Sp.
85/G2 Lhünzê, China
81/B5 Li (riv.), China
81/C4 Li (riv.), China
85/K2 Li (riv.), China
82/B3 Lian (riv.), China
52/B5 Liancourt, Fr.
78/B2 Liancourt (rocks), Japan, SKor.
81/C2 Liangcheng, China
86/D3 Liangpran (peak), Indo.
81/D4 Liang Shan (mtn.), China
81/C5 Liangzi (lake), China
81/D4 Lianyungang, China
77/J3 Liao (riv.), China
81/C3 Liaocheng, China
81/E2 Liaodong (gulf), China
77/J3 Liaoyang, China
81/F2 Liaoyuan, China
73/K3 Liāquatpur, Pak.
118/D2 Liard (riv.), Can.
122/E3 Libby, Mt,US
97/J7 Libenge, D.R. Congo
125/G3 Liberal, Ks,US
52/C3 Libercourt, Fr.
109/H6 Liberdade (riv.), Braz.
49/H3 Liberec, Czh.
98/C5 Liberia
116/D5 Liberia, CR
116/D4 Libertad, Belz.
113/F2 Libertad, Uru.
111/D1 Libertador General San Martín, Arg.
129/G2 Liberty, Ky,US
131/K7 Liberty (res.), Md,US
128/E2 Liberty, Mo,US
129/F4 Liberty, Ms,US
128/E4 Liberty, Tx,US
132/Q15 Libertyville, Il,US
87/G4 Libobo (cape), Indo.
57/K1 Liboc (riv.), Czh.
82/D5 Libon, Phil.
96/G7 Libreville (cap.), Gabon
97/J2 Libya
97/K2 Libyan (des.), Afr.
97/K1 Libyan (plat.), Libya
112/C2 Licantén, Chile
60/C4 Licata, It.
74/E2 Lice, Turk.

57/H1 **Lich**, Ger.
47/E1 **Lichfield**, Eng,UK
57/J1 **Lichtenfels**, Ger.
50/D5 **Lichtenvoorde**, Neth.
52/C1 **Lichtervelde**, Belg.
81/B5 **Lichuan**, China
126/C4 **Licking** (riv.), Ky,US
60/D2 **Licosa** (cape), It.
64/E5 **Lida**, Bela.
45/F1 **Liddell Water** (riv.), Sc,UK
119/R7 **Liddon** (gulf), NW,Can
47/F2 **Lidlington**, Eng,UK
57/K4 **Lido**, It.
60/C2 **Lido di Ostia**, It.
49/K2 **Lidzbark**, Pol.
49/L1 **Lidzbark Warmiński**, Pol.
102/E2 **Liebenbergsvlei** (riv.), SAfr.
55/F3 **Liechtenstein**
52/D2 **Liedekerke**, Belg.
53/E2 **Liège**, Belg.
53/E3 **Liège** (prov.), Belg.
42/J3 **Lieksa**, Fin.
50/C5 **Lienden**, Neth.
51/E4 **Lienen**, Ger.
57/K3 **Lienz**, Aus.
64/D4 **Liepāja**, Lat.
52/D1 **Lier**, Belg.
56/E1 **Lies** (riv.), Belg.
53/F3 **Lieser** (riv.), Ger.
42/G3 **Liesjärven Nat'l Park**, Fin.
54/D2 **Liestal**, Swi.
42/G3 **Lieto**, Fin.
52/B3 **Liévin**, Fr.
126/F2 **Lièvre** (riv.), Qu,Can
57/L3 **Liezen**, Aus.
44/B5 **Liffey** (riv.), Ire.
93/V12 **Lifou** (isl.), NCal.
46/B5 **Lifton**, Eng,UK
87/F1 **Ligao**, Phil.
57/H4 **Ligure, Appenino** (mts.), It.
57/H4 **Liguria** (reg.), It.
57/H5 **Ligurian** (sea), Eur.
85/H2 **Lijiang** (Lijiang Naxizu Zizhixian), China
104/E3 **Likasi**, D.R. Congo
122/C2 **Likely**, BC,Can
104/F3 **Likoma** (isl.), Malw.
96/J8 **Likouala** (riv.), Congo
60/A1 **L'Ile-Rousse**, Fr.
51/F2 **Lilienthal**, Ger.
85/K2 **Liling**, China
53/D1 **Lille**, Belg.
52/C2 **Lille**, Fr.
42/D3 **Lillehammer**, Nor.
52/B2 **Lillers**, Fr.
42/D4 **Lillestrøm**, Nor.
122/C3 **Lillooet**, BC,Can
122/C3 **Lillooet** (riv.), BC,Can
104/F3 **Lilongwe** (cap.), Malw.
91/G5 **Lilydale**, Austl.
62/D4 **Lim** (riv.), Yugo.
108/C6 **Lima** (cap.), Peru
58/A2 **Lima** (riv.), Port.
123/L4 **Lima** (peak), Mn,US
126/C3 **Lima**, Oh,US
112/Q9 **Limache**, Chile
110/K6 **Lima Duarte**, Braz.
49/L4 **Limanowa**, Pol.
74/J4 **Limassol**, Cyp.
44/B1 **Limavady**, NI,UK
44/A2 **Limavady** (dist.), NI,UK
112/C4 **Limay** (riv.), Arg.
52/A6 **Limay**, Fr.
60/A2 **Limbara** (peak), It.
84/B3 **Limbdi**, India
53/E2 **Limburg** (prov.), Belg.
53/E1 **Limburg** (prov.), Neth.
57/H1 **Limburg an der Lahn**, Ger.
127/Q8 **Limehouse**, On,Can
110/C2 **Limeira**, Braz.
43/A4 **Limerick**, Ire.
58/B2 **Limia** (riv.), Sp.
61/J3 **Limnos** (isl.), Gre.
56/D4 **Limoges**, Fr.
56/D4 **Limogne** (plat.), Fr.
116/E5 **Limón**, CR
125/G3 **Limon**, Co,US
56/D4 **Limousin** (mts.), Fr.
56/D4 **Limousin** (reg.), Fr.
56/E5 **Limoux**, Fr.
104/F5 **Limpopo** (riv.), Afr.
47/G4 **Limpsfield**, Eng,UK
83/E2 **Limu** (mtn.), China
82/C5 **Linapacan** (isl.), Phil.
112/C2 **Linares**, Chile
116/B3 **Linares**, Mex.
58/D3 **Linares**, Sp.
82/C2 **Linchuan**, China
112/E2 **Lincoln**, Arg.
127/R9 **Lincoln**, On,Can
115/L1 **Lincoln** (sea), Can., Grld.
45/H5 **Lincoln**, Eng,UK
126/B3 **Lincoln**, Il,US
127/G2 **Lincoln**, Me,US
125/H2 **Lincoln** (cap.), Ne,US
122/B4 **Lincoln Beach**, Or,US
122/B4 **Lincoln City**, Or,US
45/H5 **Lincoln Heath** (woodl.), Eng,UK
132/F7 **Lincoln Park**, Mi,US
131/F5 **Lincoln Park**, NJ,US
45/H5 **Lincolnshire** (co.), Eng,UK
45/H5 **Lincolnshire Wolds** (hills), Eng,UK
129/H3 **Lincolnton**, NC,US
131/F5 **Lincroft**, NJ,US
60/A2 **L'Incudine, Mont** (mtn.), Fr.
50/D3 **Linde** (riv.), Neth.
90/C3 **Lindeman** (isl.), Austl.
108/G2 **Linden**, Guy.
129/G3 **Linden**, Al,US
131/F5 **Linden**, NJ,US
55/F2 **Lindenberg im Allgäu**, Ger.
132/P15 **Lindenhurst**, Il,US
131/G5 **Lindenhurst**, NY,US
131/F6 **Lindenwold**, NJ,US
64/B4 **Lindesberg**, Swe.
101/C5 **Lindi**, Tanz.
101/C5 **Lindi** (prov.), Tanz.
43/E3 **Lindisfarne** (Holy) (isl.), Eng,UK
51/E6 **Lindlar**, Ger.
91/D3 **Lind Nat'l Park**, Austl.
126/E2 **Lindsay**, On,Can
124/C3 **Lindsay**, Ca,US
128/D2 **Lindsborg**, Ks,US
93/K4 **Line** (isls.), Kiri.
81/B3 **Linfen**, China
81/C4 **Lingchuan**, China
82/B2 **Lingchuan**, China
50/C5 **Linge** (riv.), Neth.
51/E3 **Lingen**, Ger.
47/F4 **Lingfield**, Eng,UK
86/B3 **Lingga** (isls.), Indo.
53/G6 **Lingolsheim**, Fr.
98/B3 **Linguère**, Sen.
81/D3 **Ling Xian**, China
82/B2 **Ling Xian**, China
81/E5 **Lingyang Shan** (mtn.), China
81/L8 **Lingyen Shan** (mtn.), China
81/E5 **Lingyin Si**, China
82/D2 **Linhai**, China
110/D1 **Linhares**, Braz.
42/E4 **Linköping**, Swe.
81/C3 **Linliu Shan** (mtn.), China
42/J3 **Linnansaaren Nat'l Park**, Fin.
46/A3 **Linney Head** (pt.), Wal,UK
43/C2 **Linnhe, Loch** (inlet), Sc,UK
53/F2 **Linnich**, Ger.
60/C5 **Linosa** (isl.), It.
81/C3 **Linqing**, China
110/B2 **Lins**, Braz.
103/H9 **Linta** (riv.), Madg.
47/G2 **Linton**, Eng,UK
126/C4 **Linton**, In,US
123/H4 **Linton**, ND,US
45/H5 **Linwood**, Eng,UK
81/B4 **Linyi**, China
81/D3 **Linyi**, China
81/D4 **Linyi**, China
57/L2 **Linz**, Aus.
52/E5 **Lion** (gulf), Fr.
60/D3 **Lipari** (isls.), It.
42/J3 **Liperi**, Fin.
66/F1 **Lipetsk**, Rus.
66/F1 **Lipetsk Obl.**, Rus.
108/E8 **Lipez** (range), Bol.
108/E8 **Lipez** (riv.), Bol.
47/F4 **Liphook**, Eng,UK
62/E4 **Lipljan**, Yugo.
49/K2 **Lipno**, Pol.
62/E2 **Lipova**, Rom.
50/E5 **Lippe** (riv.), Ger.
51/F5 **Lippetal**, Ger.
51/F5 **Lippstadt**, Ger.
49/K4 **Liptovský Mikuláš**, Slvk.
91/C3 **Liptrap** (cape), Austl.
75/D5 **Lipu La** (pass), India
75/D5 **Lipu Lehk Shankou** (pass), China
101/B2 **Lira**, Ugan.
104/C1 **Liranga**, Congo
60/C2 **Liri** (riv.), It.
59/E3 **Liria**, Sp.
97/K7 **Lisala**, D.R. Congo
59/P10 **Lisboa** (dist.), Port.
127/G2 **Lisbon**, Me,US
123/J4 **Lisbon**, ND,US
59/P10 **Lisbon** (Lisboa) (cap.), Port.
44/B2 **Lisburn**, NI,UK
44/B3 **Lisburn** (dist.), NI,UK
130/E2 **Lisburne** (cape), Ak,US
81/B4 **Li Shan** (mtn.), China
85/H2 **Lishe** (riv.), China
82/C2 **Lishui**, China
93/H2 **Lisianski** (isl.), Hi,US
56/D2 **Lisieux**, Fr.
46/C5 **Liskeard**, Eng,UK
132/P16 **Lisle**, Il,US
52/B5 **L'Isle-Adam**, Fr.
56/F5 **L'Isle-sur-la-Sorgue**, Fr.
91/E1 **Lismore**, Austl.
44/B3 **Lisnacree**, NI,UK
47/F4 **Liss**, Eng,UK
50/B4 **Lisse**, Neth.
51/E6 **Lister** (riv.), Ger.
126/D3 **Listowel**, On,Can
85/H2 **Litang** (riv.), China
74/K5 **Līṭānī** (riv.), Leb.
126/B4 **Litchfield**, Il,US
123/K4 **Litchfield**, Mn,US
50/C5 **Lith**, Neth.
45/F5 **Litherland**, Eng,UK
90/D2 **Lithgow**, Austl.
64/D5 **Lithuania**
64/E5 **Litovskiy Nat'l Park**, Lith.
90/D4 **Littabella Nat'l Park**, Austl.
125/J4 **Little** (riv.), Ga,US
125/J4 **Little** (riv.), La,US
129/J3 **Little** (riv.), NC,US
125/J4 **Little** (riv.), Ok,US
128/D4 **Little** (riv.), Tx,US
126/D1 **Little Abitibi** (riv.), On,Can
49/J5 **Little Alföld** (plain), Hun.
85/F5 **Little Andaman** (isl.), India
122/F4 **Little Belt** (mts.), Mt,US
122/G4 **Little Bighorn Nat'l Mon.**, Mt,US
125/H2 **Little Blue** (riv.), Ks, Ne,US
45/F4 **Littleborough**, Eng,UK
117/E4 **Little Cayman** (isl.), Cay.
124/E4 **Little Colorado** (riv.), Az,US
126/D2 **Little Current**, On,Can
126/C1 **Little Current** (riv.), On,Can
46/C5 **Little Dart** (riv.), Eng,UK
91/B3 **Little Desert Nat'l Park**, Austl.
130/E2 **Little Diomede** (isl.), Ak,US
123/K4 **Little Falls**, Mn,US
128/C3 **Littlefield**, Tx,US
123/K4 **Little Fork** (riv.), Mn,US
47/F5 **Littlehampton**, Eng,UK
117/G3 **Little Inagua** (isl.), Bahm.
102/C4 **Little Karoo** (reg.), SAfr.
127/K2 **Little Miquelon** (isl.), StP.
125/J4 **Little Missouri** (riv.), Ar,US
123/H4 **Little Missouri** (riv.), ND, SD,US
85/F6 **Little Nicobar** (isl.), India
47/G2 **Little Ouse** (riv.), Eng,UK
47/G2 **Littleport**, Eng,UK
125/J4 **Little Red** (riv.), Ar,US
128/E3 **Little Rock** (cap.), Ar,US
130/L3 **Little Salmon**, Yk,Can
98/B4 **Little Scarcies** (riv.), Gui., SLeo.
123/K5 **Little Sioux** (riv.), Ia,US
130/B5 **Little Sitkin** (isl.), Ak,US
122/D2 **Little Smoky** (riv.), Ab,Can
124/E2 **Little Snake** (riv.), Co, Wy,US
47/G4 **Little Stour** (riv.), Eng,UK
47/F2 **Little Stukeley**, Eng,UK
127/G2 **Littleton**, NH,US
126/B4 **Little Wabash** (riv.), Il,US
125/G2 **Little White** (riv.), SD,US
122/E5 **Little Wood** (riv.), Id,US
74/F3 **Little Zab** (riv.), Iraq
77/J3 **Liu** (riv.), China
77/K3 **Liu** (riv.), China
82/A3 **Liu** (riv.), China
104/D3 **Liuwa Pan Nat'l Park**, Zam.
85/J3 **Liuzhou**, China
129/H4 **Live Oak**, Fl,US
53/F6 **Liverdun**, Fr.
132/L11 **Livermore**, Ca,US
128/B4 **Livermore** (peak), Tx,US
90/G8 **Liverpool**, Austl.
127/H2 **Liverpool**, NS,Can
130/M2 **Liverpool** (bay), NW,Can
119/J1 **Liverpool** (cape), Nun.,Can
45/F5 **Liverpool**, Eng,UK
45/F5 **Liverpool** (bay), Eng,UK
45/H2 **Liverton**, Eng,UK
122/F4 **Livingston**, Mt,US
131/F5 **Livingston**, NJ,US
128/E4 **Livingston**, Tx,US
125/J5 **Livingston** (lake), Tx,US
122/E3 **Livingstone** (range), Ab,Can
104/E4 **Livingstone**, Zam.
104/B1 **Livingstone, Chutes de** (Livingstone) (falls), Congo
62/C4 **Livno**, Bosn.
66/F1 **Livny**, Rus.
42/H2 **Livojoki** (riv.), Fin.
132/F7 **Livonia**, Mi,US
57/J5 **Livorno**, It.
56/F4 **Livron-sur-Drôme**, Fr.
52/B6 **Livry-Gargan**, Fr.
125/C1 **Liwale**, Tanz
46/A7 **Lizard**, Eng,UK
46/A7 **Lizard** (pt.), Eng,UK
46/A6 **Lizard, The** (pen.), Eng,UK
62/B2 **Ljubljana** (cap.), Slov.
62/C4 **Ljubuški**, Cro.
42/F3 **Ljungan** (riv.), Swe.
42/E4 **Ljungby**, Swe.
64/C3 **Ljusdal**, Swe
42/E3 **Ljusnan** (riv.), Swe.
112/C2 **Llaillay**, Chile
112/C3 **Llaima** (vol.), Chile
108/E7 **Llallagua**, Bol.
46/B2 **Llanarth**, Wal,UK
44/D5 **Llanberis**, Wal,UK
44/D5 **Llanberis, Pass of** (pass), Wal,UK
112/C2 **Llancañelo** (lake), Arg.
46/C3 **Llandeilo**, Wal,UK
46/D3 **Llandogo**, Wal,UK
46/C3 **Llandovery**, Wal,UK
44/E6 **Llandrillo**, Wal,UK
46/C2 **Llandrindod Wells**, Wal,UK
44/E5 **Llandudno**, Wal,UK
46/C3 **Llandybie**, Wal,UK
46/B2 **Llandyssul**, Wal,UK
46/B3 **Llanelli**, Wal,UK
46/C1 **Llanelltyd**, Wal,UK
44/D6 **Llanenddwyn**, Wal,UK
44/D5 **Llanerchymedd**, Wal,UK
58/C1 **Llanes**, Sp.
46/C1 **Llanfair Caereinion**, Wal,UK
44/E5 **Llanfairfechan**, Wal,UK
44/D5 **Llanfair-Pwllgwyngyll**, Wal,UK
46/C1 **Llanfyllin**, Wal,UK
46/C2 **Llangammarch Wells**, Wal,UK
46/C3 **Llangattock**, Wal,UK
45/E6 **Llangollen**, Wal,UK
46/C2 **Llangurig**, Wal,UK
46/C2 **Llanidloes**, Wal,UK
44/D5 **Llanllyfni**, Wal,UK
46/B3 **Llannon**, Wal,UK
128/D4 **Llano**, Tx,US
125/H5 **Llano** (riv.), Tx,US
124/G4 **Llano Estacado** (plain), NM, Tx,US
46/B2 **Llanon**, Wal,UK
108/D3 **Llanos** (plain), Col., Ven.
112/B4 **Llanquihue** (lake), Chile
45/E5 **Llanrhaeadr**, Wal,UK
46/B2 **Llanrhystyd**, Wal,UK
46/A3 **Llanrian**, Wal,UK
44/E5 **Llanrwst**, Wal,UK
46/C3 **Llanthony**, Wal,UK
46/C3 **Llantrisant**, Wal,UK
46/C4 **Llantwit Major**, Wal,UK
44/E6 **Llanuwchllyn**, Wal,UK
46/C1 **Llanwnog**, Wal,UK
46/C2 **Llanwrtyd Wells**, Wal,UK
45/E5 **Llay**, Wal,UK
46/C2 **Lledrod**, Wal,UK
59/F2 **Lleida** (Lérida), Sp.
116/B3 **Llera**, Mex.
44/D6 **Lleyn** (pen.), Wal,UK
59/F1 **Llobregat** (riv.), Sp.
58/D1 **Llodio**, Sp.
59/G2 **Lloret de Mar**, Sp.
116/E6 **Llorona** (pt.), CR
131/G5 **Lloyd** (pt.), NY,US
122/F2 **Lloydminster**, Ab, Sk,Can
127/K1 **Lloyds** (riv.), Nf,Can
59/G3 **Lluchmayor**, Sp.
111/C1 **Llullaillaco** (vol.), Chile
46/C3 **Llynfi** (riv.), Wal,UK
83/D1 **Lo** (riv.), Viet.
111/C1 **Loa** (riv.), Chile
124/E3 **Loa**, Ut,US
57/H4 **Loano**, It.
59/N8 **Loaoya** (can.), Sp.
102/D2 **Lobatse**, Bots.
112/F3 **Lobería**, Arg.
104/B3 **Lobito**, Ang.
98/D5 **Lobo** (riv.), IvC.
112/F2 **Lobos**, Arg.
108/B5 **Lobos de Tierra** (isl.), Peru
112/B2 **Lobos, Punta de** (pt.), Chile
55/E5 **Locarno**, Swi.
44/D2 **Lochans**, Sc,UK
44/E1 **Locharbriggs**, Sc,UK
50/D4 **Lochem**, Neth.
43/C2 **Lochgilphead**, Sc,UK
44/E1 **Lochmaben**, Sc,UK
52/C1 **Lochristi**, Belg.
43/C2 **Lochy, Loch** (lake), Sc,UK
45/E1 **Lockerbie**, Sc,UK
128/D4 **Lockhart**, Tx,US
126/E3 **Lock Haven**, Pa,US
91/C3 **Lockington**, Austl.
132/P16 **Lockport**, Il,US
127/S9 **Lockport**, NY,US
83/D4 **Loc Ninh**, Viet.
60/E3 **Locri**, It.
125/J3 **Locust** (cr.), Ia, Mo,US
74/M9 **Lod**, Isr.
47/H1 **Loddon**, Eng,UK
47/E4 **Loddon** (riv.), Eng,UK
56/E5 **Lodève**, Fr.
64/G3 **Lodeynoye Pole**, Rus.
72/F3 **Lodge** (cr.), Mt,US
125/G2 **Lodgepole** (cr.), Ne, Wy,US
57/H4 **Lodi**, It.
132/M10 **Lodi**, Ca,US
131/F5 **Lodi**, NJ,US
104/D1 **Lodja**, D.R. Congo
101/B2 **Lodwar**, Kenya
49/K3 **Łódź**, Pol.
49/K3 **Łódź** (prov.), Pol.
59/N9 **Loeches**, Sp.
83/C2 **Loei**, Thai.
50/C4 **Loenen**, Neth.
98/C5 **Lofa** (co.), Libr.
98/C5 **Lofa** (riv.), Libr.
42/D2 **Lofoten** (isls.), Nor.
45/H2 **Loftus**, Eng,UK
91/C4 **Lofty** (range), Austl.
90/F7 **Logan**, Austl.
130/K3 **Logan** (mtn.), Yk,Can
125/G4 **Logan**, NM,US
126/D4 **Logan**, Oh,US
124/E2 **Logan**, Ut,US
126/D4 **Logan**, WV,US
44/D2 **Logan, Mull of** (pt.), Sc,UK
126/C3 **Logansport**, In,US
96/J6 **Logone** (riv.), Camr., Chad
58/D1 **Logroño**, Sp.
51/G6 **Lohfelden**, Ger.
64/E3 **Lohja**, Fin.
53/G2 **Lohmar**, Ger.
48/E2 **Lohne**, Ger.
51/F3 **Löhne**, Ger.
85/G3 **Loi Lun** (range), Myan., China
56/E2 **Loing** (riv.), Fr.
56/C3 **Loir** (riv.), Fr.
56/C3 **Loire** (riv.), Fr.
53/E5 **Loisin** (riv.), Fr.
101/B3 **Loita** (hills), Kenya
108/C4 **Loja**, Ecu.
58/C4 **Loja**, Sp.
52/D1 **Lokeren**, Belg.
104/D1 **Lokolia**, D.R. Congo
97/K8 **Lokolo** (riv.), D.R. Congo
97/J8 **Lokoro** (riv.), D.R. Congo
119/K2 **Loks** (isl.), Nun.,Can
97/L6 **Lol** (riv.), Sudan
48/F1 **Lolland** (isl.), Den.
122/E4 **Lolo** (peak), Mt,US
104/E1 **Lolo**, D.R. Congo
92/G5 **Lolua**, Tuv.
63/F4 **Lom**, Bul.
98/C4 **Loma** (mts.), Gui., SLeo.
116/B4 **Loma Bonita**, Mex.
131/C2 **Loma Linda**, Ca,US
98/C4 **Loma Mansa** (peak), SLeo.
97/K8 **Lomami** (riv.), D.R. Congo
113/S12 **Lomas de Zamora**, Arg.
132/P16 **Lombard**, Il,US
109/H3 **Lombarda** (mts.), Braz.
57/J4 **Lombardy** (reg.), It.
87/F5 **Lomblen** (isl.), Indo.
87/E5 **Lombok** (isl.), Indo.
99/F5 **Lomé** (cap.), Togo
104/D1 **Lomela**, D.R. Congo
97/K8 **Lomela** (riv.), D.R. Congo
131/B3 **Lomita**, Ca,US
56/E1 **Lomme**, Fr.
53/E1 **Lommel**, Belg.
43/C2 **Lomond, Loch** (lake), Sc,UK
87/E5 **Lompobatang** (peak), Indo.
124/B4 **Lompoc**, Ca,US
83/C2 **Lom Sak**, Thai.
49/M2 **Łomża**, Pol.
49/M2 **Łomża** (prov.), Pol.
84/B4 **Lonāvale**, India
112/B3 **Loncoche**, Chile
52/D2 **Londerzeel**, Belg.
52/A4 **Londinières**, Fr.
126/D3 **London**, On,Can
47/F3 **London** (cap.), Eng,UK
126/C4 **London**, Ky,US
47/F3 **London Colney**, Eng,UK
113/J8 **Londonderry** (isl.), Chile
44/A2 **Londonderry**, NI,UK
44/A2 **Londonderry** (dist.), NI,UK
110/B2 **Londrina**, Braz.
125/H4 **Lone Grove**, Ok,US
90/E7 **Lone Pine Sanct.**, Austl.
90/C4 **Lonesome Nat'l Park**, Austl.
117/F3 **Long** (isl.), Bahm.
123/J2 **Long** (pt.), Mb,Can
126/C1 **Long** (lake), On,Can
82/A3 **Long** (riv.), China
69/T2 **Long** (str.), Rus.
46/C1 **Long** (mtn.), Wal,UK
127/F3 **Long** (isl.), NY,US
112/C2 **Longaví**, Chile
127/R10 **Long Beach**, On,Can
131/B3 **Long Beach**, Ca,US
131/F6 **Long Beach** (isl.), NJ,US
131/G5 **Long Beach**, NY,US
45/G1 **Longbenton**, Eng,UK
129/H5 **Longboat Key**, Fl,US
131/G5 **Long Branch**, NJ,US
47/E2 **Long Buckby**, Eng,UK
83/D1 **Long Chau**, Viet.
82/C3 **Longchuan**, China
85/G3 **Longchuan**, China
47/F3 **Long Crendon**, Eng,UK
45/G6 **Long Eaton**, Eng,UK
53/E5 **Longeau** (riv.), Fr.
127/G2 **Longfellow** (mts.), Me,US
43/B4 **Longford**, Ire.
82/B2 **Longhui**, China
131/G5 **Long Island** (sound), Ct,NY,US
126/C1 **Longlac**, On,Can
46/D4 **Longleat House**, Eng,UK
81/B4 **Longmen Shan** (mtn.), China
81/C4 **Longmen Shiyao** (caves), China
125/F2 **Longmont**, Co,US
46/D1 **Long Mynd, The** (hill), Eng,UK
45/G5 **Longnor**, Eng,UK
83/D4 **Long Phu**, Viet.
127/K2 **Long Range** (mts.), Nf,Can
45/F4 **Longridge**, Eng,UK
76/E4 **Longshou** (mts.), China
45/J6 **Long Sutton**, Eng,UK
45/F2 **Longtown**, Eng,UK
52/B2 **Longuenesse**, Fr.
127/N6 **Longueuil**, Qu,Can
53/E5 **Longuyon**, Fr.
54/B3 **Longvic**, Fr.
128/E3 **Longview**, Tx,US
122/C4 **Longview**, Wa,US
53/E4 **Longwy**, Fr.
83/D4 **Long Xuyen**, Viet.
82/C2 **Longyan**, China
51/E3 **Löningen**, Ger.
56/C5 **Lons**, Fr.
54/B4 **Lons-le-Saunier**, Fr.
46/B6 **Looe**, Eng,UK
46/B6 **Looe** (isl.), Eng,UK
90/B1 **Lookout** (pt.), Austl.
129/J3 **Lookout** (cape), NC,US
101/B3 **Loolmalasin** (peak), Tanz.
122/F2 **Loon Lake**, Sk,Can
50/C5 **Loon op Zand**, Neth.
43/G7 **Loop Head** (pt.), Ire.
52/C2 **Loos**, Fr.
75/F3 **Lop** (lake), China
69/R4 **Lopatka, Mys** (cape), Rus.
83/C3 **Lop Buri**, Thai.
96/G8 **Lopez** (cape), Gabon
50/B5 **Lopik**, Neth.
97/K7 **Lopori** (riv.), D.R. Congo
42/G1 **Lopphavet** (bay), Nor.
73/J3 **Lora** (riv.), Pak.
58/C4 **Lora del Río**, Sp.
73/J3 **Lora, Hāmūn-i-** (lake), Pak.
126/D3 **Lorain**, Oh,US
73/J2 **Loralai**, Pak.
59/E4 **Lorca**, Sp.
92/E8 **Lord Howe** (isl.), Austl.
124/E4 **Lordsburg**, NM,US
53/G3 **Lorelei** (cliff), Ger.
110/H7 **Lorena**, Braz.
87/J5 **Lorentz** (riv.), Indo.
50/C2 **Lorentzsluizen** (dam), Neth.
123/J3 **Lorette**, Mb,Can
97/N7 **Lorian** (swamp), Kenya
117/F6 **Lorica**, Col.
56/B3 **Lorient**, Fr.
118/G2 **Lorillard** (riv.), Nun.,Can
62/D2 **Lorinci**, Hun.
127/Q8 **Lorne Park**, On,Can
54/D2 **Lörrach**, Ger.
53/F6 **Lorrain** (plat.), Fr.
127/N6 **Lorraine**, Qu,Can
54/C1 **Lorraine** (reg.), Fr.
45/E2 **Lorton**, Eng,UK
131/J8 **Lorton**, Va,US
131/B3 **Los Alamitos**, Ca,US
124/B4 **Los Alamos**, Ca,US
125/F4 **Los Alamos**, NM,US
112/C4 **Los Alerces Nat'l Park**, Arg.
132/K12 **Los Altos**, Ca,US
112/C2 **Los Andes**, Chile
112/B3 **Los Ángeles**, Chile
131/B2 **Los Angeles**, Ca,US
131/B2 **Los Angeles** (riv.), Ca,US
124/B3 **Los Banos**, Ca,US
58/C4 **Los Barrios**, Sp.
107/B7 **Los Chonos** (arch.), Chile
58/C1 **Los Corrales de Buelna**, Sp.
113/J7 **Los Glaciares Nat'l Park**, Arg.
53/F4 **Losheim**, Ger.
117/N8 **Los Herreras**, Mex.
49/M2 **Łosice**, Pol.
62/B3 **Lošinj** (isl.), Cro.
112/B3 **Los Lagos**, Chile
112/B4 **Los Lagos** (reg.), Chile
124/F4 **Los Lunas**, NM,US
117/N8 **Los Mochis**, Mex.
112/B4 **Los Muermos**, Chile
108/C2 **Los Orquideas Nat'l Park**, Col.
58/C4 **Los Palacios y Villafranca**, Sp.
113/J8 **Los Pingüinos Nat'l Park**, Chile
116/A4 **Los Reyes**, Mex.
117/H5 **Los Roques** (isls.), Ven.
58/B3 **Los Santos de Maimona**, Sp.
112/B3 **Los Sauces**, Chile
50/E4 **Losser**, Neth.
117/H5 **Los Teques**, Ven.
124/D1 **Lost River** (range), Id,US
46/B6 **Lostwithiel**, Eng,UK
112/C1 **Los Vilos**, Chile
58/D3 **Los Yébenes**, Sp.
56/D4 **Lot** (riv.), Fr.
112/B3 **Lota**, Chile
73/G1 **Lotfābād**, Trkm.
51/E4 **Lotte**, Ger.
81/B5 **Lou** (riv.), China
83/C2 **Louangphrabang**, Laos
104/B1 **Loubomo**, Congo
56/B2 **Loudéac**, Fr.
82/B2 **Loudi**, China
56/D3 **Loudun**, Fr.
54/B3 **Loue** (riv.), Fr.
98/A3 **Louga**, Sen.
98/B3 **Louga** (reg.), Sen.
45/G6 **Loughborough**, Eng,UK
44/B3 **Loughbrickland**, NI,UK
119/R7 **Lougheed** (isl.), Nun.,Can
44/B3 **Loughgall**, NI,UK
126/E4 **Louisa**, Va,US
92/E6 **Louisiade** (arch.), PNG
128/E4 **Louisiana** (state), US
126/C4 **Louisville**, Ky,US
129/F3 **Louisville**, Ms,US
119/J3 **Louis XIV** (pt.), Qu,Can
58/A4 **Loulé**, Port.
57/K1 **Louny**, Czh.
125/H2 **Loup** (riv.), Ne,US
44/B2 **Loup, The**, NI,UK
56/C5 **Lourdes**, Fr.
59/P10 **Loures**, Port.
58/A3 **Louriçal**, Port.
58/A3 **Lourinhã**, Port.
58/A2 **Lousã**, Port.
59/P10 **Lousa**, Port.
44/B4 **Louth** (co.), Ire.
45/H5 **Louth**, Eng,UK
61/H4 **Loutrákion**, Gre.
53/D2 **Louvain** (Leuven), Belg.
110/G8 **Louveira**, Braz.
52/A5 **Louviers**, Fr.
52/B5 **Louvres**, Fr.
52/C3 **Louvroil**, Fr.
52/B2 **Louvaart** (can.), Belg.
64/F4 **Lovat'** (riv.), Bela., Rus.
62/D4 **Lovćen Nat'l Park**, Yugo.
63/G4 **Lovech**, Bul.
63/G4 **Lovech** (reg.), Bul.
125/F2 **Loveland**, Co,US
122/F4 **Lovell**, Wy,US
124/C2 **Lovelock**, Nv,US
57/J4 **Lovere**, It.
125/F4 **Loving**, NM,US
125/G4 **Lovington**, NM,US
64/G2 **Lovozero** (lake), Rus.
119/H2 **Low** (cape), Nun.,Can
97/L8 **Lowa** (riv.), D.R. Congo
45/H6 **Lowdham**, Eng,UK
127/G3 **Lowell**, Ma,US
102/B2 **Löwen** (dry riv.), Namb.
122/D3 **Lower Arrow** (lake), BC,Can
57/L2 **Lower Austria** (prov.), Aus.
47/E2 **Lower Brailes**, Eng,UK
91/B3 **Lower Glenelg Nat'l Park**, Austl.
91/C4 **Lower Gordon-Franklin Wild Rivers Nat'l Park**, Austl.
47/E3 **Lower Heyford**, Eng,UK
123/K4 **Lower Red** (lake), Mn,US
48/E2 **Lower Saxony** (state), Ger.
68/K3 **Lower Tunguska** (riv.), Rus.
104/E4 **Lower Zambezi Nat'l Park**, Zam.
47/H2 **Lowestoft**, Eng,UK
104/E1 **Lowi** (riv.), D.R. Congo
49/K2 **Łowicz**, Pol.
44/E1 **Lowther** (hills), Sc,UK
127/Q9 **Lowville**, On,Can
51/F2 **Loxstedt**, Ger.
93/V12 **Loyalty** (isls.), NCal.
62/D3 **Loznica**, Yugo.
66/F2 **Lozovaya**, Ukr.
62/E3 **Lozovik**, Yugo.
81/C5 **Lu** (riv.), China
104/D2 **Luachimo**, Ang.
104/E1 **Lualaba** (riv.), D.R. Congo
81/J6 **Luam** (riv.), China
120/T10 **Lua Makika** (crater), Hi,US
81/D5 **Lu'an**, China
81/D2 **Luan** (riv.), China
58/C1 **Luanco**, Sp.
104/B2 **Luanda** (cap.), Ang.
83/C5 **Luang** (lag.), Thai.
83/B4 **Luang** (peak), Thai.
83/C2 **Luang Prabang** (range), Laos
101/B5 **Luangwa** (riv.), Moz., Zam.
104/E3 **Luanshya**, Zam.
81/D3 **Luan Xian**, China
104/D3 **Luao**, Ang.
101/A5 **Luapula** (prov.), Zam.
58/B1 **Luarca**, Sp.
104/D3 **Luashi**, D.R. Congo
96/G7 **Luba**, EqG.
116/D4 **Lubaantun** (ruins), Belz.
49/M3 **Lubaczów**, Pol.
49/H3 **Lubań**, Pol.
104/B3 **Lubango**, Ang.
49/M3 **Lubartów**, Pol.
49/K2 **Lubawa**, Pol.
51/F4 **Lübbecke**, Ger.
53/D2 **Lubbeek**, Belg.
128/C3 **Lubbock**, Tx,US
48/F2 **Lübeck**, Ger.
104/D1 **Lubefu**, D.R. Congo
49/M3 **Lubelska** (upland), Pol.
101/A3 **Lubero**, D.R. Congo
49/J3 **Lubin**, Pol.
49/M3 **Lublin**, Pol.
49/M3 **Lublin** (prov.), Pol.
49/K3 **Lubliniec**, Pol.
66/E2 **Lubny**, Ukr.
49/J2 **Luboń**, Pol.
49/H3 **Lubsko**, Pol.
104/E2 **Lubudi**, D.R. Congo
86/B4 **Lubuklinggau**, Indo.
86/B3 **Lubuksikaping**, Indo.
104/E3 **Lubumbashi**, D.R. Congo
104/E2 **Lubunda**, D.R. Congo
104/C2 **Lucala**, Ang.
44/B5 **Lucan**, Ire.
83/D1 **Luc An Chau**, Viet.
130/K3 **Lucania** (mtn.), Yk,Can
104/D2 **Lucapa**, Ang.
57/J5 **Lucca**, It.
44/D2 **Luce** (bay), Sc,UK
129/F4 **Lucedale**, Ms,US
110/B2 **Lucélia**, Braz.
82/D5 **Lucena**, Phil.
58/C4 **Lucena**, Sp.
49/K4 **Lučenec**, Slvk.
55/E3 **Lucerne** (Vierwaldstättersee) (lake), Swi.
48/F2 **Lüchow**, Ger.
49/G2 **Luckenwalde**, Ger.
84/D2 **Lucknow**, India
122/G3 **Lucky Lake**, Sk,Can
117/F3 **Lucrecia** (cape), Cuba
104/D3 **Lucusse**, Ang.
63/H4 **Luda Kamchiya** (riv.), Bul.
51/E6 **Lüdenscheid**, Ger.
102/A2 **Lüderitz**, Namb.
47/E4 **Ludgershall**, Eng,UK
73/L2 **Ludhiāna**, India
51/E5 **Ludinghausen**, Ger.
126/C3 **Ludington**, Mi,US
46/D2 **Ludlow**, Eng,UK
63/H4 **Ludogorie** (reg.), Bul.
63/G2 **Luduș**, Rom.
42/E3 **Ludvika**, Swe.
57/H2 **Ludwigsburg**, Ger.
49/G2 **Ludwigsfelde**, Ger.
48/F2 **Ludwigslust**, Ger.
104/D2 **Luebo**, D.R. Congo
128/E4 **Lufkin**, Tx,US
64/F4 **Luga**, Rus.
55/E6 **Lugano**, Swi.
51/G5 **Lügde**, Ger.
104/G3 **Lugenda** (riv.), Moz.
46/D2 **Lugg** (riv.), Eng,UK
44/B6 **Lugnaquillia** (mtn.), Ire.
58/B1 **Lugo**, Sp.
62/E3 **Lugoj**, Rom.
66/F2 **Luhans'k**, Ukr.
66/F2 **Luhans'ka** (obl.), Ukr.
51/H2 **Lühe** (riv.), Ger.
104/D4 **Luiana**, Ang.
57/H4 **Luino**, It.
105/X **Luitpold** (coast), Ant.
62/D3 **Lukavac**, Bosn.
104/C1 **Lukenie** (riv.), D.R. Congo
63/G4 **Lukovit**, Bul.
49/M3 **Łuków**, Pol.
92/F4 **Lukunor** (atoll), Micr.
42/G2 **Luleå**, Swe.
42/G2 **Luleälv** (riv.), Swe.
63/H5 **Lüleburgaz**, Turk.
81/B4 **Luling Guan** (pass), China
92/G5 **Lulua**, Tuv.
104/D2 **Lulua** (riv.), D.R. Congo
104/D3 **Lumai**, Ang.
75/D5 **Lumajamgdong** (lake), China
129/J3 **Lumberton**, NC,US
128/E4 **Lumberton**, Tx,US
104/H4 **Lumbo**, Moz.
122/D3 **Lumby**, BC,Can
85/F2 **Lumding**, India
53/E2 **Lummen**, Belg.
83/D3 **Lumphat**, Camb.
123/G3 **Lumsden**, Sk,Can
89/G7 **Lumsden**, NZ
104/D3 **Lunache**, Ang.
49/G1 **Lund**, Swe.
124/D3 **Lund**, Nv,US
104/F5 **Lundi** (riv.), Zim.
46/B4 **Lundy** (isl.), Eng,UK
51/F2 **Lune** (riv.), Ger.
45/F3 **Lune** (riv.), Eng,UK
51/H2 **Lüneburg**, Ger.
51/G2 **Lüneburger Heide** (reg.), Ger.
56/F5 **Lunel**, Fr.
51/E5 **Lünen**, Ger.
127/H2 **Lunenburg**, NS,Can
104/E3 **Lunga** (riv.), Zam.
85/F3 **Lunglei**, India
104/D3 **Lungue-Bungo** (riv.), Ang.
84/B3 **Luni** (riv.), India
81/B3 **Luo** (riv.), China
81/B4 **Luo** (riv.), China
81/C4 **Luohe**, China

162

Luoma – March

81/D4 Luoma (lake), China
83/C1 Luong (mts.), Viet.
81/C4 Luoyang, China
104/B1 Luozi, D.R. Congo
104/E4 Lupane, Zim.
85/H2 Lupanshui, China
63/F3 Lupeni, Rom.
85/H2 Luquan, China
73/J2 Lūrah (riv.), Afg.
126/E4 Luray, Va,US
44/B3 Lurgan, NI,UK
104/H3 Lúrio, Moz.
104/G3 Lúrio (riv.), Moz.
104/E4 Lusaka (cap.), Zam.
104/E1 Lusamba, D.R. Congo
104/D1 Lusambo, D.R. Congo
81/D3 Lu Shan (mtn.), China
81/C5 Lu Shan (peak), China
61/F2 Lushnje, Alb.
123/G5 Lusk, Wy,US
97/J7 Lutanga (riv.), D.R. Congo
131/K7 Lutherville, Md,US
50/D1 Lütjehorn (isl.), Ger.
47/F3 Luton, Eng,UK
47/F3 Luton (co.), Eng,UK
66/C2 Lutsk, Ukr.
51/F5 Lutter (riv.), Ger.
105/C Lützow-Holm (bay), Ant.
97/P7 Luuq, Som.
123/J5 Luverne, Mn,US
53/E4 Luxembourg
53/E4 Luxembourg (prov.), Belg.
53/F4 Luxembourg (cap.), Lux.
53/F4 Luxembourg (dist.), Lux.
85/J2 Lu Xian, China
100/C3 Luxor (Al Uqşur), Egypt
56/C5 Luy (riv.), Fr.
81/B3 Luya Shan (mtn.), China
110/C1 Luz, Braz.
65/L3 Luza (riv.), Rus.
54/E3 Luzern (canton), Swi.
55/E3 Luzern (Lucerne), Swi.
85/J2 Luzhou, China
109/J7 Luziânia, Braz.
82/D4 Luzon (isl.), Phil.
66/C2 L'viv, Ukr.
66/B2 L'vivs'ka Obl., Ukr.
83/C1 Lwi (riv.), Myan.
65/P3 Lyapin (riv.), Rus.
63/G4 Lyaskovets, Bul.
42/F2 Lycksele, Swe.
47/G5 Lydd, Eng,UK
105/Y Lyddan (isl.), Ant.
103/E2 Lydenburg, SAfr.
46/D3 Lydney, Eng,UK
122/F5 Lyman, Wy,US
46/C5 Lyme (bay), Eng,UK
46/D5 Lyme Regis, Eng,UK
47/E5 Lymington, Eng,UK
45/F5 Lymm, Eng,UK
49/L1 Łyna (riv.), Pol.
44/D5 Lynas (pt.), Wal,UK
131/G5 Lynbrook, NY,US
126/E4 Lynchburg, Va,US
129/H3 Lynches (riv.), SC,US
90/A2 Lynd (riv.), Austl.
47/E5 Lyndhurst, Eng,UK
131/F5 Lyndhurst, NJ,US
45/F1 Lyne (riv.), Eng,UK
42/G1 Lyngen (fjord), Nor.
127/G3 Lynn, Ma,US
129/G4 Lynn Haven, Fl,US
132/C2 Lynnwood, Wa,US
46/C4 Lynton, Eng,UK
131/B3 Lynwood, Ca,US
118/F2 Lynx (lake), NW,Can
56/F4 Lyon, Fr.
125/H3 Lyons, Ks,US
46/C4 Lype (hill), Eng,UK
92/E5 Lyra (reef), PNG
52/B2 Lys (riv.), Fr.
49/K4 Lysá (peak), Czh.
64/E5 Lysaya, Gora (hill), Bela.
49/L3 Łysica (peak), Pol.
52/C2 Lys-lez-Lannoy, Fr.
65/N4 Lys'va, Rus.
66/F2 Lysychans'k, Ukr.
46/D5 Lytchett Matravers, Eng,UK
45/E4 Lytham Saint Anne's, Eng,UK
65/X9 Lytkarino, Rus.
122/C3 Lytton, BC,Can
66/F1 Lyubertsy, Rus.
63/H5 Lyubimets, Bul.
66/E2 Lyubotin, Ukr.
66/E1 Lyudinovo, Rus.
46/C3 Lywd (riv.), Wal,UK

M

83/C1 Ma (riv.), Laos, Viet.
74/K5 Ma'alot, Isr.
100/C2 Ma'ān, Jor.
64/F2 Maanselkä (mts.), Fin.
81/D5 Ma'anshan, China
50/C6 Maarheeze, Neth.
50/C4 Maarssen, Neth.
48/D3 Maas (riv.), Eur.
50/C6 Maasbracht, Neth.
50/D6 Maasbree, Neth.
53/E1 Maaseik, Belg.
82/D5 Maasin, Phil.
53/E2 Maasmechelen, Belg.
50/B5 Maassluis, Neth.
53/E2 Maastricht, Neth.
74/N7 Ma'ayan Harod Nat'l Park, Isr.
82/D4 Mabalacat, Phil.
104/F5 Mabalane, Moz.
45/J5 Mablethorpe, Eng,UK
104/F5 Mabote, Moz.
112/B5 Macá (peak), Chile
110/D2 Macaé, Braz.
109/L5 Macaíba, Braz.
109/H3 Macapá, Braz.
108/C4 Macará, Ecu.
109/L5 Macau, Braz.
82/B3 Macau, China
92/H7 Macauley (isl.), NZ
108/D3 Macaya (riv.), Col.
117/G4 Macaya (pk.), Haiti
129/H4 Macclenny, Fl,US
45/F5 Macclesfield, Eng,UK
45/F5 Macclesfield (can.), Eng,UK
102/D3 Macdhui (peak), SAfr.
43/D2 Macduff, Sc,UK
61/G2 Macedonia
61/G2 Macedonia (reg.), FYROM, Gre.
109/L5 Maceió, Braz.
60/C1 Macerata, It.
105/E Macey (peak), Ant.
102/D3 Machache (peak), Les.
110/H6 Machado, Braz.
101/C3 Machakos, Kenya
108/C4 Machala, Ecu.
108/B4 Machalilla Nat'l Park, Ecu.
104/F5 Machanga, Moz.
44/D2 Machars, The (pen.), Sc,UK
104/F5 Machaze, Moz.
104/E5 Machemma (ruins), SAfr.
46/C3 Machen, Wal,UK
81/C5 Macheng, China
127/H2 Machias, Me,US
58/D1 Machichaco (cape), Sp.
59/V15 Machico, Madr.,Port.
79/H7 Machida, Japan
84/D4 Machilipatnam, India
117/G5 Machiques, Ven.
108/D6 Machu Picchu (ruins), Peru
108/F6 Machupo (riv.), Bol.
46/C1 Machynlleth, Wal,UK
63/J3 Măcin, Rom.
98/D3 Macina (reg.), Mali
91/D1 Macintyre (riv.), Austl.
124/E3 Mack, Co,US
90/C3 Mackay, Austl.
105/E MacKenzie (bay), Ant.
90/C3 Mackenzie (riv.), Austl.
122/C2 Mackenzie, BC,Can
130/N2 Mackenzie (riv.), NW,Can
118/C2 Mackenzie (bay), NW, Yk,Can
118/C2 Mackenzie (mts.), NW, Yk,Can
119/R7 Mackenzie King (isl.), NW,Can
126/C2 Mackinac Island, Mi,US
129/F1 Mackinaw (riv.), Il,US
126/C2 Mackinaw City, Mi,US
122/F2 Macklin, Sk,Can
90/F7 Macleay (isl.), Austl.
130/L3 Macmillan (riv.), Yk,Can
60/A2 Macomer, It.
54/A5 Mâcon, Fr.
125/K4 Macon (bayou), Ar, La,US
129/H3 Macon, Ga,US
125/J3 Macon, Mo,US
44/B1 Macosquin, NI,UK
91/C4 Macquarie (har.), Austl.
39/S8 Macquarie (isl.), Austl.
91/C1 Macquarie (riv.), Austl.
105/D Mac-Robertson Land (reg.), Ant.
108/F5 Macuim (riv.), Braz.
122/C5 Mad (riv.), Ca,US
74/K5 Ma'dabā, Jor.
103/H8 Madagascar
96/H3 Madama, Niger
63/G5 Madan, Bul.
84/C5 Madanapalle, India
92/D5 Madang, PNG
96/H1 Madanīyīn, Tun.
99/G3 Madaoua, Niger
84/F3 Mādārīpur, Bang.
126/E2 Madawaska (riv.), On,Can
127/G2 Madawaska, Me,US
108/F5 Madeira (riv.), Braz.
59/V15 Madeira (isl.), Madr., Port.
59/U14 Madeira (aut. reg.), Port.
123/L4 Madelin (isl.), Wi,US
117/N8 Madera, Mex.
116/D5 Madera (vol.), Nic.
84/C2 Madhipura, India
84/C3 Madhya Pradesh (state), India
108/E6 Madidi (riv.), Bol.
125/H4 Madill, Ok,US
104/B1 Madingo-Kayes, Congo
129/G3 Madison, Al,US
129/H4 Madison, Fl,US
126/C4 Madison, In,US
129/F3 Madison, Ms,US
122/F4 Madison (riv.), Mt,US
125/H2 Madison, Ne,US
131/F5 Madison, NJ,US
123/J4 Madison, SD,US
126/B3 Madison (cap.), Wi,US
126/D4 Madison, WV,US
132/F6 Madison Heights, Mi,US
126/C4 Madisonville, Ky,US
128/E4 Madisonville, Tx,US
86/D5 Madiun, Indo.
76/D5 Madoi, China
54/C1 Madon (riv.), Fr.
60/C4 Madonie Nebrodi (mts.), It.
73/G5 Madrakah, Ra's al (pt.), Oman
84/D5 Madras (Chennai), India
122/C4 Madras, Or,US
116/B2 Madre (lag.), Mex.
128/D5 Madre (lag.), Tx,US
107/C4 Madre de Dios (riv.), Bol., Peru
113/J7 Madre de Dios (isl.), Chile
56/E5 Madrès (mtn.), Fr.
58/C2 Madrid (aut. comm.), Sp.
59/N9 Madrid (cap.), Sp.
58/D3 Madridejos, Sp.
84/D4 Madugula, India
84/C6 Madurai, India
79/F2 Maebashi, Japan
83/C2 Mae Charim, Thai.
83/B2 Mae Ping Nat'l Park, Thai.
46/C3 Maesteg, Wal,UK
83/B2 Mae Tho (peak), Thai.
92/F6 Maewo (isl.), Van.
83/B2 Mae Ya (mtn.), Thai.
101/C4 Mafia (isl.), Tanz.
102/D2 Mafikeng, SAfr.
98/C4 Mafou (riv.), Gui.
110/B3 Mafra, Braz.
58/A3 Mafra, Port.
69/R4 Magadan, Rus.
101/C3 Magadi, Kenya
102/P12 Magalies Berg (range), SAfr.
113/K8 Magallanes (Magellan) (str.), Arg., Chile
113/K8 Magallanes y Antártica Chilena (reg.), Chile
117/G6 Magangué, Col.
82/D6 Maganoy, Phil.
99/H3 Magaria, Niger
82/D4 Magat (riv.), Phil.
125/J4 Magazine (peak), Ar,US
77/K1 Magdagachi, Rus.
127/J2 Magdalen (isls.), Qu,Can
113/T12 Magdalena, Arg.
108/D3 Magdalena (riv.), Col.
117/M7 Magdalena de Kino, Mex.
87/E3 Magdalena, Gunung (peak), Malay.
48/F2 Magdeburg, Ger.
48/F2 Magdeburger Börde (plain), Ger.
110/K7 Magé, Braz.
129/F4 Magee, Ms,US
44/C2 Magee, Island (pen.), NI,UK
86/C5 Magelang, Indo.
113/K8 Magellan (Magallanes) (str.), Arg., Chile
42/H1 Magerøya (isl.), Nor.
57/H4 Maggiore (lake), It., Swi.
100/B2 Maghāghah, Egypt
44/B2 Maghera, NI,UK
44/B2 Magherafelt, NI,UK
44/B2 Magherafelt (dist.), NI,UK
60/A5 Maghnia (peak), Tun.
45/F4 Maghull, Eng,UK
44/B1 Magilligan, NI,UK
44/B1 Magilligan (pt.), NI,UK
62/D3 Maglaj, Bosn.
62/D4 Maglić (peak), Yugo.
61/F2 Maglie, It.
126/D2 Magnetawan (riv.), On,Can
90/B2 Magnetic (passg.), Austl.
90/B2 Magnetic I. Nat'l Park, Austl.
65/N5 Magnitogorsk, Rus.
128/E3 Magnolia, Ar,US
127/F2 Magog, Qu,Can
97/N6 Mago Nat'l Park, Eth.
46/D3 Magor, Wal,UK
127/H1 Magpie (riv.), Qu,Can
85/F3 Magwe, Myan.
85/F4 Magwe (div.), Myan.
72/E1 Mahābād, Iran
84/B4 Mahād, India
93/X15 Mahaena, FrPol.
108/D2 Mahaica, Guy.
103/H8 Mahajamba (bay), Madg.
103/H7 Mahajamba (riv.), Madg.
103/H6 Mahajanga (prov.), Madg.
103/H7 Mahajilo (riv.), Madg.
87/E3 Mahakam (riv.), Indo.
104/E5 Mahalapye, Bots.
72/F2 Maḩallāt, Iran
73/G2 Māhān, Iran
84/D3 Mahānadī (riv.), India
98/D4 Mahandiabani (riv.), IvC.
84/C2 Mahārajpur, India
84/B4 Mahārāshtra (state), India
84/D3 Mahāsamund, India
83/C2 Maha Sarakham, Thai.
103/H7 Mahavavy (riv.), Madg.
84/C4 Mahbubnagar, India
73/L2 Mahe, India
39/M6 Mahé (isl.), Sey.
103/S15 Mahébourg, Mrts.
66/D1 Mahilyow, Bela.
66/D1 Mahilyowskaya (prov.), Bela.
85/G3 Mahlaing, Myan.
84/C2 Mahoba, India
59/H3 Mahón, Sp.
84/B3 Mahuva, India
131/F4 Mahwah, NJ,US
90/E6 Maiala Nat'l Park, Austl.
92/G4 Maiana (atoll), Kiri.
93/W15 Maiao (isl.), FrPol.
108/D1 Maicao, Col.
109/H3 Maicuru (riv.), Braz.
47/F3 Maidenhead, Eng,UK
46/D5 Maiden Newton, Eng,UK
44/D1 Maidens, Sc,UK
132/G7 Maidstone, On,Can
122/F2 Maidstone, Sk,Can
47/G4 Maidstone, Eng,UK
96/H5 Maiduguri, Nga.
52/B4 Maignelay-Montigny, Fr.
43/A4 Maigue (riv.), Ire.
84/D3 Maihar, India
78/E3 Maihara, Japan
97/L8 Maiko Nat'l Park, D.R. Congo
120/V13 Maili, Hi,US
73/K3 Mailsi, Pak.
57/H2 Main (riv.), Ger.
44/B2 Main (riv.), NI,UK
104/C1 Mai-Ndombe (lake), D.R. Congo
127/G3 Maine (gulf), Can., US
56/C2 Maine (hills), Fr.
43/A4 Maine (riv.), Ire.
127/G2 Maine (state), US
90/C5 Main Range Nat'l Park, Austl.
57/H2 Mainz, Ger.
112/C2 Maipo (vol.), Arg., Chile
112/Q9 Maipo (riv.), Chile
112/F3 Maipú, Arg.
112/C2 Maipú, Chile
57/G4 Maira (riv.), It.
110/G8 Mairiporã, Braz.
117/G3 Maisí (cape), Cuba
103/D3 Maitland (riv.), On,Can
105/A Maitri, Ant.
53/F5 Maizières-lès-Metz, Fr.
78/D3 Maizuru, Japan
59/N9 Majadahonda, Sp.
61/G2 Maja e Zezë (peak), Alb.
60/A4 Majardah (riv.), Tun.
62/E3 Majdanpek, Yugo.
96/J2 Majdūl, Libya
87/E4 Majene, Indo.
97/N6 Majī, Eth.
81/D3 Majia (riv.), China
59/G3 Majorca (Mallorca) (isl.), Sp.
92/G4 Majuro (atoll), Mrsh.
92/G4 Majuro (cap.), Mrsh.
104/B1 Makabana, Congo
120/V13 Makaha, Hi,US
120/V13 Makakilo City, Hi,US
74/N2 Makarov, Rus.
62/C4 Makarska, Cro.
86/E4 Makassar (str.), Indo.
93/L6 Makatea (isl.), FrPol.
103/H8 Makay (massif), Madg.
93/L6 Makemo (atoll), FrPol.
98/B4 Makeni, SLeo.
104/D5 Makgadikgadi (salt pans), Bots.
67/H4 Makhachkala, Rus.
87/G3 Makian (isl.), Indo.
92/G4 Makin (atoll), Kiri.
75/B1 Makinsk, Kaz.
66/F2 Makiyivka, Ukr.
72/C4 Makkah (Mecca), SAr.
62/E2 Makó, Hun.
96/H7 Makokou, Gabon
49/L2 Maków Mazowiecki, Pol.
73/H3 Makran (reg.), Iran, Pak.
73/K3 Makrāna, India
74/F2 Mākū, Iran
101/B5 Makumbako, Tanz.
78/B5 Makurazaki, Japan
130/E5 Makushin (vol.), Ak,US
108/C6 Mala, Peru
84/B5 Malabar (coast), India
96/G7 Malabo (cap.), EqG.
110/D1 Malacacheta, Braz.
83/B5 Malacca (str.), Malay., Thai.
49/J4 Malacky, Slvk.
122/E5 Malad City, Id,US
58/C4 Málaga, Sp.
58/D3 Malagón, Sp.
44/B5 Malahide, Ire.
92/F5 Malaita (isl.), Sol.
97/M6 Malakal, Sudan
84/D4 Malakangiri, India
117/G5 Malambo, Col.
86/D5 Malang, Indo.
104/C2 Malange, Ang.
112/C2 Malargüe, Arg.
126/E1 Malartic, Qu,Can
87/E5 Malasoro (pt.), Indo.
74/D2 Malatya, Turk.
104/F3 Malawi
83/B5 Malay (pen.), Malay.
64/G4 Malaya Vishera, Rus.
82/E6 Malaybalay, Phil.
72/E2 Malāyer, Iran
86/C2 Malaysia
65/L2 Malazemel'skaya (tundra), Rus.
74/E2 Malazgirt, Turk.
127/G2 Malbaie (riv.), Qu,Can
99/G3 Malbaza-Usine, Niger
49/K1 Malbork, Pol.
56/D5 Malcaras, Pic de (peak), Fr.
48/G2 Malchin, Ger.
76/C2 Malchin, Mong.
52/C1 Maldegem, Belg.
93/K5 Malden (isl.), Kiri.
126/B4 Malden, Mo,US
71/G9 Maldives
47/G3 Maldon, Eng,UK
113/G2 Maldonado, Uru.
113/G2 Maldonado (dept.), Uru.
71/G9 Male (cap.), Mald.
61/H4 Maléa, Akra (cape), Gre.
84/B3 Mālegaon, India
92/F6 Malekula (isl.), Van.
56/D4 Malemort-sur-Corrèze, Fr.
48/F1 Malente, Ger.
73/L2 Māler Kotla, India
67/H4 Malgobek, Rus.
59/G2 Malgrat de Mar, Sp.
97/L4 Malha Wells, Sudan
122/D5 Malheur (lake), Or,US
122/D5 Malheur (riv.), Or,US
103/S14 Malheureux (cape), Mrts.
98/E2 Mali
83/B3 Mali (isl.), Myan.
76/F4 Malian (riv.), China
131/B2 Malibu, Ca,US
97/L4 Malik (wadi), Sudan
66/D2 Malin, Ukr.
87/E3 Malinau, Indo.
101/D3 Malindi, Kenya
52/D1 Malines (Mechelen), Belg.
81/C3 Maling Guan (pass), China
103/H8 Malio (riv.), Madg.
83/D1 Malipo, China
73/J4 Malīr Cantonment, Pak.
82/E6 Malita, Phil.
97/P7 Malka Mari Nat'l Park, Kenya
63/H5 Malkara, Turk.
99/H3 Mallammaduri, Nga.
100/B3 Mallawī, Egypt
91/B2 Mallee Cliffs Nat'l Park, Austl.
112/Q10 Malloa, Chile
59/G3 Mallorca (Majorca) (isl.), Sp.
43/A4 Mallow, Ire.
42/G2 Malmberget, Swe.
53/F3 Malmédy, Belg.
102/B4 Malmesbury, SAfr.
46/D3 Malmesbury, Eng,UK
48/G1 Malmö, Swe.
49/G1 Malmöhus (co.), Swe.
65/L4 Malmyzh, Rus.
109/H5 Maloca, Braz.
92/G4 Maloelap (atoll), Mrsh.
126/F2 Malone, NY,US
49/L3 Małopolska (upland), Pol.
42/C3 Måløy, Nor.
45/F5 Malpas, Eng,UK
108/B3 Malpelo (isl.), Col.
58/A1 Malpica, Sp.
60/D5 Malta
60/D5 Malta (isl.), Malta
122/G3 Malta, Mt,US
45/G2 Maltby, Eng,UK
45/G5 Maltby, Eng,UK
127/Q8 Malton, On,Can
45/H3 Malton, Eng,UK
104/C1 Maluku, D.R. Congo
42/E3 Malung, Swe.
84/B4 Malvan, India
59/P10 Malveira, Port.
91/G5 Malvern, Austl.
128/E3 Malvern, Ar,US
46/D2 Malvern (Great Malvern), Eng,UK
113/M8 Malvinas, Islas (Falkland Islands) (dpcy.), UK
67/J2 Malyy Uzen' (riv.), Kaz.
76/D1 Malyy Yenisey (riv.), Rus.
53/F6 Malzéville, Fr.
09/M5 Mamanguape, Braz.
131/G5 Mamaroneck, NY,US
104/E4 Mamba, Zam.
82/D6 Mambajao, Phil.
97/A2 Mambasa, D.R. Congo
87/J4 Mamberamo (riv.), Indo.
96/J6 Mambéré (riv.), CAfr.
74/D3 Mambij, Syria
82/D5 Mamburao, Phil.
53/F4 Mamer, Lux.
56/D2 Mamers, Fr.
52/B2 Mametz, Fr.
99/H5 Mamfé, Camr.
126/C4 Mammoth Cave Nat'l Park, Ky,US
129/F2 Mammoth Spring, Ar,US
108/E6 Mamoré (riv.), Bol.
103/H6 Mamoutzou (cap.), May.
99/E5 Mampong, Gha.
49/L1 Mamry (lake), Pol.
87/E4 Mamuju, Indo.
104/D5 Mamuno, Bots.
109/G4 Mamuri (riv.), Braz.
81/C5 Man (riv.), China
98/D5 Man, IvC.
108/F4 Manacapuru, Braz.
46/A6 Manacle (pt.), UK
59/G3 Manacor, Sp.
87/F3 Manado, Indo.
116/D5 Managua (cap.), Nic.
116/D5 Managua (lake), Nic.
103/J8 Manakara, Madg.
131/F5 Manalapan, NJ,US
72/F3 Manama (Al Manāmah) (cap.), Bahr.
103/H7 Manambaho (riv.), Madg.
103/H7 Manambolo (riv.), Madg.
103/J7 Mananara, Madg.
103/H8 Mananara (riv.), Madg.
103/J8 Mananjary, Madg.
103/H8 Manantary (riv.), Madg.
75/D2 Manas (lake), China
75/E3 Manas (riv.), China
84/D2 Manāslu (mtn.), Nepal
131/F5 Manasquan, NJ,US
131/F5 Manasquan (riv.), NJ,US
125/F3 Manassa, Co,US
126/E4 Manassas, Va,US
61/G1 Manastir Dečani, Yugo.
61/G1 Manastir Gračanica, Yugo.
61/G1 Manastir Sopoćani, Yugo.
79/H7 Manatsuru, Japan
108/F4 Manaus, Braz.
74/B3 Manavgat, Turk.
123/H2 Manawan (lake), Sk,Can
79/H7 Manazuru-misaki (cape), Japan
44/D3 Man, Calf of (isl.), IM,UK
58/D4 Mancha Real, Sp.
84/C4 Mancherāl, India
90/E6 Manchester (lake), Austl.
45/F5 Manchester, Eng,UK
126/D4 Manchester, Ky,US
127/G3 Manchester, NH,US
129/G3 Manchester, Tn,US
77/J3 Manchuria (reg.), China
72/F3 Mand (riv.), Iran
101/B5 Manda, Tanz.
110/B2 Mandaguari, Braz.
42/C4 Mandal, Nor.
87/K4 Mandala (peak), Indo.
83/B1 Mandalay, Myan.
83/A1 Mandalay (div.), Myan.
69/L5 Mandalgovī, Mong.
72/E2 Mandalī, Iraq
123/H4 Mandan, ND,US
97/J6 Manda Nat'l Park, Chad
81/D4 Mandang Shan (mtn.), China
87/F5 Mandasavu (peak), Indo.
82/D5 Mandaue, Phil.
57/H4 Mandello del Lario, It.
53/F3 Manderscheid, Ger.
117/F4 Mandeville, Jam.
73/L2 Māndi, India
104/F4 Mandié, Moz.
87/G4 Mandiola (isl.), Indo.
84/D3 Mandla, India
48/E1 Mandø (isl.), Den.
61/L6 Mándra, Gre.
103/H9 Mandrare (riv.), Madg.
103/J6 Mandritsara, Madg.
84/C3 Mandsaur, India
89/A4 Mandurah, Austl.
61/E2 Manduria, It.
84/A3 Māndvi, India
84/C5 Mandya, India
84/C2 Mane (pass), Nepal
47/G2 Manea, Eng,UK
84/D3 Manendragarh, India
99/H5 Manéngouba, Massif du (peak), Camr.
57/J4 Manerbio, It.
72/B3 Manfalūt, Egypt
60/D2 Manfredonia, It.
60/E2 Manfredonia (gulf), It.
81/B4 Mang (riv.), China
109/J6 Mangabeiras (hills), Braz.
104/C1 Mangai, D.R. Congo
93/K7 Mangaia (isl.), CookIs.
85/F2 Mangaldai, India
82/D4 Mangaldan, Phil.
63/J4 Mangalia, Rom.
84/B5 Mangalore, India
93/M7 Mangareva (isl.), FrPol.
67/K4 Mangistauz Obl., Kaz.
87/E3 Mangkalihat (cape), Indo.
73/K2 Mangla, Pak.
108/C3 Manglares (pt.), Col.
99/F4 Mango, Togo
104/G3 Mangoche, Malw.
103/H8 Mangoky (riv.), Madg.
87/G4 Mangole (isl.), Indo.
103/J7 Mangoro (riv.), Madg.
46/D4 Mangotsfield, Eng,UK
84/B3 Māngrol, India
113/G2 Mangueira (lake), Braz.
125/H4 Mangum, Ok,US
67/J3 Mangyshlak (pen.), Kaz.
67/K4 Mangyshlak (plat.), Kaz.
125/H3 Manhattan, Ks,US
122/F4 Manhattan, Mt,US
131/B3 Manhattan Beach, Ca,US
110/D2 Manhuaçu, Braz.
110/D2 Manhumirim, Braz.
61/H4 Máni (pen.), Gre.
103/H7 Mania (riv.), Madg.
104/F4 Manica, Moz.
108/F5 Manicoré, Braz.
108/F5 Manicoré (riv.), Braz.
123/J3 Manicouagan, Mb,Can
127/G1 Manicouagan (res.), Qu,Can
127/G1 Manicouagan (riv.), Qu,Can
127/H1 Manicouagan, Petit Lac (lake), Qu,Can
90/C3 Manifold (cape), Austl.
93/L6 Manihi (isl.), FrPol.
93/J6 Manihiki (atoll), CookIs.
82/D5 Manila (cap.), Phil.
124/E2 Manila, Ut,US
103/J7 Maningory (riv.), Madg.
87/G4 Manipa (str.), Indo.
85/F3 Manipur (state), India
74/A2 Manisa, Turk.
44/D3 Man, Isle of (isl.), UK
126/C2 Manistee, Mi,US
126/C2 Manistee (riv.), Mi,US
118/G3 Manitoba (prov.), Can.
123/J3 Manitoba (lake), Mb,Can
127/H1 Manitou (riv.), Qu,Can
126/D2 Manitoulin (isl.), On,Can
128/B2 Manitou Springs, Co,US
126/C1 Manitouwadge, On,Can
126/C2 Manitowoc, Wi,US
126/F2 Maniwaki, Qu,Can
108/C2 Manizales, Col.
84/C4 Manjlegaon, India
73/L5 Mānjra (riv.), India
123/K4 Mankato, Mn,US
98/D4 Mankono, IvC.
76/F3 Manlay, Mong.
58/D2 Manlleu, Sp.
90/H8 Manly, Austl.
84/B3 Manmād, India
83/B4 Man Mia (peak), Thai.
84/C6 Mannar (gulf), India, SrL.
84/C6 Mannar, SrL.
84/C5 Mannārgudi, India
102/C4 Mannetjiesberg (peak), SAfr.
57/H2 Mannheim, Ger.
119/Q7 Manning (cape), NW,Can
129/H3 Manning, SC,US
47/H3 Manningtree, Eng,UK
98/C5 Mano (riv.), Libr., SLeo.
104/E2 Manono, D.R. Congo
131/H5 Manorville, NY,US
56/F5 Manosque, Fr.
127/G1 Manouane (lake), Qu,Can
127/G1 Manouane (riv.), Qu,Can
93/H5 Manra (Sydney) (atoll), Kiri.
59/F2 Manresa, Sp.
101/A5 Mansa, Zam.
98/B3 Mansa Konko, Gam.
87/F1 Mansalay, Phil.
119/H2 Mansel (isl.), Nun.,Can
45/G5 Mansfield, Eng,UK
128/E3 Mansfield, La,US
126/D3 Mansfield, Oh,US
45/G5 Mansfield Woodhouse, Eng,UK
108/B4 Manta, Ecu.
87/E2 Mantalingajan (mt.), Phil.
108/C6 Mantaro (riv.), Peru
124/B3 Manteca, Ca,US
110/D1 Mantena, Braz.
52/A6 Mantes-la-Jolie, Fr.
52/A6 Mantes-la-Ville, Fr.
84/C4 Manthani, India
124/E3 Manti, Ut,US
131/G5 Manticock (pt.), NY,US
110/C2 Mantiquiera (range), Braz.
81/C3 Mantou Shan (mtn.), China
57/J4 Mantova, It.
116/E3 Mantua, Cuba
65/K4 Manturovo, Rus.
42/H3 Mäntyharju, Fin.
108/E6 Manú (riv.), Peru
93/J6 Manua (isls.), ASam.
93/K6 Manuae (atoll), CookIs.
120/W13 Manuawili, Hi,US
109/J6 Manuel Alves (riv.), Braz.
86/C5 Manuk (riv.), Indo.
89/H6 Manukau, NZ
108/D6 Manú Nat'l Park, Peru
108/E6 Manuripe (riv.), Bol.
92/D5 Manus (isl.), PNG
131/F5 Manville, NJ,US
128/E4 Many, La,US
67/G3 Manych (riv.), Rus.
67/G3 Manych-Gudilo (lake), Rus.
124/E3 Many Farms, Az,US
101/B4 Manyoni, Tanz.
58/D3 Manzanares, Sp.
59/N8 Manzanares (riv.), Sp.
117/P10 Manzanillo, Mex.
128/B3 Manzano (mts.), NM,US
77/H2 Manzhouli, China
100/C2 Manzilah, Buḩayrat al (lake), Egypt
60/A4 Manzil bū Ruqaybah, Tun.
60/B4 Manzil Tamīn, Tun.
103/E2 Manzini, Swaz.
117/G4 Mao, DRep.
87/J4 Maoke (mts.), Indo.
82/B3 Maoming, China
75/D5 Mapam (lake), China
116/C4 Mapastepec, Mex.
117/P8 Mapimí, Bolsón de (val.), Mex.
127/Q8 Maple, On,Can
123/K5 Maple (riv.), Ia,US
123/J4 Maple (riv.), ND,US
122/F3 Maple Creek, Sk,Can
131/F6 Maple Shade, NJ,US
131/F5 Maplewood, NJ,US
108/G4 Mapuera (riv.), Braz.
84/B4 Mapusa, India
103/F2 Maputo (cap.), Moz.
100/D5 Maqdam, Ras (cape), Sudan
73/J2 Maqor, Afg.
75/D5 Maquan (riv.), China
104/C2 Maquela do Zombo, Ang.
125/K2 Maquoteka (riv.), Ia,US
110/B3 Mar (range), Braz.
101/B3 Mara (prov.), Tanz.
109/J5 Marabá, Braz.
109/J3 Maracá (isl.), Braz.
117/G5 Maracaibo, Ven.
117/G6 Maracaibo (lake), Ven.
109/H7 Maracaju (mts.), Braz.
117/H5 Maracay, Ven.
58/D4 Maracena, Sp.
99/G3 Maradi, Niger
99/G3 Maradi (dept.), Niger
72/E1 Marāgheh, Iran
108/E3 Marahuaca (peak), Ven.
125/J3 Marais des Cygnes (riv.), Ks, Mo,US
109/J4 Marajó, Braz.
109/J4 Marajó (bay), Braz.
107/D3 Marajó (isl.), Braz.
82/E6 Maramag, Phil.
110/K8 Marambaia (isl.), Braz.
129/F2 Maramec (riv.), Mo,US
63/F2 Maramureş (co.), Rom.
124/E4 Marana, Az,US
109/L4 Maranguape, Braz.
109/J6 Maranhão (riv.), Braz.
90/C4 Maranoa (riv.), Austl.
108/C4 Marañón (riv.), Peru
98/D5 Maraoue Nat'l Park, IvC.
86/B4 Marapi (peak), Indo.
86/C4 Maras (peak), Indo.
63/H3 Mărăşeşti, Rom.
126/C1 Marathon, On,Can
129/H5 Marathon, Fl,US
128/C4 Marathon, Tx,US
110/A4 Marau, Braz.
82/D6 Marawi, Phil.
100/B5 Marawī, Sudan
46/A6 Marazion, Eng,UK
58/C4 Marbella, Sp.
122/F5 Marbleton, Wy,US
48/E3 Marburg, Ger.
62/C2 Marcali, Hun.
104/B4 Marca, Ponta da (pt.), Ang.
47/G1 March, Eng,UK
56/D3 Marche (mts.), Fr.
57/K5 Marche (reg.), It.
53/E3 Marche-en-Famenne, Belg.
58/C4 Marchena, Sp.

163
Mar C– Mezhd

111/D3 **Mar Chiquita** (lake), Arg.
52/A2 **Marck**, Fr.
129/H5 **Marco**, Fl,US
108/C7 **Marcona**, Peru
122/E3 **Marconi** (peak), BC,Can
112/E2 **Marcos Juárez**, Arg.
52/C2 **Marcq-en-Baroeul**, Fr.
130/J3 **Marcus Baker** (mtn.), Ak,US
126/F2 **Marcy** (peak), NY,US
73/K2 **Mardān**, Pak.
113/F3 **Mar del Plata**, Arg.
47/G4 **Marden**, Eng,UK
74/E3 **Mardin**, Turk.
93/W12 **Maré** (isl.), NCal.
90/B2 **Mareeba**, Austl.
43/C2 **Maree, Loch** (lake), Sc,UK
45/H5 **Mareham le Fen**, Eng,UK
47/G5 **Maresfield**, Eng,UK
128/B4 **Marfa**, Tx,US
46/C3 **Margam**, Wal,UK
66/E3 **Marganets**, Ukr.
84/B4 **Margao**, India
117/J5 **Margarita** (isl.), Ven.
47/H4 **Margate**, Eng,UK
56/E4 **Margeride** (mts.), Fr.
101/A2 **Margherita** (peak), Ugan.
62/F2 **Marghita**, Rom.
75/B3 **Margilan**, Uzb.
75/E5 **Margog Caka** (lake), China
82/D6 **Margosatubig**, Phil.
53/E2 **Margraten**, Neth.
105/V **Marguerite** (bay), Ant.
91/D4 **Maria** (peak), Austl.
93/K7 **Maria** (isl.), FrPol.
91/D4 **Maria Island Nat'l Park**, Austl.
129/F3 **Marianna**, Ar,US
129/G4 **Marianna**, Fl,US
116/E3 **Mariano**, Cuba
57/K2 **Mariánské Lázně** (Marienbad), Czh.
122/F3 **Marias** (riv.), Mt,US
62/B2 **Maribor**, Slov.
110/L7 **Maricá**, Braz.
108/E4 **Marié** (riv.), Braz.
105/S **Marie Byrd Land** (reg.), Ant.
117/J4 **Marie-Galante** (isl.), Guad.
42/F3 **Mariehamn**, Fin.
57/K2 **Marienbad** (Mariánské Lázně), Czh.
51/E6 **Marienheide**, Ger.
42/E4 **Mariestad**, Swe.
129/G3 **Marietta**, Ga,US
126/D4 **Marietta**, Oh,US
56/F5 **Marignane**, Fr.
110/B2 **Marília**, Braz.
58/A1 **Marín**, Sp.
131/B3 **Marina del Rey**, Ca,US
52/A5 **Marines**, Fr.
126/C2 **Marinette**, Wi,US
110/B2 **Maringá**, Braz.
58/A3 **Marinha Grande**, Port.
129/G3 **Marion**, Al,US
126/B4 **Marion**, Il,US
126/C3 **Marion**, In,US
126/B4 **Marion**, Ky,US
126/C2 **Marion**, Mi,US
126/D3 **Marion**, Oh,US
129/H3 **Marion** (lake), SC,US
126/D4 **Marion**, Va,US
124/C3 **Mariposa**, Ca,US
63/H5 **Maritsa** (riv.), Bul., Turk.
66/F3 **Mariupol'**, Ukr.
65/K4 **Mariy Aut. Rep.**, Rus.
74/K5 **Marj 'Uyūn**, Leb.
50/B6 **Mark** (riv.), Belg.
76/B2 **Markakol** (lake), Kaz.
42/E4 **Markaryd**, Swe.
50/C4 **Marken** (isl.), Neth.
50/C4 **Markerwaard** (polder), Neth.
47/E1 **Market Bosworth**, Eng,UK
47/F1 **Market Deeping**, Eng,UK
45/F6 **Market Drayton**, Eng,UK
47/F2 **Market Harborough**, Eng,UK
44/B3 **Markethill**, NI,UK
45/H5 **Market Rasen**, Eng,UK
45/H4 **Market Weighton**, Eng,UK
119/J2 **Markham** (bay), Nun.,Can
127/R8 **Markham**, On,Can
49/L2 **Marki**, Pol.
124/C3 **Markleeville**, Ca,US
61/L7 **Markópoulon**, Gre.
67/H2 **Marks**, Rus.
128/E4 **Marksville**, La,US
57/K2 **Marktredwitz**, Ger.
125/J3 **Mark Twain** (lake), Mo,US
51/E5 **Marl**, Ger.
131/F5 **Marlboro**, NJ,US
47/E4 **Marlborough**, Eng,UK
52/B3 **Marles-les-Mines**, Fr.
47/F3 **Marlow**, Eng,UK
131/F6 **Marlton**, NJ,US
52/C3 **Marly**, Fr.
52/B5 **Marly-la-Ville**, Fr.
52/B5 **Marly-le-Roi**, Fr.
53/F5 **Marly-sur-Seille**, Fr.
56/D4 **Marmande**, Fr.
63/H5 **Marmara** (isl.), Turk.
63/J5 **Marmara** (sea), Turk.
74/B3 **Marmaris**, Turk.
108/F5 **Marmelos** (riv.), Braz.
126/A1 **Marmion** (lake), On,Can
57/J3 **Marmolada** (peak), It.
58/C3 **Marmolejo**, Sp.
52/C6 **Marne** (dept.), Fr.
56/E2 **Marne** (riv.), Fr.
53/D6 **Marne au Rhin, Canal de la** (can.), Fr.
46/D5 **Marnhull**, Eng,UK
96/J6 **Maro**, Chad
93/H2 **Maro** (reef), Hi,US
103/J6 **Maroantsetra**, Madg.
93/L6 **Marokau** (atoll), FrPol.
103/J8 **Marolambo**, Madg.
103/J6 **Maromokotro** (peak), Madg.
104/F4 **Marondera**, Zim.
109/H3 **Maroni** (riv.), FrG., Sur.
90/D4 **Maroochydore-Mooloolaba**, Austl.
96/H5 **Maroua**, Camr.
103/H7 **Marovoay**, Madg.
53/G5 **Marpingen**, Ger.
45/F5 **Marple**, Eng,UK
76/D5 **Marqên Gangri** (peak), China
92/D8 **Marquarie** (riv.), Austl.
93/M5 **Marquesas** (isls.), FrPol.
126/C2 **Marquette**, Mi,US
97/K5 **Marrah** (mts.), Sudan
96/D1 **Marrakech**, Mor.
101/C2 **Marsabit**, Kenya
60/C4 **Marsala**, It.
97/L1 **Marsá Matrūh**, Egypt
51/F6 **Marsberg**, Ger.
60/C1 **Marsciano**, It.
45/G4 **Marsden**, Eng,UK
50/B3 **Marsdiep** (chan.), Neth.
56/F5 **Marseille**, Fr.
128/E4 **Marsh** (isl.), La,US
122/F2 **Marshall**, Sk,Can
123/K4 **Marshall**, Mn,US
125/J3 **Marshall**, Mo,US
128/E3 **Marshall**, Tx,US
92/G3 **Marshall Islands**
123/K5 **Marshalltown**, Ia,US
125/J3 **Marshfield**, Mo,US
126/B2 **Marshfield**, Wi,US
47/E3 **Marsh Gibbon**, Eng,UK
45/G2 **Marske-by-the-Sea**, Eng,UK
83/B2 **Martaban** (gulf), Myan.
122/G2 **Martensville**, Sk,Can
127/G3 **Martha's Vineyard** (isl.), Ma,US
54/D5 **Martigny**, Swi.
56/F5 **Martigues**, Fr.
105/S **Martin** (pen.), Ant.
49/K4 **Martin**, Slvk.
129/G3 **Martin** (lake), Al,US
123/H5 **Martin**, SD,US
129/F2 **Martin**, Tn,US
60/E2 **Martina Franca**, It.
132/K10 **Martinez**, Ca,US
129/H3 **Martinez**, Ga,US
116/B3 **Martínez de la Torre**, Mex.
117/J4 **Martinique** (passage), Dom., Mart.
117/J5 **Martinique** (isl.), Fr.
110/B2 **Martinópolis**, Braz.
126/E4 **Martinsburg**, WV,US
126/C4 **Martinsville**, In,US
126/E4 **Martinsville**, Va,US
38/H7 **Martin Vaz** (isls.), Braz.
46/D2 **Martley**, Eng,UK
46/D5 **Martock**, Eng,UK
59/F2 **Martorell**, Sp.
58/D4 **Martos**, Sp.
126/F1 **Martre** (riv.), Qu,Can
123/J5 **Marty**, SD,US
78/C3 **Marugame**, Japan
79/F2 **Maruko**, Japan
50/D2 **Marum**, Neth.
78/E2 **Maruoka**, Japan
93/M7 **Marutea** (atoll), FrPol.
79/H7 **Maruyama**, Japan
72/F3 **Marv Dasht**, Iran
90/D4 **Mary** (riv.), Austl.
73/H1 **Mary**, Trkm.
90/D4 **Maryborough**, Austl.
91/B3 **Maryborough**, Austl.
129/G4 **Mary Esther**, Fl,US
123/H3 **Maryfield**, Sk,Can
98/C5 **Maryland** (co.), Libr.
126/E4 **Maryland** (state), US
131/K7 **Maryland City**, Md,US
44/E2 **Maryport**, Eng,UK
127/L2 **Marystown**, Nf,Can
125/H3 **Marysville**, Ks,US
132/H6 **Marysville**, Mi,US
132/C1 **Marysville**, Wa,US
125/J2 **Maryville**, Mo,US
129/H3 **Maryville**, Tn,US
60/D2 **Marzano** (peak), It.
96/H2 **Marzūq**, Libya
96/H3 **Marzūq, Şhrā** (des.), Libya
74/K6 **Masada** (Horvot Meẕada) (ruins), Isr.
101/C4 **Masai Steppe** (grsld.), Tanz.
101/A3 **Masaka**, Ugan.
60/B5 **Masākin**, Tun.
59/E3 **Masamagrell**, Sp.
87/F4 **Masamba**, Indo.
80/E5 **Masan**, SKor.
101/C5 **Masasi**, Tanz.
116/D5 **Masaya**, Nic.
82/D5 **Masbate**, Phil.
82/D5 **Masbate** (isl.), Phil.
96/F1 **Mascara**, Alg.
103/S15 **Mascarene** (isls.), Mrts., Reun.
117/P9 **Mascota**, Mex.
127/N6 **Mascouche**, Qu,Can
102/D3 **Maseru** (cap.), Les.
71/E6 **Mashad**, Iran
45/G3 **Masham**, Eng,UK
73/G1 **Mashhad**, Iran
73/H3 **Māshkel, Hāmūn-i-** (lake), Pak.
73/H3 **Māshkīd** (riv.), Iran
67/L1 **Masim** (peak), Rus.
73/G5 **Masira** (gulf), Oman
73/G4 **Maşīrah** (isl.), Oman
72/E2 **Masjed-e Soleymān**, Iran
43/A4 **Mask, Lough** (lake), Ire.
103/J6 **Masoala** (cape), Madg.
103/J6 **Masoala** (pen.), Madg.
126/C3 **Mason**, Mi,US
128/D4 **Mason**, Tx,US
132/A3 **Mason** (lake), Wa,US
123/K5 **Mason City**, Ia,US
59/X17 **Maspalomas**, Canl.,Sp.
59/K6 **Masquefa**, Sp.
57/J4 **Massa**, It.
127/F3 **Massachusetts** (state), US
127/G3 **Massachusetts** (bay), Ma,US
60/E2 **Massafra**, It.
131/G5 **Massapequa**, NY,US
126/F2 **Massena**, NY,US
119/S7 **Massey** (sound), Nun.,Can
104/D3 **Massibi**, Ang.
56/E4 **Massif Central** (plat.), Fr.
126/D3 **Massillon**, Oh,US
105/G **Masson** (isl.), Ant.
52/B6 **Massy**, Fr.
50/B5 **Mastgat** (chan.), Neth.
131/H5 **Mastic**, NY,US
73/J3 **Mastung**, Pak.
78/B3 **Masuda**, Japan
86/B4 **Masurai** (peak), Indo.
104/F5 **Masvingo**, Zim.
74/L4 **Maşyāf**, Syria
61/F2 **Mat** (riv.), Alb.
104/B2 **Matadi**, D.R. Congo
128/C3 **Matador**, Tx,US
116/D5 **Matagalpa**, Nic.
126/E1 **Matagami** (lake), Qu,Can
128/D4 **Matagorda** (bay), Tx,US
128/D4 **Matagorda** (isl.), Tx,US
84/D6 **Matale**, SrL.
98/B3 **Matam**, Sen.
116/A2 **Matamoros**, Mex.
116/B2 **Matamoros**, Mex.
97/K3 **Ma'ṭan as Sarra** (well), Libya
127/H1 **Matane**, Qu,Can
127/H1 **Matane** (riv.), Qu,Can
116/E3 **Matanzas**, Cuba
110/B2 **Matão**, Braz.
127/H1 **Matapedia** (riv.), Qu,Can
112/C2 **Mataquito** (riv.), Chile
72/C6 **Matara** (ruins), Egypt
84/D6 **Matara**, SrL.
87/E5 **Mataram**, Indo.
59/G2 **Mataró**, Sp.
93/L7 **Mataura**, FrPol.
92/H6 **Mata Utu** (cap.), Wall.
131/F5 **Matawan**, NJ,US
116/A3 **Matehuala**, Mex.
60/E2 **Matera**, It.
117/F3 **Maternillos** (pt.), Cuba
62/F2 **Mátészalka**, Hun.
131/C3 **Mathews** (lake), Ca,US
128/D4 **Mathis**, Tx,US
84/C2 **Mathura**, India
82/E6 **Mati**, Phil.
110/K6 **Matias Barbosa**, Braz.
116/B4 **Matías Romero**, Mex.
60/A4 **Mātir**, Tun.
45/G5 **Matlock**, Eng,UK
108/G7 **Mato Grosso**, Braz.
109/G6 **Mato Grosso** (plat.), Braz.
110/A1 **Mato Grosso do Sul** (state), Braz.
104/E5 **Matopos**, Zim.
58/A2 **Matosinhos**, Port.
73/G4 **Maţraḩ**, Oman
102/B4 **Matroosberg** (peak), SAfr.
100/A2 **Maţrūḩ**, Egypt
100/B2 **Maţrūḩ** (gov.), Egypt
103/H8 **Matsiatra** (riv.), Madg.
79/L10 **Matsubara**, Japan
79/H7 **Matsubushi**, Japan
79/H7 **Matsuda**, Japan
79/H7 **Matsudo**, Japan
78/C3 **Matsue**, Japan
77/N3 **Matsumae**, Japan
79/E2 **Matsumoto**, Japan
78/E3 **Matsusaka**, Japan
79/G1 **Matsushima**, Japan
78/E2 **Matsutō**, Japan
78/C4 **Matsuyama**, Japan
126/D1 **Mattagami** (riv.), On,Can
126/E2 **Mattawa**, On,Can
57/G4 **Matterhorn** (pk.), It., Swi.
132/Q16 **Matteson**, Il,US
130/H2 **Matthews** (mtn.), Ak,US
117/G3 **Matthew Town**, Bahm.
78/E2 **Mattō**, Japan
44/B4 **Mattock** (riv.), Ire.
126/B4 **Mattoon**, Il,US
117/J6 **Maturín**, Ven.
104/E4 **Matusadona Nat'l Park**, Zim.
87/F2 **Matutum** (mt.), Phil.
108/G3 **Maú** (riv.), Braz., Guy.
110/C2 **Mauá**, Braz.
52/C3 **Maubeuge**, Fr.
85/G4 **Ma-ubin**, Myan.
43/D2 **Maud**, Sc,UK
84/D2 **Maudaha**, India
108/G4 **Maués**, Braz.
108/G4 **Maués Açu** (riv.), Braz.
92/D3 **Maug** (isls.), NMar.
44/D3 **Maughold**, IM,UK
44/D3 **Maughold Head** (pt.), IM,UK
56/F5 **Mauguio**, Fr.
120/T10 **Maui** (isl.), Hi,US
93/K7 **Mauke** (isl.), Cookls.
52/A6 **Mauldre** (riv.), Fr.
112/B2 **Maule** (reg.), Chile
112/C1 **Maule** (riv.), Chile
56/C3 **Mauléon**, Fr.
112/B4 **Maullín**, Chile
126/C3 **Maumee** (riv.), In, Oh,US
104/D4 **Maun**, Bots.
120/U11 **Mauna Kea** (vol.), Hi,US
120/U11 **Mauna Loa** (vol.), Hi,US
93/K6 **Maupiti** (isl.), FrPol.
84/C2 **Mau Rānīpur**, India
52/A6 **Maurepas**, Fr.
127/F2 **Mauricie Nat'l Park**, Qu,Can
98/B2 **Mauritania**
103/S15 **Mauritius**
126/B3 **Mauston**, Wi,US
62/E5 **Mavrovo Nat'l Park**, FYROM
83/B4 **Maw Daung** (pass), Thai.
105/D **Mawson** (coast), Ant.
105/E **Mawson** (sta.), Ant.
116/D3 **Maxcanú**, Mex.
53/F6 **Maxéville**, Fr.
126/F4 **May** (cape), NJ,US
86/C4 **Maya** (isl.), Indo.
69/P4 **Maya** (riv.), Rus.
117/G3 **Mayaguana** (isl.), Bahm.
117/H4 **Mayagüez**, PR
73/K1 **Mayakovskogo** (peak), Taj.
117/F3 **Mayarí**, Cuba
79/L10 **Maya-san** (peak), Japan
44/D1 **Maybole**, Sc,UK
97/N5 **Maych'ew**, Eth.
53/G3 **Mayen**, Ger.
56/C2 **Mayenne**, Fr.
56/C3 **Mayenne** (riv.), Fr.
122/E2 **Mayerthorpe**, Ab,Can
126/B4 **Mayfield**, Ky,US
66/G3 **Maykop**, Rus.
47/G3 **Mayland**, Eng,UK
85/G3 **Maymyo**, Myan.
112/C5 **Mayo** (riv.), Arg.
130/L3 **Mayo**, Yk,Can
117/N8 **Mayo** (riv.), Mex.
58/D1 **Mayor** (cape), Sp.
103/H6 **Mayotte** (terr.), Fr.
117/F4 **May Pen**, Jam.
126/D4 **Maysville**, Ky,US
123/J4 **Mayville**, ND,US
132/Q16 **Maywood**, Il,US
104/E4 **Mazabuka**, Zam.
56/E5 **Mazamet**, Fr.
60/C4 **Mazara** (val.), It.
60/C4 **Mazara del Vallo**, It.
73/J1 **Mazār-e Sharīf**, Afg.
58/A1 **Mazaricos**, Sp.
58/E4 **Mazarrón**, Sp.
108/G2 **Mazaruni** (riv.), Guy.
116/C5 **Mazatenango**, Guat.
117/N9 **Mazatlán**, Mex.
64/D4 **Mažeikiai**, Lith.
90/B3 **Mazeppa Nat'l Park**, Austl.
44/B3 **Mazetown**, NI,UK
52/B3 **Mazingarbe**, Fr.
104/C2 **Mazingu**, D.R. Congo
76/D3 **Mazong** (peak), China
49/L2 **Mazury** (reg.), Pol.
66/D1 **Mazyr**, Bela.
103/E2 **Mbabane** (cap.), Swaz.
95/H6 **Mbabo** (peak), Camr.
96/J7 **Mbaïki**, CAfr.
97/H6 **Mbakaou** (lake), Camr.
101/A5 **Mbala**, Zam.
96/H7 **Mbalam**, Camr.
101/B2 **Mbale**, Ugan.
96/H7 **Mbalmayo**, Camr.
99/H5 **Mbam** (riv.), Camr.
99/H5 **Mbam, Massif du** (peak), Camr.
97/J7 **Mbandaka**, D.R. Congo
101/A3 **Mbarara**, Ugan.
97/J7 **Mbata**, CAfr.
93/Y18 **Mbengga** (isl.), Fiji
101/B5 **Mbeya**, Tanz.
101/B5 **Mbeya** (prov.), Tanz.
101/B5 **Mbeya** (range), Tanz.
104/B1 **M'Bigou**, Gabon
96/G7 **Mbini**, EqG.
96/H7 **Mbini** (riv.), EqG.
97/L6 **Mbomou** (riv.), CAfr.
98/B3 **Mboune, Vallée du** (wadi), Sen.
98/A3 **M'Bour**, Sen.
104/D2 **Mbuji-Mayi**, D.R. Congo
125/J4 **McAlester**, Ok,US
128/D5 **McAllen**, Tx,US
122/C2 **McBride**, BC,Can
122/D4 **McCall**, Id,US
128/C4 **McCamey**, Tx,US
132/C3 **McChord A.F.B.**, Wa,US
132/M9 **McClellan A.F.B.**, Ca,US
123/H4 **McClusky**, ND,US
129/F4 **McComb**, Ms,US
125/G2 **McConaughy** (lake), Ne,US
125/G2 **McCook**, Ne,US
129/H3 **McCormick**, SC,US
123/J3 **McCreary**, Mb,Can
124/C2 **McDermitt**, Nv,US
39/N8 **McDonald** (isls.), Austl.
130/F3 **McDonald** (mtn.), Ak,US
130/L2 **McDougall** (pass), NW, Yk,Can
128/F3 **McGehee**, Ar,US
129/F3 **McGehee**, Ar,US
122/D2 **McGregor** (riv.), BC,Can
132/G7 **McGregor**, On,Can
132/P15 **McHenry**, Il,US
93/H5 **McKean** (atoll), Kiri.
119/K2 **McKeand** (riv.), Nun.,Can
126/E3 **McKeesport**, Pa,US
129/F2 **McKenzie**, Tn,US
130/H3 **McKinley** (mtn.), Ak,US
130/J3 **McKinley Park**, Ak,US
122/B5 **McKinleyville**, Ca,US
128/D3 **McKinney**, Tx,US
123/H4 **McLaughlin**, SD,US
131/J8 **McLean**, Va,US
122/D2 **McLennan**, Ab,Can
122/D2 **McLeod** (riv.), Ab,Can
118/E2 **McLeod** (bay), NW,Can
122/C2 **McLeod Lake**, BC,Can
118/F1 **M'Clintock** (chan.), Nun.,Can
119/Q7 **M'Clure** (str.), NW,Can
122/C4 **McMinnville**, Or,US
129/G3 **McMinnville**, Tn,US
105/M **McMurdo**, Ant.
132/B3 **McNeil** (isl.), Wa,US
104/F3 **Mcocha**, Malw.
125/H3 **McPherson**, Ks,US
76/E5 **Mê** (riv.), China
124/D3 **Mead** (lake), Az, Nv,US
130/G2 **Meade** (riv.), Ak,US
122/F2 **Meadow Lake**, Sk,Can
127/Q8 **Meadowvale**, On,Can
124/D3 **Meadow Valley** (riv.), Nv,US
129/F4 **Meadville**, Ms,US
126/D3 **Meadville**, Pa,US
109/J5 **Mearim** (riv.), Braz.
47/E1 **Measham**, Eng,UK
130/F2 **Meat** (mtn.), Ak,US
44/B4 **Meath** (co.), Ire.
123/G2 **Meath Park**, Sk,Can
52/B6 **Meaux**, Fr.
72/C4 **Mecca** (Makkah), SAr.
52/D1 **Mechelen** (Malines), Belg.
48/F1 **Mecklenburger Bucht** (bay), Ger.
48/F2 **Mecklenburg-Western Pomerania** (state), Ger.
104/G3 **Mecuia** (peak), Moz.
84/C4 **Medak**, India
86/A3 **Medan**, Indo.
113/L7 **Medanosa** (pt.), Arg.
47/F1 **Medbourne**, Eng,UK
51/F6 **Medebach**, Ger.
108/C2 **Medellín**, Col.
50/C3 **Medemblik**, Neth.
45/G5 **Meden** (riv.), Eng,UK
131/H5 **Medford**, NY,US
122/C5 **Medford**, Or,US
126/B2 **Medford**, Wi,US
63/J3 **Medgidia**, Rom.
63/G2 **Mediaş**, Rom.
122/D4 **Medical Lake**, Wa,US
124/F2 **Medicine Bow** (range), Co, Wy,US
123/G5 **Medicine Bow**, Wy,US
122/F3 **Medicine Hat**, Ab,Can
47/E5 **Medina** (riv.), Eng,UK
123/J4 **Medina**, ND,US
126/D3 **Medina**, Oh,US
125/H5 **Medina**, Tx,US
72/C4 **Medina** (Al Madīnah), SAr.
58/C2 **Medina del Campo**, Sp.
58/C4 **Medina-Sidonia**, Sp.
39/K4 **Mediterranean** (sea)
122/F2 **Medley**, Ab,Can
67/L2 **Mednogorsk**, Rus.
67/H2 **Medveditsa, Gora** (riv.), Rus.
69/S2 **Medvezh'i** (isls.), Rus.
64/G3 **Medvezh'yegorsk**, Rus.
124/F2 **Meeker**, Co,US
51/G3 **Meerbach** (riv.), Ger.
50/D6 **Meerbusch**, Ger.
53/E1 **Meerhout**, Belg.
53/E2 **Meerssen**, Neth.
84/C2 **Meerut**, India
47/E1 **Meese** (riv.), Eng,UK
122/F4 **Meeteetse**, Wy,US
97/N7 **Mēga**, Eth.
97/P6 **Megalo**, Eth.
127/G2 **Megantic** (peak), Qu,Can
61/H3 **Mégara**, Gre.
85/F2 **Meghalaya** (state), India
74/N7 **Megiddo** (ruins), Isr.
126/E1 **Mégiscane** (lake), Qu,Can
126/E1 **Mégiscane** (riv.), Qu,Can
74/B3 **Megista** (isl.), Gre.
53/E2 **Mehaigne** (riv.), Belg.
51/G1 **Mehe** (riv.), Ger.
84/C3 **Mehkar**, India
73/F3 **Mehrān** (riv.), Iran
72/F2 **Mehriz**, Iran
84/B3 **Mehsāna**, India
82/C2 **Mei** (riv.), China
82/C3 **Mei** (riv.), China
110/B1 **Meia Ponte** (riv.), Braz.
96/H6 **Meiganga**, Camr.
119/R6 **Meighen** (isl.), Nun.,Can
77/K3 **Meihekou**, China
83/A1 **Meiktila**, Myan.
51/H4 **Meine**, Ger.
51/E6 **Meinerzhagen**, Ger.
57/J1 **Meiningen**, Ger.
81/C5 **Meishan** (res.), China
49/G3 **Meissen**, Ger.
51/G6 **Meissner** (peak), Ger.
79/M10 **Meiwa**, Japan
82/C3 **Meizhou**, China
96/H7 **Mekambo**, Gabon
97/N5 **Mek'elē**, Eth.
96/D1 **Meknès**, Mor.
71/K8 **Mekong** (riv.), Asia
87/F4 **Mekongga** (peak), Indo.
83/D4 **Mekong, Mouths of the**, Viet.
86/B3 **Melaka**, Malay.
92/E5 **Melanesia** (reg.)
84/C6 **Melappālaiyam**, India
86/D4 **Melawi** (riv.), Indo.
47/G2 **Melbourn**, Eng,UK
91/F5 **Melbourne**, Austl.
118/F2 **Melbourne** (isl.), Nun.,Can
45/G6 **Melbourne**, Eng,UK
129/H4 **Melbourne**, Fl,US
112/B5 **Melchor** (isl.), Chile
116/D4 **Melchor de Mencos**, Mex.
116/A2 **Melchor Múzquiz**, Mex.
46/D5 **Melcombe Regis**, Eng,UK
48/E1 **Meldorf**, Ger.
62/E3 **Melenci**, Yugo.
64/J5 **Melenki**, Rus.
67/K1 **Meleuz**, Rus.
119/J3 **Mélèzes** (riv.), Qu,Can
96/J5 **Melfi**, Chad
60/D2 **Melfi**, It.
123/G2 **Melfort**, Sk,Can
42/D3 **Melhus**, Nor.
96/E1 **Melilla**, Sp.
112/B5 **Melimoyu** (peak), Chile
112/Q9 **Melipilla**, Chile
61/F3 **Melissano**, It.
123/H3 **Melita**, Mb,Can
60/D4 **Melito di Porto Salvo**, It.
66/E3 **Melitopol'**, Ukr.
57/L2 **Melk**, Aus.
97/P7 **Melka Meri**, Eth.
46/D4 **Melksham**, Eng,UK
52/C2 **Melle**, Belg.
51/F4 **Melle**, Ger.
42/E4 **Mellerud**, Swe.
58/B1 **Mellid**, Sp.
45/F3 **Melling**, Eng,UK
113/J7 **Mellizo Sur** (peak), Chile
57/J1 **Mellrichstadt**, Ger.
51/F1 **Mellum** (isl.), Ger.
57/L1 **Mělník**, Czh.
113/G2 **Melo**, Uru.
132/Q16 **Melrose Park**, Il,US
51/G6 **Melsungen**, Ger.
45/G4 **Meltham**, Eng,UK
91/C3 **Melton**, Austl.
45/H6 **Melton Mowbray**, Eng,UK
56/E2 **Melun**, Fr.
90/B1 **Melville** (cape), Austl.
92/B6 **Melville** (isl.), Austl.
119/L3 **Melville** (lake), Nf,Can
119/R7 **Melville** (isl.), NW,Nun.,Can
119/H2 **Melville** (pen.), Nun.,Can
123/H3 **Melville**, Sk,Can
87/E2 **Melville** (cape), Phil.
131/G5 **Melville**, NY,US
132/F7 **Melvindale**, Mi,US
62/D2 **Mélykút**, Hun.
75/D5 **Mēmar** (lake), China
50/D1 **Memmert** (isl.), Ger.
55/G2 **Memmingen**, Ger.
83/D4 **Memot**, Camb.
86/B2 **Memphis** (ruins), Egypt
132/G6 **Memphis**, Mi,US
125/J2 **Memphis**, Mo,US
129/F3 **Memphis**, Tn,US
128/C3 **Memphis**, Tx,US
128/E3 **Mena**, Ar,US
44/D5 **Menai** (str.), Wal,UK
44/D5 **Menai Bridge**, Wal,UK
50/C2 **Menaldum**, Neth.
103/H9 **Menarandra** (riv.), Madg.
128/D4 **Menard**, Tx,US
126/B2 **Menasha**, Wi,US
103/H7 **Menavava** (riv.), Madg.
86/D4 **Mendawai** (riv.), Indo.
56/E4 **Mende**, Fr.
51/E6 **Menden**, Ger.
130/E4 **Mendenhall** (cape), Ak,US
74/B3 **Menderes, Büyük** (riv.), Turk.
110/K7 **Mendes**, Braz.
97/N6 **Mendī**, Eth.
53/G3 **Mendig**, Ger.
46/D4 **Mendip** (hills), Eng,UK
124/B3 **Mendocino**, Ca,US
120/B3 **Mendocino** (cape), Ca,US
112/C2 **Mendoza**, Arg.
112/C2 **Mendoza** (prov.), Arg.
103/H9 **Mendrare** (riv.), Madg.
62/F3 **Menedinţi** (co.), Rom.
117/G6 **Mene Grande**, Ven.
74/A2 **Menemen**, Turk.
52/C2 **Menen**, Belg.
101/C3 **Menengai Crater**, Kenya
76/H2 **Menengiyn** (plain), Mong.
60/C4 **Menfi**, It.
86/C4 **Menggala**, Indo.
58/D4 **Mengíbar**, Sp.
81/D4 **Menglianggu** (mtn.), China
91/B2 **Menindee** (lake), Austl.
112/B5 **Menlolat** (peak), Chile
132/K12 **Menlo Park**, Ca,US
126/C2 **Menominee**, Mi,US
126/B3 **Menomonee Falls**, Wi,US
126/B2 **Menomonie**, Wi,US
59/H3 **Menorca** (Minorca) (isl.), Sp.
86/A4 **Mentawai** (isls.), Indo.
86/A4 **Mentawai** (str.), Indo.
131/C2 **Mentone**, Ca,US
128/C4 **Mentone**, Tx,US
126/D3 **Mentor**, Oh,US
87/E3 **Menyapa** (peak), Indo.
130/M3 **Menzie** (mtn.), Yk,Can
47/E5 **Meon** (riv.), Eng,UK
117/N8 **Meoqui**, Mex.
87/H4 **Meos Waar** (isl.), Indo.
104/B2 **Mepala**, Ang.
67/G4 **Mepistskaro** (peak), Geo.
50/D3 **Meppel**, Neth.
51/E3 **Meppen**, Ger.
59/E2 **Mequinenzo** (res.), Sp.
125/K3 **Meramec** (riv.), Mo,US
55/H4 **Merano**, It.
86/D4 **Meratus** (mts.), Indo.
92/D5 **Merauke**, Indo.
97/P7 **Merca**, Som.
57/G4 **Mercantour Nat'l Park**, Fr.
124/B3 **Merced**, Ca,US
124/C3 **Merced** (riv.), Ca,US
112/C1 **Mercedario** (peak), Arg.
112/D2 **Mercedes**, Arg.
112/F2 **Mercedes**, Arg.
113/F2 **Mercedes**, Uru.
132/C2 **Mercer Island**, Wa,US
131/F5 **Mercerville-Hamilton Square**, NJ,US
52/D2 **Merchtem**, Belg.
127/N7 **Mercier**, Qu,Can
122/D2 **Mercoal**, Ab,Can
124/D3 **Mercury**, Nv,US
119/K2 **Mercy** (cape), Yk,Can
55/E5 **Merdellou** (mtn.), Fr.
46/D4 **Mere**, Eng,UK
113/M8 **Meredith** (cape), Falk.
128/C3 **Meredith** (lake), Tx,US
66/F2 **Merefa**, Ukr.
52/C2 **Merelbeke**, Belg.
83/D3 **Mereuch**, Camb.
77/J2 **Mergel** (riv.), China
83/B3 **Mergui**, Myan.
83/B4 **Mergui** (arch.), Myan.
52/B3 **Méricourt**, Fr.
116/D3 **Mérida**, Mex.
58/B3 **Mérida**, Sp.
117/G6 **Mérida**, Ven.
108/D2 **Mérida**, Ven.
129/F3 **Meridian**, Ms,US
128/D4 **Meridian**, Tx,US
132/C2 **Meridian-East Hill**, Wa,US
56/C4 **Mérignac**, Fr.
52/D1 **Merksem**, Belg.
50/B6 **Merksplas**, Belg.
97/M4 **Meroe** (ruins), Sudan
74/K5 **Meron, Har** (mtn.), Isr.
91/F5 **Merri** (cr.), Austl.
131/G5 **Merrick**, NY,US
126/B2 **Merrill**, Wi,US
127/G3 **Merrimack**, NH,US
46/D5 **Merriott**, Eng,UK
122/C3 **Merritt**, BC,Can
129/H4 **Merritt Island**, Fl,US
45/F5 **Mersey** (riv.), Eng,UK
45/F5 **Merseyside** (co.), Eng,UK
74/C3 **Mersin**, Turk.
86/B3 **Mersing**, Malay.
53/F5 **Merten**, Fr.
46/C3 **Merthyr Tydfil**, Wal,UK
46/C3 **Merthyr Tydfil** (co.), Wal,UK
105/K **Mertz** (glac.), Ant.
128/C4 **Mertzon**, Tx,US
52/B5 **Méru**, Fr.
101/C2 **Meru**, Kenya
52/B2 **Merville**, Fr.
50/C5 **Merwedekanaal** (can.), Neth.
53/F2 **Merzenich**, Ger.
74/C2 **Merzifon**, Turk.
53/F5 **Merzig**, Ger.
113/K7 **Mesa** (peak), Arg.
130/G3 **Mesa** (mtn.), Ak,US
124/E4 **Mesa**, Az,US
123/K4 **Mesabi** (range), Mn,US
117/M8 **Mesa del Seri**, Mex.
61/E2 **Mesagne**, It.
61/J5 **Mesarás** (gulf), Gre.
124/E3 **Mesa Verde Nat'l Park**, Co,US
128/C3 **Mescalero** (ridge), NM,US
51/F6 **Meschede**, Ger.
57/H4 **Mesco, Punta di** (pt.), It.
126/F1 **Mesgouez** (lake), Qu,Can
61/G3 **Mesolóngion**, Gre.
112/F2 **Mesopotamia** (reg.), Arg.
72/D2 **Mesopotamia** (reg.), Iraq
60/E3 **Mesoraca**, It.
128/D3 **Mesquite**, Tx,US
96/E1 **Mesrouh** (peak), Mor.
96/F1 **Messaad**, Alg.
113/J7 **Messier** (chan.), Chile
60/D3 **Messina**, It.
60/D4 **Messina** (str.), It.
104/F5 **Messina**, SAfr.
61/H4 **Messíni**, Gre.
61/H4 **Messini** (gulf), Gre.
63/F5 **Mesta** (riv.), Bul.
57/K4 **Mestre**, It.
98/C5 **Mesurado** (cape), Libr.
127/G1 **Métabetchouan**, Qu,Can
127/G1 **Métabetchouane** (riv.), Qu,Can
119/K2 **Meta Incognita** (pen.), Nun.,Can
129/F4 **Metairie**, La,US
111/D2 **Metán**, Arg.
60/E2 **Metapontum** (ruins), It.
61/G3 **Metéora**, Gre.
45/H5 **Metheringham**, Eng,UK
61/G4 **Methóni**, Gre.
62/C4 **Metković**, Cro.
126/B4 **Metropolis**, Il,US
53/D3 **Mettet**, Belg.
51/E4 **Mettingen**, Ger.
53/F5 **Mettlach**, Ger.
50/D6 **Mettmann**, Ger.
97/N6 **Metu**, Eth.
131/F5 **Metuchen**, NJ,US
53/F5 **Metz**, Fr.
52/C2 **Meulebeke**, Belg.
53/E6 **Meurthe-et-Moselle** (dept.), Fr.
53/E3 **Meuse** (riv.), Belg., Fr.
52/E6 **Meuse** (dept.), Fr.
53/E5 **Meuse, Cotes de** (uplands), Fr.
74/N9 **Mevasseret Ẕiyyon**, Isr.
45/G5 **Mexborough**, Eng,UK
128/D4 **Mexia**, Tx,US
109/J3 **Mexiana**, Braz.
117/L7 **Mexicali**, Mex.
116/A3 **Mexico**
116/B4 **México** (state), Mex.
125/J5 **Mexico** (gulf), NAm
125/K3 **Mexico**, Mo,US
116/B4 **Mexico** (cap.), Mex.
72/F2 **Meybod**, Iran
102/Q13 **Meyerton**, SAfr.
73/H1 **Meymaneh**, Afg.
74/K6 **Meẕada, Ḥorvot** (Masada) (ruins), Isr.
63/F4 **Mezdra**, Bul.
64/J2 **Mezen'** (bay), Rus.
65/K2 **Mezen'** (riv.), Rus.
68/J4 **Mezhdurechensk**, Rus.

164
Mezhd – Moret

68/E2 Mezhdusharskiy (isl.), Rus.
62/E2 Mezőberény, Hun.
62/E2 Mezőkovácsháza, Hun.
62/E2 Mezőkövesd, Hun.
62/E2 Mezőtúr, Hun.
84/C3 Mhow, India
81/D3 Mi (riv.), China
116/B4 Miahuatlán, Mex.
58/C3 Miajadas, Sp.
124/E4 Miami, Az,US
129/H5 Miami, Fl,US
125/J3 Miami, Ok,US
129/H5 Miami Beach, Fl,US
81/B4 Mianchi, China
72/E1 Mīāndoāb, Iran
72/E1 Mīāneh, Iran
131/G4 Mianus (riv.), Ct,US
73/K2 Miānwāli, Pak.
76/E5 Mianyang, China
82/B2 Miao'er (peak), China
81/E3 Miaodao (isls.), China
81/H6 Miaofeng Shan (mtn.), China
65/P5 Miass, Rus.
65/Q5 Miass (riv.), Rus.
49/J2 Miastko, Pol.
100/C5 Miberika, Sudan
122/D2 Mica Creek, BC,Can
49/L4 Michalovce, Slvk.
130/K2 Michelson (mtn.), Ak,US
126/C3 Michigan (lake), Can., US
126/C2 Michigan (state), US
126/C3 Michigan City, In,US
126/C2 Michipicoten (isl.), On,Can
116/A4 Michoacán (state), Mex.
67/G1 Michurinsk, Rus.
45/F2 Mickle Fell (mtn.), Eng,UK
45/F2 Mickleton, Eng,UK
116/E5 Mico (riv.), Nic.
117/J5 Micoud, StL.
92/E3 Micronesia (reg.)
92/D4 Micronesia, Fed. States of
99/G2 Midal (well), Niger
123/H3 Midale, Sk,Can
50/A6 Middelburg, Neth.
102/D3 Middelburg, SAfr.
103/E2 Middelburg, SAfr.
48/E1 Middelfart, Den.
50/B5 Middelharnis, Neth.
52/B1 Middelkerke, Belg.
124/C2 Middle Alkali (lake), Ca,US
85/F5 Middle Andaman (isl.), India
127/F2 Middlebury, Vt,US
128/C4 Middle Concho (riv.), Tx,US
45/G3 Middleham, Eng,UK
125/G2 Middle Loup (riv.), Ne,US
125/J2 Middle Raccoon (riv.), Ia,US
131/K7 Middle River, Md,US
126/D4 Middlesboro, Ky,US
45/G2 Middlesbrough, Eng,UK
45/G2 Middlesbrough (co.), Eng,UK
47/F4 Middlesex (reg.), Eng,UK
131/F5 Middlesex, NJ,US
122/C4 Middle Sister (peak), Or,US
45/F4 Middleton, Eng,UK
47/E2 Middleton Cheney, Eng,UK
45/F2 Middleton-in-Teesdale, Eng,UK
44/B3 Middletown, NI,UK
131/F5 Middletown, NJ,US
45/F5 Middlewich, Eng,UK
47/F5 Midhurst, Eng,UK
56/D5 Midi (can.), Fr.
56/D4 Midi-Pyrénées (reg.), Fr.
126/E2 Midland, On,Can
126/C3 Midland, Mi,US
128/C4 Midland, Tx,US
132/Q16 Midlothian, Il,US
56/C5 Midou (riv.), Fr.
82/D6 Midsayap, Phil.
46/D4 Midsomer Norton, Eng,UK
92/H2 Midway (isls.), PacUS
91/C4 Midway Point-Sorell, Austl.
125/H4 Midwest City, Ok,US
72/C3 Midyan (reg.), SAr.
74/E3 Midyat, Turk.
66/B4 Midzhur (peak), Bul.
62/F4 Midžor (peak), Yugo.
78/B4 Mie, Japan
78/E3 Mie (pref.), Japan
49/H2 Międzychód, Pol.
49/M3 Międzyrzec Podlaski, Pol.
49/H2 Międzyrzecz, Pol.
49/L3 Mielec, Pol.
96/J7 Miéle I, Congo
63/G2 Miercurea Ciuc, Rom.
58/C1 Mieres, Sp.
57/J3 Miesbach, Ger.
97/P6 Mī'ēso, Eth.
56/E3 Migennes, Fr.
116/A3 Miguel Auza, Mex.
110/B2 Miguelópolis, Braz.
110/K7 Miguel Pereira, Braz.
58/D3 Miguelturra, Sp.
78/D3 Mihama, Japan
78/C3 Mihara, Japan
79/G2 Miharu, Japan
73/J3 Mihrābpur, Pak.
59/E2 Mijares (riv.), Sp.
58/C4 Mijas, Sp.
50/B4 Mijdrecht, Neth.
79/N10 Mikawa (bay), Japan
79/N9 Mikawa-Mino (mts.), Japan
67/G4 Mikha Tskhakaya, Geo.
63/F4 Mikhaylovgrad, Bul.
62/F4 Mikhaylovgrad (reg.), Bul.
67/G2 Mikhaylovka, Rus.
79/K10 Miki, Japan
42/H3 Mikkeli, Fin.
61/J4 Míkonos (isl.), Gre.
61/G2 Mikri Prespa (lake), Gre.
79/M10 Mikuma, Japan
101/C4 Mikumi, Tanz.
101/C4 Mikumi Nat'l Park, Tanz.
78/E2 Mikuni, Japan
79/F2 Mikuni-tōge (pass), Japan
108/C4 Milagro, Ecu.
57/H4 Milan (Milano), It.
74/A3 Milas, Turk.
60/D3 Milazzo, It.
46/D5 Milborne Port, Eng,UK
47/G2 Mildenhall, Eng,UK
91/B2 Mildura, Austl.
128/C4 Miles, Tx,US
123/G4 Miles City, Mt,US
57/K1 Milešovka (peak), Czh.
123/G3 Milestone, Sk,Can
60/D2 Miletto (peak), It.
47/F4 Milford, Eng,UK
44/B3 Milford, NI,UK
128/D2 Milford (lake), Ks,US
124/D3 Milford, Ut,US
46/A3 Milford Haven, Wal,UK
47/E5 Milford on Sea, Eng,UK
92/G4 Mili (atoll), Mrsh.
49/J3 Milicz, Pol.
120/V13 Mililani Town, Hi,US
122/F3 Milk (riv.), Can., US
47/E4 Milk (hill), Eng,UK
122/E3 Milk River, Ab,Can
105/G Mill (isl.), Ant.
119/J2 Mill (isl.), Nun.,Can
56/E4 Millau, Fr.
132/K11 Millbrae, Ca,US
46/B6 Millbrook, Eng,UK
129/H3 Milledgeville, Ga,US
127/N6 Mille Iles (riv.), Qu,Can
126/B1 Mille Lacs (lake), On,Can
123/K4 Mille Lacs (lake), Mn,US
123/J4 Miller, SD,US
67/G2 Millerovo, Rus.
44/C1 Milleur (pt.), Sc,UK
56/D4 Millevaches (plat.), Fr.
127/Q9 Millgrove, On,Can
127/R8 Milliken, On,Can
127/G2 Millinocket, Me,US
44/C2 Millisle, NI,UK
45/E3 Millom, Eng,UK
123/G5 Mills, Wy,US
131/F5 Millstone (riv.), NJ,US
45/F3 Millthrop, Eng,UK
132/J11 Mill Valley, Ca,US
128/E3 Millwood (lake), Ar,US
92/E5 Milne (bay), PNG
45/F4 Milnrow, Eng,UK
98/C4 Milo (riv.), Gui.
127/G2 Milo, Me,US
61/J4 Mílos (isl.), Gre.
132/L12 Milpitas, Ca,US
57/H1 Milseburg (peak), Ger.
127/Q8 Milton, On,Can
45/F2 Milton, Eng,UK
47/G4 Milton, Eng,UK
129/G4 Milton, Fl,US
127/G3 Milton, NH,US
122/D4 Milton-Freewater, Or,US
127/Q8 Milton Heights, On,Can
47/F2 Milton Keynes, Eng,UK
47/F2 Milton Keynes (co.), Eng,UK
43/H7 Miltown Malbay, Ire.
82/B2 Miluo, China
46/C4 Milverton, Eng,UK
132/Q13 Milwaukee, Wi,US
78/B4 Mimi (riv.), Japan
56/C4 Mimizan, Fr.
82/C2 Min (riv.), China
85/H2 Min (riv.), China
124/C3 Mina, Nv,US
87/F3 Minahasa (pen.), Indo.
79/M10 Minakuchi, Japan
78/B4 Minamata, Japan
79/F3 Minami-Alps Nat'l Park, Japan
79/M10 Minamichita, Japan
92/D2 Minamiiō (isl.), Japan
92/E2 Minami-Tori-Shima (isl.), Japan
113/G2 Minas, Uru.
116/E3 Minas de Matahambre, Cuba
58/B4 Minas de Ríotinto, Sp.
110/H6 Minas Gerais (state), Braz.
85/F3 Minbu, Myan.
112/C1 Mincha, Chile
46/D3 Minchinhampton, Eng,UK
112/B4 Minchinmávida (vol.), Chile
82/D6 Mindanao (isl.), Phil.
82/D6 Mindanao (sea), Phil.
55/G1 Mindel (riv.), Ger.
51/F4 Minden, Ger.
128/E3 Minden, La,US
125/H2 Minden, Ne,US
82/D5 Mindoro (isl.), Phil.
82/D5 Mindoro (str.), Phil.
46/C4 Minehead, Eng,UK
109/H7 Mineiros, Braz.
131/G5 Mineola, NY,US
67/G3 Mineral'nye Vody, Rus.
128/D3 Mineral Wells, Tx,US
57/H5 Minerbio (pt.), Fr.
81/C3 Ming (riv.), China
67/H4 Mingäçevir, Azer.
67/H4 Mingäçevir (res.), Azer.
127/J1 Mingan (riv.), Qu,Can
73/K2 Mingāora, Pak.
83/A1 Mingun (ruins), Myan.
58/B1 Minho (riv.), Sp.
123/L3 Miniss (lake), On,Can
123/H2 Minitonas, Mb,Can
123/K4 Minneapolis, Mn,US
123/J3 Minnedosa, Mb,Can
123/K4 Minnesota (state), US
123/K4 Minnesota (riv.), Mn,US
44/D2 Minnigaff, Sc,UK
126/B1 Minnis (lake), On,Can
126/A1 Minnitaki (lake), On,Can
79/E3 Mino, Japan
79/F3 Minobu, Japan
79/N9 Mino-Mikawa (mts.), Japan
79/L10 Mino'o, Japan
79/L10 Mino'o (riv.), Japan
59/G3 Minorca (Menorca) (isl.), Sp.
123/H3 Minot, ND,US
82/C2 Minqing, China
51/F1 Minsener Oog (isl.), Ger.
66/C1 Minsk (cap.), Bela.
49/L2 Mińsk Mazowiecki, Pol.
66/C1 Minskaya (prov.), Bela.
47/G4 Minster, Eng,UK
75/B4 Mintaka (pass), China
127/H2 Minto, NB,Can
118/E1 Minto (inlet), NW,Can
130/L3 Minto, Yk,Can
60/C2 Minturno, It.
100/B2 Minūf, Egypt
68/K4 Minusinsk, Rus.
127/K2 Miquelon, StP.
108/C3 Mira (riv.), Col., Ecu.
58/A2 Mira, Port.
58/A4 Mira (riv.), Port.
127/M6 Mirabel, Qu,Can
110/D2 Miracema, Braz.
109/J5 Miracema do Norte, Braz.
112/C4 Mirador (pass), Chile
84/B4 Miraj, India
131/C2 Mira-Loma, Ca,US
61/J5 Mirambéllou (gulf), Gre.
127/H2 Miramichi, NB, Can.
131/A2 Mira Monte, Ca,US
109/G8 Miranda (riv.), Braz.
58/D1 Miranda de Ebro, Sp.
57/J4 Mirandola, It.
110/B2 Mirandópolis, Braz.
110/B2 Mirante do Paranapanema, Braz.
110/B2 Mirassol, Braz.
116/D5 Miravalles (vol.), CR
58/B1 Miravalles (mtn.), Sp.
54/C1 Mirecourt, Fr.
45/G4 Mirfield, Eng,UK
66/E2 Mirgorod, Ukr.
113/G2 Mirim (lake), Braz., Uru.
73/H3 Mirjāveh, Iran
105/G Mirnyy, Ant.
69/M3 Mirnyy, Rus.
123/H2 Mirond (lake), Sk,Can
61/H4 Mirtóön (sea), Gre.
80/E5 Miryang, SKor.
84/D2 Mirzāpur, India
97/M7 Misa, D.R. Congo
100/A4 Misâha, Bîr (well), Egypt
78/D3 Misaki, Japan
126/C3 Mishawaka, In,US
130/F2 Misheguk (mtn.), Ak,US
79/F3 Mishima, Japan
60/C3 Misilmeri, It.
117/L7 Misión del Rosario, Mex.
111/F2 Misiones (mts.), Arg.
117/L8 Misión San Fernando, Mex.
62/E1 Miskolc, Hun.
79/M10 Misono, Japan
87/H4 Misool (isl.), Indo.
123/L4 Misquah (hills), Mn,US
96/J1 Mişrātah, Libya
97/L1 Mişrātah (pt.), Libya
126/D1 Missinaibi (lake), On,Can
126/D1 Missinaibi (riv.), On,Can
128/D5 Mission, Tx,US
124/C4 Mission Viejo, Ca,US
123/M2 Missisa (lake), On,Can
126/E1 Missisicabi (riv.), Qu,Can
127/Q8 Mississauga, On,Can
121/J6 Mississippi (delta), US
121/H5 Mississippi (riv.), US
129/F3 Mississippi (state), US
92/C5 Missol (isl.), Indo.
122/E4 Missoula, Mt,US
121/G3 Missouri (riv.), US
125/J3 Missouri (state), US
128/E4 Missouri City, Tx,US
123/H3 Missouri, Coteau du (upland), Can., US
90/B3 Mistake (cr.), Austl.
127/L2 Mistaken (pt.), Can.
127/F1 Mistassibi (riv.), Qu,Can
126/F1 Mistassini, Qu,Can
126/F1 Mistassini (lake), Qu,Can
127/F1 Mistassini (riv.), Qu,Can
49/J4 Mistelbach an der Zaya, Aus.
47/H3 Mistley, Eng,UK
61/H4 Mistrás (ruins), Gre.
60/D4 Mistretta, It.
130/M4 Misty Fjords Nat'l Mon., Ak,US
79/M10 Misugi, Japan
117/N9 Mita (pt.), Mex.
79/H7 Mitaka, Japan
46/D3 Mitcheldean, Eng,UK
90/A1 Mitchell (riv.), Austl.
129/H3 Mitchell (mtn.), NC,US
125/G2 Mitchell, Ne,US
123/J5 Mitchell, SD,US
90/A1 Mitchell & Alice Rivers Nat'l Park, Austl.
74/H6 Mīt Ghamr, Egypt
84/B2 Mithankot, Pak.
73/J4 Mithi, Pak.
93/K6 Mitiaro (isl.), CookIs.
61/K3 Mitilíni, Gre.
100/C2 Mitla (pass), Egypt
116/B4 Mitla (ruins), Mex.
79/G2 Mito, Japan
96/G7 Mitra (peak), EqG.
113/L8 Mitre (pen.), Arg.
52/B6 Mitry-Mory, Fr.
103/H7 Mitsinjo, Madg.
103/J6 Mitsio, Nosy (isl.), Madg.
97/N4 Mits'iwa, Erit.
79/F2 Mitsukaidō, Japan
79/F2 Mitsuke, Japan
51/F4 Mittelland (can.), Ger.
51/E3 Mittelradde (riv.), Ger.
48/G3 Mittweida, Ger.
101/A4 Mitumba (mts.), D.R. Congo
104/E2 Mitwaba, D.R. Congo
79/H7 Miura, Japan
79/H7 Miura (pen.), Japan
116/C5 Mixco Viejo (ruins), Guat.
79/M10 Miya (riv.), Japan
79/G1 Miyagi (pref.), Japan
77/N4 Miyako, Japan
82/E3 Miyako (isl.), Japan
78/B5 Miyakonojō, Japan
78/B5 Miyanojō, Japan
79/H6 Miyashiro, Japan
78/B4 Miyazaki (pref.), Japan
78/D3 Miyazu, Japan
81/D2 Miyun, China
81/D2 Miyun (res.), China
44/B6 Mizen Head (pt.), Ire.
63/H3 Mizil, Rom.
85/F3 Mizoram (state), India
79/E3 Mizunami, Japan
42/E4 Mjölby, Swe.
42/D3 Mjøsa (lake), Nor.
96/D1 Mkorn (peak), Mor.
103/F2 Mkuze (riv.), SAfr.
57/L1 Mladá Boleslav, Czh.
62/E3 Mladenovac, Yugo.
101/B4 Mlala (hills), Tanz.
49/L2 Mława, Pol.
62/C4 Mljet (isl.), Cro.
62/C4 Mljet Nat'l Park, Cro.
42/E2 Mo, Nor.
87/G5 Moa (isl.), Indo.
98/C5 Moa (riv.), Libr., SLeo.
124/E3 Moab, Ut,US
92/H6 Moala Group (isls.), Fiji
58/A1 Moaña, Sp.
104/B1 Moanda, Gabon
72/F2 Mobārakeh, Iran
125/J3 Moberly, Mo,US
122/F4 Moberly Lake, BC,Can
79/F4 Mobile, Al,US
123/H4 Mobridge, SD,US
109/J4 Mocajuba, Braz.
104/B4 Moçâmedes, Ang.
83/D4 Moc Hoa, Viet.
102/D2 Mochudi, Bots.
108/C3 Mocoa, Col.
110/G6 Mococa, Braz.
84/B3 Modāsa, India
46/C6 Modbury, Eng,UK
102/D3 Modderrivier (riv.), SAfr.
57/J4 Modena, It.
57/G2 Moder (riv.), Fr., Ger.
124/B3 Modesto, Ca,US
60/D4 Modica, It.
96/H4 Modjigo (reg.), Niger
49/J4 Mödling, Aus.
62/D3 Modriča, Bosn.
83/E3 Mo Duc, Viet.
60/E2 Modugno, It.
91/C3 Moe, Austl.
102/A2 Moeb (bay), Namb.
56/B3 Moëlan-sur-Mer, Fr.
45/E5 Moel Fammau (mtn.), Wal,UK
45/E6 Moel Fferna (mtn.), Wal,UK
46/C1 Moelfre (mtn.), UK
46/C2 Moel Hywel (mtn.), Wal,UK
45/E6 Moel Sych (mtn.), Wal,UK
46/C2 Moel y Llyn (mtn.), UK
92/E4 Moen, Micr.
124/E3 Moenkopi (dry riv.), Az,US
93/K7 Moerai, FrPol.
50/D6 Moers, Ger.
52/C1 Moervaart (can.), Belg.
44/E1 Moffat, Sc,UK
73/L2 Moga, India
97/Q7 Mogadishu (cap.), Som.
79/G2 Mogami (riv.), Japan
58/B4 Mogent (riv.), Sp.
110/G8 Mogi das Cruzes, Braz.
110/G7 Mogi-Guaçu, Braz.
66/C2 Mogilev-Podol'skiy, Ukr.
49/J2 Mogilno, Pol.
110/F7 Mogi-Mirim, Braz.
77/H1 Mogocha, Rus.
85/G3 Mogok, Myan.
113/F3 Mogotes (pt.), Arg.
58/B4 Moguer, Sp.
62/D3 Mohács, Hun.
123/H3 Mohall, ND,US
126/F3 Mohawk (riv.), NY,US
103/G6 Mohéli (isl.), Com.
104/D4 Mohembo, Bots.
130/E3 Mohican (cape), Ak,US
51/F6 Möhne (riv.), Ger.
51/F6 Möhnestausee (res.), Ger.
63/H2 Moineşti, Rom.
75/A3 Moinkum (des.), Kaz.
99/E5 Moinsi (hills), Gha.
126/E2 Moira (riv.), On,Can
56/F4 Moirans, Fr.
119/K3 Moisie (riv.), Qu,Can
56/D4 Moissac, Fr.
59/Q10 Moita, Port.
124/C4 Mojave (des.), Ca,US
110/G7 Moji-Guaçu (riv.), Braz.
123/L3 Mojikit (lake), On,Can
108/E6 Mojos (plain), Bol.
109/J4 Moju (riv.), Braz.
79/F2 Mōka, Japan
120/W13 Mokapu (pt.), Hi,US
124/B3 Mokelumne (riv.), Ca,US
132/Q16 Mokena, Il,US
92/F4 Mokil (atoll), Micr.
83/B3 Mokochu (peak), Thai.
85/F2 Mokokchūng, India
96/H5 Mokolo, Camr.
80/D5 Mokp'o, SKor.
62/E3 Mokrin, Yugo.
67/G1 Moksha (riv.), Rus.
53/E1 Mol, Belg.
62/E3 Mol, Yugo.
60/E2 Mola di Bari, It.
62/B3 Molat (isl.), Cro.
58/E3 Molatón (mtn.), Sp.
45/E5 Mold, Wal,UK
63/H2 Moldavia (reg.), Rom.
63/G2 Moldavian Carpathians (range), Rom.
42/C3 Molde, Nor.
66/C3 Moldova
63/H2 Moldova (riv.), Rom.
62/E3 Moldova Nouă, Rom.
63/G3 Moldoveanu (peak), Rom.
47/F4 Mole (riv.), Eng,UK
102/D2 Molepolole, Bots.
60/E2 Molfetta, It.
81/F2 Molihong Shan (peak), China
112/C2 Molina, Chile
58/E3 Molina de Segura, Sp.
126/B3 Moline, Il,US
60/D2 Molise (reg.), It.
57/K3 Möll (riv.), Aus.
42/D5 Møllebjerg (peak), Den.
108/D7 Mollendo, Peru
59/F2 Mollerussa, Sp.
112/C2 Molles (pt.), Chile
59/L6 Mollet del Vallès, Sp.
59/L7 Mollins de Rei, Sp.
48/F2 Mölln, Ger.
64/E5 Molodechno, Bela.
105/D Molodezhnaya, Ant.
64/H4 Mologa (riv.), Rus.
120/T10 Molokai (isl.), Hi,US
65/L4 Moloma (riv.), Rus.
102/C2 Molopo (Moloporivier) (dry riv.), Bots., SAfr.
96/J7 Moloundou, Camr.
123/J2 Molson (lake), Mb,Can
87/H5 Molu (isl.), Indo.
87/G4 Molucca (sea), Indo.
87/G3 Moluccas (isls.), Indo.
109/K5 Mombaça, Braz.
101/C4 Mombasa, Kenya
77/N3 Mombetsu, Japan
63/G5 Momchilgrad, Bul.
87/H4 Momfafa (cape), Indo.
117/G6 Mompós, Col.
85/F3 Mon (riv.), Myan.
83/B3 Mon (state), Myan.
48/G1 Møn (isl.), Den.
117/H4 Mona (passage), DRep., PR
57/G5 Monaco
57/G5 Monaco (cap.), Mona.
44/B3 Monaghan, Ire.
44/A3 Monaghan (co.), Ire.
117/E6 Monagrillo (ruins), Pan.
128/C4 Monahans, Tx,US
122/D3 Monashee (mts.), BC,Can
90/H8 Mona Vale, Austl.
59/E3 Moncada, Sp.
57/G4 Moncalieri, It.
82/E6 Moncayo, Phil.
58/D2 Moncayo (range), Sp.
64/G2 Monchegorsk, Rus.
50/D6 Mönchengladbach, Ger.
58/A4 Monchique, Port.
58/A4 Monchique (range), Port.
129/H3 Moncks Corner, SC,US
116/A2 Monclova, Mex.
127/H2 Moncton, NB,Can
58/A2 Mondego (cape), Port.
58/A2 Mondego (riv.), Port.
58/B1 Mondoñedo, Sp.
53/F5 Mondorf-les-Bains, Lux.
57/G4 Mondovi, It.
58/B1 Mondragón, Sp.
60/C2 Mondragone, It.
58/B3 Monesterio, Sp.
125/J3 Monett, Mo,US
44/C2 Money Head (pt.), Sc,UK
44/B2 Moneymore, NI,UK
44/C2 Moneyreagh, NI,UK
57/K4 Monfalcone, It.
57/H4 Monferrato (reg.), It.
58/B1 Monforte, Sp.
110/G9 Mongaguá, Braz.
83/D1 Mong Cai, Viet.
84/E2 Monghyr, India
97/J5 Mongo, Chad
98/C4 Mongo (riv.), Gui., SLeo.
76/D2 Mongolia
97/K5 Mongororo, Chad
104/B1 Mongoungou, Gabon
104/D4 Mongu, Zam.
75/F2 Mönh Hayrhan Uul (peak), Mong.
76/E1 Mönh Sarĭdag (peak), Mong.
44/E1 Moniaive, Sc,UK
59/K6 Monistrol de Montserrat, Sp.
124/C3 Monitor (range), Nv,US
49/M2 Mońki, Pol.
104/D1 Monkoto, D.R. Congo
46/D3 Monmouth, Eng,UK
126/B3 Monmouth, Il,US
122/C4 Monmouth, Or,US
131/G5 Monmouth Beach, NJ,US
46/D3 Monmouthshire (co.), Wal,UK
46/D2 Monmow (riv.), UK
50/C4 Monnickendam, Neth.
99/F5 Mono (prov.), Ben.
99/F5 Mono (riv.), Ben., Togo
124/C3 Mono (lake), Ca,US
60/E2 Monopoli, It.
62/D2 Monor, Hun.
127/Q8 Mono Road, On,Can
59/E3 Monóvar, Sp.
60/C3 Monreale, It.
129/H3 Monroe, Ga,US
128/E3 Monroe, La,US
126/D3 Monroe, Mi,US
129/H3 Monroe, NC,US
124/D3 Monroe, Ut,US
126/B3 Monroe, Wi,US
129/G4 Monroeville, Al,US
98/C5 Monrovia (cap.), Libr.
131/C2 Monrovia, Ca,US
52/C3 Mons, Belg.
53/F2 Monschau, Ger.
57/J4 Monselice, It.
131/F4 Monsey, NY,US
50/B4 Monster, Neth.
42/F4 Mönsteras, Swe.
103/J6 Montagne d'Ambre Nat'l Park, Madg.
127/J2 Montague, PE,Can
130/L3 Montague, Yk,Can
130/J4 Montague (isl.), Ak,US
130/J4 Montague (str.), Ak,US
128/D3 Montague, Tx,US
60/E2 Montalbano Jonico, It.
122/F4 Montana (state), US
110/D1 Montanha, Braz.
56/E3 Montargis, Fr.
52/B5 Montataire, Fr.
56/D4 Montauban, Fr.
104/E6 Mont aux Sources (peak), Les.
56/F3 Montbard, Fr.
54/C2 Montbéliard, Fr.
59/L7 Montcada i Reixac, Sp.
56/F3 Montceau-les-Mines, Fr.
131/C2 Montclair, Ca,US
56/C5 Mont-de-Marsan, Fr.
52/B4 Montdidier, Fr.
116/B4 Monte Albán (ruins), Mex.
109/H4 Monte Alegre, Braz.
110/B1 Monte Alegre de Minas, Braz.
110/B2 Monte Alto, Braz.
109/K7 Monte Azul, Braz.
131/B2 Montebello, Ca,US
111/F2 Montecarlo, Arg.
110/C1 Monte Carmelo, Braz.
117/G6 Monte Carmelo, Ven.
111/E3 Monte Caseros, Arg.
117/G4 Monte Cristo, DRep.
60/B1 Montecristo (isl.), It.
58/C4 Montefrío, Sp.
117/F4 Montego Bay, Jam.
59/P10 Montelavar, Port.
56/F4 Montélimar, Fr.
58/C4 Montellano, Sp.
124/D2 Montello, Nv,US
112/D5 Montemayor (plat.), Arg.
116/B2 Montemorelos, Mex.
58/A3 Montemor-o-Novo, Port.
58/A2 Montemuro (mtn.), Port.
110/B4 Montenegro, Braz.
62/D4 Montenegro (rep.), Yugo.
60/D2 Montenero di Bisaccia, It.
48/B5 Montenoison, Butte de (mtn.), Fr.
109/L7 Monte Pascoal Nat'l Park, Braz.
56/E2 Montereau-faut-Yonne, Fr.
124/B3 Monterey, Ca,US
124/B3 Monterey (bay), Ca,US
131/B2 Monterey Park, Ca,US
117/F6 Montería, Col.
108/F7 Montero, Bol.
111/C2 Monteros, Arg.
60/C1 Monterotondo, It.
116/A2 Monterrey, Mex.
113/K7 Montes (pt.), Arg.
60/D2 Monte Sant'Angelo, It.
60/E2 Montescaglioso, It.
109/K7 Montes Claros, Braz.
60/D1 Montesilvano Marina, It.
56/F4 Monteux, Fr.
113/F2 Montevideo (cap.), Uru.
113/T12 Montevideo (dept.), Uru.
123/K4 Montevideo, Mn,US
53/E5 Montfaucon, Fr.
50/B4 Montfoort, Neth.
52/B6 Montgeron, Fr.
46/C1 Montgomery, Wal,UK
129/G3 Montgomery (cap.), Al,US
126/D4 Montgomery, WV,US
131/J7 Montgomery Village, Md,US
131/E5 Montgomeryville, Pa,US
56/E5 Montgrand (mtn.), Fr.
54/C5 Monthey, Swi.
128/F3 Monticello, Ar,US
132/K9 Monticello (dam), Ca,US
129/H4 Monticello, Fl,US
126/C3 Monticello, In,US
126/C4 Monticello, Ky,US
125/K2 Monticello, Mo,US
124/E3 Monticello, Ut,US
126/E4 Monticello, Va,US
52/B3 Montigny-en-Gohelle, Fr.
52/B6 Montigny-le-Bretonneux, Fr.
53/F5 Montigny-lès-Metz, Fr.
52/D3 Montigny-le-Tilleul, Belg.
58/A3 Montijo, Port.
58/B3 Montijo, Sp.
58/C4 Montilla, Sp.
56/D2 Montivilliers, Fr.
127/G1 Mont-Joli, Qu,Can
126/F2 Mont-Laurier, Qu,Can
56/E3 Montluçon, Fr.
127/G2 Montmagny, Qu,Can
56/D3 Montmorillon, Fr.
58/C3 Montoro, Sp.
98/D5 Mont Peko Nat'l Park, IvC.
122/F5 Montpelier, Id,US
127/F2 Montpelier (cap.), Vt,US
56/E5 Montpellier, Fr.
126/C2 Montreal (riv.), On,Can
127/N7 Montréal, Qu,Can
123/G2 Montreal (lake), Sk,Can
52/A3 Montreuil, Fr.
54/C5 Montreux, Swi.
43/D2 Montrose, Sc,UK
124/F3 Montrose, Co,US
127/N6 Mont-Royal, Qu,Can
52/B6 Montry, Fr.
127/P6 Mont-Saint-Hilaire, Qu,Can
53/E4 Mont-Saint-Martin, Fr.
126/F2 Mont-Saint-Michel, Qu,Can
56/C2 Mont-Saint-Michel, Fr.
56/C2 Mont-Saint-Michel (bay), Fr.
98/D4 Mont Sangbé Nat'l Park, IvC.
59/L6 Montseny Nat'l Park, Sp.
98/C5 Montserrado (co.), Libr.
59/F2 Montserrat (mtn.), Sp.
117/J4 Montserrat (isl.), UK
131/F5 Montville, NJ,US
125/G4 Monument Draw (cr.), NM, Tx,US
85/G3 Monywa, Myan.
57/H4 Monza, It.
104/E4 Monze, Zam.
59/F2 Monzón, Sp.
102/P13 Mool (riv.), SAfr.
90/D4 Mooloolaba-Maroochydore, Austl.
91/G5 Moorabbin, Austl.
123/G4 Moorcroft, Wy,US
127/R8 Moore (pt.), On,Can
125/H4 Moore, Ok,US
93/K6 Moorea (isl.), FrPol.
129/H5 Moore Haven, Fl,US
131/F6 Moorestown, NJ,US
129/H3 Mooresville, NC,US
123/J4 Moorhead, Mn,US
52/C2 Moorslede, Belg.
57/J2 Moosburg, Ger.
126/D1 Moose (riv.), On,Can
123/H3 Moose (mtn.), Sk,Can
126/D1 Moose Factory, On,Can
127/G2 Moosehead (lake), Me,US
130/H3 Mooseheart (mtn.), Ak,US
123/G3 Moose Jaw, Sk,Can
123/H3 Moosomin, Sk,Can
126/D1 Moosonee, On,Can
98/D3 Mopti, Mali
98/E3 Mopti (reg.), Mali
108/D7 Moquegua, Peru
62/D2 Mór, Hun.
96/H5 Mora, Camr.
58/D3 Mora, Sp.
42/E3 Mora, Swe.
125/F4 Mora, NM,US
125/F4 Mora (riv.), NM,US
61/F1 Morača (riv.), Yugo.
84/C2 Morādābād, India
109/L5 Morada Nova, Braz.
110/C1 Morada Nova de Mina, Braz.
112/C2 Morado Nat'l Park, Chile
103/H7 Morafenobe, Madg.
49/K2 Morąg, Pol.
132/K11 Moraga, Ca,US
112/B5 Moraleda (chan.), Chile
58/B2 Moraleja, Sp.
116/D4 Morales, Guat.
124/E2 Moran, Wy,US
90/C3 Moranbah, Austl.
93/M7 Morane (isl.), FrPol.
58/E3 Moratalla, Sp.
49/J4 Morava (riv.), Czh.
61/G1 Morava (riv.), Yugo.
49/J4 Moravia (reg.), Czh.
49/J4 Moravská Třebová, Czh.
49/H4 Moravské Budějovice, Czh.
53/G4 Morbach, Ger.
52/B2 Morbecque, Fr.
55/F5 Morbegno, It.
42/F4 Mörbylånga, Swe.
123/J3 Morden, Mb,Can
91/G6 Mordialloc, Austl.
67/G1 Mordovia, Rus.
123/H4 Moreau (riv.), SD,US
43/D3 Morebattle, Sc,UK
45/F3 Morecambe, Eng,UK
45/E3 Morecambe (bay), Eng,UK
91/D1 Moree, Austl.
126/D4 Morehead, Ky,US
129/J3 Morehead City, NC,US
116/A4 Morelia, Mex.
116/B4 Morelos (state), Mex.
84/C2 Morena, India
58/C3 Morena (range), Sp.
63/G3 Moreni, Rom.
131/C3 Moreno Valley, Ca,US
42/C3 Møre og Romsdal (co.), Nor.
131/B2 Morepack, Ca,US
118/C3 Moresby (isl.), BC,Can
90/F6 Moreton (bay), Austl.
90/D4 Moreton (cape), Austl.
46/C5 Moretonhampstead, Eng,UK
90/D4 Moreton I. Nat'l Park, Austl.

165
Moret – Natur

47/E3 **Moreton in Marsh,** Eng,UK
65/N2 **Moreyu** (riv.), Rus.
54/C4 **Morez,** Fr.
129/F4 **Morgan City,** La,US
126/C4 **Morganfield,** Ky,US
60/D4 **Morgantina** (ruins), It.
129/H3 **Morganton,** NC,US
126/C4 **Morgantown,** Ky,US
126/E4 **Morgantown,** WV,US
56/E3 **Morge** (riv.), Fr.
54/C4 **Morges,** Swi.
73/H1 **Morghāb** (riv.), Afg.
112/B3 **Morguilla** (pt.), Chile
76/C3 **Mori,** China
57/J4 **Mori,** It.
125/F4 **Moriarty,** NM,US
122/B2 **Morice** (lake), BC,Can
79/L10 **Moriguchi,** Japan
51/G5 **Moringen,** Ger.
122/E2 **Morinville,** Ab,Can
77/N4 **Morioka,** Japan
79/H7 **Moriya,** Japan
78/D3 **Moriyama,** Japan
56/B2 **Morlaix,** Fr.
52/D3 **Morlanwelz,** Belg.
45/G4 **Morley,** Eng,UK
84/B4 **Mormugao,** India
90/F6 **Morningside,** Austl.
113/J7 **Mornington** (isl.), Chile
73/J3 **Moro,** Pak.
82/D6 **Moro** (gulf), Phil.
96/C1 **Morocco**
101/C4 **Morogoro,** Tanz.
101/C4 **Morogoro** (prov.), Tanz.
91/C3 **Moroka-Wonnangatta Nat'l Park,** Austl.
103/G8 **Morombe,** Madg.
112/F2 **Morón,** Arg.
117/F3 **Morón,** Cuba
108/C4 **Morona** (riv.), Ecu., Peru
103/H8 **Morondara** (riv.), Madg.
103/H8 **Morondava,** Madg.
58/C4 **Morón de la Frontera,** Sp.
103/G5 **Moroni** (cap.), Com.
87/G3 **Morotai** (isl.), Indo.
87/G3 **Morotai** (str.), Indo.
101/B2 **Moroto,** Ugan.
79/H7 **Moroyama,** Japan
67/G2 **Morozovsk,** Rus.
45/G1 **Morpeth,** Eng,UK
74/J4 **Morphou,** Cyp.
74/J4 **Morphou** (bay), Cyp.
50/C3 **Morra** (lake), Neth.
125/G2 **Morrill,** Ne,US
110/B1 **Morrinhos,** Braz.
123/J3 **Morris,** Mb,Can
126/B3 **Morris,** Il,US
123/K4 **Morris,** Mn,US
115/P1 **Morris Jesup** (cape), Grld.
131/F5 **Morris Plains,** NJ,US
46/C3 **Morriston,** Wal,UK
131/F5 **Morristown,** NJ,US
129/H2 **Morristown,** Tn,US
131/F5 **Morrisville,** Pa,US
124/B4 **Morro Bay,** Ca,US
104/C3 **Morro de Môco** (peak), Ang.
110/B3 **Morro do Capão Doce** (hill), Braz.
109/K6 **Morro do Chapéu,** Braz.
53/G2 **Morsbach,** Ger.
67/G1 **Morshansk,** Rus.
67/J3 **Morskoy** (isl.), Kaz.
46/B4 **Morte** (pt.), UK
109/H6 **Mortes** (riv.), Braz.
47/E4 **Mortimer,** Eng,UK
46/D2 **Mortimers Cross,** Eng,UK
126/B3 **Morton,** Il,US
132/Q15 **Morton Grove,** Il,US
91/D2 **Morton Nat'l Park,** Austl.
52/D1 **Mortsel,** Belg.
56/E3 **Morvan** (plat.), Fr.
84/B3 **Morvi,** India
91/C3 **Morwell,** Austl.
58/A1 **Mos,** Sp.
57/H2 **Mosbach,** Ger.
59/P10 **Moscavide,** Port.
64/G5 **Moscow** (upland), Rus.
122/D4 **Moscow,** Id,US
65/X9 **Moscow** (Moskva) (cap.), Rus.
64/H5 **Moscow Obl.,** Rus.
105/H **Moscow Univ. Ice Shelf,** Ant.
53/F4 **Mosel** (riv.), Ger.
52/F5 **Moselle** (dept.), Fr.
53/F5 **Moselle** (riv.), Fr.
122/D4 **Moses Lake,** Wa,US
102/C2 **Moshaweng** (dry riv.), SAfr.
101/C3 **Moshi,** Tanz.
49/J2 **Mosina,** Pol.
42/E2 **Mosjøen,** Nor.
64/G5 **Moskva** (riv.), Rus.
65/X9 **Moskva** (Moscow) (inset) (cap.), Rus.
62/C2 **Mosonmagyaróvár,** Hun.
125/G4 **Mosquero,** NM,US
116/E6 **Mosquitos** (gulf), Pan.
116/E5 **Mosquitos, Costa de** (coast), Nic.
42/D4 **Moss,** Nor.
98/E4 **Mossi Highlands** (upland), Burk.
57/H2 **Mössingen,** Ger.
45/F4 **Mossley,** Eng,UK
44/C2 **Mossley,** NI,UK
109/L5 **Mossoró,** Braz.
129/F4 **Moss Point,** Ms,US
44/B1 **Moss-side,** NI,UK
57/K1 **Most,** Czh.
96/E1 **Mostaganem,** Alg.
62/C4 **Mostar,** Bosn.
58/D2 **Móstoles,** Sp.
45/E5 **Mostyn,** Wal,UK
74/E3 **Mosul** (Al Mawçil), Iraq
116/D4 **Motagua** (riv.), Guat.
42/E4 **Motala,** Swe.
81/E2 **Motian Ling** (mtn.), China
84/D2 **Motīhāri,** India
79/G2 **Motomiya,** Japan
42/K1 **Motovskiy** (gulf), Rus.
58/D4 **Motril,** Sp.
123/H4 **Mott,** ND,US
116/D3 **Motul,** Mex.
68/K4 **Motygino,** Rus.
98/B2 **Mougris** (well), Mrta.
98/E3 **Mouhoun** (prov.), Burk.
104/B1 **Mouila,** Gabon
96/H4 **Moul** (well), Niger
91/C2 **Moulamein** (riv.), Austl.
45/F5 **Mouldsworth,** Eng,UK
56/E3 **Moulins,** Fr.
83/B2 **Moulmein,** Myan.
96/E1 **Moulouya** (riv.), Mor.
47/G2 **Moulton,** Eng,UK
129/H4 **Moultrie,** Ga,US
129/H3 **Moultrie** (lake), SC,US
125/J3 **Mound City,** Ks,US
96/J6 **Moundou,** Chad
126/D4 **Moundsville,** WV,US
83/C3 **Moung Roessei,** Camb.
83/D3 **Mounlapamok,** Laos
90/B3 **Mount Aberdeen Nat'l Park,** Austl.
84/B3 **Mount Abu,** India
118/D2 **Mountain** (riv.), NW,Can
46/C3 **Mountain Ash,** Wal,UK
129/G3 **Mountain Brook,** Al,US
125/J3 **Mountain Grove,** Mo,US
128/E2 **Mountain Home,** Ar,US
122/E5 **Mountain Home,** Id,US
128/E3 **Mountain View,** Ar,US
132/K12 **Mountain View,** Ca,US
102/D4 **Mountain Zebra Nat'l Park,** SAfr.
129/H2 **Mount Airy,** NC,US
89/A4 **Mount Barker,** Austl.
91/A2 **Mount Barker,** Austl.
90/C5 **Mount Barney Nat'l Park,** Austl.
91/C3 **Mount Buffalo Nat'l Park,** Austl.
126/C4 **Mount Carmel,** Il,US
97/M2 **Mount Catherine** (peak), Egypt
132/G6 **Mount Clemens,** Mi,US
90/E6 **Mount Coot'tha,** Austl.
104/F4 **Mount Darwin,** Zim.
91/B3 **Mount Eccles Nat'l Park,** Austl.
90/B2 **Mount Elliot Nat'l Park,** Austl.
91/B3 **Mount Emu** (cr.), Austl.
91/C4 **Mount Field Nat'l Park,** Austl.
91/B3 **Mount Gambier,** Austl.
92/D5 **Mount Hagen,** PNG
131/F6 **Mount Holly,** NJ,US
127/Q9 **Mount Hope,** On,Can
91/D3 **Mount Imlay Nat'l Park,** Austl.
89/C3 **Mount Isa,** Austl.
91/D1 **Mount Kaputar Nat'l Park,** Austl.
131/G4 **Mount Kisco,** NY,US
132/C2 **Mountlake Terrace,** Wa,US
131/F6 **Mount Laurel,** NJ,US
90/D4 **Mount Mistake Nat'l Park,** Austl.
126/D3 **Mount Morris,** Mi,US
90/E6 **Mount Nebo,** Austl.
129/J3 **Mount Olive,** NC,US
61/H3 **Mount Parnes Nat'l Park,** Gre.
127/L2 **Mount Pearl,** Nf,Can
123/L5 **Mount Pleasant,** Ia,US
126/C3 **Mount Pleasant,** Mi,US
128/E3 **Mount Pleasant,** Tx,US
124/E3 **Mount Pleasant,** Ut,US
132/Q15 **Mount Prospect,** Il,US
131/K8 **Mount Rainier,** Md,US
122/C4 **Mount Rainier Nat'l Park,** Wa,US
122/D3 **Mount Revelstoke Nat'l Park,** BC,Can
91/B3 **Mount Richmond Nat'l Park,** Austl.
125/G2 **Mount Rushmore Nat'l Mem.,** SD,US
46/A6 **Mount's** (bay), Eng,UK
90/B2 **Mount Spec Nat'l Park,** Austl.
126/D4 **Mount Sterling,** Ky,US
126/B4 **Mount Vernon,** Il,US
126/C4 **Mount Vernon,** In,US
131/G5 **Mount Vernon,** NY,US
126/D3 **Mount Vernon,** Oh,US
131/J8 **Mount Vernon,** Va,US
122/C3 **Mount Vernon,** Wa,US
90/C4 **Mount Walsh Nat'l Park,** Austl.
91/E1 **Mount Warning Nat'l Park,** Austl.
91/D4 **Mount William Nat'l Park,** Austl.
58/B3 **Moura,** Port.
56/C5 **Mourenx,** Fr.
44/B3 **Mourne** (dist.), NI,UK
44/B3 **Mourne** (mts.), NI,UK
52/C2 **Mouscron,** Belg.
96/J5 **Moussoro,** Chad
52/B5 **Moussy-le-Neuf,** Fr.
52/C2 **Mouvaux,** Fr.
44/B3 **Moy,** NI,UK
101/C2 **Moyalē,** Eth.
96/D1 **Moyen Atlas** (mts.), Mor.
53/F5 **Moyeuvre-Grande,** Fr.
44/B2 **Moygashel,** NI,UK
44/B1 **Moyle** (dist.), NI,UK
87/E5 **Moyo** (isl.), Indo.
75/C4 **Moyu,** China
104/G4 **Mozambique**
104/G5 **Mozambique** (chan.), Afr.
64/H5 **Mozhaysk** Rus.
65/M4 **Mozhga,** Rus.
101/A4 **Mpanda,** Tanz.
104/C4 **Mpangu,** Namb.
101/A5 **Mpika,** Zam.
101/A5 **Mporokoso,** Zam.
99/E5 **Mpraeso,** Gha.
103/E5 **Mpumalanga** (prov.), SAfr.
49/L2 **Mrągowo,** Pol.
62/C3 **Mrkonjić Grad,** Bosn.
64/G4 **Msta** (riv.), Rus.
49/L4 **Mszana Dolna,** Pol.
66/F1 **Mtsensk,** Rus.
101/D5 **Mtwara,** Tanz.
101/C5 **Mtwara** (prov.), Tanz.
104/G4 **Mualama,** Moz.
83/D2 **Muang Gnommarat,** Laos
83/C2 **Muang Kerthao,** Laos
83/D3 **Muang Kheng,** Laos
83/D3 **Muang Khongxedon,** Laos
83/D3 **Muang Lakhonpheng,** Laos
83/D1 **Muang Soy,** Laos
83/C2 **Muang Thathom,** Laos
83/D2 **Muang Xamteu,** Laos
83/D2 **Muang Xepon,** Laos
86/B3 **Muar,** Malay.
86/B4 **Muarabungo,** Indo.
73/J4 **Muāri** (pt.), Pak.
96/H5 **Mubi,** Nga.
108/F3 **Mucajaí** (riv.), Braz.
53/G2 **Much,** Ger.
101/A5 **Muchinga** (mts.), Zam.
46/D1 **Much Wenlock,** Eng,UK
44/B2 **Muckamore Abbey,** NI,UK
104/H3 **Mucojo,** Moz.
74/C2 **Mucur,** Turk.
110/D1 **Mucuri** (riv.), Braz.
104/D3 **Mucussueje,** Ang.
77/K3 **Mudanjiang,** China
63/J5 **Mudanya,** Turk.
77/K2 **Muddan** (riv.), China
42/F2 **Muddas Nat'l Park,** Swe.
124/E3 **Muddy** (riv.) Ut,US
125/H4 **Muddy Boggy** (cr.), Ok,US
53/G2 **Mudersbach,** Ger.
91/D2 **Mudgee,** Austl.
122/G1 **Mudjatik** (riv.), Sk,Can
132/D3 **Mud Mountain** (lake), Wa,US
83/B2 **Mudon,** Myan.
113/J8 **Muela** (peak), Chile
74/N8 **Mufjir, Nahr** (dry riv.), WBnk.
104/E3 **Mufulira,** Zam.
58/A1 **Mugardos,** Sp.
57/K4 **Muggia,** It.
58/A1 **Mugia,** Sp.
74/B3 **Muğla,** Turk.
67/L2 **Mugodzharskoye** (mts.), Kaz.
101/A4 **Mugombazi,** Tanz.
100/D4 **Muḩammad Qawl,** Sudan
100/C3 **Muḩammad, Ra's** (pt.), Egypt
104/E2 **Muhila** (mts.), D.R. Congo
57/K2 **Mühlviertel** (reg.), Aus.
42/H2 **Muhos,** Fin.
72/C2 **Mūḩ, Sabkhat al** (lake), Syria
64/D4 **Muhu** (isl.), Est.
50/C4 **Muiden,** Neth.
43/C3 **Muirkirk,** Sc,UK
43/C2 **Muir of Ord,** Sc,UK
132/J11 **Muir Woods Nat'l Mon.,** Ca,US
80/D5 **Muju,** SKor.
66/B2 **Mukachevo,** Ukr.
100/D4 **Mukawwar** (isl.), Sudan
123/M2 **Muketei** (riv.), On,Can
74/L5 **Mukhayyam al Yarmūk,** Syria
132/C2 **Mukilteo,** Wa,US
79/L10 **Mukō,** Japan
92/D2 **Mukoshima** (isls.), Japan
83/B4 **Mu Ko Similan Nat'l Park,** Thai.
83/B4 **Mu Ko Surin Nat'l Park,** Thai.
73/K2 **Muktsar,** India
58/E3 **Mula,** Sp.
104/G4 **Mulanje,** Malw.
130/G4 **Mulchatna** (riv.), Ak,US
112/B3 **Mulchén,** Chile
48/G3 **Mulde** (riv.), Ger.
105/D **Mule** (pt.), Ant.
58/D4 **Mulhacén, Cerro de** (mtn.), Sp.
48/F3 **Mülhausen,** Ger.
50/D6 **Mülheim an der Ruhr,** Ger.
54/D2 **Mulhouse,** Fr.
81/D3 **Muling** (pass), China
77/L2 **Muling** (riv.), China
93/R9 **Mulinu'u** (cape), Samoa
73/L2 **Mulkila** (mtn.), India
44/B5 **Mullaghcleevaun** (mtn.), Ire.
44/B2 **Mullaghmore** (mtn.), NI,UK
125/G2 **Mullen,** Ne,US
86/D4 **Muller** (mts.), Indo.
54/D2 **Müllheim,** Ger.
43/B4 **Mullingar,** Ire.
129/J3 **Mullins,** SC,US
46/A6 **Mullion,** Eng,UK
104/C4 **Mulondo,** Ang.
73/K2 **Multān,** Pak.
122/C3 **Multnomah** (falls), Or,US
86/D3 **Mulu, Gunung** (peak), Malay.
100/B5 **Mulwad,** Sudan
84/B4 **Mumbai** (Bombay), India
104/C3 **Mumbué,** Ang.
104/E3 **Mumbwa,** Zam.
83/B5 **Mum Nauk** (pt.), Thai.
83/C3 **Mun** (riv.), Thai.
87/F4 **Muna** (isl.), Indo.
42/H4 **Munamägi** (hill), Est.
126/C3 **Muncie,** In,US
132/P15 **Mundelein,** Il,US
99/H5 **Mundemba,** Camr.
48/E3 **Munden,** Ger.
51/G6 **Münden,** Ger.
47/H1 **Mundesley,** Eng,UK
47/G2 **Mundford,** Eng,UK
84/C3 **Mungaolī,** India
91/B2 **Mungo Nat'l Park,** Austl.
75/F1 **Mungun-Tayga, Gora** (peak), Rus.
55/H1 **Munich** (München), Ger.
126/C2 **Munising,** Mi,US
69/L4 **Munku-Sardyk** (peak), Rus.
76/D1 **Munku-Sasan** (peak), Rus.
113/J8 **Muñoz Gamero** (pen.), Chile
51/E5 **Münster,** Ger.
51/H3 **Munster,** Ger.
43/A4 **Munster** (prov.), Ire.
132/Q16 **Munster,** In,US
51/E4 **Münsterland** (reg.), Ger.
63/F2 **Muntele Mare** (peak), Rom.
86/C4 **Muntok,** Indo.
83/D1 **Muong Khuong,** Viet.
42/G1 **Muonioälv** (riv.), Swe.
42/G1 **Muoniojoki** (riv.), Fin.
104/C4 **Mupa Nat'l Park,** Moz.
97/Q7 **Muqdisho** (Mogadishu) (cap.), Som.
57/L3 **Mur** (riv.), Aus.
62/C2 **Mura** (riv.), Slvk.
74/E2 **Muradiye,** Turk.
79/F1 **Murakami,** Japan
113/J7 **Murallón** (peak), Chile
101/C3 **Murang'a,** Kenya
74/E2 **Murat** (riv.), Turk.
66/D5 **Murat Daği** (peak), Turk.
59/E4 **Murcia,** Sp.
58/E4 **Murcia** (aut. comm.), Sp.
127/H1 **Murdochville,** Qu,Can
90/B1 **Murdock** (pt.), Austl.
63/G2 **Mureş** (co.), Rom.
63/G2 **Mureş** (riv.), Rom.
56/D5 **Muret,** Fr.
128/E3 **Murfreesboro,** Ar,US
129/G3 **Murfreesboro,** Tn,US
73/H1 **Murgab** (riv.), Trkm.
86/D5 **Muria** (peak), Indo.
110/D2 **Muriaé,** Braz.
73/G3 **Mūrī ān, Hāmūn-e Jaz** (lake), Iran
48/G2 **Müritz See** (lake), Ger.
97/N6 **Murle,** Eth.
64/G1 **Murmansk,** Rus.
64/G2 **Murmansk Obl.,** Rus.
79/M10 **Muro,** Japan
59/G3 **Muro,** Sp.
64/J5 **Murom,** Rus.
77/N3 **Muroran,** Japan
58/A1 **Muros,** Sp.
78/D4 **Muroto,** Japan
78/D4 **Muroto-zaki** (pt.), Japan
49/J2 **Murowana Goślina,** Pol.
129/G3 **Murphy,** NC,US
126/B4 **Murphysboro,** Il,US
91/D2 **Murramarang Nat'l Park,** Austl.
91/A2 **Murray** (riv.), Austl.
92/D5 **Murray** (lake), PNG
126/B4 **Murray,** Ky,US
129/H3 **Murray** (lake), SC,US
91/A2 **Murray Bridge,** Austl.
91/C2 **Murrumbidgee** (riv.), Austl.
62/C2 **Murska Sobota,** Slov.
45/G2 **Murton,** Eng,UK
93/M7 **Mururoa** (isl.), FrPol.
84/D3 **Murwāra,** India
91/E1 **Murwillumbah,** Austl.
49/H5 **Mürz** (riv.), Aus.
57/L3 **Mürzzuschlag,** Aus.
74/E2 **Muş,** Turk.
63/F4 **Musala** (peak), Bul.
73/G3 **Musandam** (pen.), Oman
79/H7 **Musashino,** Japan
73/G4 **Muscat** (Musqaţ) (cap.), Oman
131/E5 **Musconetcong** (riv.), NJ,US
131/C2 **Muscoy,** Ca,US
104/E5 **Musekwapoort** (pass), SAfr.
92/C7 **Musgrave** (ranges), Austl.
127/L1 **Musgrave Harbour,** Nf,Can
84/E3 **Mushābani,** India
74/N9 **Mushāsh, Wādī** (dry riv.), WBnk.
104/C1 **Mushie,** D.R. Congo
86/B4 **Musi** (riv.), Indo.
132/P14 **Muskego,** Wi,US
126/C3 **Muskegon,** Mi,US
126/C3 **Muskegon** (riv.), Mi,US
126/D4 **Muskingum** (riv.), Oh,US
125/J4 **Muskogee,** Ok,US
126/E2 **Muskoka** (lake), On,Can
101/B3 **Musoma,** Tanz.
73/G4 **Musqaţ** (Muscat) (cap.), Oman
127/J1 **Musquaro** (riv.), Qu,Can
92/D5 **Mussau** (isl.), PNG
122/F4 **Musselshell** (riv.), Mt,US
60/C4 **Mussomeli,** It.
74/B2 **Mustafakemalpaşa,** Turk.
84/D2 **Mustāng,** Nepal
125/H4 **Mustang,** Ok,US
57/K2 **Můstek** (peak), Czh.
112/C5 **Musters** (lake), Arg.
80/E2 **Musu-dan** (pt.), NKor.
116/D5 **Musún** (mt.), Nic.
91/D2 **Muswellbrook,** Austl.
100/B3 **Mūt,** Egypt
74/C3 **Mut,** Turk.
104/F4 **Mutare,** Zim.
87/F5 **Mutis** (peak), Indo.
103/H6 **Mutsamudu,** Com.
77/N3 **Mutsu,** Japan
110/D1 **Mutum,** Braz.
67/L4 **Muynak,** Uzb.
73/K2 **Muzaffargarh,** Pak.
84/C2 **Muzaffarnagar,** India
84/E2 **Muzaffarpur,** India
110/G6 **Muzambinho,** Braz.
75/D3 **Muzat** (riv.), China
75/D4 **Muztag** (peak), China
75/E4 **Muztag** (peak), China
75/C4 **Muztagata** (peak), China
104/C2 **Mwadi-Kalumbu,** D.R. Congo
101/B3 **Mwanza,** Tanz.
101/B3 **Mwanza** (prov.), Tanz.
43/H7 **Mweelrea** (mtn.), Ire.
104/D1 **Mweka,** D.R. Congo
104/D2 **Mwene-Ditu,** D.R. Congo
101/A5 **Mweru** (lake), D.R. Congo, Zam.
91/E2 **Myall Lakes Nat'l Park,** Austl.
85/G4 **Myanaung,** Myan.
76/C2 **Myangad,** Mong.
85/G2 **Myanmar** (Burma)
85/F4 **Myaungmya,** Myan.
85/G3 **Myingyan,** Myan.
85/G2 **Myitkyina,** Myan.
49/J4 **Myjava,** Slvk.
66/E3 **Mykolayiv,** Ukr.
66/D3 **Mykolayivs'ka** (obl.), Ukr.
46/C2 **Mynydd Eppynt** (mts.), Wal,UK
46/B2 **Mynydd Pencarreg** (mtn.), Wal,UK
85/F3 **Myohaung,** Myan.
79/F2 **Myōkō-san** (mtn.), Japan
129/J3 **Myrtle Beach,** SC,US
122/C5 **Myrtle Creek,** Or,US
42/D4 **Mysen,** Nor.
49/K4 **Myślenice,** Pol.
49/H2 **Myślibórz,** Pol.
83/E3 **My Son** (ruins), Viet.
84/C5 **Mysore,** India
49/K3 **Myszków,** Pol.
83/D4 **My Tho,** Viet.
64/H5 **Mytishchi,** Rus.
57/K2 **Mže** (riv.), Czh.
101/B5 **Mzuzu,** Malw.

N

83/C1 **Na** (riv.), Viet.
57/J2 **Naab** (riv.), Ger.
50/B5 **Naaldwijk,** Neth.
50/C4 **Naarden,** Neth.
44/B5 **Naas,** Ire.
102/B3 **Nababeep,** SAfr.
84/E3 **Nabadwīp,** India
78/E3 **Nabari,** Japan
79/M10 **Nabari** (riv.), Japan
65/M5 **Naberezhnye Chelny,** Rus.
72/D5 **Nabī Shu'ayb, Jabal an** (mtn.), Yem.
127/J1 **Nabisipi** (riv.), Qu,Can
82/D5 **Nabua,** Phil.
60/B4 **Nābul,** Tun.
60/B4 **Nābul** (gov.), Tun.
74/K5 **Nābulus,** WBnk.
78/D4 **Nachi-Katsuura,** Japan
49/J3 **Náchod,** Czh.
51/E6 **Nachrodt-Wiblingwerde,** Ger.
112/B3 **Nacimiento,** Chile
128/E4 **Nacogdoches,** Tx,US
46/D4 **Nadder** (riv.), Eng,UK
92/G6 **Nadi,** Fiji
84/B3 **Nadiād,** India
62/E2 **Nădlac,** Rom.
45/H3 **Nafferton,** Eng,UK
73/J3 **Nag,** Pak.
82/D5 **Naga,** Phil.
78/C4 **Nagahama,** Japan
78/E3 **Nagahama,** Japan
79/G1 **Nagai,** Japan
85/F2 **Nāgāland** (state), India
79/F2 **Nagano,** Japan
79/E3 **Nagano** (pref.), Japan
79/F2 **Nagaoka,** Japan
78/D3 **Nagaokakyō,** Japan
79/J7 **Nagara,** Japan
79/E3 **Nagara** (riv.), Japan
79/H7 **Nagareyama,** Japan
84/B4 **Nagar Haveli, Dadrak** (terr.), India
84/C4 **Nāgārjuna Sāgar** (res.), India
116/D5 **Nagarote,** Nic.
130/M5 **Nagas** (pt.), BC,Can
78/A4 **Nagasaki,** Japan
78/A4 **Nagasaki** (pref.), Japan
79/M9 **Nagashima,** Japan
78/B3 **Nagato,** Japan
84/B2 **Nāgaur,** India
84/C3 **Nāgda,** India
84/C6 **Nāgercoil,** India
75/F2 **Nagoonnuur,** Mong.
67/H5 **Nagorno-Karabakh Aut. Obl.,** Azer.
79/E3 **Nagoya,** Japan
84/C3 **Nāgpur,** India
76/C5 **Nagqu** (riv.), China
62/C2 **Nagyatád,** Hun.
62/E1 **Nagyhalász,** Hun.
62/E2 **Nagykálló,** Hun.
62/C2 **Nagykanizsa,** Hun.
62/D2 **Nagykáta,** Hun.
62/D2 **Nagykőrös,** Hun.
62/E1 **Nagy-Milic** (peak), Hun.
82/E2 **Naha,** Japan
118/D2 **Nahanni Nat'l Park,** NW,Can
74/K5 **Nahariyya,** Isr.
92/D2 **Nahashima** (isls.), Japan
72/E2 **Nahāvand,** Iran
53/G4 **Nahe** (riv.), Ger.
99/E4 **Nahouri** (prov.), Burk.
112/B3 **Nahuelbuta Nat'l Park,** Chile
112/C4 **Nahuel Huapí Nat'l Park,** Arg.
117/N8 **Naica,** Mex.
76/C4 **Naij Gol** (riv.), China
78/C3 **Naikai-Seto Nat'l Park,** Japan
46/D4 **Nailsea,** Eng,UK
46/D3 **Nailsworth,** Eng,UK
84/D3 **Nainpur,** India
43/D2 **Nairn,** Sc,UK
43/D2 **Nairn** (riv.), Sc,UK
101/C3 **Nairobi** (cap.), Kenya
101/C3 **Nairobi Nat'l Park,** Kenya
72/F2 **Najafābād,** Iran
72/D3 **Najd** (des.), SAr.
58/D1 **Nájera,** Sp.
84/C2 **Najībābād,** India
79/K9 **Naka,** Japan
78/D4 **Naka** (riv.), Japan
79/G2 **Naka** (riv.), Japan
79/H7 **Nakai,** Japan
79/F1 **Nakajō,** Japan
120/T10 **Nakalele** (pt.), Hi,US
79/G2 **Nakaminato,** Japan
78/C4 **Nakamura,** Japan
79/F2 **Nakano,** Japan
78/C3 **Nakano** (lake), Japan
78/B5 **Nakatane,** Japan
79/E3 **Nakatsugawa,** Japan
97/N4 **Nak'fa,** Erit.
77/L3 **Nakhodka,** Rus.
83/C3 **Nakhon Nayok,** Thai.
83/C3 **Nakhon Pathom,** Thai.
83/D2 **Nakhon Phanom,** Thai.
83/C3 **Nakhon Ratchasima,** Thai.
83/C3 **Nakhon Sawan,** Thai.
83/B4 **Nakhon Si Thammarat,** Thai.
42/G3 **Nakkila,** Fin.
49/J2 **Nakło nad Notecią,** Pol.
48/F1 **Nakskov,** Den.
80/E5 **Naktong** (riv.), SKor.
101/C3 **Nakuru,** Kenya
122/D3 **Nakusp,** BC,Can
73/J3 **Nāl** (riv.), Pak.
76/F2 **Nalayh,** Mong.
53/F5 **Nalbach,** Ger.
85/F2 **Nalbāri,** India
91/D3 **Nalbaugh Nat'l Park,** Austl.
67/G4 **Nal'chik,** Rus.
83/C2 **Nale,** Laos
84/C4 **Nalgonda,** India
63/K5 **Nallıhan,** Turk.
58/B1 **Nalón** (riv.), Sp.
96/H1 **Nālūt,** Libya
72/F2 **Namak** (lake), Iran
73/G2 **Namakzār-e Shadād** (salt dep.), Iran
75/B3 **Namangan,** Uzb.
102/B3 **Namaqualand** (reg.), SAfr.
87/J4 **Namaripi** (cape), Indo.
53/G4 **Namborn,** Ger.
90/D4 **Nambour,** Austl.
83/D4 **Nam Can,** Viet.
83/C1 **Nam Cum,** Viet.
83/D1 **Nam Dinh,** Viet.
126/B2 **Namekagon** (riv.), Wi,US
99/E3 **Namemtenga** (prov.), Burk.
79/E2 **Namerikawa,** Japan
104/B5 **Namib** (des.), Namb.
104/C5 **Namibia**
102/A2 **Namib-Naukluft Park,** Namb.
79/G2 **Namie,** Japan
84/D2 **Namja** (pass), Nepal
85/G2 **Namjagbarwa** (peak), China
83/C2 **Nam Nao Nat'l Park,** Thai.
83/B4 **Namnoi** (peak), Myan.
91/D1 **Namoi** (riv.), Austl.
92/E4 **Namonuito** (atoll), Micr.
92/F4 **Namorik** (atoll), Mrsh.
122/D5 **Nampa,** Id,US
80/C3 **Namp'o,** NKor.
104/G4 **Nampula,** Moz.
75/D6 **Namsê Shankou** (pass), China
42/D2 **Namsos,** Nor.
83/B2 **Nam Tok Mae Surin Nat'l Park,** Thai.
92/F4 **Namu** (atoll), Mrsh.
83/C2 **Nam Un** (res.), Thai.
53/D3 **Namur,** Belg.
53/D3 **Namur** (prov.), Belg.
49/J3 **Namysłów,** Pol.
81/B4 **Nan** (riv.), China
83/C2 **Nan,** Thai.
83/C2 **Nan** (riv.), Thai.
122/C3 **Nanaimo,** BC,Can
120/V13 **Nanakuli,** Hi,US
79/E2 **Nanao,** Japan
108/D4 **Nanay** (riv.), Peru
112/C2 **Nancagua,** Chile
82/C2 **Nanchang,** China
82/C2 **Nancheng,** China
53/F6 **Nancy,** Fr.
84/C4 **Nānded,** India
85/G3 **Nanding** (riv.), China
82/A4 **Nandu** (riv.), China
84/B3 **Nandurbār,** India
84/C4 **Nandyāl,** India
73/K1 **Nanga Parbat** (mtn.), Pak.
86/D4 **Nangapinoh,** Indo.
81/C3 **Nangong,** China
87/F1 **Nangtud** (mt.), Phil.
81/D4 **Nanjing,** China
78/C4 **Nankoku,** Japan
85/J3 **Nanliu** (riv.), China
77/K3 **Nanlou** (peak), China
85/J3 **Nanning,** China
79/M9 **Nannō,** Japan
44/B4 **Nanny** (riv.), Ire.
84/D2 **Nānpāra,** India
82/C2 **Nanping,** China
79/M10 **Nansei,** Japan
119/S6 **Nansen** (sound), Nun.,Can
101/B3 **Nansio,** Tanz.
79/F2 **Nantai-san** (mtn.), Japan
52/B6 **Nanterre,** Fr.
56/C3 **Nantes,** Fr.
52/B5 **Nanteuil-le-Haudouin,** Fr.
126/D3 **Nanticoke,** On,Can
122/E3 **Nanton,** Ab,Can
81/E4 **Nantong,** China
127/G3 **Nantucket** (isl.), MA,US
45/F5 **Nantwich,** Eng,UK
46/C3 **Nantyglo,** Wal,UK
131/F4 **Nanuet,** NY,US
93/Z18 **Nanuku** (chan.), Fiji
92/G5 **Nanumanga** (atoll), Tuv.
92/G5 **Nanumea** (isl.), Tuv.
110/D1 **Nanuque,** Braz.
81/C4 **Nanwon** (res.), China
81/B4 **Nanwutai** (mtn.), China
81/D4 **Nanyang,** China
81/D4 **Nanyang** (lake), China
101/C2 **Nanyuki,** Kenya
119/J3 **Naococane** (lake), Qu,Can
84/A3 **Naokot,** Pak.
77/L2 **Naoli** (riv.), China
98/D5 **Naoua** (falls), IvC.
132/K10 **Napa,** Ca,US
132/K10 **Napa** (riv.), Ca,US
126/E2 **Napanee,** On,Can
100/B5 **Napata** (ruins), Sudan
132/P16 **Naperville,** Il,US
89/H6 **Napier,** NZ
102/L11 **Napier,** SAfr.
129/H5 **Naples,** Fl,US
60/D2 **Naples** (Napoli), It.
60/D2 **Napoli** (gulf), It.
90/A4 **Nappa Merrie,** Austl.
47/E2 **Napton on the Hill,** Eng,UK
93/L6 **Napuka** (isl.), FrPol.
78/D3 **Nara,** Japan
78/D3 **Nara** (pref.), Japan
98/D3 **Nara,** Mali
73/J4 **Nāra** (riv.), Pak.
75/D5 **Nara Logna** (pass), Nepal
84/D4 **Narasannapeta,** India
79/J7 **Narashino,** Japan
83/C5 **Narathiwat,** Thai.
84/F3 **Nārāyanganj,** Bang.
84/C4 **Nārāyanpet,** India
46/B3 **Narberth,** Wal,UK
56/E5 **Narbonne,** Fr.
58/B1 **Narcea** (riv.), Sp.
61/F2 **Nardò,** It.
46/B6 **Nare** (pt.), UK
119/T7 **Nares** (str.), Nun.,Can
49/L2 **Narew** (riv.), Pol.
117/F6 **Narganá,** Pan.
103/H6 **Narinda** (bay), Madg.
113/K8 **Nariz** (peak), Chile
84/D2 **Narkatiāganj,** India
84/C3 **Narmada** (riv.), India
74/E2 **Narman,** Turk.
60/C1 **Narni,** It.
65/P2 **Narodnaya** (peak), Rus.
58/A1 **Narón,** Sp.
73/K2 **Nārowāl,** Pak.
42/G3 **Närpes,** Fin.
82/C6 **Narra,** Phil.
91/D1 **Narrabri,** Austl.
84/C3 **Narsimhapur,** India
84/C3 **Narsingarh,** India
78/D3 **Naruto,** Japan
64/F4 **Narva,** Est.
64/E4 **Narva** (riv.), Est., Rus.
82/D4 **Narvacan,** Phil.
42/F1 **Narvik,** Nor.
65/M2 **Nar'yan-Mar,** Rus.
75/C3 **Naryn,** Kyr.
75/B3 **Naryn** (riv.), Kyr.
63/G2 **Năsăud,** Rom.
47/F3 **Nash,** Eng,UK
46/C4 **Nash** (pt.), Wal,UK
127/G3 **Nashua,** NH,US
128/E3 **Nashville,** Ar,US
129/G2 **Nashville** (cap.), Tn,US
62/D3 **Našice,** Cro.
49/L2 **Nasielsk,** Pol.
84/B4 **Nāsik,** India
97/M6 **Nāşir,** Sudan
84/B2 **Nasīrābād,** India
73/J3 **Nasīrābād,** Pak.
87/F1 **Naso** (pt.), Phil.
93/Z17 **Nasorolevu** (peak), Fiji
130/N4 **Nass** (riv.), BC,Can
117/F2 **Nassau** (cap.), Bahm.
113/L8 **Nassau** (bay), Chile
93/J6 **Nassau** (isl.), CookIs.
100/C4 **Nasser** (res.), Egypt
42/E4 **Nässjö,** Swe.
119/J3 **Nastapoka** (isls.), Nun.,Can
48/F1 **Næstved,** Den.
79/F2 **Nasu-dake** (mtn.), Japan
83/B2 **Nat** (peak), Myan.
104/E5 **Nata,** Bots.
126/C1 **Natagani** (riv.), On,Can
109/L5 **Natal,** Braz.
127/J1 **Natashquan** (riv.), Qu,Can
129/F4 **Natchez,** Ms,US
128/E4 **Natchitoches,** La,US
54/D5 **Naters,** Swi.
93/Z17 **Natewa** (bay), Fiji
84/B3 **Nāthdwāra,** India
122/B2 **Nation** (riv.), BC,Can
124/C4 **National City,** Ca,US
85/G4 **Nattaung** (peak), Myan.
86/C3 **Natuna** (isls.), Indo.
124/E3 **Natural Bridges Nat'l Mon.,** Ut,US
91/D4 **Naturaliste** (cape), Austl.

166

Nauca – North

116/B4 **Naucalpan**, Mex.
102/E3 **Naudesnek** (pass), SAfr.
82/D5 **Naujan**, Phil.
64/D4 **Naujoji-Akmenė**, Lith.
102/A2 **Naukluft-Namib Game Rsv.**, Namb.
92/F5 **Nauru**
59/N8 **Navacarrada** (pass), Sp.
124/E3 **Navajo Nat'l Mon.**, Az,US
59/M9 **Navalcarnero**, Sp.
58/C3 **Navalmoral de la Mata**, Sp.
44/B4 **Navan**, Ire.
69/T3 **Navarin** (cape), Rus.
113/L8 **Navarino** (isl.), Chile
58/D1 **Navarre** (aut. comm.), Sp.
112/F2 **Navarro**, Arg.
46/A6 **Navax** (pt.), UK
58/B1 **Navia**, Sp.
58/B1 **Navia** (riv.), Sp.
112/C2 **Navidad**, Chile
109/H8 **Naviraí**, Braz.
63/J3 **Năvodari**, Rom.
68/G5 **Navoi**, Uzb.
117/N8 **Navojoa**, Mex.
117/N9 **Navolato**, Mex.
61/G3 **Návpaktos**, Gre.
61/H4 **Návplion**, Gre.
84/B3 **Navsāri**, India
119/H1 **Navy Board** (inlet), Nun.,Can
84/E3 **Nawābganj**, Bang.
84/D2 **Nawābganj**, India
73/J3 **Nawābshāh**, Pak.
73/G5 **Nawş, Ra's** (pt.), Oman
67/H5 **Naxcıvan**, Azer.
67/H5 **Naxcivan Aut. Rep.**, Azer.
61/J4 **Náxos** (isl.), Gre.
117/P9 **Nayarit** (state), Mex.
47/G3 **Nayland**, Eng,UK
76/B2 **Nayramadlïn** (peak), Mong.
75/B4 **Nayzatash, Pereval** (pass), Taj.
58/A3 **Nazaré**, Port.
52/C2 **Nazareth**, Belg.
74/K5 **Nazareth** (Nazerat), Isr.
117/P8 **Nazas** (riv.), Mex.
108/D6 **Nazca**, Peru
108/C6 **Nazca Lines** (ruins), Peru
92/B2 **Naze**, Japan
47/H3 **Naze, The** (pt.), Eng,UK
74/B3 **Nazilli**, Turk.
97/N6 **Nazrēt**, Eth.
68/H4 **Nazyvayevsk**, Rus.
101/A5 **Nchelenge**, Zam.
104/F3 **Ncheu**, Malw.
104/B2 **Ndalatando**, Ang.
97/K6 **Ndele**, CAfr.
92/F6 **Ndende** (isl.), Sol.
96/J5 **N'Djamena** (cap.), Chad
96/H8 **N'Djolé**, Gabon
104/E3 **Ndola**, Zam.
99/H5 **Ndop**, Camr.
98/B2 **Ndrhamcha, Sebkha de** (dry lake), Mrta.
56/C4 **Né** (riv.), Fr.
61/J5 **Néa Alikarnassós**, Gre.
44/B2 **Neagh, Lough** (lake), NI,UK
61/H3 **Néa Ionía**, Gre.
63/H2 **Neamţ** (co.), Rom.
130/A6 **Near** (isls.), Ak,US
46/C3 **Neath**, Wal,UK
46/C3 **Neath** (riv.), Wal,UK
46/C3 **Neath Port Talbot** (co.), Wal,UK
44/D3 **Neb** (riv.), IM,UK
67/K5 **Nebitdag**, Trkm.
90/E6 **Nebo** (mtn.), Austl.
125/G2 **Nebraska** (state), US
125/J2 **Nebraska City**, Ne,US
60/C4 **Nebrodi, Madonie** (mts.), It.
122/B2 **Nechako** (riv.), BC,Can
128/E4 **Neches** (riv.), Tx,US
97/N6 **Nechisar Nat'l Park**, Eth.
55/E1 **Neckar** (riv.), Ger.
93/J2 **Necker** (isl.), Hi,US
112/F3 **Necochea**, Arg.
60/C1 **Necropoli** (ruins), It.
58/A1 **Neda**, Sp.
50/C6 **Nederweert**, Neth.
50/D4 **Neede**, Neth.
47/H2 **Needham Market**, Eng,UK
47/F2 **Needingworth**, Eng,UK
124/D4 **Needles**, Ca,US
47/E5 **Needles, The** (seastacks), UK
126/B2 **Neenah**, Wi,US
123/J3 **Neepawa**, Mb,Can
53/E1 **Neerpelt**, Belg.
51/H2 **Neetze** (riv.), Ger.
53/F2 **Neffelbach** (riv.), Ger.
65/M4 **Neftekamsk**, Rus.
71/C7 **Nefud** (des.), SAr.
44/D6 **Nefyn**, Wal,UK
126/C2 **Negaunee**, Mi,US
97/N6 **Negēlē**, Eth.
100/D2 **Negev** (phys. reg.), Isr.
63/G3 **Negoiu** (peak), Rom.
84/C6 **Negombo**, SrL.
62/F3 **Negotin**, Yugo.
62/F5 **Negotino**, FYROM
108/B5 **Negra** (pt.), Peru
85/F4 **Negrais** (cape), Myan.
58/A1 **Negreira**, Sp.
63/H2 **Negreşti**, Rom.
112/C3 **Negro** (peak), Arg.
112/D3 **Negro** (riv.), Arg.
108/F7 **Negro** (riv.), Bol.
109/G7 **Negro** (riv.), Braz.
108/F4 **Negro** (riv.), Braz., Ven.
113/F2 **Negro** (riv.), Uru., Braz.
82/D6 **Negros** (isl.), Phil.
117/G4 **Neiba**, DRep.
103/R15 **Neiges, Piton des** (peak), Reun.
81/C4 **Neihuang**, China
81/B2 **Nei Monggol** (aut. reg.), China
76/G3 **Nei Monggol** (plat.), China
108/C3 **Neiva**, Col.
118/G3 **Nejanilini** (lake), Mb,Can
97/N6 **Nejo**, Eth.
97/N6 **Nek'emtē**, Eth.
64/G4 **Nelidovo**, Rus.
125/H2 **Neligh**, Ne,US
84/C5 **Nellore**, India
91/B3 **Nelson** (cape), Austl.
122/D3 **Nelson**, BC,Can
118/G3 **Nelson** (riv.), Mb,Can
113/J7 **Nelson** (str.), Chile
89/H7 **Nelson**, NZ
45/F4 **Nelson**, Eng,UK
46/C3 **Nelson**, Wal,UK
130/F3 **Nelson** (isl.), Ak,US
91/E2 **Nelson Bay**, Austl.
103/E2 **Nelspruit**, SAfr.
98/D2 **Néma**, Mrta.
98/D2 **Néma, Dhar** (hills), Mrta.
57/H4 **Nembro**, It.
63/H2 **Nemira** (peak), Rom.
77/J2 **Nemor** (riv.), China
56/E2 **Nemours**, Fr.
77/P3 **Nemuro**, Japan
77/J2 **Nen** (riv.), China
47/G1 **Nene** (riv.), Eng,UK
65/M2 **Nenets Aut. Okr.**, Rus.
125/J3 **Neosho** (riv.), Ks, Mo,US
125/J3 **Neosho**, Mo,US
71/H7 **Nepal**
84/D2 **Nepālganj**, Nepal
84/C3 **Nepanagar**, India
90/G8 **Nepean** (riv.), Austl.
126/F2 **Nepean**, Can.
124/E3 **Nephi**, Ut,US
43/A3 **Nephin** (mtn.), Ire.
127/H2 **Nepisiguit** (riv.), NB,Can
76/H1 **Nercha** (riv.), Rus.
64/J4 **Nerekhta**, Rus.
62/D4 **Neretva** (riv.), Bosn., Cro.
64/E5 **Neris** (riv.), Lith.
58/D4 **Nerja**, Sp.
58/B4 **Nerva**, Sp.
66/C4 **Nesebŭr**, Bul.
125/H3 **Ness City**, Ks,US
51/H6 **Nesse** (riv.), Ger.
130/M4 **Nesselrode** (mtn.), Ak,US
43/C2 **Ness, Loch** (lake), Sc,UK
45/E5 **Neston**, Eng,UK
61/J2 **Néstos** (riv.), Gre.
74/M9 **Nes Ziyyona**, Isr.
74/K5 **Netanya**, Isr.
131/F5 **Netcong**, NJ,US
51/G5 **Nethe** (riv.), Ger.
46/D3 **Netherend**, Eng,UK
50/B5 **Netherlands**
117/H5 **Netherlands Antilles** (isls.), Neth.
47/E5 **Netley**, Eng,UK
60/E3 **Neto** (riv.), It.
53/H2 **Netphen**, Ger.
50/D6 **Nette** (riv.), Ger.
51/H5 **Nette** (riv.), Ger.
53/G3 **Nettebach** (riv.), Ger.
53/F3 **Nettersheim**, Ger.
50/D6 **Nettetal**, Ger.
119/J2 **Nettilling** (lake), Nun.,Can
45/H5 **Nettleham**, Eng,UK
60/C2 **Nettuno**, It.
49/G2 **Neubrandenburg**, Ger.
54/C4 **Neuchâtel**, Swi.
54/C4 **Neuchâtel** (canton), Swi.
54/C4 **Neuchâtel** (lake), Swi.
49/G2 **Neuenhagen**, Ger.
50/D4 **Neuenhaus**, Ger.
51/E4 **Neuenkirchen**, Ger.
51/F3 **Neuenkirchen**, Ger.
51/E6 **Neuenrade**, Ger.
53/E4 **Neufchâteau**, Belg.
54/B1 **Neufchâteau**, Fr.
52/B5 **Neuilly-en-Thelle**, Fr.
52/C5 **Neuilly-Saint-Front**, Fr.
52/B6 **Neuilly-sur-Seine**, Fr.
57/J2 **Neumarkt in der Oberpfalz**, Ger.
48/E1 **Neumünster**, Ger.
62/C2 **Neunkirchen**, Aus.
53/G5 **Neunkirchen**, Ger.
53/H2 **Neunkirchen**, Ger.
53/G2 **Neunkirchen-Seelscheid**, Ger.
112/C3 **Neuquén**, Arg.
112/C3 **Neuquén** (prov.), Arg.
112/C3 **Neuquén** (riv.), Arg.
48/G2 **Neuruppin**, Ger.
129/J3 **Neuse** (riv.), NC,US
50/D6 **Neuss**, Ger.
51/G4 **Neustadt am Rübenberge**, Ger.
57/J2 **Neustadt an der Donau**, Ger.
57/H2 **Neustadt an der Weinstrasse**, Ger.
57/J1 **Neustadt bei Coburg**, Ger.
48/F1 **Neustadt in Holstein**, Ger.
48/G2 **Neustrelitz**, Ger.
55/G1 **Neu-Ulm**, Ger.
56/G2 **Neuves-Maisons**, Fr.
51/F1 **Neuwerk** (isl.), Ger.
53/G3 **Neuwied**, Ger.
67/V7 **Neva** (riv.), Rus.
58/D4 **Nevada** (mts.), Sp.
124/C3 **Nevada** (state), US
125/J3 **Nevada**, Mo,US
112/C4 **Nevado Cónico** (peak), Chile
111/C1 **Nevado de Chañi** (peak), Arg.
117/P10 **Nevado de Colima Nat'l Park**, Mex.
111/C2 **Nevado del Candado** (peak), Arg.
108/C3 **Nevado del Huila** (peak), Col.
105/C3 **Nevado del Huila Nat'l Park**, Col.
112/C2 **Nevado, Sierra del** (mts.), Arg.
64/F4 **Nevel'**, Rus.
52/C1 **Nevele**, Belg.
77/N2 **Nevel'sk**, Rus.
56/E3 **Nevers**, Fr.
62/D4 **Nevesinje**, Bosn.
67/G3 **Nevinnomyssk**, Rus.
117/J4 **Nevis** (isl.), StK.
74/C2 **Nevşehir**, Turk.
108/G3 **New** (riv.), Guy.
47/E5 **New** (for.), Eng,UK
126/D4 **New** (riv.), WV,US
44/E2 **New Abbey**, Sc,UK
126/C4 **New Albany**, In,US
129/F3 **New Albany**, Ms,US
47/E4 **New Alfresford**, Eng,UK
109/G2 **New Amsterdam**, Guy.
45/H5 **New Ancholme** (riv.), Eng,UK
132/K11 **Newark**, Ca,US
131/F5 **Newark**, NJ,US
126/D3 **Newark**, Oh,US
45/H5 **Newark-on-Trent**, Eng,UK
132/G6 **New Baltimore**, Mi,US
132/G3 **New Bedford**, Ma,US
132/P14 **New Berlin**, Wi,US
129/J3 **New Bern**, NC,US
126/C2 **Newberry**, Mi,US
129/H3 **Newberry**, SC,US
45/G1 **Newbiggin-by-the-Sea**, Eng,UK
128/D4 **New Braunfels**, Tx,US
46/C2 **Newbridge on Wye**, Wal,UK
92/D5 **New Britain** (isl.), PNG
127/F3 **New Britain**, Ct,US
127/H2 **New Brunswick** (prov.), Can.
131/F5 **New Brunswick**, NJ,US
44/A2 **New Buildings**, NI,UK
45/G2 **Newburn**, Eng,UK
47/E4 **Newbury**, Eng,UK
45/F3 **Newby Bridge**, Eng,UK
92/F6 **New Caledonia** (terr.), Fr.
93/U12 **New Caledonia** (isl.), NCal.
131/G4 **New Canaan**, Ct,US
91/D2 **Newcastle**, Austl.
127/S8 **Newcastle**, On,Can
103/E2 **Newcastle**, SAfr.
44/C3 **Newcastle**, NI,UK
126/C4 **New Castle**, In,US
126/D3 **New Castle**, Pa,US
123/G5 **Newcastle**, Wy,US
46/B2 **Newcastle Emlyn**, Wal,UK
45/F1 **Newcastleton**, Sc,UK
45/F5 **Newcastle-under-Lyme**, Eng,UK
45/G2 **Newcastle upon Tyne**, Eng,UK
131/G4 **New City**, NY,US
43/C3 **New Cumnock**, Sc,UK
84/C2 **New Delhi** (cap.), India
122/D3 **New Denver**, BC,Can
131/F5 **New Egypt**, NJ,US
91/E1 **New England Nat'l Park**, Austl.
130/F4 **Newenham** (cape), Ak,US
46/D3 **Newent**, Eng,UK
127/S9 **Newfane**, NY,US
119/K3 **Newfoundland** (prov.), Can.
127/L1 **Newfoundland** (isl.), Nf,Can
44/D1 **New Galloway**, Sc,UK
92/E5 **New Georgia** (isls.), Sol.
92/E5 **New Georgia** (sound), Sol.
127/J2 **New Glasgow**, NS,Can
127/N6 **New Glasgow**, Qu,Can
92/C5 **New Guinea** (isl.), Indo., PNG
127/G3 **New Hampshire** (state), US
92/D5 **New Hanover** (isl.), PNG
47/F5 **Newhaven**, Eng,UK
126/F3 **New Haven**, Ct,US
132/G6 **New Haven**, Mi,US
92/F6 **New Hebrides** (isls.), Van.
131/F5 **New Hope**, Pa,US
128/F4 **New Iberia**, La,US
47/G5 **Newick**, Eng,UK
92/E5 **New Ireland** (isl.), PNG
126/F3 **New Jersey** (state), US
126/E3 **New Kensington**, Pa,US
128/D2 **Newkirk**, Ok,US
132/Q16 **New Lenox**, Il,US
126/E2 **New Liskeard**, On,Can
127/F3 **New London**, Ct,US
126/B2 **New London**, Wi,US
46/A6 **Newlyn**, Eng,UK
125/K3 **New Madrid**, Mo,US
90/F6 **Newmarket**, Austl.
126/E2 **Newmarket**, On,Can
47/G2 **Newmarket**, Eng,UK
126/D4 **New Martinsville**, WV,US
122/D4 **New Meadows**, Id,US
124/F4 **New Mexico** (state), US
45/F5 **New Mills**, Eng,UK
129/G3 **Newnan**, Ga,US
46/D3 **Newnham**, Eng,UK
91/C4 **New Norfolk**, Austl.
129/F4 **New Orleans**, La,US
126/D3 **New Philadelphia**, Oh,US
89/H6 **New Plymouth**, NZ
46/F6 **Newport**, Eng,UK
45/E5 **Newport**, Eng,UK
46/B2 **Newport**, Wal,UK
46/D3 **Newport**, Wal,UK
46/D3 **Newport** (co.), Wal,UK
129/F3 **Newport**, Ar,US
126/C4 **Newport**, Ky,US
122/B4 **Newport**, Or,US
127/G3 **Newport**, RI,US
126/D5 **Newport**, Tn,US
127/F2 **Newport**, Vt,US
122/D3 **Newport**, Wa,US
131/C3 **Newport Beach**, Ca,US
126/E4 **Newport News**, Va,US
47/F2 **Newport Pagnell**, Eng,UK
129/H4 **New Port Richey**, Fl,US
117/F3 **New Providence** (isl.), Bahm.
46/A6 **Newquay**, Eng,UK
46/B2 **New Quay**, Wal,UK
46/C2 **New Radnor**, Wal,UK
127/H1 **New Richmond**, Qu,Can
131/G5 **New Rochelle**, NY,US
123/J4 **New Rockford**, ND,US
47/G5 **New Romney**, Eng,UK
45/G5 **New Rossington**, Eng,UK
44/B3 **Newry**, NI,UK
44/B3 **Newry** (can.), NI,UK
105/Z **New Schwabenland** (reg.), Ant.
69/P2 **New Siberian** (isls.), Rus.
129/H4 **New Smyrna Beach**, Fl,US
91/C2 **New South Wales** (state), Austl.
46/D2 **Newton**, Eng,UK
45/E1 **Newton**, Sc,UK
125/H3 **Newton**, Ks,US
127/G3 **Newton**, Ma,US
127/F4 **Newton**, NJ,US
128/E4 **Newton**, Tx,US
46/C5 **Newton Abbot**, Eng,UK
45/G2 **Newton Aycliffe**, Eng,UK
46/B6 **Newton Ferrers**, Eng,UK
45/F5 **Newton-le-Willows**, Eng,UK
43/C2 **Newtonmore**, Sc,UK
45/G1 **Newton on the Moor**, Eng,UK
44/D2 **Newton Stewart**, Sc,UK
91/B3 **Newtown**, Austl.
46/C1 **Newtown**, Wal,UK
123/H4 **New Town**, ND,US
131/F5 **Newtown**, Pa,US
44/C2 **Newtownabbey**, NI,UK
44/C2 **Newtownards**, NI,UK
43/B3 **Newtownbutler**, NI,UK
44/B3 **Newtownhamilton**, NI,UK
43/D3 **Newtown Saint Boswells**, Sc,UK
44/A2 **Newtownstewart**, NI,UK
46/C3 **New Tredegar**, Wal,UK
123/K4 **New Ulm**, Mn,US
127/J2 **New Waterford**, NS,Can
122/C3 **New Westminster**, BC,Can
126/F3 **New York** (state), US
131/G5 **New York**, NY,US
89/H6 **New Zealand**
105/L **New Zealand** (peak), Ant.
79/L10 **Neyagawa**, Japan
46/B3 **Neyland**, Wal,UK
73/F3 **Neyrīz**, Iran
73/G1 **Neyshābūr**, Iran
65/P4 **Neyva** (riv.), Rus.
84/C5 **Neyveli**, India
84/C6 **Neyyāttinkara**, India
66/D2 **Nezhin**, Ukr.
122/D4 **Nezperce**, Id,US
86/C3 **Ngabang**, Indo.
87/H5 **Ngabordamlu** (cape), Indo.
104/F4 **Ngabu**, Malw.
96/H5 **Ngala**, Nga.
75/D5 **Ngangla Ringco** (lake), China
75/E5 **Ngangzê** (lake), China
96/H6 **Ngaoundéré**, Camr.
91/B2 **Ngarkat Consv. Park**, Austl.
92/E4 **Ngatik** (isl.), Micr.
93/Z18 **Ngau** (isl.), Fiji
83/D2 **Nghia Dan**, Viet.
83/D1 **Nghia Lo**, Viet.
104/C4 **Ngiva**, Ang.
104/C1 **Ngo**, Congo
83/E4 **Ngoan Muc** (pass), Viet.
85/J4 **Ngoc Linh** (peak), Viet.
104/D4 **Ngonye** (falls), Zam.
77/D5 **Ngoring** (lake), China
96/H8 **Ngounié** (riv.), Gabon
96/H5 **Nguigmi**, Niger
92/C4 **Ngulu** (atoll), Micr.
83/C2 **Ngum** (riv.), Laos
83/D1 **Nguyen Binh**, Viet.
103/E2 **Ngwenya** (peak), Swaz.
108/G4 **Nhamundá** (riv.), Braz.
83/E3 **Nha Trang**, Viet.
98/E3 **Niafounke**, Mali
127/R9 **Niagara** (riv.), Can., US
127/R9 **Niagara Falls**, On,Can
127/R9 **Niagara Falls**, NY,US
99/F3 **Niamey** (cap.), Niger
99/F3 **Niamey** (dept.), Niger
98/C4 **Niandan** (riv.), Gui.
97/L7 **Niangara**, D.R. Congo
98/E3 **Niangay** (lake), Mali
81/C3 **Niangzi Guan** (pass), China
86/A3 **Nias** (isl.), Indo.
101/B5 **Niassa** (prov.), Moz.
116/D5 **Nicaragua**
116/E5 **Nicaragua** (lake), Nic.
60/E3 **Nicastro-Sambiase**, It.
57/G5 **Nice**, Fr.
129/G4 **Niceville**, Fl,US
78/B5 **Nichinan**, Japan
85/F6 **Nicobar** (isls.), India
127/F2 **Nicolet**, Qu,Can
74/J4 **Nicosia** (cap.), Cyp.
60/D4 **Nicosia**, It.
116/D5 **Nicoya**, CR
116/D6 **Nicoya** (gulf), CR
116/D6 **Nicoya** (pen.), CR
45/G4 **Nidd** (riv.), Eng,UK
57/H1 **Nidda**, Ger.
53/F2 **Nideggen**, Ger.
53/G6 **Niderviller**, Fr.
55/E4 **Nidwalden** (canton) Swi.
49/L2 **Nidzica**, Pol.
48/E1 **Niebüll**, Ger.
57/G2 **Nied** (riv.), Fr.
53/F5 **Nied** (riv.), Ger.
57/K3 **Niedere Tauern** (mts.), Aus.
49/G3 **Niederlausitz** (reg.), Ger.
53/H4 **Nieder-Olm**, Ger.
51/E1 **Niedersächsisches Wattenmeer Nat'l Park**, Ger.
62/B1 **Niederösterreich** (prov.), Aus.
53/F2 **Niederzier**, Ger.
49/L2 **Niegocin** (lake), Pol
51/G5 **Nieheim**, Ger.
49/J3 **Niemodlin**, Pol.
51/G3 **Nienburg**, Ger.
98/D5 **Niénokoué** (peak), IvC.
52/B2 **Nieppe**, Fr.
98/B3 **Niéri Ko** (riv.), Sen.
50/D5 **Niers** (riv.), Ger.
83/D4 **Niet Ban Tinh Xa**, Viet.
50/D5 **Nieuw-Bergen**, Neth.
50/C4 **Nieuwegein**, Neth.
50/B5 **Nieuwerkerk aan de IJssel**, Neth.
50/B4 **Nieuwkoop**, Neth.
50/D3 **Nieuwleusen**, Neth.
50/C4 **Nieuw-Loosdrecht**, Neth.
109/G2 **Nieuw-Nickerie**, Sur.
52/B1 **Nieuwpoort**, Belg.
50/D3 **Nieuw-Schoonebeek**, Neth.
74/C3 **Niğde**, Turk.
102/E2 **Nigel**, SAfr.
99/G2 **Niger**
99/G5 **Niger** (riv.), Afr.
99/G4 **Niger** (state), Nga.
99/G4 **Nigeria**
99/G5 **Niger, Mouths of the** (delta), Nga.
126/D1 **Nighthawk** (lake), On,Can
58/A1 **Nigrán**, Sp.
61/H2 **Nigrita**, Gre.
93/J2 **Nihoa** (isl.), Hi,US
79/G2 **Nihonmatsu**, Japan
79/F3 **Nii** (isl.), Japan
79/F2 **Niigata**, Japan
79/F2 **Niigata** (pref.), Japan
78/C4 **Niihama**, Japan
120/R10 **Niihau** (isl.), Hi,US
78/C3 **Niimi**, Japan
79/F2 **Niitsu**, Japan
79/H7 **Niiza**, Japan
58/D4 **Níjar**, Sp.
50/C4 **Nijkerk**, Neth.
52/D1 **Nijlen**, Belg.
50/C5 **Nijmegen**, Neth.
64/F1 **Nikel'**, Rus.
79/F2 **Nikkō**, Japan
79/F2 **Nikkō Nat'l Park**, Japan
69/Q4 **Nikolayevsk-na-Amure**, Rus.
67/H1 **Nikol'sk**, Rus.
66/E3 **Nikopol'**, Ukr.
74/D2 **Niksar**, Turk.
62/D4 **Nikšić**, Yugo.
93/H5 **Nikumaroro** (Gardner) (atoll), Kiri.
92/G5 **Nikunau** (isl.), Kiri.
97/M2 **Nile** (riv.), Afr.
74/H6 **Nile** (delta), Egypt
101/A2 **Nile** (prov.), Ugan.
132/Q15 **Niles**, Il,US
126/C3 **Niles**, Mi,US
126/D3 **Niles**, Oh,US
110/K7 **Nilópolis**, Braz.
42/J3 **Nilsiä**, Fin.
84/B3 **Nīmach**, India
77/L1 **Niman** (riv.), Rus.
98/C5 **Nimba** (peak), IvC.
98/C5 **Nimba** (co.), Libr.
56/F5 **Nîmes**, Fr.
105/L **Nimrod** (glac.), Ant.
53/F4 **Nimsbach** (riv.), Ger.
101/A2 **Nimule Nat'l Park**, Sudan
72/D1 **Nineveh** (ruins), Iraq
112/D4 **Ninfas** (pt.), Arg.
82/D2 **Ningbo**, China
81/C4 **Ningling**, China
81/B3 **Ningxia Huizu Zizhiqu** (aut. reg.), China
83/D1 **Ninh Binh**, Viet.
83/E3 **Ninh Hoa**, Viet.
92/D5 **Niningo** (isl.), PNG
105/K **Ninnis** (glac.), Ant.
79/H7 **Ninomiya**, Japan
52/D2 **Ninove**, Belg.
125/G2 **Niobrara** (riv.), Ne,US
98/B3 **Niokolo-Koba Nat'l Park**, Sen.
98/D3 **Niono**, Mali
98/B3 **Nioro-du-Rip**, Sen.
98/C3 **Nioro du Sahel**, Mali
56/C3 **Niort**, Fr.
123/H2 **Nipawin**, Sk,Can
126/B1 **Nipigon**, On,Can
126/B1 **Nipigon** (lake), On,Can
126/E2 **Nipissing** (lake), On,Can
112/C3 **Niquén**, Chile
79/F3 **Nirasaki**, Japan
90/H8 **Nirimba-Hmas**, Austl.
84/C4 **Nirmal**, India
62/E4 **Niš**, Yugo.
58/B3 **Nisa**, Port.
61/H1 **Nišava** (riv.), Yugo.
60/D4 **Niscemi**, It.
79/M9 **Nishiharu**, Japan
78/C3 **Nishiki** (riv.), Japan
79/L10 **Nishinomiya**, Japan
78/B5 **Nishino'omote**, Japan
79/E3 **Nishio**, Japan
78/D3 **Nishiwaki**, Japan
49/M3 **Nisko**, Pol.
132/B3 **Nisqually Reach** (str.), Wa,US
92/E5 **Nissan** (isl.), PNG
79/N9 **Nisshin**, Japan
123/K4 **Nisswa**, Mn,US
110/K7 **Niterói**, Braz.
44/E1 **Nith** (riv.), Sc,UK
44/E1 **Nithsdale** (val.), Sc,UK
75/C5 **Niti** (pass), India
49/K4 **Nitra**, Slvk.
49/K4 **Nitra** (riv.), Slvk.
65/P4 **Nitsa** (riv.), Rus.
93/H6 **Niuafo'ou** (isl.), Tonga
93/H6 **Niuatoputapu Group** (isls.), Tonga
93/J7 **Niue** (terr.), NZ
92/G6 **Niulakita** (isl.), Tuv.
85/H2 **Niulan** (riv.), China
86/C3 **Niut** (peak), Indo.
92/G5 **Niutau** (isl.), Tuv.
52/D2 **Nivelles**, Belg.
56/E3 **Nivernais** (hills), Fr.
123/J3 **Niverville**, Mb,Can
124/C3 **Nixon**, Nv,US
75/D4 **Niya** (riv.), China
78/C4 **Niyodo** (riv.), Japan
84/C4 **Nizāmābād**, India
65/M4 **Nizhnekama** (res.), Rus.
65/L5 **Nizhnekamsk**, Rus.
69/K4 **Nizhneudinsk**, Rus.
68/H3 **Nizhnevartovsk**, Rus.
67/G1 **Nizhniy Lomov**, Rus.
65/K4 **Nizhniy Novgorod** (Gor'kiy), Rus.
65/K4 **Nizhniy Novgorod Obl.**, Rus.
65/N4 **Nizhniy Tagil**, Rus.
74/D3 **Nizip**, Turk.
49/K4 **Nizke Tatry Nat'l Park**, Slvk.
101/B5 **Njombe**, Tanz.
99/H5 **Nkambe**, Camr.
104/B1 **Nkayi**, Congo
101/B5 **Nkhata Bay**, Malw.
99/H5 **Nkogam, Massif du** (peak), Camr.
99/H5 **N'Kongsamba**, Camr.
85/G2 **Nmai** (riv.), Myan.
84/F3 **Noākhāli**, Bang.
84/E3 **Noāmundi**, India
130/F2 **Noatak** (riv.), Ak,US
130/F2 **Noatak Nat'l Prsv.**, Ak,US
78/B4 **Nobeoka**, Japan
125/H4 **Noble**, Ok,US
126/C3 **Noblesville**, In,US
127/Q8 **Nobleton**, On,Can
77/N3 **Noboribetsu**, Japan
62/C5 **Noci**, It.
79/H7 **Noda**, Japan
52/B3 **Noeux-les-Mines**, Fr.
124/E5 **Nogales**, Az,US
78/B4 **Nogata**, Japan
56/D2 **Nogent-le-Rotrou**, Fr.
52/B5 **Nogent-sur-Oise**, Fr.
64/H5 **Noginsk**, Rus.
90/B4 **Nogoa** (riv.), Austl.
76/C2 **Nogoonuur**, Mong.
112/F2 **Nogoyá**, Arg.
49/K5 **Nógrád** (co.), Hun.
59/F1 **Noguera Pallarosa** (riv.), Sp.
80/E4 **Nogwak-san** (mtn.), SKor.
84/B2 **Nohar**, India
53/G4 **Nohfelden**, Ger.
126/E2 **Noire** (riv.), Qu,Can
56/B2 **Noires** (mts.), Fr.
56/B3 **Noirmoutier** (isl.), Fr.
52/B6 **Noisiel**, Fr.
52/B6 **Noisy-le-Sec**, Fr.
79/F3 **Nojima-zaki** (pt.), Japan
42/G3 **Nokia**, Fin.
87/F4 **Nokilalaki** (peak), Indo.
73/H3 **Nok Kundi**, Pak.
96/J7 **Nola**, CAfr.
91/D2 **Nomadgi Nat'l Park**, Austl.
130/F3 **Nome** (cape), Ak,US
78/B5 **Nomo-misaki** (cape), Japan
78/A4 **Nomo-zaki** (pt.), Japan
76/D2 **Nömrög**, Mong.
118/F2 **Nonacho** (lake), NW,Can
57/G4 **None**, It.
52/B5 **Nonette** (riv.), Fr.
81/F1 **Nong'an**, China
83/D2 **Nong Han** (res.), Thai.
83/C2 **Nong Het**, Laos
83/C2 **Nong Khai**, Thai.
83/C2 **Nong Pet**, Laos
53/F4 **Nonnweiler**, Ger.
92/G5 **Nonouti** (atoll), Kiri.
81/E5 **Nonri** (isl.), China
80/D4 **Nonsan**, SKor.
50/A5 **Noordbeveland** (isl.), Neth.
50/B3 **Noorderhaaks** (isl.), Neth.
50/B3 **Noordhollandsch** (can.), Neth.
50/C3 **Noordostpolder** (polder), Neth.
50/B4 **Noordwijk aan Zee**, Neth.
50/B4 **Noordwijkerhout**, Neth.
50/B4 **Noordzeekanaal** (can.), Neth.
90/D4 **Noosa-Tewantin**, Austl.
122/B3 **Nootka** (isl.), BC,Can
122/B3 **Nootka** (sound), BC,Can
116/B4 **Nopala**, Mex.
77/L1 **Nora** (riv.), Rus.
64/B4 **Nora**, Swe.
87/F2 **Norala**, Phil.
131/C3 **Norco**, Ca,US
127/M6 **Nord** (riv.), Qu,Can
52/C3 **Nord** (dept.), Fr.
52/B3 **Nord, Canal du** (can.), Fr.
51/E1 **Norden**, Ger.
51/F2 **Nordenham**, Ger.
68/K2 **Nordenskjöld** (arch.), Rus.
51/E1 **Norderney**, Ger.
51/E1 **Norderney** (isl.), Ger.
51/G1 **Norderstedt**, Ger.
48/F3 **Nordhausen**, Ger.
51/F1 **Nordholz**, Ger.
51/E4 **Nordhorn**, Ger.
42/H1 **Nordkapp** (North) (cape), Nor.
42/H1 **Nordkinn** (pt.), Nor.
51/E5 **Nordkirchen**, Ger.
101/A3 **Nord-Kivu** (prov.), D.R. Congo
42/E2 **Nordland** (co.), Nor.
42/F3 **Nordmaling**, Swe.
48/E1 **Nord-Ostsee** (can.), Ger.
99/H5 **Nord-Ouest** (prov.), Camr.
56/D1 **Nord-Pas-de-Calais** (reg.), Fr.
51/E3 **Nord-Radde** (riv.), Ger.
51/E3 **Nord-Sud** (can.), Ger.
42/E2 **Nord-Trøndelag** (co.), Nor.
51/E4 **Nordwalde**, Ger.
43/B4 **Nore** (riv.), Ire.
56/E5 **Nore, Pic de** (peak), Fr.
92/F7 **Norfolk** (isl.), Austl.
91/C4 **Norfolk** (peak), Austl.
47/G1 **Norfolk** (co.), Eng,UK
125/H2 **Norfolk**, Ne,US
126/E4 **Norfolk**, Va,US
47/H1 **Norfolk Broads** (swamp), Eng,UK
125/J3 **Norfork** (lake), Ar, Mo,US
50/D2 **Norg**, Neth.
79/E2 **Norikura-dake** (mtn.), Japan
68/J3 **Noril'sk**, Rus.
126/B3 **Normal**, Il,US
90/A2 **Norman** (riv.), Austl.
125/H4 **Norman**, Ok,US
92/E6 **Normanby** (isl.), PNG
132/C3 **Normandy Park**, Wa,US
45/G4 **Normanton**, Eng,UK
102/B3 **Norotshama** (peak), Namb.
123/H3 **Norquay**, Sk,Can
42/F2 **Norrbotten** (co.), Swe.
58/B1 **Norrea** (riv.), Sp.
52/B2 **Norrent-Fontes**, Fr.
132/Q16 **Norridge**, Il,US
129/H2 **Norris** (lake), Tn,US
131/E5 **Norristown**, Pa,US
42/F4 **Norrköping**, Swe.
42/F2 **Norrland** (reg.), Swe.
42/F4 **Norrtälje**, Swe.
112/E4 **Norte** (pt.), Arg.
113/F3 **Norte** (pt.), Arg.
108/G6 **Norte** (mts.), Braz.
109/J3 **Norte, Cabo do** (cape), Braz.
113/J6 **Norte, Campo de Hielo** (glacier), Chile
109/G6 **Nortelândia**, Braz.
51/G5 **Nörten-Hardenberg**, Ger.
91/C3 **North** (pt.), Austl.
91/C4 **North** (pt.), Austl.
126/D2 **North** (chan.), On,Can
127/J2 **North** (cape), PE,Can
41/E3 **North** (sea), Eur.
89/H6 **North** (cape), NZ
89/H6 **North** (isl.), NZ
44/C1 **North** (chan.), UK
130/D5 **North** (cape), Ak,US
130/F3 **North** (peak), Ak,US
62/D4 **North Albanian Alps** (mts.), Alb., Yugo.
45/G3 **Northallerton**, Eng,UK
89/A4 **Northam**, Austl.
46/B4 **Northam**, Eng,UK
115/* **North America**
47/F2 **Northampton**, Eng,UK
47/E2 **Northampton** (uplands), Eng,UK
126/F3 **Northampton**, Ma,US
131/E5 **Northampton**, Pa,US
47/F2 **Northamptonshire** (co.), Eng,UK
85/F5 **North Andaman** (isl.), India
119/K3 **North Aulatsivik** (isl.), Nf,Can
43/C2 **North Ballachulish**, Sc,UK
44/D3 **North Barrule** (mtn.), IM,UK
122/F2 **North Battleford**, Sk,Can
126/E2 **North Bay**, On,Can
122/B5 **North Bend**, Or,US
131/F5 **North Bergen**, NJ,US
43/D2 **North Berwick**, Sc,UK
50/C5 **North Brabant** (prov.), Neth.
132/Q15 **Northbrook**, Il,US
131/F5 **North Brunswick**, NJ,US
101/A2 **North Buganda** (prov.), Ugan.
125/H3 **North Canadian** (riv.), Ok,US
123/L2 **North Caribou** (lake), On,Can
129/H3 **North Carolina** (state), US
122/C3 **North Cascades Nat'l Park**, Wa,US
129/J3 **North Charleston**, SC,US
132/Q15 **North Chicago**, Il,US
45/H5 **North Collingham**, Eng,UK
122/C3 **North Cowichan**, BC,Can
123/H4 **North Dakota** (state), US
46/D5 **North Dorset Downs** (uplands), Eng,UK
44/C2 **North Down** (dist.), NI,UK

167
North – Opole

47/F4 North Downs (hills), Eng,UK
90/C3 North East (pt.), Austl.
117/G3 Northeast (pt.), Bahm.
130/E3 Northeast (cape), Ak,US
101/D2 North Eastern (prov.), Kenya
68/C2 Northeast Land (isl.), Sval.
45/H4 Northeast Lincolnshire (co.), Eng,UK
51/G5 Northeim, Ger.
47/G1 North Elmham, Eng,UK
89/C2 Northern (terr.), Austl.
99/E4 Northern (reg.), Gha.
74/K5 Northern (dist.), Isr.
101/B5 Northern (reg.), Malw.
98/B4 Northern (prov.), SLeo.
100/B4 Northern (reg.), Sudan
101/B2 Northern (prov.), Ugan.
101/A5 Northern (prov.), Zam.
75/B4 Northern Areas (terr.), Pak.
102/C3 Northern Cape (prov.), SAfr.
93/J6 Northern Cook (isls.), CookIs.
41/J2 Northern Dvina (riv.), Rus.
43/B3 Northern Ireland, UK
126/B1 Northern Light (lake), On,Can, Mn,US
92/D3 Northern Marianas, US
103/E6 Northern Province (prov.), SAfr.
68/G3 Northern Sos'va (riv.), Rus.
61/J3 Northern Sporades (isls.), Gre.
65/N3 Northern Ural (mts.), Rus.
65/K4 Northern Uval (hills), Rus.
68/E4 Northern Wals (upland), Rus.
123/K4 Northfield, Mn,US
47/G4 Northfleet, Eng,UK
47/H4 North Foreland (pt.), Eng,UK
129/H5 North Fort Myers, Fl,US
126/D1 North French (riv.), On,Can
48/E1 North Frisian (isls.), Den., Ger.
127/F2 North Hero, Vt,US
132/M9 North Highlands, Ca,US
132/C3 North Hill-Edgewood, Wa,US
50/B3 North Holland (prov.), Neth.
45/H5 North Hykeham, Eng,UK
65/Q5 North Kazakhstan Obl., Rus.
80/D2 North Korea
85/F2 North Lakhimpur, India
124/D3 North Las Vegas, Nv,US
45/H4 North Lincolnshire (co.), Eng,UK
128/E3 North Little Rock, Ar,US
101/B5 North Luangwa Nat'l Park, Zam.
119/R7 North Magnetic Pole, NAm
123/J2 North Moose (lake), Mb,Can
129/J3 North Myrtle Beach, SC,US
42/H1 North (Nordkapp) (cape), Nor.
67/G4 North Ossetian Aut. Rep., Rus.
127/R9 North Pelham, On,Can
46/C4 North Petherton, Eng,UK
90/E6 North Pine (riv.), Austl.
131/F5 North Plainfield, NJ,US
125/G2 North Platte (riv.), US
125/G2 North Platte, Ne,US
129/G3 Northport, Al,US
131/G5 Northport (Old Northport), NY,US
131/J7 North Potomac, Md,US
48/E3 North Rhine-Westphalia (state), Ger.
124/D3 North Rim, Az,US
122/F2 North Saskatchewan (riv.), Ab, Sk,Can
45/G2 North Shields, Eng,UK
68/K2 North Siberian (plain), Rus.
45/J5 North Somercotes, Eng,UK
46/D3 North Somerset (co.), Eng,UK
90/D4 North Stradbroke (isl.), Austl.
131/G4 North Tarrytown, NY,US
45/H5 North Thoresby, Eng,UK
47/E4 North Tidworth, Eng,UK
127/S9 North Tonawanda, NY,US
45/F1 North Tyne (riv.), Eng,UK
127/J2 Northumberland (str.), Can.
45/F1 Northumberland (co.), Eng,UK
45/F1 Northumberland Nat'l Park, Eng,UK
124/B2 North Umpqua (riv.), Or,US
118/D4 North Vancouver, BC,Can
132/F7 Northville, Mi,US
47/H1 North Walsham, Eng,UK
89/A3 North West (cape), Austl.
102/D2 North-West (prov.), SAfr.
75/B4 Northwest Frontier (prov.), Pak.
127/L1 North West Gander (riv.), Nf,Can
43/C2 North West Highlands (mts.), Sc,UK
118/E2 Northwest Territories (terr.), Can.
45/H5 North Wheatley, Eng,UK
45/F5 Northwich, Eng,UK
45/G5 North Wingfield, Eng,UK
123/J4 Northwood, ND,US
127/R8 North York, On,Can
45/H3 North York Moors Nat'l Park, Eng,UK
45/G3 North Yorkshire (co.), Eng,UK
130/F3 Norton (bay), Ak,US
130/E3 Norton (sound), Ak,US
125/H3 Norton, Ks,US
126/D4 Norton, Va,US
45/F6 Norton Bridge, Eng,UK
126/C3 Norton Shores, Mi,US
48/E1 Nortorf, Ger.
127/Q8 Norval, On,Can
105/Z Norvegia (cape), Ant.
53/F2 Nörvenich, Ger.
131/B3 Norwalk, Ca,US
131/G4 Norwalk, Ct,US
126/D3 Norwalk, Oh,US
42/B3 Norway
123/J2 Norway House, Mb,Can
119/S7 Norwegian (bay), Nun.,Can
41/D2 Norwegian (sea), Eur.
47/H1 Norwich, Eng,UK
126/F3 Norwich, NY,US
79/L10 Nose, Japan
73/K1 Noshaq (mtn.), Pak.
77/N3 Noshiro, Japan
63/H4 Nos Maslen Nos (pt.), Bul.
86/E2 Nosong (cape), Malay.
102/C2 Nosop (dry riv.), Bots.
66/D2 Nosovka, Ukr.
73/G3 Noşratābād, Iran
113/J7 Notch (cape), Chile
49/J2 Notec (riv.), Pol.
60/D4 Noto, It.
63/D4 Noto (gulf), It.
79/E2 Noto (pen.), Japan
60/D4 Noto Antica (ruins), It.
79/M9 Notogawa, Japan
127/L1 Notre Dame (bay), Nf,Can
127/G1 Notre Dame (mts.), Qu,Can
127/N7 Notre-Dame-de-l'Ile-Perrot, Qu,Can
126/F1 Nottaway (riv.), Qu,Can
119/H2 Nottingham (isl.), Nun.,Can
45/G6 Nottingham, Eng,UK
45/G6 Nottingham (co.), Eng,UK
45/H5 Nottinghamshire (co.), Eng,UK
51/E5 Nottuln, Ger.
96/B3 Nouadhibou, Mrta.
98/B2 Nouakchott (cap.), Mrta.
93/V13 Nouméa (cap.), NCal.
102/D3 Noupoort, SAfr.
52/A3 Nouvion, Fr.
53/D4 Nouzonville, Fr.
109/H8 Nova Andradina, Braz.
63/F3 Novaci, Rom.
109/L5 Nova Cruz, Braz.
49/K4 Nová Dubnica, Slvk.
110/L7 Nova Friburgo, Braz.
62/C3 Nova Gradiška, Cro.
110/K7 Nova Iguaçu, Braz.
108/G4 Nova Olinda do Norte, Braz.
62/E3 Nova Pazova, Yugo.
110/B4 Nova Prata, Braz.
57/H4 Novara, It.
55/E5 Novara (prov.), It.
127/J2 Nova Scotia (prov.), Can.
132/J10 Novato, Ca,US
62/D4 Nova Varoš, Yugo.
110/D1 Nova Venécia, Braz.
109/H6 Nova Xavantina, Braz.
66/E3 Novaya Kakhovka, Ukr.
69/R2 Novaya Sibir' (isl.), Rus.
68/E2 Novaya Zemlya (isl.), Rus.
63/H4 Nova Zagora, Bul.
59/E3 Novelda, Sp.
49/J4 Nové Mesto nad Váhom, Slvk.
49/K5 Nové Zámky, Slvk.
64/F4 Novgorod, Rus.
64/G4 Novgorod Obl., Rus.
132/F7 Novi, Mi,US
62/E3 Novi Bečej, Yugo.
63/F4 Novi Iskur, Bul.
57/H4 Novi Ligure, It.
63/H4 Novi Pazar, Bul.
62/E4 Novi Pazar, Yugo.
62/D3 Novi Sad, Yugo.
110/K6 Novo (riv.), Braz.
67/G2 Novoannenskiy, Rus.
108/F5 Novo Aripuanã, Braz.
65/K4 Novocheboksarsk, Rus.
66/G3 Novocherkassk, Rus.
66/C2 Novograd-Volynskiy, Ukr.
64/E5 Novogrudok, Bela.
110/B4 Novo Hamburgo, Braz.
110/B2 Novo Horizonte, Braz.
68/G5 Novokazalinsk, Kaz.
67/J1 Novokuybyshevsk, Rus.
68/J4 Novokuznetsk, Rus.
105/A Novolazarevskaya, Ant.
62/B3 Novo Mesto, Slov.
62/E3 Novo Miloševo, Yugo.
66/F1 Novomoskovsk, Rus.
66/E3 Novomoskovsk, Ukr.
64/F5 Novopolotsk, Bela.
66/F3 Novorossiysk, Rus.
66/F3 Novoshakhtinsk, Rus.
68/J4 Novosibirsk, Rus.
67/L2 Novotroitsk, Rus.
66/D2 Novoukrainka, Ukr.
66/C2 Novovolynsk, Ukr.
65/L4 Novovyatsk, Rus.
66/D1 Novozybkov, Rus.
62/C3 Novska, Cro.
49/K4 Nový Jičín, Czh.
67/K4 Novyy Uzen, Kaz.
49/L3 Nowa Dęba, Pol.
49/J3 Nowa Ruda, Pol.
49/M3 Nowa Sarzyna, Pol.
49/H3 Nowa Sól, Pol.
125/J3 Nowata, Ok,US
49/K2 Nowe, Pol.
49/K2 Nowe Miasto Lubawskie, Pol.
84/C2 Nowgong, India
85/F2 Nowgong, India
130/H3 Nowitna (riv.), Ak,US
130/H3 Nowitna Nat'l Wild. Ref., Ak,US
49/H2 Nowogard, Pol.
124/F1 Nowood (riv.), Wy,US
73/K2 Nowshera, Pak.
49/K1 Nowy Dwór Gdański, Pol.
49/L4 Nowy Sącz, Pol.
49/L4 Nowy Sącz (prov.), Pol.
49/L4 Nowy Targ, Pol.
49/J2 Nowy Tomyśl, Pol.
58/A1 Noya, Sp.
52/B5 Noye (riv.), Fr.
52/C4 Noyon, Fr.
104/G4 Nsanje, Malw.
99/E5 Nsawam, Gha.
76/D5 Nu (riv.), China
97/M5 Nūbah (mts.), Sudan
100/C4 Nubian (des.), Sudan
124/E3 Nucla, Co,US
128/D4 Nueces (riv.), Tx,US
118/G2 Nueltin (lake), Nun.,Can
50/C6 Nuenen, Neth.
81/E2 Nü'er (riv.), China
116/C5 Nueva Concepción, Guat.
116/E3 Nueva Gerona, Cuba
113/F2 Nueva Helvecia, Uru.
112/B3 Nueva Imperial, Chile
108/C3 Nueva Loja, Ecu.
113/S11 Nueva Palmira, Uru.
116/A2 Nueva Rosita, Mex.
117/F3 Nuevitas, Cuba
112/D4 Nuevo (gulf), Arg.
117/N7 Nuevo Casas Grandes, Mex.
117/N9 Nuevo Ideal, Mex.
116/B2 Nuevo Laredo, Mex.
116/A2 Nuevo León (state), Mex.
113/S11 Nuevo Palmira, Uru.
92/E5 Nuguria (isls.), PNG
93/J2 Nuhau (isl.), Hi,US
51/F6 Nuhne (riv.), Ger.
92/G5 Nui (atoll), Tuv.
79/N10 Nukata, Japan
130/F4 Nuklunek (mtn.), Ak,US
93/H7 Nuku'alofa (cap.), Tonga
92/G5 Nukufetau (atoll), Tuv.
93/L5 Nuku Hiva (isl.), FrPol.
92/H5 Nukulaelae (isl.), Tuv.
92/F5 Nukumanu (atoll), PNG
93/H5 Nukunonu (atoll), Tok.
92/E4 Nukuoro (isl.), Micr.
68/F5 Nukus, Uzb.
93/M6 Nukutavake (isl.), FrPol.
59/E3 Nules, Sp.
92/B8 Nullarbor (plain), Austl.
96/H6 Numan, Nga.
50/B5 Numansdorp, Neth.
79/F2 Numata, Japan
79/F3 Numazu, Japan
53/G2 Nümbrecht, Ger.
87/H4 Numfoor (isl.), Indo.
118/G2 Nunavut (terr.), Can.
91/G5 Nunawading, Austl.
47/E1 Nuneaton, Eng,UK
91/D3 Nungatta Nat'l Park, Austl.
130/E4 Nunivak (isl.), Ak,US
50/C4 Nunspeet, Neth.
45/G2 Nunthorpe, Eng,UK
77/J1 Nuomin (riv.), China
98/C5 Nuon (riv.), IvC., Libr.
60/A2 Nuoro, It.
75/B2 Nura (riv.), Kaz.
53/F3 Nürburgring, Ger.
74/D3 Nurhak, Turk.
100/B5 Nuri (ruins), Sudan
57/J2 Nürnberg, Ger.
91/C1 Nurri (peak), Austl.
57/H2 Nürtingen, Ger.
74/L4 Nuşayrīyah, Jabal an (mts.), Syria
74/E3 Nusaybin, Turk.
130/G4 Nushagak (riv.), Ak,US
73/J3 Nushki, Pak.
53/E2 Nuth, Neth.
131/F5 Nutley, NJ,US
115/M3 Nuuk (Godthåb), Grld.
93/X15 Nuupere (pt.), FrPol.
100/C2 Nuwaybi', Egypt
102/L10 Nuy (riv.), SAfr.
104/E4 Nxai Pan Nat'l Park, Bots.
131/G4 Nyack, NY,US
101/B4 Nyahua, Tanz.
75/F5 Nyainqêntanglha Feng (peak), China
97/K5 Nyala, Sudan
97/L6 Nyamlell, Sudan
64/J3 Nyandoma, Rus.
101/B3 Nyanza (prov.), Kenya
101/A4 Nyanza-Lac, Buru.
101/B5 Nyasa (Malawi) (lake), Afr.
48/F1 Nyborg, Den.
42/E4 Nybro, Swe.
49/L5 Nyiradony, Hun.
62/F2 Nyírbátor, Hun.
49/L5 Nyíregyháza, Hun.
101/C2 Nyiru (peak), Kenya
48/F1 Nykøbing, Den.
42/F4 Nyköping, Swe.
102/E2 Nylstroom, SAfr.
42/F4 Nynäshamn, Swe.
54/C5 Nyon, Swi.
57/K2 Nýřany, Czh.
49/J3 Nysa, Pol.
122/D5 Nyssa, Or,US
77/M4 Nyūdo-zaki (pt.), Japan
64/F2 Nyuk (lake), Rus.
104/E2 Nyunzu, D.R. Congo
79/E2 Nyūzen, Japan
98/C5 Nzérékoré, Gui.
98/C4 Nzérékoré (comm.), Gui.
98/D5 Nzi (riv.), IvC.

O

47/E1 Oadby, Eng,UK
123/H4 Oahe (lake), ND, SD,US
120/V13 Oahu (isl.), Hi,US
123/J3 Oakbank, Mb,Can
132/Q14 Oak Creek, Wi,US
123/J4 Oakes, ND,US
132/Q16 Oak Forest, Il,US
47/F1 Oakham, Eng,UK
126/D4 Oak Hill, WV,US
124/C3 Oakhurst, Ca,US
132/K11 Oakland, Ca,US
131/F4 Oakland, NJ,US
132/A3 Oakland (bay), Wa,US
132/Q16 Oak Lawn, Il,US
47/E3 Oakley, Eng,UK
47/F2 Oakley, Eng,UK
132/L11 Oakley, Ca,US
125/G3 Oakley, Ks,US
132/Q16 Oak Park, Il,US
132/F7 Oak Park, Mi,US
122/C5 Oakridge, Or,US
129/G2 Oak Ridge, Tn,US
127/R8 Oak Ridges, On,Can
46/D3 Oaksey, Eng,UK
131/A2 Oak View, Ca,US
127/Q9 Oakville, On,Can
89/H7 Oamaru, NZ
116/B4 Oaxaca, Mex.
116/B4 Oaxaca (state), Mex.
68/H3 Ob' (gulf), Rus.
68/G3 Ob' (riv.), Rus.
92/F6 Oba (isl.), Van.
126/D2 Obabika (lake), On,Can
78/D3 Obama, Japan
99/H5 Oban (hills), Camr., Nga.
89/G7 Oban, NZ
126/D1 Obasatika (riv.), On,Can
79/M10 Obata, Japan
111/E2 Oberá, Arg.
50/D6 Oberhausen, Ger.
49/H3 Oberlausitz (reg.), Ger.
125/G3 Oberlin, Ks,US
55/E1 Oberndorf am Neckar, Ger.
51/G4 Obernkirchen, Ger.
53/G4 Oberthal, Ger.
57/L3 Oberwölz, Aus.
87/G4 Obi (isls.), Indo.
87/G4 Obi (str.), Indo.
109/G4 Óbidos, Braz.
77/N3 Obihiro, Japan
62/E4 Obilić, Yugo.
79/J7 Obitsu (riv.), Japan
83/B2 Ob Luang Gorge, Thai.
77/L2 Obluch'ye, Rus.
64/H5 Obninsk, Rus.
97/P5 Obock, Djib.
49/J2 Oborniki, Pol.
49/J3 Oborniki Śląskie, Pol.
49/J2 Obra (riv.), Pol.
62/E3 Obrenovac, Yugo.
79/M10 Ōbu, Japan
99/E5 Obuasi, Gha.
55/E4 Obwalden (canton), Swi.
129/H4 Ocala, Fl,US
56/C5 Occabe, Sommet d' (peak), Fr.
108/E7 Occidental, Cordillera (range), SAm.
130/L4 Ocean (cape), Ak,US
131/G5 Ocean Beach, NY,US
126/F4 Ocean City, Md,US
122/B2 Ocean Falls, BC,Can
131/F5 Ocean Grove, NJ,US
92/* Oceania
124/C4 Oceanside, Ca,US
131/G5 Oceanside, NY,US
83/D4 Oc-Eo (ruins), Viet.
67/G4 Ochamchira, Geo.
77/P3 Ochiishi-misaki (cape), Japan
117/F4 Ocho Rios, Jam.
51/E4 Ochtrup, Ger.
51/F2 Ochtum (riv.), Ger.
47/E3 Ock (riv.), Eng,UK
64/C3 Ockelbo, Swe.
129/H4 Ocmulgee (riv.), Ga,US
63/F2 Ocna Mureş, Rom.
129/H3 Oconee (lake), Ga,US
129/H3 Oconee (riv.), Ga,US
116/D5 Ocotal, Nic.
116/A3 Ocotlán, Mex.
116/B4 Ocotlán, Mex.
56/C2 Octeville, Fr.
69/L1 October Revolution (isl.), Rus.
99/E5 Oda, Gha.
78/C3 Oda, Japan
79/M10 Ōdai, Japan
78/E3 Ōdaigahara-san (mtn.), Japan
100/D4 Oda, Jabal (peak), Sudan
77/N3 Ōdate, Japan
79/F3 Odawara, Japan
42/C3 Odda, Nor.
97/P7 Oddur, Som.
51/F6 Odeborn (riv.), Ger.
48/A4 Ødemira, Port.
74/A2 Ödemiş, Turk.
102/D2 Odendaalsrus, SAfr.
48/F1 Odense, Den.
51/E6 Odenthal, Ger.
131/K7 Odenton, Md,US
49/H2 Oderhaff (lag.), Ger., Pol.
49/H2 Oder (Odra) (riv.), Ger., Pol.
57/K4 Oderzo, It.
66/D3 Odesa, Ukr.
63/J2 Odes'ka (obl.), Ukr.
128/C4 Odessa, Tx,US
122/D4 Odessa, Wa,US
56/B2 Odet (riv.), Fr.
98/D4 Odienné, IvC.
64/H5 Odintsovo, Rus.
82/D5 Odiongan, Phil.
59/P10 Odivelas, Port.
63/H3 Odobeşti, Rom.
56/C2 Odon (riv.), Fr.
83/D4 Odongk, Camb.
50/D3 Odoorn, Neth.
63/G2 Odorheiu Secuiesc, Rom.
49/H2 Odra (Oder) (riv.), Ger., Pol.
62/D3 Odžaci, Yugo.
96/J7 Odzala Nat'l Park, Congo
79/L9 Ōe, Japan
50/B4 Oegstgeest, Neth.
109/K5 Oeiras, Braz.
51/F5 Oelde, Ger.
57/K1 Oelsnitz, Ger.
93/M7 Oeno (atoll), Pitc.,UK
51/E5 Oer-Erkenschwick, Ger.
53/E4 Oesling (mts.), Lux.
50/B6 Oesterdam (dam), Neth.
57/H2 Oestrich-Winkel, Ger.
61/H3 Oeta Nat'l Park, Gre.
74/E2 Of, Turk.
60/D2 Ofanto (riv.), It.
74/K6 Ofaqim, Isr.
44/A5 Offaly (co.), Ire.
57/H1 Offenbach, Ger.
54/D1 Offenburg, Ger.
57/G3 Oftringen, Swi.
77/M4 Oga, Japan
97/P6 Ogadēn (reg.), Eth.
78/E3 Ōgaki, Japan
125/G2 Ogallala, Ne,US
92/D2 Ogasawara, Japan
99/G4 Ogbomosho, Nga.
124/E2 Ogden, Ut,US
126/F2 Ogdensburg, NY,US
129/H3 Ogeechee (riv.), Ga,US
126/D2 Ogidaki (mtn.), On,Can
130/L3 Ogilvie (mts.), Yk,Can
118/C2 Ogilvie (riv.), Yk,Can
57/J4 Oglio (riv.), It.
46/C4 Ogmore by Sea, Wal,UK
54/B3 Ognon (riv.), Fr.
87/F3 Ogoamas (peak), Indo.
123/M3 Ogoki (lake), On,Can
123/L3 Ogoki (res.), On,Can
123/M3 Ogoki (riv.), On,Can
96/G8 Ogooué (riv.), Gabon
79/H7 Ogose, Japan
63/F4 Ogosta (riv.), Bul.
64/E4 Ogre, Lat.
79/M9 Oguchi, Japan
62/B3 Ogulin, Cro.
99/F5 Ogun (riv.), Nga.
99/F5 Ogun (state), Nga.
67/K5 Ogurchinskiy (isl.), Trkm.
96/G2 Ohanet, Alg.
90/G8 O'Hares (cr.), Austl.
51/E2 Ohe (riv.), Ger.
113/J7 O'Higgins (lake), Chile
125/B4 Ohio (riv.), US
125/D3 Ohio (state), US
45/F1 Oh Me Edge (hill), Eng,UK
123/H3 Ohoopee (riv.), Ga,US
57/K1 Ohře (riv.), Czh.
48/F2 Ohre (riv.), Ger.
62/E5 Ohrid (lake), Alb., FYROM
62/E5 Ohrid, FYROM
85/G2 Oi (riv.), China
79/H7 Ōi, Japan
79/F3 Ōi (riv.), Japan
109/H3 Oiapoque (riv.), Braz.
59/P10 Oieras, Port.
52/B3 Oignies, Fr.
126/E3 Oil City, Pa,US
50/C5 Oirschot, Neth.
52/B5 Oise (dept.), Fr.
52/B5 Oise (riv.), Fr.
52/C5 Oise à l'Aisne, Canal de (can.), Fr.
52/A4 Oisemont, Fr.
75/H7 Ōiso, Japan
50/C5 Oisterwijk, Neth.
52/C3 Oisy-le-Verger, Fr.
78/B4 Ōita, Japan
78/B4 Ōita (pref.), Japan
78/B4 Ōita (riv.), Japan
131/A2 Ojai, Ca,US
49/K3 Ojcowski Nat'l Park, Pol.
79/L10 Ōji, Japan
117/P8 Ojinaga, Mex.
75/F2 Ojiya, Japan
116/A3 Ojocaliente, Mex.
111/C2 Ojos del Salado (peak), Arg., Chile
117/L7 Ojos Negros, Mex.
65/J4 Oka (riv.), Rus.
119/K3 Okak (isl.), Nf,Can
122/C3 Okanagan (lake), BC,Can
122/D3 Okanagan Falls, BC,Can
104/B1 Okanda Nat'l Park, Gabon
122/D3 Okanogan, Wa,US
122/D3 Okanogan (riv.), Wa,US
73/K2 Okāra, Pak.
104/C4 Okaukuejo, Namb.
104/D4 Okavango Delta (reg.), Bots.
78/B4 Ōkawa, Japan
79/F2 Okaya, Japan
78/C3 Okayama, Japan
78/C3 Okayama (pref.), Japan
79/E3 Okazaki, Japan
129/H5 Okeechobee, Fl,US
129/H5 Okeechobee (lake), Fl,US
79/H7 Okegawa, Japan
46/C5 Okehampton, Eng,UK
46/B5 Okement (riv.), Eng,UK
51/H4 Oker (riv.), Ger.
69/Q4 Okha, Rus.
61/J3 Ókhi (peak), Gre.
69/Q4 Okhotsk (sea), Japan, Rus.
78/C2 Oki (isls.), Japan
78/C2 Oki-Daisen Nat'l Park, Japan
82/E2 Okinawa (isls.), Japan
92/C2 Okino-Tori-Shima (Parece Vela) (isl.), Japan
85/G4 Okkan, Myan.
125/H4 Oklahoma (state), US
125/H4 Oklahoma City (cap.), Ok,US
129/H4 Oklawaha (riv.), Fl,US
125/J4 Okmulgee, Ok,US
123/K5 Okoboji (lakes), Ia,US
129/F3 Okolona, Ms,US
122/E3 Okotoks, Ab,Can
100/C4 Oko, Wādī (dry riv.), Sudan
42/E2 Oksskolten (peak), Nor.
67/J1 Oktyabr'sk, Rus.
65/M5 Oktyabr'skiy, Rus.
64/G4 Okulovka, Rus.
77/M3 Okushiri (isl.), Japan
79/H7 Okutama, Japan
104/D5 Okwa (riv.), Bots.
124/C3 Olancha, Ca,US
116/D4 Olanchito, Hon.
42/F4 Öland (isl.), Swe.
42/F4 Ölands södra udde (pt.), Swe.
57/G4 Olan, Pic d' (peak), Fr.
60/D2 Olanto (riv.), It.
124/F3 Olathe, Co,US
125/J3 Olathe, Ks,US
112/E3 Olavarría, Arg.
49/J3 Oława, Pol.
51/F5 Ölbach (riv.), Ger.
60/A2 Olbia, It.
55/H1 Olching, Ger.
127/S9 Olcott, NY,US
132/D3 Old Baldy (mtn.), Wa,US
131/F5 Old Bridge, NJ,US
130/L2 Old Crow, Yk,Can
50/C4 Oldebroek, Neth.
51/F2 Oldenburg, Ger.
50/D4 Oldenzaal, Neth.
45/F4 Oldham, Eng,UK
122/E3 Oldman (riv.), Ab,Can
44/E3 Old Man of Coolston, The (mtn.), Eng,UK
47/F2 Old Nene (riv.), Eng,UK
131/G5 Old Northport (Northport), NY,US
51/F1 Oldoog (isl.), Ger.
127/G2 Old Town, Me,US
47/F4 Old Windsor, Eng,UK
123/G3 Old Wives (lake), Sk,Can
126/E3 Olean, NY,US
49/M1 Olecko, Pol.
58/A1 Oleiros, Sp.
69/N4 Olekma (riv.), Rus.
132/B2 Olele (pt.), Wa,US
64/G1 Olenegorsk, Rus.
69/N2 Olenëk (bay), Rus.
69/N2 Olenëk (riv.), Rus.
75/B1 Olenty (riv.), Kaz.
56/C4 Oléron (isl.), Fr.
59/K6 Olesa de Montserrat, Sp.
49/J3 Oleśnica, Pol.
49/K3 Olesno, Pol.
51/E5 Olfen, Ger.
76/B2 Ölgiy, Mong.
58/B4 Olhão, Port.
57/L4 Olib (isl.), Cro.
60/A2 Oliena, It.
102/B2 Olifants (dry riv.), Namb.
102/B3 Olifants (riv.), SAfr.
102/E2 Olifantsrivier (riv.), SAfr.
92/D4 Olimarao (atoll), Micr.
61/H2 Olimbos (Mount Olympus) (peak), Gre.
110/B2 Olímpia, Braz.
109/M5 Olinda, Braz.
112/E2 Oliva, Arg.
59/E3 Oliva, Sp.
58/B3 Oliva de la Frontera, Sp.
58/A3 Olivais, Port.
110/C2 Oliveira, Braz.
58/B3 Olivenza, Sp.
122/D3 Oliver, BC,Can
56/D3 Olivet, Fr.
108/E8 Ollagüe (vol.), Bol.
59/E3 Ollería, Sp.
84/C5 Ollūr, India
112/Q9 Olmué, Chile
47/F2 Olney, Eng,UK
126/B4 Olney, Il,US
131/J7 Olney, Md,US
127/J1 Olomane (riv.), Qu,Can
49/J4 Olomouc, Czh.
82/D5 Olongapo, Phil.
56/C3 Olonne-sur-Mer, Fr.
56/C5 Oloron-Sainte-Marie, Fr.
59/G1 Olot, Sp.
69/S3 Oloy (range), Rus.
51/E6 Olpe, Ger.
51/F6 Olsberg, Ger.
50/D4 Olst, Neth.
49/L2 Olsztyn, Pol.
49/L2 Olsztyn (prov.), Pol.
49/L2 Olsztynek, Pol.
63/G3 Olt (co.), Rom.
63/G4 Olt (riv.), Rom.
112/C4 Olte (mts.), Arg.
54/D3 Olten, Swi.
63/H3 Olteniţa, Rom.
63/F3 Olteţ (riv.), Rom.
74/E2 Oltu, Turk.
74/E2 Oltu (riv.), Turk.
82/D3 Oluanpi, Tai.
58/C4 Olvera, Sp.
132/B3 Olympia (cap.), Wa,US
61/G4 Olympia (Olimbía) (ruins), Gre.
122/B4 Olympic (mts.), Wa,US
122/B4 Olympic Nat'l Park, Wa,US
74/J4 Olympus (mtn.), Cyp.
122/C4 Olympus (peak), Wa,US
61/H2 Olympus, Mount (Ólimbos) (peak), Gre.
61/H2 Olympus Nat'l Park, Gre.
69/S3 Olyutorskiy (bay), Rus.
65/K2 Oma (riv.), Rus.
79/E2 Ōmachi, Japan
79/F3 Omae-zaki (pt.), Japan
44/A2 Omagh, NI,UK
44/A2 Omagh (dist.), NI,UK
125/J2 Omaha, Ne,US
122/D3 Omak, Wa,US
73/G4 Oman
73/G4 Oman (gulf), Asia
104/C4 Omatako (riv.), Namb.
87/F5 Ombai (str.), Indo.
46/D2 Ombersley, Eng,UK
104/B4 Ombombo, Namb.
104/A1 Omboué, Gabon
60/B1 Ombrone (riv.), It.
97/M4 Omdurman (Umm Durmān), Sudan
79/H7 Ōme, Japan
57/H4 Omegna, It.
116/B4 Ometepec, Mex.
79/M9 Ōmihachiman, Japan
60/E1 Omiš, Cro.
79/G2 Ōmiya, Japan
130/M4 Ommaney (cape), Ak,US
50/D3 Ommen, Neth.
76/F2 Ömnödelger, Mong.
76/C2 Ömnögovĭ, Mong.
60/A2 Omodeo (lake), It.
71/Q3 Omolon (riv.), Rus.
97/N6 Omo Nat'l Park, Eth.
97/N6 Omo Wenz (riv.), Eth.
68/H4 Omsk, Rus.
63/G3 Omul (peak), Rom.
63/H4 Omurtag, Bul.
78/B4 Ōmuta, Japan
65/M4 Omutninsk, Rus.
79/G1 Onagawa, Japan
125/J5 Onalaska, Tx,US
58/D1 Oñate, Sp.
126/C2 Onaway, Mi,US
112/E1 Oncativo, Arg.
44/D3 Onchan, IM,UK
104/B4 Oncocúa, Ang.
59/E3 Onda, Sp.
104/C4 Ondangua, Namb.
49/L4 Ondava (riv.), Slvk.
104/C4 Ondjiva, Ang.
99/G5 Ondo (state), Nga.
76/G2 Öndörhaan, Mong.
76/E2 Öndörhangay, Mong.
64/H3 Onega, Rus.
64/H2 Onega (bay), Rus.
64/G3 Onega (lake), Rus.
64/H3 Onega (pen.), Rus.
64/H3 Onega (riv.), Rus.
122/C3 One Hundred Mile House, BC,Can
126/F3 Oneida, NY,US
125/H2 O'Neill, Ne,US
126/F3 Oneonta, NY,US
76/E2 Ongiyn (riv.), Mong.
84/D4 Ongole, India
123/H4 Onida, SD,US
59/E3 Onil, Sp.
103/G8 Onilahy (riv.), Madg.
99/G5 Onitsha, Nga.
103/H7 Onive (riv.), Madg.
52/C3 Onnaing, Fr.
46/D2 Onny (riv.), Eng,UK
78/D3 Ono, Japan
78/E3 Ōno, Japan
78/B4 Onoda, Japan
78/C3 Onomichi, Japan
76/G1 Onon (riv.), Mong., Rus.
92/G5 Onotoa (atoll), Kiri.
79/E3 Ontake-san (mtn.), Japan
118/H3 Ontario (prov.), Can.
126/E3 Ontario (lake), Can., US
131/C2 Ontario, Ca,US
122/D4 Ontario, Or,US
59/E3 Onteniente, Sp.
126/B2 Ontonagon, Mi,US
92/F5 Ontong Java (isl.), Sol.
128/E2 Oologah (lake), Ok,US
50/A6 Oostburg, Neth.
50/C4 Oostelijk Flevoland (polder), Neth.
52/B1 Oostende, Belg.
50/B5 Oosterhout, Neth.
50/A5 Oosterschelde (chan.), Neth.
52/C2 Oosterzele, Belg.
52/C1 Oostkamp, Belg.
50/C4 Oostvaardersplassen (lake), Neth.
50/B4 Oostzaan, Neth.
84/C5 Ootacamund, India
123/B2 Ootsa (lake), BC,Can
104/D1 Opala, D.R. Congo
49/J2 Opalenica, Pol.
62/B3 Opatija, Cro.
49/L3 Opatów, Pol.
49/J4 Opava, Czh.
129/G3 Opelika, Al,US
128/E4 Opelousas, La,US
126/E2 Opeongo (lake), On,Can
53/E1 Opglabbeek, Belg.
50/C5 Oploo, Neth.
50/B3 Opmeer, Neth.
49/L3 Opoczno, Pol.
49/J3 Opole, Pol.
49/J3 Opole (prov.), Pol.

168

Opole – Pasad

49/L3 **Opole Lubelskie,** Pol.
129/G4 **Opp,** Al,US
42/D3 **Oppdal,** Nor.
42/D3 **Oppland** (co.), Nor.
122/D4 **Opportunity,** Wa,US
52/D2 **Opwijk,** Belg.
62/E2 **Oradea,** Rom.
62/E4 **Orahovac,** Yugo.
84/C2 **Orai,** India
67/J2 **Oral,** Kaz.
67/J2 **Oral Obl.,** Kaz.
96/E1 **Oran,** Alg.
102/B3 **Orange** (riv.), Afr.
91/D2 **Orange,** Austl.
56/F4 **Orange,** Fr.
109/H3 **Orange** (mts.), Sur.
131/C3 **Orange,** Ca,US
131/F5 **Orange,** NJ,US
128/E4 **Orange,** Tx,US
126/E4 **Orange,** Va,US
129/H3 **Orangeburg,** SC,US
129/H4 **Orange Park,** Fl,US
126/D3 **Orangeville,** On,Can
116/D4 **Orange Walk,** Belz.
98/A4 **Orango** (isl.), GBis.
49/G2 **Oranienburg,** Ger.
50/D3 **Oranjekanaal** (can.), Neth.
117/G5 **Oranjestad** (cap.), Aru.
104/E5 **Orapa,** Bots.
74/M8 **Or 'Aqiva,** Isr.
82/E5 **Oras,** Phil.
63/F3 **Orăştie,** Rom.
62/E3 **Oraviţa,** Rom.
56/E5 **Orb** (riv.), Fr.
58/C1 **Órbigo** (riv.), Sp.
128/B2 **Orchard City,** Co,US
122/E4 **Orchard Homes,** Mt,US
132/F6 **Orchard Lake Village,** Mi,US
82/D3 **Orchid** (isl.), Tai.
57/G4 **Orco** (riv.), It.
56/F3 **Or, Côte d'** (uplands), Fr.
125/H2 **Ord,** Ne,US
58/A1 **Órdenes,** Sp.
59/F1 **Ordesa y Monte Perdido Nat'l Park,** Sp.
81/B3 **Ordos** (des.), China
74/D2 **Ordu,** Turk.
125/G3 **Ordway,** Co,US
42/E4 **Örebro,** Swe.
42/E4 **Örebro** (co.), Swe.
122/C4 **Oregon** (state), US
124/B2 **Oregon Caves Nat'l Mon.,** Or,US
122/C4 **Oregon City,** Or,US
66/F1 **Orël,** Rus.
66/E2 **Orel'** (riv.), Ukr.
66/E1 **Orel Obl.,** Rus.
124/E2 **Orem,** Ut,US
67/K2 **Orenburg,** Rus.
67/K1 **Orenburg Obl.,** Rus.
58/B1 **Orense,** Sp.
61/K2 **Orestiás,** Gre.
47/H2 **Orford,** Eng,UK
47/H2 **Orford Ness** (pt.), UK
124/D4 **Organ Pipe Cactus Nat'l Mon.,** Az,US
110/L7 **Órgãos** (mts.), Braz.
63/J2 **Orgeyev,** Mol.
66/D5 **Orhaneli,** Turk.
63/J5 **Orhangazi,** Turk.
76/F2 **Orhon** (riv.), Mong.
56/C5 **Orhy, Pic d'** (peak), Fr.
111/C6 **Oriental** (val.), Arg.
108/D6 **Oriental, Cordillera** (range), SAm.
101/A2 **Orientale** (prov.), D.R. Congo
59/E3 **Orihuela,** Sp.
126/E2 **Orillia,** On,Can
132/K11 **Orinda,** Ca,US
108/F2 **Orinoco** (riv.), Col., Ven.
117/J6 **Orinoco** (delta), Ven.
132/F6 **Orion** (lake), Mi,US
84/D3 **Orissa** (state), India
60/A3 **Oristano,** It.
60/A3 **Oristano** (gulf), It.
42/H3 **Orivesi,** Fin.
109/G4 **Oriximiná,** Braz.
116/B4 **Orizaba,** Mex.
62/D4 **Orjen** (peak), Yugo.
51/F6 **Orke** (riv.), Ger.
41/D3 **Orkney** (isls.), Sc,UK
128/C4 **Orla,** Tx,US
110/C2 **Orlândia,** Braz.
129/H4 **Orlando,** Fl,US
60/D3 **Orlando, Capo d'** (cape), It.
132/Q16 **Orland Park,** Il,US
56/D2 **Orléanais** (hist. reg.), Fr.
56/D3 **Orléans,** Fr.
124/B2 **Orleans,** Ca,US
49/K4 **Orlová,** Czh.
82/D5 **Ormoc,** Phil.
129/H4 **Ormond Beach,** Fl,US
45/F4 **Ormskirk,** Eng,UK
56/F2 **Ornain** (riv.), Fr.
53/F5 **Orne** (riv.), Fr.
42/E2 **Ørnes,** Nor.
49/L1 **Orneta,** Pol.
42/F3 **Örnsköldsvik,** Swe.
117/N8 **Oro** (riv.), Mex.
55/F6 **Orobie, Alpi** (range), It.
98/D4 **Orodara,** Burk.
59/E1 **Oroel** (peak), Sp.
122/D4 **Orofino,** Id,US
93/L6 **Orohena** (peak), FrPol.
92/E4 **Oroluk** (atoll), Micr.
127/H2 **Oromocto,** NB,Can
60/A1 **Oro, Monte d'** (mtn.), Fr.
93/H5 **Orona** (Hull) (atoll), Kiri.
127/G2 **Orono,** Me,US
74/L4 **Orontes** (riv.), Asia
77/J1 **Oroqen Zizhiqi,** China
87/F2 **Oroquieta,** Phil.
60/A2 **Orosei** (gulf), It.
62/E2 **Orosháza,** Hun.
62/D2 **Oroszlány,** Hun.
124/C2 **Orovada,** Nv,US
124/E4 **Oro Valley,** Az,US
124/B3 **Oroville,** Ca,US
122/D3 **Oroville,** Wa,US
45/F4 **Orrell,** Eng,UK
52/B5 **Orry-la-Ville,** Fr.
42/E3 **Orsa,** Swe.
52/B6 **Orsay,** Fr.
64/F5 **Orsha,** Bela.
67/L2 **Orsk,** Rus.
62/F3 **Orşova,** Rom.
42/C3 **Ørsta,** Nor.
57/H4 **Orta** (lake), It.
74/C2 **Orta,** Turk.
74/B3 **Ortaca,** Turk.
60/D2 **Orta Nova,** It.
58/B1 **Ortegal** (cape), Sp.
56/C5 **Orthez,** Fr.
58/B1 **Ortigueira,** Sp.
55/G5 **Ortles** (mts.), It., Swi.
108/E6 **Ortón** (riv.), Bol.
77/H2 **Orton** (riv.), China
60/D1 **Ortona,** It.
132/F6 **Ortonville,** Mi,US
123/J4 **Ortonville,** Mn,US
51/H3 **Örtze** (riv.), Ger.
74/F3 **Orūmīyeh,** Iran
108/E7 **Oruro,** Bol.
60/C1 **Orvieto,** It.
105/V **Orville** (coast), Ant.
47/H2 **Orwell** (riv.), Eng,UK
76/H2 **Orxon** (riv.), China
63/F4 **Oryakhovo,** Bul.
74/M8 **Or Yehuda,** Isr.
65/M4 **Osa,** Rus.
125/J3 **Osage** (riv.), Mo,US
125/J3 **Osage Beach,** Mo,US
78/L10 **Ōsaka,** Japan
79/L10 **Ōsaka** (bay), Japan
78/D3 **Ōsaka** (pref.), Japan
80/D4 **Osan,** SKor.
110/G8 **Osasco,** Braz.
130/E3 **Osborn** (mtn.), Ak,US
125/H3 **Osborne,** Ks,US
129/F3 **Osceola,** Ar,US
48/F2 **Oschersleben,** Ger.
128/B3 **Oscura** (mts.), NM,US
75/B3 **Osh,** Kyr.
104/C4 **Oshakati,** Namb.
127/S8 **Oshawa,** On,Can
77/M3 **Oshima** (pen.), Japan
104/C4 **Oshivelo,** Namb.
123/H5 **Oshkosh,** Ne,US
126/B2 **Oshkosh,** Wi,US
74/F3 **Oshnovīyeh,** Iran
99/G5 **Oshogbo,** Nga.
104/C1 **Oshwe,** D.R. Congo
62/D3 **Osijek,** Cro.
57/K5 **Osimo,** It.
66/D1 **Osipovichi,** Bela.
123/K5 **Oskaloosa,** Ia,US
42/F4 **Oskarshamn,** Swe.
75/D2 **Öskemen,** Kaz.
66/F2 **Oskol** (riv.), Rus., Ukr.
42/D4 **Oslo** (cap.), Nor.
84/C4 **Osmānābād,** India
74/C2 **Osmancık,** Turk.
63/K5 **Osmaneli,** Turk.
74/D3 **Osmaniye,** Turk.
51/F4 **Osnabrück,** Ger.
52/B5 **Osny,** Fr.
110/B4 **Osório,** Braz.
112/B4 **Osorno,** Chile
122/D3 **Osoyoos,** BC,Can
90/B1 **Osprey** (reef), Austl.
50/C5 **Oss,** Neth.
91/C4 **Ossa** (peak), Austl.
61/H3 **Ossa** (mtn.), Gre.
48/B3 **Ossa** (range), Port.
99/G5 **Osse** (riv.), Nga.
45/G4 **Ossett,** Eng,UK
131/G4 **Ossining,** NY,US
64/G4 **Ostashkov,** Rus.
51/E4 **Ostbevern,** Ger.
51/G1 **Oste** (riv.), Ger.
52/B1 **Ostend** (Oostende), Belg.
48/F2 **Osterburg,** Ger.
51/F4 **Ostercappeln,** Ger.
50/D1 **Osterems** (chan.), Neth.
42/E4 **Östergötland** (co.), Swe.
57/K2 **Osterhofen,** Ger.
51/F2 **Osterholz-Scharmbeck,** Ger.
51/H5 **Osterode,** Ger.
48/F3 **Osterode am Harz,** Ger.
42/E3 **Östersund,** Swe.
42/D4 **Østfold** (co.), Nor.
51/E2 **Ostfriesland** (reg.), Ger.
42/F3 **Östhammar,** Swe.
60/C2 **Ostia Antica** (ruins), It.
57/J4 **Ostiglia,** It.
49/K4 **Ostrava,** Czh.
51/E2 **Ostrhauderfehn,** Ger.
52/C3 **Ostricourt,** Fr.
62/D4 **Oštri Rt** (cape), Yugo.
49/K2 **Ostróda,** Pol.
66/F2 **Ostrogozhsk,** Rus.
49/L2 **Ostrołęka,** Pol.
49/L2 **Ostrołęka** (prov.), Pol.
57/K1 **Ostrov,** Czh.
64/F4 **Ostrov,** Rus.
49/L3 **Ostrowiec Świętokrzyski,** Pol.
49/L2 **Ostrów Mazowiecka,** Pol.
49/J3 **Ostrów Wielkopolski,** Pol.
49/J3 **Ostrzeszów,** Pol.
51/H1 **Oststeinbek,** Ger.
60/E2 **Ostuni,** It.
61/G2 **Osum** (riv.), Alb.
63/G4 **Osŭm** (riv.), Bul.
78/B5 **Ōsumi** (isls.), Japan
78/B5 **Ōsumi** (pen.), Japan
78/B5 **Ōsumi** (str.), Japan
58/C4 **Osuna,** Sp.
110/B2 **Osvaldo Cruz,** Braz.
45/G3 **Oswaldkirk,** Eng,UK
45/F4 **Oswaldtwistle,** Eng,UK
126/E3 **Oswego,** NY,US
45/E6 **Oswestry,** Eng,UK
49/K3 **Oświęcim** (Auschwitz), Pol.
78/F2 **Ota,** Japan
78/C3 **Ōta** (riv.), Japan
78/C3 **Ōtake,** Japan
79/G2 **Ōtakine-yama** (mtn.), Japan
57/K2 **Otava** (riv.), Czh.
79/G2 **Ōtawara,** Japan
62/F3 **Oţelu Roşu,** Rom.
93/L6 **Otepa,** FrPol.
117/N8 **Oteros** (riv.), Mex.
76/D2 **Otgon,** Mong.
76/D2 **Otgon Tenger** (peak), Mong.
122/D4 **Othello,** Wa,US
52/B5 **Othis,** Fr.
61/F3 **Othonoí** (isl.), Gre.
99/F4 **Oti** (riv.), Gui.
104/C5 **Otjikango,** Namb.
104/C5 **Otjinene,** Namb.
104/C5 **Otjiwarongo,** Namb.
104/B4 **Otjokavare,** Namb.
45/G4 **Otley,** Eng,UK
81/A3 **Otog Qi,** China
123/L3 **Otoskwin** (riv.), On,Can
79/N10 **Otowa,** Japan
42/C4 **Otra** (riv.), Nor.
67/J1 **Otradnyy,** Rus.
61/F2 **Otranto** (str.), Alb., It.
49/J4 **Otrokovice,** Czh.
78/D3 **Ōtsu,** Japan
42/D3 **Otta,** Nor.
126/F2 **Ottawa** (cap.), Can.
119/H3 **Ottawa** (isls.), Nun.,Can
126/E2 **Ottawa** (riv.), On, Qu,Can
126/B3 **Ottawa,** Il,US
125/J3 **Ottawa,** Ks,US
126/C3 **Ottawa,** Oh,US
46/C5 **Otter** (riv.), Eng,UK
45/F1 **Otterburn,** Eng,UK
51/F1 **Otterndorf,** Ger.
51/G2 **Ottersberg,** Ger.
46/C5 **Ottery Saint Mary,** Eng,UK
52/D2 **Ottignies-Louvain-La-Neuve,** Belg.
57/J2 **Ottobrunn,** Ger.
123/K5 **Ottumwa,** Ia,US
53/G5 **Ottweiler,** Ger.
91/B3 **Otway** (cape), Austl.
113/J8 **Otway** (bay), Chile
113/K8 **Otway** (sound), Chile
91/B3 **Otway Nat'l Park,** Austl.
49/L2 **Otwock,** Pol.
55/G4 **Ötztal Alps** (mts.), Aus., It.
83/C1 **Ou** (riv.), Laos
128/E3 **Ouachita** (riv.), Ar, La,US
125/J4 **Ouachita** (mts.), Ar, Ok,US
96/C3 **Ouadane,** Mrta.
97/J5 **Ouaddaï** (reg.), Chad
99/E3 **Ouagadougou** (cap.), Burk.
97/K6 **Ouaka** (riv.), CAfr.
98/D2 **Oualâta, Dhar** (hills), Mrta.
56/E3 **Ouanne** (riv.), Fr.
96/C3 **Ouarane** (reg.), Mrta.
96/G1 **Ouargla,** Alg.
96/D1 **Ouarzazate,** Mor.
127/F1 **Ouasiemsca** (riv.), Qu,Can
97/J6 **Oubangui** (riv.), CAfr.
99/E3 **Oubritenga** (prov.), Burk.
79/L10 **Ōuda,** Japan
99/E3 **Oudalan** (prov.), Burk.
50/B5 **Oud-Beijerland,** Neth.
50/A5 **Ouddorp,** Neth.
50/D5 **Oude IJssel** (riv.), Neth.
52/C2 **Oudenaarde,** Belg.
50/B5 **Oudenbosch,** Neth.
52/B1 **Oudenburg,** Belg.
50/E2 **Oude Pekela,** Neth.
56/C3 **Oudon** (riv.), Fr.
102/C4 **Oudtshoorn,** SAfr.
50/B6 **Oud-Turnhout,** Belg.
98/E2 **Oued el Hadjar** (well), Mali
96/D1 **Oued Zem,** Mor.
99/F5 **Ouémé** (prov.), Ben.
99/F4 **Ouémé** (riv.), Ben.
93/V13 **Ouen** (isl.), NCal.
56/A2 **Ouessant** (isl.), Fr.
96/J7 **Ouesso,** Congo
99/H5 **Ouest** (prov.), Camr.
117/G4 **Ouest** (pt.), Haiti
96/D1 **Ouezzane,** Mor.
97/J6 **Ouham** (riv.), CAfr., Chad
52/C5 **Ouichy-le-Château,** Fr.
96/E1 **Oujda,** Mor.
42/J2 **Oulangan Nat'l Park,** Fin.
91/A2 **Oulnina** (peak), Austl.
42/H2 **Oulu,** Fin.
42/H2 **Oulun** (prov.), Fin.
42/H2 **Oulujärvi** (lake), Fin.
96/D1 **Oum er Rhia** (riv.), Mor.
97/J5 **Oum Hadjer,** Chad
64/E2 **Ounasjoki** (riv.), Fin.
47/F2 **Oundle,** Eng,UK
97/K4 **OuniangaKebir,** Chad
53/E2 **Oupeye,** Belg.
53/F4 **Our** (riv.), Eur.
54/A2 **Ource** (riv.), Fr.
52/C5 **Ourcq** (riv.), Fr.
42/H1 **Øure Anarjokka Nat'l Park,** Nor.
42/F1 **Øure Dividal Nat'l Park,** Nor.
97/J3 **Ouri,** Chad
109/K5 **Ouricuri,** Braz.
110/B2 **Ourinhos,** Braz.
99/H3 **Ourofané,** Niger
110/G7 **Ouro Fino,** Braz.
110/D2 **Ouro Preto,** Braz.
53/E3 **Ourthe** (riv.), Belg.
45/H4 **Ouse** (riv.), Eng,UK
47/G5 **Ouse** (riv.), Eng,UK
56/B3 **Oust** (riv.), Fr.
59/Q11 **Outão,** Port.
126/E2 **Outaouais** (riv.), Qu,Can
127/G1 **Outardes** (riv.), Qu,Can
127/G1 **Outardes Quatre** (res.), Qu,Can
98/D2 **Outeid Arkas** (well), Mali
43/A2 **Outer Hebrides** (isls.), Sc,UK
58/A1 **Outes,** Sp.
122/G3 **Outlook,** Sk,Can
52/A2 **Outreau,** Fr.
127/N6 **Outremont,** Qu,Can
93/V12 **Ouvéa** (atoll), NCal.
57/H4 **Ovada,** It.
93/Y18 **Ovalau** (isl.), Fiji
111/B3 **Ovalle,** Chile
58/A2 **Ovar,** Port.
53/G2 **Overath,** Ger.
50/B5 **Overflakkee** (isl.), Neth.
52/D2 **Overijse,** Belg.
50/D3 **Overijssel** (prov.), Neth.
50/D4 **Overijssels** (can.), Neth.
125/J3 **Overland Park,** Ks,US
131/K7 **Overlea,** Md,US
112/C5 **Overo** (peak), Arg.
53/E1 **Overpelt,** Belg.
47/E1 **Overseal,** Eng,UK
47/H1 **Overstrand,** Eng,UK
47/E4 **Overton,** Eng,UK
45/F6 **Overton,** Wal,UK
124/D3 **Overton,** Nv,US
42/G2 **Övertorneå,** Swe.
58/C1 **Oviedo,** Sp.
42/J1 **Øvre Pasvik Nat'l Park,** Nor.
104/C1 **Owando,** Congo
79/N9 **Owariasahi,** Japan
78/E3 **Owase,** Japan
125/J3 **Owasso,** Ok,US
123/K4 **Owatonna,** Mn,US
126/E3 **Owego,** NY,US
82/B6 **Owen** (shoal)
44/A2 **Owenkillew** (riv.), NI,UK
124/C3 **Owens** (riv.), Ca,US
126/C4 **Owensboro,** Ky,US
126/D2 **Owen Sound,** On,Can
124/C2 **Owhyee** (mts.), Id,US
131/K7 **Owings Mills,** Md,US
122/F4 **Owl Creek** (mts.), Wy,US
126/C3 **Owosso,** Mi,US
122/D5 **Owyhee** (riv.), Id, Or,US
124/C2 **Owyhee,** Nv,US
124/C2 **Owyhee** (lake), Or,US
72/E1 **Owzan** (riv.), Iran
123/H3 **Oxbow,** Sk,Can
123/K2 **Oxford** (lake), Mb,Can
47/E3 **Oxford,** Eng,UK
47/E3 **Oxford** (can.), Eng,UK
132/F6 **Oxford,** Mi,US
129/F3 **Oxford,** Ms,US
126/C4 **Oxford,** Oh,US
47/E3 **Oxfordshire** (co.), Eng,UK
90/E7 **Oxley** (cr.), Austl.
131/A2 **Oxnard,** Ca,US
131/K8 **Oxon Hill-Glassmanor,** Md,US
47/F4 **Oxted,** Eng,UK
79/E2 **Oyabe,** Japan
79/F2 **Oyama,** Japan
79/M10 **Ōyamada,** Japan
79/L10 **Ōyamazaki,** Japan
109/H3 **Oyapock** (riv.), FrG.
96/H7 **Oyem,** Gabon
122/F3 **Oyen,** Ab,Can
99/F5 **Oyo,** Nga.
99/F4 **Oyo** (state), Nga.
79/L10 **Ōyodo,** Japan
78/B5 **Ōyodo** (riv.), Japan
131/G5 **Oyster Bay,** NY,US
51/G2 **Oyten,** Ger.
82/D6 **Ozamiz,** Phil.
56/D2 **Ozanne** (riv.), Fr.
125/J3 **Ozark** (plat.), US
129/G4 **Ozark,** Al,US
128/E3 **Ozark,** Ar,US
128/E3 **Ozark** (mts.), Ar, Mo,US
125/J3 **Ozarks, Lake of the** (lake), Mo,US
62/E1 **Ózd,** Hun.
69/S4 **Ozernoy** (cape), Rus.
122/B3 **Ozette** (lake), Wa,US
123/L3 **Ozhiski** (lake), On,Can
60/A2 **Ozieri,** It.
49/K3 **Ozimek,** Pol.
52/B6 **Ozoir-la-Ferrière,** Fr.
128/C4 **Ozona,** Tx,US
49/K3 **Ozorków,** Pol.
78/C4 **Ōzu,** Japan

P

55/H1 **Paar** (riv.), Ger.
102/B4 **Paarl,** SAfr.
49/K3 **Pabianice,** Pol.
84/E3 **Pābna,** Bang.
108/F6 **Pacaás Novos** (mts.), Braz.
108/F6 **Pacaás Novos Nat'l Park,** Braz.
109/H4 **Pacajá** (riv.), Braz.
108/C5 **Pacasmayo,** Peru
60/C4 **Paceco,** It.
108/C6 **Pachacamac** (ruins), Peru
60/D4 **Pachino,** It.
84/C3 **Pachmarhī,** India
38/B4 **Pacific** (ocean)
122/B3 **Pacific** (ranges), BC,Can
132/K11 **Pacifica,** Ca,US
131/B2 **Pacifico** (mtn.), Ca,US
118/D4 **Pacific Rim Nat'l Park,** BC,Can
86/D5 **Pacinan** (cape), Indo.
86/D5 **Pacitan,** Indo.
59/P10 **Paço de Arcos,** Port.
86/B4 **Padang,** Indo.
86/B4 **Padangpanjang,** Indo.
86/A3 **Padangsidempuan,** Indo.
47/G4 **Paddock Wood,** Eng,UK
51/F5 **Paderborn,** Ger.
73/J3 **Pad Īdan,** Pak.
45/F4 **Padiham,** Eng,UK
62/E3 **Padina,** Yugo.
42/E2 **Padjelanta Nat'l Park,** Swe.
57/J4 **Padova** (Padua), It.
104/B2 **Padrão, Ponta do** (pt.), Ang.
128/D5 **Padre Island Nat'l Seashore,** Tx,US
58/A1 **Padrón,** Sp.
102/D4 **Padrone** (cape), SAfr
46/B5 **Padstow,** Eng,UK
57/J4 **Padua** (Padova), It.
126/B4 **Paducah,** Ky,US
128/C3 **Paducah,** Tx,US
80/E4 **Paektŏk-san** (mtn.), SKor.
80/D2 **Paektu-San** (mtn.), NKor.
80/C4 **Paengnyŏng** (isl.), SKor.
62/B3 **Pag** (isl.), Cro.
82/D6 **Pagadian,** Phil.
86/B4 **Pagai Selatan** (isl.), Indo.
86/A4 **Pagai Utara** (isl.), Indo.
92/D3 **Pagan** (isl.), NMar.
124/E3 **Page,** Az,US
93/H6 **Pago Pago** (cap.), ASam.
124/F3 **Pagosa Springs,** Co,US
126/C1 **Pagwachuan** (riv.), On,Can
86/B3 **Pahang** (riv.), Malay
124/D3 **Pahrump,** Nv,US
124/C3 **Pahute Mesa** (upland), Nv,US
81/C5 **Pai** (lake), China
61/L7 **Paiania,** Gre.
46/C6 **Paignton,** Eng,UK
42/H3 **Päijänne** (lake), Fin.
83/C3 **Pailin,** Camb.
120/T10 **Pailolo** (chan.), Hi,US
64/D3 **Paimio,** Fin.
112/C2 **Paine,** Chile
113/J7 **Paine** (peak), Chile
126/D3 **Painesville,** Oh,US
46/C2 **Painscastle,** Wal,UK
123/J2 **Paint** (lake), Mb,Can
124/E4 **Painted** (des.), Az,US
128/D4 **Paint Rock,** Tx,US
126/D4 **Paintsville,** Ky,US
43/C3 **Paisley,** Sc,UK
84/C4 **Paithan,** India
42/G2 **Pajala,** Swe.
49/K3 **Pajęczno,** Pol.
117/E6 **Pajonal Abajo,** Pan
86/B3 **Pakanbaru,** Indo.
91/G6 **Pakenham,** Austl.
113/J7 **Pakenham** (cape), Chile
61/J5 **Pákhnes** (peak), Gre.
65/X9 **Pakhra** (riv.), Rus.
73/H3 **Pakistan**
62/B3 **Paklenica Nat'l Park,** Cro.
85/G3 **Pakokku,** Myan.
122/F3 **Pakowki** (lake), Ab,Can
73/K2 **Pākpattan,** Pak.
85/H6 **Pak Phanang,** Thai.
62/C3 **Pakrac,** Cro.
62/D2 **Paks,** Hun.
83/D3 **Pakxe,** Laos
96/H6 **Pala,** Chad
59/N9 **Palacio Real,** Sp.
59/G2 **Palafrugell,** Sp.
60/D4 **Palagonia,** It.
60/E1 **Palagruža** (isls.), Cro.
61/F3 **Palaiokastritsa,** Gre.
84/D4 **Pālakolla,** India
59/G2 **Palamós,** Sp.
86/D4 **Palangkaraya,** Indo.
84/B3 **Pālanpur,** India
120/T10 **Palaoa** (pt.), Hi,US
104/E5 **Palapye,** Bots.
84/C5 **Palar** (riv.), India
58/B1 **Palas de Rey,** Sp.
132/P15 **Palatine,** Il,US
129/H4 **Palatka,** Fl,US
92/C4 **Palau**
82/C6 **Palawan** (isl.), Phil.
82/C5 **Palawan** (passage), Phil.
84/C6 **Pālayankottai,** India
60/D4 **Palazzolo Acreide,** It.
96/G8 **Palé,** EqG.
87/F3 **Paleleh,** Indo.
86/B4 **Palembang,** Indo.
112/B4 **Palena** (riv.), Chile
58/C1 **Palencia,** Sp.
127/Q9 **Palermo,** On,Can
60/C3 **Palermo,** It.
128/E4 **Palestine,** Tx,US
128/E3 **Palestine** (lake), Tx,US
73/K5 **Pālghar,** India
80/E4 **P'algong-san** (mtn.), SKor.
110/B3 **Palhoça,** Braz.
84/B2 **Pāli,** India
113/K8 **Pali Aike Nat'l Park,** Chile
62/D2 **Palić,** Yugo.
120/V13 **Palikea** (peak), Hi,US
92/E4 **Palikir** (cap.), Micr.
61/H3 **Palioúrion, Ákra** (cape), Gre.
131/F5 **Palisades Park,** NJ,US
84/B3 **Pālitāna,** India
62/C3 **Paljenik** (peak), Bosn.
84/C6 **Palk** (str.), India, SrL.
42/H1 **Pallas-Ounastunturin Nat'l Park,** Fin.
42/H1 **Pallastunturi** (peak), Fin.
109/J6 **Palma** (riv.), Braz.
59/G3 **Palma,** Sp.
58/C4 **Palma del Río,** Sp.
60/C4 **Palma di Montechiaro,** It.
109/L5 **Palmares,** Braz.
110/B3 **Palmas,** Braz.
98/D5 **Palmas** (cape), Libr.
117/F3 **Palma Soriano,** Cuba
129/H4 **Palm Bay,** Fl,US
90/H8 **Palm Beach,** Austl.
131/B1 **Palmdale,** Ca,US
110/B3 **Palmeira,** Braz.
109/L5 **Palmeira dos Índios,** Braz.
104/B2 **Palmeirinhas, Ponta das** (pt.), Ang.
59/Q10 **Palmela,** Port.
105/V **Palmer** (arch.), Ant.
105/V **Palmer Land** (reg.), Ant.
90/C3 **Palmerston** (cape), Austl.
93/J6 **Palmerston** (atoll), CookIs.
89/H7 **Palmerston,** NZ
90/B2 **Palmerston Nat'l Park,** Austl.
89/H7 **Palmerston North,** NZ
129/H5 **Palmetto,** Fl,US
129/H4 **Palm Harbor,** Fl,US
60/D3 **Palmi,** It.
112/C2 **Palmilla,** Chile
108/C3 **Palmira,** Col.
124/C4 **Palm Springs,** Ca,US
93/J4 **Palmyra** (isl.), PacUS
72/C2 **Palmyra** (ruins), Syria
84/E3 **Palmyras** (pt.), India
44/E2 **Palnackie,** Sc,UK
84/C5 **Palni,** India
82/D5 **Palo,** Phil.
132/K12 **Palo Alto,** Ca,US
117/M8 **Palo Bola,** Mex.
125/G3 **Palo Duro** (cr.), Ok, Tx,US
57/J4 **Palon** (peak), It.
128/D3 **Palo Pinto,** Tx,US
59/E4 **Palos, Cabo de** (cape), Sp.
132/Q16 **Palos Hills,** Il,US
131/B3 **Palos Verdes Estates,** Ca,US
116/D5 **Palo Verde Nat'l Park,** Mex.
84/D2 **Pālpa,** Nepal
111/C1 **Palpalá,** Arg.
87/G4 **Palpetu** (cape), Indo.
74/D2 **Palu,** Turk.
82/D5 **Paluan,** Phil.
86/C3 **Pamangkat,** Indo.
56/D5 **Pamiers,** Fr.
75/B4 **Pamir** (riv.), Afg., Taj.
75/B4 **Pamir** (reg.), China, Taj.
129/J3 **Pamlico** (riv.), NC,US
129/J3 **Pamlico** (sound), NC,US
128/C3 **Pampa,** Tx,US
112/E2 **Pampa Humida** (plain), Arg.
112/E3 **Pampas** (plain), Arg.
112/D3 **Pampa Seca** (plain), Arg.
108/D2 **Pamplona,** Col.
58/E1 **Pamplona,** Sp.
63/K5 **Pamukova,** Turk.
82/E6 **Panabo,** Phil.
124/D3 **Panaca,** Nv,US
84/C6 **Panadura,** SrL.
63/G4 **Panagyurishte,** Bul.
86/B5 **Panaitan** (isl.), Indo.
84/B4 **Pānāji,** India
117/E6 **Panama**
117/E6 **Panama** (can.), Pan.
117/F6 **Panamá** (cap.), Pan.
117/F6 **Panama** (gulf), Pan.
117/F6 **Panama** (isth.), Pan.
129/G4 **Panama City,** Fl,US
124/C3 **Panamint** (range), Ca,US
57/J4 **Panaro** (riv.), It.
82/D5 **Panay** (isl.), Phil.
124/C3 **Pancake** (range), Nv,US
62/E3 **Pančevo,** Yugo.
62/E4 **Pančicev vrh** (peak), Yugo.
63/H3 **Panciu,** Rom.
104/E4 **Pandamatenga,** Bots.
111/B2 **Pan de Azúcar Nat'l Park,** Chile
84/C4 **Pandharpur,** India
113/G2 **Pando,** Uru.
85/F2 **Pandu,** India
64/E5 **Panevėžys,** Lith.
75/D3 **Panfilov,** Kaz.
83/B1 **Pang** (riv.), Myan.
93/H7 **Pangai,** Tonga
61/J2 **Pangaíon** (peak), Gre.
101/C3 **Pangani** (riv.), Tanz.
47/E4 **Pangbourne,** Eng,UK
86/A3 **Pangkalanberandan,** Indo.
87/F4 **Pangkalaseang** (cape), Indo.
86/C4 **Pangkalpinang,** Indo.
124/D3 **Panguitch,** Ut,US
87/F2 **Pangutaran,** Phil.
82/D6 **Pangutaran** (isl.), Phil.
128/C3 **Panhandle,** Tx,US
87/J4 **Paniai** (lake), Indo.
120/R10 **Paniau** (peak), Hi,US
92/F7 **Panié** (peak), NCal.
84/C2 **Pānīpat,** India
73/K1 **Panj** (Pyandzh) (riv.), Afg., Taj.
84/D3 **Panna,** India
90/F7 **Pannikin** (isl.), Austl.
110/B2 **Panorama,** Braz.
45/E6 **Pant,** Eng,UK
47/G3 **Pant** (riv.), Eng,UK
109/G7 **Pantanal Matogrossense Nat'l Park,** Braz.
60/B4 **Pantelleria** (isl.), It.
52/B5 **Pantin,** Fr.
58/B1 **Pantón,** Sp.
116/B3 **Pánuco,** Mex.
116/B3 **Pánuco** (riv.), Mex.
85/H2 **Panzhihua,** China
60/E3 **Paola,** It.
125/J3 **Paola,** Ks,US
124/F3 **Paonia,** Co,US
96/J6 **Paoua,** CAfr.
83/C3 **Paoy Pet,** Camb.
62/C2 **Pápa,** Hun.
116/D5 **Papagayo** (gulf), CR
116/B3 **Papantla de Olarte,** Mex.
93/X15 **Papara,** FrPol.
93/X15 **Papeete** (cap.), FrPol.
51/E2 **Papenburg,** Ger.
50/B5 **Papendrecht,** Neth.
93/X15 **Papenoo,** FrPol.
93/X15 **Papetoai,** FrPol.
74/J4 **Paphos,** Cyp.
125/H2 **Papillion,** Ne,US
61/G2 **Papingut, Maj'e** (peak), Alb.
87/H4 **Papisoi** (cape), Indo.
92/D5 **Papua** (gulf), PNG
92/D5 **Papua New Guinea**
110/C1 **Pará** (riv.), Braz.
110/K7 **Paracambi,** Braz.
109/J7 **Paracatu,** Braz.
82/B4 **Paracel** (isls.)
71/N7 **Parace Vela** (Okino-Tori-Shima) (isl.), Japan
62/E4 **Paraćin,** Yugo.
59/N8 **Paracuellos,** Sp.
110/C1 **Pará de Minas,** Braz.
84/E3 **Paradip,** India
122/F2 **Paradise Hill,** Sk,Can
109/J4 **Paragominas,** Braz.
129/F2 **Paragould,** Ar,US
108/F6 **Paraguá** (riv.), Bol.
108/F2 **Paragua** (riv.), Ven.
110/H6 **Paraguaçu,** Braz.
109/L6 **Paraguaçu** (riv.), Braz.
110/B2 **Paraguaçu Paulista,** Braz.
109/G6 **Paraguai** (riv.), Braz.
117/G5 **Paraguaná** (pen.), Ven.
111/E2 **Paraguarí,** Par.
107/D5 **Paraguay**
110/D2 **Paraíba do Sul** (riv.), Braz.
110/H8 **Paraibuna** (riv.), Braz.
109/J6 **Paraíso do Norte de Goiás,** Braz.
110/G7 **Paraisópolis,** Braz.
99/F4 **Parakou,** Ben.
109/G2 **Paramaribo** (cap.), Sur.
108/C2 **Paramillo Nat'l Park,** Col.
109/K6 **Paramirim** (riv.), Braz.
131/B3 **Paramount,** Ca,US
131/F5 **Paramus,** NJ,US
69/R4 **Paramushir** (isl.), Rus.
110/B3 **Paraná** (state), Braz.
107/D5 **Paraná** (riv.), SAm.
110/B3 **Paranaguá,** Braz.
110/B1 **Paranaíba,** Braz.
110/B1 **Paranaiba** (riv.), Braz.
110/B2 **Paranapanema** (riv.), Braz.
110/B3 **Paranapiacaba** (range), Braz.
107/D4 **Paranatinga** (riv.), Braz.
109/H8 **Paranavai,** Braz.
87/F2 **Parang,** Phil.
110/C1 **Paraopeba,** Braz.
109/J8 **Parapanema** (riv.), Braz.
108/F7 **Parapetí** (riv.), Bol.
110/J8 **Parati,** Braz.
110/H8 **Paratinga** (riv.), Braz.
84/C4 **Parbhani,** India
48/F2 **Parchim,** Ger.
49/M3 **Parczew,** Pol.
74/M8 **Pardes Hanna-Kardur,** Isr.
84/B3 **Pārdi,** India
110/G6 **Pardo** (riv.), Braz.
49/H3 **Pardubice,** Czh.
86/D5 **Pare,** Indo.
108/F6 **Parecis** (mts.), Braz.
59/P10 **Parede,** Port.
112/C2 **Paredones,** Chile
126/E1 **Parent** (lake), Qu,Can
87/E4 **Parepare,** Indo.
59/L6 **Parets del Vallès,** Sp.
61/G3 **Párga,** Gre.
117/J5 **Paria** (gulf), Trin., Ven.
124/E3 **Paria** (riv.), Az, Ut,US
117/J5 **Paria** (pen.), Ven.
117/J6 **Pariaguán,** Ven.
86/B4 **Pariaman,** Indo.
108/E7 **Parinacota** (peak), Bol.
109/G4 **Parintins,** Braz.
52/B6 **Paris** (cap.), Fr.
128/E3 **Paris,** Ar,US
126/B4 **Paris,** Tn,US
128/E3 **Paris,** Tx,US
124/F2 **Park** (range), Co,US
124/D4 **Parker,** Az,US
125/F3 **Parker,** Co,US
126/D4 **Parkersburg,** WV,US
91/D2 **Parkes,** Austl.
47/H3 **Parkeston,** Eng,UK
126/B2 **Park Falls,** Wi,US
44/B2 **Parkgate,** NI,UK
46/A5 **Park Head** (pt.), UK
47/E5 **Parkhurst,** Eng,UK
132/C3 **Parkland,** Wa,US
123/K4 **Park Rapids,** Mn,US
132/Q15 **Park Ridge,** Il,US
131/F4 **Park Ridge,** NJ,US
123/J3 **Park River,** ND,US
131/K7 **Parkville,** Md,US
132/L9 **Parkway-Sacramento,** Ca,US
58/D2 **Parla,** Sp.
84/D4 **Parlakhemundi,** India
84/C4 **Parli,** India
57/J4 **Parma,** It.
126/D3 **Parma,** Oh,US
109/K4 **Parnaíba,** Braz.
109/K4 **Parnaíba** (riv.), Braz.
61/H3 **Parnassos Nat'l Park,** Gre.
61/H3 **Párnis** (peak), Gre.
61/H4 **Párnon** (mts.), Gre.
64/E4 **Pärnu,** Est.
91/C1 **Paroo** (riv.), Austl.
61/J4 **Páros** (isl.), Gre.
102/B4 **Parow,** SAfr.
124/D3 **Parowan,** Ut,US
112/C3 **Parral,** Chile
90/H8 **Parramatta,** Austl.
116/A2 **Parras de la Fuente,** Mex.
46/D4 **Parrett** (riv.), Eng,UK
116/E6 **Parrita,** CR
119/H2 **Parry** (bay), Nun.,Can
118/F1 **Parry** (chan.), Nun.,Can
119/R7 **Parry** (isls.), NW,Nun.,Can
126/D2 **Parry Sound,** On,Can
55/G3 **Parseierspitze** (peak), Aus.
123/H4 **Parshall,** ND,US
131/F5 **Parsippany,** NJ,US
122/C2 **Parsnip** (riv.), BC,Can
125/J3 **Parsons,** Ks,US
64/C2 **Pårtefjället** (peak), Swe.
56/C3 **Parthenay,** Fr.
60/C3 **Partinico,** It.
77/L3 **Partizansk,** Rus.
126/D1 **Partridge** (riv.), On,Can
84/C4 **Partūr,** India
109/H4 **Paru** (riv.), Braz.
84/D4 **Pārvathīpuram,** India
45/G5 **Parwich,** Eng,UK
102/D2 **Parys,** SAfr.
127/K1 **Pasadena,** Nf,Can
131/B2 **Pasadena,** Ca,US
131/K7 **Pasadena,** Md,US
128/E4 **Pasadena,** Tx,US

169
Pasaj – Pô

108/C4 Pasaje, Ecu.
83/C3 Pa Sak (riv.), Thai.
86/B3 Pasaman (peak), Indo.
129/F4 Pascagoula, Ms,US
63/H2 Paşcani, Rom.
122/D4 Pasco, Wa,US
113/J7 Pascua (riv.), Chile
52/A3 Pas-de-Calais (dept.), Fr.
52/B3 Pas-en-Artois, Fr.
82/D5 Pasig, Phil.
85/G2 Pāsighāt, India
74/E2 Pasinler, Turk.
49/K1 Pasłęk, Pol.
49/L2 Pasłęka (riv.), Pol.
62/B4 Pašman (isl.), Cro.
73/H3 Pasni, Pak.
111/E2 Paso de Los Libres, Arg.
112/C2 Paso del Planchón (peak), Chile
124/B4 Paso Robles (El Paso de Robles), Ca,US
130/M3 Pass (peak), Yk,Can
131/F5 Passaic, NJ,US
131/F5 Passaic (riv.), NJ,US
110/J7 Passa Quatro, Braz.
57/K2 Passau, Ger.
52/C2 Passendale, Belg.
60/D4 Passero (pt.), It.
111/F2 Passo Fundo, Braz.
110/A3 Passo Fundo (res.), Braz.
99/E3 Passoré (prov.), Burk.
110/C2 Passos, Braz.
57/G4 Passy, Fr.
108/C4 Pastaza (riv.), Ecu., Peru
108/C3 Pasto, Col.
130/F3 Pastol (bay), Ak,US
86/D5 Pasuruan, Indo.
62/D2 Pásztó, Hun.
112/D4 Patagonia (reg.), Arg.
86/B4 Patah (peak), Indo.
84/B3 Pātan, India
131/K7 Patapsco (riv.), Md,US
131/G5 Patchogue, NY,US
46/D3 Patchway, Eng,UK
45/G3 Pateley Bridge, Eng,UK
59/E3 Paterna, Sp.
131/F5 Paterson, NJ,US
73/L2 Pathānkot, India
122/G5 Pathfinder (res.), Wy,US
86/D5 Pati, Indo.
108/C3 Patía (riv.), Col.
73/L2 Patiāla, India
87/F2 Patikul, Phil.
84/E2 Patna, India
44/D1 Patna, Sc,UK
87/F1 Patnongon, Phil.
74/E2 Patnos, Turk.
110/A3 Pato Branco, Braz.
129/G2 Patoka (riv.), In,US
61/F2 Patos, Alb.
109/L5 Patos, Braz.
110/B4 Patos (lake), Braz.
110/C1 Patos de Minas, Braz.
61/G3 Pátrai, Gre.
61/G3 Patrai (gulf), Gre.
113/J7 Patricio Lynch (isl.), Chile
45/H4 Patrington, Eng,UK
110/C1 Patrocínio, Braz.
83/C5 Pattani, Thai.
83/C3 Pattaya, Thai.
51/G4 Pattensen, Ger.
60/D3 Patti, It.
46/D1 Pattingham, Eng,UK
84/C5 Pattukkottai, India
130/N4 Pattullo (mtn.), BC,Can
116/E4 Patuca (pt.), Hon.
116/D5 Patuca (riv.), Hon.
131/K8 Patuxent (riv.), Md,US
56/C5 Pau, Fr.
109/L7 Pau Brasil, Braz.
108/E5 Pauini (riv.), Braz.
110/F7 Paulínia, Braz.
109/L5 Paulo Afonso, Braz.
109/L5 Paulo Afonso Nat'l Park, Braz.
131/E6 Paulsboro, NJ,US
125/H4 Pauls Valley, Ok,US
46/D4 Paulton, Eng,UK
85/G4 Paungde, Myan.
75/C5 Pauri, India
57/H4 Pavia, It.
63/G4 Pavlikeni, Bul.
75/C1 Pavlodar, Kaz.
130/F4 Pavlof (vol.), Ak,US
66/E2 Pavlograd, Ukr.
64/J5 Pavlovo, Rus.
57/J4 Pavullo nel Frignano, It.
86/D4 Pawan (riv.), Indo.
125/H3 Pawhuska, Ok,US
83/B2 Pawn (riv.), Myan.
125/H3 Pawnee (riv.), Ks,US
126/C3 Paw Paw, Mi,US
127/G3 Pawtucket, RI,US
61/F3 Paxoí (isl.), Gre.
61/G3 Paxoí (Yáios), Gre.
86/B4 Payakumbuh, Indo.
112/C3 Payén, Altiplanicie del (plat.), Arg.
122/D4 Payette, Id,US
122/D5 Payette (riv.), Id,US
65/P1 Pay-Khoy (mts.), Rus.
119/J3 Payne (lake), Qu,Can
113/F2 Paysandú, Uru.
113/F1 Paysandú (dept.), Uru.
56/C3 Pays de la Loire (reg.), Fr.
124/E4 Payson, Az,US
124/E2 Payson, Ut,US
112/C3 Payún (peak), Arg.
74/D3 Pazarcık, Turk.
63/G4 Pazardzhik, Bul.
66/D5 Pazaryeri, Turk.
110/A2 Peabiru, Braz.
118/E3 Peace (riv.), Ab, BC,Can
129/H5 Peace (riv.), Fl,US
122/D1 Peace River, Ab,Can
122/D3 Peachland, BC,Can
129/G3 Peachtree City, Ga,US
45/G5 Peak District Nat'l Park, Eng,UK
120/W13 Pearl (har.), Hi,US
129/F4 Pearl (riv.), La, Ms,US
129/F3 Pearl, Ms,US
131/B1 Pearland, Ca,US
93/H2 Pearl and Hermes (reef), Hi,US
120/W13 Pearl City, Hi,US
82/B3 Pearl River (inlet), China
131/F4 Pearl River, NY,US
128/D4 Pearsall, Tx,US
119/R7 Peary (chan.), Nun.,Can
125/H4 Pease (riv.), Tx,US
47/E2 Pebworth, Eng,UK
62/E4 Peć, Yugo.
65/N2 Pechora, Rus.
65/M1 Pechora (bay), Rus.
65/M2 Pechora (riv.), Rus.
125/G5 Pecos (riv.), NM, Tx,US
128/C4 Pecos, Tx,US
125/F4 Pecos Nat'l Mon., NM,US
52/C3 Pecquencourt, Fr.
62/D2 Pécs, Hun.
117/E6 Pedasí, Pan.
91/C4 Pedder (lake), Austl.
117/G4 Pedernales, DRep.
110/B2 Pederneiras, Braz.
131/C3 Pedley, Ca,US
109/K7 Pedra Azul, Braz.
110/G7 Pedreira, Braz.
109/K5 Pedreiras, Braz.
84/D6 Pedro (pt.), SrL.
117/F4 Pedro Cays (isls.), Jam.
108/E3 Pedro II, Braz.
111/E1 Pedro Juan Caballero, Par.
110/C1 Pedro Leopoldo, Braz.
110/A4 Pedro Osório, Braz.
43/D3 Peebles, Sc,UK
90/F6 Peel (isl.), Austl.
118/G1 Peel (sound), Nun.,Can
130/L2 Peel (riv.), Yk,Can
44/D3 Peel, IM,UK
45/F1 Peel Fell (mtn.), Eng,UK
53/E1 Peer, Belg.
57/J2 Pegnitz, Ger.
57/J2 Pegnitz (riv.), Ger.
59/E3 Pego, Sp.
45/G1 Pegswood, Eng,UK
83/B2 Pegu, Myan.
83/B2 Pegu (mts.), Myan.
83/B2 Pegu (riv.), Myan.
83/B2 Pegu (Bago) (div.), Myan.
47/H4 Pegwell (bay), Eng,UK
112/E2 Pehuajó, Arg.
112/C2 Pehuenche (pass), Chile
81/B3 Peijiachuankou, China
51/H4 Peine, Ger.
42/H4 Peipus (lake), Est., Rus.
110/K6 Peixe (riv.), Braz.
110/C2 Peixoto (res.), Braz.
86/C5 Pekalongan, Indo.
86/B3 Pekan Nanas, Malay.
126/B3 Pekin, Il,US
112/C5 Pelada (plain), Arg.
60/C5 Pelagie (isls.), It.
62/F3 Peleaga, Vîrful (peak), Rom.
127/D3 Pelee (isl.), On,Can
126/D3 Pelee (pt.), On,Can
117/J5 Pelée (mt.), Mart.
127/R9 Pelham, On,Can
129/G3 Pelham, Al,US
49/H4 Pelhřimov, Czh.
122/E2 Pelican (mts.), Ab,Can
123/H2 Pelican (lake), Sk,Can
123/H2 Pelican Narrows, Sk,Can
98/A4 Pelindã, Ponta de (pt.), GBis.
62/E5 Pelister Nat'l Park, FYROM
62/C4 Pelješac (pen.), Cro.
130/M3 Pelly (riv.), Yk,Can
118/H2 Pelly Bay, Nun.,Can
130/L3 Pelly Crossing, Yk,Can
61/G3 Peloponnisos (reg.), Gre.
60/D3 Peloritani (mts.), It.
110/A4 Pelotas, Braz.
110/B3 Pelotas (riv.), Braz.
49/K2 Pelplin, Pol.
87/F5 Pemali (cape), Indo.
86/A3 Pematangsiantar, Indo.
101/C4 Pemba (isl.), Tanz.
101/C4 Pemba (prov.), Tanz.
122/C3 Pemberton, BC,Can
122/E2 Pembina (riv.), Ab,Can
123/J3 Pembina (riv.), Can., US
123/J3 Pembina, ND,US
126/E2 Pembroke, On,Can
46/B3 Pembroke, Wal,UK
46/B3 Pembrokeshire (co.), Wal,UK
112/B3 Pemuco, Chile
58/A2 Penafiel, Port.
112/G9 Peñaflor, Chile
58/D2 Peñalara (mtn.), Sp.
109/J4 Penalva, Braz.
110/B2 Penápolis, Braz.
58/C2 Peñaranda de Bracamonte, Sp.
59/E2 Peñarroya (mtn.), Sp.
58/C3 Peñarroya-Pueblonuevo, Sp.
46/C4 Penarth, Wal,UK
113/L8 Peñas (cape), Arg.
113/J6 Penas (gulf), Chile
58/C1 Peñas (cape), Sp.
112/B3 Penco, Chile
61/L6 Pendelikón (mtn.), Gre.
99/F4 Pendjari (riv.), Ben., Burk.
99/F4 Pendjari Nat'l Park, Ben.
45/F4 Pendle (hill), Eng,UK
122/D4 Pendleton, Or,US
122/D4 Pend Oreille (lake), Id,US
122/D3 Pend Oreille (riv.), Id, Wa,US
58/A2 Peneda-Gerês Nat'l Park, Port.
109/L6 Penedo, Braz.
46/C1 Penegoes, Wal,UK
126/E2 Penetanguishene, On,Can
84/C4 Penganga (riv.), India
82/C3 Penghu (Pescadores) (isls.), Tai.
110/B3 Penha, Braz.
122/E2 Penhold, Ab,Can
58/C4 Penibético, Sistema (range), Sp.
58/A3 Peniche, Port.
109/J5 Penitente (mts.), Braz.
46/D1 Penkridge, Eng,UK
44/E5 Penmaenmawr, Wal,UK
56/A3 Penmarch, Fr.
56/A3 Penmarc'h, Pointe de (pt.), Fr.
60/D1 Penna, Punta della (cape), It.
62/C5 Penne (pt.), It.
84/C5 Penner (riv.), India
126/E3 Penn Hills, Pa,US
54/D5 Pennine Alps (mts.), It., Swi.
45/F2 Pennine Chain (range), Eng,UK
131/F5 Pennington, NJ,US
131/E6 Pennsauken, NJ,US
126/E3 Pennsylvania (state), US
119/S7 Penny (str.), Nun.,Can
126/E3 Penn Yan, NY,US
126/G2 Penobscot (riv.), Me,US
117/E6 Penonomé, Pan.
44/E1 Penpont, Sc,UK
44/D5 Penrhyn Mawr (pt.), Wal,UK
93/K5 Penrhyn (Tongareva) (atoll), CookIs.
90/G8 Penrith, Austl.
45/F2 Penrith, Eng,UK
46/A6 Penryn, Eng,UK
105/X Pensacola (mts.), Ant.
129/G4 Pensacola, Fl,US
123/G3 Pense, Sk,Can
46/B5 Pensilva, Eng,UK
131/J8 Pentagon, Va,US
92/F6 Pentecost (isl.), Van.
63/H3 Penteleu (peak), Rom.
122/D3 Penticton, BC,Can
46/B5 Pentire (pt.), UK
43/D3 Pentland (hills), Sc,UK
46/C3 Pentyrch, Wal,UK
112/C2 Peñuelas Nat'l Park, Chile
46/A6 Penwith (pen.), Eng,UK
45/E6 Pen-y-Cae, Wal,UK
45/F3 Pen-y-Ghent (mtn.), Eng,UK
44/E5 Pen-y-Gogarth (pt.), Wal,UK
46/C2 Pen y Gurnos (mtn.), Wal,UK
67/H1 Penza, Rus.
46/A6 Penzance, Eng,UK
67/G1 Penza Obl., Rus.
55/H2 Penzberg, Ger.
69/S3 Penzhina (bay), Rus.
69/S3 Penzhina (riv.), Rus.
126/B3 Peoria, Il,US
53/E2 Pepinster, Belg.
131/F5 Pequannock, NJ,US
86/B4 Perabumulih, Indo.
59/M9 Perales (riv.), Sp.
127/H1 Percé, Qu,Can
56/D2 Perche (hills), Fr.
49/J4 Perchtoldsdorf, Aus.
90/C3 Percy (isls.), Austl.
59/F1 Perdido (mtn.), Sp.
108/C3 Pereira, Col.
110/B2 Pereira Barreto, Braz.
112/E2 Pergamino, Arg.
57/K5 Pergola, It.
127/G1 Péribonca (riv.), Qu,Can
56/D4 Périgueux, Fr.
117/G6 Perija, Sierra de (range), Col., Ven.
72/D6 Perim (isl.), Yem.
61/J5 Peristéra (isl.), Gre.
61/L6 Peristéri, Gre.
113/K6 Perito Moreno Nat'l Park, Arg.
84/C5 Periyakulam, India
131/E5 Perkasie, Pa,US
53/F5 Perl, Ger.
116/E5 Perlas (lag.), Nic.
116/E5 Perlas (pt.), Nic.
48/F2 Perleberg, Ger.
65/N4 Perm', Rus.
65/M4 Perm' Obl., Rus.
56/F4 Pernes-les-Fontaines, Fr.
62/F4 Pernik, Bul.
64/D3 Perniö, Fin.
52/B4 Péronne, Fr.
65/X9 Perovo, Rus.
56/E5 Perpignan, Fr.
131/C3 Perris, Ca,US
56/B2 Perros-Guirec, Fr.
127/N7 Perrot (isl.), Qu,Can
118/F2 Perry (riv.), Nun.,Can
129/H4 Perry, Fl,US
129/H3 Perry, Ga,US
125/H3 Perry, Ok,US
131/K7 Perry Hall, Md,US
128/C2 Perryton, Tx,US
125/K3 Perryville, Mo,US
52/B5 Persan, Fr.
72/F3 Persepolis (ruins), Iran
46/D2 Pershore, Eng,UK
72/E3 Persian (gulf), Asia
74/D2 Pertek, Turk.
89/A4 Perth, Austl.
126/E2 Perth, On,Can
43/D2 Perth, Sc,UK
131/F5 Perth Amboy, NJ,US
56/F5 Pertuis, Fr.
56/C3 Pertuis Breton (inlet), Fr.
60/A2 Pertusato (cape), Fr.
108/C5 Peru
126/B3 Peru, Il,US
126/C3 Peru, In,US
62/D4 Perućačko (lake), Bosn.
60/C1 Perugia, It.
110/G9 Peruíbe, Braz.
52/C2 Péruwelz, Belg.
74/E3 Pervari, Turk.
65/J5 Pervomaysk, Rus.
66/D2 Pervomaysk, Ukr.
65/N4 Pervoural'sk, Rus.
86/B4 Pesagi (peak), Indo.
57/K5 Pesaro, It.
82/C3 Pescadores (Penghu) (isls.), Tai.
60/D1 Pescara, It.
67/J4 Peschanyy, Mys (cape), Kaz.
65/L2 Pesha (riv.), Rus.
73/K2 Peshāwar, Pak.
63/G4 Peshtera, Bul.
126/B2 Peshtigo (riv.), Wi,US
56/C4 Pessac, Fr.
56/D5 Pessons, Pic dels (peak), And.
62/D2 Pest (co.), Hun.
64/G4 Pestovo, Rus.
74/K5 Petah Tiqwa, Isr.
129/F4 Petal, Ms,US
61/J4 Petalión (gulf), Gre.
132/J10 Petaluma, Ca,US
53/E4 Pétange, Lux.
116/B4 Petapa, Mex.
117/H5 Petare, Ven.
104/F3 Petauke, Zam.
126/E2 Petawawa (riv.), On,Can
126/E2 Petawawa, On,Can
123/L4 Petenwell (lake), Wi,US
126/E2 Peterborough, On,Can
47/F1 Peterborough, Eng,UK
47/F1 Peterborough (co.), Eng,UK
43/E2 Peterhead, Sc,UK
105/T Peter I (isl.), Ant.
38/E9 Peter I (isl.), Nor.
45/G2 Peterlee, Eng,UK
112/C2 Peteroa (vol.), Arg.
122/F1 Peter Pond (lake), Sk,Can
126/E4 Petersburg, Va,US
47/F5 Petersfield, Eng,UK
51/F4 Petershagen, Ger.
60/E3 Petilia Policastro, It.
127/H2 Petitcodiac, NB,Can
117/G4 Petite Riviere de l'Artibonite, Haiti
53/F5 Petite-Rosselle, Fr.
52/C6 Petit Morin (riv.), Fr.
42/J3 Petkeljärven Nat'l Park, Fin.
84/B3 Petlād, India
116/D3 Peto, Mex.
112/C2 Petorca, Chile
126/C2 Petoskey, Mi,US
69/M2 Petra (isls.), Rus.
100/C2 Petra (Baṭrā) (ruins), Jor.
59/E3 Petrel, Sp.
60/C2 Petralla (peak), It.
63/F5 Petrich, Bul.
124/E4 Petrified Forest Nat'l Park, Az,US
63/F3 Petrila, Rom.
64/F4 Petrodvorets, Rus.
63/F4 Petrokhanski Prokhod (pass), Bul.
109/K5 Petrolina, Braz.
68/G4 Petropavlovsk, Kaz.
69/R4 Petropavlovsk-Kamchatskiy, Rus.
110/K7 Petrópolis, Braz.
63/F3 Petroşani, Rom.
62/D3 Petrovaradin, Yugo.
67/H1 Petrovsk, Rus.
76/F1 Petrovsk-Zabaykal'skiy, Rus.
64/G3 Petrozavodsk, Rus.
45/F2 Petterill (riv.), Eng,UK
47/F5 Petworth, Eng,UK
62/A2 Petzeck (peak), Aus.
130/G4 Peulik (mtn.), Ak,US
112/C2 Peumo, Chile
47/G5 Pevensey, Eng,UK
132/P13 Pewaukee (lake), Wi,US
47/E4 Pewsey, Eng,UK
65/K2 Peza (riv.), Rus.
56/E5 Pézenas, Fr.
53/G5 Pfälzer Wald (for.), Ger.
51/G6 Pfieffe (riv.), Ger.
57/H2 Pforzheim, Ger.
57/H2 Pfungstadt, Ger.
83/C1 Phak (riv.), Laos
84/B2 Phalodi, India
83/C3 Phanat Nikhom, Thai.
83/B4 Phangan (isl.), Thai.
83/C3 Phang Hoei (range), Thai.
83/C3 Phanom Dongrak (mts.), Camb., Thai.
83/E4 Phan Rang, Viet.
83/E4 Phan Thiet, Viet.
128/D5 Pharr, Tx,US
83/C5 Phatthalung, Thai.
83/C2 Phaya Fo (peak), Thai.
83/B2 Phayao, Thai.
129/G3 Phenix City, Al,US
102/C2 Phepane (dry riv.), SAfr.
83/B3 Phet Buri, Thai.
83/C2 Phetchabun, Thai.
83/C2 Phichit, Thai.
129/F3 Philadelphia, Ms,US
131/E6 Philadelphia, Pa,US
72/B4 Philae (ruins), Egypt
123/H4 Philip, SD,US
52/D3 Philippeville, Belg.
126/D4 Philippi, WV,US
92/B3 Philippine (sea), Asia
82/D5 Philippines
117/J4 Philipsburg, NAnt.
122/E4 Philipsburg, Mt,US
50/B5 Philipsdam (dam), Neth.
125/H3 Phillipsburg, Ks,US
131/E5 Phillipsburg, NJ,US
83/C3 Phimai (ruins), Thai.
83/C2 Phitsanulok, Thai.
83/D4 Phnom Penh (Phnum Penh) (cap.), Camb.
83/D3 Phnum Tbeng Meanchey, Camb.
83/C5 Pho (pt.), Thai.
93/H5 Phoenix (isls.), Kiri.
124/D4 Phoenix (cap.), Az,US
129/H2 Phoenix (peak), NC,US
93/H5 Phoenix (Rawaki) (atoll), Kiri.
131/E5 Phoenixville, Pa,US
83/C1 Phongsali, Laos
83/C2 Phou Bia (peak), Laos
83/D2 Phou Huatt (peak), Viet.
83/C1 Phou Loi (peak), Laos
83/D2 Phou Xai Lai Leng (peak), Laos
83/C2 Phrae, Thai.
83/C3 Phra Nakhon Si Ayutthaya, Thai.
83/B4 Phra Thong (isl.), Thai.
83/C4 Phsar Ream, Camb.
83/D2 Phuc Loi, Viet.
85/J3 Phuc Yen, Viet.
83/C2 Phu Hin Rong Kla Nat'l Park, Thai.
83/E4 Phu Hoi, Viet.
83/B5 Phuket, Thai.
83/B5 Phuket (isl.), Thai.
83/C2 Phu Kradung Nat'l Park, Thai.
84/D3 Phulabāni, India
83/D2 Phu Loc, Viet.
83/D1 Phu Luong, Viet.
83/D1 Phu Luong (peak), Viet.
83/D1 Phu Ly, Viet.
83/D4 Phumi Banam, Camb.
83/C4 Phumi Choan, Camb.
83/D3 Phumi Kampong Trabek, Camb.
83/D4 Phumi Krek, Camb.
83/D3 Phumi Labang Siek, Camb.
83/D3 Phumi Prek Preah, Camb.
83/C3 Phumi Samraong, Camb.
83/C3 Phumi Toek Sok, Camb.
83/E3 Phu My, Viet.
83/E3 Phu Nhon, Viet.
83/D2 Phu Phan Nat'l Park, Thai.
83/C4 Phu Quoc (isl.), Viet.
83/D4 Phu Rieng Sron, Viet.
83/C2 Phu Rua Nat'l Park, Thai.
83/D1 Phu Tho, Viet.
83/D2 Phu Vang, Viet.
81/D4 Pi (riv.), China
57/H4 Piacenza, It.
60/A1 Pianosa (isl.), It.
49/L2 Piaseczno, Pol.
63/H2 Piatra Neamţ, Rom.
57/K3 Piave (riv.), It.
117/N9 Piaxtla (riv.), Mex.
60/D4 Piazza Armerina, It.
97/M6 Pibor Post, Sudan
126/C1 Pic (riv.), On,Can
117/P8 Picacho del Centinela (peak), Mex.
52/B4 Picardy (Picardie) (reg.), Fr.
129/F4 Picayune, Ms,US
60/E2 Piccolo (lag.), It.
112/C2 Pichidegua, Chile
112/C2 Pichilemu, Chile
127/R8 Pickering, On,Can
45/H3 Pickering, Eng,UK
45/H3 Pickering, Vale of (val.), Eng,UK
123/L3 Pickle Lake, On,Can
59/S12 Pico (isl.), Azor.,Port.
108/F3 Pico da Neblina Nat'l Park, Braz.
116/A4 Pico de Tancitaro Nat'l Park, Mex.
131/B3 Pico Rivera, Ca,US
139/K5 Picos, Braz.
112/D5 Pico Truncado, Arg.
52/B4 Picquigny, Fr.
126/E3 Picton, On,Can
127/J2 Pictou, NS,Can
46/D5 Piddle (riv.), Eng,UK
84/D6 Pidurutagala (peak), SrL.
57/G4 Piedmont (reg.), It.
132/K11 Piedmont, Ca,US
113/F2 Piedras (pt.), Arg.
108/D6 Piedras (riv.), Peru
49/K3 Piekary Śląskie, Pol.
102/B4 Piekenierskloof (pass), SAfr.
42/H3 Pieksämäki, Fin.
42/J3 Pielinen (lake), Fin.
49/L4 Pieniński Nat'l Park, Pol.
59/K6 Piera, Sp.
125/H2 Pierce, Ne,US
122/F2 Pierceland, Sk,Can
123/H4 Pierre (cap.), SD,US
127/N7 Pierrefonds, Qu,Can
52/C5 Pierrefonds, Fr.
56/F4 Pierrelatte, Fr.
103/E3 Pietermaritzburg, SAfr.
104/E5 Pietersburg, SAfr.
103/E2 Piet Retief, SAfr.
63/G2 Pietrosul (peak), Rom.
122/E2 Pigeon (lake), Ab,Can
123/L3 Pigeon (riv.), Can., US
126/B4 Piggott, Ar,US
116/E3 Pigs (bay), Cuba
112/E3 Pigüé, Arg.
113/C4 Pijijiapan, Mex.
50/B4 Pijnacker, Neth.
92/D4 Pikelot (isl.), Micr.
125/F3 Pikes (peak), Co,US
131/K7 Pikesville, Md,US
126/D4 Pikeville, Ky,US
82/D6 Pikit, Phil.
49/J2 Piła, Pol.
49/J2 Piła (prov.), Pol.
102/P12 Pilanesberg (range), SAfr.
111/E2 Pilar, Par.
87/F1 Pilar, Phil.
108/F8 Pilaya (riv.), Bol.
132/D1 Pilchuck (riv.), Wa,US
107/C5 Pilcomayo (riv.), SAm.
47/G3 Pilgrims Hatch, Eng,UK
82/D5 Pili, Phil.
66/B2 Pilica (riv.), Pol.
61/H3 Pilion (peak), Gre.
62/D2 Pilis, Hun.
62/D2 Pilis (peak), Hun.
49/K5 Pilisvörösvár, Hun.
84/C2 Pilkhua, India
91/C4 Pillar (cape), Austl.
132/K12 Pillar (pt.), Ca,US
129/G2 Pilot (peak), Tn,US
57/K2 Pilsen (Plzeň), Czh.
124/E4 Pima, Az,US
84/B4 Pimpri-Chinchwad, India
117/M7 Pinacote (mt.), Mex.
113/J7 Pinaculo (peak), Arg.
82/D5 Pinamalayan, Phil.
86/A2 Pinang (isl.), Malay.
74/D2 Pınarbaşı, Turk.
116/D3 Pinar del Río, Cuba
63/H5 Pınarhisar, Turk.
108/C4 Piñas, Ecu.
82/D4 Pinatubo (mt.), Phil.
123/K3 Pinawa, Mb,Can
45/H6 Pinchbeck, Eng,UK
122/E3 Pincher Creek, Ab,Can
126/D3 Pinconning, Mi,US
62/E2 Pincota, Rom.
127/N7 Pincourt, Qu,Can
49/L3 Pińczów, Pol.
110/H7 Pindamonhangaba, Braz.
109/J4 Pindaré (riv.), Braz.
109/J4 Pindaré-Mirim, Braz.
73/K2 Pindi Gheb, Pak.
61/G3 Pindos Nat'l Park, Gre.
61/G2 Pindus (mts.), Gre.
84/B3 Pindwāra, India
129/F4 Pine (hills), Ms,US
123/G4 Pine (hills), Mt,US
131/F6 Pine Barrens (reg.), NJ,US
128/E3 Pine Bluff, Ar,US
123/G5 Pine Bluffs, Wy,US
59/G2 Pineda de Mar, Sp.
122/F5 Pinedale, Wy,US
123/J3 Pine Falls, Mb,Can
64/J2 Pinega (riv.), Rus.
131/F6 Pine Hill, NJ,US
123/L2 Pineimuta (riv.), On,Can
105/T Pine Island (bay), Ant.
126/A2 Pine Island, Mn,US
102/L10 Pinelands, SAfr.
123/H5 Pine Ridge, SD,US
57/G4 Pinerolo, It.
103/E3 Pinetown, SAfr.
83/B2 Ping (riv.), Thai.
81/C4 Pingdingshan, China
81/D3 Pingdu, China
92/F4 Pingelap (atoll), Micr.
81/C5 Pingjing Guan (pass), China
81/D2 Pingquan, China
81/C3 Pingshan, China
82/D3 Pingtung, Tai.
81/C3 Pingxiang, China
82/B2 Pingxiang, China
83/D1 Pingxiang, China
81/C3 Pingxing Guan (pass), China
77/J4 Pingyang, China
67/N1 Pinhal, Braz.
59/Q10 Pinhal Novo, Port.
110/B3 Pinhão, Braz.
109/J4 Pinheiro, Braz.
110/D1 Pinheiros, Braz.
61/G3 Piniós (riv.), Gre.
61/G4 Piniós (riv.), Gre.
50/C2 Pinkegat (chan.), Neth.
124/B3 Pinnacles Nat'l Mon., Ca,US
51/G1 Pinnau (riv.), Ger.
51/G1 Pinneberg, Ger.
112/C3 Pino Hachado (pass), Arg.
132/K10 Pinole, Ca,US
124/C4 Pinos (peak), Ca,US
116/E3 Pinos (Juventud) (isl.), Cuba
58/D4 Pinos-Puente, Sp.
116/B4 Pinotepa Nacional, Mex.
87/E4 Pinrang, Indo.
92/F7 Pins, Ile des (isl.), NCal.
66/C1 Pinsk, Bela.
112/C3 Pinto, Chile
59/N9 Pinto, Sp.
124/D3 Pioche, Nv,US
60/B1 Piombino, It.
68/J2 Pioner (isl.), Rus.
49/L3 Pionki, Pol.
110/F4 Piorini (riv.), Braz.
49/K3 Piotrków (prov.), Pol.
49/K3 Piotrków Trybunalski, Pol.
84/B2 Pīpār, India
124/D3 Pipe Spring Nat'l Mon., Az,US
123/H3 Pipestone (cr.), Mb, Sk,Can
123/L2 Pipestone (riv.), On,Can
123/J4 Pipestone, Mn,US
123/J4 Pipestone Nat'l Mon., Mn,US
73/K2 Piplān, Pak.
127/G1 Pipmuacan (res.), Qu,Can
126/C3 Piqua, Oh,US
110/H7 Piquete, Braz.
110/A3 Piquiri (riv.), Braz.
110/B1 Piracanjuba, Braz.
110/C2 Piracicaba, Braz.
110/K7 Piraí, Braz.
110/B3 Piraí do Sul, Braz.
61/H4 Piraiévs, Gre.
110/B2 Pirajú, Braz.
110/B2 Pirajuí, Braz.
113/J7 Pirámide (peak), Chile
111/E2 Pirané, Arg.
110/D2 Piranga (riv.), Braz.
109/L5 Piranhas (riv.), Braz.
110/C1 Pirapora, Braz.
110/B2 Pirapózinho, Braz.
110/C2 Pirassununga, Braz.
112/C1 Pircas (peak), Arg.
110/B1 Pires do Rio, Braz.
63/F5 Pirin (mtn.), Bul.
63/F5 Pirin (mts.), Bul.
63/F5 Pirin Nat'l Park, Bul.
109/K4 Piripiri, Braz.
53/G5 Pirmasens, Ger.
49/G3 Pirna, Ger.
62/F4 Pirot, Yugo.
66/E2 Piryatin, Ukr.
57/J5 Pisa, It.
87/E2 Pisau, Tanjong (cape), Malay.
108/D2 Pisba Nat'l Park, Col.
131/F5 Piscataway, NJ,US
108/C6 Pisco, Peru
108/C6 Pisco (riv.), Peru
57/L2 Písek, Czh.
73/J2 Pishīn, Pak.
111/C2 Pissis (peak), Arg.
52/B4 Pissy, Fr.
132/P15 Pistakee (lake), Il,US
60/E2 Pisticci, It.
57/J5 Pistoia, It.
58/C1 Pisuerga (riv.), Sp.
49/L2 Pisz, Pol.
124/B2 Pit (riv.), Ca,US
108/C3 Pitalito, Col.
110/B3 Pitanga, Braz.
93/N7 Pitcairn Islands (terr.), UK
42/G2 Piteå, Swe.
42/F2 Piteälv (riv.), Swe.
63/G3 Piteşti, Rom.
56/E2 Pithiviers, Fr.
43/D2 Pitlochry, Sc,UK
131/E6 Pitman, NJ,US
43/D2 Pitmedden, Sc,UK
112/B3 Pitrufquén, Chile
90/H8 Pitt (lake), Austl.
43/D2 Pittenweem, Sc,UK
132/L10 Pittsburg, Ca,US
125/J3 Pittsburg, Ks,US
128/E3 Pittsburg, Tx,US
126/E3 Pittsburgh, Pa,US
127/F3 Pittsfield, Ma,US
127/G2 Pittsfield, Me,US
110/C2 Piũí, Braz.
108/B5 Piura, Peru
84/D2 Piuthān, Nepal
61/F1 Piva (riv.), Yugo.
66/D2 Pivdenny Buh (riv.), Ukr.
117/G5 Pivijay, Col.
62/D4 Pivsko (lake), Yugo.
65/K4 Pizhma (riv.), Rus.
60/E3 Pizzo, It.
60/C1 Pizzuto (peak), It.
102/D3 P. K. Le Rouxdam (res.), SAfr.
127/L2 Placentia (bay), Nf,Can
131/C3 Placentia, Ca,US
82/D5 Placer, Phil.
52/B5 Plailly, Fr.
83/C3 Plai Mat (riv.), Thai.
131/F5 Plainfield, NJ,US
128/C3 Plains, Tx,US
131/F5 Plainsboro, NJ,US
126/A2 Plainview, Mn,US
131/G5 Plainview, NY,US
128/C3 Plainview, Tx,US
125/H3 Plainville, Ks,US
87/E5 Plampang, Indo.
110/D1 Planalto do Brasil (plat.), Braz.
117/F6 Planeta Rica, Col.
128/D3 Plano, Tx,US
129/H5 Plantation, Fl,US
129/H4 Plant City, Fl,US
129/F4 Plaquemine, La,US
58/B2 Plasencia, Sp.
60/C4 Platani (riv.), It.
113/F2 Plata, Río de la (estuary), Arg.
99/H4 Plateau (state), Nga.
117/G6 Plato, Col.
125/J2 Platte (riv.), Mo,US
125/H2 Platte (riv.), Ne,US
123/J5 Platte, SD,US
126/B3 Platteville, Wi,US
57/K2 Plattling, Ger.
126/F2 Plattsburgh, NY,US
57/K1 Plauen, Ger.
62/D4 Plav, Yugo.
116/D4 Playa de los Muertos (ruins), Hon.
108/B4 Playas, Ecu.
124/E5 Playas (lake), NM,US
83/E3 Play Cu (Pleiku), Viet.
123/J2 Playgreen (lake), Mb,Can
132/K11 Pleasant Hill, Ca,US
132/L11 Pleasanton, Ca,US
128/D4 Pleasanton, Tx,US
132/Q14 Pleasant Prairie, Wi,US
131/G4 Pleasantville, NY,US
83/E3 Pleiku (Play Cu), Viet.
48/G3 Pleisse (riv.), Ger.
91/G5 Plenty (riv.), Austl.
123/G3 Plentywood, Mt,US
56/B2 Plérin, Fr.
49/J3 Pleszew, Pol.
127/G1 Plétipi (lake), Qu,Can
51/E6 Plettenberg, Ger.
63/G4 Pleven, Bul.
62/B3 Plitvice Lakes Nat'l Park, Cro.
57/L4 Plitvička Jezera Nat'l Park, Cro.
62/D4 Pljevlja, Yugo.
62/B4 Ploča, Rt (pt.), Yugo.
49/K2 Płock, Pol.
49/K2 Płock (prov.), Pol.
62/C4 Pločno (peak), Bosn.
56/B3 Ploemeur, Fr.
63/H3 Ploieşti, Rom.
48/F1 Plön, Ger.
122/G2 Plonge (lake), Sk,Can
49/L2 Płońsk, Pol.
49/H3 Ploučnice (riv.), Czh.
56/B2 Ploufragan, Fr.
56/A2 Plougastel-Daoulas, Fr.
63/G4 Plovdiv, Bul.
63/G5 Plovdiv (reg.), Bul.
126/B2 Plover, Wi,US
44/A2 Plumbridge, NI,UK
64/D5 Plungė, Lith.
117/J4 Plymouth (cap.), Monts.
46/B6 Plymouth, Eng,UK
46/B6 Plymouth (co.), Eng,UK
126/C3 Plymouth, In,US
127/G3 Plymouth, NH,US
126/C3 Plymouth, Wi,US
46/C2 Plynlimon (mtn.), UK
57/K2 Plzeň (Pilsen), Czh.
49/J2 Pniewy, Pol.
99/E4 Pô, Burk.

Po – Qarţā

57/J4 Po (riv.), It.
57/J4 Po (val.), It.
110/G8 Poá, Braz.
75/D3 Pobedy, Pik (peak), Kyr.
49/J2 Pobiedziska, Pol.
129/F2 Pocahontas, Ar,US
122/E5 Pocatello, Id,US
66/E1 Pochep, Rus.
57/K2 Pöcking, Ger.
92/E6 Pocklington (reef), PNG
45/H4 Pocklington, Eng,UK
110/H6 Poço Fundo, Braz.
125/J4 Pocola, Ok,US
109/G7 Poconé, Braz.
131/E4 Pocono (lake), Pa,US
110/G6 Poços de Caldas, Braz.
49/K3 Poddębice, Pol.
62/D4 Podgorica, Yugo.
49/M3 Podlasie (reg.), Pol.
64/H5 Podol'sk, Rus.
98/B2 Podor, Sen.
64/G3 Podporozh'ye, Rus.
62/C3 Podravska Slatina, Cro.
62/E4 Podujevo, Yugo.
57/J5 Poggibonsi, It.
61/G2 Pogradec, Alb.
130/F5 Pogromni (vol.), Ak,US
80/E4 P'ohang, SKor.
127/G2 Pohénégamook, Qu,Can
42/G3 Pohjanmaa (reg.), Fin.
92/E4 Pohnpei (isl.), Micr.
131/E5 Pohopoco Mtn. (ridge), Pa,US
105/H Poinsett (cape), Ant.
118/E2 Point (lake), NW,Can
129/F4 Point au Fer (isl.), La,US
117/J4 Pointe-à-Pitre, Guad.
127/N7 Pointe-Claire, Qu,Can
127/F2 Pointe-du-Lac, Qu,Can
104/B1 Pointe-Noire, Congo
59/G4 Pointe Pescade, Cap de la (cape), Alg.
117/J5 Point Fortin, Trin.
91/E1 Point Lookout (peak), Austl.
126/D3 Point Pelee Nat'l Park, On,Can
131/F5 Point Pleasant, NJ,US
126/C4 Point Pleasant, Oh,US
126/D4 Point Pleasant, WV,US
56/D3 Poitiers, Fr.
56/C3 Poitou (hist. reg.), Fr.
56/C3 Poitou-Charentes (reg.), Fr.
84/B2 Pokaran, India
84/D2 Pokhara, Nepal
67/K1 Pokhvistnevo, Rus.
83/E4 Po Klong Garai Cham Towers, Viet.
97/L7 Poko, D.R. Congo
57/L1 Polabská Nížina (reg.), Czh.
58/C1 Pola de Laviana, Sp.
58/C1 Pola de Lena, Sp.
58/C1 Pola de Siero, Sp.
66/A2 Pol'ana (peak), Slvk.
49/K2 Poland
49/L3 Połaniec, Pol.
65/P2 Polar Urals (mts.), Rus.
74/C2 Polatlı, Turk.
49/J2 Połczyn-Zdrój, Pol.
73/J1 Pol-e-Khomri, Afg.
47/E1 Polesworth, Eng,UK
62/E2 Polgár, Hun.
61/J4 Poliaigos (isl.), Gre.
60/D3 Policastro (gulf), It.
49/H2 Police, Pol.
60/E2 Policoro, It.
61/H2 Políkhni, Gre.
82/D4 Polillo (isl.), Phil.
60/E3 Polistena, It.
49/J3 Polkowice, Pol.
59/G3 Pollensa, Sp.
82/E6 Polomolok, Phil.
113/G2 Polonia (cape), Uru.
84/D6 Polonnaruwa, SrL.
66/C2 Polonnoye, Ukr.
64/F5 Polotsk, Bela.
46/B6 Polperro, Eng,UK
63/G4 Polski Trŭmbesh, Bul.
122/E4 Polson, Mt,US
66/E2 Poltava, Ukr.
66/E2 Poltavs'ka (obl.), Ukr.
64/F3 Polvijärvi, Fin.
64/G1 Polyarnyy, Rus.
93/J3 Polynesia (reg.)
110/D2 Pomba (riv.), Braz.
109/L5 Pombal, Braz.
58/A3 Pombal, Port.
49/H2 Pomerania (reg.), Pol.
49/H1 Pomeranian (bay), Ger., Pol.
110/B3 Pomerode, Braz.
44/B2 Pomeroy, NI,UK
122/D4 Pomeroy, Wa,US
92/E5 Pomio, PNG
131/C2 Pomona, Ca,US
63/H4 Pomorie, Bul.
129/H5 Pompano Beach, Fl,US
60/D2 Pompei (ruins), It.
110/C1 Pompeu, Braz.
131/F4 Pompton Lakes, NJ,US
99/E4 Pô Nat'l Park, Burk.
125/H3 Ponca City, Ok,US
117/H4 Ponce, PR
126/E1 Poncheville (lake), Qu,Can
119/J1 Pond (inlet), Nun.,Can
84/B5 Pondicherry (terr.), India
84/C5 Pondicherry (terr.), India
84/D4 Pondicherry (terr.), India
58/B1 Ponferrada, Sp.
103/E2 Pongolo (riv.), SAfr.
98/E4 Poni (prov.), Burk.
49/M3 Poniatowa, Pol.
122/E2 Ponoka, Ab,Can
64/H2 Ponoy (riv.), Rus.
52/D3 Pont-à-Celles, Belg.
109/L7 Ponta da Baleia (pt.), Braz.
59/S12 Ponta da Pico (mtn.), Azor.,Port.
59/T13 Ponta Delgada, Azor.,Port.
59/U15 Ponta do Sol, Madr.,Port.
110/B3 Ponta Grossa, Braz.
110/B1 Pontalina, Braz.
53/F6 Pont-à-Mousson, Fr.
109/G8 Ponta Porã, Braz.
46/C3 Pontardawe, Wal,UK
46/B3 Pontardulais, Wal,UK
54/C4 Pontarlier, Fr.
52/B6 Pontault-Combault, Fr.
126/E1 Pontax (riv.), Qu,Can
129/F4 Pontchartrain (lake), La,US
56/B3 Pontchâteau, Fr.
56/E4 Pont-du-Château, Fr.
60/C2 Pontecorvo, It.
58/A3 Ponte de Sor, Port.
45/G4 Pontefract, Eng,UK
45/G1 Ponteland, Eng,UK
110/D2 Ponte Nova, Braz.
46/C2 Ponterwyd, Wal,UK
46/D1 Pontesbury, Eng,UK
108/G7 Pontes e Lacerda, Braz.
58/A1 Pontevedra, Sp.
126/B3 Pontiac, Il,US
132/F6 Pontiac, Mi,US
86/C4 Pontianak, Indo.
56/B2 Pontivy, Fr.
52/B5 Pontoise, Fr.
129/F3 Pontotoc, Ms,US
46/C2 Pontrhydfendigaid, Wal,UK
46/D3 Pontrilas, Eng,UK
52/B5 Pont-Sainte Maxence, Fr.
56/F4 Pont-Saint-Esprit, Fr.
46/B3 Pontyates, Wal,UK
46/C3 Pontyclun, Wal,UK
46/C3 Pont y Cymmer, Wal,UK
46/C3 Pontypool, Wal,UK
46/C3 Pontypridd, Wal,UK
60/C2 Ponziane (isls.), It.
47/E5 Poole, Eng,UK
47/E5 Poole (bay), Eng,UK
46/D5 Poole (co.), Eng,UK
84/B4 Poona (Pune), India
108/E7 Poopó (lake), Bol.
108/C3 Popayán, Col.
52/B2 Poperinge, Belg.
91/B2 Popilta (lake), Austl.
91/B2 Popio (lake), Austl.
123/K2 Poplar (riv.), Mb, On,Can
123/G3 Poplar, Mt,US
123/G3 Poplar (riv.), Mt,US
125/K3 Poplar Bluff, Mo,US
129/F4 Poplarville, Ms,US
96/J6 Popokabaka, D.R. Congo
92/D5 Popondetta, PNG
63/H4 Popovo, Bul.
49/L4 Poprad, Slvk.
49/L4 Poprad (riv.), Slvk.
109/J6 Porangatu, Braz.
84/A3 Porbandar, India
58/C4 Porcuna, Sp.
130/K2 Porcupine (riv.), Yk,Can, Ak,US
90/B3 Porcupine Gorge Nat'l Park, Austl.
123/H2 Porcupine Plain, Sk,Can
57/K4 Pordenone, It.
42/G3 Pori, Fin.
89/H7 Porirua, NZ
64/E4 Porkhov, Rus.
117/J5 Porlamar, Ven.
46/C4 Porlock, Eng,UK
77/N2 Poronaysk, Rus.
105/J Porpoise (bay), Ant.
58/A1 Porriño, Sp.
42/H1 Porsangen (fjord), Nor.
42/D4 Porsgrunn, Nor.
74/B2 Porsuk (riv.), Turk.
108/F7 Portachuelo, Bol.
44/B3 Portadown, NI,UK
44/C3 Portaferry, NI,UK
126/C3 Portage, Mi,US
126/B3 Portage, Wi,US
123/J3 Portage la Prairie, Mb,Can
122/B3 Port Alberni, BC,Can
58/B3 Portalegre, Port.
58/B3 Portalegre (dist.), Port.
125/G4 Portales, NM,US
102/D4 Port Alfred, SAfr.
122/B3 Port Alice, BC,Can
122/C3 Port Angeles, Wa,US
117/F4 Port Antonio, Jam.
43/C2 Port Appin, Sc,UK
128/E4 Port Arthur, Tx,US
127/K1 Port au Choix, Nf,Can
89/C4 Port Augusta, Austl.
117/G4 Port-au-Prince (cap.), Haiti
44/C3 Portavogie, NI,UK
51/F4 Porta Westfalica, Ger.
85/F5 Port Blair, India
128/E4 Port Bolivar, Tx,US
98/E5 Port-Bouët, IvC.
119/K2 Port Burwell, Qu,Can
127/H1 Port-Cartier, Qu,Can
129/H5 Port Charlotte, Fl,US
131/G5 Port Chester, NY,US
126/D3 Port Clinton, Oh,US
127/R10 Port Colborne, On,Can
127/Q8 Port Credit, On,Can
127/S8 Port Darlington, On,Can
91/C4 Port Davey (har.), Austl.
117/G4 Port-de-Paix, Haiti
86/B3 Port Dickson, Malay.
130/M4 Port Edward, BC,Can
109/H4 Portel, Braz.
126/D2 Port Elgin, Can.
102/D4 Port Elizabeth, SAfr.
44/D3 Port Erin, IM,UK
102/L10 Porterville, SAfr.
124/C3 Porterville, Ca,US
56/F4 Portes-lès-Valence, Fr.
96/B3 Port-Étienne, Mrta.
56/D5 Portet-sur-Garonne, Fr.
46/B3 Port Eynon, Wal,UK
46/B3 Port Eynon (pt.), Wal,UK
104/A1 Port-Gentil, Gabon
43/C3 Port Glasgow, Sc,UK
44/B2 Portglenone, NI,UK
46/C3 Porth, Wal,UK
99/G5 Port Harcourt, Nga.
122/B3 Port Hardy, BC,Can
127/J2 Port Hawkesbury, NS,Can
46/C4 Porthcawl, Wal,UK
89/A3 Port Hedland, Austl.
46/A6 Porthleven, Eng,UK
44/D6 Porthmadog, Wal,UK
131/A2 Port Hueneme, Ca,US
132/H6 Port Huron, Mi,US
58/A4 Portimão, Port.
46/B5 Port Isaac, Eng,UK
46/D4 Portishead, Eng,UK
131/G5 Port Jefferson, NY,US
91/C4 Portland (cape), Austl.
117/F4 Portland (pt.), Jam.
46/D6 Portland (pt.), Eng,UK
130/N4 Portland (inlet), BC,Can, Ak,US
126/C3 Portland, In,US
127/G3 Portland, Me,US
122/C4 Portland, Or,US
129/G2 Portland, Tn,US
46/D5 Portland, Isle of (pen.), Eng,UK
128/D4 Port Lavaca, Tx,US
89/C4 Port Lincoln, Austl.
103/S15 Port Louis (cap.), Mrts.
91/E1 Port Macquarie, Austl.
44/B5 Portmarnock, Ire.
122/B3 Port McNeill, BC,Can
127/H1 Port-Menier, Qu,Can
92/D5 Port Moresby (cap.), PNG
127/G1 Portneuf (riv.), Qu,Can
60/A1 Porto (gulf), Fr.
58/A2 Porto, Port.
58/A2 Porto (dist.), Port.
110/B4 Pôrto Alegre, Braz.
104/B3 Porto Amboim, Ang.
57/K5 Portocivitanova, It.
60/C4 Porto Empedocle, It.
60/B1 Portoferraio, It.
110/C2 Pôrto Ferreira, Braz.
117/J5 Port-of-Spain (cap.), Trin.
57/K4 Portogruaro, It.
57/J4 Portomaggiore, It.
109/J6 Porto Nacional, Braz.
99/F5 Porto-Novo (cap.), Ben.
129/H4 Port Orange, Fl,US
60/C1 Porto San Giorgio, It.
60/B1 Porto Santo Stefano, It.
60/A2 Porto Torres, It.
110/B3 Porto União, Braz.
108/F5 Porto Velho, Braz.
108/B4 Portoviejo, Ecu.
44/C2 Portpatrick, Sc,UK
91/C3 Port Phillip (bay), Austl.
89/C4 Port Pirie, Austl.
44/B1 Portrush, NI,UK
100/C2 Port Said (Būr Sa'īd), Egypt
129/G4 Port Saint Joe, Fl,US
56/F5 Port-Saint-Louis-du-Rhône, Fr.
129/H5 Port Saint Lucie, Fl,US
44/D3 Port Saint Mary, IM,UK
47/E5 Portsea (isl.), Eng,UK
130/M4 Port Simpson, BC,Can
47/F5 Portslade by Sea, Eng,UK
47/E5 Portsmouth, Eng,UK
47/E5 Portsmouth (co.), Eng,UK
127/G3 Portsmouth, NH,US
126/D4 Portsmouth, Oh,US
126/E4 Portsmouth, Va,US
91/E2 Port Stephens (bay), Austl.
44/B1 Portstewart, NI,UK
100/D5 Port Sudan (Būr Sūdān), Sudan
46/C3 Port Talbot, Wal,UK
122/C3 Port Townsend, Wa,US
58/A3 Portugal
58/D1 Portugalete, Sp.
117/H6 Portuguesa (riv.), Ven.
92/F6 Port-Vila (cap.), Van.
131/G5 Port Washington, NY,US
126/C3 Port Washington, Wi,US
44/D2 Port William, Sc,UK
111/E2 Posadas, Arg.
58/C4 Posadas, Sp.
62/C3 Posavina (val.), Bosn., Cro.
87/F4 Poso (lake), Indo.
80/D5 Posŏng, SKor.
132/C2 Possession (sound), Wa,US
128/C3 Post, Tx,US
64/E5 Postavy, Bela.
96/F3 Poste Maurice Cortier (ruins), Alg.
96/F3 Poste Weygand (ruins), Alg.
122/D4 Post Falls, Id,US
102/C3 Postmasburg, SAfr.
62/B3 Postojna, Slov.
102/D2 Potchefstroom, SAfr.
125/J4 Poteau, Ok,US
60/D2 Potenza, It.
60/C1 Potenza (riv.), It.
122/D4 Potholes (res.), Wa,US
109/K5 Poti (riv.), Braz.
67/G4 P'ot'i, Geo.
57/J5 Poti, Alpe di (peak), It.
131/J7 Potomac, Md,US
126/E4 Potomac (riv.), Md, Va,US
108/E7 Potosí, Bol.
125/K3 Potosi, Mo,US
111/C2 Potrerillos, Chile
48/G2 Potsdam, Ger.
126/F2 Potsdam, NY,US
47/F3 Potters Bar, Eng,UK
47/F2 Potterspury, Eng,UK
47/F2 Potton, Eng,UK
84/D6 Pottuvil, SrL.
126/F3 Poughkeepsie, NY,US
44/B5 Poulaphouca (res.), Ire.
45/G5 Poulter (riv.), Eng,UK
45/F4 Poulton-le-Fylde, Eng,UK
57/G4 Pourri (mtn.), Fr.
110/H7 Pouso Alegre, Braz.
83/C3 Pouthisat, Camb.
83/C3 Pouthisat (riv.), Camb.
49/K4 Považská Bystrica, Slvk.
58/A2 Póvoa de Varzim, Port.
67/G2 Povorino, Rus.
77/L3 Povorotnyy, Mys (cape), Rus.
119/J2 Povungnituk (riv.), Qu,Can
123/G4 Powder (riv.), Mt, Wy,US
124/E3 Powell (lake), Az, Ut,US
122/F4 Powell, Wy,US
122/B3 Powell River, BC,Can
127/R9 Power (res.), NY,US
46/C2 Powys (co.), Wal,UK
46/C1 Powys, Vale (val.), Wal,UK
109/H7 Poxoréo, Braz.
82/C2 Poyang (lake), China
45/F5 Poynton, Eng,UK
58/A1 Poyo, Sp.
62/E3 Požarevac, Yugo.
116/B3 Poza Rica, Mex.
62/E4 Požega, Yugo.
49/J2 Poznań, Pol.
49/J2 Poznań (prov.), Pol.
58/D4 Pozo Alcón, Sp.
58/C3 Pozoblanco, Sp.
59/N9 Pozuelo de Alarcón, Sp.
60/D4 Pozzallo, It.
60/C1 Pozzoni (peak), It.
49/K2 Prabuty, Pol.
83/B4 Pracham Hiang (pt.), Thai.
57/L2 Prachatice, Czh.
83/C3 Prachin Buri, Thai.
83/C3 Prachin Buri (riv.), Thai.
83/B4 Prachuap Khiri Khan, Thai.
49/J3 Praděd (peak), Czh.
109/L7 Prado, Braz.
131/C3 Prado (dam), Ca,US
57/L1 Prague (Praha) (cap.), Czh.
57/L1 Praha (reg.), Czh.
63/G3 Prahova (co.), Rom.
59/S12 Praia de Victória, Azor.,Port.
110/G9 Praia Grande, Braz.
126/B3 Prairie du Chien, Wi,US
127/N6 Prairies (riv.), Qu,Can
123/J4 Prairies, Coteau des (upland), US
128/E4 Prairie View, Tx,US
83/B3 Pran Buri (res.), Thai.
84/D4 Prānhita (riv.), India
86/A3 Prapat, Indo.
83/D3 Prasat Preah Vihear, Camb.
49/K3 Praszka, Pol.
110/B1 Prata, Braz.
57/J5 Prato, It.
60/C1 Pratola Peligna, It.
113/J7 Pratt (isl.), Chile
125/H3 Pratt, Ks,US
129/G3 Prattville, Al,US
58/B1 Pravia, Sp.
46/C6 Prawle (pt.), Eng,UK
87/E5 Praya, Indo.
63/G3 Predeal, Rom.
123/H3 Preeceville, Sk,Can
45/F6 Prees, Eng,UK
45/F4 Preesall, Eng,UK
48/F1 Preetz, Ger.
49/L1 Pregolya (riv.), Rus.
126/E1 Preissac (lake), On,Can
83/D4 Prek Pouthi, Camb.
59/L7 Premiá de Mar, Sp.
49/G2 Prenzlau, Ger.
49/J4 Přerov, Czh.
55/G5 Presanella (peak), It.
45/F5 Prescot, Eng,UK
126/F2 Prescott, On,Can
124/D4 Prescott, Az,US
62/E4 Preševo, Yugo.
111/D2 Presidencia Roque Sáenz Peña, Arg.
109/K5 Presidente Dutra, Braz.
110/A2 Presidente Epitácio, Braz.
110/B2 Presidente Prudente, Braz.
112/B5 Presidente Ríos (lake), Chile
110/B2 Presidente Venceslau, Braz.
128/B4 Presidio, Tx,US
63/H4 Preslav, Bul.
52/B6 Presles-en-Brie, Fr.
49/L4 Prešov, Slvk.
49/G2 Prespa (lake), Eur.
127/G2 Presque Isle, Me,US
45/E5 Prestatyn, Wal,UK
99/E5 Prestea, Gha.
46/D2 Presteigne, Wal,UK
57/K2 Přeštice, Czh.
91/G5 Preston, Austl.
45/F4 Preston, Eng,UK
46/D5 Preston, Eng,UK
122/F5 Preston, Id,US
126/D4 Prestonsburg, Ky,US
45/F4 Prestwich, Eng,UK
43/C3 Prestwick, Sc,UK
47/F3 Prestwood, Eng,UK
109/J6 Prêto (riv.), Braz.
102/E2 Pretoria (cap.), SAfr.
51/F4 Preussisch Oldendorf, Ger.
61/G3 Préveza, Gre.
130/D4 Pribilof (isls.), Ak,US
62/D4 Priboj, Yugo.
57/L2 Příbram, Czh.
124/E3 Price, Ut,US
124/E3 Price (riv.), Ut,US
129/F4 Prichard, Al,US
58/C4 Priego de Córdoba, Sp.
102/C3 Prieska, SAfr.
122/D3 Priest (lake), Id,US
122/D3 Priest River, Id,US
58/C1 Prieta (mtn.), Sp.
49/K4 Prievidza, Slvk.
48/F2 Prignitz (reg.), Ger.
62/C3 Prijedor, Bosn.
62/D4 Prijepolje, Yugo.
67/H3 Prikaspian (plain), Kaz., Rus.
67/H3 Prikumsk, Rus.
62/E5 Prilep, FYROM
66/E2 Priluki, Ukr.
60/C2 Prima Porta, It.
113/J7 Primero (cape), Chile
47/E1 Primethorpe, Eng,UK
69/P5 Primorsk Kray, Rus.
66/F3 Primorsko-Akhtarsk, Rus.
122/F2 Primrose (lake), Ab, Sk,Can
53/F5 Prims (riv.), Ger.
118/E1 Prince Albert (pen.), NW,Can
118/E1 Prince Albert (sound), NW,Can
123/G2 Prince Albert, Sk,Can
123/G2 Prince Albert Nat'l Park, Sk,Can
118/D1 Prince Alfred (cape), NW,Can
119/J2 Prince Charles (isl.) Nun.,Can
39/L8 Prince Edward (isls.), SAfr.
127/J2 Prince Edward Island (prov.), Can.
127/J2 Prince Edward Island Nat'l Park, PE,Can
122/C2 Prince George, BC,Can
119/R7 Prince Gustav Adolf (sea), Nun.,Can
105/C Prince Harold (coast), Ant.
118/G1 Prince Leopold (isl.), Nun.,Can
50/C2 Princenhof (lake), Neth.
118/G1 Prince of Wales (isl.), Nun.,Can
118/E1 Prince of Wales (str.), NW,Can
130/M4 Prince of Wales (isl.), Ak,US
105/C Prince Olav (coast), Ant.
119/R7 Prince Patrick (isl.), NW,Can
118/G1 Prince Regent (inlet), Nun.,Can
130/M4 Prince Rupert, BC,Can
47/F3 Princes Risborough, Eng,UK
105/A Princess Astrid (coast), Ant.
90/A1 Princess Charlotte (bay), Austl.
119/S6 Princess Margaret (range), Nun.,Can
105/Z Princess Martha (coast), Ant.
105/B Princess Ragnhild (coast), Ant.
122/A2 Princess Royal (isl.), BC,Can
117/J5 Princes Town, Trin.
122/C3 Princeton, BC,Can
126/B3 Princeton, Il,US
126/C4 Princeton, In,US
126/C4 Princeton, Ky,US
123/K4 Princeton, Mn,US
131/F5 Princeton, NJ,US
126/D4 Princeton, WV,US
130/J3 Prince William (sound), Ak,US
96/G7 Príncipe (isl.), SaoT.
130/K3 Prindle (vol.), Ak,US
122/C4 Prineville, Or,US
50/B5 Prinsenbeek, Neth.
50/C2 Prinses Margriet (can.), Neth.
116/E5 Prinzapolka, Nic.
60/D4 Priolo di Gargallo, It.
58/A1 Prior (cape), Sp.
64/F3 Priozersk, Rus.
66/C2 Pripet (marshes), Bela., Ukr.
62/E4 Priština, Yugo.
48/G2 Pritzwalk, Ger.
56/F4 Privas, Fr.
67/H2 Privolzhskiy, Rus.
67/K1 Priyutovo, Rus.
62/E4 Prizren, Yugo.
62/C3 Prnjavor, Bosn.
86/D5 Probolinggo, Indo.
128/D3 Proctor (lake), Tx,US
84/C5 Proddatūr, India
53/D3 Profondeville, Belg.
116/E6 Progreso, Pan.
113/T12 Progreso, Uru.
77/K2 Progress, Rus.
67/H4 Prokhladnyy, Rus.
75/E1 Prokop'yevsk, Rus.
62/E4 Prokuplje, Yugo.
85/G4 Prome, Burma
110/B2 Promissão, Braz.
110/B2 Promissão (res.), Braz.
109/L6 Propriá, Braz.
49/J2 Prosna (riv.), Pol.
130/L3 Prospector (mtn.), Yk,Can
82/E6 Prosperidad, Phil.
49/J4 Prostějov, Czh.
49/L3 Prószowice, Pol.
63/H4 Provadiya, Bul.
57/G5 Provence (mts.), Fr.
56/F5 Provence (reg.), Fr.
57/G4 Provence-Alpes-Côte d'Azur (reg.), Fr.
108/F6 Providência (mts.), Braz.
116/E5 Providencia (isl.), Col.
56/E2 Provins, Fr.
124/E2 Provo, Ut,US
59/T13 Provoação, Azor.,Port.
122/F2 Provost, Ab,Can
62/C4 Prozor, Bosn.
110/B3 Prudentópolis, Braz.
45/G2 Prudhoe, Eng,UK
130/J1 Prudhoe (bay), Ak,US
49/J3 Prudnik, Pol.
53/F3 Prüm (riv.), Ger.
49/K1 Pruszcz Gdański, Pol.
49/L2 Pruszków, Pol.
63/J2 Prut (riv.), Eur.
105/F Prydz (bay), Ant.
128/E2 Pryor (cr.), Ok,US
49/L2 Przasnysz, Pol.
49/H3 Przemków, Pol.
49/M4 Przemyśl, Pol.
49/M4 Przemyśl (prov.), Pol.
49/M3 Przeworsk, Pol.
75/C3 Przheval'sk, Kyr.
64/C5 Przyłądek Rozewie (cape), Pol.
49/L3 Przysucha, Pol.
61/J3 Psará (isl.), Gre.
64/F4 Pskov (lake), Est., Rus.
64/F4 Pskov, Rus.
64/F4 Pskov Obl., Rus.
49/K4 Pszczyna, Pol.
61/G2 Ptolemaís, Gre.
62/B2 Ptuj, Slov.
83/C2 Pua, Thai.
108/D5 Pucallpa, Peru
132/G7 Puce, On,Can
81/B4 Pucheng, China
112/Q9 Puchuncaví, Chile
63/G3 Pucioasa, Rom.
49/K1 Puck, Pol.
47/G3 Puckeridge, Eng,UK
112/C3 Pucón, Chile
42/H2 Pudasjärvi, Fin.
46/D5 Puddletown, Eng,UK
45/G4 Pudsey, Eng,UK
85/H2 Pudu (riv.), China
84/C5 Pudukkottai, India
116/B4 Puebla, Mex.
116/B4 Puebla (state), Mex.
58/A1 Puebla del Caramiñal, Sp.
125/F3 Pueblo, Co,US
116/C5 Pueblo Nuevo Tiquisate, Guat.
112/C2 Puente Alto, Chile
58/A1 Puenteareas, Sp.
58/A1 Puente Caldelas, Sp.
58/A1 Puente-Ceso, Sp.
112/C2 Puente del Inca, Arg.
58/A1 Puentedeume, Sp.
58/C4 Puente-Genil, Sp.
58/B1 Puentes de García Rodríguez, Sp.
120/R10 Pueo (pt.), Hi,US
124/E4 Puerco (riv.), Az, NM,US
124/F4 Puerco (riv.), NM,US
112/B5 Puerto Aisén, Chile
108/C3 Puerto Asís, Col.
108/E2 Puerto Ayacucho, Ven.
116/D4 Puerto Barrios, Guat.
117/H5 Puerto Cabello, Ven.
116/E5 Puerto Cabezas, Nic.
117/H5 Puerto Cumarebo, Ven.
59/X16 Puerto de la Cruz, Canl.
58/A1 Puerto del Son, Sp.
116/B4 Puerto Escondido, Mex.
111/F2 Puerto Iguazú, Arg.
117/J5 Puerto La Cruz, Ven.
116/E4 Puerto Lempira, Hon.
58/C3 Puertollano, Sp.
58/E4 Puerto Lumbreras, Sp.
112/D4 Puerto Madryn, Arg.
108/E6 Puerto Maldonado, Peru
112/B4 Puerto Montt, Chile
116/D3 Puerto Morelos, Mex.
113/J7 Puerto Natales, Chile
117/F6 Puerto Obaldía, Pan.
117/G4 Puerto Plata, DRep.
82/C6 Puerto Princesa, Phil.
112/B4 Puerto Quellón, Chile
58/B4 Puerto Real, Sp.
117/H4 Puerto Rico (commonwealth), US
116/C5 Puerto San José, Guat.
108/G7 Puerto Suárez, Bol.
117/N9 Puerto Vallarta, Mex.
112/B4 Puerto Varas, Chile
112/C5 Pueyrredón (lake), Arg.
44/D5 Puffin (isl.), Wal,UK
67/J1 Pugachev, Rus.
132/C2 Puget (sound), Wa,US
60/E2 Puglia (reg.), It.
56/E5 Puigmal (mtn.), Fr.
59/G1 Puigsacalm (mtn.), Sp.
86/C5 Pujut (cape), Indo.
93/J6 Pukapuka (isl.), Cookls.
93/M6 Puka Puka (atoll), FrPol.
93/M6 Pukarua (isl.), FrPol.
126/C1 Pukaskwa Nat'l Park, On,Can
87/F1 Pulandita (pt.), Phil.
92/D4 Pulap (atoll), Micr.
129/G3 Pulaski, Tn,US
126/D4 Pulaski, Va,US
49/L3 Puławy, Pol.
47/F5 Pulborough, Eng,UK
50/D7 Pulheim, Ger.
87/G3 Pulisan (cape), Indo.
122/D4 Pullman, Wa,US
54/C5 Pully, Swi.
49/G3 Pulsnitz (riv.), Ger.
49/L2 Pułtusk, Pol.
92/D4 Puluwat (atoll), Micr.
46/C2 Pumpsaint, Wal,UK
85/F2 Pumu (pass), China
93/X15 Punaauia, FrPol.
108/E7 Punata, Bol.
73/K2 Pūnch, India
84/B4 Pune (Poona), India
86/B3 Punggai (cape), Malay.
104/E1 Punia, D.R. Congo
75/C5 Punjab (state), India
73/K2 Punjab (plains), Pak.
73/K3 Punjab (prov.), Pak.
108/D7 Puno, Peru
116/D4 Punta Allen, Mex.
113/K8 Punta Arenas, Chile
117/G5 Punta Cardón, Ven.
117/J6 Punta de Mata, Ven.
116/D4 Punta Gorda, Belz.
116/E5 Punta Gorda (bay), Nic.
129/H5 Punta Gorda, Fl,US
117/M7 Punta Peñasco, Mex.
116/E6 Puntarenas, CR
58/B4 Punta Umbría, Sp.
120/S10 Puolo (pt.), Hi,US
108/D6 Puquio, Peru
68/H3 Pur (riv.), Rus.
108/C3 Puracé Nat'l Park, Col.
46/D5 Purbeck, Isle of (pen.), Eng,UK
125/H4 Purcell, Ok,US
112/B3 Purén, Chile
125/G3 Purgatoire (riv.), Co,US
84/D3 Purī, India
64/E4 Purikari (pt.), Est.
50/B3 Purmerend, Neth.
84/C4 Pūrna, India
84/C3 Pūrna (riv.), India
111/B5 Purranque, Chile
47/E3 Purton, Eng,UK
108/F4 Purús (riv.), Braz.
63/G4 Pŭrvomay, Bul.
86/C5 Purwokerto, Indo.
84/C4 Pusad, India
80/E5 Pusan, SKor.
80/D5 Pusan-Jikhalsi (prov.), SKor.
86/A2 Pusat Gayo (mts.), Indo.
64/F4 Pushkin, Rus.
62/E2 Püspökladány, Hun.
112/C2 Putaendo, Chile
86/D4 Puting (cape), Indo.
116/B4 Putla, Mex.
112/B4 Putomayo (riv.), Col.
68/K3 Putorana (mts.), Rus.
112/C4 Putrachoique (peak), Arg.
84/C6 Puttalam, SrL.
52/D1 Putte, Belg.
50/C4 Putten, Neth.
50/B5 Putten (isl.), Neth.
53/F5 Püttlingen, Ger.
98/C5 Putu (range), Libr.
108/D4 Putumayo (riv.), SAm.
86/D3 Putussibau, Indo.
120/T10 Puu Kukui (peak), Hi,US
52/D1 Puurs, Belg.
81/B3 Pu Xian, China
132/C3 Puyallup, Wa,US
132/C3 Puyallup (riv.), Wa,US
81/C4 Puyang, China
56/E4 Puy de Barbier (peak), Fr.
56/E4 Puy de Sancy (peak), Fr.
112/B4 Puyehue (vol.), Chile
112/B4 Puyehue Nat'l Park, Chile
56/D5 Puymorens, Col de (pass), Fr.
59/E3 Puzal, Sp.
101/C4 Pwani (prov.), Tanz.
101/A5 Pweto, D.R. Congo
44/D6 Pwllheli, Wal,UK
73/K1 Pyandzh (Panj) (riv.), Afg., Taj.
64/F2 Pyaozero (lake), Rus.
85/G4 Pyapon, Burma
68/J2 Pyasina (riv.), Rus.
67/G3 Pyatigorsk, Rus.
56/F4 Pyfara (mtn.), Fr.
42/H3 Pyhä-Häkin Nat'l Park, Fin.
42/H3 Pyhäjärvi, Fin.
42/H2 Pyhätunturi (peak), Fin.
83/B2 Pyinmana, Burma
46/C3 Pyle, Wal,UK
80/C2 P'yŏngan-Bukto (prov.), NKor.
80/C3 P'yŏngan-Namdo (prov.), NKor.
80/D4 P'yŏngt'aek, SKor.
80/C3 P'yŏngyang (cap.), NKor.
80/C3 P'yŏngyang-Si (prov.), NKor.
130/M4 Pyramid (mtn.), BC,Can
131/B1 Pyramid (lake), Ca,US
124/C3 Pyramid (lake), Nv,US
59/E1 Pyrenees (range), Eur.
56/C5 Pyrénées Occidentales Nat'l Park, Fr.
49/H2 Pyrzyce, Pol.
65/Q4 Pyshma (riv.), Rus.
83/B2 Pyu, Burma

Q

74/L6 Qā'al Jafr (salt pan), Jor.
74/K5 Qabātiyah, WBnk.
96/H1 Qābis, Tun.
72/F1 Qā'emshahr, Iran
61/G1 Qafa e Malit (pass), Alb.
96/G1 Qafşah, Tun.
77/J2 Qagan (lake), China
81/C2 Qahar Youyi Qianqi, China
76/C4 Qaidam (basin), China
74/M8 Qalansuwa, Isr.
74/F3 Qal'at Dizah, Iraq
74/H6 Qallīn, Egypt
74/K5 Qalqīlyah, WBnk.
72/F5 Qamar, Ghubbat al (bay), Yem.
74/N8 Qanah, Wādī (dry riv.), WBnk.
73/J2 Qandahār, Afg.
75/B2 Qaraghandy, Kaz.
74/E3 Qarah Qōsh, Iraq
97/Q6 Qardho, Som.
72/E2 Qareh Chāy (riv.), Iran
75/F4 Qarqan (riv.), China
61/G2 Qarrit, Qaf'e (pass), Alb.
60/B4 Qarţājannah (ruins), Tun.

100/B2 Qārūn, Birkat (lake), Egypt
72/E2 Qasr-e-Shīrīn, Iran
100/A3 Qaşr Farāfirah, Egypt
74/L5 Qaţanā, Syria
72/F3 Qatar
100/A2 Qattara (depr.), Egypt
74/L4 Qaţţīnah (lake), Syria
84/A2 Qāzi Ahmad, Pak.
72/F1 Qazvīn, Iran
61/F2 Qendrevica (peak), Alb.
73/G3 Qeshm (isl.), Iran
72/E1 Qezel (riv.), Iran
85/J2 Qi (riv.), China
81/D4 Qian (can.), China
81/D1 Qian (riv.), China
81/D5 Qianqiu Guan (pass), China
81/E2 Qian Shan (peak), China
81/B5 Qifeng Guan (pass), China
76/D4 Qilian (mts.), China
76/D4 Qilian (peak), China
74/N9 Qilt, Wādī (dry riv.), WBnk.
75/F4 Qimantag (mts.), China
81/B4 Qin (mts.), China
81/C4 Qin (riv.), China
100/C3 Qinā, Egypt
82/B1 Qing (riv.), China
81/E3 Qingdao, China
76/D4 Qinghai (lake), China
76/D4 Qinghai (mts.), China
82/C2 Qingjiang, China
82/A2 Qingshui, China
77/H4 Qingzhou, China
81/D3 Qinhuangdao, China
81/C3 Qinyuan, China
82/B4 Qiongshan, China
77/J2 Qiqihar, China
74/K5 Qiryat Ata, Isr.
74/K5 Qiryat Bialik, Isr.
74/K6 Qiryat Gat, Isr.
74/M9 Qiryat Mal'akhi, Isr.
74/K5 Qiryat Shemona, Isr.
74/K5 Qiryat Yam, Isr.
77/L2 Qitaihe, China
81/C4 Qixing (riv.), China
77/L2 Qixing (riv.), China
72/F2 Qom, Iran
72/F2 Qom (riv.), Iran
84/E2 Qomolangma (Everest) (peak), China
73/J1 Qondūz (riv.), Afg.
67/M1 Qostanay, Kaz.
82/C2 Qu (riv.), China
127/F3 Quabbin (res.), Ma,US
47/F3 Quainton, Eng,UK
51/E3 Quakenbrück, Ger.
131/E5 Quakertown, Pa,US
76/H5 Quan (riv.), China
128/D3 Quanah, Tx,US
81/B4 Quanbao Shan (mtn.), China
83/E3 Quang Ngai, Viet.
83/D2 Quang Trach, Viet.
83/D2 Quang Tri, Viet.
46/C4 Quantocks (hills), Eng,UK
82/B2 Quanzhou, China
123/G3 Qu'Appelle, Sk,Can
123/H3 Qu'Appelle (riv.), Sk,Can
123/G3 Qu'Appelle (dam), Sk,Can
119/K2 Quaqtaq, Qu,Can
52/C3 Quaregnon, Belg.
86/E4 Quarles (mts.), Indo.
57/J5 Quarrata, It.
60/A3 Quartu Sant'Elena, It.
131/B1 Quartz Hill, Ca,US
60/A4 Quballāt, Tun.
73/G1 Qūchān, Iran
91/D2 Queanbeyan, Austl.
119/J3 Québec (prov.), Can.
127/G2 Québec (cap.), Qu,Can
110/J7 Quebra-Cangalha (mts.), Braz.
112/B4 Quedal (pt.), Chile
46/D3 Quedgeley, Eng,UK
118/C3 Queen Charlotte (isls.), BC,Can
118/C3 Queen Charlotte (sound), BC,Can
122/B3 Queen Charlotte (str.), BC,Can
128/E3 Queen City, Tx,US
119/R7 Queen Elizabeth (isls.), NW,Nun.,Can
105/G Queen Mary (coast), Ant.
105/P Queen Maud (mts.), Ant.
118/F2 Queen Maud (gulf), Nun.,Can
105/Z Queen Maud Land (reg.), Ant.
119/S7 Queens (chan.), Nun.,Can
44/E1 Queensberry (mtn.), Sc,UK
45/G4 Queensbury, Eng,UK
45/E5 Queensferry, Wal,UK
90/B3 Queensland (state), Austl.
127/R9 Queenston, On,Can
102/D3 Queenstown, SAfr.
112/B4 Queilén, Chile
109/H4 Quelimada, Braz.
104/G4 Quelimane, Moz.
58/A3 Queluz, Port.

47/E3 Quenington, Eng,UK
112/F3 Quequén, Arg.
112/F3 Quequén Grande (riv.), Arg.
116/A3 Querétaro, Mex.
116/A3 Querétaro (state), Mex.
116/E5 Quesada, CR
58/D4 Quesada, Sp.
81/C4 Queshan, China
122/C2 Quesnel, BC,Can
122/C2 Quesnel (lake), BC,Can
83/E3 Que Son, Viet.
125/E3 Questa, NM,US
73/J2 Quetta, Pak.
112/B5 Queulat Nat'l Park, Chile
108/C4 Quevedo, Ecu.
116/C5 Quezaltenango, Guat.
82/E6 Quezon, Phil.
82/D5 Quezon City, Phil.
81/D4 Qufu, China
104/B3 Quibala, Ang.
108/C2 Quibdó, Col.
56/B3 Quiberon (bay), Fr.
104/B2 Quiçama Nat'l Park, Ang.
51/L1 Quickborn, Ger.
53/G5 Quierschied, Ger.
124/D4 Quijotoa, Az,US
112/B4 Quilán (cape), Chile
112/Q9 Quilicura, Chile
123/G2 Quill (lakes), Sk,Can
108/D6 Quillabamba, Peru
108/E7 Quillacollo, Bol.
112/C3 Quillagua (pt.), Chile
112/C3 Quilleco, Chile
84/C6 Quilon, India
112/C2 Quilpué, Chile
56/A3 Quimper, Fr.
129/G4 Quincy, Fl,US
126/B4 Quincy, Il,US
127/G3 Quincy, Ma,US
122/D4 Quincy, Wa,US
83/E3 Qui Nhon, Viet.
124/C2 Quinn (riv.), Nv,US
58/D3 Quintanar de la Orden, Sp.
116/D4 Quintana Roo (state), Mex.
112/Q9 Quintero, Chile
112/D2 Quinto (riv.), Arg.
117/N8 Quiriego, Mex.
112/B3 Quirihue, Chile
101/D5 Quirimba (arch.), Moz.
110/B1 Quirinópolis, Braz.
117/J6 Quiriquire, Ven.
127/H2 Quispamsis, NB,Can
111/D2 Quitilipi, Arg.
129/F3 Quitman, Ga,US
129/F3 Quitman, Ms,US
128/E4 Quitman, Tx,US
108/C4 Quito (cap.), Ecu.
109/L5 Quixeramobim, Braz.
85/H2 Qujing, China
76/C4 Qumar (riv.), China
118/G2 Quoich (riv.), NI,UK
44/C3 Quoile (riv.), NI,UK
102/B4 Quoin (pt.), SAfr.
74/L4 Qurnat as Sawdā' (mtn.), Leb.
100/C3 Qūs, Egypt
119/T6 Quttinirpaaq Nat'l Park, Nun.,Can
76/F4 Quwu (mts.), China
83/C1 Quynh Nhai, Viet.
81/C3 Quzhou, China
52/D5 Qyteti Stalin, Alb.
68/G5 Qyzylorda, Kaz.

R

57/L3 Raab (riv.), Aus.
42/H2 Raahe, Fin.
50/D4 Raalte, Neth.
50/B5 Raamsdonk, Neth.
74/M8 Ra'anana, Isr.
119/S7 Raanes (pen.), Nun.,Can
101/D3 Raas Jumbo, Som.
62/B3 Rab (isl.), Cro.
62/C2 Rába (riv.), Hun.
74/K6 Rabat, Malta
96/D1 Rabat (cap.), Mor.
57/K4 Rabaul, PNG
57/K4 Rabbi (riv.), It.
84/C4 Rabkavi, India
127/S8 Raby (pt.), On,Can
129/F4 Raccoon (pt.), La,US
119/L4 Race (cape), Nf,Can
83/D4 Rach Gia, Viet.
83/D4 Rach Gia (bay), Viet.
49/K3 Racibórz, Pol.
132/Q14 Racine, Wi,US
62/D2 Ráckeve, Hun.
62/E4 Rădăuţi, Rom.
57/K2 Radbuza (riv.), Czh.
45/G6 Radcliffe on Trent, Eng,UK
62/A2 Radenthein, Aus.
51/E6 Radevormwald, Ger.
126/D4 Radford, Va,US
84/B3 Rādhanpur, India
122/G2 Radisson, Sk,Can
47/F3 Radlett, Eng,UK
63/G4 Radnevo, Bul.
49/L3 Radom, Pol.

47/E3 Radom (prov.), Pol.
62/F4 Radomir, Bul.
49/K3 Radomsko, Pol.
62/F5 Radoviš, FYROM
46/D4 Radstock, Eng,UK
64/D5 Radviliškis, Lith.
46/C3 Radyr, Wal,UK
49/K2 Radziejów, Pol.
49/L2 Radzymin, Pol.
49/M3 Radzyń Podlaski, Pol.
119/H3 Rae (isth.), Nun.,Can
118/E2 Rae (riv.), Nun.,Can
84/D2 Rāe Bareli, India
129/J3 Raeford, NC,US
73/J2 Raeren, Eelg.
50/D5 Raesfeld, Ger.
111/D3 Rafaela, Arg.
74/K6 Rafaḥ, Gzza
73/G2 Rafsanjān, Iran
122/E5 Raft (riv.), Id, Ut,US
97/L6 Raga, Sudan
113/J8 Ragged (pt.), Chile
44/A1 Raghtin More (mtn.), Ire.
46/D3 Raglan, Wal,UK
42/E2 Rago Nat'l Park, Nor.
60/D4 Ragusa, It.
51/F4 Rahden, Ger.
73/K3 Rahīmyār Khān, Pak.
131/F5 Rahway, NJ,US
46/B3 Raiatea (isl.), FrPol.
84/C4 Raichūr, India
123/H4 Raigarh, India
124/E3 Rainbow Bridge Nat'l Mon., Ut,US
45/F4 Rainford, Eng,UK
122/C4 Rainier (mt.), Wa,US
129/G3 Rainsville Al,US
45/G5 Rainworth, Eng,UK
123/K3 Rainy (lake), Can., US
123/K3 Rainy (riv.), Can., US
126/A1 Rainy River, On,Can
84/D3 Raipur, India
48/F1 Raisdorf, Ger.
132/E8 Raisin (riv.), Mi,US
42/G3 Raisio, Fin.
52/C3 Raismes, Fr.
93/J7 Raja (pt.), Indo.
84/D4 Rājahmundry, India
84/C5 Rājampet, India
86/D3 Rajang (riv.), Malay.
73/K3 Rājanpur, Pak.
84/C6 Rājapālaiyam, India
67/G1 Rasskazovo, Rus.
73/L3 Rajgarh, India
73/L3 Rajgarh, India
84/B3 Rājkot, India
84/D3 Rāj-Nāndgaon, India
73/L2 Rājpura, India
84/B3 Rājshāhi, Bang.
84/B3 Rājula, Ind a
93/J5 Rakahanga (atoll), Cooks.
73/K1 Rakaposhi (mtn.), Pak.
85/F4 Rakhine (state), Burma
104/D5 Rakops, Bots.
63/G4 Rakovski, Eul.
64/E4 Rakvere, Est.
129/J3 Raleigh (cap.), NC,US
92/F4 Ralik Chain (arch.), Mrsh.
122/F3 Ralston, Ab Can
109/K6 Ramalho (mts.), Braz.
74/K6 Rām Allāh, WBnk.
84/B4 Ramas (cape), India
74/K5 Ramat Gan, Isr.
74/M8 Ramat HaSharon, Isr.
93/Z17 Rambi (isl.), Fiji
52/A6 Rambouillet, Fr.
48/E2 Rame (pt.), UK
84/C6 Rāmechhāp, Nepal
84/C6 Rāmeshwaram, India
72/E2 Rāmhormoz, Iran
74/K6 Ramla, Isr.
100/C2 Ramm, Jabel (mt.), Jor.
44/A4 Ramor, Lough (lake), Ire.
85/F4 Ramree (isl.), Burma
72/F1 Ramsar (Salht Sar), Iran
45/F4 Ramsbottom, Eng,UK
47/E4 Ramsbury, Eng,UK
126/D2 Ramsey (lake), On,Can
47/F2 Ramsey, Eng,UK
44/D3 Ramsey, IM,UK
46/A3 Ramsey (isl.), Wal,UK
47/H4 Ramsgate, Eng,UK
53/G5 Ramstein-Miesenbach, Ger.
92/D5 Ramu (riv.), PNG
84/D3 Rānāghat, India
128/D5 Ranavalona, Tx,US
123/G3 Rancagua, Chile
56/B2 Rance (riv.), Fr.
110/B2 Rancharia, Braz.
122/D4 Ranchester, Wy,US
84/E3 Rānchī, India
131/C2 Rancho Cordova, Ca,US
131/B3 Rancho Palos Verdes, Ca,US
112/B4 Ranco (lake), Chile
97/P5 Randa, Djib.
44/B2 Randalstown, NI,UK

60/D4 Randazzo, It.
102/P13 Randburg, SAfr.
42/D4 Randers, Den.
131/F5 Randolph, NJ,US
49/H2 Randow (riv.), Ger.
90/H8 Randwick, Austl.
83/C2 Rang (peak), Thai.
85/F3 Rāngāmāti, Bang.
87/E4 Rangasa (cape), Indo.
124/E2 Rangely, Co,US
128/D3 Ranger, Tx,US
93/L6 Rangiroa (atoll), FrPol.
83/B2 Rangoon (Yangon) (cap.), Burma
84/B2 Rangpur, Bang.
84/C5 Rāni bennur, India
83/B4 Ranong, Thai.
53/G3 Ransbach-Baumbach, Ger.
127/S9 Ransomville, NY,US
52/D1 Ranst, Belg.
87/F4 Rantekombola (peak), Indo.
126/B3 Rantoul, Il,US
83/D2 Rao Co (peak), Laos
54/C1 Raon-L'Étape, Fr.
92/H7 Raoul (isl.), NZ
81/C3 Raoyang, China
93/L7 Rapa (isl.), FrPol.
112/Q10 Rapel (canal), Chile
112/B5 Raper (cape), Chile
123/H4 Rapid City, SD,US
123/H4 Rappahannock (riv.), Va,US
84/D3 Rapti (riv.), India
131/F5 Raritan (bay), NJ,US
131/F5 Raritan (riv.), NJ,US
93/J6 Raroia (atoll), FrPol.
93/J7 Rarotonga (isl.), Cooks.
112/E4 Rasa (pt.), Arg.
74/E3 Ra's al 'Ayn, Syria
97/J7 Ra's al Unūf, Libya
100/C2 Ras Gharib, Egypt
84/B2 Rasharkin, NI,UK
74/H6 Rashīd (Rosetta), Egypt
72/E1 Rasht, Iran
62/E4 Raška, Yugo.
118/G2 Rasmussen (basin), Nun.,Can
122/F4 Raso (pt.), Port.
132/C2 Redmond, Or,US
57/H2 Rastatt, Ger.
51/F2 Rastede, Ger.
130/B6 Rata (isl.), Ak,US
130/B6 Rata (cape), Indo.
84/B2 Ratangarh, India
83/B3 Rat Buri, Thai.
84/C2 Rāth, India
130/H3 Ratak (chain), Mrsh.
123/J3 Rathenow, Ger.
48/G2 Rathfriland, NI,UK
44/B1 Rathlin (isl.), NI,UK
44/B1 Rathlin (sound), NI,UK
92/F4 Ratik Chain (arch.), Mrsh.
84/C3 Ratlām, India
84/B4 Ratnāgiri, India
84/B4 Ratnapura, SrL.
125/F3 Raton, NM,US
42/E3 Rättvik, Swe.
48/F2 Ratzeburg, Ger.
86/B3 Raub, Malay.
112/F3 Rauch, Arg.
42/D3 Raufoss, Nor.
110/D2 Raul Soares, Braz.
84/B3 Raurkela, India
60/C4 Ravanusa, It.
52/C6 Ravels, Belg.
45/E3 Ravenglass, Eng,UK
47/H3 Raveningham, Eng,UK
45/G5 Ravenshead, Eng,UK
126/D4 Ravenswood, WV,US
73/K2 Rāvi (riv.), India, Pak.
62/B2 Ravne na Koroškem, Slov.
93/H5 Rawaki (Phoenix) (atoll), Kiri.
73/K2 Rāwalpindi, Pak.
49/L3 Rawa Mazowiecka, Pol.
49/K2 Rawicz, Pol.
122/G5 Rawlins, Wy,US
45/G5 Rawmarsh, Eng,UK
45/F4 Rawtenstall, Eng,UK
112/D4 Rawson, Arg.
84/D4 Rāyadrug, India
84/C6 Rāyagada, India
77/H2 Raychikhinsk, Rus.
84/E3 Rayleigh, Eng,UK
90/H8 Regents Park, Austl.
50/D4 Raymond, Ab,Can
128/D5 Raymondville, Tx,US
123/G3 Raymore, Sk,Can
83/C3 Rayong, Thai.
57/H4 Razdan, Arm.
63/J3 Razelm (lake), Rom.
63/G2 Razgrad, Bul.
61/K1 Razgulj (peak), Bul.
63/G3 Razlog, Bul.
56/A2 Ré, Pointe du (pt.), Fr.
110/C3 Rea (riv.), Eng,UK
58/B3 Reading, Eng,UK
47/F4 Reading, Eng,UK
83/C3 Reang Kesei, Camb.
59/M6 Reao (atoll), FrPol.
77/N2 Rebun (isl.), Japan
57/K5 Recanati, It.

53/F6 Réchicourt-le-Château, Fr.
66/D1 Rechitsa, Bela.
122/F3 Recife, Braz.
102/D4 Recife (cape), SAfr.
51/E4 Recke, Ger.
51/E5 Recklinghausen, Ger.
48/G2 Recknitz (riv.), Ger.
83/B2 Reclining Buddha (Shwethalyaung) (ruins), Burma
111/E2 Reconquista, Arg.
72/C4 Red (riv.), Afr., Asia
85/H3 Red (riv.), China, Viet.
44/B1 Red (bay), NI,UK
125/J5 Red (riv.), US
128/D2 Red (hills), Ks,US
49/K1 Reda, Pol.
131/F5 Red Bank, NJ,US
124/B2 Red Bluff, Ca,US
125/G4 Red Bluff (lake), NM, Tx,US
45/G2 Redcar, Eng,UK
45/G2 Redcar & Cleveland (co.), Eng,UK
122/F3 Redcliff, Ab,Can
90/F6 Redcliffe, Austl.
76/H2 Red Cloud, Ne,US
122/F3 Red Deer, Ab,Can
122/F3 Red Deer (riv.), Ab,Can
123/H2 Red Deer (lake), Mb,Can
123/H2 Red Deer (riv.), Mb, Sk,Can
112/C2 Redding, Ca,US
47/E2 Redditch, Eng,UK
45/F1 Rede (riv.), Eng,UK
132/F7 Redford, Mi,US
47/F4 Redhill, Eng,UK
120/T10 Red Hill (peak), Hi,US
127/K1 Red Indian (lake), Nf,Can
53/G6 Réding, Fr.
123/H4 Red Lake, On,Can
123/H4 Red Lake (riv.), Mn,US
131/J7 Redland, Md,US
90/F7 Redland Bay, Austl.
131/C2 Redlands, Ca,US
122/F4 Red Lodge, Mt,US
132/C2 Redmond, Or,US
132/C3 Redmond, Wa,US
58/A1 Redondela, Sp.
58/B3 Redondo, Port.
131/B3 Redondo Beach, Ca,US
130/H3 Redoubt (vol.), Ak,US
123/J3 Red River of the North (riv.), Can., US
96/C3 Red Rock (riv.), Ia,US
46/A6 Redruth, Eng,UK
100/A6 Red Sea (hills), Sudan
118/D2 Redstone (riv.), NW,Can
123/G2 Red Sucker (lake), Mb,Can
123/H3 Redvers, Sk,Can
99/F4 Red Volta (riv.), Burk., Gui.
52/D4 Redwater, Ab,Can
124/B3 Redway, Ca,US
86/B3 Red Willow (cr.), Ne,US
76/H2 Red Wing, Mn,US
132/K12 Redwood City, Ca,US
123/K4 Redwood Falls, Mn,US
124/A2 Redwood Nat'l Park, Ca,US
126/D3 Reed City, Mi,US
47/H4 Reedham, Eng,UK
123/G3 Reedley, Ca,US
126/B3 Reedsburg, Wi,US
122/B3 Reedsport, Or,US
90/B1 Reedy (cr.), Austl.
89/H7 Reefton, NZ
43/A4 Ree, Lough (lake), Ire.
47/H1 Reepham, Eng,UK
50/D5 Rees, Ger.
124/C3 Reese (riv.), Nv,US
50/D3 Reest (riv.), Neth.
51/F5 Reeth, Eng,UK
50/B4 Reeuwijk, Neth.
49/H2 Rega (riv.), Pol.
110/E1 Regência, Pontal de (pt.), Braz.
109/K5 Regeneração, Braz.
57/K2 Regensburg, Ger.
57/J2 Regenstauf, Ger.
96/F2 Reggane, Alg.
50/D4 Regge (riv.), Neth.
60/D4 Reggio di Calabria, It.
57/H4 Reggio nell'Emilia, It.
63/G2 Reghin, Rom.
123/G3 Regina (cap.), Sk,Can
123/G3 Regina Beach, Sk,Can
110/C3 Registro, Braz.
96/E2 Réguibat (well), Alg.
58/B3 Reguengosde Monsaraz, Port.
51/G5 Rehburg-Loccum, Ger.
51/E5 Rehlingen-Siersburg, Ger.

104/C5 Rehoboth, Namb.
74/M9 Rehovot, Isr.
53/G2 Reichshof, Ger.
122/F3 Reid (lake), Sk,Can
129/J2 Reidsville, NC,US
47/F4 Reigate, Eng,UK
52/D5 Reims, Fr.
113/J7 Reina Adelaida (arch.), Chile
51/H1 Reinbek, Ger.
123/J2 Reindeer (isl.), Mb,Can
123/H1 Reindeer (lake), Mb, Sk,Can
123/H1 Reindeer (riv.), Sk,Can
58/C1 Reinosa, Sp.
42/G1 Reisduoddarhal'di (peak), Nor.
50/D2 Reitdiep (riv.), Neth.
122/F5 Reliance, Wy,US
96/F1 Relizane, Alg.
51/G1 Rellingen, Ger.
53/G2 Remagen, Ger.
109/K5 Remanso, Braz.
86/D5 Rembang, Indo.
109/H3 Rémire, FrG.
57/H2 Rems (riv.), Ger.
51/E6 Remscheid, Ger.
81/B5 Ren (riv.), China
112/C2 Renca, Chile
129/F2 René (lake), Il,US
48/E1 Rendsburg, Ger.
54/C1 Renens, Swi.
126/E2 Renfrew, On,Can
112/C2 Rengo, Chile
65/N3 Reni, Ukr.
50/C5 Renkum, Neth.
92/F6 Rennell (isl.), Sol.
56/C2 Rennes, Fr.
57/J4 Reno (riv.), It.
124/C3 Reno, Nv,US
102/C3 Renoster (riv.), SAfr.
102/D2 Renoster (riv.), SAfr.
81/D3 Renqiu, China
126/C3 Rensselaer, In,US
58/E1 Rentería, Sp.
132/C3 Renton, Wa,US
127/P6 Repentigny, Qu,Can
45/G6 Repton, Eng,UK
50/D2 Republic, Wa,US
125/H2 Republican (riv.), Ks, Ne,US
90/C3 Repulse (bay), Austl.
108/D4 Requena, Peru
59/E3 Requena, Sp.
112/C2 Requiñoa, Chile
112/B5 Rescue (pt.), Chile
62/E5 Resen, FYROM
110/J7 Resende, Braz.
124/E4 Reserve, NM,US
111/E2 Resistencia, Arg.
62/E3 Reşiţa, Rom.
119/K2 Resolute, Nun.,Can
119/K2 Resolution (isl.), Nun.,Can
110/D1 Resplendor, Braz.
52/B4 Ressons-sur-Matz, Fr.
127/H2 Restigouche (riv.), NB,Can
132/K11 Reston, Ca,US
131/J8 Reston, Va,US
123/C2 Restoration (pt.), Wa,US
57/N4 Retalhuleu, Guat.
52/D4 Rethel, Fr.
61/J5 Réthimnon, Gre.
53/E1 Retie, Belg.
64/H5 Reutov, Rus.
56/D5 Revel, Fr.
122/D3 Revelstoke, BC,Can
90/H8 Revesby, Austl.
52/D4 Revin, Fr.
75/B4 Revolyutsii, Pik (peak), Taj.
42/G1 Revsbotn (fjord), Nor.
84/D3 Rewa, India
84/C2 Rewāri, India
130/J3 Rex (mtn.), Ak,US
122/F5 Rexburg, Id,US
52/B2 Rexpoëde, Fr.
117/F6 Rey (isl.), Pan.
47/H2 Reydon, Eng,UK
124/B3 Reyes (pt.), Ca,US
74/D3 Reyhanlı, Turk.
42/N7 Reykjanes (cape), Ice.
116/B2 Reynosa, Mex.
56/C2 Rezé, Fr.
64/E4 Rēzekne, Lat.
55/F4 Rhaetian Alps (mts.), It., Swi.
55/F3 Rhätikon (mts.), Aus., Swi.
46/C2 Rhayader, Wal,UK
51/F5 Rheda-Wiedenbrück, Ger.
50/D5 Rheden, Neth.
52/D5 Rheinberg, Ger.
51/E4 Rheine, Ger.
51/E5 Rhein-Herne (can.), Ger.
53/F4 Rhemiles (well), Alg.
50/D3 Rhenen, Neth.
61/H1 Rhine (riv.), Eur.
126/B2 Rhinelander, Wi,US

53/F3 Rhineland-Palatinate (state), Ger.
53/D3 Rhisnes, Belg.
74/C1 Rhiw (riv.), Wal,UK
127/G3 Rhode Island (state), US
74/B3 Rhodes (isl.), Gre.
74/B3 Rhodes (Ródhos), Gre.
63/H3 Rhodope (mts.), Bul.
46/C3 Rhondda, Wal,UK
46/C3 Rhondda Cynon Taff (co.), Wal,UK
57/F4 Rhône-Alpes (reg.), Fr.
56/F4 Rhône (riv.), Fr., Swi.
52/C3 Rhonelle (riv.), Fr.
45/E6 Rhosllanerchrugog, Wal,UK
44/E5 Rhossili, Wal,UK
44/E5 Rhuddlan, Wal,UK
51/H5 Rhume (riv.), Ger.
46/C2 Rhyddhywel (mtn.), Wal,UK
46/B3 Rhydowen, Wal,UK
44/E5 Rhyl, Wal,UK
46/C3 Rhymney, Wal,UK
109/K6 Riacho de Santana, Braz.
131/C2 Rialto, Ca,US
86/B3 Riau (isls.), Indo.
58/A1 Ribadavia, Sp.
58/B1 Ribadeo, Sp.
58/C1 Ribadesella, Sp.
103/H8 Riban'i Manamby (mts.), Madg.
45/F4 Ribble (riv.), Eng,UK
48/E1 Ribe, Den.
48/E1 Ribe (co.), Den.
110/L7 Ribeira, Braz.
57/J4 Ribeira (riv.), It.
110/B3 Ribeira do Pombal, Braz.
59/T13 Ribeira Grande, Azor.
110/B2 Ribeirão do Pinha, Braz.
110/C2 Ribeirão Preto, Braz.
52/C4 Ribemont, Fr.
60/C4 Ribera, It.
108/E6 Riberalta, Bol.
48/G1 Ribnitz-Damgarten, Ger.
126/E2 Rice (lake), On,Can
126/E2 Rice Lake, Wi,US
118/C2 Richards (isl.), NW,Can
127/G2 Richardson (lakes), Me,US
112/B5 Richel (isl.), Neth.
124/D3 Richfield, Ut,US
59/Q10 Rich Frio, Port.
44/B3 Richhill, NI,UK
122/D4 Richland, Wa,US
129/H3 Richland Balsam (peak), NC,US
126/B3 Richland Center, Wi,US
128/D4 Richland Creek (res.), Tx,US
91/D2 Richmond, Austl.
127/F2 Richmond, Qu,Can
132/K11 Richmond, Ca,US
126/C4 Richmond, In,US
126/C4 Richmond, Ky,US
126/E4 Richmond, Va,US
126/E4 Richmond (cap.), Va,US
132/C2 Richmond Beach-Innis Arden, Wa,US
127/R8 Richmond Hill, On,Can
90/G2 Richmond-Raaf, Austl.
47/F3 Rickmansworth, Eng,UK
50/B5 Ridderkerk, Neth.
126/E2 Rideau (lake), On,Can
124/C4 Ridgecrest, Ca,US
131/F5 Ridgewood, NJ,US
45/F2 Riding Mill, Eng,UK
123/H3 Riding Mtn. Nat'l Park, Mb,Can
53/F5 Riegelsberg, Ger.
52/E2 Riemst, Belg.
49/G3 Riesa, Ger.
113/J8 Riesco (isl.), Chile
57/G3 Riet (riv.), SAfr.
51/F5 Rietberg, Ger.
60/C1 Rieti, It.
45/G3 Riffe (lake), Wa,US
124/E3 Rifle, Co,US
101/C3 Rift Valley (prov.), Kenya
64/E4 Riga (Rīga) (cap.), Lat.
59/L6 Riga (Rīga) (gulf), Lat.
122/F3 Rigby, Id,US
73/H2 Rīgestan (reg.), Afg.
122/D4 Riggins, Id,US
84/D3 Rihand Sāgar (res.), India
77/H2 Riihimäki, Fin.
105/C Riiser-Larsen (pen.), Ant.
42/G2 Riisitunturin Nat'l Park, Fin.
62/B3 Rijeka, Cro.
50/D5 Rijnsburg, Neth.
50/D4 Rijssen, Neth.
93/M7 Rikitea, FrPol.
62/B3 Rila (mts.), Bul.
63/G3 Rila (peak), Bul.
61/H1 Rilski Manastir, Bul.

72/D3 Rīma, Wādī (dry riv.), SAr.
122/E2 Rimbey, Ab,Can
97/J5 Rimé (wadi), Chad
57/K4 Rimini, It.
63/H3 Rîmnicu Sărat, Rom.
63/G3 Rîmnicu Vîlcea, Rom.
127/G1 Rimouski, Qu,Can
76/D1 Rinchinlhümbe, Mong.
58/C4 Rincón de la Victoria, Sp.
116/D5 Rincón de la Vieja Nat'l Park, CR
117/P9 Rincón de Romos, Mex.
44/C3 Ringboy (pt.), NI,UK
42/D4 Ringkøbing, Den.
47/G5 Ringmer, Eng,UK
131/F5 Ringoes, NJ,US
44/B1 Ringsend, NI,UK
48/F1 Ringsted, Den.
50/B4 Ringvaart (can.), Neth.
42/F1 Ringvassøy (isl.), Nor.
91/G5 Ringwood, Austl.
47/E5 Ringwood, Eng,UK
131/F4 Ringwood, NJ,US
61/J4 Rinia (isl.), Gre.
44/C2 Rinns, The (pen.), Sc,UK
51/G4 Rinteln, Ger.
108/C5 Rio Abiseo Nat'l Park, Peru
108/C4 Riobamba, Ecu.
110/L7 Rio Bonito, Braz.
108/E5 Rio Branco, Braz.
113/G2 Rio Branco, Uru.
110/B3 Rio Branco do Sul, Braz.
126/C4 Rio Bravo del Norte (Rio Grande) (riv.), Mex., US
112/B4 Rio Bueno, Chile
110/D2 Rio Casca, Braz.
113/T12 Riochuelo, Arg.
112/C2 Rio Clarillo Nat'l Park, Chile
110/J7 Rio Claro, Braz.
112/D3 Rio Colorado, Arg.
112/D2 Rio Cuarto, Arg.
110/K7 Rio de Janeiro, Braz.
110/K7 Rio de Janeiro (state), Braz.
112/B5 Rio Dell, Ca,US
110/B3 Rio de Sul, Braz.
59/Q10 Rio Frio, Port.
110/G4 Rio Gallegos, Arg.
113/L8 Rio Grande, Arg.
110/A5 Rio Grande, Braz.
128/C4 Rio Grande (riv.), Mex., US
128/D5 Rio Grande City, Tx,US
110/G8 Rio Grande da Serra, Braz.
116/E5 Rio Grande de Matagalpa (riv.), Nic.
110/A4 Rio Grande do Sul (state), Braz.
117/G5 Riohacha, Col.
117/F6 Rio Hato, Pan.
108/C5 Rioja, Peru
108/F4 Rio Jaú Nat'l Park, Braz.
109/L5 Rio Largo, Braz.
56/E4 Riom, Fr.
58/A3 Rio Maior, Port.
122/D3 Riondel, BC,Can
122/C4 Rio Negro (prov.), Arg.
113/F2 Rio Negro (dept.), Uru.
113/F2 Rio Negro (riv.), Uru.
60/D2 Rionero in Vulture, It.
110/C1 Rio Paranaíba, Braz.
110/A4 Rio Pardo, Braz.
111/E2 Rio Pilcomayo Nat'l Park, Arg.
124/A4 Rio Rancho, NM,US
56/F3 Riorges, Fr.
112/E1 Rio Segundo, Arg.
112/B5 Rio Simpson Nat'l Park, Chile
112/D2 Rio Tercero, Arg.
110/B1 Rio Verde, Braz.
116/B3 Rioverde, Mex.
109/H4 Rio Verde de Mato Grosso, Braz.
62/E3 Ripanj, Yugo.
129/F3 Ripley, Ms,US
129/F2 Ripley, Tn,US
59/G1 Ripoll, Sp.
59/L6 Ripoll (riv.), Sp.
59/L6 Ripollet, Sp.
45/G3 Ripon, Eng,UK
123/L5 Ripon, Wi,US
60/D4 Riposto, It.
45/G4 Ripponden, Eng,UK
46/C3 Risca, Wal,UK
77/N2 Rishiri (isl.), Japan
74/K6 Rishon LeZiyyon, Isr.
56/D2 Risle (riv.), Fr.
62/B3 Risnjak (peak), Cro.
62/B3 Risnjak Nat'l Park, Cro.
63/F3 Rişnov, Rom.
50/D5 Rijnsburg, Neth.
50/D4 Rijssen, Neth.
93/M7 Rikitea, FrPol.
62/B3 Rila (mts.), Bul.
63/G3 Rila (peak), Bul.
79/L9 Rittō, Japan
122/D4 Ritzville, Wa,US
57/J4 Riva, It.
93/K7 Rimatara (isl.), FrPol.
49/L4 Rimavská Sobota, Slvk.

172

Rivad – Saint

112/E2 **Rivadavia,** Arg.
57/G4 **Rivarolo Canavese,** It.
116/D5 **Rivas,** Nic.
56/F4 **Rive-de-Gier,** Fr.
112/B5 **Rivera** (isl.), Chile
111/E3 **Rivera,** Uru.
113/G1 **Rivera** (dept.), Uru.
132/F7 **River Rouge,** Mi,US
122/B3 **Rivers** (inlet), BC,Can
123/H3 **Rivers,** Mb,Can
99/G5 **Rivers** (state), Nga.
102/C4 **Riversdale,** SAfr.
131/C3 **Riverside,** Ca,US
90/G8 **Riverstone,** Austl.
123/J3 **Riverton,** Mb,Can
122/F5 **Riverton,** Wy,US
127/H2 **Riverview,** NB,Can
132/F7 **Riverview,** Mi,US
129/H5 **Riviera Beach,** Fl,US
131/K7 **Riviera Beach,** Md,US
127/G2 **Rivière-du-Loup,** Qu,Can
102/L11 **Riviersonde-rendreeks** (mts.), SAfr.
66/C2 **Rivne,** Ukr.
66/C2 **Rivnens'ka Obl.,** Ukr.
57/G4 **Rivoli,** It.
52/D2 **Rixensart,** Belg.
72/E4 **Riyadh** (Ar Riyāḑ) (cap.), SAr.
74/E2 **Rize,** Turk.
81/D4 **Rizhao,** China
60/E3 **Rizzuto** (cape), It.
42/D4 **Rjukan,** Nor.
98/B2 **Rkîz** (lake), Mrta.
42/D3 **Roa,** Nor.
47/F2 **Roade,** Eng,UK
43/D2 **Roadside,** Sc,UK
117/J4 **Road Town** (cap.), BVI
124/E3 **Roan** (plat.), Co,US
45/F1 **Roan Fell** (hill), Sc,UK
129/H2 **Roan High** (peak), NC,US
56/F3 **Roanne,** Fr.
129/G3 **Roanoke,** Al,US
129/J2 **Roanoke** (riv.), NC, Va,US
126/E4 **Roanoke,** Va,US
129/J2 **Roanoke Rapids,** NC,US
116/D4 **Roatán** (isl.), Hon.
91/C4 **Robbins** (isl.), Austl.
91/B1 **Robe** (peak), Austl.
43/A4 **Robe** (riv.), Ire.
53/E6 **Robert-Espagne,** Fr.
128/C4 **Robert Lee,** Tx,US
130/E4 **Roberts** (mtn.), Ak,US
47/G5 **Robertsbridge,** Eng,UK
42/G2 **Robertsfors,** Swe.
84/D3 **Robertsganj,** India
102/B4 **Robertson,** SAfr.
127/F1 **Roberval,** Qu,Can
45/H3 **Robin Hood's Bay,** Eng,UK
126/C4 **Robinson,** Il,US
132/C3 **Robinson** (pt.), Wa,US
107/B6 **Robinson Crusoe** (isl.), Chile
90/C4 **Robinson Gorge Nat'l Park,** Austl.
123/H3 **Roblin,** Mb,Can
108/G7 **Roboré,** Bol.
122/D2 **Robson** (peak), BC,Can
128/D5 **Robstown,** Tx,US
128/C3 **Roby,** Tx,US
58/A3 **Roca, Cabo da** (cape), Port.
116/B4 **Roca Partida** (pt.), Mex.
109/M4 **Rocas,** Braz.
57/G4 **Rocciamelone** (peak), It.
56/E5 **Roc de France** (mtn.), Fr.
113/G2 **Rocha,** Uru.
113/G2 **Rocha** (dept.), Uru.
45/F4 **Rochdale,** Eng,UK
46/B6 **Roche,** Eng,UK
56/C4 **Rochefort,** Fr.
47/G4 **Rochester,** Eng,UK
126/C3 **Rochester,** In,US
132/F6 **Rochester,** Mi,US
123/K4 **Rochester,** Mn,US
127/G3 **Rochester,** NH,US
126/E3 **Rochester,** NY,US
132/F6 **Rochester Hills,** Mi,US
47/G3 **Rochford,** Eng,UK
126/B3 **Rock** (riv.), Il, Wi,US
122/C4 **Rock** (cr.), Or,US
41/C3 **Rockall** (isl.), UK
130/L3 **Rock Creek,** Yk,Can
90/H8 **Rockdale,** Austl.
105/R **Rockefeller** (plat.), Ant.
126/B3 **Rockford,** Il,US
127/G2 **Rock Forest,** Qu,Can
123/G3 **Rockglen,** Sk,Can
90/C3 **Rockhampton,** Austl.
129/H3 **Rock Hill,** SC,US
89/A4 **Rockingham,** Austl.
129/J3 **Rockingham,** NC,US
126/B3 **Rock Island,** Il,US
126/F2 **Rockland,** On,Can
127/G2 **Rockland,** Me,US
91/B3 **Rocklands** (res.), Austl.
129/H4 **Rockledge,** Fl,US
128/D4 **Rockport,** Tx,US
128/C4 **Rocksprings,** Tx,US
122/F5 **Rock Springs,** Wy,US
131/J7 **Rockville,** Md,US
131/G5 **Rockville Center,** NY,US
128/D3 **Rockwall,** Tx,US
129/G3 **Rockwood,** Tn,US
115/E4 **Rocky** (mts.), NAm
126/D4 **Rocky** (peak), Ky,US
91/C4 **Rocky Cape Nat'l Park,** Austl.
127/K1 **Rocky Harbour,** Nf,Can
126/D2 **Rocky Island** (lake), On,Can
129/J3 **Rocky Mount,** NC,US
126/E4 **Rocky Mount,** Va,US
122/E2 **Rocky Mountain House,** Ab,Can
125/F2 **Rocky Mountain Nat'l Park,** Co,US
131/H5 **Rocky Point,** NY,US
53/G5 **Rodalben,** Ger.
127/K1 **Roddickton,** Nf,Can
46/D1 **Roden** (riv.), Eng,UK
132/K10 **Rodeo,** Ca,US
56/E4 **Rodez,** Fr.
74/B3 **Ródhos** (Rhodes), Gre.
57/K2 **Roding,** Ger.
51/F4 **Rödinghausen,** Ger.
61/F2 **Rodonit, Kep i** (cape), Alb.
39/N6 **Rodrigues** (isl.), Mrts.
44/B2 **Roe** (riv.), NI,UK
50/D6 **Roer** (riv.), Neth.
50/C6 **Roermond,** Neth.
52/C2 **Roeselare,** Belg.
132/D2 **Roesiger** (lake), Wa,US
119/H2 **Roes Welcome** (sound), Nun.,Can
66/D1 **Rogachev,** Bela.
42/C4 **Rogaland** (co.), Nor.
62/D4 **Rogatica,** Bosn.
128/E2 **Rogers,** Ar,US
126/D4 **Rogers** (peak), Va,US
126/D2 **Rogers City,** Mi,US
129/H2 **Rogersville,** Tn,US
54/B1 **Rognon** (riv.), Fr.
49/J2 **Rogoźno,** Pol.
124/B2 **Rogue** (riv.), Or,US
97/L6 **Rohl** (riv.), Sudan
73/J3 **Rohri,** Pak.
83/C2 **Roi Et,** Thai.
52/C4 **Roisel,** Fr.
112/E2 **Rojas,** Arg.
116/B3 **Rojo** (cape), Mex.
117/H4 **Rojo** (cape), PR
86/B3 **Rokan** (riv.), Indo.
90/A1 **Rokeby-Croll Creek Nat'l Park,** Austl.
98/C4 **Rokel** (riv.), SLeo.
79/L10 **Rokkō-san** (peak), Japan
110/B2 **Rolândia,** Braz.
50/D3 **Rolde,** Neth.
122/C2 **Rolla,** BC,Can
125/K3 **Rolla,** Mo,US
123/J3 **Rolla,** ND,US
132/P15 **Rolling Meadows,** Il,US
90/C4 **Roma,** Austl.
56/E4 **Romagnat,** Fr.
53/E5 **Romagne-sous-Montfaucon,** Fr.
129/J3 **Romain** (cape), SC,US
119/K3 **Romaine** (riv.), Qu,Can
63/H2 **Roman,** Rom.
87/G5 **Romang** (isl.), Indo.
87/G5 **Romang** (str.), Indo.
63/F3 **Romania**
56/F4 **Romans-sur-Isère,** Fr.
130/E3 **Romanzof** (cape), Ak,US
60/C2 **Roma** (Rome) (cap.), It.
53/F5 **Rombas,** Fr.
82/D5 **Romblon,** Phil.
129/G3 **Rome,** Ga,US
126/F3 **Rome,** NY,US
132/P16 **Romeoville,** Il,US
60/C2 **Rome** (Roma) (cap.), It.
56/E2 **Romilly-sur-Seine,** Fr.
50/D6 **Rommerskirchen,** Ger.
47/G4 **Romney Marsh** (reg.), Eng,UK
66/E2 **Romny,** Ukr.
48/E1 **Rømø** (isl.), Den.
56/D3 **Romorantin-Lanthenay,** Fr.
47/E5 **Romsey,** Eng,UK
132/F7 **Romulus,** Mi,US
83/D2 **Ron,** Viet.
122/E4 **Ronan,** Mt,US
109/H6 **Roncador** (mts.), Braz.
117/F5 **Roncador Cay** (isl.), Col.
60/C1 **Ronciglione,** It.
52/C2 **Roncq,** Fr.
58/C4 **Ronda,** Sp.
42/D3 **Rondane Nat'l Park,** Nor.
109/H7 **Rondonópolis,** Braz.
85/J2 **Rong** (riv.), China
123/G2 **Ronge** (lake), Sk,Can
92/F3 **Rongelap** (atoll), Mrsh.
92/F3 **Rongerik** (atoll), Mrsh.
93/X15 **Roniu** (peak), FrPol.
131/G5 **Ronkonkoma,** NY,US
49/H1 **Rønne,** Den.
42/E4 **Ronneby,** Swe.
105/U **Ronne Entrance** (inlet), Ant.
51/G4 **Ronnenberg,** Ger.
52/C2 **Ronse,** Belg.
109/H6 **Ronuro** (riv.), Braz.
102/P13 **Roodeport-Maraisburg,** SAfr.
102/B2 **Rooiberg** (peak), Namb.
84/C2 **Roorkee,** India
50/B5 **Roosendaal,** Neth.
105/N **Roosevelt** (isl.), Ant.
108/F6 **Roosevelt** (riv.), Braz.
118/D3 **Roosevelt** (mtn.), BC,Can
124/E2 **Roosevelt,** Ut,US
130/L4 **Root** (mtn.), Ak,US
132/Q14 **Root** (riv.), Wi,US
58/D4 **Roquetas de Mar,** Sp.
108/F2 **Roraima** (peak), Guy.
123/J3 **Rorketon,** Mb,Can
112/E2 **Rosario,** Arg.
109/K4 **Rosário,** Braz.
117/N9 **Rosario,** Mex.
113/F2 **Rosario,** Uru.
111/D2 **Rosario de la Frontera,** Arg.
113/S11 **Rosario del Tala,** Arg.
111/F3 **Rosário do Sul,** Braz.
117/M8 **Rosarito,** Mex.
59/G1 **Rosas** (gulf), Sp.
108/C3 **Rosa Zárate,** Ecu.
51/G6 **Rosdorf,** Ger.
93/J6 **Rose** (isl.), ASam.
130/M4 **Rose** (pt.), BC,Can
123/J3 **Roseau** (riv.), Can., US
117/J4 **Roseau** (cap.), Dom.
123/K3 **Roseau,** Mn,US
103/S15 **Rose Belle,** Mrts.
122/C5 **Roseburg,** Or,US
131/K7 **Rosedale,** Md,US
129/F3 **Rosedale,** Ms,US
43/D2 **Rosehearty,** Sc,UK
132/P16 **Roselle,** Il,US
131/F5 **Roselle,** NJ,US
127/N6 **Rosemère,** Qu,Can
128/E4 **Rosenberg,** Tx,US
48/G5 **Rosenheim,** Ger.
59/G1 **Roses,** Sp.
60/D1 **Roseto degli Abruzzi,** It.
122/G3 **Rosetown,** Sk,Can
74/H6 **Rosetta** (Rashīd), Egypt
132/M9 **Roseville,** Ca,US
132/G6 **Roseville,** Mi,US
74/M8 **Rosh Ha'Ayin,** Isr.
74/K5 **Rosh HaNiqra** (pt.), Isr.
63/G3 **Roşiori de Vede,** Rom.
48/G1 **Roskilde,** Den.
48/F1 **Roskilde** (co.), Den.
66/E1 **Roslavl',** Rus.
50/C5 **Rosmalen,** Neth.
60/D4 **Rosolini,** It.
56/B3 **Rosporden,** Fr.
53/G2 **Rösrath,** Ger.
105/M **Ross** (isl.), Ant.
105/P **Ross** (sea), Ant.
123/J2 **Ross** (isl.), Mb,Can
57/K3 **Rossa** (peak), It.
45/E4 **Rossall** (pt.), Eng,UK
60/E3 **Rossano,** It.
92/E6 **Rossel** (isl.), PNG
105/N **Ross Ice Shelf,** Ant.
127/H2 **Rossignol** (lake), NS,Can
43/H6 **Rosskeeragh** (pt.), Ire.
122/D3 **Rossland,** BC,Can
44/A3 **Rosslea,** NI,UK
98/B2 **Rosso,** Mrta.
46/D3 **Ross on Wye,** Eng,UK
66/F2 **Rossosh',** Rus.
130/M3 **Ross River,** Yk,Can
123/G2 **Rosthern,** Sk,Can
48/G1 **Rostock,** Ger.
66/F3 **Rostov,** Rus.
67/G2 **Rostov Obl.,** Rus.
44/B3 **Rostrevor,** NI,UK
129/G3 **Roswell,** Ga,US
125/F4 **Roswell,** NM,US
55/F1 **Rot** (riv.), Ger.
92/D3 **Rota** (isl.), NMar.
58/B4 **Rota,** Sp.
51/G2 **Rotenburg,** Ger.
51/G7 **Rotenburg an der Fulda,** Ger.
53/F2 **Rötgen,** Ger.
48/E3 **Rothaargebirge** (mts.), Ger.
45/G1 **Rothbury,** Eng,UK
45/G5 **Rother** (riv.), Eng,UK
47/F5 **Rother** (riv.), Eng,UK
45/G5 **Rotherham,** Eng,UK
43/D2 **Rothes,** Sc,UK
53/E2 **Rotheux-Rimière,** Belg.
47/F2 **Rothwell,** Eng,UK
87/F6 **Roti** (isl.), Indo.
89/H6 **Rotorua,** NZ
53/D2 **Rotselaar,** Belg.
57/K2 **Rott** (riv.), Ger.
53/F6 **Rotte** (riv.), Fr.
50/B5 **Rotterdam,** Neth.
50/D2 **Rottumeroog** (isl.), Neth.
50/D2 **Rottumerplaat** (isl.), Neth.
55/E1 **Rottweil,** Ger.
92/G6 **Rotuma** (isl.), Fiji
52/C2 **Roubaix,** Fr.
56/F4 **Roubion** (riv.), Fr.
56/D2 **Rouen,** Fr.
126/F2 **Rouge** (riv.), Qu,Can
132/F6 **Rouge** (riv.), Mi,US
129/G2 **Rough** (riv.), Ky,US
90/C4 **Round Hill** (pt.), Austl.
44/B1 **Round Knowe** (mtn.), NI,UK
132/P15 **Round Lake,** Il,US
132/P15 **Round Lake Beach,** Il,US
124/C3 **Round Mountain,** Nv,US
128/D4 **Round Rock,** Tx,US
122/F4 **Roundup,** Mt,US
46/E4 **Roundway** (hill), Eng,UK
90/G8 **Rouse Hill,** Austl.
53/E5 **Rouvres-en-Woërve,** Fr.
126/E1 **Rouyn-Noranda,** Qu,Can
42/H2 **Rovaniemi,** Fin.
83/D3 **Rovieng Tbong,** Camb.
57/J4 **Rovigo,** It.
119/J2 **Rowley** (isl.), Nun.,Can
98/B4 **Roxa** (isl.), GBis.
82/C5 **Roxas,** Phil.
82/D4 **Roxas,** Phil.
87/F1 **Roxas City,** Indo.
129/J2 **Roxboro,** NC,US
117/J5 **Roxborough,** Trin.
98/A3 **Roxo** (cape), Sen.
125/F4 **Roy,** NM,US
124/D2 **Roy,** Ut,US
57/G4 **Roya** (riv.), Fr.
43/B4 **Royal** (can.), Ire.
118/H4 **Royale** (isl.), Mi,US
47/E2 **Royal Leamington Spa,** Eng,UK
47/G4 **Royal Military** (can.), Eng,UK
102/E3 **Royal Natal Nat'l Park,** SAfr.
90/H9 **Royal Nat'l Park,** Austl.
132/F6 **Royal Oak,** Mi,US
47/G4 **Royal Tunbridge Wells,** Eng,UK
56/C4 **Royan,** Fr.
47/F2 **Royston,** Eng,UK
45/F4 **Royton,** Eng,UK
62/E4 **Rožaje,** Yugo.
49/L4 **Rožňava,** Slvk.
52/D4 **Rozoy-sur-Serre,** Fr.
49/M3 **Roztoczański Nat'l Park,** Pol.
128/E3 **R.S. Kerr** (lake), Ok,US
67/G1 **Rtishchevo,** Rus.
45/E6 **Ruabon,** Wal,UK
104/B4 **Ruacana** (falls), Ang.
104/B4 **Ruacana,** Namb.
101/B2 **Ruaha Nat'l Park,** Tanz.
72/E5 **Rub' al Khali** (des.), SAr.
66/F2 **Rubezhnoye,** Ukr.
59/G2 **Rubí,** Sp.
131/C3 **Rubidoux,** Ca,US
75/D1 **Rubtsovsk,** Rus.
124/D2 **Ruby** (mts.), Nv,US
124/D2 **Ruby Valley,** Nv,US
50/B5 **Rucphen,** Neth.
49/K2 **Ruda Woda** (lake), Pol.
45/G6 **Ruddington,** Eng,UK
49/G2 **Rüdersdorf,** Ger.
49/M3 **Rudnik,** Pol.
67/M1 **Rudnyy,** Kaz.
68/F1 **Rudolf** (isl.), Rus.
48/F3 **Rudolstadt,** Ger.
72/F1 **Rūdsar,** Iran
45/H3 **Rudston,** Eng,UK
44/B1 **Rue** (pt.), NI,UK
56/D4 **Ruelle-sur-Touvre,** Fr.
62/F4 **Ruen** (Rujen) (peak), Bul., Mac.
97/M5 **Rufā'ah,** Sudan
61/F3 **Ruffano,** It.
101/C4 **Rufiji** (riv.), Tanz.
112/E2 **Rufino,** Arg.
47/E2 **Rugby,** Eng,UK
123/J3 **Rugby,** ND,US
46/E1 **Rugeley,** Eng,UK
49/G1 **Rügen** (isl.), Ger.
50/D6 **Ruhr** (riv.), Ger.
51/D6 **Ruhrgebiet** (reg.), Ger.
125/F4 **Ruidoso,** NM,US
50/D3 **Ruinen,** Neth.
117/N9 **Ruiz,** Mex.
62/F4 **Rujen** (Ruen) (peak), Bul., FYROM
97/J8 **Ruki** (riv.), D.R. Congo
101/B4 **Rukwa** (lake), Tanz.
101/A4 **Rukwa** (prov.), Tanz.
62/D3 **Ruma,** Yugo.
97/L6 **Rumbek,** Sudan
117/G3 **Rum Cay** (isl.), Bahm.
127/G2 **Rumford,** Me,US
49/K1 **Rumia,** Pol.
46/C4 **Rumney,** Wal,UK
77/N3 **Rumoi,** Japan
101/B5 **Rumphi,** Malw.
131/F5 **Rumson,** NJ,US
52/D1 **Rumst,** Belg.
44/B1 **Runabay Head** (pt.), NI,UK
45/F5 **Runcorn,** Eng,UK
97/L7 **Rungu,** D.R. Congo
101/B4 **Rungwa,** Tanz.
101/B5 **Rungwe** (peak), Tanz.
131/E6 **Runnemede,** NJ,US
131/C2 **Running Springs,** Ca,US
76/D3 **Ruo** (riv.), China
75/E4 **Ruoqiang,** China
86/B3 **Rupat** (isl.), Indo.
63/G2 **Rupea,** Rom.
52/D1 **Rupel** (riv.), Belg.
126/E1 **Rupert** (riv.), Qu,Can
122/E5 **Rupert,** Id,US
119/J3 **Rupert House** (Waskaganish), Qu,Can
53/G2 **Ruppichteroth,** Ger.
53/F1 **Rur** (riv.), Ger.
93/K7 **Rurutu** (isl.), FrPol.
104/F4 **Rusape,** Zim.
47/E4 **Rushall,** Eng,UK
123/K4 **Rush City,** Mn,US
47/F2 **Rushden,** Eng,UK
126/C4 **Rushville,** In,US
125/G2 **Rushville,** Ne,US
128/E4 **Rusk,** Tx,US
45/H5 **Ruskington,** Eng,UK
109/L4 **Russas,** Braz.
90/F7 **Russell** (isl.), Austl.
123/H3 **Russell,** Mb,Can
123/H1 **Russell** (lake), Mb,Can
118/F1 **Russell** (isl.), Nun.,Can
129/H3 **Russell** (lake), Ga, SC,US
125/H3 **Russell,** Ks,US
129/G3 **Russellville,** Al,US
128/E3 **Russellville,** Ar,US
126/C4 **Russellville,** Ky,US
68/* **Russia**
124/B3 **Russian** (riv.), Ca,US
67/H4 **Rust'avi,** Geo.
102/D2 **Rustenburg,** SAfr.
128/E3 **Ruston,** La,US
58/C4 **Rute,** Sp.
87/F5 **Ruteng,** Indo.
104/F5 **Rutenga,** Zim.
124/D3 **Ruth,** Nv,US
51/F6 **Rüthen,** Ger.
45/E5 **Ruthin,** Wal,UK
127/F3 **Rutland,** Vt,US
47/F1 **Rutland** (co.), Eng,UK
47/F1 **Rutland Water** (res.), Eng,UK
75/C5 **Rutog,** China
101/A3 **Rutshuru,** D.R. Congo
50/D4 **Ruurlo,** Neth.
60/E2 **Ruvo di Puglia,** It.
101/C5 **Ruvuma** (prov.), Tanz.
101/B5 **Ruvuma** (riv.), Tanz.
74/F3 **Ruwāndūz,** Iraq
101/A2 **Ruwenzori** (range), Ugan.
67/H1 **Ruzayevka,** Rus.
49/K4 **Ružomberok,** Slvk.
101/A3 **Rwanda**
91/D2 **Ryan** (mt.), Austl.
44/C2 **Ryan, Loch** (inlet), Sc,UK
66/F1 **Ryazan',** Rus.
64/J5 **Ryazan' Obl.,** Rus.
66/G1 **Ryazhsk,** Rus.
64/G1 **Rybachiy** (pen.), Rus.
75/C3 **Rybach'ye,** Kyr.
64/H4 **Rybinsk,** Rus.
64/H4 **Rybinsk** (res.), Rus.
49/K3 **Rybnik,** Pol.
63/J2 **Rybnitsa,** Mol.
122/D2 **Rycroft,** Ab,Can
90/H8 **Ryde,** Austl.
47/E5 **Ryde,** Eng,UK
47/G5 **Rye,** Eng,UK
47/G5 **Rye** (bay), Eng,UK
45/H3 **Rye** (riv.), Eng,UK
124/C2 **Rye Patch** (res.), Nv,US
49/L3 **Ryki,** Pol.
67/J2 **Ryn-Peski** (des.), Kaz.
79/F1 **Ryōtsu,** Japan
79/M9 **Ryōzen-yama** (peak), Japan
49/K2 **Rypin,** Pol.
66/B2 **Rysy** (peak), Slvk.
45/G2 **Ryton,** Eng,UK
47/E2 **Ryton on Dunsmore,** Eng,UK
49/H1 **Rytterknægten** (peak), Den.
79/G3 **Ryūgasaki,** Japan
79/M9 **Ryūō,** Japan
49/M3 **Rzeszów,** Pol.
49/L3 **Rzeszów** (prov.), Pol.
64/G4 **Rzhev,** Rus.

S

51/G4 **Saale** (riv.), Ger.
48/F3 **Saalfeld,** Ger.
57/K3 **Saalfelden am Steinernen Meer,** Aus.
122/C3 **Saanich,** BC,Can
53/F5 **Saar** (riv.), Ger.
53/F5 **Saarbrücken,** Ger.
64/D4 **Saaremaa** (isl.), Est.
53/F5 **Saarland** (state), Ger.
53/F5 **Saarlouis,** Ger.
83/D3 **Sab** (riv.), Camb.
117/J4 **Saba** (isl.), NAnt.
62/D3 **Šabac,** Yugo.
59/G2 **Sabadell,** Sp.
78/E3 **Sabae,** Japan
87/E2 **Sabah** (state), Malay.
86/A2 **Sabang,** Indo.
117/F6 **Sabanita,** Pan.
97/M6 **Sabat** (riv.), Eth., Sudan
73/H2 **Şāberi, Hāmūn-e** (lake), Afg.
96/H2 **Sabhā,** Libya
100/B3 **Sabie,** Egypt
103/F2 **Sabie** (Sabierivier) (riv.), Moz., SAfr.
59/E1 **Sabiñánigo,** Sp.
116/A2 **Sabinas,** Mex.
116/A2 **Sabinas** (riv.), Mex.
116/A2 **Sabinas Hidalgo,** Mex.
128/E4 **Sabine** (lake), La, Tx,US
128/E4 **Sabine** (riv.), La, Tx,US
125/J5 **Sabine Pass** (waterway), La, Tx,US
60/C1 **Sabini** (mts.), It.
110/D1 **Sabinópolis,** Braz.
72/F4 **Sabkhat Maţţī** (salt marsh), UAE
87/F1 **Sablayan,** Phil.
127/J3 **Sable** (isl.), Can.
127/H3 **Sable** (cape), NS,Can
129/H5 **Sable** (cape), Fl,US
56/C3 **Sablé-sur-Sarthe,** Fr.
58/B2 **Sabor** (riv.), Port.
87/H4 **Sabra** (cape), Indo.
105/J **Sabrina** (coast), Ant.
73/G1 **Sabzevār,** Iran
122/D4 **Sacajawea** (peak), Or,US
124/E4 **Sacaton,** Az,US
58/A3 **Sacavém,** Port.
60/C2 **Sacco** (riv.), It.
63/G3 **Săcele,** Rom.
123/L2 **Sachigo** (lake), On,Can
123/L2 **Sachigo** (riv.), On,Can
127/H2 **Sackville,** NB,Can
127/G3 **Saco,** Me,US
110/C1 **Sacramento,** Braz.
132/M9 **Sacramento** (cap.), Ca,US
124/B2 **Sacramento** (riv.), Ca,US
125/F4 **Sacramento** (mts.), NM,US
58/D4 **Sacratif** (cape), Sp.
120/W12 **Sacred** (falls), Hi,US
45/G2 **Sacriston,** Eng,UK
60/E2 **Sacro** (peak), It.
58/A1 **Sada,** Sp.
122/C2 **Saddle** (hills), Ab, BC,Can
45/G4 **Saddleworth,** Eng,UK
83/D4 **Sa Dec,** Viet.
73/K3 **Sādiqābād,** Pak.
85/G2 **Sadiya,** India
79/F2 **Sado** (isl.), Japan
58/A3 **Sado** (riv.), Port.
78/B4 **Sadowara,** Japan
84/B2 **Sādri,** India
96/H1 **Safāqis,** Tun.
72/E3 **Saffānīyah, Ra's as** (pt.), SAr.
42/E4 **Säffle,** Swe.
124/E4 **Safford,** Az,US
47/G2 **Saffron Walden,** Eng,UK
96/D1 **Safi,** Mor.
73/H2 **Safid** (mts.), Afg.
73/J1 **Safīd** (riv.), Afg.
73/K1 **Safid Khers** (mts.), Afg., Taj.
74/L4 **Şāfītā,** Syria
64/G5 **Safonovo,** Rus.
74/C2 **Safranbolu,** Turk.
84/E2 **Saga,** China
78/B4 **Saga,** Japan
78/A4 **Saga** (pref.), Japan
79/G1 **Sagae,** Japan
85/G3 **Sagaing,** Burma
85/F3 **Sagaing** (div.), Burma
79/H7 **Sagami** (bay), Japan
79/H7 **Sagami** (riv.), Japan
79/F3 **Sagami** (sea), Japan
79/F3 **Sagamihara,** Japan
79/H7 **Sagamiko,** Japan
84/C3 **Sāgar,** India
130/J2 **Sagavanirktok** (riv.), Ak,US
87/F1 **Sagay,** Phil.
126/D3 **Saginaw,** Mi,US
126/D3 **Saginaw** (bay), Mi,US
119/K3 **Saglek** (bay), Nf,Can
60/A1 **Sagone** (gulf), Fr.
58/A4 **Sagres,** Port.
75/E2 **Sagsay** (riv.), Mong.
117/F3 **Sagua de Tánamo,** Cuba
124/E4 **Saguaro Nat'l Park,** Az,US
127/G1 **Saguenay** (riv.), Qu,Can
96/C2 **Saguia el Hamra** (wadi), Mor., WSah.
59/E3 **Sagunto,** Sp.
84/E2 **Sa'gya,** China
67/K2 **Sagyz** (riv.), Kaz.
74/L6 **Saḩāb,** Jor.
100/B5 **Sahaba,** Sudan
117/F6 **Sahagún,** Col.
72/E1 **Sahand** (mtn.), Iran
96/G3 **Sahara** (des.), Afr.
73/L3 **Sahāranpur,** India
84/E2 **Saharsa,** India
84/E2 **Sāhibganj,** India
73/K2 **Sāhīwāl,** Pak.
96/H2 **Şaḩrā Awbārī** (des.), Libya
96/H3 **Şaḩrā Marzūq** (des.), Libya
97/K2 **Sahra' Rabyānah** (des.), Libya
116/A3 **Sahuayo,** Mex.
84/D2 **Sai** (riv.), India
79/E2 **Sai** (riv.), Japan
96/F1 **Saïda,** Alg.
84/D2 **Saidpur,** India
78/C2 **Saigō,** Japan
83/D4 **Saigon** (Ho Chi Minh City), Viet.
78/C4 **Saijō,** Japan
78/A4 **Saikai Nat'l Park,** Japan
78/B4 **Saiki,** Japan
84/C4 **Sailu,** India
42/J3 **Saimaa** (lake), Fin.
52/C4 **Sains-Richaumont,** Fr.
43/D3 **Saint Abb's Head** (pt.), Sc,UK
56/E5 **Saint-Affrique,** Fr.
46/A6 **Saint Agnes,** Eng,UK
127/L2 **Saint Alban's,** Nf,Can
127/F2 **Saint Albans,** Vt,US
126/D4 **Saint Albans,** WV,US
122/E2 **Saint Albert,** Ab,Can
46/D5 **Saint Aldhelm's Head** (pt.), Eng,UK
52/C3 **Saint-Amand-les-Eaux,** Fr.
56/E3 **Saint-Amand-Montrond,** Fr.
127/G1 **Saint-Ambroise,** Qu,Can
103/R15 **Saint-André,** Reun.
56/F2 **Saint-André-les-Vergers,** Fr.
43/D2 **Saint Andrews,** Sc,UK
98/B5 **Saint Ann** (cape), SLeo.
117/F4 **Saint Ann's Bay,** Jam.
56/B2 **Saint Anne,** Chl,UK
127/Q9 **Saint Anns,** On,Can
46/A3 **Saint Ann's** (pt.), UK
127/L1 **Saint Anthony,** Nf,Can
122/F5 **Saint Anthony,** Id,US
127/N6 **Saint-Antoine,** Qu,Can
52/D6 **Saint-Armand-sur-Fion,** Fr.
44/E5 **Saint Asaph,** Wal,UK
46/C4 **Saint Athan,** Wal,UK
56/B2 **Saint Aubin,** Chl,UK
127/N6 **Saint-Augustin,** Qu,Can
129/H4 **Saint Augustine,** Fl,US
46/B6 **Saint Austell,** Eng,UK
56/B3 **Saint-Avé,** Fr.
53/F5 **Saint-Avold,** Fr.
56/D5 **Saint-Barthélemy, Pic de** (peak), Fr.
44/E3 **Saint Bees,** Eng,UK
44/E2 **Saint Bees Head** (pt.), Eng,UK
127/M6 **Saint-Benoît,** Qu,Can
103/R15 **Saint-Benoît,** Reun.
127/P7 **Saint-Blaise,** Qu,Can
102/C4 **Saint Blaize** (cape), SAfr.
46/D3 **Saint Briavels,** Eng,UK
46/A3 **Saint Brides** (bay), Wal,UK
56/B2 **Saint-Brieuc,** Fr.
56/B2 **Saint-Brieuc** (bay), Fr.
127/P6 **Saint-Bruno-de-Montarville,** Qu,Can
127/M6 **Saint-Canut,** Qu,Can
127/R9 **Saint Catharines,** On,Can
117/J5 **Saint Catherine** (mt.), Gren.
47/E5 **Saint Catherine's** (pt.), Eng,UK
56/F4 **Saint-Chamond,** Fr.
132/P16 **Saint Charles,** Il,US
126/E4 **Saint Charles,** Md,US
125/K3 **Saint Charles,** Mo,US
132/G7 **Saint Clair** (lake), On,Can, Mi,US
132/H6 **Saint Clair** (riv.), On,Can, Mi,US
132/G6 **Saint Clair Shores,** Mi,US
54/B5 **Saint-Claude,** Fr.
46/B3 **Saint Clears,** Wal,UK
52/B6 **Saint-Cloud,** Fr.
123/K4 **Saint Cloud,** Mn,US
46/B6 **Saint Columb Major,** Eng,UK
127/N7 **Saint-Constant,** Qu,Can
123/K4 **Saint Croix** (riv.), Mn, Wi,US
117/H4 **Saint Croix** (isl.), USVI
130/M3 **Saint Cyr** (mtn.), Yk,Can
52/B6 **Saint-Cyr-l'École,** Fr.
46/A3 **Saint David's,** Wal,UK
46/A3 **Saint David's Head** (pt.), Wal,UK
52/B6 **Saint-Denis,** Fr.
103/R15 **Saint-Denis** (cap.), Reun.
54/C1 **Saint-Dié,** Fr.
56/F2 **Saint-Dizier,** Fr.
56/E3 **Saint-Doulchard,** Fr.
126/F2 **Sainte-Agathe-des-Monts,** Qu,Can
127/H1 **Sainte-Anne-des-Monts,** Qu,Can
127/N6 **Sainte-Anne-des-Plaines,** Qu,Can
127/G2 **Sainte-Foy,** Qu,Can
125/K3 **Sainte Genevieve,** Mo,US
52/B6 **Sainte-Geneviève-des-Bois,** Fr.
127/P6 **Sainte-Julie-de-Verchères,** Qu,Can
127/J2 **Saint Eleanors,** PE,Can
130/K3 **Saint Elias** (mts.), Can., US
130/K4 **Saint Elias** (cape), Ak,US
130/K3 **Saint Elias** (mt.), Ak,US
130/K3 **Saint Elias-Wrangell Nat'l Park and Prsv.,** Ak,US
127/H1 **Sainte-Marguerite** (riv.), Qu,Can
127/G2 **Sainte-Marie,** Qu,Can
103/J7 **Sainte Marie, Nosy** (isl.), Madg.
57/G5 **Sainte-Maxime,** Fr.
52/C5 **Saint-Erme-Outre-et-Ramecourt,** Fr.
123/J3 **Sainte Rose du Lac,** Mb,Can
56/C4 **Saintes,** Fr.
127/M6 **Sainte-Scholastique,** Qu,Can
56/E5 **Saint-Estève,** Fr.
127/N6 **Sainte-Thérèse,** Qu,Can
56/F4 **Saint-Étienne,** Fr.
56/D2 **Saint-Étienne-du-Rouvray,** Fr.
127/N6 **Saint-Eustache,** Qu,Can
127/F1 **Saint-Félicien,** Qu,Can
44/C3 **Saintfield,** NI,UK
56/E2 **Saint-Florentin,** Fr.
56/E3 **Saint-Florent-sur-Cher,** Fr.
97/K6 **Saint-Floris Nat'l Park,** CAfr.
56/E4 **Saint-Flour,** Fr.
102/D4 **Saint Francis** (cape), SAfr.
125/K4 **Saint Francis** (riv.), Ar, Mo,US
125/G3 **Saint Francis,** Ks,US
132/Q14 **Saint Francis,** Wi,US
129/F4 **Saint Francisville,** La,US
129/F2 **Saint Francois** (mts.), Mo,US
56/D5 **Saint-Gaudens,** Fr.
127/H2 **Saint George,** Nb,Can
127/K1 **Saint George** (cape), Nf,Can
130/E4 **Saint George** (isl.), Ak,US
124/A2 **Saint George** (pt.), Ca,US
129/H3 **Saint George,** SC,US
124/D3 **Saint George,** Ut,US
127/K1 **Saint George's,** Nf,Can
127/J2 **Saint Georges** (bay), NS,Can
127/G2 **Saint-Georges,** Qu,Can
117/J5 **Saint George's** (cap.), Gren.
44/C6 **Saint George's** (chan.), Ire., UK
52/B6 **Saint-Germain-en-Laye,** Fr.
52/B6 **Saint-Germain-sur-Morin,** Fr.
52/A5 **Saint-Germer-de-Fly,** Fr.
52/C3 **Saint-Ghislain,** Belg.
56/F5 **Saint-Gilles,** Fr.
56/C3 **Saint-Gilles-Croix-de-Vie,** Fr.
56/D5 **Saint-Girons,** Fr.
46/B3 **Saint Govan's Head** (pt.), Wal,UK
90/F6 **Saint Helena** (isl.), Austl.
102/B4 **Saint Helena** (bay), SAfr.
95/B6 **Saint Helena** (isl.), UK
132/J9 **Saint Helena** (mtn.), Ca,US
91/D4 **Saint Helens** (pt.), Austl.
45/F5 **Saint Helens,** Eng,UK
122/C4 **Saint Helens,** Or,US
122/C4 **Saint Helens, Mount** (vol.), Wa,US
56/B2 **Saint Helier,** Chl,UK
56/C3 **Saint-Herblain,** Fr.
127/M6 **Saint-Hermas,** Qu,Can
84/E3 **Sainthia,** India
127/G1 **Saint-Honoré,** Qu,Can
127/P7 **Saint-Hubert,** Qu,Can
127/F2 **Saint-Hyacinthe,** Qu,Can
126/C1 **Saint Ignace** (isl.), On,Can
126/C2 **Saint Ignace,** Mi,US
90/H8 **Saint Ives,** Austl.
46/A6 **Saint Ives,** Eng,UK
47/F2 **Saint Ives,** Eng,UK
127/P7 **Saint-Jacques-le-Mineur,** Qu,Can
118/C3 **Saint James** (cape), BC,Can
123/K5 **Saint James,** Mn,US
131/G5 **Saint James,** NY,US
127/G1 **Saint-Jean** (lake), Qu,Can
127/H1 **Saint-Jean** (riv.), Qu,Can
56/C4 **Saint-Jean-d'Angély,** Fr.
56/D3 **Saint-Jean-de-la-Ruelle,** Fr.
56/C5 **Saint-Jean-de-Luz,** Fr.
127/G2 **Saint-Jean-Port-Joli,** Qu,Can
127/F2 **Saint-Jean-sur-Richelieu,** Qu,Can
127/N6 **Saint-Jérôme,** Qu,Can
122/D4 **Saint Joe** (riv.), Id,US

173

Saint – Santa

127/H2 Saint John, NB,Can
127/H2 Saint John (riv.), Can., US
56/B2 Saint John, Chl,UK
117/J4 Saint John's (cap.), Anti.
127/L2 Saint John's (cap.), Nf,Can.
44/C3 Saint John's (pt.), IM,UK
124/E4 Saint Johns, Az,US
121/K6 Saint Johns (riv.), Fl,US
127/F2 Saint Johnsbury, Vt,US
126/B1 Saint Joseph (lake), On,Can
103/R15 Saint-Joseph, Reun.
126/C2 Saint Joseph (isl.), Mi,US
126/C3 Saint Joseph (riv.), Mi,US
125/J3 Saint Joseph, Mo,US
56/E5 Saint-Juéry, Fr.
56/D4 Saint-Junien, Fr.
46/A6 Saint Just, Eng,UK
46/A6 Saint Just in Roseland, Eng,UK
91/F5 Saint Kilda, Austl.
43/A2 Saint Kilda (isl.), Sc,UK
117/J4 Saint Kitts and Nevis
127/P6 Saint-Lambert, Qu,Can
123/J3 Saint Laurent, Mb,Can
127/N6 Saint-Laurent, Qu,Can
52/B3 Saint-Laurent-Blangy, Fr.
109/H2 Saint-Laurent du Maroni, FrG.
127/J1 Saint Lawrence (gulf), Can.
127/L2 Saint Lawrence, Nf,Can
127/G1 Saint Lawrence (riv.), Can, US
130/D3 Saint Lawrence (isl.), Ak,US
126/E2 Saint Lawrence Islands Nat'l Park, Can.
127/M7 Saint-Lazare, Qu,Can
91/G5 Saint Leonard (mtn.), Austl.
127/N6 Saint-Léonard, Qu,Can
103/R15 Saint-Leu, Reun.
56/C2 Saint-Lô, Fr.
127/N7 Saint Louis (lake), Qu,Can
123/G2 Saint Louis, Sk,Can
103/R15 Saint-Louis, Reun.
98/A2 Saint-Louis, Sen.
98/B3 Saint-Louis (reg.), Sen.
122/A2 Saint Louis (riv.), Mn,US
125/K3 Saint Louis, Mo,US
127/H2 Saint-Louis-de-Kent, NB,Can
117/G4 Saint-Louis du Nord, Haiti
127/P7 Saint-Luc, Qu,Can
117/J5 Saint Lucia
103/F3 Saint Lucia, Lake (lag.), SAfr.
56/C3 Saint-Maixent-L'École, Fr.
123/J3 Saint Malo, Mb,Can
56/B2 Saint-Malo, Fr.
56/B2 Saint-Malo (gulf), Fr.
56/F5 Saint-Mandrier-sur-Mer, Fr.
52/B5 Saint-Mard, Fr.
47/H4 Saint Margaret's at Cliffe, Eng,UK
122/D4 Saint Maries, Id,US
123/J3 Saint Martin (lake), Mb,Can
117/J4 Saint-Martin (isl.), Fr.
52/A2 Saint-Martin-Boulogne, Fr.
52/C6 Saint-Martin-d'Ablois, Fr.
56/F4 Saint-Martin-d'Hères, Fr.
98/A3 Saint Mary (cape), Gam.
90/G8 Saint Marys, Austl.
126/D3 Saint Mary's, Nf,Can
127/J2 Saint Marys (riv.), NS,Can
130/F3 Saint Marys, Ak,US
129/H4 Saint Marys, Ga,US
126/E3 Saint Marys, Pa,US
127/N7 Saint-Mathieu, Qu,Can
130/D3 Saint Matthew (isl.), Ak,US
129/H3 Saint Matthews, SC,US
92/E5 Saint Matthias (isls.), PNG
52/B6 Saint-Maur-des-Fossés, Fr.
126/F1 Saint-Maurice (riv.), Qu,Can
46/A6 Saint Mawes, Eng,UK
53/F6 Saint-Max, Fr.
46/C3 Saint Mellons, Wal,UK
52/D6 Saint-Memmie, Fr.
52/B6 Saint-Michel-sur-Orge, Fr.
56/B3 Saint-Nazaire, Fr.
47/F2 Saint Neots, Eng,UK
53/E2 Saint-Nicolas, Belg.
52/B2 Saint-Omer, Fr.
52/A4 Saint-Omer-en-Chaussée, Fr.
127/G2 Saint-Pamphile, Qu,Can
127/G2 Saint-Pascal, Qu,Can
38/H5 Saint Paul (isls.), Braz.
122/F2 Saint Paul, Ab,Can
39/N7 Saint Paul (isl.), FrAnt.
99/F5 Saint Paul (cape), Gha.
98/C5 Saint Paul (riv.), Gui., Libr.
103/R15 Saint-Paul, Reun.
130/E4 Saint Paul (isl.), Ak,US
125/J3 Saint Paul, Ks,US
123/K4 Saint Paul (cap.), Mn,US
56/C5 Saint-Paul-lès-Dax, Fr.
90/B1 Saint Pauls (peak), Austl.
56/F4 Saint-Paul-Trois-Châteaux, Fr.
123/K4 Saint Peter, Mn,US
109/M3 Saint Peter and Saint Paul (rocks), Braz.
56/B2 Saint Peter Port, Chl,UK
47/H4 Saint Peter's, Eng,UK
65/V7 Saint Petersburg (Leningrad), Rus.
129/H5 Saint Petersburg, Fl,US
127/P7 Saint-Philippe-de-La Prairie, Qu,Can
117/J5 Saint-Pierre, Mart.
103/R15 Saint-Pierre, Reun.
127/K2 Saint Pierre & Miquelon (dpcy.), Fr
56/D3 Saint-Pierre-des-Corps, Fr.
56/C5 Saint-Pierre-du-Mont, Fr.
123/J3 Saint Pierre-Jolys, Mb,Can
56/B2 Saint-Pol-de-Léon, Fr.
52/B1 Saint-Pol-sur-Mer, Fr.
56/E5 Saint-Pons (mtn.), Fr.
52/B5 Saint-Prix, Fr.
52/C4 Saint-Quentin, Fr.
57/G5 Saint-Raphaël, Fr.
56/F5 Saint-Rémy-de-Provence, Fr.
52/A3 Saint-Riquier, Fr.
56/B2 Saint Sampson's, Chl,UK
52/C3 Saint-Saulve, Fr.
129/H4 Saint Simons Island, Ga,US
127/H2 Saint Stephen, NB,Can
46/B6 Saint Stephen in Brannel, Eng,UK
126/D3 Saint Thomas, On,Can
117/H4 Saint Thomas (isl.), USVI
127/N7 Saint-Urbain-Premier, Qu,Can
56/F3 Saint-Vallier, Fr.
52/B2 Saint-Venant, Fr.
91/C4 Saint Vincent (pt.), Austl.
117/J5 Saint Vincent & the Grenadines
53/F3 Saint Vith, Belg.
122/F2 Saint Walburg, Sk,Can
84/D2 Sāipal (mtn.), Nepal
92/D3 Saipan (isl.), NMar.
79/F2 Saitama (pref.), Japan
78/B4 Saito, Japan
83/B3 Sai Yok Nat'l Park, Thai.
62/E1 Sajószentpéter, Hun.
102/C3 Sak (riv.), SAfr.
79/H7 Sakado, Japan
79/J7 Sakae, Japan
79/M9 Sakahogi, Japan
79/F2 Sakai, Japan
78/C3 Sakaide, Japan
78/C3 Sakaiminato, Japan
123/H3 Sakakawea (lake), ND,US
119/J3 Sakami (lake), Qu,Can
63/K5 Sakarya (prov.), Turk.
74/B2 Sakarya (riv.), Turk.
77/M4 Sakata, Japan
72/H4 Sakawa, Japan
69/Q4 Sakhalin (gulf), Rus.
69/Q4 Sakhalin (isl.), Rus.
72/F1 Sakht Sar (Ramsar), Iran
67/H4 Şaki, Azer.
66/E3 Šaki, Ukr.
82/D3 Sakishima (isls.), Japan
67/L1 Sakmara (riv.), Rus.
83/D2 Sakon Nakhon, Thai.
73/J3 Sakrand, Pak.
79/F2 Saku, Japan
79/J7 Sakura, Japan
79/L10 Sakurai, Japan
67/G3 Sal (riv.), Rus.
49/J4 Šal'a, Slvk.
42/F4 Sala, Swe.
60/D2 Sala Consilina, It.
111/E2 Saladas, Arg.
112/F2 Saladillo, Arg.
112/D3 Salado (riv.), Arg.
112/D3 Salado (riv.), Arg.
116/B2 Salado (riv.), Mex.
107/C5 Salado del Norte (riv.), Arg
99/E4 Salaga, Gha.
87/G4 Salahatu (mtn.), Indo.
62/F2 Sălaj (co.), Rom.
96/J5 Salal, Chad
100/D4 Şalālah, Sudan
112/D5 Salamanca (plain), Arg.
112/C1 Salamanca, Chile
116/A3 Salamanca, Mex.
58/C2 Salamanca, Sp.
126/E3 Salamanca, NY,US
97/J6 Salamat (riv.), Chad
61/H3 Salamís, Gre.
61/L7 Salamís (isl.), Gre.
74/L4 Salamīyah, Syria
83/C1 Sala Mok Laos
58/B1 Salas, Sp.
67/K1 Salavat, Rus.
92/B5 Salayar (isl.), Indo.
38/D7 Sala y Gomez (isls.), Chile
56/E3 Salbris, Fr.
46/C6 Salcombe, Eng,UK
91/C3 Sale, Austl.
96/D1 Salé, Mor.
45/F5 Sale, Eng,UK
87/G3 Salebabu (isl.), Indo.
68/G3 Salekhard, Rus.
84/C5 Salem, India
126/C4 Salem, In,US
125/K3 Salem, Mo,US
127/G3 Salem, NH,US
122/C4 Salem (cap.), Or,US
126/D4 Salem, Va,US
60/C4 Salemi, It.
60/F2 Salentina (pen.), It.
60/D2 Salerno, It.
60/D2 Salerno (gulf), It.
47/G3 Sales (pt.), UK
45/F5 Salford, Eng,UK
62/D1 Salgótarján, Hun.
109/L5 Salgueiro, Braz.
125/F3 Salida, Co,US
74/B2 Salihli, Turk.
66/C1 Salihorsk, Bela.
104/F3 Salima, Malw.
100/B4 Salīmah (oasis), Sudan
58/B1 Salime (res.), Sp.
117/G3 Salina (pt.), Bahm.
60/D3 Salina (isl.), It.
125/H3 Salina, Ks,US
124/E3 Salina, Ut,US
116/B4 Salina Cruz, Mex.
109/K7 Salinas, Braz.
116/A3 Salinas, Mex.
124/B3 Salinas, Ca,US
124/B3 Salinas (riv.), Ca,US
59/G3 Salinas, Cabo de (cape), Sp.
125/F4 Salinas Nat'l Mon., NM,US
60/D2 Saline (marsh), It.
125/J4 Saline (riv.), Ar,US
125/G3 Saline (riv.), Ks,US
109/J4 Salinópolis, Braz.
119/J2 Salisbury (isl.), Nun.,Can
47/E4 Salisbury, Eng,UK
46/D4 Salisbury (plain), Eng,UK
126/F4 Salisbury, Md,US
129/H3 Salisbury, NC,US
42/J2 Salla, Fin.
57/G4 Sallanches, Fr.
50/D4 Salland (reg.), Neth.
98/B4 Sallatouk (pt.), Gui.
52/B3 Sallaumines, Fr.
59/F2 Sallent, Sp.
125/J4 Sallisaw, Ok,US
100/D5 Sallūm, Sudan
84/D2 Sallyāna, Nepal
44/B5 Sally Gap (pass), Ire.
53/F3 Salm (riv.), Ger.
74/F2 Salmās, Iran
122/D4 Salmon (riv.), Id,US
122/D3 Salmon Arm, BC,Can
124/D2 Salmon Falls (riv.), Id, Nv,US
122/E4 Salmon River (mts.), Id,US
42/G3 Salo, Fin.
54/B2 Salon (riv.), Fr.
56/F5 Salon-de-Provence, Fr.
97/K8 Salonga Nat'l Park, D.R. Congo
61/H3 Salonika (Thermaic) (gulf), Gre.
61/H2 Salonika (Thessaloníki), Gre.
62/E2 Salonta, Rom.
58/B3 Salor (riv.), Sp.
98/B3 Saloum, Vallée du (wadi), Sen.
67/G3 Sal'sk, Rus.
60/C4 Salso (riv.), It.
102/C3 Salt (riv.), SAfr.
124/E4 Salt (riv.), Az,US
111/C1 Salta, Arg.
46/B6 Saltash, Eng,UK
45/H2 Saltburn, Eng,UK
43/B4 Saltee (isls.), Ire.
42/E2 Saltfjorden (fjord), Nor.
46/D4 Saltford, Eng,UK
129/H4 Saltilla (riv.), Ga,US
116/A2 Saltillo, Mex.
124/E2 Salt Lake City (cap.), Ut,US
112/E2 Salto, Arg.
110/C2 Salto, Braz.
60/C1 Salto (riv.), It.
111/E3 Salto, Uru.
113/F1 Salto (dept.), Uru.
111/E3 Salto Grande (res.), Arg., Uru.
124/C4 Salton Sea (lake), Ca,US
110/A3 Salto Santiago (res.), Braz.
129/H3 Saluda (riv.), SC,US
82/D6 Salug, Phil.
84/D4 Sālūr, India
109/H2 Salut (isls.), FrG.
57/G4 Saluzzo, It.
113/J7 Salvación (bay), Chile
109/L6 Salvador, Braz.
58/A3 Salvaterra de Magos, Port.
58/A1 Salvatierra de Miño, Sp.
71/J8 Salween (riv.), Asia
67/J5 Sal'yany, Azer.
126/D4 Salyersville, Ky,US
49/H5 Salza (riv.), Aus.
51/E4 Salzbergen, Ger.
57/K3 Salzburg, Aus.
57/K3 Salzburg (prov.), Aus.
51/H4 Salzgitter, Ger.
51/G4 Salzhemmendorf, Ger.
51/F5 Salzkotten, Ger.
48/F2 Salzwedel, Ger.
58/C1 Sama, Sp.
86/C4 Samak (cape), Indo.
87/F2 Samales (isls.), Phil.
84/D4 Sāmalkot, India
100/B2 Samālūt, Egypt
117/H4 Samaná (cape), DRep.
74/C3 Samandağı, Turk.
74/H6 Samannūd, Egypt
82/E5 Samar (isl.), Phil.
67/J1 Samara, Rus.
67/K1 Samara (riv.), Rus.
67/J1 Samara Obl., Rus.
77/M2 Samarga (riv.), Rus.
74/N8 Samaria (reg.), WBnk.
74/N8 Samaria Nat'l Park, WBnk.
61/H5 Samarias Gorge Nat'l Park, Gre.
87/E4 Samarinda, Indo.
68/G6 Samarkand, Uzb.
72/D2 Sāmarrā', Iraq
73/K3 Samasata, Pak.
84/D3 Sambalpur, India
104/C2 Samba Lucala, Ang.
103/H7 Sambao (riv.), Madg.
86/D4 Sambar (cape), Indo.
86/C3 Sambas, Indo.
103/J6 Sambava, Madg.
66/B2 Sambor, Ukr.
113/F2 Samborombón (bay), Arg.
83/D3 Sambor Prei Kuk (ruins), Camb.
52/C3 Sambre (riv.), Belg.,Fr.
52/C4 Sambre à l'Oise, Canal de (can.), Fr.
80/E4 Samch'ŏk, SKor.
101/C4 Same, Tanz.
83/C4 Samit (cape), Camb.
83/C3 Samkos (peak), Camb.
132/C2 Sammamish (lake), Wa,US
80/E5 Samnangjin, SKor.
93/H6 Samoa
62/B3 Samobor, Cro.
63/F4 Samokov, Bul.
59/Q10 Samora Correia, Port.
74/A3 Sámos, Gre.
61/J2 Samothráki (isl.), Gre.
112/D2 Sampacho, Arg.
86/D4 Sampit, Indo.
86/D4 Sampit (riv.), Indo.
128/E4 Sam Rayburn (res.), Tx,US
83/C1 Sam Sao (mts.), Laos, Viet.
90/E6 Samson (mtn.), Austl.
83/D2 Sam Son, Viet.
90/E6 Samsonvale (lake), Austl.
74/D2 Samsun, Turk.
83/B4 Samui (isl.), Thai.
79/H7 Samukawa, Japan
67/J4 Samur (riv.), Azer., Rus.
83/C3 Samut Prakan, Thai.
83/C3 Samut Sakhon, Thai.
83/C3 Samut Songkhram, Thai.
83/D3 San (riv.), Camb.
77/H5 San (riv.), China
98/D3 San, Mali
49/M3 San (riv.), Pol.
62/C3 Sana (riv.), Bosn.
72/D5 Sanaa (Şan'a) (cap.), Yemen
58/A1 San Adrián, Cabo de (cape), Sp.
105/Z Sanae IV, Ant.
82/E6 San Agustin (cape), Phil.
59/N8 San Agustin de Guadalix, Sp.
130/F5 Sanak (isl.), Ak,US
82/G4 Sanama (isl.), Indo.
107/B5 San Ambrosio (isl.), Chile
72/E1 Sanandaj, Iran
132/K11 San Andreas (lake), Ca,US
116/F5 San Andrés, Col.
116/E5 San Andrés (isl.), Col.
124/F4 San Andres (mts.), NM,US
113/S12 San Andrés de Giles, Arg.
58/C1 San Andrés del Rabanedo, Sp.
116/B4 San Andrés Tuxtla, Mex.
128/C4 San Angelo, Tx,US
132/J11 San Anselmo, Ca,US
113/F3 San Antonio (cape), Arg.
112/C2 San Antonio, Chile
117/M9 San Antonio, Mex.
131/C2 San Antonio (mt.), Ca,US
124/F4 San Antonio, NM,US
128/D4 San Antonio, Tx,US
128/D4 San Antonio (riv.), Tx,US
59/F3 San Antonio Abad, Sp.
112/F2 San Antonio de Areco, Arg.
117/J5 San Antonio del Golfo, Ven.
112/D4 San Antonio Oeste, Arg.
128/E4 San Augustine, Tx,US
84/C3 Sānāwad, India
60/D2 San Bartolomeo in Galdo, It.
60/C1 San Benedetto del Tronto, It.
131/C2 San Bernardino, Ca,US
131/C2 San Bernardino (mts.), Ca,US
112/C2 San Bernardo, Chile
117/F6 San Bernardo (pt.), Col.
117/N8 San Blas, Mex.
129/G4 San Blas (cape), Fl,US
128/E3 San Bois (mts.), Ok,US
57/J4 San Bonifacio, It.
108/E6 San Borja, Bol.
127/S9 Sanborn, NY,US
132/K11 San Bruno, Ca,US
116/A2 San Buenaventura, Mex.
131/A2 San Buenaventura (Ventura), Ca,US
112/C3 San Carlos, Chile
116/A2 San Carlos, Mex.
116/E5 San Carlos, Nic.
82/D4 San Carlos, Phil.
113/G2 San Carlos, Uru.
124/E4 San Carlos (lake), Az,US
132/K11 San Carlos, Ca,US
117/H6 San Carlos, Ven.
112/C4 San Carlos de Bariloche, Arg.
117/G6 San Carlos del Zulia, Ven.
61/F2 San Cataldo, It.
112/C2 San Clemente, Chile
58/D3 San Clemente, Sp.
124/C4 San Clemente (isl.), Ca,US
111/D3 San Cristóbal, Arg.
116/E3 San Cristóbal, Cuba
116/D5 San Cristobal (vol.), Nic.
92/F6 San Cristobal (isl.), Sol.
108/D2 San Cristóbal, Ven.
116/C4 San Cristóbal de las Casas, Mex.
117/F3 Sancti Spíritus, Cuba
122/F2 Sand (riv.), Ab,Can
102/D3 Sand (riv.), SAfr.
125/G2 Sand (hills), Ne,US
78/D3 Sanda, Japan
44/C1 Sanda (isl.), Sc,UK
83/D3 Sandan, Camb.
63/F5 Sandanski, Bul.
45/F5 Sandbach, Eng,UK
51/F2 Sande, Ger.
42/D4 Sandefjord, Nor.
105/Q Sanders (coast), Ant.
128/C4 Sanderson, Tx,US
129/H3 Sandersville, Ga,US
90/F6 Sandgate, Austl.
44/D2 Sandhead, Sc,UK
127/Q8 Sandhill, On,Can
47/F4 Sandhurst, Eng,UK
113/L8 San Diego (cape), Arg.
124/C4 San Diego, Ca,US
128/D5 San Diego, Tx,US
74/B2 Sandıklı, Turk.
131/C2 San Dimas, Ca,US
60/D4 San Dimitri, Ras (pt.), Malta
116/E3 Sandino, Cuba
87/E3 Sandkan, Malay.
42/C4 Sandnes, Nor.
42/E2 Sandnessjøen, Nor.
104/D2 Sandoa, D.R. Congo
49/L3 Sandomierz, Pol.
57/K4 San Donà di Piave, It.
98/B3 Sandougou (riv.), Gam., Sen.
47/E5 Sandown, Eng,UK
122/D3 Sandpoint, Id,US
91/F5 Sandringham, Austl.
47/G1 Sandringham, Eng,UK
126/D3 Sandusky, Mi,US
126/D3 Sandusky, Oh,US
42/D4 Sandvika, Nor.
42/F3 Sandviken, Swe.
90/B2 Sandwich (cape), Austl.
47/H4 Sandwich, Eng,UK
90/D4 Sandy (cape), Austl.
123/K2 Sandy (lake), On,Can
47/F2 Sandy, Eng,UK
124/E2 Sandy, Ut,US
123/H2 Sandy Bay, Sk,Can
131/F5 Sandy Hook (bay), NJ,US
129/G3 Sandy Springs, Ga,US
53/E4 Sanem, Lux.
60/C2 San Felice Circeo, It.
112/C2 San Felipe, Chile
117/M7 San Felipe, Mex.
108/E1 San Felipe, Ven.
107/A5 San Félix (isl.), Chile
113/S12 San Fernando, Arg.
112/C2 San Fernando, Chile
116/B3 San Fernando, Mex.
82/D4 San Fernando, Phil.
58/B4 San Fernando, Sp.
131/B2 San Fernando, Ca,US
117/H6 San Fernando de Apure, Ven.
59/N9 San Fernando-de-Henares, Sp.
42/E3 Sånfjällets Nat'l Park, Swe.
130/K3 Sanford (mtn.), Ak,US
129/H4 Sanford, Fl,US
127/G3 Sanford, Me,US
129/J3 Sanford, NC,US
111/D3 San Francisco, Arg.
117/M7 San Francisco, Mex.
82/E6 San Francisco, Phil.
124/E4 San Francisco (riv.), Az, NM,US
132/K11 San Francisco, Ca,US
132/K11 San Francisco (bay), Ca,US
117/G5 San Francisco, Ven.
116/D5 San Francisco de la Paz, Hon.
117/N8 San Francisco del Oro, Mex.
117/G4 San Francisco de Macorís, DRep.
112/C2 San Francisco de Mostazal, Chile
131/B2 San Gabriel, Ca,US
131/B2 San Gabriel (mts.), Ca,US
131/C2 San Gabriel (riv.), Ca,US
84/B4 Sangamner, India
126/B3 Sangamon (riv.), Il,US
73/H2 Sangān (mtn.), Afg.
108/C4 Sangay Nat'l Park, Ecu.
58/A1 Sangenjo, Sp.
81/C2 Sanggan (riv.), China
86/D3 Sanggau, Indo.
96/J7 Sangha (riv.), CAfr., Congo
73/J3 Sanghar, Pak.
87/F3 Sangihe (isls.), Indo.
108/D2 San Gil, Col.
60/E2 San Giorgio Ionico, It.
60/C4 San Giovanni Gemini, It.
60/E3 San Giovanni in Fiore, It.
57/J4 San Giovanni in Persiceto, It.
75/D2 Sangiyn Dalay (lake), Mong.
80/E4 Sangju, SKor.
87/E3 Sangkulirang, Indo.
84/B4 Sāngli, India
96/H7 Sangmélima, Camr.
79/L10 Sangō, Japan
124/C4 San Gorgonio (peak), Ca,US
125/F3 Sangre de Cristo (mts.), Co, NM,US
117/J5 Sangre Grande, Trin.
60/D2 Sangro (riv.), It.
108/G6 Sangue (riv.), Braz.
99/E4 Sanguie (prov.), Burk.
117/M8 San Hipólito (pt.), Mex.
102/E3 Sani (pass), SAfr.
116/D4 San Ignacio, Belz.
108/E6 San Ignacio, Bol.
103/F7 San Ignacio, Bol.
112/B3 San Ignacio, Chile
117/M8 San Ignacio, Mex.
117/N9 San Ignacio, Mex.
78/D3 San'in Kaigin Nat'l Park, Japan
117/F6 San Jacinto, Col.
131/C3 San Jacinto (riv.), Ca,US
112/C2 San Javier, Chile
59/E4 San Javier, Sp.
79/F2 Sanjō, Japan
108/F6 San Joaquín, Bol.
124/B3 San Joaquin (val.), Ca,US
112/E1 San Jorge, Arg.
112/D5 San Jorge (cape), Arg.
112/D5 San Jorge (gulf), Arg.
117/M7 San Jorge (bay), Mex.
55/F2 San Jorge (gulf), Sp.
112/D4 San José (gulf), Arg.
116/D4 San Jose, Belz.
116/E6 San José (cap.), CR
117/M8 San José (isl.), Mex.
82/D4 San Jose, Phil.
59/F3 San José, Sp.
113/F2 San José (dept.), Uru.
113/T11 San José (riv.), Uru.
132/L12 San Jose, Ca,US
117/G5 San José, Ven.
117/J6 San José de Amacuro, Ven.
82/D5 San Jose de Buenavista, Phil.
108/F7 San José de Chiquitos, Bol.
117/M8 San José de Gracia, Mex.
117/J6 San José de Guanipa, Ven.
117/H6 San José de Guaribe, Ven.
111/C3 San José de Jáchal, Arg.
117/N9 San José del Cabo, Mex.
112/Q9 San José de Maipo, Chile
113/F2 San José de Mayo, Uru.
117/M8 San José de Pimas, Mex.
112/C1 San Juan, Arg.
113/M8 San Juan (cape), Arg.
112/C1 San Juan (prov.), Arg.
111/C3 San Juan (riv.), Arg.
116/E5 San Juan (riv.), CR, Nic.
117/G4 San Juan, DRep.
117/H4 San Juan (cap.), PR
124/F3 San Juan (mts.), Co,US
124/E3 San Juan (riv.), Co, Ut,US
128/A2 San Juan (basin), NM,US
111/E2 San Juan Bautista, Par.
59/E3 San Juan de Alicante, Sp.
58/B4 San Juan de Aznalfarache, Sp.
117/P10 San Juan de Lima (pt.), Mex.
116/E5 San Juan del Norte, Nic.
117/P9 San Juan de los Lagos, Mex.
117/H6 San Juan de los Morros, Ven.
113/K7 San Julián, Gran Bajo de (val.), Arg.
111/D3 San Justo, Arg.
98/C4 Sankanbiriwa (peak), SLeo.
98/C4 Sankoroni (riv.), Gui., Mali
57/L3 Sankt Andrä, Aus.
53/G2 Sankt Augustin, Ger.
55/F3 Sankt Gallen, Swi.
55/F3 Sankt Gallen (canton), Swi.
53/G5 Sankt Ingbert, Ger.
57/K3 Sankt Johann im Pongau, Aus.
57/K3 Sankt Johann in Tirol, Aus.
57/L2 Sankt Pölten, Aus.
57/L3 Sankt Veit an der Glan, Aus.
53/G5 Sankt Wendel, Ger.
117/M9 San Lázaro (cape), Mex.
132/K11 San Leandro, Ca,US
108/E6 San Lorenzo, Bol.
112/C2 San Lorenzo (peak), Chile
108/C3 San Lorenzo, Ecu.
108/B4 San Lorenzo (cape), Ecu.
60/A3 San Lorenzo (cape), It.
117/N8 San Lorenzo, Mex.
132/K11 San Lorenzo, Ca,US
58/C2 San Lorenzo de El Escorial, Sp.
58/B4 Sanlúcar de Barrameda, Sp.
117/N9 San Lucas, Mex.
117/N9 San Lucas (cape), Mex.
112/D2 San Luis, Arg.
112/D2 San Luis (mts.), Arg.
112/D2 San Luis (prov.), Arg.
117/F3 San Luis, Cuba
116/D4 San Luis, Guat.
128/B2 San Luis (val.), Co,US
124/B4 San Luis Obispo, Ca,US
116/A3 San Luis Potosi, Mex.
116/A3 San Luis Potosí (state), Mex.
117/M7 San Luis Río Colorado, Mex.
124/E4 San Manuel, Az,US
117/F6 San Marcos, Col.
116/B4 San Marcos, Mex.
128/D4 San Marcos, Tx,US
82/D4 San Mariano, Phil.
57/K5 San Marino
57/K5 San Marino (cap.), SMar.
112/C2 San Martín, Arg.
113/J7 San Martín (lake), Arg.
108/F6 San Martín (riv.), Bol.
112/C4 San Martín de los Andes, Arg.
99/E3 Sanmatenga (prov.), Burk.
132/K11 San Mateo, Ca,US
128/B3 San Mateo (mts.), NM,US
112/D4 San Matías (gulf), Arg.
108/G7 San Matías, Bol.
81/B4 Sanmenxia, China
108/F6 San Miguel (riv.), Bol.
116/D5 San Miguel, ESal.
116/A3 San Miguel de Allende, Mex.
112/F2 San Miguel del Monte, Arg.
111/C2 San Miguel de Tucumán, Arg.
82/C2 Sanming, China
79/L9 Sannan, Japan
97/M5 Sannār, Sudan
60/D2 Sannicandro Garganico, It.
124/C4 San Nicolas (isl.), Ca,US
112/E2 San Nicolás de los Arroyos, Arg.
116/A2 San Nicolás de los Garzas, Mex.
69/P2 Sannikova (str.), Rus.
79/F2 Sano, Japan
49/M4 Sanok, Pol.
112/B4 San Pablo, Chile
82/D5 San Pablo, Phil.
132/K11 San Pablo, Ca,US
132/K10 San Pablo (bay), Ca,US
112/F2 San Pedro, Arg.
116/D4 San Pedro, Belz.
112/C2 San Pedro, Chile
111/C1 San Pedro (vol.), Chile
98/D5 San Pédro, IvC.
111/E1 San Pedro, Par.
58/B3 San Pedro (range), Sp.
124/E4 San Pedro (riv.), Az,US
131/B3 San Pedro (bay), Ca,US
116/C4 San Pedro Carchá, Guat.
116/A2 San Pedro de las Colinas, Mex.
108/C5 San Pedro de Lloc, Peru
59/E4 San Pedro del Pinatar, Sp.
117/H4 San Pedro de Macorís, DRep.
116/B4 San Pedro Pochutla, Mex.
116/D4 San Pedro Sula, Hon.
60/A3 San Pietro (isl.), It.
44/E1 Sanquhar, Sc,UK
108/C3 Sanquianga Nat'l Park, Col.
117/L7 San Quintín, Mex.
117/L7 San Quintín (cape), Mex.
112/C2 San Rafael, Arg.
132/J11 San Rafael, Ca,US
124/E3 San Rafael (riv.), Ut,US
117/G5 San Rafael, Ven.
113/G2 San Ramón, Uru.
132/L11 San Ramon, Ca,US
111/D1 San Ramón de la Nueva Orán, Arg.
57/G5 San Remo, It.
58/C4 San Roque, Sp.
112/B3 San Rosendo, Chile
128/D4 San Saba, Tx,US
125/H5 San Saba (riv.), Tx,US
116/D5 San Salvador (cap.), ESal.
113/S11 San Salvador (riv.), Uru.
111/C1 San Salvador de Jujuy, Arg.
117/G3 San Salvador (Watling) (isl.), Bahm.
60/D1 San Salvo, It.
58/E1 San Sebastián, Sp.
58/D2 San Sebastián de los Reyes, Sp.
57/J4 San Sebastiano, It.
60/D2 San Severo, It.
76/F2 Sant, Mong.
116/D5 Santa Ana, ESal.
117/M7 Santa Ana, Mex.
131/C3 Santa Ana, Ca,US
131/C3 Santa Ana (mts.), Ca,US
117/H5 Santa Ana, Ven.
110/D1 Santa Bárbara, Braz.
112/B3 Santa Bárbara, Chile
116/D5 Santa Bárbara, Hon.
117/N8 Santa Bárbara, Mex.
131/A2 Santa Barbara, Ca,US
131/A2 Santa Barbara (chan.), Ca,US
108/E3 Santa Bárbara, Ven.
110/C2 Santa Bárbara d'Oeste, Braz.
82/D6 Santa Catalina, Phil.
124/C4 Santa Catalina (gulf), Ca,US
124/C4 Santa Catalina (isl.), Ca,US
110/B3 Santa Catarina (isl.), Braz.
110/B3 Santa Catarina (state), Braz.
110/B3 Santa Cecília, Braz.
117/F3 Santa Clara, Cuba
58/A4 Santa Clara (res.), Port.
132/L12 Santa Clara, Ca,US
131/B2 Santa Clara (riv.), Ca,US
117/J6 Santa Clara, Ven.
131/B2 Santa Clarita, Ca,US
59/G2 Santa Coloma de Farners, Sp.
59/L7 Santa Coloma de Gramanet, Sp.
58/A1 Santa Comba, Sp.
113/K7 Santa Cruz (prov.), Arg.
113/K7 Santa Cruz (riv.), Arg.
108/F7 Santa Cruz, Bol.
112/C2 Santa Cruz, Chile
116/D5 Santa Cruz, CR
82/D5 Santa Cruz, Phil.

Santa – Sethā

82/E6 Santa Cruz, Phil.
92/F6 Santa Cruz (isls.), Sol.
124/B3 Santa Cruz, Ca,US
131/A2 Santa Cruz (isl.), Ca,US
59/S12 Santa Cruz da Graciosa, Azor.,Port.
59/R12 Santa Cruz das Flores, Azor.,Port.
116/C4 Santa Cruz del Quiché, Guat.
117/F3 Santa Cruz del Sur, Cuba
59/X16 Santa Cruz de Tenerife, Canl.
110/B2 Santa Cruz do Rio Pardo, Braz.
111/F2 Santa Cruz do Sul, Braz.
59/L7 Sant Adrià de Besòs, Sp.
112/D5 Santa Elena (peak), Arg.
116/D5 Santa Elena (cape), CR
58/A1 Santa Eugenia de Ribeira, Sp.
59/F3 Santa Eulalia del Río, Sp.
112/E1 Santa Fé, Arg.
112/E2 Santa Fé (prov.), Arg.
58/D4 Santa Fé, Sp.
129/H4 Santa Fe (riv.), Fl,US
125/F4 Santa Fe (cap.), NM,US
110/B2 Santa Fe do Sul, Braz.
60/D3 Sant'Agata di Militello, It.
110/B1 Santa Helena de Goiás, Braz.
109/J4 Santa Inês, Braz.
113/J8 Santa Inés (isl.), Chile
110/G8 Santa Isabel, Braz.
116/E5 Santa Isabel, Col.
92/E5 Santa Isabel (isl.), Sol.
96/G7 Santa Isabel, Pico de (peak), EqG.
113/F2 Santa Lucía, Uru.
113/G2 Santa Lucía (riv.), Uru.
109/J4 Santa Luzia, Braz.
110/D1 Santa Luzia, Braz.
112/E2 Santa Magdalena, Arg.
117/M8 Santa Magdalena (isl.), Mex.
117/M9 Santa Margarita (isl.), Mex.
111/F2 Santa Maria, Braz.
112/C2 Santa María, Chile
112/B3 Santa María (isl.), Chile
59/T13 Santa Maria (isl.), Azor.,Port.
124/B4 Santa Maria, Ca,US
58/B4 Santa María, Cabo de (cape), Port.
60/D2 Santa Maria Capua Vetere, It.
109/K6 Santa Maria da Vitória, Braz.
61/F3 Santa Maria di Leuca (cape), It.
110/D1 Santa Maria do Suaçí, Braz.
117/G5 Santa Marta, Col.
110/B4 Santa Marta Grande, Cabo de (cape), Braz.
131/B2 Santa Monica, Ca,US
131/B3 Santa Monica (bay), Ca,US
131/B2 Santa Monica Mts. Nat'l Rec. Area, Ca,US
109/K6 Santana, Braz.
59/P11 Santana, Port.
59/V15 Santana, Madr.,Port.
111/E3 Santana do Livramento, Braz.
108/C3 Santander, Col.
58/D1 Santander, Sp.
60/A3 Sant'Antioco, It.
131/A2 Santa Paula, Ca,US
59/E3 Santa Pola, Sp.
59/E3 Santa Pola, Cabo de (cape), Sp.
109/H4 Santarém, Braz.
58/A3 Santarém, Port.
58/A3 Santarém (dist.), Port.
109/L5 Santa Rita, Braz.
110/H7 Santa Rita do Sapucaí, Braz.
112/D3 Santa Rosa, Arg.
112/D4 Santa Rosa (val.), Arg.
111/F2 Santa Rosa, Braz.
108/C4 Santa Rosa, Ecu.
124/B3 Santa Rosa, Ca,US
124/B4 Santa Rosa (isl.), Ca,US
125/F4 Santa Rosa, NM,US
124/C2 Santa Rosa (range), Nv,US
112/D2 Santa Rosa de Calamuchita, Arg.
116/D5 Santa Rosa de Copán, Hon.
110/C2 Santa Rosa de Viterbo, Braz.
117/M8 Santa Rosalía, Mex.
117/H6 Santa Rosalía, Ven.
116/D5 Santa Rosa Nat'l Park, CR
131/B2 Santa Susana (mts.), Ca,US
109/J6 Santa Teresa (riv.), Braz.
113/G2 Santa Teresa Nat'l Park, Uru.
109/H6 Santa Teresinha, Braz.
113/F3 Santa Teresita, Arg.
110/B1 Santa Vitória, Braz.
113/G2 Santa Vitória do Palmar, Braz.
59/L7 Sant Boi de Llobregat, Sp.
59/F2 Sant Carles de la Ràpita, Sp.
59/G2 Sant Celoni, Sp.
59/G2 Sant Cugat del Vallès, Sp.
129/H3 Santee (dam), SC,US
129/J3 Santee (riv.), SC,US
117/P10 San Telmo (pt.), Mex.
57/J4 Santerno (riv.), It.
60/D3 Sant'Eufemia (gulf), It.
59/G2 Sant Feliu de Guíxols, Sp.
59/G2 Sant Feliu de Llobregat, Sp.
59/F1 Sant Gervàs (peak), Sp.
111/F2 Santiago, Braz.
112/Q9 Santiago (cap.), Chile
113/J7 Santiago (cape), Chile
117/G4 Santiago, DRep.
128/B5 Santiago (riv.), Mex.
116/E6 Santiago, Pan.
116/E6 Santiago (mt.), Pan.
82/D4 Santiago, Phil.
131/C3 Santiago (peak), Ca,US
128/C4 Santiago (mts.), Tx,US
58/A1 Santiago de Compostela, Sp.
117/F4 Santiago de Cuba, Cuba
111/D2 Santiago del Estero, Arg.
117/N9 Santiago Ixcuintla, Mex.
116/B4 Santiago Jamiltepec, Mex.
117/N8 Santiago Papasquiaro, Mex.
112/Q9 Santiago, Región Metropolitana de (reg.), Chile
55/F3 Säntis (peak), Swi.
59/K6 Sant Jeroni (mtn.), Sp.
59/K6 Sant Llorenc del Munt Nat'l Park, Sp.
79/K9 Santō, Japan
110/G8 Santo Amaro (isl.), Braz.
110/B2 Santo Anastácio, Braz.
110/G8 Santo André, Braz.
111/F2 Santo Ângelo, Braz.
96/G7 Santo António, SaoT.
110/D2 Santo Antônio de Pádua, Braz.
117/H4 Santo Domingo (cap.), DRep.
108/C4 Santo Domingo de los Colorados, Ecu.
59/E3 Santomera, Sp.
58/D1 Santoña, Sp.
61/J4 Santoríni (Thíra), Gre.
110/G8 Santos, Braz.
110/K6 Santos Dumont, Braz.
117/L7 Santo Tomás, Mex.
117/N8 Santo Tomás, Mex.
112/E1 Santo Tomé, Arg.
59/K7 Sant Pere de Ribes, Sp.
59/K7 Sant Sadurní d'Anoia, Sp.
58/D1 Santurce-Antiguo, Sp.
59/K6 Sant Vincenç de Castellet, Sp.
59/L7 Sant Vincenç dels Hort, Sp.
112/B5 San Valentín (peak), Chile
112/C2 San Vicente, Chile
116/D5 San Vicente, ESal.
117/L7 San Vicente, Mex.
58/B3 San Vicente de Alcántara, Sp.
108/C6 San Vicente de Cañete, Peru
59/E3 San Vicente del Raspeig, Sp.
60/B1 San Vincenzo, It.
60/C3 San Vito (cape), It.
83/E2 Sanya, China
85/J4 Sanya, China
110/G8 São Bernardo do Campo, Braz.
111/E2 São Borja, Braz.
110/B1 São Domingos (riv.), Braz.
110/D2 São Fidélis, Braz.
111/G2 São Francisco (isl.), Braz.
109/L5 São Francisco (riv.), Braz.
110/B3 São Francisco do Sul, Braz.
110/B4 São Fransisco de Paula, Braz.
111/F3 São Gabriel, Braz.
110/D1 São Gabriel da Palha, Braz.
110/K7 São Gonçalo, Braz.
110/H6 São Gonçalo do Sapuçaí, Braz.
110/C1 São Gotardo, Braz.
110/C2 São Joachim da Barra, Braz.
109/K4 São João, Braz.
108/F5 São João (mts.), Braz.
110/D2 São João da Barra, Braz.
110/G6 São João da Boa Vista, Braz.
58/A2 São João da Madeira, Port.
59/P10 São João das Lampas, Port.
110/C2 São João del Rei, Braz.
110/K7 São João de Meriti, Braz.
109/K5 São João do Piauí, Braz.
110/K6 São João Nepomuceno, Braz.
110/B4 São Joaquim, Braz.
110/B4 São Joaquim Nat'l Park, Braz.
59/S12 São Jorge (isl.), Azor.,Port.
110/B3 São José, Braz.
110/A5 São José do Norte, Braz.
110/G6 São José do Rio Pardo, Braz.
110/B2 São José do Rio Preto, Braz.
110/H8 São José dos Campos, Braz.
110/B3 São José dos Pinhais, Braz.
110/B4 São Leopoldo, Braz.
110/H7 São Lourenço, Braz.
109/G7 São Lourenço (riv.), Braz.
110/B4 São Lourenço do Sul, Braz.
104/C3 São Lucas, Ang.
109/K4 São Luís, Braz.
110/B2 São Manoel, Braz.
109/K4 São Marcos (bay), Braz.
110/E1 São Mateus, Braz.
110/B3 São Mateus do Sul, Braz.
59/T13 São Miguel (isl.), Azor.,Port.
110/C2 São Miguel Arcanjo, Braz.
54/A4 Saône (riv.), Fr.
54/B4 Saône-et-Loire (dept.), Fr.
110/G8 São Paulo, Braz.
110/H8 São Paulo (state), Braz.
108/E4 São Paulo de Olivença, Braz.
110/D2 São Pedro da Aldeia, Braz.
79/M9 Saori, Japan
107/F3 São Roque (cape), Braz.
59/S12 São Roque do Pico, Azor.,Port.
110/H8 São Sebastião, Braz.
104/G5 São Sebastião (pt.), Moz.
110/C2 São Sebastião do Paraíso, Braz.
110/B1 São Simão (res.), Braz.
58/A4 São Teotónio, Port.
110/C2 São Tiago, Braz.
107/E5 São Tomé (cape), Braz.
96/G7 São Tomé (cap.), SaoT.
96/F7 São Tomé and Príncipe
96/E1 Saouru (dry riv.), Alg.
110/G8 São Vicente, Braz.
58/A4 São Vicente, Cabo de (cape), Port.
63/K5 Sapanca, Turk.
61/H1 Sapareva Banya, Bul.
129/H4 Sapelo (isl.), Ga,US
61/G4 Sapiéndza (isl.), Gre.
50/D2 Sappemeer, Neth.
77/N3 Sapporo, Japan
60/D2 Sapri, It.
110/H7 Sapucaí (riv.), Braz.
72/E1 Saqqez, Iran
62/E4 Şar (mts.), Yugo.
72/E1 Sarāb, Iran
83/C3 Sara Buri, Thai.
59/E2 Saragossa (Zaragoza), Sp.
62/D4 Sarajevo (cap.), Bosn.
129/F4 Saraland, Al,US
86/D4 Saran (peak), Indo.
75/B2 Saran', Kaz.
126/F2 Saranac Lake, NY,US
61/L6 Sarandapótamos (riv.), Gre.
61/G3 Sarandë, Alb.
113/G2 Sarandí Del Yi, Uru.
84/C3 Sārangpur, India
67/H1 Saransk, Rus.
65/M4 Sarapul, Rus.
129/H5 Sarasota, Fl,US
132/K12 Saratoga, Ca,US
122/G5 Saratoga, Wy,US
126/F3 Saratoga Springs, NY,US
67/H2 Saratov, Rus.
67/J1 Saratov (res.), Rus.
67/H2 Saratov Obl., Rus.
86/D3 Sarawak (state), Malay.
74/B3 Sarayköy, Turk.
74/C2 Sarayönü, Turk.
62/D2 Sárbogárd, Hun.
52/B5 Sarcelles, Fr.
84/B2 Sardārshahar, India
60/A2 Sardegna (reg.), It.
57/G5 Sardinaux, Cap de (cape), Fr.
60/A2 Sardinia (isl.), It.
125/K4 Sardis (lake), Ms,US
125/J4 Sardis (lake), Ok,US
42/F2 Sareks Nat'l Park, Swe.
42/F2 Sarektjåkko (peak), Swe.
87/E4 Sarempaka (peak), Indo.
73/K2 Sargodha, Pak.
97/J6 Sarh, Chad
72/F1 Sārī, Iran
87/J4 Saribi (cape), Indo.
92/D3 Sarigan (isl.), NMar.
74/E2 Sarıkamış, Turk.
74/C2 Sarıkaya, Turk.
54/D4 Sarine (riv.), Swi.
97/K2 Sarīr Kalanshiyū (des.), Libya
97/J3 Sarīr Tibastī (des.), Libya
128/D5 Sarita, Tx,US
62/E2 Sarkad, Hun.
67/L4 Sarkamyshskoye (lake), Trkm., Uzb.
68/H5 Sarkand, Kaz.
74/B2 Şarkîkaraağaç, Turk.
74/D2 Şarkışla, Turk.
63/H5 Şarköy, Turk.
56/D4 Sarlat-La-Canéda, Fr.
113/K8 Sarmiento (peak), Chile
55/E4 Sarnen, Swi.
132/H6 Sarnia, On,Can
66/C2 Sarny, Ukr.
61/H4 Saronic (gulf), Gre.
61/L7 Saronikós (gulf), Gre.
63/H5 Saros (gulf), Turk.
62/E1 Sárospatak, Hun.
53/F6 Sarre (riv.), Fr.
53/G6 Sarrebourg, Fr.
53/G5 Sarreguemines, Fr.
58/B1 Sarria, Sp.
51/G4 Sarstedt, Ger.
69/P3 Sartang (riv.), Rus.
56/C3 Sarthe (riv.), Fr.
52/B6 Sartrouville, Fr.
62/D2 Sárvíz (riv.), Hun.
75/C2 Sary Ishikotrau (des.), Kaz.
75/B2 Saryshagan, Kaz.
75/A2 Sarysu (riv.), Kaz.
57/H4 Sarzana, It.
123/K3 Sasaginnigak (lake), Mb,Can
84/D3 Sasarām, India
79/L9 Sasayama, Japan
79/L9 Sasayama (riv.), Japan
78/A4 Sasebo, Japan
118/F3 Saskatchewan (prov.), Can.
122/F3 Saskatchewan (riv.), Can.
122/G2 Saskatoon, Sk,Can
116/D5 Saslaya (mt.), Nic.
67/G1 Sasovo, Rus.
98/D5 Sassandra, IvC.
98/D5 Sassandra (riv.), IvC.
60/A2 Sassari, It.
51/F5 Sassenberg, Ger.
50/B4 Sassenheim, Neth.
49/G1 Sassnitz, Ger.
57/J4 Sassuolo, It.
50/A6 Sas Van Gent, Neth.
75/D2 Sasykkol (lake), Kaz.
78/B5 Sata-misaki (cape), Japan
84/B4 Sātāra, India
92/E4 Satawan (atoll), Micr.
108/D6 Satipo, Peru
45/G2 Satley, Eng,UK
84/D3 Satna, India
62/E1 Sátoraljaújhely, Hun.
75/A2 Satpayev, Kaz.
84/C3 Satpura (range), India
62/F2 Satu Mare, Rom.
62/F2 Satu Mare (co.), Rom.
83/C5 Satun, Thai.
93/R9 Satupaitea, Samoa
112/E3 Sauce Grande (riv.), Arg.
72/D4 Saudi Arabia
57/F4 Sauer (riv.), Ger., Lux.
53/F1 Sauerland (reg.), Ger.
108/G6 Sauêruiná (riv.), Braz.
123/K4 Sauk (riv.), Mn,US
123/K4 Sauk Centre, Mn,US
123/K4 Sauk Rapids, Mn,US
56/D3 Sauldre (riv.), Fr.
126/C2 Sault Sainte Marie, On,Can
126/C2 Sault Sainte Marie, Mi,US
53/E6 Saulx (riv.), Fr.
90/D3 Saumarez (reefs), Austl.
56/C3 Saumur, Fr.
46/B3 Saundersfoot, Wal,UK
104/D2 Saurimo, Ang.
132/K11 Sausalito, Ca,US
62/C3 Sava (riv.), Eur.
60/E2 Sava, It.
93/H6 Savai'i (isl.), Samoa
127/G1 Savane (riv.), Qu,Can
129/H3 Savannah, Ga,US
129/H3 Savannah (riv.), Ga, SC,US
129/F3 Savannah, Tn,US
85/H4 Savannaket, Laos
83/D2 Savannakhet, Laos
117/F4 Savanna-la-Mar, Jam.
126/B1 Savant (lake), On,Can
84/B4 Sāvantvādi, India
104/C4 Savate, Ang.
104/F5 Save (riv.), Moz., Zim.
72/F1 Sāveh, Iran
63/H2 Săveni, Rom.
53/G6 Saverne, Fr.
57/G4 Savigliano, It.
57/K4 Savignano sul Rubicone, It.
52/B6 Savigny, Fr.
57/K5 Savio (riv.), It.
122/C3 Savona, BC,Can
57/H4 Savona, It.
42/J3 Savonlinna, Fin.
54/C6 Savoy Alps (mts.), Fr.
42/E4 Sävsjö, Swe.
87/F5 Savu (sea), Indo.
86/B4 Sawahlunto, Indo.
100/D5 Sawākin, Sudan
83/B2 Sawankhalok, Thai.
79/G3 Sawara, Japan
79/F2 Sawasaki-bana (pt.), Japan
124/F3 Sawatch (range), Co,US
47/G3 Sawbridgeworth, Eng,UK
96/J2 Sawdā (mts.), Libya
72/D5 Sawdā', Jabal (mtn.), SAr.
97/L5 Sawdirī, Sudan
87/H4 Saweba (cape), Indo.
44/A2 Sawel (mtn.), NI,UK
100/B3 Sawhāj, Egypt
100/B3 Sawhāj (gov.), Egypt
85/F6 Sāwi, India
72/G5 Sawqirah, Ghubbat (bay), Oman
47/G2 Sawston, Eng,UK
91/E1 Sawtell, Austl.
122/E4 Sawtooth (range), Id,US
87/F6 Sawu (isls.), Indo.
59/E3 Sax, Sp.
45/H5 Saxilby, Eng,UK
47/H2 Saxmundham, Eng,UK
49/G3 Saxony (state), Ger.
48/F3 Saxony-Anhalt (state), Ger.
79/F3 Sayama, Japan
116/D3 Sayil (ruins), Mex.
53/G2 Saynbach (riv.), Ger.
75/D3 Sayram (lake), China
131/F5 Sayreville, NJ,US
131/G5 Sayville, NY,US
61/F2 Sazan (isl.), Alb.
57/L2 Sázava (riv.), Czh.
45/E3 Scafell Pikes (mtn.), Eng,UK
45/H3 Scalby, Eng,UK
60/D3 Scalea, It.
57/J5 Scandicci, It.
82/C4 Scarborough (shoal)
127/R8 Scarborough, On,Can
45/H3 Scarborough, Eng,UK
52/B3 Scarpe (riv.), Fr.
131/G4 Scarsdale, NY,US
44/E1 Scar Water (riv.), Sc,UK
52/D2 Schaerbeek, Belg.
55/E2 Schaffhausen, Swi.
55/E2 Schaffhausen (canton), Swi.
50/B3 Schagen, Neth.
50/C5 Schaijk, Neth.
51/E6 Schalksmühle, Ger.
91/C3 Schanck (cape), Austl.
51/F1 Scharhorn (isl.), Ger.
132/P15 Schaumburg, Il,US
50/D2 Scheemda, Neth.
51/G2 Scheessel, Ger.
52/C2 Schelde (Scheldt) (riv.), Belg.
124/D3 Schell Creek (range), Nv,US
51/H4 Schellerten, Ger.
126/F3 Schenectady, NY,US
51/G1 Schenefeld, Ger.
132/R16 Schererville, In,US
50/D5 Schermbeck, Ger.
50/C3 Scherpenzeel, Neth.
50/B5 Schiedam, Neth.
51/G5 Schieder-Schwalenberg, Ger.
50/D2 Schiermonnikoog (isl.), Neth.
53/G5 Schiffweiler, Ger.
50/C5 Schijndel, Neth.
52/D1 Schilde, Belg.
50/D2 Schildmeer (lake), Neth.
51/F1 Schillighörn (cape), Ger.
53/G6 Schiltigheim, Fr.
53/E2 Schinnen, Neth.
50/D4 Schipbeek (riv.), Neth.
61/G2 Schkumbin (riv.), Alb.
51/F5 Schlangen, Ger.
53/F2 Schleiden, Ger.
48/E1 Schleswig, Ger.
51/H1 Schleswig-Holstein (state), Ger.
48/E1 Schleswig-Holsteinisches Wattenmeer Nat'l Park, Ger.
51/F5 Schloss Holte-Stukenbrock, Ger.
57/H1 Schlüchtern, Ger.
48/F3 Schmalkalden, Ger.
51/F6 Schmallenberg, Ger.
53/F5 Schmelz, Ger.
53/F3 Schneifel (upland), Ger.
51/G2 Schneverdingen, Ger.
130/V12 Schofield Barracks, Hi,US
113/L7 Scholl, Cerro (mtn.), Arg.
48/F2 Schönebeck, Ger.
48/F2 Schöningen, Ger.
50/D3 Schoonebeek, Neth.
50/B5 Schoonhoven, Neth.
50/B3 Schoorl, Neth.
51/E1 Schortens, Ger.
52/D1 Schoten, Belg.
91/D4 Schouten (isl.), Austl.
92/C5 Schouten (isls.), Indo.
50/A5 Schouwen (isl.), Neth.
56/D5 Schrader (peak), Fr.
55/E1 Schramberg, Ger.
126/C1 Schreiber, On,Can
102/B2 Schroffenstein (peak), Namb.
128/D4 Schulenburg, Tx,US
51/H4 Schunter (riv.), Ger.
51/E4 Schüttorf, Ger.
131/E5 Schuylkill (riv.), Pa,US
57/J2 Schwabach, Ger.
55/E1 Schwäbische Alb (range), Ger.
57/H2 Schwäbisch Hall, Ger.
53/F5 Schwalbach, Ger.
51/G6 Schwalm (riv.), Ger.
50/D6 Schwalmtal, Ger.
57/K2 Schwandorf im Bayern, Ger.
86/D4 Schwaner (mts.), Indo.
51/F2 Schwanewede, Ger.
49/G3 Schwartz Elster (riv.), Ger.
102/B2 Schwartzerberg (peak), Namb.
51/H2 Schwarzenbek, Ger.
53/F3 Schwarzer Mann (peak), Ger.
57/J3 Schwaz, Aus.
49/J4 Schwechat, Aus.
49/H2 Schwedt, Ger.
57/J1 Schweinfurt, Ger.
51/E6 Schwelm, Ger.
48/F2 Schwerin, Ger.
48/F2 Schweriner (lake), Ger.
51/E6 Schwerte, Ger.
51/G1 Schwinge (riv.), Ger.
51/G5 Schwülme (riv.), Ger.
55/E3 Schwyz, Swi.
55/E3 Schwyz (canton), Swi.
60/C4 Sciacca, It.
60/D4 Scicli, It.
126/D4 Scioto (riv.), Oh,US
123/G3 Scobey, Mt,US
47/G1 Scolt (pt.), UK
60/D4 Scordia, It.
45/G3 Scotch Corner, Eng,UK
131/F5 Scotch Plains, NJ,US
105/W Scotia (sea), Ant.
43/C2 Scotland, UK
105/M Scott, Ant.
105/L Scott (coast), Ant.
118/D3 Scott (cape), BC,Can
119/R7 Scott (cape), NW,Can
118/F2 Scott (lake), NW,Can
125/G3 Scott City, Ks,US
45/F1 Scottish Borders (reg.), Sc,UK
125/G2 Scottsbluff, Ne,US
125/F2 Scotts Bluff Nat'l Mon., Ne,US
129/G3 Scottsboro, Al,US
126/C4 Scottsburg, In,US
124/E4 Scottsdale, Az,US
91/C4 Scotts Peak (dam), Austl.
126/C4 Scottsville, Ky,US
126/C3 Scottville, Mi,US
45/H4 Scunthorpe, Eng,UK
62/D4 Scutari (lake), Alb., Yugo.
121/K5 Sea (isls.), Ga,US
47/G5 Seaford, UK
44/C3 Seaforde, NI,UK
45/G2 Seaham, Eng,UK
119/H2 Seahorse (pt.), Nun.,Can
118/G3 Seal (riv.), Mb,Can
112/B5 Seal (pt.), Chile
102/C4 Seal (cape), SAfr.
131/B3 Seal Beach, Ca,US
45/H3 Seamer, Eng,UK
124/D4 Searchlight, Nv,US
128/F3 Searcy, Ar,US
44/E3 Seascale, Eng,UK
122/C4 Seaside, Or,US
132/C3 SeaTac, Wa,US
46/C5 Seaton, Eng,UK
46/B6 Seaton (riv.), Eng,UK
45/G2 Seaton Carew, Eng,UK
45/G1 Seaton Valley, Eng,UK
132/C2 Seattle, Wa,US
129/H5 Sebastian, Fl,US
117/M8 Sebastián Vizcaíno (bay), Mex.
91/B3 Sebastopol, Austl.
86/D4 Sebayan (peak), Indo.
63/F3 Sebeş, Rom.
74/D2 Şebinkarahisar, Turk.
62/F2 Şebiş, Rom.
49/H3 Sebnitz, Ger.
87/F2 Seboto (pt.), Phil.
129/H5 Sebring, Fl,US
87/E4 Sebuku (isl.), Indo.
57/J4 Secchia (riv.), It.
108/B5 Sechura, Peru
108/B5 Sechura (bay), Peru
108/B5 Sechura (des.), Peru
52/C2 Seclin, Fr.
113/L7 Seco (riv.), Arg.
84/C4 Secunderābād, India
108/E7 Securé (riv.), Bol.
125/J3 Sedalia, Mo,US
53/D4 Sedan, Fr.
83/B3 Sedaung (mtn.), Burma
45/F3 Sedbergh, Eng,UK
100/B4 Seddenga Temple (ruins), Sudan
74/K6 Sederot, Isr.
45/G2 Sedgefield, Eng,UK
130/L2 Sedgwick (mtn.), Yk,Can
98/B3 Sedhiou, Sen.
57/L1 Sedlo (peak), Czh.
124/E4 Sedona, Az,US
49/L3 Sędziszów, Pol.
56/C2 Sée (riv.), Fr.
102/D3 Seekooi (riv.), SAfr.
51/H5 Seesen, Ger.
51/G2 Seeve (riv.), Ger.
86/B3 Segamat, Malay.
63/F3 Segarcea, Rom.
60/C4 Segesta (ruins), It.
64/G3 Segezha, Rus.
59/E3 Segorbe, Sp.
98/D3 Ségou, Mali
98/D3 Ségou (reg.), Mali
58/C2 Segovia, Sp.
64/G3 Segozero (lake), Rus.
56/C3 Segré, Fr.
59/F2 Segre (riv.), Sp.
130/D5 Seguam (isl.), Ak,US
96/H3 Séguédine, Niger
98/D5 Séguéla, IvC.
128/D4 Seguin, Tx,US
58/D3 Segura (riv.), Sp.
104/D5 Sehithwa, Bots.
84/C3 Sehore, India
73/J3 Sehwān, Pak.
79/L10 Seika, Japan
125/H3 Seiling, Ok,US
53/F6 Seille (riv.), Fr.
42/G3 Seinäjoki, Fin.
123/L3 Seine (riv.), On,Can
56/C2 Seine (bay), Fr.
56/D2 Seine (riv.), Fr.
52/B5 Seine-et-Marne (dept.), Fr.
52/B6 Seine-Saint-Denis (dept.), Fr.
42/G3 Seitsemisen Nat'l Park, Fin.
79/M10 Seiwa, Japan
79/E3 Seki, Japan
79/M9 Sekigahara, Japan
79/H6 Sekiyado, Japan
99/E5 Sekondi, Gha.
122/C4 Selah, Wa,US
60/A3 Selargius, It.
87/H5 Selaru (isl.), Indo.
86/D4 Selatan (cape), Indo.
130/F2 Selawik (lake), Ak,US
87/F5 Selayar (isl.), Indo.
57/K1 Selb, Ger.
45/G4 Selby, Eng,UK
123/H4 Selby, SD,US
131/G5 Selden, NY,US
60/D2 Sele (riv.), It.
104/E5 Selebi-Phikwe, Bots.
77/L1 Selemdzha (riv.), Rus.
76/F1 Selenga (riv.), Rus.
76/E2 Selenge, Mong.
76/E2 Selenge (riv.), Mong.
54/D1 Sélestat, Fr.
75/B1 Selety (riv.), Kaz.
75/B1 Seletyteniz (lake), Kaz.
64/G4 Seliger (lake), Rus.
124/D4 Seligman, Az,US
60/C4 Selinunte (ruins), It.
122/D3 Selkirk (mts.), BC,Can
123/J3 Selkirk, Mb,Can
43/D3 Selkirk, Sc,UK
124/E5 Sells, Az,US
46/E2 Selly Oak, Eng,UK
51/E5 Selm, Ger.
129/G3 Selma, Al,US
129/F3 Selmer, Tn,US
130/M3 Selous (mtn.), Yk,Can
47/F5 Selsey, Eng,UK
47/F5 Selsey Bill (pt.), Eng,UK
56/C2 Sélune (riv.), Fr.
108/E5 Selvas (for.), Braz.
57/H2 Selz (riv.), Ger.
96/C2 Semara, WSah.
86/D5 Semarang, Indo.
74/F3 Şemdinli, Turk.
65/K4 Semenov, Rus.
86/D5 Semeru (peak), Indo.
75/D1 Semey, Kaz.
130/G4 Semidi (isls.), Ak,US
66/F2 Semiluki, Rus.
122/G5 Seminoe (res.), Wy,US
129/G4 Seminole (lake), Ga,US
128/C3 Seminole, Tx,US
130/B5 Semisopochnoi (isl.), Ak,US
86/D4 Semitau, Indo.
72/F1 Semnān, Iran
56/C3 Semnon (riv.), Fr.
53/E4 Semois (riv.), Belg.
53/D4 Semoy (riv.), Fr.
64/B2 Semskefjellet (peak), Nor.
83/D3 Sen (riv.), Camb.
83/C3 Sena, Thai.
82/C6 Senaja, Malay.
104/D4 Senanga, Zam.
129/F3 Senatobia, Ms,US
47/E2 Sence (riv.), Eng,UK
78/B5 Sendai, Japan
79/G1 Sendai (bay), Japan
78/B5 Sendai (riv.), Japan
78/D3 Sendai (riv.), Japan
51/E5 Senden, Ger.
51/E5 Sendenhorst, Ger.
49/J4 Senec, Slvk.
52/D2 Seneffe, Belg.
98/B3 Senegal
98/B2 Sénégal (riv.), Afr.
102/D3 Senekal, SAfr.
49/H3 Senftenberg, Ger.
75/D5 Sênggê (riv.), China
112/C5 Senguerr (riv.), Arg.
109/L6 Senhor do Bonfim, Braz.
49/J4 Senica, Slvk.
57/K5 Senigallia, It.
74/B2 Senirkent, Turk.
60/E2 Senise, It.
62/B3 Senj, Cro.
42/F1 Senja (isl.), Nor.
52/B5 Senlis, Fr.
79/L10 Sennan, Japan
97/M5 Sennar (dam), Sudan
52/D2 Senne (riv.), Belg.
126/E1 Senneterre, Qu,Can
46/C3 Sennybridge, Wal,UK
99/F3 Séno (prov.), Burk.
56/E2 Sens, Fr.
62/E3 Senta, Yugo.
104/E2 Sentery, D.R. Congo
122/C2 Sentinel (peak), BC,Can
92/E4 Senyavin (isls.), Micr.
84/C3 Seoni, India
84/C3 Seonī Mālwā, India
80/D4 Seoul-Jikhalsi (prov.), SKor.
80/D4 Seoul (Sŏul) (cap.), SKor.
110/K8 Sepetiba (bay), Braz.
92/D5 Sepik (riv.), PNG
49/J2 Sępólno Krajeńskie, Pol.
63/G4 Septemvri, Bul.
127/H1 Sept-Îles, Qu,Can
132/A1 Sequim (bay), Wa,US
124/C3 Sequoia Nat'l Park, Ca,US
53/E2 Seraing, Belg.
86/C5 Serang, Indo.
86/C3 Serasan (str.), Indo., Malay.
62/E4 Serbia (rep.), Yugo.
67/H1 Serdobsk, Rus.
130/D2 Serdtse-Kamen, Mys (pt.), Rus.
74/C2 Şereflikoçhisar, Turk.
56/F3 Serein (riv.), Fr.
86/B3 Seremban, Malay.
101/B3 Serengeti (plain), Tanz.
101/B3 Serengeti Nat'l Park, Tanz.
104/F3 Serenje, Zam.
65/K5 Sergach, Rus.
68/J2 Sergeya Kirova (isls.), Rus.
64/H4 Sergiyev Posad, Rus.
86/D3 Seria, Bru.
57/H4 Seriate, It.
61/J4 Sérifos (isl.), Gre.
74/B3 Serik, Turk.
109/H5 Seringa (mts.), Braz.
74/B3 Serinhisar, Turk.
87/G5 Sermata (isl.), Indo.
68/G4 Serov, Rus.
104/E5 Serowe, Bots.
58/B4 Serpa, Port.
60/A3 Serpeddi (peak), It.
98/C3 Serpent, Vallée du (wadi), Mali
64/H5 Serpukhov, Rus.
110/D2 Serra, Braz.
110/J8 Serra da Bocaina Nat'l Park, Braz.
110/C2 Serra da Canastra Nat'l Park, Braz.
109/K5 Serra de Capivara Nat'l Park, Braz.
110/D1 Serra do Cipo Nat'l Park, Braz.
110/K7 Serra dos Órgãos Nat'l Park, Braz.
61/H2 Sérrai, Gre.
60/E3 Serralta di San Vito (peak), It.
60/A3 Serramanna, It.
117/F5 Serrana (bank), Col.
108/E3 Serranía de la Neblina Nat'l Park, Ven.
117/F4 Serranilla (bank), Col.
60/A4 Serrat (cape), Tun.
109/L5 Serra Talhada, Braz.
52/C4 Serre (riv.), Fr.
109/L6 Serrinha, Braz.
58/A3 Sertã, Port.
110/C2 Sertãozinho, Braz.
76/C4 Serteng (mts.), China
86/D4 Seruyan (riv.), Indo.
100/B4 Sesebi (ruins), Sudan
57/H4 Sesia (riv.), It.
58/A3 Sesimbra, Port.
58/D1 Sestao, Sp.
57/J5 Sesto Fiorentino, It.
57/H4 Sesto San Giovanni, It.
60/A3 Sestu, It.
62/C3 Sesvete, Cro.
56/E5 Sète, Fr.
109/K4 Sete Cidades Nat'l Park, Braz.
110/C1 Sete Lagoas, Braz.
73/J3 Sethārja, Pak.

175

Sétif – Sodan

96/G1 **Sétif,** Alg.
79/E3 **Seto,** Japan
78/C3 **Seto-Naikai Nat'l Park,** Japan
57/G4 **Settimo Torinese,** It.
123/J2 **Setting** (lake), Mb,Can
45/F3 **Settle,** Eng,UK
79/L10 **Settsu,** Japan
58/A3 **Setúbal,** Port.
59/Q11 **Setúbal** (bay), Port.
58/A3 **Setúbal** (dist.), Port.
56/C4 **Seudre** (riv.), Fr.
56/C4 **Seugne** (riv.), Fr.
126/A1 **Seul** (lake), On,Can
67/H4 **Sevan** (lake), Arm.
66/E3 **Sevastopol',** Ukr.
43/G7 **Seven Hogs, The** (isls.), Ire.
47/G4 **Sevenoaks,** Eng,UK
123/L2 **Severn** (riv.), On,Can
46/D3 **Severn** (riv.), Eng,UK
131/K7 **Severn,** Md,US
131/K7 **Severna Park,** Md,US
65/P3 **Severnaya Sos'va** (riv.), Rus.
71/K2 **Severnaya Zemlya** (arch.), Rus.
46/C4 **Severn, Mouth of the** (estuary), Eng,UK
65/Q2 **Severnyy,** Rus.
49/G3 **Severočeský** (reg.), Czh.
66/F2 **Severodonetsk,** Ukr.
64/H2 **Severodvinsk,** Rus.
69/R4 **Severo-Kuril'sk,** Rus.
49/J4 **Severomoravský** (reg.), Czh.
64/G1 **Severomorsk,** Rus.
65/N3 **Severoural'sk,** Rus.
124/D3 **Sevier** (des.), Ut,US
124/D3 **Sevier** (riv.), Ut,US
129/H3 **Sevierville,** Tn,US
58/C4 **Seville,** Sp.
63/G4 **Sevlievo,** Bul.
98/C5 **Sewa** (riv.), SLeo.
130/E2 **Seward** (pen.), Ak,US
125/H2 **Seward,** Ne,US
130/M5 **Sewell Inlet,** BC,Can
122/D2 **Sexsmith,** Ab,Can
39/M6 **Seychelles**
74/B3 **Seydişehir,** Turk.
74/C2 **Seyhan** (riv.), Turk.
91/C3 **Seymour,** Austl.
128/D3 **Seymour,** Tx,US
52/C6 **Sézanne,** Fr.
58/A3 **Sezimbra,** Port.
60/C2 **Sezze,** It.
63/G3 **Sfîntu Gheorghe,** Rom.
50/C4 **'s-Graveland,** Neth.
50/B5 **'s-Gravendeel,** Neth.
50/B4 **'s-Gravenhage** (The Hague) (cap.), Neth.
43/C2 **Sgurr Mór** (mtn.), Sc,UK
81/C4 **Sha** (riv.), China
81/B4 **Shaanxi** (prov.), China
97/P7 **Shabeelle, Webi** (riv.), Som.
104/E1 **Shabunda,** D.R. Congo
105/M **Shackleton** (coast), Ant.
105/G **Shackleton Ice Shelf,** Ant.
65/P4 **Shadrinsk,** Rus.
128/B4 **Shafter,** Tx,US
46/D4 **Shaftesbury,** Eng,UK
75/C2 **Shagan** (riv.), Kaz.
73/J3 **Shāhdādkot,** Pak.
73/J3 **Shāhdādpur,** Pak.
84/D3 **Shahdol,** India
97/K1 **Shaḩḩāt,** Libya
84/C2 **Shāhjahānpur,** India
73/K3 **Shahpura,** India
84/A2 **Shāhpur Chākar,** Pak.
100/C3 **Shā'ib al Banāt, Jabal** (mtn.), Egypt
84/C3 **Shājāpur,** India
73/L2 **Shakargarh,** Pak.
104/D4 **Shakawe,** Bots.
68/H5 **Shakhtinsk,** Kaz.
66/G3 **Shakhty,** Rus.
64/K4 **Shakhun'ya,** Rus.
67/H4 **Shalbuzdag, Gora** (peak), Rus.
46/C5 **Shaldon,** Eng,UK
101/B4 **Shama** (riv.), Tanz.
74/J6 **Shamal Sīnā'** (gov.), Egypt
123/M2 **Shamattawa** (riv.), On,Can
84/C3 **Shāmgarh,** India
84/C2 **Shāmli,** India
72/D3 **Shammar, Jabal** (mts.), SAr.
130/L3 **Shamrock** (mtn.), Yk,Can
128/C3 **Shamrock,** Tx,US
83/B1 **Shan** (plat.), Burma
83/B1 **Shan** (state), Burma
97/M4 **Shandī,** Sudan
81/D3 **Shandong** (pen.), China
81/C5 **Shangcheng,** China
81/L8 **Shanghai,** China
81/C4 **Shangqiu,** China
82/C2 **Shangrao,** China
47/E5 **Shanklin,** Eng,UK
43/A4 **Shannon** (riv.), Ire.
69/P4 **Shantar** (isls.), Rus.
82/C3 **Shantou,** China
82/B3 **Shaoguan,** China
82/D2 **Shaoxing,** China
82/B2 **Shaoyang,** China
45/F2 **Shap,** Eng,UK
105/L **Shapeless** (peak), Ant.
65/M2 **Shapkina** (riv.), Rus.
74/F3 **Shaqlāwah,** Iraq
73/G5 **Sharbatāt, Ra's ash** (pt.), Oman
100/C3 **Sharm ash Shaykh,** Egypt
47/F2 **Sharnbrook,** Eng,UK
126/D3 **Sharon,** Pa,US
123/K2 **Sharpe** (lake), Mb,Can
123/J4 **Sharpe** (lake), SD,US
65/K4 **Shar'ya,** Rus.
97/N6 **Shashemenē,** Eth.
81/C5 **Shashi,** China
124/B2 **Shasta** (dam), Ca,US
124/B2 **Shasta** (peak), Ca,US
66/B2 **Shatskiy Nat'l Park,** Ukr.
96/G1 **Shaţţ al Jarīd** (dry lake), Tun.
125/H3 **Shattuck,** Ok,US
122/F3 **Shaunavon,** Sk,Can
47/E4 **Shaw,** Eng,UK
126/B2 **Shawano,** Wi,US
127/M6 **Shawbridge,** Qu,Can
46/D1 **Shawbury,** Eng,UK
127/F2 **Shawinigan,** Qu,Can
125/H4 **Shawnee,** Ok,US
74/E3 **Shaykhān,** Iraq
66/C1 **Shchara** (riv.), Bela.
66/F1 **Shchekino,** Rus.
65/X9 **Shchelkovo,** Rus.
66/F2 **Shchigry,** Rus.
75/B1 **Shchuchinsk,** Kaz.
97/P6 **Shebelē Wenz** (riv.), Eth.
73/J1 **Sheberghān,** Afg.
126/C3 **Sheboygan,** Wi,US
127/H2 **Shediac,** NB,Can
44/A4 **Sheelin, Lough** (lake), Ire.
130/F2 **Sheep** (mtn.), Ak,US
50/D5 **'s-Heerenberg,** Neth.
45/G5 **Sheffield,** Eng,UK
129/G3 **Sheffield,** Al,US
47/F2 **Shefford,** Eng,UK
97/P6 **Shēh Husēn,** Eth.
113/K7 **Shehuen** (riv.), Arg.
126/C1 **Shekak** (riv.), On,Can
73/K2 **Shekhūpura,** Pak.
69/T2 **Shelagskiy** (cape), Rus.
127/H3 **Shelburne,** NS,Can
129/F3 **Shelby,** Ms,US
122/F3 **Shelby,** Mt,US
129/H3 **Shelby,** NC,US
129/F2 **Shelbyville** (lake), Il,US
126/C4 **Shelbyville,** In,US
129/G3 **Shelbyville,** Tn,US
69/R3 **Shelekhov** (gulf), Rus.
130/H4 **Shelikof** (str.), Ak,US
123/G2 **Shellbrook,** Sk,Can
126/B2 **Shell Lake,** Wi,US
123/K5 **Shell Rock** (riv.), Ia,US
132/A3 **Shelton,** Wa,US
67/J4 **Shemakha,** Azer.
130/A5 **Shemya** (isl.), Ak,US
123/K5 **Shenandoah,** Ia,US
126/E4 **Shenandoah Nat'l Park,** Va,US
98/B5 **Shenge** (pt.), SLeo.
75/E3 **Shengli Daban** (pass), China
81/B5 **Shennongjia,** China
47/E1 **Shenstone,** Eng,UK
77/J3 **Shenyang,** China
85/K3 **Shenzhen,** China
84/B2 **Sheoganj,** India
84/C2 **Sheopur,** India
66/C2 **Shepetovka,** Ukr.
128/E4 **Shepherd,** Tx,US
92/F6 **Shepherd** (isls.), Van.
47/G4 **Sheppey** (isl.), Eng,UK
47/E1 **Shepshed,** Eng,UK
46/D4 **Shepton Mallet,** Eng,UK
119/H1 **Sherard** (cape), Nun.,Can
46/D5 **Sherborne,** Eng,UK
98/B5 **Sherbro** (isl.), SLeo.
127/G2 **Sherbrooke,** Qu,Can
45/G2 **Sherburn,** Eng,UK
99/H4 **Shere** (hill), Nga.
84/D3 **Sherghāti,** India
128/E3 **Sheridan,** Ar,US
122/G4 **Sheridan,** Wy,US
47/H1 **Sheringham,** Eng,UK
128/D3 **Sherman,** Tx,US
50/C5 **'s-Hertogenbosch,** Neth.
122/E2 **Sherwood Park,** Ab,Can
41/D2 **Shetland** (isls.), Sc,UK
81/D4 **Sheyang** (riv.), China
123/J4 **Sheyenne** (riv.), ND,US
81/C4 **Shi** (riv.), China
132/E6 **Shiawassee** (riv.), Mi,US
79/F2 **Shibata,** Japan
100/B2 **Shibīn al Kaum,** Egypt
123/L2 **Shibogama** (lake), On,Can
78/B5 **Shibushi** (bay), Japan
75/B1 **Shiderty** (riv.), Kaz.
78/D3 **Shido,** Japan
46/D1 **Shifnal,** Eng,UK
79/L9 **Shiga,** Japan
78/E3 **Shiga** (pref.), Japan
79/M10 **Shigaraki,** Japan
81/C3 **Shigu Shan** (mtn.), China
75/E3 **Shihezi,** China
61/F2 **Shijak,** Alb.
81/C3 **Shijiazhuang,** China
73/J3 **Shikārpur,** Pak.
79/M9 **Shikatsu,** Japan
79/H7 **Shiki,** Japan
78/C4 **Shikoku** (isl.), Japan
78/C4 **Shikoku** (mts.), Japan
77/P3 **Shikotan** (isl.), Rus.
45/G2 **Shildon,** Eng,UK
76/H1 **Shilka,** Rus.
77/H1 **Shilka** (riv.), Rus.
73/L2 **Shilla** (mtn.), India
74/N8 **Shillo, Nahal** (dry riv.), WBnk.
85/F2 **Shillong,** India
76/D2 **Shilüüstey,** Mong.
79/M10 **Shima** (pen.), Japan
78/B4 **Shimabara,** Japan
78/D3 **Shimamoto,** Japan
78/C3 **Shimane** (pref.), Japan
77/K1 **Shimanovsk,** Rus.
79/M9 **Shimasahi,** Japan
97/Q5 **Shimber Berris** (peak), Som.
85/H2 **Shimian,** China
79/F3 **Shimizu,** Japan
79/F3 **Shimoda,** Japan
79/F2 **Shimodate,** Japan
84/C5 **Shimoga,** India
79/L10 **Shimoichi,** Japan
78/A5 **Shimo-koshiki** (isl.), Japan
78/B4 **Shimonoseki,** Japan
79/F2 **Shinano** (riv.), Japan
73/H2 **Shindand,** Afg.
78/D4 **Shingū,** Japan
78/C3 **Shinji** (lake), Japan
77/N4 **Shinjō,** Japan
79/M9 **Shinkawa,** Japan
79/E2 **Shinminato,** Japan
79/M9 **Shinsei,** Japan
101/B3 **Shinyanga,** Tanz.
101/B3 **Shinyanga** (prov.), Tanz.
79/G1 **Shiogama,** Japan
78/D4 **Shio-no-misaki** (cape), Japan
45/G4 **Shipley,** Eng,UK
127/H2 **Shippegan,** NB,Can
79/M9 **Shippo,** Japan
124/E3 **Shiprock,** NM,US
47/E2 **Shipston on Stour,** Eng,UK
75/C5 **Shipuqi Shankou** (pass), China
72/F2 **Shīr** (mtn.), Iran
79/H8 **Shirahama,** Japan
78/E3 **Shirakawa-tōge** (pass), Japan
79/F3 **Shirane-san** (mtn.), Japan
79/H6 **Shiraoka,** Japan
72/F3 **Shīrāz,** Iran
74/H6 **Shirbīn,** Egypt
45/G1 **Shiremoor,** Eng,UK
81/C5 **Shirjiu** (lake), China
79/J7 **Shiroi,** Japan
79/G2 **Shiroishi,** Japan
79/F2 **Shirone,** Japan
79/H7 **Shiroyama,** Japan
73/G1 **Shīrvān,** Iran
81/D2 **Shi San Ling,** China
130/F5 **Shishaldin** (vol.), Ak,US
76/D1 **Shishhid** (riv.), Mong.
81/C5 **Shishou,** China
79/J7 **Shisui,** Japan
84/C2 **Shivpurī,** India
81/B4 **Shiyan,** China
76/F4 **Shizuishan,** China
77/N3 **Shizunai,** Japan
79/F3 **Shizuoka,** Japan
79/F3 **Shizuoka** (pref.), Japan
61/F1 **Shkodër,** Alb.
61/G2 **Shkumbin** (riv.), Alb.
130/C2 **Shmidta, Mys** (pt.), Rus.
91/D2 **Shoalhaven** (riv.), Austl.
123/H3 **Shoal Lake,** Mb,Can
90/C3 **Shoalwater** (bay), Austl.
78/C3 **Shōbara,** Japan
78/D3 **Shōdo** (isl.), Japan
47/G3 **Shoeburyness,** Eng,UK
84/C4 **Sholāpur,** India
74/N8 **Shomron** (ruins), WBnk.
79/M9 **Shonai** (riv.), Japan
79/J7 **Shōnan,** Japan
84/C4 **Shorāpur,** India
47/F5 **Shoreham by Sea,** Eng,UK
132/P16 **Shorewood,** Il,US
132/Q13 **Shorewood,** Wi,US
73/K2 **Shorkot,** Pak.
90/F6 **Shorncliffe,** Austl.
129/G3 **Short** (peak), Tn,US
92/E5 **Shortland** (isl.), Sol.
47/E5 **Shorwell,** Eng,UK
124/C3 **Shoshone** (mts.), Nv,US
122/F4 **Shoshone** (riv.), Wy,US
122/F5 **Shoshoni,** Wy,US
66/E2 **Shostka,** Ukr.
47/H3 **Shotley,** Eng,UK
45/G2 **Shotton,** Eng,UK
79/H7 **Shōwa,** Japan
124/E4 **Show Low,** Az,US
66/D2 **Shpola,** Ukr.
128/E3 **Shreveport,** La,US
46/D1 **Shrewsbury,** Eng,UK
46/D1 **Shropshire** (co.), Eng,UK
45/F6 **Shropshire Union** (can.), Eng,UK
81/D4 **Shu** (riv.), China
81/D5 **Shu** (riv.), China
77/K3 **Shuangyang,** China
77/L2 **Shuangyashan,** China
74/H6 **Shubrā Khīt,** Egypt
74/K6 **Shu'fāţ,** WBnk.
81/D5 **Shuiyang** (riv.), China
73/K3 **Shujāābād,** Pak.
76/D4 **Shule** (riv.), China
130/G4 **Shumagin** (isls.), Ak,US
63/H4 **Shumen,** Bul.
65/K5 **Shumerlya,** Rus.
75/B2 **Shunak, Gora** (peak), Kaz.
81/C3 **Shuo Xian,** China
73/G2 **Shūr** (riv.), Iran
104/F4 **Shurugwi,** Zim.
75/F1 **Shushenskoye,** Rus.
72/E2 **Shūshtar,** Iran
122/D3 **Shuswap** (lake), BC,Can
97/N5 **Shuwak,** Sudan
64/J4 **Shuya,** Rus.
83/A1 **Shwebo,** Burma
83/B2 **Shwemawdaw Pagoda** (ruins), Burma
75/C5 **Shyok** (riv.), India
73/H2 **Siāh** (mts.), Afg.
86/B3 **Siak** (riv.), Indo.
73/K2 **Siālkot,** Pak.
82/E6 **Siargao** (isl.), Phil.
82/D6 **Siasi,** Phil.
87/F2 **Siaton** (pt.), Phil.
87/G3 **Siau** (isl.), Indo.
64/D5 **Šiauliai,** Lith.
82/D5 **Sibalom,** Phil.
67/L1 **Sibay,** Rus.
62/B4 **Šibenik,** Cro.
68/K3 **Siberia** (reg.), Rus.
73/J3 **Sibi,** Pak.
101/C1 **Sibiloi Nat'l Park,** Kenya
104/B1 **Sibiti,** Congo
63/G3 **Sibiu,** Rom.
63/G2 **Sibiu** (co.), Rom.
47/G3 **Sible Hedingham,** Eng,UK
86/A3 **Sibolga,** Indo.
85/F2 **Sibsāgar,** India
87/F2 **Sibuco,** Phil.
87/F2 **Sibuko,** Phil.
87/F1 **Sibuyan** (isl.), Phil.
82/D5 **Sibuyan** (sea), Phil.
122/D3 **Sicamous,** BC,Can
85/H2 **Sichuan** (prov.), China
60/C4 **Sicilia** (reg.), It.
60/C3 **Sicily** (isl.), It.
60/B4 **Sicily** (str.), It., Tun.
116/D4 **Sico** (riv.), Hon.
108/D6 **Sicuani,** Peru
62/D3 **Šid,** Yugo.
84/C4 **Siddipet,** India
60/E3 **Siderno Marina,** It.
110/B4 **Sideròpolis,** Braz.
131/C1 **Sidewinder** (mtn.), Ca,US
61/F3 **Sidhári,** Gre.
84/D3 **Sidhi,** India
61/H2 **Sidhirókastron,** Gre.
84/B3 **Sidhpur,** India
100/A2 **Sīdī Barrānī,** Egypt
96/E1 **Sidi Bel-Abbes,** Alg.
60/A5 **Sīdī Bū Zayd** (gov.), Tun.
96/C2 **Sidi Ifni,** Mor.
74/H6 **Sīdī Sālim,** Egypt
105/R **Sidley** (mtn.), Ant.
90/A1 **Sidmouth** (cape), Austl.
46/C5 **Sidmouth,** Eng,UK
122/C3 **Sidney,** BC,Can
123/G4 **Sidney,** Mt,US
125/G2 **Sidney,** Ne,US
126/C3 **Sidney,** Oh,US
129/G3 **Sidney Lanier** (lake), Ga,US
74/K5 **Sidon** (Şaydā), Leb.
96/J1 **Sidra** (gulf), Libya
51/F3 **Siede** (riv.), Ger.
49/M2 **Siedlce,** Pol.
49/L2 **Siedlce** (prov.), Pol.
53/G2 **Sieg** (riv.), Ger.
53/G2 **Siegburg,** Ger.
53/H2 **Siegen,** Ger.
49/M2 **Siemianówka** (lake), Pol.
49/M2 **Siemiatycze,** Pol.
83/D3 **Siempang,** Camb.
83/C3 **Siemreab,** Camb.
57/J5 **Siena,** It.
56/C2 **Sienne** (riv.), Fr.
49/K3 **Sieradz,** Pol.
49/K3 **Sieradz** (prov.), Pol.
53/F5 **Sierk-les-Bains,** Fr.
49/K2 **Sierpc,** Pol.
128/B4 **Sierra Blanca,** Tx,US
108/D3 **Sierra de la Macarena Nat'l Park,** Col.
116/A2 **Sierra del Carmen Nat'l Park,** Mex.
117/M7 **Sierra de San Pedro Mártir,** Mex.
112/D4 **Sierra Grande,** Arg.
98/B4 **Sierra Leone**
98/B4 **Sierra Leone** (cape), SLeo.
131/B2 **Sierra Madre,** Ca,US
116/B4 **Sierra Madre del Sur** (mts.), Mex.
117/N8 **Sierra Madre Occidental** (range), Mex.
116/B3 **Sierra Madre Oriental** (mts.), Mex.
116/A2 **Sierra Mojada,** Mex.
124/B3 **Sierra Nevada** (range), Ca,US
117/G5 **Sierra Nevada de Santa Marta,** Col.
117/G6 **Sierra Nevada Nat'l Park,** Ven.
124/E5 **Sierra Vista,** Az,US
54/D5 **Sierre,** Swi.
59/M8 **Siete** (peak), Sp.
112/C2 **Siete Tazas Nat'l Park,** Chile
61/J4 **Sífnos** (isl.), Gre.
63/F2 **Sighetu Marmaţiei,** Rom.
63/G2 **Sighişoara,** Rom.
45/F1 **Sighty Crag** (hill), Eng,UK
86/A2 **Sigli,** Indo.
55/F1 **Sigmaringen,** Ger.
64/C4 **Sigtuna,** Swe.
84/D3 **Sihorā,** India
42/H3 **Siilinjärvi,** Fin.
74/E3 **Siirt,** Turk.
118/D3 **Sikanni Chief** (riv.), BC,Can
84/C2 **Sīkar,** India
98/D4 **Sikasso,** Mali
98/D4 **Sikasso** (reg.), Mali
125/K3 **Sikeston,** Mo,US
77/M2 **Sikhote-Alin'** (mts.), Rus.
61/J4 **Síkinos** (isl.), Gre.
84/E2 **Sikkim** (state), India
62/D3 **Siklós,** Hun.
58/B1 **Sil** (riv.), Sp.
55/G4 **Silandro** (Schlanders), It.
116/A3 **Silao,** Mex.
82/D5 **Silay,** Phil.
85/F3 **Silchar,** India
63/J5 **Şile,** Turk.
47/E1 **Sileby,** Eng,UK
49/H3 **Silesia** (reg.), Pol.
96/F3 **Silet,** Alg.
74/C3 **Silifke,** Turk.
84/E2 **Silīguri,** India
75/E5 **Siling** (lake), China
93/H6 **Silisili** (peak), Samoa
63/H3 **Silistra,** Bul.
63/J5 **Silivri,** Turk.
42/D4 **Silkeborg,** Den.
45/G2 **Silksworth,** Eng,UK
59/E3 **Silla,** Sp.
64/E4 **Sillamäe,** Est.
58/A1 **Silleda,** Sp.
45/E2 **Silloth,** Eng,UK
128/E2 **Siloam Springs,** Ar,US
72/D1 **Silopi,** Turk.
128/E4 **Silsbee,** Tx,US
45/G4 **Silsden,** Eng,UK
96/J4 **Siltou** (well), Chad
49/L1 **Šilutė,** Lith.
74/E2 **Silvan,** Turk.
84/B3 **Silvassa,** India
122/D5 **Silver** (cr.), Or,US
124/B2 **Silver** (lake), Or,US
123/L4 **Silver Bay,** Mn,US
124/E4 **Silver City,** NM,US
130/L3 **Silver Creek,** Yk,Can
45/F3 **Silverdale,** Eng,UK
132/B2 **Silverdale,** Wa,US
132/C2 **Silver Lake-Fircrest,** Wa,US
131/J8 **Silver Spring,** Md,US
47/E2 **Silverstone,** Eng,UK
46/C5 **Silverton,** Eng,UK
124/F3 **Silverton,** Co,US
122/C4 **Silverton,** Or,US
128/C3 **Silverton,** Tx,US
58/A4 **Silves,** Port.
60/D1 **Silvi,** It.
124/C2 **Silvies** (riv.), Or,US
55/G4 **Silvretta** (mts.), Aus., Swi.
60/A4 **Silyānah** (gov.), Tun.
86/D3 **Simanggang,** Malay.
126/E2 **Simard** (lake), Qu,Can
74/B2 **Simav,** Turk.
67/H1 **Simbirsk Obl.,** Rus.
126/D3 **Simcoe,** On,Can
126/E2 **Simcoe** (lake), On,Can
97/N5 **Simēn** (mts.), Eth.
62/F3 **Simeria,** Rom.
86/A3 **Simeulue** (isl.), Indo.
66/E3 **Simferopol',** Ukr.
81/E5 **Siming** (mtn.), China
63/F5 **Simitli,** Bul.
131/B2 **Simi Valley,** Ca,US
73/L2 **Simla,** India
62/F2 **Şimleu Silvaniei,** Rom.
55/D4 **Simme** (riv.), Swi.
53/F2 **Simmerath,** Ger.
53/G4 **Simmerbach** (riv.), Ger.
116/C4 **Simojovel,** Mex.
122/D2 **Simonette** (riv.), Ab,Can
102/B4 **Simonstown,** SAfr.
50/D1 **Simonszand** (isl.), Neth.
86/A3 **Simpang-kiri** (riv.), Indo.
53/E2 **Simpelveld,** Neth.
118/H2 **Simpson** (pen.), Nun.,Can
118/G2 **Simpson** (riv.), Nun.,Can
49/H1 **Simrishamn,** Swe.
87/E3 **Simunul,** Phil.
97/Q6 **Sinadhago,** Som.
72/B3 **Sinafir** (isl.), SAr.
100/C2 **Sinai** (pen.), Egypt
117/N8 **Sinaloa** (state), Mex.
117/F6 **Sincelejo,** Col.
129/H3 **Sinclair** (lake), Ga,US
122/G5 **Sinclair,** Wy,US
84/C2 **Sind** (riv.), India
73/J3 **Sind** (prov.), Pak.
82/D6 **Sindañgan,** Phil.
86/C5 **Sindangbarang,** Indo.
57/H2 **Sindelfingen,** Ger.
58/A4 **Sines,** Port.
58/A4 **Sines, Cabo de** (cape), Port.
98/D5 **Sinfra,** IvC.
86/B3 **Singapore**
86/B3 **Singapore** (cap.), Sing.
83/C3 **Sing Buri,** Thai.
55/E2 **Singen,** Ger.
63/G2 **Sîngeorz-Băi,** Rom.
101/B4 **Singida,** Tanz.
101/B4 **Singida** (prov.), Tanz.
61/H2 **Singitic** (gulf), Gre.
87/F4 **Singkang,** Indo.
86/C3 **Singkawang,** Indo.
86/B4 **Singkep** (isl.), Indo.
91/D2 **Singleton,** Austl.
60/A2 **Siniscola,** It.
97/M5 **Sinjah,** Sudan
74/E3 **Sinjār,** Iraq
100/D5 **Sinkāt,** Sudan
52/C3 **Sin-le-Noble,** Fr.
84/B4 **Sinnar,** India
60/E2 **Sinni** (riv.), It.
62/E2 **Sînnicolau Mare,** Rom.
100/B2 **Sinnūris,** Egypt
98/C5 **Sino** (co.), Libr.
63/J3 **Sinoe** (lake), Rom.
109/G6 **Sinop,** Braz.
74/C1 **Sinop,** Turk.
86/D3 **Sintang,** Indo.
52/D2 **Sint-Genesius-Rode,** Belg.
52/D1 **Sint-Gillis-Waas,** Belg.
52/D1 **Sint-Katelijne-Waver,** Belg.
52/C1 **Sint-Laureins,** Belg.
117/J4 **Sint Maarten** (isl.), NAnt.
50/C5 **Sint-Michielsgestel,** Neth.
52/D1 **Sint-Niklaas,** Belg.
50/C5 **Sint-Oedenrode,** Neth.
128/D4 **Sinton,** Tx,US
52/D2 **Sint-Pieters-Leeuw,** Belg.
58/A3 **Sintra,** Port.
59/P10 **Sintra** (mts.), Port.
53/E2 **Sint-Truiden,** Belg.
117/F6 **Sinú** (riv.), Col.
83/C2 **Sinŭiju,** NKor.
53/G2 **Sinzig,** Ger.
62/D2 **Sió** (riv.), Hun.
87/F2 **Siocon,** Phil.
62/D2 **Siófok,** Hun.
104/D4 **Sioma Ngwezi Nat'l Park,** Zam.
54/D5 **Sion,** Swi.
56/E4 **Sioule** (riv.), Fr.
123/J5 **Sioux City,** Ia,US
123/J5 **Sioux Falls,** SD,US
126/B1 **Sioux Lookout,** On,Can
60/E1 **Šipan** (isl.), Cro.
81/F2 **Siping,** China
123/J2 **Sipiwesk** (lake), Mb,Can
105/Q **Siple** (coast), Ant.
105/R **Siple** (isl.), Ant.
129/G3 **Sipsey** (riv.), Al,US
86/A4 **Sipura** (isl.), Indo.
110/B2 **Siqueira Campos,** Braz.
116/E5 **Siquia** (riv.), Nic.
42/C4 **Sira** (riv.), Nor.
60/D4 **Siracusa** (Syracuse), It.
84/E3 **Sirājganj,** Bang.
122/C2 **Sir Alexander** (peak), BC,Can
74/D2 **Şiran,** Turk.
63/H2 **Siret,** Rom.
63/H3 **Siret** (riv.), Rom.
86/D3 **Sirik** (cape), Malay.
83/C2 **Sirikit** (res.), Thai.
85/H4 **Sirit** (res.), Thai.
130/B5 **Sirius** (pt.), Ak,US
118/D2 **Sir James MacBrien** (peak), NW,Can
73/G3 **Sīrjan,** Iran
91/D4 **Sir John** (cape), Austl.
74/E3 **Şırnak,** Turk.
84/B3 **Sirohi,** India
84/C3 **Sironj,** India
61/J4 **Síros** (isl.), Gre.
84/C2 **Sirsa,** India
84/B5 **Sirsi,** India
62/C3 **Sisak,** Cro.
83/D3 **Sisaket,** Thai.
85/H4 **Si Sa Ket,** Thai.
83/B2 **Si Satchanalai** (ruins), Thai.
123/H2 **Sisipuk** (lake), Mb, Sk,Can
83/C3 **Sisophon,** Camb.
123/J4 **Sisseton,** SD,US
99/E4 **Sissili** (prov.), Burk.
129/H2 **Sissonville,** WV,US
85/F3 **Sitākunda,** Bang.
59/F2 **Sitges,** Sp.
61/H2 **Sithoniá** (pen.), Gre.
61/K5 **Sitía,** Gre.
130/M2 **Sitidgi** (lake), NW,Can
130/L4 **Sitka,** Ak,US
49/K4 **Sitno** (peak), Slvk.
83/B2 **Sittang** (riv.), Burma
50/C7 **Sittard,** Neth.
47/G4 **Sittingbourne,** Eng,UK
85/F3 **Sittwe** (Akyab), Burma
62/D3 **Sivac,** Yugo.
84/C6 **Sivakāsi,** India
74/D2 **Sivas,** Turk.
74/D3 **Siverek,** Turk.
74/B2 **Sivrihisar,** Turk.
52/D3 **Sivry-Rance,** Belg.
97/L2 **Sīwah,** Egypt
84/D2 **Siwān,** India
44/A2 **Sixmilecross,** NI,UK
130/K3 **Sixtymile,** Yk,Can
76/G3 **Siziwang,** China
42/D5 **Sjælland** (isl.), Den.
62/E4 **Sjenica,** Yugo.
42/M6 **Sjónfridh** (peak), Ice.
42/P7 **Skaftafell Nat'l Park,** Ice.
42/D4 **Skagen,** Den.
42/D4 **Skagens** (cape), Den.
42/D4 **Skagerrak** (str.), Eur.
42/P6 **Skálfandafljót** (riv.), Ice.
49/J4 **Skalica,** Slvk.
57/K2 **Skalice** (riv.), Czh.
61/J3 **Skantzoura** (isl.), Gre.
42/E4 **Skaraborg** (co.), Swe.
49/L3 **Skarżysko-Kamienna,** Pol.
49/K4 **Skawina,** Pol.
118/D3 **Skeena** (range), BC,Can
122/A2 **Skeena** (riv.), BC,Can
45/J5 **Skegness,** Eng,UK
42/F2 **Skellefteälven** (riv.), Swe.
42/G2 **Skellefteå,** Swe.
45/G4 **Skelmanthorpe,** Eng,UK
45/F4 **Skelmersdale,** Eng,UK
45/H2 **Skelton,** Eng,UK
45/G2 **Skerne** (riv.), Eng,UK
44/B4 **Skerries,** Ire.
61/G4 **Skhiza** (isl.), Gre.
125/H3 **Skiatook,** Ok,US
45/E2 **Skiddaw** (mtn.), Eng,UK
42/D4 **Skien,** Nor.
49/L3 **Skierniewice,** Pol.
49/K3 **Skierniewice** (prov.), Pol.
96/G1 **Skikda,** Alg.
61/G4 **Skinári, Ákra** (cape), Gre.
45/H4 **Skipsea,** Eng,UK
45/F4 **Skipton,** Eng,UK
45/F3 **Skirfare** (riv.), Eng,UK
61/J3 **Skíros** (isl.), Gre.
42/D4 **Skjeberg,** Nor.
64/B2 **Skjelåtinden** (peak), Nor.
42/D5 **Skjern,** Den.
46/A3 **Skokholm** (isl.), Wal,UK
132/Q15 **Skokie,** Il,US
46/A3 **Skomer** (isl.), Wal,UK
83/D3 **Skon,** Camb.
61/H3 **Skópelos** (isl.), Gre.
66/F1 **Skopin,** Rus.
62/E5 **Skopje** (cap.), FYROM
42/E4 **Skövde,** Swe.
77/J1 **Skovorodino,** Rus.
127/G2 **Skowhegan,** Me,US
130/L3 **Skukum** (mtn.), Yk,Can
125/K2 **Skunk** (riv.), Ia,US
49/H2 **Skwierzyna,** Pol.
132/D2 **Skykomish** (riv.), Wa,US
113/J8 **Skyway** (sound), Chile
42/D5 **Slagelse,** Den.
45/F4 **Slaidburn,** Eng,UK
49/L4 **Slaná** (riv.), Slvk.
43/B4 **Slaney** (riv.), Ire.
64/F4 **Slantsy,** Rus.
63/G3 **Slatina,** Rom.
115/F3 **Slave** (riv.), Can.
99/F5 **Slave Coast** (reg.), Afr.
122/E2 **Slave Lake,** Ab,Can
75/C1 **Slavgorod,** Rus.
62/C3 **Slavonia** (reg.), Cro.
62/C3 **Slavonska Požega,** Cro.
62/D3 **Slavonski Brod,** Cro.
66/C2 **Slavuta,** Ukr.
66/F3 **Slavyansk-na-Kubani,** Rus.
49/J1 **Sławno,** Pol.
123/K5 **Slayton,** Mn,US
45/H6 **Sleaford,** Eng,UK
50/D3 **Sleen,** Neth.
119/H3 **Sleeper** (isls.), Nun.,Can
123/K4 **Sleepy Eye,** Mn,US
44/A4 **Sliabh na Caillighe** (mtn.), Ire.
129/F4 **Slidell,** La,US
50/B5 **Sliedrecht,** Neth.
60/D5 **Sliema,** Malta
44/A3 **Slieve Beagh** (mtn.), NI,UK
44/C3 **Slieve Binnian** (mtn.), NI,UK
44/C3 **Slieve Croob** (mtn.), NI,UK
44/C3 **Slieve Donard** (mtn.), NI,UK
44/B3 **Slieve Gullion** (mtn.), NI,UK
44/A1 **Slieve Snaght** (mtn.), Ire.
43/A3 **Sligo,** Ire.
43/A3 **Sligo** (bay), Ire.
63/H4 **Sliven,** Bul.
62/F4 **Slivnitsa,** Bul.
127/S10 **Sloan,** NY,US
65/L4 **Slobodskoy,** Rus.
63/H3 **Slobozia,** Rom.
50/D2 **Slochteren,** Neth.
66/C1 **Slonim,** Bela.
50/C3 **Slotermeer** (lake), Neth.
47/F4 **Slough,** Eng,UK
49/K4 **Slovakia**
62/B3 **Slovenia**
62/B2 **Slovenska Bistrica,** Slov.
49/L4 **Slovenské Rudohorie** (mts.), Slvk.
66/F2 **Slov'yans'k,** Ukr.
49/J1 **Słowiński Nat'l Park,** Pol.
49/H2 **Słubice,** Pol.
66/C2 **Sluch'** (riv.), Ukr.
49/J2 **Słupca,** Pol.
49/J1 **Słupia** (riv.), Pol.
49/J1 **Słupsk,** Pol.
49/J1 **Słupsk** (prov.), Pol.
66/C1 **Slutsk,** Bela.
76/E1 **Slyudyanka,** Rus.
47/F4 **Smallfield,** Eng,UK
119/K3 **Smallwood** (res.), Nf,Can
123/G2 **Smeaton,** Sk,Can
62/E3 **Smederevo,** Yugo.
62/E3 **Smederevska Palanka,** Yugo.
42/E3 **Smedjebacken,** Swe.
66/D2 **Smela,** Ukr.
50/D3 **Smilde,** Neth.
105/V **Smith** (pen.), Ant.
122/B3 **Smith** (inlet), BC,Can
119/J2 **Smith** (isl.), Nun.,Can
122/F4 **Smith** (riv.), Mt,US
122/B2 **Smithers,** BC,Can
129/J3 **Smithfield,** NC,US
124/E2 **Smithfield,** Ut,US
126/E4 **Smith Mtn.** (lake), Va,US
126/E2 **Smiths Falls,** On,Can
131/G5 **Smithtown,** NY,US
127/Q9 **Smithville,** On,Can
125/J4 **Smithville,** Ok,US
91/E1 **Smoky** (cape), Austl.
122/D2 **Smoky** (riv.), Ab,Can
125/H3 **Smoky** (hills), Ks,US
125/G3 **Smoky Hill** (riv.), Ks,US
122/E2 **Smoky Lake,** Ab,Can
42/C3 **Smøla** (isl.), Nor.
64/G5 **Smolensk,** Rus.
64/F5 **Smolensk Obl.,** Rus.
61/G2 **Smólikas** (peak), Gre.
63/G5 **Smolyan,** Bul.
105/U **Smyley** (isl.), Ant.
129/G3 **Smyrna,** Ga,US
44/D3 **Snaefell** (mtn.), IM,UK
130/M2 **Snake** (riv.), Yk,Can
122/D4 **Snake** (riv.), US
125/G2 **Snake** (riv.), Ne,US
50/C2 **Sneek,** Neth.
50/C2 **Sneekermeer** (lake), Neth.
102/D3 **Sneeuberg** (mts.), SAfr.
102/B4 **Sneeuberg** (peak), SAfr.
127/Q8 **Snelgrove,** On,Can
47/G1 **Snettisham,** Eng,UK
49/H3 **Sněžka** (peak), Czh.
62/B3 **Snežnik** (peak), Yugo.
49/L2 **Śniardwy** (lake), Pol.
47/G4 **Snodland,** Eng,UK
42/D3 **Snøhetta** (peak), Nor.
132/C2 **Snohomish,** Wa,US
132/C2 **Snohomish** (riv.), Wa,US
132/D2 **Snoqualmie** (riv.), Wa,US
42/E2 **Snøtind** (peak), Nor.
44/D5 **Snowdon** (mtn.), Wal,UK
44/D5 **Snowdonia Nat'l Park,** Wal,UK
124/E4 **Snowflake,** Az,US
123/H2 **Snow Lake,** Mb,Can
130/K2 **Snowy** (peak), Ak,US
91/D3 **Snowy River Nat'l Park,** Austl.
128/C3 **Snyder,** Tx,US
103/H7 **Soalala,** Madg.
103/J7 **Soanierana-Ivongo,** Madg.
45/G6 **Soar** (riv.), Eng,UK
57/L2 **Soběslav,** Czh.
87/K4 **Sobger** (riv.), Indo.
73/J3 **Sobhādero,** Pak.
109/K6 **Sobradinho** (res.), Braz.
109/K4 **Sobral,** Braz.
79/M9 **Sobue,** Japan
49/L2 **Sochaczew,** Pol.
66/F4 **Sochi,** Rus.
93/K6 **Society** (isls.), FrPol.
110/G7 **Socorro,** Braz.
124/F4 **Socorro,** NM,US
128/B4 **Socorro,** Tx,US
71/E8 **Socotra** (isl.), Yem.
83/D4 **Soc Trang,** Viet.
58/D3 **Socuéllamos,** Sp.
42/H2 **Sodankylä,** Fin.

176

Soda S – Suir

122/F5 **Soda Springs**, Id,US
79/H7 **Sodegaura**, Japan
42/F3 **Söderhamn**, Swe.
42/F4 **Södertälje**, Swe.
97/N6 **Sodo**, Eth.
51/F5 **Soest**, Ger.
50/C4 **Soest**, Neth.
51/E3 **Soeste** (riv.), Ger.
103/J6 **Sofia** (riv.), Madg.
63/F4 **Sofia (Sofiya)** (cap.), Bul.
62/F4 **Sofiya** (reg.), Bul.
108/D2 **Sogamoso**, Col.
42/B3 **Sognafjorden** (fjord), Nor.
42/C3 **Sogn og Fjordane** (co.), Nor.
96/J4 **Sogollé** (well), Chad
77/K5 **Sŏgwip'o**, SKor.
47/G2 **Soham**, Eng,UK
52/D2 **Soignies**, Belg.
52/C5 **Soissons**, Fr.
78/C3 **Sōja**, Japan
84/B2 **Sojat**, India
80/C3 **Sŏjosŏn** (bay), NKor.
67/J1 **Sok** (riv.), Rus.
83/C3 **Sok** (pt.), Thai.
79/H7 **Sōka**, Japan
80/E3 **Sokch'o**, SKor.
74/A3 **Söke**, Turk.
76/F1 **Sokhor** (peak), Rus.
67/G4 **Sokhumi**, Arm.
62/E4 **Sokobanja**, Geo.
99/F4 **Sokodé**, Togo
64/J4 **Sokol**, Rus.
49/M2 **Sokółka**, Pol.
57/K1 **Sokolov**, Czh.
49/M2 **Sokołów Podlaski**, Pol.
99/G4 **Sokoto** (plains), Nga.
99/G4 **Sokoto** (riv.), Nga.
99/G3 **Sokoto** (state), Nga.
42/C4 **Sola**, Nor.
82/D4 **Solana**, Phil.
108/C2 **Solano** (pt.), Col.
58/C4 **Sol, Costa del** (coast), Sp.
59/P10 **Sol, Costa do** (reg.), Port.
125/J2 **Soldier** (riv.), Ia,US
117/G5 **Soledad**, Col.
131/B2 **Soledad** (canyon), Ca,US
117/J6 **Soledad**, Ven.
116/A3 **Soledad Diez Guiterrez**, Mex.
110/A4 **Soledade**, Braz.
47/E5 **Solent** (chan.), Eng,UK
53/E4 **Soleuvre** (mtn.), Lux.
74/E2 **Solhan**, Turk.
47/E2 **Solihull**, Eng,UK
65/N4 **Solikamsk**, Rus.
67/K2 **Sol'-Iletsk**, Rus.
51/E6 **Solingen**, Ger.
42/F3 **Sollefteå**, Swe.
59/G3 **Sóller**, Sp.
51/G5 **Solling** (mts.), Ger.
42/D3 **Søln** (peak), Nor.
54/B5 **Solnan** (riv.), Fr.
86/D5 **Solo** (riv.), Indo.
86/B4 **Solok**, Indo.
116/C5 **Sololá**, Guat.
92/E5 **Solomon** (sea), PNG, Sol.
128/D2 **Solomon** (riv.), Ks,US
92/E6 **Solomon Islands**
67/L4 **Solonchak Goklenkui** (salt marsh), Trkm.
54/D3 **Solothurn**, Swi.
54/D3 **Solothurn** (canton), Swi.
64/G2 **Solovetskiy** (isls.), Rus.
59/F2 **Solsona**, Sp.
62/D2 **Solt**, Hun.
62/B4 **Šolta** (isl.), Cro.
51/G3 **Soltau**, Ger.
62/D2 **Soltvadkert**, Hun.
62/E5 **Solunska** (peak), FYROM
46/A3 **Solva** (riv.), Wal,UK
124/B4 **Solvang**, Ca,US
42/E4 **Sölvesborg**, Swe.
44/E2 **Solway Firth** (inlet), Eng, Sc,UK
104/E3 **Solwezi**, Zam.
79/G2 **Sōma**, Japan
74/A2 **Soma**, Turk.
52/C3 **Somain**, Fr.
97/Q6 **Somalia**
127/F1 **Somaqua** (riv.), Qu,Can
62/D3 **Sombor**, Cro.
117/P9 **Sombrerete**, Mex.
110/B4 **Sombrio**, Braz.
45/G5 **Somercotes**, Eng,UK
50/C6 **Someren**, Neth.
42/G3 **Somero**, Fin.
122/E3 **Somers**, Mt,US
118/G1 **Somerset** (isl.), Nun.,Can
46/D4 **Somerset** (co.), Eng,UK
126/C4 **Somerset**, Ky,US
131/F5 **Somerset**, NJ,US
127/S9 **Somerset**, NY,US
91/C4 **Somerset-Burnie**, Austl.
102/D4 **Somerset East**, SAfr.
102/B4 **Somerset West**, SAfr.
47/F2 **Somersham**, Eng,UK
127/G3 **Somersworth**, NH,US
46/D4 **Somerton**, Eng,UK
124/D4 **Somerton**, Az,US
131/F5 **Somerville**, NJ,US
125/H5 **Somerville** (lake), Tx,US
63/F2 **Someş** (riv.), Rom.
63/G2 **Someşul Mare** (riv.), Rom.
56/D1 **Somme** (bay), Fr.
52/B4 **Somme** (dept.), Fr.
52/A3 **Somme** (riv.), Fr.
52/D6 **Somme** (riv.), Fr.
52/D5 **Somme-Soude** (riv.), Fr.
62/C2 **Somogy** (co.), Hun.
116/D5 **Somoto**, Nic.
47/F5 **Somptin**, Eng,UK
42/D5 **Sønderborg**, Den.
102/L11 **Sonderend** (riv.), SAfr.
48/E1 **Sønderjylland** (co.), Den.
55/F5 **Sondrio**, It.
84/C2 **Sonepat**, India
84/D3 **Sonepur**, India
83/E3 **Song Cau**, Viet.
83/D4 **Song Dinh**, Viet.
55/F5 **Sondrio** (prov.), It.
101/B5 **Songea**, Tanz.
81/F1 **Songhua** (riv.), China
75/B3 **Song-Kel'** (lake), Kyr.
83/C5 **Songkhla**, Thai.
83/C2 **Songkhram** (riv.), Thai.
77/J2 **Songling**, China
83/C1 **Song Ma**, Viet.
104/F4 **Songo**, Moz.
81/C4 **Song Shan** (peak), China
80/D4 **Songt'an**, SKor.
81/C5 **Songzi Guan** (pass), China
83/E3 **Son Ha**, Viet.
76/G3 **Sonid Youqi**, China
76/G3 **Sonid Zuoqi**, China
83/C1 **Son La**, Viet.
73/J3 **Sonmiāni** (bay), Pak.
57/J1 **Sonneberg**, Ger.
47/F4 **Sonning**, Eng,UK
48/G5 **Sonntagshorn** (peak), Ger.
109/J5 **Sono** (riv.), Braz.
78/D3 **Sonobe**, Japan
132/K10 **Sonoma**, Ca,US
132/J10 **Sonoma** (mts.), Ca,US
117/M8 **Sonora** (riv.), Mex.
117/M8 **Sonora** (state), Mex.
124/B3 **Sonora**, Ca,US
128/C4 **Sonora**, Tx,US
117/M7 **Sonoyta** (riv.), Mex.
72/E2 **Sonqor**, Iran
50/D5 **Sonsbeck**, Ger.
58/D3 **Sonseca**, Sp.
116/D5 **Sonsonate**, ESal.
92/C4 **Sonsorol** (isls.), Palau
62/D3 **Sonta**, Yugo.
83/D1 **Son Tay**, Viet.
51/G6 **Sontra**, Ger.
87/G3 **Sopi** (cape), Indo.
83/C1 **Sopka**, Laos
73/K2 **Sopore**, India
63/G4 **Sopot**, Bul.
49/K1 **Sopot**, Pol.
62/C2 **Sopron**, Hun.
46/D3 **Sör** (riv.), Wal,UK
60/C2 **Sora**, It.
80/E3 **Sŏrak-san** (mtn.), SKor.
127/F2 **Sorel**, Qu,Can
74/M9 **Soreq, Nabel** (dry riv.), Isr.
57/H4 **Soresina**, It.
56/F5 **Sorgues**, Fr.
74/C2 **Sorgun**, Turk.
58/D2 **Soria**, Sp.
113/F2 **Soriano** (dept.), Uru.
86/A3 **Sorikmerapi** (peak), Indo.
67/K3 **Sor Karatuley** (salt pan), Kaz.
67/K3 **Sor Kaydak** (salt marsh), Kaz.
67/K3 **Sor Mertvyy Kultuk** (salt marsh), Kaz.
52/D4 **Sormonne** (riv.), Fr.
48/F1 **Sorø**, Den.
110/C2 **Sorocaba**, Braz.
67/K1 **Sorochinsk**, Rus.
63/J1 **Soroki**, Mol.
92/D4 **Sorol** (atoll), Micr.
87/H4 **Sorong**, Indo.
101/B2 **Soroti**, Ugan.
42/G1 **Sørøya** (isl.), Nor.
42/G1 **Sørøysundet** (chan.), Nor.
51/E6 **Sorpestausee** (res.), Ger.
58/A3 **Sorraia** (riv.), Port.
60/D2 **Sorrento**, It.
104/B5 **Sorris-Sorris**, Namb.
60/A2 **Sorso**, It.
82/D5 **Sorsogon**, Phil.
64/F3 **Sortavala**, Rus.
64/D4 **Sõrve** (pt.), Est.
51/H5 **Söse** (riv.), Ger.
66/F1 **Sosna** (riv.), Rus.
112/C2 **Sosneado** (peak), Arg.
65/M3 **Sosnogorsk**, Rus.
65/L4 **Sosnovka**, Rus.
49/K3 **Sosnowiec**, Pol.
117/G4 **Sosúa**, DRep.
52/D6 **Soude** (riv.), Fr.
117/J4 **Soufrière** (mt.), Guad.
117/J5 **Soufrière** (mt.), StV.
96/G1 **Souk Ahras**, Alg.
53/G1 **Soultz-sous-Forets**, Fr.
99/E3 **Soum** (prov.), Burk.
53/E2 **Soumagne**, Belg.
102/E3 **Sources, Mont aux** (peak), Les.
109/J4 **Soure**, Braz.
58/A2 **Soure**, Port.
123/H3 **Souris**, Mb,Can
127/J2 **Souris**, PE,Can
123/H3 **Souris** (riv.), Can., US
98/E3 **Sourou** (prov.), Burk.
96/D2 **Sous** (wadi), Mor.
109/L5 **Sousa**, Braz.
58/B3 **Sousel**, Port.
102/C3 **Sout** (riv.), SAfr.
90/G8 **South** (cr.), Austl.
127/H2 **South** (mts.), NS,Can
119/H2 **South** (bay), Nun.,Can
89/G7 **South** (cape), NZ
89/H7 **South** (isl.), NZ
104/D6 **South Africa**
47/E2 **Southam**, Eng,UK
107/* **South America**
119/H2 **Southampton** (cape), Nun.,Can
119/H2 **Southampton** (isl.), Nun.,Can
126/D2 **Southampton**, On,Can
47/E5 **Southampton**, Eng,UK
47/E5 **Southampton** (co.), Eng,UK
85/F5 **South Andaman** (isl.), India
129/J2 **South Anna** (riv.), Va,US
129/H3 **South Augusta**, Ga,US
119/K3 **South Aulatsivik** (isl.), Nf,Can
89/C3 **South Australia** (state), Austl.
129/F3 **Southaven**, Ms,US
44/D1 **South Ayrshire** (reg.), Sc,UK
44/D3 **South Barrule** (mtn.), IM,UK
126/C3 **South Bend**, In,US
47/G4 **Southborough**, Eng,UK
126/E4 **South Boston**, Va,US
47/F5 **Southbourne**, Eng,UK
46/C6 **South Brent**, Eng,UK
101/A3 **South Buganda** (prov.), Ugan.
127/F2 **South Burlington**, Vt,US
129/H3 **South Carolina** (state), US
71/L8 **South China** (sea), Asia
123/H4 **South Dakota** (state), US
46/D5 **South Dorset Downs** (uplands), Eng,UK
47/F5 **South Downs** (hills), Eng,UK
39/S8 **South East** (cape), Austl.
91/C3 **South East** (pt.), Austl.
117/G3 **Southeast** (pt.), Bahm.
130/E3 **Southeast** (cape), Ak,US
132/P16 **South Elgin**, Il,US
45/G4 **South Elmsall**, Eng,UK
44/C1 **Southend**, Sc,UK
47/G3 **Southend-on-Sea**, Eng,UK
74/K6 **Southern** (dist.), Isr.
98/B5 **Southern** (prov.), SLeo.
101/A3 **Southern** (prov.), Ugan.
93/J6 **Southern Cook** (isls.), CookIs.
118/G3 **Southern Indian** (lake), Mb,Can
129/J3 **Southern Pines**, NC,US
44/D1 **Southern Uplands** (mts.), Sc,UK
47/G1 **Southery**, Eng,UK
91/C4 **South Esk** (riv.), Austl.
132/F7 **Southfield**, Mi,US
47/H4 **South Foreland** (pt.), Eng,UK
124/F3 **South Fork**, Co,US
129/F3 **South Fulton**, Tn,US
131/B3 **South Gate**, Ca,US
132/F7 **Southgate**, Mi,US
105/X **South Georgia** (isl.), UK
46/D3 **South Gloucestershire** (co.), Eng,UK
46/C6 **South Hams** (plain), Eng,UK
47/F5 **South Hayling**, Eng,UK
126/E4 **South Hill**, Va,US
50/B5 **South Holland** (prov.), Neth.
132/Q16 **South Holland**, Il,US
45/G4 **South Kirkby**, Eng,UK
80/D4 **South Korea**
124/C3 **South Lake Tahoe**, Ca,US
104/F3 **South Luangwa Nat'l Park**, Zam.
105/K **South Magnetic Pole**, Ant.
132/Q14 **South Milwaukee**, Wi,US
47/G3 **Southminster**, Eng,UK
46/C4 **South Molton**, Eng,UK
123/J2 **South Moose** (lake), Mb,Can
130/M5 **South Moresby Nat'l Park Rsv.**, BC,Can
45/G5 **South Normanton**, Eng,UK
105/W **South Orkney** (isls.), UK
67/G4 **South Ossetian Aut. Obl.**, Geo.
47/F3 **South Oxhey**, Eng,UK
46/D5 **South Petherton**, Eng,UK
90/E6 **South Pine** (riv.), Austl.
131/F5 **South Plainfield**, NJ,US
125/G2 **South Platte** (riv.), Co, Ne,US
105/A **South Pole**, Ant.
45/E4 **Southport**, Eng,UK
129/J3 **Southport**, NC,US
131/F5 **South River**, NJ,US
105/Y **South Sandwich** (isls.), UK
132/K11 **South San Francisco**, Ca,US
122/F3 **South Saskatchewan** (riv.), Ab, Sk,Can
105/W **South Shetland** (isls.), UK
45/G2 **South Shields**, Eng,UK
125/H2 **South Sioux City**, Ne,US
84/E3 **South Suburban**, India
45/F2 **South Tyne** (riv.), Eng,UK
87/F2 **South Ubian**, Phil.
45/H5 **Southwell**, Eng,UK
91/C4 **South West** (cape), Austl.
91/C4 **South West Nat'l Park**, Austl.
47/H2 **Southwold**, Eng,UK
47/G3 **South Woodham Ferrers**, Eng,UK
90/C4 **Southwood Nat'l Park**, Austl.
45/G5 **South Yorkshire** (co.), Eng,UK
63/G2 **Sovata**, Rom.
60/E3 **Soverato Marina**, It.
49/L1 **Sovetsk**, Rus.
64/D5 **Sovetsk**, Rus.
64/L4 **Sovetsk**, Rus.
77/N2 **Sovetskaya Gavan'**, Rus.
45/G4 **Sowerby Bridge**, Eng,UK
102/D2 **Soweto**, SAfr.
64/J2 **Soyana** (riv.), Rus.
80/D4 **Soyang** (lake), SKor.
56/D4 **Soyaux**, Fr.
105/E **Soyuz**, Ant.
66/D1 **Sozh** (riv.), Eur.
53/E3 **Spa**, Belg.
105/U **Spaatz** (isl.), Ant.
58/C2 **Spain**
45/H6 **Spalding**, Eng,UK
132/C3 **Spanaway**, Wa,US
117/F4 **Spanish Town**, Jam.
124/C3 **Sparks**, Nv,US
129/H2 **Sparta**, NC,US
131/F4 **Sparta**, NJ,US
129/G3 **Sparta**, Tn,US
126/B3 **Sparta**, Wi,US
129/H3 **Spartanburg**, SC,US
61/H4 **Sparta (Spárti)**, Gre.
60/A3 **Spartivento** (cape), It.
60/E4 **Spartivento** (cape), It.
122/E3 **Sparwood**, BC,Can
77/L3 **Spassk-Dal'niy**, Rus.
61/H5 **Spátha, Ákra** (cape), Gre.
42/C2 **Spean** (riv.), Sc,UK
43/C2 **Spean Bridge**, Sc,UK
123/H4 **Spearfish**, SD,US
45/F5 **Speke**, Eng,UK
92/C8 **Spencer** (gulf), Austl.
130/E2 **Spencer** (pt.), Ak,US
123/K5 **Spencer**, Ia,US
51/F4 **Spenge**, Ger.
45/G2 **Spennymoor**, Eng,UK
61/H3 **Sperkhios** (riv.), Gre.
44/A3 **Sperrin** (mts.), NI,UK
43/D2 **Spey** (riv.), Sc,UK
57/H2 **Speyer**, Ger.
127/Q8 **Speyside**, On,Can
60/E3 **Spezzano Albanese**, It.
119/H2 **Spicer** (isl.), Nun.,Can
51/E1 **Spiekeroog** (isl.), Ger.
54/D4 **Spiez**, Swi.
50/B5 **Spijkenisse**, Neth.
130/K2 **Spike** (mtn.), Ak,US
62/A2 **Spilimbergo**, It.
45/J5 **Spilsby**, Eng,UK
60/A2 **Spina, Bruncu** (peak), It.
73/J2 **Spin Būldak**, Afg.
53/E5 **Spincourt**, Fr.
122/D2 **Spirit River**, Ab,Can
122/G2 **Spiritwood**, Sk,Can
49/L4 **Spišská Nová Ves**, Slvk.
47/E5 **Spithead** (chan.), Eng,UK
68/B2 **Spitsbergen** (isl.), Sval.
57/K3 **Spittal an der Drau**, Aus.
123/K2 **Split** (lake), Mb,Can
62/C4 **Split**, Cro.
55/F4 **Splugenpass** (pass), It., Swi.
122/D4 **Spokane** (riv.), Id, Wa,US
122/D4 **Spokane**, Wa,US
60/C1 **Spoleto**, It.
126/B3 **Spoon** (riv.), Il,US
126/B2 **Spooner**, Wi,US
123/K3 **Sprague**, Mb,Can
50/C5 **Sprang-Capelle**, Neth.
82/B5 **Spratly** (isls.)
49/H2 **Spree** (riv.), Ger.
57/K4 **Spresiano**, It.
53/E3 **Sprimont**, Belg.
129/G4 **Spring** (cr.), Ga,US
128/E4 **Spring**, Tx,US
127/K1 **Springdale**, Nf,Can
128/E2 **Springdale**, Ar,US
51/G4 **Springe**, Ger.
125/F3 **Springer**, NM,US
124/E4 **Springerville**, Az,US
125/G3 **Springfield**, Co,US
126/B4 **Springfield** (cap.), Il,US
127/F3 **Springfield**, Ma,US
125/J3 **Springfield**, Mo,US
126/D4 **Springfield**, Oh,US
122/C4 **Springfield**, Or,US
129/G2 **Springfield**, Tn,US
131/J8 **Springfield**, Va,US
127/F3 **Springfield**, Vt,US
127/H2 **Springhill**, NS,Can
128/E3 **Springhill**, La,US
102/E2 **Springs**, SAfr.
123/H3 **Springside**, Sk,Can
91/G5 **Springvale**
123/K5 **Spring Valley**, Mn,US
131/F4 **Spring Valley**, NY,US
51/E6 **Sprockhövel**, Ger.
47/H1 **Sprowston**, Eng,UK
126/E4 **Spruce** (peak), WV,US
131/E5 **Spruce Run** (res.), NJ,US
50/B5 **Spui** (riv.), Neth.
45/J4 **Spurn Head** (pt.), Eng,UK
122/C3 **Squamish**, BC,Can
60/E3 **Squillace** (gulf), It.
61/F2 **Squinzano**, It.
62/D3 **Srbobran**, Yugo.
83/C4 **Sre Ambel**, Camb.
62/D3 **Srebrenica**, Bosn.
63/G4 **Sredna** (mts.), Bul.
63/G4 **Srednogorie**, Bul.
83/D3 **Sre Khtum**, Camb.
49/J2 **Śrem**, Pol.
62/E3 **Sremčica**, Yugo.
62/D3 **Sremska Mitrovica**, Yugo.
83/C3 **Sreng** (riv.), Camb.
83/D3 **Sre Noy**, Camb.
83/D3 **Srepok** (riv.), Camb.
77/H1 **Sretensk**, Rus.
73/K3 **Sri Dungargarh**, India
73/K3 **Sri Gangānagar**, India
84/D4 **Srikākulam**, India
84/D6 **Sri Lanka**
73/K2 **Srīnagar**, India
84/B4 **Srīvardhan**, India
49/J3 **Środa Śląska**, Pol.
49/J2 **Środa Wielkopolska**, Pol.
90/A2 **Staaten River Nat'l Park**, Austl.
42/H1 **Stabbursdalen Nat'l Park**, Nor.
50/B6 **Stabroek**, Belg.
51/G1 **Stade**, Ger.
52/C2 **Staden**, Belg.
50/D3 **Stadskanaal**, Neth.
51/G4 **Stadthagen**, Ger.
50/D5 **Stadtlohn**, Ger.
55/E3 **Stäfa**, Swi.
49/G1 **Staffanstorp**, Swe.
45/F6 **Stafford**, Eng,UK
46/D2 **Stafford & Worcester** (can.), Eng,UK
45/F5 **Staffordshire** (co.), Eng,UK
60/B4 **Stagnone** (isls.), It.
45/G2 **Staindrop**, Eng,UK
47/F4 **Staines**, Eng,UK
132/M12 **Stakes** (mtn.), Ca,US
66/F2 **Stakhanov**, Ukr.
46/D5 **Stalbridge**, Eng,UK
47/H1 **Stalham**, Eng,UK
119/S6 **Stallworthy** (cape), Nun.,Can
49/M3 **Stalowa Wola**, Pol.
45/F5 **Stalybridge**, Eng,UK
63/G4 **Stamboliyski**, Bul.
47/F1 **Stamford**, Eng,UK
131/G4 **Stamford**, Ct,US
45/H4 **Stamford Bridge**, Eng,UK
42/E1 **Stamsund**, Nor.
44/B4 **Stamullin**, Ire.
102/E2 **Standerton**, SAfr.
45/F4 **Standish-with-Langtree**, Eng,UK
47/G4 **Stanford le Hope**, Eng,UK
42/D3 **Stange**, Nor.
103/E3 **Stanger**, SAfr.
45/F2 **Stanhope**, Eng,UK
131/F5 **Stanhope**, NJ,US
124/B3 **Stanislaus** (riv.), Ca,US
63/F4 **Stanke Dimitrov**, Bul.
91/C4 **Stanley** (peak), Austl.
127/H2 **Stanley**, NB,Can
84/C5 **Stanley** (res.), India
45/G2 **Stanley**, Eng,UK
123/H3 **Stanley**, ND,US
97/L8 **Stanley** (falls), D.R. Congo
62/E4 **Stanovo**, Yugo.
59/N4 **Stanovoy** (range), Rus.
47/G3 **Stansted Mountfitchet**, Eng,UK
47/G2 **Stanton**, Eng,UK
131/C3 **Stanton**, Ca,US
126/D4 **Stanton**, Ky,US
128/C3 **Stanton**, Tx,US
50/D3 **Staphorst**, Neth.
47/E4 **Stapleford**, Eng,UK
47/G4 **Staplehurst**, Eng,UK
49/L3 **Starachowice**, Pol.
62/E3 **Stara Pazova**, Yugo.
62/F3 **Stara Planina** (mts.), Yugo.
64/F4 **Staraya Russa**, Rus.
63/G4 **Stara Zagora**, Bul.
93/K5 **Starbuck** (isl.), Kiri.
90/B1 **Starcke Nat'l Park**, Austl.
49/H2 **Stargard Szczeciński**, Pol.
29/H4 **Starke**, Fl,US
129/F3 **Starkville**, Ms,US
66/F3 **Staroderevyan-kovskaya**, Rus.
66/E1 **Starodub**, Rus.
49/K2 **Starogard Gdański**, Pol.
66/F3 **Staroshcher-binovskaya**, Rus.
46/C6 **Start** (bay), Eng,UK
46/C6 **Start** (pt.), Eng,UK
49/L3 **Staszów**, Pol.
126/E3 **State College**, Pa,US
131/F5 **Staten** (isl.), NY,US
129/H3 **Statesboro**, Ga,US
129/H3 **Statesville**, NC,US
48/E3 **Staufenberg**, Ger.
46/D3 **Staunton**, Eng,UK
126/E4 **Staunton**, Va,US
46/D2 **Staunton on Wye**, Eng,UK
42/C4 **Stavanger**, Nor.
45/F3 **Staveley**, Eng,UK
45/G5 **Staveley**, Eng,UK
67/G3 **Stavropol'**, Rus.
67/G3 **Stavropol' Kray**, Rus.
91/B3 **Stawell**, Austl.
122/C4 **Stayton**, Or,US
124/F2 **Steamboat Springs**, Co,US
51/H3 **Stederau** (riv.), Ger.
91/F5 **Steele** (cr.), Austl.
123/J4 **Steele**, ND,US
103/E2 **Steelpoortrivier** (riv.), SAfr.
50/B5 **Steenbergen**, Neth.
124/C2 **Steens** (mtn.), Or,US
119/J1 **Steensby** (inlet), Nun.,Can
50/D3 **Steenwijk**, Neth.
123/G1 **Steephill** (lake), Sk,Can
46/C4 **Steep Holm** (isl.), Eng,UK
45/J5 **Steeping** (riv.), Eng,UK
130/J2 **Steese Nat'l Rec. Area**, Ak,US
118/F1 **Stefansson** (isl.), Nun.,Can
112/C5 **Steffen** (peak), Chile
54/D4 **Steffisburg**, Swi.
62/A2 **Steiermark** (prov.), Aus.
57/J2 **Steigerwald** (for.), Ger.
48/F4 **Stein**, Ger.
53/E2 **Stein**, Neth.
123/J3 **Steinbach**, Mb,Can
51/F5 **Steinhagen**, Ger.
51/G5 **Steinheim**, Ger.
51/G4 **Steinhuder Meer** (lake), Ger.
42/D2 **Steinkjer**, Nor.
52/D1 **Stekene**, Belg.
127/J2 **Stellarton**, NS,Can
102/B4 **Stellenbosch**, SAfr.
51/H2 **Stelle**, Ger.
57/H5 **Stello** (mtn.), Fr.
55/G4 **Stelvio Nat'l Park**, It.
48/F2 **Stendal**, Ger.
63/G4 **Steneto Nat'l Park**, Bul.
42/D4 **Stenungsund**, Swe.
91/B1 **Stephens Creek**, Austl.
127/K1 **Stephenville**, Nf,Can
128/D3 **Stephenville**, Tx,US
125/G2 **Sterling**, Co,US
128/C4 **Sterling City**, Tx,US
132/F6 **Sterling Heights**, Mi,US
67/K1 **Sterlitamak**, Rus.
122/E2 **Stettler**, Ab,Can
126/D3 **Steubenville**, Oh,US
47/F3 **Stevenage**, Eng,UK
123/J2 **Stevenson** (lake), Mb,Can
130/H4 **Stevenson** (str.), Ak,US
126/B2 **Stevens Point**, Wi,US
122/E4 **Stevensville**, Mt,US
50/C3 **Stevinsluizen** (dam), Neth.
130/L3 **Stewart** (riv.), Yk,Can
130/L3 **Stewart Crossing**, Yk,Can
130/L3 **Stewart River**, Yk,Can
44/B2 **Stewartstown**, NI,UK
123/K5 **Stewartville**, Mn,US
47/F5 **Steyning**, Eng,UK
57/L2 **Steyr**, Aus.
57/L3 **Steyr** (riv.), Aus.
50/C2 **Stiens**, Neth.
125/J4 **Stigler**, Ok,US
130/M4 **Stikine** (riv.), BC,Can
123/K4 **Stillwater**, Mn,US
124/C3 **Stillwater** (range), Nv,US
125/H3 **Stillwater**, Ok,US
125/J4 **Stilwell**, Ok,US
44/D1 **Stinchar** (riv.), Sc,UK
128/C3 **Stinnett**, Tx,US
62/F5 **Štip**, FYROM
53/F5 **Stiring-Wendel**, Fr.
43/D2 **Stirling**, Sc,UK
127/L2 **St. John's** (cap.), Nf,Can
42/D3 **Stjørdal**, Nor.
47/E4 **Stockbridge**, Eng,UK
49/J4 **Stockerau**, Aus.
42/F4 **Stockholm** (cap.), Swe.
45/F5 **Stockport**, Eng,UK
45/F4 **Stocks** (res.), Eng,UK
45/G5 **Stocksbridge**, Eng,UK
132/M11 **Stockton**, Ca,US
125/J3 **Stockton** (lake), Mo,US
128/C4 **Stockton** (plat.), Tx,US
45/G2 **Stockton-on-Tees**, Eng,UK
45/G2 **Stockton-on-Tees** (co.), Eng,UK
83/D3 **Stoeng Treng**, Camb.
46/B6 **Stoke** (pt.), Eng,UK
45/F5 **Stoke-on-Trent**, Eng,UK
45/F5 **Stoke-on-Trent** (co.), Eng,UK
91/B4 **Stokes** (pt.), Austl.
62/C4 **Stolac**, Bosn.
53/F2 **Stolberg**, Ger.
69/P2 **Stolbovoy** (isl.), Rus.
102/K10 **Stompneuspunt** (pt.), SAfr.
45/F6 **Stone**, Eng,UK
43/D2 **Stonehaven**, Sc,UK
47/E4 **Stonehenge** (ruins), Eng,UK
46/D3 **Stonehouse**, Eng,UK
123/J3 **Stonewall**, Mb,Can
127/Q9 **Stoney Creek**, On,Can
123/J2 **Stony** (pt.), Mb,Can
131/G5 **Stony Brook**, NY,US
123/J3 **Stony Mountain**, Mb,Can
131/G4 **Stony Point**, NY,US
68/K3 **Stony Tunguska** (riv.), Rus.
126/D1 **Stooping** (riv.), On,Can
119/S7 **Stor** (isl.), Nun.,Can
51/G1 **Stör** (riv.), Ger.
42/F2 **Stora Sjöfallets Nat'l Park**, Swe.
42/F2 **Storavan** (lake), Swe.
48/F1 **Store Bælt** (chan.), Den.
42/D3 **Støren**, Nor.
91/C4 **Storm** (bay), Austl.
123/K5 **Storm Lake**, Ia,US
44/C2 **Stormont**, NI,UK
47/F5 **Storrington**, Eng,UK
42/F1 **Storsteinsfjellet** (peak), Nor.
48/F1 **Storstrøm** (co.), Den.
47/G3 **Stort** (riv.), Eng,UK
42/F2 **Storuman**, Swe.
122/G4 **Story**, Wy,US
113/J7 **Stosch** (isl.), Chile
47/F2 **Stotfold**, Eng,UK
123/H3 **Stoughton**, Sk,Can
46/D5 **Stour** (riv.), Eng,UK
47/E2 **Stour** (riv.), Eng,UK
47/H3 **Stour** (riv.), Eng,UK
47/H4 **Stour** (riv.), Eng,UK
46/D2 **Stourbridge**, Eng,UK
47/G4 **Stour, Great** (riv.), Eng,UK
46/D2 **Stourport on Severn**, Eng,UK
47/G2 **Stowmarket**, Eng,UK
47/E3 **Stow on the Wold**, Eng,UK
44/A2 **Strabane** (dist.), NI,UK
43/D2 **Strachan**, Sc,UK
43/C2 **Strachur**, Sc,UK
57/H4 **Stradella**, It.
50/D6 **Straelen**, Ger.
57/K2 **Strakonice**, Czh.
63/H4 **Straldzha**, Bul.
48/G1 **Stralsund**, Ger.
102/B4 **Strand**, SAfr.
44/C3 **Strangford**, NI,UK
44/C3 **Strangford Lough** (inlet), NI,UK
64/C4 **Strängnäs**, Swe.
44/B1 **Stranocum**, NI,UK
44/C2 **Stranraer**, Sc,UK
123/G3 **Strasbourg**, Sk,Can
54/D1 **Strasbourg**, Fr.
126/D3 **Stratford**, On,Can
89/H6 **Stratford**, NZ
131/E6 **Stratford**, NJ,US
47/E2 **Stratford upon Avon**, Eng,UK
43/C3 **Strathaven**, Sc,UK
122/E3 **Strathmore**, Ab,Can
46/B5 **Stratton**, Eng,UK
57/K2 **Straubing**, Ger.
42/M6 **Straumnes** (pt.), Ice.
57/G3 **Strausberg**, Ger.
131/B2 **Strawberry** (peak), Ca,US
132/P15 **Streamwood**, Il,US
47/E3 **Streatley**, Eng,UK
126/B3 **Streator**, Il,US
57/L2 **Středočeská Žulová Vrchovina** (mts.), Czh.
57/L2 **Středočeský** (reg.), Czh.
49/K4 **Středoslovenský** (reg.), Slvk.
46/D4 **Street**, Eng,UK
127/Q8 **Streetsville**, On,Can
63/F3 **Strehaia**, Rom.
64/H2 **Strel'na** (riv.), Rus.
45/F5 **Stretford**, Eng,UK
47/G2 **Stretham**, Eng,UK
50/B5 **Strijen**, Neth.
61/H2 **Strimón** (gulf), Gre.
61/H2 **Strimónas** (riv.), Gre.
113/K7 **Strobel** (lake), Arg.
61/G4 **Strofádhes** (isls.), Gre.
60/D3 **Stromboli** (isl.), It.
42/D4 **Strømmen**, Nor.
42/D4 **Strömstad**, Swe.
42/E3 **Strömsund**, Swe.
49/J3 **Stronie Śląskie**, Pol.
46/D3 **Stroud**, Eng,UK
42/E5 **Struga**, FYROM
102/C4 **Struisbaai** (bay), SAfr.
44/A2 **Strule** (riv.), NI,UK
61/H2 **Struma** (riv.), Bul., Gre.
46/A2 **Strumble Head** (pt.), UK
62/F5 **Strumica**, FYROM
42/C3 **Stryn**, Nor.
49/J3 **Strzegom**, Pol.
49/H2 **Strzelce Krajeńskie**, Pol.
90/A5 **Strzelecki** (cr.), Austl.
91/D4 **Strzelecki** (peak), Austl.
49/J3 **Strzelin**, Pol.
49/L4 **Strzyżów**, Pol.
122/B2 **Stuart** (lake), BC,Can
122/B2 **Stuart** (riv.), BC,Can
129/H5 **Stuart**, Fl,US
126/E4 **Stuarts Draft**, Va,US
49/G1 **Stubbenkammer** (pt.), Ger.
47/E5 **Studland**, Eng,UK
47/E2 **Studley**, Eng,UK
49/J4 **Stupava**, Slvk.
64/H5 **Stupino**, Rus.
123/J3 **Sturgeon** (bay), Mb,Can
126/B1 **Sturgeon** (lake), On,Can
126/C2 **Sturgeon Bay**, Wi,US
126/E2 **Sturgeon Falls**, On,Can
126/C3 **Sturgis**, Mi,US
123/H4 **Sturgis**, SD,US
46/D5 **Sturminster Newton**, Eng,UK
47/H4 **Sturry**, Eng,UK
90/A5 **Sturt** (des.), Austl.
91/B1 **Sturt** (peak), Austl.
91/B1 **Sturt Nat'l Park**, Austl.
102/D4 **Stutterheim**, SAfr.
57/H2 **Stuttgart**, Ger.
129/F3 **Stuttgart**, Ar,US
66/C2 **Styr** (riv.), Ukr.
57/L3 **Styria** (prov.), Aus.
110/D1 **Suaçui Grande** (riv.), Braz.
100/D5 **Suakin** (arch.), Sudan
82/D3 **Suao**, Tai.
86/C5 **Subang**, Indo.
60/C1 **Subasio** (peak), It.
86/C3 **Subi** (isl.), Indo.
62/D2 **Subotica**, Yugo.
131/F5 **Succasunna-Kenvil**, NJ,US
63/H2 **Suceava**, Rom.
63/G2 **Suceava** (co.), Rom.
49/L3 **Suchedniów**, Pol.
43/A4 **Suck** (riv.), Ire.
108/E7 **Sucre** (cap.), Bol.
108/G5 **Sucunduri** (riv.), Braz.
110/B2 **Sucuriú** (riv.), Braz.
64/H4 **Suda** (riv.), Rus.
97/L5 **Sudan**
96/H5 **Sudan** (phys. reg.), Afr.
126/D2 **Sudbury**, On,Can
47/G2 **Sudbury**, Eng,UK
51/H2 **Sude** (riv.), Ger.
49/H3 **Sudeten** (mts.), Czh., Pol.
101/A3 **Sud-Kivu** (prov.), D.R. Congo
50/D5 **Südlohn**, Ger.
99/H5 **Sud-Ouest** (prov.), Camr.
97/L6 **Sue** (riv.), Sudan
59/E3 **Sueca**, Sp.
63/G4 **Süedinenie**, Bul.
100/C2 **Suez** (can.), Egypt
100/C2 **Suez** (gulf), Egypt
100/C2 **Suez (As Suways)**, Egypt
74/K5 **Sūf**, Jor.
131/F4 **Suffern**, NY,US
47/G2 **Suffolk** (co.), Eng,UK
126/E4 **Suffolk**, Va,US
125/K2 **Sugar** (riv.), Il, Wi,US
128/E4 **Sugar Land**, Tx,US
46/C3 **Sugar Loaf** (mtn.), Wal,UK
129/H2 **Sugarloaf** (peak), Ky,US
76/F1 **Sühbaatar**, Mong.
57/J1 **Suhl**, Ger.
74/B2 **Şuhut**, Turk.
82/B3 **Sui** (riv.), China
83/B4 **Sui** (pt.), Thai.
109/H6 **Suia-Missu** (riv.), Braz.
77/L2 **Suibin**, China
77/L3 **Suifenhe**, China
77/K2 **Suihua**, China
77/K2 **Suileng**, China
52/D5 **Suippe** (riv.), Fr.
43/B4 **Suir** (riv.), Ire.

177

Suisu – Tecum

132/K10 Suisun City, Ca,US
79/L10 Suita, Japan
131/K8 Suitland-Silver Hill, Md,US
76/G5 Suizhou, China
84/B2 Sūjāngarh, India
86/C5 Sukabumi, Indo.
86/C4 Sukadana, Indo.
86/C4 Sukadana (bay), Indo.
79/G2 Sukagawa, Japan
66/E1 Sukhinichi, Rus.
64/J4 Sukhona (riv.), Rus.
83/B2 Sukhothai, Thai.
73/J3 Sukkur, Pak.
78/C4 Sukumo, Japan
87/G4 Sula (isls.), Indo.
65/L2 Sula (riv.), Rus.
73/J3 Sulaimān (range), Pak.
87/E4 Sulawesi (Celebes) (isl.), Indo.
100/B4 Sulb Temple (ruins), Sudan
44/D3 Sulby (riv.), IM,UK
49/H2 Sulechów, Pol.
49/H2 Sulęcin, Pol.
49/L2 Sulejówek, Pol.
51/F3 Sulingen, Ger.
76/D4 Sulin Gol (riv.), China
42/F2 Sulitjelma (peak), Nor.
108/B4 Sullana, Peru
122/F3 Sullivan (lake), Ab,Can
126/C4 Sullivan, In,US
126/E1 Sullivan Mines, Qu,Can
46/C4 Sully, Wal,UK
60/C1 Sulmona, It.
125/J4 Sulphur (riv.), Ar, Tx,US
128/E4 Sulphur, La,US
125/H4 Sulphur, Ok,US
128/E3 Sulphur Springs, Tx,US
87/E2 Sulu (sea), Malay., Phil.
82/D6 Sulu (arch.), Phil.
74/C2 Suluova, Turk.
97/K1 Sulūq, Libya
53/G2 Sülz (riv.), Ger.
53/G5 Sulzbach, Ger.
57/J2 Sulzbach-Rosenberg, Ger.
105/P Sulzberger (bay), Ant.
105/Q Sulzberger Ice Shelf, Ant.
62/E3 Šumadija (reg.), Yugo.
108/D3 Sumapaz Nat'l Park, Col.
86/B4 Sumatra (isl.), Indo.
86/E5 Sumba (isl.), Indo.
87/E5 Sumba (str.), Indo.
67/L5 Sumbar (riv.), Trkm.
86/E5 Sumbawa (isl.), Indo.
87/E5 Sumbawa Besar, Indo.
101/A5 Sumbawanga, Tanz.
104/B3 Sumbe, Ang.
76/F2 Sümber, Mong.
130/M4 Sumdum (mtn.), Ak,US
62/C2 Sümeg, Hun.
86/D5 Sumenep, Indo.
45/G3 Summer Bridge, Eng,UK
122/D3 Summerland, BC,Can
127/J2 Summerside, PE,Can
126/D4 Summersville, WV,US
129/G3 Summerville, Ga,US
129/H3 Summerville, SC,US
131/F5 Summit, NJ,US
132/C3 Sumner, Wa,US
78/D3 Sumoto, Japan
49/J4 Šumperk, Czh.
67/J4 Sumqayıt, Azer.
66/E2 Sums'ka (obl.), Ukr.
129/H3 Sumter, SC,US
66/E2 Sumy, Ukr.
122/E4 Sun (riv.), Mt,US
79/M9 Sunami, Japan
91/C3 Sunbury, Austl.
47/F4 Sunbury on Thames, Eng,UK
80/D5 Sunch'ŏn, SKor.
124/D4 Sun City, Az,US
131/C3 Sun City, Ca,US
127/G3 Suncook, NH,US
86/B5 Sunda (str.), Indo.
123/G4 Sundance, Wy,US
84/E3 Sundarbans (reg.), Bang., India
84/B3 Sundargarh, India
73/L2 Sundarnagar, India
102/D4 Sundays (riv.), SAfr.
45/G2 Sunderland, Eng,UK
51/F6 Sundern, Ger.
91/D1 Sundown Nat'l Park, Austl.
122/E3 Sundre, Ab,Can
42/F3 Sundsvall, Swe.
86/B4 Sungaipenuh, Indo.
86/B2 Sungai Petani, Malay.
74/C2 Sungurlu, Turk.
128/B4 Sunland Park, NM,US
42/D3 Sunndalsøra, Nor.
42/E4 Sunne, Swe.
47/F4 Sunninghill, Eng,UK
132/K12 Sunnyvale, Ca,US
79/H8 Su-no-saki (cape), Japan
126/B3 Sun Prairie, Wi,US
131/B3 Sunset Beach, Ca,US
91/B2 Sunset Country (reg.), Austl.
124/E4 Sunset Crater Nat'l Mon., Az,US
91/F5 Sunshine, Austl.
69/P3 Suntar-Khayata (mts.), Rus.
51/G4 Süntel (mts.), Ger.
99/E5 Sunyani, Gha.
101/A5 Sunzu (peak), Zam.
78/B4 Suo (sea), Japan
83/D1 Suoi Rut, Viet.
42/H3 Suomenselkä (reg.), Fin.
83/D4 Suong, Camb.
108/C6 Supe, Peru
126/C2 Superior (lake), Can., US
124/E4 Superior, Az,US
122/E4 Superior, Mt,US
126/A2 Superior, Wi,US
126/B2 Superior (upland), Wi,US
83/C3 Suphan Buri, Thai.
87/J4 Supiori (isl.), Indo.
72/E2 Sūq ash Shuyūkh, Iraq
74/L4 Şuqaylabīyah, Syria
81/D4 Suqian, China
113/F3 Sur (pt.), Arg.
53/E4 Sûr (riv.), Belg.
124/B3 Sur (pt.), Ca,US
67/H1 Sura (riv.), Rus.
86/D5 Surabaya, Indo.
84/D4 Surada, India
86/D5 Surakarta, Indo.
82/D6 Surallah, Phil.
49/K4 Šurany, Slvk.
84/B3 Surat, India
84/B2 Suratgarh, India
83/B4 Surat Thani, Thai.
53/G6 Surbourg, Fr.
113/J7 Sur, Campo de Hielo (glacier), Chile
62/E3 Surčin, Yugo.
62/F4 Surdulica, Yugo.
53/E4 Sûre (riv.), Belg., Lux.
84/B3 Surendranagar, India
56/C3 Surgères, Fr.
68/H3 Surgut, Rus.
84/E3 Sūri, India
59/F2 Súria, Sp.
82/E6 Surigao, Phil.
83/C3 Surin, Thai.
109/G3 Suriname
75/A4 Surkhob (riv.), Taj.
131/K8 Surrattsville (Clinton), Md,US
122/C3 Surrey, BC,Can
47/F4 Surrey (co.), Eng,UK
96/J1 Surt, Libya
42/D3 Sur-Trøndelag (co.), Nor.
74/K5 Şūr (Tyre), Leb.
74/D3 Sürüç, Turk.
79/F3 Suruga (bay), Japan
60/B5 Sūsah, Tun.
60/B5 Sūsah (gov.), Tun.
78/C4 Susaki, Japan
72/E2 Sūsangerd, Iran
124/B2 Susanville, Ca,US
74/D2 Suşehri, Turk.
81/B4 Sushui (riv.), China
130/J3 Susitna (riv.), Ak,US
79/F3 Susono, Japan
126/E3 Susquehanna (riv.), US
127/H2 Sussex, NB,Can
47/F4 Sussex, Vale of (val.), Eng,UK
50/C6 Susteren, Neth.
69/Q3 Susuman, Rus.
90/H9 Sutherland, Austl.
62/D4 Sutjeska Nat'l Park, Bosn.
73/K2 Sutlej (riv.), India, Pak.
45/H6 Sutterton, Eng,UK
45/J6 Sutton Bridge, Eng,UK
47/E1 Sutton Coldfield, Eng,UK
45/G5 Sutton in Ashfield, Eng,UK
45/J5 Sutton on Sea, Eng,UK
45/H5 Sutton on Trent, Eng,UK
102/D4 Suurberge (mts.), SAfr.
92/G6 Suva (cap.), Fiji
79/F2 Suwa, Japan
49/M1 Suwałki, Pol.
49/M2 Suwałki (prov.), Pol.
129/H4 Suwannee (riv.), Fl,US
93/J6 Suwarrow (atoll), Cookls.
74/K5 Şuwaylih, Jor.
81/D4 Suzhou, China
81/E5 Suzhou, China
79/E2 Suzu, Japan
78/E3 Suzuka, Japan
79/M10 Suzuka (range), Japan
79/E2 Suzu-misaki (cape), Japan
57/J4 Suzzara, It.
68/C2 Svalbard (arch.), Nor.
83/D4 Svay Rieng, Camb.
42/E4 Svealand (reg.), Swe.
48/F1 Svendborg, Den.
119/S7 Svendsen (pen.), Nun.,Can
42/E4 Svenljunga, Swe.
65/P4 Sverdlovsk (Yekaterinburg), Rus.
65/P4 Sverdlovsk Obl., Rus.
119/S7 Sverdrup (chan.), Nun.,Can
119/R7 Sverdrup (isls.), Nun.,Can
68/H2 Sverdrup (isl.), Rus.
66/D1 Svetlogorsk, Bela.
67/G3 Svetlograd, Rus.
62/E4 Svetozarevo, Yugo.
42/P7 Svíahnúkar (peak), Ice.
62/E3 Svilajnac, Yugo.
63/H5 Svilengrad, Bul.
63/G4 Svishtov, Bul.
49/J4 Svitavy, Czh.
77/K1 Svobodnyy, Rus.
63/F4 Svoge, Bul.
42/E1 Svolvær, Nor.
69/Q2 Svyatyy Nos (cape), Rus.
47/E1 Swadlincote, Eng,UK
47/G1 Swaffham, Eng,UK
90/D3 Swain (reefs), Austl.
129/H3 Swainsboro, Ga,US
93/H5 Swains Island (atoll), ASam.
104/C2 Swa-Kibula, D.R. Congo
104/B5 Swakopmund, Namb.
45/G3 Swale (riv.), Eng,UK
47/H4 Swalecliffe, Eng,UK
47/G4 Swale, The (chan.), Eng,UK
50/D6 Swalmen, Neth.
122/D2 Swan (hills), Ab,Can
123/H2 Swan (riv.), Mb, Sk,Can
116/E4 Swan (isls.), Hon.
47/E5 Swanage, Eng,UK
91/B2 Swan Hill, Austl.
47/G4 Swanley-Hextable, Eng,UK
123/H2 Swan River, Mb,Can
46/C3 Swansea, Wal,UK
46/C3 Swansea (bay), Wal,UK
46/B3 Swansea (co.), Wal,UK
131/E6 Swarthmore, Pa,US
102/D3 Swart Kei (riv.), SAfr
49/J2 Swarzędz, Pol.
102/B2 Swarzrand (mts.), Namb.
44/B2 Swatragh, NI,UK
47/E5 Sway, Eng,UK
103/E2 Swaziland
42/E3 Sweden
122/C4 Sweet Home, Or,US
128/C3 Sweetwater, Tx,US
122/F5 Sweetwater (riv.), Wy,US
102/C4 Swellendam, SAfr.
49/J3 Świdnica, Pol.
49/M3 Świdnik, Pol.
49/H2 Świdwin, Pol.
49/J3 Świebodzice, Pol.
49/H2 Świebodzin, Pol.
49/K2 Świecie, Pol.
122/G3 Swift Current, Sk,Can
47/E3 Swindon, Eng,UK
47/E3 Swindon (co.), Eng,UK
45/H6 Swineshead, Eng,UK
49/H2 Świnoujście, Pol.
45/G5 Swinton, Eng,UK
54/D4 Swiss (plat.), Swi.
53/F2 Swist Bach (riv.), Ger.
54/D4 Switzerland
44/B5 Swords, Ire.
64/G3 Syamozero (lake), Rus.
49/J3 Syców, Pol.
90/H8 Sydney, Austl.
127/J2 Sydney, NS,Can
93/H5 Sydney (Manra) (atoll), Kiri.
127/J2 Sydney Mines, NS,Can
51/F3 Syke, Ger.
65/L3 Syktyvkar, Rus.
129/G3 Sylacauga, Al,US
42/E3 Sylarna (peak), Swe.
85/F3 Sylhet, Bang.
48/E1 Sylt (isl.), Ger.
65/N4 Sylva (riv.), Rus.
126/D3 Sylvania, Oh,US
132/F6 Sylvan Lake, Mi,US
61/L6 Syntagma Square, Gre.
131/G5 Syosset, NY,US
105/C Syowa, Ant.
125/G3 Syracuse, Ks,US
126/E3 Syracuse, NY,US
60/D4 Syracuse (Siracusa), It.
68/G5 Syrdar'ya (riv.), Asia
72/C1 Syria
85/G4 Syriam, Burma
65/L3 Sysola (riv.), Rus.
47/E1 Syston, Eng,UK
67/J1 Syzran', Rus.
62/E1 Szabolcs-Szatmár-Bereg (co.), Hun.
49/J2 Szamotuły, Pol.
62/E2 Szarvas, Hun.
62/D2 Százhalombatta, Hun.
49/H2 Szczecin, Pol.
49/H2 Szczecin (prov.), Pol.
49/J2 Szczecinek, Pol.
49/L2 Szczytno, Pol.
62/E2 Szeged, Hun.
62/D2 Szeghalom, Hun.
62/E2 Szegvár, Hun.
62/D2 Székesfehérvár, Hun.
62/D2 Szekszárd, Hun.
62/D2 Szentendre, Hun.
62/E2 Szentes, Hun.
62/E1 Szerencs, Hun.
49/M1 Szeskie (peak), Pol.
62/C2 Szigetvár, Hun.
62/E2 Szolnok, Hun.
62/C2 Szombathely, Hun.
49/H3 Szprotawa, Pol.
49/K2 Sztum, Pol.
49/J2 Szubin, Pol.
49/L3 Szydłowiec, Pol.

T

82/D5 Tabaco, Phil.
73/G2 Tabas, Iran
116/C4 Tabasco (state), Mex.
109/K6 Tabatinga (mts.), Braz.
122/E3 Taber, Ab,Can
59/E3 Tabernes de Valldigna, Sp.
92/G5 Tabiteuea (atoll), Kiri.
82/D5 Tablas (isl.), Phil.
102/B4 Table (bay), SAfr.
102/L10 Table (mtn.), SAfr.
125/J3 Table Rock (lake), Ar, Mo,US
58/B1 Taboada, Sp.
57/L2 Tábor, Czh.
101/B4 Tabora, Tanz.
101/B4 Tabora (prov.), Tanz.
98/D5 Tabou, IvC.
93/K4 Tabuaeran (Fanning) (atoll), Kiri.
82/D4 Tabuk, Phil.
72/C3 Tabūk, SAr.
92/F6 Tabwemasana (mtn.), Van.
117/F6 Tacarcuna (mt.), Pan.
75/D2 Tacheng, China
82/D3 Tachia (riv.), Tai.
78/A4 Tachibana (bay), Japan
79/F3 Tachikawa, Japan
82/D3 Tachoshui, Tai.
57/K2 Tachov, Czh.
82/E5 Tacloban, Phil.
108/D7 Tacna, Peru
132/C3 Tacoma, Wa,US
108/E7 Tacora (vol.), Chile
59/X16 Tacoronte, Canl.,Sp.
113/G1 Tacuarembó, Uru.
113/G2 Tacuarembó (dept.), Uru.
79/F2 Tadami (riv.), Japan
79/L10 Tadaoka, Japan
45/G4 Tadcaster, Eng,UK
96/F2 Tademaït (plat.), Alg.
84/D4 Tādepallegūdem, India
93/V12 Tadine, NCal.
47/E4 Tadley, Eng,UK
72/C2 Tadmur, Syria
79/M9 Tado, Japan
78/C3 Tadotsu, Japan
84/C5 Tādpatri, India
96/H2 Tadrart (mts.), Alg., Libya
80/D3 T'aebaek (mts.), NKor., SKor.
80/D4 Taech'ŏn, SKor.
80/D3 Taegang-got (pt.), NKor.
80/E5 Taegu, SKor.
80/E5 Taegu-Jikhalsi (prov.), SKor.
80/D4 Taejŏn, SKor.
46/B3 Taf (riv.), Wal,UK
58/E1 Tafalla, Sp.
46/C3 Taff (riv.), Wal,UK
111/C2 Tafí Viejo, Arg.
72/F2 Taft, Iran
73/H3 Taftān (mtn.), Iran
79/M9 Taga, Japan
66/F3 Taganrog, Rus.
66/F3 Taganrog (gulf), Rus., Ukr.
98/C2 Tagant (reg.), Mrta.
73/G1 Tagarav (peak), Trkm.
78/B4 Tagawa, Japan
82/D6 Tagbilaran, Phil.
57/G5 Taggia, It.
96/E1 Taghit, Alg.
130/M3 Tagish, Yk,Can
57/K3 Tagliamento (riv.), It.
52/D5 Tagnon, Fr.
87/F2 Tagolo (pt.), Phil.
109/J7 Taguatinga, Braz.
87/G4 Tagula (isl.), PNG
82/E6 Tagum, Phil.
65/P4 Tagun (riv.), Rus.
58/B3 Tagus (riv.), Port., Sp.
86/B3 Tahan (peak), Malay.
79/N10 Tahara, Japan
96/G3 Tahat (peak), Alg.
93/L6 Tahenea (atoll), FrPol.
93/L6 Tahiti (isl.), FrPol.
128/E3 Tahlequah, Ok,US
130/J3 Tahneta (pass), Ak,US
124/C3 Tahoe (lake), Ca, Nv,US
128/C3 Tahoka, Tx,US
99/G3 Tahoua, Niger
99/G3 Tahoua (dept.), Niger
122/B3 Tahsis, BC,Can
100/B3 Tahta, Egypt
93/L6 Tahuata (isl.), FrPol.
87/G3 Tahulandang (isl.), Indo.
81/L8 Tai (lake), China
77/H4 Tai'an, China
93/X15 Taiarapu (pen.), FrPol.
81/C3 Taibai Shan (mtn.), China
82/D3 T'aichung, Tai.
81/C3 Taihang (mts.), China
82/D3 Taihsi, Tai.
79/L10 Taima, Japan
43/C2 Tain, Sc,UK
82/D3 T'ainan, Tai.
61/H4 Tainaron, Ákra (cape), Gre.
98/D5 Taï Nat'l Park, IvC.
93/L5 Taiohae, FrPol.
82/D2 T'aipei (cap.), Tai.
77/J2 Taiping (peak), China
86/B3 Taiping, Malay.
78/C3 Taisha, Japan
79/L10 Taishi, Japan
82/C2 Taishun, China
112/B5 Taitao (pen.), Chile
82/D3 Taitung, Tai.
82/D3 Taiwan
82/C3 Taiwan (str.), China, Tai.
61/H4 Taíyetos (mts.), Gre.
81/C3 Taiyuan, China
81/D4 Taizhou, China
81/E2 Taizi (riv.), China
86/C4 Tajam (peak), Indo.
96/H3 Tajarhī, Libya
68/H6 Tajikistan
79/F2 Tajima, Japan
79/E3 Tajimi, Japan
79/L10 Tajiri, Japan
58/C3 Tajo (Tagus) (riv.), Sp.
72/F1 Tajrīsh, Iran
116/C4 Tajumulco (vol.), Guat.
58/D2 Tajuña (riv.), Sp.
83/B2 Tak, Thai.
79/G2 Takahagi, Japan
78/D3 Takahama, Japan
78/C3 Takahashi, Japan
78/C3 Takahashi (riv.), Japan
79/G2 Takahata, Japan
79/L10 Takaishi, Japan
78/D3 Takamatsu, Japan
79/M10 Takami-yama (peak), Japan
78/B4 Takanabe, Japan
79/E2 Takaoka, Japan
89/H6 Takapuna, NZ
79/L10 Takarazuka, Japan
93/L6 Takaroa (isl.), FrPol.
79/F2 Takasaki, Japan
79/M9 Takashima, Japan
79/L10 Takatori, Japan
78/D3 Takatsuki, Japan
79/E2 Takayama, Japan
78/E3 Takefu, Japan
78/C3 Takehara, Japan
72/E1 Tākestān, Iran
78/B4 Taketa, Japan
79/M10 Taketoyo, Japan
83/D4 Takev, Camb.
85/H4 Ta Khli, Thai.
97/R2 Takht-e Jamshīd (Persepolis) (ruins), Iran
79/M10 Taki, Japan
118/E2 Takijuq (lake), Nun.,Can
77/N3 Takikawa, Japan
79/K10 Takino, Japan
122/B2 Takla (lake), BC,Can
75/D4 Takla Makan (des.), China
99/E5 Takoradi, Gha.
74/H6 Talā, Egypt
45/E5 Talacre, Wal,UK
112/Q9 Talagante, Chile
84/B3 Talāja, India
99/G2 Talak (reg.), Niger
104/C2 Tala Mugongo, Ang.
86/B4 Talang (peak), Indo.
53/F5 Talange, Fr.
54/A3 Talant, Fr.
108/B4 Talara, Peru
75/B3 Talas (riv.), Kaz.
74/C2 Talas, Turk.
87/G3 Talaud (isls.), Indo.
58/C3 Talavera de la Reina, Sp.
84/D6 Talawakele, SrL.
97/M5 Talawdī, Sudan
58/C3 Talayuela, Sp.
112/C2 Talca, Chile
112/B3 Talcahuano, Chile
84/E3 Tālcher, India
75/C3 Taldyqorghan, Kaz.
56/C4 Talence, Fr.
68/H5 Talgar, Kaz.
46/C3 Talgarth, Wal,UK
87/F4 Taliabu (isl.), Indo.
97/M6 Tali Post, Sudan
87/E5 Taliwang, Indo.
74/H6 Talkhā, Egypt
129/G3 Talladega, Al,US
74/E3 Tall 'Afar, Iraq
129/G4 Tallahassee (cap.), Fl,US
129/F3 Tallahatchie (riv.), Ms,US
74/N9 Tall 'Āsūr (Ba'al Hazor) (mtn.), WBnk.
131/E6 Talleyville, De,US
64/E4 Tallinn (cap.), Est.
74/E3 Tall Kayf, Iraq
129/H3 Tallulah (falls), Ga,US
129/F3 Tallulah, La,US
97/N5 Talo (peak), Eth.
84/B3 Taloda, India
73/J1 Tāloqān, Afg.
111/B2 Taltal, Chile
118/E2 Taltson (riv.), NW,Can
83/C4 Talumphuk (pt.), Thai.
73/L2 Talwāra, India
79/H7 Tama, Japan
79/H7 Tama (riv.), Japan
79/M10 Tamaki, Japan
99/E4 Tamale, Gha.
92/G5 Tamana (atoll), Kiri.
96/G3 Tamanghasset, Alg.
46/B5 Tamar (riv.), Eng,UK
62/D2 Tamási, Hun.
116/B3 Tamazunchale, Mex.
79/L9 Tamba, Japan
79/L9 Tamba (hills), Japan
98/B3 Tambacounda, Sen.
98/B3 Tambacounda (reg.), Sen.
98/C3 Tambaoura, Falaise de (escarp.), Mali
86/C3 Tambelan (isls.), Indo.
87/E5 Tambora (peak), Indo.
91/C3 Tamboritha (peak), Austl.
67/G1 Tambov, Rus.
67/G1 Tambov Obl., Rus.
58/A1 Tambre (riv.), Sp.
97/L6 Tambura, Sudan
47/E1 Tame (riv.), Eng,UK
58/B2 Tâmega (riv.), Port.
99/H2 Tamgak (peak), Niger
98/B3 Tamgue, Massif du (reg.), Gui., Sen.
84/C5 Tamil Nadu (state), India
83/E3 Tam Ky, Viet.
83/D2 Tam Le, Viet.
129/H5 Tampa, Fl,US
42/G3 Tampere, Fin.
116/B3 Tampico, Mex.
86/A3 Tampulonanjing (peak), Indo.
116/B3 Tamuín, Mex.
116/B3 Tamaulipas (state), Mex.
91/D1 Tamworth, Austl.
47/E1 Tamworth, Eng,UK
85/K3 Tan (riv.), China
97/N5 Tana (lake), Eth.
101/C3 Tana (riv.), Kenya
42/H1 Tana (riv.), Nor.
78/D4 Tanabe, Japan
110/B2 Tanabi, Braz.
42/J1 Tanafjorden (fjord), Nor.
130/C6 Tanaga (isl.), Ak,US
60/D2 Tanagro (riv.), It.
79/G2 Tanagura, Japan
83/C5 Tanah Merah, Malay.
83/D4 Tan An, Viet.
130/J3 Tanana (riv.), Ak,US
57/H4 Tanaro (riv.), It.
84/C2 Tānda, India
84/D2 Tānda, India
98/D3 Tanda (lake), Mali
97/M5 Tandaltī, Sudan
63/H3 Țăndărei, Rom.
112/F3 Tandil, Arg.
73/J3 Tando Ādam, Pak.
73/J3 Tando Allāhyār, Pak.
73/J3 Tando Muhammad Khān, Pak.
91/B2 Tandou (lake), Austl.
44/B3 Tandragee, NI,UK
78/B5 Tanega (isl.), Japan
83/B2 Tanem (range), Burma, Thai.
96/E3 Tanezrouft (des.), Alg., Mali
81/C3 Tang (riv.), China
81/C4 Tang (riv.), China
101/C4 Tanga, Tanz.
101/C4 Tanga (prov.), Tanz.
103/H8 Tangainony, Madg.
101/A4 Tanganyika (lake), Afr.
109/G6 Tangará da Serra, Braz.
130/G1 Tangent (pt.), Ak,US
48/F2 Tangerhütte, Ger.
75/E5 Tanggula (mts.), China
75/F5 Tanggula Shankou (pass), China
96/D1 Tangier (Tanger), Mor.
132/B3 Tanglewilde-Thompson Place, Wa,US
75/E5 Tangra (lake), China
62/D6 Tangub, Phil.
87/H5 Tanimbar (isls.), Indo.
82/D6 Tanjay, Phil.
86/A3 Tanjungbalai, Indo.
86/C5 Tanjungkarang-Telukbetung, Indo.
86/C4 Tanjungpandan, Indo.
86/A3 Tanjungpura, Indo.
73/K2 Tānk, Pak.
92/F6 Tanna (isl.), Van.
79/L9 Tannan, Japan
75/F1 Tannu-Ola (mts.), Mong., Rus.
99/E5 Tano (riv.), Ghana, IvC.
74/H6 Ţanţā, Egypt
97/M1 Ţanţā, Egypt
96/C2 Tan-Tan, Mor.
116/B3 Tantoyuca, Mex.
84/D4 Tanuku, India
101/B4 Tanzania
79/H7 Tanzawa-yama (peak), Japan
82/B2 Tao (riv.), China
83/B4 Tao (isl.), Thai.
77/J2 Tao'er (riv.), China
63/D4 Taormina, It.
125/F3 Taos, NM,US
96/E3 Taoudenni, Mali
82/B2 Taoyuan, China
82/D3 Taoyuan, Tai.
64/E4 Tapa, Est.
116/C5 Tapachula, Mex.
109/G4 Tapajós (riv.), Braz.
109/G3 Tapanahoni (riv.), Sur.
108/E5 Tapauá (riv.), Braz.
82/D5 Tapaz, Phil.
110/B4 Tapejara, Braz.
110/B4 Tapes, Braz.
86/B3 Tapis (peak), Malay.
99/F3 Tapoa (prov.), Burk.
62/C2 Tapolca, Hun.
126/E4 Tappahannock, Va,US
131/G4 Tappan, NY,US
131/G4 Tappan Zee (reach), NY,US
132/C3 Tapps (lake), Wa,US
84/B3 Tāpti (riv.), India
100/B5 Taqab, Sudan
100/D5 Taqātu' Hayyā, Sudan
110/B4 Taquara, Braz.
110/B4 Taquari, Braz.
109/G7 Taquari (riv.), Braz.
110/B2 Taquaritinga, Braz.
110/B2 Taquarituba, Braz.
75/B3 Tar (riv.), Kyr.
62/D4 Tara (riv.), Bosn., Yugo.
68/H4 Tara, Rus.
99/H4 Taraba (riv.), Nga.
74/K4 Ţarābulus (Tripoli), Leb.
96/H1 Ţarābulus (Tripoli) (cap.), Libya
44/B4 Tara, Hill of (hill), Ire.
87/E3 Tarakan, Indo.
58/D2 Tarancón, Sp.
101/B3 Tarangire Nat'l Park, Tanz.
60/E2 Taranto, It.
60/E3 Taranto (gulf), It.
108/C5 Tarapoto, Peru
56/F4 Tarare, Fr.
56/F5 Tarascon, Fr.
108/D5 Tarauacá, Braz.
93/M7 Taravai (isl.), FrPol.
92/G4 Tarawa (atoll), Kiri.
92/G4 Tarawa (cap.), Kiri.
58/E2 Tarazona, Sp.
58/E3 Tarazona de la Mancha, Sp.
75/D2 Tarbagatay (mts.), Kaz.
73/K2 Tarbela (res.), Pak.
56/D5 Tarbes, Fr.
129/J3 Tarboro, NC,US
62/A2 Tarcento, It.
56/E3 Tardes (riv.), Fr.
56/D4 Tardoire (riv.), Fr.
77/M2 Tardoki-Jani (peak), Rus.
91/E1 Taree, Austl.
100/C2 Ţarfā', Wādī al (dry riv.), Egypt
100/B4 Tarfāwī, Bi'r (well), Egypt
44/D2 Tarf Water (riv.), Sc,UK
96/H1 Tarhūnah, Libya
58/C4 Tarifa, Sp.
108/F8 Tarija, Bol.
87/J4 Tariku (riv.), Indo.
87/J4 Tariku-taritatu (plain), Indo.
76/B4 Tarim (basin), China
75/D3 Tarim (riv.), China
73/J2 Tarin (riv.), Afg.
87/J4 Taritatu (riv.), Indo.
66/E3 Tarkhankut, Mys (cape), Ukr.
99/E5 Tarkwa, Gha.
82/D4 Tarlac, Phil.
108/C6 Tarma, Peru
56/D5 Tarn (riv.), Fr.
76/E2 Tarna (riv.), Mong.
73/J2 Tarnak (riv.), Afg.
49/L3 Tarnobrzeg, Pol.
49/L3 Tarnobrzeg (prov.), Pol.
49/L3 Tarnów, Pol.
49/L3 Tarnów (prov.), Pol.
75/D5 Taro (lake), China
57/J4 Taro (riv.), It.
96/D1 Taroudannt, Mor.
129/H4 Tarpon Springs, Fl,US
45/F5 Tarporley, Eng,UK
60/B1 Tarquinia, It.
59/F2 Tarragona, Sp.
59/F2 Tàrrega, Sp.
131/G4 Tarrytown, NY,US
74/C3 Tarsus, Turk.
64/E4 Tartu, Est.
74/K4 Ţarţūs, Syria
74/K4 Ţarţūs (dist.), Syria
79/M9 Tarui, Japan
78/B5 Tarumizu, Japan
83/B5 Tarutao Nat'l Park, Thai.
76/D2 Tarvagatay (mts.), Mong.
45/F5 Tarvin, Eng,UK
83/D3 Ta Seng, Camb.
75/E2 Tashanta, Rus.
68/F5 Tashauz, Trkm.
67/L4 Tashauz Obl., Trkm.
75/A3 Tashkent (cap.), Uzb.
75/B3 Tash-Kumyr, Kyr.
86/C5 Tasikmalaya, Indo.
74/C3 Taşkent, Turk.
74/C2 Taşköprü, Turk.
92/E8 Tasman (sea)
91/C4 Tasman (pen.), Austl.
91/C4 Tasman Head (cape), Austl.
91/C4 Tasmania (state), Austl.
62/F2 Tăşnad, Rom.
62/D2 Tata, Hun.
96/D2 Tata, Mor.
62/D2 Tatabánya, Hun.
126/D2 Tatachikapika (riv.), On,Can
93/M6 Tatakoto (isl.), FrPol.
76/D4 Tatalin (riv.), China
77/N2 Tatar (str.), Rus.
65/L5 Tatarstan Aut. Rep., Rus.
68/H4 Tatarsk, Rus.
96/H1 Tatāwīn, Tun.
79/F3 Tateyama, Japan
79/E2 Tate-yama (mtn.), Japan
118/E2 Tathlina (lake), NW,Can
98/B2 Tatilt (well), Mrta.
118/G3 Tatnam (cape), Mb,Can
99/H3 Tatokou, Niger
49/K4 Tatranský Nat'l Park, Slvk.
49/K4 Tatrzański Nat'l Park, Pol.
47/G4 Tatsfield, Eng,UK
79/E3 Tatsuno, Japan
45/H5 Tattershall, Eng,UK
74/E2 Tatvan, Turk.
109/K5 Tauá, Braz.
110/H8 Taubaté, Braz.
57/H2 Tauberbischofsheim, Ger.
57/K3 Tauern, Hohe (mts.), Aus.
57/K2 Taufkirchen, Ger.
125/K3 Taum Sauk (peak), Mo,US
85/G3 Taungdwingyi, Burma
83/B1 Taunggyi, Burma
73/K2 Taunsa, Pak.
127/S8 Taunton, On,Can
46/C4 Taunton, Eng,UK
127/G3 Taunton, Ma,US
57/H1 Taunusstein, Ger.
89/H6 Taupo, NZ
49/M1 Tauragė, Lith.
89/H6 Tauranga, NZ
56/D3 Taurion (riv.), Fr.
74/C3 Taurus (mts.), Turk.
58/E2 Tauste, Sp.
56/C2 Taute (riv.), Fr.
93/X15 Tautira, FrPol.
92/E5 Tauu (isls.), PNG
124/E3 Tavaputs (plat.), Ut,US
129/H4 Tavares, Fl,US
74/B3 Tavas, Turk.
65/Q4 Tavda (riv.), Rus.
47/H1 Taverham, Eng,UK
52/B5 Taverny, Fr.
93/Z17 Taveuni (isl.), Fiji
58/B4 Tavira, Port.
46/B5 Tavistock, Eng,UK
83/B3 Tavoy, Burma
77/L3 Tavrichanka, Rus.
74/B2 Tavşanlı, Turk.
46/B5 Tavy (riv.), Eng,UK
46/B4 Taw (riv.), Eng,UK
126/D2 Tawas City, Mi,US
79/L10 Tawaramoto, Japan
87/E3 Tawau, Malay.
46/C3 Tawe (riv.), Wal,UK
82/C6 Tawi-tawi (isl.), Phil.
100/D5 Ţawkar, Sudan
96/G1 Tawzar, Tun.
116/B4 Taxco, Mex.
73/K2 Taxila (ruins), Pak.
75/C4 Taxkorgan (Taxkorgan Tajik Zizhixian), China
43/D2 Tay (riv.), Sc,UK
43/C2 Tay, Loch (lake), Sc,UK
125/H2 Taylor, Ne,US
126/B4 Taylorville, Il,US
69/L2 Taymyr (lake), Rus.
68/K2 Taymyr (pen.), Rus.
68/K2 Taymyr (riv.), Rus.
68/J2 Taymyr Aut. Okr., Rus.
83/D4 Tay Ninh, Viet.
68/K4 Tayshet, Rus.
82/C5 Taytay, Phil.
68/J3 Taz (riv.), Rus.
96/B1 Taza, Mor.
129/H2 Tazewell, Tn,US
126/D4 Tazewell, Va,US
97/K2 Tāzirbū (oasis), Libya
116/D5 Tazumal (ruins), ESal.
67/H4 T'bilisi (cap.), Geo.
104/B1 Tchibanga, Gabon
96/H6 Tcholliré, Camr.
49/K1 Tczew, Pol.
108/E4 Tea (riv.), Braz.
45/H5 Tealby, Eng,UK
89/G7 Te Anau, NZ
131/F5 Teaneck, NJ,US
116/C4 Teapa, Mex.
86/B4 Tebak (peak), Indo.
96/G1 Tébessa, Alg.
99/F2 Tebesselamane (well), Mali
111/E2 Tebicuary (riv.), Par.
86/A3 Tebingtinggi, Indo.
67/H4 Tebulos-mta (peak), Rus.
59/E5 Tech (riv.), Fr.
63/J3 Techirghiol, Rom.
112/C4 Tecka (riv.), Arg.
117/P10 Tecomán, Mex.
117/N9 Tecuala, Mex.
63/H3 Tecuci, Rom.
132/G7 Tecumseh, On,Can
126/D3 Tecumseh, Mi,US

178

Tecum – Torre

125/H2 Tecumseh, Ne,US
73/H1 Tedzhen, Trkm.
68/G6 Tedzhen (riv.), Trkm.
45/G2 Tees (bay), Eng,UK
45/G2 Tees (riv.), Eng,UK
108/F4 Tefé, Braz.
108/E4 Tefé (riv.), Braz.
86/C5 Tegal, Indo.
50/D6 Tegelen, Neth.
96/H2 Tegheri (well), Libya
44/E6 Tegid, Llyn (lake), Wal,UK
99/H3 Tégouma (wadi), Niger
116/D5 Tegucigalpa (cap.), Hon.
118/G2 Tehek (lake), Nun.,Can
72/F1 Tehrān (cap.), Iran
75/C5 Tehri, India
116/B4 Tehuacán, Mex.
116/C4 Tehuantepec (gulf), Mex.
116/C4 Tehuantepec (isth.), Mex.
59/X16 Teide (peak), Canl.,Sp.
46/B2 Teifi (riv.), Wal,UK
97/L4 Teiga (plat.), Sudan
46/C5 Teignmouth, Eng,UK
58/B3 Tejo (Tagus) (riv.), Port.
125/H2 Tekamah, Ne,US
89/H6 Te Kao, NZ
116/D3 Tekax, Mex.
75/C3 Tekeli, Kaz.
75/D3 Tekes (riv.), China
72/C6 Tekezē Wenz (reg.), Eth.
97/N5 Tekezē Wenz (riv.), Eth., Sudan
75/D4 Tekiliktag (peak), China
63/H5 Tekirdağ, Turk.
84/D4 Tekkali, India
84/D3 Tel (riv.), India
116/D4 Tela, Hon.
67/H4 Telavi, Geo.
74/K5 Tel Aviv (dist.), Isr.
74/K5 Tel Aviv-Yafo, Isr.
59/X17 Telde, Canl.
98/E2 Télé (lake), Mali
75/G2 Telem (lake), Mong.
110/B3 Telemaco Borba, Braz.
42/D4 Telemark (co.), Nor.
87/E3 Telen (riv.), Indo.
63/G4 Teleorman (co.), Rom.
96/G3 Telertheba (peak), Alg.
109/G5 Teles Pires (riv.), Braz.
46/D1 Telford, Eng,UK
45/F6 Telford and Wrekin (co.), Eng,UK
54/H3 Telfs, Aus.
51/E5 Telgte, Ger.
98/B4 Télimélé, Gui.
74/N9 Tel Jericho Nat'l Park, WBnk.
122/B2 Telkwa, BC,Can
126/C4 Tell City, In,US
84/C5 Tellicherry, India
124/F3 Telluride, Co,US
74/N7 Tel Megiddo Nat'l Park, Isr.
76/D2 Telmen (lake), Mong.
86/B3 Telok Anson, Malay.
75/E1 Telotskoye (lake), Rus.
64/D5 Telšiai, Lith.
49/G2 Teltow (reg.), Ger.
99/E5 Tema, Gha.
126/D2 Temagami (lake), On,Can
102/E2 Tembisa, SAfr.
117/J6 Temblador, Ven.
104/C2 Tembo, D.R. Congo
46/D2 Teme (riv.), Eng,UK
62/D3 Temerin, Yugo.
86/B3 Temerloh, Malay.
75/B1 Temirtau, Kaz.
127/F1 Témiscamie (riv.), Qu,Can
126/E2 Témiscaming, Qu,Can
76/E1 Temnik (riv.), Rus.
93/M7 Temoe (isl.), FrPol.
124/E4 Tempe, Az,US
60/A2 Tempio Pausania, It.
128/D4 Temple, Tx,US
44/B2 Templepatrick, NI,UK
91/G5 Templestowe, Austl.
49/G2 Templin, Ger.
116/B3 Tempoal, Mex.
104/C3 Tempué, Ang.
66/F3 Temryuk, Rus.
52/D1 Temse, Belg.
112/B3 Temuco, Chile
96/D5 Tena Kourou (peak), Burk.
84/D4 Tenāli, India
83/B3 Tenasserim (range), Burma
83/B4 Tenasserim (Thanintharyi) (div.), Burma
50/D2 Ten Boer, Neth.
46/D2 Tenbury, Eng,UK
46/B3 Tenby, Wal,UK
97/P5 Tendaho, Eth.
79/G1 Tendō, Japan
96/G3 Ténéré du Tafassasset (des.), Niger
99/H2 Ténéré, 'Erg du (des.), Niger
59/X16 Tenerife (isl.), Canl.
59/L6 Tenes (riv.), Sp.
83/B1 Teng (riv.), Burma
87/E4 Tenggarong, Indo.
76/E4 Tengger (des.), China
75/A1 Tengiz (lake), Kaz.
57/G4 Tenibres (peak), It.
111/D1 Teniente Enciso Nat'l Park, Par.
62/D3 Tenja, Cro.
99/E4 Tenkodogo, Burk.
129/F2 Tennessee (riv.), US
129/G3 Tennessee (state), US
112/C2 Teno, Chile
42/H1 Tenojoki (riv.), Fin.
116/C4 Tenosique, Mex.
79/L10 Tenri, Japan
79/E3 Tenryū (riv.), Japan
47/G4 Tenterden, Eng,UK
83/B2 Ten Thousand Buddhas, Cave of, Burma
87/F3 Tentolomatinan (peak), Indo.
58/A1 Teo, Sp.
116/A3 Teocaltiche, Mex.
110/A2 Teodoro Sampaio, Braz.
110/D1 Teófilo Otoni, Braz.
117/P9 Tepatitlán de Morelos, Mex.
117/P9 Tepic, Mex.
49/G3 Teplice, Czh.
117/M7 Tepoca (cape), Mex.
93/L6 Tepoto (isl.), FrPol.
117/P9 Tequila, Mex.
59/G1 Ter (riv.), Sp.
99/F3 Téra, Niger
58/B1 Tera (riv.), Sp.
50/B4 Ter Aar, Neth.
93/K4 Teraina (Washington) (atoll), Kiri.
60/C1 Teramo, It.
74/E2 Tercan, Turk.
59/S12 Terceira (isl.), Azor.,Port.
112/E2 Tercero (riv.), Arg.
63/K2 Terderovsk (bay), Ukr.
67/H4 Terek (riv.), Rus.
109/K5 Teresina, Braz.
110/L7 Teresópolis, Braz.
52/C4 Tergnier, Fr.
76/D4 Tergun Daba (mts.), China
50/B5 Terheijden, Neth.
64/G1 Teriberskiy, Mys (pt.), Rus.
50/C2 Terkaplesterpoelen (lake), Neth.
63/H5 Terkirdağ (prov.), Turk.
73/J1 Termez, Uzb.
60/C4 Termini Imerese, It.
116/C4 Términos (lag.), Mex.
124/B2 Termo, Ca,US
60/D1 Termoli, It.
46/D1 Tern (riv.), Eng,UK
87/G3 Ternate, Indo.
50/A6 Terneuzen, Neth.
60/C1 Terni, It.
56/F3 Ternin (riv.), Fr.
52/B3 Ternoise (riv.), Fr.
66/C2 Ternopil', Ukr.
66/C2 Ternopil's'ka (obl), Ukr.
77/N2 Terpeniya (bay), Rus.
122/A2 Terrace, BC,Can
126/C1 Terrace Bay, On,Can
60/C2 Terracina, It.
127/Q8 Terra Cotta, On,Can
60/A3 Terralba, It.
127/L1 Terra Nova Nat'l Park, Nf,Can
59/G2 Terrassa, Sp.
56/D4 Terrasson-la-Villedieu, Fr.
127/N6 Terrebonne, Qu,Can
129/G2 Terre Haute, In,US
90/H8 Terrey Hills, Austl.
47/G1 Terrington Saint Clement, Eng,UK
123/G4 Terry, Mt,US
75/A1 Tersakkan (riv.), Kaz.
50/C2 Terschelling (isl.), Neth.
59/E2 Teruel, Sp.
83/B5 Terutao (isl.), Thai.
63/H4 Tervel, Bul.
57/K3 Terza Grande (peak), It.
76/C1 Tes, Mong.
76/D2 Tes, Mong.
56/D5 Tescou (riv.), Fr.
130/G1 Teshekpuk (lake), Ak,US
77/N3 Teshio-dake (mtn.), Japan
76/D2 Tesiyn (riv.), Mong.
76/C1 Tes-Khem (riv.), Rus.
62/C3 Teslić, Bosn.
118/C3 Teslin (lake), BC,Can
130/M3 Teslin, Yk,Can
118/C2 Teslin (riv.), Yk,Can
99/G3 Tessaoua, Niger
53/E1 Tessenderlo, Belg.
47/E4 Test (riv.), Eng,UK
59/G1 Têt (riv.), Fr.
46/D3 Tetbury, Eng,UK
57/G4 Tête de l'Estrop (peak), Fr.
63/G4 Teteven, Bul.
45/H5 Tetford, Eng,UK
93/L6 Tetiaroa (isl.), FrPol.
53/F5 Teting-sur-Nied, Fr.
130/K3 Tetlin Nat'l Wild. Ref., Ak,US
122/F4 Teton (riv.), Mt,US
96/D1 Tétouan, Mor.
62/E4 Tetovo, FYROM
59/N9 Tetuan, Sp.
111/D1 Teuco (riv.), Arg.
60/A3 Teulada (cape), It.
123/J3 Teulon, Mb,Can
51/F4 Teutoburger Wald (for.), Ger.
57/K5 Tevere (Tiber) (riv.), It.
74/K5 Teverya (Tiberias), Isr.
43/D3 Teviot (riv.), Sc,UK
90/D4 Tewantin-Noosa, Austl.
46/D3 Tewkesbury, Eng,UK
128/E3 Texarkana, Ar, Tx,US
128/C4 Texas (state), US
128/E4 Texas City, Tx,US
50/B2 Texel (isl.), Neth.
125/G3 Texoma, Ok,US
64/J4 Teykovo, Rus.
116/B4 Teziutlán, Mex.
85/F2 Tezpur, India
83/C1 Tha (riv.), Laos
118/G2 Tha-anne (riv.), Nun.,Can
102/E3 Thabana-Ntlenyana (peak), Les.
103/E2 Thabankulu (peak), SAfr.
102/D2 Thabazimbi, SAfr.
83/B3 Tha Chin (riv.), Thai.
83/B4 Thaen (pt.), Thai.
83/D1 Thai Binh, Viet.
83/C3 Thailand
83/C4 Thailand (gulf), Thai.
83/D1 Thai Nguyen, Viet.
73/K2 Thal, Pak.
75/B5 Thal (des.), Pak.
83/C5 Thaleban Nat'l Park, Thai.
72/E6 Thamar, Jabal (mtn.), Yem.
47/F3 Thame, Eng,UK
47/F3 Thame (riv.), Eng,UK
126/D3 Thames (riv.), On,Can
47/G3 Thames (riv.), Eng,UK
84/B4 Thāna, India
47/H4 Thanet, Isle of (isl.), Eng,UK
85/J5 Thang Duc, Viet.
83/D2 Thanh Hoa, Viet.
85/J4 Thanh Lang Xa, Viet.
83/D4 Thanh Phu, Viet.
83/D4 Thanh Tri, Viet.
83/B4 Thanintharyi (Tenasserim) (div.), Burma
84/C5 Thanjavur, India
73/J3 Thar (des.), India, Pak.
84/B3 Tharād, India
85/G4 Tharrawaddy, Burma
61/J2 Thásos (isl.), Gre.
47/E4 Thatcham, Eng,UK
83/D1 That Khe, Viet.
83/B2 Thaton, Burma
85/H4 Tha Uthen, Thai.
47/G3 Thaxted, Eng,UK
49/H4 Thaya (riv.), Aus.
85/G4 Thayetmyo, Burma
85/G3 Thazi, Burma
47/E4 Theale, Eng,UK
100/C3 Thebes (ruins), Egypt
128/C3 The Caprock (cliffs), NM,US
122/C4 The Dalles, Or,US
91/B3 The Grampians (mts.), Austl.
50/B4 The Hague (s'-Gravenhage) (cap.), Neth.
91/C3 The Lakes Nat'l Park, Austl.
118/F2 Thelon (riv.), NW,Nun.,Can
44/B2 The Loup, NI,UK
123/H3 Theodore, Sk,Can
124/E4 Theodore Roosevelt (lake), Az,US
123/G4 Theodore Roosevelt Nat'l Park, ND,US
123/H2 The Pas, Mb,Can
52/B5 Thérain (riv.), Fr.
61/H3 Thermaic (Salonika) (gulf), Gre.
61/H3 Thermopílai (Thermopylae) (pass), Gre.
122/F5 Thermopolis, Wy,US
126/D2 Thessalon, On,Can
61/H2 Thessaloníki (Salonika), Gre.
61/H3 Thessaly (reg.), Gre.
47/G2 Thet (riv.), Eng,UK
47/G2 Thetford, Eng,UK
127/G2 Thetford Mines, Qu,Can
53/E2 Theux, Belg.
117/J4 The Valley (cap.), Angu.
47/G1 The Wash (bay), Eng,UK
47/G4 The Weald (reg.), Eng,UK
128/E4 The Woodlands, Tx,US
46/D1 The Wrekin (hill), Eng,UK
61/G3 Thíamis (riv.), Gre.
129/F4 Thibodaux, La,US
123/J3 Thief River Falls, Mn,US
122/C5 Thielsen (peak), Or,US
83/D4 Thien Ngon, Viet.
56/E4 Thiers, Fr.
98/A3 Thiès, Sen.
98/A3 Thiès (reg.), Sen.
101/C3 Thika, Kenya
84/E2 Thimphu (cap.), Bhu.
42/N7 Thingvellir Nat'l Park, Ice.
53/F5 Thionville, Fr.
61/J4 Thíra (isl.), Gre.
45/E2 Thirlmere (lake), Eng,UK
45/G3 Thirsk, Eng,UK
42/D4 Thisted, Den.
42/P6 Thistilfjördhur (bay), Ice.
130/L3 Thistle (mtn.), Yk,Can
93/Z18 Thithia (isl.), Fiji
82/B5 Thitu (isl.)
61/H3 Thívai, Gre.
42/N7 Thjórsa (riv.), Ice.
118/G2 Thlewiaza (riv.), Nun.,Can
83/D4 Thoi Binh, Viet.
50/B5 Tholen, Neth.
50/B5 Tholen (isl.), Neth.
53/G5 Tholey, Ger.
129/G3 Thomaston, Ga,US
129/G4 Thomasville, Al,US
129/H4 Thomasville, Ga,US
129/H3 Thomasville, NC,US
122/C3 Thompson (riv.), BC,Can
123/J2 Thompson, Mb,Can
125/J2 Thompson (riv.), Ia, Mo,US
122/E4 Thompson Falls, Mt,US
132/B3 Thompson Place-Tanglewilde, Wa,US
118/E1 Thomsen (riv.), NW,Can
90/A4 Thomson (riv.), Austl.
129/H3 Thomson, Ga,US
83/C3 Thon Buri, Thai.
85/J4 Thon Cam Lo, Viet.
83/B2 Thongwa, Burma
83/E4 Thon Lac Nghiep, Viet.
54/C5 Thonon-les-Bains, Fr.
83/E4 Thon Song Pha, Viet.
124/E4 Thoreau, NM,US
122/E2 Thorhild, Ab,Can
52/B6 Thorigny, Fr.
45/G2 Thornaby-on-Tees, Eng,UK
46/D3 Thornbury, Eng,UK
45/H4 Thorne, Eng,UK
127/R8 Thornhill, On,Can
44/E1 Thornhill, Sc,UK
45/G2 Thornley, Eng,UK
45/G3 Thornthwaite, Eng,UK
45/E4 Thornton Cleveleys, Eng,UK
45/H3 Thornton Dale, Eng,UK
127/R9 Thorold, On,Can
47/H3 Thorpe le Soken, Eng,UK
45/G2 Thorpe Thewles, Eng,UK
56/C3 Thouars, Fr.
56/C3 Thouet (riv.), Fr.
131/B2 Thousand Oaks, Ca,US
66/C4 Thracian (sea), Gre., Turk.
122/F4 Three Forks, Mt,US
130/L4 Three Guardsmen (mtn.), BC,Can
122/E3 Three Hills, Ab,Can
91/C4 Three Hummock (isl.), Austl.
92/G8 Three Kings (isls.), NZ
83/B3 Three Pagodas (pass), Burma
99/E5 Three Points (cape), Gha.
126/C3 Three Rivers, Mi,US
128/D3 Throckmorton, Tx,US
46/B5 Thrushel (riv.), Eng,UK
46/D2 Thruxton, Eng,UK
83/D4 Thu Dau Mot, Viet.
83/D4 Thu Duc, Viet.
52/D3 Thuin, Belg.
56/E5 Thuir, Fr.
119/T7 Thule Air Base, Grld.
54/D4 Thun, Swi.
126/B1 Thunder Bay, On,Can
83/C2 Thung Salaeng Luang Nat'l Park, Thai.
55/E2 Thur (riv.), Swi.
55/F2 Thurgau (canton), Swi.
57/H1 Thüringer Wald (for.), Ger.
48/F3 Thuringia (state), Ger.
47/E2 Thurlaston, Eng,UK
43/B4 Thurles, Ire.
105/T Thurston (isl.), Ant.
116/B4 Tiacolula, Mex.
108/E7 Tiahuanco (ruins), Bol.
130/M5 Tian (pt.), BC,Can
109/K4 Tianguá, Braz.
81/D3 Tianjin, China
81/D3 Tianjin (prov.), China
81/C5 Tianmen, China
81/K9 Tianmu (mts.), China
68/H5 Tian Shan (range), Asia
76/F5 Tianshui, China
81/C5 Tiantangzhai (mtn.), China
96/F1 Tiaret, Alg.
93/S9 Tiavea, Samoa
110/B2 Tibaji (riv.), Braz.
96/H6 Tibati, Camr.
45/F6 Tibberton, Eng,UK
98/C4 Tibé, Pic de (peak), Gui.
74/K5 Tiberias (Sea of Galilee) (lake), Isr., Syria
74/K5 Tiberias (Teverya), Isr.
57/K5 Tiber (Tevere) (riv.), It.
96/J3 Tibesti (mts.), Chad, Libya
75/D5 Tibet (Xizang) Aut. Reg., China
57/L7 Tibidabo (peak), Sp.
96/H1 Ţīb, Ra's aţ (Cape Bon) (cape), Tun.
45/G5 Tibshelf, Eng,UK
117/G4 Tiburon (cape), Haiti
117/M8 Tiburón (isl.), Mex.
132/K11 Tiburon, Ca,US
47/G4 Ticehurst, Eng,UK
132/P14 Tichigan (lake), Wi,US
98/C2 Tichīt, Dhar (hills), Mrta.
96/C3 Tichla, WSah.
57/H4 Ticino (riv.), It.
55/E5 Ticino (canton), Swi.
45/G5 Tickhill, Eng,UK
126/F3 Ticonderoga, NY,US
116/D3 Ticul, Mex.
42/E4 Tidaholm, Swe.
45/G5 Tideswell, Eng,UK
96/F2 Tidikelt (plain), Alg.
98/C2 Tidjikdja, Mrta.
87/G3 Tidore (isl.), Indo.
98/A2 Tidra (isl.), Mrta.
59/X16 Tiede Nat'l Park, Canl.
50/C5 Tiel, Neth.
77/J3 Tieling, China
59/N9 Tielmes, Sp.
52/C1 Tielt, Belg.
53/D2 Tielt-Winge, Belg.
98/D4 Tiemba (riv.), IvC.
75/E3 Tiemen Guan (pass), China
53/D2 Tienen, Belg.
71/H5 Tien Shan (range), China
83/D1 Tien Yen, Viet.
83/D2 Tien Yen, Viet.
96/J3 Tieroko (peak), Chad
42/F3 Tierp, Swe.
124/F3 Tierra Amarilla, NM,US
113/L8 Tierra del Fuego (isl.), Arg., Chile
113/L8 Tierra del Fuego, Antártida e Islas del Atlántico Sur (prov.), Arg.
113/K8 Tierra del Fuego Nat'l Park, Arg.
58/C2 Tiétar (riv.), Sp.
110/B2 Tietê (riv.), Braz.
96/C2 Tifariti, WSah.
126/D3 Tiffin, Oh,US
129/H4 Tifton, Ga,US
93/V12 Tiga (isl.), NCal.
96/H6 Tignère, Camr.
113/S12 Tigre, Arg.
108/C4 Tigre (riv.), Peru
117/J6 Tigre (riv.), Ven.
72/D1 Tigris (riv.), Iraq, Turk.
96/J4 Tigui (well), Chad
99/G2 Tiguidit, Falaise de (escarp.), Niger
116/B3 Tihuatlán, Mex.
42/J3 Tiilikkajärven Nat'l Park, Fin.
98/B1 Tijirīt (reg.), Mrta.
117/L7 Tijuana, Mex.
110/K8 Tijuca Nat'l Park, Braz.
110/B3 Tijucas, Braz.
110/B1 Tijuco (riv.), Braz.
116/C4 Tikal Nat'l Park, Guat.
84/C3 Tīkamgarh, India
130/G3 Tikchik (lakes), Ak,US
93/L6 Tikehau (atoll), FrPol.
66/G3 Tikhoretsk, Rus.
64/G4 Tikhvin, Rus.
61/H2 Tikveš (lake), FYROM
50/C5 Tilburg, Neth.
47/G4 Tilbury, Eng,UK
128/D4 Tilden, Tx,US
45/H5 Till (riv.), Eng,UK
122/C4 Tillamook, Or,US
54/B3 Tille (riv.), Fr.
42/D4 Tilst, Den.
43/D2 Tilt (riv.), Sc,UK
112/Q9 Tiltil, Chile
65/L2 Timan (ridge), Rus.
89/H7 Timaru, NZ
66/F3 Timashevsk, Rus.
109/L5 Timbaúba, Braz.
123/H4 Timber Lake, SD,US
110/B3 Timbó, Braz.
98/E2 Timbuktu (Tombouctou), Mali
87/H4 Timbuni (riv.), Indo.
61/G3 Timfristós (peak), Gre.
96/F2 Timimoun, Alg.
98/A2 Timiris (cape), Mrta.
62/E3 Timiş (co.), Rom.
62/E3 Timiş (riv.), Rom.
62/E3 Timişoara, Rom.
99/G2 Ti-m-Mershoï (wadi), Niger
126/D1 Timmins, On,Can
126/B2 Timms (hill), Wi,US
109/K5 Timon, Braz.
131/K7 Timonium, Md,US
89/B2 Timor (sea)
87/F5 Timor (isl.), Indo.
110/D1 Timóteo, Braz.
69/N4 Timpton (riv.), Rus.
42/F3 Timrå, Swe.
129/G3 Tims Ford (lake), Tn,US
102/E3 Tina (riv.), SAfr.
82/E6 Tinaca (pt.), Phil.
84/C5 Tindivanam, India
96/D2 Tindouf, Alg.
58/B1 Tineo, Sp.
82/C2 Ting (riv.), China
90/F7 Tingalpa (res.), Austl.
91/D3 Tingaringy Nat'l Park, Austl.
96/H2 Tinghert (upland), Libya
98/C4 Tingi (mts.), Gui., SLeo.
130/F2 Tingmerkpuk (mtn.), Ak,US
108/C5 Tingo María, Peru
112/C2 Tinguirrica (vol.), Chile
109/L6 Tinharé, Braz.
109/L6 Tinharé (isl.), Braz.
83/D2 Tinh Gia, Viet.
92/D3 Tinian (isl.), NMar.
98/C4 Tinkisso (riv.), Gui.
132/Q16 Tinley Park, Il,US
111/C2 Tinogasta, Arg.
61/J4 Tinos (isl.), Gre.
52/C5 Tinqueux, Fr.
96/G2 Tinrhert (plat.), Alg.
96/D1 Tinrhir, Mor.
85/G2 Tinsukia, India
46/B5 Tintagel, Eng,UK
58/B4 Tinto (riv.), Sp.
131/F5 Tinton Falls, NJ,US
45/G5 Tintwistle, Eng,UK
96/F4 Ti-n-Zaouâten, Alg.
123/H3 Tioga, ND,US
86/B3 Tioman (isl.), Malay.
47/G3 Tiptree, Eng,UK
84/C5 Tiptūr, India
93/L6 Tiputa, FrPol.
109/J4 Tiracambu (mts.), Braz.
100/C2 Tiran (str.), Egypt
61/F2 Tiranë (cap.), Alb.
100/C3 Tiran, Jazīrat (isl.), Egypt
55/G5 Tirano, It.
63/J2 Tiraspol', Mol.
74/A2 Tire, Turk.
66/F4 Tirebolu, Turk.
99/F1 Tirest (well), Mali
63/G3 Tîrgovişte, Rom.
63/H3 Tîrgu Bujor, Rom.
63/F3 Tîrgu Cărbuneşti, Rom.
63/H2 Tîrgu Frumos, Rom.
63/F3 Tîrgu Jiu, Rom.
63/F2 Tîrgu Lăpuş, Rom.
63/G2 Tîrgu Mureş, Rom.
63/H2 Tîrgu Neamţ, Rom.
63/H2 Tîrgu Ocna, Rom.
63/H3 Tîrgu Secuiesc, Rom.
73/K1 Tirich Mīr (mtn.), Pak.
63/G2 Tîrnava Mare (riv.), Rom.
63/G2 Tîrnava Mică (riv.), Rom.
63/G2 Tîrnăveni, Rom.
61/H3 Tírnavos, Gre.
55/G3 Tirol (prov.), Aus.
46/C1 Tir Rhiwiog (mtn.), Wa,UK
57/K2 Tirschenreuth, Ger.
60/A2 Tirso (riv.), It.
84/C5 Tiruchchendūr, India
84/C5 Tiruchchirāppalli, India
84/C6 Tiruchendūr, India
84/C6 Tirunelveli, India
84/C5 Tirupati, India
84/C5 Tiruppattūr, India
84/C5 Tiruppūr, India
84/C5 Tirūr, India
84/C5 Tiruvannāmalai, India
66/B2 Tisa (riv.), Eur.
46/D4 Tisbury, Eng,UK
123/G2 Tisdale, Sk,Can
125/H4 Tishomingo, Ok,US
62/E2 Tisza (riv.), Hun.
62/E2 Tiszaföldvár, Hun.
62/E2 Tiszafüred, Hun.
62/E2 Tiszakécske, Hun.
62/E1 Tiszalök, Hun.
62/E2 Tiszavasvári, Hun.
62/E3 Titel, Yugo.
108/E7 Titicaca (lake), Bol., Peru
84/D3 Titlagarh, India
55/E4 Titlis (peak), Swi.
62/D4 Titovo Užice, Yugo.
62/E5 Titov Veles, FYROM
62/E5 Titov vrh (peak), FYROM
63/G3 Titu, Rom.
129/H4 Titusville, Fl,US
98/A3 Tivaouane, Sen.
62/D4 Tivat, Yugo.
46/C5 Tiverton, Eng,UK
116/D3 Tizimín, Mex.
73/L1 Tiznap (riv.), China
96/D2 Tiznit, Mor.
50/C3 Tjeukemeer (lake), Neth.
117/P8 Tlahualilo de Zaragoza, Mex.
116/B4 Tlalnepantla, Mex.
116/B4 Tlapa, Mex.
116/B4 Tlaxcala, Mex.
116/B4 Tlaxcala (state), Mex.
96/E1 Tlemcen, Alg.
96/J2 Tmassah, Libya
63/G2 Toaca (peak), Rom.
103/J7 Toamasina, Madg.
103/J7 Toamasina (prov.), Madg.
132/B2 Toandos (pen.), Wa,US
93/L6 Toau (atoll), FrPol.
122/B3 Toba (inlet), BC,Can
76/D5 Toba, China
86/A3 Toba (lake), Indo.
79/E3 Toba, Japan
117/J5 Tobago (isl.), Trin.
73/J2 Toba Kākar (range), Pak.
58/E3 Tobarra, Sp.
75/B5 Toba Tek Singh, Pak.
44/B2 Tobermore, NI,UK
109/L6 Tobias Barreto, Braz.
123/H2 Tobin (lake), Sk,Can
127/H2 Tobique (riv.), NB,Can
65/Q4 Tobol (riv.), Kaz., Rus.
68/G4 Tobol'sk, Rus.
97/K1 Tobruk, Libya
131/E4 Tobyhanna (lake), Pa,US
65/L2 Tobysh (riv.), Rus.
109/J5 Tocantinópolis, Braz.
109/J5 Tocantins (riv.), Braz.
129/H3 Toccoa, Ga,US
55/E5 Toce (riv.), It.
79/F2 Tochigi, Japan
79/F2 Tochigi (pref.), Japan
79/F2 Tochio, Japan
58/C4 Tocina, Sp.
111/B1 Tocopilla, Chile
117/F6 Tocumen, Pan.
117/H5 Tocuyito, Ven.
117/H5 Tocuyo (riv.), Ven.
79/H7 Toda, Japan
84/C2 Toda Bhīm, India
47/F3 Toddington, Eng,UK
60/C1 Todi, It.
45/F4 Todmorden, Eng,UK
94/C4 Todos os Santos (bay), Braz.
109/G3 Toekomstig (res.), Sur.
122/E2 Tofield, Ab,Can
42/E3 Töfsingdalens Nat'l Park, Swe.
93/H6 Tofua (isl.), Tonga
98/C2 Togba (well), Mrta.
130/G4 Togiak Nat'l Wild. Ref., Ak,US
99/F4 Togo
79/N9 Tōgō, Japan
124/E4 Tohatchi, NM,US
93/X15 Tohivea (peak), FrPol.
79/F2 Tōhoku (prov.), Japan
79/F3 Toi, Japan
79/M9 Tōin, Japan
124/C3 Toiyabe (range), Nv,US
78/C3 Tojō, Japan
79/L10 Tōjō, Japan
79/E3 Tōkai, Japan
79/F2 Tōkamachi, Japan
100/D5 Tokar, Sudan
92/B1 Tokara (isls.), Japan
100/D5 Tokar Game Rsv., Sudan
74/D2 Tokat, Turk.
93/H5 Tokelau (terr.), NZ
79/N9 Toki, Japan
79/N9 Toki (riv.), Japan
79/H6 Tokigawa, Japan
79/M10 Tokoname, Japan
89/H6 Tokoroa, NZ
79/F3 Tokorozawa, Japan
76/B2 Toksun, China
75/B3 Toktogul (res.), Kyr.
78/D3 Tokushima, Japan
78/C4 Tokushima (pref.), Japan
79/H7 Tokyo (bay), Japan
79/H7 Tōkyō (cap.), Japan
103/H9 Tôlanaro, Madg.
63/H4 Tolbukhin, Bul.
111/F1 Toledo, Braz.
82/D5 Toledo, Phil.
58/C3 Toledo, Sp.
58/C3 Toledo (mts.), Sp.
126/D3 Toledo, Oh,US
128/E4 Toledo Bend (res.), La, Tx,US
60/C1 Tolentino, It.
112/C3 Tolhuaca Nat'l Park, Chile
75/D2 Toli, China
103/G8 Toliara, Madg.
103/H8 Toliara (prov.), Madg.
87/F3 Tolitoli, Indo.
44/B5 Tolka (riv.), Ire.
62/A2 Tolmezzo, It.
62/D2 Tolna, Hun.
62/D2 Tolna (co.), Hun.
87/F4 Tolo (gulf), Indo.
58/D1 Tolosa, Sp.
132/D2 Tolt (riv.), Wa,US
112/B3 Toltén, Chile
112/B3 Toltén (riv.), Chile
116/B4 Toluca, Mex.
67/J1 Tol'yatti, Rus.
68/J4 Tom' (riv.), Rus.
126/B3 Tomah, Wi,US
77/N3 Tomakomai, Japan
92/G6 Tomanivi (peak), Fiji
58/A3 Tomar, Port.
61/G3 Tómaros (peak), Gre.
49/M3 Tomaszów Lubelski, Pol.
49/L3 Tomaszów Mazowiecki, Pol.
43/D2 Tomatin, Sc,UK
108/G6 Tombador (mts.), Braz.
97/M6 Tombe, Sudan
129/F4 Tombigbee (riv.), Al, Ms,US
104/B2 Tomboco, Ang.
98/E2 Tombouctou (Timbuktu), Mali
124/E5 Tombstone, Az,US
104/B4 Tombua, Ang.
112/B3 Tomé, Chile
56/B2 Tomé (isl.), Fr.
49/G1 Tomelilla, Swe.
58/D3 Tomelloso, Sp.
87/F4 Tomini (gulf), Indo.
58/A2 Tomiño, Sp.
79/H7 Tomiura, Japan
69/N4 Tommot, Rus.
108/E2 Tomo (riv.), Col.
126/C4 Tompkinsville, Ky,US
68/J4 Tomsk, Rus.
131/F6 Toms River, NJ,US
130/K3 Tom White (mtn.), Ak,US
122/D3 Tonasket, Wa,US
127/S9 Tonawanda, NY,US
47/G4 Tonbridge, Eng,UK
79/L10 Tondabayashi, Japan
87/F3 Tondano, Indo.
42/D5 Tønder, Den.
97/K6 Tondou (mts.), CAfr.
79/J7 Tone, Japan
79/G3 Tone (riv.), Japan
46/C4 Tone (riv.), Eng,UK
72/F1 Tonekābon, Iran
76/F5 Tong (riv.), China
93/H7 Tonga
93/K5 Tongareva (Penrhyn) (atoll), Cookls.
93/H7 Tonga-tapu (isl.), Tonga
76/F4 Tongchuan, China
53/E2 Tongeren, Belg.
82/B2 Tonggu, China
77/K3 Tonghua, China
87/E5 Tongo (peak), Indo.
85/J2 Tongren, China
84/F2 Tongsa (riv.), Bhu.
76/D5 Tongtian (riv.), China
122/G4 Tongue (riv.), Mt, Wy,US
50/D6 Tönisvorst, Ger.
97/L6 Tonj, Sudan
84/C2 Tonk, India
125/H3 Tonkawa, Ok,US
83/D1 Tonkin (gulf), China, Viet.
98/D5 Tonkoui (peak), IvC.
83/C3 Tonle Sap (lake), Camb.
56/D4 Tonneins, Fr.
124/D4 Tonopah, Az,US
124/C3 Tonopah, Nv,US
78/D3 Tonoshō, Japan
104/E5 Tonota, Bots.
42/D4 Tønsberg, Nor.
124/E4 Tonto Nat'l Mon., Az,US
124/D2 Tooele, Ut,US
91/G6 Toomuc (cr.), Austl.
90/C4 Toowoomba, Austl.
131/B2 Topanga, Ca,US
125/J3 Topeka (cap.), Ks,US
122/B2 Topley, BC,Can
63/G2 Toplita, Rom.
49/K4 Topol'čany, Slvk.
63/G3 Topoloveni, Rom.
63/H4 Topolovgrad, Bul.
64/F2 Topozero (lake), Rus.
122/C4 Toppenish, Wa,US
46/C5 Topsham, Eng,UK
97/M6 Tor, Eth.
79/M9 Torahime, Japan
108/D7 Torata, Peru
87/G3 Torawitan (cape), Indo.
74/A2 Torbalı, Turk.
73/G1 Torbat-e Ḩeydarīyeh, Iran
56/B1 Torbay, Eng,UK
130/H3 Torbert (mtn.), Ak,US
48/E1 Törder, Den.
59/L6 Tordera (riv.), Sp.
58/C2 Tordesillas, Sp.
59/G1 Torelló, Sp.
46/C3 Torfaen (co.), Wal.,UK
49/G2 Torgelow, Ger.
52/C1 Torhout, Belg.
79/J7 Toride, Japan
79/E3 Torii-tōge (pass), Japan
58/A1 Toriñana (cape), Sp.
57/G4 Torino (Turin), It.
92/D1 Tori-Shima (isl.), Japan
97/M7 Torit, Sudan
73/H1 Torkestān (mts.), Afg.
58/C2 Tormes (riv.), Sp.
45/H4 Torne (riv.), Eng,UK
51/G1 Tornesch, Ger.
62/D4 Tornik (peak), Yugo.
42/G2 Torniojoki (Torneälven) (riv.), Fin., Swe.
58/C2 Toro, Sp.
111/C2 Toro, Cerro del (peak), Arg.
62/E2 Törökszentmiklós, Hun.
61/H2 Toronaic (gulf), Gre.
127/R8 Toronto (cap.), On,Can
64/F4 Toropets, Rus.
101/B2 Tororo, Ugan.
59/N8 Torote (riv.), Sp.
46/B6 Torpoint, Eng,UK
46/C6 Torquay, Eng,UK
131/B3 Torrance, Ca,US
58/D4 Torre del Campo, Sp.
58/D4 Torredonjimeno, Sp.

179
Torre – Uraya

58/D2 Torrejón de Ardoz, Sp.
58/C1 Torrelavega, Sp.
59/N8 Torrelodones, Sp.
90/B3 Torrens (cr.), Austl.
89/C4 Torrens (lake), Austl.
59/E3 Torrente, Sp.
117/P8 Torreón, Mex.
59/E4 Torre-Pacheco, Sp.
58/D3 Torreperogil, Sp.
92/D6 Torres (str.), Austl.
110/B4 Tôrres, Braz.
92/F6 Torres (isls.), Van.
113/J7 Torres del Paine Nat'l Park, Chile
58/A3 Torres Novas, Port.
58/A3 Torres Vedras, Port.
59/E4 Torrevieja, Sp.
44/B1 Torr Head (pt.), NI,UK
46/B5 Torridge (riv.), Eng,UK
58/C3 Torrijos, Sp.
123/G5 Torrington, Wy,US
58/D4 Torrox, Sp.
41/D2 Tórshavn, Den.
56/B2 Torteval, ChI,UK
117/J4 Tortola (isl.), BVI
60/A3 Tortolì, It.
57/H4 Tortona, It.
59/F2 Tortosa, Sp.
59/F2 Tortosa (cape), Sp.
75/C3 Torugart, Pereval (pass), Kyr.
49/K2 Toruń, Pol.
49/K2 Toruń (prov.), Pol.
43/A3 Tory (isl.), Ire.
49/L4 Torysa (riv.), Slvk.
64/G4 Torzhok, Rus.
78/C4 Tosa, Japan
78/C4 Tosa (bay), Japan
78/C4 Tosashimizu, Japan
104/B5 Toscanini, Namb.
57/J4 Tosco-Emiliano (range), It.
76/D4 Toson (lake), China
76/D2 Tosontsengel, Mong.
55/E3 Töss (riv.), Swi.
45/G1 Tosson (hill), Eng,UK
111/D2 Tostado, Arg.
51/G2 Tostedt, Ger.
78/B4 Tosu, Japan
74/C2 Tosya, Turk.
58/E4 Totana, Sp.
47/E5 Totland, Eng,UK
46/C6 Totnes, Eng,UK
116/A4 Totolapan, Mex.
112/E2 Totoras, Arg.
105/H Totten (glac.), Ant.
45/F4 Tottington, Eng,UK
47/E5 Totton, Eng,UK
78/D3 Tottori, Japan
78/C3 Tottori (pref.), Japan
96/D1 Toubkal, Jebel (peak), Mor.
82/D3 Toucheng, Tai.
123/G3 Touchwood (hills), Sk,Can
98/E3 Tougan, Burk.
96/G1 Touggourt, Alg.
53/E6 Toul, Fr.
127/H1 Toulnustouc (riv.), Qu,Can
56/F5 Toulon, Fr.
56/D5 Toulouse, Fr.
96/H3 Toumo (well), Niger
98/D5 Toumodi, IvC.
82/D3 Tounan, Tai.
83/B2 Toungoo, Burma
98/D5 Toura (mts.), IvC.
52/C2 Tourcoing, Fr.
56/C5 Tourettes, Pic de (peak), Fr.
58/A1 Touriñan (cape), Sp.
56/C2 Tourlaville, Fr.
52/C2 Tournai, Belg.
54/A4 Tournus, Fr.
56/D3 Tours, Fr.
59/E3 Tous (res.), Sp.
56/B2 Toussaines, Signal de (peak), Fr.
96/J3 Toussidé (peak), Chad
97/K6 Toussoro (peak), CAfr.
102/C4 Touws (riv.), SAfr.
117/G6 Tovar, Ven.
47/E2 Tove (riv.), Eng,UK
76/E2 Tövshrüüleh, Mong.
79/G2 Towada, Japan
47/F2 Towcester, Eng,UK
45/G2 Tow Law, Eng,UK
123/H3 Towner, ND,US
122/F4 Townsend, Mt,US
132/A2 Townsend (mt.), Wa,US
90/C3 Townshend (cape), Austl.
90/B2 Townsville, Austl.
73/H1 Towraghondi, Afg.
131/K7 Towson, Md,US
87/F4 Towuti (lake), Indo.
75/C3 Toxkan (riv.), China, Kyr.
128/C4 Toyah, Tx,US
128/C4 Toyahvale, Tx,US
79/E2 Toyama, Japan
79/E2 Toyama (bay), Japan
79/E2 Toyama (pref.), Japan
79/N9 Toyoake, Japan
79/E3 Toyohashi, Japan
79/E3 Toyokawa, Japan
79/L10 Toyonaka, Japan
79/L10 Toyono, Japan
78/D3 Toyo'oka, Japan
79/M9 Toyosato, Japan
79/E2 Toyoshina, Japan
79/E3 Toyota, Japan
79/M9 Toyoyama, Japan
130/H2 Tozi (mtn.), Ak,US
83/E3 Tra Bong, Viet.
74/D2 Trabzon, Turk.
127/H2 Tracadie, NB,Can
83/D4 Tra Cu, Viet.
127/F2 Tracy, QU,Can
132/M11 Tracy, Ca,US
58/B4 Trafalgar (cape), Sp.
59/P10 Trafaria, Port.
112/B3 Traiguén, Chile
122/D3 Trail, BC,Can
57/L3 Traisen (riv.), Aus.
49/J4 Traiskirchen, Aus.
43/A4 Tralee, Ire.
83/D1 Tra Linh, Viet.
110/B4 Tramandaí, Braz.
83/E3 Tra Mi, Viet.
125/G3 Tramperos (cr.), NM, Tx,US
42/E4 Tranås, Swe.
53/D4 Tranet (mtn.), Fr.
83/B5 Trang, Thai.
87/H5 Trangan (isl.), Indo.
60/E2 Trani, It.
105/W Transantarctic (mts.), Ant.
62/F2 Transylvania (reg.), Rom.
62/F3 Transylvanian Alps (range), Rom.
83/D4 Tra On, Viet.
60/C3 Trapani, It.
83/D3 Trapeang Veng, Camb.
122/E4 Trapper (peak), Mt,US
52/B6 Trappes, Fr.
91/C3 Traralgon, Austl.
98/B2 Trarza (reg.), Mrta.
60/C1 Trasimeno (lake), It.
58/B2 Trás-os-Montes e Alto Douro (dist.), Port.
102/E2 Trasvaal (prov.), SAfr.
83/C3 Trat, Thai.
57/L2 Traun, Aus.
57/L2 Traun (riv.), Aus.
57/K3 Traunreut, Ger.
57/K3 Traunsee (lake), Aus.
57/K3 Traunstein, Ger.
48/F2 Trave (riv.), Ger.
91/B2 Travellers (lake), Austl.
130/G2 Traverse (peak), Ak,US
123/J4 Traverse (lake), SD,US
126/C2 Traverse City, Mi,US
83/D4 Tra Vinh, Viet.
128/D4 Travis (lake), Tx,US
62/C3 Travnik, Bosn.
46/C2 Trawsalt (mtn.), Wal,UK
44/E6 Trawsfynydd, Wal,UK
44/E6 Trawsfynydd, Llyn (lake), Wal,UK
62/B2 Trbovlje, Slov.
57/H4 Trebbia (riv.), It.
48/G1 Trebel (riv.), Ger.
49/H4 Třebíč, Czh.
62/D4 Trebinje, Bosn.
60/E3 Trebisacce, It.
57/L2 Třeboň, Czh.
58/B4 Trebujena, Sp.
46/C3 Tredegar, Wal,UK
46/C2 Trefeglwys, Wal,UK
44/E5 Trefnant, Wal,UK
46/C2 Tregaron, Wal,UK
113/G2 Treinta y Tres, Uru.
113/G2 Treinta y Tres (dept.), Uru.
57/G4 Tré-la-Tête (mtn.), Fr.
56/C3 Trélazé, Fr.
46/B3 Trelech, Wal,UK
112/D4 Trelew, Arg.
56/D4 Trélissac, Fr.
48/G1 Trelleborg, Swe.
44/D6 Tremadoc (bay), Wal,UK
44/B4 Tremblestown (riv.), Ire.
122/B2 Trembleur (lake), BC,Can
53/D2 Tremelo, Belg.
60/D1 Tremiti (isls.), It.
124/D2 Tremonton, Ut,US
127/F1 Trenche (riv.), Qu,Can
49/K4 Trenčín, Slvk.
112/E2 Trenque Lauquen, Arg.
45/H5 Trent (riv.), Eng,UK
45/F6 Trent and Mersey (can.), Eng,UK
57/J3 Trentino-Alto Adige (reg.), It.
55/H5 Trento, It.
55/H5 Trento (prov.), It.
126/E2 Trenton, On,Can
129/H4 Trenton, Fl,US
129/G3 Trenton, Ga,US
132/F7 Trenton, Mi,US
125/J2 Trenton, Mo,US
131/F5 Trenton (cap.), NJ,US
129/F3 Trenton, Tn,US
46/C3 Treorchy, Wal,UK
61/F2 Trepuzzi, It.
113/T11 Tres Arboles, Uru.
112/E3 Tres Arroyos, Arg.
110/H6 Três Coraçoes, Braz.
110/B2 Três Irmãos (res.), Braz.
111/D2 Tres Isletas, Arg.
110/B2 Três Lagoas, Braz.
110/C1 Três Marias, Braz.
110/C1 Três Marias (res.), Braz.
117/N9 Tres Marías (isls.), Mex.
112/B5 Tres Montes (cape), Chile
112/C4 Tres Picos (peak), Arg.
112/E3 Tres Picos (peak), Arg.
110/H6 Três Pontas, Braz.
112/D5 Tres Puntas (cape), Arg.
110/K7 Três Rios, Braz.
57/J2 Treuchtlingen, Ger.
48/G2 Treuenbrietzen, Ger.
57/H4 Treviglio, It.
57/K4 Treviso, It.
46/A5 Trevose Head (pt.), Eng,UK
131/J7 Triadelphia (res.), Md,US
90/B2 Tribulation (cape), Austl.
61/F3 Tricase, It.
84/C5 Trichūr, India
87/J4 Tricora (peak), Indo.
82/B5 Trident (shoal)
52/A5 Trie-Château, Fr.
53/F4 Trier, Ger.
60/E2 Triggiano, It.
63/G4 Triglav (peak), Bul.
62/A2 Triglav (peak), Slov.
62/A2 Triglav Nat'l Park, Slov.
60/D2 Trigno (riv.), It.
58/B4 Trigueros, Sp.
61/G3 Trikala, Gre.
61/G3 Trikhonis (lake), Gre.
54/D3 Trimbach, Swi.
45/G2 Trimdon, Eng,UK
84/D6 Trincomalee, SrL.
109/J7 Trindade, Braz.
49/K4 Třinec, Czh.
47/F3 Tring, Eng,UK
112/E3 Trinidad (isl.), Arg.
108/F6 Trinidad, Bol.
113/J7 Trinidad (gulf), Chile
113/F2 Trinidad, Uru.
125/F3 Trinidad, Co,US
117/J5 Trinidad and Tobago
109/N8 Trinidade, Braz.
127/L2 Trinity (bay), Nf,Can
130/H4 Trinity (isls.), Ak,US
124/B2 Trinity (riv.), Ca,US
124/D2 Trinity (range), Nv,US
128/E4 Trinity (riv.), Tx,US
100/D5 Trinkitat, Sudan
103/S15 Triolet, Mrts.
61/G3 Tripolis, Gre.
96/H1 Tripolitania (reg.), Libya
74/K4 Tripoli (Ṭarābulus), Leb.
96/H1 Tripoli (Ṭarābulus) (cap.), Libya
84/C6 Tripunittura, India
85/F3 Tripura (state), India
38/J7 Tristan da Cunha (isls.), StH.
98/B4 Tristao (isls.), Guin.
112/D4 Triste (peak), Arg.
83/D4 Tri Ton, Viet.
51/H1 Trittau, Ger.
84/C6 Trivandrum, India
49/J4 Trnava, Slvk.
92/E5 Trobriand (isls.), PNG
52/A5 Troesne (riv.), Fr.
57/L3 Trofaiach, Aus.
59/Q11 Tróia, Port.
53/G2 Troisdorf, Ger.
53/G6 Troisfontaines, Fr.
127/G1 Trois-Pistoles, Qu,Can
127/F2 Trois-Rivières, Qu,Can
65/P5 Troitsk, Rus.
42/E4 Trollhättan, Swe.
109/G4 Trombetas (riv.), Braz.
39/M6 Tromelin (isl.), Reu.
42/F1 Troms (co.), Nor.
42/F1 Tromsø, Nor.
112/C4 Tronador (peak), Arg., Chile
42/D3 Trondheim, Nor.
60/C1 Tronto (riv.), It.
74/J4 Troodos (mts.), Cyp.
44/D1 Trool, Loch (lake), Sc,UK
43/C3 Troon, Sc,UK
60/D3 Tropea, It.
124/D3 Tropic, Ut,US
44/B1 Trostan (mtn.), NI,UK
118/D2 Trout (lake), NW,Can
123/K3 Trout (lake), On,Can
45/F4 Troutbeck, Eng,UK
122/E1 Trout Lake, BC,Can
46/D4 Trowbridge, Eng,UK
129/G4 Troy, Al,US
132/F6 Troy, Mi,US
126/F3 Troy, NY,US
129/G1 Troy, Oh,US
63/G4 Troyan, Bul.
63/G4 Troyanski Prokhod (pass), Bul.
53/D6 Troyes, Fr.
61/K3 Troy (Ilium) (ruins), Turk.
62/E4 Trstenik, Yugo.
130/M3 Truitt (peak), Yk,Can
116/D4 Trujillo, Hon.
108/C5 Trujillo, Peru
58/C3 Trujillo, Sp
117/G6 Trujillo, Ven.
92/E4 Truk (isls.), Micr.
131/G4 Trumbull, Ct,US
46/D2 Trumpet, Eng,UK
83/D1 Trung Khanh, Viet.
127/J2 Truro, NS,Can
46/A6 Truro, Eng,UK
124/F4 Truth Or Consequences, NM,US
49/H3 Trutnov, Czh.
56/E4 Truyère (riv.), Fr.
44/D6 Trwyn Cilan (pt.), Wal,UK
63/G4 Tryavna, Bul.
42/E3 Trysil, Nor.
49/J3 Trzcianka, Pol.
49/H1 Trzebiatów, Pol.
49/J3 Trzebnica, Pol.
49/J2 Trzemeszno, Pol.
62/B2 Tržič, Slov.
76/D3 Tsagaan Bogd (peak), Mong.
76/G2 Tsagaan-Ovoo, Mong.
76/E1 Tsagaan-Üür, Mong.
103/J6 Tsaratanana Massif (plat.), Madg.
102/B2 Tsarisberge (mts.), Namb.
75/F2 Tsast Uul (peak), Mong.
102/E3 Tsatsana (peak), Les.
104/D5 Tsau, Bots.
101/C3 Tsavo, Kenya
101/C3 Tsavo East Nat'l Park, Kenya
101/C3 Tsavo West Nat'l Park, Kenya
76/F2 Tsenhermandal, Mong.
76/D2 Tsetsen-Uul, Mong.
104/B1 Tshela, D.R. Congo
104/D2 Tshibwika, D.R. Congo
104/D2 Tshikapa, D.R. Congo
97/K8 Tshuapa (riv.), D.R. Congo
65/L2 Tsil'ma (riv.), Rus.
67/G2 Tsimlyansk (res.), Rus.
103/H9 Tsiombe, Madg.
103/H7 Tsiribihina (riv.), Madg.
103/H7 Tsiroanomandidy, Madg.
102/C4 Tsitsikamma Forest & Coastal Nat'l Park, SAfr.
67/G4 Ts'khinvali, Geo.
64/G4 Tsna (riv.), Rus.
76/D2 Tsogt, Mong.
76/F3 Tsogt-Ovoo, Mong.
76/F3 Tsogttsetsiy, Mong.
76/F2 Tsöh (riv.), Mong.
102/D3 Tsomo (riv.), SAfr.
78/E3 Tsu, Japan
78/A3 Tsu (isls.), Japan
79/F2 Tsubame, Japan
78/E2 Tsubata, Japan
79/G2 Tsuchiura, Japan
79/M10 Tsuchiyama, Japan
77/M3 Tsugaru (str.), Japan
79/L10 Tsuge, Japan
79/H7 Tsukui, Japan
78/B4 Tsukumi, Japan
104/C4 Tsumeb, Namb.
79/K10 Tsuna, Japan
79/F3 Tsuru, Japan
78/E3 Tsuruga, Japan
79/F2 Tsurugashima, Japan
79/E2 Tsurugi, Japan
78/D4 Tsurugi-san (mtn.), Japan
79/M9 Tsushima, Japan
78/D3 Tsuyama, Japan
86/C5 Tua (cape), Indo.
58/B2 Tua (riv.), Port.
112/B4 Tuamapu (chan.), Chile
93/L6 Tuamotu (arch.), FrPol.
81/B4 Tuan (riv.), China
86/A3 Tuan (pt.), Indo.
83/C1 Tuan Giao, Viet.
86/A3 Tuangku (isl.), Indo.
83/D2 Tuan Thuong, Viet.
82/D4 Tuao, Phil.
66/F3 Tuapse, Rus.
124/E3 Tuba City, Az,US
86/D5 Tuban, Indo.
72/D6 Tuban (riv.), Yem.
110/B4 Tubarão, Braz.
50/D4 Tubbergen, Neth.
55/E1 Tübingen, Ger.
52/D2 Tubize, Belg.
98/C5 Tubmanburg, Libr.
92/H6 Tubou, Fiji
97/K1 Ṭubruq (Tobruk), Libya
93/K7 Tubuaï (isls.), FrPol.
93/K7 Tubuaï (isl.), FrPol.
49/J2 Tuchola, Pol.
124/E4 Tucson, Az,US
125/G4 Tucumcari, NM,US
117/H6 Tucupido, Ven.
117/J6 Tucupita, Ven.
109/J4 Tucuruí, Braz.
109/H4 Tucuruí (res.), Braz.
58/E1 Tudela, Sp.
56/E5 Tude, Rochers de la (mtn.), Fr.
102/E3 Tugela (falls), SAfr.
103/E3 Tugela (riv.), SAfr.
129/H2 Tug Fork (riv.), WV,US
82/D4 Tuguegarao, Phil.
87/F5 Tukangbesi (isls.), Indo.
64/D4 Tukums, Lat.
86/D4 Tukung (peak), Indo.
132/C3 Tukwila, Wa,US
116/B3 Tula, Mex.
66/F1 Tula, Rus.
75/F4 Tulagt Ar (riv.), China
116/B3 Tulancingo, Mex.
66/F1 Tula Obl., Rus.
124/C3 Tulare, Ca,US
125/F4 Tularosa, NM,US
125/F4 Tularosa (val.), NM,US
102/L10 Tulbagh, SAfr.
108/C3 Tulcán, Ecu.
63/J3 Tulcea, Rom.
63/J3 Tulcea (co.), Rom.
128/C3 Tulia, Tx,US
130/E5 Tulik (vol.), Ak,US
92/E5 Tulin (isls.), PNG
74/K5 Ṭūlkarm, WBnk.
129/G3 Tullahoma, Tn,US
43/B4 Tullamore, Ire.
56/D4 Tulle, Fr.
49/J4 Tulln, Aus.
64/G1 Tuloma (riv.), Rus.
125/J3 Tulsa, Ok,US
108/C3 Tuluá, Col.
69/L4 Tulun, Rus.
116/D5 Tuma (riv.), Nic.
124/E5 Tumacacori Nat'l Mon., Az,US
109/H3 Tumac-Humac (mts.), Braz.
108/C3 Tumaco, Col.
82/D4 Tumauini, Phil.
97/J8 Tumba (lake), D R. Congo
108/B4 Tumbes, Peru
83/C3 Tumbot (peak), Camb.
77/K3 Tumen, China
117/J6 Tumeremo, Ven.
84/C5 Tumkūr, India
43/C2 Tummel (riv.), Sc,UK
77/M1 Tumnin (riv.), Rus.
86/B2 Tumpat, Malay.
87/F4 Tumpu (peak), Indo.
91/D2 Tumut, Austl.
132/B3 Tumwater, Wa,US
74/D2 Tunceli, Turk.
101/B5 Tunduma, Tanz.
101/C5 Tunduru, Tanz.
75/C1 Tundyk (riv.), Kaz.
62/H4 Tundzha (riv.), Bul., Turk.
84/C4 Tungabhadra (res.), India
84/C4 Tungabhadra (riv.), India
91/C3 Tungamah, Austl.
68/K3 Tunguska, Lower (riv.), Rus.
68/K3 Tunguska, Stony (riv.), Rus.
60/B4 Tūnis (cap.), Tun.
60/B4 Tunis (gov.), Tun.
60/B4 Tunis (gulf), Tun.
96/G1 Tunisia
108/D2 Tunjá, Col.
119/K3 Tunungayualuk (isl.), Nf,Can
112/C2 Tunuyán, Arg.
112/C2 Tunuyán (riv.), Chile
124/B3 Tuolumne (riv.), Ca,US
83/D2 Tuong Duong, Viet.
85/J3 Tuoniang (riv.), China
75/F5 Tuotuo (riv.), China
110/B2 Tupã, Braz.
110/B1 Tupaciguara, Braz.
93/K6 Tupai (isl.), FrPol.
129/F3 Tupelo, Ms,US
110/B2 Tupi Paulista, Braz.
108/E8 Tupiza, Bol.
126/F2 Tupper Lake, NY,US
112/C2 Tupungato (peak), Arg., Chile
84/F2 Tura, India
65/Q4 Tura (riv.), Rus.
77/L1 Turana (mts.), Rus.
68/G5 Turan Lowland (plain), Uzb.
117/F5 Turbaco, Col.
73/H3 Turbat, Pak.
117/F6 Turbo, Col.
62/F2 Turda, Rom.
93/M7 Tureia (atoll), FrPol.
49/K2 Turek, Pol.
68/G4 Turgay Obl., Kaz.
126/E1 Turgeon (riv.), Qu,Can
63/H4 Türgovishte, Bul.
74/A2 Turgutlu, Turk.
74/D2 Turhal, Turk.
59/E3 Turia (riv.), Sp.
57/G4 Turin (Torino), It.
101/C2 Turkana (lake), Eth., Kenya
75/A3 Turkestan, Kaz.
62/E2 Túrkeve, Hun.
74/C2 Turkey
67/K5 Türkmenbashi, Trkm.
68/F6 Turkmenistan
117/G3 Turks and Caicos (isls.), UK
42/G3 Turku (Åbo), Fin.
124/B3 Turlock, Ca,US
117/H5 Turmero, Ven.
44/D4 Turnberry, Sc,UK
116/D4 Turneffe (isls.), Belz.
50/B6 Turnhout, Belg.
122/F1 Turnor Lake, Sk,Can
49/H3 Turnov, Czh.
63/G4 Turnu Măgurele, Rom.
76/B3 Turpan, China
75/E3 Turpan (depr.), China
116/F4 Turquino (pk.), Cuba
43/D2 Turriff, Sc,UK
98/B5 Turtle (isls.), SLeo.
122/F2 Turtleford, Sk,Can
45/F4 Turton, Eng,UK
75/C3 Turugart Shankou (pass), China
110/J6 Turvo (riv.), Braz.
129/G3 Tuscaloosa, Al,US
60/B1 Tuscano (arch.), It.
57/J5 Tuscany (reg.), It.
124/C2 Tuscarora, Nv,US
129/G3 Tuskegee, Al,US
131/C3 Tustin, Ca,US
49/K3 Tuszyn, Pol.
64/H4 Tutayev, Rus.
45/G6 Tutbury, Eng,UK
84/C6 Tuticorin, India
62/E4 Tutin, Yugo.
86/D3 Tutong, Bru.
63/H3 Tutrakan, Bul.
125/H3 Tuttle Creek (lake), Ks,US
93/H6 Tutuila (isl.), ASam.
130/F2 Tututalak (mtn.), Ak,US
76/F2 Tuul (riv.), Mong.
42/H3 Tuusula, Fin.
68/K4 Tuva Aut. Rep., Rus.
92/G5 Tuvalu
72/E4 Ṭuwayq, Jabal (mts.), SAr.
45/H5 Tuxford, Eng,UK
117/N9 Tuxpan, Mex.
116/B4 Tuxtepec, Mex.
116/C4 Tuxtla Gutiérrez, Mex.
58/A1 Túy, Sp.
83/D2 Tuyen Hoa, Viet.
83/D1 Tuyen Quang, Viet.
83/E3 Tuy Hoa, Viet.
65/M5 Tuymazy, Rus.
72/E2 Tūysarkān, Iran
74/C2 Tuz (lake), Turk.
124/D4 Tuzigoot Nat'l Mon., Az,US
72/D2 Ṭūz Khurmātū, Iraq
62/D3 Tuzla, Bosn.
64/G4 T'ver, Rus.
64/G4 T'ver Obl., Rus.
64/G4 Tvertsa (riv.), Rus.
63/G4 Tvŭrditsa, Bul.
49/J3 Twardogóra, Pol.
43/D3 Tweed (riv.), UK
91/E1 Tweed Heads, Austl.
50/D4 Twente (can.), Neth.
50/D4 Twente (reg.), Neth.
127/Q9 Twenty Mile (riv.), On,Can
125/G5 Twin Buttes (res.), Tx,US
122/E5 Twin Falls, Id,US
51/G6 Twiste (riv.), Ger.
51/F3 Twistringen, Ger.
125/G3 Two Buttes (riv.), Co,US
91/D3 Twofold (bay), Austl.
123/L4 Two Harbors, Mn,US
122/F2 Two Hills, Ab,Can
126/C2 Two Rivers, Wi,US
47/E1 Twycross, Eng,UK
47/F4 Twyford, Eng,UK
46/C1 Twymyn (riv.), Wal,UK
44/D2 Twynholm, Sc,UK
49/K3 Tychy, Pol.
47/G1 Tydd Saint Giles, Eng,UK
126/E2 Tyendinaga, On,Can
129/H3 Tyger (riv.), SC,US
45/F4 Tyldesley, Eng,UK
128/E3 Tyler, Tx,US
77/N1 Tymovskoye, Rus.
57/L2 Týn, Czh.
125/H2 Tyndall, SD,US
43/C2 Tyndrum, Sc,UK
45/F2 Tyne (riv.), Eng,UK
45/G2 Tyne & Wear (co.), Eng,UK
45/G1 Tynemouth, Eng,UK
72/C2 Tyre, Leb.
74/K5 Tyre (Ṣūr), Leb.
77/L2 Tyrma (riv.), Rus.
67/G4 Tyrnyauz, Rus.
91/B2 Tyrrell (cr.), Austl.
91/B2 Tyrrell (lake), Austl.
60/B2 Tyrrhenian (sea), It.
131/J8 Tysons Corner, Va,US
67/J3 Tyub-Karagan (pt.), Kaz.
67/J3 Tyuleni (isls.), Kaz.
67/H3 Tyuleniy (isl.), Rus.
65/Q4 Tyumen', Rus.
65/Q4 Tyumen' Obl., Rus.
75/C3 Tyup, Kyr.
46/B3 Tywi (riv.), Wal,UK
46/B1 Tywyn, Wal,UK
104/F5 Tzaneen, SAfr.

U

93/M5 Ua Huka (isl.), FrPol.
93/L5 Ua Pou (isl.), FrPol.
108/G4 Uatumã (riv.), Braz.
108/E3 Uaupés (riv.), Braz.
62/E3 Ub, Yugo.
110/D2 Ubá, Braz.
53/F2 Übach-Palenberg, Ger.
65/Q5 Ubagan (riv.), Kaz.
97/J7 Ubangi (riv.), D.R. Congo
109/L6 Ubatã, Braz.
110/H8 Ubatuba, Braz.
82/D5 Ubay, Phil.
57/F4 Ubaye (riv.), Fr.
50/C5 Ubbergen, Neth.
78/B4 Ube, Japan
58/D3 Úbeda, Sp.
108/G7 Uberaba (lake), Bol.
110/C1 Uberaba, Braz.
53/F5 Überherrn, Ger.
110/B1 Uberlândia, Braz.
87/J4 Ubia (peak), Indo.
83/D3 Ubon Ratchathani, Thai.
58/C4 Ubrique, Sp.
108/D5 Ucayali (riv.), Peru
48/C3 Uccle, Belg.
65/N5 Uchaly, Rus.
65/X8 Uchinskoye, Rus.
77/N3 Uchiura (bay), Japan
48/F2 Uchte (riv.), Ger.
69/P4 Uchur (riv.), Rus.
53/F5 Uckange, Fr.
49/G2 Uckermark (reg.), Ger.
47/G5 Uckfield, Eng,UK
122/B3 Ucluelet, BC,Can
76/F1 Uda (riv.), Rus.
84/B3 Udaipur, India
42/D4 Uddevalla, Swe.
42/F2 Uddjaure (lake), Swe.
50/C5 Uden, Neth.
50/C5 Udenhout, Neth.
84/C4 Udgīr, India
73/L2 Udhampur, India
57/K3 Udine, It.
84/B5 Udipi, India
65/L4 Udmurt Aut. Rep., Rus.
83/C2 Udon Thani, Thai.
49/H2 Ueckermünde, Ger.
79/F2 Ueda, Japan
97/K7 Uele (riv.), D.R. Congo
51/H3 Uelzen, Ger.
79/F3 Uenohara, Japan
51/G1 Uetersen, Ger.
51/H4 Uetze, Ger.
65/M5 Ufa, Rus.
65/N5 Ufa (riv.), Rus.
47/E3 Uffington, Eng,UK
101/B2 Uganda
61/F3 Ugento, It.
57/G4 Ugine, Fr.
77/N2 Uglegorsk, Rus.
64/H4 Uglich, Rus.
57/L4 Ugljan (isl.), Cro.
66/E1 Ugra (riv.), Rus.
76/F2 Ugtaaltsaydam, Mong.
49/J4 Uherské Hradiště, Czh.
57/K2 Úhlava (riv.), Czh.
104/C2 Uíge, Ang.
67/K2 Uil (riv.), Kaz.
102/L11 Uilkraal (riv.), SAfr.
67/G4 Uilpata, Gora (peak), Rus.
124/E2 Uinta (mts.), Ut,US
80/E4 Ŭisŏng, SKor.
102/D4 Uitenhage, SAfr.
50/B3 Uitgeest, Neth.
50/B4 Uithoorn, Neth.
92/F4 Ujae (atoll), Mrsh.
92/F4 Ujelang (atoll), Mrsh.
62/E2 Újfehértó, Hun.
79/L10 Uji, Japan
79/L10 Ujitawara, Japan
84/C3 Ujjain, India
87/E5 Ujung Pandang, Indo.
65/M3 Ukhta, Rus.
124/B3 Ukiah, Ca,US
64/E5 Ukmergė, Lith.
66/D2 Ukraine
76/F2 Ulaanbaatar (cap.), Mong.
76/C2 Ulaangom, Mong.
76/B2 Ulaanhus, Mong.
76/F1 Ulan-Burgasy (mts.), Rus.
77/J2 Ulanhot, China
76/F1 Ulan-Ude, Rus.
75/F5 Ulan Ul (lake), China
101/C4 Ulaya, Tanz.
80/E4 Ulchin, SKor.
62/D5 Ulcinj, Yugo.
76/G2 Uldz (riv.), Mong.
77/H2 Ulgain (riv.), China
84/B4 Ulhāsnagar, India
76/D2 Uliastay, Mong.
97/L8 Ulindi (riv.), D.R. Congo
92/D3 Ulithi (atoll), Micr.
58/A1 Ulla (riv.), Sp.
91/D2 Ulladulla, Austl.
42/F1 Ullsfjorden (fjord), Nor.
45/F2 Ullswater (lake), Eng,UK
78/B2 Ullŭng (isl.), SKor.
55/F1 Ulm, Ger.
80/E5 Ulsan, SKor.
44/A3 Ulster (reg.), Ire.
116/D4 Ulúa (riv.), Hon.
72/D1 Uludoruk (peak), Turk.
74/C3 Ulukışla, Turk.
76/B2 Ulungur (lake), China
76/B2 Ulungur (riv.), China
92/C7 Uluru (Ayers Rock) (peak), Austl.
75/A2 Ulutau, Gora (peak), Kaz.
45/E3 Ulverston, Eng,UK
91/C4 Ulverstone, Austl.
64/F4 Ul'yanovka, Rus.
67/J1 Ul'yanovsk, Rus.
128/C2 Ulysses, Ks,US
116/D3 Umán, Mex.
66/D2 Uman', Ukr.
84/D4 Umarkot, India
73/L2 Umāsi La (pass), India
92/D5 Umboi (isl.), PNG
60/C1 Umbria (reg.), It.
57/K5 Umbro-Marchigiano, Appenino (range), It.
68/B3 Ume (riv.), Swe.
42/G3 Umeå, Swe.
42/F2 Umeälven (riv.), Swe.
103/E3 Umfolozi (riv.), SAfr.
103/E3 Umgeni (riv.), SAfr.
73/F4 Umm as Samīm (salt dep.), Oman
97/M4 Umm Durmān (Omdurman), Sudan
74/K5 Umm el Fahm, Isr.
100/C4 Umm Hibal, Bi'r (well), Egypt
97/M5 Umm Ruwābah, Sudan
130/E5 Umnak (isl.), Ak,US
122/C5 Umpqua (riv.), Or,US
102/E3 Umtata, SAfr.
111/F1 Umuarama, Braz.
102/E3 Umzimvubu (riv.), SAfr.
62/B3 Una (riv.), Bosn., Cro.
109/J7 Unaí, Braz.
130/E5 Unalaska (isl.), Ak,US
72/C2 'Unāzah, Jabal (mtn.), SAr.
124/E3 Uncompahgre (plat.), Co,US
123/H4 Underwood, ND,US
93/Z17 Undu (pt.), Fiji
66/E1 Unecha, Rus.
130/F4 Unga (isl.), Ak,US
101/D3 Ungama (bay), Kenya
119/K3 Ungava (bay), Qu,Can
119/J2 Ungava (pen.), Qu,Can
66/C3 Ungeny, Mol.
109/K4 União, Braz.
110/B3 União da Vitória, Braz.
109/L5 União dos Palmares, Braz.
130/E4 Unimak (isl.), Ak,US
108/F4 Unini (riv.), Braz.
125/K3 Union, Mo,US
131/F5 Union, NJ,US
122/D4 Union, Or,US
129/H3 Union, SC,US
132/K11 Union City, Ca,US
131/F5 Union City, NJ,US
129/F2 Union City, Tn,US
116/E3 Unión de Reyes, Cuba
129/G3 Union Springs, Al,US
126/E4 Uniontown, Pa,US
127/R8 Unionville, On,Can
125/J2 Unionville, Mo,US
72/F4 United Arab Emirates
43/* United Kingdom
118/* United States
119/T6 United States (range), Nun.,Can
122/F2 Unity, Sk,Can
128/D4 Universal City, Tx,US
84/B3 Unjha, India
51/E5 Unna, Ger.
84/D2 Unnāo, India
48/F3 Unstruct (riv.), Ger.
54/E4 Unterwalden (canton), Swi.
74/D2 Ünye, Turk.
78/A4 Unzen-Amakusa Nat'l Park, Japan
78/B4 Unzen-dake (mtn.), Japan
65/K4 Unzha (riv.), Rus.
79/E2 Uozu, Japan
117/J6 Upata, Ven.
104/E2 Upemba Nat'l Park, D.R. Congo
102/C3 Upington, SAfr.
84/B3 Upleta, India
120/U10 Upolu (pt.), Hi,US
93/H6 Upolu (isl.), Samoa
124/C2 Upper (lake), Ca,US
129/H1 Upper Arlington, Oh,US
122/D3 Upper Arrow (lake), BC,Can
57/K2 Upper Austria (prov.), Aus.
131/E6 Upper Darby, Pa,US
47/G5 Upper Dicker, Eng,UK
99/E4 Upper East (reg.), Gha.
89/H7 Upper Hutt, NZ
125/J2 Upper Iowa (riv.), Ia,US
122/C5 Upper Klamath (lake), Or,US
44/B2 Upperlands, NI,UK
126/C2 Upper Peninsula (pen.), Mi,US
123/L5 Upper Peoria (lake), Il,US
123/K3 Upper Red (lake), Mn,US
47/E3 Upper Thames (val.), Eng,UK
99/E4 Upper West (reg.), Gha.
47/F1 Uppingham, Eng,UK
42/F4 Uppsala, Swe.
42/F3 Uppsala (co.), Swe.
130/D3 Upright (cape), Ak,US
90/B2 Upstart (bay), Austl.
123/G4 Upton, Wy,US
46/D2 Upton upon Severn, Eng,UK
72/E2 Ur (ruins), Iraq
79/H7 Uraga (chan.), Japan
68/F5 Ural (mts.), Rus.
68/F5 Ural (riv.), Rus.
118/F3 Uranium City, Sk,Can
108/F3 Uraricoera (riv.), Braz.
79/F3 Urawa, Japan
68/G3 Uray, Rus.
79/H7 Urayasu, Japan

180

Urban – Volog

126/B3 Urbana, Il,US
126/D3 Urbana, Oh,US
45/G3 Ure (riv.), Eng,UK
116/E6 Ureña, CR
124/E5 Ures, Mex.
79/M10 Ureshino, Japan
74/D3 Urfa, Turk.
51/G6 Urft (riv.), Ger.
68/G5 Urgench, Uzb.
42/H1 Urho Kekkosen Nat'l Park, Fin.
55/E4 Uri (canton), Swi.
108/F2 Urimáan, Ven.
117/N8 Urique (riv.), Mex.
50/C3 Urk, Neth.
74/A2 Urla, Turk.
63/H3 Urlaţi, Rom.
77/L2 Urmi (riv.), Rus.
72/D1 Urmia (lake), Iran
45/F5 Urmston, Eng,UK
62/E4 Uroševac, Yugo.
44/E1 Urr Water (riv.), Sc,UK
109/J6 Uruaçu, Braz.
116/A4 Uruapan, Mex.
108/D6 Urubamba (riv.), Peru
108/G4 Urubu (riv.), Braz.
109/K5 Uruçuí (mts.), Braz.
109/J7 Uruçuia (riv.), Braz.
111/E2 Uruguaiana, Braz.
111/E3 Uruguay
111/E2 Uruguay (riv.), SAm.
76/B3 Ürümqi, China
69/R5 Urup (isl.), Rus.
110/B4 Urussanga, Braz.
77/H1 Uryumkan (riv.), Rus.
67/G2 Uryupinsk, Rus.
63/H3 Urziceni, Rom.
78/B4 Usa, Japan
65/N2 Usa (riv.), Rus.
74/B2 Uşak, Turk.
113/N7 Usborne (peak), Falk.
78/B4 Ushibuka, Japan
79/J7 Ushiku, Japan
75/C2 Ushtobe, Kaz.
113/K8 Ushuaia, Arg.
84/C6 Usilampatti, India
46/D3 Usk, Wal,UK
46/D3 Usk (riv.), Wal,UK
63/J5 Üsküdar, Turk.
51/G5 Uslar, Ger.
66/F1 Usman', Rus.
76/E1 Usol'ye-Sibirskoye, Rus.
82/D5 Uson, Phil.
112/C2 Uspallata (pass), Arg., Chile
54/C5 Ussel, Fr.
54/C5 Usses (riv.), Fr.
77/L2 Ussuri (Wusuli) (riv.), Rus., China
77/L3 Ussuriysk, Rus.
60/C3 Ustica (isl.), It.
69/L4 Ust'-Ilimsk, Rus.
49/H3 Ústí nad Labem, Czh.
49/J1 Ustka, Pol.
69/S4 Ust'-Kamchatsk, Rus.
69/L4 Ust'-Kut, Rus.
76/E1 Ust'-Ordynskiy, Rus.
49/M4 Ustrzyki Dolne, Pol.
65/K3 Ust'ya (riv.), Rus.
67/K4 Ustyurt (plat.), Kaz., Uzb.
75/D3 Usu, China
78/B4 Usuki, Japan
116/D5 Usulután, ESal.
116/C4 Usumacinta (riv.), Mex.
124/E3 Utah (state), US
124/D2 Utah (lake), Ut,US
79/L10 Utano, Japan
125/G3 Ute (cr.), NM,US
64/E5 Utena, Lith.
83/C3 Uthai Thani, Thai.
126/F3 Utica, NY,US
58/E3 Utiel, Sp.
123/K2 Utik (lake), Mb,Can
122/E2 Utikuma (lake), Ab,Can
92/G3 Utirik (atoll), Mrsh.
92/G5 Utiroa, Kiri.
84/D2 Utraulā, India
50/C4 Utrecht, Neth.
50/C4 Utrecht (prov.), Neth.
58/C4 Utrera, Sp.
79/F2 Utsunomiya, Japan
83/C2 Uttaradit, Thai.
75/C5 Uttarkashi, India
84/C2 Uttar Pradesh (state), India
45/G6 Uttoxeter, Eng,UK
117/H4 Utuado, PR
92/F6 Utupua (isl.), Sol.
93/K6 Uturoa, FrPol.
76/G2 Uulbayan, Mong.
76/E1 Üür (riv.), Mong.
76/C1 Üüreg (lake), Mong.
76/C1 Uus (lake), Mong.
108/E3 Uva (riv.), Col.
128/D4 Uvalde, Tx,US
65/K4 Uval, Northern (hills), Rus.
67/G2 Uvarovo, Rus.
75/F1 Uvs Nuur (lake), Mong.
78/C4 Uwajima, Japan
97/L6 Uwayl, Sudan
81/B3 Uxin Qi, China
116/D3 Uxmal (ruins), Mex.
65/P5 Uy (riv.), Kaz., Rus.
76/E2 Uyanga, Mong.
76/C2 Uyench, Mong.
108/E8 Uyuni, Bol.
68/G5 Uzbekistan
66/B2 Uzhhorod, Ukr.
66/F1 Uzlovaya, Rus.
63/H5 Uzunköprü, Turk.

V

102/C3 Vaal (riv.), SAfr.
102/E2 Vaaldam (res.), SAfr.
53/F2 Vaals, Neth.
53/E2 Vaalsberg (hill), Neth.
42/G3 Vaasa (Vasa), Fin.
50/C4 Vaassen, Neth.
62/D2 Vác, Hun.
132/K10 Vaca (mts.), Ca,US
110/B4 Vacaria, Braz.
132/L10 Vacaville, Ca,US
119/J2 Vachon (riv.), Qu,Can
55/F3 Vaduz (cap.), Lcht.
64/J3 Vaga (riv.), Rus.
62/B3 Vaganski vrh (peak), Cro.
65/R4 Vagay (riv.), Rus.
42/E4 Vaggeryd, Swe.
49/J4 Váh (riv.), Slvk.
93/M6 Vahitahi (isl.), FrPol.
73/K5 Vaijāpur, India
125/F3 Vail, Co,US
52/C5 Vailly-sur-Aisne, Fr.
92/G5 Vaitupu (isl.), Tuv.
74/D2 Vakfıkebir, Turk.
68/J3 Vakh (riv.), Rus.
73/K1 Vākhān (mts.), Afg.
73/J1 Vakhsh (riv.), Trkm.
54/D5 Valais (canton), Swi.
50/C5 Valburg, Neth.
64/G4 Valdai (hills), Rus.
53/F6 Val-de-Bide, Fr.
58/C3 Valdecañas (res.), Sp.
52/B6 Val-de-Marne (dept.), Fr.
42/F4 Valdemarsvik, Swe.
59/M8 Valdemorillo, Sp.
58/D3 Valdepeñas, Sp.
58/C2 Valderaduey (riv.), Sp.
112/E4 Valdés (pen.), Arg.
112/B3 Valdivia, Chile
52/A5 Val-d'Oise (dept.), Fr.
126/E1 Val d'Or, Qu,Can
129/H4 Valdosta, Ga,US
58/A1 Valdoviño, Sp.
122/D5 Vale, Or,US
122/D2 Valemount, BC,Can
110/K7 Valença, Braz.
59/E3 Valencia, Sp.
59/E3 Valencia (aut. comm.), Sp.
59/F3 Valencia (gulf), Sp.
117/H5 Valencia, Ven.
58/B3 Valencia de Alcántara, Sp.
52/C3 Valenciennes, Fr.
63/H3 Vălenii de Munte, Rom.
125/G2 Valentine, Ne,US
128/B4 Valentine, Tx,US
57/H4 Valenza, It.
46/C3 Vale of Glamorgan (co.), Eng,UK
117/G6 Valera, Ven.
64/E4 Valga, Est.
110/G7 Valhinos, Braz.
56/D5 Valier (mtn.), Fr.
60/A2 Valinco (gulf), Fr.
62/D3 Valjevo, Yugo.
53/E2 Valkenburg, Neth.
50/C6 Valkenswaard, Neth.
116/D3 Valladolid, Mex.
58/C2 Valladolid, Sp.
59/E3 Vall de Uxó, Sp.
59/N9 Vallecas, Sp.
57/G5 Vallecrosia, It.
57/G4 Valle d'Aosta (reg.), It.
117/L7 Valle de Guadalupe, Mex.
117/H6 Valle de la Pascua, Ven.
59/M8 Valle de los Caídos, Sp.
117/N8 Valle de Zaragoza, Mex.
117/G5 Valledupar, Col.
108/F7 Vallegrande, Bol.
59/X16 Vallehermoso, Canl.,Sp.
50/C4 Valleikanaal (can.), Neth.
132/K10 Vallejo, Ca,US
111/B2 Vallenar, Chile
53/G3 Vallendar, Ger.
117/L7 Valle San Telmo, Mex.
60/D5 Valletta (cap.), Malta
123/J4 Valley City, ND,US
131/G4 Valley Cottage, NY,US
126/D2 Valley East, On,Can
127/M7 Valleyfield, Qu,Can
131/E5 Valley Forge Nat'l Hist. Park, Pa,US
131/G5 Valley Stream, NY,US
122/D2 Valleyview, Ab,Can
112/E3 Vallimanca (riv.), Arg.
59/F2 Valls, Sp.
122/G3 Val Marie, Sk,Can
59/M8 Valmayor (res.), Sp.
51/F6 Valme (riv.), Ger.
64/E4 Valmiera, Lat.
61/F2 Valona (bay), Alb.
84/C5 Vālparai, India
112/C2 Valparaíso, Chile
112/C2 Valparaíso (reg.), Chile
117/P9 Valparaíso, Mex.
129/G4 Valparaiso, Fl,US
126/C3 Valparaiso, In,US
62/D3 Valpovo, Cro.
56/F4 Valréas, Fr.
102/D2 Vals (riv.), SAfr.
84/B3 Valsād, India
102/B4 Valsbaai (bay), SAfr.
66/F2 Valuyki, Rus.
131/B2 Val Verde, Ca,US
58/B4 Valverde del Camino, Sp.
42/G3 Vammala, Fin.
74/E2 Van, Turk.
74/E2 Van (lake), Turk.
67/H4 Vanadzor, Arm.
93/L7 Vanavaro (isl.), FrPol.
128/E3 Van Buren, Ar,US
127/H2 Van Buren, Me,US
125/K3 Van Buren, Mo,US
122/C3 Vancouver, BC,Can
122/B3 Vancouver (isl.), BC,Can
122/C4 Vancouver, Wa,US
130/L3 Vancouver (mtn.), Yk,Can, Ak,US
105/L Vanda, Ant.
126/B4 Vandalia, Il,US
125/K3 Vandalia, Mo,US
102/D2 Vanderbijl Park, SAfr.
122/B2 Vanderhoof, BC,Can
53/F6 Vandoeuvre-lès-Nancy, Fr.
42/E4 Vänern (lake), Swe.
42/E4 Vänersborg, Swe.
103/H8 Vangaindrano, Madg.
50/C2 Van Harinxmakanaal (can.), Neth.
83/D1 Van Hoa, Viet.
128/B4 Van Horn, Tx,US
119/R7 Vanier (isl.), Nun.,Can
92/F6 Vanikoro (isl.), Sol.
87/K4 Vanimo, PNG
77/N2 Vanino, Rus.
42/F3 Vännäs, Swe.
56/E2 Vanne (riv.), Fr.
56/B3 Vannes, Fr.
83/E3 Van Ninh, Viet.
57/G4 Vanoise Nat'l Park, Fr.
102/E3 Vanreenenpas (pass), SAfr.
87/J4 Van Rees (mts.), Indo.
119/H2 Vansittart (isl.), Nun.,Can
42/H3 Vantaa, Fin.
92/G6 Vanua Levu (isl.), Fiji
92/F6 Vanuatu
126/C3 Van Wert, Oh,US
83/D1 Van Yen, Viet.
57/G5 Var (riv.), Fr.
72/F1 Varāmīn, Iran
84/D2 Vārānasi, India
42/J1 Varangerfjorden (fjord), Nor.
42/J1 Varangerhalvøya (pen.), Nor.
60/D2 Varano (lake), It.
62/C2 Varaždin, Cro.
57/H4 Varazze, It.
42/E4 Varberg, Swe.
62/E5 Vardar (riv.), FYROM
48/E1 Varde, Den.
51/F2 Varel, Ger.
127/P6 Varennes, Qu,Can
52/A4 Varennes (riv.), Fr.
56/E3 Varennes-Vauzelles, Fr.
62/D3 Vareš, Bosn.
57/H4 Varese, It.
110/G6 Vargem do Sul, Braz.
109/K5 Vargem Grande, Braz.
110/H6 Varginha, Braz.
42/C4 Varhaug, Nor.
42/H3 Varkaus, Fin.
42/E3 Värmland (co.), Swe.
63/H4 Varna, Bul.
63/H4 Varna (reg.), Bul.
42/E4 Värnamo, Swe.
62/D2 Várpalota, Hun.
74/E2 Varto, Turk.
44/B5 Vartry (res.), Ire.
44/B5 Vartry (riv.), Ire.
110/C1 Várzea da Palma, Braz.
109/G7 Várzea Grande, Braz.
64/H2 Varzuga (riv.), Rus.
62/C2 Vas (co.), Hun.
109/L5 Vasa Barris (riv.), Braz.
49/M4 Vásárosnamény, Hun.
42/G3 Vasa (Vaasa), Fin.
65/K2 Vashka (riv.), Rus.
132/C3 Vashon (isl.), Wa,US
66/D2 Vasil'kov, Ukr.
63/H2 Vaslui, Rom.
63/H2 Vaslui (co.), Rom.
126/D3 Vassar, Mi,US
61/G4 Vassés (Bassae) (ruins), Gre.
110/K7 Vassouras, Braz.
42/F4 Västerås, Swe.
42/F2 Västerbotten (co.), Swe.
42/F4 Västerhaninge, Swe.
42/F3 Västernorrland (co.), Swe.
42/F4 Västervik, Swe.
42/E3 Västmanland (co.), Swe.
64/C3 Vastmanland (co.), Swe.
60/D1 Vasto, It.
42/E5 Vaterstetten, Ger.
60/C2 Vatican City
42/P7 Vatnajökull (glac.), Ice.
63/G2 Vatra Dornei, Rom.
42/E4 Vättern (lake), Swe.
93/Y18 Vatukoula, Fiji
54/C4 Vaud (canton), Swi.
127/M7 Vaudreuil, Qu,Can
127/Q8 Vaughan, On,Can
125/F4 Vaughn, NM,US
56/F4 Vaulx-en-Velin, Fr.
56/F5 Vauvert, Fr.
52/D4 Vaux (riv.), Fr.
122/E3 Vauxhall, Ab,Can
52/B3 Vaux-Vraucourt, Fr.
93/H6 Vava'u Group (isls.), Tonga
84/D6 Vavuniya, SrL.
42/E4 Växjö, Swe.
68/F3 Vaygach (isl.), Rus.
110/C1 Vazante, Braz.
110/G8 Vázea Paulista, Braz.
64/G5 Vazuza (res.), Rus.
50/D4 Vecht (riv.), Neth.
56/F3 Vechta, Ger.
51/E4 Vechte (riv.), Ger.
62/D2 Vecsés, Hun.
63/G3 Vedea (riv.), Rom.
112/E2 Vedia, Arg.
50/D2 Veendam, Neth.
50/C4 Veenendaal, Neth.
50/A5 Veerse Meer (res.), Neth.
42/D2 Vega (isl.), Nor.
130/B6 Vega (pt.), Ak,US
42/D2 Vegafjorden (fjord), Nor.
50/C5 Veghel, Neth.
61/G2 Vegorítis (lake), Gre.
122/E2 Vegreville, Ab,Can
42/H3 Vehkalahti, Fin.
58/C4 Vejer de la Frontera, Sp.
43/E1 Vejle, Den.
43/E1 Vejle (co.), Den.
117/G5 Vela (cape), Col.
59/S12 Velas, Azor,Port.
50/E6 Velbert, Ger.
57/L3 Velden am Wörthersee, Aus.
50/C6 Veldhoven, Neth.
50/C6 Velen, Ger.
62/B2 Velenje, Slov.
58/C4 Vélez-Málaga, Sp.
58/D4 Vélez-Rubio, Sp.
110/C1 Velhas (Araguari) (riv.), Braz.
62/C3 Velika Gorica, Cro.
62/E3 Velika Plana, Yugo.
64/F4 Velikaya (riv.), Rus.
64/F4 Velikiye Luki, Rus.
64/K3 Velikiy Ustyug, Rus.
63/G4 Veliko Tŭrnovo, Bul.
63/G4 Velingrad, Bul.
49/J4 Velké Meziříčí, Czh.
49/K4 Vel'ký Krtíš, Slvk.
60/D2 Velletri, It.
51/G6 Vellmar, Ger.
59/N8 Vellón (res.), Sp.
84/C5 Vellore, India
64/J3 Vel'sk, Rus.
50/C4 Veluwe (reg.), Neth.
50/C4 Veluwemeer (lake), Neth.
50/C4 Veluwezoom Nat'l Park, Neth.
123/H3 Velva, ND,US
112/E2 Venado Tuerto, Arg.
60/D2 Venafro, It.
110/A4 Venâncio Aires, Braz.
57/G4 Venaria, It.
57/G5 Vence, Fr.
110/B2 Venceslau Brás, Braz.
58/A3 Vendas Novas, Port.
56/D3 Vendôme, Fr.
59/F2 Vendrell, Sp.
57/J4 Veneto (reg.), It.
57/K4 Venezia (gulf), It.
57/K4 Venezia (Venice), It.
108/E2 Venezuela
117/G5 Venezuela (gulf), Col., Ven.
84/B4 Vengurla, India
130/G4 Veniaminof (vol.), Ak,US
129/H5 Venice, Fl,US
57/K4 Venice (Venezia), It.
56/F4 Vénissieux, Fr.
84/C5 Venkatagiri, India
50/D6 Venlo, Neth.
42/C4 Vennesla, Nor.
60/D2 Venosa, It.
50/C5 Venray, Neth.
64/D4 Venta (riv.), Lat., Lith.
58/C2 Venta de Baños, Sp.
93/L6 Vent, Iles du (isls.), FrPol.
93/K6 Vent, Iles sous le (isls.), FrPol.
47/E5 Ventnor, Eng,UK
64/D4 Ventspils, Lat.
131/A2 Ventura (San Buenaventura), Ca,US
60/B1 Venturina, It.
93/X15 Vénus (pt.), FrPol.
116/C4 Venustiano Carranza, Mex.
111/D2 Vera, Arg.
116/B4 Veracruz, Mex.
116/B3 Veracruz (state), Mex.
113/B4 Veranópolis, Braz.
84/B3 Verāval, India
57/H4 Verbania, It.
57/H4 Vercelli, It.
42/D3 Verdal, Nor.
110/B1 Verdão (riv.), Braz.
112/E3 Verde (bay), Arg.
110/H6 Verde (riv.), Braz.
117/N8 Verde (riv.), Mex.
111/E1 Verde (riv.), Par.
96/B5 Verde (cape), Sen.
124/E4 Verde (riv.), Az,US
58/B1 Verde, Costa (coast), Sp.
109/K7 Verde Grande (riv.), Braz.
51/G3 Verden, Ger.
125/J3 Verdigris (riv.), Ks, Ok,US
110/B1 Verdinho (riv.), Braz.
56/F5 Verdon (riv.), Fr.
127/N7 Verdun, Qu,Can
53/E5 Verdun-sur-Meuse, Fr.
102/D2 Vereeniging, SAfr.
65/M4 Vereshchagino, Rus.
49/M4 Veretskiy Pereval (pass), Ukr.
98/B4 Verga (cape), Gui.
58/D1 Vergara, Sp.
127/F2 Vergennes, Vt,US
61/H2 Vergina (ruins), Gre.
58/B2 Verín, Sp.
64/F1 Verkhnetulomskiy (res.), Rus.
69/N3 Verkhoyansk (range), Rus.
51/F5 Verl, Ger.
52/C4 Vermand, Fr.
122/F2 Vermilion, Ab,Can
122/F2 Vermilion (riv.), Ab,Can
125/K2 Vermilion (riv.), Il,US
123/K4 Vermillion (range), Mn,US
123/J5 Vermillion, SD,US
125/H2 Vermillion (riv.), SD,US
127/F2 Vermont (state), US
124/E2 Vernal, Ut,US
56/D2 Verneuil-sur-Avre, Fr.
102/C3 Verneukpan (salt pan), SAfr.
122/D3 Vernon, BC,Can
52/A5 Vernon, Fr.
128/D3 Vernon, Tx,US
132/Q15 Vernon Hills, Il,US
53/F5 Verny, Fr.
129/H5 Vero Beach, Fl,US
61/H2 Véroia, Gre.
57/J4 Verona, It.
52/B6 Verrières-le-Buisson, Fr.
52/B6 Versailles, Fr.
126/C4 Versailles, Ky,US
66/E2 Verskla (riv.), Rus., Ukr.
51/F4 Versmold, Ger.
58/E1 Vert (riv.), Fr.
55/G4 Vertana (peak), It.
56/C3 Vertou, Fr.
53/E2 Verviers, Belg.
47/E5 Verwood, Eng,UK
46/B6 Veryan (bay), Eng,UK
53/F2 Vesdre (riv.), Belg.
67/G3 Veselyy (res.), Rus.
52/D5 Vesle (riv.), Fr.
54/D2 Vesoul, Fr.
42/C4 Vest-Agder (co.), Nor.
42/E1 Vesterålen (isls.), Nor.
42/E2 Vestfjorden (fjord), Nor.
42/D4 Vestfold (co.), Nor.
48/F1 Vest-Sjælland (co.), Den.
42/E1 Vestvågøya (isl.), Nor.
62/C2 Veszprém, Hun.
62/C2 Veszprém (co.), Hun.
62/E2 Vészto, Hun.
102/D3 Vet (riv.), SAfr.
42/E4 Vetlanda, Swe.
65/K4 Vetluga (riv.), Rus.
60/C1 Vetralla, It.
56/D3 Veude (riv.), Fr.
52/B1 Veurne, Belg.
54/C5 Vevey, Swi.
53/F2 Veybach (riv.), Ger.
56/D4 Vézère (riv.), Fr.
74/C2 Vezirköprü, Turk.
108/E7 Viacha, Bol.
109/K4 Viana, Braz.
58/B1 Viana del Bollo, Sp.
58/A2 Viana do Castelo, Port.
58/A2 Viana do Castelo (dist.), Port.
50/C5 Vianen, Neth.
83/C2 Viangchan (Vientiane) (cap.), Laos
58/C4 Viar (riv.), Sp.
57/J5 Viareggio, It.
56/E4 Viaur (riv.), Fr.
42/D4 Viborg, Den.
60/E3 Vibo Valentia, It.
59/G2 Vic, Sp.
58/D4 Vicar, Sp.
113/S12 Vicente López, Arg.
57/J4 Vicenza, It.
64/J4 Vichuga, Rus.
56/E3 Vichy, Fr.
129/F3 Vicksburg, Ms,US
60/C1 Vico (lake), It.
110/D2 Viçosa, Braz.
61/G3 Vicou Gorge Nat'l Park, Gre.
52/C5 Vic-sur-Aisne, Fr.
53/F6 Vic-sur-Seille, Fr.
101/B3 Victoria (lake), Afr.
112/E2 Victoria, Arg.
91/C3 Victoria (state), Austl.
116/D4 Victoria (peak), Belz.
85/F3 Victoria (peak), Burma
122/C3 Victoria (cap.), BC,Can
118/E1 Victoria (isl.), NW,Nun.,Can
118/F2 Victoria (str.), Nun.,Can
127/Q8 Victoria, On,Can
112/B3 Victoria, Chile
82/B3 Victoria, China
87/E2 Victoria (peak), Phil.
63/G3 Victoria, Rom.
128/D4 Victoria, Tx,US
117/F3 Victoria de las Tunas, Cuba
105/L Victoria Land (reg.), Ant.
101/B2 Victoria Nile (riv.), Ugan.
127/G2 Victoriaville, Qu,Can
131/C1 Victorville, Ca,US
103/F3 Vidal (cape), SAfr.
129/H3 Vidalia, Ga,US
129/F4 Vidalia, La,US
110/B3 Videira, Braz.
63/G3 Videle, Rom.
62/F4 Vidin, Bul.
84/C3 Vidisha, India
128/E4 Vidor, Tx,US
56/E5 Vidourle (riv.), Fr.
56/C3 Vie (riv.), Fr.
112/C4 Viedma, Arg.
113/J7 Viedma (lake), Arg.
58/C1 Vieja (mtn.), Sp.
128/B4 Vieja (mts.), Tx,US
53/E3 Vielsalm, Belg.
51/H5 Vienenburg, Ger.
131/J8 Vienna, Va,US
126/D4 Vienna, WV,US
49/J4 Vienna (Wien) (cap.), Aus.
56/F4 Vienne, Fr.
56/D3 Vienne (riv.), Fr.
83/C2 Vientiane (Viangchan) (cap.), Laos
53/D6 Viere (riv.), Fr.
50/D5 Vierlingsbeek, Neth.
53/E4 Vierre (riv.), Fr.
50/D6 Viersen, Ger.
56/E3 Vierzon, Fr.
60/E2 Vieste, It.
83/D2 Vietnam
83/D1 Viet Tri, Viet.
52/C3 Vieux-Condé, Fr.
117/J5 Vieux Fort, StL.
82/D5 Viga, Phil.
82/D4 Vigan, Phil.
57/H4 Vigevano, It.
109/J4 Vigia, Braz.
60/C2 Viglio (peak), It.
56/C5 Vignemale (mtn.), Fr.
52/B6 Vigneux, Fr.
57/J4 Vignola, It.
58/A1 Vigo, Sp.
53/F5 Vigy, Fr.
73/K2 Vihāri, Pak.
42/H3 Viitasaari, Fin.
84/D4 Vijayawada, India
61/F2 Vijosë (riv.), Alb.
42/D4 Vikersund, Nor.
63/F5 Vikhren (peak), Bul.
122/F2 Viking, Ab,Can
59/G2 Viladecans, Sp.
59/V14 Vila de Porto Santo, Madr.,Port.
104/G4 Vila de Sena, Moz.
58/A2 Vila do Conde, Port.
59/T13 Vila do Porto, Azor,Port.
59/K7 Vilafranca del Penedès, Sp.
58/A3 Vila Franca de Xira, Port.
59/T13 Vila Franca do Campo, Azor.,Port.
56/B3 Vilaine (riv.), Fr.
103/H7 Vilanandro (cape), Madg.
58/A2 Vila Nova de Gaia, Port.
59/F2 Vilanova i la Geltrú, Sp.
59/K7 Vilanova i la Geltru, Sp.
58/B2 Vila Real, Port.
58/B2 Vila Real (dist.), Port.
58/B4 Vila Real de Santo António, Port.
110/D2 Vila Velha Argolas, Braz.
63/F3 Vîlcea (co.), Rom.
42/F2 Vilhelmina, Swe.
108/F6 Vilhena, Braz.
64/E5 Viliya (riv.), Bela.
64/E4 Viljandi, Est.
69/K2 Vil'kitsogo (str.), Rus.
112/Q9 Villa Alemana, Chile
111/D2 Villa Ángela, Arg.
58/E1 Villaba, Sp.
58/B1 Villablino, Sp.
117/H6 Villa Bruzual, Ven.
112/E4 Villa Cañas, Arg.
58/D3 Villacañas, Sp.
111/D3 Villa Carlos Paz, Arg.
58/D3 Villacarrillo, Sp.
57/K3 Villach, Aus.
112/E2 Villa Constitución, Arg.
58/A1 Villa de Cruces, Sp.
58/C4 Villa del Río, Sp.
111/C3 Villa Dolores, Arg.
116/C4 Villa Flores, Mex.
58/B3 Villafranca de los Barros, Sp.
116/A2 Villa Frontera, Mex.
58/A1 Villagarcía, Sp.
128/E4 Village Mills, Tx,US
113/F3 Villa Gesell, Arg.
112/F1 Villaguay, Arg.
116/C4 Villahermosa, Mex.
117/N7 Villa Hidalgo, Mex.
59/E3 Villajoyosa, Sp.
58/B1 Villalba, Sp.
58/B2 Villalcampo (res.), Sp.
112/E2 Villa María, Arg.
58/C4 Villamartín, Sp.
108/F8 Villa Montes, Bol.
116/D4 Villanueva, Hon.
58/A1 Villanueva de Arosa, Sp.
58/C3 Villanueva de Córdoba, Sp.
58/D3 Villanueva del Arzobispo, Sp.
58/C3 Villanueva de la Serena, Sp.
58/D3 Villanueva de los Infantes, Sp.
131/C3 Villa Park, Ca,US
132/Q16 Villa Park, Il,US
112/D3 Villa Regina, Arg.
59/E3 Villarreal de los Infantes, Sp.
112/B3 Villarrica, Chile
112/B3 Villarrica (lake), Chile
111/E2 Villarrica, Par.
112/C3 Villarrica Nat'l Park, Chile
58/D3 Villarrobledo, Sp.
58/D3 Villarrubia de los Ojos, Sp.
112/F2 Villa San José, Arg.
108/F7 Villa Serrano, Bol.
111/F2 Villa Unión, Arg.
117/N9 Villa Unión, Mex.
108/D3 Villavicencio, Col.
58/C1 Villaviciosa, Sp.
59/N9 Villaviciosa de Odón, Sp.
108/E8 Villazón, Bol.
56/E4 Villefranche-de-Rouergue, Fr.
56/F4 Villefranche-sur-Saône, Fr.
52/B6 Villejuif, Fr.
59/E3 Villena, Sp.
52/C2 Villeneuve-d'Ascq, Fr.
56/F5 Villeneuve-lès-Avignon, Fr.
52/B6 Villeneuve-Saint-Georges, Fr.
56/D4 Villeneuve-sur-Lot, Fr.
56/D5 Villeneuve-Tolosane, Fr.
52/B6 Villeparisis, Fr.
128/E4 Ville Platte, La,US
52/C5 Villers-Cotterêts, Fr.
53/F6 Villers-lès-Nancy, Fr.
52/C3 Villers-Outreaux, Fr.
53/E5 Villerupt, Fr.
55/E1 Villingen-Schwenningen, Ger.
84/C5 Villupuram, India
49/N1 Vilnius (cap.), Lith.
42/H3 Vilppula, Fin.
57/K2 Vils (riv.), Ger.
57/K2 Vilshofen, Ger.
52/D2 Vilvoorde, Belg.
69/M3 Vilyuy (range), Rus.
69/N3 Vilyuy (riv.), Rus.
55/H4 Vipiteno (Sterzing), It.
58/B1 Vimianzo, Sp.
42/E4 Vimmerby, Swe.
52/B3 Vimy, Fr.
96/H6 Vina (riv.), Camr.
112/C2 Viña del Mar, Chile
57/G5 Vinaigre (mtn.), Fr.
59/F2 Vinaroz, Sp.
105/H Vincennes (bay), Ant.
52/B6 Vincennes, Fr.
126/C4 Vincennes, In,US
131/B2 Vincent, Ca,US
42/F2 Vindeln, Swe.
127/R9 Vineland, On,Can
126/F4 Vineland, NJ,US
83/D2 Vinh, Viet.
110/G8 Vinhedo, Braz.
83/D4 Vinh Long, Viet.
83/D4 Vinh Quoi, Viet.
83/E3 Vinh Thanh, Viet.
83/D1 Vinh Yen, Viet.
62/F5 Vinica, FYROM
125/J3 Vinita, Ok,US
62/F3 Vînju Mare, Rom.
62/D3 Vinkovci, Cro.
66/D2 Vinnytsya, Ukr.
66/D2 Vinnyts'ka (obl.), Ukr.
66/B2 Vinogradov, Ukr.
38/E9 Vinson (peak), Ant.
52/A5 Viosne (riv.), Fr.
55/H4 Vipiteno (Sterzing), It.
82/D5 Virac, Phil.
74/D3 Viranşehir, Turk.
84/B4 Virār, India
123/H3 Virden, Mb,Can
56/C2 Vire, Fr.
104/B4 Virei, Ang.
111/C7 Virgenes (cape), Arg.
127/R9 Virgil, On,Can
117/J4 Virgin (isls.), UK, US
124/D3 Virgin (riv.), US
126/E5 Virginia (state), US
123/K4 Virginia, Mn,US
126/F4 Virginia Beach, Va,US
124/C3 Virginia City, Nv,US
83/D3 Virochey, Camb.
52/D3 Viroin (riv.), Belg.
126/B3 Viroqua, Wi,US
62/C3 Virovitica, Cro.
53/E4 Virton, Belg.
84/C6 Virudunagar, India
52/B6 Viry-Châtillon, Fr.
60/D1 Vis (isl.), Cro.
84/D4 Visākhapatnam, India
124/C3 Visalia, Ca,US
82/D5 Visayan (sea), Phil.
51/F3 Visbek, Ger.
42/F4 Visby, Swe.
110/D2 Visconde do Rio Branco, Braz.
119/R7 Viscount Melville (sound), NW,Nun.,Can
53/E2 Visé, Belg.
62/D4 Višegrad, Bosn.
58/B2 Viseu, Port.
58/B2 Viseu (dist.), Port.
63/G2 Vişeu de Sus, Rom.
65/N3 Vishera (riv.), Rus.
102/B4 Vishoek, SAfr.
84/B3 Visnagar, India
62/D3 Višnjevac, Cro.
62/D4 Visoko, Bosn.
51/G3 Visselhövede, Ger.
124/C4 Vista, Ca,US
61/J2 Vistonís (lake), Gre.
49/K2 Vistula (Wisła) (riv.), Pol.
63/G4 Vit (riv.), Bul.
123/J3 Vita, Mb,Can
57/J5 Vitalba (peak), It.
60/C1 Viterbo, It.
83/D4 Vi Thanh, Viet.
92/G6 Viti Levu (isl.), Fiji
76/G1 Vitim (plat.), Rus.
76/G1 Vitim (riv.), Rus.
110/D2 Vitória, Braz.
58/D1 Vitoria, Sp.
109/K6 Vitória da Conquista, Braz.
109/L5 Vitória de Santo Antão, Braz.
63/F4 Vitosha Nat'l Park, Bul.
56/C2 Vitré, Fr.
56/F5 Vitrolles, Fr.
52/D6 Vitry-le-François, Fr.
52/B6 Vitry-sur-Seine, Fr.
64/F5 Vitsyebsk, Bela.
64/E5 Vitsyebskaya (prov.), Bela.
60/D4 Vittoria, It.
57/K4 Vittorio Veneto, It.
56/F4 Vivarais (mts.), Fr.
58/B1 Vivero, Sp.
63/H5 Vize, Turk.
65/K2 Vizhas (riv.), Rus.
84/D4 Vizianagaram, India
50/B5 Vlaardingen, Neth.
62/F2 Vlădeasa (peak), Rom.
67/H4 Vladikavkaz, Rus.
64/J4 Vladimir, Rus.
64/J5 Vladimir Obl., Rus.
66/C2 Vladimir-Volynskiy, Ukr.
77/L3 Vladivostok, Rus.
51/E2 Vlagtwedde, Neth.
63/G2 Vlăhiţa, Rom.
62/E4 Vlajna (peak), Yugo.
62/D3 Vlasenica, Bosn.
49/H4 Vlašim, Czh.
62/F4 Vlasotince, Yugo.
50/B2 Vlieland (isl.), Neth.
50/C2 Vliestroom (chan.), Neth.
50/C5 Vlijmen, Neth.
50/A6 Vlissingen, Neth.
61/F2 Vlorë, Alb.
51/F4 Vlotho, Ger.
57/L1 Vltava (riv.), Czh.
57/K2 Vöcklabruck, Aus.
64/H3 Vodlozero (lake), Rus.
50/D5 Voerde, Ger.
57/H1 Vogelsberg (mts.), Ger.
57/H4 Voghera, It.
62/D4 Vogošća, Bosn.
57/J1 Vogtland (reg.), Ger.
93/U12 Voh, NCal.
57/K2 Vohenstrauss, Ger.
103/H9 Vohimena (cape), Madg.
103/G7 Vohipeno, Madg.
101/C3 Voi, Kenya
56/F4 Voiron, Fr.
56/D2 Voise (riv.), Fr.
119/K3 Voisey (bay), Nf,Can
52/B5 Voisne (riv.), Fr.
62/D5 Vojosë (riv.), Alb.
62/D3 Vojvodina (aut. prov.), Yugo.
53/F5 Völklingen, Ger.
92/C2 Volcano (isls.), Japan
42/C3 Volda, Nor.
50/C4 Volendam, Neth.
41/J3 Volga (riv.), Rus.
64/H3 Volga-Baltic Wtwy., Rus.
67/G3 Volgodonsk, Rus.
67/H2 Volgograd, Rus.
67/H2 Volgograd (res.), Rus.
67/G2 Volgograd Obl., Rus.
50/B5 Volkerakdam (dam), Neth.
57/L3 Völkermarkt, Aus.
64/G4 Volkhov, Rus.
64/F4 Volkhov (riv.), Rus.
53/F5 Völklingen, Ger.
51/G6 Volkmarsen, Ger.
49/N2 Volkovysk, Bela.
103/E2 Volksrust, SAfr.
53/G5 Volmunster, Fr.
64/H4 Vologda, Rus.
64/J3 Vologda Obl., Rus.
54/C1 Vologne (riv.), Fr.

181

Vólos – Whitw

61/H3 Vólos, Gre.
61/H3 Volos (gulf), Gre.
67/H1 Vol'sk, Rus.
99/E4 Volta (lake), Gha.
99/F5 Volta (reg.), Gha.
99/F5 Volta (riv.), Gha.
110/J7 Volta Redonda, Braz.
57/J5 Volterra, It.
60/D2 Volturno (riv.), It.
61/H2 Vólvi (lake), Gre.
65/L5 Volzhsk, Rus.
67/H2 Volzhskiy, Rus.
130/H3 Von Frank (mtn.), Ak,US
56/D3 Vonne (riv.), Fr.
50/B4 Voorburg, Neth.
50/B5 Voorne (isl.), Neth.
50/B4 Voorschoten, Neth.
50/D4 Voorst, Neth.
55/F3 Vorarlberg (prov.), Aus.
50/D4 Vorden, Neth.
55/E4 Vorderrhein (riv.), Swi.
56/F4 Voreppe, Fr.
65/Q2 Vorkuta, Rus.
67/G1 Vorona (riv.), Rus.
66/F2 Voronezh, Rus.
66/F1 Voronezh (riv.), Rus.
67/G2 Voronezh Obl., Rus.
64/G1 Voron'ya (riv.), Rus.
53/E1 Vorst, Belg.
64/E4 Võru, Est.
54/C1 Vosges (dept.), Fr.
54/C2 Vosges (mts.), Fr.
64/H5 Voskresensk, Rus.
42/C3 Voss, Nor.
105/V Vostock (cape), Ant.
105/H Vostok, Ant.
93/K6 Vostok (isl.), Kiri.
65/M4 Votkinsk, Rus.
65/M4 Votkinsk (res.), Rus.
110/C2 Votorantim, Braz.
110/B2 Votuporanga, Braz.
58/B2 Vouga (riv.), Port.
61/H5 Voúxa, Ákra (cape), Gre.
123/K3 Voyageurs Nat'l Park, Mn,US
105/J Voyeykov Ice Shelf, Ant.
65/M3 Voy-Vozh, Rus.
64/H3 Vozhe (lake), Rus.
66/D3 Voznesensk, Ukr.
63/H3 Vrancea (co.), Rom.
71/S2 Vrangelya (isl.), Rus.
62/E4 Vranje, Yugo.
49/L4 Vranov nad Teplou, Slvk.
63/F4 Vratsa, Bul.
62/C3 Vrbas (riv.), Bosn.
62/D3 Vrbas, Yugo.
102/E2 Vrede, SAfr.
50/D4 Vreden, Ger.
102/B4 Vredenburg, SAfr.
57/L4 Vrhnika, Slov.
50/D2 Vries, Neth.
50/D4 Vriezenveen, Neth.
48/B5 Vrin (riv.), Fr.
84/C2 Vrindāban, India
62/E4 Vrnjačka Banja, Yugo.
62/E3 Vršac, Yugo.
102/D2 Vryburg, SAfr.
103/E2 Vryheid, SAfr.
49/K4 Vsetín, Czh.
130/E5 Vsevidof (mtn.), Ak,US
49/K4 Vtáčnik (peak), Slvk.
62/E4 Vučitrn, Yugo.
50/C5 Vught, Neth.
62/D3 Vukovar, Cro.
122/E3 Vulcan, Ab,Can
63/F3 Vulcan, Rom.
60/D3 Vulcano (isl.), It.
63/F4 Vŭlchedrŭm, Bul.
60/B1 Vulci (ruins), It.
83/D2 Vu Liet, Viet.
83/D4 Vung Tau, Viet.
92/G7 Vunisea, Fiji
130/K2 Vuntut Nat'l Park, Yk,Can.
64/E1 Vuotso, Fin.
63/F4 Vŭrshets, Bul.
84/B3 Vyāra, India
65/L4 Vyatka (riv.), Rus.
65/L4 Vyatskiye Polyany, Rus.
77/L2 Vyazemskiy, Rus.
64/G5 Vyaz'ma, Rus.
64/F3 Vyborg, Rus.
65/K3 Vychegda (riv.), Rus.
49/H3 Východočeský (reg.), Czh.
49/L4 Východoslovenský (reg.), Slvk.
64/G3 Vygozero (lake), Rus.
49/M4 Vyhorlat (peak), Slvk.
64/J5 Vyksa, Rus.
65/L3 Vym' (riv.), Rus.
46/C1 Vyrnwy (riv.), Wal,UK
64/G4 Vyshniy Volochek, Rus.
49/J4 Vyškov, Czh.

W

99/E4 Wa, Gha.
50/C5 Waal (riv.), Neth.
50/C6 Waalre, Neth.
50/C5 Waalwijk, Neth.
52/C1 Waarschoot, Belg.
122/E2 Wabasca, Ab,Can
118/E3 Wabasca (riv.), Ab,Can
126/C4 Wabash (riv.), Il, In,US
126/C3 Wabash, In,US
51/G6 Wabern, Ger.
123/K3 Wabigoon (lake), On,Can
123/J2 Wabowden, Mb,Can
49/K2 Wąbrzeźno, Pol.
81/D4 Wabu (lake), China
79/L9 Wachi, Japan
52/C1 Wachtebeke, Belg.
50/D6 Wachtendonk, Ger.
128/D4 Waco, Tx,US
128/D2 Waconda (lake), Ks,US
123/K4 Waconia, Mn,US
91/D3 Wadbilliga Nat'l Park, Austl.
96/J2 Waddān, Libya
50/C2 Waddenzee (sound), Neth.
122/B3 Waddington (mtn.), BC,Can
45/F4 Waddington, Eng,UK
45/H5 Waddington, Eng,UK
50/B4 Waddinxveen, Neth.
90/D4 Waddy (pt.), Austl.
46/B5 Wadebridge, Eng,UK
123/H3 Wadena, Sk,Can
123/K4 Wadena, Mn,US
55/E3 Wädenswil, Swi.
53/F4 Wadern, Ger.
51/F5 Wadersloh, Ger.
53/F5 Wadgassen, Ger.
47/G4 Wadhurst, Eng,UK
74/K6 Wādī As Sīr, Jor.
100/B4 Wādī Ḥalfā', Sudan
97/M5 Wad Medanī, Sudan
49/K4 Wadowice, Pol.
77/J4 Wafangdian, China
51/F3 Wagenfeld-Hasslingen, Ger.
50/C5 Wageningen, Neth.
118/G2 Wager (bay), Nun.,Can
91/C2 Wagga Wagga, Austl.
49/J2 Wągrowiec, Pol.
73/K2 Wāh, Pak.
87/G4 Wahai, Indo.
100/B4 Wāḥat Salīmah (well), Sudan
120/V12 Wahiawa, Hi,US
125/H2 Wahoo, Ne,US
123/J4 Wahpeton, ND,US
124/D3 Wah Wah (range), Ut,US
84/B4 Wai, India
120/V13 Waianae, Hi,US
57/L3 Waidhofen an der Ybbs, Aus.
87/H3 Waigeo (isl.), Indo.
87/E5 Waikabubak, Indo.
89/H7 Waikari, NZ
120/T10 Wailuku, Hi,US
120/V12 Waimea (falls), Hi,US
127/R10 Wainfleet, On,Can
45/J5 Wainfleet All Saints, Eng,UK
84/C3 Waingangā (riv.), India
87/F5 Waingapu, Indo.
122/F2 Wainwright, Ab,Can
120/V13 Waipahu, Hi,US
120/U10 Waipio, Hi,US
89/H6 Wairoa, NZ
89/H6 Waitemata, NZ
93/Z17 Waiyevu, Fiji
79/E2 Wajima, Japan
101/D2 Wajir, Kenya
87/G4 Waka (cape), Indo.
78/D3 Wakasa, Japan
78/D3 Wakasa (bay), Japan
123/G2 Wakaw, Sk,Can
78/D3 Wakayama, Japan
78/D4 Wakayama (pref.), Japan
92/F3 Wake (isl.), PacUS
128/D2 Wakeeney, Ks,US
45/G4 Wakefield, Eng,UK
126/B2 Wakefield, Mi,US
85/G4 Wakema, Myan.
78/D3 Waki, Japan
77/N2 Wakkanai, Japan
79/H7 Wakō, Japan
126/D1 Wakwayowkastic (riv.), On,Can
63/G3 Walachia (range), Rom.
63/G3 Walachia (reg.), Rom.
49/J3 Wałbrzych, Pol.
49/J3 Wałbrzych (prov.), Pol.
47/E4 Walbury (hill), Eng,UK
50/A5 Walcheren (isl.), Neth.
52/D3 Walcourt, Belg.
49/J2 Wałcz, Pol.
53/G2 Waldbröl, Ger.
51/G6 Waldeck, Ger.
125/F2 Walden, Co,US
122/G2 Waldheim, Sk,Can
54/D1 Waldkirch, Ger.
57/L2 Waldviertel (reg.), Aus.
87/F4 Walea (str.), Indo.
87/F4 Waleabahi (isl.), Indo.
119/H2 Wales (isl.), Nun.,Can
43/C4 Wales, UK
105/T Walgreen (coast), Ant.
123/J3 Walhalla, ND,US
129/H3 Walhalla, SC,US
90/A2 Walikale, D.R. Congo
102/L11 Walker (bay), SAfr.
124/C3 Walker (lake), Nv,US
124/C3 Walker (riv.), Nv,US
126/D2 Walkerton, On,Can
122/E4 Wallace, Id,US
132/H6 Wallaceburg, On,Can
45/E5 Wallasey, Eng,UK
122/D4 Walla Walla, Wa,US
132/F6 Walled (lake), Mi,US
132/F6 Walled Lake, Mi,US
51/F4 Wallenhorst, Ger.
52/C3 Wallers, Fr.
47/E3 Wallingford, Eng,UK
93/H6 Wallis (isls.), Wall.
92/G6 Wallis & Futuna (terr.), Fr.
122/D4 Wallowa (mts.), Or,US
45/G2 Wallsend, Eng,UK
45/E3 Walney, Isle of (isl.), Eng,UK
131/C2 Walnut, Ca,US
124/E4 Walnut Canyon Nat'l Mon., Az,US
132/K11 Walnut Creek, Ca,US
129/F2 Walnut Ridge, Ar,US
130/F4 Walrus (isls.), Ak,US
46/E1 Walsall, Eng,UK
119/K2 Walsingham (cape), Nun.,Can
47/G1 Walsingham, Eng,UK
51/G3 Walsrode, Ger.
129/H3 Walterboro, SC,US
129/G4 Walter F. George (res.), Al, Ga,US
47/G3 Waltham Holy Cross, Eng,UK
45/F4 Walton-le-Dale, Eng,UK
47/F4 Walton on Thames, Eng,UK
47/H3 Walton on the Naze, Eng,UK
51/E5 Waltrop, Ger.
104/B5 Walvis Bay, Namb.
104/C3 Wama, Ang.
97/L7 Wamba, D.R. Congo
50/C5 Wamel, Neth.
45/E2 Wampool (riv.), Eng,UK
122/G5 Wamsutter, Wy,US
81/D5 Wan (riv.), China
131/F4 Wanaque, NJ,US
131/F4 Wanaque (res.), NJ,US
77/L2 Wanda (mts.), China
85/G3 Wanding, China
83/B2 Wang (riv.), Thai.
89/H7 Wanganui, NZ
91/C3 Wangaratta, Austl.
55/F2 Wangen, Ger.
51/E1 Wangerooge (isl.), Ger.
87/F6 Wanggamet (peak), Indo.
83/B4 Wang Hip (peak), Thai.
81/E5 Wangpan (bay), China
87/F4 Wani (peak), Indo.
79/M9 Wanouchi, Japan
75/D5 Wanquan (lake), China
45/G1 Wansbeck (riv.), Eng,UK
47/E3 Wantage, Eng,UK
76/F5 Wanxian, China
53/E2 Wanze, Belg.
126/C3 Wapakoneta, Oh,US
123/G2 Wapawekka (lake), Sk,Can
122/D2 Wapiti (riv.), Ab, BC,Can
87/J4 Wapoga (riv.), Indo.
125/K3 Wappapello (lake), Mo,US
123/K5 Wapsipinicon (riv.), Ia,US
79/H7 Warabi, Japan
84/C4 Warangal, India
47/F2 Warboys, Eng,UK
51/G6 Warburg, Ger.
53/F3 Warche (riv.), Belg.
47/G4 Warden (pt.), Eng,UK
51/F2 Wardenburg, Ger.
84/C3 Wardha, India
45/F3 Ward's Stone (mtn.), Eng,UK
47/F3 Ware, Eng,UK
52/C2 Waregem, Belg.
46/D5 Wareham, Eng,UK
53/E2 Waremme, Belg.
48/G2 Waren, Ger.
51/E5 Warendorf, Ger.
47/F3 Wargrave, Eng,UK
83/D3 Warin Chamrap, Thai.
44/B3 Waringstown, NI,UK
45/F1 Wark, Eng,UK
49/L3 Warka, Pol.
46/D2 Warley, Eng,UK
123/G2 Warman, Sk,Can
102/E2 Warmbad, SAfr.
51/G6 Warmebach (riv.), Ger.
51/H5 Warme Bode (riv.), Ger.
49/K1 Warmia (reg.), Pol.
46/D4 Warminster, Eng,UK
131/E5 Warminster, Pa,US
124/B2 Warner (mts.), Ca,US
129/H3 Warner Robins, Ga,US
48/G2 Warnow (riv.), Ger.
50/D4 Warnsveld, Neth.
91/G5 Warrandyte, Austl.
90/B4 Warrego (range), Austl.
90/B4 Warrego (riv.), Austl.
130/M2 Warren (pt.), NW,Can
128/E3 Warren, Ar,US
132/F6 Warren, Mi,US
123/J3 Warren, Mn,US
131/F5 Warren, NJ,US
126/D3 Warren, Oh,US
126/E3 Warren, Pa,US
44/B3 Warrenpoint, NI,UK
125/J3 Warrensburg, Mo,US
102/D3 Warrenton, SAfr.
126/E4 Warrenton, Va,US
132/P16 Warrenville, Il,US
45/F5 Warrington, Eng,UK
129/G4 Warrington, Fl,US
91/B3 Warrnambool, Austl.
123/K3 Warroad, Mn,US
91/D1 Warrumbungle Nat'l Park, Austl.
126/C3 Warsaw, In,US
125/J3 Warsaw, Mo,US
49/L3 Warsawa (prov.), Pol.
49/L2 Warsaw (Warszawa) (cap.), Pol.
49/H5 Warscheneck (peak), Aus.
45/G5 Warslow, Eng,UK
45/G5 Warsop, Eng,UK
51/F6 Warstein, Ger.
49/H2 Warta (riv.), Pol.
90/D5 Warwick, Austl.
47/E2 Warwick, Eng,UK
127/G3 Warwick, RI,US
47/E2 Warwickshire (co.), Eng,UK
124/E2 Wasatch (range), Ut,US
124/C4 Wasco, Ca,US
123/K4 Waseca, Mn,US
118/F1 Washburn (lake), Nun.,Can
45/G4 Washburn (riv.), Eng,UK
123/M3 Washi (lake), On,Can
45/H5 Washingborough, Eng,UK
45/G2 Washington, Eng,UK
122/C4 Washington (state), US
131/B8 Washington (cap.), DC,US
126/B3 Washington, Il,US
126/C4 Washington, In,US
129/J3 Washington, NC,US
127/G3 Washington (mtn.), NH,US
131/F5 Washington, NJ,US
126/D3 Washington, Pa,US
132/C2 Washington (lake), Wa,US
126/C2 Washington (isl.), Wi,US
126/D4 Washington Court House, Oh,US
93/K4 Washington (Teraina) (atoll), Kiri.
125/H4 Washita (riv.), Ok, Tx,US
47/G1 Wash, The (bay), Eng,UK
49/M2 Wasilków, Pol.
126/E1 Waskaganish (Rupert House), Qu,Can
130/G4 Waskey (mtn.), Ak,US
50/B4 Wassenaar, Neth.
50/D6 Wassenberg, Ger.
57/H1 Wasserkuppe (peak), Ger.
120/C4 Wassuk (range), Nv,US
45/E3 Wast Water (lake), Eng,UK
126/E1 Waswanipi (lake), Qu,Can
87/E4 Watampone, Indo.
79/M10 Watarai, Japan
79/F2 Watarase (riv.), Japan
79/G1 Watari, Japan
46/C4 Watchet, Eng,UK
47/E3 Watchfield, Eng,UK
47/G2 Waterbeach, Eng,UK
127/F3 Waterbury, Ct,US
127/Q9 Waterdown, On,Can
129/H3 Wateree (lake), SC,US
129/H3 Wateree (riv.), SC,US
43/B4 Waterford, Ire.
132/F6 Waterford, Mi,US
46/A6 Watergate (bay), Eng,UK
123/J2 Waterhen (lake), Mb,Can
122/F2 Waterhen (riv.), Sk,Can
52/D2 Waterloo, Belg.
126/D3 Waterloo, On,Can
125/J2 Waterloo, Ia,US
126/B4 Waterloo, Il,US
52/D2 Waterloo Battlesite, Belg.
47/E5 Waterlooville, Eng,UK
52/D2 Watermael-Boitsfort, Belg.
122/E3 Waterton Lakes Nat'l Park, Ab,Can
126/F3 Watertown, NY,US
123/J4 Watertown, SD,US
126/B3 Watertown, Wi,US
103/E2 Waterval-Bo, SAfr.
127/G2 Waterville, Me,US
122/C4 Waterville, Wa,US
47/F3 Watford, Eng,UK
123/H4 Watford City, ND,US
45/G5 Wath-upon-Dearne, Eng,UK
117/G3 Watling (San Salvador) (isl.), Bahm.
47/F3 Watlington, Eng,UK
83/B2 Wat Mahathat, Thai.
125/H4 Watonga, Ok,US
87/G3 Watowato (peak), Indo.
83/D3 Wat Phu, Laos
123/G3 Watrous, Sk,Can
101/A2 Watsa, D.R. Congo
126/C3 Watseka, Il,US
118/D2 Watson Lake, Yk,Can
124/B3 Watsonville, Ca,US
57/J3 Wattens, Aus.
52/C2 Wattignies, Fr.
47/G1 Watton, Eng,UK
52/C2 Wattrelos, Fr.
83/C2 Wat Xieng Thong, Laos
129/H5 Wauchula, Fl,US
132/P15 Wauconda, Il,US
132/Q15 Waukegan, Il,US
132/P13 Waukesha, Wi,US
46/C3 Waun Fâch (mtn.), Wal,UK
46/C1 Waun Oer (mtn.), Wal,UK
126/B3 Waupun, Wi,US
125/H4 Waurika, Ok,US
126/B2 Wausau, Wi,US
126/C3 Wauseon, Oh,US
132/P13 Wauwatosa, Wi,US
47/H2 Waveney (riv.), Eng,UK
45/E2 Waver (riv.), Eng,UK
91/G5 Waverly, Austl.
129/G2 Waverly, Tn,US
52/D2 Wavre, Belg.
52/B2 Wavrin, Fr.
97/L6 Wāw, Sudan
126/C2 Wawa, On,Can
126/E1 Wawagosic (riv.), Qu,Can
128/D3 Waxahachie, Tx,US
53/F3 Waxweiler, Ger.
129/H4 Waycross, Ga,US
132/F7 Wayne, Mi,US
125/H2 Wayne, Ne,US
131/F5 Wayne, NJ,US
129/H3 Waynesboro, Ga,US
129/F4 Waynesboro, Ms,US
126/E4 Waynesboro, Pa,US
126/E4 Waynesboro, Va,US
125/J3 Waynesville, Mo,US
129/H3 Waynesville, NC,US
52/C3 Waziers, Fr.
79/L10 Wazuka, Japan
48/K2 Wda (riv.), Pol.
99/F3 W du Niger Nat'l Park, Afr.
86/A2 We (isl.), Indo.
47/G4 Weald, The (reg.), Eng,UK
45/G2 Wear (riv.), Eng,UK
45/F2 Wear Head, Eng,UK
125/H4 Weatherford, Ok,US
128/D3 Weatherford, Tx,US
45/F5 Weaver (riv.), Eng,UK
124/B2 Weaverville, Ca,US
123/J4 Webster, SD,US
123/K5 Webster City, Ia,US
101/B2 Webuye, Kenya
105/W Weddell (sea), Ant.
113/M7 Weddell (isl.), Falk.
91/C2 Weddin Mountains Nat'l Park, Austl.
51/G1 Wedel, Ger.
51/G3 Wedemark, Ger.
46/D4 Wedmore, Eng,UK
46/D1 Wednesbury, Eng,UK
46/D1 Wednesfield, Eng,UK
124/B2 Weed, Ca,US
47/E2 Weedon Bec, Eng,UK
129/H4 Weeki Wachee Springs, Fl,US
46/B5 Week Saint Mary, Eng,UK
50/D4 Weerselo, Neth.
50/C6 Weert, Neth.
50/C4 Weesp, Neth.
50/D6 Wegberg, Ger.
49/L1 Węgorzewo, Pol.
49/M2 Węgrów, Pol.
51/G6 Wehre (riv.), Ger.
77/H4 Wei (riv.), China
77/H3 Weichang, China
48/G3 Weida, Ger.
57/K2 Weiden, Ger.
81/D3 Weifang, China
77/J4 Weihai, China
57/H1 Weilburg, Ger.
53/F2 Weilerswist, Ger.
55/H2 Weilheim, Ger.
48/F3 Weimar, Ger.
55/F2 Weingarten, Ger.
49/J4 Weinviertel (reg.), Aus.
126/D3 Weirton, WV,US
122/D4 Weiser, Id,US
122/D4 Weiser (riv.), Id,US
81/D4 Weishan (lake), China
53/F4 Weiskirchen, Ger.
129/G3 Weiss (lake), Al,US
57/J2 Weissenburg im Bayern, Ger.
48/F3 Weissenfels, Ger.
53/G3 Weissenthurm, Ger.
53/F3 Weisser Stein (peak), Ger.
55/G4 Weisskugel (mt.), Aus., It.
54/E5 Weissmies (peak), Swi.
49/H3 Weisswasser, Ger.
57/L3 Weiz, Aus.
85/J3 Weizhou (isl.), China
49/K1 Wejherowo, Pol.
126/D4 Welch, WV,US
97/N5 Weldiya, Eth.
47/F2 Weldon, Eng,UK
97/M6 Welel (peak), Eth.
47/E4 Welford, Eng,UK
47/F3 Welham Green, Eng,UK
84/D6 Weligama, SrL.
53/E2 Welkenraedt, Belg.
102/D3 Welkom, SAfr.
127/R10 Welland, On,Can
127/R10 Welland (can.), On,Can
47/F1 Welland (riv.), Eng,UK
127/R10 Wellandport, On,Can
53/E2 Wellen, Belg.
47/F2 Wellingborough, Eng,UK
91/C3 Wellington (inlet), Austl.
119/S7 Wellington (chan.), Nun.,Can
113/J7 Wellington (isl.), Chile
89/H7 Wellington (cap.), NZ
102/B4 Wellington, SAfr.
46/C5 Wellington, Eng,UK
46/D2 Wellington, Eng,UK
128/D2 Wellington, Ks,US
128/C3 Wellington, Tx,US
122/C2 Wells, BC,Can
46/D4 Wells, Eng,UK
122/E5 Wells, Nv,US
47/G1 Wells-next-the-Sea, Eng,UK
126/D4 Wellston, Oh,US
57/L2 Wels, Aus.
46/C1 Welshpool, Wal,UK
51/E5 Welver, Ger.
47/F3 Welwyn, Eng,UK
47/F3 Welwyn Garden City, Eng,UK
45/F6 Wem, Eng,UK
101/B4 Wembere (riv.), Tanz.
122/D2 Wembley, Ab,Can
46/B6 Wembury, Eng,UK
119/J3 Wemindji, Qu,Can
52/D2 Wemmel, Belg.
122/C4 Wenatchee, Wa,US
82/B4 Wenchang, China
99/E5 Wenchi, Gha.
51/H4 Wendeburg, Ger.
53/G2 Wenden, Ger.
47/F3 Wendover, Eng,UK
124/D2 Wendover, Nv,US
46/A6 Wendron, Eng,UK
46/D2 Wenlock Edge (ridge), Eng,UK
51/F6 Wenne (riv.), Ger.
51/G4 Wennigsen, Ger.
45/F3 Wennington, Eng,UK
45/F3 Wensleydale (val.), Eng,UK
47/H1 Wensum (riv.), Eng,UK
45/G4 Went (riv.), Eng,UK
82/D2 Wenzhou, China
48/G3 Werdau, Ger.
97/Q6 Werdēr, Eth.
51/E6 Werdohl, Ger.
50/B5 Werkendam, Neth.
51/E5 Werl, Ger.
51/E3 Werlte, Ger.
51/E6 Wermelskirchen, Ger.
51/E5 Werne an der Lippe, Ger.
57/J2 Werneck, Ger.
51/H5 Wernigerode, Ger.
91/D2 Werong (peak), Austl.
51/G6 Werra (riv.), Ger.
51/F4 Werre (riv.), Ger.
91/E1 Werrikimbe Nat'l Park, Austl.
45/F5 Werrington, Eng,UK
51/E5 Werse (riv.), Ger.
57/H2 Wertheim, Ger.
51/F4 Werther, Ger.
50/C3 Wervershoof, Neth.
52/C2 Wervik, Belg.
50/D5 Wesel, Ger.
51/E5 Wesel-Datteln-Kanal (can.), Ger.
51/F2 Weser (riv.), Ger.
51/G4 Wesergebirge (ridge), Ger.
128/D5 Weslaco, Tx,US
46/D4 Wessex (reg.), Eng,UK
123/J4 Wessington Springs, SD,US
91/C4 West (pt.), Austl.
132/P13 West Allis, Wi,US
129/H3 West Augusta, Ga,US
131/G5 West Babylon, NY,US
74/K5 West Bank (occ. zone)
126/B3 West Bend, Wi,US
84/E3 West Bengal (state), India
47/G3 West Bergholt, Eng,UK
126/C2 West Branch, Mi,US
45/G6 West Bridgford, Eng,UK
47/E1 West Bromwich, Eng,UK
46/D4 Westbury, Eng,UK
131/G5 Westbury, NY,US
132/P16 West Chicago, Il,US
46/B3 West Cleddau (riv.), Wal,UK
129/H3 West Columbia, SC,US
45/G2 West Cornforth, Eng,UK
131/C2 West Covina, Ca,US
50/A6 Westdorpe, Neth.
64/E5 West Dvina (riv.), Eur.
128/B2 West Elk (mts.), Co,US
50/D3 Westerbork, Neth.
51/E4 Westerkappeln, Ger.
48/E1 Westerland, Ger.
53/D1 Westerlo, Belg.
100/B3 Western (des.), Egypt
99/E5 Western (reg.), Gha.
101/B2 Western (prov.), Kenya
98/B4 Western (area), SLeo.
101/A2 Western (prov.), Ugan.
89/B3 Western Australia (state), Austl.
102/P4 Western Cape (prov.), SAfr.
78/A3 Western Channel (str.), Japan, SKor.
84/B4 Western Ghats (mts.), India
96/B3 Western Sahara
76/C1 Western Sayan (mts.), Rus.
50/A6 Westerschelde (chan.), Neth.
51/E2 Westerstede, Ger.
126/D3 Westerville, Oh,US
50/C5 Westervoort, Neth.
53/G2 Westerwald (for.), Ger.
51/F4 Westfalica, Porta (pass), Ger.
113/M8 West Falkland (isl.), Falk.
123/J4 West Fargo, ND,US
92/D4 West Fayu (isl.), Micr.
131/F5 Westfield, NJ,US
52/B2 West Flanders (prov.), Belg.
126/B4 West Frankfort, Il,US
50/C2 West Frisian (isls.), Neth.
47/F1 West Glen (riv.), Eng,UK
131/G4 West Haverstraw, NY,US
129/F3 West Helena, Ar,US
43/D2 Westhill, Sc,UK
45/F4 Westhoughton, Eng,UK
127/Q8 West Humber (riv.), On,Can
117/F4 West Indies (isls.), NAm.
131/G5 West Islip, NY,US
124/E2 West Jordan, Ut,US
45/E5 West Kirby, Eng,UK
127/F7 Westland, Mi,US
122/E2 Westlock, Ab,Can
104/E3 West Lunga Nat'l Park, Zam.
44/A4 Westmeath (co.), Ire.
129/F3 West Memphis, Ar,US
47/G3 West Mersea, Eng,UK
47/E2 West Midlands (co.), Eng,UK
131/F4 West Milford, NJ,US
131/B3 Westminster, Ca,US
132/Q16 Westmont, Il,US
131/E6 Westmont (Haddon), NJ,US
45/F3 Westmoreland (reg.), Eng,UK
127/N7 Westmount, Qu,Can
125/J3 Weston, Mo,US
126/D4 Weston, WV,US
102/P13 Westonaria, SAfr.
46/D4 Weston-super-Mare, Eng,UK
46/D4 Weston Zoyland, Eng,UK
131/F5 West Orange, NJ,US
129/H5 West Palm Beach, Fl,US
129/G4 West Pensacola, Fl,US
125/K3 West Plains, Mo,US
129/G3 West Point (lake), Al, Ga,US
129/F3 West Point, Ms,US
125/H2 West Point, Ne,US
131/G4 Westport, Ct,US
122/B2 West Road (riv.), BC,Can
132/L9 West Sacramento, Ca,US
127/S10 West Seneca, NY,US
68/H3 West Siberian (plain), Rus.
47/F4 West Sussex (co.), Eng,UK
124/E2 West Valley City, Ut,US
122/C3 West Vancouver, BC,Can
126/D4 West Virginia (state), US
46/B4 Westward Ho!, Eng,UK
131/F5 Westwood, NJ,US
45/G4 West Yorkshire (co.), Eng,UK
128/B2 Wet (mts.), Co,US
87/G5 Wetar (isl.), Indo.
87/G5 Wetar (str.), Indo.
122/E2 Wetaskiwin, Ab,Can
101/C4 Wete, Tanz.
126/E1 Wetetnagami (riv.), Qu,Can
45/F2 Wetheral, Eng,UK
45/G4 Wetherby, Eng,UK
91/B2 Wetherell (lake), Austl.
51/E6 Wetter, Ger.
52/C1 Wetteren, Belg.
51/E4 Wettringen, Ger.
52/C2 Wevelgem, Belg.
92/D5 Wewak, PNG
125/H4 Wewoka, Ok,US
43/B4 Wexford, Ire.
44/B6 Wexford (co.), Ire.
47/H1 Weybourne, Eng,UK
123/H3 Weyburn, Sk,Can
46/D5 Weymouth, Eng,UK
46/D5 Weymouth (bay), Eng,UK
89/H6 Whakatane, NZ
45/F5 Whaley Bridge, Eng,UK
45/F4 Whalley, Eng,UK
89/H6 Whangarei, NZ
45/G3 Wharfe (riv.), Eng,UK
128/D4 Wharton, Tx,US
123/G5 Wheatland, Wy,US
47/E3 Wheatley, Eng,UK
132/P16 Wheaton, Il,US
46/D1 Wheaton Aston, Eng,UK
131/J7 Wheaton-Glenmont, Md,US
129/G3 Wheeler (lake), Al,US
125/F3 Wheeler (peak), NM,US
124/D3 Wheeler (peak), Nv,US
132/Q15 Wheeling, Il,US
126/D3 Wheeling, WV,US
45/F3 Whernside (mtn.), Eng,UK
45/G2 Whickham, Eng,UK
132/B1 Whidbey (isl.), Wa,US
124/B2 Whiskeytown-Shasta-Trinity Nat'l Rec. Area, Ca,US
45/G2 Whitburn, Eng,UK
127/S8 Whitby, On,Can
45/H3 Whitby, Eng,UK
45/F6 Whitchurch, Eng,UK
47/E4 Whitchurch, Eng,UK
47/F3 Whitchurch, Eng,UK
46/C4 Whitchurch, Wal,UK
105/D White (isl.), Ant.
127/K1 White (bay), Nf,Can
126/C1 White (lake), On,Can
64/H2 White (sea), Rus.
130/L4 White (pass), Ak,US
129/F3 White (riv.), Ar,US
124/E2 White (riv.), Co, Ut,US
126/C4 White (riv.), In,US
125/J5 White (lake), La,US
125/K4 White (riv.), La, Mo,US
125/G2 White (riv.), Ne, SD,US
124/D3 White (riv.), Nv,US
128/C3 White (riv.), Tx,US
126/D4 White (peak), Va,US
127/K1 White Bear (riv.), Nf,Can
123/G3 White City, Sk,Can
122/E2 Whitecourt, Ab,Can
45/E1 White Esk (riv.), Sc,UK
123/K4 Whiteface (riv.), Mn,US
45/F4 Whitefield, Eng,UK
126/C2 Whitefish (bay), On,Can, Mi,US
122/E3 Whitefish, Mt,US
130/L2 Whitefish Station, Yk,Can
46/B3 Whiteford (pt.), Wal,UK
123/G2 White Fox, Sk,Can
122/E4 Whitehall, Mt,US
131/E5 Whitehall (Fullerton), Pa,US
44/E2 Whitehaven, Eng,UK
44/C2 Whitehead, NI,UK
130/L3 Whitehorse (cap.), Yk,Can
47/E3 Whitehorse (hill), Eng,UK
131/K7 White Marsh, Md,US
130/J2 White Mountains Nat'l Rec. Area, Ak,US
123/K3 Whitemouth (riv.), Mb,Can
97/M5 White Nile (riv.), Sudan
131/K7 White Oak, Md,US
126/A1 White Otter (lake), On,Can
131/G4 White Plains, NY,US
126/C1 White River, On,Can
124/E4 Whiteriver, Az,US
128/B3 White Rock, NM,US
124/F4 White Sands, NM,US
124/F4 White Sands Nat'l Mon., NM,US
113/K8 Whiteside (chan.), Chile
122/F4 White Sulphur Springs, Mt,US
126/D4 White Sulphur Springs, WV,US
129/J3 Whiteville, NC,US
99/E4 White Volta (riv.), Burk., Gha.
123/L3 Whitewater (lake), On,Can
123/H3 Whitewood, Sk,Can
44/D2 Whithorn, Sc,UK
46/B3 Whitland, Wal,UK
45/G1 Whitley Bay, Eng,UK
124/C3 Whitney (mtn.), Ca,US
125/H4 Whitney (lake), Tx,US
46/B6 Whitsand (bay), Eng,UK
47/H4 Whitstable, Eng,UK
90/C3 Whitsunday I. Nat'l Park, Austl.
131/B3 Whittier, Ca,US
47/F1 Whittlesey, Eng,UK
45/G5 Whitwell, Eng,UK